Tax Rate Schedules for 2015

Tax Rate for Corporations

Taxable Income		Pay	+	% on Excess	of the amount over
Over	But Not Over				
$0	$ 50,000	$0		15%	$0
50,000	75,000	7,500		25	50,000
75,000	100,000	13,750		34	75,000
100,000	335,000	22,250		39	100,000
335,000	10,000,000	113,900		34	335,000
10,000,000	15,000,000	3,400,000		35	10,000,000
15,000,000	18,333,333	5,150,000		38	15,000,000
18,333,333	—	6,416,667		35	18,333,333

Tax Rate for Estates and Trusts

Taxable Income		Pay	+	% on Excess	of the amount over
Over	But Not Over				
$0	$2,500	$0.00		15%	$0
2,500	5,900	375.00		25	2,500
5,900	9,050	1,225.00		28	5,900
9,050	12,300	2,107.00		33	9,050
12,300	—	3,179.50		39.6	12,300

2016

CCH FEDERAL TAXATION
Basic Principles

GENERAL EDITORS

Ephraim P. Smith
California State University

Philip J. Harmelink
University of New Orleans

James R. Hasselback
Clarion University

CONTRIBUTING AUTHORS

Ted D. Englebrecht
Louisiana Tech University

Philip J. Harmelink
University of New Orleans

Robert Ricketts
Texas Tech University

Christopher J. Fenn
Georgia State University

James R. Hasselback
Clarion University

Ephraim P. Smith
California State University

Edward C. Foth
DePaul University

Thomas M. Porcano
Miami University (Ohio)

Larry Tunnell
New Mexico State University

Wolters Kluwer

Chapters 1–14, 17, and 18 also appear in *2016 CCH Federal Taxation—Comprehensive Topics.*

Revision Author and Consultant: David L. Gibberman, J.D.
CCH® Study MATE™ Author: David L. Gibberman, J.D.

EDITORIAL STAFF
Production: Jennifer Schencker, Craig Arritola
Cover Design: Laila Gaidulis

ISBN 978-0-8080-4075-0

4025 W. Peterson Ave.
Chicago, IL 60646-6085
800 248 3248
CCHGroup.com

Printed in the United States of America

SUSTAINABLE FORESTRY INITIATIVE
Certified Chain of Custody
Promoting Sustainable Forestry
www.sfiprogram.org
SFI-00712

Preface

CCH Federal Taxation—Basic Principles introduces the student of accounting to the complex and absorbing study of federal taxation. *Basic Principles* focuses on the basic forms and structures of federal taxation and delves particularly into those aspects that affect individual taxpayers.

The field of federal taxation has developed from several separate disciplines, chiefly accounting and law. Thus, there is no single source document that fully defines, in a clear, consistent, and comprehensive manner, all the elements involved in federal taxation (both the theoretical and practical aspects). This book is written to interpret and demystify the extensive body of knowledge that must be understood by any student who wishes to pursue a career in the field of federal taxation or by any individual who desires a clearer understanding of federal taxation for personal use.

Basic Principles covers these topics: Individual Taxation, Gross Income (two chapters), Deductions (three chapters), Tax Credits, Property Transactions (three chapters), Partnerships and Corporations, Trusts and Estates, and Tax Planning for Individuals. As cornerstones for the foundation of federal taxation, these topics constitute the basic extensive outline of the field; this book distills the major ideas and operational techniques for dealing with problems encountered in these areas.

The thirty-second edition of *CCH Federal Taxation—Basic Principles* has been prepared to ensure that all material presented is complete and reflects all tax acts, issued regulations, and case developments through March 2015. The evolution of the income tax laws to their present state has been periodically accelerated by many reforms, including the comprehensive Tax Reform Act of 1986, which led to the redesignation of the tax code as the Internal Revenue Code of 1986. Predictably, changes soon followed and, in almost every year since 1986, a new tax bill has been signed into law. Reformation of the tax law continues to be the trend, and for this reason information on the tax law must be monitored and revised. Thus, extensive research and review have gone into the preparation of each annual edition of this book.

This edition continues the practice instituted last year of using Tax Return Problems. The problems are highlighted as such in the Problems section of the following chapters: 4-7, 10-12, and 17-18. For faculty teaching the course in the fall semester of 2015, draft copies of Form 1040 and accompanying schedules are usually available in September.

This volume can stand alone, and the format is flexible enough so that individual segments can stand alone as well. Therefore, instructors can adapt the use of this text to a wide range of interests and to fit a number of time constraints. It will still offer a balanced approach to the overall topic.

This book was not prepared as a restatement of the Internal Revenue Code and related tax law. Many such works currently exist. It was designed as a learning device to present federal tax information in a way that will stimulate thought and planning as well as aid in mastery of the difficult, tightly interwoven intricacies of federal tax law. Various sections of the book present topics of federal tax law in a sequence different from that in the Code. This was done so that common ideas and underlying similarities could be linked in the mind of the student and unifying characteristics could be drawn together to present a clearer and more functional picture of the whole.

The contributing authors of the volume wish to thank many of their colleagues for helpful suggestions and for the time and energy they have given in improving the manuscript.

March 2015   Ephraim P. Smith

How to Use This Book

CCH Federal Taxation—Basic Principles has been organized to make it easy to study the fundamental concepts of federal tax laws affecting individuals. Special features, end-of-chapter materials, an appendix, and supplementary materials are provided to further assist in the learning process.

CHAPTER OPENINGS

All chapters begin with the same elements: a list of the learning objectives and an overview. This information provides a framework for understanding the material that will be studied in the chapter.

SPECIAL FEATURES

Special features—Keystone Problems, Planning Pointers, and Tax Blunders—appear throughout the book. Their purpose is to make familiar the specific applications of the tax law, suggest tax-saving strategies, and illustrate methods of avoiding undesired tax consequences. Additionally, vivid and realistic examples to illustrate salient points are included within the chapters to show application of the law and accounting techniques.

END-OF-CHAPTER MATERIALS

Every chapter ends with a summary of the material covered. Questions and Problems follow for applying the principles learned and allowing the instructor to evaluate and recall the main ideas discussed in the chapter. The problems are sequenced in the order in which the topics are presented in the chapter. Also included are Comprehensive Problems and Research Problems. Comprehensive Problems are designed to develop computational skills, while the purpose of the Research Problems is to provide an opportunity to learn and utilize the methodology of tax research.

END-OF-BOOK MATERIALS

In addition to the Topical Index, other useful research materials are found at the end of the book. The Appendix covers various Tax Rate Schedules, and the Glossary of Tax Terms contains over 200 definitions. In addition, the Finding Lists and Table of Cases detail the textbook's citations by Internal Revenue Code Sections, Regulation Sections, Revenue Procedures, Revenue Rulings, and court cases.

SUPPLEMENTARY MATERIALS

A *Study Manual,* sold separately, outlines and highlights the in-depth textbook presentation and contains Objective Questions (and Answers) for self-evaluation. It also includes a series of Tax Return Problems designed to complement conceptual study of federal taxation and to provide exposure to various aspects of tax return preparation.

To order the *Study Manual* for this volume *(CCH Federal Tax Study Manual, 2016),* contact your bookstore or write or call: Wolters Kluwer, 4025 W. Peterson Ave., Chicago, Illinois 60646-6085 (800-248-3248; CCHGroup.com).

ACCESS UPDATES

CCH has created a special webpage to keep you up to date with changing tax laws and new developments. This page will also hold any revised content that may be created before the next edition is released.

Visit *CCHGroup.com/CTBP* to find information on updates to the book and latest developments!

FREE ONLINE AIDS

CCH® Study MATE™ is an online learning center for college students. The *Study MATE Fundamental Tax Topics* library was created to supplement this textbook by providing an easy online tutor to help students with difficult concepts and test them on their knowledge. Each course contains online learning features to capture student attention and "Test Your Knowledge" questions to aid comprehension. At the end of each course, a 15-question final exam is presented. Students have the opportunity to take the exam three times. After passing the exam, students can e-mail a completion certificate to their professor.

Professors and students who use CCH textbooks have free access to the Fundamental Tax Topics library for a full year! To view the courses available, visit *www.cchstudymate.com*. To enroll, follow the instructions provided on the tear-out instruction card bound into the book and use the access code as payment.

Anyone with questions, comments, or feedback can contact us at *studymate@cch.com*.

Contents

A detailed Table of Contents for each chapter begins on page ix.

		PAGE
Chapter 1	Introduction to Federal Taxation and Understanding the Federal Tax Law	1-1
Chapter 2	Tax Research, Practice, and Procedure	2-1
Chapter 3	Individual Taxation—An Overview	3-1
Chapter 4	Gross Income	4-1
Chapter 5	Gross Income—Exclusions	5-1
Chapter 6	Deductions: General Concepts and Trade or Business Deductions	6-1
Chapter 7	Deductions: Business/Investment Losses and Passive Activity Losses	7-1
Chapter 8	Deductions: Itemized Deductions	8-1
Chapter 9	Tax Credits, Prepayments, and Alternative Minimum Tax	9-1
Chapter 10	Property Transactions: Determination of Basis and Gains and Losses	10-1
Chapter 11	Property Transactions: Nonrecognition of Gains and Losses	11-1
Chapter 12	Property Transactions: Treatment of Capital and Section 1231 Assets	12-1
Chapter 13	Tax Accounting	13-1
Chapter 14	Deferred Compensation and Education Savings Plans	14-1
Chapter 15	Tax Planning for Individuals	15-1
Chapter 16	Partnerships, Corporations, and S Corporations	16-1
Chapter 17	Federal Estate Tax, Federal Gift Tax, and Generation-Skipping Transfer Tax	17-1
Chapter 18	Income Taxation of Trusts and Estates	18-1

Appendix	A-1
Tax Table	T-1
Glossary of Tax Terms	G-1
Finding Lists	F-1
Table of Cases	C-1
Topical Index	I-1

Table of Contents

PARAGRAPH

CHAPTER 1 **INTRODUCTION TO FEDERAL TAXATION AND UNDERSTANDING THE FEDERAL TAX LAW**

FUNDAMENTAL ASPECTS OF FEDERAL TAXATION

Sources of Revenue 1101

Tax Collection and Penalties 1121

Taxpayer Obligations 1131

Brief History of the Federal Income Tax 1151

Federal Tax Legislative Process 1161

Tax Reform 1165

UNDERLYING RATIONALE OF THE FEDERAL INCOME TAX

Objectives of the Tax Law 1171

Economic Factors 1175

Social Factors 1181

Political Factors 1185

Tax Policy and Reform Measures 1187

BASIC TAX CONCEPTS

Essential Tax Terms Defined 1195

CHAPTER 2 **TAX RESEARCH, PRACTICE, AND PROCEDURE**

TAX REFERENCE MATERIALS

Classification of Materials 2001

PRIMARY SOURCE MATERIALS

Statutory Authority 2021

Administrative Authority 2035

Judicial Authority 2055

SECONDARY SOURCE MATERIALS

Analysis of Tax Law Sources 2075

RESEARCH METHODOLOGY

Types of Tax Research Situations 2125

Research Model 2135

Research Cases and Examples 2147

TAX ADMINISTRATION

Organization of the IRS 2211

Representation of Taxpayers 2215

PARAGRAPH

Rulings Programs 2225

Taxpayer Compliance Assistance 2245

TAX PRACTICE AND PROCEDURE

Examination of Returns 2301

Appeals Process 2311

Settlement Agreements 2315

Refunds 2325

Interest on Under/Overpayments 2333

Statute of Limitations 2355

Penalties 2365

Disclosure of a Position on a Return 2370

Ethics Rules for Practitioners 2375

CHAPTER 3   INDIVIDUAL TAXATION—AN OVERVIEW

Components of the Tax Formula 3001

Gross Income 3011

Deductions for Adjusted Gross Income 3015

Adjusted Gross Income 3025

Itemizing v. Standard Deduction 3035

Personal Exemptions 3045

Tax Rates 3055

Tax Credits and Prepayments 3065

Net Tax Due or Refund 3075

Classification of Taxpayers 3085

PERSONAL EXEMPTIONS

Taxpayer and Spouse 3201

Dependents 3225

High-Income Phaseout of Exemptions 3227

FILING STATUS AND REQUIREMENTS

Married Individuals Filing Jointly 3301

Married Individuals Filing Separately 3315

Single Individuals 3325

Heads of Households 3345

Surviving Spouses 3355

Tax Returns of Dependents 3365

Filing Requirements 3375

PARAGRAPH

Tax Tables 3385

Tax Rate Schedules 3395

Self-Employment Tax and Medicare Surtaxes 3405

CHAPTER 4 GROSS INCOME

THE CONCEPT OF INCOME

Economic Income 4001

The Legal/Tax Concept of Income 4015

Accounting Income 4025

ECONOMIC BENEFIT, CONSTRUCTIVE RECEIPT, AND ASSIGNMENT OF INCOME DOCTRINES

Economic Benefit Doctrine 4101

Constructive Receipt Doctrine 4125

Assignment of Income Doctrine 4201

Community Property Income 4215

Tenancy by the Entirety 4225

Joint Tenants and Tenants in Common 4235

ITEMS INCLUDED IN GROSS INCOME

List of Income Items 4301

Compensation for Services 4315

Compensation v. Gift 4325

Jury Duty Pay 4331

Prizes and Awards 4335

Scholarships and Fellowships 4345

Gross Income Derived from Business 4355

Partnerships and S Corporations 4375

Interest 4385

Rent and Royalty Income 4395

Dividend Income 4401

Divorce and Separation 4451

Discharge of Debt 4485

STOCK OPTION PLANS

Restricted Stock Plans 4601

Incentive Stock Option (ISO) Plans 4615

Employee Stock Purchase Plans 4625

Nonstatutory Stock Option Plans 4655

PARAGRAPH

CHAPTER 5 GROSS INCOME—EXCLUSIONS

COMMON EXCLUSIONS FROM GROSS INCOME

Gifts and Inheritances 5001

Life Insurance Proceeds 5015

Sale of Residence 5025

Recovery of Tax Benefit Items 5035

Retirement Income 5055

Interest on Government Obligations 5075

EMPLOYEE BENEFITS

Fringe Benefits 5101

Group-Term Life Insurance 5115

Annuities 5125

Adoption Expenses 5140

Compensation for Injuries and Sickness 5145

Accident and Health Plans 5155

Qualified Long-Term Care Insurance 5165

Meals and Lodging 5185

Cafeteria Plans 5195

Educational Assistance Plans 5201

Tuition Reduction Plans 5215

Dependent Care Assistance Programs 5235

Military Benefits 5255

CHAPTER 6 DEDUCTIONS: GENERAL CONCEPTS AND TRADE OR BUSINESS DEDUCTIONS

CATEGORIES OF ALLOWABLE DEDUCTIONS

Classification of Tax Deductions 6001

Deductions "For" vs. "From" AGI 6101

Deductions "For" AGI 6115

Deductions "From" AGI—Itemized Deductions 6125

TRADE OR BUSINESS DEDUCTIONS

Overview—Code Sec. 162 6201

General Criteria 6205

Expense Must Be Incurred in a Trade or Business Activity 6215

Expense Must Be Ordinary and Necessary 6225

PARAGRAPH

Expense Must Be Reasonable..6235

Expense Must Be Paid or Incurred During the Taxable Year 6245

EXPENSES INCURRED FOR THE PRODUCTION OF INCOME

Code Sec. 212—Production of Income or Protection of Assets 6301

Investment Expense Deductions..6315

Tax Planning and Compliance Expenses..6325

DEDUCTIONS FOR LOSSES

Code Sec. 165 6401

OTHER ALLOWABLE DEDUCTIONS "FOR" AGI

Business Investigation Start-Up and Organizational Costs..6505

Business Gifts..6515

Transportation Expenses...6535

Travel Expenses 6545

Moving Expenses...6560

Qualified Higher Education Expenses 6565

Student Loan Interest...6570

Health Insurance and Health Savings Accounts..6575

Manufacturing Deduction..6585

EMPLOYEE BUSINESS EXPENSES

Employee Business Expenses—In General..6601

LIMITATIONS ON THE DEDUCTIBILITY OF EXPENSES

Certain Deductions Limited or Disallowed 6701

Hobby Expenses and Losses 6715

Personal Deductions..6725

Public Policy Restrictions 6735

Lobbying and Political Contributions..6745

Meals and Entertainment Expenses 6755

Expenses and Interest Relating to Tax-Exempt Income..6765

Related Party Transactions..6775

Payment of Another Taxpayer's Obligation 6785

Capital Expenditures..6795

BUSINESS DEDUCTIONS RELATED TO CAPITAL EXPENDITURES

Depreciation of Tangible Property...6801

Alternative MACRS System 6805

Depreciation of Real Property 6815

PARAGRAPH

Code Sec. 179 Election to Expense Certain Depreciable Assets 6825

Bonus Depreciation...6835

Depreciation of Automobiles...6845

Property Converted from Personal to Business Use..6855

Amortization 6865

Research and Experimental Expenditures 6875

Depletion of Natural Resources...6885

Substantiation of Tax Deductions...6901

CHAPTER 7   DEDUCTIONS: BUSINESS/INVESTMENT LOSSES AND PASSIVE ACTIVITY LOSSES

TAX SHELTERS AND AT-RISK RULES

Tax Shelters 7001

At-Risk Rules 7125

PASSIVE ACTIVITY LOSS RULES

Application of Rules 7201

Classification of Income 7205

Disallowance of Passive Losses and Credits 7211

Suspended Losses 7215

Disposition of a Passive Activity 7225

Taxpayers Affected by Passive Losses 7231

Material Participation 7235

Identifying an Activity 7261

Rental Activities 7273

Rental Real Estate Activities 7281

Change of Activity Status 7287

BUSINESS AND INVESTMENT LOSSES

Business Casualty and Theft Losses 7301

Net Operating Losses (NOLs) 7331

Hobby Losses 7345

Home Office Expenses 7351

Vacation Home Expenses 7371

Manufacturing Deduction under Code Section 199 7375

PARAGRAPH

CHAPTER 8   # DEDUCTIONS: ITEMIZED DEDUCTIONS

MEDICAL EXPENSES

Requirements for the Deduction 8001

Medical Care Expenses 8015

Capital Expenditures 8025

Transportation and Lodging Expenses 8035

Hospital and Other Institutional Care 8045

Medicines and Drugs 8055

Medical Insurance Premiums 8065

TAXES

Summary of Deductible Taxes 8101

Property Taxes 8105

Income Taxes 8115

INTEREST

Requirements for Deduction 8201

Personal (Consumer) Interest 8205

Qualified Education Loan Interest 8210

Qualified Residence Interest 8215

Investment Interest 8225

Trade or Business Interest 8235

Passive Investment Interest 8245

Payments for Services 8255

Prepaid Interest 8265

Mortgage Insurance Premiums 8275

CHARITABLE CONTRIBUTIONS

Qualified Organizations 8301

Valuation of Charitable Donations 8315

Limitations on Charitable Contributions 8325

Filing and Substantiation Requirements 8355

PERSONAL CASUALTY AND THEFT LOSSES

Casualty Losses 8501

Theft Losses 8525

MISCELLANEOUS ITEMIZED DEDUCTIONS

Employee Business Expenses 8601

Reimbursed Employee Expenses 8603

PARAGRAPH

Unreimbursed Employee Expenses 8605

Job-Seeking Expenses 8655

Education Expenses 8665

Work Clothes and Uniforms 8675

Tax Counsel and Return Preparer Fees 8680

INVESTMENT EXPENSES

Rent and Royalty Expenses 8701

Miscellaneous Investment Expenses 8745

Wagering Losses 8775

Unrecovered Investment in Annuity 8785

CHAPTER 9   TAX CREDITS, PREPAYMENTS, AND ALTERNATIVE MINIMUM TAX

NONREFUNDABLE TAX CREDITS

Types of Credits 9001

Household and Dependent Care Credit 9015

Elderly and Disabled Persons Credit 9025

American Opportunity Tax and Lifetime Learning Credits 9031

Child Tax Credit 9032

Credit for Qualified Retirement Savings 9033

Adoption Assistance Credit 9034

Foreign Tax Credit 9035

Residential Credits 9042

General Business Credit 9045

REFUNDABLE TAX CREDITS

Withholding of Tax on Wages Credit 9105

Social Security Tax Refunds Credit 9115

Earned Income Credit 9125

Withholding of Tax at Source Credit 9135

Gasoline and Special Fuels Tax Credit 9155

Estimated Tax Payments Credit 9165

ALTERNATIVE MINIMUM TAX

Imposition of Tax 9401

Adjustments to Taxable Income 9415

Tax Preference Items 9425

Exemption Amount 9435

Tax Credits 9445

PARAGRAPH

Carryover of Credit 9455

Alternative Minimum Tax Planning 9475

CHAPTER 10 PROPERTY TRANSACTIONS: DETERMINATION OF BASIS AND GAINS AND LOSSES

FACTORS IN DETERMINING GAIN OR LOSS

Definition of Realized Gain or Loss 10,001

Amount Realized 10,015

Adjusted Basis 10,025

Holding Period...10,030

Recognition and Nonrecognition of Gain or Loss 10,035

DETERMINATION OF BASIS

Cost 10,101

Basis Allocation 10,115

Stock Dividends...10,125

Stock Rights...10,130

Fair Market Value 10,135

Property Acquired by Gift 10,145

Property Acquired from Decedent 10,175

Stock Transactions 10,201

Personal-Use Property Conversion 10,215

Related Parties 10,225

Installment Reporting 10,245

CHAPTER 11 PROPERTY TRANSACTIONS: NONRECOGNITION OF GAINS AND LOSSES

SALE OF A PERSONAL RESIDENCE

The General Rules 11,001

Principal Residence 11,005

Special Provisions 11,015

Definitions Related to Residence 11,025

LIKE-KIND EXCHANGES

Definition 11,201

Qualifying Property 11,215

Receipt of Boot 11,225

PARAGRAPH

Giving Boot 11,235

Assumption of Liabilities 11,245

Basis of Acquired Property 11,255

Holding Period 11,265

Three-Party Exchanges 11,275

INVOLUNTARY CONVERSIONS

Definition of an Involuntary Conversion 11,301

Involuntary Conversion Rules for Property Damaged in Disaster 11,305

Replacement Property—Mandatory Rules 11,315

Replacement Property—Elective Rules 11,325

Severance Damages 11,335

Qualifying Replacement Property 11,345

Condemnation of Real Property—Special Rule 11,355

Time Limit 11,365

Reporting Requirements 11,385

Depreciation Rules...11,395

OTHER TRANSACTIONS INVOLVING NONRECOGNITION

Corporate and Partnership Exchanges 11,401

Stock-for-Stock Exchanges 11,405

Insurance Contract Exchanges 11,415

U.S. Obligations Exchanges 11,435

Reacquisitions of Real Property 11,455

CHAPTER 12　PROPERTY TRANSACTIONS: TREATMENT OF CAPITAL AND SECTION 1231 ASSETS

SPECIAL RULES AND LIMITATIONS ON TRANSACTIONS

Background 12,001

Capital Asset Definition 12,025

SPECIAL SITUATIONS IN CAPITAL v. ORDINARY TREATMENT

Inventory 12,101

Sale of a Business 12,115

Patents 12,125

Franchises 12,135

Lease Cancellation Payments 12,155

Options 12,165

PARAGRAPH

HOLDING PERIOD

Computation of Holding Period 12,201

Special Rules for Holding Period 12,215

INDIVIDUAL TAXPAYERS

Determination of Taxable Income 12,301

Capital Loss Carryovers 12,315

Corporate Taxpayers Distinguished 12,401

SPECIAL PROVISIONS FOR CERTAIN INVESTMENTS

Nonbusiness Bad Debts 12,501

Worthless Securities 12,515

Small Business Stock 12,525

Gains on Small Business Stock 12,530

Dealers in Securities 12,535

Subdivided Real Estate 12,545

SECTION 1231 ASSETS AND PROCEDURE

Background 12,601

Definition of Section 1231 Assets 12,615

Computational Procedures 12,645

Personal Casualty and Theft Gains and Losses 12,655

DEPRECIATION RECAPTURE—SECTION 1245

Purpose of Rules 12,701

Definition of Section 1245 Property 12,715

Computational Procedures 12,725

Depreciation Methods 12,735

ACRS or MACRS Property 12,745

Summary: Section 1245 Recapture 12,755

DEPRECIATION RECAPTURE—SECTION 1250

Definition of Section 1250 Property 12,801

Purpose of Rules 12,815

Nonresidential Real Property—Pre-1981 Acquisitions 12,825

Nonresidential Real Property—ACRS 12,835

Nonresidential Real Property—MACRS 12,841

Residential Real Property—Pre-1981 Acquisitions 12,845

Residential Real Property—ACRS 12,855

Residential Real Property—MACRS 12,861

PARAGRAPH

Low-Income Housing—Pre-1987 Acquisitions 12,865

Summary: Section 1250 Recapture 12,875

RECAPTURE RULES IN OTHER EVENTS

Gifts and Inheritances 12,901

Like-Kind Exchanges and Involuntary Conversions 12,915

Charitable Contributions 12,925

Installment Sales 12,935

CHAPTER 13   TAX ACCOUNTING

TAXABLE INCOME AND TAX LIABILITY FOR VARIOUS ENTITIES

Recapitulation of Taxable Income and Tax Liability 13,001

ACCOUNTING PERIODS

The Tax Year 13,007

Election of the Tax Year 13,015

CHANGE OF ACCOUNTING PERIODS

IRS Permission or Consent 13,101

Exceptions to Permission Requirements 13,115

Short Tax Years 13,165

Accounting Period Tax Planning 13,175

Special Rules—The Tax Year 13,180

ACCOUNTING METHODS

Overall Methods 13,201

Cash Method 13,215

Limitations on Use of Cash Method 13,225

Special Rules—Cash Method 13,230

Accrual Method 13,235

Accrual Method Tax Planning 13,240

Separate Sources of Income 13,245

Hybrid Methods 13,265

Tangible Property Regulations...13,275

CHANGE OF ACCOUNTING METHODS

IRS Permission or Consent 13,301

Adjustment—Voluntary/Required Change 13,325

Time and Form of Application 13,355

Accounting Method Tax Planning 13,365

Timeliness 13,375

INVENTORIES

Use of Inventories 13,401

Valuation of Inventory 13,415

Cost Methods 13,425

Uniform Capitalization Rules 13,435

Lower-of-Cost-or-Market (LCM) Method 13,445

Valuation of Inventory Items 13,453

Dollar-Value LIFO Method 13,473

Simplified Dollar-Value LIFO Method 13,481

Estimates of Inventory Shrinkage 13,485

LONG-TERM CONTRACTS

Alternative Accounting Methods 13,501

Comparison of the Methods 13,515

Capitalization of Expenses 13,535

Special Rules 13,540

INSTALLMENT SALES

Use of Installment Method 13,601

Computation of Gain 13,655

Electing Out of Installment Reporting 13,675

Dispositions of Installment Obligations 13,685

Repossessions 13,695

Interest on Deferred Payment Sales 13,699

Advantages and Disadvantages of Installment Method 13,710

CHAPTER 14 DEFERRED COMPENSATION AND EDUCATION SAVINGS PLANS

EMPLOYER-SPONSORED DEFERRED COMPENSATION PLANS: "QUALIFIED" AND "NONQUALIFIED"

Qualified Employer-Sponsored Plans 14,001

Nonqualified Employer-Sponsored Plans..14,015

BASIC TYPES OF EMPLOYER-SPONSORED QUALIFIED RETIREMENT PLANS

Defined Contribution Plans 14,101

Defined Benefit Plans...14,110

Profit-Sharing Plans...14,115

Stock Bonus Plans..14,120

Employee Stock Ownership Plans (ESOPs)...14,125

Money Purchase Pension Plans 14,130

PARAGRAPH

QUALIFIED PLAN REQUIREMENTS

Sources of Legislative Authority..14,201

Nondiscrimination Requirements..14,205

Limitations on Contributions to a Defined Contribution Plan.............................14,215

Limitations on Benefits Provided by a Defined Benefit Plan................................14,225

Required Minimum Distribution Rules...14,235

Early Withdrawal Restrictions...14,245

Participation Requirements..14,255

Coverage Requirements..14,265

Vesting Requirements...14,275

"Exclusive Benefit of the Employee" Requirement...14,285

TAX CONSEQUENCES TO EMPLOYER AND EMPLOYEE

Contributions and Distributions: Basic Terminology...14,301

Contributions and Deductions—General Rules...14,305

Earnings on Contributions..14,315

Partial Distributions—Computing Tax Liability..14,325

Lump-Sum Distributions—Computing Tax Liability..14,335

Rollovers..14,345

Loans..14,355

COMMON RETIREMENT PLANS FOR LARGE BUSINESSES

401(k) Plans..14,401

Roth 401(k) Plans..14,405

Qualified Annuity (403(a)) Plans...14,415

Tax-Sheltered Annuity (403(b)) Plans..14,425

Section 457(b) Deferred Compensation Plans...14,435

Retirement Plans for Federal and Postal Employees...14,445

COMMON RETIREMENT PLANS FOR SMALL BUSINESSES

Plans for Small Businesses—Basic Concepts..14,501

Solo 401(k) Plans...14,515

Keogh Plans..14,525

Simplified Employee Pension (SEP) Plans..14,535

SIMPLE Plans..14,545

"DB/K" Plans...14,555

PARAGRAPH

PERSONAL RETIREMENT PLANS FOR WORKING INDIVIDUALS

Common Rules for Traditional and Roth IRAs 14,601

Specific Rules for Traditional IRAs 14,625

Rules Specific for Roth IRAs 14,635

NONQUALIFIED DEFERRED COMPENSATION PLANS

Nonqualified Plans—Basic Concepts 14,701

Rabbi Trusts 14,705

Employee Stock Purchase Plans 14,715

Incentive Stock Options (ISOs) 14,725

Nonqualified Stock Options (NSOs) 14,735

Restricted Stock Plans 14,745

Variable Annuity Contracts 14,755

Short-Term Informal Arrangements 14,765

EDUCATION SAVINGS VEHICLES

Coverdell Education Savings Accounts 14,801

529 Plans 14,815

CHAPTER 15 TAX PLANNING FOR INDIVIDUALS

GENERAL PRINCIPLES OF TAX PLANNING

Avoiding Income Recognition 15,001

Deferral or Acceleration of Income 15,015

Acceleration or Deferral of Deductions 15,025

Itemized or the Standard Deduction 15,035

SELF-EMPLOYED v. EMPLOYEE TAX PLANNING

Health Insurance Plans 15,101

Trade or Business Expenses 15,115

FAMILY TAX PLANNING

Income-Shifting 15,201

College Planning 15,225

Divorce Settlements 15,255

FIXED AND OTHER ASSETS TAX PLANNING

Expensing Election 15,401

Leasing v. Buying 15,411

Like-Kind Exchanges 15,425

Residence Sale 15,435

PARAGRAPH

Involuntary Conversions 15,445

Section 1231 Assets 15,465

DEDUCTION TAX PLANNING

Itemized Deductions—Two-Tier System 15,501

Checklist of Itemized Deductions 15,515

Medical Expenses 15,525

State and Local Taxes 15,535

Charitable Contributions 15,545

Charitable Gifting 15,547

Personal Interest 15,555

Qualified Residence Interest 15,565

Investment Interest 15,575

Business Meals and Entertainment 15,585

Business and Educational Travel 15,595

Hobby Losses 15,601

Home Office Expenses 15,605

RETIREMENT PLANNING

Individual Retirement Accounts (IRAs) 15,701

Section 401(k) Plans 15,715

Retirement Plan Distributions 15,725

CHAPTER 16   PARTNERSHIPS, CORPORATIONS, AND S CORPORATIONS

CHOICE OF BUSINESS ORGANIZATION

General Considerations 16,001

Limitation of Liability 16,005

CHARACTERISTICS OF A PARTNERSHIP

Organizing a Partnership 16,101

Organization Expense & Start-Up Costs 16,109

Partner's Basis in the Partnership 16,115

Partnership Income and Deductions 16,120

Reporting Requirements 16,125

Related Parties 16,133

Contributions to the Partnership 16,141

Debts 16,149

Partnership Liabilities—Contributed Property 16,157

Basis Allocations by Partners 16,165

PARAGRAPH

Admission of a New Partner 16,171

Partnership Distributions 16,175

Sale or Exchange of Partnership Interest 16,181

Estimated Income Tax 16,187

Family Partnerships 16,195

CHARACTERISTICS OF A CORPORATION

Corporate Formation 16,215

Corporate Income, Deductions, and Credits 16,225

Charitable Contributions 16,235

Corporate Distributions 16,241

Regular Rates and Graduated Scale 16,245

Personal Service Corporations 16,250

Corporate Alternative Minimum Tax 16,255

Minimum Tax Computation 16,265

Penalty Taxes 16,275

Corporate Liquidations 16,285

S CORPORATIONS

Tax Treatment 16,301

S Corporation Election 16,315

Taxable Year 16,325

Termination of Election 16,335

Tax on S Corporation Income 16,345

Allocation of Income, Deductions, and Credits 16,355

Treatment of Losses 16,365

Treatment of Distributions 16,375

Accumulated Adjustments Account 16,385

CHAPTER 17 FEDERAL ESTATE TAX, FEDERAL GIFT TAX, AND GENERATION-SKIPPING TRANSFER TAX

IMPACT OF ECONOMIC GROWTH AND TAX RELIEF RECONCILIATION ACT OF 2001, TAX RELIEF ACT OF 2010, AND AMERICAN TAXPAYER RELIEF ACT OF 2012

ASSESSMENT OF THE 2010 TAX RELIEF ACT

LEGAL TERMS COMMON TO ESTATES AND TRUSTS

PARAGRAPH

COMPUTATION AND PAYMENT OF ESTATE TAX

Estate Tax Computation—Summary 17,001

Applicable Credit Amount 17,009

Unified Rate Schedule 17,015

Payment of Tax and Returns 17,025

Credits Against Tax 17,035

GROSS ESTATE

Property Includible in Gross Estate 17,101

CONSERVATION EASEMENT

Code Section 2031(c) Exclusion..17,105

Present and Future Interests in Property 17,109

Gifts Within Three Years of Death 17,117

Retained Life Estates 17,125

Reversions 17,133

Revocable Transfers 17,141

Annuities 17,149

Co-Ownerships of Property 17,157

Powers of Appointment 17,165

Life Insurance 17,173

Part-Sale, Part-Gift Transfers 17,175

VALUATION OF GROSS ESTATE

General Principles 17,181

Specific Properties 17,185

Listed Securities 17,187

Closely Held Stock 17,191

Buy-Sell Agreements 17,193

Special Use Valuation for Farmland and Closely Held Business Realty 17,195

DEDUCTIONS FROM THE GROSS ESTATE

Expenses, Debts, and Losses 17,201

Marital Deduction 17,217

Charitable Contributions 17,225

State Death Taxes 17,230

Disclaimers 17,255

PARAGRAPH

FEDERAL GIFT TAX

Definition of Transfers by Gift 17,301

Basis of Property Transferred by Gift 17,315

Present v. Future Interests 17,325

EXCLUSIONS

General Considerations 17,341

Marital Deduction 17,345

Charitable Deduction 17,355

Valuation of Gifts 17,365

Nontaxable Transfers 17,375

Co-Ownerships of Property 17,385

Powers of Appointment 17,395

Liability for Tax 17,405

Gift Tax Computation—Summary 17,415

GENERATION-SKIPPING TRANSFER (GST) TAX

Nature and Purpose of Tax 17,501

Overview 17,515

Taxable Events 17,525

Exemptions from Tax 17,535

Rate of Tax 17,545

Tax Computations 17,555

Payment of Tax 17,565

Credits and Deductions 17,575

CHAPTER 18   INCOME TAXATION OF TRUSTS AND ESTATES

TAXATION OF ESTATES

Decedent's Final Income Tax Return 18,001

Income and Deductions on Final Return 18,015

Federal Income Tax Concerns of an Estate 18,025

Fiduciary Responsibilities 18,035

Estate Federal Income Tax Return 18,045

TAXATION OF TRUSTS

Nature of Trusts 18,209

Trust Federal Income Tax Return 18,215

FEDERAL INCOME TAXATION SCHEME—ESTATES AND TRUSTS

Distributable Net Income (DNI) System 18,301

DNI Computations—Simple Trusts 18,325

Depreciation and Depletion Deductions 18,331

DNI Computations—Complex Trusts and Estates 18,345

Charitable Contributions—Complex Trusts and Estates 18,357

Tax Return Special Rules 18,365

Alternative Minimum Tax 18,371

Gifts, Legacies, and Bequests 18,373

Property Distributions 18,381

Termination of Estate or Trust 18,387

TAXATION OF TRUSTS—SPECIAL RULES

Multiple Trusts 18,503

Grantor Trusts 18,525

PAGE

APPENDIX

Tax Rate Schedules for 2015 .... A–1

TAX TABLE
.... T–1

GLOSSARY OF TAX TERMS
.... G–1

FINDING LISTS

Internal Revenue Code Sections Cited F–1

Private Letter Rulings Cited F–10

Regulations Sections Cited F–10

Revenue Procedures Cited F–13

Revenue Rulings Cited F–13

TABLE OF CASES
.... C–1

TOPICAL INDEX
.... I–1

Chapter

1

Introduction to Federal Taxation and Understanding the Federal Tax Law

OBJECTIVES

After completing Chapter 1, you should be able to:

1. Identify types of taxes used by federal and state governments to raise revenues.
2. Understand the methods of tax collection and the trends shown by tax collection statistics.
3. Differentiate between tax avoidance and tax evasion.
4. Recall the underlying rationale of the federal income tax and its historical development.
5. Describe the route a tax bill takes until enacted into law.
6. Define the basic tax concepts and terms of federal income taxation.

INTRODUCTION

Federal taxation is the fuel by which Americans power their "Ship of State." The tax structure which supports our federal government has gone from quill and ink records of revolutionary assessments to lightning speed computers which calculate and validate millions of income tax returns submitted by individuals and corporations. Federal taxes, in addition to the income tax, include a variety of other taxes covering estates, gifts, and customs, as well as excise taxes, and other minor categories of tax. Our governments can thus select among a variety of tax alternatives to produce the revenues required to operate national programs and carry out national policies.

Taxes are big business. Unfortunately, many business decisions are made in the United States today without regard to federal tax consequences. Individuals are concerned with personal income tax decisions and gift and estate tax decisions, while corporations concern themselves with corporate taxes, personal holding company taxes, and accumulated earnings tax decisions. Further, businesspersons must concern themselves with the choice of business entity: corporation, partnership, or S corporation. Differences in tax costs can be considerable. Advantages and disadvantages are virtually unlimited. This book presents information which is required knowledge if you make business decisions.

While most businesspersons (and many advisors) think about how to make decisions in nontax terms, the tax accountant bears the burden of introducing tax considerations. The topics presented in this book must be viewed in terms of decision-making—therefore, tax planning and tax research are of the utmost importance. Tax decisions are not made in a vacuum. Lawyers, accountants, financial managers, and a host of other experts work as a team in the decision-making process. This book is intended to serve as a guide for accounting students and for MBA students interested in gaining insight into and expertise in the tax complexities of business decision-making.

OVERVIEW

This chapter presents information on the magnitude of federal taxes collected and on taxpayer obligations. Then, a brief historical account is presented of federal tax collections prior to and after the adoption of the Sixteenth Amendment to the Constitution, which enabled Congress to levy "taxes on incomes, from whatever source derived." Following this is an introductory discussion of the federal legislative process and an analysis of the social, political, and economic rationale underlying the federal tax law. Finally, basic tax concepts are explained.

Fundamental Aspects of Federal Taxation

¶1101   ## SOURCES OF REVENUE

Types of Taxes

From the very beginning, with the ratification of the Sixteenth Amendment to the Constitution, through various Revenue Acts and many court cases, a set of tax laws has evolved that raised $2.49 trillion, net of refunds, on the 240 million tax returns processed by the IRS in 2013. This was higher than the $2.151 trillion raised in 2012. The federal government uses a number of different types of taxes to generate the cash flow it needs for operating the government. The following is a listing of the various types of federal taxes:

Income taxes	Corporations, individuals, fiduciaries
Employment taxes	Old age, survivors, disability, and hospital insurance (federal insurance contributions, self-employment insurance contributions), unemployment insurance, railroad retirement
Estate and gift taxes	Estate, gift, and generation-skipping transfers
Excise and customs taxes	Alcohol, tobacco, gasoline, other

Over the years individuals have borne the burden in the arena of tax payments. Individual taxes account for approximately 50.19 percent of total tax collections. Corporate income tax collections account for approximately 10.86 percent of total tax receipts.

Historically, Americans have been staunch supporters of the federal government's tax efforts. The rate of participation and compliance is one of the highest in the world. Realistically, the impact of estimating withholding provisions and the threat of government audits have aided in the outstanding record of the Internal Revenue Service.

Individual Income Taxes

Presently the United States government taxes income, transfers, and several transaction-type items (excise, customs, etc.). The major source of revenues is the tax on individuals (see Table 2). In 2013, individuals contributed 50.19 percent of the gross internal revenue collected. Since 1943, the U.S. has been on a pay-as-you-go system. Income taxes withheld by employers increased from $1.035 trillion in 2012 to $1.123 trillion in 2013. In 2013, 118 million individual taxpayers received a tax refund which totaled almost $312.8 billion.

Corporate Income Taxes

Corporate income taxes accounted for 10.86 percent of the total revenue collected by the U.S. government in 2013. The Tax Reform Act of 1986 reduced the top corporate income tax rate from 46 percent to 34 percent. The Revenue Reconciliation Act of 1993 raised the corporate income tax rate to 35 percent. The American Jobs Creation Act of 2004 created many business incentives. The corporate tax rate has changed from 1 percent in 1913 to a high of 52 percent between 1952 and 1962. Generally, corporations are subject to tax based on net income without regard to dividends distributed to their shareholders.

Estate and Gift Taxes

Estate and gift taxes accounted for only 0.75 percent of the total revenue collected by the government in 2013. The estate tax, as we know it today, was enacted on September 8, 1916, and is levied on the transfer of property. The gift tax was originally enacted in 1924, was repealed in 1926, and then was restored in 1932.

Excise and Customs Taxes

Excise and customs taxes are levied on transactions, not on income or wealth. Examples of excise taxes are the taxes on alcohol, tobacco, and gasoline. The government collects the tax, usually at an early stage of production. In 2013, 2.4 percent of the government's revenue, or $59.9 billion, came from excise taxes.

Customs taxes are levied on certain goods entering the country. There are several reasons why the government levies this tax but by far the most important reason is the protection of U.S. industry from foreign competition.

State and Local Taxes

Just as the federal government needs an ever-increasing amount of dollars to satisfy its requirements, so do the states and local communities. State and local taxes are also big business. The major source of revenue for state governments is the income tax and the sales tax. For local communities, the property tax is a major source of revenue. Combined state and local collections totalled over $3.4 trillion in 2011 as was reported by the U.S. Census Bureau. California collected the most in state taxes followed by New York and Texas.

Value-Added Tax

The value-added tax (VAT) is of fairly recent origin and much more popular overseas than in the United States. The concept of a VAT was first proposed by a German industrialist and government consultant, Dr. Wilhelm von Siemens, in 1918. In the next three decades much discussion took place. France was the first major country to adopt the VAT. In 1919, France instituted a general sales tax. This stayed in place until 1948, when it was replaced with a tax on production at each stage of the manufacturing process.

There are many forms of taxation, but basically all taxes can be categorized as direct taxes or indirect taxes. The federal income tax on individuals and corporations is a direct tax. Indirect taxes are those levied on producers or distributors with the expectation that these taxes will be passed on to the ultimate consumer. The VAT is an example of an indirect tax. It is merely a sales tax assessed at any or all levels of production and distribution. It is applied only on the value added to the product in an early stage of production or distribution. Notice that the VAT is a tax on products, not on business entities. The major drawback of the VAT is that it is extremely regressive.

EXAMPLE 1.1	A sweater is produced at a cost of $10. If the VAT is 5 percent, then each taxpayer, regardless of income level or ability to pay, must pay the fifty cents for VAT.

The VAT continues to be discussed as an attractive source of revenue in the United States. Each 1 percent of VAT would be expected to raise $12 billion. Even with the exclusions for food and medicine, $7.6 billion would be raised per percentage point of tax. Despite these attractions, the VAT worries many Americans. First, it is a very regressive tax. Second, there is some concern that ultimately the VAT will partially replace the personal income tax. Proponents of the VAT, however, maintain that its use would help shrink the "tax gap" (discussed at ¶1121). That is, the element of the population not currently paying taxes would have to pay a VAT tax, since it is a layered sales tax.

Flat Tax

The past several years have seen heated discussions about using a flat tax. Proponents of a flat tax point to the lower cost of administration and the ease of preparation by Americans as the major benefits. A flat tax would take an individual's total income minus an allowance for family size and apply one tax rate. This rate would apply to all individuals. There would be no deductions.

Various senators and representatives have presented proposals for consideration. A flat tax has been proposed composed of two tax forms—one for individuals and one for businesses. Their proposal would tax individuals on total income minus an allowance based on family size and then apply a 17 percent tax rate. For businesses, the tax rate would be the same 17 percent, but it would be applied against the firm's gross revenue minus costs of purchases, wages, salaries, capital equipment, structures, land, and pensions. To date, none of these proposals has been successful.

Fair Tax

The Fair Tax is a consumption tax. The proponents of the fair tax would replace the Internal Revenue Code with a consumption tax. In many respects it would resemble the sales tax that many states now collect. Proponents suggest that low income individuals would receive a rebate from the government as a way to reduce the regressive nature of the tax.

KEYSTONE PROBLEM	The federal government currently uses many forms of taxation, both direct and indirect, to raise revenue. Would it not be more effective and less burdensome just to employ a single tax? What would you consider to be a more effective and efficient system of raising revenue?

CCH Study**MATE**™
Your Personal Online Tax "Tutor"—24/7!

If you find taxes difficult, you're not alone!

Now you have CCH StudyMATE™, a personal online "tutor." With StudyMATE you can plug into online learning any time of day or night. CCH StudyMATE walks you through the most important concepts covered in your textbook using individual learning sessions designed to make learning as easy as possible.

CCH Study MATE is easy to use, and since you've bought our book, you have free access to our Fundamental Tax Topics Library for a full year! CCH StudyMATE courses are designed with web learning in mind, so you can navigate your way through them independently. They are relatively short, but each course covers a substantial amount of material—including the top concepts covered in your textbook.

These are student-centered courses with presentations that are different than those found in the text, so they give you another voice—another opportunity for concepts to sink in.

How Many Courses Do I Take?

Your instructor may want you to access all the courses in the fundamental series, you may be asked to take selective courses on certain topics, or your instructor may leave it up to you to use StudyMATE as you choose.

Access CCH Study MATE at www.cchstudymate.com

For your records, print your User ID and Password below:

User ID: _____

Password: _____

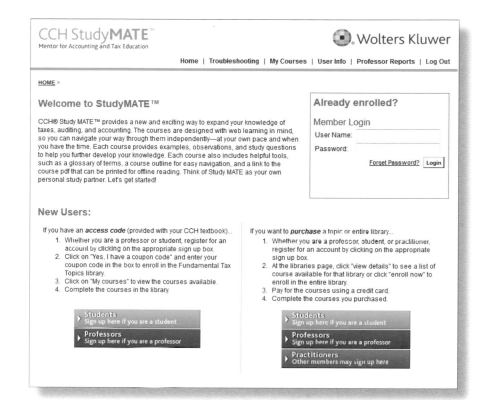

So, How Do I Get In?

Getting started is easy.

1. Go to www.cchstudymate.com and follow the instructions for New Users with an ACCESS CODE to sign up for a free account. Fill in the information on the registration page including a user ID and password of your choice.

2. Continue following the online instructions to enter your access code (provided below).

3. Click on MY COURSES to view the list of online courses, then click on the course title to begin.

ACCESS CODE:

CCHSM_15_BASIC_1_056521

Technical Support: 866-798-5897 • support@learning.net

Wolters Kluwer • 4025 West Peterson Ave. • Chicago, IL 60646-6085

Take advantage of all the CCH StudyMATE courses offered!

The Fundamental Topics library covers the most important federal tax concepts typically covered in a one- or two-semester tax course.

- Accumulated Earnings and Personal Holding Company Taxes
- Alternative Minimum Tax
- Business Deductions
- Calculating Gain or Loss Realized from a Disposition of Property
- Characterization of Gain or Loss from a Disposition of Property
- Deductions for Losses and Bad Debts
- Deductions for an Individual's Personal and Investment Expenses
- Distributions Liquidating a C Corporation
- Distributions by C Corporations to Their Shareholders
- Education Savings Plans and Other Tax Breaks for Educational Expenses
- Estate Tax
- Federal Income Taxation—An Overview
- Federal Tax Practice and Procedure
- Generation-Skipping Transfer Tax
- Gift Tax
- Gross Income
- Gross Income—Exclusions
- Income Tax Credits
- Income Taxation of Trusts, Estates, and Their Beneficiaries
- Multijurisdictional Taxation: International and State and Local Transactions
- Nonrecognition of Gain or Loss from a Disposition of Property
- Organization and Income of C Corporations
- Partnerships-Distributions to Partners and Sales of Partnership Interests
- Partnerships—Formation and Operation
- Qualified and Nonqualified Retirement Plans (Including IRAs)
- Reorganization of a C Corporation
- S Corporations
- Tax Accounting

Wolters Kluwer

¶1121 TAX COLLECTION AND PENALTIES

Returns

The Internal Revenue Service processed 240 million federal tax returns and supplementary documents in 2013—a 1.5 percent increase from the 237.3 million processed in 2012. This is in comparison to 143 million tax returns processed in 1980. It collected $2.491 trillion in 2013, a slight increase from 2012. Taxes and tax collections are indeed big business. Table 1, derived from the 1980 Annual Report of the Commissioner of the Internal Revenue Service and the 2013 Internal Revenue Service Data Book, details the magnitude of work required to support our government. Approximately 60.8 percent of all returns are filed by individuals. In 2013, individuals filed 146 million returns, for a total of approximately $1.25 trillion. In 2013, corporate collections increased to $270 billion.

Table 1. NUMBER OF RETURNS FILED BY PRINCIPAL TYPE OF RETURN
(Figures in Thousands)

Type of Return	1980	2012	2013	Increase or Decrease Between 1980 and 2013	
				Amount	Percent
Grand total	143,446	237,245	240,076	96,630	67.36
Income tax, total	107,827	182,336	185,035	77,208	71.60
Individual	93,143	146,244	145,997	52,854	56.75
Declaration of estimated tax	8,699	22,158	24,806	16,107	185.16
Fiduciary	1,877	3,461	3,733	1,856	98.88
Partnership	1,390	3,626	3,686	2,296	165.18
Corporation	2,718	6,843	6,814	4,096	150.70
Estate tax	148	27	32	(116)	(78.38)
Gift tax	216	249	313	97	44.91
Employment tax	26,499	25,590	29,958	3,459	13.05)
Exempt organizations	444	1,367	1,463	1,019	229.50
Excise tax	909	1,197	909	0	0.00
Supplemental documents	6,064	22,583	22,365	16,301	268.82

Sources: 1980 Annual Report of the Commissioner of the Internal Revenue Service and Internal Revenue Service Data Books 2012 and 2013.

Tax Collections

Tax collections have increased dramatically between 1980 and 2013. This was due in part to the growth in the economy. Table 2 gives data on tax collections from 1980, 2012, and 2013. Obviously, the increase in tax collections from 1980 to 2013 is staggering—$1,451,955,152,000. Now, notice the detail. Corporate taxes have increased 274 percent between 1980 and 2013, while individual income taxes have increased 335 percent. Estate and gift taxes have increased 189 percent in the same period. Keep these figures in mind as you read the chapters that follow.

Just as the dollar amounts have increased in tax collections, so has the number of returns filed. From 1980 to 2013, the number of corporate income tax returns increased by 150.7 percent. During the same time period, the number of individual income tax returns increased by 57 percent. The number of individuals requesting an individual income tax refund decreased slightly in 2013 to 118 million.

Table 2. GROSS INTERNAL REVENUE COLLECTIONS (net of refunds)
(Figures in Thousands)

Source	Percent of 2013 Collections	1980	2012	2013	Increase or Decrease Between 1980 and 2013	
					Amount	Percent
Grand total	100.00	$519,375,273	$2,150,891,380	$2,490,705,698	$1,971,330,425	379.56
Income taxes, total	61.05	359,927,392	1,301,267,256	1,520,555,543	1,160,628,151	322.46
Corporation	10.86	72,379,610	237,491,187	270,424,731	198,045,121	273.62
Individual	50.19	287,547,782	1,063,776,069	1,250,130,812	962,583,030	334.76
Employment taxes, total	35.79	128,330,480	780,667,222	891,471,426	763,140,946	594.67
Old-age, survivors, disability, and hospital insurance	35.26	122,486,499	768,848,709	878,283,901	755,797,402	617.05
Unemployment insurance	0.31	3,309,000	7,053,053	7,749,247	4,440,247	134.19
Railroad retirement	0.22	2,534,981	4,689,621	5,438,277	2,903,296	114.53
Estate and gift taxes, total	0.75	6,498,381	13,945,618	18,782,819	12,284,438	189.04
Excise taxes, total	2.40	24,619,021	55,011,283	59,895,910	35,276,889	143.29

Sources: 1980 Annual Report of the Commissioner of the Internal Revenue Service and Internal Revenue Service Data Books 2012 and 2013.

Tax Audits and Penalties

The U.S. tax system is a voluntary compliance tax system. The total number of federal tax returns filed in 2013 was 240,076,000, of which 145,997,000 were filed by individual taxpayers. The IRS conducted examinations of 1,558,057 returns, and on the basis of these examinations, it recommended additional tax and penalties of $37.1 billion.

Although audits of individual returns made up the bulk of the examinations (1,404,931 returns), they resulted in only $14.0 billion of the total recommended collections, while audits of corporate returns yielded $16.7 billion. Of course, audits do not always favor the IRS, as evidenced by the fact that, of the individual returns examined, 39,300 resulted in additional refunds; this amount was down from 54,000 in 2012.

Until recently, there had been an upsurge in the number of taxpayers who illegally sought, either openly or covertly, to reduce or eliminate their tax obligation. However, the IRS has responded to the challenge by taking advantage of the developing computer technology. Computers already scrutinize tax returns, check errors, and perform a number of routine, repetitive tasks with speed, efficiency, and great accuracy. The IRS continues to match almost all information returns that businesses are required to submit on magnetic media to verify that correct amounts are reported on taxpayers' returns. Information returns include W-2 Forms listing salary and 1099 Forms listing other income.

In 2013, the IRS audited over 1.4 million individual income tax returns or 1.0 percent of all individual tax returns. The percentage of returns audited was approximately the same as the previous year. Table 3 presents information on the percentage of returns audited by type of return.

For years, the audit rate for individual returns had been declining. For fiscal year 2013, the audit rate for individual returns was 1.0 percent. In FY 1997 it was 1.28 percent, and in FY 1995 it was 1.67 percent.

Table 3. PERCENTAGE OF RETURNS AUDITED

Type of Return	Percentage Audited	
	2012	2013
Individual	1.0	1.0
Partnership	0.5	0.4
Corporation	1.6	1.4
Estate	29.9	11.6
Gift	1.4	1.1
Excise	3.3	1.6
Employment	0.2	0.2

Sources: Internal Revenue Service Data Books 2012 and 2013.

Because of severe budget deficits during the late 1980s and 1990s, the personnel needed to audit the growing number of returns filed have not been added. A major reason for the decline in audit rates has been staff reduction at the IRS and the movement of IRS personnel to focus on customer service. Since the late 1980's, staff in the examinations division was reduced by over 30 percent. Table 4 graphically depicts the percentage of returns audited by the Internal Revenue Service.

Table 4. PERCENTAGE OF RETURNS AUDITED—1980—2013

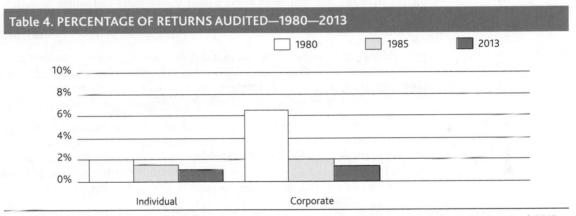

Sources: 1980 Annual Report of the Commissioner of the Internal Revenue Service and Internal Revenue Service Data Book 2013.

Naturally, for certain types of taxpayers and those with higher incomes, the probability of audit is much greater. Individuals with income of over $100,000 were most likely to be audited.

The Internal Revenue Service has acknowledged that the problem of tax evasion is indeed a serious one. The "tax gap," that is, the total revenue lost through tax evasion, has increased from $81 billion in 1981 to $345 billion in 2001 and to $450 billion in 2006. IRS officials estimate that enforcement activities along with late payments have recovered $65 billion of the tax gap for 2006 resulting in a net tax gap in 2006 of $385 billion. The IRS estimated that 61 percent of the tax gap was caused by individuals and the remainder by corporations. Today, the voluntary compliance rate is estimated by the Commissioner of Internal Revenue to be 83 to 85 percent. Each percentage point of noncompliance costs the government $26 billion in lost revenue.

The Tax Reform Act of 1986 closed many of the loopholes associated with tax shelters. Since 1988 the IRS has been using a revised audit-selection formula that is aimed at high-income returns. Further, the Tax Acts of 1986 and 1987, the Technical and Miscellaneous Revenue Act of 1988, and the Revenue Reconciliation Acts of 1989, 1990, and 1993 changed the penalties imposed on taxpayers for not complying with the tax laws.

The Improved Penalty and Compliance Act, which was incorporated into the Revenue Reconciliation Act of 1989, revamped the civil tax penalty provisions of the Internal Revenue Code. The goal was to create a fairer, less complex, and more effective penalty system. The Act made changes in the following broad areas:

1. Document and information return penalties
2. Accuracy-related penalties
3. Preparer, promoter, and protestor penalties
4. Penalties for failures to file or pay tax

¶1131

TAXPAYER OBLIGATIONS

Tax accountants, lawyers, and businesspersons, since the inception of the first federal income tax law, have concerned themselves with choosing among the various forms a transaction may take. There is an acute awareness among tax accountants that tax consequences of an action may differ depending upon procedural variations and alternative approaches to a business decision. The increasing complexity of the modern tax laws serves only to accentuate the problem.

Because of the extreme difficulty experienced in trying to differentiate between tax avoidance and tax evasion, Congress enacted, in the 1954 Internal Revenue Code, a provision which illustrates circumstances that constitute prima facie evidence of the tainted purpose. The 1986 Code contends with the problem of criminal tax evasion in Section 7201, entitled "Attempt to Evade or Defeat Tax." It reads:

> Any person who willfully attempts in any manner to evade or defeat any tax imposed by this title or the payment thereof shall, in addition to other penalties provided by law, be guilty of a felony and, upon conviction thereof, shall be fined not more than $100,000 ($500,000 in the case of a corporation), or imprisoned not more than five years, or both, together with the costs of prosecution.

The goal of every businessperson should be profit maximization. The government endorses this goal. Tax avoidance is legal and a legitimate pursuit of a business entity.

Tax Avoidance

All citizens have the prerogative to arrange their transactions and affairs in such a manner as to reduce their tax liabilities. A good businessperson is obligated to search out those transactions and to time those events which will lower the tax liability. Judge Learned Hand, in S.R. Newman, declared many years ago:

> Over and over again courts have said that there is nothing sinister in so arranging one's affairs as to keep taxes as low as possible. Everybody does so, rich or poor; and all do right, for nobody owes any public duty to pay more than the law demands: taxes are enforced extractions, not voluntary contributions. To demand more in the name of morals is mere cant. CA-2, 47-1 USTC ¶9175, 159 F.2d 848.

There is a clear demarcation between tax avoidance and tax evasion. The saving of tax dollars requires specific actions so as to avoid the tax liability prior to the time it would have occurred according to law. It requires the proper handling of affairs so that items of income are subjected to a lower tax rate than would apply if no action had been taken. In some instances, it requires the postponing of income which is subject to taxation until a time when the individual's tax bracket would be lower.

Tax Evasion

To be guilty of evading taxes, the individual must already have a tax liability. All actions must be definitely complete, and in spite of this liability, the taxpayer does not report income. The courts have ruled that it is not wrong to find a form of a transaction that does not lead to any tax liability. However, there is a legal obligation to disclose a tax liability based on completed transactions, and the refusal to report the tax liability is illegal.

The Tax Court in *Berland's Inc. of South Bend* (16 TC 182, acq., 1951-2 CB 1, Dec. 18,057) said that the purpose of tax evasion must be the "principal" purpose, and the taxpayer is not guilty of tax evasion merely because the tax consequences of the particular transaction are considered. Furthermore, the Tax Court said:

> The consideration of the tax aspects of the plan was no more than should be expected of any business bent on survival under the tax rates then current. Such consideration is only part of ordinary business prudence.

What frequently distinguishes tax avoidance from tax evasion is the intent of the taxpayer. The intent to evade tax occurs when a taxpayer knowingly misrepresents the facts. Intent is a mental process, a state of mind. A taxpayer's intent is judged by his or her actions. The taxpayer who knowingly understates income leaves evidence in the form of identifying earmarks, referred to as "badges" of fraud. Internal revenue agents are on the lookout for these badges of fraud. The more common badges are:

1. Understatement of income. The IRS considers the failure to report entire sources of income, such as tips, or specific items where similar items are included in income, such as dividends received, as an indication that there may have been an understatement of income. Other such indications include the unexplained failure to report substantial amounts of income determined by the IRS to have been

received, the concealment of bank accounts or other property, and the failure to deposit receipts to a business account contrary to normal practices.

2. Claiming of fictitious or improper deductions. To the IRS, a substantial overstatement of deductions is a badge of fraud that could warrant a further look at the taxpayer's books. Other indications of improper deductions are the inclusion of obviously unallowable items in unrelated accounts and the claiming of fictitious deductions or dependency deductions for nonexistent, deceased, or self-supporting persons.

3. Accounting irregularities. Accounting practices that are considered a badge of fraud include the keeping of two sets of books or no books, false entries, backdated or postdated documents, inadequate records, and discrepancies between book and return amounts.

4. Allocation of income. The distribution of profits to fictitious partners and the inclusion of income or deductions in the return of a related taxpayer with a lower tax rate than that of the taxpayer are indications of an intentional misstatement of taxable income.

5. Acts and conduct of the taxpayer. Aside from the improper reporting of income or deductions, a taxpayer's conduct can give the IRS reason to question the propriety of a return. For example, false statements, attempts to hinder an examination of a return, the destruction of books or records, the transfer of assets for purposes of concealment, or the consistent underreporting of income over a period of years are badges of fraud.

The presence of one or more of these badges of fraud does not in itself mean that the return is fraudulent. However, it should alert an examiner that additional probing and inquiry are necessary. Internal Revenue Manual, Sec. 4.10.

Corporate Tax Avoidance

Normally, the Commissioner and the courts accept a corporation as being distinct from its shareholders. However, if it appears that a sham transaction has taken place, then the Commissioner has grounds for taking action. Judge Learned Hand, in summarizing many cases on the subject of tax avoidance v. tax evasion, stated in *National Investors Corp. v. Hoey*:

> To be a separate jural person for purposes of taxation, a corporation must engage in some industrial, commercial, or other activity besides avoiding taxation: in other words, that the term "corporation" will be interpreted to mean a corporation which does some "business" in the ordinary meaning; and that escaping taxation is not "business" in the ordinary meaning. 44-2 USTC ¶9407, 144 F.2d 466, 467-68 (CA-2 1944).

Section 269 of the Internal Revenue Code provides the Commissioner with a very important tool in judging whether or not a corporate acquisition is tax avoidance or merely a sham. If the Commissioner feels that there is no principal purpose for the tax-free acquisition, "such deduction, credit, or other allowance" may be disallowed. The key defense by the taxpayer is to substantiate that there was indeed a "principal purpose." If there is a principal purpose, nothing stops the taxpayer from having other purposes, such as the saving of taxes. *Kershaw Mfg. Co., Inc.*, 24 TCM 228, TC Memo. 1965-44, Dec. 27,268(M).

Taxpayer's Assessment of Tax Liability

In order to decrease potential tax liability, the taxpayer must choose the action that will allow the greatest tax savings. An example of a tax savings device is investment in municipal bonds instead of corporate bonds. The interest derived from corporate bonds is taxable income, whereas the interest received from municipal bonds is tax free. In the above example, the taxpayer does not have to hide the fact that there is a lower tax liability on the profit.

When contemplating a transaction, the taxpayer makes an assessment of the tax liability. Naturally, any doubtful issues are resolved in the taxpayer's own favor. Certainly, there is nothing fraudulent about using this procedure. On the other hand, if the taxpayer knowingly overstates expenses, thereby reducing the tax liability, then the taxpayer is guilty of tax evasion.

¶1151

BRIEF HISTORY OF THE FEDERAL INCOME TAX

The origin of taxation in the United States dates back to the Constitution and, therefore, the Constitution is the ultimate source of the power to tax. Originally, the Constitution empowered Congress "to lay and collect taxes, duties, imports and excises, to pay the debts and provide for the common defense and general welfare of the United States." In granting this power, Congress also limited the power of taxation in that "all duties, imports, and excises shall be uniform throughout the United States, that direct taxes should be laid in proportion to the population." It was within these confinements that many cases tested the constitutionality of the early tax laws—a test many of the taxes did not pass. During the late 1800s, the terms "uniform" and "direct taxes" were very important concepts.

Income Tax Law of 1894

In the late 1880s, support was mounting at the state level for an income tax. In Ohio, the State Democratic Convention approved a graduated income tax in the summer of 1891. Reflecting on the mood of the country at that time, William Jennings Bryan supported an income tax as preferential to a tax on tobacco and beer which he felt would put an unfair hardship on the poor. Although this proposed tax and others like it were never passed, they encouraged others to investigate the possibilities of a federal income tax. Ultimately this led to the actual passage of the Wilson Tariff Bill of 1894. This bill was not an income tax bill; however, an amendment was attached to the bill which allowed for an income tax. The provisions of this income tax law stated that the tax would commence on January 1, 1895, and continue until January 1, 1900. It was a 2 percent tax on all "gains, profits, and income" over $4,000 "derived from any kind of property, rents, interest, dividends, or salaries, or from any profession, trade, employment, or vocation." Income was defined to include interest on all securities except federal bonds which were exempt by law of their issuance from any federal taxation. The Act also imposed a 2 percent tax on net profits of corporations but not on partnerships.

There was much criticism of this law. Concerns arose that provisions such as the $4,000 exemption made the law discriminatory against certain groups. Consequently, many cases were brought before the courts. The major point raised by opponents of the Act was whether or not such a tax on income derived from property was a "direct tax" in the sense commonly understood in the Constitution. A direct tax was held to be a tax on the land and, therefore, had to be apportioned among the states.

The Supreme Court declared the law unconstitutional in the famous *Pollock v. Farmers' Loan & Trust Co.* case, 157 U.S. 429, 15 S.Ct. 673 (1895). It characterized the income tax as a "direct tax" and stated that the Constitution provides that "no direct tax shall be laid, unless in proportion to the census or enumeration hereinbefore directed to be taken." Therefore, the Court invalidated a significant portion of the law and rendered income tax apportionment impossible. Further, the Court considered the property tax a direct tax and excise and duties taxes as indirect taxes. The Court stated, in a five-to-four decision, that a tax on real estate and on personal property is a direct tax and, therefore:

> unconstitutional and void, because not apportioned according to representation, all these sections constituting one entire scheme of taxation, are necessarily invalid.

The Court expressed, in one of its longest opinions, no opinion on whether or not the income tax provisions were unconstitutional. Thus, with this decision, the first federal income tax law since the Civil War in the United States was declared to be unconstitutional.

Corporation Excise Tax of 1909

Support for an income tax was growing even though the courts had voided all attempts made by Congress. Government was becoming more costly and new sources of revenue were essential. The Spanish American War produced a great need for funds, and many believed that an income tax was the only solution. In the Pollock decision, the Supreme Court voted five to four that the tax was unconstitutional. By late 1908, it was abundantly clear that only by passage of a constitutional amendment would the government receive the power needed to impose a federal income tax. Therefore, an amendment was passed by Congress in 1909. However, because of the length of time required to ratify a constitutional amendment, Congress simultaneously passed the Corporation Excise Tax of 1909. The Supreme Court had ruled in the Pollock case that an "excise tax" was not required to be apportioned. Further, the Court indicated in several cases that an income tax on corporations would be upheld if it were deemed an excise tax levied on corporations for the privilege of carrying on or doing business as a corporation, granted the amount of tax due was based upon the net income of the corporation.

The Tax Act of 1909 was the first Act to be upheld by the courts that taxed corporate profits. Prior to this time, corporate profits were tax free except for a short period of time during the Civil War. The 1909 Act provided that corporations would pay an annual special excise tax. This tax amounted to 1 percent on net income over $5,000 exclusive of dividends from other corporations.

As can be imagined, many influential people objected to the 1909 Act. By 1910, fifteen cases challenging the Act had reached the Supreme Court. In a unanimous decision, the Supreme Court upheld that the Tax Act of 1909 was not a direct tax, but an indirect tax and "an excise upon the particular privilege of doing business as a corporate entity."

The Revenue Act of 1909 was a tax for the privilege of doing business as a corporation, even though the assessment was on the net income of the corporation. A unanimous Supreme Court upheld the law in *Flint v. Stone Tracy Co.*, 220 U.S. 107, 31 S.Ct. 342 (1911).

When examining the differences between the 1895 law which was held to be unconstitutional and the 1909 law which was upheld as constitutional, the difference is indeed in only a few words, changing a tax upon income to a tax measured by income. Justice Day wrote the opinion for the Supreme Court and stated that the difference was "not merely nominal, but rests upon substantial difference between the mere ownership of property and the actual doing of business in a certain way."

Sixteenth Amendment and the Revenue Act of 1913

Taxation laws as we know them today derive their authority from the Sixteenth Amendment as passed by Congress on July 12, 1909. The amendment stated:

> The Congress shall have power to lay and collect taxes on incomes, from whatever source derived, without apportionment among the several States, and without regard to any census or enumeration.

Alabama became the first state to ratify the amendment in the same year that it was passed—1909. On February 25, 1913, the final vote for ratification was received.

Congress now was given the clear authority to enact a tax on income from whatever source derived. Taxes could be either direct or indirect and could be imposed without regard to any census or enumeration.

On October 3, 1913, pursuant to the power granted by the Sixteenth Amendment, Congress enacted the Revenue Act of 1913 which imposed a tax on the net income of individuals and corporations. The Revenue Act of 1913 was retroactive to March 1, 1913. This date is important for tax purposes because this is the date which is sometimes used as a basis for computing gains and losses. Simultaneous to the enactment of the Revenue Act, the Corporation Excise Tax was repealed.

The Revenue Act of 1913 serves as the basis for the income tax laws of the United States. However, it would never have been passed without its two precedents, the Income Tax Law of 1894 and the Corporation Excise Tax of 1909. These two laws laid the foundation and framework for an income tax. The Supreme Court ruling in the Pollock case made it mandatory that an amendment to the Constitution be passed to allow for a direct tax on income.

1913 to Date

Following the passage of the Sixteenth Amendment, there have been many changes in the tax law. Many of the more important changes in our federal taxing system are outlined below. Some of the data for 1916–1962 came from World Tax Series: Taxation in the United States, CCH (Commerce Clearing House), 1963, pp. 117–118.

1913 The Revenue Act of 1913—Normal tax and surtax approved. Personal exemptions established.

1916 The Revenue Act of 1916—Established the estate tax.

1917 Charitable contributions granted tax deductible status. Federal income taxes were disallowed as a tax deduction. Credit for dependents allowed for first time.

1918 Tax preferences and exemptions established. Tax credit was granted for foreign income taxes paid. Carryforward provisions adopted for net operating losses. Depletion deductions for mines and oil and gas wells were instituted. Tax-free corporate mergers and other reorganizations permitted.

1921 Capital gains rates established. Profit-sharing and pension trusts exempted from tax.

1924 Gift tax enacted to prevent avoidance of the estate tax.

1926 January 1, 1926—Gift tax repealed.

1932 Gift tax restored in more effective form.

1934 The personal exemption and exemption for dependents were made deductible in determining net income for the purpose of surtax as well as normal tax.

1935 Federal Social Security Act enacted.

1936 Mutual investment companies allowed deduction for dividends distributed by them.

1938 LIFO adopted as an acceptable inventory method.

1939 Internal Revenue Code of 1939—Set out to codify separately the Internal Revenue laws.

1942 Net operating losses were allowed to be carried back. Provisions were made or changed for medical expenses, alimony, capital gains, and a standard deduction in lieu of itemized deductions.

1943 Current Tax Payment Act—Pay-as-you-go system adopted.

1948 Marital deduction originated for estate and gift tax. Split-income treatment approved for married couples.

1950 Self-employment tax enacted.

1954 Internal Revenue Code of 1954—Successor to the 1939 Code. Completely overhauled federal tax laws. Largest piece of federal legislation enacted to date. Broad changes were made in an attempt to codify income, estate, gift, and excise tax laws along with administration and procedure rules into one document.

1962 The Revenue Act of 1962—Granted a tax credit of 7 percent for investment in Section 38 Property. Further, the concept of "depreciation recapture" was introduced.

1964 The Revenue Act of 1964—Intended to stimulate sagging economy. Largest corporate and individual tax rate reduction since the Act of 1913.

The Act extended depreciation recapture to business realty. Foreign investment income subjected to increased taxation.

1966 The Tax Adjustment Act of 1966—Suspended the 7 percent investment credit. It was reinstituted six months later.

Graduated withholding replaced flat-rate. Corporations required to pay estimated tax more quickly.

1969 The Tax Reform Act of 1969—Investments in commercial and industrial buildings were significantly affected when depreciation allowances were reduced and the recapture rules changed. Investment tax credit repealed.

1971 The Revenue Act of 1971—Restored investment credit at 7 percent.

1974 Employee Retirement Income Security Act of 1974 (ERISA)—Major changes to the entire private pension system.

1975 The Tax Reduction Act of 1975—Reduced taxes for both individuals and corporations. Changed the investment tax credit from seven to 10 percent for a two-year period.

1976 The Tax Reform Act of 1976—Established at-risk rules for tax shelters and eliminated many tax shelters. Also, the Act made extensive changes in the treatment of foreign income.

1977 The Tax Reduction and Simplification Act of 1977—Attempted to simplify the system. Established zero-bracket amount exemption deductions.

1978 The Revenue Act of 1978—Revised corporate rate structures. New structure taxes the first $100,000 of income on a graduated scale, ranging from 17 to 40 percent, and at a 46 percent rate on all taxable income over $100,000. The Act made the 10 percent investment credit permanent.

The Act also made changes to capital gains, tax shelter rules, employee benefits, and estate and gift taxes.

1978 The Energy Tax Act of 1978—Instituted a tax credit for residential energy savings.

1980 The Bankruptcy Act of 1980—Added a seventh type of tax-free reorganization, the "G" type. Clarified rules for tax treatment of bad debts.

1980 The Windfall Profit Tax Act—Excise tax levied on domestic oil.

1980 The Installment Sales Revision Act of 1980—Revised installment sales rules.

1981 Economic Recovery Tax Act (ERTA)—Largest tax cut bill ever passed. Top individual tax rates decreased from 70 to 50 percent. All property placed in service after December 31, 1980, eligible for the Accelerated Cost Recovery System (ACRS). Increased allowable contributions to Keoghs, SEPs, and other retirement systems. Permitted two-earner married couples a deduction to reduce the inequity of the "marriage penalty." Extended the investment credit to include a wider array of investments.

1982 Tax Equity and Fiscal Responsibility Act (TEFRA)—Largest revenue-raising bill ever passed. Tightened up on itemized deductions. New rules on partial liquidations and for the taxation of distributed appreciated property. Tightened up pension rules. Corporate deductions for certain tax preferences cut by 15 percent. Required that basis of depreciated property must be reduced by 50 percent of investment credit. ACRS modified for 1985 and 1986 and Federal Unemployment Tax Act (FUTA) notes increased.

1982 Technical Corrections Act of 1982—Made changes to: ACRS, the investment credit, targeted jobs credit, the credit for research costs, and incentive stock options. Made changes to the Windfall Profit Tax Act.

1982 Subchapter S Revision Act of 1982—Enacted many new provisions for S corporations.

1983 Social Security Act Amendments of 1983—Bailed out the Social Security System.

1984 Deficit Reduction Act of 1984—Composed of two parts: first, the Tax Reform Act of 1984 and second, the Spending Reduction Act of 1984. The Tax Reform Act of 1984 provided for reducing the holding period on capital gains from more than one year to more than six months, extending the ACRS recovery period for 15-year real property to 18 years, taxing interest-free loans between family members, and drastically slashing the income-averaging provisions.

1986 The Tax Reform Act of 1986—The most significant and complex tax revision in the history of this country. The scope of the changes was so comprehensive that the tax law was redesignated the Internal Revenue Code of 1986.

1987 Revenue Act of 1987—Focused primarily on business tax rules. Areas affected included accounting for long-term contracts, limitations on the use of the installment method, application of corporate tax rates to master limited partnerships, and changes in the estimated tax rules for corporations. The Act postponed for five years the reduction to 50 percent of the top estate and gift tax rate.

1988 Family Support Act of 1988—Provided for major reform in the area of modifying the principal welfare program, Aid to Families with Dependent Children (AFDC). Also included in the Act was the modification of employee business expense reimbursement rules. Beginning in 1989 additional amounts will have to be deducted as miscellaneous itemized deductions.

1988 Technical and Miscellaneous Revenue Act of 1988—TAMRA contained a number of substantive provisions. Included in the Act were the taxpayer's bill of rights, limitations on the completed-contract accounting method, and extension of the exclusions for employee-provided educational assistance and the business energy credits.

1989 P.L. 101-140. Repealed Code Sec. 89. The nondiscrimination and qualification rules for employee benefit plans were repealed. Prior law nondiscrimination rules were reinstated.

1989 Medicare Catastrophic Coverage Repeal Act of 1989—Repealed the medicare surtax retroactively.

1989 Revenue Reconciliation Act of 1989—The Act achieved a deficit reduction of about $17.8 billion and accelerated the rate of collection of withholding and payroll tax. The Act also changed the partial interest exclusion on ESOPs. Modifications were also made to the like-kind exchange rules.

1990 Revenue Reconciliation Act of 1990—The Act contained a number of significant changes, including a deficit reduction of about $40 billion in 1991. The Act also increased from two to three the number of statutory rates, 15 percent, 28 percent, and 31 percent. Also, a maximum capital gain rate of 28 percent was established.

1991 Tax Extension Act of 1991—The Act extended, for six months only, 11 tax provisions that were to expire on December 31, 1991.

1992 Energy Policy Act of 1992—The Act greatly increased the amount of employer-provided transportation benefits excludable by employees.

1993 Revenue Reconciliation Act of 1993—The Act raised the tax rates for high-income earners. Changes also were made to the AMT, passive losses, and Section 179. Corporate tax rates increased by 1 percent.

1994 Social Security Domestic Employment Reform Act of 1994—The Act raised the threshold for paying Social Security and federal unemployment taxes on domestic workers from $50 per quarter to $1,000 annually, retroactive to the beginning of 1994.

1994 General Agreement on Tariffs and Trade (GATT)—To offset the loss of revenue from the reduction in tariffs, Congress passed several tax and revenue provisions. The major revenue items were: estimated tax treatment for Code Sec. 936 and subpart F income; increased premiums for employers with underfunded pension plans; and reduced interest rates on large corporate tax refunds.

1996 Taxpayer Bill of Rights 2—The Act included more than 40 separate provisions, many of which provided useful tools for tax practitioners representing clients before the IRS.

1996 Small Business Job Protection Act—The major portion of tax law changes passed in 1996 was contained in this Act. It also contained many technical corrections. The balance of the Act was divided into four major categories: small business provisions, S corporation reform, pension simplification, and revenue-raising offsets.

1996 Health Insurance Portability and Accountability Act—The focus of this Act was on portability of health insurance. However, this Act contained tax provisions that focus on a variety of health-related issues, as well as several revenue-raising provisions unrelated to health care.

1996 Personal Responsibility and Work Opportunity Reconciliation Act—The tax impact of this Act was primarily limited to the earned income tax credit.

1997 Taxpayer Relief Act of 1997—The Act provided significant tax cuts for many taxpayers. Major features included a reduction in capital gains tax rates, expanded IRAs, educational tax incentives, estate tax relief, and a child tax credit.

1998 IRS Restructuring and Reform Act of 1998—The major intent of the Act was to rein in the Internal Revenue Service. Two of the most important provisions of the Act dealt with changing the holding period for a capital asset to be classified as long-term so as to receive the most favored capital gain rate from more than 18 months down to more than 12 months. The second important area of the Act was the "technical corrections" section, which clarified many of the key provisions in the Taxpayer Relief Act of 1997. There were over seventy technical corrections contained in the Act.

1998 Tax and Trade Relief Extension Act of 1998—This Act included extensions of several expiring tax credits through June 30, 2000. The major extensions provided for in this legislation include the research tax credit, the work opportunity credit, and the welfare-to-work credit.

1999 Tax Relief Extension Act of 1999—This Act extended the time period for which tax credits and exclusions continued to be available.

2000 FSC Repeal and Extraterritorial Income Exclusion Act of 2000; the Consolidated Appropriations Act, 2001; the Installment Tax Correction Act of 2000—The year 2000 saw the passage of three important tax bills that contain many provisions impacting taxpayers. The Community Renewal Tax Relief Act of 2000 was contained in the Consolidated Appropriations Act, 2000. This Act renewed provisions designed to enhance investment in low and moderate-income, rural and urban communities. The Act also extended for two years medical savings accounts (MSAs). Also included was a provision expanding innocent spouse relief. The Installment Tax Correction Act of 2000 reinstated the availability of the installment method of accounting for accrual basis taxpayers.

2001 Economic Growth and Tax Relief Reconciliation Act of 2001—The largest tax cut since 1981. The Economic Growth and Tax Relief Reconciliation Act of 2001 (P.L. 107-16) was estimated to provide tax savings of $1.35 trillion over the next 10 years. The Act contained over 440 Code changes and numerous phase-in and transitional rules. The wide range of changes primarily affected individuals, from cuts in marginal income tax rates to changes in contribution limits for retirement plans.

2002 The Job Creation and Worker Assistance Act of 2002 was passed in March 2002. This Act contained a number of general business incentives, special relief for New York City, individual incentives, extenders, and some technical corrections.

2003 Jobs and Growth Tax Relief Reconciliation Act of 2003—The third largest tax cut in U.S. history. The purpose of the tax bill was to jump-start the U.S. economy. The bill contained ten major provisions. Half of the provisions accelerated tax cuts originally scheduled not to take effect until 2006.

2004 Working Families Tax Relief Act of 2004—The primary focus of this $146 billion package was on offering the middle class tax relief.

2004 American Jobs Creation Act of 2004—The primary focus of this $145 billion package was on business incentives.

2005 Energy Policy Act of 2005—The $14.5 billion energy package contained incentives for oil, gas, electric, nuclear and alternative fuel industries.

2005 The Safe, Accountable, Flexible, Efficient Transportation Equity Act: A Legacy for Users—This $286.5 billion, six-year, highway and mass transit bill authorized funds for federal-aid highways, highway safety programs and transit programs.

2005 The Katrina Emergency Tax Relief Act of 2005 (KETRA)—Signed into law by President Bush on September 23, 2005. KETRA provided $6.1 billion in emergency tax relief for victims of Hurricane Katrina. Another major provision of the bill was that it provided tax incentives for charitable giving.

2005 Gulf Opportunity Zone Act of 2005—The hurricane relief act is an $8.6 billion package of tax incentives primarily aimed at the gulf region. Major provisions included creation of Gulf Opportunity (GO) Zones, fifty percent bonus depreciation related to rebuilding in the zones, expansion of Code Sec. 179 expensing for investments in the GO Zone, enhancements of low-income housing and rehabilitation credits within the zones, and expanded tax-exempt bond limits within the zones.

2006 Pension Protection Act of 2006—Provided for significant strengthening of traditional pension plans. Specific focus was on the funding rules for defined benefit plans and strengthening the reporting rules for plan administrators. Further, the Act made permanent the retirement savings enacted under the Economic Growth and Tax Relief Act of 2001.

2006 Tax Relief and Health Care Act of 2006—The Act extended a number of provisions including the higher education tuition deduction, state and local sales tax deduction, welfare to work tax credit, teacher classroom expenses and tax credits for research and development.

2007 Small Business and Work Opportunity Tax Act of 2007—Provided for incentives for small businesses together with an increase in the federal minimum wage. The Act extended the work opportunity tax credit through August 31, 2011. Further, the Act enhanced the Section 179 deduction, extending it through 2010 and indexing it for inflation.

2007 Mortgage Forgiveness Debt Relief Act of 2007—The Mortgage Forgiveness Debt Relief Act was a way of giving tax relief for debt forgiveness on mortgages and continuing the deduction for mortgage insurance payments.

2008 Economic Stimulus Act of 2008—The Act was designed to jump start the U.S. economy. The centerpiece of the Act provided for rebates to individuals reaching as high as $600 and $1,200 for married couples. Beyond the rebates to individuals, the Act also provided for $44.8 billion in business incentives. The major business incentive was the enhanced Code Section 179 expensing. It raised Code Section 179 expensing from $128,000 in 2008 to $250,000 and increased the threshold for reducing the deduction from $510,000 to $800,000.

2008 Farm and Military Acts of 2008—The Food, Conservation and Energy Act of 2008 provided benefits to farmers, ranchers and timber producers. The Military Tax Relief Bill provided benefits to members of the armed forces who are receiving combat pay, saving for retirement, or purchasing a new home.

2008 Housing Assistance Act of 2008—This Act provided first-time homebuyers with a refundable credit of 10% of the purchase of a new home up to $7,500, subject to certain phase-out rules. Furthermore, it provided taxpayers who claim the standard deduction an additional deduction up to $500 or $1,000 on a joint return for state and local property taxes. It also provided an increase for low-income housing tax credits.

2008 Emergency Economic Stabilization Act of 2008—The centerpiece of the legislation was the $700 billion which was made available to stabilize the economy. The Act also included AMT (alternative minimum tax) relief along with the extension of numerous tax provisions that were set to expire.

2009 The American Recovery and Reinvestment Act of 2009—The $789 billion new law contained nearly $300 billion in tax relief. Major provisions included: Making Work Pay Credit, enhancements to the child tax credit, a 2009 Alternative Minimum Tax (AMT) patch, many energy incentives, and extension of bonus depreciation and Section 179 expensing.

2009 Worker, Homeownership, and Business Assistance Act of 2009—The major provisions of the Act were that it extended and expanded the first-time homebuyer credit, it allowed for up to $2,400 in unemployment benefits to be tax-free in 2009, and it allowed for enhanced credits for the years 2009 and 2010 for the earned income credit and the child tax credit.

2010 The Hiring Incentives to Restore Employment Act—This bill is referred to as the HIRE Act. The HIRE Act greatly expanded Code Section 179 expensing, COBRA premium assistance extended through March 31, 2010, and an employer's payroll tax holiday and retention credit for employers hiring workers who were unemployed.

2010 Small Business Jobs Act of 2010—The bill contained several important tax provisions. The Act significantly increased the maximum expensing under Section 179 to $500,000 and increased the beginning of the phase-out range to $2 million for tax years beginning in 2010 and 2011. Also, the Act extended the 50 percent bonus first year depreciation for one year.

2010 Tax Relief, Unemployment Insurance Reauthorization, and Job Creation Act of 2010—The 2010 Tax Relief Act extended for two years the Bush-era tax cuts including the capital gains and dividend tax cuts. Further it cut payroll taxes two percentage points in 2011, placed a two-year patch on the alternative minimum tax and revived the estate tax.

2012 American Taxpayer Relief Act of 2012—The Act allows all Bush-era tax cuts to sunset after 2012 for individuals with income over $400,000 and $450,000 for couples. Also, the Act permanently patches the alternative minimum tax, increased capital gains rates to 20 percent for those individuals making over $400,000 and extended for five years the American Opportunity Tax Credit.

2014 The Tax Increase Prevention Act of 2014 was signed into law by President Obama on December 19, 2014. H.R. 5771 extends temporarily over 50 expired provisions. The law also creates Achieving a Better Life Experience (ABLE) which affords benefits for persons with disabilities.

¶1161 FEDERAL TAX LEGISLATIVE PROCESS

When reviewing the tax acts since the mid to late 1970s, it becomes obvious that tax reform is a yearly event. Tax bills are passed for numerous reasons (i.e., revenue needs, incentive for economic development, or to affect the economy). Further, each year certain provisions of the Internal Revenue Code expire and must be renewed. Tax bills in this country have not followed a uniform path. Normally, major tax legislation originates with the President sending a message to Congress. An alternative approach is for congressional initiative on a tax bill.

The Constitution requires that revenue legislation originate in the House of Representatives. Therefore, the first step is for hearings before the House of Representatives Ways and Means Committee. Many influential bodies present recommendations to this Committee—the Secretary of the Treasury, the Office of Management and Budget, etc. After meeting with various bodies, the Committee meets in executive session, and a tax bill is transmitted by means of a Committee report to the House.

The House of Representatives debates the bill usually under a "closed rule" procedure, which permits amendments to come only if approved by the Ways and Means Committee. If the bill is defeated it may be referred back to committee; if it passes, it is sent to the Senate where it is first discussed in the Senate Finance Committee.

Hearings are held by the Finance Committee which might result in amendments to the House bill. The amendments may range from insignificant to totally changing the bill. The bill is then transmitted to the whole Senate. One significant difference between the House and the Senate is that, in the Senate, any Senator may offer amendments from the floor of the Senate. After passage, if there are any differences between the House and Senate versions of the bill, it goes to the Joint Conference Committee, which is composed of ranking members of the House Ways and Means Committee (seven members) and the Senate Finance Committee (five members) for resolution. The Conference Committee version of the bill must be accepted or rejected—it cannot be changed by either the House or the Senate. Assuming passage by the House and the Senate, the bill becomes law when approved by the President. If it is vetoed, both the Senate and the House must vote affirmatively by a two-thirds majority to override the President's veto.

Exhibit 1 illustrates the sequence of events whereby a tax bill is introduced before the House Ways and Means Committee, passes through the House of Representatives, the Senate Finance Committee, and the Senate. As indicated in the final portion of Exhibit 1, if approved by the President, the tax bill will be incorporated into the Internal Revenue Code.

Exhibit 1. THE LEGISLATIVE PROCESS

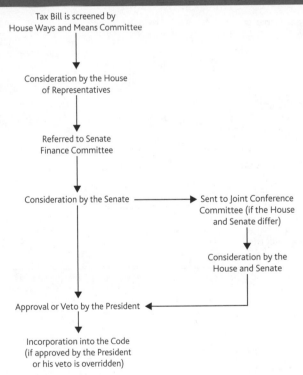

Tax Bill is screened by House Ways and Means Committee

Consideration by the House of Representatives

Referred to Senate Finance Committee

Consideration by the Senate → Sent to Joint Conference Committee (if the House and Senate differ)

Consideration by the House and Senate

Approval or Veto by the President

Incorporation into the Code (if approved by the President or his veto is overridden)

TAX REFORM

Tax reform acts are passed by Congress and signed into law by the President quite regularly. Several tax reform acts stand out because of the magnitude of the act. The year 1986 was a most interesting year for tax legislation. Both political parties, Democrats and Republicans, were "demanding" tax reform. The Treasury Department presented to President Reagan a massive tax reform plan that would impact the tax liability of most individuals and corporations. President Reagan, in his 1986 budget, called for a tax system that would be "simpler, more neutral, and more conducive to economic growth."

Tax Reform Act of 1986

The Senate passed a bill with only two rate brackets, 15 and 27 percent (28 percent was the final figure approved). Like that of the House of Representatives, their bill called for the removal of many tax deductions. One new feature added in the Senate bill was the drastic reduction in the number of people eligible for Individual Retirement Accounts (IRAs). After much debate, compromising, and political maneuvering, the Tax Reform Act of 1986 was passed and signed into law by President Reagan on October 22, 1986. The Tax Reform Act of 1986 carries the label of the most extensive overhaul of the U.S. tax code in almost 40 years, as well as the most fundamental reform of the U.S. tax structure. The scope of the changes was so comprehensive that the tax code was renamed the Internal Revenue Code of 1986.

One of the measures adopted in the Tax Reform Act of 1986 was that inflation adjustments would be provided annually for several specific items such as the standard deduction, tax brackets, personal exemption amounts, and the earned income credit. Indexing was designed to protect individuals from "bracket creep"—that is, where an individual's income increases only by the inflationary rate but the taxpayer moves into a higher tax bracket. Table 5 presents comparative data for the inflation-indexed items for 2014 and 2015.

Table 5. 2014-2015 PARTIAL COMPARISON OF TAX CHANGES FOR INDIVIDUALS

Item

Filing requirements		2014	2015
If filing status is:		A return is required if gross income was at least:	A return is required if gross income was at least:
Single	Under 65	$10,150	$10,300
	65 or older	11,700	11,850
Head of Household	Under 65	$13,050	$13,250
	65 or older	14,600	14,800
Married Filing Jointly	Both under 65	$20,300	$20,600
	One spouse 65 or older	21,500	21,850
	Both 65 or older	22,700	23,100
	Not living with spouse at end of year (or on date spouse died)	$3,950	$4,000
Married Filing Separately	All	$3,950	$4,000
Qualifying Widow(er)	Under 65	$16,350	$16,600
	65 or older	17,550	17,850

Note: Children and other dependents should see Chapter 3 for special rules.

Table 5. 2014-2015 PARTIAL COMPARISON OF TAX CHANGES FOR INDIVIDUALS—Continued

Item

Tax rates		2014			2015	
Married filing jointly or surviving spouse	10%	0	$18,150	10%	0	$18,450
	15%	$18,150	to $73,800	15%	$18,450	to $74,900
	25%	$73,800	to $148,850	25%	$74,900	to $151,200
	28%	$148,850	to $226,850	28%	$151,200	to $230,450
	33%	$226,850	to $405,100	33%	$230,450	to $411,500
	35%	$405,100	to $457,600	35%	$411,500	to $464,850
	39.6%	Over	$457,600	39.6%	Over	$464,850
Single	10%	0	to $9,075	10%	0	to $9,225
	15%	$9,075	to $36,900	15%	$9,225	to $37,450
	25%	$36,900	to $89,350	25%	$37,450	to $90,750
	28%	$89,350	to $186,350	28%	$90,750	to $189,300
	33%	$186,350	to $405,100	33%	$189,300	to $411,500
	35%	$405,100	to $406,750	35%	$411,500	to $413,200
	39.6%	Over	$406,750	39.6%	Over	$413,200
Married filing separately	10%	0	to $9,075	10%	0	to $9,225
	15%	$9,075	to $36,900	15%	$9,225	to $37,450
	25%	$36,900	to $74,425	25%	$37,450	to $75,600
	28%	$74,425	to $113,425	28%	$75,600	to $115,225
	33%	$113,425	to $202,550	33%	$115,225	to $205,750
	35%	$202,550	to $228,800	35%	$205,750	to $232,425
	39.6%	Over	$228,800	39.6%	Over	$232,425
Head of household	10%	0	to $12,950	10%	0	to $13,150
	15%	$12,950	to $49,400	15%	$13,150	to $50,200
	25%	$49,400	to $127,550	25%	$50,200	to $129,600
	28%	$127,550	to $206,600	28%	$129,600	to $209,850
	33%	$206,600	to $405,100	33%	$209,850	to $411,500
	35%	$405,100	to $432,200	35%	$411,500	to $439,000
	39.6%	Over	$432,200	39.6%	Over	$439,000
Social Security wage base	The maximum amount of taxable and creditable annual earnings subject to the Social Security and self-employment income tax is $117,000.			The maximum amount for 2015 is $118,500.		

Table 5. 2014-2015 PARTIAL COMPARISON OF TAX CHANGES FOR INDIVIDUALS—Continued

Item	2014	2015
Personal Exemptions	$3,950 in 2014, indexed for inflation; phased out at high income levels.	$4,000, indexed for inflation; reduced or eliminated at high income levels.
	Phaseout begins:	The personal exemptions for high-income taxpayers whose adjusted gross income exceeds the threshold amount tied to filing status ($309,900—joint returns or surviving spouses; $284,050—heads of households, $258,250—single taxpayers, and $154,950—married persons filing separate return) are reduced by two percent for each $2,500 by which AGI exceeds the threshold amount.
	$305,050 Joint returns or surviving spouses	
	279,650 Head of households	
	254,200 Single taxpayers	
	152,525 Married persons filing separate returns	

Standard deduction		
Basic standard deduction		
Single	$6,200	$6,300
Head of household	9,100	9,250
Married filing jointly or qualifying widow(er)	12,400	12,600
Married filing separately	6,200	6,300
Additional standard deduction for blindness or 65		
Married (filing jointly or separately) or qualifying widow(er)	$1,200	$1,250
Single or head of household	$1,550	$1,550
Dependent's standard deduction	Cannot exceed the greater of (A) $1,000 or (B) earned income plus $350 (limited to $6,200).	Cannot exceed the greater of (A) $1,050 or (B) earned income plus $350 (limited to $6,300).
Nanny Tax	Wage threshold for paying Social Security and federal unemployment taxes on domestic workers is $1,900 annually.	Wage threshold for paying Social Security and federal unemployment taxes on domestic workers is $1,900 annually.

Tax Relief, Unemployment Insurance Reauthorization, and Job Creation Act of 2010

In mid-December 2010, Congress passed and President Obama signed a tax bill that will cost approximately $857 billion. It reduces individual tax rates, provides a more generous $1,000 child tax credit, tax breaks for students, a two-year alternative minimum tax patch, a two percentage point payroll tax cut, and 100 percent bonus depreciation, enhances jobless benefits for people unemployed, and revives the estate tax for decedents dying after December 31, 2009.

American Taxpayer Relief Act of 2012

The "fiscal cliff" was averted. The Act allowed the Bush-era tax cuts to sunset for taxpayers with incomes over $400,000 and for couples with income over $450,000. Many tax breaks that were to expire were extended. It permanently patches the alternative minimum tax and provides for a maximum estate tax of 40 percent with a $5 million exclusion.

Other highlights of the Act include: raising the tax on incomes over $400,000 (individuals) and $450,000 (filing jointly) to 39.6 percent; raising the maximum capital gains tax to 20 percent; five year extension on the American Opportunity Tax Credit; and a two year extension on certain business tax items.

The Act also extends all marriage penalty relief provisions. However, the Act reinstates the limitation on itemized deductions and revives the personal exemption phaseout.

Expired Tax Provisions—Tax Extenders

At the end of 2014, President Obama signed into law the Tax Increase Prevention Act of 2014 which extended 51 tax provisions. These provisions are referred to as extenders. It is the usual procedure of Congress to pass a bill that renews the expired provisions each year. Below is a listing of the most important extenders that are covered in the book.

- Deduction for certain expenses of elementary and secondary school teachers
- Exclusion from gross income of discharge of qualified principal residence indebtedness
- Parity for exclusion from income for employer-provided mass transit and parking benefits
- Mortgage insurance premiums treated as qualified residence interest
- Deduction of State and local general sales taxes
- Above-the-line deduction for qualified tuition and related expenses
- Tax-free distributions from individual retirement lpans for charitable purposes
- Research credit
- Work opportunity tax credit
- 15-year straight-line cost recovery for qualified leasehold improvements, qualified restaurant building and improvements, and qualified retail improvements
- Bonus depreciation
- Increased expensing limitations and treatment of certain real property as section 179 property
- Temporary exclusion of 100 percent of gain on certain small business stock
- Basis adjustment to stock of S corporations making charitable contributions of property
- Reduction in S corporation recognition period for built-in gains tax

Underlying Rationale of the Federal Income Tax

¶1171

OBJECTIVES OF THE TAX LAW

The federal income tax is comprised of a complicated and continually evolving blend of legislative provisions, administrative pronouncements, and judicial decisions. The primary purpose of the tax law is obviously to raise revenue, but social, political, and economic objectives are also extremely important. These various objectives, which frequently work at cross-purposes with the revenue raising objective of the law, must be examined and understood to gain an appreciation of the rationale underlying the immense multipurpose body of law known as the federal income tax.

It is easy to criticize the entire tax law for being too complex. However, any time one law attempts to raise revenue and achieve a variety of social, political, and economic objectives, while simultaneously attempting to be equitable to all income levels and administratively feasible for the government to enforce, it cannot avoid being complex.

Tax loopholes are frequently attacked as being counterproductive to the revenue raising objective of the Treasury because they cost the U.S. government billions of dollars in lost revenue. However, some of these so-called loopholes can be thought of as tax incentives, enacted by Congress to encourage certain types of investment, or to achieve specified social, economic, or political objectives.

For example, the tax law provides that interest from municipal bonds is generally excluded from gross income, while interest received from all other sources, including savings accounts and corporate obligations, is subject to taxation. The municipal bond provision thus offers excellent tax benefits for individuals with available resources to invest, but these bonds typically provide a lower yield than corporate obligations.

Primarily because of this tax benefit, municipal bonds are a popular type of investment for wealthy taxpayers. To better evaluate the criticism that municipal bonds are a tax loophole, the probable tax consequences of this type of investment can be examined in the case of a taxpayer in the 39.6 percent marginal tax bracket.

EXAMPLE 1.2

Cliff, a 39.6% bracket taxpayer, has $50,000 available to invest. After evaluating the pros and cons of stocks, bonds, money market certificates, and other types of investments, his decision is limited to the following two choices:

		Freemont	Data-Search
Freemont Highway municipal bonds, rate of interest			9%
Data-Search Inc., corporate bonds, rate of interest			12%
Interest income (before taxes)		$4,500	$6,000
Income taxes		0	2,376
Yield (after taxes)		$4,500	$3,624

Result. Cliff will select the Freemont municipal bonds. Even with a lower rate of interest than the corporate obligations, Freemont provides a larger after-tax yield.

A common but simplistic criticism of this tax provision is that the wealthy individual has used a loophole to avoid $1,782 of taxes ($4,500 interest × 39.6 percent tax rate), thereby depriving the U.S. government of a corresponding amount of revenue. However, this criticism must be weighed against the underlying purpose of the municipal bond provision which is encouraging taxpayers to invest in state and local obligations and allowing the various municipalities to compete for resources in the bond market at a lower rate of interest than corporate bonds.

¶1175

ECONOMIC FACTORS

Over the years, numerous provisions of the tax law have been employed to help stimulate the economy, to encourage capital investment, or to direct resources to selected business activities. Perhaps the most well-known provision of the tax law, designed to serve as a stimulus to the economy, was the investment tax credit. This credit, which served to encourage investment in qualified property, primarily tangible personal property used in a trade or business, had been suspended for a period of time, repealed, reinstated, and again repealed.

Similar to its use of the investment credit, Congress has used depreciation write-offs as a means of controlling the economy. Viewed as a popular stimulus for business investment is the tax benefit resulting from the accelerated cost recovery methods of depreciation. Additionally, the related election to expense allows the taxpayer to deduct as much as $25,000 (in 2015) of the cost of qualifying property in the year of purchase. However, where the cost of qualified property placed in service during the year exceeds $200,000, the $25,000 ceiling is reduced by the amount of such excess. Prior law allowed taxpayers to deduct as much as $500,000 (in 2014). Notice the drop from up to $500,000 in 2014 to a maximum of $25,000 in 2015. This is indeed one of the "tax extenders" taxpayers are watching closely.

Various other tax provisions have been employed to help stimulate selected industries. Thus, unique tax benefits, such as the provisions for percentage depletion, apply to the mining of natural resources. Correspondingly, farming activities benefit from special elections to expense rather than capitalize soil and water conservation expenditures under an approved conservation plan.

Small business investment has been encouraged by various provisions. For example, certain types of small businesses may elect to file as an S corporation, which essentially provides the limited liability protection of corporate status, while treating most items of income as if the entity were a partnership. Correspondingly, a special rule allows ordinary loss treatment for small business stock.

Even the tax rate structure for regular corporations encourages small business. The current corporate tax brackets are as follows:

Taxable Income					
Over	But not over:	Pay	+	%	of Excess over:
$ 0	$ 50,000	$ 0		15	$ 0
50,000	75,000	7,500		25	50,000
75,000	100,000	13,750		34	75,000
100,000	335,000	22,250		39	100,000
335,000	10,000,000	113,900		34	335,000
10,000,000	15,000,000	3,400,000		35	10,000,000
15,000,000	18,333,333	5,150,000		38	15,000,000
18,333,333	—	6,416,667		35	18,333,333

An additional 5 percent rate is incorporated into the rate schedule above in order to phase out benefits of the graduated rates up to 34 percent. Thus, the graduated rate benefits are phased out between $100,000 and $335,000 of taxable income by increasing the maximum 34 percent rate to 39 percent. Similarly, to phase out the benefit of the 34 percent bracket, the tax rate on income between $15,000,000 and $18,333,333 increases from the maximum rate of 35 percent to 38 percent.

¶1181   SOCIAL FACTORS

Numerous tax provisions can best be explained in light of their underlying social objectives. For example, premiums paid by an employer on group-term insurance plans are not treated as additional compensation to the employees. This provision encourages business investment in group-term insurance and provides benefits to the family of a deceased employee. Also, social considerations provide the rationale for excluding employer-paid premiums on accident and health plans or the premiums on medical benefit plans from an employee's gross income.

Deferred compensation plans allow an individual to defer taxation on current income until retirement. The preferential tax treatment is an attempt to encourage private retirement plans to supplement the Social Security benefits. Other socially motivated tax provisions include the deduction for charitable contributions, the child care credit for working parents, and the credit for the elderly.

Frequently, social considerations help to explain a tax provision that discourages certain types of activities. For example, even though an individual may have incurred a fine or a penalty while engaged in a regular business activity, no deduction is allowed for this type of expenditure. The basis underlying this Congressional policy is that by allowing such a deduction, the law would be implicitly condoning and encouraging such activities. Correspondingly, bribes to government officials and illegal kickbacks or rebates are not deductible, even if related to the active conduct of one's trade or business.

¶1185   POLITICAL FACTORS

Since the tax law is created by Congress, and Congress consists of several hundred elected officials, political factors play a major role in the development of tax legislation. Special interest groups frequently seek to influence tax legislation, while Congressmen themselves are often likely to introduce legislation which would be of particular benefit to their own district or, perhaps, to selected constituents. Of course, special interest legislation does invite widespread criticism if it does not also serve a useful economic or social objective.

As with the economic and social objectives, many politically inspired provisions have been designed in a negative context to discourage certain types of activities. Thus, provisions such as the alternative minimum tax, which imposes an alternative tax rate on taxable income increased by tax preference items, the limitation on investment interest expense, or the accumulated earnings restrictions on corporations can be explained on this basis.

¶1187   TAX POLICY AND REFORM MEASURES

If there has been a trend through the years in tax statutes, it has been toward reform. The word "reform" itself first appeared in the popular name of the tax act entitled Tax Reform Act of 1969, but the concept of reform had begun to take shape long before and the enactment of reform measures has continued unabated through the years.

During the later part of the 1980s, various changes in the tax law, especially the passage of the Tax Reform Act of 1986, have resulted in the most dramatic tax modifications in tax policy since the enactment of the Internal Revenue Code of 1913. For the first time in 73 years, Congress attempted to address the broad public-policy implications of the entire tax law. In undertaking the revision of 1986, Congress sorted through a massive panorama of loopholes, inequities, and antiquated provisions and eliminated provisions that had lost much of their original social, political, or economic purpose.

Clearly, the tax policy implications of the 1986 revision will be under examination for some time to come. A major impact can be expected on the manner in which individuals and businesses save, invest, earn, and spend their money. For example, with the curtailment of the deduction for contributions to individual retirement accounts (IRAs), high-yield securities such as dividend-paying blue chip stocks, corporate bonds, and "municipals" might become more attractive investments than growth stocks. In fact, many wage earners may find it advantageous to pay taxes on their entire salary, rather than investing in a deferred compensation plan if they anticipate future increases in their marginal tax rates. Correspondingly, with the elimination of the consumer interest deduction, many individuals may shift to making cash purchases instead of incurring nondeductible obligations. Of course, some homeowners may be tempted to circumvent these restrictive provisions by using home equity loans to finance consumer purchases.

The Taxpayer Relief Act of 1997 cut taxes in a fashion that had not been seen since 1981. The reduction of capital gains tax rates will have a significant impact on investment strategies.

The student of tax law can anticipate frequent if not annual changes to the way individuals and businesses are taxed. The source of tax revenue to finance the operation of the federal government during the next decade will be a hotly debated issue. Some tax policymakers will promote new taxation schemes, such as a consumption tax, while others will advocate a tax policy that is revenue-neutral and neutral as to its impact on various income groups.

Basic Tax Concepts

¶1195   ESSENTIAL TAX TERMS DEFINED

When studying federal income taxation, it is important to keep in mind several basic tax concepts. By understanding these basic concepts unique to federal taxation, the course will be more interesting and meaningful. Because some of the terms set out below have definitions peculiar to income taxation, it is advisable that they be carefully examined before proceeding to the discussion of specific topics. Refer to the Glossary of Tax Terms in the back of the book for a comprehensive listing of tax terms discussed throughout the text.

Accrual basis of accounting

The accrual basis is distinguished from the cash basis. On the accrual basis, income is accounted for as and when it is earned, whether or not it has been collected. Expenses are deducted when they are incurred, whether or not paid in the same period. In determining when the expenses of an accrual-basis taxpayer are incurred, the all-events test is applied. Such test provides that the expenses are deductible in the year in which all of the events have occurred that determine the fact of liability and the amount of the liability can be determined with reasonable accuracy. Generally, all of the events that establish liability for an amount, for the purpose of determining whether such amount has been incurred, are treated as not occurring any earlier than the time that economic performance occurs.

Assignment of income doctrine

The assignment of income by an individual who retains the right of ownership to the property has generally proved ineffective as a tax-shifting procedure. For the assignment to be effective, a gift of the property would be necessary. For example, Ben is preparing to attend Major State College. As a means of paying for room and board, his father assigns to Ben his salary. This is an invalid assignment of income and Ben's father would be liable for the tax. In *Lucas v. Earl*, 2 USTC ¶496, 281 U.S. 111-115, 50 S.Ct. 241 (1930), the Supreme Court ruled that the government could "tax salaries to those who earned them and provide that the tax could not be escaped by anticipatory arrangements and contracts however skillfully devised to prevent the salary when paid from vesting even for a second in the man who earned it." Also, in this case the Court stated that "no distinction can be taken according to the motives leading to the arrangement by which the fruits are attributed to a different tree from that on which they grew."

Basis

The basis of property is the cost of such property. It usually means the amount of cash paid for the property and the fair market value of other property provided in the transaction.

EXAMPLE 1.3	An individual paid cash of $20,000 for an automobile and assumed a $7,500 loan on the car; thus, the basis in the automobile is $27,500.

EXAMPLE 1.4

An individual paid $500,000 for a tract of land and a building. Purchase commissions, legal and recording fees, surveys, transfer taxes, title insurance, and charges for installation of utilities amounted to $70,000. The basis of the property would be $570,000. Any amounts owed by the seller and assumed by the buyer are included in the basis of the property.

The definition and the determination of "basis" are of utmost importance because it is that figure which is usually used for depreciation and the determination of gain or loss. If property was acquired by gift, inheritance, or in exchange for other property, special rules for finding its basis apply.

Business purpose

When a transaction occurs it must be grounded in a business purpose other than tax avoidance. Tax avoidance is not a proper motive for being in business. The concept of business purpose was originally set forth in *Gregory v. Helvering*, 35-1 USTC ¶9043, 293 U.S. 465, 55 S.Ct. 266 (1935). In this case, the Supreme Court ruled that a transaction aiming at tax-free status had no business purpose. Further, the Court stated that merely transferring assets from one corporation to another under a plan which can be associated with neither firm was invalid. This was merely a series of legal transactions that when viewed by the Court in its entirety had no business purpose.

Capital asset

Everything owned and used for personal purposes, pleasure, or investment is a capital asset. Examples of capital assets are stocks, bonds, a residence, household furnishings, a pleasure automobile, gems and jewelry, gold, silver, etc. Capital assets do not include inventory, accounts or notes receivable, depreciable property, real property, works created by personal efforts (copyrights), and U.S. publications.

Cash basis

The cash basis is one of the two principal recognized methods of accounting. It must be used by all taxpayers who do not keep books. As to all other taxpayers (except corporations, certain partnerships, and tax-exempt trusts) it is elective, except that it may not be used if inventories are necessary in order to reflect income. On the cash basis, income is reported only as it is received, in money or other property having a fair market value, and expenses are deductible only in the year that they are paid.

Claim of right

The term claim of right asks whether cash or property received by an individual to which the individual does not have full claim and which the individual might have to return in the future must be included in income. The question here is whether the taxpayer must report the income when received or wait until the taxpayer has full right to it. In *North American Oil Consolidated v. Burnet*, 3 USTC ¶943, 286 U.S. 417 (1932), the Supreme Court resolved the question by stating that amounts received by an individual under a claim of right must be included in gross income even though the individual might have to refund the amount at a later time.

Conduits

Some entities are not tax paying. They pass through their income (loss) to owners (beneficiaries). A partnership is an example of a conduit. Partnerships do not pay taxes; they merely report the partnership's taxable income or losses. The income (loss) flows directly to the partners. However, partnerships do compute partnership taxable income. Other types of conduits are grantor trusts and S corporations.

Constructive-receipt doctrine

When a cash-basis individual receives income, or it is credited to an account the individual may draw upon, or it is set aside for the individual, the courts have ruled that the individual has constructively received the income. This concept was developed to stop taxpayers from choosing the year in which to recognize income. Once an individual has an absolute right to the income, it must be recognized. A good example of the constructive receipt doctrine is interest earned on a bank account. If interest is credited to the taxpayer's account, it is of no consequence that the taxpayer does not withdraw the money. The day the interest is credited to the account is the day the taxpayer must include the amount in income.

Entity

Generally, for tax purposes there are four types of entities: individuals, corporations, trusts, and estates. Each entity determines its own tax and files its own tax return. Each tax entity has its specific rules to follow for the determination of taxable income. Basically the concept of "entity" answers the question "Who is the taxpayer?" Note that partnerships were not in the list of entities. For tax purposes, partnerships are not tax-paying entities. The income (loss) flows directly to the partners.

Gross income

Gross income, for income tax purposes, refers to all income that is taxable. The law enumerates specific items of income that are not to be included in gross income and, therefore, are nontaxable. With these exceptions, all income is includible in gross income.

Holding period

The holding period of property is the length of time that the property has been held by the taxpayer, or the length of time that the taxpayer is treated for income tax purposes as having held it. The term is most important for income tax purposes as it relates to capital gains transactions. Whether capital gain or loss is short or long term depends on whether the asset sold or exchanged has been held by the taxpayer for more than 12 months.

Income

The fundamental concept of income is set forth in the Sixteenth Amendment—"incomes, from whatever source derived." It is the gain derived from capital, labor, or both. For tax purposes the term "income" is not used alone. The most common usages are gross income, adjusted gross income, and taxable income.

Income-shifting

Income-shifting is the transfer of income from one family member to another who is subject to a lower tax rate or the selection of a form of business that decreases the tax liability for its owners.

Pay-as-you-go tax system

The American tax system is often referred to as a pay-as-you-go tax system. Much of the federal government's tax collections come from withholdings and estimated taxes. The various types of taxpayers pay tax throughout the year, not just at year-end. The United States has been on a pay-as-you-go system since 1943.

Realized v. recognized gain or loss

A gain or loss is realized when a transaction is completed. However, not all realized gains and losses are taxed (recognized). A recognized gain or loss occurs when a taxpayer is obligated to pay tax on a completed transaction.

Substance v. form

Individuals should arrange their financial transactions in a manner that will minimize their tax liability. If a transaction is all it purports to be and not merely a transaction to avoid taxes, then it is valid. If the transaction is solely to avoid taxes and there is no business purpose to the transaction, then it is invalid. The fact that a taxpayer uses one form of transaction rather than another to minimize taxes does not invalidate the transaction. A good example of when substance v. form is a significant issue is in the area of leases. Payments under a lease are tax deductible. Payments under a purchase agreement are not tax deductible. Therefore, it is of utmost importance to determine the true "substance" of this type of transaction. Questions to be asked might include: Do any equity rights transfer to the lessee at the end of the lease period? May the lessee buy the property at a nominal purchase price? With a lease transaction it is immaterial that the parties refer to the transaction as a lease. The true substance of the transaction controls over the form.

Tax benefit rule

A recovery is includible in income only to the extent that the deduction reduced tax in any prior year by any amount. Therefore, where a deduction reduced taxable income but did not reduce tax, the recovery amount is excludable from income. This rule applies to both corporate and noncorporate taxpayers.

Taxable income

Taxable income for a corporation is gross income minus all deductions allowable, including special deductions such as the one for dividends received. Taxable income for individuals who itemize deductions is equal to adjusted gross income minus personal exemptions, minus the greater of itemized deductions or the standard deduction amount. For taxpayers who do not itemize, taxable income is adjusted gross income minus personal exemptions minus the standard deduction.

Wherewithal to pay

The concept that the taxpayer should be taxed on a transaction when he or she has the means to pay the tax. For example, a taxpayer owns property that is increasing in value. The IRS does not tax the increased value until the taxpayer sells the property. At the time of sale, the taxpayer has the wherewithal to pay.

SUMMARY

- Taxes are indeed big business. The Internal Revenue Service collected $2,490,705,698,000 in 2013.
- Individuals contributed over 50.19 percent of all taxes raised by the IRS.
- Corporations contributed approximately 10.86 percent of all taxes raised by the IRS.
- A basic understanding of tax terminology will help business leaders run their corporations.

QUESTIONS

1. Clearly, individuals are carrying a much heavier tax burden than corporations. Is this justified?

2. Some economists have argued that corporate taxes should be eliminated and only individuals should be taxed. Explain.

3. Discuss excise tax when used as a measure for social control (i.e., tax on alcohol and gasoline).

4. Why is the value-added tax (VAT) considered regressive?

5. How might the VAT be used to balance the budget?

6. What is the test which distinguishes between tax avoidance and tax evasion?

7. If your interest is in tax avoidance, name several types of investments that will lower your tax liability.

8. "The tax evader is a criminal." Support or refute this statement.

9. Discuss the badges of fraud.

10. What is meant by the term "tax gap"?

11. Why is income-shifting considered such a major tax planning concept?

12. What was the constitutional impediment to income taxation prior to the Sixteenth Amendment?

13. The federal taxing system has tried to reflect changes in society and lifestyles. Give three examples.

14. What was the purpose of the Sixteenth Amendment?

15. Of what importance is the date March 1, 1913?

16. Where must revenue legislation originate?

17. Which committees of Congress are responsible for revenue legislation?

18. What is the purpose of the Joint Conference Committee?

PROBLEMS

19. The legislative process of a tax bill begins with the:
    a. House Ways and Means Committee
    b. President
    c. Senate Finance Committee
    d. Any of the above

20. The Sixteenth Amendment granted Congress the right to:
    a. Create progressive tax rates
    b. Create a value-added tax
    c. Tax income from whatever source derived
    d. Impose a national property tax

21. The value-added tax has great appeal to politicians because:
    a. It has the potential to raise large sums of money.
    b. It taxes the rich and not the poor.
    c. It is progressive in nature.
    d. All of the above.

22. An attractive characteristic of the personal income tax is:
    a. It does not tax the poor.
    b. It is equitable.
    c. It is free from loopholes.
    d. It has the ability to raise a considerable amount of money.

23. The Tax Reform Act of 1986:
    a. Amended the Internal Revenue Code of 1954
    b. Replaced the Internal Revenue Code of 1954 with the Internal Revenue Code of 1986
    c. Replaced the Internal Revenue Code of 1954 with the Internal Revenue Code of 1987
    d. Was found to be unconstitutional by the Supreme Court in 1987

24. The American Recovery and Reinvestment Act of 2009 did all of the following except:
    a. Enhanced the child care credit
    b. Expanded energy incentives
    c. Created a homebuyer credit
    d. Lowered personal income tax rates for the wealthy

25. When approving a tax bill and there are differences between the House and Senate versions, the differences are resolved by the:
    a. President
    b. Speaker of the House
    c. President of the Senate
    d. Joint Conference Committee

26. Net capital gains are:
    a. Taxed at a maximum rate of 31 percent.
    b. Taxed at a maximum rate of 28 percent.
    c. Taxed at a maximum rate of 20 percent
    d. Taxed at a maximum rate of 15 percent.

27. The American Taxpayer Relief Act of 2012 did all of the following except:
    a. Permanently patched the Alternative Minimum Tax
    b. Sunset the Bush-era tax cuts
    c. Installed a maximum 20 percent capital gains tax rate
    d. Extended the American Opportunity Tax Credit

28. Which item listed below is not a capital asset?
    a. Stocks
    b. Pleasure automobile
    c. Bonds
    d. Depreciable property

29. Major features of conduits are:
    a. Pass through their income to owners
    b. Need not file income tax returns
    c. Need not pay taxes
    d. Both (a) and (c) above

30. What are several major provisions of the Emergency Economic Stabilization Act of 2008?

31. **Research Problem.** The following case highlights the right of the taxpayer to select among legitimate business alternatives in order to avoid taxes. Read the case and prepare a written brief.

Peterson & Pegau Baking Co., 2 BTA 637 (1925), Dec. 775.

Chapter

2

Tax Research, Practice, and Procedure

OBJECTIVES

After completing Chapter 2, you should be able to:

1. Identify the primary authoritative sources of the tax law and understand the relative weight of these authorities.
2. Explain the role of the court system as a forum for both the taxpayer and the government.
3. Develop a familiarity with the various forms of judicial citations.
4. Understand the general organization of a loose-leaf tax service and the importance of a citator service and other types of secondary reference materials.
5. Describe the organization of the Internal Revenue Service and selected rules relating to practice before the IRS.
6. Discuss the examination of returns, including correspondence examinations, office examinations, and field examinations.
7. Explain the appeals process, both within the IRS and through the court system.
8. Understand the possible communications between the IRS and taxpayers, including private rulings, determination letters, and technical advice.
9. Describe some of the more common penalties to which taxpayers and tax preparers might be subject.
10. Understand ethics as related to the tax practitioner.

OVERVIEW

To the general public, the tax practitioner is often viewed simply as a preparer of tax returns. However, from a broader, more professional perspective, tax practice also involves extensive research, creative tax planning, and effective representation of clients before the audit or appellate divisions of the Internal Revenue Service.

Tax research is the process whereby one systematically searches for the answer to a tax question, using the various primary and secondary sources of tax-related information. This involves reviewing and evaluating appropriate Internal Revenue Code sections, Treasury Regulations, Internal Revenue Service Rulings, and court decisions. Research into this voluminous material is typically facilitated by the use of one of the loose-leaf tax services, which are organized and cross-referenced in such a manner as to assist the researcher in the confusing trek through the overwhelming mass of authoritative data. Also, due to rapid technological advances made in computer-assisted tax research, the researcher may access the most complete and up-to-date authoritative data with online tax research services.

The tax specialist needs to understand the organizational structure of the IRS and its administrative procedures to provide fully informed tax consulting services to taxpayers involved in disputes with the IRS. Thus, this chapter includes a discussion of the internal organization of the IRS and how its various administrative groups function, the rules relating to practice before the IRS, and the procedures for examination of returns, including service center examinations, office examinations, and field examinations.

What actions can a taxpayer take if there is an adverse decision by the tax auditor or revenue agent? To provide an answer to this question, this chapter details and explains the appeals process, both within the IRS and through the court system. Another approach available to the taxpayer is the right to request advice from the IRS on the tax consequences of a particular transaction. This chapter discusses the various communications between the IRS and taxpayers, including private letter rulings, determination letters, and technical advice.

Some of the more common penalties to which taxpayers and tax preparers might be subject are also discussed. Tax practitioners should be familiar with the code of professional ethics of their profession since a violation of these standards might mean that "due care" has not been exercised and the practitioner might be subject to charges of negligence.

Tax Reference Materials

¶2001 ## CLASSIFICATION OF MATERIALS

Tax reference materials are usually classified as primary "authoritative" sources or secondary "reference" sources. Primary source materials include the Internal Revenue Code (Statutory Authority), Treasury Regulations and Internal Revenue Service Rulings (Administrative Authority), and the various decisions of the trial courts and the appellate courts (Judicial Authority).

Secondary reference materials consist primarily of the various loose-leaf tax reference services. Additional secondary materials include periodicals, textbooks and treatises, published papers from tax institutes and symposia, and newsletters.

Reminder. While the editorial opinions included in the secondary reference materials are extremely knowledgeable and comprehensive, neither the IRS nor the courts will afford any authoritative weight to these opinions. One exception is Mertens, *Law of Federal Income Taxation*. This tax service is often quoted in judicial decisions.

Both primary and secondary sources can be accessed through one of the computer-assisted research services. These electronic data bases are updated daily and contain many source documents not normally found in the traditional tax library.

Primary Source Materials

¶2021 ## STATUTORY AUTHORITY

Statutory authority is primarily the Internal Revenue Code, but it also includes the U.S. constitution and tax treaties. The authority of the U.S. government to raise revenue through a federal income tax is derived from the Sixteenth Amendment to the Constitution. Following ratification of this Amendment, the federal income tax law was enacted on October 3, 1913, and was made retroactive to March 1, 1913. Various other revenue acts were soon enacted. From these provisions, a loose and disconnected body of tax law emerged, making it virtually impossible to systematically engage in tax research. Accordingly, to facilitate a convenient form of organization, the various revenue acts that were legislated between 1913 and 1939 were codified into Title 26 of the United States Code, known as the Internal Revenue Code of 1939.

In subsequent years, with the growing complexity of the tax law, the Code was revised and rewritten as the Internal Revenue Code of 1954. During the next thirty-two years numerous tax laws were incorporated as amendments into the 1954 Code. Accordingly, the Economic Recovery Tax Act of 1981 (ERTA), the Tax Equity and Fiscal Responsibility Act of 1982 (TEFRA), and the Tax Reform Act of 1984 were included as part of the Internal Revenue Code of 1954, as amended. However, in 1986, as a result of the sweeping changes made by the Tax Reform Act of 1986, Congress changed the name of the tax law to the Internal Revenue Code of 1986.

Organization of the Code

The Internal Revenue Code of 1986 is comprised of nine subtitles (A-I), each consisting of individual, consecutively numbered chapters (1-98). The subtitles most commonly encountered by the tax practitioner that form the basis of this book are Subtitle A, "Income Taxes," including Chapters 1–6, and Subtitle B, "Estate and Gift Taxes," including Chapters 11–13. The remaining subtitles relate to topics such as employment taxes, excise taxes, alcohol and tobacco taxes, etc. Portions of Subtitle F, "Procedure and Administration," including Chapters 61–80, are also examined in this text.

The major portion of the Code dealing with federal income tax is located in Chapter 1 of Subtitle A. This extremely important Chapter, entitled "Normal Taxes and Surtaxes," is further divided into Subchapters (A–Y), and each Subchapter is then generally divided into parts and subparts, which are then divided into sections. These sections are typically referred to as "Code Sections."

The following exhibit (Exhibit 1) provides a Table of Contents for Chapter 1 of Subtitle A of the Internal Revenue Code of 1986.

Exhibit 1. INTERNAL REVENUE CODE OF 1986—SELECTED TABLE OF CONTENTS
Subtitle A—Income Taxes
Chapter 1—Normal Taxes and Surtaxes

Subchapter		Beginning Section Number
A	Determination of Tax Liability	1
B	Computation of Taxable Income	61
C	Corporate Distributions and Adjustments	301
D	Deferred Compensation, Etc.	401
E	Accounting Periods and Methods of Accounting	441
F	Exempt Organizations	501
G	Corporations Used to Avoid Income Tax on Shareholders	531
H	Banking Institutions	581
I	Natural Resources	611
J	Estates, Trusts, Beneficiaries, and Decedents	641
K	Partners and Partnerships	701
L	Insurance Companies	801
M	Regulated Investment Companies and Real Estate Investment Trusts	851
N	Tax Based on Income from Sources Within or Without the United States	861
O	Gain or Loss on Disposition of Property	1001
P	Capital Gains and Losses	1201
Q	Readjustment of Tax Between Years and Special Limitations	1301
S	Subchapter S: Tax Treatment of S Corporations and Their Shareholders	1361
T	Cooperatives and Their Patrons	1381
U	Designation and Treatment of Empowerment Zones, Enterprise Communities, and Rural Development Investment Areas	1391
V	Title 11 Cases	1398
W	District of Columbia Enterprise Zone	1400
X	Renewal Communities	1400E
Y	Short-Term Regional Benefits	1400L

Citing the Code

Code Sections, particularly those found within Chapter 1 of Subtitle A, are cited by detailed reference to section, subsection, paragraph, and subparagraph. On occasion, the reference is even broken down to inferior subdivisions, such as a clause.

For example, Section 453(e)(3)(A)(i) might serve as an illustration.

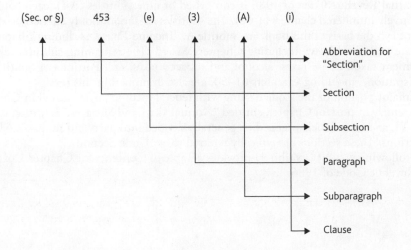

Throughout this text, references to Code Sections are in the form explained above. Unless otherwise noted, references to Code Sections relate to the Internal Revenue Code of 1986. References to the 1939 or 1954 Code are specifically noted.

Congressional Committee Reports

Congressional Committee Reports are the minutes or official statements made by members of the House Ways and Means Committee, Senate Finance Committee, and Conference Committee on their intention in passing a specific piece of legislation. Unlike Treasury Regulations, Revenue Rulings, and Revenue Procedures issued by the IRS that are not binding on the courts, congressional intent expressed in Committee Reports very often is binding as these Committee Reports are regarded as very high authority. Committee Reports are published in the *Cumulative Bulletin* and by private publishers, including Wolters Kluwer, CCH and Research Institute of America. Additionally, the *Congressional Record* reports floor debates in the House of Representatives and in the Senate.

Blue Books

As stated in the House Committee Report to the Revenue Reconciliation Act of 1989 (P.L. 101-239), "Blue Books" have been added to the list of authorities on which taxpayers may rely for interpretation of the tax law (see discussion at ¶2035). Blue Books are prepared by the Staff of the Joint Committee on Taxation for major tax acts. Although Blue Books are generally based on Committee Reports for an act, they often contain additional interpretative information. The IRS has used this interpretative information in numerous rulings as the basis for a particular position. Blue Books are published by Wolters Kluwer, CCH.

¶2035 ADMINISTRATIVE AUTHORITY

As a result of congressional authority, the Secretary of the Treasury or a delegate, the Commissioner of Internal Revenue, is authorized to provide administrative interpretation of the tax law. As noted in Section 7805(a):

> Except where such authority is expressly given by this title to any person other than an officer or employee of the Treasury Department, the Secretary or his delegate shall prescribe all needful rules and regulations for the enforcement of this title, including all rules and regulations as may be necessary by reason of any alteration of law in relation to internal revenue.

Treasury Regulations

Treasury Regulations have generally been classified into three broad categories: legislative, interpretative, and procedural. Legislative regulations are those which are issued by the Treasury under a specific grant of authority by Congress to prescribe the operating rules for a statute. Generally, legislative regulations have the force and effect of law. Interpretative regulations are issued pursuant to the general rule-making power granted to the Commissioner under Code Sec. 7805(a) and provide taxpayers with guidance in order to comply with a statute. Although interpretative regulations do not have the force and effect of law, the courts customarily accord them substantial weight. Procedural regulations are considered to be directive rather than mandatory and, thus, do not have the force and effect of law. They explain the IRS's position and provide the mechanics for compliance with the various federal income tax laws, as for example the making and filing of tax elections.

The Regulations are organized in a sequential system consistent with the Code. Additionally, the Regulations are prefixed by a number which designates the applicable area of taxation to which they refer. For example, following are the more important Regulation prefixes:

Part	1.	Final income tax regulations
Part	20.	Estate Tax
Part	25.	Gift Tax
Part	31.	Withholding taxes
Part	301.	Procedure and Administration
Part	601.	Statement of Procedural Rules

Accordingly, an "Income Tax" Regulation relating to Section 453 of the Code would be cited as Reg. §1.453, followed by a dash, then the sequential number of issue, with subparts added for more detailed reference.

Proposed Regulations

New Regulations and changes to existing Regulations usually are issued in proposed form before they are finalized. During the interval between the publication of the Notice of Proposed Rulemaking and finalization of the Regulation, taxpayers and other interested parties are permitted to file objections or suggestions. Proposed Regulations do not have the same weight as Temporary Regulations. Tax law publishers such as Wolters Kluwer, CCH and Thomson Reuters provide a comprehensive listing of these Proposed Regulations, showing the date of their proposal and date of adoption and also publish the text of the Proposed Regulations.

Temporary Regulations

Sometimes Temporary Regulations are issued by the Treasury Department. Their purpose is to provide interim guidance regarding recent tax legislation until final Regulations are adopted. Temporary Regulations (issued after November 20, 1988) must also be issued as Proposed Regulations and must undergo public and administrative scrutiny during a comment period as do Proposed Regulations. Every Temporary Regulation issued after November 20, 1988, will expire three years from the date of issuance. Prior to its expiration, a Temporary Regulation has the same weight as a Final Regulation.

Final Regulations

Finalized Regulations are published in the *Federal Register* as are the Proposed Regulations and Temporary Regulations. All tax Regulations are also published in the *Internal Revenue Bulletin*. Final Regulations and Temporary Regulations are designated as Treasury Decisions (T.D.s) and are assigned a sequential number in order of issuance for the year. The effective date and date of adoption are significant.

Final Regulations as well as Proposed and Temporary Regulations are reproduced in major tax services.

Revenue Rulings and Revenue Procedures

Revenue Rulings, the official pronouncements of the IRS, are similar to Treasury Regulations in that they represent administrative interpretations of the internal revenue laws. Revenue Rulings are issued with respect to a particular issue and insure that this issue will be handled uniformly throughout the country, both in planning and in auditing. Revenue Rulings, however, do not have the same authoritative weight as regulations. Every issue of the *Internal Revenue Bulletin* includes the following statement:

> Rulings and procedures reported in the Bulletin do not have the force and effect of Treasury Department Regulations, but they may be used as precedents. Unpublished rulings will not be relied on, used, or cited as precedents by Service personnel in the disposition of other cases. In applying published rulings and procedures, the effect of subsequent legislation, regulations, court decisions, rulings, and procedures must be considered, and Service personnel and others concerned are cautioned against reaching the same conclusions in other cases unless the facts and circumstances are substantially the same.

Revenue Procedures are published official statements of procedure issued by the IRS that affect either the rights or the duties of taxpayers or other members of the public under the Internal Revenue Code and related statutes and regulations. Revenue Procedures usually reflect the contents of internal management documents. A statement of the IRS position on a substantive tax issue will not be included in a Revenue Procedure. Revenue Procedures are directive and not mandatory.

Both Revenue Rulings and Revenue Procedures are originally published in the weekly issues of the *Internal Revenue Bulletin,* printed by the U.S. Government. However, through 2008, on a semiannual basis, the bulletins were compiled, reorganized by Code section classification, and published in a bound volume designated the *Cumulative Bulletin.* Once published in the *Cumulative Bulletin,* a Revenue Ruling or Revenue Procedure receives a permanent citation as shown below:

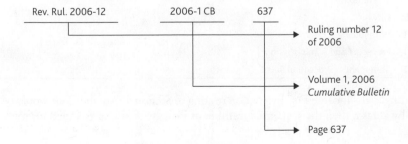

After 2008, a Revenue Ruling, such as Rev. Rul. 2014-12, would be cited as Rev. Rul. 2014-12, 2014-15 I.R.B. 923. This is the 12th Rev. Rul. of 2014 in the 15th weekly issue of the Internal Revenue Bulletin on page 923. The citation for a Revenue Procedure is identical, except the abbreviation "Rev. Proc." is used in place of "Rev. Rul."

Other Administrative Pronouncements

In addition to substantive rulings (Revenue Rulings and Revenue Procedures) published to promote a uniform application of the tax laws, the IRS issues communications to individual taxpayers and IRS personnel in three primary ways: (1) Private Letter Rulings, (2) Determination Letters, and (3) Technical Advice Memoranda. These documents are part of the IRS rulings program, which is discussed in detail at ¶2225.

Digests of Private Letter Rulings may be found in *Private Letter Rulings* (published by Research Institute of America), BNA *Daily Tax Reports,* and Tax Analysts & Advocates *Tax Notes. IRS Letter Rulings Reports* (published by Wolters Kluwer, CCH) contains both digests and the full texts of all Private Letter Rulings. These documents may also be accessed electronically through CCH's CD-ROM and Online computer software. Determination Letters are not published; however, the IRS is now required to make individual rulings available for public inspection. Technical Advice Memoranda are available similar to Private Letter Rulings.

Technical Information Releases (TIRs) and Announcements are periodically distributed by the IRS to advise the public of various technical matters. While these pronouncements are published weekly in the *Internal Revenue Bulletin*, they are not usually included in the *Cumulative Bulletin*.

IRS List of Substantial Authority for Taxpayer Reliance

The IRS has provided guidance on (1) adequate disclosure of items and positions taken on tax returns for purposes of avoiding the accuracy related penalty for understatement of tax, Rev. Proc. 94-36, 1994-1 CB 682, and (2) a listing of substantial authority that may be relied on to avoid imposition of that penalty. Reg. §1.6662-4(d)(3). In addition, the IRS issues a list of positions for which there is not substantial authority. This list must be issued by the Secretary of the Treasury (and revised not less frequently than annually) and published in the *Federal Register.* Code Sec. 6662(d)(2)(D).

The purpose of the list is to assist taxpayers in determining whether a position should be disclosed in order to avoid the substantial understatement penalty. House Committee Report, Revenue Reconciliation Act of 1989. Thus, a taxpayer could choose to disclose that position to avoid the imposition of the accuracy-related penalty. However, inclusion of a position on this list is not conclusive as to whether or not substantial authority exists with respect to that position.

Prior to 1990, the list of substantial authority was restricted to: (1) the Internal Revenue Code, (2) final and temporary regulations, (3) court cases, (4) IRS administrative pronouncements, (5) tax treaties, and (6) congressional intent reflected in committee reports accompanying legislation. Reg. §1.6661-3.

The list of substantial authority now includes (1) the Joint Committee on Taxation's General Explanation of tax legislation (i.e., the "Blue Book"); (2) proposed regulations; (3) information or press releases; (4) notices, announcements, and other similar documents published in the *Internal Revenue Bulletin;* (5) private letter rulings; (6) technical advice memoranda; (7) actions on decisions; and (8) general counsel memoranda. Reg. §1.6662-4(d)(3)(iii). "Authority" does not include conclusions reached in treatises, legal periodicals, and opinions rendered by tax professionals.

With respect to the test for "substantial authority," the IRS continues to apply the principle that there is substantial authority for the tax treatment of an item only if the weight of authorities supporting such treatment is substantial in relation to the weight of authorities supporting contrary tax treatment. The type of document providing the authority affects the weight to be accorded an authority. Reg. §1.6662-4(d)(3)(i) and (ii).

¶2055 JUDICIAL AUTHORITY

The ultimate test in the interpretation of the Code, in determining the validity of Regulations, and in applying the "law" to the facts of a given case takes place in the courts. The court system provides the taxpayer with the opportunity to test before a neutral forum both the position taken by the taxpayer and that taken by the Commissioner with respect to any issue. The courts historically have played a substantial role in the interpretation, application, and enforcement of the tax law. Exhibit 2 outlines the trial and appellate court alternatives for federal tax litigation.

Trial Court System

There are three tribunals that have original jurisdiction to hear and decide tax cases arising under the Internal Revenue Code. A taxpayer can file a petition with the United States Tax Court, in which event assessment and collection of the deficiency will be stayed until the Tax Court's decision becomes final. But the taxpayer may, if he or she prefers, pay the deficiency and then sue for a refund in a U.S. District Court or the United States Court of Federal Claims.

Exhibit 2. JUDICIAL APPEALS ALTERNATIVES

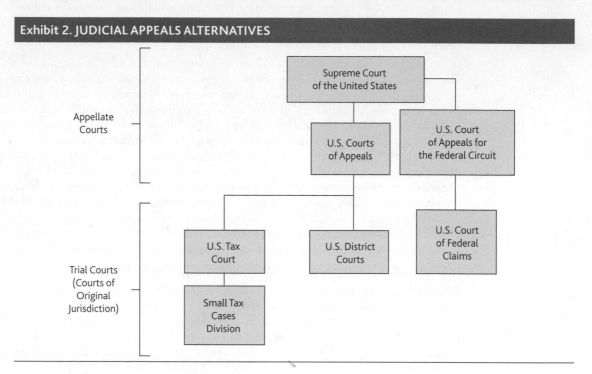

U.S. Tax Court

The United States Tax Court consists of 19 judges appointed by the President for 15-year terms. It is a special court whose jurisdiction is limited almost exclusively to litigation under the Internal Revenue Code. Prior to 1943, the Tax Court was known as the Board of Tax Appeals. Although the Tax Court is a single court located in Washington, D.C., hearings are held in several cities throughout the nation, usually with only a single judge present who submits his opinion to the chief judge. Only rarely does the chief judge decide that a full review is necessary by all 19 judges.

Decisions of the Tax Court are issued as either "regular" or "memorandum" decisions. "Regular" decisions are those which require an interpretation of the law. In theory, "memorandum" decisions concern only well-established principles of law and require only a determination of facts. However, on occasion, the courts have cited "memorandum" decisions. Hence, both kinds of Tax Court decisions should be regarded as having precedent value.

Viewing itself as a national court hearing cases from all parts of the country, for many years the Tax Court had followed a policy of deciding cases on what it thought the result should be. The Tax Court has abandoned its "national law" view, under which it applied its own rule on a nationwide basis without limitation by rules of the circuits in which tax controversies arose. The Tax Court has adopted the position that it will follow precedents of the Circuit Court of Appeals of jurisdiction (known as the *Golsen* rule). As a result, it is entirely possible that the Tax Court will rule differently on identical fact patterns for two taxpayers residing in different circuits in the event of inconsistent holdings between the various Circuit Courts.

The Tax Court is the only court to which a taxpayer may take a case without first paying the tax. Consequently, taxpayers resort to it in many instances; and because it is a court of limited jurisdiction dealing primarily with tax matters, its decisions are accorded considerable weight. This is particularly true of decisions in which the Commissioner of Internal Revenue has acquiesced.

Historically, the policy of the IRS has been to announce in the *Internal Revenue Bulletin* the determination of the Commissioner to acquiesce or not acquiesce in most of the regular decisions of the Tax Court. An announcement of acquiescence (cited Acq.) indicates that the IRS has accepted the conclusion reached in the case but not necessarily the reasons given by the court in its opinion. An announcement of nonacquiescence (cited Nonacq.) usually means that the IRS will continue to litigate the issue if it arises again. Since 1991, the IRS has indicated acquiescences or nonacquiescences for memorandum decisions of the Tax Court as well as for decisions of other courts. An announcement of acquiescence is not legally binding on the IRS and thus can be retroactively withdrawn at any time. If a case is being relied upon, it is important to determine whether it has been acquiesced in by the Commissioner, the extent of the acquiescence (if any), and whether the initial acquiescence may have been withdrawn at a later date.

Additionally, a procedure is used in the Tax Court for cases involving disputes of $50,000 or less. The taxpayer who uses the "small tax case" procedures should be aware that the decision may not be appealed. The advantage to using this procedure is the fact that the formal procedures of the Tax Court are relaxed and made informal.

Judicial Citations—Tax Court Regular Decisions. Regular and memorandum decisions of the Tax Court are reported separately. The Government Printing Office publishes bound volumes of only the regular decisions under the title *United States Tax Court Reports* (cited TC).

Permanent Citation: *Microsoft Corporation,* 115 TC 228 (2000).

Thus, the decision appears in Volume 115 of the *United States Tax Court Reports,* page 228, issued in 2000.

Because there is usually a time lag between the date a decision is rendered and the date it appears in bound form, a temporary citation is used until a permanent citation can be substituted.

Temporary Citation: *Gilda A. Petrane v. Commissioner,* 129 TC —, No. 1 (July 2007).

Thus, the temporary citation identified that the decision appeared in Volume 129 of the *United States Tax Court Reports,* page left blank, 1st regular decision issued by the Tax Court since Volume 128 was issued. Once Volume 129 was issued, the permanent citation incorporating the page was substituted and the number of the case is not used.

Permanent Citation: *Gilda A. Petrane v. Commissioner,* 129 TC 1 (2007).

Judicial Citations—Tax Court Memorandum Decisions. The government provides only photocopies of the memorandum decisions. However, memorandum decisions are published by both Wolters Kluwer, CCH and Thomson Reuters in bound volumes separate from those in which they report other tax cases. The Tax Court memorandum decisions are published by Wolters Kluwer, CCH under the title *Tax Court Memorandum Decisions* (cited TCM), while the RIA series is called *RIA Memorandum Decisions* (cited TC Memo).

CCH Citation: *Harvey D. Perry, Jr. v. Commissioner,* 84 TCM 1, T.C. Memo. 2002-165 (2002).

Thomson Reuters Citation: *Harvey D. Perry, Jr. v. Commissioner,* 2002 TC Memo ¶2002-165.

Although presented in a different way, the reference in both citations indicates that the memorandum decision was the 165th memorandum decision issued by the Tax Court in 2002.

Both regular and memorandum decisions for years prior to 1943 were published by the government under the title *United States Board of Tax Appeals Reports.*

Citation: *J.E. Burke,* 19 BTA 743 (1930).

Thus, the decision appears in Volume 19 of the *United States Board of Tax Appeals Reports,* page 743, issued in 1930.

U.S. District Courts

The U.S. District Courts were the main courts of original jurisdiction for tax cases prior to the establishment of the Board of Tax Appeals which later became the Tax Court. A taxpayer can take a case to the U.S. District Court for the district in which the taxpayer resides only if the taxpayer first pays the tax deficiency assessed by the IRS and then sues for a refund. Each state has at least one District Court in which both tax and nontax litigation are heard. Only in a District Court can one obtain a jury trial, and even there a jury can decide only questions of fact—not those of law.

Judicial Citations—U.S. District Courts Decisions. Published decisions of the U.S. District Courts, including both tax and all other types of litigation, are reported in the *Federal Supplement* (cited F.Supp.) published by West Publishing Company. In addition, the tax decisions of the District Courts are also published in the two special tax reporter series, CCH *United States Tax Cases* (cited USTC) and Thomson Reuters *American Federal Tax Reports* (cited AFTR).

West Citation: *Eugene B. Glick,* 96 F.Supp. 2d 850 (DC Ind., 3/14/00).

The order of citation is volume number, reporter, page number.

CCH Citation: *Eugene B. Glick,* 2000-1 USTC ¶50,372 (DC Ind., 3/14/00).

Paragraph reference rather than a page number gives the location of the case.

Thomson Reuters Citation: *Eugene B. Glick,* 86 AFTR 2d 2000-5083 (DC Ind., 3/14/00).

The prefix "2000" preceding the page number indicates the year the case was decided.

U.S. Court of Federal Claims

The U.S. Court of Federal Claims is a single court consisting of 16 judges appointed by the President. The court resides in Washington, D.C. and the decision to travel is made on a case-by-case basis and is heard by the trial judge to whom the case has been assigned. Prior to October 29, 1992, the court was known as the U.S. Claims Court, and prior to October 1, 1982, the court was known as the U.S. Court of Claims whose decisions were appealed directly to the Supreme Court.

In federal tax matters, the U.S. Court of Federal Claims has concurrent jurisdiction with the U.S. District Courts. The Court of Federal Claims is a constitutional court and has jurisdiction in judgment on any claim against the United States which is:

1. Based on the Constitution
2. Based on any Act of Congress
3. Based on any regulation of an executive department

Judicial Citations—U.S. Court of Federal Claims Decisions. Since 1992, decisions of the Court of Federal Claims have been reported by West Publishing Company in the *Federal Claims Reporter* (cited FedCl). The decisions of the Claims Court from October 1982 until 1992 were reported by West Publishing Company in a series designated the *U.S. Claims Court Reporter* (cited ClCt). Decisions of the predecessor Court of Claims were published by the U.S. Government Printing Office in a separate series of volumes entitled the *U.S. Court of Claims Reports* (cited CtCl). The decisions of the predecessor Court of Claims were also published by West Publishing Company from May 1960 through September 1982 in the *Federal Reporter* 2d Series (cited F.2d), while decisions between 1932 and 1960 were reported in the *Federal Supplement* (cited F.Supp.).

In addition, the tax decisions of the Court of Federal Claims (and the predecessor Claims Court and Court of Claims) are also published in the CCH *United States Tax Cases* (cited USTC) and Thomson Reuters *American Federal Tax Reports* (cited AFTR).

West Citation:	*Katz v. U.S.,* 22 ClCt 714 (ClCt, 1991).
	Scott v. U.S., 354 F.2d 292 (CtCl, 1965).
	Betz v. U.S., 40 Fed Cl 286 (Fed Cl, 1998).
CCH Citation:	*Katz v. U.S.,* 91-1 USTC ¶50,289 (ClCt, 1991).
	Scott v. U.S., 66-1 USTC ¶9169 (CtCl, 1965).
	Betz v. U.S., 98-1 USTC ¶50,199 (Fed Cl, 1998).
Thomson Reuters Citation:	*Katz v. U.S.,* 67 AFTR2d 91-733 (ClCt, 1991).
	Scott v. U.S., 16 AFTR2d 6087 (CtCl, 1965).
	Betz v. U.S., 81 AFTR2d 98-611 (Fed Cl, 1998).

Appeals Court System

If either the taxpayer or the IRS is not satisfied with a trial court decision, an appellate court may be asked to review that decision. There are two levels of courts that handle appeals from the three courts of original jurisdiction. Appeals may be taken to the United States Courts of Appeals of jurisdiction or the U.S. Court of Appeals for the Federal Circuit. As a final step, the controversy may be appealed from the appellate courts to the Supreme Court.

The authority of decisions of all Courts of Appeals stands above that of the Tax Court, a District Court, or the Court of Federal Claims. The United States Supreme Court is, of course, the final authority as to what a statute means or as to any question of federal law.

U.S. Circuit Courts of Appeals

Appeals in tax cases may be taken from the U.S. District Courts or the Tax Court by either the IRS or the taxpayer to the United States Courts of Appeals of jurisdiction. Jurisdiction is based upon the location of the taxpayer's residence. There are eleven numbered circuits and additional unnumbered circuits for the District of Columbia Circuit and the Federal Circuit. See Exhibit 3.

Normally, a Circuit Court's review, made by a panel of three judges is limited to the application of law—not the determination of facts. In this process, the appellate court of any circuit is obligated to follow the findings of the Supreme Court but not those of the other Circuit Courts. When conflicts develop between circuits, District Courts of each individual circuit are required to follow any precedent set by the appellate court of their own circuit (i.e., the Circuit Court to which their decisions may be appealed). Also, as noted earlier, pursuant to the *Golsen* rule, the Tax Court follows the policy of observing precedent set by the appellate court of the circuit in which the taxpayer resides. In this way, consistency in the application of law is maintained between the Tax Court and the District Court of jurisdiction even though there may exist an inconsistency in the law's application to taxpayers residing in various circuits.

Judicial Citations—U.S. Circuit Courts of Appeals Decisions. All decisions, both tax and nontax, of the various Circuit Courts are published by West Publishing Company in the *Federal Reporter* including 2nd and 3rd Series (cited F.2d and F.3d). In addition, tax decisions of the Circuit Courts are also contained in CCH's *United States Tax Cases* (cited USTC) and Thomson Reuters *American Federal Tax Reports* (cited AFTR). Citations indicate not only the volume and page, but also the particular court.

West Citation: *Diane S. Blodgett v. Commissioner,* 394 F.3d 1030 (CA-8, 2005).

CCH Citation: *Diane S. Blodgett v. Commissioner,* 2005-1 USTC ¶50,146 (CA-8, 2005).

Thomson Reuters Citation: *Diane S. Blodgett v. Commissioner,* 95 AFTR2d 2005-448 (CA-8, 2005).

U.S. Court of Appeals for the Federal Circuit

On October 1, 1982, the seven judges of the Court of Claims and the five judges of the Court of Customs and Patent Appeals became the 12 judges of the newly created Court of Appeals for the Federal Circuit (CA-FC). The IRS and taxpayers appeal decisions from the U.S. Court of Federal Claims to this court. The court is empowered to sit in various locations around the country and can be expected to make an effort to hold sessions in the major cities where its business arises.

U.S. Supreme Court

Appeals to the U.S. Supreme Court from the Circuit Courts of Appeals and the Court of Appeals for the Federal Circuit may be made generally by a petition for certiorari. The Supreme Court may grant certiorari at its discretion; further, the Supreme Court is not required to give reasons for its refusal to review. However, past experience has shown that the Court generally grants certiorari only if:

1. The issue has resulted in conflicting decisions in the Circuit Court of Appeals or
2. The issue involved raises an important and continuing problem in the administration of the tax law.

If the Supreme Court declines to review the decision, it will formally deny the petition for certiorari.

Judicial Citations—U.S. Supreme Court Decisions. All Supreme Court decisions are published by the U.S. Government Printing Office in the *United States Supreme Court Reports* (cited U.S.), West Publishing Co. in the *Supreme Court Reporter* (cited S.Ct.), and the Lawyer's Co-Operative Publishing Co. in the *United States Reports, Lawyer's Edition* (cited L.Ed.). Like all other federal tax cases (except those rendered by the U.S. Tax Court), tax-related Supreme Court decisions are reported by CCH in *United States Tax Cases* (cited USTC) and Thomson Reuters in *American Federal Tax Reports* (cited AFTR).

GPO Citation: *Drye, Jr. v. U.S.,* 528 U.S. 49 (1999).

West Citation: *Drye, Jr. v. U.S.,* 120 S.Ct. 474 (1999).

Lawyer's Ed. Citation: *Drye, Jr. v. U.S.,* 145 L.Ed.2d 466 (1999).

CCH Citation: *Drye, Jr. v. U.S.,* 99-2 USTC ¶51,006 (1999).

Thomson Reuters Citation: *Drye, Jr. v. U.S.,* 84 AFTR2d 99-7160 (1999).

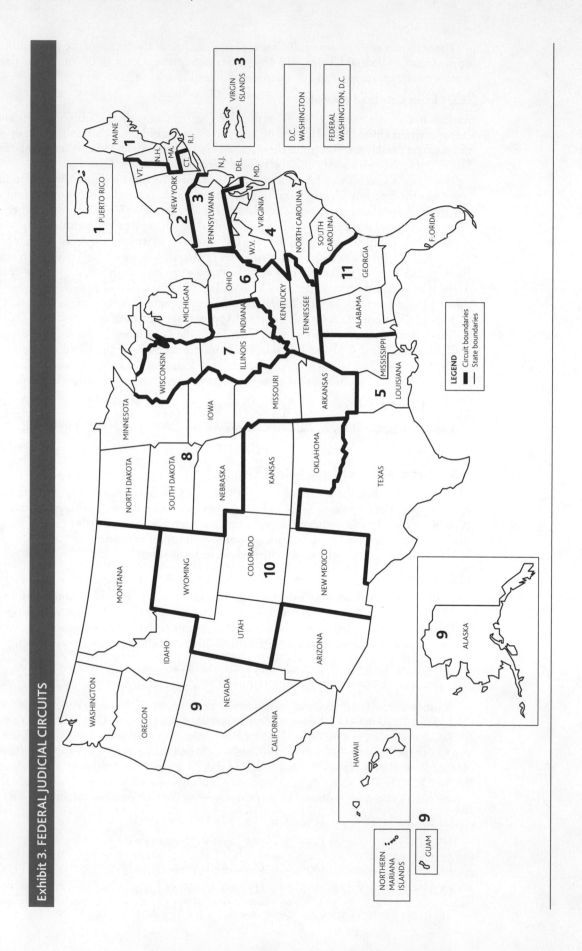

Exhibit 3. FEDERAL JUDICIAL CIRCUITS

Secondary Source Materials

¶2075   ## ANALYSIS OF TAX LAW SOURCES

The voluminous bulk and complexity of our tax law make it extremely difficult to systematically research all of the statutory and administrative provisions associated with a given set of tax issues. The problem is further compounded when one also attempts to analyze, evaluate, and update the leading court cases that impact on these issues. Fortunately, secondary reference materials provide a convenient cross-referenced and continuously updated road map to guide the practitioner in the complicated task of wading through a growing maze of primary tax authority.

Tax Research Services

There are various tax research services that are published with the specific purpose of providing comprehensive reference information on the ever-changing tax law and on-going developments in administrative rulings and case decisions. The use of any particular tax research service is best described in materials made available to users by the representatives of the tax research services. However, there are some general points to be made on the use of these tax research services. First, it is important to check for the latest developments on any topic, issue, or case being researched under a specific statute, regulation, or ruling. Second, editorial analysis, be it a synopsis or digest, provided by the tax research services for case decisions or administrative rulings is an interpretative commentary. Such editorial commentary, no matter how knowledgeable, is not intended to be a substitute for the authoritative primary source document.

Internet Based Research Systems

The role of electronic research systems cannot be overstated. To say that most print materials are also available online does not describe the increasingly integrated and comprehensive search capabilities of online research systems. Users can access computerized tax law data banks with their personal computers by using various tax research publisher's online internet based research systems. Whatever format the researcher uses, all data bases are now integrated with primary and secondary source materials from which the researcher can retrieve full text documents or search for key words or phrases. Publishers' computerized tax research systems can also be used to access citation information to locate all judicial decisions that have cited a particular decision or statute. These online citators are more current than was possible in print format.

Wolters Kluwer, CCH Tax Products on the Internet

As an example of an electronic tax research system, CCH's IntelliConnect® offers a completely integrated suite of tax research materials including primary source documents, i.e., the Internal Revenue Code, Treasury Regulations, Revenue Rulings, tax case decisions, administrative guidance and more. In addition to primary source material, Intelliconnect includes editorial analysis and content including fully searchable versions of most CCH products including the Standard Federal Tax Reporter. The Standard Federal Tax Reporter is a comprehensive Federal tax resource and the organization of this resource is described more fully below, following this discussion of internet based research systems.

In addition to the Standard Federal Tax Reporter, CCH research products online include *CCH Practical Tax Expert*, which provides tax research, focusing on the topics that matter most to the small firm preparer, such as individual and small business taxation. It provides practical explanations of tax law, including examples, comments, planning notes and compliance notes, as well as a variety of tools and practice aids. It includes discussions of source material including the Internal Revenue Code, Treasury Regulations, Rulings and other IRS material, all properly cited and linked for further research.

Practical Tax Professional provides tax research, focusing on the topics that matter most to the small firm practitioner, such as individual and small business taxation, while also providing coverage of a full range of federal tax research issues.

CCH Tax Research Consultant is another tax research product available on IntelliConnect®. Tax Research Consultant covers all tax topics, not just income, and it is arranged by topic rather than Code section. This service is updated weekly.

IntelliConnect® includes many other tax research resources and is organized by overall category including Federal Tax, State Tax, Financial and Estate Planning, Accounting, etc. Within each category, various resources and products are available for research and practice assistance. The electronic format of the internet-based tax research services provides an opportunity to include automated tools and calculators, which makes the tax research systems ideal not only for tax research but also to find quick answers and practice aids. IntelliConnect® includes Smart Charts on many topics as well as calculators, decision tools and more. In addition to these features, the internet-based research systems provide an opportunity for the most current information that can be updated more frequently than the print resources. IntelliConnect® includes the CCH daily news service, Tax Day, current journals and newsletters, the latest CCH briefings on major tax developments, a Case Citator that is current to date and many other electronic products including CCH's well-regarded Law, Explanation and Analysis books on current legislation. Subscribers to internet based tax research systems receive log in information providing access to the full array of resources anytime and virtually anyplace.

In addition to the internet-based tax research systems, new applications are being continuously developed by most tax research services. Wolters Kluwer, CCH offers tax research information specifically designed for mobile devices including iPhones and iPads. Some of these applications include CCH Mobility, eBooks, current journals and newsletters.

It must be noted here that despite the encompassing nature of electronic research and search methods, students are well advised to have a firm understanding of the nature, basis and authority of the documents they are using to support a tax position and how the various sources of authority are interrelated and linked. Therefore, following the internet screen shots below on the Wolters Kluwer internet based system, a more detailed description of the organization of various tax research products is included with the understanding that these original research resources are still available in print format and are now also available through the electronic research systems.

Complete, current, and reliable tax information is on the Internet from Wolters Kluwer, CCH at CCHGroup.com. Many tax research products are also available on mobile applications.

Researching a Topic

In the Internet browser's Address bar, go to *http://intelliconnect.cch.com*. You will be taken to the Log In page where you can enter your User ID and Password in order to reach the IntelliConnect® home page where you can initiate a search.

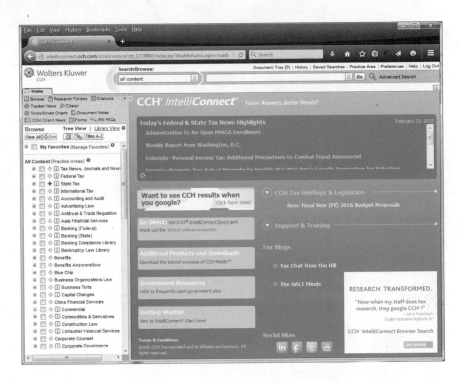

Type your search term or phrase in the navigation bar at the top of the screen. For purposes of illustration look for the "nanny tax threshold for 2015" and click Go. On the left side of the screen you can choose to Narrow Your Results. For this example click the plus next to "by Document Type" and when the list expands, click on Explanations.

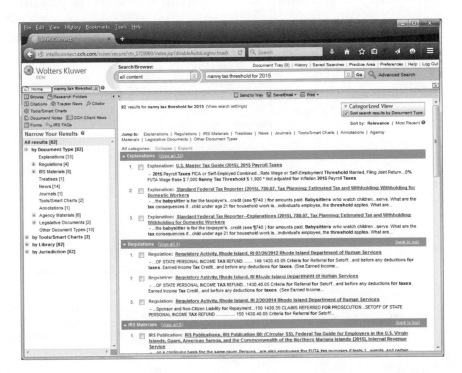

This screen displays the results that best match your query. Click on the first document and the screen will split so that the document will appear at the bottom.

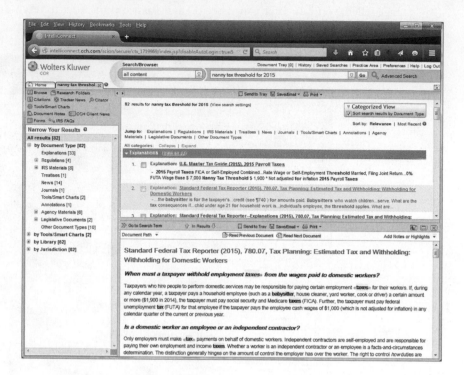

Review the document to see if it contains the information with respect to the nanny tax threshold for 2015. In this example the first item listed contains information on the nanny tax threshold for 2015. The nanny tax increases to $1,900 for 2015. Cash amounts paid for a nanny are not subject to FICA taxes if less than $1,900 during 2015.

Once you have found the information you were searching for you might want to email it to yourself. There are several options in the middle of the Tri-screen. Click on Save/Email and choose Email document from the drop down list. Enter the required information and click send.

The only way to become proficient at using an electronic data base is through practice and experience. The tax student is encouraged to experiment with CCH online software by searching for the answer to a tax question. Once the art of electronic searching is mastered, it will be obvious how much more comprehensive and efficient it is than a traditional paper search. For example, what authority can you find to justify a deduction for home office expense by a college professor? What authority can you find that would deny the deduction?

IRS Homepage

The IRS homepage on the World Wide Web (*http://www.irs.gov*) went online on January 8, 1996. During its first 24 hours of operation, close to one million "hits" were recorded. Features on the IRS homepage include the following: Tax Stats, About IRS, Careers, Freedom of Information Act (FOIA), The Newsroom, Accessibility, Site Map, Español, and Help.

One very useful aspect of the IRS homepage is the ability to retrieve the latest in tax news. Use the IRS Newsroom to access information on important topics (as shown below). From the IRS homepage, click on News & Events.

Across the top of the page the tabs provided are: Filing, Payments, Refunds, Credits & Deductions, News & Events, Forms & Pubs, Help & Resources and for Tax Pros. Besides retrieving tax news from the IRS, tax forms and publications may be downloaded. The sixth item listed across the top of the page is Forms and Publications. By clicking on Forms and Publications, the Forms and Publications page appears. All IRS tax forms may be retrieved from this site. Please note that forms and publications from prior years are available back to 1992.

By clicking on the "Current Forms & Pubs" link, *http://apps.irs.gov/app/picklist/list/formsPublications.html* appears. All IRS tax forms may be retrieved from this site.

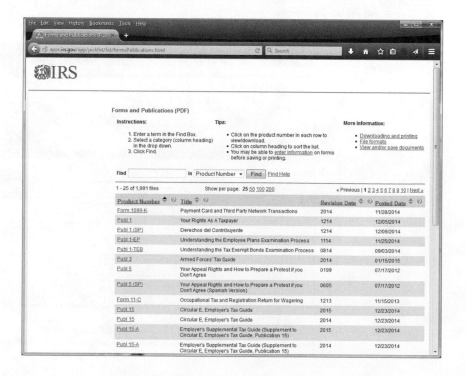

Searching the Internet

A good way to search the Internet is by using search engines. A search engine allows you to type in a term or phrase which describes your area of interest. For example, open your Internet browser's search screen and type in the phrase "tax history." Once the search is complete, all of the finds are listed and linked to millions of useful sources (sample screens shown below).

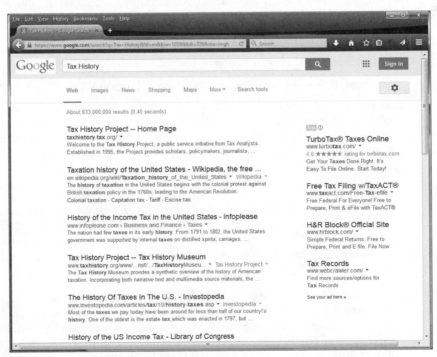

Standard Federal Tax Reporter, Wolters Kluwer, CCH

Wolters Kluwer, CCH publishes loose-leaf reporters in all major federal tax areas. These reporters are also available on CCH's tax research system, IntelliConnect®. The most comprehensive of these tax reference services is the *Standard Federal Tax Reporter,* frequently referred to as the *Standard* or *Fed.* Other specialized tax services include the *Federal Excise Tax Reporter* and the *Federal Estate and Gift Tax Reporter.* The *Federal Tax Guide,* also published by Wolters Kluwer, CCH, is a two-volume service covering many of the same topics that are included in the *Standard.*

The *Standard Reporter* consists of 25 coordinated and cross-referenced loose-leaf volumes that provide comprehensive coverage of the income tax law. The service also provides weekly supplements presenting current federal court decisions, new rulings, and changes in the law or regulations, digests of Tax Court decisions, as well as reviews of the significant legislative changes, and editorial comments which provide tax planning ideas related to current developments.

The major portion of the *Standard,* Volumes 1 through 18, compiles the legislative, administrative, and judicial aspects of the income tax law. The volumes are arranged in Code Section order and reflect the current income tax law and accompanying related regulatory texts (including proposed amendments to the Regulations) as well as legislative Committee Reports, followed by "CCH Explanations" and supplemented with digests of associated administrative rulings and judicial decisions. Volume 19, "New Matters," is used to retain current developments such as digests of Tax Court decisions, full texts of rulings, current tables of decisions and rulings, and the Supreme Court Docket.

The *Standard* also includes the "U.S. Tax Cases Advance Sheets" Volume in which are reported the full texts of new income tax decisions from the federal courts, including the U.S. Supreme Court and the U.S. Court of Federal Claims. In the two Internal Revenue Code Volumes may be found the current internal revenue statutes. The two Citator Volumes access the basic Compilations by case name and document number. The Index Volume leads to the basic contents by subject through the Topical Index and also features a tax calendar, rate tables and tax rate schedules, tax planning information, checklists, and special tables.

United States Tax Reporter, Thomson Reuters

United States Tax Reporter, published by Thomson Reuters, consists of 18 coordinated loose-leaf volumes organized by Code sections and updated on a weekly basis. The service is similar to Wolters Kluwer's and also includes a two-volume Internal Revenue Code, a seven-volume Citator, a one-volume Index, a one-volume Table of Cases, Rulings, and Tax Tables, a Recent Developments volume, an Advance Sheets volume for AFTR2d cases and a volume of proposed amendments to Federal Tax Regulations. Thomson Reuters also publishes loose-leaf tax services for excise taxes and for estate and gift taxes. This service is included in the Thomson Reuters Checkpoint online service.

Mertens, Law of Federal Income Taxation, Thomson West

Merten's *Treatise on the Law of Federal Income Taxation,* published by Thomson West, is an intensive, annotated work, providing excellent in-depth discussions of general concepts of tax law. However, unlike services such as those of Wolters Kluwer, CCH and Thomson Reuters, Mertens is not generally used as a comprehensive, self-contained reference service. Rather, it is typically regarded as a useful complement to the traditional reference services.

Tax Management Portfolios, Bureau of National Affairs

Tax Management Portfolios, published by the Bureau of National Affairs (BNA), is a useful supplement to a tax library. Each portfolio ranges in length from 50 to 200 pages and deals exclusively with a special tax topic, covering Code, Regulations, reference to primary authorities, and extensive editorial discussion, including numerous tax planning ideas. BNA Portfolios are available online.

Federal Tax Coordinator, Thomson Reuters

The *Federal Tax Coordinator,* published by Thomson Reuters, is somewhat similar in organization to CCH's *Standard Federal Tax Reporter* and Thomson Reuters's *United States Tax Reporter,* with compilation volumes and an elaborate cross-reference system of indexation. However, the 26-volume service is organized by topic rather than by Code section. Popular features of the *Tax Coordinator* are the editorial explanations, illustrations, planning ideas, and warnings of potential tax traps. This service is included in the Thomson Reuters Checkpoint online service.

The Citator

Probably the most comprehensive method for evaluating and updating case law is through the use of a citator. The *CCH Citator,* published annually as a two-volume loose-leaf reference service, contains an alphabetical listing of the Tax Court (formerly the Board of Tax Appeals) and federal court decisions since 1913. The Current Citator Table is updated annually in print. It is updated currently online in Intel-liConnect®. Additionally, the *CCH Citator* indicates a paragraph reference where each case is digested in the Compilation Volumes of the *Standard Federal Tax Reporter.* More than one paragraph reference will be given if a case involves several tax issues. The *Citator* is available on IntelliConnect® and offers instant linking to the cases cited.

Each listing outlines the judicial history of a selected case beginning with the highest court to have ruled on that issue. Then, in descending order, the actions of lower courts are also cited and described. Finally, under each listing, the *CCH Citator* refers to other court cases, which helps to evaluate a given decision as a precedent.

The *Citator 2nd,* published by Thomson Reuters, is a seven-volume service with monthly and annual cumulative supplements organized in a manner somewhat consistent with that of the *CCH Citator.* Essentially, Thomson Reuters provides an alphabetical list of court cases followed by a descriptive legislative history of each case. However, in those cases involving more than one issue, the Thomson Reuters citator also cross-references its descriptive system of judicial references according to the various issues. Citators are included in the online services of Wolters Kluwer, CCH and Thomson Reuters.

To illustrate the usefulness of the citator to the researcher, the CCH Citator will be explained in greater detail. Refer to Exhibit 4, a sample taken from the CCH Citator and locate the *Atlas Life Insurance Co.* case. The case name is followed by paragraph (¶) references to the Compilation Volumes in which the decision appears as an annotation to the law, regulations, and other cases in point. The black dot preceding each court action in the case permits the researcher to quickly scan the judicial history of the case. *Atlas Life Insurance Co.* was decided on appeal in the Supreme Court in 1965, which reversed the decision of the Court of Appeals for the Tenth Circuit. The Court of Appeals decision reversed the ruling of the District Court of Oklahoma.

Exhibit 4. CCH CITATOR—COURT CASES SAMPLE SECTION

Atlas, Inc.—continued
Mervis Industries, Inc., DC-Ind, 94-2 USTC ¶ 50,324, 866 FSupp 1143
TMG II, DC-DofC, 91-2 USTC ¶ 50,513, 778 FSupp 37
Newgard, Jr., Trust, L.A., DC-ND, 89-2 USTC ¶ 9395
Carter, DC-Calif, 82-1 USTC ¶ 9314
Viva Ltd., DC-Colo, 81-1 USTC ¶ 9169, 490 FSupp 1002
Vavrina v. Koch, DC-Md, 80-2 USTC ¶ 9697
Waite, Inc., DC-Pa, 80-1 USTC ¶ 9128, 480 FSupp 1235
Atlas Insurance Company . . . . ¶ 12,014.311, 12,014.3205
  • CA-5—(aff'g unreported DC per curiam), 64-2 USTC ¶ 9828; 338 F2d 334
Atlas Leasing, Inc. (See Central De Gas De Chihuahua, S.A.)
Atlas Life Insurance Co. . . . . . . ¶ 25,736.60, 25,913.74
  • SCt—(rev'g CA), 65-1 USTC ¶ 9407; 381 US 233; 85 SCt 1379; Ct D 1903; 1965-2 CB 220
Bankers Life and Casualty Co., CA-7, 98-1 USTC ¶ 50,346, 142 F3d 973
American Mutual Life Ins. Co., FedCl, 2000-1 USTC ¶ 50,314, 46 FedCl 445
Standard Life & Accident Ins. Co., SCt, 77-2 USTC ¶ 9480, 433 US 148, 97 SCt 2523, Ct D 1986, 1977-2 CB 230
Consumer Life Ins. Co., SCt, 77-1 USTC ¶ 9364, 430 US 725, 97 SCt 1440, Ct D 1985, 1977-1 CB 178
Boli, CA-FC, 87-2 USTC ¶ 9566, 831 F2d 276
Goldin, CA-2, 87-1 USTC ¶ 9128, 809 F2d 187
Reserve Life Insurance Co., CtCls, 81-1 USTC ¶ 9147, 640 F2d 368
Investors Diversified Services, Inc., CtCls, 78-1 USTC ¶ 9379, 216 CtCls 192, 575 F2d 843
Group Life & Health Ins. Co., CA-5, 70-2 USTC ¶ 9683, 434 F2d 115
Franklin Life Ins. Co., CA-7, 68-2 USTC ¶ 9459, 399 F2d 757
Northwestern Mutual Life Ins. Co., ClsCt, 85-1 USTC ¶ 9233, 7 ClsCt 501
Union Mutual Life Ins. Co., DC-Me, 76-2 USTC ¶ 9661, 420 FSupp 1181
Jefferson Standard Life Ins. Co., CA-4, 69-1 USTC ¶ 9278, 408 F2d 842
Franklin Life Ins. Co., DC-Ill, 67-2 USTC ¶ 9515
Union Central Life Ins. Co., TC, Dec. 38,339, 77 TC 845
Ball, TC, Dec. 30,153, 54 TC 1200
Allstate Fire Ins. Co., TC, Dec. 28,197, 47 TC 237
  • CA-10—(rev'g DC), 64-2 USTC ¶ 9510; 333 F2d 389
  • DC-Okla—63-1 USTC ¶ 9452; 216 FSupp 457

Atlas Mixed Mortar Co. . . . . ¶ 21,817.636
  • BTA—Dec. 6956; 23 BTA 245
Harrold, CA-4, 52-1 USTC ¶ 9107, 192 F2d 1002
Levin, TC, Dec. 20,224, 21 TC 996
Jenkins, TC, Dec. 20,125(M), 13 TCM 61
Vincent, TC, Dec. 19,366, 19 TC 501
Patsch, TC, Dec. 19,288, 19 TC 189
Harrold, TC, Dec. 18,045, 16 TC 134
Atlas, Nicholas (See Lester, Emanuel)
Atlas Oil & Refining Corp. . . . . ¶ 44,432.01
  • TC—Dec. 24,943; 36 TC 675; A. 1962-2 CB 3
Adkins-Phelps, Inc., CA-8, 68-2 USTC ¶ 9609, 400 F2d 737
Wisconsin Central Railroad Co., CtCls, 62-1 USTC ¶ 9121, 155 CtCls 781, 296 F2d 750
Atlas Oil and Refining Corp. ¶ 38,963.32, 38,963.59, 38,967.626
  • TC—Dec. 20,387; 22 TC 552; NA. 1955-1 CB 7
Simpson Est., TC, Dec. 49,836(M), 67 TCM 2938, TC Memo. 1994-207
Union Texas International Corp., TC, Dec. 52,710, 110 TC 321
Atkinson, TC, Dec. 46,340(M), 58 TCM 1257, TC Memo. 1990-37
Woods, TC, Dec. 45,602, 92 TC 776
Century Data Systems, Inc., TC, Dec. 42,872, 86 TC 157
Reef Corp., TC, Dec. 27,309(M), 24 TCM 379, TC Memo. 1965-72
Pollack, TC, Dec. 26,693(M), 23 TCM 433, TC Memo. 1964-63
Rose, TC, Dec. 21,160, 24 TC 755
Harlan, TC, Dec. 54,209, 116 TC 31
Atlas Oil & Refining Corp. . . . . ¶ 20,307.20
  • TC—Dec. 18,601; 17 TC 733; A. 1952-1 CB 1
Miles Production Co., TC, Dec. 47,265, 96 TC 595
Century Data Systems, Inc., TC, Dec. 42,872, 86 TC 157
Atlas Tool Co., TC, Dec. 35,124, 70 TC 86
Dougherty, TC, Dec. 32,138, 60 TC 917
Reef Corp., TC, Dec. 27,309(M), 24 TCM 379, TC Memo. 1965-72
Rose, TC, Dec. 21,160, 24 TC 755
Rev. Rul. 58-256
Atlas Plaster & Fuel Co. . . . . . . ¶ 8637.681, 42,201.57
  • CA-6—(aff'g BTA), 1932 CCH ¶ 9067; 55 F2d 802; Ct D 541; XI-2 CB 323
Tumwater Lbr. Mills Co., CA-9, 1933 CCH ¶ 9403, 65 F2d 675
Bluegrass Plant Foods, Inc., TC, Dec. 22,918(M), 17 TCM 271, TC Memo. 1958-53
  • BTA—Dec. 5821; 18 BTA 1123
Atlas Plywood Co. . . . . . . ¶ 11,075.5135, 11,075.6044,

In addition to the historical record of the case, citations are given for the court actions taken in a particular case which show where the full text of the decision may be found. A citation to *U.S. Tax Cases* (USTC), for example, refers to an expansive series of volumes published by Wolters Kluwer, CCH that cover tax-related court opinions issued since 1913. The volumes, published twice a year, cover Supreme Court, Courts of Appeals, District Courts, and Court of Federal Claims cases. The Thomson Reuters citator would refer to the *American Federal Tax Reports* (AFTR), the comparable Thomson Reuters series of federal court cases. Memorandum decisions of the Tax Court are published by Wolters Kluwer, CCH under the title *Tax Court Memorandum Decisions* (cited TCM), while the Thomson Reuters series is called *TC Memorandum Decisions* (cited TC Memo).

The Citator typically gives even further research information than already discussed. For each case listed in the Citator there is given the "cited record" of that case. These "cited records" list the names and citations of later cases which discussed and distinguished the main case. Thus, the "cited record" permits the researcher to evaluate the judicial authority of the related case.

For the very latest developments in any case, the researcher using the CCH Citator should consult the Current Citator Table. Following this procedure, the researcher must be sure to check the "Case Table" (for the current year) in Volume 19, the "New Matters" volume of the *Standard*. Appeals to higher courts, IRS acquiescences or nonacquiescences, and government decisions on whether to appeal federal court cases are shown in the "Case Table" (for the current year) for all cases. (Where Supreme Court action is indicated in the Case Table, more information on the case may be obtained from the Supreme Court Docket located in the New Matters Volume.) The "Finding Lists" section of the CCH Citator allows the researcher to determine the status of Revenue Rulings and Revenue Procedures.

Books

In addition to the loose-leaf reference services and the bound volumes of tax-related court cases published in the special reporter series *U.S. Tax Cases* (USTC) available from Wolters Kluwer, CCH or the *American Federal Tax Reports* (AFTR) available from Thomson Reuters, a well-equipped tax library should contain numerous leading tax textbooks.

Following are selected, highly recommended tax books:

Price on Contemporary Estate Planning, John R. Price and Samuel A. Donaldson (Wolters Kluwer, CCH)

Federal Tax Practitioner's Guide, Susan Flax Posner (Wolters Kluwer, CCH)

Federal Income Taxation of Corporations and Shareholders, Boris I. Bittker and James I. Eustice (Thomson/WG&L)

S Corporation Taxation, Robert W. Jamison (Wolters Kluwer, CCH)

Practical Guide to Partnerships and LLCs, Robert Ricketts and Larry Tunnell (Wolters Kluwer, CCH)

Practical Guide to S Corporations, Michael Schlesinger (Wolters Kluwer, CCH)

Partnership Taxation, Arthur B. Willis, John S. Pennell, and Philip F. Postlewaite (Thomson/WG&L)

Tax Institutes

Current tax topics are discussed and technical papers presented at the various tax institutes and symposia held annually at universities and other locations throughout the United States. The well-known tax institutes such as New York University and the National Tax Association—Tax Institute of America publish their annual proceedings. The papers of the Annual University of Chicago Federal Tax Conference are published in the March issue of *TAXES—The Tax Magazine* as are the proceedings of the Tax Council Policy Institute (TCPI) annual meeting published in the June issue. The papers from the annual UCLA Tax Controversy Institute are published each year in the December-January issue of the *Journal of Tax Practice and Procedure.*

Tax Periodicals

Several monthly and quarterly journals contain current articles dealing exclusively with technical tax matters. Some of these magazines cover a broad range of tax topics, while others specialize in a particular area of taxation.

Following are some of the more popular tax periodicals:

Corporate Taxation (Thomson/WG&L)

CPA Journal (New York State Society of Certified Public Accountants)

Estate Planning (Thomson/WG&L)

International Tax Journal (Wolters Kluwer, CCH)

Journal of the American Taxation Association (American Accounting Association)

Journal of Passthrough Entities (Wolters Kluwer, CCH)

Journal of Tax Practice and Procedure (Wolters Kluwer, CCH)

Journal of Taxation (Thomson/WG&L)

Journal of Taxation of Financial Products (Wolters Kluwer, CCH)

National Tax Journal (National Tax Association—Tax Institute of America)

Practical Tax Strategies (Thomson/WG&L)

Tax Adviser (American Institute of Certified Public Accountants)

Tax Executive (Tax Executive Institute)

Tax Law Review (New York University)

Tax Lawyer (American Bar Association)

Taxes—The Tax Magazine (Wolters Kluwer, CCH)

Trusts and Estates (Penton Media, Inc.)

Newsletters

The practitioner needs to stay on top of current developments in the tax field and for this purpose finds that weekly and even daily updates of pertinent tax law information is needed. Daily reporting is available both electronically through on-line computer legal research systems from tax publishers and through the mail. There is the CCH daily *Tax Day News* and *Federal Tax Weekly,* published by Wolters Kluwer, CCH; the BNA *Daily Tax Report,* available from the Bureau of National Affairs; and Tax Analysts' *Tax Notes Today.* The most popular weekly newsletters are *Federal Tax Weekly,* published by Wolters Kluwer, CCH; the *Federal Taxes Weekly Alert,* published by Thomson Reuters; and Tax Analysts' weekly *Tax Notes.* CCH's *Tax Day News* is available on the CCHGroup.com site and can be customized and delivered via RSS feed.

Research Methodology

¶2125

TYPES OF TAX RESEARCH SITUATIONS

Essentially, there are two types of tax research cases or situations. The "closed-fact" case, sometimes referred to as ex post facto research, involves the legal interpretation of historical events. In such cases, the taxable transactions have already occurred and can no longer be altered, although various tax elections and alternatives might still be available. Two common examples of "closed-fact" situations are preparation of a tax return after the taxable year is completed and representation of a taxpayer before the Audit Division of the IRS on the examination of a previously filed tax return.

In contrast, the "open-fact" case typically involves events that have not yet been finalized (i.e., controllable facts). Thus, this type of research relates primarily to future planning decisions. However, whether the primary focus of a research engagement is for tax compliance or tax planning, the underlying methods and techniques should be systematic, thorough, properly documented, and effectively communicated to the client.

¶2135

RESEARCH MODEL

The following research model presents a five-step systematic format that can be applied to a "closed-fact" or an "open-fact" case:

1. Gathering the facts and identifying the tax issues to be researched.
2. Locating and studying the primary and secondary authorities relevant to the enumerated tax issues.
3. Updating and evaluating the weight of the various authorities.
4. Reexamining various facets of the research.
5. Arriving at conclusions and communicating these conclusions to the client.

STEP 1: Gathering the Facts and Identifying the Tax Issues to Be Researched

During this difficult part of the research process it is necessary to elicit a comprehensive, unbiased report from the client. Difficulty stems from the fact that taxpayers often tend to have a simple perspective of the tax issues related to their problem. They fail to see the multiple issues that might be involved in what they perceive as a single, straightforward issue.

EXAMPLE 2.1

Mary Jones, a single taxpayer, moved from New York to Miami in 2015. Accordingly, she sold her residence in New York at a gain well in excess of $400,000. In preparation of her 2015 tax return, since the gain on the sale of this residence is quite substantial, the researcher must examine the facts and explore the tax-savings elections.

Mary is asked to provide all information related to these events, and she supplies the real estate closing statement reflecting the sale of the New York residence. As far as Mary is concerned, she has supplied "all" information necessary to resolve this issue. However, the following facts must still be ascertained:

1. What was the cost of the New York residence?
2. Should any improvements be capitalized as part of the basis of the New York residence?
3. Were there any selling costs involved with the sale?
4. Over the years, were there any property assessments that should be capitalized as part of the basis of the New York residence?
5. Was any portion of the New York residence depreciated as a home office deduction on prior tax returns?
6. Is Mary eligible for the $250,000 tax-free exclusion?

STEP 2: Locating and Studying the Secondary and Primary Authorities Relevant to the Enumerated Tax Issues

For each issue enumerated in Step 1, the research might begin with a thorough reading of the compilation materials found in the tax services whether in print format (loose-leaf and books) or electronic format (CD-ROM, online, or the Internet). The editorial explanations and observations provide useful insights and help direct the research process. Additionally, the research should continue with a review of the applicable Code sections, Regulations, and digests of selected judicial decisions. Those cases which seem particularly appropriate to the research should be cited to facilitate reference for subsequent follow-up study. Finally, before leaving the tax services, it is imperative to refer to the "Current Developments" section to examine the impact of recent actions.

STEP 3: Updating and Evaluating the Weight of the Various Authorities

The statutory and administrative authorities selected in Step 2 must now be evaluated to determine relative weight. Additionally, the relevant court cases must be assessed in terms of their value as judicial precedent. Before relying upon a particular decision, it is essential to refer to one of the loose-leaf citator services and review the history and current status of that case.

It is not uncommon to discover conflicting interpretations of similar issues by different courts. In place of a national law policy, the Tax Court has adopted the position that better judicial administration requires it to follow a Court of Appeals decision. Nevertheless, courts at the same level of jurisdiction may issue conflicting opinions; whereas, the Internal Revenue Service is not obligated to adhere to either decision on a nationwide basis. Accordingly, a District or Circuit Court decision favorable to a taxpayer has significant precedent value only within that district or circuit.

STEP 4: Reexamining Various Facets of the Research

After studying and evaluating the various statutory, administrative, and judicial authorities, it often becomes necessary to reexamine the original tax problem. It may even become necessary to seek additional facts and modify or expand the research process.

Additionally, if there are any authorities in conflict with the projected conclusions, it is essential to study them carefully. The researcher must not only be able to support his or her own research conclusions, but also must be prepared to defend these conclusions in light of conflicting authorities.

During this phase of the research, it may sometimes be useful to clarify the meanings of unfamiliar or highly technical words or terms. A standard dictionary may provide some guidance, but if the words are not generally used in a nonlegal context, *Black's Law Dictionary* should be consulted.

STEP 5: Arriving at Conclusions and Communicating the Conclusions to the Client

Communicating the conclusions of the tax research to the client requires professional judgment. The client should be advised of the potential benefits and risks associated with the recommended actions. Since the communication will be in writing, it is essential to determine how much or how little detail should be noted. Additionally, the communication must be expressed at the client's level of sophistication. This sometimes presents a difficult task, especially when the research involves complex issues and highly technical reasoning.

Essentially, the communication should be concise, well-structured, and should follow an organized format that includes:

1. A review of the facts
2. An enumeration of the various tax issues
3. The conclusions
4. A discussion of the reasoning and authorities supporting the conclusions

While the client might be concerned only with the section dealing with conclusions, the professional substance of the communication is contained in the reasoning and authority. It is in this section of the report that the various authorities are discussed and evaluated. Finally, it is in this section that the client is supplied with authoritative support, should it ever become necessary to defend against a challenge by the Internal Revenue Service.

¶2147   RESEARCH CASES AND EXAMPLES

The following cases and examples illustrate the *step-by-step* application of selected aspects of research methodology. Additionally, details are outlined to highlight the *trial-and-error* nature of tax research and the need for patience, perseverance, and creativity.

CASE 1. (Illustrating a Code Section approach to tax research.)

TAX PROBLEM

Sue Wilson had her personal automobile stolen in 2015 and received an insurance reimbursement in 2016. In preparing her 2015 tax return, the preparer must ascertain how much of a theft loss may be claimed and in which year it should be deducted.

FACTS

The automobile was acquired in 2013 at a cost of $20,000 and was stolen on June 14, 2015. The fair market value at the time of theft was $10,000. On January 15, 2016, the insurance company paid $7,500 to Wilson as a "full reimbursement" for the theft.

ISSUES

Is the theft deductible since the vehicle is used exclusively for personal use? If deductible, how much of a loss may be claimed? In which year, 2015 or 2016, should the loss be claimed?

RESEARCH

On determining that Section 165 of the Internal Revenue Code deals with Deductions for Losses, the researcher using the CCH *Standard* tax service (whether in print or electronic format) should refer to the Compilation Volumes where the texts of the Code sections and Regulations, both with all amendments to date, and CCH Explanations, plus digests of applicable rulings and decisions are located. Code section reference is facilitated by referring to the backbone of the various loose-leaf volumes. Section 165(h) provides authoritative support for deducting a *personal* casualty loss or theft and outlines details of the $100 and 10 percent of adjusted gross income limitations for this deduction.

Regulation §1.165-1(d)(2)(ii), which is located in the CCH *Standard* Compilations immediately following Section 165, is reprinted in Exhibit 5. The illustration provided in this Regulation is similar to the Wilson facts.

Accordingly, it would appear that, to the extent Sue can claim a theft loss, it will be deductible in 2015. However, a major question relates to the calculation of the loss. Is the loss measured by the $20,000 original cost of the automobile or by the $10,000 fair market value?

Reg. §1.165-7(b)(1) gives the general rule to be followed in determining the amount deductible for casualty losses:

> . . . the amount of loss to be taken into account . . . shall be the lesser of either—(i) The amount which is equal to the fair market value of the property immediately before the casualty reduced by the fair market value of the property immediately after the casualty; or (ii) The amount of the adjusted basis prescribed [by regulation] for determining the loss from the sale or other disposition of the property involved.

Exhibit 5. CCH STANDARD FEDERAL TAX REPORTS—COMPILATION SAMPLE PAGE: Regulations

Regulations

[¶9803] §1.165-1 Losses.—* * *

(d) *Year of deduction.* (1) A loss shall be allowed as a deduction under section 165(a) only for the taxable year in which the loss is sustained. For this purpose, a loss shall be treated as sustained during the taxable year in which the loss occurs as evidenced by closed and completed transactions and as fixed by identifiable events occurring in such taxable year. For provisions relating to situations where a loss attributable to a disaster will be treated as sustained in the taxable year immediately preceding the taxable year in which the disaster actually occurred, see section 165(h) and §1.165-11.

(2)(i) If a casualty or other event occurs which may result in a loss and, in the year of such casualty or event, there exists a claim for reimbursement with respect to which there is a reasonable prospect of recovery, no portion of the loss with respect to which reimbursement may be received is sustained, for purposes of section 165, until it can be ascertained with reasonable certainty whether or not such reimbursement will be received. Whether a reasonable prospect of recovery exists with respect to a claim for reimbursement of a loss is a question of fact to be determined upon an examination of all facts and circumstances. Whether or not such reimbursement will be received may be ascertained with reasonable certainty, for example, by a settlement of the claim, by an adjudication of the claim, or by an abandonment of the claim. When a taxpayer claims that the taxable year in which a loss is sustained is fixed by his abandonment of the claim for reimbursement, he must be able to produce objective evidence of his having abandoned the claim, such as the execution of a release.

(ii) If in the year of the casualty or other event a portion of the loss is not covered by a claim for reimbursement with respect to which there is a reasonable prospect of recovery, then such portion of the loss is sustained during the taxable year in which the casualty or other event occurs. For example, if property having an adjusted basis of $10,000 is completely destroyed by fire in 1961, and if the taxpayer's only claim for reimbursement consists of an insurance claim for $8,000 which is settled in 1962, the taxpayer sustains a loss of $2,000 in 1961. However, if the taxpayer's automobile is completely destroyed in 1961 as a result of the negligence of another person and there exists a reasonable prospect of recovery on a claim for the full value of the automobile against such person, the taxpayer does not sustain any loss until the taxable year in which the claim is adjudicated or otherwise settled. If the automobile had an adjusted basis of $5,000 and the taxpayer secures a judgment of $4,000 in 1962, $1,000 is deductible for the taxable year 1962. If in 1963 it becomes reasonably certain that only $3,500 can ever be collected on such judgment, $500 is deductible for the taxable year 1963.

The Regulation further provides that if the property is used in a trade or business or is held for the production of income and is totally destroyed, the amount of loss is measured exclusively by the adjusted basis of the property.

In preparing Wilson's 2015 tax return, the theft loss will be computed as follows:

1.	Original cost	$20,000
2.	Fair market value (before theft)	10,000
3.	Fair market value (after theft)	0
4.	Loss in value, caused by theft	10,000
5.	Basis for loss: lesser of line 1 or line 4	10,000
6.	Less: Insurance recovery	7,500
7.	Sustained loss	2,500
8.	Less: Section 165(h) limitation	100
9.	Deductible amount (before 10 percent of AGI limitation)	$2,400

The $2,400 loss, calculated at line 9, should be combined with all other casualty or theft losses incurred in 2015. The aggregate will be deductible to the extent that it exceeds 10 percent of Wilson's 2015 adjusted gross income.

CASE 2. (Illustrating a topical index approach to tax research.)

TAX PROBLEM

Philip Davis, a full-time electrician employed by the Exeter Hotel, hires a preparer to prepare his 2015 tax return. Davis works exclusively at the hotel but feels that he is entitled to deduct the cost of operating his personal vehicle. Davis transports several thousand pounds of electrical parts, equipment, and tools to work each day.

FACTS

The Exeter Hotel does not provide a convenient, well-protected location for Davis to store the various electrical items. Accordingly, the van has a customized interior with appropriate shelves and cabinets for the electrical items. The van, which is also used by Davis as a personal vehicle, was purchased on April 1, 2015, at a cost of $19,000, which includes $2,000 for the customized interior.

ISSUE

Can Davis claim a full or partial transportation expense deduction even though the cost of commuting is not deductible?

RESEARCH

The subject indexes to the CCH Compilation Volumes (whether in print or electronic format) are located in a separate volume entitled the Index Volume. The researcher determines a few key topics under which the relevant references might be found.

First attempt. Locate the term "Transportation." The heading "expenses for" refers the searcher to the topic "Traveling expenses." Under this listing are numerous headings, but the entry at "automobile expenses" leading to "Automobiles: expenses" seems to be the most relevant reference.

Second attempt. Locate the topic "Automobiles" and the term "expenses." Under this listing, the following subheadings seem appropriate for additional research:

.. equipment transported   8590.04; 8590.25

.. tools transported   8590.04; 8590.25

The paragraph reference 8590.25 given in the Index leads to Code Section 162 in the CCH Compilations Volume and thereunder to a digest of the *Fausner* case (*Fausner v. Commissioner,* 73-2 USTC ¶9515), a 1973 Supreme Court decision that disallowed a transportation deduction. In examining this digest, reprinted below, it would appear that Davis cannot deduct any part of his transportation expense.

Exhibit 6. CCH STANDARD FEDERAL TAX REPORTS—COMPILATION SAMPLE PAGE: Annotations

TRADE OR BUSINESS EXPENSES §162 [¶8590]

.25 Equipment and tool transportation.—An individual could not deduct any part of his automobile expenses where he used his car to transport bulky equipment to and from his places of employment because storage facilities were lacking where it was shown that the individual would have used his car to commute to work in any event. Under this circumstance, it was held that it was not possible to allocate the automobile expenses between nondeductible commuting expenses and deductible business expenses incurred in transporting the tools nor had the existence of any additional expense been shown, with the result that the entire cost of traveling to and from the taxpayer's work constituted commuting expenses.

D. Fausner, Sup. Ct., per curiam, 73-2 USTC ¶9515, 413 US 838, aff'g CA-5, per curiam, 73-1 USTC ¶9180, 472 F2d 561.

Code §162 ¶8540.25

However, following the *Fausner* decision, the IRS issued Rev. Rul. 75-380, 1975-2 CB 59, superseding Rev. Rul. 56-25, 1956-2 CB 152, and revoking Rev. Rul. 63-100, 1963-1 CB 34. The full text of Rev. Rul. 75-380 is given at paragraph 8540.2501. Of particular importance to Davis is the following observation in Rev. Rul. 75-380:

Therefore, in situations where a taxpayer can establish that additional expenses were incurred for transporting work implements to and from work, a reasonable and feasible method of allocation within the scope of the Supreme Court's opinion in *Fausner* would be to allow an ordinary and necessary business expense deduction for only the portion of the cost of transporting the work implements by the mode of transportation used which is in excess of cost of commuting by the same mode of transportation without the work implements. The fact that a taxpayer might have or would have used a less expensive mode of transportation if it had not been necessary to carrying the work implements is immaterial.

Based on this logic, it would seem that Davis may, at least, claim a depreciation deduction for the $2,000 that he spent to install shelves and cabinets in his van. However, he would not be entitled to claim a deduction for the cost of transportation to and from work.

Subsequently, following Rev. Rul. 75-380, the Tax Court found in *H.A. Pool,* 36 TCM 93, Dec. 34,233(M), T.C. Memo. 1977-20, that a transportation deduction was allowed for the excess cost of driving a truck rather than a car, since it was necessary to transport tools to work, and the car would not have been able to carry that weight. Following the reasoning in *Pool,* we might also be able to contend that the excess cost of acquiring a van, rather than a passenger automobile, is eligible for a transportation deduction. Of course, in this instance, we are taking a somewhat aggressive position, and our client must be advised of the inherent risk of being challenged by the Internal Revenue Service. The final decision, whether or not to claim this deduction, rests with the client.

Tax Administration

¶2211

ORGANIZATION OF THE IRS

The administration and enforcement of federal internal revenue taxes are required to be performed under the supervision of the Secretary of the Treasury. Code Sec. 7801(a). The Internal Revenue Service, a division of the Department of the Treasury, has been delegated the operational aspects of the determination, assessment, and collection of all internal revenue taxes. The Commissioner of Internal Revenue, the official in charge, is appointed by the President and serves under the Secretary of the Treasury. Code Sec. 7802.

The Internal Revenue Service (IRS) consists of a National Office, headquartered in Washington, D.C., and an extensive field organization composed of over a hundred thousand revenue agents, revenue officers, and support personnel. The main task of the National Office is to develop uniform policies for the nationwide administration of the tax law and coordinate the various operations of the IRS.

Internal Revenue Service Restructuring and Reform Act of 1998

In accordance with the Internal Revenue Service Restructuring and Reform Act of 1998, the IRS modified its entire structure. The structure divides the IRS into four operating divisions. Each operating division is responsible for serving a group of similar taxpayers. The structure is organized to reflect specific types of taxpayers and common issues associated with these taxpayers. See Exhibit 7.

Exhibit 7. IRS ORGANIZATION CHART

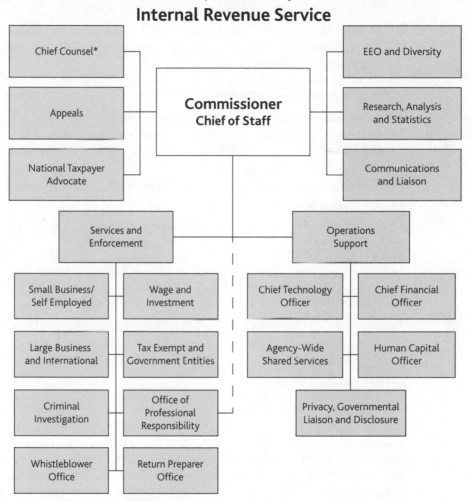

U.S. Department of Treasury

Internal Revenue Service

* With respect to tax litigation and the legal interpretation of tax law, the Chief Counsel also reports to the General Counsel of the Treasury Department. On matters solely related to tax policy, the Chief Counsel reports to the Treasury General Counsel.

The IRS's mission is to:

Provide America's taxpayers top quality service by helping them understand and meet their tax responsibilities and by applying the tax law with integrity and fairness to all.

The four operating divisions are supported by two agency-wide service organizations: (1) Information Systems; and (2) Agency-Wide Shared Services. In addition, the IRS Appeals Office, the Taxpayer Advocate Service, the Office of the Chief Counsel and Criminal Investigation are nationwide organizations that provide separate specialized services.

The Operating Divisions

Wage and Investment Income Division (W&I)

W&I covers individual taxpayers who only receive wage and/or investment income, which includes approximately 88 million filers. Most of these taxpayers only deal with the IRS when filing their tax returns each year. Compliance matters are limited to such issues as dependency exemption, credits, filing status, and deductions. Much of the income earned by W&I taxpayers is reported by third parties (such as employers, banks, brokerage firms) and the income is generally collected through third party withholding. Thus, this group is generally highly compliant. Most of these taxpayers earn under $50,000 a year.

Within the W&I group, there are three operating units:

1. Communications, Assistance, Research and Education—The primary role is education;
2. Customer Account Services—The role is to process returns submitted by taxpayers and validate that the proper taxes have been paid;
3. Compliance—The role is to address the limited compliance and collection issues that may arise with respect to this group of taxpayers.

Small Business and Self-Employed Division (SB/SE)

SB/SE is comprised of fully or partially self-employed individuals and small businesses. It includes corporations and partnerships with assets less than or equal to $10 million. Also, estate and gift taxpayers, fiduciary returns and all individuals who file international returns are examined by this group, which includes approximately 45 million filers. Typical taxpayers from this group interact with the IRS 4 to 60 times per year.

Large Business and International Division (LB&I)

LB&I includes businesses with assets over $10 million or about 210,000 filers. Many complex matters such as tax law interpretation, accounting and regulation issues are common. The largest taxpayers in this group deal with the IRS on an almost continuous basis. The LB&I is aligned by six industry groupings and one examination support function as follows: financial services; natural resources and construction; heavy manufacturing and transportation; communications, technology and media; retailers, food, pharmaceuticals, and healthcare; global high wealth; and field specialists.

Tax-Exempt Organizations and Governmental Entities Division (TE/GE)

TE/GE includes pension plans, exempt organizations and the governmental entities, and is comprised of about 24 million filers.

Other Units

Criminal Investigation (CI)

The CI unit reports directly to the Service Commissioner and Deputy Commissioner. It operates as a nationwide unit with 35 Special Agent In Charge Offices. CI's mission is to the serve the public by investigating potential criminal violations of the Internal Revenue Code and related financial crimes. The new CI will focus more on tax administration issues and less on nontax crimes (such as drug cases). It will provide a streamlined investigative review process and a geographic alignment that is more consistent with the location of the various United States Attorney's Offices.

IRS Appeals Office

The IRS Appeals Office is headquartered in Washington, D.C., but will maintain the geographic location of current offices. The field staff has been realigned to closely mirror the new operating structure. Thus, within a particular office, Appeals Officers will be designated to work on cases from a particular operating division. Three appeals operating units will manage operations for each of the taxpayer segments as follows: (1) Appeals—Large and Mid-Size Businesses; (2) Appeals—Small Business/Self-Employed and Exempt/Governmental Entities; and (3) Appeals—Wage and Investment.

National Taxpayer Advocate (NTA)

The NTA was designed to help taxpayers who have problems with the IRS, and who were not able to get them resolved through the normal administrative process. The NTA is organized around two major functions: (1) the casework function—to resolve all individual taxpayer problems; and (2) the systemic analysis and the advocacy function—to work with the operating divisions to identify systemic problems, analyze root causes, implement solutions, and proactively identify potential problems with new systems and procedures. The NTA will be physically located in geographic locations to allow contact with local taxpayers. A local NTA within each operating division will help to identify system problems in the division.

Office of Chief Counsel

Within the Office of Chief Counsel there is a Division Counsel for each operating division. The Division Counsel provides legal advice and representation, and participates in the plans and activities of the operating division management. The main focus of the Operating Division Counsel is to provide legal services to the operating divisions, take part in planning the strategic use of litigation resources and assist the operating divisions in developing compliance approaches and new taxpayer service initiatives.

Field Counsel will provide litigation services and legal advice on locally managed cases. Field Counsel will consist of attorney groups that will report to an assigned Operating Division counsel.

Office of Professional Responsibility

The Office of Professional Responsibility establishes and enforces consistent standards of competence, integrity, and conduct for tax professionals

Whistleblower Office

The IRS Whistleblower Office processes tips received from individuals who spot tax problems in their workplace, while conducting day-to-day personal business or anywhere else they may be encountered. The Whistleblower Office is responsible for assessing and analyzing the tips and after determining their degree of credibility, the case is assigned to the appropriate IRS office for further investigation.

Communications and Liaison

The Communications and Liaison Division attempts to ensure that communications with customers, Congress, and stakeholders are consistent and coordinated. The Division also attempts to ensure that there is a quality work environment that is operationally efficient and effective, including an emphasis on automating business processes. It attempts to ensure that there is appropriate collection, use, and protection of information to accomplish IRS business objectives.

Office of Privacy, Governmental Liaison and Disclosure

This Division is intended to preserve and enhance public confidence by advocating for the protection and proper use of identity information.

Return Preparer Office

This office's mission is to improve compliance by providing comprehensive oversight and support of tax professionals. Its goal is to improve the compliance and accuracy of tax returns prepared by tax return preparers.

¶2215   REPRESENTATION OF TAXPAYERS

Rules for persons representing taxpayers before the IRS are published in Treasury Department Circular No. 230. See 31 CFR Part 10. The phrase "practice before the IRS" includes all matters connected with presentation to the IRS relating to a client's rights, privileges, or liabilities under laws or regulations administered by the IRS. Circular No. 230, Sec. 10.2.

Neither the preparation of a return nor the appearance as a witness for the taxpayer is considered practice before the IRS. Attorneys or certified public accountants who are not under suspension or disbarment may practice before the IRS, as may any person enrolled as an agent. The latter individual, however, must demonstrate special competence in tax matters by written examination administered by the IRS. Treasury Department Circular No. 230, Sec. 10.4.

In certain situations, other persons may represent taxpayers. Individuals may appear on their own behalf, and, in addition, Treasury Department Circular No. 230, Sec. 10.7, states a number of situations where individuals may appear on behalf of others without enrollment:

1. An individual may represent another individual who is his or her full-time employer, a partnership of which he or she is a general partner or a full-time employee, or a family member.
2. Corporations, associations, or organized groups may be represented by bona fide officers or full-time employees.
3. Trusts, receiverships, guardianships, or estates may be represented by their trustees, receivers, guardians, administrators, or executors or full-time employees.
4. An individual who prepares the taxpayer's return as a preparer may represent the taxpayer before officers and employees of the Examination Division of the IRS.

EXAMPLE 2.2

> Sam Spaulding is being audited by the IRS for tax years 2013 and 2014. He prepared his own 2013 return, but ABC Tax Return Preparation Service prepared his 2014 return. ABC could represent Sam on matters relating to the 2014 return but only at the agent or examining officer level, not at the higher level of the Appeals Division.

Circular No. 230, Secs. 10.20 to 10.30, states a number of rules relative to practice before the IRS by tax preparers:

1. They shall not neglect or refuse promptly to submit records or information requested by the IRS.
2. They shall advise the client promptly of any noncompliance, error, or omission that may have been on any return or document submitted to the IRS.
3. They shall exercise due diligence in preparing returns and documents and in determining the correctness of oral or written representations made by them to the IRS and to clients.
4. They shall not unreasonably delay the prompt disposition of any matter before the IRS.
5. They shall not in any IRS matter knowingly and directly or indirectly employ or accept assistance from any person who is under disbarment or suspension from practice before the IRS.
6. They shall not charge an unconscionable fee for representation of a client in any matter before the IRS.
7. They shall not represent clients with conflicting interests.
8. They shall not use or participate in the use of any form of public communication containing false, fraudulent, misleading, or unfair statements or claims.

¶2225   RULINGS PROGRAMS

Since passage of the first income tax laws, the IRS has engaged in major publication efforts to provide taxpayers and their advisors with the most current interpretive views of all areas of federal income tax law. The *Internal Revenue Bulletin* is the authoritative instrument of the IRS for announcing official rulings (Revenue Rulings and Revenue Procedures) and for publishing Treasury Decisions, Executive Orders, Tax Conventions, legislation, and other items of general interest. Since publication invites reliance, taxpayers must be aware of the degree of authoritative weight that may be accorded such documents. See detailed discussion at ¶2035.

In addition, Technical Information Releases (TIRs) and Announcements are periodically distributed by the IRS to advise the public of various technical matters. While these pronouncements are published weekly in the *Internal Revenue Bulletin,* they are not usually included in the *Cumulative Bulletin.*

The IRS also issues communications to individual taxpayers and IRS personnel in three primary ways: (1) letter rulings, (2) determination letters, and (3) technical advice memoranda. These documents are part of the IRS Rulings Program, which includes published rulings appearing in the *Internal Revenue Bulletin.*

Letter Rulings

A letter ruling is a "written determination issued to a taxpayer that interprets and applies the tax laws to that taxpayer's specific set of facts." Rev. Proc. 2015-1, Sec. 2.01, 2015-1 IRB. Letter rulings generally are issued on uncompleted, actual (rather than hypothetical) transactions or on transactions that have been completed before the filing of the tax return for the year in question. Thus, the emphasis of the letter rulings program is upon the questions or problems of the taxpayer, in contrast to the published rulings program, where the emphasis is centered on uniformity of interpretation of the tax law.

It is the policy of the IRS, however, not to issue letter rulings in a number of general areas:

1. Results of transactions that lack bona fide business purposes or have as their principal purpose the reduction of federal taxes.
2. Matters on which a court decision adverse to the government has been handed down and the question of following the decision or litigating further has not yet been resolved.
3. Matters involving the prospective application of the estate tax to the property or the estate of a living person.
4. Matters involving alternate plans of proposed transactions or involving hypothetical situations.
5. Matters involving the federal tax consequences of any proposed federal, state, local, or municipal legislation.
6. Whether a proposed transaction would subject the taxpayer to a criminal penalty.

Further, it is the policy of the IRS to provide revised lists of those areas of the Internal Revenue Code in which advanced rulings or determination letters will not or will "not ordinarily" be issued. ("Not ordinarily" connotes that unique and compelling reasons must be demonstrated to justify a ruling or determination letter.) Additions or deletions to the revised lists are made as needed to reflect the current policy of the IRS and are set out in several Revenue Procedures. For example, no ruling will be issued to determine whether compensation is reasonable in amount and therefore allowable as a deduction under Code Sec. 162. This is but one of over 50 areas identified by the IRS for nonissuance of letter rulings. There is also a listing of over 50 areas in which rulings will not ordinarily be issued. Rev. Proc. 2015-3, Sec. 3 and 4, 2015-1 IRB. Areas in international transactions for which rulings will not be issued are also listed. Rev. Proc. 2015-7, Sec. 3, 2015-1 IRB.

The issuance of rulings serves to reduce the number of disputes with revenue agents. A favorable ruling generally will avoid any controversy with an agent in the event of a later audit. For the taxpayer, rulings reduce the uncertainty of tax consequences of a particular action. On the other hand, a ruling request has some disadvantages. Cost is a factor since, under the IRS user fee program, a taxpayer will have to pay fees to have a request prepared. Code Sec. 7805. Rev. Proc. 2015-8, Sec. 6, 2015-1 IRB. Also, there is often delay in obtaining a ruling, which could be difficult for the taxpayer if time is a significant factor.

Detailed instructions as to the information that a taxpayer should submit in requesting a ruling are given in Rev. Proc. 2015-1, *supra*.

PLANNING POINTER	Although there may be advantages to obtaining a ruling, it may not always be desirable to request a ruling. If the tax results are uncertain but the taxpayer wants to go ahead with a proposed transaction, it might be unwise to request a ruling. Also, if time is a crucial factor and the proposed transaction is so complex that a long time might pass before a response to a ruling request would be given, it might be unwise to request a ruling.

Determination Letters

The determination letter program is part of the letter rulings program. Determination Letters are not published; however, the IRS is now required to make individual rulings available for public inspection. A determination letter is a written statement issued by a Director in response to an inquiry by an individual or an organization. It applies to the particular facts involved and is based upon principles and precedents previously announced by the National Office to a specific set of facts. Rev. Proc. 2015-1, Sec. 2.03, *supra*. Determination letters are issued in response to taxpayers' requests submitted to the Director, whereas letter rulings are issued by the National Office. The most important use of determination letters in prospective transactions is in the qualification of pension plans and the determination of the tax-exempt status of an organization.

PLANNING POINTER	It is advisable for taxpayers to request a determination letter in connection with pension plans; otherwise, the taxpayer may later find out that the plan does not qualify and deductions might be disallowed.

A Director may not issue a determination letter in response to an inquiry relating to a question specifically covered by statute, regulations, rulings, etc. published in the *Internal Revenue Bulletin* where (1) it appears that the taxpayer has directed a similar inquiry to the National Office; (2) the identical issue involving the same taxpayer is pending in a case before the Appeals Office; (3) the determination letter is requested by an industry, trade, or similar group; or (4) the request involves an industry-wide problem. Reg. §601.201(c)(4). The form for a request for a determination letter is the same as that for a ruling. Rev. Proc. 2015-1, *supra*.

Technical Advice Memoranda

A technical advice memorandum is advice or guidance furnished by the National Office upon request of a District or an Appeals Office in response to any technical or procedural question that develops during the examination or appeals process. Rev. Proc. 2015-2, Sec. 3, 2015-1 IRB. Both the taxpayer and the District or Appeals Office may request technical advice. The taxpayer may request advice where there appears to be a lack of uniformity in the application of law or where the issue is unusual or complex. Technical advice adverse to the taxpayer and furnished to an Appeals Office does not preclude the possibility of settlement. Technical advice can also be advantageous from the IRS's viewpoint in that it serves to establish consistent holdings in field offices. Responses to requests for technical advice memoranda sometimes become the basis for a Revenue Ruling.

User Fee Program

The payment of user fees is required for all requests to the IRS for rulings, opinion letters, determination letters, and similar requests. The IRS issues schedules of fees and procedures for the collection of the fees along with other guidelines as prescribed by the Revenue Act of 1987. The fee schedules range from $200 to $20,000. Rev. Proc. 2015-8, Sec. 6, 2015-1 IRB.

¶2245   TAXPAYER COMPLIANCE ASSISTANCE

In order to assist taxpayers, individuals, corporations, partnerships, and other legal entities to be in compliance with requirements of the Internal Revenue Code and regulations, the IRS develops and issues IRS Publications that address a variety of general and special topics of concern to taxpayers. A typical IRS Publication highlights changes in the tax law in a specific area (for example, Pub. No. 508, Educational Expenses), explains the purpose of the law, defines terminology, lists exemptions, provides several examples, and includes sample worksheets and filled-in forms. As to taxpayer reliance, the IRS warns in every IRS Publication that information provided covers only the most common tax situation and is not intended to replace the law or change its meaning. Even though IRS Publications do not bind the IRS, the information contained in IRS Publications provides essential guidance for tax law compliance, particularly in technical or specialized areas.

Tax Practice and Procedure

¶2301   EXAMINATION OF RETURNS

Selection of Returns

The selection of returns for examination begins at the service centers. Returns can be selected by computer programs or by manual selection. The IRS uses the Discriminant Inventory Function (DIF) system, which involves computer scoring using mathematical formulas to select tax returns with the highest probability of errors. Returns with the highest scores are then manually examined by district classifiers, who determine whether a return should be subject to examination. *Internal Revenue Manual,* Sec. 4.1.5.1.1. Taxpayers are divided into classes, including such classifications as business versus nonbusiness; total positive income of varying amounts for nonbusiness returns; and total gross receipts of varying amounts for business returns. Total Positive Income (TPI) is defined as the sum of positive income items on the return such as wages, interest, dividends, and other income items, with losses treated as zero.

Returns are sometimes chosen at random for the National Research Program (NRP). NRP is a program for measuring taxpayer compliance through specialized audits of individual tax returns. The principal uses of NRP data are to measure the levels of compliance and tax administration gaps necessary for formulation of the IRS's long-term enforcement policies, to determine changes in compliance levels over a period of time in order to properly direct enforcement programs, to develop and improve return selection procedures and changes in the DIF scores, to identify alternative methods of operation, and to achieve greater operating economies.

Other events that might give rise to an examination are:

1. Total positive income is above specified amounts.
2. Another IRS office or a non-IRS party might provide information (e.g., a tip from a bitter former spouse).
3. A claim for refund may result in a closer examination of the return.
4. A return of a related party (family member, partner) might be examined to determine the correctness of the taxpayer's return.

EXAMPLE 2.3   Arthur and Beverly Saunders were divorced in 2015. During their marriage, Arthur had not reported some consulting income he received beyond his regular salary. Beverly, still upset about the divorce, reports Arthur to the IRS. This may result in an audit.

EXAMPLE 2.4   In 2015, Charles Regus files an amended return with a sizeable refund claim as a result of educational expense deductions that he could have taken on his 2013 return, but which he failed to take because he was uncertain as to whether they would qualify. It is possible that close examination of his 2013 return might occur as a result of this claim for refund. However, if Charles believes he has a good case, he should file the amended return.

Correspondence Examinations

Correspondence examinations involve relatively simple problems that can generally be resolved by mail. These examinations would include mathematical errors, broadly defined in Code Sec. 6213(g)(2) to mean (1) an error in addition, subtraction, multiplication, or division shown on any return; (2) an incorrect use of any IRS table if such incorrect use is apparent from other information on the return; (3) inconsistent entries on the return; (4) an omission of information required to be supplied on the return to substantiate a return item; and (5) a deduction or credit that exceeds a statutory limit that is either a specified monetary amount or a percentage, ratio, or fraction—if the items entering into the application of such limit appear on the return.

EXAMPLE 2.5   James Judson, single, incorrectly determines his tax liability because he used the joint rate schedule rather than the single rate schedule. This correction and adjustment can be resolved by mail.

The Service Center personnel might also question specific items under the Unallowable Items Program. For example, a deduction of Social Security taxes by the taxpayer would result in notification by the Service Center. Such a contact is considered to be an examination in contrast to a mathematical/clerical error notification, which is not considered to be an examination. (If it is an examination, one is entitled to a notice of deficiency and to administrative appeal.) The IRS also matches information returns of some taxpayers with income tax returns. If there is a discrepancy, the return will be corrected, or the file might be referred for examination and possibly criminal investigation.

District Office Examinations

A District Office examination of a return is conducted by a tax auditor of the Audit Division either by correspondence or by interview. Sometimes the matters are so simple they can be handled by correspondence. Verification of particular itemized deductions such as interest, taxes, or charitable contributions might be handled by correspondence. *Internal Revenue Manual,* Sec. 4.10.2 and 3.

Returns selected for interview examinations generally require some analysis and judgment as well as verification. Examples of types of issues which lend themselves to interview examinations are income items that are not subject to withholding, deductions for travel and entertainment, items such as casualty and theft losses that involve the use of fair market value, education expenses, deductions for business-related expenses, and determination of basis of property. Also, if the taxpayer's income is low in relation to financial responsibilities as indicated on the return through the number of dependents or interest expense, or if the taxpayer's occupation is of the type that required only a limited formal education, an office interview might be deemed appropriate. Certain business activities or occupations reported may lend themselves to office interview examinations (e.g., auto repair shops, restaurants, service stations, professional persons, farmers, motels, and others).

EXAMPLE 2.6   Edward Egars, an outside salesperson, reports income of $25,000 and takes travel and entertainment deductions before application of the 50 percent limit on meals and entertainment of $15,000. Edward could be called in for an office examination to verify his travel and entertainment expenses.

EXAMPLE 2.7	Jane Judson has adjusted gross income of $15,000 and gives $7,000 in cash contributions to her church. Since her contributions exceed the norm for her bracket and approach the maximum limitation for her income level, she could be called in to verify her charitable contributions.

PLANNING POINTER	In an office examination, the taxpayer or a representative should provide only information or support for items that are requested of the taxpayer by the IRS; otherwise, the tax auditor might open up other areas for investigation. Situations may vary, but some practitioners believe that it is better for the taxpayer, assuming there is a representative such as a CPA or a lawyer, not to be present because the representative can keep better control over the interview and also maintain a less emotional atmosphere.

When there is a disagreement after an office examination, if practicable, the taxpayer is given an opportunity for an interview with the tax auditor's immediate supervisor or for a conference with an Appeals Officer. Reg. §601.105(c)(1)(ii). If these actions are not feasible, the taxpayer will be sent a 30-day letter from the District Office indicating the proposed adjustments and the courses of action. If the taxpayer agrees with the adjustment, the taxpayer can sign the agreement form. If the taxpayer disagrees, an Appeals Office conference may be requested within 30 days or the taxpayer may ignore the 30-day letter and wait for the 90-day letter, which allows the taxpayer to file a petition in the Tax Court. Reg. §601.105(c)(1)(ii) and (d)(1)(iv).

Field Examinations

Field examinations are conducted by revenue agents and involve more complex issues than do office examinations. Field audits take place in the taxpayer's or the taxpayer's representative's office or home. The revenue agent must identify items that may need adjustment, gather the appropriate evidence, and apply the applicable Code provisions, Regulations, and other interpretative rulings. Techniques have been developed by the IRS to try to ensure that revenue agents consider all areas necessary for a proper calculation of the tax liability. An agent has power to subpoena all books and records and to compel the attendance of witnesses. Code Sec. 7602.

The agent completes a report called the Revenue Agent Report (RAR). In agreed cases, a copy of the RAR is sent to the taxpayer before review. If the taxpayer agrees with the revenue agent's adjustments and proposals, the taxpayer can sign Form 870 (Waiver of Restrictions on Assessment and Collection of Deficiency in Tax). In unagreed cases, the taxpayer does not receive the RAR until after review by the Review Staff.

PLANNING POINTER	The revenue agent should be treated courteously and should be promptly furnished information and substantiation relating to applicable tax return items. Although the cooperation of the taxpayer (or the taxpayer's representative) is important, the taxpayer should respond only to questions asked by the agent. Disclosing unnecessary information could cause problems for the taxpayer.
	There are some advantages to settling with the revenue agent. In addition to being less costly than settling at higher levels, negotiations with the revenue agent are generally more informal than negotiations at higher levels and less demanding on technical aspects. Also, if questionable issues exist but were not raised at the agent level, it may be wise to settle at that level in order to avoid the possibility of persons at higher levels raising those questionable issues. Similarly, there is an advantage to the revenue agent to have an agreed case because it involves more effort and time to write a report on an unagreed case than on an agreed case.

Audit Reconsideration

The audit reconsideration is a procedure that is used when a taxpayer has ignored a statutory notice of deficiency or where there has been a breakdown in communication between the taxpayer and the IRS. *Internal Revenue Manual,* Sec. 4.13.4.4. An audit reconsideration is permitted when a new notice was not sent to the taxpayer's new address, the taxpayer had not received any notification from the IRS on any assessment, and the taxpayer had not been given an opportunity to submit any required substantiation or necessary documentation.

¶2311   APPEALS PROCESS

Administrative Process

If the taxpayer and the agent do not agree, the taxpayer will be sent a 30-day letter that explains the appellate procedures and urges the taxpayer to reply within 30 days either by signing the waiver or by requesting a conference. If the taxpayer does not respond to the 30-day letter, a statutory notice of deficiency (90-day letter) will be sent giving the taxpayer 90 days to file a petition with the Tax Court. Thus, if the taxpayer and agent do not agree, the taxpayer has several options:

1. The taxpayer may request a conference in the IRS Appeals Office.
2. After receiving the statutory notice of deficiency, the taxpayer may file a petition in the Tax Court within the 90-day period.
3. The taxpayer could wait for the 90-day period to expire, pay the assessment, and start a refund suit in the District Court or the Court of Federal Claims.

If the IRS and the taxpayer agree, the statutory notice of deficiency issued by the IRS (90-day letter) may be rescinded. The rescinded notice voids the limitations regarding credits, refunds, and assessments, and the taxpayer will have no right to petition the Tax Court based on such notice. Rescinding the deficiency notice will allow for resolution of the controversy within the IRS.

IRS Appeals Office

If an appeal is made within the IRS, an appropriate request must be made. The request must be accompanied by a written protest unless:

1. The proposed increase or decrease in tax or claimed refund is not more than $2,500 for any of the tax periods involved in field examination cases.
2. The examination was conducted by a tax auditor (i.e., an office examination) or by correspondence. (See IRS Publication No. 5, Appeal Rights and Preparation of Protests for Unagreed Cases.)

If a protest is required, it should be sent within the 30-day period granted in the letter containing the examination report. The protest should contain:

1. A statement that the taxpayer wants to appeal the findings of the examiner to the Appeals Office
2. Taxpayer's name and address
3. The date and symbols from the letter transmitting the proposed adjustments and findings the taxpayer is protesting
4. The tax periods or years involved
5. An itemized schedule of the adjustments with which the taxpayer does not agree
6. A statement of facts supporting the taxpayer's position in any contested factual issue
7. A statement outlining the law or other authority on which the taxpayer is relying

A taxpayer may go to the Appeals Office at two different times: (1) if the protest is filed within the 30-day period as stated in the 30-day letter, or (2) if the 30-day period passes and the taxpayer files a petition in the Tax Court within 90 days after receipt of a statutory notice of deficiency.

Exhibit 8 shows graphically the income tax appeal procedures within the IRS (as described above) and through the court system (as described on the following pages).

Exhibit 8. INCOME TAX APPEAL PROCEDURE

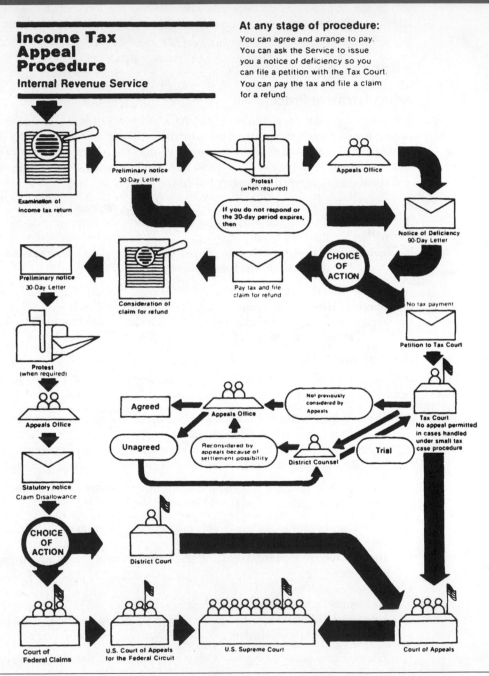

There are a number of important factors to consider in filing a protest and going to the Appeals Office. It is less expensive than litigation and yet the taxpayer leaves open the opportunity to file a petition in the Tax Court or to sue for refund in a District Court or the Court of Federal Claims. In addition, a taxpayer is often able to gather more information about the IRS position in the event the taxpayer needs to carry the case further, and there may be a chance that the taxpayer can convince the Appeals Officer that the IRS was incorrect at the agent level. The Appeals Officer may be at some disadvantage in that the case was not personally prepared and the Appeals Officer is relying on the information presented by the revenue agent, which could be an advantage to the taxpayer.

On the other hand, there may be some disadvantages to having an Appeals Conference. New issues might be raised in an Appeals Conference, although the IRS's policy is to avoid raising an issue unless the grounds for such action are "substantial" and the potential effect upon tax liability is "material." 26 CFR Sec. 601.106(d)(1). The Appeals Officer must have a strong reason for raising an issue. The *Internal Revenue Manual,* Sec. 8.6.1.4, has given the following example in the past:

EXAMPLE 2.8

> If a District Director disallowed a claimed farm loss solely on the ground that it was a hobby loss and stated nothing concerning the items making up the loss, there would not be substantial grounds for raising a new issue concerning the amount of the loss merely because the Appeals Officer suspected that the items had not been verified. On the other hand, if the examiner had indicated in the report that the items had not been verified, there would be good reason for the Appeals Officer to refer the case back to the District Director if it was believed such action was necessary. If the District Director stated that some of the items of claimed expense were personal in nature, this would constitute substantial grounds for the Appeals Officer to raise a new issue or to refer the case back to the District Director for further information and investigation.

Taxpayers may represent themselves at the Appeals Conference or be represented by an attorney, CPA, or person enrolled to practice before the IRS. The Appeals Officer, who actually handles the appeals, reports to the Regional Director of Appeals who, in turn, reports to the Regional Commissioner. Proceedings before the Appeals Officer are informal and are held in the District Office. The Appeals Officer may request that the taxpayer submit additional information, which could involve additional conferences.

The Appeals Officer may resolve controversies between the taxpayer and the IRS by considering the "hazards of litigation." The *Internal Revenue Manual,* Sec. 8.1.1.3, states that a fair and impartial resolution "reflects on an issue-by-issue basis the probable result in event of litigation, or one which reflects mutual concessions for the purpose of settlement based on the relative strength of the opposing positions where there is a substantial uncertainty of the result in event of litigation." If there is uncertainty as to the application of the law, the Appeals Officer will consider a settlement in view of the hazards that would exist if the case were litigated. Thus, the Appeals Officer, in evaluating a case for settlement, will objectively assess how a court might look at the case rather than attempt to obtain the best results for the IRS. The Appeals Officer considers the value of the evidence that would be presented, the witnesses, the uncertainty as to an issue of fact and the uncertainty as to a conclusion considering the court in which the case might be litigated or appealed.

If a satisfactory settlement of the issue is reached after consideration by the Appeals Office, the taxpayer will be requested to sign Form 870-AD. By signing Form 870-AD, the taxpayer waives restrictions on the assessment and collection of any deficiency. Form 870-AD does not stop the running of interest when filed. It is merely the taxpayer's offer to waive restrictions, and interest will run until 30 days after the IRS has accepted the offer. If the taxpayer does not agree with the decision at the Appeals level, a notice of deficiency will be issued by the Appeals Office after consideration by the Regional Counsel of the memorandum recommending a notice of deficiency.

Taxpayer's Rights

The Taxpayer Bill of Rights is a series of provisions which require the Treasury Department to outline in "simple and nontechnical terms the rights of a taxpayer and the obligations of the IRS during an audit." Additionally, the IRS is required to inform taxpayers of their administrative and appeals rights in the event of an adverse decision, as well as the procedures related to refund claims, taxpayer complaints, collection assessments, levies, and tax liens. The Treasury Department has prepared and released the required information statement, IRS Publication No. 1, Your Rights as a Taxpayer.

The Taxpayer Bill of Rights is divided into four major categories:

1. Taxpayer rights and IRS obligations
2. Levy and lien provisions
3. Proceedings by taxpayers
4. Authority of the Tax Court

Most significantly, the law requires abatement of penalties resulting from reliance on erroneous written IRS advice, authorizes recovery of damages for failure of the IRS to remove a lawful lien, permits the filing of an application for hardship relief with the IRS Taxpayer Advocate, and outlines provisions whereby a taxpayer, who substantially prevails in an administrative or court proceeding against the IRS, may recover reasonable administrative and litigation costs. Additionally, the law allows a taxpayer or an IRS representative to make an audio recording of an in-person interview regarding the determination or collection of any tax.

To ensure the effective administration of the Taxpayer Bill of Rights, an Office for Taxpayer Services has been established, under the direction of an Assistant Commissioner for Taxpayer Services. Responsibilities of this office include: telephone, walk-in and taxpayer educational services, and the design and production of tax and informational forms. Also, there is a Taxpayer Advocate, holding the rank of Assistant to the Commissioner, who may act, under the Problem Resolution Program, on behalf of the taxpayer during the audit or collection process.

Appeal Through the Court System

Within 90 days of mailing of a notice of deficiency, the taxpayer may petition the Tax Court for re-determination of the deficiency. Code Sec. 6213(a). If the 90-day deficiency notice was issued by the Appeals Office, it is possible to arrange for pretrial settlement with the Regional Counsel of the IRS even after the case has been docketed in the Tax Court. Taxpayers filing a petition with the Tax Court may have their cases handled under less formal rules applicable to "small tax cases" if the amount of the deficiency or claimed overpayment is not greater than $50,000. However, "small tax cases" are not appealable and are not to be treated as precedents for any other cases. Code Sec. 7463(a) and (b). If the taxpayer does not file a petition with the Tax Court within 90 days, the opportunity to appeal to the Tax Court is lost.

The taxpayer can pay the deficiency and file a claim for refund by filing Form 1040X (Amended U.S. Individual Income Tax Return) and mailing it to the IRS Center where the taxpayer filed the original return. A claim for refund must be filed within three years from the date the return was filed or within two years from the date the tax was paid, whichever is later. Code Sec. 6511(a). If the return was filed before the due date, the three-year period starts to run from the date the return was due.

A suit to recover may not be started until after six months from the date the taxpayer filed the claim for refund, unless a decision on the claim for refund was made before then. A suit for refund must be started before the end of two years from the date of mailing of a notice to the taxpayer disallowing part or all of the claim. Code Sec. 6532(a).

Federal Court System

There are three trial courts or courts of original jurisdiction: the U.S. Tax Court, the U.S. District Courts, and the U.S. Court of Federal Claims. Appeal from a decision of the Tax Court of the U.S. District Court may be taken by either side to the federal Court of Appeals for the circuit in which the taxpayer resides or the corporation has its principal place of business. A review of a decision of the U.S. Court of Federal Claims is taken to the U.S. Court of Appeals for the Federal Circuit. The Supreme Court has jurisdiction to hear appeals or review decisions of the federal Court of Appeals and the U.S. Court of Appeals for the Federal Circuit. (See Exhibit 9.) For a detailed discussion of the trial court system, see ¶2055.

Choice of Tax Forum

There are a number of factors to consider in deciding whether to litigate a case and where to litigate.

1. **Jurisdiction.** The Tax Court handles only income, estate, gift, and excess profits tax cases. The District Court and the Court of Federal Claims can litigate all areas of internal revenue taxes.
2. **Payment of tax.** In the Tax Court, payment of tax is not generally allowed. Section 6213(b)(4) allows the taxpayer to pay the tax after receiving a 90-day letter and still sue in the Tax Court. This feature can be used by the taxpayer to stop the accrual of interest on the deficiency while still choosing the Tax Court forum. In the District Court and the Court of Federal Claims, payment of tax is required. Thus, whether the taxpayer has the money to pay the tax may be a factor in the choice of tax forum.
3. **Jury trial.** A jury trial is available only in the District Court. Often, tax cases do not make good jury cases because of their complexity. Also, sometimes jurors may be prejudiced against a taxpayer who is wealthier than they are.
4. **Rules of evidence.** The rules of evidence are most strict in jury trials where efforts must be made to keep the jurors from hearing inappropriate evidence. The evidence rules are most lenient in the Tax Court.
5. **Expertise of judges.** Since the Tax Court hears only tax cases, the judges are all very knowledgeable in tax law. The District Court judges are generally the least technically oriented since the District Court hears many types of cases.
6. **Publicity.** There will likely be the most publicity in the District Court since such suit is brought in the district in which the taxpayer lives.

7. **Legal precedent.** The court decisions by which the particular forum will be bound may also be a consideration. The Tax Court is bound by Tax Court decisions (unless the Court of Appeals of the circuit to which the case might be appealed held differently), by the Court of Appeals to which the case might be appealed, and by the U.S. Supreme Court. (See *J.E. Golsen,* 54 TC 757, Dec. 30,049 (1970), aff'd, 71-2 ustc ¶9497, 445 F.2d 985 (CA-10 1971), cert. denied, 404 U.S. 940, 92 S.Ct. 284.) The District Court is bound by decisions of the Court of Appeals for the circuit to which the decision would be appealed, and by the U.S. Supreme Court. The Court of Federal Claims is bound by decisions of the Court of Appeals for the Federal Circuit and by U.S. Supreme Court decisions.

8. **Factual precedent.** In certain types of cases, one court may be more favorable to the taxpayer than another court. For example, regarding the characterization of voluntary payments to employees' widows as a gift or as compensation, the Tax Court decisions have consistently been unfavorable to the taxpayer, while results in the Courts of Appeals have been more balanced. 2015 CCH Standard Federal Tax Reports ¶5507.4741.

9. **Statute of limitations.** The statute of limitations is suspended in a filing in the Tax Court whereas suit in the Court of Federal Claims and the District Court does not suspend the statute of limitations. Suspension of the statute of limitations means that the IRS can raise new issues and claims for additional taxes.

10. **Discovery.** In the District Court and the Court of Federal Claims, both parties (i.e., taxpayer and IRS) have available to them discovery tools that allow them access to the other party's evidence prior to trial. In the Tax Court, the parties are expected "to attain the objectives of discovery through informal consultation or communication" and no depositions are permitted (except in very limited circumstances). Tax Court Rule 70.

PLANNING POINTER	It is important for taxpayers to be aware of the characteristics of the courts so that an appropriate choice can be made if the taxpayer decides to go to court. A taxpayer, having made a decision to go to the District Court, for example, cannot later decide to go to the Tax Court.
	The taxpayer must think very seriously before taking a case to court. Not only may the economic costs be high, but the psychological and emotional costs may be high. The taxpayer must consider whether the tax savings will be worth the legal fees, time, and psychological costs.
	A taxpayer, in deciding to which court to take a case, should not look simply at the statistics on taxpayer winnings in the various courts. Statistics like that have some value only if winnings by taxpayers on similar issues are being examined.

KEYSTONE PROBLEM	If a taxpayer is called up for an office examination, what should the taxpayer do? If the taxpayer and the tax auditor do not agree, what steps should be taken? What factors would be considered in deciding whether or not to pursue the matter?

¶2315 SETTLEMENT AGREEMENTS

Where a taxpayer and the appeals officer have reached an agreement as to some or all of the issues in controversy, generally the appeals officer will request that the taxpayer sign a Form 870, the same agreement that is used at the district level. However, when neither party with justification is willing to concede in full the unresolved area of disagreement and a resolution of the dispute involves concessions for the purposes of settlement by both parties, a mutual concession settlement is reached, and a Form 870-AD type of agreement is to be used. Form 870 becomes effective as a waiver of restrictions and assessment when received by the Internal Revenue Service, whereas the Form 870-AD is effective upon acceptance by or on behalf of the Commissioner of Internal Revenue.

¶2325 REFUNDS

Claims for refund of individual income taxes are to be made on Form 1040X (Amended U.S. Individual Income Tax Return) and on Form 1120X for corporate income tax refunds. The claim for refund must be filed no later than three years from the date the return was filed or no later than two years from the date the tax was paid, whichever period expires later. Code Sec. 6511(a). If the return was filed before the due date, the three-year period starts to run from the date the return was due. There is a special seven-year period of limitation on a claim for refund based on a debt that became wholly worthless or on a worthless security. If the refund claim relates to a net operating loss, capital loss, or credit carryback, the refund claim may be filed within three years after the time for filing the tax return for the year of the loss (or unused credit). Code Sec. 6511(d).

Any tax deducted or withheld at the source during any calendar year shall be deemed to be paid on the 15th day of the fourth month following the close of the taxable year. Code Sec. 6513(b). Thus, a refund for taxes withheld must be filed within three years of the due date of the return (including extensions). Code Sec. 6511(b).

EXAMPLE 2.9

In 2015, Joe, a college student, worked part-time during the summer. He earned $3,000 and had income tax withheld of $400. He did not file a 2015 tax return by April 15, 2016. If he does not file his 2015 tax return by April 15, 2019, he cannot obtain the refund of $400.

¶2333 INTEREST ON UNDER/OVERPAYMENTS

The interest rate that taxpayers must pay for underpayment of taxes is equal to the federal short-term rate plus three percentage points. In the case of overpayment of taxes, the amount of interest owed by the Treasury is equal to the federal short-term rate plus three percentage points. Code Sec. 6621(a). These interest rates are adjusted quarterly, with the new rates becoming effective two months after the date of each adjustment.

Interest is also paid by the IRS on overpayments of tax. However, if any overpayment of tax is refunded within 45 days after the due date of the return (or filing date if later), no interest is allowed. If any overpayment results from a carryback (net operating loss, capital loss, or credit) through filing an amended return, interest is paid only if the overpayment is not refunded within the 45-day period. Code Sec. 6611(e) and (f).

¶2355 STATUTE OF LIMITATIONS

Assessment of any tax must be made within three years after the return was filed or after the due date for filing, whichever is later. Code Sec. 6501(a). After making an assessment of tax, the IRS has 10 years in which to initiate collection proceedings. Code Sec. 6502(a).

EXAMPLE 2.10

Fred Forbes filed his 2015 return on February 20, 2016. The government may not assess any additional tax for 2015 after April 15, 2019. If, on the other hand, he had filed his 2015 return on October 8, 2016, the statute of limitations would expire on October 8, 2019.

There are some exceptions to the general rule:

1. There is no limitation on the period for assessment in three cases: (1) false return, (2) willful attempt to evade tax, and (3) no return. Code Sec. 6501(c)(1)-(3).

EXAMPLE 2.11

Linda Lord failed to file tax returns in 2004 and 2005 when she had $20,000 gross income. If the government discovered in 2015 that the returns were not filed, it could assess 2004 and 2005 taxes against Linda.

---

2. If the taxpayer omits from gross income an amount that is in excess of 25 percent of the amount of gross income stated on the return, the tax may be assessed at any time within six years after the return is filed or the due date for filing, if later. In computing gross income, revenues from the sale of goods or services are not to be reduced by cost of goods sold. Code Sec. 6501(e)(1). Gross income also includes capital gains but is not reduced by capital losses.

EXAMPLE 2.12

On her 2014 return filed on March 20, 2015, Vera Vaughn reported her salary of $35,000 and taxable interest of $5,000. She failed to report a $9,000 capital gain. Since the $9,000 omission does not exceed $10,000 (25 percent of $40,000), the statute of limitations expires on April 15, 2018. If the omitted capital gain had been $11,000, the statute of limitations would expire on April 15, 2021.

EXAMPLE 2.13 As a sole proprietor, George Ganger had $50,000 sales and $20,000 cost of goods sold, which were reported on his 2014 tax return filed on March 14, 2015. Through an oversight he failed to report $8,000 interest. Since $8,000 interest does not exceed $12,500 (25 percent of $50,000), the statute of limitations expires on April 15, 2018.

3. Where both the taxpayer and the IRS agree, the statute of limitations may be extended for a specific period. The extension must be executed before the expiration of the applicable limitation period. Code Sec. 6501(c)(4).

4. Certain taxpayers may request a prompt assessment. The period of assessment may be shortened to 18 months in the case of a decedent, the estate of a decedent, or a corporation that is dissolved or contemplating dissolution. Code Sec. 6501(d). The purpose of this rule is to allow an estate or corporation to settle its affairs early without having to make contingent plans for later possible tax assessments.

5. If a personal holding company fails to file with its return a schedule regarding its status as a personal holding company, the tax may be assessed at any time within six years after the return is filed. Code Sec. 6501(f).

6. In the case of a deficiency attributable to the application of a carryback (capital loss, net operating loss, or credit), the statute of limitations runs from the year of the loss rather than the carryback year. Code Sec. 6501(h) and (j).

Sections 1311 through 1314 contain provisions to mitigate the effect of the statute of limitations where inequitable results might occur.

¶2365   PENALTIES

Penalties are treated as additions to federal internal revenue taxes and are, therefore, not deductible for federal income tax purposes.

Delinquency Penalties

The penalty for *failure to file* a return on the due date (determined with regard to any extension of time for filing) is 5 percent of the amount of tax due if the failure is for not more than one month, with an additional 5 percent for each additional month or fraction thereof, but not exceeding 25 percent in the aggregate. Code Sec. 6651(a)(1). The penalty is imposed on the net amount due—the difference between (1) the amount required to be shown on the return and (2) the amount paid on or before the due date and the amount of credit that may be claimed on the return. Effective for returns due after December 31, 1989, in case of a fraudulent failure to file a return, the failure to file penalty is increased to 15 percent if the net amount of tax due for each month the return is not filed up to a maximum of five months or 75 percent. Code Sec. 6651(f). The failure to file penalty is reduced by the 0.5 percent failure to pay penalty for any month in which both apply.

The penalty for *failure to pay* the amount of tax due on a tax return or for failure to pay an assessed tax within 10 days of the date of notice is one-half of one percent of the tax for one month or less and an additional one-half of one percent per month or part thereof until the penalty reaches 25 percent. An additional one-half of one percent per month is assessed if the taxpayer fails to pay a deficiency within 10 days after a notice is issued. Code Sec. 6651(a)(2) and (3) and (d). The penalty is imposed on the net amount due.

Either or both of the penalties can be avoided if the taxpayer can show that failure to file and/or pay was due to reasonable cause and not to willful neglect. Code Sec. 6651(a)(1), (2), and (3). The burden of establishing these facts is on the taxpayer. The *Internal Revenue Manual,* Sec. 20.1.7.9.1, gives some indication of what would be considered as reasonable cause for purposes of the delinquency penalties:

1. A return mailed in time but returned for insufficient postage.
2. A return filed within the legal period but in the wrong district.
3. Death or serious illness of the taxpayer or in the immediate family.
4. Unavoidable absence of the taxpayer.
5. Destruction of the taxpayer's business or business records by fire or other casualty.
6. Erroneous information given the taxpayer by an IRS official, or a request for proper blanks or returns not furnished by the IRS in sufficient time to permit the filing of the return by the due date.
7. The taxpayer made an effort to obtain assistance or information necessary to complete the return by a personal appearance at an IRS office but was unsuccessful because the taxpayer, through no fault, was unable to see an IRS representative.

8. The taxpayer is unable to obtain the records necessary to determine the amount of tax due for reasons beyond the taxpayer's control.
9. The taxpayer contacts a competent tax adviser, furnishes the necessary information, and then is incorrectly advised that the filing of a return is not required.

If the cause does not fall within one of the reasonable causes listed above, the District Director will decide whether the taxpayer established a reasonable cause for delinquency. *Internal Revenue Manual,* Sec. 20.1.7.9.1.

Accuracy-Related and Fraud Penalties

The penalties relating to the accuracy of tax returns are consolidated into one accuracy-related penalty equal to 20 percent of the portion of the underpayment to which the penalty applies. The penalty applies to the portion of underpayment attributable to one or more of the following five areas:

1. Negligence
2. Substantial understatement of income tax
3. Substantial valuation misstatement
4. Substantial overstatement of pension liabilities
5. Substantial estate or gift tax valuation understatement
6. Understatements resulting from listed and reportable transactions

The penalty does not apply to any portion of an underpayment attributable to a penalty for fraud. Code Sec. 6662(a) and (b).

For purposes of the consolidated penalty, "underpayment" means the amount by which any tax exceeds the excess of (1) the sum of (a) the amount shown as the tax by a taxpayer on the return, plus (b) amounts not shown as tax that were previously assessed, over (2) the amount of rebates made. Code Sec. 6664(a).

The accuracy-related penalties will not be imposed if it is shown that there was a reasonable cause for the underpayment and that the taxpayer acted in good faith with respect to the underpayment. Code Sec. 6664(c)(1).

Negligence Penalty

A 20 percent penalty is imposed for underpayment of tax due to negligence or disregard of rules and regulations. Code Sec. 6662(a).

EXAMPLE 2.14   Due to negligence, Steven Stover underpaid his taxes for 2015 by $30,000. His penalty is $6,000 (20% × $30,000).

The term "negligence" includes any failure to make a reasonable attempt to comply with the provisions of the Code, and the term "disregard" includes any careless, reckless, or intentional disregard. The definition of negligence is not limited only to the items specified. Thus, all behavior that is considered negligent under present law continues to be within the scope of the negligence penalty. Also, any behavior that is considered negligent by the courts but that is not specifically included within the definition is subject to the penalty.

In an effort to provide guidance as to the scope of the term "negligence," the *Internal Revenue Manual,* Sec. 4.10.6.2.1, states that it is "the omission to do something which a reasonable person, guided by those considerations which ordinarily regulate the conduct of human beings, would do, or doing something which a reasonable person would not do." According to the *Manual,* Sec. 4.10.6.2.1, the following are examples of cases in which negligence may exist:

1. Taxpayer continues year after year to make substantial errors in reporting income and claiming deductions even though these mistakes have been called to the taxpayer's attention in previous reports.
2. Taxpayer fails to maintain proper records after being advised through inadequate record procedures to do so and subsequent returns containing substantial errors are filed.
3. Taxpayer took careless and exaggerated deductions unsubstantiated by facts.
4. Taxpayer failed to give any explanation for the understatement of income and for failure to keep books and records.

Substantial Understatement of Tax Liability

If there is a substantial understatement of income tax, an amount equal to 20 percent of the amount of the understatement can be assessed. A substantial understatement of income tax occurs when the understatement exceeds the greater of 10 percent of the tax required to be shown on the return or $5,000. Code Sec. 6662(d)(1). In the case of a corporation (except for an S corporation or a personal holding company), the understatement must exceed the greater of 10 percent of the tax required to be shown on the return or $10,000. The amount of the understatement is equal to the excess of the tax required to be shown on the return over the amount of tax that is actually shown on the return.

The penalty can be avoided if there was substantial authority for the tax treatment; if relevant facts affecting the treatment are adequately disclosed in the return or a statement attached to the return; and in the case of tax shelter items, if the taxpayer reasonably believed that the tax treatment of such item was more likely than not the proper treatment. Code Sec. 6662(d)(2)(B) and (C). The penalty can be waived on showing of reasonable cause and that the taxpayer acted in good faith. Code Sec. 6664(c).

Substantial Valuation Misstatement Penalty

All taxpayers having an underpayment of tax attributable to a valuation misstatement are subject to this 20 percent penalty. Code Sec. 6662(e). There is a substantial valuation misstatement if the value of any property (or the adjusted basis of any property) is 150 percent or more of the amount determined to be the correct amount of the valuation or adjusted basis of the property. If the portion of the underpayment that is subject to the penalty is attributable to one or more gross valuation misstatements, the penalty will be applied at the rate of 40 percent. A gross valuation misstatement occurs if the value of the property (or the adjusted basis) was 200 percent or more of the correct amount of the valuation of the adjusted basis of the property. Code Sec. 6662(h)(2)(A). No penalty will be imposed on a taxpayer for a substantial valuation misstatement unless the portion of the underpayment attributable to substantial valuation misstatements exceeds $5,000, or $10,000 in the case of a corporation other than an S corporation or a personal holding company.

EXAMPLE 2.15	Bert Barge gives a painting he purchased three years ago to his alma mater and takes a charitable contribution deduction in the amount of $50,000, the value placed on it by his art professor friend. If the actual value was only $20,000 and if the tax underpayment is $10,000, Bert would be subject to a $4,000 valuation misstatement penalty (40 percent of $10,000). The valuation was more than 200 percent of the correct valuation.

Although valuation misstatements of charitable property resulting in understatements of tax are subject to the accuracy penalty provisions, the charitable deduction penalty waiver for qualified appraisers is still possible. No penalty will be imposed for an underpayment of tax resulting from a substantial or gross misstatement of charitable deduction property if it can be shown that there was a reasonable cause for the underpayment and that the taxpayer acted in good faith.

Substantial Overstatement of Pension Liabilities

The 20 percent penalty for substantial overstatement of pension liabilities applies only if the actuarial determination of pension liabilities is 200 percent or more of the amount determined to be correct. Code Sec. 6662(f). If a portion of the substantial overstatement to which the penalty applies is attributable to a gross valuation misstatement of 400 percent or more, the penalty is doubled to 40 percent of the underpayment. Code Sec. 6662(h). No penalty is imposed if the underpayment for the tax year attributable to substantial overstatements of pension liabilities is $1,000 or less.

Estate or Gift Tax Valuation Understatements

A 20 percent penalty is imposed for estate or gift tax valuation understatement if the value of any property claimed on an estate or gift tax return is 65 percent or less of the amount determined to be the correct amount of the valuation. Code Sec. 6662(g). If the understatement is attributable to a gross valuation misstatement of 40 percent or less of the correct amount, the penalty amount is 40 percent of the underpayment. Code Sec. 6662(h)(2)(C). This penalty applies only if the underpayment attributable to the understatement exceeds $5,000 for a tax period with respect to gift tax (or with respect to the estate in the case of estate tax).

Understatements Resulting from Listed and Reportable Transactions

An accuracy-related penalty was added by the American Jobs Creation Act of 2004 for understatements resulting from listed and reportable transactions. Code Sec. 6662A. The penalty applies to understatements attributable to (1) any listed transaction, and (2) any reportable transaction with a significant tax avoidance purpose. The penalty is generally 20 percent of the understatement if the taxpayer disclosed the transaction, and 30 percent if the transaction was not disclosed.

The listed and reportable transactions penalty is coordinated with three other penalties; (1) The Code Sec. 6662 accuracy-related penalty; (2) Code Sec. 6663 fraud penalty; and (3) The valuation misstatement penalties under Code Sec. 6662(e) and 6662 (h). There is a "reasonable cause" exception, although it is more demanding than the reasonable cause exception to the accuracy-related (Code Sec. 6662) and fraud (Code Sec. 6663) penalties.

Penalty for Aiding Understatement of Tax Liability

Any person who aids in the preparation or presentation of any tax document in connection with matters arising under the internal revenue laws with the knowledge that the document will result in the understatement of tax liability of another person is subject to a penalty of $1,000 ($10,000 for a corporation) for a taxable period. Code Sec. 6701.

Civil Fraud Penalty

If any part of an underpayment is due to fraud, the penalty imposed is 75 percent of the underpayment (the "civil fraud" penalty). Code Sec. 6663(a). Once the IRS establishes that any portion of an underpayment is due to fraud, the entire underpayment is assumed to be attributable to fraud, unless the taxpayer proves otherwise. Code Sec. 6663(b). The 20 percent accuracy-related penalty does not apply to any portion of an underpayment on which the fraud penalty is imposed. However, the accuracy-related penalty may be applied to any portion of the underpayment not attributable to fraud.

EXAMPLE 2.16	Beth Barrett owes a $50,000 deficiency, all due to civil fraud. In addition to the $50,000 tax deficiency, Beth will be liable for a $37,500 (75 percent of $50,000) civil fraud penalty.

Criminal Fraud Penalty

In addition to the civil fraud penalty, criminal fraud penalties may be imposed. Section 7201 provides that "any person who willfully attempts in any manner to evade or defeat any tax imposed by this title or the payment thereof shall, in addition to other penalties provided by law, be guilty of a felony. . . ." In order for there to be criminal fraud, the attempt to evade or defeat tax must be willful, which implies a "voluntary intentional violation of a known legal duty." *C.J. Bishop,* 73-1 USTC ¶9459, 412 U.S. 346, 93 S.Ct. 2009 (1973). Thus, an individual's behavior could not be willful if the actions are done through carelessness, or genuine misunderstanding of what the law requires.

A taxpayer convicted of criminal fraud is subject to a fine of up to $100,000 ($500,000 in the case of a corporation) or imprisonment of up to five years, or both, together with the costs of prosecution. Code Sec. 7201. The more important fraud provisions include the following:

1. Any person who willfully fails to collect or pay over withholding tax is guilty of a felony and, upon conviction, will be fined not more than $10,000, or imprisoned not more than five years, or both, together with the costs of prosecution. Code Sec. 7202.
2. Any person who willfully fails, when required, to pay estimated tax, to file a return, to keep records, or to supply information will be guilty of a misdemeanor and, upon conviction, will be fined not more than $25,000 ($100,000 in the case of a corporation) or imprisoned not more than one year, or both, together with the costs of prosecution. Code Sec. 7203.
3. Any person who willfully furnishes a false or fraudulent statement or who willfully fails to supply an employee with a statement of wages and withholdings will, if convicted, be fined not more than $1,000 or imprisoned not more than one year, or both. Code Sec. 7204.
4. Any person who willfully supplies false or fraudulent information regarding exemptions will, if convicted, be fined not more than $1,000 or imprisoned for not more than one year, or both. Code Sec. 7205.
5. Any person who is convicted under the fraud and false statement statute will be fined not more than $100,000 ($500,000 in the case of a corporation) or imprisoned not more than three years, or both, together with the costs of prosecution. Code Sec. 7206. This statute includes:

a. Making a false declaration that is made under the penalties of perjury
b. Aiding or assisting in preparation or presentation of returns, claims, or other documents that are false as to any material matter
c. Simulating or falsely executing any bond or other document required by the internal revenue laws
d. Removing, depositing, or concealing any property with intent to evade or defeat assessment or collection of any tax
e. Concealing property or withholding, falsifying, or destroying records relating to the financial condition of the taxpayer in connection with an offer in compromise or a closing agreement

6. Any person who willfully delivers or discloses any list, return, statement or other document known to that person to be fraudulent or false as to any material matter will be fined not more than $10,000 ($50,000 in the case of a corporation) or imprisoned not more than one year, or both. Code Sec. 7207.

Estimated Taxes and Underpayment Penalties

All taxpayers are generally required to make interim tax payments of substantially all of their accrued tax liability for the current year. For individuals, this is generally accomplished through withholding. Where withholding is insufficient, however, as is frequently the case with self-employed individuals, the taxpayer must file a declaration of estimated tax and may have to make quarterly estimated tax payments. The specific requirements are set forth in ¶9165.

If the total amount of tax paid through withholding and estimated tax payments is not enough, an underpayment penalty is imposed. The underpayment is computed on a quarterly basis and the interest penalty is then applied to these quarterly underpayments. Code Sec. 6654(d)(1). The charge runs until the amount is paid or until the due date of the return, whichever is earlier. An individual taxpayer can avoid the penalty for underpayment if the payments of estimated tax are at least as large as any one of the following:

1. 90 percent of the tax shown on the return or 100 percent (110 percent if adjusted gross income for 2002 and later exceeds $150,000) of the tax shown on the return for the preceding taxable year (assuming it showed a tax liability and covered a taxable year of 12 months). Code Sec. 6654(d)(1)(A) and (B).
2. An amount equal to 90 percent of the tax for the taxable year computed by annualizing the taxable income received for the months in the taxable year ending before the month in which the installment is required to be paid. Code Sec. 6654(d)(2).

The underpayment penalty can be waived if the underpayment is due to casualty, disaster, or other unusual circumstances, or occurs during the first two years after a taxpayer retired after reaching age 62, or became disabled. Code Sec. 6654(e)(3).

A penalty is also imposed on corporations by Code Sec. 6655 for any underpayment of estimated corporate tax. However, no penalty is imposed if the corporation pays estimated tax at least as large as any one of the following:

1. The tax shown on the return of the corporation for the preceding year
2. The tax based on the prior year's income but determined under the current year's rates
3. The tax shown on the return of the corporation for the current year.
4. An amount equal to at least 100 percent of the tax due on the current year's taxable income for specified cutoff periods and on an annualized basis. Code Sec. 6655(d)(1)(B)(ii) and (e).

Note: Large corporations (those with taxable income of $1 million or more in any one of the three preceding tax years) do not qualify for the first two exceptions.

Failure to Make Deposits of Taxes

Employers are liable for payment of the tax that must be withheld. Code Sec. 3402. Unless underpayment is due to reasonable cause and not due to willful neglect, a penalty of as much as 15 percent of the amount of the underpayment may be imposed. Code Sec. 6656(a) and (b).

Tax Preparer Penalties

If an income tax return preparer, in preparing a tax return with an understatement of tax liability, takes a frivolous position or one for which there is not a realistic possibility of being sustained on its merits, the penalty is the greater of $1,000 or 50 percent of the income derived by the tax return preparer with respect to the return. Code Sec. 6694(a). An "income tax return preparer" is any person who prepares for compensation or who employs one or more persons to prepare for compensation any return of tax or any claim for refund of tax. Code Sec. 7701(a)(36). No more than one individual associated with a firm will qualify as a preparer with respect to the same return or refund claim. Under the "one-preparer-per-firm" rule, should more than one member of a firm be involved in providing advice, the individual with supervisory responsibility for the matter will be subject to the penalty as a nonsigning preparer. Reg. §1.6694-1. A preparer is not subject to penalty for failure to follow a rule or regulation if the preparer in good faith and with a reasonable basis takes the position that the rule or regulation does not accurately reflect the Code.

A penalty of the greater of $5,000 or 50 percent of the income derived by the tax return preparer with respect to the return applies if any part of any understatement of liability as to a return or claim for refund is due to a willful attempt to understate the liability or to any reckless or any intentional disregard of the rules or regulations. Code Sec. 6694(b).

EXAMPLE 2.17	A guarantee of a specific amount of refund by a preparer is an example of an action that would give rise to this penalty. Or if the preparer intentionally disregards information given by the taxpayer in order to reduce the taxpayer's liability, the preparer is guilty of a willful attempt to understate tax liability.

PLANNING POINTER	This does not mean that the preparer may not rely in good faith on the information furnished by the taxpayer. However, the preparer must make reasonable inquiries if the information furnished by the taxpayer appears to be incorrect or incomplete.

A $50 penalty applies each time a preparer (1) fails to furnish a copy of the return to the taxpayer, (2) fails to sign the return, or (3) fails to furnish an identifying number. Code Sec. 6695(a)-(c). The maximum amount for each of these penalties is limited to $25,000. Any preparer who fails to retain a copy of the returns prepared or a list of the returns prepared is liable for a penalty of $50 for each such failure, with a maximum fine of $25,000 applicable to any one return period. Code Sec. 6695(d). A penalty of $50 applies for each failure to retain and make available to the IRS upon request a list of the preparers employed during a return period and $50 for each failure to set forth a required item in the information list (to a maximum of $25,000 for any single return period). Code Sec. 6695(e). Any preparer who endorses or otherwise negotiates a refund check issued to a taxpayer for a return or claim for refund prepared by the preparer is liable for a penalty of $500 with respect to each such check. Code Sec. 6695(f).

¶2370   DISCLOSURE OF A POSITION ON A RETURN

The taxpayer may avoid the substantial-understatement penalty and the tax return preparer may avoid the penalty for taking a position for which there is not a realistic possibility of being sustained on its merits by disclosing the item on Form 8275, Disclosure Statement. To avoid the accuracy-related penalty, the taxpayer must disclose any nonfrivolous position for which there is not substantial authority but which has a reasonable basis. Code Sec. 6662(d)(2)(B)(ii). Similarly, the tax return preparer may avoid the $1,000 Code Sec. 6694(a) penalty if any nonfrivolous position that does not have a realistic possibility of being sustained on its merits is disclosed on Form 8275. The "realistic possibility" standard is treated in the regulations as being identical to the "substantial authority" standard in Code Sec. 6662(d)(2)(B)(i). Reg. §1.6694-2(b)(1). Thus, the requirement for disclosure in order to avoid the accuracy-related penalty is identical for both taxpayers and tax preparers, even though the statutory language differs somewhat. Once adequate disclosure has been made, tax preparers are not subject to the penalty as long as the position taken is not frivolous (i.e., not patently improper). Reg. §1.6694-2(c)(1) and (2). For taxpayers, however, the position taken must have a "reasonable basis," in order to avoid the penalty. Code Sec. 6662(d)(2)(B)(ii)(II). The regulations treat this standard as "significantly higher than the not frivolous standard applicable to preparers." Reg. §§1.6662-3(b)(3)(ii) and 1.6662-4(e)(2)(i).

¶2375   ETHICS RULES FOR PRACTITIONERS

CPAs and attorneys must practice according to the code of professional ethics of their professions. The codes are similar to Treasury Department Circular No. 230. The Tax Committee of the American Institute of Certified Public Accountants (AICPA) also issued 10 statements on selected topics between 1964 and 1977. The first two statements were withdrawn in 1982. The eight remaining statements were revised in 1988 and in 2001. Prior to 2001, they were advisory opinions of the Committee as to what are appropriate standards of conduct in certain situations. Effective October 31, 2001, the Statements are enforceable standards for AICPA members. Effective January 1, 2010, the new sixth standard combined the previous sixth and seventh standards to give seven standards. Summaries of the current seven "Statements on Standards for Tax Services" follow.

1. With respect to tax return positions, a CPA should comply with the following standards:
    a. A CPA should not recommend to a client that a position be taken with respect to the tax treatment of any item on a return unless the CPA has a good faith belief that the position has a realistic possibility of being sustained administratively or judicially on its merits if challenged.
    b. A CPA should not prepare or sign a return if the CPA knows that the return takes a position that the CPA could not recommend under the standard expressed in paragraph 1(a).
    c. A CPA may recommend a position that the CPA concludes is not frivolous so long as the position is adequately disclosed on the return.
    d. In recommending tax return positions and in signing returns, a CPA should, where relevant, advise the client as to the potential penalty consequences of the recommended tax return position, and the opportunity, if any, to avoid such penalties through disclosure.

    The CPA should not recommend a tax return position that exploits the Internal Revenue Service audit selection process or serves as a mere "arguing" position solely to obtain leverage in the bargaining process of settlement negotiation with the Internal Revenue Service.

2. The CPA should make a reasonable effort to obtain from the client, and provide, appropriate answers to all questions on a tax return before signing as a preparer.

    Statement No. 2 indicates that reasonable grounds may exist for omitting an answer:
    a. The information is not readily available and the answer is not significant in terms of taxable income or loss or the tax liability shown on the return.
    b. Genuine uncertainty exists regarding the meaning of a question in relation to the particular return.
    c. The answer to the question is voluminous; in such cases, assurance should be given on the return that the data will be supplied upon an examination.

3. In preparing a return, the CPA may in good faith rely without verification upon information furnished by the client. The CPA should make reasonable inquiries if the information furnished appears to be incorrect, incomplete, or inconsistent either on its face or on the basis of other facts known to the CPA. The CPA should refer to the client's returns for proper years whenever feasible.

    Where the Internal Revenue Code or income tax regulations impose a condition with respect to deductibility or other tax treatment of an item, the CPA should make appropriate inquiries to determine whether such condition has been met.

4. A CPA may prepare tax returns involving the use of the taxpayer's estimates if it is impracticable to obtain exact data, and the estimated amounts are reasonable under the facts and circumstances known to the CPA. When estimates are used, they should be presented in a way that avoids the implication of greater accuracy than exists. Estimated amounts should not be presented in a manner which provides a misleading impression as to the degree of factual accuracy.

    There are unusual circumstances where disclosure that an estimate is used is necessary to avoid misleading the Internal Revenue Service regarding the degree of accuracy of the return. Some examples of unusual circumstances are as follows:
    a. The taxpayer has died or is ill at the time the return must be filed.
    b. The taxpayer has not received a K-1 for a flow-through entity at the time the return must be filed.
    c. There is litigation pending which bears on the return.
    d. Fire or computer failure destroyed relevant records.

5. The recommendation of a position to be taken concerning the tax treatment of an item in the preparation of a tax return should be based upon the facts and the law as they are evaluated at the time the return is prepared. Unless the taxpayer is bound as to tax treatment in a later year, the disposition of an item in an administrative proceeding does not govern the taxpayer in the treatment of a similar item in a later year's return. Therefore, if the CPA follows the standards of Statement No. 1, the CPA may recommend a tax return position, or prepare a tax return that departs from the treatment of an item as concluded in an administrative proceeding or a court decision regarding a prior year's return.

6. The CPA should inform the client promptly upon learning of an error in a previously filed return, an error in a return that is the subject of an administrative proceeding, or upon learning of a client's

failure to file a required return. The CPA should recommend the measures to be taken and such recommendation may be given orally. The CPA should not inform the IRS, and may not do so without the client's permission, except where required by law.

If the CPA is requested to prepare the current year's return and the client has not taken appropriate action to correct an error in a prior year's return, the CPA should consider whether to withdraw from preparing the return. If the CPA does prepare the current year's return, the CPA should take reasonable steps to ensure that the error is not repeated.

When the CPA is representing a client in an administrative proceeding with respect to a return which contains an error known to the CPA, the CPA should require the client's agreement to disclose the error to the IRS. Lacking such agreement, the CPA should consider whether to withdraw from representing the client and whether to continue a professional relationship with the client.

7. In providing tax advice to clients, the CPA should use professional judgment to ensure that the advice reflects competence and appropriately serves the client's needs. No standard format or guidelines need be followed in communicating written or oral advice to a client.

The CPA may communicate with a client when subsequent developments affect advice previously provided with respect to significant matters. However, the CPA cannot be expected to communicate later developments except while assisting a client in implementing procedures or plans associated with the advice provided or unless the CPA undertakes this obligation by specific agreement with the client.

TAX BLUNDERS

1. Laura Lerner found out that taxpayers have either partially or completely won around 50 percent of cases brought to the Tax Court. Therefore, she decides on litigation in the Tax Court, where she thinks she has a fairly good chance of being successful. However, in looking at the tax issue with which Laura is concerned, a tax researcher discovers that the taxpayer has never won a case like hers. Laura should not have relied on the overall statistics.

2. Edward Enders decides to take his case to the Tax Court because then he does not have to pay the tax before litigation. After some time has passed, someone tells him that a jury would probably have looked favorably on his case, and now he wants to go to District Court. Having gone to the Tax Court, Edward cannot now take his case to District Court.

3. Vera Vokel, known for her temper, her frugality, and her dislike for the IRS, is requested to come in to the local IRS office for an office examination. Although she had a CPA prepare her return, she decides she would like to save the fees it might cost her to have the CPA represent her and, therefore, decides to go in alone for the examination. In the course of the discussion, she becomes furious at the auditor and is disallowed her items at issue. Vera should have had her CPA represent her and she should probably not have been present herself so that the audit could be conducted in a businesslike and unemotional manner.

SUMMARY

- The primary authoritative sources of the law are statutory, administrative, and judicial.

- The taxpayer can appeal within the IRS and/or decide to go to Tax Court, the District Court, or the Court of Federal Claims, and then attempt to appeal to the Court of Appeals and the Supreme Court.

- A tax researcher can use loose-leaf tax services, a citator, other types of secondary reference materials, or electronic tax research systems and the internet in the research process.

- The Internal Revenue Service consists of the national office, and an extensive organization consisting of 4 operating divisions and other units.

- The examination of tax returns can be as simple as a correspondence examination or a more involved office examination or field examination.

- A tax practice can involve tax compliance and tax planning.

- Communications between the IRS and taxpayers can include private letter rulings, determination letters, and technical advice.

- There are numerous penalties to which taxpayers and tax preparers may be subject.

- The knowledge and use of ethics is very important for the tax practitioner.

QUESTIONS

1. Does the Internal Revenue Code of 1986 include pre-1986 tax law?

2. In which Subtitle and Chapter of the Internal Revenue Code is the majority of the income tax law found?

3. Are the federal courts bound to follow Treasury Regulations when deciding a tax case?

4. Do Regulations have higher authority in federal tax law than Revenue Rulings?

5. List the various "administrative" sources of tax law.

6. How is the manner of citing a Revenue Ruling or a Revenue Procedure affected by the passage of time?

7. In which Judicial Circuit is the District of Columbia?

8. List the three trial courts that have jurisdiction over tax cases.

9. What are the primary differences between Regular and Memorandum decisions of the U.S. Tax Court?

10. Is an announcement of acquiescence by the Commissioner of Internal Revenue legally binding upon the IRS?

11. What do the following abbreviations represent? CCH, BTA, USTC, AFTR, AFTR2d, S.Ct., CA-3, TCM.

12. Which tax service is known for its willingness to take a stand on controversial issues not covered by legislation or tax law?

13. Which tax service is frequently quoted in judicial decisions?

14. Refer to the Sue Wilson research illustration in the chapter (Case #1). Assume, at the time of filing her 2015 tax return, Sue Wilson believed she would receive a recovery on a claim for the full value of the automobile. However, in August 2016, Sue received only $8,000 from the insurance company. How much of a loss will she claim in 2015? In 2016? (Give your answer before consideration of the 10 percent of AGI limitation.)

15. Which computer-based research system contains the text of tax treaties?

16. Where can the historical record of a court case be found?

17. Describe the organization of the Internal Revenue Service.

18. Who may practice before the Internal Revenue Service?

19. Define and distinguish between a Private Letter Ruling, a Determination Letter, and a Technical Advice Memorandum.

20. Define DIF; NRP.

21. What events might cause an IRS examination?

22. What kind of taxpayer errors could be solved by mail?

23. What types of tax issues lend themselves to an interview or office examination?

24. Why might a taxpayer in a field examination want to make every effort to settle with the revenue agent?

25. Define 30-day letter; 90-day letter.

26. Describe the appeals process within the IRS.

27. Describe the trial and appellate court system for federal tax litigation.

28. What factors should a taxpayer consider in choosing a tax forum?

29. What are the two delinquency penalties?

30. What could constitute "reasonable cause" for purposes of the delinquency penalties?

31. What is the negligence penalty?

32. What two parties might be subject to the understatement of tax liability penalty?

33. Describe the valuation overstatement penalty.

34. How may an individual avoid a penalty for underpayment of tax liability?

35. Jim files his return one month after the due date and pays the remaining $8,000 of tax owed by him. What are his delinquency penalties?

36. Due to negligence, Rose underpaid her taxes by $20,000. What is her negligence penalty?

37. Olivia is being audited by the IRS. The revenue agent determines that certain expenses that were deducted on her return are not valid, and he accordingly makes adjustments to her tax liability. Upon receipt of her 30-day letter, she phones you, a CPA, for advice regarding possible future action on the matter. What options would you discuss with Olivia?

PROBLEMS

38. Based upon the organization of the Internal Revenue Code, what general topic would be covered in Code Sec. 731?
    a. Capital gains and losses
    b. Partners and partnerships
    c. Exempt organizations
    d. Insurance companies

39. Which of the following is published in the *Federal Register*?
    a. Technical Information Releases
    b. Revenue Rulings
    c. Revenue Procedures
    d. Treasury Regulations

40. To read an IRS Revenue Ruling that was issued within the past week which source should be used?
    a. Internal Revenue Code
    b. Cumulative Bulletin
    c. Federal Register
    d. Internal Revenue Bulletin

41. Which of the following publications includes the memorandum decisions of the United States Tax Court?
    a. Federal Register
    b. Cumulative Bulletin
    c. Internal Revenue Bulletin
    d. Tax Court Memorandum Decisions (TCM) (published by Wolters Kluwer)
    e. U.S. Tax Cases (USTC) (published by Wolters Kluwer)

42. Which of the following publications includes the regular decisions of the United States Tax Court?
    a. Federal Register
    b. Internal Revenue Bulletin
    c. United States Tax Court Reports
    d. Tax Court Memorandum Decisions (TCM) (published by Wolters Kluwer)
    e. U.S Tax Cases (USTC) (published by Wolters Kluwer)

43. Matthew, a sole proprietor, employs Timothy as his full-time employee. Timothy's 2014 tax return is being audited by the IRS. Because of Timothy's high regard for Matthew's knowledge and judgment, Timothy has asked Matthew to represent him in the audit. May Matthew represent Timothy?

44. Marvin filed his 2013 tax return on August 15, 2014, having obtained an automatic extension of time to file. However, not having the money to pay the tax bill at that time, he arranged with the IRS to pay his tax liability six months later. On February 15, 2015, Marvin paid the tax. Subsequently, on November 13, 2015, he discovered a deduction that he neglected to take on his 2013 return and he wishes to file a claim for a refund. May he do so?

45. Your client, Steve, is an engineer whose income has doubled over the past four years. He feels that by incorporating he could reduce his tax significantly. However, he can demonstrate no business purpose for incorporating as he is employed by an international oil company and he does no outside work. He asks you to request a ruling from the IRS regarding his proposed incorporation. Would you request a ruling for him?

46. Ron mailed his 2014 federal tax return on April 15, 2015, attaching only a first-class postage stamp. However, the postage should have been higher since the return weighed three ounces. His return is sent back to him on April 22, 2015, at which time he pays the additional postage. Will Ron be required to pay a delinquency penalty?

47. Karen engaged Joe, a CPA, to prepare her tax return. Karen received a refund check of $300 from the IRS. She endorsed the check and mailed it to Joe as payment for the preparation of her return. Joe took the check to his bank and deposited the amount in his bank account. Describe the possible consequences of this situation.

48. Jim, a retail merchant, reported the following on his 2014 return:

Sales	$200,000
Cost of goods sold	$80,000
Gross profit	$120,000

What amount must be omitted from income for the six-year statute of limitations to apply?

49. Andrea, a CPA, is representing her client, Rodney, in an administrative proceeding. In the course of this engagement, she discovers an error in the return that may result in a material understatement of tax liability. What, if anything, should Andrea do with regard to this discovery?

50. Mary, a CPA, prepared Gordon's tax return for the current year. In preparing his return, she took a deduction that is contrary to the Code. She feels that he is entitled to this deduction because of her belief that possible conflicts exist between two sections of the Internal Revenue Code. Is Mary in conflict with the AICPA "Statements on Responsibilities in Tax Practice"?

51. An individual files an income tax return for the calendar-year 2014 on September 20, 2015, and pays $1,200, which is the balance of the tax due. Disregarding interest, how much in delinquency penalties would he have to pay?

52. Tommy gives a painting to a church and takes a charitable contribution deduction in the amount of $50,000. If the actual value was only $20,000 and if the tax underpayment is $12,000, how much valuation overstatement penalty should he pay?

53. Sandy had the following items on her timely filed 2014 income tax return:

Gross receipts	$400,000
Cost of goods sold	($300,000)
Capital gain	$20,000
Capital loss	($30,000)

Sandy inadvertently omitted some income on her 2014 return. What is the statute of limitations if she omitted $100,000 of income on the return? What if she omitted $120,000 of income?

54. On February 15, 2013, Brent filed his 2012 income tax return (due April 15, 2013), and he paid a tax of $15,000 at that time. On June 10, 2014, he filed an amended 2012 return showing an additional $3,000 of tax which was then paid. In 2015, Brent found that he should claim a refund of $6,000 because he failed to take some deductions to which he was entitled. What amount can he recover if he files the claim for refund on March 14, 2016? What if he files the claim on May 15, 2016?

55. Angela filed her 2014 income tax return on February 14, 2015, showing gross income of $20,000. She mistakenly deducted a $6,000 casualty loss that in good faith she considered deductible. By what date must the IRS assert a notice of deficiency?
    a. February 14, 2018
    b. April 15, 2018
    c. February 14, 2021
    d. April 15, 2021

56. Harold and Maude filed a joint return for 2014 reporting:

Gross business income	$400,000
Net business income	80,000
Net capital gain	40,000

Maude inadvertently omitted some income from this return. The six-year statute applies only if Maude's omitted gross income exceeds:
    a. $20,000
    b. $30,000
    c. $100,000
    d. $110,000

57. Reginald filed his 2014 income tax return on January 15, 2015. On November 1, 2015, he learned that his investment of $10,000 in 1,000 shares of Ultimate Corp. had become worthless in 2014. What is the last day on which he must file an amended 2014 return to claim this loss?
    a. January 15, 2018
    b. April 15, 2018
    c. November 1, 2018
    d. April 15, 2022

58. If a practitioner who is authorized to practice before the IRS knows that a client has not complied with the revenue laws of the United States with respect to a matter administered by the IRS, the practitioner is required to:
    a. Advise the client of the noncompliance
    b. Immediately notify the IRS
    c. Do nothing
    d. Advise his client and immediately notify the IRS

59. Anna's 2013 individual tax return was examined and the IRS proposed changes resulting in additional tax. Anna wishes to bypass the IRS's appeal system and file a refund suit in the United States Court of Federal Claims on contested income tax issues. Your advice to Anna should be:
    a. Request that her return be reexamined
    b. Pay all of the additional tax and file another Form 1040 tax return
    c. Pay all of the additional tax, then file a claim for refund and request in writing that the claim be immediately rejected
    d. File a claim for refund and do nothing else

60. Peter's return was examined and the result was additional tax of $16,000 due to unreported lottery winnings. Peter has received a letter notifying him of his right to appeal the proposed changes within 30 days. Which of the following should Peter do in preparing his appeal?
    a. Call the examiner and request a conference
    b. Provide a brief written statement of the disputed issues
    c. Submit a written protest within the time limit specified
    d. Submit a written protest explaining additional expenses not previously claimed

61. Which of the following statements is not correct in respect to tax return preparer penalties?
    a. The penalty for an understatement due to the preparer's negligent or intentional disregard of one or more rules or regulations is $250; for willful understatement of liability the penalty is $1,000.
    b. If a preparer in good faith and with reasonable basis takes the position that a rule or regulation does not accurately reflect the Code, he or she is not subject to either penalty.
    c. The IRS has the burden of proof that a preparer has negligently or intentionally disregarded a rule or regulation.
    d. Many Code sections require the existence of specific facts and circumstances. In order to avoid a penalty, a preparer shall make appropriate inquiries of the taxpayer to determine that the requirements have been met incident to claiming a deduction.

62. **Research Problem.** What is the current status of Rev. Rul. 57-82?

63. **Research Problem.** Code Sec. 303(b)(2)(A)(ii) makes reference to two other Code sections. What are they?

64. **Research Problem.** Which Rev. Rul. does Rev. Rul. 76-74 supersede?

65. **Research Problem.** What is the date of IRS Letter Ruling 8302032?

66. **Research Problem.** On what date was Reg. §1.274-8 adopted?

67. **Research Problem.** What Code Section immediately follows Code Sec. 280?

68. **Research Problem.** Refer to a citator and locate the following case: *New York Life Insurance Co. v. Edwards.*
    a. What happened on appeal to the Court of Appeals?
    b. What happened on appeal to the Supreme Court?

69. **Research Problem.** What Code sections cover the standard deduction, trade or business expenses, losses, medical expenses, and moving expenses?

70. **Research Problem.** What two Code sections are referred to in Code Sec. 56(f)(2)(F)(ii)(II)?

71. **Research Problem.** Refer to the *Pennsylvania Indemnity Co.* case in a citator. What was the disposition of the case on appeal to the Supreme Court from the Court of Appeals?

72. **Research Problem.** Reg. §1.212-1(n) refers to two Code Sections. What are they?

73. **Research Problem.** Refer to *Black's Law Dictionary* or a similar legal reference book and ascertain the definition of the following words or terms: annotated, certiorari, remanded, dictum, acquiesced.

74. **Research Problem.** A taxpayer has a cellular telephone, used 45 percent for business and 55 percent for personal use. Is the MACRS depreciation method allowable?

75. **Research Problem.** What is the effective date of Code Sec. 1031(f)?

76. **Research Problem.** A borrower is personally liable on a real estate mortgage with an outstanding balance of $1.5 million. Borrower's basis in the property is $1 million and the property has a current fair market value of $1.2 million. The property is repossessed by the bank.
    a. If the borrower is insolvent both before and after the repossession, what taxable gain, if any, is recognized by borrower?
    b. Does your answer to (a) change if the borrower is not personally liable on the mortgage (i.e., a nonrecourse debt)? Why or why not?

77. **Research Problem.** Anthony Antunicci, a Massachusetts lawyer, has tired of the long, cold New England winters. He recently spent three months in Florida where he took a Florida bar review course which enabled him to successfully pass the Florida bar exam. He has since opened a second law office in Coral Gables and plans to work in that office from January through March each year. His younger brother, Joey, will operate their Boston office in his absence.

Can Anthony deduct the cost of the Florida bar review course as an education expense since he has already established himself in the profession of being a lawyer by previously passing the Massachusetts bar exam?

(**Hint:** to answer this question using CCH Online, use the search term: (lawyer or attorney) and (bar review course and second state).)

78. **Research Problem.** Jane was notified by the IRS that she should appear at the local IRS district office with records supporting travel expense deductions taken on her 2012 tax return. Because she had to meet with some clients, she did not appear at the IRS office, nor did she bother to make an appointment for an alternative time. To what penalty or penalties could Jane be subject?

79. **Research Problem.** A corporate client was the target of a hostile takeover by a corporate raider. In successfully thwarting the hostile takeover, the Board of Directors incurred legal fees of $100,000.
    a. What is the proper tax treatment of these fees?
    b. Assume that the takeover was friendly. Does this change your answer? If so, explain why your answer is different

80. An oil tanker collided with a ship in Tampa Bay. The resulting oil spill severely curtailed the fishing business for two months. The Franklin Fishing Boat Co. made a claim against the tanker's owner for impairment of Franklin's revenue during the two-month period. Mr. Franklin received an initial payment of $50,000 from the tanker's owner, $20,000 of which was for lost revenue and $30,000 of which was for punitive damages allowed by state law from a handler of hazardous substances. How much of the award, if any, is taxable?

Chapter

3

Individual Taxation—An Overview

OBJECTIVES

After completing Chapter 3, you should be able to:

1. Understand the components of the tax formula.
2. Apply the standard deduction to each filing status.
3. Determine whether an individual qualifies as a personal exemption.
4. Distinguish among the five different filing statuses.
5. Apply the tax tables and the tax rate schedules to taxable income.

OVERVIEW

This chapter discusses the components of the tax formula and studies the implications of the standard deduction to the taxpayer. Additionally, the qualifications for the personal exemption are analyzed. Finally, the basic filing statuses are examined as well as the role of the tax tables and the tax rate schedules.

¶3001   COMPONENTS OF THE TAX FORMULA

Taxable income is computed using one of the two overall accounting methods, the cash method or the accrual method. It is also possible to use a combination of the two overall methods. Under the cash method, income is reported when it is received and deductions are taken when the expense is paid. The accrual method requires income to be reported when all the events necessary to fix the right to receive payment have occurred and there is reasonable certainty regarding the amount. Likewise, accrual basis taxpayers usually claim a deduction in the year in which all events that fix the liability have occurred, provided the amount of the liability is reasonably determinable.

A basic understanding of the method used to calculate the tax liability is a necessity in the study of federal income taxation. That method is as follows:

	Gross Income
−	Deductions for Adjusted Gross Income
=	Adjusted Gross Income
−	Greater of Itemized Deductions or Standard Deduction
−	Personal Exemptions
=	Taxable Income
×	Tax Rate
=	Tax Liability
−	Tax Credits and Prepayments
=	Net Tax Due or Refund

¶3011   GROSS INCOME

Gross income includes all items of income from whatever source unless specifically excluded. Examples of gross income include compensation for services, interest, rents, royalties, dividends, and annuities. An individual's income from business is included in gross income after deducting the cost of goods sold.

The receipt of income can be in different forms such as cash, property, services, or even a forgiveness of an indebtedness. However, income is not reported by a taxpayer until it is realized.

Gross income and inclusions and exclusions will be discussed in further detail in Chapters 4 and 5.

¶3015   DEDUCTIONS FOR ADJUSTED GROSS INCOME

To arrive at adjusted gross income, all deductions specifically allowed by law are subtracted from gross income. Some of the items allowed as deductions for adjusted gross income include:

1. Trade or business expenses, such as advertising, depreciation, and utilities.
2. Certain reimbursed employee expenses, such as travel, transportation, and entertainment expenses.
3. Moving expenses.
4. Losses from sale or exchange of property.

These deductions are sometimes referred to as "deductions from gross income" or, since almost all the allowable deductions in this section are business expenses, the deductions are sometimes referred to as "business deductions." These deductions are discussed in Chapter 6.

¶3025   ADJUSTED GROSS INCOME

In the tax formula there are deductions for adjusted gross income and then deductions from adjusted gross income. It is important to take these deductions in the proper categories. Adjusted gross income is an important subtotal because certain other items are based on the amount of adjusted gross income. The credit for child and dependent care expenses along with itemized deductions for medical expenses, charitable contributions, personal casualty losses, and miscellaneous expenses are all based on adjusted gross income. The phaseout of itemized deductions and personal exemptions are also based on adjusted gross income.

¶3035   ITEMIZING v. STANDARD DEDUCTION

Itemized deductions are certain expenses of a personal nature that are specifically allowed as a deduction. Items included in this group are: medical expenses, state and local income taxes, property taxes, home mortgage interest, charitable contributions, personal casualty losses, and miscellaneous employee expenses.

Taxpayers receive the benefit of a minimum amount of itemized deductions called the standard deduction. The standard deduction is a fixed amount used to simplify the computation of the tax liability. It is also designed to eliminate lower-income individuals from the tax rolls. All taxpayers subtract the larger of their itemized deductions or the standard deduction.

The standard deduction is based on the filing status of the taxpayer and is made up of the "basic standard deduction" plus any "additional standard deduction." The standard deduction is adjusted annually, if necessary, for inflation.

Filing Status	Basic Standard Deduction 2015
Single	$6,300
Married Filing Jointly	12,600
Married Filing Separately	6,300
Head of Household	9,250
Surviving Spouse	12,600

The standard deduction is of principal benefit to moderate and low income level taxpayers since the amount is usually more than the total itemized deductions, which means that such taxpayers need not report their itemized deductions. Thus, the need to audit such returns by the IRS is substantially reduced since the opportunities for error or misstatement of taxable income are lessened.

Overall Limitation on Itemized Deductions

For tax years beginning after 1990, an individual whose adjusted gross income exceeds a threshold amount is required to reduce the amount allowable for itemized deductions by 3 percent of the excess over that threshold. For 2015, the threshold amount is $309,900 for married filing jointly, $284,050 for head of household, $258,250 for single, and $154,950 for married filing separately. These thresholds are indexed for inflation. There was no phaseout for 2010 through 2012.

In no event, however, may the reduction be more than 80 percent of allowable itemized deductions, not counting the deductions for medical expenses, investment interest, casualty losses, or wagering losses to the extent of wagering gains. The reduction is applied only after first taking into account the other Code provisions that determine how much of a particular type of expense may be deducted, such as the 2 percent limitation on miscellaneous deductions.

EXAMPLE 3.1

Mark and Sylvia Ward are married taxpayers who file a joint return. In 2015, they have adjusted gross income of $359,900 and preliminary itemized deductions of $18,000. Their itemized deductions consist of medical expenses ($8,000), state and local taxes ($7,000), and charitable contributions ($3,000). Their adjusted itemized deductions on their return would be $16,500, computed as follows:

Medical expenses		$8,000
State and local taxes	$7,000	
Charitable contributions	3,000	
	$10,000	
Less: 3% of AGI in excess of $309,900	1,500	8,500
Adjusted itemized deductions		$ 16,500

Additional Standard Deduction for Age and Blindness

An additional standard deduction is allowed for aged or blind taxpayers. The additional standard deduction is the total of the additional amounts allowed for age and blindness. The dollar value of an additional amount will depend on the taxpayer's filing status. The extra standard deductions effective for 2015 are shown below. The amounts are adjusted for inflation.

Filing Status	Dollar Value of One Additional Filing Status Amount 2015
Single	$1,550
Married Filing Jointly	1,250
Married Filing Separately	1,250
Head of Household	1,550
Surviving Spouse	1,250

Taxpayers can receive an additional standard deduction for being both aged and blind. Thus, a married couple, both of whom are aged and blind, receive an additional standard deduction of $5,000 ($1,250 × 4).

EXAMPLE 3.2

Rebecca Greene, 55, qualifies as a head of household in 2015. Her basic standard deduction is $9,250. She is not entitled to an additional standard deduction.

EXAMPLE 3.3

Assume the same facts as in Example 3.2, except that Rebecca is 67 and legally blind. Her basic standard deduction for 2015 is $9,250. She is also entitled to an additional standard deduction of $3,100 ($1,550 for her age and $1,500 for her blindness). Her total standard deduction is $12,350.

EXAMPLE 3.4

Jeffrey and Donna Dirk are both 72 and file a joint return for 2015. Donna is blind. Their basic standard deduction is $12,600. They are entitled to an additional standard deduction of $3,750 ($1,250 × 2 for their age plus $1,250 for Donna's blindness). Their total standard deduction is $16,350.

To qualify for the old-age additional standard deduction, the taxpayer and/or spouse must be age 65 before the close of the year. For purposes of the old-age additional standard deduction, an individual attains the age of 65 on the day preceding the 65th birthday. Thus, an individual whose 65th birthday falls on January 1 in a given year attains the age of 65 on the last day of the calendar year immediately preceding.

A person is considered blind for the extra standard deduction if that person's central visual acuity does not exceed 20/200 in the better eye with correcting lenses, or if visual acuity is greater than 20/200 but is accompanied by a limitation in the fields of vision such that the widest diameter of the visual field subtends an angle no greater than 20 degrees.

If the taxpayer or spouse dies during the year, the number of additional standard deduction amounts for age or blindness is determined as of the date of death. Thus, the additional standard deduction for age will not be allowed for an individual who dies before attaining the age of 65 even though the individual would have been 65 before the close of the year.

The additional standard deductions for age 65 or older and blindness apply only to taxpayers and their spouses. No additional standard deduction amounts are allowed to taxpayers who claim an exemption for dependents who are aged or blind.

EXAMPLE 3.5

Darren Davidson is single and fully supports his 70-year-old father. Darren qualifies as a head of household. Darren's regular standard deduction is $9,250 for 2015. Darren may claim a dependency exemption for his father but may not claim the additional standard deduction amount for his dependent father.

Married Taxpayers Filing Separately

All taxpayers may not be able to take the larger of itemized deductions or the standard deduction. Rules require both spouses to either itemize or use the standard deduction. If one spouse takes itemized deductions the other spouse is required to also itemize even if itemized deductions are less than the standard deduction for married individuals filing separately.

EXAMPLE 3.6	Joe and Mary Bloome are married but decide to file separate returns for 2015. Joe has adjusted gross income of $30,000 and $6,400 of itemized deductions, while Mary has $25,000 of adjusted gross income and $3,300 of itemized deductions. Joe and Mary can elect not to itemize, in which case they will each use the standard deduction of $6,300. However, if they decide to itemize, Joe will have itemized deductions of $6,400 and Mary will have $3,300 of itemized deductions. Since Joe itemizes, Mary is also required to itemize.

PLANNING POINTER	In situations where total itemized deductions are approximately equal to the standard deduction, it is possible for cash basis taxpayers to obtain a deduction for itemized deductions in one year and to use the standard deduction the next year by proper timing of payments. For example, an individual may pay two years' church pledges in one year and nothing the next year. It may also be possible to pay real estate or city and state income tax estimated payments prior to the end of the year.

¶3045 PERSONAL EXEMPTIONS

The personal exemption for 2015 is $4,000. From 1979 through 1984, the personal exemption was $1,000. The application of the index for inflation raised the personal exemption to $1,040 for 1985 and $1,080 for 1986. The Tax Reform Act of 1986 raised the personal exemption to $1,900 for 1987, $1,950 for 1988, and $2,000 for 1989. The personal exemption as adjusted for inflation after 1989 was raised to $2,050 for 1990, $2,150 for 1991, $2,300 for 1992, $2,350 for 1993, $2,450 for 1994, $2,500 for 1995, $2,550 for 1996, $2,650 for 1997, $2,700 for 1998, $2,750 for 1999, $2,800 for 2000, $2,900 for 2001, $3,000 for 2002, $3,050 for 2003, $3,100 for 2004, $3,200 for 2005, $3,300 for 2006, $3,400 for 2007, $3,500 for 2008, $3,650 for 2009 and 2010, $3,700 for 2011, $3,800 for 2012, $3,900 for 2013, and $3,950 for 2014.

No personal exemption amount is allowable on the return of an individual who is eligible to be claimed as a dependent on another taxpayer's return. For example, a child will not be allowed the personal exemption on his or her own return if that child is eligible to be claimed on the parent's return.

The deduction for personal exemptions is reduced or even eliminated for certain high-income taxpayers. Taxpayers whose adjusted gross income exceeds the appropriate threshold amount (based on filing status) have to reduce exemptions by 2 percent for each $2,500 of adjusted gross income or fraction thereof in excess of the threshold amount. The phaseout of the tax benefit for personal exemptions began in 1991, and the threshold amounts are adjusted for inflation (cost-of-living index adjustment).

¶3055 TAX RATES

The tax formula implies that the "Taxable Income" figure is multiplied by the appropriate tax rate to arrive at the "Tax Liability." In reality, the "Tax Liability" is either derived from the appropriate column of the tax tables or is computed from the appropriate line in the tax rate schedules.

Prior to 1986 the maximum tax rate was 50 percent. The tax rate schedules for 1987 ranged from 11 percent to 38.5 percent. The tax rate schedules (reproduced in the Appendix) include six tax brackets for 2015: 10 percent, 15 percent, 25 percent, 28 percent, 33 percent, 35 percent, and 39.6 percent.

¶3065 TAX CREDITS AND PREPAYMENTS

Any tax credits are applied against the income tax. It is significant to note the difference between a credit and a tax deduction. A deduction reduces income to which the rate applies and indirectly reduces the tax liability. A credit directly reduces the tax liability.

The principal credits include the earned income credit, child tax credit, credit for the elderly, general business credit, dependent care credit, education credits, and foreign tax credit. These credits will be discussed in further detail in Chapter 9.

The tax liability is further reduced by the amounts withheld on income and by any estimated payments made during the year. Income taxes may be withheld on the various sources of income that a taxpayer receives during the year. Employers are required to withhold income tax on compensation paid to their employees. In addition, estimated payments may be necessary if enough taxes have not been withheld.

¶3075   **NET TAX DUE OR REFUND**

The tax result after applying the credits and prepayments to the "Tax Liability" is the amount that must be paid to the Internal Revenue Service or the amount overpaid and to be refunded to the taxpayer.

¶3085   **CLASSIFICATION OF TAXPAYERS**

The Internal Revenue Code defines the term "taxpayer" as any person subject to any internal revenue act. The term "person" includes an individual, a trust, estate, partnership, association, company, or corporation. A "partnership" includes a syndicate, group, pool, joint venture, or other unincorporated venture, through or by means of which any business, financial operation, or venture is carried on and which is not a trust or estate or a corporation. The term "corporation" is not defined but is stated to include associations, joint-stock companies, and insurance companies.

A proper classification of taxpayers is essential in determining the type of tax return to be filed. Individuals have little trouble choosing the right tax return, but problems often arise with artificial entities such as trusts, estates, partnerships, corporations, and associations.

Taxpayers are usually classified according to the type of tax return that they are required to file. Excluding most information returns (which are not tax returns in the strict sense of the term) and returns for organizations exempt from income tax, almost all tax returns will fall into one of the following four categories:

Type Of Return	Form	Filed By
Individual	1040	Every natural person with income of statutory minimums
Corporation	1120	Corporations, including organizations taxed as corporations
Fiduciary	1041	Trusts and estates with income in excess of statutory minimums
Partnership	1065	Partnerships or joint ventures (information return only)

Personal Exemptions

In computing taxable income an individual is allowed a deduction for each personal exemption allowed. The personal exemption is $4,000 for 2015. After 1989, the personal exemption amount is indexed for inflation.

Such exemptions are (1) the exemptions for an individual taxpayer and spouse, and (2) the exemptions for dependents of the taxpayer. However, no personal exemption amount is allowed on the return of an individual who is eligible to be claimed as a dependent on another taxpayer's return.

¶3201   **TAXPAYER AND SPOUSE**

Since there are two taxpayers on a joint return, two exemptions are allowed on the return even though there may be only one individual earning income. Where a joint return is filed by the taxpayer and spouse, no other person is allowed an exemption for the spouse even if the spouse otherwise qualifies as a dependent of another person.

The taxpayer is allowed an exemption for the spouse of the taxpayer if a joint return is not filed. However, the spouse must have no income for the year and must not be the dependent of another taxpayer. Thus, a taxpayer is not entitled to an exemption for the spouse on a separate return for the year in which the spouse has any gross income even though the income is not sufficient to require the spouse to file a return.

Exemptions	6a ☐ **Yourself.** If your parent (or someone else) can claim you as a dependent on his or her tax return, **do not** check box 6a.				No. of boxes checked on 6a and 6b _____
	b ☐ **Spouse**				No. of your children on 6c who:
	c **Dependents:**	**(2)** Dependent's social security number	**(3)** Dependent's relationship to you	**(4)** ✓ if qualifying child for child tax credit (see page 19)	• lived with you _____
	(1) First name Last name				• did not live with you due to divorce or separation (see page 19) _____
If more than six dependents, see page 19.	_____	┊ ┊		☐	
	_____	┊ ┊		☐	Dependents on 6c not entered above _____
	_____	┊ ┊		☐	
	_____	┊ ┊		☐	Add numbers entered on lines above ▶ ☐
	d Total number of exemptions claimed				

Source: Form 1040

¶3225 DEPENDENTS

Taxpayers are allowed to claim a personal exemption and receive a $4,000 deduction in 2015 for each dependent.

The statutory definition of a dependent has been rewritten to categorize each dependent as a qualifying child or a qualifying relative. The definition also creates a uniform definition of child for dependency exemption, child credit, earned income tax credit, dependent care credit, and head of household filing status.

Qualifying Child

A child is a qualifying child of a taxpayer if the child satisfies each of four tests:

Principal Abode. The child has the same principal place of abode as the taxpayer for more than one half the taxable year. Temporary absences due to special circumstances, including absences due to illness, education, business, vacation, or military service, are not treated as absences.

Relationship. The child has specified relationship to the taxpayer. The child must be the taxpayer's son, daughter, stepson, stepdaughter, brother, sister, stepbrother, stepsister, or a descendant of any such individual. An individual legally adopted by the taxpayer, or an individual who is lawfully placed with the taxpayer for adoption by the taxpayer, is treated as a child of such taxpayer by blood. A foster child who is placed with the taxpayer by an authorized placement agency or by judgment, decree, or other order of any court of competent jurisdiction is treated as the taxpayer's child.

Age. The child has not yet attained a specified age. In general, a child must be under age 19 (or 24 in the case of a full-time student) in order to be a qualifying child. In general, no age limit applies with respect to individuals who are totally and permanently disabled at any time during the calendar year. The prior-law requirements are retained that a child must be under age 13 for purposes of the dependent care credit, and under age 17 for purposes of the child tax credit.

A tie-breaking rule applies if more than one taxpayer claims a child as a qualifying child. First, if only one of the individuals claiming the child as a qualifying child is the child's parent, the child is deemed the qualifying child of the parent. Second, if both parents claim the child and the parents do not file a joint return, then the child is deemed a qualifying child first with respect to the parent with whom the child resides the longest period of time, and second with respect to the parent with the highest adjusted gross income. Third, if the child's parents do not claim the child, then the child is deemed a qualifying child with respect to the claimant with the highest adjusted gross income.

The prior-law support and gross income tests (discussed below) for determining dependency do not apply to a child who meets the requirements of the uniform definition of qualifying child.

Support. A child who provides over half of his or her own support is not considered a qualifying child of another taxpayer.

Qualifying Relative

Taxpayers generally may claim an individual who does not meet the uniform definition of qualifying child with respect to any individual who is a qualifying relative. A qualifying relative must meet all of the following tests:

1. Relationship or member of household
2. Gross income
3. Support
4. Not a qualifying child

Relationship or Member of the Household Test

The dependent must be a relative of the taxpayer or a member of the taxpayer's household. Individuals considered to be related to the taxpayer and eligible for the dependency exemption include: a child or a descendant of a child; a brother, sister, stepbrother, or stepsister; the father or mother, or an ancestor of either; a stepfather or stepmother; a son or daughter of a brother or sister of the taxpayer; a brother or sister of the father or mother of the taxpayer; and a son-in-law, daughter-in-law; father-in-law, mother-in-law, brother-in-law, or sister-in-law. A nonrelated person must be a member of the taxpayer's household for the entire year to qualify as a dependent. The taxpayer must maintain and occupy the household. An individual is not a member of the taxpayer's household if any time during the year the relationship between the individual and the taxpayer is in violation of local law.

Gross Income Test

A taxpayer is allowed an exemption for each dependent whose gross income for the year is less than the personal exemption amount ($4,000 for 2015).

EXAMPLE 3.7	Colleen Drew, age 21, earned $4,300 working part-time while attending school full-time. Colleen's lives the entire year with her friend who pays more than one-half of Colleen's support. Colleen's friend will not be able to claim Colleen as a dependent since Colleen made more than $4,000.

The gross income amount is determined before the deduction of any expenses, such as materials, taxes, and depreciation. Thus, a taxpayer would not be able to claim his grandmother for 2015 if she received $4,100 in rental income, even though her expenses reduced the net income to less than $4,000. However, cost of goods sold is subtracted from gross receipts to determine gross income. Receipts which are excludable from gross income are not counted in applying the gross income test.

Support Test

Over one-half of the support of a dependent must be furnished by the taxpayer. In determining whether the taxpayer has provided over half of the support, the support received from the taxpayer as compared to the entire amount of support which the individual receives from all sources, including support which the individual supplies, will be taken into account.

In computing the amount which is contributed for the support of an individual, there must be included any amount which is contributed by the individual for his or her own support, including receipts which are excludable from gross income, such as benefits received under Social Security or money withdrawn from a savings account. However, it is only the amount actually spent on support which is taken into consideration, not the total amount available for support.

The term "support" includes food, shelter, clothing, medical and dental care, education, and similar items. Generally, the amount of an item of support will be the amount of expense incurred by the one furnishing the item. If the item of support furnished by an individual is in the form of property or lodging, it will be necessary to measure the amount of the item of support in terms of its fair market value. The value of personal services is not included in support determination. *F. Markarian,* 65-2 USTC ¶10,755, 352 F.2d 870 (CA-7 1965), cert. denied, 384 U.S. 988, 86 S.Ct. 1886.

Where the taxpayer owns the home in which the dependent lives, the fair rental value of the lodging furnished is part of the total support. However, this does not mean an equal allocation between taxpayers and dependents. It is recognized that an adult has certain minimum base housing costs which cannot be treated as equal to the minimum housing costs of minor children. In one case, the court allocated 60 percent of the housing costs to the mother and 40 percent to be divided equally among three children. *J.D.M. Cameron,* 33 TCM 725, Dec. 32,654(M), T.C. Memo. 1974-166. Amounts paid to others to care for children while working are included as part of support. *T. Lovett,* 18 TC 477, Dec. 19,018 (1952), Acq., 1952-2 CB 2. The amount paid may also qualify for the dependent care credit.

Some capital expenditures may qualify as items of support. The cost of an automobile is counted in determining who furnished over half of a dependent's support. A television set furnished and set apart in the child's bedroom is also an item of support. Rev. Rul. 77-282, 1977-2 CB 52.

Welfare payments made by a state agency to or on behalf of a dependent are attributable to the agency rather than the taxpayer. *H. Johnson,* 33 TCM 659, Dec. 32,630(M), T.C. Memo. 1974-150; *H.M. Lutter,* 75-1 USTC ¶10,439, 514 F.2d 1095 (CA-7 1975), cert. denied, 423 U.S. 931, 96 S.Ct. 283. This may deny a dependency exemption to the taxpayer since the agency may have provided more than half the support of a child. However, amounts expended by a state for training and education of handicapped children are not taken into account in determining support. This rule applies only if the institution qualifies as an "educational institution" and the residents qualify as "students." Rev. Rul. 59-379, 1959-2 CB 51, clarified by Rev. Rul. 60-190, 1960-1 CB 51. Social Security Medicare benefits are disregarded in the computation of support. Rev. Rul. 79-173, 1979-1 CB 86.

Amounts received as scholarships for study at an educational institution are not considered in determining whether the taxpayer furnishes more than one-half the support of the student. Amounts received for tuition payments and allowances by a veteran are not considered scholarships in determining the support test.

EXAMPLE 3.8	John has a cousin who lives with John and who receives a $5,000 scholarship to Academic University for one year. John contributes $4,100, which constitutes the balance of the cousin's support for that year. John may claim the cousin as a dependent, as the $5,000 scholarship is not counted in determining the support of the cousin and, therefore, John is considered as providing all the support of the cousin.

Not a Qualifying Child Test

An individual who is a qualifying child of the taxpayer or of any other taxpayer cannot be a qualifying relative.

Special Rules Applying to Dependents

The taxpayer and the dependent will be considered as occupying the household for the entire year notwithstanding temporary absences from the household due to special circumstances. A nonpermanent failure to occupy the common abode by reason of illness, education, business, vacation, military service, or a custody agreement under which the dependent is absent for less than six months in the tax year, will be considered temporary absence due to special circumstances.

The fact that the dependent dies during the year will not deprive the taxpayer of the deduction if the dependent lived in the household for the entire part of the year preceding death. Similarly, the period during the year preceding birth of an individual will not prevent the individual from qualifying as a dependent.

No exemption will be allowed for any dependent who has filed a joint return with the dependent's spouse. However, the dependency exemption will still be allowed where a joint return is filed by a dependent and spouse merely as a claim for refund and where no tax liability would exist for either spouse on the basis of separate returns. Rev. Rul. 65-34, 1965-1 CB 86.

The term "dependent" does not include an individual who is not a citizen or national of the United States unless such individual is a resident of the United States or a country contiguous to the United States. This exception does not apply to any child that has the same principal place of abode as the taxpayer and is a member of the taxpayer's household and the taxpayer is a citizen or national of the United States.

The term "student" means an individual who, during each of five calendar months during the calendar year, is a full-time student at an educational institution, or is pursuing a full-time course of instructional on-farm training. A full-time student is one who is enrolled for some part of five calendar months for the number of hours or courses which is considered to be full-time attendance. The five calendar months need not be consecutive. School attendance exclusively at night does not constitute full-time attendance. However, full-time attendance may include some attendance at night in connection with a full-time course of study.

Dependents will not be allowed to claim exemptions for dependents in any year they are themselves a dependent.

Social Security numbers are required for all individuals who are claimed as dependents. Failure to include the Social Security number or other required information can result in the loss of the exemption.

Multiple Support Agreements

Special rules allow a taxpayer to be treated as having contributed over half of the support of an individual where two or more taxpayers contributed to the support of the individual if (1) no one person contributed over half of the individual's support, (2) each member of the group which collectively contributed more than half of the support of the individual would have been entitled to claim the individual as a dependent except for the fact that they did not contribute more than one-half of the support, (3) the member of the group claiming the individual as a dependent contributed more than 10 percent of the individual's support, and (4) each other person in the group who contributed more than 10 percent of the support files a written declaration that they will not claim the individual as a dependent for the year.

EXAMPLE 3.9	Brothers Alfred, Bill, Chuck, and Don contributed the entire support of their mother in the following percentages: Alfred, 30 percent; Bill, 20 percent; Chuck, 29 percent; and Don, 21 percent. Any one of the brothers, except for the fact that he did not contribute more than half of her support, would have been entitled to claim his mother as a dependent. Consequently, any one of the brothers could claim a deduction for the exemption of the mother provided a written declaration from each of the brothers is attached to the return of the individual taking the exemption. If, on the other hand, Don were a neighbor instead of a brother, he would not qualify as a member of the group for multiple support agreement purposes. He would not be eligible to claim the mother since she was not a member of Don's household. Don would not be required to sign the multiple support agreement.

Divorced or Separated Parents

When taxpayers are divorced, legally separated, or never married, special rules apply to determine which one is entitled to exemptions for their children. These rules may result in a taxpayer who did not provide more than half of the support of the child being entitled to the exemption.

To qualify, the parents must be divorced or legally separated under a decree of divorce or separate maintenance, separated under a written separation agreement, or lived apart at all times during the last six months of the year. In addition, both parents together must provide more than one-half of the child's support. The child must be in the custody of one or both parents for more than one-half of the calendar year. Thus, a dependency exemption may not be claimed by one of the parents if a person other than the parents provides one-half or more for the support of the child during the year or has custody of the child for one half or more of the year.

As a general rule, a child will be treated as receiving over half of the support from the parent having custody for the greater number of nights for the year. If the parents of the child are divorced or separated for only a portion of a year after having joint custody for the prior portion of the year, the parent who has custody for the greater number of nights of the remainder of the year after divorce or separation will be treated as having custody for a greater portion of the year.

EXAMPLE 3.10	Bill, a child of Jim and Cathy Durell, who were divorced on June 1, received $5,000 for support during the year, of which $2,200 was provided by Jim and $1,950 by Cathy. No multiple support agreement was entered into. Prior to the divorce, Jim and Cathy jointly had custody of Bill. For the remainder of the year, Jim had custody of Bill for the months of October through December, while Cathy had custody of Bill for the months of June through September. Since Cathy had custody for four of the seven months following the divorce, she had custody for the greater number of nights and is the custodial parent for the year and is allowed the personal exemption.

Post-1984 Divorces

For divorces taking place in years after 1984, the custodial parent is entitled to the exemption in all cases unless he or she expressly waives the right to the exemption. This may be done by the custodial parent signing a written declaration that he or she will not claim the exemption. The noncustodial parent is required to attach this declaration to his or her tax return each year when claiming the exemption. Failure to attach Form 8332, Release of Claim to Exemption for Child of Divorced or Separated Parents, means that the noncustodial parent cannot claim the exemption, regardless of the amount of support furnished.

Form **8332**		Release/Revocation of Release of Claim	OMB No. 1545-0074

Form **8332**
(Rev. February 2009)
Department of the Treasury
Internal Revenue Service

Release/Revocation of Release of Claim to Exemption for Child by Custodial Parent

► Attach a separate form for each child.

OMB No. 1545-0074

Attachment
Sequence No. **115**

Name of noncustodial parent

Noncustodial parent's
social security number (SSN) ►

Part I   Release of Claim to Exemption for Current Year

I agree not to claim an exemption for _____
Name of child

for the tax year 20____ .

_____   _____   _____
Signature of custodial parent releasing claim to exemption   Custodial parent's SSN   Date

Note. If you choose not to claim an exemption for this child for future tax years, also complete Part II.

Part II   Release of Claim to Exemption for Future Years (If completed, see **Noncustodial parent** on page 2.)

I agree not to claim an exemption for _____
Name of child

for the tax year(s)_____ .
(Specify. See instructions.)

_____   _____   _____
Signature of custodial parent releasing claim to exemption   Custodial parent's SSN   Date

Part III   Revocation of Release of Claim to Exemption for Future Year(s)

I revoke the release of claim to an exemption for _____
Name of child

for the tax year(s)_____ .
(Specify. See instructions.)

_____   _____   _____
Signature of custodial parent revoking the release of claim to exemption   Custodial parent's SSN   Date

EXAMPLE 3.11

Mike and Jennifer are divorced. Mike pays over half of the support of their child, Amanda. Amanda resides with Jennifer for the greater part of the year. Mike is unable to claim Amanda as a dependent on his return because he does not have a signed Form 8332 from Jennifer.

KEYSTONE PROBLEM

The personal exemption reduces taxable income by $4,000 in 2015. In certain situations, such as multiple support agreements and children of divorced parents, it is possible to assign the personal exemption for a dependent to one of the eligible parties. What should be taken into consideration in determining which party should receive the personal exemption?

¶3227   HIGH-INCOME PHASEOUT OF EXEMPTIONS

For tax years beginning after 1990, the deduction for personal exemptions is reduced or even eliminated for certain high-income taxpayers. If a taxpayer's adjusted gross income exceeds the appropriate threshold amount (based on filing status) below, the deduction for exemptions is reduced by 2 percent for each $2,500 or fraction thereof by which the adjusted gross income exceeds the threshold amount. In the case of a married person filing separately, the exemption deduction is reduced by 2 percent for each $1,250 or fraction thereof by which such adjusted gross income exceeds the threshold amount. In no case will the deduction for exemptions be reduced by more than 100 percent.

For 2015, the threshold amounts (adjusted annually for inflation) are as follows:

Joint return or a surviving spouse	$309,900
Head of household	284,050
Single taxpayer	258,250
Married person filing a separate return	154,950

The deduction for personal exemptions will be fully eliminated when adjusted gross income exceeds the threshold amount by more than $122,500.

| EXAMPLE 3.12 | Assume a married couple with four personal exemptions has $353,400 in adjusted gross income. The couple's personal exemption deduction would be computed as follows: |

Adjusted gross income	$353,400
Threshold for phaseout	309,900
Excess over threshold	$43,500
Each $2,500	÷ 2,500
Number of $2,500s	17.4
Number of $2,500s or fractions thereof	18
Phaseout rate	2%
Reduction in personal exemptions	36%
Personal exemption amount	$4,000
Personal exemptions (4)	× 4
Initial personal exemption deduction	$16,000
Personal exemption percent allowed	× 64%
Personal exemption deduction	$10,240

Filing Status and Requirements

The tax liability of an individual not only varies with the amount of income but also depends upon marital status. Taxpayers must determine their income tax liability from among five different filing statuses:

1. Married individuals filing jointly
2. Married individuals filing separate returns
3. Single individuals
4. Heads of households
5. Surviving spouses

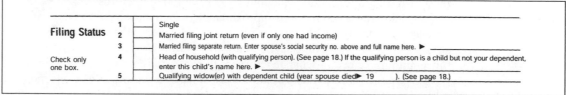

Source: Form 1040

A married taxpayer meeting the "abandoned spouse" requirements may be considered as an unmarried person for tax purposes. These requirements are: (1) the taxpayer must file a separate return, (2) the taxpayer's spouse cannot be a member of the household during the last six months of the year, (3) the taxpayer must furnish over half the cost of maintaining the taxpayer's home, and (4) the taxpayer's home must be the principal residence of a dependent child for more than one-half of the year.

| EXAMPLE 3.13 | Melvin Moore left Esther and their two children on April 15, 2015, and has not been heard from since. Esther furnishes the entire cost of the household and the support of the two children for the remainder of the year. For 2015, Esther would qualify as an abandoned spouse and thus be considered as unmarried. If Melvin had left during the last half of the year, or if there were no children, Esther would not qualify as unmarried under the abandoned spouse rules. She would file as married filing separately. |

An individual qualifying as an abandoned spouse will qualify for head of household status. Head of household status provides the spouse with a lower rate than the tax rate for a married person filing a separate return or a single individual.

Married persons are taxed at the lowest rate if they file jointly, and at the highest rates if they file separately. Unmarried taxpayers who are heads of households use a set of rates between those for single people and those for married couples filing jointly. Surviving spouses use the same rates as those married filing jointly. All unmarried taxpayers who do not qualify for another filing status must file as single taxpayers.

¶3301   MARRIED INDIVIDUALS FILING JOINTLY

A married couple may file a joint return including their combined incomes, or each spouse may file a separate return reflecting his or her income only. A joint return is not allowed if either the husband or wife is a nonresident alien at any time during the tax year, or if the husband and wife have different tax years. However, if at the end of a tax year one spouse is a U.S. citizen or a resident alien and the other spouse is a nonresident alien, a special election may be made to treat the nonresident spouse as a U.S. resident. If no election is made, the taxpayer's status is married filing separately unless there is a dependent which would allow head of household status to be used.

Joint returns were originally enacted to establish equity for married taxpayers in common law states since in community property states married taxpayers are able to split their income. Therefore, the progressive rates are constructed upon the assumption that income is earned equally by the two spouses. A joint return may be filed and the splitting device may be used even if one spouse has no income.

If a joint return is filed, the income and deductions of both spouses are combined. The exemptions to which either spouse is entitled are combined, and both spouses sign the return. In a joint return, the general rule is that both spouses are jointly and severally liable for any deficiency in tax, interest, and penalties.

A joint return may be made for the survivor and a deceased spouse or for both deceased spouses. The tax year of such spouses must begin on the same day and end on different days only because of the death of either or both spouses. The surviving spouse must not remarry before the close of the tax year and the spouses must have been eligible to file a joint return on the date of death.

The determination of whether an individual is married is made as of the close of the tax year, unless the spouse dies during the year, in which case the determination will be made as of the time of death. A married couple does not have to be living together on the last day of the tax year in order to file a joint return, but an individual legally separated under a decree of divorce or separate maintenance will not be considered married.

¶3315   MARRIED INDIVIDUALS FILING SEPARATELY

If a husband and wife file separate returns, they should each report only their own income and claim only their own exemptions and deductions on their individual returns.

Separate returns will result in approximately the same tax liability as a joint return where both spouses have approximately equal amounts of income. However, when the incomes are unequal, it is generally advantageous for married taxpayers in noncommunity property states to file a joint return since the combined amount of tax on separate returns is higher than the tax on a joint return.

Special circumstances may warrant the use of separate returns. Where one spouse incurs significant medical expenses, the smaller adjusted gross income of a separate return results in a larger medical deduction since medical expenses are allowed only to the extent they exceed 10 percent (7.5 percent if over 65) of adjusted gross income. It may be desirable to file separate returns to protect against a potential deficiency on the other spouse's return where there is some concern over the tax liability or there is a questionable item on the return itself.

In community property states, a married couple's income is treated as earned equally by the two spouses. Income earned on capital investment made from a spouse's separate property in most community property states remains the separate property of that spouse. There are three community property states in which income from separate property is treated as community property (Texas, Idaho, and Louisiana). See discussion of the "Texas Rule" at ¶4215. Community property income and deductions must be accounted for on the same basis. Deductions pertaining to the separate property of one spouse must be taken by that spouse. However, where the income from that property is taxable one-half to each spouse, the deductions must be divided between the husband and wife.

The Code places numerous limitations upon deductions, credits, etc., where married taxpayers file separately. If both husband and wife have income, they should generally figure their tax both jointly and separately to insure they are using the method resulting in less tax.

If an individual has filed a separate return for a year for which a joint return could have been filed and the time for filing the return has expired, a joint return by the husband and wife may still be filed. The joint return must be filed within three years of the due date of the original return for which a change is requested. All payments, credits, refunds, or other payments made or allowed on the separate return of either spouse are taken into account in determining the extent to which the tax based on the joint return has been paid.

If a joint return has been filed for a year, the spouses may not thereafter file separate returns for that year after the time for filing the return for that year has expired.

¶3325   SINGLE INDIVIDUALS

A single individual for tax purposes is an unmarried person who does not qualify as head of household. Generally, if only one of the two individuals is working, it is advantageous from a tax standpoint to enter into marriage. However, where the incomes are approximately equal, the total tax will be smaller if they are not married.

¶3345   HEADS OF HOUSEHOLDS

Unmarried individuals who maintain a household for qualifying children or dependents are entitled to use the head of household rates. The definition of a dependent for purposes of head of household status is the same as the uniform definition contained in the dependency exemption rules. The dependent must be a qualifying child or a qualified relative of the taxpayer. Over one-half of the cost of maintaining the household must be furnished by the taxpayer. The household must be the principal abode for more than one-half of the year. A qualifying relative must qualify as the taxpayer's dependent. A dependent relative who is a dependent only because of a multiple-support agreement cannot qualify a taxpayer for head of household status. A legally adopted child of a taxpayer is considered a child of the taxpayer by blood. A dependent foster child is treated like a dependent blood son or daughter, rather than as an unrelated individual. However, the foster child must be a dependent to enable the parent to use head of household status. Rev. Rul. 84-89, 1984-1 CB 5. A taxpayer with a qualifying child is not required to claim the qualifying child as a dependent in order to qualify for head of household status. A nonrelative cannot qualify an individual for head of household status.

EXAMPLE 3.14   Sara Shuster is unmarried and maintains a household in which she and her son reside. The son is claimed by his father as a dependent. Since Sara is not required to claim the dependency exemption on her child, she may use the head-of-household tax rate schedule. If the son is married, Sara must be able to claim him as a dependent in order to file as head of household.

The taxpayer's dependent parents need not live with the taxpayer to enable the taxpayer to qualify as a head of household. The household maintained by the taxpayer must actually constitute the principal place of abode of the father or mother or both of them. The father or mother must occupy the household for the entire year. A rest home or home for the aged qualifies as a household for this purpose.

EXAMPLE 3.15   Meg Morgan, an unmarried individual living in Baltimore, maintains a household in Los Angeles for her dependent mother. Meg may use the head-of-household tax rate schedule even though her mother does not live with her.

Although generally a married couple cannot file a joint return if one of them is a nonresident alien, the taxpayer who is a U.S. citizen will qualify as a head of household if the taxpayer is the one providing the maintenance of the household and if there is a related dependent living with the taxpayer the entire year. The law provides that, for purposes of the head of household status, the taxpayer is treated as unmarried.

A taxpayer does not qualify for head of household status if the only other person living in his household is a nonresident alien spouse because the spouse does not qualify as a dependent. However, a taxpayer having a nonresident alien spouse may qualify if an unmarried dependent or unmarried stepchild lives with the taxpayer. Rev. Rul. 55-711, 1955-2 CB 13, amplified by Rev. Rul. 74-370, 1974-2 CB 7.

A physical change in the location of a home will not prevent a taxpayer from qualifying as a head of household. The fact that the individual qualifying the taxpayer for head of household status is born or dies within the tax year will not block a claim for head of household status. The household must have been the principal place of abode of the individual for the remaining or preceding part of the year.

A nonpermanent failure to occupy the common abode by reason of illness, education, business, vacation, military service, or a custody agreement under which a child or stepchild is absent for less than six months in a year will not bar the head of household status. However, it must be reasonable to assume that the household member will return to the household and the taxpayer continues to maintain the household or a substantially equivalent household in anticipation of such return.

The costs of maintaining a household are the expenses incurred for the mutual benefit of the occupants. They include property taxes, mortgage interest, rent, utility charges, upkeep and repairs, property insurance, and food consumed on the premises. Such expenses do not include the cost of clothing, education, medical treatment, vacations, life insurance, and transportation. In addition, the cost of maintaining a household does not include any amount which represents the value of services rendered in the household by the taxpayer or by a person qualifying the taxpayer as a head of household. The taxpayer, for example, cannot impute a value for services provided by the taxpayer for cooking, cleaning, and doing laundry.

It is possible for a household to be a portion of a home. The Tax Court held that a widow and her unmarried daughter occupying one level of a four-level house and sharing two levels constituted a household. *J.F. Fleming Est.,* 33 TCM 619, Dec. 32,611(M), T.C. Memo. 1974-137. Since the widow paid more than one-half of the household maintenance expenses attributable to her and her daughter, she qualified as a head of household.

¶3355 SURVIVING SPOUSES

Special tax benefits are extended to a surviving spouse. In addition to the right to file a joint return for the year in which a spouse dies, a taxpayer whose spouse died in either of the two years preceding the tax year, and who has not remarried, may file as a surviving spouse provided the surviving spouse maintains a household for a dependent child or stepchild.

Surviving spouses use the same tax rate schedules and tax tables as married taxpayers filing joint returns. The surviving spouse provisions do not authorize the surviving spouse to file a joint return; they only make the joint return tax rates available.

The surviving spouse must provide over half the cost of maintaining the household in which both the surviving spouse and dependent live. Of course, an exemption for the deceased spouse is available in the year of death but is not available on the return of the surviving spouse in the two years following death.

EXAMPLE 3.16	Albert Olm's wife died in 2015, leaving a child who qualifies as Albert's dependent. In the year of death, Albert and his deceased wife are entitled to file a joint return and claim three exemptions—one each for Albert, his deceased spouse, and the dependent child. If the child continues to live with Albert in a household provided by him and be his dependent, Albert will be allowed to file as a surviving spouse for 2016 and 2017. Only two exemptions will be allowed in those years—one for Albert and one for the dependent child.

¶3365 TAX RETURNS OF DEPENDENTS

For 2015, the standard deduction for an individual who can be claimed as a dependent on the tax return of another taxpayer is the greater of the individual's earned income plus $350 (up to the maximum allowable standard deduction) or $1,050. However, an individual over 18 or a full-time student over 23 will not qualify as a dependent if income exceeds $4,000.

An individual may not claim a personal exemption if the individual can be claimed as a dependent on another taxpayer's return. It does not matter whether the other taxpayer actually claims the exemption.

EXAMPLE 3.17	Michael Turner, who is single, is claimed as a dependent on his parents' 2015 tax return. He receives $1,500 in interest income from a savings account. In addition, he earns $1,800 while working part-time after school. The standard deduction for a single individual for 2015 is $6,300. However, Michael is limited to a standard deduction of $2,150, the larger of his earned income of $1,800 plus $350 or $1,050.

EXAMPLE 3.18 Sonya Ross is single and claimed as a dependent on her parents' 2015 tax return. She has $1,200 in interest income and also earns $400 from part-time employment. Her standard deduction is limited to $1,050, the larger of her earned income of $400 plus $350 or $1,050.

EXAMPLE 3.19 Tom Moss, a 22-year-old, full-time college student, is claimed as a dependent on his parents' 2015 return. Tom is married and files a separate return. Tom has $1,500 in interest income and wages of $6,500. His standard deduction is $6,300, because the greater of $1,050 or his earned income ($6,500) plus $350 is $6,850, but his standard deduction cannot be more than the $6,300 maximum allowable standard deduction.

Kiddie Tax

If a dependent child is subject to the kiddie tax and has more than $2,100 of net unearned (investment) income for the year, his or her net unearned income is taxed to the child at the additional rate of tax that the parent would be required to pay if the child's net unearned income were included in the parents' taxable income. This applies regardless of the source of the assets creating the child's net unearned income as long as the child has at least one living parent as of the close of the tax year and does not file a joint return. The income of the custodial parent is used for the tax computation in the case of parents that are not married. The parent with the greater taxable income is to be used when married parents file separately.

The kiddie tax applies in the following circumstances:

1. 17-year old or younger—subject to the kiddie tax regardless of the amount of his or her earned income.
2. 18-year old—subject to the kiddie tax unless the child has earned income exceeding one-half of their support.
3. 19- to 23-year old full-time student—subject to the kiddie tax unless the child has earned income exceeding one-half of their support.

Net unearned income is unearned income (such as interest, dividends, capital gains, and certain trust income) less the sum of $1,050 (referred to as the first $1,050 clause) and the greater of: (1) $1,050 of the standard deduction or $1,050 of itemized deductions, or (2) the amount of allowable deductions which are directly connected with the production of unearned income. Thus, unearned income is reduced by $2,100 unless the child has itemized deductions connected with the production of unearned income exceeding $1,050. The amount of net unearned income cannot exceed taxable income for the year.

The child in each of the following examples is subject to the kiddie tax. In each of the examples no personal exemption is allowed since the child is a dependent of another taxpayer.

EXAMPLE 3.20 Amy Acorn has $300 of unearned income and no earned income. Amy will have no tax liability since her standard deduction of $1,050 will reduce taxable income to zero.

EXAMPLE 3.21 Bill Barnes has $1,300 of unearned income and no earned income. Bill will have $250 of taxable income ($1,300 gross income – $1,050 standard deduction). His net unearned income is reduced to zero by the first $1,050 clause and the $1,050 standard deduction. The $250 taxable income is taxed at Bill's tax rate.

EXAMPLE 3.22 Charles Clewis has $2,300 of unearned income and no earned income. His $1,050 standard deduction reduces taxable income to $1,250. The $2,300 of unearned income is reduced by (1) the first $1,050 clause and (2) the $1,050 standard deduction, leaving $200 of net unearned income. The $200 of net unearned income is taxed at the additional rate of the parents while the remaining $1,050 of taxable income is taxed at Charles's rate.

EXAMPLE 3.23 Dave Drummer has $800 of earned income and $400 of unearned income. Dave's standard deduction is $1,150 (the amount of earned income plus $350). His taxable income is $50 ($1,200 gross income – $1,150 standard deduction). Since the unearned income is less than $2,100, there is no net unearned income. The taxable income is taxed at Dave's tax rate.

EXAMPLE 3.24	Frank Fisher has $450 of earned income and $2,200 of unearned income. His taxable income is $1,600 ($2,650 gross income – $1,050 standard deduction). Frank's $2,200 unearned income is reduced by $2,100 (the first $1,050 clause + the $1,050 standard deduction), leaving $100 of net unearned income. The $100 of net unearned income is taxed at the parent's rate. Frank is taxed at his rate on the remaining $1,500 taxable income ($1,600 taxable income – $100 taxed at parent's rate).

EXAMPLE 3.25	Gene Gambol has $1,100 of earned income plus $3,000 of unearned income. He has $1,100 of itemized deductions (net of the 2 percent floor) which are directly connected with the production of the unearned income. Gene has $450 of other itemized deductions. His taxable income is $2,550 ($4,100 gross income – $1,550 of itemized deductions). Gene's net unearned income of $850 is taxed at his parents' rate. The unearned income is reduced by $2,150 (the first $1,050 clause + the entire $1,100 of deductions relating to the production of unearned income since it exceeds $1,050). Gene is taxed at his rate on $1,700 ($2,550 taxable income – $850 taxed at his parents' rate).

PLANNING POINTER	Parents can avoid having a dependent's income taxed at their rate by making gifts to children of assets that will not generate income until after the child's income no longer qualifies for the kiddie tax. The tax on the income would then be taxed at the child's tax rate. Examples of such assets include single premium ordinary life insurance policies, Series EE savings bonds, and property expected to appreciate over time.

A parent may elect to include on his or her return the unearned income of a child whose income is between $1,050 and $10,500. The child's income must consist solely of interest and dividends. The child is treated as having no gross income and does not have to file a tax return if the election is made.

The electing parent must include the gross income of the child in excess of $2,100 on the parent's tax return for the year, resulting in the taxation of that income at the parent's highest marginal rate. There is an additional tax liability equal to the lesser of (1) $105 or (2) 10 percent of the child's income exceeding $1,050. This liability reflects the child's unearned income from $1,050 to $2,100 that would otherwise be taxed to the child at the 10 percent tax rate.

¶3375   FILING REQUIREMENTS

The obligation to file a return depends on the amount of gross income, marital status during the year, and age. Only income which is taxable is included in the computation of gross income in order to determine whether or not a return must be filed.

With certain exceptions, the gross income level at which taxpayers must file returns is determined by adding the standard deduction to the personal exemptions allowed for the taxpayer. Because married individuals filing separately must both itemize or both use the standard deduction, the standard deduction amount is not added to the personal exemption to determine the gross income filing figure. The old-age additional standard deduction entitles an individual to increase the gross income level filing requirement by $1,250 or $1,550. However, no increase is permitted for blindness or for exemptions for dependents.

For 2015, Code Sec. 6012 requires a tax return to be filed if gross income for the year is at least as much as the amount shown for the categories in the following table.

Filing Status	Gross Income
Single	
Under 65 and not blind	$10,300
Under 65 and blind	10,300
65 or older	11,850
Dependent with unearned income	1,050
Dependent with no unearned income	6,300
Married Filing Joint Return	
Both spouses under 65 and neither blind	$20,600
Both spouses under 65 and one or both spouses blind	20,600
One spouse 65 or older	21,850
Both spouses 65 or older	23,100
Married Filing Separate Return	
All—whether 65 or older or blind	$4,000
Head of Household	
Under 65 and not blind	$13,250
Under 65 and blind	13,250
65 or older	14,800
Surviving Spouse	
Under 65 and not blind	$16,600
Under 65 and blind	16,600
65 or older	17,850

Even if the aforementioned gross income requirements are not met, a return nevertheless must be filed if an individual had net earnings from self-employment of $400 or more.

A return should be filed by any taxpayer eligible for the earned income credit even though the taxpayer does not meet any of the above filing requirements. A refund can result even if no income tax has been withheld.

Taxpayers must record their identifying number (Social Security number) on their returns. Returns filed by taxpayers claiming exemptions for dependents must include the dependents' Social Security numbers.

¶3385   TAX TABLES

The tables are based on taxable income. The tables apply to taxpayers with taxable income of less than $100,000. Separate tables are provided for single taxpayers, married taxpayers filing jointly and surviving spouses, married taxpayers filing separately, and heads of households.

Each line of the tax tables represents an interval of taxable incomes. Under $3,050 the intervals are $25 and above $3,050 the intervals are $50. The tax given in the tables is based on the midpoint taxable income of each interval. Thus, the tax from the tables for the interval $40,000—$40,050 is the same as the tax determined from the tax rate schedules for $40,025.

The tax tables may not be used by the following taxpayers:

1. Estates or trusts
2. Taxpayers claiming the exclusion for foreign earned income
3. Taxpayers who file a short period return
4. Taxpayers whose income exceeds the ceiling amount

It is expected that 95 percent of all individual taxpayers will be able to determine their tax liability from the tables.

To find the income tax from the tax tables, the taxpayer must (1) find the line that includes the taxable income and (2) read down the column until the taxable income line is reached. For a married couple filing jointly with taxable income of $72,623, the income tax would be $9,744.

Sample Tax Table For 2015					
At Least	But Less Than	Single	Married Filing Jointly	Married Filing Separately	Head of a Household
$72,600	$72,650	$13,950	$9,744	$13,861	$12,479
72,650	72,700	13,963	9,756	13,875	12,491
72,700	72,750	13,975	9,769	13,889	12,504
72,750	72,800	13,988	9,781	13,903	12,516

The 2014 Tax Tables are provided in the Appendix.

¶3395   TAX RATE SCHEDULES

Taxpayers using the tax rate schedules must compute their tax based on taxable income. The tax rate schedules are used by those not eligible to use the tax tables. The tax rate schedules are presented in the Appendix and inside the front cover.

¶3405   SELF-EMPLOYMENT TAX AND MEDICARE SURTAXES

The tax on net self-employment income is levied to provide the self-employed with the same benefits that employees receive through their payment of the Social Security tax (FICA). In general, the tax is levied, assessed, and collected as part of the regular income tax.

The tax is imposed for the purposes of insuring the self-employed individual for old-age, survivors, and disability benefits and for hospitalization benefits under the Social Security program. For 2015, the tax rate is 15.3 percent, made up of two parts: (1) an old-age, survivors, and disability insurance (OASDI) rate of 12.4 percent and (2) a Medicare hospital insurance (HI) rate of 2.9 percent. The self-employed individual is considered both the employer and the employee.

In general, net self-employment income equals the gross income derived by an individual from a trade or business carried on as a sole proprietor, less any allowable deductions, plus the distributive share of a partnership's net income. If a self-employed individual has more than one business, the net self-employment income is the total of the net earnings of all businesses. A loss in one business is deductible from the earnings of the other businesses.

Not all self-employment income is subject to tax. Remuneration paid for the services of a newsboy under age 18 is exempt from the tax. Dividends are included only by a dealer in stock and securities. Interest is included only if on business loans. Rental income is included only by a real estate dealer or in cases in which services are rendered to the occupants. Generally, self-employment income does not include any item that is excluded from gross income. Wages received by a child under 18 from a parent are not subject to the self-employment tax.

The self-employment tax is imposed on "net earnings from self-employment." Net earnings from self-employment is net self-employment income less a special deduction. The actual deduction, however, is not subtracted from a taxpayer's net self-employment income in computing net earnings from self-employment. Instead, a taxpayer reduces net self-employment income by an amount (termed a "deemed deduction") equal to net self-employment income multiplied by one-half of the self-employment tax rate, or 7.65 percent. This deduction is incorporated into Schedule SE by multiplying the net self-employment income by .9235. (This gives the same deduction as multiplying net self-employment income by .0765 and then subtracting the result.)

A taxpayer is allowed a deduction for the employer's portion of the self-employment tax (currently one-half) as a deduction from gross income.

EXAMPLE 3.26

In 2015, Pierre Painter, a self-employed artist, had $45,000 in self-employment income. His deductible business expenses amounted to $15,000. Pierre's self-employment tax is computed as follows:

Gross income from self-employment	$45,000
Less: Business expense deductions	15,000
Net self-employment income	$30,000
Less: Deemed deduction ($30,000 × 7.65%)	2,295
Net earnings from self-employment	$27,705
Self-employment tax ($27,705 × 15.3%)	$ 4,239

On Form 1040, Schedule SE, Pierre would simply multiply his net self-employment income of $30,000 by .9235.

The cap on wages and self-employment income that is taken into account in calculating the portion of the FICA tax applicable to old-age, survivors, and disability insurance (OASDI) is $118,500 for 2015. This also applies to wages, self-employment income, and income derived under the Railroad Retirement Act. There is no longer a cap on wages and self-employment income that is taken into account in calculating the Medicare hospital insurance (HI) portion of the self-employment tax.

EXAMPLE 3.27

Katie Adams has $150,000 in self-employment income for the year. Her net earnings from self-employment is $138,525 ($150,000 × .9235). She will be subject to an OASDI tax of $14,694 ($118,500 × 12.4%) and an HI tax of $4,017.23 ($138,525 × 2.9%). Thus, her total self-employment tax is $18,711.23.

Thus, self-employment and Social Security (FICA) tax rate parity is achieved between self-employed persons and employees. Both employees and their employers are liable for Social Security tax and the employer must contribute 6.2 cents per dollar earned by the employee up to the cap limitation ($118,500 for 2015) for OASDI and another 1.45 cents per dollar without a cap for HI.

The net earnings from self-employment subject to the OASDI portion of the self-employment tax are limited to the self-employment base ($118,500 for OASDI and unlimited for HI in 2015) less any wages from which Social Security tax was withheld during the year. Thus, the tax is applied to the lesser of (1) the self-employment base ($118,500) minus income subject to Social Security taxes or (2) the net earnings from self-employment.

EXAMPLE 3.28

In 2015, Margaret Moore has $120,500 in income from self-employment and receives $8,900 in wages that are subject to Social Security taxes. Margaret's net earnings from self-employment are $111,282 ($120,500 × .9235). Her net earnings from self-employment subject to OASDI self-employment tax for the year are $109,600 ($118,500 − $8,900, the wages on which Social Security tax was withheld), which is less than net earnings from self-employment. Her net earnings from self-employment subject to the HI self-employment tax are $111,282, the full amount of the net earnings from self-employment. Thus, her total self-employment tax is $16,817.58 ($109,600 × 12.4% + $111,282 × 2.9%).

The employer portion of the self-employment tax liability for the year is allowed as a deduction on the tax return. This deduction is taken as a deduction from gross income on the front of Form 1040.

EXAMPLE 3.29

Jim Jergens has $40,000 in self-employment income. His net earnings from self-employment are $36,940 ($40,000 × .9235). The self-employment tax is $5,651.82 ($36,940 × 15.3%). The employer portion of this amount, $2,825.91 ($36,940 × 7.65%), is allowed as a deduction from gross income.

If the net earnings from self-employment are less than $400, there is no self-employment tax. However, this does not mean that the first $400 of net earnings from self-employment is not subject to the self-employment tax.

EXAMPLE 3.30   Sylvia Knight's only source of income for 2015 is $433.14 from self-employment. The net earnings from self-employment are $400 ($433.14 × .9235). The self-employment tax is $61.20 ($400 × 15.3%). Sylvia has a deduction from gross income for the employer portion of the self-employment tax, or $30.60 ($400 × 7.65%). If Sylvia had managed to earn less than $433.14, there would have been no self-employment tax.

An optional method of computing self-employment income may be used by persons whose net income from a trade or business is relatively low. The details are omitted, but the method enables taxpayers to obtain greater credit for Social Security benefits than their income would normally allow.

Additional Medicare Tax on Earned Income

A 0.9% Additional Medicare Tax applies to wages and net self-employment income for tax years after 2012. The tax applies to wages exceeding $200,000 for single, head-of-household, or surviving spouse; $250,000 for married filing jointly; $125,000 for married filing separately. The applicable thresholds are not adjusted for inflation.

The tax applies to the employee's share of wages. The tax does not apply to the employer's employment taxes. Box 5 of the W-2 is used for determining the Additional Medicare Tax and withholding.

There are no special rules for nonresident aliens and U.S. citizens living abroad for purposes of the Additional Medicare Tax. Wages, other compensation, and self-employment income that are subject to Medicare tax will also be subject to the Additional Medicare Tax if in excess of the applicable threshold.

The threshold amount for the Additional Medicare Tax applies separately to the FICA and the Railroad Retirement Tax Act (RRTA). Therefore, the amount of RRTA compensation taken into account in determining the Additional Medicare Tax under the RRTA will not reduce the threshold amounts under Section 1401(b)(2)(A) for determining the Additional Medicare Tax under the SECA.

The Additional Medicare Tax on earned income is part of the employer's overall withholding. The employee reconciles the final total of any Additional Medicare Tax when they file their Form 1040 for the tax year.

Employers are required to apply the additional withholding at $200,000 of wages, including taxable fringe benefits, bonuses, tips, commissions, or other supplemental payments, the total amount of taxable Box 5. It does not matter what filing status is shown on Form W-4. The employer applies the $200,000 threshold to each spouse in applying the Additional Medicare Tax. In effect the employer disregards the amount of wages received by the other spouse in computing the Additional Medicare Tax for each spouse.

EXAMPLE 3.31   One spouse received $210,000 of wages, while the other spouse earns $35,000 of either W-2 wages or net self-employment income. The employer of the first spouse is required to withhold an additional 0.9% Additional Medicare Tax on the last $10,000 of taxable wages (i.e., $90) even though the couple will not owe the 0.9% Additional Medicare Tax when they file their 2015 Form 1040. They will receive a tax credit against any other type of tax that may be owed.

If an employer fails to withhold the 0.9% Additional Medicare tax, and the tax is subsequently paid by the employee, the IRS will *not* collect the tax from the employer. The employer will remain subject to any applicable *penalties* on additions to tax for failure to withhold the 0.9% Additional Medicare tax as required. Code Sec. 3102(f)(3). The employee is personally responsible if the employer fails to withhold the 0.9% additional Medicare tax. Code Sec. 3102(f)(2).

The self-employed does not receive an income tax deduction for one-half of the 0.9% Additional Medicare Tax on earned income. Any deduction comes from the employer's portion of employment taxes.

EXAMPLE 3.32   A husband and wife each have "Box 5 Medicare wages" of $150,000 listed on their respective W-2s. The combined $300,000 "earned income" will be shown on Form 8959 for calculating the 0.9% Additional Medicare Tax. The couple will owe a 0.9% Additional Medicare Tax of $450 (($300,000 – $250,000 threshold) x 0.9%) which will be included as "Other Taxes" on page 2 of Form 1040.

EXAMPLE 3.33	A husband has $150,000 of "Box 5 Medicare wages" listed on his W-2. His wife has a K-1 from her law firm listing Box 14 net earnings from self-employment of $162,426 ($150,000 net self-employment income). The couple will owe $450 of Additional Medicare Tax on their collective earned income.
EXAMPLE 3.34	A husband has $150,000 of "Box 5 Medicare wages" listed on his W-2. His wife has a K-1 from her law firm with net earnings from self-employment of $150,000. The wife also has a $50,000 loss from the start-up of a new Schedule C business. Since the self-employment income of the wife would now be only $100,000, when it is added to the $150,000 in W-2 wages of the husband, the couple is not above the "applicable threshold" of $250,000 for married filing jointly. Therefore, no Additional Medicare Tax on their collective earned income would be due..
EXAMPLE 3.35	A husband and wife each have "Box 5 Medicare wages" of $150,000 listed on their respective W-2s. The wife also has a $50,000 loss from the start-up of a new Schedule C business. The couple would still owe $450 of Additional Medicare Tax. The self-employment loss is not permitted to offset W-2 wages.
EXAMPLE 3.36	The husband has $190,000 in wages subject to Medicare tax and the wife has $150,000 in compensation subject to RRTA taxes. The husband and wife do not combine their wages and RRTA compensation to determine whether they are in excess of the $250,000 threshold for a joint return. The husband and wife are not liable to pay Additional Medicare Tax because the husband's wages are not in excess of the $250,000 threshold and the wife's RRTA compensation is not in excess of the $250,000 threshold.
EXAMPLE 3.37	C, a single filer, has $130,000 in wages and $145,000 in net earnings from self-employment. C's wages are not in excess of the $200,000 threshold for single filers, so C is not liable for the Additional Medicare Tax on these wages. Before calculating the Additional Medicare Tax on self-employment income, the $200,000 threshold for single filers is reduced by C's $130,000 in wages, resulting in a reduced self-employment income threshold of $70,000. C is liable to pay the Additional Medicare Tax on $75,000 of self-employment income; $145,000 in self-employment income minus the reduced threshold of $70,000.

Net Investment Income Tax

After 2012, a 3.8% "Net Investment Income Tax" is imposed on individuals and estate and trusts. Code Sec. 1411. The Net Investment Income Tax will be calculated on Form 8960 and shown as "Other Taxes" on page 2 of Form 1040.

For individuals, the tax is imposed on the lesser of:

a. An individual's "net investment income" for the tax year, or
b. Any excess of "modified adjusted gross income" (MAGI) for the tax year over a threshold amount. Code Sec.1411(a)(1).

The "threshold amount" is $200,000 for single taxpayers and heads-of-households; $250,000 for married filing jointly and surviving spouses; $125,000 for married filing separately. Code Sec. 1411(b). MAGI means an individual's adjusted gross income for the tax year increased by otherwise excludable foreign earned income or foreign housing costs under Sec. 911 as reduced by any deduction, exclusion, or credits properly allocable to or chargeable against such foreign earned income. Code Sec. 1411(d).

| EXAMPLE 3.38 | Elmer, a single individual, earns $190,000 in wages and/or net self-employment income and also has $40,000 of "net investment income" for the year. Assuming a $230,000 MAGI, he will have to pay a 3.8% Net Investment Income Tax on the lesser of his (1) $40,000 of net investment income, or (2) $30,000 ($230,000 MAGI – $200,000 threshold). Elmer will pay a $1,140 ($30,000 × 3.8%) Net Investment Income Tax for the year. |

EXAMPLE 3.39   During the year, an unmarried taxpayer received no wages or self-employment income, but lives strictly off of her $1 million in "net investment income" from a stock and bond portfolio. Assuming a $1 million MAGI, she will have to pay a 3.8% Net Investment Income Tax on the lesser of her (1) $1 million net investment income or (2) $800,000 ($1 million – $200,000 threshold). As a result, she will pay a $30,400 ($800,000 x 3.8%) Net Investment Income Tax for the year.

The Net Investment Income Tax does not apply to a non-resident alien or to a trust "all the unexpired interests in which are devoted to charitable purposes." The tax does not apply to a trust that is exempt under Sec. 501 or a charitable remainder trust exempt from tax under Sec. 664.

"Net investment income" is defined as: [Code Sec. 1411(c)(1) and (c)(2)]

1. Gross income from interest, dividends, annuities, royalties, and rents (unless such income is "derived in the ordinary course of any trade or business");
2. Other gross income from any passive trade or business; or
3. Net gain included in computing taxable income that is attributable to the disposition of property other than property held in any trade or business that is not a "passive trade or business."

"Income derived in the ordinary course of a trade or business" does not include any trade or business that is either a passive activity of the taxpayer, or involves trading in financial instruments and commodities. The passive activity and trading in financial instruments and commodities are defined as "passive business investment income" for purposes of the 3.8% Medicare tax.

Financial Instruments include: Equity interest such as stock, Proof of indebtedness, Options, Notional principal contracts, Other derivatives, and Other evidence of an interest in one of the foregoing items.

A passive investor's share of Form 1065 or Form 1120S from Box 1 on Schedule K-1 would be "other gross income from any passive trade or business."

A Sec. 1231 gain reported on a K-1 from the sale of assets used in a trade or business that the taxpayer "materially participates" would not be treated as "net investment income" subject to the 3.8% Net Investment Income Tax. However, it would be "net investment income" to a passive investor.

"Net investment income" includes any income, gain, or loss that is attributable to an investment of working capital. Income or gain from investment in working capital is treated as not derived in the ordinary course of a trade or business. Code Sec. 1411(c)(3). For example, a business puts some of its excess working capital into an income-producing investment such as a certificate of deposit or interest-bearing account, or stocks that pay dividends or result in capital gains or losses when sold.

Net investment income does not include: Code Sec. 1411(c)(6).

1. Any distribution from qualified employee benefit plan or retirement arrangements;
2. Any distributions from a regular IRA or Roth IRA;
3. Social security benefits;
4. Any item excluded from gross income.
5. Any item taken into account in determining self-employment income for the tax year on which an individual pays self-employment tax under Sec. 1401(b).

The K-1 profits reported in Box 1 of a materially participating shareholder are not considered "unearned income" for purposes of the 3.8% Medicare tax.

EXAMPLE 3.40   John is an owner of a business that rents equipment and machinery. He also materially participates in that business. Regardless of the business being operated as an S corporation, LLC/partnership, or a sole proprietorship, any net income or loss therefrom would not be considered for purposes of the 3.8% Net Investment Income Tax calculation. However, a Schedule C sole proprietor or the K-1 recipient of "Box 1—Trades or Business Income" from an LLC/partnership would still have the potential for the 0.9% Medicare tax on earned income.

EXAMPLE 3.41   John leases a building to his rental business. This is a self-rental situation and self-rentals are not classified as passive income. The gross rental income will be deemed to be derived in the ordinary course of a trade or business and, therefore, exempt from the Net Investment Income Tax. Gain or loss from the property will also be treated as gain or loss from the disposition of property held in a nonpassive trade or business.

If a taxpayer is a "real estate professional" and they also "materially participate" in their rental activities, then Sec. 469 passive loss rules do not apply. Any rental income or loss derived from such rental activities will not factor into the taxpayer's calculation of the 3.8% Net Investment Income Tax if they meet the definition of trades or business for Section 162. The IRS has provided a safe harbor for the trades or business definition: If a taxpayer qualifies as a real estate professional and also spends more than 500 hours participating in either a separate or grouped rental activity, the IRS will treat those rental activities as trades or businesses. Reg. §1.1411-4(g)(7)(i).

EXAMPLE 3.42   John is a "real estate professional" for purposes of the passive loss rules. He also "materially participates" in the rental activities that he owns. The Net Investment Income Tax would not apply to the rental activities if his "rental activities" are treated as "trades or business" under Sec. 162. The income would not be subject to any self-employment tax under Sec. 1402. However, assume the rental activities are not "trades or business" for Sec. 162. As a result, any net rental income or loss would be part of his 3.8% Net Investment Income Tax calculation.

For purposes of the Net Investment Income Tax, the definition allows the reduction for any otherwise allowable deductions "properly allocable to such income or gain."

1. Deductions under Sec. 62 related to gross income
2. Itemized deductions under Sec. 63
3. Loss deductions under Sec. 165

A large capital loss in excess of any capital gain for a particular tax year can only offset up to $3,000 of other "net investment income." A large advisory fee for managing a stock portfolio can only offset "net investment income" to the extent it exceeds 2% of AGI as a miscellaneous itemized deduction. Investment interest expense can only be used to offset "net investment income" to the extent otherwise allowed on Form 4952. Any state or local tax attributable to the sources of net investment income may be deducted in computing net investment income. Any otherwise allowable deductions must also be reduced by the itemized deduction phaseout.

Employment Taxes for Household Employers

If a taxpayer hires someone to do household work and was able to control what work he or she did and how he or she did it, the taxpayer has a household employee. The taxpayer has to have an employer identification number (EIN) and pay employment taxes.

A Form W-2, Wage and Tax Statement, must be filed for each household employee paid $1,900 or more in cash wages in 2015 that are subject to social security and Medicare taxes. If the wages were not subject to these taxes but the employee wishes to have federal income taxes withheld, a W-2 must be filed for that employee. A Form W-3, Transmittal of Wage and Tax Statements, must also be filed if one or more W-2s are required to be filed.

If cash wages are paid of $1,000 or more in any calendar quarter of 2014 or 2015 to household employees for 2015, the taxpayer may also be subject to federal and state unemployment taxes.

In the case of persons performing domestic services in a private home of the employer and person performing agricultural labor, if the employer pays the employee's liability for FICA taxes or state unemployment taxes without deduction from the employee's wages, those payments are not wages for FICA purposes. Code Sec. 3121(a)(6).

¶3405

TAX BLUNDERS

1. Sara Michaels and Tommy Tooks marry on December 31. Sara earned $120,000 for the year, and Tommy earned $100,000. If Sara and Tommy had waited until the beginning of the following year to marry they would have realized a significant tax savings. Each filing as single taxpayers will result in less total tax than filing jointly.

2. Assume Sara earned $95,000 and Tommy earned $5,000 because he attended school most of the year and they marry at the beginning of the next year. There would be a significant tax savings in marrying at the end of the first year and filing jointly over each filing as single taxpayers.

3. Sara and Tommy decide to file as married filing separately. Sara has $7,000 in itemized deductions and Tommy has $2,500 in itemized deductions. Since Sara itemized on her return Tommy is required to itemize. They may be better off to have both take the standard deduction since the total standard deductions would be $12,600 while itemizing only results in a $9,500 total deduction.

SUMMARY

- The standard deduction eliminates low- to moderate-level taxpayers from the tax rolls. The standard deduction is made up of two parts: the basic standard deduction and the additional standard deduction. Both of these parts are adjusted each year for inflation. The standard deduction differs depending upon filing status.

- Taxpayers are allowed a personal exemption for themselves and their spouse, plus an exemption for each qualified dependent. Taxpayers who are dependents are not allowed a personal exemption for themselves.

- Taxpayers must determine their tax liability from among five different filing statuses.

- Special taxation rules are imposed on returns filed by individuals that are dependents of other taxpayers.

- In general, filing requirements are based on a taxpayer's gross income, filing status, and age.

- Self-employed individuals are required to pay a self-employment tax that is equivalent to the Social Security taxes paid by employees.

- Taxpayers could potentially be subject to a 0.9% Additional Medicare Tax and the Net Investment Income Tax.

QUESTIONS

1. What is the purpose in knowing and understanding the components of the tax formula?

2. What is the distinction between deductions for adjusted gross income and deductions from adjusted gross income?

3. How does a tax deduction differ from a tax credit?

4. What other terms are used to describe deductions for adjusted gross income?

5. Analyze any differences between increasing the standard deduction and increasing the exemption allowed.

6. Explain the rationale behind an individual's arranging financial affairs to use the standard deduction one year and itemized deductions in another year.

7. What is the reason that some taxpayers are not entitled to the standard deduction or are entitled to only part of it? Explain.

8. How is the standard deduction computed for a dependent child with unearned income?

9. George files a separate return. His wife's only source of income is $600 in interest income. Can George claim an exemption for his wife on his separate return?

10. Are taxpayers allowed to claim the additional old-age or blindness standard deduction for dependents?

11. In determining the dependency exemption, how is the value of lodging provided a dependent computed for the support test?

12. Bill and Becky had a child born on April 15. The child died within three hours of birth. Can they claim an exemption for the child?

13. Can a student attending a class in night school qualify as a full-time student?

14. Rhoda and Mike are both full-time students who married late in the year. Rhoda had $1,800 in wages from a part-time job and Mike had $950 in dividend income. They filed a joint return and received a refund of the $175 that had been withheld on Rhoda's wages. Rhoda's parents paid over one-half of Rhoda's support. Can Rhoda's parents claim her as a dependent?

15. Explain the concept of the "multiple support agreement." What are the requirements for such an agreement?

16. During the year, Alice Johnson was supported by her four sons, Amos, Luther, Bennet, and Ivan, in the following percentages:

Amos	8%
Luther	32%
Bennet	18%
Ivan	42%

Which of the brothers is entitled to claim his mother as a dependent, providing a multiple support agreement exists?

17. Homer and Wilma received a divorce in 2009. During the year, Homer contributed $950 support for their only child in the custody of Wilma. Absent any written agreement relative to the receipt of the dependency exemption, who should be entitled to the exemption?

18. What conditions must exist in Problem 17 for Homer to take the dependency exemption?

19. Tom and Jane were legally separated during the preceding year under a written separation agreement. Jane had custody of their two children for the entire year while Tom contributed $2,000 support for each child. Absent any written agreement relative to the receipt of the dependency exemption, who should be entitled to the exemptions?

20. What form is used to grant an exemption to the noncustodial parent?

21. Calculate the number of exemptions and the standard deduction that the taxpayer is entitled to take in 2015 in each of the following independent cases:

   a. John, age 66, and his wife, age 64, file a joint return.

   b. Jack, age 62 and blind, and his wife, who became 65 on January 1 of the following year, file a joint return.

   c. Jim and Mary, both 52, contribute more than half the support for Jim's father, who lives with them. Jim's father is 72 and blind. Jim and Mary file a joint return.

   d. Harry, age 66, is a widower who maintains a home for himself and his 22-year-old son who attends college full time. Harry provided more than one half of his son's support.

   e. Jackson is 28 and his wife, Joan, is 27. They have two children, one three-year-old and the other seven years old. On March 29 of this year, Joan gave birth to a daughter, who died the next day. Jackson and Joan file a joint return.

   f. Joe, age 65, and his wife, JoAnne, age 64, maintain a home for their unmarried daughter, age 23, who earned $4,000 and attends college on a part-time basis. Joe and JoAnne contributed $6,000 toward her support. Joe and JoAnne file a joint return.

   g. William, a 42-year-old bachelor, pays $450 per month support for his 75-year-old mother who is disabled and is living in a rest home. She receives a taxable pension of $100 per month and uses the entire $550 per month for routine living expenses.

   h. Same as (g), except William's mother also receives $400 per month from dividends on stock she owns. She also uses this amount for routine living expenses.

   i. Billy Bob and his wife, Mary Sue, both 45, maintain a home for Mary Sue's friend, Jackie Jo, age 17, who came to dinner one night several years ago and has lived with them since. Jackie Jo attends school and has no income. Billy Bob and Mary Sue file a joint return.

   j. Benson, a 45-year-old widower, maintains a home for his 22-year-old son, Chester, who attends college full-time on a $4,000-per-year scholarship. Chester also works part-time while at school, earning $1,500 per year. Benson contributes $2,000, which constitutes the balance of Chester's support for the year.

   k. Same as (j), except Chester contributes the $4,000 per year from his savings account instead of receiving it from the scholarship award.

   l. Richard, a bachelor under 65, maintains a home in which a son of a deceased friend has lived the entire year. Richard furnishes over one half of the support of the young man, who attends school. The young man also works part time after school, earning $2,800 per year.

   m. Dan and his wife, Pam, maintain a household for and completely support three foster children. The children have been living in Dan and Pam's home all year. On December 31 of the tax year, Pam gives birth to a son.

22. What is meant by filing status?

23. What filing status options are available to Darlene, assuming she separated from her husband in March? Darlene is the sole support of her daughter, who lives with Darlene.

24. How do head of household expenses differ from the expenses used in the support test?

25. Are all individuals required to file an income tax return?

26. Charles has interest income of $1,100 and no other income. He is claimed as a dependent by his parents. Is he required to file an income tax return?

27. Why might an individual file an income tax return even though not required to do so?

28. Under what circumstances must a return be filed by an individual even though there is only $800 in taxable income?

29. What is the difference between the tax tables and the tax rate schedules?

30. What is the limit for self-employment tax?

PROBLEMS

31. Tom and Linda are married taxpayers who file a joint return. They have itemized deductions of $12,950 and four exemptions. Assuming an adjusted gross income of $40,000, what is their taxable income for 2015?

32. Compute Marie's taxable income for 2015, assuming she is single and claims two dependent children. Her adjusted gross income is $70,000, and she has itemized deductions of $9,500.

33. Which of the following taxpayers should itemize? Explain.
    a. Robert is a single taxpayer. He has itemized deductions of $6,500.
    b. Jane qualifies as head of household. Her itemized deductions total $8,450.
    c. Brian is married and files a separate return. He has itemized deductions of $6,500.
    d. Lisa is a surviving spouse. Her itemized deductions are $12,300.

34. Compute the taxable income for 2015 under each of the following circumstances:
    a. Jim is married and files a joint return. Jim and his wife have two dependent children. They have adjusted gross income of $30,000 and itemized deductions of $12,300.
    b. Jim is single with no dependents. His adjusted gross income is $20,000 with itemized deductions of $3,800.
    c. Jim is a full-time college student under 24 supported by his father. Jim earned $2,600 from a part-time job and had $500 of interest income. His itemized deductions were $600.
    d. Jim is married but files separately and claims two dependent children. His adjusted gross income is $65,000 and he claims $8,900 of itemized deductions. Jim's wife also itemizes on her return.
    e. Assume the same situation as in (d), but Jim's itemized deductions are only $1,500.

35. Duke and Pat Collins have adjusted gross income of $358,000. They have itemized deductions of $20,000 consisting of $8,000 in medical expenses that exceed 10% of adjusted gross income, $3,000 in property taxes, $4,000 in housing interest, and $5,000 in miscellaneous itemized deductions that exceed 2 percent of adjusted gross income. What is the amount of their itemized deductions?

36. What is Mary's taxable income for 2015, assuming she has $6,100 of earned income and $800 of unearned income and is claimed as a dependent by her parents?

37. Compute Stanley's taxable income for 2015, assuming he has $1,000 in wages from working in a grocery store and $2,200 in interest income from some bonds he owns. Stanley, age 16, is claimed as a dependent on his parents' return.

38. Bradford is 12 years old and is claimed as a dependent on his parents' return. In 2015, he received unearned income of $2,200. Bradford's itemized deductions totaled $150. Determine Bradford's taxable income.

39. What is the standard deduction and the number of exemptions that a married couple will be allowed, assuming that they are not over 65 or blind, that they fully support the husband's 82-year-old blind mother, and that they have no other dependents?

40. Has Jodi provided more than 50 percent of the support in the following situations?
    a. Jodi contributed $4,200 to her mother's support during the year. Her mother received $5,300 in Medicare payments that were used to pay her medical expenses.
    b. Jodi's daughter was a full-time student. Jodi paid $2,000 towards her daughter's living expenses. The daughter earned $1,800 from a part-time job and spent that plus $600 from her savings to help support herself.

41. Margaret is attending school full-time for the year. Her parents paid $3,000 toward her support. She earned $2,000 from a part-time job which she used toward her support. In addition, Margaret withdrew $1,500 from her savings account to help in her support. Have her parents provided over one-half of Margaret's support?

42. Myrtle is fully supported by her three children and Fred, a close friend of the family. Mark paid $4,000 toward Myrtle's support, while Nancy, Opel, and Fred paid $3,200, $800, and $2,000, respectively. Which individuals are eligible to claim Myrtle under a multiple support agreement?

43. Annie was divorced in 2000. She provided over half the cost of maintaining the home that she and her 22-year-old son lived in the entire year. Her former husband provided more than half of the son's total support, and he claims the son as a dependent. What is Annie's best filing status for the year?

44. A single taxpayer with one dependent (nonrelative) has $358,000 of adjusted gross income. What is the amount of the deduction for personal exemptions allowed this taxpayer?

45. What is the best filing status in each of the following situations?
    a. Phillip and Catherine were married on December 31, 2015.
    b. John and Sandra were married in 2014. John left Sandra in March 2015, and she has not heard from him since that time.
    c. Melody and Werner were married during the year. Werner is a resident and citizen of Germany.

46. What is the taxpayer's filing status for 2015 in each of the following situations?
    a. Bill's wife died in 2014. Bill maintained a household for his two dependent children in 2015.
    b. Bill is unmarried and lives in an apartment. He supported his aged parents, who live in a separate home. Bill provided over half of the cost of maintaining his parents' home and also provided over half of each of his parents' support.
    c. Bill is unmarried and maintains a household for his 18-year-old daughter and her husband. Bill pays over half of the support of his daughter. The daughter files a joint return with her husband.

47. Indicate the filing status and the number of exemptions allowed to Sandy for 2015, 2016, 2017, and 2018, assuming her husband died in 2015 and Sandy has been the sole support of her son since that time.

48. Mike and Ellen Evans decide to part in April. Mike moves into an apartment two blocks away. The children spend each weekend with Mike. What filing statuses are available to Mike and Ellen, assuming they are not divorced before the end of the year?

49. Which of the following individuals are required to file a tax return for 2015? Assume no tax has been withheld.
    a. Rebecca, single and with no dependents, earned $6,650 for the year.
    b. Hugh and Jane are married and file a joint return. They have four children. Their gross income is $17,000 and they have itemized deductions of $8,000.
    c. Peter has self-employment income of $450. He is a full-time college student and is claimed as a dependent on his parents' return.

50. Julian and Georgia file a joint return. They have adjusted gross income of $112,000 and itemized deductions of $12,800. Are they required to use the Tax Rate Schedules or the Tax Tables in computing their income tax?

51. Eric is single and has no dependents for 2015. He earned $30,000 and had deductions from gross income of $1,800 and itemized deductions of $6,500. Compute Eric's income tax for the year using the Tax Rate Schedules.

52. Allen has taxable income of $75,475 for 2015. Using the Tax Rate Schedules in the Appendix, compute Allen's income tax liability before tax credits and prepayments for each of the following filing statuses.
    a. Married filing jointly
    b. Married filing separately
    c. Single
    d. Head of household

53. Determine the amount of self-employment tax due for 2015, assuming that Lynette earned $30,000 in wages and also earned $20,000 from a business that she owned.

54. A husband and wife who earned Box 5 Medicare wages of $175,000 and $125,000, respectively. Determine the amount of withholding for the Additional Medicare Tax and the amount of tax that they would owe on their final Form 1040.

55. A single taxpayer has $150,000 in wages and $180,000 in net self-employment income. What is the amount of Additional Medicare Tax that would be due on Form 1040 for the year?

56. What is the amount of the net investment income tax for a single individual that has $250,000 of modified adjusted gross income and $25,000 of net investment income?

57. Melvin leases a building that he owns to his wholly-owned S corporation for $30,000 for the year. Melvin materially participates in the S corporation. What amount does Melvin have to report as net investment income for the year from the $30,000?

58. Mr. Smith died early in the year. Mrs. Smith remarried in December and, therefore, was unable to file a joint return with Mr. Smith. What is the filing status of the decedent, Mr. Smith?
    a. Single
    b. Married filing separate return
    c. Married filing joint return
    d. Head of household
    e. Surviving spouse

59. Which of the following is not considered when determining the total support test for a child?
    a. Fair rental value of lodging
    b. Medical insurance premiums
    c. Birthday presents
    d. Scholarship
    e. Recreation

60. Which relative does not have to live in the same household of the taxpayer claiming head of household filing status?
    a. Aunt
    b. Son
    c. Granddaughter
    d. Father
    e. Brother

61. To qualify for head of household rates, which of the following must be present?
    a. You must be unmarried on the last day of your tax year.
    b. You must maintain a household and contribute over 50 percent of the cost of maintaining the household.
    c. The person for whom the household is maintained has to be a relative.
    d. (a) and (b).
    e. All of the above.

62. **Comprehensive Problem.** What is the total tax due for 2015, including self-employment tax, for Stuart, assuming that he earned $20,000 in wages, earned $24,000 in self-employment income from his first business, had a loss of $10,000 from his second business, received $3,000 in interest income, and had $5,100 in nonqualified dividend income?

63. **Comprehensive Problem.** Richard and Jennifer were married in 2006. They have a five-year-old child and a son born November 15, 2015. Richard's 67-year-old father lived in a nursing home until his death on May 23, 2015. Richard and Jennifer provided all of his support until his death. Richard earned $43,000 in salary during the year. They also received $2,100 in interest from the credit union. They incurred $7,800 in itemized deductions during the year. Compute Richard and Jennifer's income tax for 2015 using the Tax Rate Schedules.

64. **Comprehensive Problem.** Scott and Glenna are married with two dependent children. They have $74,000 in wage income and $4,600 in interest income on some bonds they own. They have deductions for adjusted gross income of $4,000 and itemized deductions of $12,800. Neither of the children has any income. Determine the tax savings for the family if Scott and Glenna were to transfer the bonds to the children, both under 18.

65. **Research Problem.** Sidney and Angelene were married in 2011. During 2015, they were both employed, each earning $32,000 for the year. They discovered that there was a significant tax savings if they could file as single taxpayers and thus arranged a vacation trip and a divorce before the end of the year. Early in 2016 they remarried. What is their filing status for 2015? See Rev. Rul. 76-255.

Chapter

4

Gross Income

OBJECTIVES

After completing Chapter 4, you should be able to:

1. Define and distinguish among the various concepts of income: economic, accounting, and legal.
2. Recognize the various items included in gross income.
3. Determine when items are included in income.
4. Understand the rules governing alimony.
5. Differentiate alimony from child support.
6. Comprehend the rules for recapturing alimony.
7. Understand the rules governing the discharge of indebtedness for both solvent and insolvent taxpayers.

OVERVIEW

Gross income, according to the Internal Revenue Code, includes all income unless specifically exempted by law. This comprehensive definition requires a more probing discussion of what must be included in income. Further, we must concern ourselves with "how much" must be included in income and what portion of total income may be excluded.

The Concept of Income

A frustrating characteristic of the English language is that a single term can be used to express a variety of concepts. Take the concept of income: economists, the courts, and accountants use this term, but for each, the definition imparts a singular *view*.

¶4001
ECONOMIC INCOME

The economic concept of income is more general than the accounting definition. The most commonly accepted definition of economic income is that of J. R. Hicks. He defines economic income as being "the maximum amount a person can consume during a week and still expect to be as well-off at the end of the week as he was at the beginning." J. R. Hicks, *Value and Capital* (Oxford: Clarendon Press, 1946), p. 172. This assumes that there were no capital contributions or withdrawals during the period measured. The economist's definition is not practical for tax purposes because the concept of "well-being" is not capable of objective measurement. The economic concept of income places a heavy emphasis on the future. No objective rules exist for determining well-being at any moment in time. Economists must deal in terms of real wealth, which includes holding gains and losses rather than monetary wealth alone. H. C. Simons maintained, "The precise, objective measurement of income implies the existence of perfect markets from which one, after ascertaining quantities, may obtain the prices necessary for routine valuation of all possible inventories of commodities, services, and property rights." *Personal Income Taxation* (Chicago: University of Chicago Press, 1921), p. 50. Since no such markets exist where the necessary prices for valuation may be obtained, the economic concept is an inappropriate measure of taxable income.

¶4015
THE LEGAL/TAX CONCEPT OF INCOME

The legal concept of income is also less precise than that of the accountant. Congress has not defined income, but has specified how particular items of income are to be taxed. The concept of income has crystalized through a series of court cases. The legal concept is different from the economic and accounting concepts. Gross income includes "all income from whatever source derived" unless specifically exempted by law. Code Sec. 61(a).

Eisner v. Macomber

In the case of *Eisner v. Macomber*, 1 USTC ¶32, 252 U.S. 189, 40 S.Ct. 189 (1920), the Supreme Court dealt at great length with the problem of defining income. The Court stated:

> After examining dictionaries in common use . . . , we find little to add to the succinct definition adopted in two cases arising under the Corporation Tax Act of 1909 . . . "Income may be defined as the gain derived from capital, from labor, or from both combined," provided it be understood to include profit gained through sale or conversion of capital assets. . . .

> Here we have the essential matter: *not* a gain *accruing* to capital; not a *growth* or *increment* of value in the investment; but a gain, a profit, something of exchangeable value, *proceeding* from the property, severed from the capital, however invested or employed, and *coming in*, being "*derived* "—that is, *received* or *drawn* by the recipient (the taxpayer) for his separate use, benefit and disposal; that is income derived from property.

> The same fundamental conception is clearly set forth in the Sixteenth Amendment—"incomes, from whatever source derived"—the essential thought being expressed with a conciseness and lucidity entirely in harmony with the form and style of the Constitution.

> Like the accountants' concept, the legal concept does not embrace holding gains or losses. The legal definition of income is close to the accountants', but not identical, as will be highlighted in the remainder of the chapter.

EXAMPLE 4.1	Rachel owned 300 shares of Imperial Soap which she purchased for $1,000. She sold the stock this year for $1,200. Rachel realized a gain of $200, not the $1,200 proceeds she received from the sale. Only the $200 is included in gross income. The $1,000 is Rachel's return of capital.

¶4025   ACCOUNTING INCOME

The accountant desires to measure income over a specified period of time. Income, from an accounting point of view, is the excess of revenues over the costs incurred in producing those revenues. The emphasis for the accountant is on completed transactions. Therefore, unlike the economist, the accountant does not recognize holding gains. The accountant deals exclusively with objectively measurable forms such as monetary transactions.

Realization of Income

As in financial accounting all gains must be "realized" before they are includible in income. This usually occurs at the time of an arm's-length transaction.

EXAMPLE 4.2	Tom Spears buys a parcel of real estate for $10,000 in 2002. In 2015, he has it appraised and finds that the property's market value is $15,000. He has a paper gain of $5,000, but he has no taxable income. Also in 2015, he sells the property for $15,000, at which time the income is "realized" and "recognized."

Under the accrual method of accounting, income is recognized when a transaction is consummated. Under the cash method of accounting, income is recognized only when cash is received. The cash method and accrual method of accounting are discussed in Chapter 13. To prevent cash basis taxpayers from choosing the year in which to recognize income, the Internal Revenue Service applies the constructive receipt doctrine.

Economic Benefit, Constructive Receipt, and Assignment of Income Doctrines

This chapter discusses three doctrines: the economic benefit doctrine, the constructive receipt doctrine, and the assignment of income doctrine. The doctrines focus on the following questions: what is income, when is it taxable, and to whom is it taxable?

In determining "what" is income and "when" an item must be included in the taxable income of a cash basis taxpayer, two concepts were conceived: the economic benefit doctrine and the constructive receipt doctrine. Over time the courts have tended to blur the distinction between these two doctrines. *F. Bowden*, 61-1 USTC ¶9382, 289 F.2d 20 (CA-5 1961), reversing 32 TC 853 (1959).

¶4101   ECONOMIC BENEFIT DOCTRINE

The economic benefit doctrine addresses the "what" and the constructive receipt doctrine addresses the "when." Any amount of compensation granted or paid to the individual for services rendered, be it cash, bonus, profit sharing, compensation in kind, or any other ingenious method of payment, must be included in gross income. Gross income is defined under the broad language of Code Sec. 61(a) of the Internal Revenue Code as "all income from whatever source derived." Thus, taxable income may consist of cash, receivables, property, land, or any other form of economic benefit.

¶4125   CONSTRUCTIVE RECEIPT DOCTRINE

The second doctrine, that of constructive receipt, was defined in the case of *Ross*. In this case, the Circuit Court of Appeals stated that the doctrine of constructive receipt was conceived "in order to prevent the taxpayer from choosing the year in which to reduce it (income) to possession." *L.W. Ross*, 48-2 USTC ¶9341, 169 F.2d 483 (CA-1 1948).

The Regulations explain the doctrine of constructive receipt, based upon the fact that income is:

> credited to [the taxpayer's] account, or set apart for him, or otherwise made available so that he may draw upon it at any time. . . . However, income is not constructively received if the taxpayer's control of its receipt is subject to substantial limitations or restrictions. Reg. §1.451-2.

A distinctive feature of the constructive receipt doctrine is that it affects only cash basis taxpayers, since they are deemed to have received income prior to the time of actual receipt. Because the accrual basis taxpayer is assumed to have recognized income at the moment it is "earned," there is no need to apply the constructive receipt doctrine. It is of no consequence if an individual refuses compensation. The courts have ruled that once the individual has an "absolute right" to the compensation, the amount of the remuneration must be included in the taxpayer's income. However, where the individual has only a conditional right, the courts hold that no present income was received. Generally, any compensation granted to an individual to which the individual has an absolute right is regarded as constructively received income. The taxpayer must include in current income any amounts of compensation which the taxpayer has refused to accept.

EXAMPLE 4.3	Leah was an employee of Loss Leaders Inc. On December 2, 2015, Loss Leaders announced a year-end bonus for all employees. Checks would be available for pickup at the cashier's desk December 29, 2015. Leah called in sick on December 29, 2015, and she did not stop by the cashier's desk until January 5, 2016. Leah must include her bonus on her 2015 tax return. She had a right to the bonus on December 29, 2015. It is immaterial that she chose not to collect her bonus on December 29, 2015.

As between the two doctrines, economic benefit and constructive receipt, logically the applicability of the economic benefit doctrine comes first. If the taxpayer has not received economic benefit, then it is not necessary to determine whether the taxpayer is in constructive receipt of income. Now that the concepts of "what" is income and "when" an item must be included in taxable income have been explained, it is necessary to determine "to whom" the income is taxable.

¶4201   ASSIGNMENT OF INCOME DOCTRINE

The assignment of income doctrine means that income is taxed to the individual who earned it, even if the right to the income has been transferred to another individual prior to recognition. Compensation, interest, rents, dividends, and other forms of income usually must be included in the gross income of the recipient. A tax problem arises when an individual attempts to limit tax liability by assigning income. For example, a taxpayer has the employer forward a portion of the salary to one of the taxpayer's creditors instead of to the taxpayer. The taxpayer would have to recognize this as income inasmuch as the taxpayer received benefit from the proceeds and had control of the income.

In *Helvering v. Horst,* 40-2 USTC ¶9787, 311 U.S. 112, 61 S.Ct. 144 (1940), the Supreme Court ruled that a father who gave his son interest coupons, detached from bonds prior to their maturity, was liable for the tax on the interest even though the interest was received by his son. The Court stated:

> Income is "realized" by the assignor because he, who owns or controls the source of income, also controls the disposition of that which he could have received himself and diverts the payment from himself to others as the means of procuring the satisfaction of his wants. The taxpayer has equally enjoyed the fruits of his labor or investment and obtained the satisfaction of his desires whether he collects and uses the income to procure those satisfactions, or whether he disposes of his right to collect it as the means of procuring them.

In the preceding case, if the father wished to avoid the tax liability, he would have had to transfer the property which produced the income.

Generally, the courts have felt that a person should not be allowed to reduce tax liability by the voluntary assignment of income. This is referred to as the "fruit-of-the-tree" doctrine. Income (fruit) is taxable to the individual who has earned it. Thus, assignment of income will be disregarded, for tax purposes, unless the source of the income (tree) is also assigned. In *Lucas v. Earl,* 2 USTC ¶496, 281 U.S. 111, 50 S.Ct. 241 (1930), the Court stated that the "fruit" may not be "attributed to a different tree from that on which it grew."

If a person only has physical possession over the income of another person, he or she has no tax liability. Regardless of whether or not the person received it as an agent or creditor, it is taxed to the owner of the property. The rules which govern the assignment of income apply both to income from property as well as to income from services.

EXAMPLE 4.4	Jack Smith owns a warehouse complex and assigns the rents to his daughter Linda. Jack remains liable for the tax on the rental income, even though Linda is receiving the rental income.

EXAMPLE 4.5	Linda Katz, a recent college graduate, earns $350 per week. In an effort to repay a college loan to her uncle she assigns half of her pay to him. Linda is taxed on the full $350 per week.

¶4215   COMMUNITY PROPERTY INCOME

The question of tax liability for married persons filing separate returns arises frequently during discussions concerning to whom is income taxable. Various states treat this problem differently so that there is no solution which is universally applicable. The existence of community property laws in several states requires treatment of tax liability which is significantly different from those states in which there are no community property laws.

In the eight community property states (Arizona, California, Idaho, Louisiana, Nevada, New Mexico, Texas, and Washington), all property acquired by a husband and wife *after* marriage is considered as owned by them in community, and, as such, is referred to as community property. Any income from these properties is automatically considered joint or community income, and if taxpayers are filing separate tax returns, the income would be shared equally between them on their separate returns. In 1985, Wisconsin implemented a marital property act; therefore, for federal income tax purposes it is considered a community property state. In 1998, Alaska became a community property state. Alaska adopted an optional system, whereby a couple can choose to opt-in to the community property system.

Property acquired *before* marriage or inherited by one spouse during marriage is considered to be that spouse's separate property. In California, Arizona, Nevada, New Mexico, Washington, and Wisconsin, any income from these separate properties is considered separate income; thus, if the spouses are filing separately, the income would not be shared and would be reported on that spouse's separate return. This is called the "California Rule." Conversely, in Texas, Idaho, and Louisiana, income from these separate properties is considered community income; thus, if the spouses are filing separately, the income would be shared between them on their separate returns. This is called the "Texas Rule."

Section 66 of the Internal Revenue Code sets forth a specific rule for treatment of community income where the spouses live apart. Section 66 was passed by Congress in 1980 and was effective 1981 and thereafter. The need for this section arose because in community property states each spouse is liable for one-half the tax on income. Generally, when spouses are living apart, the spouse that earns the income will keep it.

If two individuals are married to each other at some time during a calendar year, but live apart for the *entire* tax year, do not file a joint return, and one or both have earned income, none of which is transferred between them, the following rules cover the reporting of income on their separate tax returns:

1. Earned income (other than trade or business income and partnership income) is treated as income of the spouse who rendered the personal services.
2. Trade or business income is treated as the husband's income unless the wife exercises substantially all of the management and control of the business.
3. Community income derived from the separate property of one spouse is treated as the income of such spouse.
4. All other community income is taxed in accordance with the applicable community property law. Code Sec. 879(a).

¶4225   TENANCY BY THE ENTIRETY

If property is held by a married couple as tenants by the entirety, all income from the property must be included by the husband in his return or must be shared equally by husband and wife, depending on state law. In states which have abolished the common law rule, such as Delaware, Florida, Indiana, Maryland, Michigan, Missouri, New York, Oregon, Pennsylvania, and the District of Columbia, one-half of the income is reported on the husband's tax return and one-half on the wife's tax return.

¶4235   JOINT TENANTS AND TENANTS IN COMMON

Parties holding property as joint tenants each report income from the property in direct proportion to their interest in the property. When one of the parties dies, the interest in the property is automatically passed to the surviving joint tenant. Upon the death of a tenant in common, the deceased's interest is automatically transferred to the heirs. Parties holding property as tenants in common are taxed on their proportionate share of income based on their contribution of ownership of the property.

Items Included in Gross Income

Having discussed the concept of income, what it is, when it is taxable, and to whom it is taxable, attention now will be focused on the types of items which are included in gross income.

¶4301 LIST OF INCOME ITEMS

As has been explained, the concept of income is broad and general. Section 61(a) of the Code simply lists fifteen items which must be included in gross income. Remember, gross income is in no way limited to these fifteen income items.

1. Compensation for services, including fees, commissions, fringe benefits, and similar items
2. Gross income derived from business
3. Gain derived from dealings in property (discussed in Chapters 10–12)
4. Interest
5. Rents
6. Royalties
7. Dividends
8. Alimony and separate maintenance payments
9. Annuities (discussed in Chapter 5)
10. Income from life insurance and endowment contracts
11. Pensions
12. Income from discharge of indebtedness
13. Distributive share of partnership gross income
14. Income in respect of a decedent
15. Income from an interest in an estate or trust

Section 61(a) clearly points out that gross income is not limited to these items, but that these are merely the most typical sources of income. It is irrelevant whether or not the above items are received in money, goods, or services. Note that items such as gifts or inheritances are not included. On the other hand, illegal gains such as gambling gains and income from swindling or extortion must be included in income. Sections 71–90 of the Internal Revenue Code concern themselves with items to be included as gross income. Obviously there are a number of items that are specifically exempted from gross income. Chapter 5 discusses these items. They can be found in Sections 101–139 of the Internal Revenue Code.

¶4315 COMPENSATION FOR SERVICES

All compensation received by the individual is included in gross income. This would include salary, bonuses, tips, commissions, director's fees, and any other amounts received for personal services. This compensation is taxed when received and not when earned unless the individual reports income under the accrual method. Generally, the individual includes as income the fair market value of property received. If the taxpayer receives corporate stock as compensation for services, the fair market value of the stock, at the time of transfer, must be included in gross income.

EXAMPLE 4.6

Charlotte Moss, a cash basis taxpayer, received a paycheck on Friday, January 2, 2016. The pay period covered is for the previous two weeks' work. This money is included on her 2016 tax return, not her 2015 return. However, if Charlotte had had the option of receiving her paycheck on December 31, 2015, by simply requesting it, then, under the constructive receipt doctrine, her salary would have been taxed in 2015.

Year-end bonuses are included in the tax return for the year they are received. Voluntary payments such as severance pay and Christmas bonuses also must be included. Meals and living quarters which an employee receives constitute gross income unless they are furnished for the convenience of the employer. Further, they must be furnished on the employer's premises. With respect to lodging, it must be a condition of employment. See ¶5185 for a complete discussion of meals and lodging as compensation.

EXAMPLE 4.7   Charlotte's employer, IBC Inc. informed employees on December 15, 2015, that a 5 percent cash bonus, based on 2015 earnings, would be paid to all employees on February 9, 2016. Charlotte would have to include her bonus in her 2016 tax return.

Bartering is becoming a more common practice in the United States today. Bartering is the exchange of your property or services for another's property or services. The fair market value of property or services received must be included in gross income.

EXAMPLE 4.8   Robert Jones, owner of Jones' Dry Cleaning, was discussing his income tax problems with one of his best customers, Sam Owen. Sam is an accountant and is self-employed. During the course of their conversation, they struck a deal. Jones would do all of Owen's cleaning and Owen would do Jones's accounts and tax returns. No money would exchange hands. In this instance, both Jones and Owen must include in their income the fair market value of services received.

Small items given by the employer to the employee, such as a turkey at Thanksgiving or a ham at Christmas, are not taxable to the employee even though the employer is allowed a deduction for the item as a business expense. However, a small cash stipend, such as a $20 bill at Christmas or a gift certificate, would be considered as taxable and includible in gross income.

¶4325   COMPENSATION v. GIFT

Section 102(a) explicitly excludes the value of property acquired by gift from being included in gross income. However, Section 102(b) does not exclude the income earned on the property after it is received.

In determining whether or not a payment or transfer is in the form of compensation or a gift, the Supreme Court has said that it is necessary to consider all the relevant surrounding circumstances and especially to determine the intent of the parties involved. *A.G. Bogardus*, 37-2 USTC ¶9534, 302 U.S. 34, 58 S.Ct. 61 (1937). The Fifth Circuit Court of Appeals said that a gift is "not intended as a return of value or made because of any intent to repay another what is his due, but bestowed only because of personal affection or regard or pity, or from general motives of philanthropy or charity." *C. Schall*, 49-1 USTC ¶9298, 174 F.2d 893 (CA-5 1949).

A payment or transfer can be considered compensation by one party and a gift by the other. However, the Supreme Court stated in *Bogardus:*

> The statute definitely distinguishes between compensation on the one hand and gifts on the other hand, the former being taxable and the latter free from taxation. The two terms are, and were meant to be, mutually exclusive; and a bestowal of money cannot, under the statute, be both a gift and a payment of compensation.

When determining if the payment was compensation or a gift, the courts look to see if the transferor took a tax deduction for the payment. If the transferor did, then it indicates that the payment was meant to be compensation. On the other hand, if the transferor did not take a tax deduction for the sum, it is not conclusive, but it is evidence that a gift was intended. The mere fact that an employer was not legally obliged to make a payment is not, in itself, evidence of a gift. Code Sec. 102(c).

In the landmark case of *Duberstein,* the Supreme Court reiterated the statement that a gift proceeds from "detached and disinterested generosity." *M. Duberstein*, 60-2 USTC ¶9519, 363 U.S. 278, 80 S.Ct. 1190 (1960). Duberstein received a Cadillac from the president of a company with whom he had done business for quite some time. Duberstein had on several occasions given business leads to this other company. Naturally, the Commissioner insisted Duberstein must include the fair market value in gross income and Duberstein insisted it was a gift. The Supreme Court stated:

> despite the characterization of the transfer of the Cadillac by the parties and the absence of any obligation, even of a moral nature, to make it, it was at bottom a recompense for Duberstein's past services, or an inducement for him to be of further service in the future.

The *Duberstein* case concludes with the general premise that corporations ordinarily just do not make gifts without receiving some economic benefit in return.

¶4331 ## JURY DUTY PAY

Jury duty pay must be included in gross income. However, any jury duty pay remitted to an employer in exchange for compensation for the period the employee was on jury duty is deductible from gross income. Code Sec. 62(a)(13).

¶4335 ## PRIZES AND AWARDS

Gross income includes amounts received as prizes and awards from radio and television give-away and quiz shows, lotteries, door prizes, and awards from contests. Where the prize or award is not made in money but in the form of property, the fair market value of such property must be included in gross income.

Scientific and Charitable Prizes and Awards

Prizes and awards in the fields of science, charity, and the arts (such as the Pulitzer Prize and the Nobel Peace Prize) are includible in gross income unless the recipient assigns the prize or award to a governmental agency or tax-exempt charitable organization. This assignment must be made prior to the recipient's using the item that is awarded. To be eligible for the exclusion the recipient (1) must have been selected without any action on the recipient's part to enter the contest and (2) must not be required to render any substantial future services as a condition to receiving the prize or award. Code Sec. 74(b). If a proper assignment is made, none of the winnings need be included in the recipient's gross income. However, the recipient is not allowed a charitable contribution deduction.

Employee Achievement Awards

Employee awards for length of service or safety achievement are excludable from gross income by the employee and are deductible by the employer if they are awarded as part of a meaningful presentation, and:

1. The awards do not exceed a total of $400 for all *nonqualified plan awards* received by any one employee during the tax year, or
2. The awards do not exceed $1,600 for all *qualified plan awards* received by any one employee during the tax year.

However, the $1,600 limitation applies in the aggregate. Thus, the $400 limitation and the $1,600 limitation cannot be added together to allow deductions exceeding $1,600. Code Sec. 274(j)(2).

A qualified plan award is one awarded as part of an established written plan or program by the employer that does not discriminate in favor of highly compensated employees. An employee achievement award will not be considered a qualified plan award if the average cost of all employee achievement awards provided by the employer during the tax year exceeds $400. The average cost does not include awards of nominal value. Code Sec. 274(j)(3)(B). The following example illustrates the tax status of employee achievement awards.

EXAMPLE 4.9

> Ben Smith received three employee achievement awards during 2016. Two were qualified awards of a tennis racket valued at $200 and a television/stereo valued at $1,300. The third was a nonqualified award of a briefcase valued at $250. Ben's employer satisfies all the requirements for qualified plan awards. Inasmuch as Ben's total of awards received exceeds $1,600, he must include the excess $150 ($1,750 – $1,600) in gross income.

A length of service award does not qualify if it was received by an employee within the first five years of employment or if the recipient received a length of service award within the previous four years. Safety achievement awards cannot be given to more than 10 percent of the employees. Managers, administrators, clerical employees, and other professional employees are not eligible for safety achievement awards.

¶4345 ## SCHOLARSHIPS AND FELLOWSHIPS

Generally, gross income does not include any amount received as a qualified scholarship by an individual who is a degree candidate at an educational organization. A qualified scholarship is the amount received by a degree candidate that is excludable up to the aggregate amount incurred by the candidate for tuition and course-related expenses, such as books, supplies, and equipment. No exclusion is allowed for room, board, or incidental expenses. Also, no exclusion is allowed if payments received are a result of services.

Non-degree candidates must include in income scholarships and fellowships. The exclusion provision applies only to degree candidates. Under special rules the exclusion provision extends to tuition reductions provided for the education of employees of an educational institution. The rules do not affect the exclusion for employer-provided educational assistance to an employee (see ¶5201).

EXAMPLE 4.10	Mary Smart is a full-time undergraduate student at State University. Mary is an honor student and received a $3,000-per-year scholarship. The scholarship award pays for Mary's tuition ($2,000), books ($200), equipment ($300), and incidental expenses ($500). Mary would have to include in her gross income only the $500 for incidental expenses.

¶4355   GROSS INCOME DERIVED FROM BUSINESS

Gross income is defined by the Code as including gross income derived from a business. Gross income means total sales revenues less cost of goods sold, plus income from investments and any other incidental income. The Regulations state that gross income shall be determined as follows:

> without subtraction of selling expenses, losses or other items not ordinarily used in computing costs of goods sold . . . . The cost of goods sold should be determined in accordance with the method of accounting consistently used by the taxpayer. Reg. §1.61-3(a).

EXAMPLE 4.11

The income statement of ABC, a manufacturing enterprise, shows the following information:

Gross Sales		$162,000
Less: Cost of Goods Sold:		
Inventory, January 1	$30,000	
Purchases	160,000	
Goods Available for Sale	$190,000	
Less: Inventory, December 31	45,000	
Cost of Goods Sold		$145,000
Gross Profit (Gross Income)		$17,000

The taxpayer, in this example, would include $17,000 in gross income. The net profit or loss of a business is determined by subtracting from gross profit (income) all selling, as well as general and administrative, expenses. Continuing on from the previous calculations:

Gross Profit (Income)		$17,000
Less: Selling Expenses	$4,000	
General and Administrative Expenses	8,000	
Total Operating Expenses		$12,000
Net Profit (Income)		$5,000

In the determination of penalties and additional tax due to the omission of items of income, gross income is defined in Code Sec. 6501(e)(1)(A)(i) as total income received or accrued "prior to diminution by the cost of such sales."

¶4375   PARTNERSHIPS AND S CORPORATIONS

Partnerships and S corporations are not taxed, but their taxable income is taxed to the individual partners or shareholders. Each partner or shareholder absorbs a proportionate share of the firm's income, whether or not distributed. An S corporation is a small business corporation desiring not to be taxed at the corporate level. A corporation desiring S corporation status must meet various requirements, including valid stockholder approval of S status.

¶4385   INTEREST

Interest received by a taxpayer or credited to the taxpayer must be included in gross income. Interest income includes interest on bank accounts, loans, notes, corporate bonds, and U.S. savings bonds. Interest income received on obligations of states, territories, or a possession of the United States is generally wholly exempt from taxation.

EXAMPLE 4.12

> Leo Lionstone has a savings account at First National Bank that pays him interest on June 30 and December 31 of each year. In 2015, $25 of interest income was credited to his account in June and $28 of interest income on December 31. Even though Leo makes no withdrawals during the year, he must include $53 of interest income in his 2015 gross income. He had an absolute right to the money; therefore, he must recognize the income.

A cash basis taxpayer reports interest income when received. Interest earned on bank accounts is considered received, under the constructive receipt doctrine, when credited to the account. An accrual basis taxpayer reports interest income as it accrues. Interest on U.S. Series EE savings bonds may be reported each year or the taxpayer may elect to report the entire amount in the year that the bond matures. Once the taxpayer chooses a method, all of the taxpayer's Series EE savings bonds must be reported in the same manner. Code Sec. 454.

Banks and other financial institutions often hand out inexpensive gifts, such as flashlights, tote bags, or mouse pads, to attract new deposits or induce customers to add to their existing accounts. Under a IRS revenue procedure, a noncash gift is a de minimis premium, and thus taxfree, if it does not have a value of more than $10 for a deposit of less than $5,000, or $20 for a deposit of $5,000 or more. The value is based on the cost of the premium to the financial institution . The financial institution that hands out such a gift is not required to treat it as interest for information-reporting purposes. [Rev. Proc. 2000-30.]

Below-Market Interest Loans

A below-market interest demand loan is defined as a demand loan with an interest rate below the applicable federal short-term rate. For many years, individuals have been making use of below-market interest rate loans. This was especially popular among family members. To remedy this tax-avoidance scheme, the Tax Reform Act of 1984 imputed interest on interest-free or below-market demand and term loans. A demand loan is defined as any loan payable in full on demand of the lender. A term loan is a below-market loan if the amount loaned exceeds the present value of all payments due under the loan. Imputed interest is computed by using the statutory federal rate of interest. The federal rate is adjusted monthly and published by the IRS. In an effort to simplify the computation of forgone interest on below-market demand loans, the IRS established a "blended annual rate." For the year 2014, the blended annual rate is up slightly at 0.28 percent compared to 2013. The IRS usually announces the blended annual rate for each year during the summer.

Section 7872(c), relating to loans with below-market interest rates, applies to:

1. Gift loans;
2. Compensation-related loans;
3. Corporation-shareholder loans;
4. "Tax-avoidance" loans (i.e., tax avoidance being the principal purpose of the loan); and
5. Other below-market loans in which the interest arrangements have a significant effect on federal tax liability.

A below-market loan is treated as a gift, dividend, contribution to capital, payment of compensation, or other payment depending on the substance of the transaction. For below-market loans that are not gift loans, "forgone interest" is deductible by the borrower and must be included in the lender's gross income. In an employer-employee relationship it is treated as additional compensation. With respect to a corporation-shareholder relationship it is treated as if the corporation paid a dividend. The forgone interest on a gift loan is treated as a taxable gift. Forgone interest may be defined as the additional interest which would have been paid had the loan been granted at "the market rate" rather than at the artificially low rate created for the below-market rate loan.

Gift, Employee, and Commercial Loans

The rules for below-market loans do not apply to:

1. Gift loans between individuals if:
   a. the aggregate outstanding amount of loans between such individuals does not exceed $10,000, and
   b. the loan is not attributable to the purchase or carrying of income-producing assets; or
2. Compensation-related or corporation-shareholder loans if:
   a. the aggregate outstanding amount of loans between the borrower and the lender does not exceed $10,000, and
   b. the avoidance of federal tax is not a principal purpose of the loan. Code Sec. 7872(c).

Special rules exist for gift loans between individuals that do not exceed $100,000. The imputed interest is limited to the borrower's net investment income for the tax year. However, if the borrower uses the proceeds for investment purposes and the borrower's investment income is in excess of $1,000, interest is imputed. If the borrower has net investment income of $1,000 or less for the year, the borrower's net investment income is deemed to be zero.

Some loans are specifically excluded from the rules for below-market loans, such as:

1. Loans made available by lenders to the general public on the same terms and conditions;
2. Loans subsidized by a federal, state, or municipal government that are made available to the general public;
3. Certain employee-relocation loans;
4. Loans to or from a foreign person, unless the interest would be effectively connected with the conduct of a U.S. trade or business and not exempt from U.S. tax under an income tax treaty; and
5. Loans on which the interest arrangement can be shown to have no significant effect on the federal tax liability of the lender or the borrower.

If a taxpayer structures a transaction to be similar to a loan not subject to the rules and one of the principal purposes of structuring the transaction is the avoidance of federal tax, the loan will be considered a tax-avoidance loan and subject to the rules for below-market loans.

Whether an interest arrangement has a significant effect on the federal tax liability (item 5, above) will be determined by all the facts and circumstances. Some factors to be considered are:

1. Whether items of income and deduction generated by the loan offset each other;
2. The amount of such items;
3. The cost of complying with the below-market loan provisions if they applied; and
4. Any reasons, other than taxes, for structuring the transaction as a below-market loan.

These rules apply to term loans made after June 6, 1984, and to demand loans outstanding after that date.

Bond Transactions

When a bond is sold between interest dates and the accrued interest is added to the selling price, the seller must recognize the interest as income. All interest earned from the date of purchase is taxable to the buyer.

| EXAMPLE 4.13 | Aaron Adams purchases a $1,000 bond of the Rhody Corporation from Baron Ziegler at face value. Interest is paid at a rate of 9 percent on April 1 and October 1. The bond was purchased on June 1 for $1,015 ($15 representing accrued interest). Baron, the seller, must report $15 as interest income. On October 1 Aaron will receive $45 interest of which $30 ($45 – $15) will be taxable. |

"Flat" Basis Bonds

Occasionally, a taxpayer will buy a bond with defaulted interest included in the purchase price. In this case, the entire amount is considered a capital investment. However, if after the purchase date interest accrues on the bond, this would be considered interest income when received. Recovery of defaulted interest on a flat bond results in no income. All interest in excess of basis, but less than the face amount of the bonds, is taxable as a capital gain.

EXAMPLE 4.14

Aaron Adams purchases a $1,000 bond of the Rhody Corporation for $700 "flat." Interest is paid at the rate of 9 percent on April 1 and October 1. On June 1, when Adams bought the bond, there was $105 accrued interest in default. On October 1, Adams received $135 interest from Rhody Corporation. The $105 of defaulted interest is considered a return of investment and the $30 ($135–$105) is interest income. Adams's basis in the bond is now $595 ($700–$105).

¶4395   RENT AND ROYALTY INCOME

Rental income is the amount received by the owner of property for allowing someone else to use it. Rental income must be included in gross income. All expenses (i.e., depreciation, taxes, repairs, and other ordinary and necessary expenses attributable to the rental property) are deductible from gross income. If the tenant instead of paying rent pays off obligations of the landlord, then this amount must be included in the gross income of the landlord. However, the landlord may deduct these expenses if they would otherwise be deductible. For example, if the tenant pays the property taxes in lieu of rent, the landlord may deduct this sum from gross income. However, the landlord may deduct this sum from gross income in the year received, whether the taxpayer is on the cash or accrual basis, but anticipated expenses may not be deducted until actually paid. The tenant, if rent is paid in advance, is not allowed a tax deduction for rent expense until the year in which the payment is due even though the cash basis is used. Rent received in advance is always taxable when received.

Security deposits received from tenants are not included in gross income if they are to be returned to the tenant. If the security deposit is to be used as a final payment of rent, then it is advance rent and must be included in gross income when it is received.

EXAMPLE 4.15

Makayla rents an apartment for $1,000 per month. Eric, the landlord, requires Makayla to put down a $500 security deposit. If there is no damage to the apartment when Makayla moves out her security deposit will then be returned. Eric does not include the $500 in his gross income because the security deposit is to be returned.

Royalty income received for allowing someone the use of copyrights, patents, licenses, and rights to oil, gas, or other mineral properties is includible in gross income.

Lessee Improvements

Improvements made by the lessee are not income to the lessor either at the time the improvements are made or upon termination of the lease. Code Sec. 1019. Gain or loss will be recognized only at the time the property is sold.

However, where the lessee makes repairs which are the responsibility of the lessor or makes improvements in lieu of rent, the lessor has rental income to the extent of the market value of the improvements.

EXAMPLE 4.16

Robert Wolf entered into a 50-year lease with Cleveland Inc. on January 7, 1995. Wolf remodeled the building at a cost of $50,000. The building has a book value of $20,000 to Cleveland Inc. In 2015, Wolf defaulted and Cleveland Inc. took back the building. The improvements made by Wolf are not income to Cleveland Inc. in 2015. Only when the building is sold would Cleveland Inc. recognize gain on the improvements.

EXAMPLE 4.17

Robert Wolf and Cleveland Inc. agreed that Mr. Wolf would make improvements to the building amounting to $10,000. In exchange for making these improvements, Cleveland Inc. will not charge Mr. Wolf rent of $10,000 in 2015. In this case, Cleveland Inc. has $10,000 of rental income for 2015.

Lease Cancellations and Bonuses

Bonuses received for the granting of a lease are considered rental income. Also, payments received by a landlord to cancel or modify a lease must be included in gross income. However, payments made to a tenant to cancel a lease are considered as "amounts received in exchange for such lease or agreement." Code Sec.

1241. Further, Section 1241 applies to amounts received for the cancellation of a distributor's agreement if the distributor has a substantial capital investment in the distributorship. Usually, the payment received by a tenant results in capital gain income because the lease is considered a capital asset (see ¶12,155).

¶4401   DIVIDEND INCOME

The term "dividend" means "any distribution of property made by a corporation to its shareholders out of its earnings and profits." Code Sec. 316(a). In the above definition, dividends were defined in terms of "property." The term property is defined as "money, securities, and any other property." Code Sec. 317(a). Notice, it does not include stock or rights to acquire stock.

The Jobs and Growth Tax Relief Reconciliation Act of 2003 reduced the top marginal federal tax rate on dividends to 15 percent (5 percent for those with income on the 10 or 15 percent brackets). The Tax Increase Prevention Act of 2005 further reduced the five percent tax on qualified dividends to zero percent for 2008, 2009, and 2010. The 2010 Tax Relief Act extended the Bush-era tax cuts including the special lower rates for qualified dividends through 2012. The tax rates apply only to qualified dividends paid to shareholders by a domestic corporation or a qualified foreign corporation. Prior to the passage of the 2003 Tax Act dividends were taxed as ordinary income.

The American Taxpayer Relief Act of 2012 raises the top marginal federal tax rate on dividends to 20 percent, up from 15 percent. For 2015, the 20 percent tax rate applies to individuals whose income exceeds $413,200 (individuals), $464,850 (filing jointly) and $439,000 (heads of households). Taxpayers whose income level is below the above stated amounts will be taxed at a maximum rate of 15 percent.

For taxpayers whose ordinary income is taxed below 25 percent, dividends will be subject to a zero percent rate.

EXAMPLE 4.18   Clifford, a single taxpayer, has taxable income of $100,000. Included in this amount is $5,000 of qualified dividends. Clifford's marginal tax rate is 28 percent. However, on the dividend income of $5,000, his tax rate is 15 percent.

Distributions from a corporation in the form of a dividend only come after they have been authorized by the board of directors. The distribution may take the form of cash or other assets, but a true dividend must come from earnings accumulated after February 28, 1913. Code Sec. 316; Reg. §1.316-1. Retained earnings are the corporation's taxable income that has been retained in the business and not previously distributed. Usually, the directors, when desiring to make a distribution to the stockholders, award cash. Basically there are two common types of dividends:

1. Cash
2. Stock (dividends and rights)

Cash Dividend

When dealing with dividends, one must be cognizant of four dates:

1. Declaration
2. Record
3. Payment
4. Receipt

EXAMPLE 4.19	The board of directors of the Rhody Corporation declares on March 3, 2015, a cash dividend of $1.00 per share to be paid on May 27, 2015, to each stockholder of record as of April 28, 2015. The stockholder received the dividend on June 9, 2015. The four dates in the example were:

1. Declaration Date—March 3, 2015
2. Record Date—April 28, 2015
3. Payment Date—May 27, 2015
4. Receipt Date—June 9, 2015

Anyone who owns shares of stock of Rhody Corporation on April 28, 2015, is entitled to a $1.00 per share cash dividend. Therefore, the market value of the stock from March 3 until April 28 should reflect the $1.00 per share dividend. If a share of stock is sold on May 5, 2015, the stockholder still will receive the dividend because he or she was a shareholder on the date of record. The person receiving the cash dividend must recognize ordinary income for that amount. However, corporate dividends received by individuals are taxed at a maximum rate of 15/20 percent. The shareholder having the unqualified right to demand payment must recognize taxable income. Reg. §1.301-1. The date the dividend is received by the taxpayer, not the date the dividend is declared, determines taxability. Unlike accrued interest income on bonds, no part of the purchase may be allocated to dividend income.

Although from a theoretical viewpoint in the above example, the $1.00 dividend can be identified from the purchase price, in reality this is not always the case. With interest on bonds, the interest can be readily determined at any time. A person who has a stockbroker collect the dividend is still required to pay tax on it under the rules of the constructive receipt doctrine. Also, if a dividend is declared and a person dies before the payment date, the dividend income is not included in the final income tax return, but in the estate income tax return. *M. Putnam Est.,* 57-1 USTC ¶9200, 352 U.S. 82, 77 S.Ct. 175 (1956).

Mutual Funds

Individuals holding an interest in a mutual fund may receive any combination of three types of distribution: ordinary dividends, return of capital, and capital gains dividends. Taxpayers are notified within 45 days after the close of the tax year of the distribution into the above three classes from dividends distributed during the year. For example, the stockholders will be informed of the portion of the dividends received to be treated as a long-term capital gain. Further, they will be apprised of the portion of the mutual fund's established capital gains they must report as long-term capital gains even though the company has retained them. Ordinary dividends of a mutual fund are reported as dividend income to the recipient.

Life Insurance and Annuity Contracts

Dividends on life insurance and annuity contracts are excludable from gross income and are considered a reduction in the cost of the policy. Code Sec. 301. If it is a fully paid-up life insurance policy and the dividend exceeds the net premiums paid, then the excess is fully taxable. Also, once payment of the proceeds under the contract has commenced, then any dividend received is fully taxable.

EXAMPLE 4.20	Leah Lambert and her husband receive the following dividends during 2015:

	Leah	Husband
Able Auto Parts	$300	
Get Rich REIT		$450
Canadian Exploration	$250	
Live Long Insurance		$200

For the year 2015, all of the above-listed dividends are includible in gross income except the dividend from Live Long Insurance, which is considered a reduction in premium cost. Therefore, Leah has $550 of dividend income and her husband has $450 in dividend income, for a total of $1,000. This total amount of $1,000 must be included in gross income.

EXAMPLE 4.21	Leah and her husband purchased a 10-year endowment policy. The policy commences payments on January 1, 2016. Therefore, any dividends issued by the company in 2015 would not be taxable. Any dividends issued by the company after January 1, 2016, would be fully taxable.

EXAMPLE 4.22	Assume in Example 4.21 that Leah and her husband paid $25,000 for the policy. Over the years, they had received $2,200 in dividends. Therefore, their basis in the policy is $22,800 ($25,000 – $2,200).

The above rules concerning life insurance and annuity contracts apply regardless of whether the taxpayer receives the dividend in cash or lets it accumulate to purchase additional insurance.

Stock Dividends

A stock dividend is defined as a distribution by a corporation of its own stock, including treasury stock. Reg. §1.305-1. Stock dividends usually are not included in the gross income of the recipient. However, there are certain exceptions to this rule. They are as follows:

1. Distributions in lieu of money. If the stockholder has the option of receiving stock in lieu of money, then the corporate distribution is taxable to the recipient.
2. Disproportionate distributions. If some shareholders receive property and other shareholders receive stock so as to alter the individual stockholder's proportionate interest in the corporation, then the distribution is included as gross income.
3. Distributions of common and preferred stock. If some stockholders receive common stock and other stockholders receive preferred stock, then the distribution is considered part of gross income.
4. Distributions on preferred stock. A stock dividend on preferred stock is taxable to the recipient unless it increases the conversion ratio of convertible preferred stock made specifically to take into account a stock dividend or stock split on the convertible preferred stock in which case it is tax free. Code Sec. 305(b)(4).
5. Distributions of convertible preferred stock. A distribution of convertible preferred stock is taxable to the recipient unless it can be proven to the Commissioner that the individual stockholder's equity in the corporation remains constant.

Upon receipt of a nontaxable stock dividend, the stockholder must allocate the original cost over all the shares the stockholder presently owns.

EXAMPLE 4.23	Aaron Adams owns 100 shares of Rhody Corporation common stock which he purchased for $11 per share in 2010 for a total cost of $1,100. Rhody Corporation pays a 10 percent stock dividend in June 2015, and Aaron receives 10 shares (10 percent of 100 shares) of stock. Therefore, he now owns 110 shares of stock and his basis remains at $1,100 or $10 per share ($1,100/110 shares). At the time any of the 110 shares is sold, its basis is $10 per share.

EXAMPLE 4.24

If, in Example 4.23, instead of receiving the common stock, Aaron received 20 shares of Rhody Corporation preferred stock as a stock dividend and it had a fair market value of $10 per share and the 100 original shares of Rhody Corporation common stock at this time had a fair market value of $2,000, then the following computations would be necessary:

Computations:

Basis of original stock	$1,100
Fair market value of original stock	$2,000
Fair market value of the new preferred stock	200
Fair market value of preferred and common	$2,200
Basis of original 100 shares after stock dividend 1,100 × 2,000/2,200	$1,000
Basis of new stock after the dividend 1,100 × 200/2,200	$100

To determine whether or not the sale should be treated as a long-term capital gain, the date when the original shares were purchased is the controlling factor. To be classified as a long-term gain, a capital asset must be held for more than one year. For 2015, the tax on capital gains is a maximum of 20 percent if held greater than 12 months (28 percent for collectibles and section 1202 gains) and the taxpayer's income is over $413,200 if single, $464,850 for joint filers.

The new shares take on the basis of the old shares. If lots of the old shares were purchased on different dates and the dividend shares cannot be identified with any particular lot, then the new shares take the basis of the earliest purchased stock. Reg. §1.1012-1(c).

Stock Rights

A stock right is defined as a distribution by a corporation to its shareholders of *rights* to purchase corporate stock. Usually, the shareholder has a right to buy the stock at less than fair market value. Therefore, the stock rights have a market value. The stockholder receiving the rights has three alternative courses of action. The stockholder may exercise, sell, or hold the stock rights.

If the market value of the stock rights is less than 15 percent of the market value of the stock with respect to which it is distributed, then the basis of the rights is zero unless the shareholder irrevocably elects to allocate the basis between the stock and the rights. Code Sec. 307(b)(1). Where the market value of the rights is 15 percent or greater, the basis must be allocated between the stock and rights according to their respective values on the date on which the rights are distributed to the stockholder, not the record date. In Chapter 10, at ¶10,125, a full discussion appears on the allocation of basis for taxable and nontaxable stock rights.

¶4451 DIVORCE AND SEPARATION

There are two sets of rules depending on when the divorce took place. The first set is for divorces occurring before 1985 and the second set is for divorces occurring after 1984.

Pre-1985 Agreements

Although this is an old law, some individuals are still covered by it. Prior to the Tax Reform Act of 1984, Code Sec. 71 defined alimony as a series of support payments received after divorce or legal separation. If the following four conditions exist, then the recipient must include the alimony payments in gross income and the person making the payments is entitled to a tax deduction for adjusted gross income. The conditions are as follows:

1. Payments are required under the terms of the decree of divorce or separate maintenance or a written separation agreement or a decree of support.
2. Payments must be to discharge the legal obligation of support.
3. Payments must be periodic.
4. Payments must not be for child support.

The following payments would not qualify:

1. Lump-sum settlements,
2. Payments not required under the decree or agreement,
3. Payments not arising out of a marital relationship (repayment of a loan), and
4. Payments made before the decree.

Determining whether or not payments are periodic or lump-sum in nature can be quite difficult. If the installments are to be paid over an indefinite period of time, or where the period of time exceeds 10 years, by the terms of the decree, then the payments will qualify. It is not necessary that the payments come in regular intervals. However, only 10 percent of the total sum specified qualifies for alimony treatment. If more than 10 percent is paid in any year, that excess is considered a property settlement.

EXAMPLE 4.25

The decree provides for the wife to receive $280,000 over 40 years at a rate of $7,000 per year. The $7,000 payment each year would qualify as alimony and the husband would receive the tax deduction. However, assume the wife received $58,800 in each of the first two years and the remaining $162,400 ($280,000 – $117,600) equally ($4,274 per year) over the following 38 years. The husband, in this situation, can deduct only $28,000 (10% of $280,000) in each of the first two years. During the remaining years, he may deduct $4,274 a year.

If the payments are in installments over a period of 10 or fewer years, then they do not qualify as alimony. However, there is an exception to this 10-year rule when payments are subject to certain contingencies. The payments will qualify for a tax deduction if state law or the divorce decree specifies that alimony will cease at the death of either spouse, remarriage of the spouse receiving alimony, or a change of economic status of either spouse.

Alimony and separate maintenance payments received by the taxpayer are included in gross income. Further, the payer is allowed a tax deduction in the year the payment is made.

Post-1984 Agreements

Payments under instruments executed after December 31, 1984, that meet the following requirements are deductible as alimony:

1. Payments must be made in cash.
2. Payments must be made under a divorce or separation instrument.
3. Parties must live in separate households after a divorce or separation decree is entered.
4. Alimony must end at the payee's death.
5. Parties involved may not file a joint return.
6. Payments must not be for child support.

A special feature was added that the parties could designate by written agreement payments otherwise qualifying as alimony payments as excludable by the payee and nondeductible by the payer. Code Sec. 71(b)(1)(B).

The Tax Reform Act of 1986 changed only a few rules with respect to divorces. However, because of the lower tax rates and increased exemptions for dependents, tax planning for pending divorces is essential and tax planning for divorces executed after 1986 is highly recommended.

Alimony Termination on Payee's Death

Under the 1986 law, the requirement that the "instrument must state" that payments must terminate on the payee's death has been repealed. This amendment is effective for divorce or separation instruments executed after December 31, 1984.

Front-Loading Limitation

The Tax Reform Act of 1986 fixed the amount of annual payments exempt from recapture at $15,000. The front-loading requirement under the recapture rules was set at three post-separation years.

Recapture Rules

Under the revised recapture rules the tax treatment of past payments has been changed to require the inclusion of previously deducted alimony or separate maintenance payments in income. The revised recapture rules also allow the recipient spouse, who previously included the alimony in income, to deduct the recaptured amount.

Under the recapture rules adopted by the Tax Reform Act of 1986, payments will be recaptured if:

1. Payments made in the second post-separation year exceed the payments in the third post-separation year by more than $15,000, and/or
2. Payments made in the first post-separation year exceed the average of (the alimony payments of the second post-separation year and the third post-separation year less the year 2 recapture) by more than $15,000.

The excess amounts in the first and second post-separation years only may be recaptured in the third post-separation year. The following examples illustrate the alimony recapture rules.

EXAMPLE 4.26

Bob and Mary Barnsen were divorced on January 13, 2015. Mary pays Bob the following amounts of alimony under the terms of her divorce decree.

Year	Amount
2015 (1st post-separation year)	$70,000
2016 (2nd post-separation year)	40,000
2017 (3rd post-separation year)	20,000

Mary computes her amount to be recaptured as follows:

Year 2 Calculation	Amount
Payments in the second year	$40,000
Less: Payments in the third year	20,000
	20,000
Less: $15,000	15,000
Amount of second-year payments subject to recapture in 2017	$5,000

The amount of second-year payments used in computing the recapture for the first post-separation year is $35,000 ($40,000 – $5,000).

Year 1 Calculation	Amount
Payments in the first year	$70,000
Less: Average payments made in the second and third year (($35,000 + $20,000) ÷ 2)	27,500
	$42,500
Less: $15,000	15,000
Amount of first-year payments subject to recapture in 2017	$27,500

In calculating the recapture account for the first year, only $35,000, rather than $40,000, is treated as paid in the second year. This is because the average of payments made in the second and third years does not include the $5,000 payment made in the second year that is recaptured in the third year. Bob has gross income of $70,000 and $40,000 in 2015 and 2016, respectively. In 2017, the recapture of $32,500 exceeds the $20,000 alimony received; therefore, Bob has a deduction of $12,500. Mary deducts alimony of $70,000 in the first post-separation year and $40,000 in the second. In year three, she must recapture $32,500 ($5,000 + $27,500) which exceeds her third year payment of $20,000. Therefore, she has income of $12,500 in 2017.

EXAMPLE 4.27

Bill and Alice Bailey were divorced on January 6, 2015. Bill makes the following alimony payments to Alice under a divorce decree.

Year	Amount
2015 (1st post-separation year)	$50,000
2016 (2nd post-separation year)	18,000
2017 (3rd post-separation year)	0
Year 2 Calculation	
Payments in the second year	$18,000
Less: Payments in the third year	0
	$18,000
Less: $15,000	15,000
Amount of second-year payments subject to recapture in 2017	$3,000
Year 1 Calculation	
Payments in the first year	$50,000
Less: Average payments made in the second and third year (($15,000 + $0) ÷ 2)	7,500
	$42,500
Less: $15,000	15,000
Amount of first-year payments subject to recapture in 2017	$27,500

In calculating the recapture amount for the first year, only $15,000, rather than $18,000, is treated as paid in the second year. This is because the average of payments made in the second and third years does not include the $3,000 payment made in the second year that is recaptured in the third year.

Bill will show $30,500 as income on his 2017 tax return and Alice will show a tax deduction of $30,500 on her 2017 tax return.

Bill deducts as alimony $50,000 in 2015 and $18,000 in 2016 and Alice includes in her gross income $50,000 and $18,000 in those two years.

Exceptions to the Recapture Rule

There are three exceptions to the recapture rule (in addition to the $15,000 floor).

1. Payments cease by reason of death or remarriage prior to the end of the third post-separation year.
2. Payments received under a temporary support order before the divorce or separation.
3. Payments pursuant to a continuing liability to pay a fixed part of your income from a business or property or from compensation for employment or self-employment.

If the payer stops or reduces the amount of alimony or separate maintenance during any of the first three post-separation years for any other than the above listed reasons then the payments are subject to recapture.

EXAMPLE 4.28

Randy Reeves is required under the terms of a divorce decree to make payments to Candy of $50,000 in 2015, $30,000 in 2016, and $35,000 in 2017. Randy makes the first payment in 2015 and one-half the second payment when Candy remarries. Randy immediately stops making alimony payments. The recapture rule does not apply.

Exemption for Dependent Child

Under prior law, the spouse who had custody of the child was generally entitled to the personal exemption, provided the parents together furnished over half of the child's support. For years beginning after 1984, the custodial parent is entitled to the exemption unless the right to claim it is expressly waived. Code Sec. 152(e). For the custodial parent to transfer the exemption, the custodial parent must sign a written declaration transferring the exemption to the noncustodial parent. This written declaration may be made annually, for more than one year, or permanently. Even when the custodial parent transfers the exemption to the noncustodial parent, the custodial parent is still eligible for head of household filing status, the earned income credit, and the child and dependent care credit.

TAX BLUNDERS

1. Bob and Judy are in the middle of a divorce case. After the divorce Judy will be in the 28 percent tax bracket, and Bob will be in the 15 percent bracket. Judy wants to pay Bob $20,000 per year as alimony. Bob is insisting he receive $10,000 as alimony and $10,000 as child support. Bob will be the custodial parent. In this case it would benefit Judy to pay Bob's tax on the additional $10,000 alimony. She will save $1,300 by counting all $20,000 as alimony ($2,800 tax savings less $1,500 payment of Bob's tax on $10,000).

2. Same facts as above. Judy would be wise to pay Bob for the personal exemption for the child. The savings to Bob is at the 15 percent rate. Judy would benefit from the 28 percent rate.

3. The lower tax rates drastically reduce the net after-tax value for alimony payments. The payer's net after-tax cost of alimony increases as the individual's tax bracket decreases.

   Assume Frank and Robin Forkes were divorced in 1982. Frank makes annual alimony payments of $15,000. In 1987, Frank had $90,000 of taxable income, which placed him in the 38.5 percent tax bracket. Therefore, his net after-tax cost for alimony was $9,225. In 2015, with the same taxable income his after-tax cost for alimony payments increased to $10,800 because Frank is in the 28 percent tax bracket in 2015.

   Just as the lower tax rates prove disadvantageous to the payer of alimony, the increased exemption for dependents ($4,000 in 2015) makes the dependency exemption all the more important. Under present law, the custodial parent is automatically entitled to the dependency exemption.

Legal Fees

If a spouse is collecting alimony, legal fees incurred to enforce the payment are deductible as an itemized deduction by that spouse. Legal fees incurred in arranging the divorce settlement are not deductible. The payer-spouse cannot deduct any legal fees for the arrangement of the divorce or for the adjustment of alimony payments.

Payment in Arrears

Payments of amounts in arrears are deductible when paid. When a lump-sum settlement occurs for payment in arrears, even this is deductible.

Medical and Dental Expenses

Payments made for medical and dental expenses of the payee-spouse by the payer-spouse must be included in the gross income of the payee-spouse if they qualify as alimony. In addition, the payee-spouse is allowed to deduct these two expenses if the payee-spouse itemizes deductions.

Payments made for medical expenses of children of divorced parents may be deducted by the spouse making the payment. In this case, the children will be treated as dependents of both parents.

Transfer of Property Between Spouses

Under prior law, property transfers between divorcing spouses were taxable when they involved the release of support or marital rights. The 1984 tax law provides that no gain or loss will be recognized for property transfers between spouses during marriage, or former spouses incident to a divorce on transfers taking effect after July 18, 1984. The basis the property will carry is the same in the hands of the receiving spouse as it was in the hands of the transmitting spouse. Incident to a divorce means the transfer must occur within one year after the marriage ceases or is related to the cessation of the marriage.

EXAMPLE 4.29

Tom and Roberta Thorne are finishing up the terms of their divorce settlement. Roberta insists Tom turn over to her stock Tom purchased three years ago at a cost of $5,000. The current fair market value of this stock is $9,000. Under the pre-1985 tax law, Tom would have a $4,000 taxable gain, but under the 1984 tax law, the transfer of property between spouses results in no tax liability. Roberta will assume the stock with a tax basis of $5,000.

Child Support

Payments made by one spouse which are specifically identified for the support of minor children are not taxable to the other spouse and are not deductible by the first spouse. The support must be for the children of the parent making the payment. The custodial parent is entitled to the exemption unless he or she signs a waiver.

EXAMPLE 4.30	By the terms of the divorce settlement, Bob Barter is directed to pay alimony of $1,600 per month and child support of $800 per month. Assume that $800 per month is more than 50 percent of the child's support. Bob is not allowed an exemption for support of his child. The custodial parent is entitled to the exemption. The $800 is not included in income nor deductible by Bob.

When the instrument sets forth one amount for alimony and one amount for child support and a particular payment is less than the total of the two, the payment will first apply towards the child support. Child support payments, if in arrears, must be paid before any future amounts may be considered as alimony.

Where the divorce decree, for example, requires the husband to pay $1,000 a month to his divorced wife and $500 a month for the support of a minor child and the husband pays only $500, it is nevertheless considered to be payment for the support of the child. Reg. §1.71-1(e).

Reporting Requirements

The taxpayer paying alimony must furnish the payee's taxpayer identification number on the tax return. Code Sec. 215(c). A $50 penalty in a calendar year will be levied for failure to comply with the reporting requirement unless it can be shown that failure to comply was due to reasonable cause and not to willful neglect. Code Sec. 6724(d)(3).

¶4485   DISCHARGE OF DEBT

When a debt is cancelled for a consideration, in whole or in part, the debtor realizes taxable income for the amount of the debt discharged. Code Sec. 61(a)(12). For example, if the debtor performed a personal service for the creditor and the debt was fully or partially cancelled, the debtor would have to realize as income the cancelled amount as compensation for services. Reg. §1.61-12(a).

Creditor's Gifts

If a creditor gratuitously cancels a debt, then the amount forgiven is not income but a nontaxable gift. Code Sec. 102(a). The Supreme Court ruled that the cancellation of a debt by the creditor for "no consideration" is a gift and, therefore, no taxable income is involved. *Helvering v. American Dental Co.*, 43-1 USTC ¶9318, 318 U.S. 322, 63 S.Ct. 577 (1935). However, where consideration of any kind or amount is given for cancellation of the debt, it may be extremely difficult to prove the cancellation was gratuitous.

Bankruptcy and Insolvency

Generally, income from a nongratuitous discharge of indebtedness is includible in gross income unless it is excludable under Code Sec. 108. For discharges after 1986, two types of exclusions are provided in the following priority order (Code Sec. 108(a)):

1. The discharge occurs in a bankruptcy case under Title 11 of the U.S. Code.
2. The discharge occurs when the taxpayer is insolvent outside of bankruptcy. An insolvent taxpayer is one who has an excess of liabilities over the fair market value of assets immediately prior to the discharge. The exclusion is limited to the insolvent amount.

Discharge or reduction of debt in bankruptcy does not generate income. If the debt was incurred in connection with property used in a trade or business, the amount of debt that was discharged reduces certain tax attributes that could otherwise provide benefits in the future. Section 108(b)(5) allows the taxpayer to elect to apply any portion of the cancellation of debt to reduce the basis in depreciable property before reducing other tax attributes. This election by the taxpayer is available regardless of whether the debt is evidenced by a security. If the taxpayer does not elect to reduce the basis in depreciable property, then the amount excluded from gross income (the portion of the debt that was cancelled) reduces tax attributes in the order given in Code Sec. 108(b)(2)):

1. Net operating losses and carryovers
2. General business credit
3. Capital loss carryovers
4. Reduction of basis of the property of the taxpayer
5. Foreign tax credit carryovers

Tax attributes other than credit carryovers are reduced one dollar for each dollar of debt discharge excluded. Code Sec. 108(b)(3)(A). Where a taxpayer excludes income from the discharge of indebtedness in a Title 11 bankruptcy case or the discharge occurs when the taxpayer is insolvent and the taxpayer is required to apply such excluded income to reduce its tax attributes, the reduction for post-1986 tax years in foreign tax credit, research credit, and the general business credit carryovers is to be made at a rate of 33 1/3 cents per dollar excluded. Code Sec. 108(b)(3)(B).

An insolvent taxpayer is allowed to exclude from gross income any discharge of indebtedness except that the amount excluded cannot exceed the amount by which the taxpayer is insolvent. Code Sec. 108(a)(3).

| EXAMPLE 4.31 | Mike Merchant has assets of $50,000 and liabilities of $85,000. If one of Mike's creditors forgives him of $40,000 worth of debt, then Mike must recognize $5,000 ($50,000 – ($85,000 – $40,000)) of taxable income. |

Mortgage Debt Forgiveness

The Mortgage Forgiveness Debt Relief Act of 2007 offers distressed homeowners with a limited tax exclusion for debt forgiveness and mortgage insurance payments. Generally, homeowners will be able to exclude up to $2 million of mortgage debt forgiveness. This exclusion will be available from January 1, 2007 through 2014. The Emergency Economic Stabilization Act of 2008 extended this provision for three more years. A taxpayer whose principal residence has declined in market value will be able to refinance the loan without incurring a tax on the debt forgiveness. The American Taxpayer Relief Act of 2012 extended this provision through December 31, 2013. The Tax Increase Prevention Act of 2014 extended this provision through December 31, 2014.

Purchase Money Debts

If a debt owed to the seller for the purchase of property is reduced by the seller, then no income is recognized by the purchaser. The reduction is a purchase price adjustment, not a discharge in indebtedness. Consequently, the purchaser recognizes no income even though the obligation has been reduced. In order for this rule to apply, there must be a "pure" cancellation of indebtedness income; the only relationship between the parties must be that of debtor and creditor, and the debt forgiveness must not simply be the method by which the creditor makes a payment to the debtor for services or property. Code Sec. 108(e)(5).

Corporate Debts

A shareholder's gratuitous forgiveness of the corporation's indebtedness or cancellation of the corporation's indebtedness to the shareholder is usually considered a contribution of capital to the corporation to the extent of the principal debt. Code Sec. 108(e)(6); Reg. §1.61-12(a).

| EXAMPLE 4.32 | Benjamin Warren is sales manager and shareholder of Cleveland Widget Inc. The company is in bankruptcy and Benjamin has not been paid for several months. Benjamin agrees to cancel the debt for the unpaid wages. Cleveland Widget Inc. recognized no income; instead, the cancellation is treated as a contribution of capital. Benjamin, who is on the cash basis, recognizes no income from the unpaid wages. |

Student Loans

A special income exclusion applies to the discharge of all or part of a student loan under a governmental agency student loan program if, pursuant to the loan agreement, the discharge is made because the individual works for a specified period of time in certain geographical areas for certain classes of employers (e.g., as a doctor or nurse in a rural area). Code Sec. 108(f). The amount of the loan that is forgiven is excluded from gross income.

KEYSTONE PROBLEM

Roy and Ann are students at one of the country's finest state universities and wish to marry in the near future. Roy has inherited a potato farm from his late grandfather. Both have scholarships and part-time jobs. They will receive as gifts, property (a small house), and some stocks and bonds. Further, both have cash from savings and investments (about $10,000). Roy is also in debt ($5,000) to his uncle for a defunct rock band he had started as a freshman. His uncle will forgive the debt if Roy marries and settles down. The young couple have come to you for advice on financial planning. What are the principal considerations you feel they would need to take into account in planning their financial future? What steps would you advise them to take in setting up their affairs? Consider such concerns as terms of property ownership, whether to file a tax return jointly or separately, whether to choose the cash or accrual basis for paying tax, how to minimize tax liability, and other factors which you feel are relevant to the problem.

Stock Option Plans

¶4601   RESTRICTED STOCK PLANS

Stock or other property that is transferred by an employer as compensation for services rendered but that, when received, is subject to certain restrictions that affect its value, is governed by the rules contained in Code Sec. 83. As a general rule, the value of any property transferred in connection with services rendered is taxable as compensation, whether the property is goods, common stock, a partnership interest, or any other property. An exception is provided for unsecured, unfunded promises to pay. Code Sec. 83(a); Reg. §1.83-3(c).

Property Substantially Vested

The property is taxable whenever the right to it is "substantially vested," which means it is either transferable or not subject to a substantial risk of forfeiture. It is to be valued without regard to any such restriction unless it is one that will never lapse. Code Sec. 83(a)(1).

EXAMPLE 4.33

A corporation, through its bonus plan, gave one of its vice-presidents 2,660 shares of common stock with a value of $76,000 at the time. There were no conditions attached. The vice-president has compensation of $76,000 with an offsetting deduction to the corporation. The result would be the same if the stock were transferred directly to a trust for the vice-president's minor children. If the vice-president had to pay $26,000 for the stock, only $50,000 is taxable. His basis is $76,000. A subsequent sale will result in a short- or long-term capital gain or loss. If the stock is subject to a substantial risk of forfeiture, *e.g.*, it is nontransferable for five years, no income results until the restriction lapses.

The general rule is that compensation results if property is transferred "in connection with" services rendered. Thus, it does not matter whether:

1. Services are rendered as an employee or independent contractor.
2. The property was transferred by the employer or another person, such as a shareholder.
3. The property was transferred to the compensated person or to anyone else, *e.g.*, a beneficiary, a trust, a corporation, or other agent. Any income received, *e.g.*, dividends, before the property is substantially vested is also treated as compensation.

If the property is sold before it is substantially vested, ordinary income results in the amount of the proceeds. But if the property is forfeited *before* it is substantially vested, no tax loss is incurred (except for amounts paid). If the property is forfeited *after* it is substantially vested and the value was reported as compensation, an ordinary loss results. Reg. §1.83-1(b)(1) and (2). This could happen if the property was transferable, but subject to a substantial risk of forfeiture.

Property Not Substantially Vested

If property transferred in connection with services rendered is not "substantially vested," *i.e.*, it is subject to a substantial risk of forfeiture, an election may nevertheless be made to include the current fair market value of the property in gross income. Code Sec. 83(b). The election is irrevocable and must be filed with the IRS within 30 days with a copy to the employer. Making the election locks in a basis equal to the fair market value included in gross income and starts the holding period running. Section 83(h) includes a matching principle: The employer's deduction is taken whenever the property is included in the employee's gross income and in the same amount.

There are two advantages of making the election:

1. Any future appreciation will qualify as a capital gain, historically taxed at rates lower than ordinary income.
2. The appreciation between the date of transfer and the date of substantial vesting is not taxed until the eventual disposition of the property in a taxable sale or exchange.
3. There will be no self-employment tax on the increase in value.

EXAMPLE 4.34	Cornelius Track received $5,000 worth of stock from his employer on condition that he worked in the same position the next four years, which he did. At the time the stock vested it was worth $12,000. Cornelius waited another six years before selling the stock for $19,000. If Cornelius did *not* make the Section 83(b) election, he would have taxable compensation of $12,000 when the stock vested (with an offsetting deduction to the employer), and an additional $7,000 of capital gain in the year of sale. Had he made the election he would have had $5,000 of compensation up front (offsetting deduction to the employer), *no* income at the time of vesting, and $14,000 of capital gain at the sale 10 years after the initial transfer.

The disadvantages of making the Section 83(b) election include the early outlay of cash to pay tax as well as the unavailability of a loss deduction should the property be forfeited before it becomes substantially vested.

The election should therefore be made only if the property has good appreciation potential *and* it is likely that any required conditions will be met.

Substantial Risk of Forfeiture

A substantial risk of forfeiture exists if a person's rights to full enjoyment of such property are conditioned upon the future performance of substantial services by an individual. Code Sec. 83(c). The following are examples of substantial risks of forfeiture:

1. The property must be returned unless earnings go up.
2. Substantial services must be rendered.
3. A successful completion of "going public" is a condition.

Conditions not constituting substantial risks include:

1. The person is being discharged for cause or for committing a crime.
2. The person accepts a job with a competitor.
3. The employer must pay the full market value upon forfeiture.

PLANNING POINTER	An executive receives $20,000 worth of restricted stock from his employer, conditional upon five years of service. Under the general rules, the executive will have no income for five years, at which time the then fair market value will be ordinary income. If the executive signs a promissory note for $20,000, he can make a Section 83(b) election without recognizing income. This will start the holding period running and lock in a basis of $20,000. Five years later, the corporation tears up the note, resulting in $20,000 of compensation to the executive and a business deduction of $20,000 to the corporation. If the stock is sold for $50,000 upon the lapse, for example, then or later, the executive will report a long-term capital gain of $30,000. In the absence of a note and the election, the full $50,000 would have been ordinary income (with an offsetting deduction to the employer).

¶4615   INCENTIVE STOCK OPTION (ISO) PLANS

Incentive stock options (ISOs) are the latest development in statutory stock option arrangements, replacing the restricted and qualified stock option provisions that previously existed. The term "incentive stock option" means an option granted by a corporation to an individual to purchase stock of the corporation if certain requirements are met. Code Sec. 422(b). The employee must have received the option for some reason connected with employment and must remain employed by the corporation (including a parent or subsidiary) issuing the option from the time of issuance until three months before it is exercised (one year in the case of a disabled employee).

Incentive stock options may be received and exercised by the employee of a corporation without recognizing any gross income. Income is reported only after a taxpayer disposes of the stock. However, for purposes of computing the alternative minimum tax, the taxpayer generally must include the amount by which the fair market value of the stock exceeds the exercise price at the time the taxpayer's rights to the stock are either freely transferable or not subject to a substantial risk of forfeiture. Code Sec. 56(b)(3).

The employee must hold the stock for a minimum of two years after the option is granted and for one year after the option is exercised. If the requisite holding period is not met, the bargain element (value less exercise price) is ordinary income to the employee in the year of sale with an offsetting deduction to the employer. The value on exercise becomes the employee's cost basis. The sale will result in short- or long-term capital gain or loss under the general rules. If the requisite holding period is met, long-term capital gain or loss on the disposition of the stock will be realized to the extent of the difference between the option price and the amount for which the stock is sold.

EXAMPLE 4.35

On April 1, Year 1, Gumballs, Inc. granted Juan an ISO to purchase 1,000 shares of its stock for $30 a share (its fair market value) for the next five years. On March 28, Year 2, Juan exercised the option and paid $30,000 when the stock sold for $42 a share. On September 17, Year 3, Juan sold the stock for $57,000. Gumballs, Inc. receives no deduction upon grant, exercise, or sale. Juan reports a long-term capital gain of $27,000. For purposes of the alternative minimum tax only, he has an adjustment item in the year of exercise of $12,000 ($42,000 – $30,000). Had Juan sold the stock for $53,000 on March 31, Year 3, the special two-year holding period would *not* have been met. As a result Juan, in Year 3, would have had $12,000 of ordinary income and $11,000 of long-term capital gain. He still would have an AMT adjustment item of $12,000. In Year 3, the year of the sale, Gumballs, Inc. would have compensation expense of $12,000 in this case.

PLANNING POINTER

Long-term capital gains generally are taxed at a maximum of 20 percent. Meeting the holding period requirements of the ISO would also be advantageous to the shareholder if the shareholder had capital losses that would otherwise not be deductible and have to be carried over. The shareholder meeting the holding period requirements would also cause the corporation to lose the compensation deduction. Therefore, the employer should, if necessary, offer a cash bonus to employees who are still in a position to violate the one- or two-year holding period, so as to secure a deduction for the employer. The bonus, after taxes, must, of course, be less than the tax savings resulting from the compensation deduction.

For options to qualify as ISOs the following requirements must be met:

1. The term of the option may not exceed 10 years.
2. The option price must be no less than the fair market value of the stock on the date of issuance.
3. The option must be transferable by inheritance only.
4. The option plan must specify the aggregate number of shares that may be issued and the employees eligible to receive the option.
5. The option must be granted within 10 years of the earlier of the date of adoption of the plan or the date it was approved by the shareholders.
6. If the employee owns more than 10 percent of the company, the option price must be at least 110 percent of the market value and its term may not exceed five years. Code Sec. 422(b) and (c).

To the extent that the aggregate fair market value of stock with respect to which ISOs are exercisable for the first time by an individual during any calendar year exceeds $100,000, such options are not considered ISOs. Code Sec. 422(d). Further, an option granted after 1986 will not be treated as an ISO if the terms of the option at the time it is granted provide that it will not be treated as an incentive stock option. Code Sec. 422(b).

¶4625 EMPLOYEE STOCK PURCHASE PLANS

An employee stock option plan is, generally, one permitting employees to buy stock in the employer corporation at a discount. Options issued under an employee stock purchase plan qualify for special tax treatment. Code Sec. 423. No income is recognized under such a plan at the time the option is granted; the recognition is deferred until stock acquired under the plan is disposed of.

If stock acquired under such a plan is disposed of after being held for the required period, the employee will realize ordinary income to the extent of the excess of the fair market value of the stock at the time the option was granted over the option price. Any further gain is a capital gain. If the stock is disposed of when its value is less than its value at the time the option was granted, the amount of ordinary income will be limited to the excess of current value over the option price.

An employee stock purchase plan must provide that only employees may be granted options and must be approved by the stockholders of the granting corporation within 12 months before or after the date the plan is adopted. Code Sec. 423(b). Other conditions that must be met either by the plan or in the stock offering are:

1. The option price may not be less than the smaller of (a) 85 percent of fair market value of the stock when the option is granted or (b) 85 percent of the fair market value at exercise.
2. The option must be exercisable within five years from the date of grant where the option price is not less than 85 percent of the fair market value of the stock at exercise. If the option price is stated in any other terms, the option must not be exercisable after 27 months from the date of the grant.
3. No options may be granted to owners of five percent or more of the value or voting power of all classes of stock of the employer or its parent or subsidiary.
4. No employee may be able to purchase more than $25,000 of stock in any one calendar year.
5. The option may not be transferable (other than by will or laws of inheritance) and may be exercisable only by the employee to whom it is granted.
6. If the exercise price was less than the value of the stock upon grant and the option was exercised, the employee may have compensation income (with an offsetting deduction by the employer) upon disposition, including a transfer at death. The compensation equals the lesser of fair market value at grant or at exercise, less the exercise price, and is added to the stock basis. There is no offsetting deduction by the employer.

EXAMPLE 4.36

Brenda Tripper was given a Section 423 option to buy 500 shares of Zoom, Inc. stock for $45 a share when it was selling for $51. She exercised the option two years later when the stock was selling for $58 and sold the stock after another three years for $71 a share. The lesser of $58 or $51, less $45 a share, or $6 a share, is compensation in the year of sale, i.e., $3,000. Brenda's basis is increased by $6 a share to $51. Thus, her long-term capital gain is $20 per share ($71 – $51), or $10,000. If Brenda had died, rather than sold the shares, her final return would show $3,000 in compensation but no capital gain. (Her basis increase of $6 a share would be irrelevant, since her death results in a fair market value basis.)

¶4655 NONSTATUTORY STOCK OPTION PLANS

The term "nonstatutory stock options" refers to those options that do not qualify for the favorable tax treatment accorded options that are covered by a specific Code provision as are qualified stock options, incentive stock options, employee stock purchase plans, and restricted stock options. Code Secs. 421-425. While statutory options generally are not taxed until the taxpayer disposes of the options and any gains on the dispositions are taxed at capital gains rates, nonstatutory stock options usually are taxed at ordinary income rates at the time they are granted, the options being considered compensation for services rendered by the employee. Generally, if an option is acquired under a nonstatutory program, the employee may be taxed when (1) the option is granted, (2) the option is exercised, (3) the option is sold, or (4) the restrictions on the disposition of the option-acquired stock lapse. Reg. §1.83-7(a).

EXAMPLE 4.37

> Joseph Barkin is granted a nonmarketable, nonstatutory option to buy 10,000 shares of his employer's stock at $40 per share for five years at the time the stock is selling for $36 per share. Four years later, Joseph exercises the option when the stock is selling for $47 per share. Joseph has no income, and his employer receives no deduction at the time the option is granted. Upon exercise of the option, Joseph has ordinary compensation of $70,000, the bargain element, and his employer receives a corresponding deduction. Joseph's basis in the stock is $470,000. Upon a later sale, Joseph generates a short- or long-term capital gain or loss with the holding period starting at the time the option is exercised.

The taxation of a nonstatutory stock option will depend upon the date when the option was granted. Generally, if the nonstatutory option was granted after April 21, 1969, its taxation will be determined by Code Sec. 83 and Reg. §1.83-7. Thus, if the option has a readily ascertainable fair market value at the time it is granted in connection with the performance of services, the person who performed the services realizes compensation either (1) when the rights in the option become transferable, or (2) when the right in the option is not subject to a substantial risk of forfeiture. If the option does not have an ascertainable fair market value at the time when it is granted, taxation occurs when the right to receive the stock is unconditional. The difference between the option cost and the fair market value of the stock at the time the optionee has a right to receive it is taxed as compensation.

SUMMARY

- The economic benefit doctrine and the constructive receipt doctrine were conceived to explain what constitutes income and when an item of income is taxable.

- Under the accrual method of accounting, income is recognized when a transaction is consummated; under the cash method of accounting, income is recognized only when cash is received or constructively received.

- Section 61(a) of the Internal Revenue Code provides a list of 15 items that are includible in gross income. Gross income, however, is not limited to these items. (See checklist on the next page.)

- Several rules, including the alimony recapture rules, govern when alimony payments should be included in the recipient's gross income and when they are deductible by the payer.

- Alimony is support payment made from one spouse to the other after divorce or legal separation. Child support consists of payments made by one spouse that are specifically identified for the support of minor children. Alimony and child support payments are subject to different tax treatments.

- When a debt is cancelled for a consideration, the debtor realizes taxable income for the amount of the debt discharged. Special rules govern the discharge of indebtedness for insolvent taxpayers.

CHECKLIST

Inclusions in Gross Income

Agreement not to Compete	Gambling Winnings
Alimony	Hobby Income
Annuities	Illegal Transactions (gains from gambling, betting, lotteries, embezzlement, protection money, etc.)
Awards	Insider's Profits
Back Pay	Interest
Bad Debt Recoveries	Jury Duty Fees
Bargain Purchase from Employer	Kickbacks
Bonuses	Mileage Allowance
Breach of Contract Damages	Military Pay
Buried Treasure	Notary Fees
Business Income	Partnership Income
Cancellation of Debts	Pensions
Cancellation of Lease	Per Diem Allowance
Christmas Bonuses	Prizes
Commissions	Professional Fees
Compensation for Personal Services	Punitive Damages
Debts Forgiven	Rents
Director's Fees	Retirement Pay
Discounts	Rewards
Dividends	Royalties
Embezzlement Proceeds	Salaries
Employee Death Benefits	Severance Pay
Employee's Awards	Social Security Benefits for the
Employee's Bonuses	Well-to-Do
Estate and Trust Income	Supplemental Unemployment
Benefits	Tips and Gratuities
Executor's Fees	Travel Allowances
Fees	Unemployment Compensation
Gain from Sale of Property	U.S. Savings Bonds (interest)
Gain from Sale of Securities (including government securities)	Wages

QUESTIONS

1. Explain and differentiate between the three concepts of income: economic, legal, and accounting.

2. Compare and contrast the economic benefit doctrine and the constructive receipt doctrine.

3. Explain the fruit-of-the-tree doctrine and why it was established by the courts.

4. Ilana is short of money, so he asks his boss for an advance of $25. Is this taxable income to Ilana?

5. Mr. Chen directs his employer to deduct $50 per week from his pay for the purchase of U.S. savings bonds. Can Mr. Chen exclude this amount from his gross income? Explain.

6. Distinguish between compensation and gifts and identify the tax consequence associated with each.

7. Under what conditions will scholarships or fellowships granted by an educational institution not be included in gross income.

8. Are selling and administrative expenses of a business deducted before or after gross income?

9. In a rental agreement, when are improvements to the property made by the lessee regarded as income?

10. Describe under what terms a stock dividend would not be included in gross income.

11. An elderly woman gives stocks and bonds to her son for management and safekeeping. She keeps the stocks and bonds in her own name. He is to manage the portfolio at his choosing. To whom are the dividends and capital gains taxable at year-end?

12. Under what conditions are alimony payments from divorces included in the recipient's gross income?

13. Give some examples of payments not qualifying as alimony.

14. Describe the intent of the "front-loading" provisions with respect to alimony payments.

15. Explain the tax status of child support payments.

16. Are payments for a life insurance policy that is owned by a former spouse who is the beneficiary of the policy deductible as alimony by the payer?

17. John and Jane divorced in 2015. They have two children, ages 6 and 11. The divorce decree requires John to pay $800 a month to Jane and does *not* specify the use of the money. According to the decree, the payments will stop after the children reach 18 or graduate from high school, whichever comes first. May John deduct the payments as alimony?

18. All of the following would be *excluded* from income as a qualified scholarship by an individual who is a candidate for a degree at a qualified educational institution, except:
    a. Tuition
    b. Student fees
    c. Course books
    d. Room and board

19. On January 1, 2014, John made a loan of $6,000 to his neighbor. The loan was evidenced by a written promise to repay the principal within three years and was to bear interest at a rate of 6% per annum. John's neighbor paid interest for the first year only and then his financial condition deteriorated. In 2015, John learned that he would only be able to recover $3,000 of the loan. The loan was *not* made in the course of John's business. May John deduct $3,000 of the loan on his tax return?

20. If another person cancels or pays your debts, but not as a loan or gift, have you constructively received this amount, and generally must you include it in your gross income for the year?

PROBLEMS

21. Leah Sarah is employed at Cleveland Inc. at an annual salary of $45,000. Leah received $35,000 in salary in 2015 from Cleveland Inc., a prosperous company. They credited the unpaid salary to Leah Sarah's account. Leah only had to stop by the payroll office to receive her money. In January 2016, Leah Sarah requested and received the remaining $10,000 of her salary. How much income must Leah Sarah report on her 2015 income tax return?

22. Cal Corey and his wife are living in Las Vegas, Nevada, and own an apartment house from which they receive $20,000 a year in net rental income. Cal's wife also owns an apartment house, which she purchased as an investment while she was working before their recent marriage. The net rental income from this building is $15,000 a year. If the Coreys file separate returns what would each file for rental income on their tax returns?

23. Fred Miller, a teacher, had several additional sources of income during 2015. He received a $500 gift as a result of his helping a friend build a house, and he was assigned $300 of interest due his uncle on bonds his uncle owns. He also had the use of a van (value of $1,000) for the year from his parents who were traveling. Further, he received free, $600 of gasoline for the van because he tutored the son of the station owner free of charge. What of the additional income must be included in his income tax return?

24. Helen Troy, a student seeking a Master's degree in accounting, was awarded a 50 percent scholarship to graduate school (valued at $3,000) and a $6,000 per year teaching assistantship (not required of Master's level students). She also, because of her great beauty, won first prize in the Miss International Beauty Pageant. The prize included $14,000 in cash, a $25,000 car, a $10,000 scholarship, and travel expenses of $2,000 relating to the pageant. What must she include as gross income?

25. Billy Dent, as the owner of an apartment building, receives and makes the following payments during 2015:

Received in January 2015 rent that was due in December 2014	$5,000
Received in December 2015 rent not due until January 2016	4,000
Security deposit which is to be refunded when tenant vacates the apartment	500

How much rental income must Billy Dent include on his 2015 income tax return?

26. Abby, a cash basis taxpayer, is paid an annual salary of $250,000 plus a percentage of net profits. The additional compensation for 2015 was $50,000. This sum is payable to her on February 9, 2016 after the annual audit had been completed. However, a tentative credit of $10,000 was entered to her drawing account on December 1, 2015 and was immediately available to her. Abby comes to your office and asks you how much compensation must be included in her gross income for 2015. What will you tell her? Why?

27. Judd Harrison owns 200 shares of stock in the Widget Company for which he paid $1,600 in 1999. The board of directors of the company decided to pay a 10 percent stock dividend in April 2015, for which Judd received 20 shares of stock. Was this a taxable stock dividend? Explain.

28. Joe and Mabel, a married couple filing a joint return, have modified adjusted gross income of $385,000. Included in this sum is $100,000 of net investment income. Are Joe and Mabel subject to the 3.8 percent Medicare Tax?

29. Abby is a single taxpayer with $250,000 of modified adjusted gross income which includes $80,000 of net investment income. Abby owes 3.8 percent Medicare Tax on what amount of her income?

30. In January 2016, Judd Harrison decides to sell 100 shares in the Widget Company. Since April 2015, no stock dividends had been paid by the company. On the date the stock is sold the market price is $12 a share. What is the basis per share that Judd must use in computing any gains or losses? (Refers back to Problem 27.)

31. In 2015, Ollie Lingo and his wife have several endowment life insurance policies. On the first, which begins payment in 2016, but was fully paid by 2010, a dividend of $200 is declared and paid. On the second, which began payment in 2014, a $500 dividend is paid. On the third, which has two more years before it is paid up, a dividend of $100 is paid. How much of dividends received, if anything, is to be excluded from gross income? (In none of the cases cited above has the taxpayer received dividends in excess of premiums paid.)

32. For each independent situation, determine the amount, if any, that is includible in the gross income of the employee.
    a. The employee of a motel has the choice of free lodging on the premises (fair market value $400 per week) or extra cash compensation. He is not required to live on premises. He chooses the lodging.
    b. An employee arranges to have his annual bonus, $1,000, paid directly to his son. His objective is to make a wedding gift to the son.
    c. An employee earns a salary of $500 per week. Pursuant to a court order, $100 of his salary goes to his ex-wife for child support.

33. R.E. Lee entered into a 10-year lease in 2009 with Mr. Grant. In addition to the $18,000 a year rent he paid in 2015, he prepaid two months of 2016 rent totaling $3,000. Also, in 2015, Mr. Lee remodeled the kitchen at a cost of $4,500. How much rental income must Mr. Grant include in gross income in 2015? What is the tax status to Mr. Grant of the remodeling work completed by Mr. Lee?

34. Arnold and Barbara Cane were divorced in June 2015. Pursuant to the divorce decree, Arnold is obliged to perform as follows:
    a. Transfer title of their personal home to Barbara. They purchased the house in 1998 and their basis today is $400,000. The fair market value of the house is $500,000. The house is subject to a 25-year, $250,000 mortgage.
    b. Arnold is to continue making payments on the house until it is fully paid off. In 2015, Arnold made payments totaling $18,000.
    c. Arnold is to make $3,000 per month payments to Barbara. Of this amount one-half is for child support. The divorce decree further states that alimony is to cease upon the death of the wife. In 2015, he made six payments.

How do the transactions in the divorce agreement affect Arnold's and Barbara's taxable income?

35. John and Mary Johnson were divorced in January 2015. By terms of their divorce decree John had to pay alimony to Mary at the rate of $50,000 in 2015, $25,000 in 2016, and zero in 2017. For the first three years of the agreement, determine what portions of the payments are deductible by John and includible in Mary's gross income.

36. Roy Rainer will pay his wife, Mae, alimony according to the following schedule:

Year 1	$50,000
Year 2	$40,000
Year 3–Year 8	$20,000

Roy and Mae were divorced on January 6, 2015.

For the first three years of the agreement, what portions are excludable and includible in Mae's gross income?

37. Richard and Sally Murphy were divorced in 2013. By the terms of their decree Richard pays Sally $1,000 a month for alimony and child support. When Jane, their 14-year-old daughter, reaches age 18, the payments will be reduced by $300 per month.

Explain to Richard and Sally their tax status for 2015.

38. An individual performed special valuable services not called for by his employment, in consideration for which his employer agreed to pay him a bonus in an amount to be determined later. After due consideration, however, the firm prefers instead to cement the employee's relation to it by selling him, without any restriction, a block of its stock worth $5,000 for $1,000 cash. Has the employee thereby received any amount includible in his gross income for the year?

39. A married taxpayer, age 57, has the following receipts:

Salary	$50,000
Dividends from stock of domestic corporation	1,300
Interest on state toll road bonds	750
Gambling winnings	110
Rents	5,600

The taxpayer's employer paid the premiums on an $80,000 group-term life insurance policy on his life. His spouse is the beneficiary. Annual cost per $1,000 of coverage is assumed to be $5.16. During the tax year, the taxpayer pays $2,200 in taxes on his rental property and $2,650 for its operation and maintenance. He had gambling losses of $65. He made no charitable contributions. Calculate the taxpayer's gross income and adjusted gross income.

40. Robert Reed, a bachelor, maintains his parents in a nursing home. They have no income of their own and are completely dependent on their son. His parents are 75 and 72 years of age. Robert has the following sources of income:

Salary	$45,000
Interest on Municipal Bonds	750
Interest on Bank Accounts	800
Dividends on Common Stock of U.S. Corporation	500

Robert has itemized deductions of $12,000. Robert owns several apartment buildings. His net rental income was $3,000 for the year. Then, on December 31 one of his best tenants brought in a check for $500. This money covers the months of December and January. Robert is confused on how to account for this rental income. It is not included in the $3,000 listed above. Compute Robert's taxable income.

41. Fran Finery's boutique has assets of $100,000 and liabilities of $140,000. Fran's major creditor cancels $50,000 in liabilities.

Discuss the tax ramifications of this forgiveness of debt. Assume the majority of Fran's assets are depreciable property. Discuss the tax ramifications facing the Finery Corporation assuming it is not in bankruptcy. Then, discuss the ramifications assuming the Finery Corporation is in bankruptcy.

42. If Mack Mudd becomes insolvent with assets of $35,000 and liabilities of $65,000 and one of his creditors cancels a debt of $10,000, what amount must Mack recognize as income?

43. Faraway Travel, Inc. granted its vice-president, Chris Best, an incentive stock option on 1,000 shares of Faraway stock at $25 a share, its fair market value, on July 22, Year 1. Chris exercised the option on October 31, Year 2, at $42 a share and sold the stock for $47 a share on December 15, Year 3.
    a. What were the tax consequences to Chris?
    b. To Faraway?
    c. What difference, if any, does it make if Chris sold the stock on October 31, Year 3?

44. **IRS Adapted Problem.** Mr. Garcia, a cash-basis taxpayer, owns an apartment building. His records reflect the following information for 2015:

Tenant G paid cost of floor repairs that were Mr. Garcia's responsibility	$950
Security deposits to be returned to tenants upon expiration of their leases in 2017	1,350
Advance rents received in December for the first six months of 2016	3,000

What is the amount of gross rental income Mr. Garcia should include in his gross income?
a. $2,300
b. $3,000
c. $3,950
d. $4,350
e. $5,300

45. **IRS Adapted Problem.** Roger signed for a ten-year lease to rent office space from Doug. In the first year, Roger paid Doug $5,000 for the first year's rent and $5,000 as rent for the last year of the lease. How much must Doug include in income in the first year of the lease?
a. $0
b. $5,000
c. $5,500
d. $10,000

46. **IRS Adapted Problem.** Each of the following would be one of the requirements for a payment to be alimony under instruments executed after 1984 except:
a. Payments are required by a divorce or separation instrument.
b. Payments can be a noncash property settlement.
c. Payments are *not* designated in the instrument as *not* alimony.
d. Payments are *not* required after death of the recipient spouse.

47. **IRS Adapted Problem.** Robert divorced Laura in 2011. During 2015, per the divorce decree, Robert made the following payments:

The entire mortgage payment on house (jointly owned, and payments with stop after death of the recipient spouse)	$10,800
Tuition for their child	$6,000
Child support	$4,500
Life insurance policy premiums on policy owned by Laura	$3,000

What is the amount Robert can deduct as alimony on his 2015 tax return?
a. $3,000
b. $5,400
c. $8,400
d. $10,800

48. The "fruit-of-the-tree" concept is associated with which doctrine regarding income:
a. Constructive Receipt Doctrine
b. Assignment of Income Doctrine
c. Economic Benefit Doctrine
d. All of the above
e. None of the above.

49. Which of the following item(s) must be included in an individual's return as income?
a. Compensation for services
b. Prizes and awards
c. Inheritance
d. (a) and (b)
e. All of the above.

50. **IRS Adapted Problem.** In which of the following situations will the divorced custodial parent be entitled to the dependency exemption for the child?
a. The noncustodial parent provides $1,500 of support for the child and the custodial parent provides $1,200.
b. The custodial and noncustodial parent both provide $1,500 of support for the child.
c. The custodial parent provides $1,500 of support for the child and the noncustodial parent provides $1,200.
d. All of the above.

51. **IRS Adapted Problem.** Which of the following is not considered "constructive receipt" income in 2015?
a. Andrew Mason was informed that his check for services rendered was available on December 15, 2015, but he waited until January 16, 2016, to pick up the check.
b. A payment on a sale of real property placed in escrow on December 16, 2015, but not received by Benjamin Miles until January 12, 2016, when the transaction was closed.
c. Earned income of Candice Cord was received by her agent on December 30, 2015, but was not received by her until January 5, 2016.
d. Daniel Dryer received a check on December 30, 2015, for services rendered, but was unable to make a deposit until January 5, 2016.
e. Ellen Elks received stock on December 30, 2015, for services rendered, but was unable to find a buyer for the stock until January 20, 2016.

52. **IRS Adapted Problem.** A distribution of stock or stock rights is generally considered a taxable dividend unless it is which of the following:
    a. A distribution in lieu of money
    b. A proportionate distribution
    c. A distribution with respect to preferred stock
    d. A distribution of convertible preferred stock

53. **Comprehensive Problem (Tax Return Problem).** David and Doris Kelley were divorced on February 3, 2015. They lived apart during 2015. The divorce decree required David to make the following payments:
    a. Transfer full title to their jointly owned family home to Doris. Fair market value of the home is $180,000, basis $150,000.
    b. $1,000 per month mortgage payments on the house, above. The mortgage has 20 years remaining before being fully paid off, but the payments would end on her death.
    c. $2,000 per month for 10 years' support payments to Doris, of which $600 per month is child support.
    d. Doris insisted that the children attend private schools. In 2015, David paid $1,500 in tuition for the children's private high school.

    David paid his lawyer $5,000 to represent him in the divorce proceedings. David and Doris agreed that Doris would maintain a home for the children. Further, Doris agreed to allow David to claim one child as a dependency exemption. This agreement was put in writing and signed by Doris.

    Besides the divorce, David has had a big year financially. He owns an apartment house and he requires each new tenant to place a $750 security deposit with him before moving into the apartment. When the tenant ultimately vacates the apartment, David will refund the deposit. In 2015, David collected $3,750 in security deposits and rental income of $15,000.

    David entered a local raffle in 2015. David won first prize, which was a new automobile with a window price of $20,000. He checked with several local car dealers and was positive that if he had purchased a similar car on his own, the price would have been $18,200.

    David loaned his sister Lois $5,000. Lois was repaying the loan at $100 per month plus interest of $40. Since Lois was about to depart on an extended vacation on December 2, 2015, she gave David $200 plus interest of $80 to cover the months of December and January.

    David has a good job that pays an annual salary of $50,000. In 2015, business was very good and in December 2015 bonuses were announced for the employees. David earned a $4,000 bonus for 2015. Bonuses would be mailed to the employees during the first week of January 2016. David has itemized deductions of $20,000.

    Determine David's 2015 taxable income.

54. **Comprehensive Problem (Tax Return Problem).** Bert and Barbara Longfelt support in nursing homes both Bert's parents and Barbara's parents. Bert's parents are 70 and 68 years of age respectively and have no income except for the $3,600 in Social Security they receive annually. Barbara's parents, both 72 years of age, have the following sources of income:

Social Security	$9,800
Interest Income (Joint Ownership)	$2,600
Dividend Income	$900

Bert's annual salary is $45,000 and his wife's annual salary is $55,000.

They have two small children who live at home. Also, they own an apartment house from which they derive $6,000 net rental income. Two items from their rental property confused them so they did not include them in their rental income:

Security deposits received and to be used against final month's rent	$500
Two tenants paid rent in advance in December 2015. The rent was due January 1, 2016	$600

Barbara owned stock prior to her marriage to Bert and received the following cash dividends:

General Corp. nonqualified common stock dividend (U.S. corporation)	$300
Live Forever Life Insurance Co. (dividends on life insurance policy)	$100

Bert and Barbara have several sources of interest income:

Interest income from savings accounts	$850
Interest income from State of Tennessee Highway Bonds	$400

Barbara entered the local area bake-off, won first place for her cherry pie, and received a $1,000 cash prize.

Bert, who is an accountant, made an arrangement with Harold the dentist. Bert would do Harold's tax work if Harold would take care of Bert and his family's dental work. During the year, Bert estimated that the value of his services to Harold was $500 and that Harold gave Bert and his family $600 worth of dental services. In December, Bert did a consulting assignment on a weekend and received $700. No Social Security or taxes were withheld.

During the year, they had $15,000 withheld for federal taxes.

During 2015, Bert and Barbara have $14,000 of itemized deductions. Compute Bert and Barbara's net tax due, including self-employment tax. Assume dividends are taxed at ordinary rates.

55. **Research Problem.** Robert Olsen was a very successful college basketball player. Knowing that he would be offered a multimillion dollar contract, he established a corporation assigning to it his services in professional sports in exchange for a monthly salary. Upon audit the IRS challenged this assignment of contract. Who will prevail? See *C. Johnson,* 78 TC 882, Dec. 39,069 (1982).

Chapter

5

Gross Income—Exclusions

OBJECTIVES

After completing Chapter 5, you should be able to:

1. List the items specifically excluded from gross income.
2. Distinguish between exclusions and deductions.
3. Determine the nontaxable portion of life insurance and annuities.
4. Determine the nontaxable portion of Social Security benefits.
5. Distinguish between taxable and nontaxable interest income.
6. Determine the tax status of various fringe benefits.
7. Understand the tax status of various educational assistance plans.

OVERVIEW

Gross income is defined in the Internal Revenue Code as including "all income from whatever source derived." It includes all income unless expressly exempted by law. The exempted classes are referred to as "exclusions from gross income." This chapter discusses those items that have been specifically excluded from gross income. In addition to several cash considerations, a major portion of the chapter will be dedicated to a discussion of various types of fringe benefits. Finally, the tax status of these elements of income and their relative value to employees will be discussed.

No matter what the type of job, taxes take a significant portion of each weekly paycheck. Therefore, the proper arrangement of income to derive the greatest benefit from sources which are includible and excludable in gross income is of great importance.

Sections 101 through 139 of the Internal Revenue Code list "Items Specifically Excluded from Gross Income." Selected sections are as follows:

Sec. 101.	Certain death benefits
Sec. 102.	Gifts and inheritances
Sec. 103.	Interest on state and local bonds
Sec. 104.	Compensation for injuries or sickness
Sec. 105.	Amounts received under accident and health plans
Sec. 106.	Contributions by employer to accident and health plans
Sec. 107.	Rental value of parsonages
Sec. 108.	Income from discharge of indebtedness
Sec. 109.	Improvements by lessee on lessor's property
Sec. 110.	Qualified lessee construction allowances for short-term leases.
Sec. 111.	Recovery of tax benefit items
Sec. 112.	Certain combat zone compensation of members of the Armed Forces
Sec. 115.	Income of States, municipalities, etc.
Sec. 117.	Qualified scholarships
Sec. 118.	Contributions to the capital of a corporation
Sec. 119.	Meals or lodging furnished for the convenience of the employer
Sec. 120.	Amounts received under qualified group legal services plans
Sec. 121.	Exclusion of gain from sale of principal residence
Sec. 122.	Certain reduced uniformed services retirement pay
Sec. 123.	Amounts received under insurance contracts for certain living expenses
Sec. 125.	Cafeteria plans
Sec. 126.	Certain cost-sharing payments
Sec. 127.	Educational assistance programs
Sec. 129.	Dependent care assistance programs
Sec. 130.	Certain personal injury liability assignments
Sec. 131.	Certain foster care payments
Sec. 132.	Certain fringe benefits
Sec. 134.	Certain military benefits
Sec. 135.	Income from United States savings bonds used to pay higher education tuition and fees
Sec. 136.	Energy conservation subsidies provided by public utilities
Sec. 137.	Adoption assistance programs
Sec. 138.	Medicare Advantage MSA
Sec. 139.	Disaster relief payments
Sec. 139A.	Federal subsidies for prescription drug plans
Sec. 139B.	Benefits provided to volunteer firefighters and emergency medical responders.
Sec. 139C.	COBRA premium assistance
Sec. 139D.	Indian health care benefits
Sec. 139E.	Indian general welfare benefits
Sec. 140.	Cross references to other Acts

Note that the items listed are exclusions from gross income. Do not confuse exclusions from gross income with deductions from gross income, a subject discussed in later chapters. Basically, an exclusion does not appear on the individual's tax return, whereas deductions must appear. It should be noted that even though some income sources may be considered exclusions and are not reported on an individual's 1040 tax return, they may still be subject to tax (i.e., a gift which requires a gift tax return by the donor). This chapter provides an overview of commonly encountered exclusions. Not all types of exclusions are discussed in this chapter. For example, Sections 107 and 118 are not discussed. The exclusions from income which will be discussed more fully include cafeteria plans, life insurance, fringe benefits, and retirement plans.

Common Exclusions from Gross Income

¶5001   GIFTS AND INHERITANCES

A gift, bequest, or inheritance is excluded from gross income. Code Sec. 102(a). Therefore, it follows that the donor does not receive a tax deduction for the property transmitted. A gift transpires when there is a valid transfer of property from one individual to another for no consideration. If property received by gift or inheritance later produces income, the income is taxable. Although the recipient of a gift pays no tax on receipt of the gift, the donor may be required to pay a transfer tax, known as the gift tax.

¶5015   LIFE INSURANCE PROCEEDS

Generally, life insurance proceeds received by the beneficiary are not included in gross income if such amounts are paid by reason of death of the insured. Code Sec. 101(a)(1). Premiums on life insurance policies are not deductible by the insured; therefore, it logically follows that the proceeds from the policy would be excluded from gross income. It is immaterial who the beneficiary is or whether the policy was part of a "group" life insurance plan or was individually purchased. If, however, the payment is delayed and the total amount when received includes some interest, the interest is taxable.

When the proceeds are received for reasons other than death, such as surrender of a life insurance policy, the insured is allowed to recover tax free the amount actually paid for the contract. Code Sec. 72(e)(2)(B). If the cost of the policy exceeds the proceeds, the loss is not deductible. *London Shoe Co., Inc.,* 35-2 USTC ¶9664, 80 F.2d 230 (CA-2 1935), cert. denied, 298 U.S. 663, 56 S.Ct. 747.

In computing the premiums paid under the policy, all dividends received must be subtracted from the amounts paid in.

EXAMPLE 5.1	Ralph Rogers surrendered an endowment policy and received $25,000 from the insurance company. Over time, Ralph had paid in $14,500 in premiums. He must recognize $10,500 ($25,000 – $14,500) of income. He may exclude from income only the amount of his total premiums paid.

Amounts received under a life insurance contract after December 31, 1996, on the life of the insured, terminally or chronically ill individual may be excluded from gross income.

¶5025   SALE OF RESIDENCE

Gross income may not include all the gain realized from the sale or exchange of a principal residence. The gain to be excluded is limited to a maximum of $500,000 ($250,000 for married individual filing a separate return). For detailed discussion, see Chapter 11.

¶5035   RECOVERY OF TAX BENEFIT ITEMS

Gross income includes amounts received that were part of an ealier year deduction or credit. This is considered a recovery and generally must be included in gross income in the year received. Common types of recoveries are refunds, such as state tax tax refunds, and reimbursements or rebates. Chapter 8, ¶8115, discusses state income tax refunds and the tax benefit rule.

¶5055   RETIREMENT INCOME

Historically, Social Security benefits, both monthly and lump-sum, had been excluded from tax. The exclusion extended to benefits received under the Railroad Retirement Act. Benefits received from retirement systems of other countries are not excluded from the federal income tax.

A portion of the Social Security benefits or railroad retirement benefits must be included in taxable income for taxpayers whose provisional income exceeds a base of $25,000 for a single taxpayer ($32,000 for a married taxpayer filing a joint return and zero for a married person filing a separate return). Provisional income equals modified adjusted gross income plus one-half the Social Security benefits received. Modified adjusted gross means adjusted gross income plus interest on tax-exempt bonds, interest on U.S. savings bonds used to pay higher education tuition and fees, employer adoption assistance, the interest deduction on higher education loans, the deduction for qualified education expenses, and the foreign income exclusion. The amount of Social Security benefits includible in taxable income is the lesser of one-half of the benefits or one half of the excess of the taxpayer's provisional income over the base.

EXAMPLE 5.2

Bill and Linda Peterson, both over age 65, have the following sources of income:

Interest Income (taxable)	$19,000
Dividend Income	4,000
Net Rental Income	6,000
Adjusted Gross Income	$29,000
Social Security Benefits	$10,500
Computations:	
Adjusted Gross Income	$29,000
1/2 of Social Security Benefits	5,250
Provisional Income	$34,250
Base Amount for Married Couple	32,000
Excess	$2,250
50 Percent of Excess	$1,125

Of the $10,500 Bill and Linda received in Social Security benefits, they must include $1,125 in their gross income. Remember, the maximum amount to be included in gross income is the lesser of 50 percent of the "excess" or 50 percent of the Social Security benefit received.

EXAMPLE 5.3

Assume the same facts as in Example 5.2, except that Bill and Linda also have $9,000 of interest income from tax-exempt bonds.

Computations:	
Adjusted Gross Income from Example 5.2	$29,000
Plus: Tax-Exempt Interest	9,000
1/2 of Social Security Benefits	5,250
Provisional Income	$43,250
Less: Base Amount for Married Couples	32,000
Excess	$11,250
50 Percent of Excess	$5,625

In this instance, Bill and Linda must include $5,250 in their gross income. This is because 50 percent of their Social Security benefits is the maximum amount that can be included in gross income.

Social Security benefits are taxable to the individual who receives the benefits. Therefore, if a child receives Social Security benefits, the benefits are taxable to the child using the same formulas that are discussed above.

The Revenue Reconciliation Act of 1993 created a second threshold for years after 1993. This second threshold applies to taxpayers with provisional income greater than $34,000 for a single taxpayer and $44,000 for a married taxpayer filing a joint return. Taxpayers with provisional income exceeding the second threshold will be taxed up to 85 percent of their Social Security benefits.

Taxpayers with provisional income exceeding these amounts will include the lesser of:

A. 85 percent of the taxpayer's Social Security benefits, or
B. the total of the following calculation:
1. 85 percent of the amount that provisional income exceeds the new threshold amounts, plus
2. the smaller of: (a) the amount of Social Security benefits included under prior law; or (b) $4,500 for an unmarried taxpayer, or $6,000 for married taxpayers filing jointly.

Married taxpayers filing separate returns have no base amount and must include in gross income the lesser of: (a) 85 percent of their Social Security benefits; or (b) 85 percent of their provisional income. For illustrations when provisional income exceeds the thresholds, see Examples 5.6 through 5.9.

EXAMPLE 5.4

Linda, a single taxpayer, has AGI of $26,000 and Social Security benefits of $8,000. Linda's provisional income is $30,000 and she must include in her AGI $2,500 of her Social Security benefits. Inasmuch as her provisional income is below the threshold amount ($34,000), she includes in AGI the lesser of 50 percent of her Social Security benefits or one-half the excess of combined income over the base.

EXAMPLE 5.5

Philip and Linda, a married couple filing a joint return, have AGI of $30,000 and Social Security benefits of $14,000. Therefore their provisional income is $37,000. Philip and Linda must include in their AGI $2,500 of their Social Security benefits. Inasmuch as provisional income, $37,000, does not exceed the threshold amount ($44,000), only $2,500 is included in the AGI of Philip and Linda.

EXAMPLE 5.6

Pat, a single taxpayer, has modified AGI of $36,000 and she received $10,000 in Social Security benefits. Pat's provisional income is therefore $41,000. Pat must include in her AGI $8,500 of her Social Security benefits. This is computed as follows:

A. $10,000 × 85% = $8,500
B. [($41,000 − $34,000) × 85%] + $4,500 = $10,450

EXAMPLE 5.7

Steve and Marla, a married couple filing a joint return, have modified AGI of $50,000 and Social Security benefits of $14,000. Steve and Marla have provisional income of $57,000. They must include $11,900 of their Social Security benefits in their gross income. This is computed as follows:

A. $14,000 × 85% = $11,900
B. [($57,000 − $44,000) × 85%] + $6,000 = $17,050

EXAMPLE 5.8

Ron, a single taxpayer, has AGI of $32,000 of income and $8,000 of Social Security benefits. Ron's provisional income is $36,000 and he must include $5,700 of his Social Security benefits in his income. This is computed as follows:

A. $8,000 × 85% = $6,800
B. [($36,000 − $34,000) × 85%] + $4,000* = $5,700
*$8,000 × 50% = $4,000 maximum includible under prior law

¶5055

EXAMPLE 5.9	Norm and Pat, a married couple filing a joint return, have AGI of $40,000 and Social Security benefits of $12,000. Norm and Pat have provisional income of $46,000 and they must include $7,700 of Social Security benefits in their AGI. This is computed as follows: A. $12,000 × 85% = $10,200 B. [($46,000 – $44,000) × 85%] + $6,000* = $7,700 *$12,000 × 50% = $6,000 maximum includible under prior law

¶5075   INTEREST ON GOVERNMENT OBLIGATIONS

Savings Bonds

Interest earned on United States savings bonds is fully taxable. On Series EE bonds, no interest per se is paid each year, but the bond is issued at a discount and each year increases in value until maturity. The difference between the purchase price of the bond and the redemption value is taxable interest income. Cash basis taxpayers have the choice of reporting interest income on a yearly basis or reporting all interest income when the bonds finally mature, while accrual basis taxpayers must accrue the increase in the redemption value each year as interest. If cash basis taxpayers exercise the election to report the interest currently, all such bonds owned by them must be similarly treated for all subsequent years.

Taxpayers who elected to defer recognizing income until the bonds mature may change their method of reporting income to a yearly basis without permission from the IRS. However, in the year of change all interest accrued to date, not previously reported, must be included in gross income.

Series EE bonds were first issued in 1980. Prior to 1980, Series E bonds were issued. Series HH bonds replaced Series H bonds in 1980, as well. Series HH and Series H bonds are treated identically for tax purposes. August 2004 was the last date that Series HH bonds were issued. After that date taxpayers will no longer be able to reinvest series HH bonds or exchange series EE bonds for HH bonds. These bonds are issued at face value and interest is paid twice a year by check. Cash basis taxpayers must report interest income in the year it is received.

Taxpayers who owned Series E bonds prior to 1980 and did not report interest income on a yearly basis could trade their E bonds for Series H bonds and not realize taxable income unless they received cash on the trade. The same rules hold for Series EE bonds as for Series HH bonds today. On the E/EE bonds, the taxpayer defers the recognition of income until the taxpayer disposes of the bonds or they mature. Then the taxpayer reports as interest income the difference between the redemption value and the total cost of traded bonds, plus any amount received at the time of trade.

EXAMPLE 5.10	Robert and Mary Moore had the following interest income in 2015: 1. Interest on Series EE bonds, $300 2. Interest on bank savings account, $400 3. Interest on municipal bond, $500 Robert and Mary have taxable interest income of $700. If they elect, they can defer the recognition of income on the Series EE bonds until the bonds mature. In that case, then total interest to be included in gross income totals $400.

Educational Savings Bonds

A tax exclusion is provided for interest earned on U.S. savings bonds used to finance the higher education of the taxpayer, the taxpayer's spouse, or dependents. Code Sec. 135. The bonds must have been purchased after December 31, 1989, and the exclusion is available only to the individual who purchased the bonds. The purchaser of the bonds must have reached the age of 24 and be the sole owner of the bonds. The bonds must be redeemed during the same tax year in which the qualified educational expenses are incurred by the taxpayer, the taxpayer's spouse, or any dependents.

Qualified higher education expenses include tuition and fees, net of scholarships and other tuition reduction amounts. Qualified higher education expenses must be further reduced by expenses taken into account for the American Opportunity Tax Credit and Lifetime Learning credits. Books, supplies, room and board and expenses incurred for sports, games, or hobbies other than as part of a degree program are not covered.

The key to computing the exclusion is the amount of qualified higher education expenses that the individual incurs in the year the bonds are redeemed. If these expenses exceed the aggregate redemption amount (principal plus interest), then all of the interest may be excluded, subject to an income-linked phase-out discussed below. If the redemption amount is larger than the qualified educational expenses, however, the exclusion is reduced on a pro rata basis.

EXAMPLE 5.11

During 2015, Mary Adams, age 50, redeems Series EE bonds and receives $5,000 of principal and $2,500 of accrued interest. Mary's daughter attends college and has qualified expenses of $8,000. Mary may exclude from her gross income the entire $2,500 of interest.

EXAMPLE 5.12

Same facts as in Example 5.11, except Mary's daughter incurred only $6,000 in qualified expenses. Mary may exclude from gross income only $2,000. This is calculated as follows:

$$\frac{\text{Qualified Expenses}}{\text{Series EE Proceeds}} = \text{Percentage Exclusion}$$

Percentage Exclusion × Series EE Interest = Interest Exclusion

Percentage Exclusion = $6,000/$7,500 = 80%

Interest Exclusion $2,500 × 80% = $2,000

The exclusion for accrued interest is subject to phaseout provisions. The phaseout ranges for 2015 are as follows:

Filing Status	Modified AGI
Married filing jointly	$115,750—$145,750
Single (including head of household)	$77,200—$92,200

Married individuals filing separately are not eligible for the exclusion.

For those falling within the phaseout range, the amount of interest otherwise excludable will be reduced (but not below zero) by multiplying that interest by a fraction that is determined by dividing the excess of modified AGI (that is, the excess of modified AGI over the bottom figure of the phaseout range) by the number of dollars in the phaseout range ($30,000 for joint returns and $15,000 for single taxpayers).

EXAMPLE 5.13

Same facts as in Example 5.11, but also assume that Mary is a single mother and that her modified AGI is $89,200. Mary may exclude from her gross income $500. This amount is computed as follows:

$2,500 – ($2,500 × $12,000/$15,000) = $500

The $12,000 is the excess of modified AGI over the phaseout range.

State and Municipal Bonds

Interest received on state and local government bonds is generally excludable from gross income. Code Sec. 103(a). The term "state or local bond" means an obligation of a state or political subdivision, and the term "state" includes the District of Columbia and any possession of the U.S. Code Sec. 103(c). Tax-exempt bonds are an attractive investment for many well-to-do investors because the after-tax return on such bonds is considerably higher than taxable bonds.

EXAMPLE 5.14	Kayla, a highly paid corporate executive, was in the 39.6 percent marginal tax bracket. She was contemplating buying some bonds, but could not decide whether to buy corporate bonds, paying 12 percent interest, or a municipal bond, paying 9 percent. Since Kayla is in the 39.6 percent marginal tax bracket, the 12 percent corporate bond nets Kayla only 7.248 percent. Therefore, the 9 percent tax-free interest income from the municipal bonds is a better decision.

EXAMPLE 5.15	Sam Roberts, a well-to-do banker, has the following securities in his portfolio:

1. One $5,000, 10 percent corporate bond, annual interest income, $500
2. Ten shares of ABC Inc. stock, no dividends paid
3. One $10,000 bond issued by the Port Authority of N.Y. in 2006 at 6 percent
4. Dividend on life insurance policy, $100
5. One $10,000, 9 percent State of Ohio bond issued in 2004, annual interest, $900

Of the items listed above, the interest on the corporate bond must be included in gross income. The shares of stock paid no dividend; therefore, there is no dollar amount to be included in gross income. However, if a dividend had been paid, it would have been includible in Sam Roberts's gross income. The $800 interest on the Port Authority bond is fully tax-exempt as is the interest on the State of Ohio bond. The life insurance dividend is considered a reduction in premium and is not includible in gross income.

Interest received on state or local bonds is generally excludable from gross income when bond proceeds are used exclusively for traditional government purposes. However, interest on state and local bonds used to benefit other persons is not tax free when it is from (1) private activity bonds that are not exempt, (2) state or local bonds that have not been issued in registered form, or (3) arbitrage bonds.

Private Activity Bonds

Private activity bonds are issued by state and local governments to help finance private business. Private activity bonds that qualify for tax exemption include (1) exempt-facility bonds (e.g., proceeds used to finance airports, water facilities, waste disposal facilities, electric energy or gas facilities), (2) qualified mortgage bonds (proceeds used to finance certain owner-occupied residences), (3) qualified veteran's mortgage bond (issued only by five states), (4) qualified small issue bonds (face amount of bond issue is $1 million or less), (5) qualified student loan bonds, (6) qualified redevelopment bonds (proceeds used to redevelop blighted areas), or (7) qualified tax-exempt organization bonds. Code Sec. 141(e). Tax-exempt interests received by the taxpayer is not included for the regular tax computation but is included in the alternative minimum tax calculation.

Registered Bonds

In order to restrict the number of long-term bearer obligations and to maintain liquidity in the financial markets, certain obligations must be issued in a registered form in order to be tax-exempt. This applies to certain bonds issued after August 15, 1986. A registration-required bond means any bond other than a bond which (1) is not of a type offered to the public, (2) has a maturity (at issue) of not more than one year, or (3) is issued abroad with safeguards to ensure that the obligations are sold and resold only to persons who are not U.S. persons and that no interest or principal is payable to any U.S. person. Code Sec. 149.

Arbitrage Bonds

Arbitrage bonds are generally denied tax-exempt status unless a special tax or rebate is paid to the United States. Code Sec. 148. Arbitrage bonds are used for speculative purposes by state or local issuing authorities. A bond issue becomes an arbitrage issue if the proceeds are used to buy other obligations, frequently federal obligations, that have a higher yield than the state issue.

Employee Benefits

¶5101   ## FRINGE BENEFITS

In the United States today fringe benefits are a very significant part of the worker's compensation package. Compensation experts maintain that approximately one-third of a worker's gross compensation is composed of fringe benefits. From a tax viewpoint, there are two types of fringe benefits: statutory and nonstatutory. A statutory fringe benefit is specifically excluded by some provision of the law. An example of a statutory fringe benefit would be employees' accident and health plans, which are covered by Section 105 of the Internal Revenue Code. A nonstatutory fringe benefit is one not specifically mentioned in the law. Examples of nonstatutory fringe benefits are free parking for employees and an employer-subsidized cafeteria. In an effort to clear the air concerning fringe benefits, the Tax Reform Act of 1984 codified the tax treatment of a number of nonstatutory fringe benefits. Gross income specifically does not include:

1. No-additional-cost services
2. Qualified employee discounts
3. Working condition fringe benefits
4. De minimis fringe benefits (property or service, the value of which is so small as to make the accounting for it unreasonable or administratively impracticable)

Nondiscrimination rules, as set forth in Section 132, must be met for the above-listed fringe benefits.

No-Additional-Cost Services

The value of no-additional-cost services provided to employees or their spouses or dependent children by employers is excludable from income. This exclusion applies whether the service is provided directly for no charge, at a reduced price, or through a cash rebate of all or part of the amount paid for the service. Reg. §1.132-2. In order for the exclusion to apply, however, the employer must not incur any significant additional costs in providing the service to the employee (disregarding any amounts paid by the employee for the service) and the service provided to the employee must be one that is offered for sale to customers in the ordinary course of the line of business of the employer for which the employee is working.

For determining whether a fringe benefit qualifies as an excludable no-additional-cost service, transportation of passengers by air and transportation of cargo by air are treated as the same service. Thus, an employee performing services in the air cargo industry may receive air travel as a no-additional-cost service. This also includes passenger travel provided through reciprocal agreements with other airlines. Code Sec. 132(h)(8).

In determining the cost of a service, the employer must include revenue that is forgone because the service is provided to an employee rather than to a nonemployee.

EXAMPLE 5.16   Regional Airlines provides its employees with seats on flights it runs. Assuming Regional provides these seats only if, at the time the plane is ready to depart, there are empty seats for the employees to occupy, no cost is attributed to this service because of forgone revenue. However, if Regional permits its employees to book no-additional-cost seats in advance of a flight's departure and then does not offer these seats for sale to the public, forgone revenue would be attributed to the cost of providing this benefit.

In addition, an employer must include the cost of labor incurred in providing no-additional-cost services to employees for purposes of determining whether substantial additional costs have been incurred. However, labor cost is not included if the services are merely incidental to the primary services being provided.

The no-additional-cost services exclusion is available to employees of one employer for services provided to them by an unrelated employer (another employer not under common control) under a reciprocal arrangement between the two employers. For the services to qualify they must be: (1) of the same type, (2) under a written reciprocal agreement between employers, and (3) no substantial additional cost to either employer.

An employee working for an employer in multiple lines of business is limited to the line of business of the employer for which the employee works. For example, a company that owns both an airline and a hotel could not offer an employee of the airline a free hotel room. However, an important exception exists to employees who service more than one line of business. Therefore, the C.E.O. of the company or the V.P. for Finance could exclude fringes from both lines of business since they both render service to both businesses.

Examples of no-additional-cost services are excess capacity services such as hotel accommodations, telephone services, and transportation by aircraft, train, bus, subway, and cruise line.

Services that are not eligible for treatment as no-additional-cost services are nonexcess capacity services such as the use of a stock brokerage firm or a mutual fund to purchase stock or an interest in the mutual fund. However, if you receive nonexcess capacity services, the value of the benefit may be a qualified employee discount.

Qualified Employee Discounts

Certain employee discounts provided to employees on the selling price of qualified property or services of the employer are excludable from gross income. In order to be excludable, the discounts must be available to employees on a nondiscriminating basis. The employee discount may not exceed the gross profit percentage normally offered by the employer to customers. In the case of qualified services, the excludable amount cannot exceed 20 percent of the price offered to nonemployee customers.

EXAMPLE 5.17	Abigail's Cut-Rate had total sales of $1,000,000 for 2015. The cost of merchandise for this period was $500,000. Therefore, the gross profit percentage was 50 percent. The employees were offered a 60 percent discount on merchandise purchased from the company. In this case, the employees had to include 10 percent of the value of the merchandise they purchased in their gross income.

EXAMPLE 5.18	Mary Ray works for a computer manufacturer. She bought a portable computer from a local computer store and received the usual employee discount. Mary also received a one-year parts and labor warranty. Normally, the computer shop does not give one-year warranties on machines. Mary need not include the value of the discount in her income but she must include the value of the warranty.

The value of the discounts can be excluded from the income of officers, owners, or highly compensated employees only if these discounts are made available on substantially the same terms to each member of a group of employees which is defined under a reasonable classification set up by the employer that does not discriminate in favor of officers, owners, or highly compensated employees. Code Sec. 132(j).

Working Condition Fringe Benefits

The fair market value of any property or service provided to an employee by an employer as a working condition fringe benefit is excludable from the gross income of the employee to the extent that the employer can deduct the costs as an ordinary and necessary business expense.

The following are examples of working condition fringe benefits that would be excludable:

1. Value of use of an employer-provided car or plane for business purposes
2. Subscriptions to business periodicals by an employer for employees
3. Safety precautions provided by an employer for employees
4. Employer expenditures for on-the-job training or travel by an employee
5. Fair market value of the use of consumer products manufactured for sale to nonemployee customers but provided to employees for product testing and evaluation outside the employer's workplace

Qualified Transportation Fringe Benefits

Generally, transportation expenses of an employee are not deductible. However, transit passes provided to employees at a discount, not to exceed $130 per month for 2015, may be excluded from an employee's gross income. Further, employer-provided parking valued at up to $250 per month, even if it is chosen instead of cash, may be excluded from gross income.

Prior law afforded parity between transit passes and employer-provided parking. Again, this is one of the "tax extenders" taxpayers are watching.

De Minimis Fringe Benefits

De minimis fringes result when the value of the property or service provided to the employee is so minimal that accounting for it would be unreasonable. Examples of *de minimis* fringes include:

1. Typing of personal letters by company secretaries
2. Occasional personal use of the company copying machine
3. Occasional parties or picnics for employees
4. Traditional holiday gifts (small fair market value)
5. Tickets occasionally given out for entertainment events
6. Coffee and donuts furnished to employees
7. Occasional supper money or taxi fare due to overtime work

While many of these employee benefits are typically not included in an employee's gross income, in most circumstances, the employer is allowed a deduction for costs incurred.

Any cash benefit or its equivalent (such as the use of a company credit card) cannot be excluded as a de minimis benefit under any circumstances. In addition, season tickets to sporting or theatrical events, the commuting use of an employer-provided car or other vehicle more than once a month, membership in a private country club or athletic facility, and use of employer-owned or leased facilities, such as an apartment or hunting lodge, for a weekend are never excludable as de minimis fringe benefits.

¶5115 GROUP-TERM LIFE INSURANCE

An employee is allowed to exclude from gross income all of the cost of a group-term life insurance policy provided by an employer if the face amount of the policy does not exceed $50,000. Code Sec. 79. When over $50,000 of group-term life insurance is purchased, the cost of the premium for the amount of insurance over $50,000 must be included in compensation of the employee.

The $50,000 coverage limitation is eliminated and the total cost of group-term life insurance coverage in any amount is excluded from the gross income of the employee where (1) the employee is disabled, (2) the employer is directly or indirectly the beneficiary of the insurance, or (3) a charitable organization is the sole beneficiary. Some retired employees may also be entitled to a full exclusion.

For a group-term policy to be covered by Code Sec. 79, it must not discriminate in favor of highly compensated employees. It is perfectly acceptable to have a group plan where coverage is directly proportional to salary.

The cost of group-term life insurance provided to an employee during any taxable period for inclusion in the employee's gross income is to be determined under the uniform premium table method. Under this method the cost of group-term life insurance protection in excess of the excludable amount is determined on the basis of uniform premiums by five-year age brackets. The age of the employee for purposes of the age brackets used in the table is the employee's age on the last day of the tax year. The amount that must be included under the uniform premium table is generally less than the actual cost of the insurance. If the employee contributes an amount to purchase group-term life insurance, the amount is subtracted from what would otherwise be included in the employee's gross income.

EXAMPLE 5.19 Nine Lives Corp. purchased group-term life insurance for all its employees. The company pays 100 percent of the premiums for all employees, equal to twice the employee's salary. Otto Olson, age 52 and vice president of Nine Lives, earns $37,500 per year. Therefore, the company paid premiums on a $75,000 group-term policy. For an individual 50–54 years of age, the premium is assumed to be $2.76 (see Table 1) per $1,000 of coverage.

Total coverage	$75,000
Tax-free group insurance	50,000
Insurance subject to tax	$25,000
Cost per thousand dollars per year of insurance for 52-year-old	$2.76
Taxable income to Otto (25 × $2.76)	$69

Table 1. UNIFORM PREMIUMS FOR $1,000 OF GROUP-TERM LIFE INSURANCE PROTECTION	
5-Year Age Bracket	**Cost Per $1,000 of Protection for 1-Month Period**
Under 25	$ .05
25 to 29	.06
30 to 34	.08
35 to 39	.09
40 to 44	.10
45 to 49	.15
50 to 54	.23
55 to 59	.43
60 to 64	.66
65 to 69	1.27
70 and above	2.06

Source: Table 1, Reg. §1.79-3(d)(2).

EXAMPLE 5.20

Assume in Example 5.19, that Otto contributes 50 cents per thousand dollars of protection per year. The amount includible in his gross income is $31.50 ($69 cost of $75,000 coverage less employee contribution of $37.50).

A company may have a group term life insurance plan where the employee pays the entire premium. If the employees are charged a uniform premium, it is still possible that some of the older workers will be subject to tax on coverage over $50,000.

EXAMPLE 5.21

Alfred Ajax is 62 years old and elects group-term insurance of $100,000 and there are no employer contributions. His employer established a uniform rate of $.25 per $1,000 per month. Alfred would have to include $96 in his gross income. The cost of the coverage over the $50,000 group policy is $396 ($0.66 × 12 months × 50). Alfred's annual contribution is $300 (.25 × 12 months × 100).

PLANNING POINTER

The fact that premiums on group-term insurance for coverage of over $50,000 are taxable to the employee need not mean that such compensation is not valuable. Usually group plans are far more attractive than policies that can be obtained individually, and therefore, may be extremely beneficial as part of a total employee compensation package.

¶5125   ANNUITIES

An annuity is a contract that pays a fixed income at set regular intervals for a specific period of time. The amount of income depends upon the premium paid, the life expectancy of the annuitant, and the number of years payments are to be received. When income is received as an annuity under an annuity, endowment, or life insurance contract, the amount received generally consists of two separate parts: (1) a nontaxable return of the annuitant's investment in the contract and (2) a taxable amount representing a gain on the investment (interest). Code Sec. 72(a).

Under special rules for the taxation of amounts received as an annuity and paid out for reasons other than the death of the insured, the tax-free portion of annuity income is spread evenly over the annuitant's lifetime. This annuity method is not limited to payments that are to be received during the taxpayer's lifetime. It also applies to payments that are to be made for a prescribed number of years.

Exclusion Ratio Formula

The excludable portion of an annuity payment is the annuity payment times the exclusion ratio. The exclusion ratio is the "investment in the contract" divided by the "expected return" under the contract as of the "annuity starting date." These terms are further defined below. The formula for determining the excludable portion may be stated as follows:

$$\text{Amount of exclusion} \quad = \quad \text{Total payment for the year} \quad \times \quad \frac{\text{Investment in the contract}}{\text{Expected return for life of contract}}$$

The following example illustrates the computation of the exclusion ratio.

EXAMPLE 5.22

Makayla Perez purchased an annuity contract that provided for payments of $100 per month. She paid $12,650 for the annuity. Makayla's expected return under the contract is assured to be $16,000.

Annual annuity payments	($100 × 12)	$1,200
Investment in the contract		12,650
Expected return		16,000
Exclusion ratio	$\dfrac{\$12,650}{\$16,000}$	79.1%
Monthly exclusion	($100 × 79.1%)	79.10
Monthly amount to be included in gross income		20.90

Once the exclusion ratio is determined, one of two sets of rules is applied depending on the taxpayer's annuity starting date.

1. **Annuity starting date before 1987.** The exclusion ratio is applied every year there is a payment, regardless of whether the annuitant lives beyond the life expectancy. If this happens, the annuitant may exclude, over the life of the contract, more than the cost. On the other hand, if the annuitant dies at an age earlier than that of the life expectancy, the total of the yearly exclusions will be less than the cost.

2. **Annuity starting date after 1986.** The exclusion ratio is applied to payments until the total exclusions equal the investment in the contract. All later payments are fully taxable. On the other hand, if the annuitant dies before the investment in the contract is fully recovered tax free through the annuity exclusion, an itemized deduction is provided for the last tax year in an amount equal to the unrecovered portion of the investment.

Annuity Starting Date Defined

The annuity starting date is the first day of the first period for which an amount is received as an annuity under the contract. The first day of the first period for which an amount is received as an annuity is the later of (1) the date upon which the obligations of the contract become fixed or (2) the first day of the period that ends on the date of the first annuity payment.

EXAMPLE 5.23

Henry Li purchased a deferred single life annuity on January 1, 2015, payable in monthly installments on the first of each month, beginning August 1 of that year for the preceding calendar month. The August 1 payment is for the period beginning July 1. The annuity starting date is July 1.

Investment in the Contract Defined

The investment in the contract is, generally, the total amount of premiums or other consideration paid for the contract less amounts, if any, received prior to the annuity starting date that are excludable from gross income. Accordingly, if a taxpayer paid premiums of $5,000 for an annuity contract and had recovered $1,000 tax free as of the annuity starting date, the investment in the contract for purposes of the exclusion ratio formula would be $4,000. Once payments have started and the tax-free amount of each annuity payment is determined then any increases in annuity payments are fully taxable.

Expected Return Under the Contract

The expected return under the contract is limited to amounts receivable as an annuity or as annuities. If no life expectancy is involved (as in the case of installment payments for a fixed number of years), the expected return is found by multiplying the total amount payable from the annuity installments by the number of payments to be received. Code Sec. 72(c)(3); Reg. §1.72-5(c) and (d).

To determine the expected return under contracts involving life expectancy, actuarial tables prescribed by the IRS must be used (see Tables 2–6 following Example 5.30). The tables provide a multiplier (based on life expectancy) that is applied to the annual payment in order to obtain the expected return under the contract. This procedure can become quite complex since annuities may be based, variously, on one life, joint lives only, joint lives and continuing to the last survivor, and for life or term certain.

Single Life Annuities

To demonstrate the general principles note the following example of a single life annuity.

EXAMPLE 5.24

Marvin Mariner retires at age 65. His annuity contract provides for him to receive $100 per month for life. His total premiums under the policy had been $14,400.

Annual annuity payment	($100 × 12 months)	$1,200
Multiple from Table 2, Age 65		20.0
Expected return	($1,200 × 20.0)	$24,000

Marvin had an investment cost of $14,400 in the annuity and an expected return of $24,000. Therefore, the exclusion ratio was $14,400/$24,000 = 60%. Since he receives $1,200 a year, he may exclude from gross income $720 ($1,200 × 60%). Where payments are made quarterly, semiannually, or annually, the applicable multiple shown in Table 5 may be used.

If Marvin received his first semiannual payment six full months after the annuity starting date, the adjusted multiple would be 19.8 (20.0 – .2). If Marvin were to receive $600 six months after his annuity starting date, his expected return would be $23,760 ($1,200 × 19.8). See Table 5.

Joint and Survivor Annuities

Under a joint and survivor annuity two individuals receive periodic payments for life. Some policies adjust the amount of the payment after the death of the first annuitant.

EXAMPLE 5.25

Robert and Betty Moss purchased a joint and survivorship annuity contract. The contract provided for the couple to receive $200 per month for life. Upon the death of one spouse, the surviving spouse would continue to receive $200 per month. Robert Moss was 69 years old and his wife was 66. The cost of the policy was $36,825.

Computations:

Annual annuity payments	($200 × 12)	$2,400
Multiple from Table 3		22.9
Expected return	($2,400 × 22.9)	$54,960
Investment in annuity contract		$36,825
Exclusion ratio	$\dfrac{\$36,825}{\$54,960}$ = 67%	
Annual exclusion	($2,400 × 67%)	$1,608

EXAMPLE 5.26

Assume the same facts as in Example 5.25, except that when the first spouse dies the surviving spouse will receive only $150 per month. The cost of the annuity is $29,450.

Computations:

Multiple from Table 3, Ages 69 and 66		22.9
Multiple from Table 4		13.1
Expected return after first death	($1,800 × 22.9)	$41,220
Expected return differential after first death	($600 × 13.1)	$7,860
Expected return from annuity		$49,080
Cost of annuity		$29,450

Exclusion ratio $\dfrac{\$29,450}{\$49,080}$ = 60%

Therefore, while both individuals are alive they can exclude $120 ($200 × 60%) per month. After the death of one spouse, the exclusion will be only $90 ($150 × 60%).

EXAMPLE 5.27

Assume the same facts as in Example 5.26, except that Robert purchases the annuity and the annuity contract provides that if Robert dies first, Betty will receive only $150 per month instead of $200. The cost of the annuity is $29,450.

Computations:

Multiple from Table 3		22.9
Multiple from Table 2		16.8
Multiple applicable to second annuitant		6.1
Expected return (first annuitant)	($2,400 × 16.8)	$40,320
Expected return (second annuitant)	($1,800 × 6.1)	$10,980
Expected return from annuity		$51,300

Exclusion ratio $\dfrac{\$29,450}{\$51,300}$ = 57.4%

Therefore, while both individuals are alive, they can exclude $114.80 ($200 × 57.4%) per month. After the death of Robert, the exclusion will be $86.10 ($150 × 57.4%) per month.

EXAMPLE 5.28   Assume the same facts as in Example 5.27, except that Robert purchases the annuity and the annuity contract provides that if Betty dies first, Robert will receive only $150 per month instead of $200. The cost of the annuity is $29,450.

Computations:

Multiple from Table 3		22.9
Multiple from Table 2		19.2
Multiple applicable to second annuitant		3.7
Expected return (first annuitant)	($2,400 × 19.2)	$46,080
Expected return (second annuitant)	($1,800 × 3.7)	$6,660
Expected return from annuity		$52,740

$$\text{Exclusion ratio} \quad \frac{\$29,450}{\$52,740} \quad = \quad 55.8\%$$

Therefore, while both individuals are alive, they can exclude $111.60 ($200 × 55.8%) per month. After the death of Betty, the exclusion will be $83.70 ($150 × 55.8%) per month.

Employee Annuities

If the employer paid in all of the cost of the pension or annuity, the payments received by the employee are fully taxable to the employee. If the employee made contributions, the total amount that an employee may exclude from income is the total amount of the employee's contributions. The employee uses the exclusion ratio until the investment in the contract is recovered. Thereafter, all proceeds are included in income. Also, if the employee's benefits cease prior to the date the employee's total contributions have been recovered, the amount of unrecovered contributions is allowed as a deduction on the annuitant's last tax return.

The Small Business Job Protection Act of 1996 provides for a simplified method for determining the portion of an annuity distribution from a qualified retirement plan.

Refund Annuities

When payments are received under a guaranteed refund provision, the value of such payments reduces the investment in the contract. Obviously, where a refund has been received, an adjustment to the "investment in the contract" must be made so as to determine the excludable portion. The adjustment required to the "investment in the contract" is determined as follows:

1. Divide maximum amount guaranteed by the amount to be received annually and round off to the nearest whole year.
2. Refer to the actuarial table entitled "Percent Value of Refund Feature" to determine the appropriate percentage figure to be employed (see Table 6).
3. Multiply percentage found in the table by the smaller of (a) original investment in the contract, or (b) the total amount guaranteed.
4. Subtract the amount determined in Step 3 from the original "investment in the contract."

The following example illustrates the above provisions.

EXAMPLE 5.29

Joseph Jacobs, 65, purchased for $25,000 an immediate installment refund annuity, payable $100 per month for life. The contract provided that, in the event the husband did not live long enough to recover the full purchase price, payments were to be made to his wife until the total payments under the contract equaled the purchase price. Joe's investment in the contract adjusted for the purpose of determining the exclusion ratio is computed in the following manner:

Investment in Contract

Cost of the annuity contract (investment in the contract, unadjusted)	$25,000
Amount to be received annually	$1,200
Number of years for which payment guaranteed ($25,000 divided by $1,200)	20.8
Rounded to nearest whole number of years	21
Percentage located in Table 6 for age 65 (age of the annuitant as of the annuity starting date) and 21 (the number of whole years)	20%
Subtract value of the refund feature to the nearest dollar (20% of $25,000)	$5,000
Investment in the contract adjusted for the present value of the refund feature without discount for interest	$20,000

Monthly Exclusion

Adjusted investment in contract	$20,000
Annual payments	1,200
Multiple from Table 2, Age 65	20.0
Expected return ($1,200 × 20)	24,000

Exclusion ratio $\dfrac{\$20,000}{\$24,000}$ = 83.3%

Monthly exclusion (83.3% of $100)	$83.33

IRS Actuarial Tables

Gender-neutral annuity tables used to compute that portion of an annuity that is includible in gross income have been adopted. These tables apply to amounts received as an annuity after June 30, 1986.

Table 2. ORDINARY LIFE ANNUITIES—ONE LIFE—EXPECTED RETURN MULTIPLES			
Age	Multiple	Age	Multiple
57	26.8	72	14.6
58	25.9	73	13.9
59	25.0	74	13.2
60	24.2	75	12.5
61	23.3	76	11.9
62	22.5	77	11.2
63	21.6	78	10.6
64	20.8	79	10.0
65	20.0	80	9.5
66	19.2	81	8.9
67	18.4	82	8.4
68	17.6	83	7.9
69	16.8	84	7.4
70	16.0	85	6.9
71	15.3	86	6.5

Source: Table V, Reg. §1.72-9.

¶5125

Table 3. ORDINARY JOINT LIFE AND LAST SURVIVOR ANNUITIES—TWO LIVES—EXPECTED RETURN MULTIPLES

Age	65	66	67	68	69	70	71	72	73	74
65	25.0	24.6	24.2	23.8	23.4	23.1	22.8	22.5	22.2	22.0
66	24.6	24.1	23.7	23.3	22.9	22.5	22.2	21.9	21.6	21.4
67	24.2	23.7	23.2	22.8	22.4	22.0	21.7	21.3	21.0	20.8
68	23.8	23.3	22.8	22.3	21.9	21.5	21.2	20.8	20.5	20.2
69	23.4	22.9	22.4	21.9	21.5	21.1	20.7	20.3	20.0	19.6
70	23.1	22.5	22.0	21.5	21.1	20.6	20.2	19.8	19.4	19.1
71	22.8	22.2	21.7	21.2	20.7	20.2	19.8	19.4	19.0	18.6
72	22.5	21.9	21.3	20.8	20.3	19.8	19.4	18.9	18.5	18.2
73	22.2	21.6	21.0	20.5	20.0	19.4	19.0	18.5	18.1	17.7
74	22.0	21.4	20.8	20.2	19.6	19.1	18.6	18.2	17.7	17.3
75	21.8	21.1	20.5	19.9	19.3	18.8	18.3	17.8	17.3	16.9
76	21.6	20.9	20.3	19.7	19.1	18.5	18.0	17.5	17.0	16.5
77	21.4	20.7	20.1	19.4	18.8	18.3	17.7	17.2	16.7	16.2
78	21.2	20.5	19.9	19.2	18.6	18.0	17.5	16.9	16.4	15.9
79	21.1	20.4	19.7	19.0	18.4	17.8	17.2	16.7	16.1	15.6
80	21.0	20.2	19.5	18.9	18.2	17.6	17.0	16.4	15.9	15.4

Source: Table VI, Reg. §1.72-9.

Table 4. ANNUITIES FOR JOINT LIFE ONLY—TWO LIVES—EXPECTED RETURN MULTIPLES

Age	65	66	67	68	69	70	71	72	73	74
65	14.9	14.5	14.1	13.7	13.3	12.9	12.5	12.0	11.6	11.2
66	14.5	14.2	13.8	13.4	13.1	12.6	12.2	11.8	11.4	11.0
67	14.1	13.8	13.5	13.1	12.8	12.4	12.0	11.6	11.2	10.8
68	13.7	13.4	13.1	12.8	12.5	12.1	11.7	11.4	11.0	10.6
69	13.3	13.1	12.8	12.5	12.1	11.8	11.4	11.1	10.7	10.4
70	12.9	12.6	12.4	12.1	11.8	11.5	11.2	10.8	10.5	10.1
71	12.5	12.2	12.0	11.7	11.4	11.2	10.9	10.5	10.2	9.9
72	12.0	11.8	11.6	11.4	11.1	10.8	10.5	10.2	9.9	9.6
73	11.6	11.4	11.2	11.0	10.7	10.5	10.2	9.9	9.7	9.4
74	11.2	11.0	10.8	10.6	10.4	10.1	9.9	9.6	9.4	9.1
75	10.7	10.5	10.4	10.2	10.0	9.8	9.5	9.3	9.1	8.8
76	10.3	10.1	9.9	9.8	9.6	9.4	9.2	9.0	8.8	8.5
77	9.8	9.7	9.5	9.4	9.2	9.0	8.8	8.6	8.4	8.2
78	9.4	9.2	9.1	9.0	8.8	8.7	8.5	8.3	8.1	7.9
79	8.9	8.8	8.7	8.6	8.4	8.3	8.1	8.0	7.8	7.6
80	8.5	8.4	8.3	8.2	8.0	7.9	7.8	7.6	7.5	7.3

Source: Table VI A, Reg. §1.72-9.

Table 5. MULTIPLE ADJUSTMENTS

If the number of whole months from the annuity starting date to the first payment date is—

	0–1	2	3	4	5	6	7	8	9	10	11	12
And payments under the contract are to be made:												
Annually	+0.5	+0.4	+0.3	+0.2	+0.1	0	0	−0.1	−0.2	−0.3	−0.4	−0.5
Semi-annually	+.2	+.1	0	0	−.1	−.2	...	...	...	...	...	...
Quarterly	+.1	0	−.1	...	...	...	...	...	...	...	...	...

Source: Reg. §1.72-5(a)(2)(i).

Table 6. PERCENT VALUE OF REFUND FEATURE

Years—

Age	21	22	23	24	25	26	27	28	29	30
55	8	9	9	10	11	12	13	14	15	16
56	9	9	10	11	12	13	14	15	16	18
57	9	10	11	12	13	14	15	17	18	19
58	10	11	12	13	14	16	17	18	19	21
59	11	12	13	15	16	17	18	20	21	22
60	12	14	15	16	17	19	20	21	23	24
61	14	15	16	17	19	20	22	23	25	26
62	15	16	18	19	20	22	23	25	27	28
63	16	18	19	21	22	24	25	27	29	30
64	18	19	21	23	24	26	28	29	31	33
65	20	21	23	25	26	28	30	31	33	35
66	21	23	25	27	28	30	32	34	35	37
67	23	25	27	29	31	32	34	36	38	40
68	25	27	29	31	33	35	37	38	40	42
69	28	29	31	33	35	37	39	41	43	44
70	30	32	34	36	38	40	42	43	45	47
71	32	34	36	38	40	42	44	46	47	49
72	35	37	39	41	43	45	46	48	50	51
73	37	39	41	43	45	47	49	51	52	54
74	40	42	44	46	48	50	51	53	54	56
75	42	44	46	48	50	52	54	56	57	58
76	45	47	49	51	53	54	56	58	59	60
77	47	50	51	53	55	57	58	60	61	62
78	50	52	54	56	57	59	61	62	63	64
79	53	55	56	58	60	61	63	64	65	66
80	55	57	59	60	62	63	65	66	67	68

Source: Table VII, Reg. §1.72-9.

¶5140 ADOPTION EXPENSES

There is a limited exclusion from gross income of up to $13,400, for 2015, of adoption expenses per child, where such expenses are paid or incurred by the taxpayer's employer under a qualified adoption assistance program. This exclusion is available for all children, with or without special needs. To be eligible, the child must be under the age of 18. Qualified adoption expenses include ordinary and necessary adoption expenses, court costs, attorney fees, and other expenses incurred for the principal purpose of the legal adoption of an eligible child. This exclusion is available for tax years beginning after 1996. An exclusion for adoption expenses must be coordinated with the adoption credit. (See ¶9031.) The employer-provided adoption expenses are available to eligible taxpayers who have modified adjusted gross income below $201,010. The exclusion is phased out between an adjusted gross income of $201,010 and $241,010.

If the adoption involves a citizen or resident of the United States, then the expenses are excludable from gross income in the year incurred. If the adoption involves a non-U.S. child, then the expenses are excludable in the year the adoption is finalized.

EXAMPLE 5.30	Ron and Roberta begin adoption proceedings in 2015 for an infant through a U.S.-based agency. During 2015, they incurred $3,000 of legal fees. During 2016, they incur $2,000 of additional adoption fees, and on November 16, 2016, they finalize the adoption. The $5,000 in expenses were incurred through Ron's employer's adoption assistance program. Ron and Roberta have $80,000 of adjusted gross income in 2016. They may exclude from gross income the $3,000 in 2015 and $2,000 paid by Ron's employer in 2016.

¶5145   COMPENSATION FOR INJURIES AND SICKNESS

The law specifically excludes from gross income:

1. Amounts received under workers' compensation acts as compensation for personal injuries or sickness
2. Amount of any damages received (whether by suit or agreement and whether as lump sums or as periodic payments) on account of personal injuries or sickness
3. Amounts received for personal injuries or sickness through accident and health insurance which the worker purchased
4. Amounts received as a pension, annuity, or similar allowance for personal injuries or sickness resulting from active service in the armed forces of any country or in the Coast and Geodetic Survey or the Public Health Service, or as a disability annuity payable under the provisions of Section 808 of the Foreign Service Act of 1980
5. Amounts received as disability income attributable to injuries incurred as a direct result of violent attack which the Secretary of State determines to be a terrorist attack and which occurred while such individual was an employee of the United States engaged in the performance of official duties outside the United States (Code Sec. 104(a))

Note the above-mentioned exclusions from gross income under workers' compensation acts cover occupational injury and sickness. Nonoccupational injuries and sicknesses are *not* covered. Further, payments received in excess of applicable workers' compensation laws are *not* excludable. However, benefits received under an accident and health insurance plan due to taxpayer's contributions are excludable from gross income. "No fault" insurance disability benefits received under the owner's insurance policy are excluded from gross income as well.

EXAMPLE 5.31	Lucy Kim worked for Cleveland Inc. for many years and was covered by workers' compensation and an accident and health plan that she personally purchased. On April 15, Lucy was seriously injured when a light fixture fell and broke her neck. She collected $4,000 for medical expenses incurred and $3,000 from her insurance company for her lost wages. Lucy may exclude from her gross income both the $4,000 received for medical expenses incurred and the $3,000 from her insurance company.

Damages compensating an injured person for personal injuries or sickness are excludable from gross income. These damages are often excludable even when measured by the amount of wages that might have been earned but for the injuries. Damages received for nonphysical injuries are not excludable from gross income. However, an exclusion from gross income is allowed to the extent damages received are used to pay medical expenses attributable to emotional distress.

Punitive damages are taxable as ordinary income, regardless of whether or not they are derived from physical or nonphysical injury. This restriction is effective for amounts received after August 20, 1996, but does not apply to punitive damages awarded in wrongful death actions if applicable state law in effect on September 13, 1995, provides that only punitive damages may be awarded.

Damages received from actions based on age, injury to reputation, emotional distress, race, or sex discrimination violations are includible in gross income if the tort occurred after August 20, 1996.

EXAMPLE 5.32	Joan Jacobs was seriously injured in an automobile accident. The driver of the other car was charged and convicted of reckless driving. Joan received the following payments.

Reimbursement for medical and hospital expenses	$6,500
Loss of income reimbursement due to accident	2,500
Punitive damages	8,000
Payments for pain and suffering	3,000
Total payments received	$20,000

From the above payments, Joan includes the $8,000 received for punitive damages in her income.

The entire amount of damages received by the individual in connection with physical injuries or physical sickness are excludable from income. See Rev. Rul. 85-97. Where the awards by the court, or, for that matter, the damages received in an out-of-court settlement, are really for lost profits in a business, then the amounts are excluded from income if the award is received on account of a personal physical injury. When reimbursement for medical expenses incurred is received, the individual cannot take an itemized deduction for the same expenses. Further, if, for example, the taxpayer incurred medical expenses in 2015 and deducted them on the 2015 tax return and in June 2016 received reimbursement for the same expenses, the reimbursement must be included in gross income to the extent of the previous deduction.

¶5155 ACCIDENT AND HEALTH PLANS

Benefits received by an employee under an accident and health plan where premiums are paid by the employer are excludable from gross income if they come under the following conditions:

1. Permanent injury or loss of bodily function if amounts are paid on the nature of the injury and not on work time lost by employee
2. Reimbursement for medical expenses of employee, spouse, or dependents (Code Sec. 105(b) and (c))

To qualify the plan must not discriminate in favor of highly compensated executives, shareholders, or certain officers. Further, reimbursements are deductible only to the extent of actual medical expenses.

EXAMPLE 5.33	Bea Safe was seriously injured while working on the job in June 2015. During the course of the year she received the following payments on account of her injury:

Workers' compensation	$750
Medical expense reimbursement	6,000
Damages for loss of limb	10,000

In the example, all three items are excluded from gross income.

The premiums the employer pays to fund an accident and health plan for employees are not taxed to the employee. It is immaterial whether or not payment is for an insured plan. Further, the plan can cover the employee for personal injuries or sickness, the employee's spouse, or any dependents. Code Sec. 106; Reg. §1.106-1.

It does not matter if the employer contributions for health and accident insurance are purchased as a group policy or an individual policy. However, if the policy provides for benefits beyond health and accident insurance then only the portion of the employer's contribution associated with the health and accident insurance is excluded.

Amounts received by the employee for sickness or injury through the employer-paid health and accident plan are excluded from gross income as long as they are for medical care reimbursement. Amounts paid under the plan that are not medical care reimbursement must be included in the employee's gross income.

¶5165   QUALIFIED LONG-TERM CARE INSURANCE

After 1996, qualified long-term care insurance contracts are generally treated as accident and health insurance contracts. Amounts received as benefits under the contract may be excluded from gross income as amounts received for personal injury or sickness.

¶5185   MEALS AND LODGING

Meals furnished to an employee or the employee's family are considered compensation to the employee. However, employees may exclude the value of meals furnished by the employer if (1) the meals are furnished on the business premises of the employer, and (2) they are furnished for the convenience of the employer. Code Sec. 119(a)(1). For example, a waitress in a luncheonette works from 6 a.m. to 2 p.m. Her employer provides for her breakfast and lunch at the luncheonette free of charge. Further, she is required to have her meals on the premises. Under the circumstances, the meals are not income to the waitress. If the waitress had the right to free lunches on her days off, they would be included in her gross income.

The value of lodging may be excluded from gross income if (1) the lodging is on the employer's premises, (2) the lodging is for the convenience of the employer, and (3) the employee must accept the lodging as a condition of employment. Code Sec. 119(a)(2). Normally such lodging is provided for employees who must be available to respond to emergencies, as in the case of ambulance drivers. The required lodging must be a condition of employment to be excluded from gross income. If the above tests are not met, the value of the meals and lodging is income to the employee. Reg. §1.61-2(d)(3).

EXAMPLE 5.34   Dr. Bruce Lee works at Metro General Hospital and is required to be on the premises because he is on call from Friday at 6:00 p.m. to Monday at 8:00 a.m. Dr. Lee is not required to report the value of meals and lodging received while on duty.

Qualified campus lodging furnished by an educational institution to faculty and other employees may be eligible for exclusion from gross income where an adequate rental is charged. For rental to be considered adequate, applicable appraisal tests must be met. Code Sec. 119(d).

¶5195   CAFETERIA PLANS

Cafeteria plans are employer-sponsored benefit packages that offer employees a choice between taking cash and qualified benefits (such as accident and health coverage or group-term life insurance coverage). Code Sec. 125; Reg. §1.125-1. No amount is included in the gross income of a cafeteria plan participant solely because he or she may choose among the benefits of the plan; but, if the participant chooses cash, it would be includible in gross income as compensation. If qualified benefits are chosen, they are excludable to the extent allowed by the law.

The cafeteria plan must limit its offering of benefits only between cash and qualified benefits to employees. A qualified benefit is any benefit that is not includible in the gross income of the employee by reason of an express provision of the law. The only taxable benefit that a cafeteria plan may offer is cash. The menu of items in the plan might include such nontaxable benefits as group-term life insurance, disability benefits, and accident and health benefits. This is not meant to be an exhaustive list of benefits includible in a cafeteria plan. Other fringes which may be included are dental plans, vacation days, and qualified dependent care assistance. Unused benefits from one plan year may not be accumulated by an employee and carried over to succeeding years.

However, the following plans have been expressly prohibited from inclusion: qualified scholarships (Code Sec. 117), educational assistance programs (Code Sec. 127), or excludable fringe benefits (Code Sec. 132). An exception is made for employer contributions to profit-sharing or stock bonus plans under a qualified cash or deferred arrangement as defined by Code Sec. 401(k)(2). The beauty of the cafeteria approach to fringe benefit management is that the employer is allowed a tax deduction for providing the fringe benefits offered in the plan while the employee participants recognize no income if they choose the nontaxable benefits. Further, the employees select fringe benefits they desire and need and not benefits of no interest to them or benefits already available to their spouses.

Participation in the cafeteria plan must be restricted to employees. The maximum number of years that can be required by the employer of the employee before allowing an employee to partake in the plan is three years. Further, the rules must be the same for all employees. The plan must not discriminate in favor of highly compensated individuals, shareholders owning more than 5 percent of the voting power or value of the stock, or certain key employees. Unless the cafeteria plan meets the above-stated anti-discrimination rules, the highly paid individuals or shareholders must include in gross income the maximum benefits they are entitled to receive. However, the plan will remain intact for the participants not included in the prohibited class. Code Sec. 125(b) and (e).

The reporting requirements for cafeteria plans are quite stringent. Employers must report to the IRS the name and address of and the amount of benefits provided to highly compensated employees. Also, they must report the number of highly compensated employees, along with a list of the number eligible to participate in the plan, the number who actually participate, and the amount of fringe benefits includible in income, and the total cost of the plan during the year.

EXAMPLE 5.35	Ralph Jones works for Lorain Inc. and earns $30,000 per year. His employer has a basic cafeteria plan. Prior to the beginning of the benefit year, the employee must select the coverage desired. Ralph may choose among the following: $2,000 in cash or medical coverage up to $2,000 for the year, group-term life insurance, and day care facilities. Any unused benefit is forfeited. Therefore, if Ralph selects medical coverage and uses only $1,200, he forfeits the remaining $800. Why choose medical coverage over cash? If Ralph chooses to receive the $2,000 in cash, he will immediately be taxed on the amount. Then, when he purchases a medical plan, he would be using after-tax dollars. Usually, group plans are considerably less expensive than privately purchased plans. By selecting group medical coverage, Ralph recognizes no income; therefore, he is selecting a nontaxable benefit plan with before-tax dollars. Remember this risk—if Ralph does not use all of his $2,000 covered medical expenses, he loses the dollars.
PLANNING POINTER	Cafeteria plans prove quite advantageous for married couples. If both spouses work for companies having cafeteria plans, they should arrange their affairs so as to provide themselves with full coverage. Typically, married couples find themselves with two medical plans and no dental plan. Cafeteria plans correct this drawback and are of great benefit to families.

¶5201 EDUCATIONAL ASSISTANCE PLANS

Payments of up to $5,250 per year received by an employee for tuition, fees, books, and supplies under an employer's assistance program may be excluded from gross income. Code Sec. 127. Any excess is includible in the employee's gross income and is subject to employment and income tax withholding.

The Economic Growth and Tax Relief Reconciliation Act of 2001 extended the exclusion to include graduate education. The graduate education exclusion became effective after December 31, 2001. This provision applies whether or not the educational courses are work-related. The Tax Relief Act of 2010 extends these provisions through December 31, 2012. The American Taxpayer Relief Act of 2012 extends permanently the exclusion of up to $5,250.

Expenses disallowed because they exceed the $5,250 limit may be excludable if they meet the working condition fringe benefit rules under Code Sec. 132. Excludable assistance payments may not cover tools or supplies that the employee retains after completion of the course or the cost of meals, lodging, or transportation. Although the courses covered by the plan need not be job-related, courses involving sports, games, or hobbies may be covered only if they involve the employer's business. Reg. §1.127-2(c).

The plan must be written. The employer may pay the expenses directly, reimburse the employees for their expenses, or provide the education directly. The plan need not be funded and prior approval of the plan by the IRS is not required, but the plan must not discriminate in favor of highly compensated employees. Further, not more than 5 percent of the total amount paid out during the year may be paid to or for employees who are shareholders or owners who own at least 5 percent of the business. An employer who maintains an educational plan must maintain records and file a return with respect to the plan. Code Sec. 6039D.

¶5215 TUITION REDUCTION PLANS

Qualified tuition reductions (QTRs) made available to employees (and their families) of qualified educational institutions are excludable from the employee's gross income. A QTR is the amount of reduction in tuition for education that is furnished by an educational institution to an employee (or an employee's dependent children or certain other individuals) provided certain requirements are met. The tuition reduction must be for education below the graduate level. Code Sec. 117(d). However, under a special rule, tuition reduction benefits paid to graduate teaching and research assistants employed by qualified educational institutions may be excluded from gross income. Code Sec. 117(d)(5).

Qualified Tuition Program

A qualified tuition program (QTP), also known as a Code Section 529 Plan, is a program that allows an individual to purchase tuition credits or make cash contributions to an account on behalf of a beneficiary for payment of qualified higher education expenses. Generally for years after 2001, no amount is included in gross income of a beneficiary or contributor with respect to any distribution from a QTP used by qualified education expenses.

To receive this tax benefit the program must be established by a state government or agency. For years after 2002, they may also be established and maintained by eligible educational institutions, such as, colleges, vocational schools or other post-secondary educational institutions.

¶5235 DEPENDENT CARE ASSISTANCE PROGRAMS

An employee receiving dependent care assistance payments provided under an employer's written non-discriminatory plan generally may exclude such payments from gross income. Code Sec. 129. The exclusion for employer-provided dependent care assistance is limited to $5,000 a year ($2,500 in the case of a separate return by a married individual). Also, the exclusion is subject to an earned income limitation. Thus, an unmarried taxpayer may not exclude from gross income more than his or her earned income for the tax year, and a married taxpayer may not exclude more than the lesser of his or her earned income or the spouse's earned income. In applying the earned income test for a married taxpayer, the earned income of an incapacitated or student spouse is deemed to be $250 per month if one qualifying dependent is involved or $500 if two or more qualifying dependents are involved.

The employer's plan must be for the exclusive use of its employees and must not discriminate in favor of employees who are officers, owners, or highly compensated employees or their dependents. The purpose of the service provided must be to enable an individual to work. An employee who excludes the value of child or dependent care services from income may not claim any income tax deduction or credit with respect to such amounts.

Qualifying expenses include amounts paid for household services and care of the qualifying person. A qualifying person is any child under age 13, a disabled spouse, or any disabled person, provided that the qualifying person is a dependent of the taxpayer. The person who provides the care may not be the taxpayer's spouse or a person claimed by the taxpayer as a dependent. Further, if the taxpayer's child provides the care, the child must be age 19 or older by the end of the tax year.

The exclusion for employer-provided dependent care assistance may not be claimed unless the taxpayer reports the dependent care provider's correct name, address, and taxpayer identification number on the tax return. The exclusion may be claimed even though the information is not provided if it can be shown that the taxpayer exercised due diligence in attempting to provide this information. Code Sec. 129(e)(9). Similar information reporting requirements also apply to employers that provide dependent care programs for their employees. The exclusion for dependent care assistance programs must be coordinated with the dependent care credit. (Chapter 9)

¶5255 MILITARY BENEFITS

Qualified military benefits are excluded from gross income. Qualified military benefits are benefits that are received either in cash or in kind by members of the armed services or their dependents by reason of military service and that, as of September 9, 1986, were excludable from gross income by law, regulation, or administrative practice. However, the personal use of a car is not excludable as a qualified military benefit. Code Sec. 134.

Military retirement pay based on years of service and/or age must be included in gross income. Code Sec. 61(a)(11). However, veterans' benefits administered by the Veterans Administration are excludable from gross income. This includes amounts paid to veterans or their families in the form of educational, training, or subsistence allowances, disability compensation and pension payments for disabilities, and veterans' pensions.

TAX BLUNDERS

1. Harry and Rachel are both retired and have $33,500 of interest income and receive social security benefits of $12,000. This year they decided to redeem two Series EE bonds with accumulated interest of $3,500 each. This transaction boosts their provisional income to $46,500. Since they passed the $44,000 threshold, the proceeds from the sales of the second bond required them to include in gross income a larger portion of their social security benefits. Harry and Rachel should cash one bond in year one and one bond in year two.

2. Robert is single and collects social security. This year his provisional income exceeded $34,000. It was composed of $32,000 of interest income and $12,000 of social security benefits. In an effort to reduce his taxes, he sold several of his taxable bonds and bought tax-exempt bonds. This did not solve his problem. In the calculation of provisional income, tax-exempt interest income is included.

3. Orange County, Inc. provided their employees with a physical fitness center on their premises. They decided in a cost cutting move to close the center and buy memberships for all their employees and their families at the local fitness club. This was cheaper for Orange County, Inc. than maintaining their own facility. By closing their facility and buying memberships in a health club, the company could no longer treat the expenditure as a de minimis fringe benefit. The employees now had income for the cost of the membership.

KEYSTONE PROBLEM	Commonwealth Medicine Company, a hospital supply firm, has had difficulty attracting new personnel, particularly at the executive level. They feel that the company is competitive in the area of salary, but that total compensation packages should be examined more carefully. Of course, many factors will determine the final list. However, you are asked to examine one consideration in developing these packages, which is to reduce the tax impact on the employee. Therefore, you wish to devise a plan that will provide benefits for employees that will not be included in their taxable income. Include in your examination the concept of cafeteria plans. Also investigate the consequences of limiting the plans to selected levels of personnel.

SUMMARY

- Sections 101 through 139 of the Internal Revenue Code list "Items Specifically Excluded from Gross Income."

- A portion of Social Security benefits must be included in taxable income for taxpayers who meet certain requirements described by the Revenue Reconciliation Act of 1993.

- A tax exclusion is provided for interest earned on U.S. savings bonds used to finance the higher education of the taxpayer, the taxpayer's spouse, or the taxpayer's dependents.

- Certain employee discounts provided to employees on the selling price of qualified property or services of the employer are excludable from gross income, provided that the discount meets certain qualifications.

- Cafeteria plans offer employees a choice between taking cash and qualified benefits, which are any benefits that are not includible in the gross income of the employee by reason of an express provision of law.

- Educational assistance plans are subject to a number of tax status rules for determining exclusion.

From Gross Income to Taxable Income—Simplified

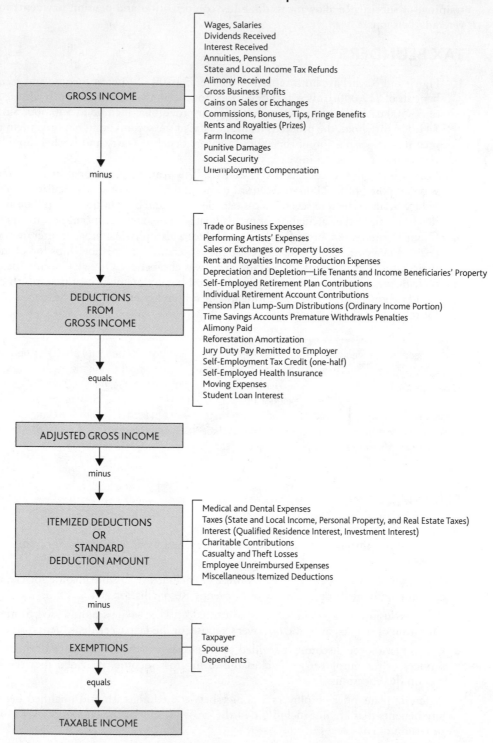

GROSS INCOME

Wages, Salaries
Dividends Received
Interest Received
Annuities, Pensions
State and Local Income Tax Refunds
Alimony Received
Gross Business Profits
Gains on Sales or Exchanges
Commissions, Bonuses, Tips, Fringe Benefits
Rents and Royalties (Prizes)
Farm Income
Punitive Damages
Social Security
Unemployment Compensation

minus

DEDUCTIONS FROM GROSS INCOME

Trade or Business Expenses
Performing Artists' Expenses
Sales or Exchanges or Property Losses
Rent and Royalties Income Production Expenses
Depreciation and Depletion—Life Tenants and Income Beneficiaries' Property
Self-Employed Retirement Plan Contributions
Individual Retirement Account Contributions
Pension Plan Lump-Sum Distributions (Ordinary Income Portion)
Time Savings Accounts Premature Withdrawls Penalties
Alimony Paid
Reforestation Amortization
Jury Duty Pay Remitted to Employer
Self-Employment Tax Credit (one-half)
Self-Employed Health Insurance
Moving Expenses
Student Loan Interest

equals

ADJUSTED GROSS INCOME

minus

ITEMIZED DEDUCTIONS OR STANDARD DEDUCTION AMOUNT

Medical and Dental Expenses
Taxes (State and Local Income, Personal Property, and Real Estate Taxes)
Interest (Qualified Residence Interest, Investment Interest)
Charitable Contributions
Casualty and Theft Losses
Employee Unreimbursed Expenses
Miscellaneous Itemized Deductions

minus

EXEMPTIONS

Taxpayer
Spouse
Dependents

equals

TAXABLE INCOME

CHECKLIST

Exclusions from Gross Income

Accident and Health Insurance Proceeds

Annuities (amounts contributed by taxpayer)

Awards for Noncompetitive Achievements

Bequests and Devises

Car Pool Receipts

Casualty Insurance Proceeds

Child Support Payments

Cost-of-Living Allowances Paid to U.S. Employees Stationed Outside the U.S.

Damages Received for: Personal Injuries or Sickness

Disability and Death Payments

Dividends on Life Insurance

Educational Assistance Plans

Federal Employees' Compensation Act Payments

Federal Income Tax Refunds

Fringe Benefits (group plans, premiums paid by employer)

Gains: Sale of Residence (up to $500,000)

Gifts, Bequests, and Inheritances

Group-Term Life Insurance (if coverage is up to $50,000)

Inheritances

Interest on Tax-Free Securities

Lessee's Improvements

Life Insurance Proceeds

Long-Term Care Insurance

Meals and Lodging (for convenience of employer)

Military Allowances

Moving Expenses

Old Age, Disability, and Survivor's Payments (Social Security Actor Railroad Retirement Act)

Payments to Beneficiary of Deceased Employee

Political Campaign Contributions (limited)

Railroad Retirement Act Pensions

Relocation Payments

Rental Allowance of Clergymen

Scholarships (limited amount)

Social Security Payments (depending on gross income)

Tuition Paid by Employer (job-related only)

Veterans' Benefits

Workers' Compensation and Similar Payments

QUESTIONS

1. How does a tax exclusion differ from a tax deduction?

2. An individual surrenders, for $20,000, an endowment life insurance policy in which he had a $15,000 investment. How much of the $20,000 of proceeds must be included in gross income?

3. What effect does interest on tax-exempt bonds have on the taxation of social security benefits?

4. How is the amount of Social Security benefits included in taxable income calculated?

5. On Series EE U.S. savings bonds, what different tax consequences arise from the two choices in reporting interest?

6. List several social justifications for issuing private activity bonds.

7. What is an annuity, and what features determine the amount of income associated with such a contract?

8. How is the excludable portion of an annuity calculated?

9. What five categories of compensation for injuries and sickness are excluded from gross income?

10. How are employer contributions to accident and health and group legal services plans treated by employees on their own income tax returns?

11. Describe the elements of a cafeteria plan and what are the beneficial aspects of such a plan for employers and employees.

12. How does a joint and survivor annuity differ from a single person annuity? How is the computation of the exclusion different for the joint annuity?

13. Name two types of fringe benefits, discussed in this chapter, that cannot be included in a cafeteria plan?

14. Indicate whether the following income sources must be included or may be excluded from gross income:
   a. Insurance proceeds for loss of finger
   b. Prizes
   c. Embezzlement proceeds
   d. Interest on all savings deposits
   e. Child support
   f. Interest on Series HH bonds
   g. Receipt of alimony by divorced husband
   h. Income produced from property acquired by gift
   i. Gifts and inheritances
   j. Scholarship grants for tuition
   k. Compensation for injuries or sickness
   l. Interest income on bonds issued by State of Ohio
   m. Life insurance proceeds from a group plan

15. Give an example of when meals provided to an employee by an employer may be excluded form income.

16. Mindy is a candidate for a bachelor's degree at a local state university. She received a grant that covered the following expenses:

Tuition	$4,000
Books and Supplies	1,000
Payment for Research Services	2,000

Mindy's tuition this year was $8,000. She spent the entire $7,000 award on tuition. What amount must Mindy include in her gross income?

17. Abigail received $6,000 from her employer as reimbursement for her expenditures on tuition, fees, and books while attending State University. Abigail is working toward a graduate degree in business administration. Must Abigail recognize the $6,000 as income?

18. If an employee is covered by a group-term life insurance plan that pays the entire premium of the policy, must the employee include the premium coverage in income if her salary is over $50,000 per year?

PROBLEMS

19. In January 2015, Leon McLeod received a gift of a beach cottage valued at $250,000 from his great-uncle who owned a number of such buildings. The cottage was rented each year to college students who occupied it during the school year. The annual net rental income received is $20,000 per year. The 2015 tax return of McLeod would include what elements of this transaction?

20. The Hightown Council refused to increase the town budget. Robert Read was laid off from work on August 4, 2015. Earlier in the year he had been temporarily disabled from a job-related injury and had received disability benefits. At year-end Robert Read and his wife have the following sources of income:

Disability income	$ 2,500
Unemployment compensation	5,000
Salary—	
January 1—August 4, 2015	10,000
Wife's salary	9,000
Supplemental unemployment compensation—	
employer provided	3,000

What amount of Read's family income was includible in gross income?

21. In 2015, Windsor Knott, an employee of the Victoria Tie Company, was seriously injured in the factory stockroom. He was hospitalized for 30 days and lost partial use of his left hand. During his hospitalization and recovery period, he received the following:

Workers' compensation	$ 9,000
Medical expenses reimbursement	10,000
Disability insurance benefits (insurance paid by taxpayer)	4,000
Accident and health insurance benefits (company policy benefits based on the degree of permanent injury)	9,500

Determine Knott's tax liability with regard to these payments. If the medical expenses had been deducted from Knott's 2015 tax return and reimbursement was received in 2016, how would the reimbursement be reflected in the 2016 return?

22. David and Renee Kimberly, ages 75 and 65, respectively, have the following sources of income:

Private pension receipts	$20,000
Social Security	12,000
Interest on bank deposits	2,500
Dividends from domestic corporations	2,000
Interest on tax-exempt securities	700

Their itemized deductions total $11,000. Compute their taxable income.

23. Hi Tech Accounting Services changed its fringe benefit package as of the first of this year. Employees are now eligible to receive group term life insurance equal to twice their annual salary up to $100,000. Harry's salary is $90,000 per year. Prior to this year employees received group term life insurance up to $50,000. Harry is 52 years of age and has adjusted gross income of $78,000. Does Harry suffer any tax consequences because of this change in policy?

24. Charles Adams, who is single, retired on March 3, 2015, at the age of 65. For the year 2015, he receives the following income:

Salary	$14,000
Interest income	2,000
Dividend income	1,000
Tax-exempt income	1,000
Social Security benefits	5,000
Net rental income	6,000

What amount, if any, of his Social Security benefits must Charles include in his 2015 gross income? What is Charles' taxable income for 2015?

25. Felix Boots, a 35-year-old male, is vice president of the Kitty-Lit Pet Products Company and earns $50,000 per year. The company provides paid group-term life insurance of twice the officers' salaries for all officers of the company. The cost of the policy to the company for Mr. Boots is $650 per year. How much of the $650 must Felix include in his gross income? If Kitty-Lit changed its policy so as to enable all employees to be covered at twice their annual salary, what would Felix have to include in his gross income?

26. A. Fluent, an investor in stocks and bonds, wanted to increase his portfolio but wanted to minimize his tax liability on the income from the bonds. He is presented with the following alternative investments: U.S. Series EE bonds, bonds for industrial development for mass transit, and qualified veterans' mortgage bonds. Which should he choose for his investment? Why?

27. Norm and Pat, a married couple filing a joint return, have the following sources of income:

Wages	$35,000
Interest income	4,000
Dividend income	3,000
Social Security benefits	9,000

Both Norm and Pat are over 65 years of age. Determine their taxable income.

28. Ron and Gayle, both over 65 years of age, have the following sources of income:

Consulting income	$36,000
Interest income	4,000
Tax-exempt interest	4,000
Social Security benefits	12,000

Ron and Gayle have itemized deductions of $16,000. Compute their taxable income.

29. Robert Provider purchases a joint and survivor annuity providing for payments of $200 per month for his life and upon his death for his wife, Robin, for the remainder of her life. As of the annuity starting date Robert is 68 and Robin is 66. The annuity cost Robert $36,000. Determine the exclusion ratio for the annuity.

30. On September 23, 2015, Mary Jones bought an annuity contract for $22,050 that will give her $125 a month for life, beginning October 30. Mary is 61 years old. Determine the exclusion ratio and the amount of the annuity to be included in Mary Jones's 2015 gross income.

31. Don Smith's wife died in January while still employed and, as her beneficiary, he began receiving an annuity of $147 per month. There was no investment in the contract after June 30, 2009. The investment in the contract was $7,938. Don Smith, age 65, received his first monthly annuity check as of February 3, 2015. Determine the amount of his pension to be included in his gross income.

32. Assume the same facts as in Problem 31, except that in January 2016, because of a cost-of-living increase, Don's annuity payment was increased to $175 per month. Determine the amount of the 2016 annuity payment to be included in Don's gross income.

33. Philip Southerly purchases a joint and survivor annuity providing for payments of $200 per month for his life and, after his death, $100 per month for his wife's life. As of the annuity starting date he is 70 years old and his wife is 67. The annuity cost Philip $28,000. Determine the exclusion ratio for the annuity Philip purchased and the amount of the pension to be included in gross income.

34. Peter Seaman, at age 45, purchased an annuity which will pay him $250 a month for life once he reaches age 65. He paid in $25,000. At retirement, he will have quarterly payments from the annuity. Peter receives his first annuity payment three months after the starting date (January 20). Perform the calculations and determine what amount he may exclude from gross income. What was the exclusion ratio? What was the adjusted multiple used to calculate the exclusion?

35. Beth, who is single, redeems her Series EE bonds. She receives $12,000, consisting of $8,000 principal and $4,000 interest. Beth's qualified educational expenses total $16,500. Further, Beth's adjusted gross income for the year is $40,000. Determine what, if any, interest income Beth must include in her gross income.

36. Linda Sue Carr worked for a large food brokerage firm. In January of this year she was terminated. After a court battle Linda Sue was reinstated in her job and received from the firm in November $7,500 in punitive damages. Must Linda Sue include the $7,500 in punitive damages in her 2015 gross income?

37. Steven Spokesman, a high school teacher in a local school district, was fired for publicly criticizing the local school district. The court ruled that Steven's freedom of speech had been violated and the school district was required to pay $24,000 in damages. Steven paid his lawyer $8,000 to defend him. Determine: (1) whether Steven must include the $24,000 in gross income and (2) whether he can deduct the $8,000 in legal fees?

38. Actress Nola Talent sued her coworker, actor Burt Dirt, for slander, citing his speech at a press interview where he labeled her a "floozy" and an "incompetent excuse for an actress." In her suit she claimed that as a consequence of this slander she not only felt degraded but was denied further acting roles. The court awarded her $100,000 in compensatory damages for damage to her acting career and $1,000 in punitive damages for the slander of her character. How is this reflected in her income tax return?

39. Robert Careless was injured while working on the production line on July 8, 2015. He received the following payments as a result of his serious injury:

Workers' compensation	$6,000
Medical expense reimbursement	2,000
Damages for personal injury	5,000

During 2015, Robert earned $16,000 in wages. How much of the above-listed amounts must Robert include in his gross income?

40. Roger Corby, a student, was employed seven nights a week at the Campus Inn as a desk clerk. He was required to be on duty from 11 p.m. to 6 a.m. and on call at various other hours, although he was rarely called after 12 a.m. His employer also required that he live on the premises and furnished him with a room free of charge, adjacent to the desk. Roger used the room as his permanent living quarters. Roger also ate all his meals free in the Inn dining room. Roger excluded the value of all these benefits from his tax return. What was the response of the IRS examiner?

41. On May 1, 2015, Anthony was in an automobile accident while on his way to work. Following doctor's advice, Anthony stayed home for six months to recover from his injuries. While at home, Anthony filed a lawsuit against the other driver. On December 1, 2015, the lawsuit was settled and Anthony received the following amounts:

Compensation for lost wages	$30,000
Personal injury damages (none of which was for punitive damages)	50,000

How much of the settlement must Anthony include in ordinary income on his 2015 tax return?

42. **IRS Adapted Problem.** Ms. Green is single and over 65 years old. She received the following income in 2015:

Interest from certificates of deposit	$3,000
Tax-exempt interest	6,000
Taxable dividends	5,000
Taxable pension	15,000
Wages from consulting work	9,000
Social Security	14,000

She did not have any adjustments to income. What is the taxable amount of Ms. Green's Social Security?
a. $7,000
b. $9,350
c. $11,000
d. $11,900
e. $13,850

43. **IRS Adapted Problem.** All of the following fringe benefits can be excluded from the employee's income except:
    a. Transportation up to $130 per month for combined commuter highway vehicle transportation and transit passes, and $250 per month for qualified parking.
    b. Holiday gifts, other than cash, with a low fair market value.
    c. Qualified employee discounts given employees on certain property and services offered to customers in the ordinary course of the line of business in which the employees perform services.
    d. Memberships to municipal athletic facilities for employees, their spouses, and their dependent children.

44. **IRS Adapted Problem.** In December 2015, Mr. Stone cashed qualified Series EE U.S. Savings Bonds, which he had purchased in January 2007. The proceeds were used for his son's college education. All of the following statements are correct concerning the exclusion of the interest received except:
    a. He cannot file as married filing separate.
    b. Eligible expenses include room and board.
    c. If the proceeds are *more* than the expenses, he will be able to exclude only part of the interest.
    d. Before he figures his interest exclusion, he must reduce his qualified higher education expenses by certain benefits.

45. On January 4, 2015, Ralph Stuart, an employee of Hard Manufacturing Inc., enrolled for the spring semester at State University where he is a candidate for an undergraduate degree in accounting. His employer reimbursed him for the following expenses: $2,000 for tuition, $600 for books and $100 for transportation to State University. What amount should Ralph exclude from his gross income in 2015?
    a. $0
    b. $2,000
    c. $2,600
    d. $2,700

46. **IRS Adapted Problem.** Mr. Hines received a $6,200 grant from a local university for the fall of 2015. Mr. Hines was a candidate for a degree, and was required to be a research assistant, for which services he received payment under the grant. The $6,200 grant provided the following:

Tuition	$3,600
Books and supplies	500
Pay for services as research assistant	2,100

Mr. Hines spent the entire $6,200 on tuition, books, and supplies. What amount must Mr. Hines include in his income for 2015?
    a. $2,100
    b. $2,600
    c. $3,200
    d. $3,600

47. **IRS Adapted Problem.** The following items were received as court awards and damages during 2015. All should be included in ordinary income for 2015 by the taxpayer who received them except:
    a. Compensation for lost wages due to slander
    b. Compensatory damages for physical injury
    c. Damages for breach of contract
    d. Interest on damages for breach of contract

48. Jose Reyes surrendered an endowment policy and received $50,000 from the ABC Insurance Company. Over time Jose had paid $35,000 in premiums. In addition, over time Jose had collected $5,000 of dividends on the policy. How much gain (loss), if any, must Jose recognize from surrendering the endowment policy?
    a. $50,000
    b. $15,000
    c. $20,000
    d. 0
    e. $10,000

49. Jacob is 69 years old and elects group-term life insurance of $200,000. The employer pays 60 percent of the cost of the life insurance plan; and employees pay at a uniform rate of $0.35 per $1,000 per month to cover the other 40 percent of the plan cost. How much, if any, would Jacob have to include in his gross income?
    a. $2,286
    b. $1,446
    c. $1,372
    d. $914
    e. $2,236

50. Ilana is a successful sole proprietor who owns a cosmetic store. She was injured in a car accident. The driver of the other car was found to be at fault for the accident. Ilana received the following payments:
    I. Hospital expenses
    II. Payments for pain and suffering
    III. Punitive damages
    IV. Loss of income from not being able to work in the cosmetic store
    V. Medical expenses

    Of the following payments, which one(s) is (are) includable in Ilana's gross income?
    a. I, and III.
    b. II and III.
    c. III.
    d. III and IV.
    e. None of the above.

51. **Comprehensive Problem (Tax Return Problem).** Rodney and Alice Jones have three small children, ranging in age from 5 to 10. One child is blind and needs special care. Rodney works as an accountant for a large CPA firm and has gross income of $45,000. Alice is a lawyer with a national law firm and earns $48,000. Rodney's parents are quite old, and he and his two brothers entirely support them according to the following percentages:

Rodney	45%
Steven	40%
Robert	15%

The brothers decide that in 2015 Rodney should be allowed to declare his parents as dependents.

Rodney's employer provides group-term life insurance at twice the employee's annual salary. Rodney is 40 years of age.

During 2015, Rodney and Alice receive the following dividends on their jointly held investments:

Dividends from Mexico Inc. (Mexican Corp.)	$700
Dividends from Widget Steel Corp.	150

They received interest income from the following investments:

Interest on State of Ohio highway bonds	$800
Interest on deposits in savings and loans	400

The Joneses have itemized deductions of $15,000. Compute their taxable income.

52. **Comprehensive Problem (Tax Return Problem).** Mr. and Mrs. Sam Morris retired on February 10, 2015, and call you in for tax advice. Both Sam and his wife Sarah have worked for many years. Sam is 66 years of age and his wife is 63.

Facts:	
Dependent child: Age 21	
Social Security Benefits	$9,900
Salaries:	
Sam (January 1—February 10)	7,000
Sarah (January 1—February 10)	5,500
Interest Income:	
Port Authority of N.Y. Bonds	300
Interest from Bank Deposits	1,400
Corporate Bonds	900
Highway Bonds of Ohio	100
Dividend Income:	
Microsoft Common Stock	4,000
General Electric Common Stock	2,000
AGA Ltd. of England	1,000
Net Rental Income	4,000

One of their tenants moved out on July 14, 2015, and Sam determines that they had damaged the stove, and therefore returned only $50 of their $150 security deposit.

The Morrises' daughter borrowed $10,000 two years ago to purchase a new automobile. She has made payments to her parents and on September 1, 2015, only $2,500 was still outstanding on the loan. On their daughter's birthday, they told her she no longer had to make payments.

Sam was Vice President of a very large corporation. As part of his fringe benefit package, the corporation purchased for him $50,000 of group-term life insurance. The corporation continues to pay for his life insurance even after retirement.

The Morrises' three children gave their parents a gala retirement party. Many friends and relatives were invited. Gifts valued at over $1,000 were received by the couple.

In October, Mrs. Morris entered a contest being run by a local bank. She submitted drawings for a bank logo. Her drawing was selected and she received $500.

Many years ago, Sam purchased an annuity policy for $9,000. Starting on March 3, 2015, he began receiving lifelong monthly payments of $60.

The Morrises' 21-year-old daughter is in college. She worked during the summer and earned $2,500. Interest on her savings accounts amounted to $500. Her parents paid for the college tuition of $4,000.

The Morrises have itemized deductions of $14,000.

Determine the Morrises' taxable income for 2015.

53. **Research Problem.** Larry Sorich, as part of his estate planning, assigned his $100,000 group-term life insurance policy to his niece. Larry's employer provided for only $50,000 of coverage; therefore, the niece paid for the premiums on the supplemental insurance. Larry did not include in gross income the premiums for the supplemental insurance. Larry's accountant challenged him on this arrangement. Who prevailed? See Rev. Rul. 71-587, 1971-2 CB 89.

Chapter

6

Deductions: General Concepts and Trade or Business Deductions

OBJECTIVES

After completing Chapter 6, you should be able to:

1. Name the four categories of deductions allowable to individual taxpayers: (1) trade or business, (2) production of income, (3) losses, and (4) personal.
2. List allowable deductions for losses.
3. Discuss criteria for determining whether taxpayer expenditures are deductible.
4. Explain common business deductions, such as advertising, salaries and wages, fringe benefits, bad debts, etc.
5. Identify allowable business deductions related to capital expenditures, such as depreciation, amortization, depletion, repairs, and improvements, etc.
6. Understand restricted business deductions for lobbying activities and business start-up costs.
7. Discuss allowable deductions for transportation, travel, entertainment, employee moving expenses, and student loan interest.

OVERVIEW

Deductions allowable to individual taxpayers fall into four categories: trade or business deductions (including business-related expenses of employees), production of income deductions, losses, and personal deductions. This chapter examines the general concepts of taxation underlying each of these categories of allowable deductions for individuals and includes an introduction to trade or business deductions, including allowable deductions for transportation, travel, entertainment, and employee moving expenses.

Section 162 allows as a deduction all the ordinary and necessary expenses paid or incurred during the taxable year in carrying on any trade or business. Although Code Sec. 162 appears to be all-inclusive in allowing all business expenditures as tax deductions, the requirements for the deductibility of business expenditures place well-defined limitations on business deductions. For this reason, a basic knowledge of allowable business deductions is of value to an informed businessperson.

With some notable exceptions, trade or business deductions are the same for all business taxpayers regardless of whether the business is organized as a corporation, partnership, or sole proprietorship. Although the income tax form used to report deductions is different, the allowable deductions generally are the same. This chapter is concerned mainly with business deductions as they appear on a sole proprietor's Schedule C, which is included as part of the taxpayer's individual income tax return.

Categories of Allowable Deductions

¶6001 ## CLASSIFICATION OF TAX DEDUCTIONS

Generally speaking, four categories of expenses may be deductible by individual taxpayers:

1. **Trade or business expenses.** Deductions applicable to trade or business including the business-related expenses of employees (Code Sec. 162).
2. **Expenses incurred for the production of income.** Deductions related to the production of investment income: (1) incurred for the production or collection of income; (2) for the management, conservation, or maintenance of property held for the production of income; and (3) in connection with the determination, collection, or refund of any tax (Code Sec. 212).
3. **Deductions for losses.** In addition to expenses incurred in trade or business activities, and investment (production of income) activities, taxpayers are allowed to deduct certain losses incurred on the sale or other disposition of property used in a trade or business activity or an investment activity. Losses related to property used for personal purposes are generally not deductible unless caused by theft or other casualty.
4. **Personal expenses.** Most personal expenses are not deductible. A number of exceptions, however, have been created by Congress over the years, allowing taxpayers to claim itemized deductions for a variety of personal expenses. Other personal expenses are allowable as "adjustments" to gross income, which have the same effect as deductions.

¶6101 ## DEDUCTIONS "FOR" vs. "FROM" AGI

Once the deductibility of an item is established, the tax formula for individuals requires that the deduction be classified as either a deduction *for* adjusted gross income (AGI) or a deduction *from* AGI (itemized deduction). In short, the deduction process requires that two questions be asked. First, is the expense deductible? Second, is the deduction *for* or *from* adjusted gross income (AGI)?

Classification is significant for several reasons. First, itemized deductions may be deducted only to the extent they exceed the standard deduction. Thus, a taxpayer whose itemized deductions do not exceed the standard deduction receives no tax benefit from his/her itemized deductions. In contrast, deductions *for* AGI may be claimed *in addition to* the standard deduction (or itemized deductions if greater).

A second reason for properly classifying deductions concerns the treatment of certain itemized deductions. Medical expenses, for example, are deductible only to the extent they exceed 10% of the taxpayer's adjusted gross income (7.5% if age 65 or older). Similarly, miscellaneous itemized deductions are deductible only to the extent they exceed 2% of AGI. Charitable contributions are subject to a ceiling, rather than a floor, based on AGI. As discussed in Chapter 8, depending on the type of property contributed, the charitable contributions deduction cannot exceed 20, 30, or 50 percent of AGI. Thus, classification of a deduction as "above the line" (i.e., "for" AGI) reduces AGI and may indirectly affect the deductible portion of other expenses which are deducted "below the line" (i.e., "from" AGI).

EXAMPLE 6.1 | Jamie Dean owns and operates a small business. During 2015, she paid property taxes of $20,000 and suffered a personal casualty loss of $10,000. She also had other itemized deductions in an amount above the standard deduction. Her adjusted gross income, before considering the above expenses, was $90,000. If the property taxes are deductible "from" AGI, she will be allowed to deduct $1,000 of her casualty loss (the amount by which the $10,000 loss exceeds 10% of her AGI). However, if she can deduct the property taxes "above the line" ("for" AGI), her adjusted gross income will be $70,000 and her deductible casualty loss will increase by $2,000 (10% of the $20,000 reduction in AGI) to $3,000. Deducting the property taxes "for" rather than "from" AGI reduced Jamie's taxable income by $2,000.

Aside from the effect on AGI, taxpayers also have an incentive to classify non-personal expenses as deductions "for" AGI rather than as miscellaneous itemized deductions in order to avoid the floor on deductibility of these expenses. If the taxpayer can properly deduct such expenses as business expenses deductible "for" AGI, the full amount of the expense will be deductible. If the taxpayer is required to deduct it instead as a miscellaneous itemized deduction, some or all of the expense will not be deductible, depending on the size of the taxpayer's AGI.

Adjusted gross income for Federal income tax purposes also serves as the tax base or the starting point for computing taxable income for many state income taxes. Several states do not allow the taxpayer to itemize deductions. Consequently, misclassification may also affect the taxpayer's state income tax liability.

Still another reason for properly classifying expenses concerns the self employment tax. Under the Social Security and Medicare programs, self employed individuals are required to make an annual contribution based on their net earnings from self employment. Net earnings from self employment include gross income from the taxpayer's trade or business less allowable trade or business deductions attributable to that income. Failure to properly classify a deduction as a deduction for AGI attributable to self employment income will increase the taxpayer's self-employment tax liability.

¶6115   DEDUCTIONS "FOR" AGI

"Above the line" deductions allowable in computing AGI (i.e., deductions "for" AGI) are governed by Code Secs. 62, 162, and 212. Deductions *for* AGI are listed in Table 1:

Table 1. DEDUCTIONS "FOR" AGI

Trade or business deductions (e.g., expenses of a sole proprietorship or self employed business person, including farmers, normally reported on Schedule C of Form 1040)

Losses from sale or exchange of business or investment property (reported on Schedule D of Form 1040, or on Form 4797)

Deductions attributable to rents or royalties (reported on Schedule E of Form 1040)

Certain employee business expenses (reported on Form 2106):

  Expenses that are reimbursed by an employee's employer (and included in the employee's income);

  Certain business expenses of reservists;

  Expenses incurred by a qualified performing artist (see below);

  Expenses incurred by an official of a state or local government who is compensated on a fee basis

Deductions for eligible contributions to Health savings accounts (HSAs)

Moving expenses, subject to certain limitations (reported on Form 3903)

Deduction for employer portion (50%) of self employment tax paid by self employed persons

Deductions for contributions to Individual Retirement Accounts or Keogh retirement plans

Deduction for health insurance premiums for eligible self-employed taxpayers

Deductions for penalties imposed for premature withdrawal of funds from a savings account

Alimony payments

Deduction for qualified payments of student loan interest and qualified tuition and fees paid during the taxable year

Domestic production activities deduction

¶6125   DEDUCTIONS "FROM" AGI—ITEMIZED DEDUCTIONS

As seen above, relatively few non-business expenses are deductible *for* AGI. Most personal expenses are not deductible, but those that are must be deducted *from* AGI as itemized deductions. In addition, most investment expenses, as well as most job-related expenses of employees, must be deducted from AGI, typically as *miscellaneous itemized deductions*. Miscellaneous itemized deductions, which are deductible only to the extent they exceed 2% of AGI, are discussed in more depth in Chapter 8.

The miscellaneous itemized deductions category is comprised primarily of *unreimbursed* employee business expenses, investment expenses, and deductions related to taxes such as tax preparation fees. Examples of these (assuming they are not reimbursed by the employer) are listed in Table 2:

Table 2. COMMON DEDUCTIONS "FROM" AGI
Employee travel away from home (including meals and lodging)
Employee transportation expenses
Outside salesperson's expenses [except that "statutory employees" (e.g., full time life insurance salespersons, certain agent or commission drivers, and traveling salespersons) are allowed to report their income and expenses on a separate Schedule C and avoid the 2% of AGI limitation]
Employee entertainment expenses
Employee home office expenses
Union dues
Professional dues and memberships
Subscriptions to business journals
Job seeking expenses (in the same business) or employment seeking expenses
Education expenses
Investment expenses, including expenses for an investment newsletter, investment advice, and rentals of safety deposit boxes
Tax preparation fees or other tax related advice including that received from accountants or attorneys, tax seminars, and books about taxes

With respect to the last item above, the IRS allows taxpayers who own a business, farm, or rental real estate or who have royalty income to allocate a portion of the total cost of preparing their tax return to the cost of preparing Schedule C (trade or business income), Schedule E (rental and royalty income), or Schedule F (farm income) and deduct these costs "for" AGI. Rev. Rul. 92-29, 1992-1 CB 20. The same holds true for expenses incurred in resolving tax controversies, including expenses relating to IRS audits of business or rental activities.

Trade or Business Deductions

¶6201

OVERVIEW—CODE SEC. 162

Two provisions in the Internal Revenue Code provide the authority for the deduction of most expenses: Code Sec. 162 governs the deductibility of trade or business expenses and Code Sec. 212 governs the tax treatment of expenses incurred "for the production of income." Numerous other provisions of the Code pertain to deductions. These other provisions, however, normally build on the basic rules contained in Code Secs. 162 and 212. For this reason, the importance of these two provisions cannot be overstated.

Code Sec. 162(a), which governs the deductibility of trade or business expenses reads, in part, as follows:

In General.—There shall be allowed as a deduction all the ordinary and necessary expenses paid or incurred during the taxable year in carrying on any trade or business, including—

(1) a reasonable allowance for salaries or other compensation for personal services actually rendered;
(2) traveling expenses (including amounts expended for meals and lodging other than amounts which are lavish or extravagant under the circumstances) while away from home in the pursuit of a trade or business;
(3) rentals or other payments required to be made as a condition to the continued use or possession, for purposes of the trade or business, of property to which the taxpayer has not taken or is not taking title or in which he has no equity.

Although Code Sec. 162(a) specifically enumerates three items that are deductible, the provision's primary importance lies in its general rule: all *ordinary* and *necessary* expenses of carrying on a trade or business are deductible. This is true, with some exceptions, whether the taxpayer is a sole proprietor, a partner in a partnership, or a corporation. The income tax form used to report the deductions is different, but the allowable deductions are generally the same. Typical trade or business deductions allowable to a sole proprietor and reported on Schedule C of Form 1040 are listed in Table 3.

Table 3. TYPICAL BUSINESS DEDUCTIONS ALLOWABLE TO SOLE PROPRIETOR— REPORTED ON SCHEDULE C OF FORM 1040
(Subject to various limitations)

Advertising

Bad debts from sales or services

Bank service charges

Car and truck expenses

Commissions

Cost of goods sold

Depletion

Depreciation

Dues and publications

Employee benefit programs

Freight charges

Insurance

Interest on indebtedness

Legal and professional services

License fees

Office expenses

Pension and profit-sharing plans

Rent on business property

Repairs

Supplies

Taxes

Travel, meals, and entertainment (limited)

Utilities and telephone

Wages

¶6205   GENERAL CRITERIA

An examination of the language of Code Sec. 162 indicates that an expenditure must satisfy four criteria to be properly classified as a trade or business expense:

1. It must be related to carrying on a trade or business activity;
2. It must be ordinary and necessary;
3. It must be reasonable; *and*
4. It must be paid or incurred during the taxable year.

All four of the above requirements must be satisfied or the expense is not deductible as a trade or business expense (though it might still be deductible as an itemized deduction from AGI). However, in some cases, expenses may not be deductible even where they do satisfy all of the above requirements. Other provisions in the Code often operate to prohibit or limit a deduction otherwise allowable under Code Sec. 162. For example, an expense may be ordinary, necessary, and related to carrying on a trade or business, but if it is also related to producing tax-exempt income, Code Sec. 265 prohibits a deduction. This limitation, and others, will be discussed later in this chapter.

¶6215   EXPENSE MUST BE INCURRED IN A TRADE OR BUSINESS ACTIVITY

Whether an expense is deductible depends in part on the type of activity in which it was incurred. A deduction is authorized by Code Sec. 162 only if the expenditure is paid or incurred in an activity that constitutes a trade or business. The purpose of this requirement is to deny deductions for expenses incurred in activities that are primarily personal in nature. For example, the costs incurred in pursuing "hobby" activities, such as collecting antiques or racing automobiles, normally would be considered nondeductible personal expenditures. Of course, this assumes that such activities do not constitute a trade or business. (The rules governing the deduction of "hobby" losses are discussed in more detail in Chapter 7).

The Code provides few clues as to when an activity will be considered a trade or business activity rather than a personal activity. Over the years, however, two criteria have emerged from the many court decisions addressing the issue. The first requirement that must be satisfied in order for an activity to be treated as a trade or business activity is a legitimate *profit motive*. *Doggett v. Burrett*, 3 USTC ¶1090, 12 AFTR 505, 65 F.2d 192 (CA-D.C., 1933). In other words, for the taxpayer's expenses to be deductible, they must be motivated by a genuine hope for a profit. For example, taxpayers who collect antiques or race automobiles can deduct all of the expenses related to these activities only if they are able to demonstrate that their activities were motivated primarily by the hope of producing income. If the required profit motive is lacking, expenses of the activity generally are deductible *only* to the extent of income generated by the activity.

EXAMPLE 6.2	Don Feen is an avid bowler. He is a member of several bowling leagues and often bowls in tournaments. During the past year, he won $1,200 in prize money from his tournament play. He spent $3,500 on travel, bowling supplies and entry fees for tournaments. Although he incurred a net loss of ($2,300) in his bowling activity, he does not mind. He does not bowl with the intent of making a profit. Accordingly, only $1,200 of his bowling expenses are deductible.

The second requirement imposed by the courts before an activity qualifies as a *trade or business* relates to the level of the taxpayer's involvement in the activity. Business status requires both a profit motive and a sufficient degree of taxpayer involvement in the activity to distinguish the activity from a passive investment. No clear guidelines have emerged indicating when a taxpayer's activities rise to the level of carrying on a business. The courts, however, generally have permitted business treatment where the taxpayer has devoted a major portion of time to the activities or the activities have been regular or continuous. *Grier v. U.S.*, 55-1 USTC ¶9184, 46 AFTR 1536, 218 F.2d. 603 (CA-2, 1955).

EXAMPLE 6.3	Charles Green owns multiple rental units, including several condominiums and townhouses. He manages his rental properties entirely by himself. His management activities include seeking new tenants, supplying furnishings, cleaning and preparing the units for occupancy, advertising, and bookkeeping. In this case, Charles' involvement with the rental activities is sufficiently continuous and systematic to constitute a business. *Edwin R. Curphey*, 73 TC 766 (1980). If the rental activities were of a more limited nature, they might not qualify as a trade or business. The determination ultimately depends on the facts of the particular situation.

EXAMPLE 6.4	Helen Thompson owns a sizable portfolio of stocks and bonds. Her managerial activities related to these securities consist primarily of maintaining records and collecting dividends and interest. She rarely trades in the market. Her activities are those normally associated with a passive investor, and accordingly would not constitute a trade or business under Code Sec. 162. *Higgins v. Comm.*, 41-1 USTC ¶9233, 25 AFTR 1160, 312 U.S. 212 (UCSC, 1941).
	On the other hand, if Helen had a substantial volume of transactions, made personal investigations of the corporations whose stock she was interested in purchasing, and devoted virtually every day to such work, her activities could constitute a trade or business. *Samuel B. Levin v. U.S.*, 79-1 USTC ¶9331, 43 AFTR2d 79-1057, 597 F.2d 760 (Ct. Cls., 1979). Again, however, the answer depends on the specific circumstances of the taxpayer's activity.

¶6225   EXPENSE MUST BE ORDINARY AND NECESSARY

The second test for deductibility is whether the expense is ordinary and necessary. An expense is *ordinary* if it is normally incurred in the type of business in which the taxpayer is involved. *Deputy v. DuPont*, 40-1 USTC ¶9161, 23 AFTR 808, 308 U.S. 488 (USSC, 1940). This is not to say that the expense is habitual or recurring. *Dunn and McCarthy, Inc. v. Comm.*, 43-2 USTC ¶9688, 31 AFTR 1043, 139 F.2d 242 (CA-2, 1943). In fact, the expense may be incurred only once in the taxpayer's lifetime and be considered ordinary. The test is whether other taxpayers in similar businesses or income producing activities would customarily incur the same type of expense.

EXAMPLE 6.5

> Pete has been in the newspaper business for 35 years. Until this year, his paper had never been sued for libel. However, this year, the paper was sued by a citizen whose alleged crimes were covered in a front page story. To protect the reputation of the newspaper, Pete incurred substantial legal costs related to the libel suit. Although the paper has never incurred legal expenses of this nature before, the expenses are ordinary since it is common in the newspaper business to incur legal expenses to defend against such charges.

It is interesting to note that the "ordinary" criterion normally becomes an issue in circumstances that are, in fact, unusual. For example, in *Goedel*, 39 B.T.A. 1 (1939), a stock dealer paid premiums for insurance on the life of the President of the United States, fearing that his death would disrupt the stock market and his business. The Court denied the deduction on the grounds that the payment was not ordinary but unusual or extraordinary.

A deductible expense must be not only ordinary, but also *necessary*. An expense is necessary if it is appropriate, helpful, or capable of making a contribution to the taxpayer's profit seeking activities. The necessary criterion, however, is rarely applied to deny a deduction. The courts have refrained from such a practice since to do so would require overriding the judgment of the taxpayer. The courts apparently feel that it would be unfair to judge *currently* whether a previous expenditure was necessary at the time it was incurred.

It should be emphasized that not all *necessary* expenses are *ordinary* expenses. Some expenses may be appropriate and helpful to the taxpayer's business but may not be normally incurred in that particular business. In such cases, no deduction is allowed.

EXAMPLE 6.6

> James Kincaid was the sole owner of Kincaid Corporation when it went bankrupt three years ago. A number of creditors lost significant amounts of money due to the bankruptcy. This year, James set up a new business and incorporated it as the Second Time Around Corporation. In order to establish good credit, James had the new corporation pay in full all the former creditors of Kincaid Corporation who lost money in the previous bankruptcy. James had no legal obligation to make these payments. The Second Time Around Corporation deducted these payments on its tax return as ordinary and necessary business expenses. James could argue that the payments made to the former creditors of Kincaid Corporation were necessary payments in order to establish credit for the new corporation, but he probably would have difficulty establishing that the payments were ordinary since they were not typical expenditures that would be made by other taxpayers in a similar situation. Example based on facts in *Welch v. Helvering,* 3 USTC ¶1164, 290 US 111, 54 S.Ct. 8 (1933). However, see *Harold L. and Temple M. Jenkins v. Commissioner*, 47 TCM 238, TC Memo 1983-667 for a case where the deduction was allowed in similar circumstances. Although the IRS disagreed with this decision, it chose not to appeal (AOD 1984-022, March 23, 1984).

TAX BLUNDER

In Example 6.6, James Kincaid made business payments that were, in his opinion, necessary business expenditures. They were not, however, ordinary business expenditures. If James had discussed his plans with a competent tax adviser before making the payments, he may well have taken a different course of action.

¶6235   EXPENSE MUST BE REASONABLE

The third requirement for a deduction is that the expense be reasonable in amount. An examination of Code Sec. 162(a) reveals that the term "reasonable" is used only in conjunction with compensation paid for services (e.g., a reasonable allowance for salaries). The courts have held, however, that reasonableness is implied in the phrase "ordinary and necessary." *Lincoln Electric Co.*, 49-2 USTC ¶9388, 176 F.2d 815 (CA-6 1949), cert. denied, 338 U.S. 949, 70 S.Ct. 488. In practice, the reasonableness standard is most often applied in situations involving salary payments made by a closely held corporation to a shareholder who also is an employee. In these situations, if the compensation paid exceeds that ordinarily paid for similar services—that which is reasonable—the excessive payment may represent a nondeductible dividend distribution. The distinction between reasonable compensation and dividend income is critical because dividends, unlike salaries, are not deductible by the corporation, although both are taxable to the recipient.

EXAMPLE 6.7	Joann Mason is the president and sole owner of Sign Corporation. During the year, Sign Corporation paid Joann a salary of $300,000. Sign Corporation claimed a tax deduction on its tax return for the full salary payment. The Internal Revenue Service (IRS), when auditing Sign Corporation's tax return, could argue that the salary payment to Joann was unreasonable in amount and that a portion of it should be treated as a disguised dividend. The rationale behind the IRS's argument is that dividend payments are not an allowable deduction for a corporation. It may be that by paying an unreasonably high salary to Joann, Sign Corporation was attempting to get a tax deduction for a payment which, in effect, was a nondeductible dividend payment. The same logic could also apply to unreasonably large lease payments and rental payments to stockholders in closely held corporations.

EXAMPLE 6.8	Larry Gill purchased a race car which he used to advertise his closely held company. In addition to driving and maintaining his own car, he also sponsored another driver. Over a two year period, his company spent about $25,000 and $40,000, respectively, maintaining Larry's race car and another $3,000 in each year to sponsor the other driver. The Tax Court ruled that such advertising was ordinary and necessary, but that the amounts expended on his own car were not reasonable – given the relatively small cost of sponsoring another driver, the $65,000 spent on his own car constituted an excessive, and thus unreasonable, expenditure for advertising. The excess of the amounts spent on his own car over those spent to sponsor the other driver were reclassified as nondeductible dividends to Mr. Gill. *Gill v. IRS*, 67 TCM 2311, TC Memo 1994-92, aff'd CA-6, 96-1 USTC ¶50,138.

PLANNING POINTER	In order to lessen the chance of a tax deduction being considered unreasonable by the IRS, the officials of a closely held corporation should substantiate the reasonableness of deductible payments made to owners of the corporation. The reasonableness of an expenditure could be substantiated by documenting similar payments made to shareholder employees by other closely held corporations of comparable size and type. If other comparable businesses are paying similar amounts, the reasonableness of the payments would appear more evident.

¶6245   EXPENSE MUST BE PAID OR INCURRED DURING THE TAXABLE YEAR

Code Secs. 162 and 212 both indicate that an expense is allowable as a deduction only if it is "paid or incurred during the taxable year." Use of both terms, "paid" and "incurred," is necessary because the year in which deductions are allowable depends on the method of accounting used by the taxpayer. Code Sec. 461(a). The term *paid* refers to taxpayers using the cash method of accounting while the term *incurred* refers to taxpayers using the accrual method of accounting. Accordingly, the year in which a deduction is allowed usually depends on whether the cash or accrual method of accounting is used.

Determining when other expenses, such as taxes and bad debts, are incurred is dependent on the nature of the underlying transaction, and the extent to which the expense may be recoverable. Deductibility also depends on the nature of the expense itself – for example, federal income taxes are not deductible at all.

Accrual Method Taxpayers

An accrual method taxpayer deducts expenses when they are incurred. Code Sec. 461(h) provides that for this purpose, an expense is considered incurred when the *all events test* is satisfied and *economic performance* has occurred. Two requirements must be met under the all events test: (1) all events establishing the existence of a liability must have occurred (i.e., the liability is fixed); and (2) the amount of the liability can be determined with reasonable accuracy. Therefore, before the liability may be accrued and deducted it must be fixed and determinable.

EXAMPLE 6.9

In *Hughes Properties, Inc.*, 86-1 USTC ¶9440, 58 AFTR2d 86-5015, 106 S. Ct. 2092 (USSC, 1986), an accrual method corporation owned a gambling casino in Reno, Nevada. The casino operated progressive slot machines that paid a large jackpot about every four months. The increasing amount of the jackpot was maintained and shown by a meter. Under state gaming regulations, the jackpot amount could not be turned back until the amount had been paid to a winner. In addition, the corporation had to maintain a cash reserve sufficient to pay all the guaranteed amounts. At the end of each taxable year, the corporation accrued and deducted the liability for the jackpot as accrued at year end. The IRS challenged the accrual, alleging that the all events test had not been met, and that the amount should be deducted only when paid. It argued that payment of the jackpot was not fixed but contingent, since it was possible that the winning combination may never be pulled. Moreover, the Service pointed out the potential for tax avoidance: the corporation was accruing deductions for payments that may be paid far in the future, and thus—given the time value of money—was overstating the amount of the deduction. The Supreme Court rejected these arguments, stating that the probability of payment was not a remote and speculative possibility. The Court noted that not only was the liability fixed under state law, but it also was not in the interest of the taxpayer to set unreasonably high odds, since customers would refuse to play and would gamble elsewhere.

Cash Method Taxpayers

Determining when a cash method taxpayer has paid an expense is generally not difficult. A cash method taxpayer "pays" the expense when cash, check, property, or service is transferred. Neither a promise to pay nor a note evidencing such a promise is considered payment. Consequently, when a cash method taxpayer buys on credit, no deduction is allowed until the debts are paid. However, if the taxpayer borrows cash and then pays the expense, the expense is deductible when paid. For this reason, a taxpayer who charges expenses to a credit card is deemed to have borrowed cash and made payment when the charge is made. Thus, the deduction is claimed when the charge is actually made and not when the bank makes payment or when the taxpayer pays the bill. Rev. Rul. 78-39, 1978-1 CB 73. When the taxpayer pays by mail, payment is usually considered made when the payment is mailed (i.e., dropped in the post office box). Rev. Rul. 73-99, 1973-1 CB 412.

Restrictions on Use of the Cash Method

Under the general rule, a cash method taxpayer deducts expenses when paid. Without restrictions, however, aggressive taxpayers could liberally interpret this provision to authorize not only deductions for routine items, but also deductions for capital expenditures and other expenses that benefit future periods (e.g., supplies, prepaid insurance, prepaid rent, and prepaid interest). To preclude such an approach, a number of limitations have been imposed on the cash method of accounting.

Provisions of both the Code and the Regulations limit the potential for deducting capital expenditures, prepaid expenses, and the like. For example, Code Sec. 263 provides that no current deduction is allowed for a capital expenditure, such as the costs of purchasing equipment, vehicles, and buildings. These costs must be recovered over the useful life of the acquired property, through the allowance for depreciation.

The Regulations—at least broadly—deal with other expenditures that are not capital expenditures per se but that also benefit future periods. According to the Regulations, any expenditure resulting "in the creation of an asset having a useful life which extends *substantially beyond the close of the taxable year* may not be deductible when made, or may be deductible only in part." Reg. §1.446-1(a)(1). In this regard, the courts agree that "substantially beyond" means a useful life of more than one year. *Martin J. Zaninovich*, 69 TC 605, *rev'd* in 80-1 USTC ¶9342, 45 AFTR2d 80-1442, 616 F.2d 429 (CA-9, 1980). Perhaps the simplest example of this rule as so interpreted concerns payments for supplies. Assuming the supplies would be exhausted before the close of the following tax year, a deduction should be allowable when payment is made. In regard to other prepayments, however, the application of this principle has spawned a hodgepodge of special rules.

Prepaid Rent

The 9th Circuit Court of Appeals' decision in *Zaninovich* above held that a cash method taxpayer's prepayments for rents or services may be deducted in the year paid when two conditions are present: (1) the period for which the payment is made does not exceed one year following the end of the current tax year, and (2) the taxpayer is contractually obligated to prepay an amount for a period extending beyond the close of the year. *Martin J. Zaninovich, supra*. If either of these conditions is not satisfied, advanced payment of rent is not deductible until the subsequent year(s).

EXAMPLE 6.10

> Rick Hatfield, a farmer, is a cash method calendar-year taxpayer. In 2015, he leased farm land for the twenty year period December 1, 2015 to November 30, 2035. The lease agreement provides that annual rent for the period December l to November 30 is payable on December 20 each year. The yearly rent is $24,000. On December 20, 2015, Rick paid the $24,000 rental for the next year. The prepayment is deductible because it is for a period not exceeding a year and Rick is obligated to pay for the entire year in advance on December 20. However, if the lease agreement required only monthly rentals of $2,000 each (instead of an annual payment of $24,000), only $2,000 would be deductible (representing the rent allocable to the month of December) because the remainder of the payment was voluntary. *Bonaire Development Co.*, 82-2 USTC ¶9428, 679 F.2d 159 (CA-9, 1983), *aff'g*, 76 TC 789 (1981).

Prepaid Insurance

Prepayments of insurance premiums normally are not deductible when paid. Instead, the IRS holds that this expense must be prorated over the period actually covered by the insurance policy. Rev. Rul. 70-413, 1970-2 CB 103. However, the "one year" exception noted above with respect to prepaid rent may also apply here.

EXAMPLE 6.11

> On December 15, 2015, Thelma purchased an insurance policy covering theft of her inventory. The policy cost $3,000 and covered the period 2016-2018. Thelma may not deduct any portion of the cost of the insurance policy in 2015. The cost will be deductible $1,000 per year in each of the next three years.

Prepaid Interest

Code Sec. 461(g) expressly denies the deduction of prepaid interest. Prepaid interest must be capitalized and deducted ratably over the period of the loan. The same is true for any costs associated with obtaining the loan. The sole exception is for "points" paid for a debt incurred by the taxpayer to purchase his or her *principal* residence. "Points" are a form of prepaid interest often charged to a borrower by a mortgage lender as a condition of making the loan. For example, a mortgage lender may charge 1.5 "points," or 1.5 percent of the amount being borrowed, as a fee to extend a mortgage loan. Points paid by a taxpayer to obtain a mortgage to *purchase* his or her *principal* residence can be deducted in the year paid. This treatment does not apply to points paid on a loan incurred to refinance the taxpayer's existing mortgage. The IRS has ruled that points paid on refinancing must be capitalized and amortized over the life of the loan the same as other types of prepaid interest. Rev. Rul. 87-22, 1987-1 CB 146.

EXAMPLE 6.12

> Karen applied for a loan for the purchase of a new house costing $200,000. The bank agreed to make her a loan of 80% of the purchase price, or $160,000 (80% of $200,000) for thirty years at a cost of two points (two percentage "points" of the loan obtained). Thus, she must pay $4,000 (2% of $200,000) to obtain the loan. Assuming it is established business practice in her area to charge points in consideration of the loan, the $4,000 in points (prepaid interest) are deductible. However, if the house is not Karen's principal residence, then the points must be deducted ratably (amortized) over the 30 year loan period. Similarly, if the loan had been incurred to *refinance* the original mortgage on the home, the points would not be currently deductible, but would be amortized over the term of the loan (30 years in this case).

Other Prepayments

Perhaps the Service's current view of the proper treatment of most prepayments is best captured in a ruling concerning prepayment for animal feed. In this ruling, the taxpayer, a cattle rancher, purchased a substantial amount of feed prior to the year in which it would be used. The purchase was made in advance because the price was low due to a depressed market. The IRS granted a deduction for the prepayment because there was a business purpose for the advanced payment, the payment was not merely a deposit, and it did not materially distort income. Based on this ruling and related cases, prepayments normally should be deductible if the asset will be consumed by the close of the following year, there is a business purpose for the expenditure, and there is no material distortion of income. Rev. Rul. 79-229, 1979-2 CB 210.

Taxes

Most taxes incurred by a trade or business (with the exception of federal income taxes) are deductible for tax purposes as business expenses. Federal income taxes are not deductible on the federal income tax return since the return is being prepared to compute the amount of federal income taxes due.

Payroll taxes paid by an employer are fully deductible, but taxes withheld from employee wages such as federal, state, and local income taxes payable and F.I.C.A. taxes are not. The latter type of tax expense (withholdings from employees' wages) is not *incurred* by the employer, but by the employee. Accordingly, the employer is not allowed a deduction for these expenditures.

Similarly, while property taxes are generally deductible by the taxpayer who pays them, if business property is sold during the year, the property taxes related to the property must be allocated between the buyer and the seller based on the number of days during the tax year that each party held the property. Code Sec. 164(d). The seller is treated as paying the tax up to, but not including, the date of sale. This allocation is required regardless of which party actually pays the property tax and regardless of the method of accounting used by the two parties. The rationale is that the buyer *incurs* the property tax for the period during which he or she owns the property. To the extent that tax has previously been paid by the seller, a portion of the purchase price paid by the buyer is treated as compensation for the buyer's share of the previously paid property tax. The seller, having been reimbursed for this portion of the property taxes, is allowed to deduct only the portion attributable to the period during which he or she owned the property, and the buyer deducts the rest.

EXAMPLE 6.13

On October 1, Joe purchased a tract of land from Kelly for $138,000. Kelly had previously paid annual property taxes on the land in the amount of $8,030. Assuming a 365 day year, Joe has owned the land for 92 days (Oct. 1 through Dec. 31), and Kelly for 273 days. Thus, $2,024 of the property tax for the year of the sale is allocable to Joe (92 days/365 days). Joe, not Kelly, will be allowed to claim a deduction for this portion of the annual property taxes, and the deemed selling price of the land will be $135,976 ($138,000 - $2,024). Note that while Kelly will be allowed to deduct only $6,006 of the property taxes paid during the year (the part deemed to be "incurred" by her), she will also be deemed to have sold the land for only $135,976 (rather than the $138,000 actual selling price), reducing any gain she may recognize on the sale by an amount equal to the foregone property tax deduction.

Bad Debts

The determination of whether a bad debt loss has been incurred can be difficult. Several issues must be considered. First, the taxpayer must be able to establish that an actual debt existed. This is generally rather easy for business debts, but can be quite difficult for debts between family members, friends, or other related parties. If the nature of the underlying transaction is not a valid debt – for example, if the taxpayer did not really intend to collect the debt, or if collection was to occur only in the event that the borrower was able to repay the purported loan, the transaction will be recharacterized as a gift rather than a loan and no deduction will be allowed.

The second issue to be considered is the amount of the loss, if any, actually incurred. Generally speaking, the amount of a bad debt deduction is limited to the adjusted basis of the debt in the hands of the taxpayer. For a business taxpayer using the cash method of accounting, the adjusted basis of business accounts receivable is normally zero; the receivables have not been recognized for tax purposes because income is recorded only when cash is collected. Since the income from the receivables has yet to be realized, no loss is incurred in the event the receivables are not collected.

EXAMPLE 6.14

On September 16, 2015, Roscoe Accounting Services, a cash method taxpayer, sells $300 of accounting services to Ron Ranger on credit. One month later, Ron is declared bankrupt and cannot pay any of the $300 debt to Roscoe. Since Roscoe uses the cash method of accounting, income is not recognized for tax purposes until cash is collected and, therefore, its accounts receivable have a zero basis. Roscoe is not entitled to a bad debt deduction for the $300 bad account receivable since the receivable has a zero basis for tax purposes.

Finally, assuming the taxpayer has a tax basis in a valid debt, the taxpayer must be able to establish that the debt is not collectible. A business bad debt deduction can be taken by proving only partial worthlessness of a debt while full worthlessness of a debt must be proven in order to claim a nonbusiness bad debt deduction. Worthlessness of a debt is established by reviewing the facts existing in each case. Reg. §1.166-2(b). The debtor's bankruptcy, death of the debtor, or unsuccessful court action against the debtor to collect the debt may be indications of the worthlessness of a debt. A taxpayer does not necessarily have to take legal action against a debtor to prove worthlessness of a debt. The facts may suggest that legal action would not have resulted in recovery of any of the debt.

Business Bad Debts

The deductibility of a bad debt further depends on the character of the underlying debt. Generally speaking, business bad debts are fully deductible by the taxpayer from gross income as an ordinary business expense in the year they become either partially or wholly worthless. (If the debt is not wholly worthless, only the amount not expected to be collected can be deducted.) Non-business bad debts, in contrast, can be deducted for tax purposes only if the debt is completely worthless. Moreover, worthlessness of a nonbusiness bad debt is always treated as a short-term capital loss and is subject to the $3,000 limitation applicable to the deduction for net capital losses (discussed in greater detail in Chapter 12). Code Sec. 166(d)(1)(B).

In contrast, when a taxpayer can demonstrate that a business debt has become wholly or partially worthless, the taxpayer can claim a deduction from *gross* income (i.e., a deduction "for" AGI) for the full amount not expected to be collected. A business debt is a debt (1) created or acquired in connection with the taxpayer's trade or business, or (2) the worthlessness of which has been incurred in the taxpayer's trade or business. Reg. §1.166-5(b). Amounts advanced to a corporation in exchange for a bond, debenture, note or other evidence of indebtedness are investments, rather than business debts. Accordingly, the partial or total worthlessness of such investments is *not* deductible as a business bad debt (although it may be deductible as a nonbusiness bad debt). Similarly, amounts advanced to a corporation by a shareholder to be used by the corporation to pay its debts are not business loans, regardless of how they are structured.

EXAMPLE 6.15	Susan Sanford owes $1,000 to the Sioto Lumber Company, an accrual method taxpayer, for lumber purchased from the company. Sioto Lumber Co. estimates that it will eventually collect from Susan only $300 of the $1,000 debt. Since the debt to Sioto is a business debt, Sioto is entitled to a $700 bad debt deduction this year for partial worthlessness of the business debt.

A cash method taxpayer can deduct a business bad debt only if an actual cash loss has been sustained or if the amount to be deducted was previously included in income. Nearly all accrual method taxpayers must use the specific charge-off method to deduct business bad debts; the reserve method for computing and deducting bad debts may be used only by small banks and thrift institutions. Under the specific charge-off method, when a specific debt, or portion thereof, becomes worthless, it is written off as an ordinary deduction for tax purposes.

Since the tax treatment accorded business bad debts and nonbusiness bad debts differs, the taxpayer must show that the dominant motivation in making the loan was business related in order to obtain the more favorable tax treatment. Specific charge-off is based on actual worthlessness and is not applicable merely because the taxpayer gives up attempts to collect. A worthless debt arising from unpaid rent, interest, or a similar item is not deductible unless the income that such item represents has been reported for income tax purposes by a taxpayer using the accrual method of accounting.

Nonbusiness Bad Debts

Nonbusiness bad debts are debts that are not created or acquired in connection with a trade or business. Loans to relatives and friends are the most common type of nonbusiness debt. Nonbusiness bad debts can be deducted for tax purposes only if full worthlessness of the debt has been determined and then only by the specific charge-off method. The deduction is allowed in the year when full worthlessness takes place, regardless of how old the debt is. In contrast to a business bad debt which is deductible as an ordinary loss in the year incurred, a nonbusiness bad debt deduction is always treated as a short-term capital loss and is subject to the $3,000 limitation applicable to the deduction for capital losses (discussed in greater detail in Chapter 12). Code Sec. 166(d)(1)(B).

Expenses Incurred for the Production of Income

¶6301   CODE SEC. 212—PRODUCTION OF INCOME OR PROTECTION OF ASSETS

Prior to enactment of Code Sec. 212, many investment related expenses were not deductible because the activities did not rise to the level of a trade or business activity. Congress enacted Code Sec. 212 in 1942, allowing for the deduction of expenses related to the "production or collection of income." As a result, the question of deductibility (assuming the other requirements discussed above are met) is effectively reduced to a single important question: Is the expense related to an activity engaged in for profit?

Production of income expenses are deductible if they are incurred:

1. For the production or collection of income;
2. For the management, conservation, or maintenance of property held for the production of income; or
3. In connection with the determination, collection, or refund of any tax.

Generally speaking, expenses related to the production of income consist primarily of those expenses incurred in rental and investment activities as well as tax planning and compliance expenses. To be deductible, such expenses must be ordinary, necessary, and reasonable. Unlike trade or business expenses, expenses related to the production of income are generally deductible as miscellaneous itemized deductions with the exception of rents and royalty expenses which are deductible for AGI on Schedule E. Code Sec. 62(a)(4).

¶6315   INVESTMENT EXPENSE DEDUCTIONS

Typical investment expenses which are deductible include safe deposit box rentals, rent and royalty expenses, investment counsel fees, subscriptions to investment-related journals, newspapers, and other publications, investment custodial fees, legal and accounting fees related to investments, and investment-related clerical fees and office rent. Code Sec. 212. The Code also allows an annual investment-related interest expense deduction which is limited to net investment income. This deduction is discussed in Chapter 8. Code Sec. 163(d).

¶6325   TAX PLANNING AND COMPLIANCE EXPENSES

All expenses incurred by individual taxpayers in connection with the determination, collection, or refund of any tax are deductible under Code Sec. 212 as nonbusiness expenses. Deductions in this area apply to tax planning expenses and tax compliance expenses of individuals and are properly classified as miscellaneous itemized deductions on the tax return. Businesses classify tax planning and compliance expenses as trade or business deductions. The cost of having a tax return prepared by a CPA or tax service is deductible as well as the legal fees incurred in contesting a tax liability in court. Deductions for tax planning and compliance expenses are not limited to the income tax area but also extend to gift and estate tax returns. Fees paid for tax advice regarding estate planning as well as divorce proceedings are also deductible. Rev. Rul. 72-545, 1972-2 CB 179.

TAX BLUNDER

In Example 6.17, assume that Barbara receives a bill from her lawyer that states "Legal Services — $3,000." If she does not request a breakout of the portion of the legal fee relating to tax planning advice, Barbara will lose the opportunity for a tax planning advice deduction on her tax return.

Deductions for Losses

¶6401 CODE SEC. 165

Code Sec. 165 establishes the general framework governing the deductibility of losses. This statute permits a deduction for the following categories of losses so long as they are not compensated for by insurance or otherwise (for example by settlement of a lawsuit):

1. Losses incurred in a trade or business (deductible without limitation);
2. Losses incurred in transactions entered into for profit, though not connected with a trade or business (deductible as capital losses); and
3. Losses of property not connected with a trade or business if such losses arise from fire, storm, shipwreck, or other casualty, or from theft (deductible as itemized deductions, subject to certain limitations discussed in Chapter 8).

Losses cannot be deducted unless attributable to a closed and completed transaction. Mere declines in value or other unrealized losses cannot be deducted. Normally, for the loss to qualify as a deduction, the property must be sold, abandoned, or scrapped. In some cases, (e.g., stock in a bankrupt company), a taxpayer may not be able to sell property because it has become completely worthless. In such cases, if the taxpayer can demonstrate the worthlessness of the property, a deduction will be allowed for the loss. The amount of the loss for tax purposes cannot exceed the taxpayer's basis in the property.

Note that personal losses—other than those attributable to a casualty or theft—are not deductible. For example, a loss incurred on the sale of a personal residence is not deductible.

EXAMPLE 6.18   Janet owns 100 shares of Clinton Corporation stock which she purchased on January 4, 2015, for $84 per share. On December 31, 2015, Clinton Corporation stock was selling at $52 per share. Janet cannot deduct the $32 per share decline in value on her 2015 tax return since it is an unrealized loss. Janet would have to sell her stock before year end in order to recognize a loss for tax purposes.

Examples of losses that can be deducted by individual taxpayers are listed in Table 4. Tax losses are discussed in greater detail in Chapter 7.

Table 4. LOSSES DEDUCTIBLE ON AN INDIVIDUAL'S TAX RETURN (SUBJECT TO VARIOUS LIMITATIONS)
Losses deductible for AGI
Business net operating loss carryback or carryforward
Business or investment-related casualty or theft loss
Loss on sale or exchange of business property
Loss on sale or exchange of investment property
Worthless securities
Losses deductible from AGI
Gambling losses but only to extent of gambling winnings
Personal casualty or theft loss

Other Allowable Deductions "For" AGI

¶6505   **BUSINESS INVESTIGATION START-UP AND ORGANIZATIONAL COSTS**

Business investigation expenses are those costs of seeking and reviewing prospective businesses prior to reaching a decision to acquire or enter any business. For example, expenses incurred to analyze potential markets, products, the availability of workers, transportation facilities, etc. before entering into a new business would constitute business investigation expenses. Once the taxpayer has decided to enter the new business, additional costs may be incurred for pre-opening advertising, employee training, lining up distributors, suppliers, or potential customers, legal and accounting fees, etc. These expenses, incurred after the decision to acquire a business, but before such business actually begins operations, are called "start-up" expenses.

For many years, the deductibility of expenses of business investigation and start up turned solely on whether the taxpayer was "carrying on" a business at the time the expenditures were incurred. Notwithstanding some modifications, the basic rule still remains: when the taxpayer is in the same or similar business as the one he or she is starting or investigating, the costs of investigation and start up are wholly deductible in the year paid or incurred. *The Colorado Springs National Bank v. U.S.*, 74-2 USTC ¶9809, 34 AFTR2d 74-6166, 505 F.2d 1185 (CA-10, 1974). The deduction is allowed whether or not the taxpayer ultimately decides to expand his/her business. *York v. Comm.*, 58-2 USTC ¶9952, 2 AFTR2d 6178, 261 F.2d 421 (CA-4, 1958). However, this rule often forces taxpayers to litigate to determine whether a business existed at the time the expenses were incurred. Prior to the enactment of Code Sec. 195, if the taxpayer could not establish the existence of a business, the expenditures normally were treated as capital expenditures with indeterminable lives. *Morton Frank*, 20 TC 511 (1953). As a result, the taxpayer could only recover the expenditure if and when he or she disposed of or abandoned the business.

EXAMPLE 6.19   Selma owns and operates an ice cream shop on the north side of the city. A new shopping mall is opening on the south side of the city, and the developers have approached her about locating a second ice cream shop in their mall. Last year, Selma paid a consulting firm $1,000 for a survey of the potential market on the south side. Because Selma was in the ice cream business when the expense was incurred, the entire $1,000 is deductible whether or not she decides to open a second ice cream shop in the southside mall.

Code Sec. 195, implemented in 1980, allows taxpayers to elect to deduct up to $5,000 of start-up expenditures in the tax year in which their trade or business begins. The $5,000 amount must be reduced by the amount by which the start-up expenditures exceed $50,000. The remainder of any start-up expenditures must be amortized over a 180 month period beginning with the month in which the active trade or business begins. It is important to recognize that Code Sec. 195 is elective. Expenses for research and development, interest payments, and taxes are not considered start up expenditures. Code Sec. 195(c)(1). Consequently, these costs are not subject to Code Sec. 195 and may be deducted under normal rules.

EXAMPLE 6.20   Jerry, a calendar year, cash method taxpayer, recently graduated with a degree in restaurant, hotel and institutional management. Jerry paid an accountant $1,200 in September to review the financial situation of a small restaurant he was thinking of buying. In December, Jerry purchased the restaurant and began actively participating in its management. Jerry may deduct the full $1,200 accountant's fee on his tax return for the current year as a start-up expenditure.

EXAMPLE 6.21

Until February, Carlos Aguirre worked for a home builder in Ohio. In March, he left his job and started his own construction company. While his new offices were under construction, he set up shop in a trailer on the construction site. He hired two outside sales representatives who began establishing their customer networks, and an architect to work in the design phase of the business. He paid a printer to print brochures for the new company, and began advertising in local media. All told, he spent $45,000 on these items before the new company opened its doors to the public. Under Code Sec. 195, he can deduct the first $5,000 of these expenses, and must amortize the remaining $40,000 over 180 months beginning in the first month the company begins doing business. Assume the company began actual business operations in July. Carlos' deduction for start-up expenses in its first year of operations will be $6,333, consisting of the $5,000 first-year deduction plus $222.22 per month ($40,000 ÷ 180 months) for 6 months (July—December). Note that if Carlos had spent $52,000 in start-up expenses, rather than $45,000, the amount deductible in the current year would have been only $3,000 plus $272.22 ($49,000 ÷ 180 months) per month for 6 months. The $5,000 first year deduction would be reduced by the excess of total start-up expenses incurred over $50,000.

As suggested above, the taxpayer must enter the business to qualify for amortization. No deduction is allowed for costs incurred to investigate a *new* business that the taxpayer decides not to pursue.

Similar rules apply to "organizational" expenses incurred in forming a new corporation [Code Sec. 248] or partnership [Code Sec. 709(b)]. The first $5,000 of such expenses may be deducted on the corporation's or partnership's first tax return, with any amounts in excess of $5,000 amortized over 180 months. As with start-up expenses, the $5,000 deduction is reduced (but not below zero) by the amount by which total organizational expenditures exceed $50,000. Organizational expenditures include expenditures for legal and accounting services, filing fees paid to the state for legal recognition of the new entity, expenditures on directors' fees paid to temporary directors, and expenditures on organizational meetings of directors, shareholders or partners.

¶6515 BUSINESS GIFTS

Code Sec. 274(b) allows a deduction for business gifts in amounts up to $25 per recipient per year. The expenses are deductible "for" AGI as business expenses for self-employed taxpayers. Taxpayers working as employees can deduct such expenditures as miscellaneous itemized deductions. A business gift normally does not have to be included in the gross income of the recipient. The following items are specifically excluded from the definition of business gifts:

1. Items costing $4 or less which have the name of the taxpayer permanently imprinted on them
2. Signs, display racks, and other promotional materials to be used on the business premises of the recipient; and
3. Tangible personal property awarded to an employee by reason of length of service or safety achievement that does not exceed $400 in value (nonqualified plans) or $1,600 in value if awarded according to a qualified plan award where the average award does not exceed $400.

EXAMPLE 6.22

During the current year, the salesperson for ABC Vending Co. gave the owner of Video Games Co. a total of five bottles of high quality wine as business gifts at various times during the year. The five bottles of wine were purchased by ABC Vending Co. for a total of $150. ABC Vending Co. is entitled to a maximum deduction of $25 for the business gifts. The remaining $125 cost of the gifts is not deductible for tax purposes.

¶6535 TRANSPORTATION EXPENSES

Transportation expenses are defined for tax purposes as the costs of transporting a taxpayer from one location to another when the taxpayer is not travelling away from home overnight for business. Reg. §1.62-1(g). Transportation expenses include air fares, taxi fares, automobile expenses, parking fees, turnpike tolls, etc.

Transportation expenses of a self-employed taxpayer are deductible for AGI as trade or business expenses. Unreimbursed employee transportation expenses are deductible from AGI as miscellaneous itemized deductions subject to the 2 percent of AGI limitation (see discussion in Chapter 8). In order for transportation expenses to be deductible by an employee, however, the expenses must be paid or incurred in connection with services performed as an employee. Commuting expenses of an employee going from home to work and back have generally been held to be nondeductible expenses. The length of commute is considered a matter of personal preference and therefore irrelevant for tax purposes. If a taxpayer has a temporary work assignment beyond the general work area, however, and chooses to return home each night, the transportation expenses related to the round trip are deductible if not reimbursed by the employer. Work assignments with a duration in excess of one year are considered nontemporary and related transportation costs are nondeductible commuting expenses. Code Sec. 162.

EXAMPLE 6.23   John Rinaldo is the manager of a retail store in the city of Clyde. He drives 10 miles to and from work each day. Transportation costs associated with his drive to and from work each day would not be deductible since they are ordinary commuting expenses. In August, John's employer requested that he be the temporary manager for two weeks at the company store in Sidney while the regular manager took vacation. The Sidney store is approximately 120 miles round-trip from John's home. His employer did not reimburse him for his transportation expenses in going to the Sidney store. The transportation expenses incurred by John during his two-week assignment in Sidney are deductible on John's tax return as transportation expenses incurred in going to a temporary work assignment beyond his general work area.

Another deductible employee transportation expense is the expense of going from one job to another job during the same workday. The costs of going to the first job and home from the second job are not deductible, but the costs of traveling from the first job to the second job are deductible. *R. Paolini,* 43 TCM 513, Dec. 38,784(M), T.C. Memo. 1982-69. Where an employee incurs additional transportation expenses beyond what would normally be incurred in commuting to work because the employee has to transport heavy and bulky tools to work, these additional expenses are also deductible as transportation expenses. Rev. Rul. 75-380, 1975-2 CB 59.

Computing Automobile Expenses

Automobile expenses are deductible as transportation expenses if incurred in connection with a trade or business or by an employee in connection with employment duties to the extent not reimbursed by the employer. Two methods are available for computing automobile expenses: the taxpayer can keep records of the actual operating costs of the automobile, including an allowance for depreciation, or, in certain instances, can deduct a standard mileage rate.

If the taxpayer uses the actual operating cost method of determining deductible automobile expenses, records must be kept of the actual costs of operation of the automobile, which include gas, oil, repairs, insurance, depreciation, licenses, and other costs. The taxpayer deducts the portion of these expenses that applies to the business use of the automobile.

The other method for calculating automobile expenses is the standard mileage rate method. Under this method, the taxpayer keeps track of the number of miles driven in the car in connection with his or her business activities and claims a standard cost per mile. For 2015, the standard mileage rate is 57.5 cents per mile. Notice 2014-79, IRB 2014-53, Dec. 29, 2014. Parking fees, tolls, and state and local property taxes paid on the automobile can be deducted in addition to the standard mileage rate. However, other actual expenses (gasoline, repairs, depreciation, etc.) cannot. In lieu of depreciation, taxpayers using the standard mileage rate must reduce the tax basis of the automobile by 24 cents per business mile.

Note that the standard mileage rate cannot be used if the taxpayer has previously used the actual expense method and claimed a depreciation deduction in excess of straight line in the first year the automobile was used for business. The reverse is not true, however; a taxpayer opting to use the standard mileage method in the first year the auto is used for business may change to the actual operating costs method in a subsequent year.

PLANNING POINTER   The actual cost method of calculating automobile expenses will usually result in a larger deduction for tax purposes than the standard mileage rate method. The disadvantage of the actual cost method as compared to the standard mileage rate method is the additional recordkeeping requirements that are required.

¶6535

¶6545   TRAVEL EXPENSES

Code Section 162(a)(2) allows a deduction for all the ordinary and necessary expenses paid or incurred during the taxable year in carrying on any trade or business, including travel expenses incurred while the taxpayer is away from home overnight. Travel expenses consist of the costs of transportation (airfare, taxi fare, etc.), amounts spent for meals and lodging other than amounts which are lavish or extravagant under the circumstances, and other incidental expenses such as laundry and dry cleaning expenses. Self-employed taxpayers deduct travel expenses for AGI as trade or business expenses. Unreimbursed employee travel expenses are deductible from AGI as miscellaneous itemized deductions, subject to the 2% floor.

To be deductible, travel expenses must be incurred while the taxpayer is "away from home" overnight. Overnight does not mean a full 24-hour period, but a period substantially longer than a normal work day where it is reasonable to need sleep or rest to meet normal job requirements. Rev. Rul. 75-168, 1975-1 CB 58.

EXAMPLE 6.24	Linda James, a CPA, drives from Columbus, Ohio to Cincinnati, Ohio, a distance of 100 miles, on Thursday night in order to attend a business meeting in Cincinnati on Friday morning at 9 a.m. The meeting ends at 11 a.m. and Linda drives back to Columbus. Linda can deduct the travel expenses related to her trip even though it did not cover a 24-hour period.

The travel deduction is available for taxpayers who incur expenses to engage in business at locations distant from the taxpayer's "tax home." For this purpose, however, a taxpayer's tax home is deemed to be located at the location of the taxpayer's "principal place of business." If a taxpayer chooses to live in an area other than where he or she works, that choice is deemed to be a personal preference not mandated by business considerations. In such cases, no deduction is allowed for costs incurred in travel between the taxpayer's residence and his or her principal place of business.

Questions regarding the location of a taxpayer's "home" for tax purposes often arise in two situations. The first is when a taxpayer works in more than one location. In such cases, the IRS considers the following three factors in determining which of the taxpayer's multiple work locations is his or her "principal" place of business: (1) length of time spent at each location; (2) degree of business activity at each location; and (3) amount of income derived from each location. The more important location when measured against these three criteria is the taxpayer's principal place of business. No deduction is allowable for travel to that location.

EXAMPLE 6.25	Larry Robinson, a CPA and a single taxpayer, works for a CPA firm in Cleveland, Ohio, from June through October each year and works for a CPA firm in Miami, Florida, from November through May. Larry makes approximately $20,000 in salary from his work in Cleveland and approximately $35,000 in salary from his work in Miami. Which area is Larry's tax home, Cleveland or Miami? Consideration of the length of time spent at each location indicates Miami as the tax home (seven months versus five months). Amount of income derived from each location also indicates Miami as the tax home ($35,000 versus $20,000). Since Miami is Larry's tax home, living costs in the Miami area are not deductible on Larry's tax return. Travel expenses incurred when traveling to and from and working in Cleveland are deductible as temporary living expenses. Another factor to consider in this case is that the IRS might argue that Larry has two tax homes, Cleveland and Miami. This issue could be refuted, however, if Larry can demonstrate that his travel expenses in Cleveland duplicate some of the living expenses he incurs in Miami when he is living in Cleveland. Apartment or motel expenses incurred in Cleveland while, at the same time, Larry still maintains an apartment in Miami are duplicate living expenses.

Questions also arise when the taxpayer's business or employer requires that he or she work in a distant location for a lengthy period of time. A deduction for travel expenses, including duplicate living expenses (lodging, utilities, food, etc.) is available where the work away from the taxpayer's home is temporary—i.e., where it is not indefinite (the taxpayer does not know how long it will last) and it does not last for more than one year. Even if the taxpayer does not incur duplicate living expenses, he or she may take a business deduction for daily transportation expenses paid or incurred in traveling between the taxpayer's residence and a temporary work location, regardless of the distance traveled. Rev. Rul. 90-23, 1990-1 CB 28. Because the alternative work location is temporary, travel between the taxpayer's home and that location is not treated as a commuting expense, which is ordinarily nondeductible.

Where the assignment is not temporary, however, no deduction for travel from the taxpayer's residence to his or her work location is allowed. If the assignment is indefinite, or lasts more than one year, the assigned location becomes the taxpayer's principal place of business. A taxpayer cannot deduct the cost of meals and lodging while performing duties at a principal place of business, even though the taxpayer maintains a permanent residence elsewhere. Congress did not intend to allow as a business expense those outlays that are not caused by the exigencies of the business but by the action of the taxpayer in having a home, for the taxpayer's convenience, at a distance from the business. Such expenditures are not essential for the conduct of the business and were not within the contemplation of Congress, which proceeded on the assumption that a person engaged in business would live within reasonable proximity of the business. *Barnhill v. Commissioner*, 148 F.2d 913 (4th Cir. 1945), 1945 CB 96; *Commissioner v. Stidger*, 386 U.S. 237 (1967), 1967-1 CB 32.

Combining Business and Personal Travel

Travel expenses are deductible for tax purposes if a taxpayer is away from home in pursuit of a trade or business including employment activities and attending a convention. A person may, however, combine personal activities such as sightseeing with a business trip. If the primary purpose of the trip is business, travel expenses including all transportation expenses are deductible as business expenses even though some time is spent on personal activities. Any direct costs associated with the personal activity, however, are not deductible. If the primary purpose of the trip is personal, travel expenses are not deductible even though some business activities are conducted during the trip. Direct costs of any business activity conducted on a personal trip such as renting a car to attend a business meeting are deductible by the taxpayer. Costs associated with taking a spouse along on a business trip are not deductible unless it can be shown that the presence of the spouse had a business purpose and the spouse is also employed by the person paying or reimbursing the expenses. Reg. §1.162-2(c).

More restrictive travel requirements apply to travel outside of the United States. Travel expenses, including transportation expenses incurred on foreign trips, must be allocated between business and personal activities unless travel outside of the United States does not exceed seven days or time attributable to personal activities is less than 25 percent of the total travel time. Code Sec. 274(c). Additional travel restrictions apply to attendance at foreign conventions and attendance at business meetings on cruise ships. Code Sec. 274(h).

Substantiation of Travel Expenses

Taxpayers must substantiate expenditures for travel and transportation expenses by adequate records or by sufficient evidence corroborating the taxpayer's statements as to (1) amount, (2) time and place, (3) business purpose, and (4) business relationship to the taxpayer. Taxpayers must have documentary evidence for any lodging expense while traveling away from home and for any other expenditure of $75 or more, except transportation charges if documentary evidence is not readily available.

In lieu of substantiating actual travel-related meal and lodging costs, employers and employees may utilize optional IRS per diem allowances. The federal per diem rate is equal to the sum of the federal lodging expense allowance and the federal meal and incidental expense (M&IE) rate for the locality of travel. For travel occurring after October 1, 2014, the M&IE rates are $65 per day for any high-cost locality and $52 per day for other localities within the United States. The M&IE rate for travel outside the United States is equal to 40 percent of the per diem rate for the locality of travel. The maximum per diem rate is $259 for high-cost localities ($194 for lodging plus $65 for M&IE), while for all other localities the maximum per diem rate is $172 ($120 for lodging and $52 for M&IE). Notice 2014-57, IRB 2014-41, September 19, 2014. The per diem amount is subject to the 50 percent limit on meals and entertainment expenses, which is discussed in ¶6755. IRS Pub. 1542.

¶6560   MOVING EXPENSES

A deduction is allowed for moving expenses paid or incurred in connection with the commencement of work by a taxpayer as an employee or as a self-employed individual at a new principal place of work. Code Sec. 217. In order to qualify for the moving expense deduction, a taxpayer must move because of a new job location. It is not necessary that the taxpayer have a prior job location. Moving expenses incurred without changing job locations are not deductible.

Time and Distance Requirements

In order for moving expenses to be deductible, the taxpayer also must meet a time requirement and a distance requirement. The time requirement states that an employee must work full-time at the new job location for at least 39 weeks in the 12-month period following the move in order for the moving expenses to be deductible. If self-employed, the taxpayer must work in the new location for 78 weeks during the two-year period following the move for the expenses to be deductible with 39 of the weeks required to be in the first 12 months. The time requirement does not apply if a worker dies, is discharged from work, becomes disabled, or is transferred by the employer. Reg. §1.217-2(d)(1).

If a taxpayer has not completed the time requirement when filing an income tax return, the moving expense deduction can be taken in the year the expenses are paid assuming that the taxpayer will meet the time requirement in the following tax year. If the time requirement is not met in the following year, the moving expense deduction taken in the prior year normally must be recognized as income in the year the time requirement is not met. Alternatively, the taxpayer may file an amended return for the prior year to delete the moving expense deduction for that year.

The distance requirement states that the distance between the taxpayer's old residence and new job location must be at least 50 miles farther than the distance between the old residence and the old job location. If the taxpayer has no old job location (new worker, unemployed), the distance test is met if the new job location is at least 50 miles from the old residence. Code Sec. 217(c)(1).

EXAMPLE 6.26	Robert Long is transferred by his employer from Kenton to Westchester. Robert also moves his family from Kenton to Westchester. Robert's old residence was 10 miles from his old job location. Robert's new job location is 75 miles from his old residence. Robert satisfies the 50-mile distance requirement since the distance between his old residence and new job location is 65 miles farther than the distance between the old residence and the old job location.

Classification of Moving Expenses

The tax law allows a deduction for two categories of moving expenses: (1) expenses incurred to move household goods and personal effects and (2) travel and lodging expenses incurred by the taxpayer in moving the family from the old residence to the new residence. The cost of meals is not deductible. If family travel to the new residence is accomplished by automobile, the taxpayer can deduct actual car expenses or an optional allowance of 23 cents per mile.

EXAMPLE 6.27	Robert Long incurs the following moving expenses in connection with his move from Kenton to Westchester:	
	Expenses of moving household goods	$3,500
	Travel and lodging for family in moving from old residence to new location	450
	Pre-move house-hunting trips	1,400
	Temporary living expenses in new location	1,200
	Real estate commission on sale of old home	4,000
	Total moving expenses	$10,550
	The expenses of moving household goods and of moving Robert's family to the new location are deductible in full. Pre-move house-hunting trips, temporary living expenses, and selling expenses incurred in selling the taxpayer's old house are not deductible. The overall moving expense deduction is $3,950 ($3,500 + $450).	

Year of Deduction

The moving expense deduction generally is taken by a cash basis taxpayer in the year the expenses are paid. The moving expense deduction is treated as a deduction from gross income to arrive at adjusted gross income. Code Sec. 62(a). Qualified moving expenses reimbursed by an employer are excludable from an employee's gross income as a qualified fringe benefit to the extent they meet the requirements for a qualified moving expense reimbursement. Qualified moving expense reimbursements include any amount received, directly or indirectly, by an employee from an employer as a payment for, or a reimbursement of, expenses that would be deductible as moving expenses under Code Sec. 217 if directly paid or incurred by the employee. Qualified moving expense reimbursements do not include payments for, or reimbursements of, expenses that were deducted by the taxpayer in a prior tax year.

¶6560

¶6565   QUALIFIED HIGHER EDUCATION EXPENSES

Under Code Sec. 222, taxpayers can claim an "above the line" deduction (deduction for AGI) for qualified higher education expenses. The maximum deduction is $4,000. Single taxpayers with adjusted gross incomes below $65,000 ($130,000 for married filing jointly) can claim the deduction. Taxpayers whose adjusted gross income falls between $65,000 and $80,000 ($130,000 and $160,000 for joint filers) may deduct $2,000. Married individuals filing a separate return are not eligible for this deduction. The tuition deduction cannot be taken in the same year as an Amercian Opportunity or Lifetime Learning Credit for the same student. See ¶9031.

¶6570   STUDENT LOAN INTEREST

Interest payments on student loans are deductible "above-the-line." That means that a taxpayer can deduct the interest whether or not he or she itemizes deductions. Eligible taxpayers may deduct up to $2,500 of interest expense on a qualified education loan under Code Sec. 221. The deduction is phased out for single taxpayers with adjusted gross income between $65,000 and $80,000 and for joint filers with adjusted gross income between $130,000 and $160,000. Married taxpayers filing separately may not take the deduction. Also, an individual is not entitled to the deduction if the taxpayer can be claimed as a dependent by another taxpayer for the tax year beginning in the calendar year in which the individual's tax year begins.

EXAMPLE 6.28

In 2015, Jamie paid $1,800 interest on a qualified education loan. Her modified AGI (AGI before subtracting deductions for education expenses, domestic production activities, and the foreign earned income exclusion) was $71,000. Jamie is single, so her deduction for qualified student loan interest is phased out by the ratio of her excess AGI ($6,000), divided by $15,000. In this case, her deduction for student loan interest is reduced by 40% ($6,000/$15,000). Note that unlike other phase-out provisions of the Code, the phase-out rules for student loan interest apply to the deduction itself, rather than to the limitation on that deduction. Jamie would have been entitled to an $1,800 deduction (the lesser of the interest actually paid or $2,500). Reducing this deduction by 40%, she will be allowed a deduction of $1,080 (60% times $1,800).

To be eligible for the deduction the education loan must be used to pay for any of the following expenses: tuition, fees, room and board, books and supplies, and other related expenses.

¶6575   HEALTH INSURANCE AND HEALTH SAVINGS ACCOUNTS

The tax law has long allowed employers to treat costs incurred for employee health insurance as a fringe benefit, deductible by the employer but not taxable to the employee. Such beneficial treatment of employer health insurance plans is designed to make health insurance affordable and to increase the portion of the population that is covered by health insurance. To equalize the tax treatment of self-employed taxpayers and employees, Code Sec. 162(l)(6) allows *self-employed* taxpayers to deduct premiums paid for health insurance above the line, as a deduction in computing AGI. For those taxpayers who are not self-employed, health insurance premiums are deductible as part of the itemized deduction for medical expenses, discussed in chapter 8.

The Internal Revenue Code also provides incentives for taxpayers to self-insure. To this end, Code Sec. 223 allows taxpayers who are covered by so-called "high deductible" plans to establish a "Health Savings Account" (HSA). HSAs, similar to IRAs, allow taxpayers to make tax-deductible contributions to an account which will be allowed to accumulate tax-free and fund future medical expenses of the taxpayer and/or dependents. The account is designed for taxpayers who are covered only by "high-deductible" health insurance plans. The premiums on high-deductible insurance plans are much lower than for more standard insurance coverage. Eligible taxpayers (or their employers) can use the difference to fund their HSAs. These plans provide particular advantages for those taxpayers who do not expect to use the full amount in the account for medical expenses since the unspent balance remaining in the account belongs to the taxpayer.

Health insurance plans typically require the insured to pay for a portion of the cost of his or her medical care (the "deductible" amount), with the insurance company paying for costs in excess of this amount. As the name implies, a "high deductible" plan is one where these "deductible" amounts are high relative to more standard insurance plans. Note that the term "deductible" in this context refers not to the tax treatment of the insurance premiums, but to the amount of medical expenses that will not be covered by insurance (i.e., that will be "deducted" from the insurance reimbursement).

Self-employed taxpayers can claim a deduction "for" AGI for HSA contributions up to $6,650 for 2015. Rev. Proc. 2014-30, IRB 2014-20, April 24, 2014. The contribution limit is $3,350 if the taxpayer has "self-only" coverage as opposed to family coverage. Individuals who have reached the age of 55 may contribute an additional $1,000 beyond these limits each year. Taxpayers working for small employers (typically under 50 employees) may exclude a like amount of employer contributions to their HSAs as nontaxable fringe benefits. A "high deductible plan" for purposes of HSA eligibility is a plan with an annual deductible of at least $1,300 for self-only coverage or $2,600 for family coverage, and which limits the taxpayer's annual "out-of-pocket expenses" (deductibles, co-payments, but not premiums) to no more than $6,450 for self-only coverage or $12,900 for family coverage. Taxpayers whose health insurance plans do not meet these requirements may not make contributions to an HSA, nor can taxpayers who are eligible for Medicare. Likewise, taxpayers who do not have health insurance may not make contributions to an HSA.

HSA distributions are tax-free to the extent used to pay qualified medical expenses of the taxpayer or his or her dependents. Distributions for non-medical purposes are fully taxable. Moreover, in addition to the income tax, taxable distributions are also subject to a 10% penalty unless made after the beneficiary reaches the age of 65, dies, or becomes disabled. Medical expenses paid with HSA distributions cannot be deducted by the taxpayer. Note that one benefit of HSA accounts is that they can serve double duty as retirement accounts: distributions received after the taxpayer reaches age 65 are taxable, but are not subject to the 10% penalty.

¶6585 MANUFACTURING DEDUCTION

The American Jobs Creation Act of 2004 created a new deduction for manufacturers. The deduction effectively reduces the corporate income tax rate for domestic manufacturing three percentage points from a top rate of 35 percent down to 31.85 percent. Domestic manufacturers who qualify for the deduction include not only traditional manufacturers but also domestic producers in the areas of construction, engineering, energy production, computer software, films and videotape, and processing of agricultural products.

The manufacturing deduction on qualified production activities is equal to nine percent of the lesser of qualified production activities income or taxable income for the year. The deduction started at a transition percentage of three percent for 2005 and 2006 and increased to six percent for 2007 through 2009. For 2010 and later years, the deduction percentage is 9%. The deduction is limited to 50 percent of the W-2 wages paid by the taxpayer during the tax year.

Corporations, individuals, S corps, partnerships, estates, trusts, and cooperatives can take advantage of the new deduction. Taxpayers can also use the new deduction for AMT purposes. The manufacturing deduction is discussed in greater detail in Chapter 7.

Employee Business Expenses

¶6601 EMPLOYEE BUSINESS EXPENSES—IN GENERAL

The definition of *trade or business* does not include the performance of services as an employee. Code Sec. 62(a)(1). However, ordinary and necessary expenses incurred by an employee in connection with his or her employment are deductible under Code Sec. 162 as business expenses. In order to be deductible by the employee, however, an employment-related expense must be directly related to the performance of employment duties or be required by an employment agreement. Code Sec. 62; *F.M. Magill*, 4 BTA 272, Dec. 1499 (1926).

Unreimbursed employee business expenses are allowed as miscellaneous itemized deductions. Miscellaneous deductions are only deductible to the extent they exceed 2 percent of the taxpayer's adjusted gross income. Business expenses incurred by an employee under a reimbursement arrangement with the employer are normally not shown on the tax return. The reimbursement arrangement must require the employee to substantiate the expenses to the employer and must not allow the employee to keep the excess reimbursement. If full reimbursement is not made, the unreimbursed expenses are only allowable as miscellaneous itemized deductions, limited to amounts in excess of 2 percent of the taxpayer's adjusted gross income. See ¶8601 for an expanded discussion.

Commuting expenses incurred going to and from work are assumed to be personal expenses incurred by all employees and, therefore, are not deductible. Work uniforms suitable for everyday use, such as a suit and tie, are also considered to be personal expenses and not deductible since they can be used by taxpayers at other times besides work. Expenses incurred in purchasing work uniforms which are not suitable for everyday use, such as a fire fighter's uniform or a police officer's uniform, are proper tax deductions.

If an employee accounts to an employer for business-related expenses and is reimbursed by the employer, the employee does not normally have to report the expenses on the tax return.

Table 5. TYPICAL EMPLOYMENT-RELATED EXPENSES DEDUCTIBLE AS TRADE OR BUSINESS DEDUCTIONS (SUBJECT TO VARIOUS LIMITATIONS)
Expenses not shown on return
Reimbursed expenses
Expenses deductible from AGI (miscellaneous itemized deductions subject to 2% of AGI limitation)
Away-from-home travel expenses
Employment agency fees
Employment-related education
Entertainment expenses (limited)
Job-hunting expenses
Office at home (limited)
Outside salesperson's expenses
Professional society dues
Small tools and supplies
Subscriptions to professional journals
Transportation expenses
Union dues
Work clothes and uniforms

An important and often controversial issue with respect to employment-related expenses is the question of whether an individual is in fact an employee or can instead be classified as a self-employed "independent contractor." If a taxpayer is self-employed, all trade or business expenses are deductible for AGI, whereas, if the individual is an employee, any unreimbursed employment-related trade or business expenses are deductible as miscellaneous itemized deductions subject to the 2 percent limitation. In determining whether an individual is an employee or is self-employed, an analysis should be made of the individual's employment activity. Factors such as the following should be considered: (1) does the individual work for many firms or clients or just work for one firm or client, (2) are the individual's services available to the public, (3) does the individual determine work hours and schedules, and (4) does the individual receive regular payments from one firm or from a variety of firms? To determine whether an individual is an employee or is self-employed no one factor should be considered as controlling, but rather all these factors should be reviewed.

EXAMPLE 6.29	Susan is a lawyer who has practiced law for over 10 years. During this period, she has served many clients but, for the past several years, she has spent most of her time with only one client, Randall Corporation. In fact, in 2015 she did not receive fees from any client other than Randall, she moved her office into the Randall Corporation headquarters building, and she abides by the Randall Corporation full-time work schedule. Also, she no longer seeks business from other clients. Is Susan still self-employed in 2015 or is she now an employee of Randall Corporation? An analysis of the facts in this example would seem to indicate that Susan is now an employee of Randall. She receives fees from only one source (Randall), she no longer seeks business from other clients, and she spends her full time at Randall Corporation.

Limitations on the Deductibility of Expenses

¶6701 CERTAIN DEDUCTIONS LIMITED OR DISALLOWED

Some provisions of the Code specifically prohibit or limit the deduction of certain expenses and losses despite their apparent relationship to the taxpayer's business or profit seeking activities. These provisions operate to disallow or limit the deduction for various expenses unless such expenses are specifically authorized by the Code. As a practical matter, these provisions have been enacted to prohibit abuses identified in specific areas. Several of the more fundamental limitations are considered below.

¶6715 HOBBY EXPENSES AND LOSSES

A taxpayer must establish that he or she pursues an activity with the objective of making a profit before the expense is deductible as a business or production of income expense. When the profit motive is absent, the deduction is governed by Code Sec. 183 as an activity not engaged in for profit (i.e., a hobby). Code Sec. 183 generally provides that hobby expenses of an individual taxpayer or S corporation are deductible only to the extent of the gross income from the hobby. Thus, no deduction is allowed for net losses incurred from the conduct of activities deemed by the IRS to constitute "hobbies," where the taxpayer lacks a genuine intent to make a profit. The factors considered by the IRS and the courts in determining whether a taxpayer's activities rise to the level of a trade or business rather than a hobby are explained further in Chapter 7.

¶6725 PERSONAL DEDUCTIONS

Personal, living, and family expenses are not deductible on a tax return unless expressly permitted. Code Sec. 262. Table 6 summarizes the general types of personal expenses and how they are treated for tax purposes.

Although many personal expenditures are not deductible for tax purposes, there is some logic and rationale behind allowing a deduction or credit for certain personal expenditures on an individual's tax return. Some personal deductions are allowed as tax deductions because they are involuntary payments which place a burden on the taxpayer's finances and inhibit the ability to pay income taxes. Deductions allowed for medical and dental expenses, casualty and theft losses, and alimony fall into this category. Other personal deductions and credits are allowed in order to encourage certain types of behavior on the part of taxpayers. For example, the allowance of a charitable deduction for tax purposes encourages the giving of gifts to charity and thereby promotes the public good. Certainly the deduction for state and local income taxes lessens to some degree the problems associated with double and triple taxation of the same income.

Table 6. TYPICAL PERSONAL EXPENDITURES DEDUCTIBLE OR NOT DEDUCTIBLE ON TAX RETURN (SUBJECT TO VARIOUS LIMITATIONS)

Expenditures deductible for AGI	
Alimony	Interest paid on qualified education loans
Individual retirement accounts (IRAs) (limited)	Penalty on early withdrawal of savings
Moving expenses	Jury duty fees paid to employer
Expenditures deductible from AGI (itemized deductions)	
Charitable contributions	Medical and dental expenses
Gambling losses (to extent of gambling winnings)	Personal casualty and theft losses
Hobby expenses (to extent of hobby income)	State and local taxes
Interest expense (limited)	
Expenditures eligible for tax credit	
Adoption expenses	Tuition, books and other course expenses
Child and disabled dependent care expenses	
Expenditures not deductible	
Commuting expenses	Household living expenses
Depreciation on property held for personal use	Life insurance premiums
Funeral expenses	Political contributions
Losses on sales of property held for personal purposes (e.g., house, car, etc.)	

The disallowance of personal expenditures by Code Sec. 262 complements the general criteria allowing a deduction. Recall that the general rules of Code Secs. 162 and 212 permit deductions for ordinary and necessary expenses incurred in a *profit seeking activity*. Where the taxpayer's motive is personal, rather than for profit, no deduction is allowed. Some of the items specifically disallowed by Code Sec. 262 are summarized in the last section of Table 6.

Legal expenses related to divorce actions and the division of income producing properties are often a source of conflict. Prior to clarification by the Supreme Court, several decisions held that divorce expenses incurred primarily to protect the taxpayer's income producing property or his or her business were deductible. The Supreme Court, however, has ruled that deductibility depends on whether the expense arises in connection with the taxpayer's profit seeking activities. That is, the origin of the expense determines deductibility. *U.S. v. Talbot Patrick et al.,* 63-1 USTC ¶9286, 372 U.S. 53, 83 S Ct. 618 (S Ct., rev'g CA-4, 1963). Under this rule, if the spouse's claim arises from the marital relationship—a personal matter—then no deduction is allowed. Division of income producing property would only be incidental to or a consequence of the marital relationship.

Legal expenses related to a divorce action may be deductible where the expense is for advice concerning the tax consequences of the divorce. Rev. Rul. 72-545, 1972-2 CB 179. The portion of the legal expense allocable to counsel on the tax consequences of a property settlement, the right to claim children as dependents, and the creation of a trust for payment of alimony are deductible.

Note that this rule applies to all legal expenses incurred by taxpayers, not just those associated with divorce proceedings. If the origin of the legal issue is inherently personal, the associated legal fees are not deductible even if they may provide the taxpayer with some economic benefit.

EXAMPLE 6.30	Gary is the president of a local bank. Last year, he was charged with driving while intoxicated. He hired a good lawyer at a cost of several thousand dollars, and the charges were dropped. Gary may well have lost his job at the local bank had the charges been made public. He certainly would have lost his job had he been convicted. Nonetheless, his legal fees are not deductible since the underlying cause of his legal difficulties was personal and not related to his trade or business of working at the bank.

PLANNING POINTER	Tax work performed for a business by a CPA and legal work performed by an attorney may be of importance to the business and, at the same time, be of personal significance to the owner of the business. To the extent possible, fees associated with the business portion of a professional service should be kept separate from the personal portion of a professional service on any billing prepared by a professional person rendering a professional service. Documentation of the business portion of a professional service versus the personal portion may be beneficial in substantiating a business tax deduction for professional services.

¶6735   PUBLIC POLICY RESTRICTIONS

Although an expense may be entirely appropriate and helpful, and may contribute to the taxpayer's profit seeking activities, it is not deductible if the allowance of a deduction would frustrate well-defined public policy. The courts established this longstanding rule on the theory that to allow a deduction for expenses such as fines and penalties would encourage violations by diluting the cost of the penalty. *Hoover Motor Express Co., Inc. v. U.S.,* 58-1 USTC ¶9367, 1 AFTR2d 1157, 356 U.S. 38 (USSC, 1958). Historically, however, the IRS and the courts were free to restrict deductions of any type of expense where, in their view, it appeared that the expenses were contrary to public policy—even if the policy had not been clearly enunciated by some governmental body. As a result, taxpayers were often forced to go to court to determine if their expense violated public policy.

Recognizing the difficulties in applying the public policy doctrine, Congress amended Code Sec. 162, adding provisions which are specifically designed to limit its use. The rules identify and disallow a deduction for specific types of expenditures considered contrary to public policy. Specifically, Code Sec. 162(f) now disallows deductions for fines, penalties, and illegal payments.

Fines and Penalties

Under Code Sec. 162(f), no deduction is allowed for any fine or similar penalty paid to a government for the violation of any law.

EXAMPLE 6.31	Taylor is a sales representative for an office supply company. While calling on customers this year, she received parking tickets totalling $100. No deduction is allowed for payment of these tickets because the violations were against the law.

EXAMPLE 6.32	Upon audit of Murray's tax return, the IRS determined that he neglected to report $10,000 of tip income from his job as a waiter, resulting in additional tax of $3,000. Murray was also assessed a negligence penalty on his tax return for intentional disregard of the rules. The penalty—20% of the tax due—is not deductible.

Under Code Sec. 162(g), the term "fines" includes any amounts paid in settlement of the taxpayer's actual or potential liability for a fine, penalty, or related charge. For example, if a company agrees to pay a settlement to the government in order to avoid being fined or penalized, the settlement is treated as a nondeductible fine or penalty for tax purposes. This is true even if the company admits no wrongdoing. Note, however, that while payments in settlement of potential fines or penalties are not deductible, payments incurred to remedy the underlying problem that resulted in the dispute are deductible. Reg. §1.162-21(c) Example (3). For example, if a company is fined $100,000 and ordered to clean up a site following an environmental accident, the costs of cleaning up the site are deductible, while the $100,000 fine is not.

Similarly, no deduction is allowed for two thirds of treble damage payments made due to a violation of antitrust laws. Reg. §1.162-21(b). Thus, only one third of fines incurred for violation of government antitrust provisions is deductible; the remaining two-thirds is treated as a fine or penalty for which no deduction is allowed.

Illegal Kickbacks, Bribes, and Other Payments

Code Sec. 162(c) also disallows any deduction for four categories of illegal payments:

1. Kickbacks or bribes to U.S. government officials and employees if illegal;
2. Payments to governmental officials or employees of foreign countries if such payments would be considered illegal under the U.S. Foreign Corrupt Practices Act;
3. Kickbacks, bribes, or other illegal payments to any other person if illegal under generally enforced U.S. or state laws that provide a criminal penalty or loss of license or privilege to engage in business; and
4. Kickbacks, rebates, and bribes, although legal, made by any provider of items or services under Medicare and Medicaid programs.

Kickbacks or bribes not described above will be deductible if the taxpayer can demonstrate that they are ordinary and necessary.

EXAMPLE 6.33	Randy travels all over the world, looking for unique items for his gift shop. Occasionally when going through customs in foreign countries, he is forced to "bribe" the customs official to do the necessary paperwork and get him through customs as quickly as possible. These so called grease payments to employees of foreign countries are deductible unless they violate the Foreign Corrupt Practices Act. In general, such payments are not considered to be illegal.

Expenses of Illegal Business

Expenses incurred in conducting an illegal business are generally deductible. *Max Cohen v. Comm.*, 49-2 USTC ¶9358, 176 F.2d 394 (CA-10, 1949) and *Neil Sullivan v. Comm.*, 58-1 USTC ¶9368, AFTR2d 1158, 356 U.S. 27 (USSC, 1958). Similar to the principle governing taxation of income from whatever source derived (including income illegally obtained), the tax law is not concerned with the lawfulness of the activity in which the deductions arise. No deduction is allowed, however, if the expense itself constitutes an illegal payment as discussed above. Moreover, Code Sec. 280E creates a significant exception to this policy, prohibiting the deduction of any expenses related to trafficking in controlled substances (i.e., drugs).

EXAMPLE 6.34

In a 2007 Tax Court case (*Californians Helping to Alleviate Medical Problems, Inc. v. Commissioner*, 128 TC 173, No. 14, May 15, 2007), the IRS challenged the deductions claimed by a corporation in connection with its activity of purchasing medical marijuana and distributing it to its members suffering from AIDS and other debilitating diseases. The corporation in question was formed to provide caregiving services to its members, who paid a membership fee to join the organization. A secondary purpose was to provide its members with medical marijuana and to instruct them on how to use medical marijuana to benefit their health. Members were prohibited from reselling marijuana obtained from the corporation, and violation of this prohibition resulted in expulsion of the member from the group.

The IRS initially disallowed any deduction for expenses incurred by the organization, including those incurred in purchasing the medical marijuana distributed to its members. The Service argued that such expenses were not deductible under Code Sec. 280E, as the corporation was engaged in the activity of trafficking in a controlled substance. The Service subsequently acknowledged that the company's cost of goods sold (i.e., the cost of purchasing the marijuana) was deductible, leaving as the sole issue before the court the question of whether the company's other expenses were deductible. The state of California had legalized the use of marijuana for medical purposes in 1996; such use, however, remained illegal under federal law. The court ruled that Code Sec. 280E did apply to expenses incurred in the distribution of marijuana to the corporation's members, but not to expenses incurred in performing the company's other caregiving services. An allocation of expenses between these two activities was required, and only those expenses allocable to the distribution of medical marijuana were disallowed.

¶6745   LOBBYING AND POLITICAL CONTRIBUTIONS

Although expenses for lobbying and political contributions may be closely related to the taxpayer's business, Congress has traditionally limited their deduction. These restrictions usually are supported on the grounds that it is not in the public's best interest for government to subsidize efforts to influence legislative matters.

Lobbying

Lobbying expenditures are deductible only if incurred for the purpose of influencing legislation at the *local* level. Therefore, the expense of influencing national and state legislation (including the costs of hiring lobbyists to represent the taxpayer in these matters) is not deductible. This prohibition is extended to the costs of any direct communication with executive branch officials in an attempt to influence official actions or positions of such official.

Even at the local level, the taxpayer must have a direct interest in the local legislation before lobbying expenses may be deducted. Although the definitional boundaries of the term "direct" are vague, a taxpayer is considered as having satisfied the test if it is reasonable to expect that the local legislative matter affects or will affect the taxpayer's business. However, a taxpayer does not have a direct interest in the nomination, appointment, or operation of any local legislative body. Reg. §1.162-20(b).

No deduction is allowed for any expenditure incurred to influence the general public on legislative matters, elections, or referendums, whether the issue is a local, state, or national issue. Code Sec. 162(e)(2). The Internal Revenue Service has suggested the following examples of nondeductible lobbying activities aimed at influencing the public:

1. Advertising in magazines and newspapers concerning legislation of direct interest to the taxpayer. Rev. Rul. 78-112, 1978-1 CB 42. This prohibition presumably extends to radio and television as well. However, expenses for "goodwill" advertising presenting views on economic, financial, social, or similar subjects of a general nature, or encouraging behavior such as contributing to the Red Cross, are deductible. Reg. §1.162-20(a)(2).
2. Preparing and distributing to a corporation's shareholders pamphlets focusing on certain legislation affecting the corporation and urging the shareholders to contact their representatives in Congress. Rev. Rul. 74-407, 1974-2 CB 45, as amplified by Rev. Rul. 78-111, 1978-1 CB 41.

EXAMPLE 6.35

Wanda owns a restaurant in Austin, Texas. Legislation has been introduced by the City Council to impose a sales tax on food and drink sold in Austin, to be used for funding a dome stadium. Wanda placed an ad in the local newspaper stating reasons why the legislation should not be passed. She testified in front of the City Council on the proposed legislation on several occasions. She also paid dues to the Austin Association of Restaurant Owners organization, which estimates that 60% of its activities were devoted to lobbying for local legislation related to restaurant owners. Wanda may deduct the cost of travel and 60% of the dues to the Restaurant Owners' Association since the local legislation is of direct interest to her. She may not deduct amounts spent to purchase the newspaper ad since it was intended to influence the general public.

Political Contributions

No deduction is permitted for any contributions, gifts, or any other amounts paid to a political party, action committee, or group or candidate related to a candidate's campaign. Code Sec. 162(e). This rule also applies to indirect payments, such as payments for advertising in a convention program and admission to a dinner, hall, or similar affair where any of the proceeds benefit a political party or candidate. Code Sec. 276.

¶6755 MEALS AND ENTERTAINMENT EXPENSES

Under regular rules, entertainment expenses are deductible by a taxpayer if the expenditures can be substantiated and are "directly related to" or "associated with" a taxpayer's business. Code Sec. 274(a). An entertainment expenditure is directly related to a taxpayer's business if the taxpayer can show that there was some general expectation of deriving some income or specific benefit from the expenditure and business was discussed or engaged in during the entertainment. A taxpayer can also show that an entertainment expenditure is directly related to the business if it is provided in a clear business setting where the guest may recognize the business motive of the taxpayer in incurring the expenditure. An entertainment expenditure is associated with a taxpayer's business if the entertainment immediately precedes or is followed by a substantial business discussion. Reg. §1.274-2(d)(1).

EXAMPLE 6.36

Linda James, an insurance agent, takes Paul Mason, president of Mason Furniture Co., to dinner in order to discuss new types of insurance coverage. Linda pays the bill for dinner. Linda can deduct the dinner expense as an entertainment expense directly related to her business. If, after the dinner, Linda takes Paul to see a professional baseball game and pays for the tickets, the cost of the tickets is deductible by Linda as an entertainment expense associated with her business since the entertainment followed a substantial business discussion.

A business entertainment activity where substantial distractions occur such as a professional sporting event or night club entertainment usually does not qualify under the regular rules as being directly related to the taxpayer's business since the presumption is that the distractions preclude the conduct of business activity. Expenditures for activities of this type usually qualify as entertainment expense deductions only if such activities are associated with the taxpayer's business and immediately precede or follow substantial business discussions as noted in the preceding example. The "immediately preceding or following" requirement is generally met if the entertainment activity takes place on the same day as the business discussion.

Only 50 percent of the amount of otherwise allowable meals and entertainment expenses is deductible subject to certain exceptions. The exceptions allowing full deductibility include meal and entertainment expenses fully taxed as compensation to the recipient, traditional recreational expenses paid by employers for employees, and expenditures for samples and promotional items made available to the general public. Items subject to the percentage limitations are food, beverages, taxes, tips, tickets, and cover charges. Transportation expenses such as taxicab fares are 100 percent deductible. Entertainment expenses of a self-employed taxpayer are deductible for AGI as trade or business expenses subject to the 50 percent rule. Entertainment expenses incurred by the taxpayer as an employee and not reimbursed by an employer are deductible from AGI as itemized deductions subject to the 50 percent limitation and the 2 percent floor on miscellaneous itemized deductions.

Entertainment Facilities

Expenditures by a taxpayer relating to the ownership of entertainment facilities such as yachts, hunting lodges, and fishing camps are generally not deductible as entertainment expenses. Out-of-pocket costs related to the use of entertainment facilities of this type, however, if directly related to or associated with the taxpayer's business are deductible for tax purposes. In addition, deductions for club dues are no longer allowed. This restriction applies to any club, whether organized for business, pleasure, recreation, or any other social purpose. The restriction, however, does not apply to professional organizations such as bar associations, business organizations such as trade associations, and civic organizations such as Kiwanis, Lions, and Rotary.

Substantiation of Entertainment Expenses

No entertainment deduction is allowed for tax purposes unless the taxpayer substantiates by adequate records or by other sufficient evidence corroborating the taxpayer's own statements the amount of the expense, the time and place of the entertainment, the business purpose of the entertainment, and the business relationship of the persons entertained to the taxpayer. Adequate substantiation for the entertainment expense deduction includes an account book or expense statement with all pertinent information maintained by the taxpayer during the year and documentary evidence including itemized receipts, paid bills, etc., for each expenditure of $75 or more made during the year. Reg. §1.274-5.

¶6765   EXPENSES AND INTEREST RELATING TO TAX-EXEMPT INCOME

Code Sec. 265 sets forth several rules generally disallowing deductions for expenses relating to tax exempt income. These provisions prohibit taxpayers from taking advantage of the tax law to secure a double tax benefit: tax exempt income and deductions for the expenses that help to produce it. The best known rule prohibits the deduction for any *interest* expense or non-business expense related to tax exempt *interest* income. Code Sec. 265(2). Without this rule, taxpayers in high tax brackets could borrow at a higher rate of interest than could be earned and still have a profit on the transaction.

EXAMPLE 6.37

Carla, an investor in the 28% tax bracket with substantial investment income, borrows funds at 9% and invests them in tax exempt bonds yielding 7%. If the interest expense were deductible, the after tax cost of borrowing would be 6.48% [(100% - 28% = 72%) × 9%]. Since the interest income is nontaxable, the after tax yield on the bond remains 7%, or .52 percentage points higher than the effective cost of borrowing. Code Sec. 265, however, denies the deduction for the interest expense, thus eliminating the feasibility of this arrangement. It should be noted, however, that *business* expenses other than interest related to tax exempt interest income may be deductible.

If the income that is exempt is not interest, none of the related expenses are deductible. Code Sec. 265(1).

EXAMPLE 6.38

Eduardo operates a minor league baseball team. The team paid premiums for disability insurance under which the company would receive proceeds under the policy in the event a player is injured. Proceeds received under a disability policy are not taxable. Accordingly, the premiums on the policy are not deductible even though the policy is presumably an ordinary and necessary business expense. Rev. Rul. 66-262, 1966-2 CB 105.

Similar to the insurance premiums in the example above, Code Sec. 264 provides that no deduction is allowed for life insurance premiums paid on policies covering the life of any officer, employee, or any other person who may have a financial interest in the taxpayer's trade or business, if the taxpayer is the *beneficiary* of the policy. Like the disability insurance proceeds in the preceding example, life insurance proceeds are excludible from the recipient's taxable income. Thus, premiums paid by a business on a key-person life insurance policy *where the company is the beneficiary* are not deductible. In contrast, payments made by a business on group-term life insurance policies where the *employees* are the beneficiaries are deductible.

¶6775   RELATED PARTY TRANSACTIONS

Without restrictions, related taxpayers (such as husbands and wives, shareholders and their corporations, etc.) could arrange transactions creating deductions for expenses and losses that do not actually affect their economic position. For example, a husband and wife could create a deduction simply by having one spouse sell property to the other at a loss. In this case, the loss is artificial because the property remains within the family and their financial situation is unaffected. Although the form of ownership has been altered, there is no substance to the transaction. To guard against the potential abuses inherent in transactions between related taxpayers, Congress designed specific safeguards contained in Code Sec. 267.

Related Taxpayers

The transactions that are subject to restriction are only those between persons who are considered "related" as defined in Code Sec. 267(b). The following taxpayers are deemed to be related for purposes of Code Sec. 267:

1. The following family members – brothers and sisters (including half blood), spouses, ancestors (i.e., parents and grandparents), and lineal descendants (i.e., children and grandchildren);
2. An individual and a corporation if the individual owns, either directly or *indirectly*, more than 50 percent of the corporation's stock;
3. An individual and a partnership in which the partner owns more than a 50% interest;
4. A personal service corporation and an employee owner (whether or not he or she owns more than 50% of the corporation's stock): a personal service corporation is a corporation whose principal activity is the performance of personal services that are performed by the employee owners;
5. Certain other relationships involving regular corporations, S corporations, partnerships, estates, trusts, and individuals.

Disallowed Losses

The taxpayer is not allowed to deduct any loss realized on a sale or exchange of property directly or indirectly to a related taxpayer (as defined above). However, any loss disallowed on the sale may be used to offset gain (if any) realized on the subsequent sale of the property by the related taxpayer to an unrelated third party.

EXAMPLE 6.39	A father owns land that he purchased as an investment for $20,000. He sells the land to his daughter for $15,000, producing a $5,000 loss. The $5,000 loss is not deductible by the father because the transaction is between related taxpayers. Assume, however, that the daughter later sells the property for $22,000. She realizes a $7,000 gain ($22,000 sales price - $15,000 basis). She is allowed to deduct the $5,000 loss previously disallowed to her father, so that she recognizes a gain of only $2,000 ($7,000 realized gain - $5,000 previously disallowed loss).
EXAMPLE 6.40	Assume the same facts as in the previous example, except that the daughter sold the property for only $19,000, rather than $22,000. In this case, she realizes a gain on the sale of $4,000 ($19,000 - $15,000). Again, she is allowed to offset this gain with the disallowed loss previously realized by her father. This reduces her taxable gain to zero (his disallowed loss was $5,000, which is greater than her realized gain of $4,000). Note, however, that the $5,000 disallowed loss is used only to the extent of the daughter's $4,000 gain. The remaining portion of the disallowed loss ($1,000) cannot be deducted.
EXAMPLE 6.41	Susan owns 100% of Equinox Corporation. She sells stock with a basis of $100 to her good friend Teri for $75, generating a $25 loss for Susan. Teri, in turn, sells the stock to Equinox Corporation for $75, thus recouping the amount she paid Susan with no gain or loss. In effect, this transaction is between Susan and her wholly owned corporation —the sale to the corporation is indirect, passing through her friend Teri. Consequently, Susan will not be allowed to deduct her $25 loss on the sale.

Unpaid Expenses and Interest

Prior to enactment of Code Sec. 267, another tax avoidance device used by related taxpayers involved the use of different accounting methods by each taxpayer. In the typical scheme, a taxpayer's corporation would adopt the accrual method of accounting while the taxpayer reported on the cash method. The taxpayer could lend money, lease property, provide services, etc., to the corporation and charge the corporation for whatever was provided. As an accrual method taxpayer, the corporation would accrue the expense and create a deduction. The cash method individual, however, would report no income until the corporation's payment of the expense was actually received. As a result, the corporation could accrue large deductions without ever having to make a disbursement and, moreover, without the taxpayer recognizing any offsetting income. The Code now prohibits this practice between "related taxpayers" as defined above. Code Sec. 267(a)(2) provides that an accrual method taxpayer can deduct an accrued expense payable to a related cash method taxpayer only in the period in which the payment is included in the recipient's income. This rule effectively places all accrual method taxpayers on the cash method of accounting for purposes of deducting such expenses.

| EXAMPLE 6.42 | Barry owns 100% of X Corporation, which manufactures electric razors. Barry uses the cash method of accounting while the corporation uses the accrual method. Both are calendar year taxpayers. On December 27, the corporation accrues a $10,000 bonus for Barry. However, due to insufficient cash flow, X Corporation is not able to pay the bonus until January 10 of the subsequent year. The corporation may not deduct the accrued bonus this year, but must wait until next year when Barry includes the payment in his income. |

| EXAMPLE 6.43 | Assume the same facts as above, except that X is a personal services corporation (e.g., a medical practice) in which Barry owns only 20% of the outstanding stock. The results are the same as above because Barry and X are still related parties: a personal service corporation and an employee owner. |

¶6785   PAYMENT OF ANOTHER TAXPAYER'S OBLIGATION

As a general rule, a taxpayer is not permitted to deduct the payment of expenses incurred by another taxpayer. A deduction is allowed only for those expenditures satisfying the taxpayer's own obligations or arising from such obligations.

| EXAMPLE 6.44 | Quentin lost his job several weeks ago. This month, he received a bill from the state for property tax on his farm. Since he did not have the money to pay the taxes, his daughter, Emily, paid them. Although Emily paid the property taxes, she will not be allowed a deduction because the property taxes were the obligation of her father. |

| PLANNING POINTER | Note that while Emily cannot deduct the property taxes paid on her father's behalf in the above example, if her father itemizes deductions, he may be able to claim the deduction. In a 2010 Memorandum Decision, the Tax Court applied the "substance–over–form" doctrine to allow a taxpayer to claim itemized deductions for medical expenses and taxes paid by her mother on her behalf. The court ruled that although the taxpayer's mother paid the expenses directly, in substance she should be treated as having transferred the funds to the taxpayer, who then transferred them to the creditors. The court noted that there was no risk of double deductions because the mother did not claim and was not entitled to either deduction. The taxpayer, who was treated as having paid the expenses with money received from her mother, was entitled to claim the deductions. Lang, TC Memo. 2010-286. |

| EXAMPLE 6.45 | Percy is the majority stockholder of Rancid Corporation. During the year, the corporation had financial difficulty and was unable to make an interest payment on an outstanding debt. To protect the goodwill of the corporation, Percy paid the interest. The payment is not deductible, and Percy will be treated as having made a contribution to the capital of the corporation in the amount of the payment. |

An exception to the general rule is provided with respect to payment of medical expenses of a dependent. To qualify as a dependent for this purpose, the person needs only to meet the relationship, support, and citizen tests. Code Sec. 213(a)(1). If the taxpayer pays the medical expenses of a person who qualifies as a dependent under the modified tests, the expenses are treated as if they were the taxpayer's expenses and are deductible subject to limitations applicable to the taxpayer.

¶6795   CAPITAL EXPENDITURES

A capital expenditure is ordinarily defined as an expenditure providing benefits that extend beyond the close of the taxable year. It is a well established rule in case law that a business expense, though ordinary and necessary, is not deductible in the year paid or incurred if it can be considered a capital expenditure. Normally, a capital expenditure may be deducted ratably over the period for which it provides benefits. For example, the Code authorizes deductions for depreciation or cost recovery, amortization, and depletion where the asset has a determinable useful life. Code Secs. 167, 168, 169, 178, 185, 188, and 611.

Capital expenditures creating assets that do not have a determinable life, however, generally cannot be depreciated, amortized or otherwise deducted. For example, land is considered as having an indeterminable life and thus cannot be depreciated or amortized. The same is true for stocks and bonds. Expenditures for these types of assets are recovered (i.e., deducted) only when there is a disposition of the asset through sale, exchange, abandonment, or other disposition. At that point, the cost of the asset can be offset against the amount realized (if any).

As a general rule, assets with a useful life of one year or less need not be capitalized. For example, taxpayers can write off short lived assets with small costs such as supplies (e.g., stationery, pens, pencils, calculators), books (e.g., the Internal Revenue Code), and small tools (e.g., screwdrivers, rakes, and shovels).

Capital Expenditures vs. Repairs

The general rule of case law disallowing deductions for capital expenditures has been codified for expenditures relating to property. Code Sec. 263 provides that deductions are not allowed for any expenditure for new buildings or for permanent improvements or betterments made to increase the value of property. Additionally, expenditures substantially prolonging the property's useful life, adapting the property to a new or different use, or materially adding to the value of the property are not deductible. Reg. §1.263(a)-1(b). Conversely, the cost of incidental repairs that do not materially increase the value of the property nor appreciably prolong its life, but maintain it in a normal operating state, may be deducted in the current year. Reg. §1.162-4. For example, costs of painting, inside and outside, and papering are usually considered repairs. *Louis Allen*, 2 BTA 1313 (1925). However, if the painting is done in conjunction with a general reconditioning or overhaul of the property, it is treated as a capital expenditure. *Joseph M. Jones*, 57-1 USTC ¶9517, 50 AFTR 2040, 242 F.2d 616 (CA-5, 1957).

EXAMPLE 6.46	Louis operates his own limousine business. Expenses for a tune up such as the cost of spark plugs and labor would be deductible as routine repairs and maintenance since such costs do not significantly prolong the car's life. In contrast, if Louis had the transmission replaced, allowing him to drive the limousine for another few years, the cost must be capitalized.

Acquisition Costs

As a general rule, costs related to the acquisition of property must be capitalized. For example, freight paid to acquire new equipment or commissions paid to acquire land must be capitalized. In addition, Code Sec. 164 requires that state and local general sales taxes related to the purchase of property must be capitalized. The costs of demolition or removal of an old building prior to using the land in another fashion must be capitalized as part of the cost of the land. Code Sec. 280B. Costs of defending or perfecting the title to property, such as legal fees, are normally capitalized. Reg. §1.263(a)-2. Similarly, legal fees incurred for the recovery of property must be capitalized unless the recovered property is investment property or money that must be included in income if received. Reg. §1.212-1(k).

Business Deductions Related to Capital Expenditures

A capital expenditure for tax purposes is an expenditure which is expected to benefit more than one tax year. Generally, capital expenditures do not qualify as tax deductions in the year the expenditures are made but must be allocated to the tax years which will receive some benefit from the expenditures. This process of allocating the cost of a capital expenditure to various tax periods is called depreciation, amortization, or depletion depending on the type of capital expenditure involved in the allocation process. The term "depreciation" is usually connected with tangible (physical presence) property, "amortization" with intangible (no physical presence) property, and "depletion" with natural resources.

¶6801   DEPRECIATION OF TANGIBLE PROPERTY

Depreciation is the process of allocating the cost of a tangible asset to expense over its estimated useful life. To be depreciable, tangible property must have a limited life. Tangible property can be divided into two parts: real property and personal property. Real property is land, land improvements, buildings, and building improvements. Land does not have a limited life; therefore, it does not qualify for depreciation. Personal property is usually business machinery and equipment and office furniture and fixtures. The term "personal property" should not be confused with property owned by an individual for personal use.

A tax deduction for depreciation of the cost of tangible property has been allowed for tax purposes since the inception of the federal income tax in 1913. In 1981, the tax depreciation system was dramatically changed and simplified by adoption of the Accelerated Cost Recovery System (ACRS).

Accelerated Cost Recovery System (ACRS)

ACRS applies to most tangible property, new or used, placed in service for business or investment purposes after 1980 and before 1987. Property which is not eligible for ACRS includes property placed in service before 1981, property depreciated using a method not expressed in terms of years (units of production method), property which is amortized, and certain public utility property. Code Sec. 168(e). ACRS was substantially modified by the Tax Reform Act of 1986. Thus, most tangible property placed in service after 1986 must now be depreciated under the Modified Accelerated Cost Recovery System (MACRS).

Modified Accelerated Cost Recovery System (MACRS)

MACRS applies to most tangible property, new or used, placed in service for business or investment purposes after 1986. The general MACRS rules classify property based on class life for purposes of determining the applicable depreciation method, the applicable recovery period, and applicable convention. Absent an election out of MACRS, the IRS-established class lives must be used to determine the applicable MACRS recovery period even when the taxpayer may prefer a longer period. Rev. Proc. 87-56, 1987-2 CB 674, clarified and modified by Rev. Proc. 88-22, 1988-1 CB 785; IRS Letter Ruling 9015014, January 9, 1990. Salvage value is disregarded in computing the MACRS deduction. Asset recovery classifications are provided by statute. Code Sec. 168(c).

1. **3-year property.** This class includes over-the-road tractor units, dies, molds, and small tools.
2. **5-year property.** This class includes autos, light-duty trucks, computers, and office equipment, such as typewriters, or calculators.
3. **7-year property.** This class includes most manufacturing equipment, furniture, and fixtures.
4. **10-year property.** This class includes mainly public utility property.
5. **15-year property.** This class includes public utility personal property.
6. **20-year property.** This class includes public utility personal property.
7. **27.5-year property.** This class includes residential rental property.
8. **39-year property.** This class includes nonresidential real property, such as office buildings, hotels, shopping centers, warehouses, and manufacturing facilities.
9. **50-year property.** Railroad gradings or tunnel bores.

MACRS also specifies the standard cost recovery method for each of the above asset classes. The cost of property in the 3-, 5-, 7-, and 10-year classes is recovered using the 200 percent declining-balance method of depreciation. Fifteen- and 20-year assets are depreciated using the 150 percent declining-balance depreciation method. The cost of 27.5-year and 39-year real property assets is recovered using the straight-line depreciation method. For all asset classes, the cost of the property or unadjusted basis is not reduced by salvage value in making the depreciation computation. When the declining-balance method is used, a switch to the straight-line method is allowed at the appropriate time to maximize the tax deduction.

Instead of computing MACRS depreciation in the above manner, optional MACRS depreciation tables are available for taxpayer use. These tables contain annual percentage depreciation rates which can be applied to the unadjusted basis of property in each tax year. An example of a MACRS depreciation table for 3-, 5-, 7-, 10-, 15-, and 20-year life property is shown in Table 7.

Averaging Conventions for Depreciation

Under MACRS, a half-year averaging convention applies to personal property. Under this convention, property placed in service or disposed of during a taxable year is considered placed in service or disposed of at the midpoint of that year. Table 7 uses the half-year convention. A midquarter convention applies when more than 40 percent of the cost of all personal property is placed in service during the last quarter of the taxable year. Under the midquarter convention, personal property is treated as placed in service (or disposed of) in the middle of the quarter in which it was actually placed in service. An example of a MACRS depreciation table for 5-year and 7-year property under the midquarter convention is shown in Table 8. In determining whether 40 percent of the aggregate basis of MACRS property is placed in service during the last three months of a tax year, property placed in service and disposed of within the same tax year is disregarded. Code Sec. 168(d)(3). For real property, both residential and nonresidential, depreciation is based on the number of months the property is in service during the taxable year with a midmonth convention applying in the first month of service and in the last month of service. The averaging convention that is used in the year when property is placed in service must also be used in the year when the property is disposed of.

Table 7. MACRS DEPRECIATION TABLE

General Depreciation System

Applicable Depreciation Method: 200 or 150 Percent

Declining Balance Switching to Straight Line

Applicable Recovery Periods: 3, 5, 7, 10, 15, 20 years

Applicable Convention: Half-year

| | and the Recovery Period is: | | | | | |
| | 3-year | 5-year | 7-year | 10-year | 15-year | 20-year |
If the Recovery Year is:	the Depreciation Rate is:					
1	33.33	20.00	14.29	10.00	5.00	3.750
2	44.45	32.00	24.49	18.00	9.50	7.219
3	14.81	19.20	17.49	14.40	8.55	6.677
4	7.41	11.52	12.49	11.52	7.70	6.177
5		11.52	8.93	9.22	6.93	5.713
6		5.76	8.92	7.37	6.23	5.285
7			8.93	6.55	5.90	4.888
8			4.46	6.55	5.90	4.522
9				6.56	5.91	4.462
10				6.55	5.90	4.461
11				3.28	5.91	4.462
12					5.90	4.461
13					5.91	4.462
14					5.90	4.461
15					5.91	4.462
16					2.95	4.461
17						4.462
18						4.461
19						4.462
20						4.461
21						2.231

Source: Rev. Proc. 87-57, 1987-2 CB 117, Table 1.

Table 8. MACRS 5-YEAR AND 7-YEAR RECOVERY RATES
(Mid-Quarter Convention)

	Placed in Service During:							
	1st Quarter		2nd Quarter		3rd Quarter		4th Quarter	
Year	5-Year	7-Year	5-Year	7-Year	5-Year	7-Year	5-Year	7-Year
1	35.00%	25.00%	25.00%	17.85%	15.00%	10.71%	5.00%	3.57%
2	26.00	21.43	30.00	23.47	34.00	25.51	38.00	27.55
3	15.60	15.31	18.00	16.76	20.40	18.22	22.80	19.68
4	11.01	10.93	11.37	11.97	12.24	13.02	13.68	14.06
5	11.01	8.75	11.37	8.87	11.30	9.30	10.94	10.04
6	1.38	8.74	4.26	8.87	7.06	8.85	9.58	8.73
7		8.75		8.87		8.86		8.73
8		1.09		3.34		5.53		7.64

EXAMPLE 6.47

In 2015, Max Book Company, a calendar year taxpayer, purchased the following assets:

1. April 10—Business equipment, cost $28,000, salvage value $3,000
2. July 7—Car, cost $14,000, salvage value $2,000
3. September 12—Office building, cost $85,000

Ignoring the Section 179 deduction and bonus depreciation, MACRS depreciation for 2015 on these assets would be:

Depreciation

1. Business equipment ($28,000 cost × 2/7ths × 1/2 or 14.29% from the table) (7-year life, 200% DB)	$4,000
2. Car ($14,000 cost × 2/5ths × 1/2 or 20% from the table) (5-year life, 200% DB)	2,800
3. Office building ($85,000 cost/39-year life × 3 1/2 months/12 months) (straight-line depr.)	636
Total	$7,436

EXAMPLE 6.48

Refer to Example 6.47 and assume the business equipment purchased in April 2015 was instead purchased in November 2015. Based on these facts, depreciation on all personal property purchased in 2015 would be based on the midquarter convention since more than 40 percent of all personal property placed in service was placed in service during the last quarter of the taxable year. MACRS depreciation for 2015 on the assets in Example 6.47 would now be:

Depreciation

1. Business equipment ($28,000 cost × 2/7ths × 1/8) (7-year life, 200% DB) (or $28,000 × 3.57% from Table 8)	$1,000
2. Car ($14,000 × 2/5ths × 3/8) (5-year life, 200% DB) (or $14,000 × 15% from Table 8)	2,100
3. Office building (Same as Example 6.47)	636
Total	$3,736

¶6805   ALTERNATIVE MACRS SYSTEM

MACRS deductions are reduced for certain property by requiring that an alternative MACRS method, based on the Asset Depreciation Range System (ADR) class lives, be used for (1) tangible property used predominantly outside the United States, (2) tax-exempt use property, (3) tax-exempt bond-financed property, (4) property imported from a foreign country for which an Executive Order is in effect because the country maintains trade restrictions or engages in other discriminatory acts, and (5) property for which an alternative MACRS election has been made (see below). Mixed-use property (property used for both business and personal purposes) that is used 50 percent or more for personal use is also required to be depreciated under the alternative MACRS rules. Code Sec. 168(g). Under the alternative MACRS rules, the applicable depreciation method for all property is the straight-line method. The deduction is computed by applying the straight-line method (without regard to salvage value), the applicable convention, and the applicable prescribed longer recovery period for the respective class of property.

Special Election

Instead of the regular MACRS deduction, taxpayers may irrevocably elect to apply the alternative MACRS system to any class of property for any tax year and depreciate assets using the straight-line method or the 150 percent declining method of depreciation. Table 9 lists alternative MACRS system 5-year and 7-year recovery rates (half-year convention) using straight-line depreciation. If elected, the alternative system applies to all property in the MACRS class placed in service during the tax year of the election. For residential rental property and nonresidential real property, the election may be made on a property-by-property basis.

Table 9. ALTERNATIVE MACRS SYSTEM		
5-Year and 7-Year Recovery Rates		
(Half-Year Convention)		
Straight-Line Depreciation		
Recovery Year	**5-Year Property**	**7-Year Property**
1	10.00%	7.14%
2	20.00	14.29
3	20.00	14.29
4	20.00	14.28
5	20.00	14.29
6	10.00	14.28
7		14.29
8		7.14

EXAMPLE 6.49

In September, Max Cracker Co., a calendar-year taxpayer, purchased two pieces of equipment. One piece of equipment cost $25,000 and had a salvage value of $4,000. The other piece of equipment cost $20,000 and had a salvage value of $2,000. Max Cracker Co. elects to depreciate the equipment using the alternative depreciation system and to depreciate the assets over the MACRS class lives using straight-line depreciation. Both pieces of equipment are seven-year assets under MACRS. Salvage value is ignored in the depreciation computation and only one-half-year depreciation is allowed in the year of acquisition. Thus, depreciation for the two pieces of property is $3,214 ($45,000 cost/7 years × 1/2).

¶6815   DEPRECIATION OF REAL PROPERTY

As noted in ¶6801, the method of depreciation used for tax purposes depends on the nature of the property being depreciated. Generally speaking, most tangible business-use property other than real estate is depreciated under MACRS using accelerated depreciation methods, while eligible real property is depreciated using the straight-line method. Historically, realty has been divided into two categories for tax purposes: residential and non-residential. While both categories are depreciated using the straight-line method, residential realty is generally depreciated over a shorter period than non-residential realty—27.5 years vs. 39 years—so that the tax burden on returns from investment in residential real estate is substantially lower.

Real property is classified as residential realty if at least 80% of the gross rental income from the building is attributable to rental income from dwelling units. Code Sec. 168(e)(2)(A). A dwelling unit is a house, apartment, etc. used to provide living accommodations on a long-term basis; hotel or motel rooms rented on a transient basis are not dwelling units for this purpose. Generally speaking, a unit is rented on a transient basis if the average rental term is less than 30 days.

EXAMPLE 6.50

Kingsbury Corp. is developing an "extended stay" hotel on a parcel of real estate in a mid-sized city. The company expects to spend $20,000,000 on the project and is uncertain whether the property will be classified as residential or non-residential realty. If the building is residential real estate, the company will be allowed a deduction for depreciation of $727,273 (rounding up) per year for each full year the property is used for business purposes. If, instead, the building is classified as non-residential (because less than 80% of the rental income from the property is from customers staying at least 30 days), the allowable annual depreciation deduction will be only $512,821 (rounding up).

Special Rules for Qualified Leasehold Improvement, Retail Improvement, or Restaurant Property

The *American Jobs Creation Act of 2004* temporarily reduced the depreciable lives of 3 categories of depreciable real estate from 39 to 15 years. The reduced depreciable life, intended as economic stimulus, applied to qualified leasehold improvement property, qualified retail improvement property and qualified restaurant property. The shorter depreciable lives were initially applicable to qualified property investments incurred between January 1 2004 and December 31, 2007, with the expectation that the economy would have recovered from recession by 2008. When the recession unexpectedly deepened in 2008, Congress implemented the first of a series of extensions. In December 2014, Congress passed legislation extending the 15-year depreciation provisions through December 31, 2014. Further extension through at least 2015 seems likely, but until such legislation is implemented, taxpayers should be aware that improvements to leasehold or retail property, as well as restaurant property placed in service after 2014, may be recoverable over the 39-year depreciable life applicable to non-residential real estate.

Qualified Property

There are three categories of real property that are eligible to be depreciated over 15 years. *Qualified leasehold improvement property* is any improvement to the interior of non-residential real property leased between unrelated parties if the improvements are in a portion of the building used exclusively by the lessee (i.e., the person to whom the property is being leased), and are made more than 3 years after the building was first placed in service. Code Sec. 168(k)(3). Note that the improvements may be made by either the lessee or lessor—whichever party pays for the improvements is allowed the depreciation deduction. Moreover, although the building must be at least 3 years old, the lease agreement may be brand new. Indeed, many leasehold improvements are made by the landlord to an older building in order to entice a new tenant to lease the property. In other cases, tenants will make improvements to leased property prior to moving in so that the property will fit their needs before they begin operations from that location.

The following types of improvements are not qualified for the shorter depreciable life for tax purposes:

- enlargement of the building;
- elevators or escalators;
- improvements to a structural component of the building that benefits a common area; or
- improvements to the internal structural framework of the building. Code Sec. 168(k)(3)(B).

EXAMPLE 6.51

Outdoor Inc. sells camping and outdoor gear to the public. In September, 2014 it leased space in a shopping mall, signing a ten-year lease agreement. Prior to beginning operations in the mall, the company paid $2,000,000 to install hard-wood flooring, rustic wall coverings, and new lighting in the space to be used for retail operations. Assuming that the mall was more than 3 years old when the lease was signed, that the leased space will be used solely by Outdoor Inc. for its retail operations, and that no other special expensing or cost recovery deductions were available, the company will be allowed a depreciation deduction of $133,333 on its 2015 corporate tax return:

Cost of leasehold improvements	$2,000,000
Depreciable life	÷ 15 yrs
Annual depreciation deduction (after first year)	$ 133,333

EXAMPLE 6.52 Assume the same facts as in Example 6.51, except that Outdoor Life placed the leasehold improvements into service in February 2015, rather than September 2014. Further assume that Congress does not pass extender legislation for 2015. Because the property was placed into service after December 31, 2014 it must be depreciated using the straight-line method over 39 years rather than 15. Thus, the company's 2015 depreciation deduction will be $44,872, computed as follows:

Cost of leasehold improvements	$2,000,000
Depreciable life	÷ 39 yrs
Annual depreciation deduction	$ 51,282
Adjustment for mid-month convention	× 10.5/12
2015 depreciation deduction	$ 44,872

Note that the applicable convention for 39-year realty placed in service in the current tax year is the mid-month convention, rather than the half-year convention applicable to shorter-lived depreciable property. Under the mid-month convention, the leasehold improvements are deemed to have been placed in service at the mid-point of the month in which they were actually placed in service--in this case, February 15. Thus, Outdoor Life will be entitled to claim a depreciation deduction for 10.5 months in 2015 (12 months less the full month of January and half the month of February).

Qualified retail improvement property is similarly defined as any improvement to the interior of a non-residential building that is open to the general public and is used "in the retail trade or business of selling tangible personal property to the general public." As with qualified leasehold improvement property, the building must have been placed in service more than 3 years prior to the date the improvements are made. Code Sec. 168(e)(8). Improvements may be made by the owner of the building or by a tenant; the depreciation deductions will be available to the taxpayer who pays for them. As above, escalators, elevators, enlargement of the building, improvements to the internal structure of the building, and improvements to "common areas" of the building (e.g., not used for retail trade) do not qualify.

The final category of property eligible for depreciation over 15 years is *qualified restaurant property*. Restaurant property is defined much more broadly than either of the above two categories. Qualified restaurant property includes any building or improvements to a building if more than 50 percent of the building's square footage is devoted to the preparation of, and on-premises seating for the consumption of prepared meals. Code Sec. 168(e)(7). There are no requirements regarding the age of the building, and no restrictions on the type of expenditures that qualify for the reduced depreciable life. Thus, the entire cost of a building used as a restaurant may be depreciated over 15 years beginning with the first year in which the building is placed in service by the taxpayer (so long as the building was placed in service before January 1, 2014).

EXAMPLE 6.53 Taste Buds Inc. opened a new restaurant in a building purchased in October, 2014. The purchase price of the building was $3,000,000, and the restaurant opened for business on December 4, 2014. Assuming this is the only qualified restaurant property purchased by the company that year, Taste Buds could claim a depreciation deduction of $25,000 on its 2014 corporate tax return:

Cost of the building	$3,000,000
Depreciable life	÷ 15 yrs
Annual depreciation deduction	$ 200,000
Adjustment for mid-quarter convention	× 1.5/12 mo
2013 depreciation deduction	$ 25,000

Because the building was placed in service in the 4th quarter of the year, it was subject to the mid-quarter convention. Under the mid-quarter convention, the taxpayer is assumed to have placed the property in service in the middle of the quarter in which it was actually placed in service. In this case, the company acquired and placed the building in service in the fourth quarter of the year. Thus, it is assumed to have placed the building in service on November 15 and was allowed 1 ½ months depreciation expense for 2014 (half of November and all of December).

EXAMPLE 6.54

Assume the same facts as in Example 6.53, except that Taste Buds placed the building into service in February 2015, rather than December 2014. Further assume that Congress does not pass extender legislation for 2015. Because the company opened the restaurant after 2014, it must depreciate the building over 39 years rather than 15. Thus, the company's annual depreciation deduction will be $76,923, rather than $200,000. For 2015, the company must apply the mid-month convention, limiting the deduction to $67,309, computed as follows:

Cost of qualified restaurant property	$3,000,000
Depreciable life	÷ 39 yrs
Annual depreciation deduction	$ 76,923
Adjustment for mid-month convention	× 10.5/12
2014 depreciation deduction	$ 67,309

As in Example 6.52, Taste Buds must reduce the annual depreciation deduction by a full month for January and a half-month for February.

¶6825 CODE SEC. 179 ELECTION TO EXPENSE CERTAIN DEPRECIABLE ASSETS

Development and General Rules

Accelerated depreciation, which increases the rate at which taxpayers are allowed to "recover" the costs of business-use property against their taxable incomes, is one of the easiest and most common business incentives used by Congress. In general, the faster the recovery period, the larger the tax benefit and the lower the net cost of the newly acquired property. This is particularly true for property that is purchased with borrowed money. For example, if a taxpayer pays ten percent of the cost of a new equipment purchase in the first year, and receives a tax benefit equal to 35% of the cost of that purchase, the net out-of-pocket cost in the year of purchase is negative—the tax benefits received by the taxpayer are greater than the cash paid (in the current year) to purchase the asset. The taxpayer actually receives more money in the form of tax savings than it spent to acquire the asset. For this reason, Congress is constantly changing the tax rules with regard to depreciation and the deductibility of new equipment purchases.

An area of particular interest to Congress is Code Sec. 179 which allows taxpayers to immediately expense a portion of the cost of newly acquired depreciable property rather than depreciating it over multiple years. When first enacted, the statute allowed taxpayers to expense up to $5,000 of depreciable equipment in the year of acquisition. The cost of purchases in excess of this amount was subject to depreciation. Between 1997 and 2003, the amount that could be expensed in the first year was gradually increased to $25,000. Beginning in 2003, the Sec. 179 amount was increased to $100,000 and indexed for inflation. In 2007, the first-year deduction was increased to $125,000, and for 2008 and 2009 it was increased to $250,000. Beginning in 2010 and extending through the end of 2014, Congress increased the amount that could be expensed under Code Sec. 179 to $500,000, allowing taxpayers to immediately expense up to $500,000 of eligible property placed in service in each of those years (with any remaining cost depreciable under MACRS).

As of the end of 2014, Congress had not extended the $500,000 increase beyond December 31, 2014—if it does not act to extend the increased first year deduction, the Code Sec. 179 deduction will revert back to $25,000 effective January 1, 2015. Note that Congress often passes so-called "extenders legislation" retroactively. For example, Congress did not pass the 2014 extension until December 15, 2015. It is very likely that Congress will again extend the $500,000 Sec. 179 cap before 2016. If it does not, however, the deduction reverts back to its pre-2003 level of $25,000.

Limitations

The Code Sec. 179 deduction is phased out as the taxpayer's equipment acquisitions exceed an overall investment limit. For 2014, the $500,000 deduction begins to be phased out at $2 million in eligible property acquisitions. For example, if a taxpayer's total investment in eligible property equals $2,100,000, the first year deduction is reduced to $400,000 (the total investment exceeds the overall limit by $100,000, thus reducing the first year deduction by this amount).

If the larger $500,000 Code Sec. 179 deduction is not extended for 2015, and reverts back to $25,000, the overall investment limit will decline from $2,000,000 to $200,000. Thus, absent extenders legislation, the Code Sec. 179 deduction will be reduced when the total investment in eligible property reaches $200,000 and will be fully phased out at $225,000 of eligible property acquisitions.

The deduction is further limited to the taxpayer's taxable trade or business income for the current year. For this purpose, trade or business income is measured before the Sec. 179 deduction and includes income and expenses from *all* of the trade or business activities in which the taxpayer is engaged, rather than just the income from the trade or business in which the purchased property is used. For example, a self-employed taxpayer whose spouse is employed by another business can count both the spouse's employment earnings and the net income from the taxpayer's trade or business in computing the taxable income limitation (assuming the taxpayer and her spouse file a joint return). To the extent the taxpayer's Sec. 179 deduction is limited by the taxable income limitation, any unused deduction can be carried forward into subsequent tax years.

EXAMPLE 6.55

In 2014, Ginger Gilmore purchased $2,100,000 in depreciable equipment for use in her commercial nursery business. The nursery's business income before accounting for the Code Sec. 179 deduction (but *after* accounting for depreciation expense with respect to that portion of the acquisition not expensed under Sec. 179) was $385,000. Assume that Ginger had no other source of income. Ginger's allowable deduction under Sec. 179 for 2014 was calculated as follows:

Code Sec. 179 deduction, before limitations		$500,000
Total investment in eligible property (in 2014)	$2,100,000	
Overall investment limit	(2,000,000)	
Reduction in Sec. 179 deduction		(100,000)
Allowable Sec. 179 deduction before application of taxable income limit		$400,000
Taxable income before Sec. 179 deduction		385,000
Allowable Sec. 179 deduction (lesser of $400,000 or $385,000)		$385,000
Sec. 179 carryover to 2015		$ 15,000

Note that the carryover to 2015 does *not* include the $100,000 phase-out reduction. Only the portion of the otherwise allowable deduction that exceeds the net taxable income limitation can be carried forward.

Assume that Congress does not extend the $500,000 cap for 2015. Further assume that Ginger purchases $18,000 in eligible property in 2015, and that her taxable income before the Sec. 179 deduction is $350,000. Her allowable Sec. 179 deduction for 2015 would be $33,000, computed as follows:

Maximum allowable Sec. 179 deduction for 2015 acquisitions assuming no extender legislation passes	$ 25,000
Actual investment in eligible property in 2015	18,000
Allowable Sec. 179 deduction for 2015 property acquisitions	$ 18,000
Carryforward from 2014	15,000
Total deduction under Code Sec. 179 for 2015	$ 33,000

¶6835   BONUS DEPRECIATION

"Bonus" depreciation, provided for the first time in 2008, is another approach used by Congress to stimulate business activity. For 2008, 2009 and 2010, Congress allowed businesses to take an additional depreciation deduction, referred to as "bonus" depreciation, equal to 50 percent of the cost of depreciable property placed in service in those years (with the remainder of the cost of such property being recovered under MACRS depreciation). Congress increased the rate of bonus depreciation to 100 percent of the cost of eligible property acquired in 2011, but allowed the rate to fall back to 50 percent beginning on January 1, 2012. The rate remains at 50% for property acquisitions made before the end of 2014. Unless Congress extends the bonus depreciation provisions for 2015, bonus depreciation will not be available for property acquired after December 31, 2014.

The combination of bonus depreciation and the Code Sec. 179 deduction provides a powerful incentive to increase investment in depreciable property, especially since the remaining cost of the property remains eligible for accelerated depreciation under MACRS. It is important, however, that taxpayers apply these provisions in the proper order. Under Treasury Regulation 1.168-1(d)(3) Example 2, taxpayers must deduct the Code Sec. 179 deduction first, then bonus depreciation. MACRS depreciation is then calculated on the remaining balance of the property acquisition.

EXAMPLE 6.56	Wilder Manufacturing, Inc. purchased new equipment in December 2014 at a total cost of $1,200,000. The property is 5-year depreciable property under MACRS and was eligible for both the Sec. 179 deduction and 50 percent bonus depreciation. The company opted to take both of those deductions, and to depreciate the remaining cost under MACRS. Its depreciation and Sec. 179 deductions with respect to this property acquisition for 2014 and 2015 are calculated as follows:

	2014	2015
Original cost of the property	$1,200,000	N/A
Code Sec. 179 deduction	(500,000)	N/A
Remaining cost	700,000	N/A
Bonus depreciation (50 percent)	(350,000)	N/A
Depreciable cost	$ 350,000	$350,000
MACRS depreciation rate (Table 8, mid-quarter convention)	5%	38%
MACRS depreciation deduction	17,500	133,000
Code Sec. 179 deduction (per above)	500,000	0
Bonus depreciation (per above)	350,000	0
Total deduction (MACRS, Sec. 179 and bonus depr.)	**$867,500**	**$133,000**

In the example above, note that Wilder was able to deduct over 72 percent of the cost of the equipment in year of purchase (2014). Had the company waited until January 2015 to purchase the equipment, the availability of bonus depreciation and the larger Sec. 179 deduction would be uncertain. Assuming Congress does not extend either of these provisions through 2015, the Sec. 179 deduction would be only $25,000, bonus depreciation would not be allowed, and the MACRS depreciation deduction would be 20 percent assuming the mid-quarter convention would not apply (because the purchase would be made in the first, rather than the last, quarter of the year). The total deduction would be only $235,000 ($25,000 plus 20% of $1,175,000—see Table 7).

Bonus depreciation could be claimed for all purchases of "eligible" property in 2014. Eligible property for this purpose consists of machinery, equipment or other tangible personal property, most computer software, and qualified leasehold improvements. Moreover, to be eligible for bonus depreciation, the property must be new—that is, its original use had to begin with the taxpayer

¶6845   DEPRECIATION OF AUTOMOBILES

Limitations on Depreciation of Passenger Cars

Calculation of depreciation expense for business-use automobiles is subject to a complex set of rules. In general, automobiles are eligible for both MACRS depreciation and bonus depreciation (when available). However, depreciation deductions with respect to a business-use automobile are generally limited to the amount that would be available for an auto costing around $16,000 or less. Automobiles costing more than this amount are labeled "luxury" automobiles, and depreciation deductions are generally not allowable on the excess cost.

This limitation is expressed in the form of overall limitations on the depreciation deduction allowable for automobiles. Code Sec. 280F. Automobiles are classified as five-year MACRS property, and limitations are imposed on the amount of depreciation that may be claimed in each year of the life of the vehicle as indicated in Table 10.

Table 10. DEPRECIATION LIMITS FOR BUSINESS-USE AUTOMOBILES		
	Passenger Cars	Trucks and Vans
Year placed in service	$3,160	$3,460
Second year	$5,100	$5,600
Third year	$3,050	$3,350
Succeeding years	$1,875	$1,975
Note: vehicles can be depreciated beyond five years if they continue to be used for business purposes and cost has not yet been fully recovered as of the end of the fifth year.		

As indicated in Table 10, the depreciation limits for trucks and vans are slightly higher than those for passenger automobiles, reflecting Congress' view that such vehicles cost a little more than passenger cars. It is very important to note that these limitations apply only to vehicles that are suitable for use as passenger cars. Automobiles with a gross vehicle weight (GVW) in excess of 6,000 pounds are not considered to be passenger cars, nor are ambulances, taxis or limousines. Accordingly, cars and trucks with a GVW in excess of 6,000 pounds are not subject to these limitations.

Business Use

If the automobile is used less than 100 percent for business purposes, the depreciation deduction limitations are determined by multiplying the limitation amount by the business-use percentage. If the business-use percentage of the car is less than 50 percent in any year, MACRS depreciation must be computed using the alternative MACRS method (straight-line method over a five-year life).

Bonus Depreciation

In years in which bonus depreciation is allowed, the first year depreciation limitation is increased by $8,000. Thus, if bonus depreciation is extended to 2015, the year 1 limitation for a passenger car placed in service in 2015 will be $11,160 ($11,460 for trucks and vans). Note that the bonus depreciation increases the year 1 limitation, but does not affect the limitations applicable to subsequent years. Thus, bonus depreciation effectively increases the price at which a car will be classified as a luxury automobile for federal income tax purposes. By increasing the first year limitation without changing the limitation applicable to any subsequent years, the taxpayer not only is allowed a larger deduction in year 1, but is allowed to increase the total depreciation deductions claimed with respect to the purchase by $8,000.

EXAMPLE 6.57

On January 23, 2015, Lucille purchased a new car for $35,000. Assuming she uses the car 100% for business purposes, she will be allowed the following depreciation deductions for years 2015-2019:

	Bonus Depreciation Extended to 2015	Bonus Depreciation *not* Extended
Depreciation allowed in:		
2015 (half-year)	$11,160	$3,160
2016	5,100	5,100
2017	3,050	3,050
2018	1,875	1,875
2019	1,875	1,875
Total depreciation deductions	$23,060	$15,060

Note that if Lucille continues to use the car for business in years after 2019, she will be allowed to deduct up to $1,875 in depreciation expense (reduced for non-business use) each year that she continues to use the car. .

Section 179

While Code Sec. 179 can be used to expense a portion of the cost of automobiles in the year of acquisition, the deduction is treated as depreciation expense and is generally subject to the luxury automobile depreciation limitations summarized in Table 10. Code Sec. 280F(d)(1). Thus, taxpayers usually do not claim a Sec. 179 deduction with respect to autos because it does not increase the allowable deduction.

As noted above, however, the limitations of Sec. 280F do not apply to automobiles, trucks or vans with gross vehicle weights in excess of 6,000 pounds. Prior to 2004, these vehicles could be fully expensed under Sec. 179, subject only to the overall limitation on the annual Sec. 179 write-off. Thus, for example, a taxpayer purchasing an SUV with a gross vehicle weight in excess of 6,000 pounds in 2003 could write off the lesser of the cost of the vehicle or $100,000 in that year. This provision generated substantial criticism as it provided an incentive to automobile manufacturers to make SUVs bigger and heavier and thus less fuel efficient. In response to these criticisms, the *American Jobs Creation Act of 2004* implemented an additional limitation the applicability of Code Sec. 179 to passenger vehicles with a GVW between 6,000 and 14,000 pounds.

The new limitation provides that no more than $25,000 of the cost of a sports utility vehicle (SUV) with a GVW between 6,000 and 14,000 pounds may be deducted in the year of acquisition under Sec. 179. Code Sec. 179(b)(5). Because the limitation is intended to apply only to non-commercial vehicles, it does not apply to vehicles designed to have a seating capacity of more than 9 persons behind the driver's seat (e.g., buses), vehicles with a cargo area of at least 6 feet in interior length (e.g., commercial trucks), or vehicles that have seating rearward of the driver's seat (e.g., delivery vans).

If a taxpayer purchases a qualified SUV at a cost greater than $25,000, the amount spent above $25,000 may be depreciated under the MACRS and bonus depreciation rules (if available). Because the limitations under Code Sec. 280F apply only to vehicles with GVW of 6,000 pounds or less, depreciation of the excess cost (over $25,000) of an eligible vehicle is not subject to the luxury auto limitations.

EXAMPLE 6.58

In 2015, Gabrielle purchased a new SUV for $70,000. The vehicle has a gross vehicle weight of 8,000 pounds and is therefore eligible for the Sec. 179 deduction. In addition, because its GVW exceeds 6,000 pounds, the SUV is not subject to the depreciation limitations of Code Sec. 280F. Assuming the vehicle is used 100% for business, Gabrielle will be able to deduct the following amount in 2015, depending on whether or not Congress extends bonus depreciation and the $500,000 Sec. 179 deduction:

	Bonus Depreciation Extended to 2015	Bonus Depreciation *not* Extended
Original cost of the SUV	$70,000	$70,000
Code Sec. 179 deduction	(25,000)[a]	(25,000)
Remaining basis	$45,000	$45,000
Bonus depreciation	(22,500)	0[b]
Depreciable basis for MACRS	$22,500	$45,000
MACRS 1st yr rate (Table 7)	20%	20%
MACRS depreciation	$ 4,500	$ 9,000
Add: Sec. 179	25,000	25,000
Bonus depreciation	22,500	0
Total deduction 2015	**$52,000**	**$34,000**

[a] Sec. 179 deduction limited to $25,000 for SUVs regardless of overall maximum allowed under statute.

[b] No deduction for bonus depreciation if Congress does not pass extension legislation for 2015.

The language of Code Sec. 179(b)(5) provides that the $25,000 limitation applies to the cost of each SUV purchased and placed in service during the tax year. Thus, if a taxpayer purchases more than one qualified vehicle in a given year, a $25,000 deduction under Code Sec. 179 will be available for *each* vehicle purchased.

EXAMPLE 6.59

In 2015, Mendoza Corp purchased two new SUVs for $35,000 each (total expenditure $70,000). The vehicles each had a GVW of 8,000 pounds and were therefore eligible for the Code Sec. 179 deduction. As in the above example, the remaining cost of each vehicle after taking the Sec. 179 deduction is eligible for both bonus (if available) and MACRS depreciation. Assuming that the vehicles are both used 100% for business, Mendoza can deduct a total will be able to deduct the following amount in 2015, depending on whether or not Congress extends bonus depreciation and the $500,000 Sec. 179 deduction:

	Bonus Depreciation and Sec. 179 Extended to 2015	Bonus Depreciation and Sec. 179 *not* Extended
Original cost of the SUVs	$70,000	$70,000
Code Sec. 179 deduction	(50,000)[a]	(50,000)
Remaining basis	$20,000	$20,000
Bonus depreciation	(10,000)	0[b]
Depreciable basis for MACRS	$10,000	$20,000
MACRS 1st yr rate (Table 7)	20%	20%
MACRS depreciation	$ 2,000	$ 4,000
Add: Sec. 179	50,000	50,000
Bonus depreciation	10,000	0
Total deduction 2015	**$62,000**	**$54,000**

[a] Sec. 179 deduction limited to $25,000 for each SUV regardless of overall maximum allowed under statute.
[b] No deduction for bonus depreciation if Congress does not pass extension legislation for 2015.

¶6855   PROPERTY CONVERTED FROM PERSONAL TO BUSINESS USE

As noted above, conversion of property from business to non-business use will create tax issues with respect to depreciation and Code Sec. 179 deductions previously claimed. However, it is also relatively common for taxpayers to convert property from personal use to business use. For example, a taxpayer may move to another city and decide to convert his or her personal residence into rental property. Similarly, a taxpayer starting her own business may convert a personal use auto to business use property in connection with the new business.

In such cases, Reg. §1.167(g)-1 provides that the tax basis of the asset for tax purposes will be equal to the lesser of the fair market value of the property at the date of conversion to business (or investment) use or its adjusted tax basis at the date of conversion. This will be the taxpayer's tax basis for purposes of computing depreciation expense and loss (if any) from a subsequent sale of the asset. If the asset is later sold for a profit, the original basis of the asset, adjusted for depreciation, will be used to calculate the taxable gain. With respect to depreciation, the asset will be treated as having first been placed in service in the year of conversion to business-use property. The appropriate convention will apply under MACRS (mid-year, mid-quarter, or mid-month). Note that in most cases, no deduction will be allowed under Code Sec. 179 for property converted from personal to business use. Unlike depreciation under MACRS, Code Sec. 179 applies to property "purchased" by the taxpayer from an unrelated seller during the taxable year for use in a trade or business. Code Sec. 179(d)(1) and (2). Since the conversion of property from personal to business use does not involve a purchase transaction, Code Sec. 179 will not be applicable.

EXAMPLE 6.60

Javier and Maria Gonzales purchased a new home in September, 2006 for $425,000. They used the home as their personal residence until July 2015, when Maria was transferred by her employer to another city. The real estate market had declined rather substantially and the Gonzales decided not to sell their home, but to place it on the rental market instead. They placed the home for rent on August 1, 2015. After a brief period of showing the home, it was rented in October, 2015. At that date, an independent appraisal estimated the value of the home to be $300,000. Allocating 5% of the value of the home to land, the Gonzales will be allowed to depreciate $285,000 of the home under MACRS. It is 27.5 year property and is depreciated using the mid-month convention. Moreover, it was converted to business use on August 1, 2015, the date it was placed on the rental market. It does not matter that the home was not rented until October of that year. For 2015, the Gonzales will be allowed to claim a depreciation deduction of $3,886 ($285,000 depreciable basis of the home ÷ 27.5 years x 4.5 months/12 months).

KEYSTONE PROBLEM

The property ledger used for tax purposes by Able Garment Co., a calendar year taxpayer, is shown below. Compute the amount of the 2015 and 2016 depreciation deductions allowable to Able Garment Co. for these assets on its tax returns based on regular MACRS depreciation percentage rates (ignore bonus depreciation and the Section 179 deduction).

Able Garment Co.

Property Ledger as of December 31, 2015

Asset	Year Purchased	Cost	Salvage Value
1. Car	2015	$19,000	$1,000
2. Car	2015	22,000	1,500
3. Office furniture	2015	14,250	1,000
4. Business equipment	2015	38,950	5,000
5. Building (Office)	Sept. 2015	95,000	—

¶6865   AMORTIZATION

In financial accounting, the term "amortization" is normally defined as the process of allocating the cost of an intangible asset to expense over its estimated useful life. The Code is not as precise in the use of the term "amortization." The Regulations actually refer to the process of allocating the cost of an intangible asset to expense as depreciation instead of amortization. Reg. §1.167(a)-3. In other sections of the Code, reference is made to amortizing the cost of tangible assets, a process which is usually referred to as depreciation in financial accounting.

Intangible Assets

Intangible assets used in a trade or business and having limited useful lives subject to reasonable estimation can be amortized over an appropriate useful life. The straight-line depreciation method is used to compute the amortization deduction. Code Sec. 197 provides for a 15-year amortization period for specified intangible assets referred to as "section 197" intangibles. A section 197 intangible includes goodwill, going concern value, licenses or permits granted by a governmental agency, covenants not to compete, franchises, trademarks, trade names, patents, and copyrights.

Other Allowable Amortization Deductions

In some instances, amortization deductions are allowed for capital expenditures which are more favorable to a taxpayer than the normal depreciation allowances applicable to the property. These amortization deductions are provided to taxpayers as tax incentives to participate in investment activities which are considered to have some public interest attached to them. For example, taxpayers may elect to amortize the cost of pollution control facilities over a 60-month period. Code Sec. 169.

¶6875   RESEARCH AND EXPERIMENTAL EXPENDITURES

The term "research and experimental" expenditures (R&E) includes all experimental and laboratory costs connected with the development of an experimental or pilot model, plant process, product, formula, invention, or similar property. It does not include expenditures for ordinary testing or inspection of materials or products for quality control or for efficiency surveys, management studies, consumer surveys, advertising, or promotion. Reg. §1.174-2(a). R&E connected with a trade or business can be treated as a current deduction for tax purposes or, if elected by the taxpayer, be deferred and amortized over a period of not less than 60 months starting in the period when benefits from the R&E are first realized. Code Sec. 174(a) and (c). Subsequent changes in treatment require approval of the IRS. Any R&E involving the purchase of property which would normally be subject to depreciation such as equipment or the purchase of land cannot be deducted immediately but must be handled in accordance with its regular treatment for tax purposes. Code Sec. 174(c).

EXAMPLE 6.61

In 2015, Jones Ribbon Co. incurs R&E for the first time. R&E included the following amounts:

R&E Salaries	$350,000
R&E Materials	150,000
Total R&E	$500,000

Jones Ribbon Co. could choose to treat all R&E incurred in 2015 as a current deduction of $500,000.

If Jones Ribbon Co. elects to capitalize and amortize 2015 R&E, the monthly amortization deduction, assuming a 60-month amortization period, would be:

$500,000/60 = $8,333.33 per month amortization in 2015 starting with the month when benefits from the R&E are first realized.

PLANNING POINTER

Generally, immediate expensing of R&E is advantageous to a taxpayer for tax purposes as compared to capitalization and amortization of R&E. This is true because immediate expensing results in larger tax deductions in earlier years and lower tax payments.

¶6885   DEPLETION OF NATURAL RESOURCES

Depletion is normally defined as the process of allocating the cost of a natural resource to expense over its estimated useful life. For tax purposes, however, it is possible that depletion deductions for a natural resource may exceed the cost of the natural resource. Some natural resources which are subject to depletion include metals such as gold, silver, and copper, and minerals like coal, clay, sand, and oil.

The owner of a natural resource is entitled to the depletion deduction. Reg. §1.611-1(b). Land on which the natural resource is located is not subject to depletion.

Two methods are available to taxpayers for computing the depletion deduction: the cost depletion method and the percentage depletion method. The taxpayer would normally compute the proper deductions using both depletion methods and then claim the higher deduction for tax purposes. Reg. §1.611-1(a).

Cost Depletion Method

The cost depletion computation involves dividing the basis of the natural resource by the estimated units to be recovered from the natural resource to determine the depletion amount per unit. The depletion amount per unit is then multiplied by the units of the natural resource sold during the year which gives the cost depletion deduction for the tax year.

EXAMPLE 6.62

In 2015, Basil Natural Resource Development Company acquires the rights to a natural resource for $5,000,000. The estimated recoverable units from the natural resource at the time of purchase amount to 250,000 units. The depletion amount per unit is $5,000,000/250,000 = $20 depletion amount per unit. If 40,000 units of the natural resource were sold during 2015, the depletion deduction using the cost depletion method would be $800,000 (40,000 units sold during year × $20 depletion amount per unit).

Percentage Depletion Method

Percentage depletion is computed by taking a specified depletion percentage and applying it to the gross income for the year derived from the sale of the natural resource. Some depletion percentages specified in the Code include 5 percent for sand and gravel, 10 percent for coal, 15 percent for gold, silver, and copper, and 22 percent for uranium. Code Sec. 613. The deduction for percentage depletion with respect to a particular property cannot exceed 50 percent of the taxpayer's net taxable income derived from the natural resource produced from that property (before accounting for the depletion deduction) for the taxable year.

EXAMPLE 6.63

Referring to the previous example, Basil Natural Resource Development Company sells 40,000 units of its natural resource during 2015 at an average price of $160 per unit. Assuming a specified depletion percentage of 15 percent stated for the natural resource and operating expenses of $115 per unit of natural resource, the percentage depletion deduction is computed as follows:

1. Gross income derived from natural resource	
(40,000 units × $160)	$6,400,000
Code specified depletion percentage	15%
Percentage depletion deduction subject to limitation	$960,000
2. Taxable income limitation	
Gross income	$6,400,000
Operating expenses before depletion (40,000 units × $115)	4,600,000
Taxable income before depletion deduction	$1,800,000
Limitation percentage	50%
Percentage depletion deduction limitation	$900,000
Percentage depletion deduction, lesser of (1) or (2)	$900,000

As mentioned earlier, a taxpayer should compare the computed cost depletion deduction with the computed percentage depletion deduction and deduct the higher amount. In the two examples, the cost depletion deduction was $800,000 and the percentage depletion deduction was $900,000. Thus, taxpayer would deduct the $900,000 percentage depletion deduction amount.

A taxpayer's tax basis in the natural resource is reduced, but not below zero, by the amounts of depletion deductions taken by the taxpayer. If the basis of the natural resource property is reduced to zero, after being reduced by depletion deductions, depletion can still be claimed by a taxpayer using the percentage depletion method since it is not based on the cost of the taxpayer's investment in natural resource property.

¶6901   SUBSTANTIATION OF TAX DEDUCTIONS

As noted earlier, tax deductions are allowed to taxpayers only if they are specifically authorized. In addition, taxpayers must be able to substantiate the deductions claimed on their tax returns if requested by the IRS through the audit process. Taxpayers can normally substantiate tax deductions by providing documentary evidence such as receipts, invoices, and cancelled checks. In some instances, oral testimony of the taxpayer or other persons in support of the taxpayer may be of some value. In the past, the IRS has argued in court that if a taxpayer fails to substantiate a deduction, then the entire deduction should be disallowed. In an important trend-setting case, however, the court held that if substantiation for a tax deduction was lacking but it was reasonable to assume that some amount of expense had been incurred, then it is reasonable to assume that some estimated tax deduction should be allowed. *G.M. Cohan,* 2 USTC ¶489, 39 F.2d 540 (CA-2 1930). The reasoning applied in the *Cohan* case to justify a reasonable deduction when substantiation for a deduction is lacking has become known as the *Cohan* rule for tax purposes. The *Cohan* rule applies to all tax deductions with the exception of travel and entertainment expenses, business gifts, charitable contributions, and a few other expenditures where substantiation is required before a deduction will be allowed.

EXAMPLE 6.64

> Lavelle attends church each Sunday and always puts a twenty-dollar bill in the church collection basket. Lavelle does not use church envelopes and does not make a charitable contribution by check. She claims charitable contributions to her church of $1,040 on her 2015 tax return. In an audit of her 2015 tax return by the IRS, Lavelle is questioned on the amount of her charitable contributions. She has no documentary evidence to support her charitable contribution deduction of $1,040. Starting in 2007, the *Cohan* rule no longer applies to charitable contributions and Lavelle will be denied a charitable contribution deduction due to the lack of substantiation.

TAX BLUNDER

In Example 6.64, Lavelle should have used church envelopes and had the church notify her in writing of her total charitable contributions at the end of the year. Alternatively, had she paid her contributions by check, she would have the cancelled checks to substantiate her gifts.

A taxpayer must be able to substantiate tax deductions claimed on the return. If a tax return is audited by the IRS, documentary evidence such as invoices, paid receipts, and cancelled checks are very important in substantiating deductions. Oral evidence of other individuals may be of some value. Oral evidence of the taxpayer may also be of some value, but the IRS is certainly aware that many taxpayers, when questioned, merely declare that their deductions were computed correctly. The *Cohan* rule is of some use to taxpayers in that it generally provides a floor for tax deductions. The *Cohan* rule, however, will rarely result in a taxpayer's being allowed a tax deduction equal to the amount originally claimed. Also, the *Cohan* rule is no longer applicable with respect to a number of deductions, as discussed above.

SUMMARY

- Allowable tax deductions are divided into four categories: trade or business, production of income, losses and personal. Basic personal living expenses of an individual taxpayer normally are not deductible with the exception of certain personal expenditures that have been allowed by Congress for various reasons as itemized deductions.

- In order to be deductible, trade or business expenditures must (1) be ordinary and necessary, (2) be reasonable in amount, and (3) be related to an activity which is deemed to be a trade or business. Some expenditures which meet all these requirements, however, may still be disallowed if they are contrary to public policy, or were incurred to generate tax-exempt income. Other expenses may be denied if they were incurred in connection with a personal transaction. Thus, for example, legal expenses may not be deductible even if ordinary, necessary to preserve a taxpayer's business assets, and reasonable in amount if they are attributable to a dispute arising from a personal transaction, such as divorce. Finally, it is important to distinguish between expenses and capital expenditures. The latter are not currently deductible but must be capitalized and recovered over time.

- Certain employment related expenses of employees are deductible as trade or business deductions if they are directly related to the performance of the employees' duties or are required by an employment agreement.

- More common trade or business deductions allowable under the criteria discussed above include advertising, bad debts, salaries, interest payments, rental payments, insurance, and legal fees. Allowable business deductions related to capital expenditures include depreciation, amortization, and depletion. Business start-up expenditures and business gifts are restricted deductions.

- Expenses incurred to produce income must meet the same requirements as those incurred in a trade or business in order to be deductible, with the exception of the requirement that they be incurred in a trade or business activity. This category of deductions includes investment expenses and tax planning and preparation expenses.

- All expenses incurred by individual taxpayers in connection with the determination, collection, or refund of any tax are deductible.

- Individual taxpayers are allowed deductions for business losses, investment losses, and casualty or theft losses. Personal losses other than casualty and theft losses are not deductible. With the exception of some selected expenditures, basic personal living expenses of a taxpayer are not deductible.

■ Some additional factors that may affect the amount of an allowable tax deduction are tax accounting method used, substantiation of deductions, and deductible amounts paid on behalf of another taxpayer.

QUESTIONS

1. Tax deductions for an individual taxpayer can be divided into what three categories?

2. What are production of income tax deductions? What allowable deductions are included in the production of income deductions category?

3. Explain the difference between a deduction for AGI and a deduction from AGI. Which type of deduction would be more advantageous for tax purposes?

4. How might an improper classification of a deduction as for or from AGI affect the itemized deductions on a taxpayer's return? How might this improper classification have an effect on a taxpayer's state income tax liability?

5. List the criteria that must be met before an expenditure can be considered as an allowable trade or business tax deduction.

6. Explain why the IRS would be interested in the reasonableness of a salary payment to an employee/owner of a closely held corporation.

7. If an activity of a taxpayer is determined to be a hobby for tax purposes, what tax deductions are available to the taxpayer? Are there any limitations on these deductions?

8. If an expenditure is part business-related and part personal, how does the taxpayer determine the business-related amount that is deductible for tax purposes?

9. What is the logical argument that supports the statutory disallowance of a deduction for any expenditure related to tax-exempt income?

10. Explain the difference between an employee and an independent contractor from a tax standpoint. What difference does it make for tax purposes if someone is characterized as an employee or independent contractor?

11. What losses are tax deductible for individual taxpayers?

12. How can a taxpayer substantiate a tax deduction if called on to do so by the IRS in an audit of the taxpayer's return?

13. What is the difference between a business and nonbusiness bad debt for tax purposes?

14. What are the basic requirements for a bad debt deduction on a tax return? Do any of these requirements differ between business and nonbusiness bad debts?

15. Can a current tax deduction for salaries and wages include payments for services performed in past years and for services to be performed in future years? Why is a sole proprietor not entitled to a tax deduction for salary payments to himself or herself?

16. Is salvage value ever considered when using MACRS depreciation? When using MACRS, is depreciation ever allowed on an asset in the year of disposal?

17. To qualify for the immediate expensing election (Code Sec. 179), an asset must meet what qualifications?

18. What is the difference between the cost depletion method and the percentage depletion method for tax purposes? Which method does a taxpayer use if the taxpayer is eligible for both methods?

19. What restrictions apply to tax deductions for business gifts?

20. Define the term "transportation expenses" as used for tax purposes. Give three examples of transportation expenses which are deductible by employees.

21. Define the term "travel expenses" as used for tax purposes. Define the term "away from home" as interpreted by the IRS.

22. In order for entertainment expenses to be deductible, the expenses must be "directly related to" or "associated with" a taxpayer's business. Define the terms "directly related to" and "associated with."

23. With regard to moving expenses paid or incurred by a taxpayer in connection with the commencement of work, what time and distance requirements must be met by the taxpayer in order to justify a moving expense deduction?

PROBLEMS

24. For the current year, Al Johnson used his personal car for both business and personal purposes. He drove 18,000 miles in the car during the year: 10,000 miles were for business-related purposes and 8,000 miles were for personal purposes. He incurred the following car expenses during the year:

Expense	Amount
Gas	$7,900
Maintenance	900
Repairs and depreciation	900
Car washes	500
Total	$10,200

Based on this information, what part of the above car expenses is deductible as business-related expenses on Al's current year income tax return?

25. Refer to the facts in Problem 24 and assume that Al's total car expenses amounted to only $6,700. What is the amount of Al's car expense deduction on his current year tax return?

26. Indicate whether the following expenditures are trade or business deductions (T), production of income deductions (PI), personal deductions (P), or are not deductible (X). Also indicate if the deductible expenditures are deductible "for" or "from" AGI.
    a. Business advertising
    b. Interest expense on home mortgage
    c. Union dues of employee
    d. Bank service charges on business checking account
    e. Entertainment expenses of employee not reimbursed by employer

27. Indicate whether the following expenditures are trade or business deductions (T), production of income deductions (PI), personal deductions (P), or are not deductible (X). Also indicate if the deductible expenditures are deductible "for" or "from" AGI.
    a. Interest expense on business loan
    b. Hobby expenses in excess of hobby income
    c. Commuting expenses of individual taxpayer
    d. Rent payments by illegal gambling business
    e. Payment to bribe government official made by a business

28. Are any of the following losses deductible on an individual's income tax return? If so, is the loss deductible "for" or "from" AGI? Explain each loss.

Loss	Amount
Loss on sale of stock by individual's business	$4,000
Hobby loss in excess of hobby gross income	3,000
Gambling losses in excess of gambling winnings	8,000
Loss on sale of stock on individual's investment portfolio	9,000
Decline in value of stock held in individual's investment portfolio	7,000
Loss on sale of personal automobile	2,000
Total	$33,000

29. Which of the following trade or business expenditures of Ajax Inc. are deductible on its current year tax return? If an expenditure is not deductible, explain why it is not a valid deduction.

Expenditure	Amount
Salaries and wages to employees	$400,000
Purchase of new office building	250,000
Payment of illegal parking fines of President	1,400
Payment of wedding expenses for President's daughter's wedding	16,000
Entertainment expenses related to company business	25,000
Interest on money borrowed to buy tax-exempt securities	9,000
Total expenditures	$700,400

30. Indicate whether the following expenditures are deductible for AGI or from AGI.
    a. Medical expenses of individual taxpayer
    b. Safe deposit box rental for business
    c. Interest expense on business loan
    d. Investment counseling fees incurred by individual investor
    e. Gambling losses to extent of gambling winnings of individual gambler not involved in gambling business

31. Indicate whether the following expenditures are deductible for AGI or from AGI.
    a. Entertainment expenses of employee not reimbursed by employer
    b. Moving expenses of employee
    c. Transportation expenses of employee not reimbursed by employer
    d. Hobby losses to extent of hobby income

32. Are any of the following expenditures deductible on an individual taxpayer's income tax return? Explain each item.

Expenditure	Amount
Cost of having income tax return prepared by a CPA	$100
Legal fee for divorce proceeding of which 20 percent related to tax planning advice	3,000
Lost wages for time missed from work while having income tax return prepared	250
Legal fee for estate planning advice of which 35 percent related to tax planning advice	900
Cost of having federal gift tax return prepared by a CPA	100
Total expenditures	$4,350

33. Two years ago, Jack Peters borrowed $150,000 from the First National Bank which he used to buy equipment used in his business. Business slowed considerably this year, and Jack was unable to make payments on the loan. To keep the bank from foreclosing on the note and putting his son out of business, Jack's father made several payments on the loan during the year. Of the total payments he made on the loan, $10,000 was attributable to interest and the remainder was applied to reduce the principal balance.

Can Jack's father deduct the $10,000 in interest expense he paid on Jack's loan? Explain.

34. For the current month, Jackson Cement Co. incurred payroll expenses as follows:

Gross salaries and wages	$675,000
Payroll taxes:	
OASDI (Social Security Tax)—employer's share	41,850
HI (Medicare tax)—employer's share	9,788
	726,638
Amounts withheld and paid to the government:	
Employee income taxes withheld	(108,990)
OASDI—employees' share	(41,850)
HI—employees' share	(9,788)

    a. What amount can Jackson claim as a tax deduction for salary and wage expense?
    b. How much can Jackson deduct as tax expense?

35. Bevis Bag Co. purchased a tract of land on August 31 of the current year, paying $225,000. Prior to the sale, the seller paid property taxes of $18,000 on the property. The taxes covered the calendar year period January 1 through December 31.
    a. Will Bevis be allowed to deduct any portion of the property taxes paid by the seller prior to the sale? If so, how much?
    b. What will be Bevis' tax basis in the land?

36. Compute MACRS depreciation for the following qualified assets for the calendar years 2015 and 2016: (Ignore bonus depreciation and the Section 179 deduction.)

Asset	Year Purchased	Cost	Salvage Value
Business equipment (7-year property)	March 2015	$85,500	$10,000
Car	May 2015	14,000	1,000
Office furniture (7-year property)	July 2015	18,050	3,000
Building (Office)	January 2015	185,000	5,000

37. Refer to the facts in Problem 36 and assume that the straight-line method under the alternative MACRS system was elected over the MACRS recovery period for all the assets listed. Based on these facts, compute the 2015 and 2016 depreciation deductions for each of the assets listed. (Ignore bonus depreciation and the Section 179 deduction.)

38. Refer to the facts in Problem 36 and assume that the office building purchased in January 2015 and the car purchased in 2015 were both sold in June 2016. How much depreciation can be claimed as a deduction on these two assets in 2016 for the portion of the year they were held by the taxpayer? Assume MACRS depreciation is used.

39. Refer to the facts in Problem 36 and assume the business equipment purchased in March was instead purchased in November. Based on these facts, compute the MACRS depreciation for the business equipment, car, and office furniture for calendar years 2015 and 2016. (Ignore bonus depreciation and the Section 179 deduction.)

40. In 2015, Jason Products Co., a calendar year taxpayer, purchased business equipment (7-year property) for $2,150,000. No other personal property was purchased during the year. Jason wants to take the largest possible tax deduction in 2015 related to this property. Compute the largest tax deduction possible in 2015 for the business equipment. (Consider bonus depreciation and the Code Sec. 179 deduction).

41. LB Corporation purchased a business car in June 2015 for $42,000. The car weighs 4,000 pounds and will be used 100 percent of the time in the business. Compute the largest depreciation deduction possible in 2015. No other property purchases were made during the year. (Consider bonus depreciation and the Section 179 deduction, if applicable.)

42. Refer to the facts in Problem 41 and assume the business car purchased is an SUV weighing 8,000 pounds. Compute the largest depreciation deduction possible in 2015. (Consider bonus depreciation and the Section 179 deduction, if applicable.)

43. LCD Corporation purchased residential real property for $385,000 (exclusive of land cost) and placed it in service on August 16, 2015. Compute MACRS depreciation on the property for 2015 and 2016.

44. Refer to the facts in Problem 43 and assume the property purchased is nonresidential rental property. Compute MACRS depreciation on the property for 2015 and 2016, assuming the property is not qualified leasehold improvement, retail improvement or restaurant property.

45. In March, Gary Parker started a new career as a real estate agent. He established Gary Parker Company, LLC on March 11 and began seeking clients. He listed his first property on March 21, and closed his first sale on April 9. Gary used his SUV, purchased three years ago and previously used for personal purposes, as his business auto. Once he began business as a real estate agent, he used the vehicle 100 percent for business purposes. Gary purchased the SUV three years ago for $42,000. At the date he started his real estate practice, it was worth approximately $28,000.
    a. What is the maximum amount Gary can claim as a first-year deduction under Code Sec. 179 this year with respect to the vehicle?
    b. What is the maximum amount of depreciation expense Gary can claim with respect to the vehicle on the current year tax return?

46. Assume the same facts as in Problem 46. Further assume that next year, Gary sells the SUV for $20,000.
    a. How much depreciation expense can Gary deduct as a business deduction with respect to the SUV on next year's tax return?
    b. How much gain or loss will Gary recognize for tax purposes in connection with the sale of the vehicle next year?

47. In the current year, James Jar Co., a calendar year taxpayer, incurred the following research and experimentation expenditures (R&E): Salaries—$150,000; and Materials—$100,000.
    a. If James Jar Co. treats R&E as a current deduction, what is the amount of the current year deduction?
    b. If James Jar Co. capitalizes R&E and amortizes it over a 60-month period, what is the amount of deduction on a monthly basis that James can take, starting with the month when benefits from the R&E are first realized?

48. At the beginning of the year, NRD Company purchased the rights to a natural resource for $10,000,000. The estimated recoverable units from the natural resource amount to 3,500,000 units. During the year, NRD sold 1,000,000 units of the natural resource for $10 per unit and incurred operating costs other than depletion of $5 per unit. Based on these facts:
    a. Compute NRD's depletion deduction using the cost depletion method.
    b. Compute the company's depletion deduction using the percentage depletion method. Assume a 15 percent specified depletion percentage.
    c. Which depletion deduction, cost or percentage, will NRD use this year?

49. In 2015, Mary Kelly drove her personal car 2,800 miles for business purposes. She also incurred $182 in parking fees and $191 in turnpike tolls connected with her business trips. None of her automobile expenses were reimbursed by her employer. Compute Mary's deduction for automobile expenses on her current year tax return, assuming all of the above expenses are valid and she elects to use the standard mileage allowance method to figure her automobile expenses.

50. Herman Welbe owns one car dealership in Ohio and one in Florida. Each year, Herman lives eight months in Ohio and four months in Florida. In the current year, Herman received $900,000 net income from his Ohio dealership and $250,000 net income from his Florida dealership. Based on these facts, is Herman entitled to any travel expenses for tax purposes in relation to his trips between his two dealerships and for living expenses incurred at either location? Explain.

51. On Monday, Harvey Leonard travels from Chicago to New York on a business trip. The trip lasts five days. Three days of the trip are spent conducting business activities and two days are spent on personal sightseeing activities. Harvey incurs $550 in airfare costs in going to and returning from New York, $50 a day in expenses for meals, and $100 a day for lodging while in New York.
    a. What amount is deductible on Harvey's tax return for travel expenses related to the above activities? Assume Harvey is self-employed.
    b. Assume Harvey is an employee and is reimbursed $700 by his employer for the trip. What amount is deductible on Harvey's tax return for unreimbursed travel expenses related to the above activities?

52. This year, Peter Poppins incurred the following employment-related moving expenses:

Expenses related to moving household goods	$4,000
Expenses to drive from old location to new location	60
Temporary living expenses in new location	1,800
Real estate commission on sale of old home	2,200
Total expenses	$8,060

Peter received no reimbursement from his employer for his moving expenses. Based on the above facts, and assuming that Peter meets the time and distance requirements, compute Peter's moving expense deduction that would appear on his current year tax return.

53. For an individual taxpayer, expenses connected with rents and royalties are normally deducted:
    a. For AGI
    b. From AGI
    c. Either for or from AGI
    d. For AGI but limited to a maximum percentage amount

54. An ordinary trade or business expenditure is one which is:
    a. Reasonable in amount
    b. Commonly incurred by other businesses
    c. Appropriate for a particular business
    d. Not a capital expenditure

55. A necessary trade or business expenditure is one which is:
    a. Reasonable in amount
    b. Commonly incurred by other businesses
    c. Appropriate for a particular business
    d. Not a capital expenditure

56. In 2015, the maximum amount of capital expenditures eligible for immediate expensing is:
    a. $139,000
    b. $25,000
    c. $500,000
    d. $2,000,000

57. **Comprehensive Problem (Tax Return Problem).** John Stantus, single, is the sole owner of Stantus Accounting Services, Co. He started the company, which is organized as a sole proprietorship, on February 10 of the current year. For this year, Stantus Accounting Services reported the following amounts of income and expenses:

Fee revenues	$540,000
Expenses:	
Employee wages	(125,000)
Payroll taxes	(9,563)
Advertising	(3,600)
Insurance	(2,400)
Utilities	(7,200)
Rent	(10,000)
Supplies	(5,000)
Selling expenses	(35,000)

- John purchased a car on February 1 of the current year for $24,000. He uses the car for both business and personal purposes. Mileage logs indicate that John put 40,000 miles on the car this year. Of that total, 28,000 miles were business related and the remaining 12,000 were related to personal travel. John wants to deduct the maximum amount allowable for business use of his car.

- John also purchased office equipment, computers and other five-year property for use in the business. He purchased $285,000 worth of such depreciable assets in March. He wants to deduct the maximum amount allowable under Code Sec. 179 and depreciate the remaining cost (if any) under the MACRS system. Assume that the Sec. 179 deduction and bonus depreciation are not extended past 2014.

- Selling expenses include $6,000 spent for meals and entertainment incurred on John's sales calls during the year.

- Selling expenses also include $12,000 in illegal payments to city officials paid to secure a lucrative contract with the city. John was uncomfortable making this payment, but reasoned that the contract was important to get his business off to a good start.

- Selling expenses also include gasoline, parking fees, and other documented auto expenses totaling $2,500 attributable to John's sales calls.

Assume that John reports the revenue and expenses of Stantus Accounting Services on Schedule C, that he uses the cash method of accounting, and that he has no other taxable income, deductions or credits other than the items listed above. As noted above, he is single, with no dependents. He lives at 105 1st Street in Jackson, Mississippi (zip code = 39201). His social security number is 555-33-4444. His business address is 501 19th Street, Jackson, MS 39201. Skipping Schedule SE (on which you would ordinarily calculate the self-employment tax), prepare John's 2014 Individual Income Tax Return. (Note: you may have to use 2014 forms.)

58. **Comprehensive Problem.** Peter Nerf, a single taxpayer, is an accountant employed by a large corporation. This year, he was transferred from the company's headquarters office to an office in another state. For the year, he had the following items of income and expense:

Wages received from his employer		$75,000
Moving expenses:		
Expenses to move household furniture	$3,000	
Travel from old residence to new location	700	
Temporary living expenses in new location	2,100	
Real estate commission on sale of old home	5,000	10,800
Medical expenses		6,600
Charitable contributions		5,000
Job related expenses (subscriptions, licenses, etc.) not reimbursed by Peter's employer		2,350

Peter's moving expenses were not reimbursed by his employer. Assuming that he had no other taxable income, deductions or credits other than those listed above, calculate Peter's taxable income for the current year.

59. **Research Problem.** The following selected court cases have helped to shape the tax law in regard to allowable trade or business tax deductions. Read the following court cases and prepare a brief written abstract for each case.
a. *New Colonial Ice Co.,* 4 USTC ¶1292, 292 U.S. 435.
b. *T.H. Welch v. Helvering,* 3 USTC ¶1164, 290 U.S. 111.

60. **Research Problem.** Prepare a brief written abstract for each of the following additional selected court cases relating to allowable trade or business deductions.
a. *A. Trujillo,* 68 TC 670, Dec. 34,554.
b. *Illinois Terminal Railroad Co.,* 67-1 USTC ¶9374, 179 Ct.Cls. 674, 375 F.2d 1016 (Ct.Cls. 1967).
c. *I.R. Wharton,* 53-2 USTC ¶9597, 207 F.2d 526 (CA-5 1953).

Chapter

7

Deductions: Business/Investment Losses and Passive Activity Losses

OBJECTIVES

After completing Chapter 7, you should be able to:

1. Determine the amount and classification of losses originating from business operations.
2. Ascertain the amount and classification of losses from investment-related activities.
3. Understand tax shelters and the rationale for at-risk rules.
4. Achieve a thorough understanding of the intricacies of the passive activity rules.
5. Identify and determine the amount of allowable business and theft losses.
6. Calculate the amount of a net operating loss and determine the amounts to be carried back and forward.
7. Understand the allowable home office expenses and determine the limitation on the deduction for such losses.
8. Achieve an understanding of the vacation home rental rules and the limitation on such losses.
9. Understand the benefits and calculations related to the new manufacturing deduction under Code Sec. 199.

OVERVIEW

Deductions are provided in the Code for losses resulting from unprofitable investment-related activities, dispositions of certain assets, and unprofitable business operations. In each of these cases certain limitations or adjustments may apply, thus limiting the amount of deductible loss. Generally, deductible losses from a business, property held for production of income, or investment property are deductible for adjusted gross income. Losses derived from personal-use property, if deductible, are usually deducted from adjusted gross income as itemized deductions.

This chapter deals with losses originating from business operations and certain investment-related activities. Tax shelters, at-risk rules, passive activity rules, business casualty and theft losses, net operating losses, hobby losses, home office expenses, and vacation homes are among the topics addressed. Casualty losses derived from personal-use properties are discussed in Chapter 8, and losses resulting from the sale of capital assets (e.g., stocks and bonds) and business-use assets (Code Sec. 1231) are discussed in Chapter 12.

Tax Shelters and At-Risk Rules

¶7001   TAX SHELTERS

A tax shelter is an activity providing deductions and/or credits to an investor which will reduce tax liability with respect to income from other sources. Prior to the Tax Reform Act of 1986, tax shelters played an unreasonably influential role in the financial planning of many individuals. A Treasury study revealed that in 1983, 21 percent of tax returns reporting total positive income greater than $250,000 paid taxes equaling *10 percent or less* of total positive income (which is composed of salary, interest, dividends, and income from profitable businesses and investments). S. Rept. No. 313, 99th Cong., 2d Sess. (1986), p. 714.

Congress recognized the undesirable consequences that tax shelters created, which included declining federal tax revenues, diverting investment capital from productive activities to tax avoidance schemes, and perhaps most importantly, the loss of faith in the federal tax system. The Senate Finance Committee went so far as to say: "Extensive shelter activity contributes to public concerns that the tax system is unfair and to the belief that tax is paid only by the naive and unsophisticated." The reason Congress had allowed tax shelters to exist in the first place was to encourage investment in certain areas in order to promote economic growth.

EXAMPLE 7.1

Arthur Johnson, a corporate executive, had income of $275,000 during 1983 (before passive loss rules). He took advantage of the tax laws (legally) by purchasing a shopping center in January 1983. The price was $500,000. He paid $25,000 down and financed the balance over 20 years. Rental income averaged $3,500 a month, while payment on the $475,000 note was $6,000 a month. Maintenance, taxes, and repairs averaged $1,500 a month. Initially, it appears that Mr. Johnson was losing $4,000 a month ($3,500 − $6,000 − $1,500) during his first year of ownership ($48,000 a year). But after considering his tax bracket (50 percent) and depreciation (12 percent for 1983), his net cash flow actually increased by $5,000 for the year because of preferential tax rules:

Net Cash Flow Before Tax Benefit	$(48,000)
Depreciation (12% × $500,000)	(60,000)
Principal Payment Adjustment*	2,000
Net Deductible Loss	$(106,000)
Times Tax Bracket	× .50
Tax Benefit	$53,000
Net Cash Flow Before Tax Benefit	(48,000)
Net Cash Flow	$5,000

* $2,000 of the note payments were applied to principal (i.e., not deductible), all other monthly expenses were deductible.

Notice that the tax benefit in the preceding example was treated as an immediate cash inflow. It simply reduced the taxpayer's tax liability by the tax benefit amount, which, essentially, represented taxes that would have been paid on income from other sources, such as salary, dividends, interest, etc. When coupled with the possibility that the property could increase in value, this was a popular form of investment and an easy concept for tax shelter salesmen to sell. However, most such investments never provided a net cash flow as illustrated in the example.

Practically all tax shelters were formed as limited partnerships. Limited partnerships were used because they allowed losses and credits to be passed through to the partners' individual tax returns. A limited partner is a partner who is not personally liable for the debts of the partnership. More importantly, a limited partner can utilize deductions and/or credits that "flow through" from the partnership. Some examples of the activities tax shelter limited partnerships engaged in included equipment leasing, real estate, oil and gas, movie productions, cattle breeding, cattle feeding, and farming. Even though most tax shelters never made a profit, thousands of taxpayers bought into them for the sole purpose of avoiding income taxes. Thus, genuine economic value was rarely considered in making an investment decision to acquire an interest in a tax shelter activity.

The Tax Reform Act of 1986 significantly impacted such investment decisions with the passage of the passive activity rules. Code Sec. 469. *Essentially all limited partnership investments, rental properties, and businesses in which an owner does not materially participate have been affected.* The general rule is that losses arising from a passive activity are not deductible, except against income from a passive activity. The unused portion of the loss, however, is not lost but is suspended (i.e., carried over) until offset by passive income in a future tax year or until the entire activity is disposed of in a fully taxable transaction.

EXAMPLE 7.2

Assume the same facts as in the preceding example, except that if Arthur Johnson purchased the shopping center in 2015, his investment would fall under the passive activity rules, which would allow no deduction (i.e., no tax benefit) for the loss in 2015. The entire disallowed loss would become a suspended loss until passive income is later received or he appropriately disposes of the rental property. For instance, if in 2016 the shopping center yields $25,000 in income, then the loss from 2015 would be used to offset the income and any unused balance of suspended loss would be carried over to 2017.

¶7125   AT-RISK RULES

Prior to the 1986 Act, Congress made a rather weak attempt to curb tax shelter abuse by enacting the at-risk provisions (Code Sec. 465) in 1976. The at-risk rules disallow losses that are in excess of an investor's amount at risk. In a general sense, at risk is the amount of investment that an investor could possibly lose. The rules apply to individuals as well as closely held corporations. An investor's amount at risk is computed as follows:

Cash invested
- \+ Adjusted basis of other property invested
- \+ Borrowings for which investor is personally liable
- \+ Borrowings for which investor has pledged collateral
- \+ Allocated portion of income
- \− Allocated portion of losses
- \− Withdrawals
- \= Amount at risk

The formula does not indicate to what extent the allocated losses are deductible for tax purposes, because the amount at risk is reduced (but not below zero) regardless of the extent to which the losses are deductible. The deductible portion of any possible losses is calculated *after* applying the at-risk rules.

An investor is not at risk for nonrecourse borrowings, stop-loss arrangements, no-loss guarantees, or borrowings in which the lender has an interest (as in seller financing). Code Sec. 465. A nonrecourse loan is a loan that is secured by the property purchased, rather than the personal assets of the borrower (i.e., the borrower is not personally liable). A recourse loan, on the other hand, is one where the borrower is personally liable for repayment.

EXAMPLE 7.3

Betty Smith gave $10,000 cash, pledged $10,000 for security of a partnership loan, and gave a computer with an adjusted basis of $5,000 for her interest in a limited partnership. Her amount at risk is $25,000. The activity allocated a $40,000 loss (passive loss) to her. Only $25,000 (the amount at risk) of the $40,000 loss can be used to offset income from other passive activities during the year. Since she is not at risk for the remaining $15,000, it is carried over into a future tax year until she becomes at risk, which would then free up this amount to be offset against passive income.

EXAMPLE 7.4

Assume Betty Smith gave $10,000 cash and signed a nonrecourse note for property that the limited partnership was acquiring. Ms. Smith would only be at risk for her $10,000 cash investment, and, consequently, only $10,000 of the $40,000 could be used to offset income from other passive activities. The remaining $30,000 is carried over until she becomes at risk.

Generally, taxpayers are not considered at risk with regard to nonrecourse loans. However, a partner is considered to be at risk for certain *qualified* nonrecourse loans on real property. A qualified nonrecourse loan is one acquired from:

1. a person who is actively and regularly engaged in the business of lending money, or
2. any federal, state, or local government (including loans guaranteed by such governments) (Code Sec. 465(b)(6)(B))

An exception to this rule applies for loans acquired from:

1. Related parties,
2. The seller of the property, or
3. A person who receives a fee due to the taxpayer's investment in the property.

A partner would not be at risk for such loans. Code Sec. 49(a)(1)(D)(iv).

Because losses reduce the amount at risk, such losses usually may be recaptured if the investor's amount at risk is less than zero at the close of a taxable year. Code Sec. 465(e). Thus, when an individual's amount at risk drops below zero, the taxpayer will include in gross income the amount of the excess. A drop in at risk, for example, can occur when a debt arrangement is changed from recourse to nonrecourse.

TAX BLUNDER

Lynn R. and Wade L. Moser et al., the taxpayers, entered into a leveraged computer leasing transaction with Finalco Inc. Finalco entered into leases with end-users, purchased the equipment, financed the purchase with a lending institution, and then resold the equipment in a sale and leaseback transaction to Lease Pro Inc., a company engaged in the purchase, sale, and leasing of computer equipment. The taxpayers then purchased the equipment from Lease Pro and leased it back to Finalco. The fixed monthly rental payment that Finalco owed to the taxpayers was the same amount as the monthly installments that the taxpayers owed to Lease Pro that, in term, was identical to the monthly installments Lease Pro owed to Finalco. As a result, in making payments, no cash was exchanged because the amount owed by each group equaled the amount each group was due. From 1981 to 1983, the taxpayers reported net losses totaling $300,937. However, these losses were disallowed because the court held that the taxpayers were not at risk under Code Sec. 465(b)(4). That is, this section suspends at-risk treatment where a transaction is structured, by whatever technique, to remove any realistic possibility that the taxpayer will suffer an economic loss if the transaction turns out to be unprofitable. *W.L. Moser*, 90-2 USTC ¶50,498, 914 F.2d 1040 (CA-8 1990). Whenever the circular nature of the taxpayers' obligations effectively shields the taxpayers from economic loss, Code Sec. 465(b)(4) will hold that the taxpayers are not at risk for any portion of the notes underlying the transaction.

Passive Activity Loss Rules

¶7201 ## APPLICATION OF RULES

The at-risk rules are still in effect and are applied before passive loss restrictions. Once the at-risk rules are satisfied, a passive loss can then be used in the following ways: offset passive income, offset other income (under certain conditions), and/or become suspended. Passive income and losses are "before AGI" items.

EXAMPLE 7.5

Bob McKeown contributed $35,000 cash and signed a $15,000 nonrecourse note to invest in Limited Partnership A (LPA). He is at risk for $35,000 in the partnership. Bob is also at risk for $50,000 in Limited Partnership B (LPB). Both activities are considered to be passive activities. During the year, LPA experienced a loss and allocated to him his portion of the loss, $65,000. LPB had a better year and allocated $25,000 of income to Bob. Because Bob is at risk for only $35,000 for LPA, only $35,000 of the $65,000 loss is considered as a passive loss. As a result, $25,000 of the $35,000 passive loss from LPA can be used to offset the $25,000 of passive income (before AGI) from LPB. Ten thousand dollars ($35,000 – $25,000) of the passive loss from LPA is suspended under the passive loss rules. At the end of the year, Bob's amount at risk for LPA will be zero ($35,000 – $35,000). The remaining $30,000 ($65,000 – $35,000) loss from LPA is carried over under the at-risk rules until Bob increases his amount at risk in LPA. Once Bob satisfies the at-risk rules, this amount will become a passive loss and may be used to offset future passive gains. Bob will be at risk for $75,000 ($50,000 + $25,000) for LPB at the end of the year.

Partnership	Initial Amount At Risk	Allocated Gain (Loss)	Loss Passive Income (Loss)	Carryover Under At-Risk Rules	Suspended Passive Loss	Ending Amount At Risk
A	$35,000	($65,000)	($35,000)	($30,000)	($10,000)	$0
B	$50,000	$25,000	$25,000	—	—	$75,000

If Bob had received $45,000 of passive income from LPB (instead of $25,000), his results would be different. He could offset the passive income with $35,000 of passive losses from LPA, resulting in $10,000 of net passive income, and have no suspended passive loss. His amount at risk for LPA is still zero and he still has a loss carryover under the at-risk rules of $30,000. His ending amount at risk for LPB would be $95,000 ($50,000 + $45,000).

Partnership	Initial Amount At Risk	Allocated Gain (Loss)	Passive Income (Loss)	Loss Carryover Under At-Risk Rules	Suspended Passive Loss	Ending Amount At Risk
A	$35,000	($65,000)	($35,000)	($30,000)	$0	$0
B	$50,000	$45,000	$45,000	—	—	$95,000

¶7205 CLASSIFICATION OF INCOME

Because of the passive activity rules, income is required to be classified as active, passive, or portfolio. Ordinarily, active income is attributable to the direct efforts of the taxpayer, such as salary, commissions, wages, etc. Passive income is income derived from a passive activity. Portfolio income is interest, dividends, annuities, and royalties not derived in the ordinary course of a trade or business. The gain from the sale of property that produces portfolio income (e.g., stocks and bonds) is also classified as portfolio income. Code Sec. 469(e). The reason for the classification is to keep separate the types of income that passive losses can offset. As previously mentioned, passive losses can only offset passive income and cannot be used as a deduction against active or portfolio income (except in certain instances). Similarly, tax credits from passive activities can only offset taxes incurred from passive income.

Portfolio income received by a limited partnership and allocated to the partners is not passive income, and the partners cannot offset the portfolio income by passive losses from this partnership or any other passive activity. Thus, limited partnerships that receive portfolio income and experience net income (or loss) from operations must separately allocate income (loss) generated from operations and portfolio income to its partners.

¶7211 DISALLOWANCE OF PASSIVE LOSSES AND CREDITS

For tax years after 1990, no passive activity losses or credits may be deducted against active and portfolio income. Interests in passive activities acquired by the taxpayer on or before October 22, 1986 (the date on which the Tax Reform Act of 1986 was enacted), were eligible for a special deduction and credit phaseout of losses for a five-year period. Code Sec. 469(m)(2). Thus, after 1990, passive losses in excess of passive gains are not deductible and must be carried forward.

¶7215 SUSPENDED LOSSES

Generally, any loss or credit from a passive activity which is disallowed by the passive loss rules is treated as a deduction or credit allocable to such activity in the next taxable year. Code Sec. 469(b). Suspended losses can become deductible against future income from passive activities or against nonpassive income upon the fully taxable disposition of an entire interest. Keeping suspended losses for each passive activity separate is necessary in order to determine the amount of an activity's deductible portion of suspended loss whenever an event qualifying for the deduction occurs (e.g., a fully taxable disposition).

EXAMPLE 7.6

Linda Helmsly owned the following passive activities during 2015 (all were acquired after 1986, and she was at risk for all losses):

Activity		Income/ (Loss)	Suspended (Loss)*
ABC		$35,000	$0
XYZ		(45,000)	(20,000)
BBD		(60,000)	(80,000)
		$(70,000)	

* Suspended losses from previous years.

The amount of net loss experienced in 2015, $70,000, is not deductible but is suspended. It must be allocated, however, between all activities showing a loss for the year (XYZ and BBD):

Activity	Allocation	Suspended (Loss)	Total Suspended (Loss)
ABC	N/A	$0	$0
XYZ	$45,000/$105,000 × $70,000	(30,000)	(50,000)
BBD	$60,000/$105,000 × $70,000	(40,000)	(120,000)

APPLICATION OF THE AT-RISK AND PASSIVE LOSS RULES

Step 1. Determine the amount at risk for each passive activity (before considering gain or loss for that year).

Step 2. Determine whether each passive activity results in a gain or loss for the tax year.

Step 3. If an activity results in a gain:

    (a)   Increase the amount at risk for that activity.

    (b)   Treat gain as passive gain.

Step 4. If an activity results in a loss:

    (a)   Reduce the amount at risk for that activity (but not below zero) by the amount of the loss.

    (b)   Any excess losses are carried over under the at-risk rules.

    (c)   Treat losses (except for amounts carried over) as passive losses.

Step 5. Add up all passive gains.

Step 6. Add up all passive losses.

Step 7. Reduce passive gains (but not below zero) by passive losses and any passive loss credits. Include any net passive gain in gross income.

Step 8. Carry over excess passive losses as suspended passive losses.

    (a)   If more than one activity results in a passive loss, allocate suspended passive losses between the activities in proportion to the amount of their passive losses.

    (b)   In future tax years, use suspended passive losses to offset passive income.

¶7225 DISPOSITION OF A PASSIVE ACTIVITY

If a passive activity is disposed of in a fully taxable transaction, any losses (including suspended losses from prior years) may be recognized by the taxpayer in the year of disposition. Such losses can offset active and portfolio income (nonpassive income). However, losses from the sale of passive activities to related parties generally are not deductible. See Chapter 10.

The excess of the sum of Items 1 + 2 over 3 will be treated as a loss which is not from a passive activity (i.e., deductible against nonpassive income):

1. Any loss from the activity for the tax year, including suspended losses from prior years, plus
2. Any loss realized from the disposition of the activity, over
3. Net income or gain from all passive activities (determined without regard to losses from the disposition or losses from the activity). Code Sec. 469(g)(1).

Passive activity interests that are capital assets and are appropriately disposed of are subject to the capital asset rules for losses (Code Sec. 1211) after applying the passive loss rules. See Chapter 12. A limited partnership interest held as an investment is a capital asset.

EXAMPLE 7.7

Rob Williams had gross income of $125,000 in 2015 and owned the following passive activities during the year:

Activity	Gain/(Loss)	Suspended (Loss)
ZZZ	$15,000	$(50,000)
XXX	(10,000)	(28,000)
YYY	(22,500)	(45,000)

All activities were acquired after 1986, and Rob was at risk for all losses. He sold his entire interest in ZZZ in a fully taxable transaction. ZZZ was a limited partnership in which Rob was a limited partner. He acquired the limited partnership interest in 1987. The selling price was $22,000, while his basis in the interest was $55,000. The result is computed as follows:

Selling price	$22,000
Adjusted basis	(55,000)
Realized loss	$(33,000)

The $50,000 of suspended losses will first offset the $15,000 gain from ZZZ, and the balance ($35,000) will be deductible against active and portfolio income. The $33,000 realized loss resulting from the sale of the limited partnership interest will become a long-term capital loss.

Death, Gift, and Other Transfers

If an interest in a passive activity is transferred by reason of death, suspended losses are deductible on a decedent's income tax return to the extent that the excess of the stepped-up basis in the hands of the transferee over the decedent's adjusted basis is less than the amount of suspended loss.

EXAMPLE 7.8

Zeb McFarland died and left a passive activity to his nephew. Zeb's basis in the activity was $25,000, while the nephew's basis was "stepped up" to $40,000. Suspended losses amounted to $21,000. The amount of passive loss deduction that can offset nonpassive income is $6,000, the $21,000 suspended loss minus the $15,000 step-up in basis.

If an interest in a passive activity is transferred by gift, the suspended losses are not deductible but are added to the recipient's basis.

EXAMPLE 7.9

Jennie Franklin gave her daughter a limited partnership interest in a real estate activity. Suspended losses amounted to $20,000. The mother's adjusted basis at the time of the gift was $30,000. The daughter's basis would be the mother's adjusted basis plus the amount of suspended losses, or $50,000 (assuming fair market value was greater than $30,000).

¶7231 TAXPAYERS AFFECTED BY PASSIVE LOSSES

The passive loss limitations apply to individuals, estates, trusts, closely held corporations, and personal service corporations. Code Sec. 469(a)(2). This list describes taxpayers that would otherwise be entitled to the tax benefits of losses or credits from a passive activity. Partnerships and S corporations are not included. Limitations on losses or credits from activities operated by these entities are passed through and applied at the level of the partners and shareholders, respectively.

Personal Service Corporations

The application of the passive activity loss rules to personal service corporations is intended to prevent taxpayers from sheltering personal service income simply by incorporating as a personal service corporation and acquiring passive activity investments at the corporate level. In general, a corporation is a personal service corporation if (1) it is a C corporation, (2) its principal activity is the performance of personal services, (3) the services are substantially performed by employee-owners, and (4) such employee-owners own more than 10 percent of the fair market value of the corporation's outstanding stock. Whether these qualifications are satisfied is determined during a testing period for the tax year, which is generally the corporation's prior tax year. Temp. Reg. §1.469-1T(g)(2).

Closely Held Corporations

A closely held corporation's losses and credits from a passive activity may be limited if (1) it is a C corporation that is not a personal service corporation, and (2) more than 50 percent of its stock is owned directly or indirectly by (or for) not more than five individuals. Noting the distinction between taxpayers is worthwhile because closely held corporations are able to offset passive losses with net active income, but not portfolio income. Code Sec. 469(e)(2). Consequently, a closely held corporation is the only entity affected by the passive loss rules that can deduct losses from a passive activity that it owns.

EXAMPLE 7.10

Jasper Corporation, a closely held corporation, generated $150,000 of income from operations during the year. It also received passive losses of $200,000 and interest of $30,000. (Jasper Corporation was fully at risk for the amount of loss.) The corporation's taxable income is $30,000 because it can offset passive losses with active income, but not with portfolio income. The remaining $50,000 of passive losses will become suspended.

Oil and Gas Working Interests

A working interest which a taxpayer holds in oil and gas properties is not subject to the passive activity rules. Code Sec. 469(c)(3). The working interest cannot be held through any entity that limits the taxpayer's liability (e.g., limited partnership interest or stock in a corporation). A working interest is a working or operating mineral interest in any tract or parcel of land. Temp. Reg. §1.469-1T(e)(4)(iv).

¶7235 MATERIAL PARTICIPATION

A passive activity is defined as "any activity which involves the conduct of a trade or business, and in which the taxpayer does not materially participate." Code Sec. 469(c)(1). Also included in the definition are rental activities, without regard to the extent of taxpayer participation. Temp. Reg. §1.469-1T(e)(1)(ii). As a consequence, trade or business activities in which a taxpayer does materially participate are not passive activities. Nevertheless, rental of real estate properties is generally classified as a passive activity regardless of the level of participation.

"Material participation" requires a taxpayer to be involved in the operations of the activity on a regular, continuous, and substantial basis. Code Sec. 469(h)(1). When making this rule, Congress was aware that many taxpayers would accumulate suspended losses from tax shelter investments as a result of the passive loss rules. Moreover, some of these taxpayers might own profitable businesses that could be turned into passive activities (which would then be used to offset passive losses). The change from an active business to a passive activity could possibly be achieved by lowering a taxpayer's level of participation in the active business. The result of such maneuvering would impede the overall effectiveness of the passive loss provisions. Material participation, then, was devised to include virtually all "passive" business owners but at the same time exclude certain "active" business owners from being brought into the passive loss arena.

On the other hand, a business in which an individual materially participates is not a passive activity. Therefore, if the business experiences a loss, the loss will be deductible against all other types of income (passive, active, and/or portfolio) without regard to the passive loss restrictions. Additional guidance in making the determination as to who qualifies as a material participant is provided under the regulations by furnishing seven tests. Temp. Reg. §1.469-5T(a). Thus, an individual will be treated as materially participating in an activity for the tax year if any of the following tests apply:

Test 1.	The individual participates in the activity for more than 500 hours during the tax year.
Test 2.	The individual's participation in the activity constitutes substantially all of the participation in such activity of all individuals (including individuals who are not owners) for the tax year.
Test 3.	The individual participates in the activity for more than 100 hours during the tax year, and such individual's participation for the tax year is not less than the participation in the activity of any other individual (including nonowners) for the tax year.
Test 4.	The activity is a "significant participation" activity for the tax year, and the individual's aggregate participation in all significant participation activities during such year exceeds 500 hours (see below).
Test 5.	The individual materially participated in the activity for any five tax years, whether or not consecutive, during the 10 tax years that immediately preceded the tax year.
Test 6.	The activity is a personal service activity and the individual materially participated in the activity for any three tax years, whether or not consecutive, preceding the tax year.
Test 7.	Based on all of the facts and circumstances, the individual participates in the activity on a regular, continuous, and substantial basis during the tax year.

Also note that in determining whether a taxpayer materially participates, the participation of a taxpayer's spouse will be taken into account. Code Sec. 469(h)(5).

Significant Participation

An individual is treated as significantly participating in an activity for a tax year if and only if the individual participates in the activity for more than 100 hours during the year. A significant participating activity is a trade or business in which an individual significantly participates, but not to the extent of material participation as determined by the other six tests. Temp. Reg. §1.469-5T(c). In other words, an individual may have ownership interests in several businesses, but participates infrequently (less than material participation in each). If the hours of participation for each activity exceed 100, and the total number of hours in all such businesses exceeds 500, then the individual is treated as materially participating in all such businesses.

EXAMPLE 7.11	David Jones owns an interest in six businesses. His level of participation is as follows:	
	Activity	**Hours**
	A	100
	B	125
	C	90
	D	135
	E	140
	F	100
	Total	690

David is not a material participant in any one of the activities above. In addition, he is not significantly participating in activities A, C, and F (not more than 100 hours of participation in each). The aggregate amount of participation in the significant participating activities is 400 hours from activities B, D, and E. Therefore, David is not treated as materially participating under Test 4, and all activities fall under the passive loss rules.

EXAMPLE 7.12	Assume the same facts as in Example 7.11, except that activity C had 105 hours of participation. Because the number of participation hours is in excess of 100, activity C is a significant participation activity. This brings the aggregate number of hours in significant participating activities to 505. David would now be considered to be a material participant, and therefore only activities A and F would fall under the passive loss rules.

Limited Partners

Limited partners, by the very nature of their relationship to the partnership, are not considered to be material participants. As a general rule, limited partners are not involved in the day-to-day management of partnership affairs. However, if limited partners participate in the activity, they may become material participants in the partnership if one of the following applies:

1. The limited partner holds a general partnership interest at all times during the partnership's tax year ending with or within the individual's tax year (or the portion of the partnership's tax year during which the individual—directly or indirectly—owns such limited partnership interest).
2. The limited partner participates more than 500 hours (Test 1).
3. The limited partner participates for any five years during the 10 tax years immediately preceding the tax year at issue (Test 5).
4. For a personal service activity, the limited partner materially participated in the activity for any three years preceding the year at issue (Test 6). Temp. Reg. §1.469-5T(e).

Participation Standard

The Internal Revenue Service considers an individual to be participating when any work is done by such individual in connection with an activity in which the individual owns an interest at the time the work is done. Individuals are not considered as participating in the following situations:

1. Work not customarily done by an owner if one of the principal purposes for the work is to avoid the disallowance of any loss or credit from such activity under the passive loss rules.
2. Work done in the individual's capacity as an investor (such as studying and reviewing financial statements of the activity, preparing or compiling summaries or analyses of the finances or operations of the activity for the individual's own use, and monitoring the finances or operations in a nonmanagerial role). Temp. Reg. §1.469-5T(f).

¶7261

IDENTIFYING AN ACTIVITY

Determining the scope of a particular activity is important for identifying whether a taxpayer has two or more separate activities or one activity having two or more undertakings. Two situations in which this determination is vital occur when material participation is involved and upon disposition of the activity. For example, if an owner is involved in an activity that has two separate and distinct undertakings, such as rental property and retail sales, then a determination must be made as to whether the two undertakings will be treated as one activity or two activities. If the sales/rental business is treated as one activity, then the individual will only have to satisfy the material participation rules for one activity. A disposition of one of the undertakings, however, will not qualify as a "disposition of an entire interest" for purposes of recognizing a loss against nonpassive income. But if the sales/rental business is treated as two separate activities, then the material participation requirements must be met for each separate activity. In addition, because each undertaking is a separate activity, a disposition of an entire interest is allowed if one of the undertakings (now an activity) is sold.

Proposed Regulations were issued in 1992 which provide guidance for grouping a taxpayer's trade or business activities and rental activities under the passive activity rules. The regulations define trade or business activities as activities that:

1. Involve the conduct of a trade or business (within the meaning of Code Sec. 162);
2. Are conducted in anticipation of the commencement of a trade or business; or
3. Involve research or experimental expenditures that are deductible under Code Sec. 174 (or would be deductible if the taxpayer adopted the method described in Code Sec. 174(a)). Prop. Reg. §1.469-4(b)(1).

Rental activities are defined as activities constituting rental activities within the meaning of Temporary Regulation §1.469-1T(e)(3). They are discussed in detail in the next section of this chapter.

Under the Regulations, a taxpayer may treat one or more trade or business activities or rental activities as a single activity. To qualify for such treatment, the activities must constitute an appropriate economic unit for determining gain or loss for purposes of Code Sec. 469.

A facts and circumstances approach is used to determine whether or not various activities may be treated as a single activity. Any reasonable method of applying the relevant facts and circumstances may be used for this purpose. Certain factors are considered the most important in determining whether separate activities constitute an appropriate economic unit. However, not all factors need be present. They are:

1. Similarities and differences in types of businesses;
2. The extent of common control;
3. The extent of common ownership;
4. Geographical location; and
5. Interdependence between activities.

Interdependence between activities may exist if firms buy or sell goods to one another, have customers in common, provide products or services together, share employees, or are accounted for on the same set of books and records. Reg. §1.469-4(c)(1) and (2).

EXAMPLE 7.13	Ernie operates a bookstore and a restaurant in a shopping mall in Atlanta and a bookstore and a restaurant in Miami. Depending upon how Ernie applies the facts and circumstances test, he may end up with one to four activities for purposes of the passive activity rules. Both bookstores and restaurants could be grouped into one activity. Alternatively, he may have two separate activities, one constituting the bookstores and one constituting the restaurants. He may also have an Atlanta activity and a Miami activity. Finally, he may treat each business as a separate activity. Reg. §1.469-4(c)(3)

EXAMPLE 7.14	Ted owns a large retail business. He is the sole proprietor of a firm that provides bookkeeping services to businesses. The retail business is the primary client of the bookkeeping firm. Because the two activities are under common control, Ted could treat the retail activity and the bookkeeping activity as a single activity. Reg. §1.469-4(c)(3).

The Regulations generally prohibit the grouping of rental activities with nonrental trade or business activities. However, such groupings are permissible if the income generated by one activity is insubstantial in relation to the income generated by the other activity. No guidance is provided in the Proposed Regulations on the meaning of the word "insubstantial" in this context. Reg. §1.469-4(d). But prior temporary regulations indicate that an activity providing 20 percent or less of the total revenue of two activities may be considered insubstantial.

Two separate rental activities, one involving personal property and the other involving real property, may not be grouped into one activity. An exception to this rule arises when personal property is rented in connection with real property. Reg. §1.469-4(e).

Limited partners in partnerships are generally prohibited from grouping the limited partnership activity with other activities. However, such groupings are permitted with other activities in which the taxpayer is a limited partner and which carry on the same type of business. If the taxpayer is not a limited partner in the second activity, the grouping may still be achieved by applying the facts and circumstances test. Reg. §1.469-4(f)(1) and (2).

Activities that have been grouped under any of the above criteria may not be regrouped in subsequent taxable years unless it can be demonstrated that the original grouping was clearly inappropriate. Alternatively, a material change in the facts and circumstances (such as a change in ownership) may occur that would justify a regrouping of activities. Reg. §1.469-4(g).

The Commissioner has the authority to regroup a taxpayer's activities. This will occur if the grouping does not result in appropriate economic units under the facts and circumstances test and one of the primary purposes of the taxpayer's grouping is to avoid the passive loss rules. Reg. §1.469-4(h).

EXAMPLE 7.15

Bob and three friends each own separate retail businesses, and they invested in limited partnerships years ago that generate annual passive losses. Bob and his friends acquire limited partner interests in a partnership created to provide janitorial services to their respective retail businesses. The janitorial service is run by a general partner selected by Bob and the others. The janitorial service is set up to insure that it generates a profit. The four limited partners plan to treat the janitorial service as a separate activity and use losses from their other limited partnership to offset the net profit from the janitorial service.

Applying the facts and circumstances test, each partner's interest in the janitorial service and the partner's respective business would constitute one appropriate economic activity, rather than two. In addition, it is obvious that the partners created the janitorial service and treated it as a separate activity in order to circumvent the passive loss rules. Hence, the Commissioner would likely require the partners to treat their respective interests in the janitorial service and their individual businesses as one activity instead of two. Penalties may also be levied against them under Code Sec. 6662. Reg. §1.469-4(h).

Activities carried on by a partnership or S corporation are first grouped by the partnership or S corporation by applying these rules. After the activities are grouped by the partnership or corporation, the individual partner or shareholder then groups the activities with other activities, as appropriate, in which the partner or shareholder is personally involved. Reg. §1.469-4(j).

Under certain circumstances, a taxpayer who disposes of a substantial part of an activity during a taxable year may treat the part disposed of as a separate activity. To do so, the taxpayer must establish the following with reasonable certainty:

1. The amount of disallowed deductions and credits carried over from prior years that are allocable to that part of the activity for the taxable year; and
2. The amount of gross income and any other deductions and credits allocable to that part of the activity for the taxable year. Reg. §1.469-4(k).

¶7273 RENTAL ACTIVITIES

An activity is a rental activity if during the year: (1) tangible property held in connection with the activity is used by customers or is held for use by customers, and (2) gross income attributable to the conduct of the activity represents amounts paid principally for the use of the property. Temp. Reg. §1.469-1T(e)(3). Generally, any rental activity is a passive activity, without regard to material participation. Code Sec. 469(c)(2) and (4).

The following tests and examples are exceptions to rental activity status (i.e., if any test is met, then the activity is not a rental activity);

1. The average period of customer use for rental property is seven days or less.

EXAMPLE 7.16

George Lee owns a home video movie rental store. The average period of customer use is two days. The store is not a rental activity.

2. The average period of customer use is 30 days or less, and significant personal services are provided by or on behalf of the owner in connection with making the property available for use by customers. Significant personal services include services performed by individuals. In making the determination, factors such as the frequency with which the service is provided, type and amount of labor required, and the value of the services relative to the amount charged for the use of property will be weighed.

EXAMPLE 7.17

Monica Sellers owns a computer leasing service. The average period of customer use is more than seven days but less than 30 days. Pursuant to the lease agreements, skilled technicians and programming consultants employed by her maintain and service malfunctioning equipment as well as implement programs for no additional charge. The value of the maintenance, repair, and implementation services exceeds 50 percent of the amount charged for the use of the equipment. Significant personal services are provided and the activity is not a passive activity.

3. Extraordinary personal services are provided by or on behalf of the owner in connection with making the property available for use by customers. Extraordinary personal services are services provided to customers so that use of the property is actually incidental to the receipt of such services.

EXAMPLE 7.18   The use of a hospital's boarding facilities generally is incidental to the receipt of personal services provided by the hospital's medical staff. The hospital's boarding operations are not rental activities.

4. The rental of such property is treated as incidental to a nonrental activity of the taxpayer.

EXAMPLE 7.19   Bob Townson owns 3,000 acres of unimproved land for the principal purpose of realizing gain from appreciation. In order to defray the cost of carrying the land, he leases it to a rancher who allows cattle to graze on it. If the gross rental income is less than 2 percent of the lesser of the land's fair market value or the adjusted basis (incidental to the nonrental activity), then the land is not a rental activity. Assuming that the land is worth $600,000 and his adjusted basis is $450,000, the rent must be less than $9,000 (2% × $450,000) in order for it to be incidental.

5. The taxpayer customarily makes the property available during defined business hours for nonexclusive use by various customers.

EXAMPLE 7.20   Operating a golf course that is available during prescribed business hours for nonexclusive use by various golfers is not a rental activity.

6. The taxpayer provides property for use in an activity conducted by a partnership, S corporation, or joint venture in which the taxpayer owns an interest, but the activity is not a rental activity. Temp. Reg. §1.469-1T(e)(3)(B)(ii).

EXAMPLE 7.21   Patricia Bowers is a partner in a law firm. She provides to the firm the use of expensive, sophisticated audio equipment for the purpose of analyzing a case. The equipment is unloaded in the firm's office and used for a specified period of time for a fee. The law firm is not engaged in a rental activity. None of her fees from the audio equipment will be considered as income from a rental activity.

PLANNING POINTER   Even though an activity is not classified as a rental activity, it may still fall into passive activity status if the material participation requirements are not met.

¶7281   RENTAL REAL ESTATE ACTIVITIES

An individual is allowed to avoid the passive loss limitations for all rental real estate activities in which the individual *actively participates*. A $25,000 offset against nonpassive income can be attained if the taxpayer's modified adjusted gross income (AGI computed without regard to any passive activity loss, taxable Social Security benefits, or deductions for IRA contributions) is $100,000 or less. Code Sec. 469(i). The offset is before AGI.

EXAMPLE 7.22   Alex Alexander owned three rental houses and had modified AGI of $77,500 for the year. The combined loss of the rental houses was $28,000. He was an active participant in the management of the rental properties. Alex qualifies for the $25,000 offset and will be able to reduce nonpassive income by that amount. The remaining $3,000 loss will become a suspended loss and will be allocated among all properties experiencing a loss.

Active participation, as opposed to material participation, need not be regular, continuous, and substantial. Active participation by an individual can include making some of the management decisions (such as approving prospective tenants, setting the terms of rental arrangements, and approving the costs of repairs or capital improvements). An outside property management firm, then, can be hired to provide appropriate management services on a day-to-day basis without jeopardizing active participation status. In addition, a taxpayer must hold a 10 percent or more interest in the property at all times during the year to be an active participant. Generally, a limited partner does not actively participate in a rental real estate activity that is owned through an interest in a limited partnership. As in the case of material participation, the participation of a taxpayer's spouse will be taken into account in determining whether the taxpayer actively participated.

Single individuals and married taxpayers filing jointly can qualify for the maximum $25,000 amount. Married individuals who live apart from their spouses at all times during the year can qualify for $12,500 each. Married individuals who do not live apart for the entire year and file separately cannot qualify for any part of the $25,000 offset.

The maximum level of modified AGI is $100,000 in qualifying for the full $25,000 ($12,500 for qualified married individuals filing separately) deduction. However, when modified AGI exceeds $100,000, the excess is subject to a phaseout of the full offset: For every dollar of modified AGI in excess of $100,000, the $25,000 ($12,500) offset is reduced by 50 cents (or 50 percent of the excess). Thus, the $25,000 offset is fully phased out at a modified AGI of $150,000.

EXAMPLE 7.23	Ron Reingold owned two rental properties during the year and actively participated in the management of the properties. His modified AGI was $140,000. Ron's loss from the rental activities is $10,000. Ron is entitled to a $5,000 offset. Ron's deduction is limited to the $5,000 offset, and the remaining $5,000 becomes a suspended loss, figured as follows:

Modified AGI	$140,000
Maximum level allowed	(100,000)
Excess	$40,000
Excess	$40,000
Times reduction %	× .50
Offset reduction	$20,000
Maximum offset	$25,000
Offset reduction	(20,000)
Offset after phaseout	$5,000

Revenue Reconciliation Act of 1993 Changes to Benefit Real Estate Professionals

Additional relief was provided by the Revenue Reconciliation Act of 1993 for individuals and closely held C corporations that materially participate in rental real estate activities. After 1993, provided certain requirements are met, losses and credits from rental real estate activities will not be subject to the passive loss limitations. These requirements are designed to demonstrate that the taxpayer is a material participant in the activity, and commits a minimum amount of time, on an annual basis, to the activity.

Individuals are eligible if:

1. more than one-half of the personal services performed in trades or businesses by the taxpayer during such taxable year are performed in real property trades or businesses in which the taxpayer materially participates, and
2. such taxpayer performs more than 750 hours of services during the taxable year in real property trades or businesses in which the taxpayer materially participates.

For closely held C corporations to qualify:

1. The corporation must materially participate in rental real estate activities; and
2. The corporation must derive more than 50 percent of its gross receipts for the taxable year from such activities.

The criteria for determining material participation are the same as under previous law. Furthermore, as under prior law, a limited partner in a limited partnership is generally not considered to be a material participant in the partnership.

These changes in the law were intended to benefit real estate professionals, those who commit the majority of their time to performing real estate activities. Thus, the average passive investor in such activities will not qualify for relief under these provisions.

However, a couple filing jointly could benefit from the new rules if at least one spouse satisfies the requirements. For example, one spouse may work as a real estate broker or as a real estate leasing agent and the other spouse could own rental property. Losses incurred on the rental property may be treated as losses from an activity in which the taxpayer materially participates (i.e., not as passive losses) if the real estate broker spouse satisfies the new requirements.

EXAMPLE 7.24   During 2015, Beth Miller participated in the following personal service activities: 800 hours as a personal estate planner, 450 hours in rental real estate activities, and 600 hours as a real estate broker. Beth devoted more than one-half of her personal services to real property trades or businesses, and her material participation in those real estate activities exceeded 750 hours. Hence, any loss incurred by Beth in either real estate activity will not be subject to the passive loss rules. She will be able to offset any losses from either real estate activity against active or portfolio income.

¶7287   CHANGE OF ACTIVITY STATUS

Under the passive activity rules, it is quite possible for an activity to change from passive to nonpassive. For example, an individual may not materially participate in a business for a previous tax year, but in later years may become a material participant. Thus, while the taxpayer was not a material participant, the business was a passive activity. Then when the taxpayer becomes a material participant, circumstances would appear to terminate the application of passive activity rules. A passive activity could become a "former passive activity" if any of the following apply:

1. The taxpayer qualifies as a material participant.
2. The activity no longer qualifies as a trade or business or rental activity.

EXAMPLE 7.25   Fred Manson's real estate activities consisted of five rental properties located on a 25-acre tract. For each rental property, an acre was carved out of the larger tract and was sold last year, leaving Fred with 20 acres of unproductive land. His real estate activities no longer qualify as a rental activity for the current year and, therefore, will be characterized as a former passive activity.

Generally, the passive loss rules do not apply to a former passive activity, except for the former passive activity's suspended losses. A former passive activity's suspended losses will continue to be suspended, but can be offset against (1) passive income from other passive activities or (2) nonpassive income from the former passive activity. Code Sec. 469(f).

EXAMPLE 7.26   Sally Dennison was not a material participant for the past few years in SSS, a partnership. The partnership was engaged in the business of selling, constructing, maintaining, and repairing fireplaces, fireplace equipment, and chimneys. Sally became a partner in the business during 2006, and her share of allocated losses for 2006–2014 was $55,000. Because she owned no other passive activities, the $55,000 was a suspended loss. In 2015, she became a material participant, and SSS significantly improved its operating position. Her share of the net income amounted to $29,500 for the year, which is now characterized as nonpassive income. The $55,000 suspended loss will offset the $29,500 of nonpassive income from SSS, while the remaining $25,500 continues to be suspended.

Business and Investment Losses

¶7301   BUSINESS CASUALTY AND THEFT LOSSES

Business and investment casualty losses which receive similar tax treatment are discussed in this section. Personal casualty losses are reviewed in greater detail at ¶8501.

The following losses can be deducted by an individual taxpayer (Code Sec. 165(c)):

1. Losses incurred in a trade or business;
2. Losses incurred in any transaction entered into for profit though not connected with a trade or business; or
3. Losses of property not connected with a trade or business, if such losses arise from fire, storm, shipwreck, or other casualty, or from theft.

Casualty losses usually are losses from fire, storm, or other catastrophe. Theft losses are losses arising from robbery, embezzlement, or larceny. Reg. §1.165-8(d). Generally, all casualty and theft losses are deductible if incurred in a trade or business or in connection with an investment with the exception of losses caused by a taxpayer's willful act or willful negligence. Reg. §1.165-7(a)(3)(i).

Proper Year of Deduction

A casualty loss is normally deductible in the year it occurs. If a casualty loss is incurred in an area designated as a disaster area by the President of the United States, the taxpayer can elect to deduct the casualty loss in the tax year preceding the year of the loss. The intent behind permitting a taxpayer to deduct a disaster area casualty loss in the tax year preceding the loss is to lessen the immediate tax burden on the taxpayer and, thereby, lessen the financial burden related to the casualty loss.

EXAMPLE 7.27   Greenwood Paper Co. incurred a casualty loss of $10,000 in 2015. The $10,000 loss is normally deductible on Greenwood's 2015 income tax return. Because the casualty occurred in an area designated as a disaster area by the President of the United States, Greenwood may elect to deduct the casualty loss on its 2014 tax return. Since the 2014 tax return was already filed, an amended return would be filed for 2014 to claim a tax refund.

No casualty loss can be taken in the year of loss if a reasonable prospect exists that full reimbursement of the loss from insurance or other source will be received in some future tax year. Reg. §1.165-1(d)(2)(i). The casualty loss deduction is limited to the actual expected loss after expected insurance reimbursement. If the actual insurance reimbursement is less than the amount anticipated in past tax years, the difference can be deducted as a casualty loss deduction in the year the claim is settled.

A theft loss is different from a casualty loss in that a theft loss is deductible in the year the theft is discovered (which may not necessarily be the same as the year of theft). As with casualty losses, a theft loss deduction is limited to the actual expected loss after expected reimbursement. If the reimbursement is less than the amount anticipated in past tax years, the difference can be deducted in the year the claim is settled.

Computation of Deduction

A deduction resulting from the *partial destruction* of business property is limited to the lesser of the following:

1. The adjusted basis of the casualty property, or
2. The decline in fair market value of the casualty property.

Any insurance or other form of compensation will reduce the amount deductible. If such property is *completely destroyed or stolen,* the deductible loss is the adjusted basis of the property less any reimbursement (regardless of decline in the fair market value).

As a general rule, if reimbursement is less than the property's adjusted basis, then no gain can be realized. If reimbursement is less than adjusted basis but more than the amount of loss (computed using decline in FMV), then a taxpayer experiences neither a gain nor a loss.

EXAMPLE 7.28

The following casualty and theft losses occurred at Turnkey Construction Company during 2015:

Event	Adjusted Basis	Fair Market Value Before Casualty	Fair Market Value After Casualty	Insurance Reimburse
1. Stolen Equip.	$12,000	$6,000	$ 0	$6,000
2. Fire—Bldg.	$77,000	$95,000	$45,000	$35,000
3. Wreck—Truck	$21,000	$18,500	$10,000	$10,000

The loss deduction for each casualty and theft is figured as follows:

1.   Stolen equipment (theft loss—treated the same way as complete casualty loss)

Adjusted basis	$12,000
Less: Insurance	6,000
Theft loss deduction	$6,000

2.   Fire in building (partial business casualty—lesser of adjusted basis or decline in fair market value)

Decline in FMV	$50,000
Less: Insurance	35,000
Casualty loss deduction	$15,000

3.   Wrecked truck (partial business casualty with insurance proceeds greater than amount of loss)

Decline in FMV	$8,500
Less: Insurance	10,000
Net	$(1,500)

The net amount of $1,500 is not a realized gain because the property's adjusted basis was $21,000 (the formula used to compute realized gain is insurance proceeds less adjusted basis, which would provide a $11,000 loss). On the other hand, the difference between the property's adjusted basis and insurance proceeds ($11,000 loss) is not a deductible loss because a partial casualty loss deduction requires the lesser of adjusted basis or decline in FMV in determining the amount of loss. Thus, a partial casualty where insurance proceeds are greater than the amount of loss yields neither a gain nor a loss (because the property's adjusted basis is greater than the insurance proceeds).

In some instances, however, a casualty or theft may result in a taxpayer realizing a gain. This could occur when the insurance coverage, which is normally based on fair market value, exceeds the cost basis of the property (i.e., insurance proceeds less adjusted basis equals realized gain).

Basis Adjustment

Whenever a taxpayer has a partial or complete casualty, the following items will reduce the property's adjusted basis if there was no gain realized:

1.   Amount of reimbursement
2.   Amount of deductible loss

EXAMPLE 7.29

Jack Caldwell's business office was partially destroyed by a tornado. His adjusted basis in the building was $210,000, and the decline in FMV was $150,000. Insurance proceeds amounted to $100,000. Mr. Caldwell's adjusted basis in the property is computed as follows:

Decline in FMV	$150,000
Less: Insurance	100,000
Deductible loss	$50,000
Adjusted basis before casualty	$210,000
Less: Insurance	100,000
Less: Deductible loss	50,000
Adjusted basis after casualty	$60,000

In determining a casualty property's decline in value, appraisals establishing the property's fair market value before the casualty as well as after the casualty are important evidence for defending the amount of a casualty loss deduction. The cost of repairs to restore the casualty property to its condition before the casualty may also be sufficient evidence to indicate the amount of the loss deduction. Reg. §1.165-1(d)(2)(ii).

¶7331 NET OPERATING LOSSES (NOLS)

Prior to the Taxpayer Relief Act of 1997, a business that had a net operating loss in one taxable year could carry the loss back to offset taxable income in the three preceding tax years or carry the loss forward to offset future taxable income for up to 15 years. Code Sec. 172.

For tax years beginning after August 5, 1997, the NOL carryback period is shortened to two years, and the NOL carryforward period is extended to 20 years. (Special carryback rules exist in relation to: (1) real estate investment trusts that do not receive carrybacks; (2) specified liability losses that are subject to a ten-year carryback; (3) excess interest losses that do not receive carrybacks; (4) farming losses that may be carried back for five years; and (5) corporate capital losses that are not affected by the changes.)

Further, the three-year carryback period is retained for the portion of the NOL that relates to casualty and theft losses of individual taxpayers and to NOLs that are attributable to Presidentially declared disasters *and* are incurred by taxpayers engaged in farming or by a small business (gross receipts of $5 million or less for a three-tax-year period).

Further, a five-year NOL carryback period applies for qualified disaster losses (Code Sec. 172(b)(1)(J), as added by the Emergency Economic Stabilization Act of 2008 (P.L. 110-343)). Also, a farming loss may be carried back for five years (Code Sec. 172(b)(1)(G) and (i)), and it does not include a qualified disaster loss.

EXAMPLE 7.30

Able Box Company has a net operating loss of $50,000 in 2015. The loss can be carried back to offset previous taxable income in 2013 and 2014. If any of the 2015 net operating loss remains after being carried back two years, the remainder can be carried forward to offset future taxable income for up to 20 years (2016–2035).

The objective of the net operating loss deduction is to increase tax fairness regarding the taxation of business income. A 12-month tax accounting period is an arbitrary period of time to tax business enterprises. Business affairs cannot be arranged into arbitrary 12-month periods. In order to alleviate the arbitrariness of a 12-month accounting period, the net operating loss deduction allows a business to offset tax losses against taxable income over a longer period of time which would normally include an entire business cycle of up and down periods.

The net operating loss deduction is available only for losses connected with a trade or business. An excess of nonbusiness and personal deductions over nonbusiness and personal income, with the exception of personal casualty and theft losses, is not eligible for NOL treatment. Personal casualty and theft losses, however, are considered to be business losses for purposes of computing the net operating loss deduction. The three-year carryback period is retained for the portion of the NOL that relates to casualty and theft losses of individual taxpayers.

Carryback and Carryforward Procedures

A business incurring a net operating loss in a taxable year can carry the loss back two years and forward 20 years. The net loss shown on a taxpayer's return usually requires adjustment in several ways before becoming a net operating loss. A business can elect to forgo the NOL carryback and carry it forward only.

PLANNING POINTER	In deciding whether to carry a net operating loss back or to just carry it forward, the taxpayer has to analyze the advantages and disadvantages of each approach. A carryback results in an immediate tax refund. Due to the time value of money, it is advantageous to forgo a carryback in favor of a carryforward only when the estimated marginal tax rate to be applied to future income is expected to be substantially higher than the tax rate which applied to the income subject to the carryback.

If a net operating loss is carried back, it must be carried back two years first. Next, if any NOL remains it is carried forward to the next year. Then if any balance remains, it is carried forward until used up or lost because of the passage of time.

EXAMPLE 7.31	Able Box Company has a net operating loss in 2015. If Able elects to carry back the NOL, it must carry back the loss to 2013. If any NOL remains, then the balance is applied against 2014 income and so on until it is used up or expires.

Taxpayers are required to file amended returns for the tax years in which they carry back net operating losses. The operating loss deduction is a deduction for adjusted gross income. Certain itemized deductions which are limited by adjusted gross income such as medical expenses and certain miscellaneous itemized deductions may have to be recomputed in the carryback year due to the change in adjusted gross income caused by the inclusion of the NOL. Charitable contributions are excluded from recomputation due to the carryback of a NOL. Code Sec. 170(b).

Computation of Net Operating Loss

The term "net operating loss" is defined as the "excess of deductions over gross income." Code Sec. 172(c). This excess of deductions over gross income is subject to modifications which limit the net operating loss to only business losses. A loss reported on a tax return by an individual taxpayer with business income is modified in the following ways in order to determine a net operating loss deduction:

Taxable Income/Loss

+ Any NOL deduction from another year

+ Deductions for personal and dependency exemptions

+ Nonbusiness capital losses exceeding nonbusiness capital gains

+ Nonbusiness deductions in excess of nonbusiness income

= Net operating loss

Nonbusiness deductions include all itemized deductions (less personal casualty and theft losses and unreimbursed employee business expenses) plus self-employed retirement plan contributions. Nonbusiness income is all income not derived from a trade or business, such as dividends, interest, and nonbusiness capital gains. Salary and wages are considered to be trade or business income for purposes of computing an NOL.

EXAMPLE 7.32

Larry Watkins owns and operates a pizza parlor. In 2015, Larry had the following income and deductions listed on his individual tax return.

Business income	$45,000	
Salary from second job	15,000	
Interest	5,000	
Dividends	2,000	
Long-term capital gain (LTCG)	1,000	$68,000
Less:		
Business deductions	$70,000	
Personal exemption	4,000	
Itemized deductions (included $10,000 personal casualty)	19,000	93,000
Taxable income		($25,000)

Larry's net operating loss for 2015 is computed as follows:

Taxable income (negative amount)			($25,000)
Add:			
Personal exemption		$4,000	
Nonbusiness deductions in excess of nonbusiness income:			
Itemized deductions	$19,000		
Less: Personal casualty	10,000		
Nonbusiness deductions	$9,000		
Less: Nonbusiness income			
Interest	5,000		
Dividends	2,000		
LTCG	1,000	1,000	
			5,000
Net operating loss deduction			($20,000)

If only the "business-related" items were considered, then the NOL could be figured as follows:

Business income	$45,000	
Salary from second job	15,000	
Total business income		$60,000
Business deductions	$70,000	
Personal casualty loss	10,000	
Total business deductions		$80,000
Net operating loss deduction		($20,000)

Recomputation of Tax Liability in Carryback Year

After the net operating loss is computed for the tax year in which the loss is incurred, the loss is then carried back two years to the appropriate tax year unless an election is made to only carry the loss forward. As previously mentioned, adjustments may have to be made for items relying on adjusted gross income in determining their deduction.

If including the net operating loss deduction in the carryback year results in a tax loss in the carryback year, required adjustments have to be made to the tax loss to determine the amount of net operating loss deduction that can be carried forward to the next year. The required adjustments are similar to the adjustments discussed previously which were required to determine the original amount of the net operating loss.

¶7345   HOBBY LOSSES

Special rules apply to expenses and losses incurred in pursuing an activity not engaged in for profit. Hobby expenses are generally deductible only to the extent of income produced by the activity. Under Code Sec. 183, expenses that are otherwise deductible under the Code without regard to the existence of a business or profit motive (taxes, interest, casualty losses, etc.) are still deductible regardless of the amount of hobby income. However, such deductions reduce the amount of hobby income available to offset other hobby deductions. Other hobby expenses are deductible in an amount equal to the excess of hobby income over deductions otherwise allowable without regard to profit motive.

In determining whether an activity is engaged in for profit, reference is made to objective standards, taking into account the facts and circumstances of each case. Although a reasonable expectation of profit is not required, the circumstances should indicate that the taxpayer entered into, or continued, the activity with the objective of making a profit.

Among the factors considered in determining whether activities are engaged in for profit are (Reg. §1.183-2(b)):

1. The taxpayer's history of income or losses with respect to the activity.
2. The amount of occasional profits, if any, which are earned.
3. The cause of the losses.
4. The success of the taxpayer in carrying on other similar or dissimilar activities.
5. The financial status of the taxpayer.
6. The time and effort expended by the taxpayer in carrying on the activity.
7. The expertise of the taxpayer or advisors.
8. The manner in which the taxpayer carries on the activity.
9. Expectation of profit by the taxpayer.
10. Expectation that assets used in the activity may appreciate in value.
11. Elements of personal pleasure or recreation.

If any activity is not engaged in for profit, deductions are allowable in the following order and only to the following extent (Reg. §1.183-1(b)(1)):

1. Amounts deductible without regard to whether the activity giving rise to such amounts was engaged in for profit are allowable in full. Examples of these expenses include interest under Code Sec. 163 and realty taxes under Code Sec. 164.
2. Amounts deductible if the activity had been engaged in for profit, but only if the deduction does not result in an adjustment to the basis of property. Such deductions are allowed only to the extent the gross income of the activity exceeds the deduction under (1).
3. Amounts which result in an adjustment to the basis of property are deductible only to the extent that income exceeds the deductions allowed under (1) and (2). Deductions falling within this category include such items as depreciation, partial losses with respect to property, partially worthless debts, amortization, and amortizable bond premiums. If such expenses exceed the remaining hobby income, then the deductible amount (equal to remaining hobby income) is prorated among such properties in the ratio of the bases of all property. Basis of the property is reduced only by the amount actually deductible under Code Sec. 183.

The deduction for the allowed hobby expenses is an itemized deduction subject to the 2 percent floor on miscellaneous itemized deductions. For example, the feed expense incurred by a person who earns hobby income from the breeding, training, and showing of dogs is deductible only to the extent that the deduction, when aggregated with other miscellaneous deductions, exceeds 2 percent of the taxpayer's adjusted gross income. Hobby expenses that are deductible without reference to whether they are incurred in an activity designed to produce income, such as certain taxes, remain fully deductible. The gross receipts from the hobby are reported on line 21 of Form 1040.

TAX BLUNDER

Thomas O. and Carol J. Elliott, taxpayers, conducted an Amway distributorship in the evenings and on weekends from 1979 to 1983. They claimed deductions for various business expenses that were allegedly necessary to the Amway distributorship. Taxpayers submitted records to support their claimed deductions consisting of a notebook with incomplete entries and many unannotated receipts. Consequently, taxpayers conducted the Amway distributorship in an unbusinesslike fashion. As a result, the Elliotts failed to show that they engaged in the Amway distributorship with the actual and honest objective of making a profit, and, therefore, taxpayers improperly claimed deductions for business expenses. Furthermore, they are liable for additions to tax and negligent penalties for underpayment of tax. *T.O. Elliott,* 90 TC 960 (1988). A taxpayer who maintains good books and records for his/her activity is more likely to have the requisite profit intent required to escape the hobby loss rules.

EXAMPLE 7.33	Gene Allison operates a fishing boat during three months of the year and is not engaged in this activity for profit. He used the boat for his own personal use for one month and leased it to another person for two months. He has income from such operations of $3,000, taxes of $1,400, utilities of $900, maintenance expenses of $600, and depreciation of $1,200. His deductions are limited to $3,000, the amount of the income from the boat, as follows:

Category 1—Taxes	$1,400
Category 2—Two-thirds of $1,500 utilities and maintenance	1,000
Category 3—Two-thirds of $1,200 depreciation limited to excess of $3,000 boat income over $2,400 total of Category 1 and 2 deductions	600
Total deductions	$3,000

The $1,400 is itemized as part of the taxes deduction, and the $1,600 is placed in the miscellaneous itemized deduction section of Schedule A that is reduced by 2 percent of adjusted gross income.

If profit results from the activity in three out of five consecutive years ending with the tax year in question, a rebuttable presumption is created that an activity was not engaged in as a hobby. This permits the taxpayer to avoid the restrictions on the deduction of hobby losses. In the case of horse racing, breeding, and showing, a rebuttable presumption is created if profit results from the activity in two out of seven consecutive years.

A taxpayer may elect to delay a determination as to whether the presumption applies until the close of the fourth (or sixth, in the case of horse racing, breeding, or showing) tax year after the tax year in which the taxpayer first engages in the activity. A taxpayer is required to execute a waiver of the statute of limitations in order to make the election.

PLANNING POINTER	Remember the eleven factors from the regulations can work either for or against the taxpayer(s). For example, in Budin v. Comm. (T.C. Memo 1994-185), the taxpayers were engaged in horse breeding, training, and jumping activities. Significant losses were incurred by the taxpayers during the years in question. The court noted that Elbert and Shirley Budin did not conduct their horse activity in a business like manner. Specifically, the Budin's avowed purpose was horse breeding; however, they had acquired geldings, which were incapable of breeding. Therefore, the true spirit of the regulations must be adhered to for tax purposes.

¶7351 HOME OFFICE EXPENSES

If a taxpayer uses a portion of a personal residence for business-related activities, expenses allocable to the portion of the home used for business purposes may qualify as a tax deduction. For personal home expenses to be tax deductible, however, a portion of the home must be used exclusively on a regular basis as:

1. The principal place of business for any trade or business of the taxpayer;
2. A place of business which is used by patients, clients, or customers in meeting or dealing with the taxpayer in the normal course of a trade or business; or
3. In the case of a separate structure which is not attached to the dwelling unit, in connection with the taxpayer's trade or business (Code Sec. 280A(c)).

For tax years beginning after December 31, 1998, the Taxpayer Relief Act of 1997 expands the definition of a "principal place of business." A home office qualifies as a taxpayer's principal place of business under the Act if:

1. The office is used by the taxpayer to conduct administrative or management activities of the taxpayer's trade or business; and
2. There is no other fixed location of the trade or business where the taxpayer conducts substantial administrative or management activities of the trade or business.

If the taxpayer is an employee, the exclusive use test mentioned above must be for the convenience of the employer and not merely for the convenience of the employee. In other words, if an employee has an office on the employer's premises, then the likelihood of having a home office for the same purpose in a personal residence is greatly reduced.

The exclusive use test means that if the portion of the home used for business activities is also used for personal (nonbusiness) activities, then no deduction will be allowed. An exception to the exclusive use test applies when personal residences are used to provide day care services for children, handicapped individuals, and elderly persons. The day care facility exception applies only if the taxpayer has applied for, been granted, or is exempt from having a license, certification, registration, or approval under applicable state law. Personal family use of the day care facilities is acceptable but, in determining the allowable deduction, expenses allocable to the personal use time are not deductible. Code Sec. 280A(c). The regular basis test means that the portion of the home used for business purposes must be used for business on a regular basis, not occasionally.

EXAMPLE 7.34	Roger Blaine, a physician, uses a portion of his personal home as his principal medical office on an exclusive and regular basis. Expenses related to the portion of the home used for business purposes are deductible on Roger's tax return. If Roger occasionally meets patients in the family living room, which is also used regularly for family activities, then none of the expenses allocable to the living room are deductible since the room is not used exclusively and on a regular basis for business.

PLANNING POINTER	Exclusive use of a portion of a home for business purposes is required to qualify for a business use of home deduction. Exclusive use for business purposes does not require, however, that the portion of the home used for business purposes be physically separated from the remainder of the home. A specified space within a room can qualify for the deduction as long as the exclusive use test is met. G. Weightman, 42 TCM 104, CCH Dec. 37,986(M), T.C. Memo. 1981-301.

Typical expenses deductible for a portion of a personal home used for business activities are heating, water, electricity, maintenance and repairs, depreciation, real estate taxes, and interest on a home mortgage. The portion of these expenses allocated to the business use of the home usually is based on the square feet used for business in relation to the total square feet available in the home. In no instance can the deduction for the business use of a home exceed the gross income derived from the business activities carried on at home and from the amount of income generated from rental activity of the home reduced by all related tax deductions other than the business use of home deduction. If the expenses of the business use of the home exceed the gross income derived from the business activity less related deductions, expenses normally allowable as deductions to all taxpayers (such as real estate taxes and interest on a home mortgage loan) are deducted first. If any income remains, other expenses are then deducted to the extent of the remaining income, with depreciation taken last.

Any excess expenses that are not deductible in the current year can be carried forward to offset income from the same home office business activities in succeeding years. Code Sec. 280A(c). Also, for any home office deduction related to work as an *employee,* the deduction is categorized as a miscellaneous itemized deduction subject to the 2 percent of adjusted gross income limitation which applies to miscellaneous itemized deductions (except for mortgage interest and property taxes, which are fully deductible).

EXAMPLE 7.35

Esther Simcox, a self-employed management consultant, maintains an office in her home on an exclusive and regular basis. The business office space accounts for one-fifth of the total space in her home. In 2015, Esther had gross income of $25,000 from her consulting business. Deductions related to her management consulting income, other than the business use of home deduction, amounted to $5,000. During 2015, Esther incurs the following home expenses:

Real estate taxes	$3,600	
Interest on mortgage loan	4,200	
Tax deductions normally allowable to all taxpayers		$7,800
Maintenance on home	$1,200	
Utilities (water, electricity, gas, sewer)	2,500	
Other expenses (repairs, maid service, etc.)	3,000	
Operating expenses		6,700
Total depreciation (straight-line)		2,500
Total		$17,000

Esther's home office deduction for 2015 is $3,400, determined by taking the $17,000 of home expenses times 1/5, the portion of the home used for business purposes. If Esther's gross income from the consulting business less related deductions, other than the business use of home deduction, amounted to only $2,000 in 2015, then the business use of home deduction is limited to $2,000. In calculating the business use of home deduction, tax deductions normally allowable to all taxpayers are deducted first.

Impact of Revenue Procedure 2013-13(1/15/13)

The IRS announced a simplified, optional method of claiming a home office deduction.Specifically, the new optional deduction is limited to $1,500 per year based on $5 per square foot for up to 300 square feet. Taxpayers using this new option will not be able to depreciate the portion of their home used in their trade or business. However, they can still claim allowable mortgage interest, real estate taxes, and casualty losses on their home as itemized deductions on Schedule A of Form 1040.

    Comparison to Example 7.35-Above. Assume that the above office space of one-fifth amounted to 300 square feet. Under Rev. Proc. 2013-13, the deduction for the qualified business use of her home is $1,500 (300 sq.ft. × $5). Esther can deduct the real estate taxes and mortgage interest on her Schedule A and the business expenses of $5,000 on Schedule C. But she cannot deduct the depreciation of $2,500. It appears that taxpayers with large deductions should first figure the deductions out under the old method ($3,400) and then compare that figure to the new method's maximum of $1,500. Also, it should be noted that the home office deduction goes on Form 8829 and is then carried to Schedule C. In contrast, deductions that are itemized are not worth as much as Schedule C deductions. Also, since the taxpayer did not take any depreciation on her home, then her basis is higher and less gain will be reported under Sec. 1231. Naturally, these considerations are just some of the variables to guage with the client before adopting this new procedure when filing tax returns.

¶7371   VACATION HOME EXPENSES

Special rules limit the amount of rental expense deductions that may be taken by an individual taxpayer (investor) on a residence that is rented out for part of a year and used for personal purposes during other parts of the year. Code Sec. 280A. If a personal residence is rented out for less than 15 days during the year, any rental income received is excluded from gross income and no rental expense deductions are allowed. Code Sec. 280A(g). However, regular expense deductions attributable to all personal residences (such as mortgage interest, property taxes, and personal casualty losses) are still available. If a residence is rented out during the year for more than 14 days, then the property will either be a personal residence (personal-use property) or rental property (which could provide a deductible loss subject to the passive loss rules).

    A vacation home becomes a personal residence when its owner uses it excessively for personal purposes. Excessive personal use is measured by the greater of 14 days or 10 percent of the number of rental days. That is, if the owner personally uses the residence *more than the greater of* (1) 14 days or (2) 10 percent of rental days, then the dwelling will be a personal residence and rental losses are not deductible. If rental expenses exceed rental income, then regular expenses (mortgage interest, property taxes, and casualty losses) are deducted first. (Any remaining regular expenses are deductible as itemized deductions.) Other rental expense deductions (maintenance, repairs, depreciation, etc.) are limited to the remaining amount of rental income (after it is reduced by the amount of regular expenses that were deducted first).

| EXAMPLE 7.36 | Joel Harris owned a condo in a resort area. During the year, he personally used it for 17 days, and it was rented for 100 days. Because he used the condo for more than either 14 days or 10 percent of rental days (10 days), the vacation home will be treated as a personal residence and losses will not be allowed. |

However, if an individual rents out a vacation home for more than 14 days and does not use it excessively for personal purposes, then it will be treated as rental property. That is, if the taxpayer does not use it for personal purposes for the greater of 14 days or 10 percent of rental days, then losses are allowed to be deducted for AGI (subject to the passive activity rules). If an individual actively participates in the rental real estate activity, then up to $25,000 of losses can be used to offset nonpassive income.

| EXAMPLE 7.37 | John Henderson owns a vacation home in Palm Springs. His expenses related to the home during the year are as follows: |

Mortgage interest and taxes	$20,000
Utilities, maintenance, and repairs	5,000
Depreciation	15,000
Total expenses	$40,000

Assume Mr. Henderson rents out the home for less than 15 days during the year and uses it personally for more than 14 days. He receives rental income of $4,000. None of the rental income is reported on his income tax return, and no rental expenses are deductible on his tax return. The mortgage interest and taxes of $20,000, however, are allowable.

In determining rental expense deductions, the allocation formulas used to compute rental expenses differ depending on the type of expense being allocated and interpretation of the tax law by the Tax Court and the IRS. For regular expenses allowable to all taxpayers, the Tax Court allocation formula is based on a full year (365 days). *D.D. Bolton*, 82-2 USTC ¶9699, 694 F.2d 556 (CA-9 1982). The IRS prefers to allocate regular expenses based on total usage of the residence. For other expenses, the allocation formula is based on total usage of the residence.

| EXAMPLE 7.38 | Assume Mr. Henderson rents out the vacation home for 25 days during the year and receives rental income of $10,000. He uses the dwelling for personal purposes for 30 days during the year. Under these assumptions, the rental income of $10,000 is included in his income because he rented the home out for more than 14 days. The dwelling will be treated as a personal residence because he used it for personal purposes for the greater of (1) 14 days, or (2) 10 percent of the rental days. The rental expense deductions are computed using both the IRS method and the Tax Court method as follows: |

	Tax Court	IRS
Rental income	$10,000	$10,000
Less: Mortgage interest payments and property taxes		
($20,000 × 25 rental days/365 days a year)	1,370	
($20,000 × 25 rental days/55 total use days)		9,091
Less: Utility expenses, maintenance, and repair expenses, etc.		
($5,000 × 25 rental days/55 total use days)	2,272	
($5,000 × 25 rental days/55 total use days, but limited to $909—cannot create a loss)		909
Amount remaining for depreciation	$6,358	$0
Less: Depreciation		
($15,000 × 25 rental days/55 total use days = $6,818, but limited to $6,358)	6,358	0
Net Rental Loss	$0	$0

EXAMPLE 7.39

Assume Mr. Henderson rents out the home for 25 days during the year and receives rental income of $10,000. He uses the home for personal purposes for seven days during the year. Under these assumptions, all rental income is recognized on his income tax return since the dwelling was rented out for more than 14 days. Because the residence will be treated as rental property (personal use was less than 14 days or 10 percent of rental days), losses are allowed. His rental income and rental expenses are computed as follows:

	Tax Court	IRS
Rental income	$10,000	$10,000
Less: Mortgage interest and property taxes		
($20,000 × 25 rental days/365 days a year)	1,370	
($20,000 × 25 rental days/32 total use days)		15,625
Less: Utility expenses, maintenance, and repair expenses, etc.		
($5,000 × 25 rental days/32 total use days)	3,906	3,906
Income or loss before depreciation	$4,724	($9,531)
Less: Depreciation		
($15,000 × 25 rental days/32 total use days)	11,718	11,718
Net Rental Loss	($6,994)	($21,249)

Under either the Tax Court or the IRS approach, the loss is less than the $25,000 loss allowed for rental property in which there is active participation. In this case, the remainder of the mortgage interest is not deductible because the vacation home is not considered a second residence. Therefore, the IRS approach is more favorable to the taxpayer.

Personal use days of a vacation home by an owner generally include the following: days of personal use by the owner or by a member of the owner's family including spouse, ancestors, lineal descendants, children, brothers, and sisters; and days of use under an arrangement to exchange one residence for another for a period of time; and days of use by any individual if not rented at a fair rental. Code Sec. 280A(d)(2)(A). Time spent at a vacation home by an owner while making repairs usually does not count as days of personal use if at least two-thirds of each day, up to eight hours a day, is spent making repairs.

KEYSTONE PROBLEM

Kim Boles, single and 38 years old, owned the following passive activities during 2015:

Activity	2015 Gain/(Loss)	Acquired
XYZ	($10,000)	10/05/86
LMN	($12,500)	06/22/87
TUV	$11,000	09/01/88

She was the sole proprietor of a small business that had gross revenues of $35,000 and expenses of $72,000. She participated in the business 2,000 hours. The business had a computer stolen from its office. The computer's basis was $12,000, and its fair market value was $7,500 at the time of the theft. The amount of the theft is not included in expenses as stated above.

Kim also owned a condo in Vail, Colorado. She used it 17 days for personal purposes and rented it 150 days. Gross rentals were $1,300, while all expenses other than interest and taxes were $1,700. Interest and taxes amounted to $6,500.

Kim received $15,400 salary from a part-time job, received $1,500 in dividends, and had total itemized deductions of $3,000. Compute Kim's taxable income for 2015 and any other tax consequences that are appropriate under the IRS method.

¶7375   MANUFACTURING DEDUCTION UNDER CODE SECTION 199

Code Sec. 199 was enacted by The American Jobs Creation Act of 2004 to help U.S. manufacturers stay competitive with their foreign rivals and to replace certain export tax benefits that were previously repealed. H. R. Conf. Rep. No. 108-755. For tax years beginning after 2004, these goals are achieved by allowing a deduction equal to a statutory percentage multiplied by the lesser of (1) a taxpayer's qualified production activities income (hereafter referred to as QPAI) for a tax year or (2) a taxpayer's taxable income for that tax year. Code Sec. 199(a)(1) and (2). When the taxpayer is an individual, the limitation noted in item (2) is adjusted gross income as derived in Code Sec. 199(d)(2). The deduction started at a transition percentage of three percent for 2005 and 2006 and rose to six percent for 2007 through 2009. By 2010, the manufacturing deduction was nine percent of the lesser of QPAI for the year or taxable income for the year. Also, the deduction may not exceed fifty percent of the W-2 wages paid by the taxpayer to the taxpayer's employees during the year. Code Sec. 199(b)(1).

In order to appreciate the above new terms and benefits, several definitions and illustrations are warranted.

Qualified Production Activities Income

Under Code Sec. 199(c)(1), QPAI means the enterprise's domestic gross receipts reduced by the sum of:

1. The costs of goods sold that are allocable to domestic production gross receipts;
2. Other deductions, expenses, or losses that are directly allocable to domestic production gross receipts (such as selling and marketing expenses); and
3. A proper share of other deductions, expenses, and losses not directly allocable to domestic production gross receipts or another class of income (such as general and administrative expenses allocable to selling and marketing expenses).

Domestic Production Gross Receipts

Domestic production gross receipts (hereafter referred to as DPGR) are defined under Code Sec. 199(c)(4) to include gross receipts from the following sources:

1. Any sale, exchange or other disposition, or any lease, rental or license, of qualifying production property that was manufactured, produced, grown or extracted by the enterprise in whole or in significant part within the United States (certain agriculture-related receipts also qualify). "Qualifying production property" generally includes any tangible personal property, computer software, or sound recordings.
2. Any sale, exchange or other disposition, or any lease, rental or license, of a qualified film produced by the enterprise. "Qualified film" includes any motion picture film or videotape (including live or delayed television programming, but not including certain sexually explicit productions) if 50% or more of the total compensation relating to the production of the film (including compensation in the form of residuals and participations) is compensation for services performed in the United States by actors, production personnel, directors, and producers.
3. Any sale, exchange or other disposition of electricity, natural gas, or potable water produced by the taxpayer in the United States.
4. Construction activities performed in the United States (including activities directly related to the construction or substantial renovation of residential and commercial buildings and infrastructure).
5. Engineering or architectural services performed in the United States for construction projects located in the United States.

Limitations. DPGR does not include the gross receipts of the taxpayer derived from:

1. The sale of food and beverages prepared by the taxpayer at a retail establishment. Code Sec. 199(c)(4)(B)(i).
2. The transmission or distribution of electricity, natural gas, or potable water. Code Sec. 199(c)(4)(B).
3. Property leased, licensed, or rented by the taxpayer for use by a related person. Code Sec. 199(c)(7)(A).

Wages-Paid Limitation

Pursuant to Code Sec. 199(b), the term wages means the wages paid for withholding tax purpose plus certain elective deferrals for retirement contributions and salary reduction arrangements. Because there is no single box on the Form W-2 that satisfies Code Sec. 199(b)(2)'s definition of wages, the IRS has provided in Notice 2005-14, Sec. 4.02(2)(b) for the following methods: (1) the unmodified box method; (2) the modified box one method; or (3) the tracking wages method. Due to the complexity of the three methods, only the unmodified box method will be illustrated. This method allows the taxpayer to use the lesser of:

1. The total entries in Box 1 (wages subject to federal income tax) of the W-2s for all employees of the taxpayer; or
2. The total entries in Box 5 (wages subject to Medicare) of the W-2s for all employees of the taxpayer.

Also, it should be noted, for purposes of Code Sec. 199(b), wages do not include any amounts paid to independent contractors or any amounts paid to partners. Consider carefully the following depiction of the new rules under Code Sec. 199.

EXAMPLE 7.40	Company X is a C corporation with three equal owners, all of whom are full-time employees. X has no other employees. It pays the owner/employees each $200,000 in salary. Assume that the salaries are considered reasonable compensation. The wage-based cap on the deduction for the manufacturing deduction is $300,000 (50% of the total wages of $600,000).

EXAMPLE 7.41	Assume the same facts as in the above example except that Company X is a limited liability company treated as a partnership for tax purposes. Under the IRS's position (Notice 2005-14), none of the $600,000 paid to the owners is wages. As a result, no manufacturing deduction would be available.

EXAMPLE 7.42	LA Drilling Company has taxable income in 2015 of $8 million, $5 million of which came from a qualified production activity. The company paid its employees wages subject to federal income tax (Box 1) of $3 million. The Medicare wages (Box 5) were $2 million. Eligible wages under the unmodified box method would be the lesser of $3 million or $2 million. The company's manufacturing deduction is the lesser of:

    1. $1 million of wages ($2 million x .50), or
    2. 9% of the lesser of :
       a. $8 million of taxable income
       b. $5 million of taxable income from the qualified production activities.

Thus, the manufacturing deduction is $450,000 ($5 million x .09).

Tax Policy Considerations

Because the manufacturing deduction definition is very broad, many domestic producers will qualify for the new deduction. That is, the Code Sec. 199 deduction is not limited to traditional manufacturing, but includes the following: construction, engineering, energy production, computer software, films and videotape, and processing of agricultural products. As a result, the issue of states losing money from this deduction should be considered. Specifically, times are tough for many states and giving up tax revenue via the manufacturing deduction may be something that they are unwilling to do. Therefore, it may be that a number of the states will not follow the federal statutes with respect to this deduction.

Since outsourcing has become a way of life in many businesses, will the Code Sec. 199 deduction discourage the use of independent contractors that do not qualify for wages on Form W-2?

Because sole proprietors do not pay themselves W-2 wages, then any deduction earned under Code Sec. 199 is eliminated by the W-2 wage limitation. Could this direct partnerships, sole proprietors, and single-member limited liability companies to incorporate as C or S corporations to secure the manufacturing deduction?

SUMMARY

- Deductions arising from tax shelters are subject to the at-risk rules and the passive activity rules. The at-risk provisions are structured to deny taxpayers from deducting losses in excess of their actual economic investment in the endeavor. In general, deductions or expenses incurred by passive activities can only be deducted against passive income, and any unused passive losses are suspended and carried forward to future years to offset passive income in those years.

- Net operating losses from business endeavors may be carried back two years and forward 20 years.

- Hobby losses require that expenses can only be deducted up to the amount of gross income derived from the activity.

- Business casualty or theft losses are the lesser of the decline in fair market value or the adjusted basis, but will equal adjusted basis when the property is totally destroyed. The three-year carryback period is retained for the portion of the NOL that relates to casualty and theft losses of individual taxpayers.

- Losses from ownership of a vacation home may be deductible if the home qualifies as rental property. The excessive use test is used in making the rental property determination (i.e., the greater of 14 days or 10 percent of the rental days). Once a home is determined to be rental, the losses are subject to the passive loss rules.

QUESTIONS

1. What is a tax shelter? Generally, what two limitations apply to the deductibility of most tax shelter loss deductions?

2. Why were tax shelters popular before the Tax Reform Act of 1986? Briefly explain why tax shelter investments are not as popular today.

3. Generally, what is "at risk"?

4. What is a nonrecourse loan? Will a nonrecourse loan given by the seller of real estate to the buyer increase the amount the buyer has at risk? Explain.

5. What is the general rule for the deductibility of passive losses?

6. Briefly, how do the at-risk rules and passive activity rules function together?

7. Differentiate between the following: active income, passive income, and portfolio income.

8. On what date was the Tax Reform Act of 1986 enacted, and what significance does this date have for losses derived from passive activities in 2015?

9. What is a "suspended loss"? How can suspended losses offset nonpassive income?

10. Generally, how will a suspended loss attributable to a passive activity that is transferred by reason of death be treated for federal income tax purposes?

11. Generally, how will a suspended loss attributable to a passive activity that is transferred by gift be treated for federal income tax purposes?

12. What type of taxpayers (entities) are affected by the passive loss rules? What is the significance of a closely held corporation with regard to the deductibility of passive losses?

13. Briefly, what is "material participation"? Why is the determination of whether a taxpayer materially participates important?

14. What are the seven tests that help to establish material participation?

15. What is "significant participation," and why is it notable?

16. What is an undertaking? What is a "separate source of income production," and why is this meaningful?

17. How are both business and rental operations usually treated when carried on at the same location by the same owner? How can both undertakings be treated as one activity?

18. How can a taxpayer combine real estate undertakings?

19. How can nonrental undertakings be combined?

20. Identify the six tests concerning rental properties that help to establish a nonrental activity.

21. What relief from passive loss restrictions is provided to help taxpayers deduct losses from rental real estate activities? What are the qualifications?

22. What is "active participation"?

23. What consequences does a taxpayer face when one of several activities is no longer a passive activity?

24. Explain the tax treatment of the following business casualty losses: complete destruction of the property and partial destruction of the property.

25. How does an expected insurance reimbursement for a business casualty loss affect the amount of a casualty loss deduction? Does it make a difference whether an expected insurance reimbursement for business casualty loss differs from the actual insurance reimbursement when the claim is settled?

26. How will a business property's basis be adjusted as a result of a casualty loss?

27. Generally, are net operating losses available for personal-use expenditures? Explain.

28. What carryback and carryforward procedures apply to business net operating losses?

29. What qualifications must be met before a taxpayer is allowed a home office deduction?

30. How can a vacation home become rental property? What is the difference between "rental property" and "personal residence"?

PROBLEMS

31. Billy Bob is at risk for $10,000 in Partnership A and $22,000 in Partnership B on January 1, 2015. Both partnerships are passive activities to Billy Bob. Billy Bob's share of net income from Partnership A during 2015 was $8,000. His share of losses from Partnership B was $12,000. What are the tax consequences to Billy Bob for 2015? How much is he at risk for each activity on January 1, 2016? Does he have any loss carryovers under the at-risk rules? Does he have any suspended losses under the passive loss rules?

32. What would be your answer to Problem 31 if Billy Bob's share of net income from Partnership A was $9,000 and his loss from Partnership B was $25,000?

33. In 2015, Wilmah Lansing invested in the Triple-K Limited Partnership by paying $15,000 cash and signing a $40,000 nonrecourse note. She also pledged $25,000 worth of securities for a loan obtained by the partnership. Her basis in the securities was $10,000. What amount does Wilmah have at risk in Triple-K as of January 1, 2016, if the partnership broke even (no income or loss)?

34. Refer to the facts in Problem 33 and assume that Triple-K allocated to Wilmah net income of $10,000 from operations in 2015. What amount does Wilmah have at risk as of January 1, 2016? Would your answer be different if she also withdrew $5,000? Explain.

35. Refer to the facts in Problem 33 and assume instead that Triple-K allocated to her a loss of $60,000 in 2015. What amount does Wilmah have at risk as of January 1, 2016?

36. In 2003, Keith Jackson invested in a partnership known as Astonishing Discoveries, Ltd. He was a limited partner. Mr. Jackson paid $25,000 cash and, along with all other partners, signed a nonrecourse note with which Astonishing Discoveries acquired an office park. The loan was made by the seller, a large financial institution that customarily made such loans. Jackson's allocated portion of the note was $100,000. In 2015, he received a $45,000 allocated loss from the partnership and had net passive income of $35,000 from other passive activities for the year. His adjusted gross income for 2015 was $145,000. Compute the following items for 2015:
   a. Amount at risk
   b. Passive loss deductions (against nonpassive income)
   c. Suspended loss.

37. Tammy Faye Jones owned three passive activities in 2015 (she had no suspended losses prior to 2015):

Activity	Date Acquired	2015 Allocated Gain/(Loss)
One	7/20/87	(60,000)
Two	9/01/87	40,000
Three	3/10/88	(30,000)

How much is her passive loss deduction (against nonpassive income) and suspended loss for each activity and the manner in which it is allocated?

38. Brent Fullback owned four passive activity interests in 2015:

Activity	Date Acquired	2015 Allocated Gain/(Loss)	Pre-2015 Suspended Loss
A-1	11/22/92	14,000	(27,000)
B-2	01/25/95	(22,000)	(25,000)
C-3	07/03/97	(5,000)	(8,000)
D-4	08/01/99	(3,000)	(1,000)

On March 2, 2015, Fullback sold his entire interest in A-1 for $15,000. His basis in the activity on January 1, 2015, was $11,000. Compute the following:
   a. Gain or loss realized from the sale of A-1
   b. Passive loss deduction (against nonpassive income) and type (i.e., ordinary income (loss) or capital income (loss))
   c. Suspended losses and how they are allocated

39. Jean Kelley owned three limited partnership interests in 2015:

Partnership	Date Acquired	2015 Allocated Gain/(Loss)	Pre-2015 Suspended Loss
MNO	05/03/97	(4,000)	(14,000)
OSD	10/14/97	10,000	(3,000)
CMP	11/15/98	(6,000)	(2,000)

How much is her passive loss deduction (against nonpassive activities) and suspended loss for each activity?

40. Thomas Settleton owned an interest as a general partner in LBO partnership. Settleton was not a material participant in the activity. His basis was $25,000 on the date he gifted the LBO partnership interest to his son, Willard. Suspended losses amounted to $40,000 as of that date. What are the federal income tax consequences of the gift to the son?

41. Teri Frazier owned three businesses and rental properties in 2015. During the year, her hair salon business experienced a $32,000 net loss. She participated 200 hours in the hair salon business. All of the salon's employees worked more than 600 hours for 2015. Her second business was a coin-operated laundry. She did not participate over 100 hours in the laundry operation. It had a net loss of $14,500. The third business was a flower shop, which had net income of $45,000 for 2015. She participated well over 1,000 hours in the flower shop business. None of the activities was located within one-half mile of each other. She also received dividends of $12,000 from her IBM stock, and interest of $14,000 from her AT&T bonds. In addition, Frazier had a net loss of $18,000 from her real estate rentals (where she was an active participant). Compute her adjusted gross income.

42. Darian Basemore owned an interest in five businesses in 2015. His level of participation and percentage of ownership in each enterprise is as follows:

Activity	Hours of Participation	Ownership Percentage
Ven-Tale	180	22%
MovERent	88	17
AZ Airlines	950	33
Sadd Books	135	12
Kingdom Autos	185	25

In which activity, if any, will Darian be considered a material participant?

43. Janice Hoplin, MD, owned her own medical clinic. She also owned the office building in which the clinic was located. The medical activity generated $125,000 of net income. She managed the building, which had 15 other medical professionals (tenants), from her medical office. The office rental activity provided her with a $12,000 net loss for the year. What is Janice's adjusted gross income?

44. Dave Eichoff had adjusted gross income for 2015 of $122,000 before any passive losses or other rental activities. He owned a mountain cabin in Idaho, which he rented for 125 days and which was not used by him at all during the year. The property will experience a net loss of $12,500. He also had a limited partnership interest that was purchased in 1985 and yielded a loss of $22,000. What is Dave's adjusted gross income after considering the passive activity and rental losses?

45. Diane Parker acquired an interest in a movie theater in June 2003. The theater broke even from 2003 to 2010. Parker did not actively participate in the activity during those years. She participated in the activity for 350, 400, 450, and 420 hours during 2011, 2012, 2013, and 2014, respectively. This was well below all other employees. The theater had losses allocated to her of $21,000, $6,000, $19,000, and $12,000 for 2011, 2012, 2013, and 2014, respectively. In 2015, however, she participated 750 hours in the business, and her share of the movie theater net income was $24,000. Her income from other sources (portfolio income) was $27,500. What are the income tax consequences to Diane for 2015?

46. Mary Beth is a CPA, devoting 3,000 hours per year to her practice. She also owns an office building in which she rents out space to tenants. She devotes none of her time to the management of the office building. She has a property management firm make all management decisions for her. During 2015, she incurred a loss, for tax purposes, of $30,000 on the office building. How must Mary Beth treat this loss on her 2015 tax return?

47. Assume the same facts as in Problem 46, except that Mary Beth is a real estate agent. She works 1,000 hours per year as a real estate agent and 1,200 hours per year managing her office building. How may she treat the loss on the office building?

48. Max Computer Center incurred the following casualty and theft losses in 2015:

Event		
a.	=	Robbery-Equip.
b.	=	Fire-Truck
c.	=	Fire-Equip.

	FAIR Market Value			
Event	Adjusted Basis	Before Casualty	After Casualty	Insurance Reimburse
a.	$8,000	$9,000	$0	$7,500
b.	$4,000	$5,000	$2,000	$3,500
c.	$9,000	$6,000	$0	$6,000

Compute the casualty and theft loss for each item listed.

49. In 2015, Mary Jackson had the following income and deductions listed on her individual income tax return:

Business income	$25,150
Interest income on personal investments	2,000
Less: Business expenses	45,000
Less: Personal exemption	4,000
Less: Nonbusiness deductions	3,000
Loss shown on tax return	$(24,850)

Compute the amount of Mary's 2015 net operating loss.

50. Ralph Sample had the following income and deductions listed on his 2015 income tax return:

Salary	$25,150
Business income	65,000
Interest income on personal investments	10,000
Less: Business expenses	102,000
Less: Personal exemption	4,000
Less: Nonbusiness deductions	12,000
Loss shown on tax return	$(17,850)

Compute the amount of Ralph's 2015 net operating loss.

51. During 2015, Jane Mason incurred the following home expenses:

Real estate taxes	$4,000
Interest on home mortgage	7,000
Maintenance on home	2,000
Other home expenses including depreciation	4,000
Total	$17,000

Assume that Jane qualified for the home office deduction, all of the above expenditures qualified for the deduction as home office expenses, 8 percent of the space in the home was used for the business activity, and Jane earned $9,000 in 2015 after all deductions other than home office expenses.

a. Compute Jane's home office deduction for 2015.

b. Assume instead that Jane earned only $1,000 after all deductions other than home office expenses. What is her home office deduction?

52. In 2015, Joan Cannon incurred the following expenses relating to her vacation home:

Mortgage interest	$6,000
Property taxes	4,000
Utility expenses	4,000
Depreciation	6,000
Total expenses	$20,000

During 2015, Joan personally used the vacation home for 20 days. Determine the rental expense deduction that she is entitled to claim on her 2015 tax return in each of the following cases. Use the Tax Court method of allocating normal expenses allowable to all taxpayers.

a. Joan rents out the vacation home for 10 days during the year and receives $800 in rental income.

b. Joan rents out the vacation home for 30 days during the year and receives $1,500 in rental income.

c. Joan rents out the vacation home for 230 days during the year and receives $9,000 in rental income.

53. Refer to Problem 52, Part (c) and assume the IRS approach to allocating normal expenses allowable to all taxpayers is used. Based on these facts, what rental expense deductions are allowable in 2015?

54. Which of the following is not a passive activity?
    a. Owning a limited partnership interest in an oil and gas limited partnership
    b. Having rental residential properties
    c. Owning a business and not materially participating
    d. Being a material participant in a small-tool rental business (averaging three days use)

55. Benson Company experienced partial destruction of a warehouse from a tornado. The warehouse had a basis of $200,000 at the time of the casualty. Its fair market value before the accident was $1,000,000 and afterward, $600,000. How has this event changed the basis of the warehouse?
    a. No effect
    b. Decrease by $200,000
    c. Decrease by $400,000
    d. Decrease by $100,000 plus insurance proceeds received

56. Which of the following taxpayers would be least likely to qualify for a home office deduction?
    a. Self-employed individual
    b. Employee with an office on the employer's premises
    c. Owner of property held for production of income
    d. Employee whose home office is for the employer's convenience

57. Net operating losses can be increased by which of the following?
    a. Personal casualty losses
    b. Business casualty losses
    c. Unreimbursed employee business expenses
    d. All of the above

58. Bob White owned a cabin in the Great Smoky Mountains. He used it for 16 days and rented it out for 190 days during the year. Which of the following is true?
    a. All allocated expenses are deductible (subject to the passive loss rules).
    b. Only allocated expenses up to gross rentals are deductible.
    c. The vacation home qualifies as a principal residence.
    d. All rentals are received tax free and no expenses, other than taxes and interest, are deductible.

59. John Malley owns an S corporation wherein he is a full-time employee. The S corporation manufactures a unique part for drilling bits used in off-shore oil rigs. In 2015, he has AGI of $720,000 and QPAI of $800,000. Compute the following for 2015:
    a. Manufacturers' deduction under Code Sec. 199 (assume that the W-2 wage limit is not a problem).
    b. John's new AGI.

60. John Henderson's portable sawmill was completely destroyed by a fire and he carried no insurance on the property. The adjusted basis for depreciation of the sawmill building and equipment at the time of the fire was $65,000, and its fair market value was $50,000. The value of the equipment after the fire was only scrap value, amounting to $200. How much is Mr. Henderson's deductible casualty loss?

61. Assume that the sawmill in Problem 60 was damaged by the fire but not completely destroyed. Just before the fire the sawmill had a fair market value of $50,000 and immediately after the fire its fair market value was $3,500.
    a. Under these facts, John's loss is limited to how much?
    b. Had the fair market value of the sawmill been $80,000 just before the fire and $10,000 just afterward, how much is John's deductible casualty loss?

62. Travis Goggans grows, manufactures, and sells veneer logs and strips. In 2015, he has QPAI of $4 million and taxable income of $5 million. Because Travis uses almost exclusively independent contractors, his W-2 wage base is only $200,000. How much is Travis Goggans' manufacturing deduction under Code Sec. 199?

63. **Comprehensive Problem (Tax Return Problem).** Harvey and Betty Duran, both age 37, are married with one dependent child. Determine their taxable income from the following information for 2014, and their tax liability. Both the ABC and XYZ partnerships are passive activities. Assume dividends are taxed as ordinary income.

Harvey's salary	$45,000
Betty's salary	62,000
Dividends received from domestic corporations (nonqualified)	11,000
Interest	7,000
Itemized deductions	6,920
Net loss from ABC Partnership (acq. 1983)	(14,200)
Net loss from XYZ Partnership (acq. 1988)	(6,000)
Harvey's business income (moonlighting)	7,700
Harvey's business deductions (before home office expenses)	22,000
Harvey's home office expenses	10,500
Net loss on rental property	(31,000)
Federal Income tax withheld	9,600

64. **Comprehensive Problem.** Michael Rambo, single and calendar year taxpayer, is the sole owner of Slice-It Pizza Company, a sole proprietorship. Michael materially participated in the activity. In 2015, Slice-It Pizza reported revenues of $600,000 and deductions of $410,000, exclusive of a net operating loss deduction of $150,000.

The NOL was carried forward from 2014. For tax purposes, Michael reports revenues and expenses of Slice-It Pizza on Schedule C of Form 1040—Individual Income Tax Return. If Michael has no other taxable income, deductions or credits in 2015, other than those listed above, what tax effect does the $150,000 NOL have on his 2015 tax return? Ignore liability for self-employment taxes.

65. **Research Problem.** Clients Buddy and Debbie Jamison are considering converting their private vacation home to rental property. They have asked for advice as to the tax aspects of owning such property. The only real estate they own is their principal residence and the vacation home. Some of the following sources may prove to be helpful in preparing a report for the clients: Code Sec. 280A; Code Sec. 469; Reg. §1.165-9(b); *A.B. Wood*, (CA-5) 52-2 USTC ¶9374, 197 F.2d 859; *E.G. McKinney*, 42 TCM 468, Dec. 36,077(M), T.C. Memo. 1981-377, aff'd (CA-10) 83-2 USTC ¶9655; *T.B. Jefferson*, 50 TC 963, Dec. 29,153; *L.M. McAuley*, 35 TCM 1236, Dec. 34,005(M), T.C. Memo. 1976-276.

66. **Research Problem.** The taxpayer, Hugh Ames, has been engaged in the general practice of medicine for more than 30 years. In 1991, he took over the operation of his family farm and decided to convert the farm into a cattle farm. He employed full-time help on the farm, but he himself did much of the physical work involved in improving the farm. In formulating his plans and in carrying them out, Dr. Ames had the advice and assistance of the local farm agent, an expert cattleman, and an expert farm machinery mechanic.

Dr. Ames raised cattle as well as catfish and quarter horses. However, after encountering technical and demand problems, he discontinued the raising of catfish and horses. He was presently raising thoroughbreds and was confident that this venture would prove more profitable.

During the period from 1991 through 2015, Dr. Ames' farming operation resulted in substantial losses, averaging approximately $15,000 per year. During the taxable years of 2014 and 2015, his farm losses totaled $30,000 and $25,000 respectively. The evidence showed Dr. Ames had not made a profit, on a year-to-year basis, during this entire period, although his testimony to the IRS agent was that he always had operated and still operated his farm with a profit motive. Can Dr. Ames deduct the losses? See *Gregory, Jr. v. U.S.* (37 AFTR2d 76-785) and *Loy D. Mercer v. Comm'r*, (67-1 USTC ¶9390).

Chapter

8

Deductions: Itemized Deductions

OBJECTIVES

After completing Chapter 8, you should be able to:

1. List items making up the medical expense deduction.
2. Apply rules for the interest expense deduction.
3. Explain the requirements for the charitable contribution deduction.
4. Explain the requirements for the personal casualty and theft losses deduction.
5. Identify deductions for employee business expenses and investment expenses, as well as other miscellaneous itemized deductions.

OVERVIEW

In computing taxable income, personal, living, or family expenses are generally disallowed. However, tax rules do allow some deductions for expenses which are essentially personal in nature. These types of expenses are deductible from adjusted gross income, referred to as itemized deductions, and deducted on Schedule A of the individual tax return.

This chapter discusses those expenses that are specifically allowed as itemized deductions. These deductions include: medical expenses, taxes, interest, charitable contributions, casualty and theft losses, employee business expenses, investment expenses, and other miscellaneous itemized deductions.

While these itemized deductions are allowed by law, there is an overall limitation on the amount of itemized deductions that can be taken. High-income taxpayers whose AGI exceeds a certain threshold amount are required to reduce the allowable itemized deductions by a designated percent. This provision is detailed in Chapter 3.

Medical Expenses

¶8001 REQUIREMENTS FOR THE DEDUCTION

Individuals can deduct many types of medical expenses as itemized deductions. The deduction is allowable only to individuals and only for medical expenses actually paid during the year, regardless of when the expenses were incurred or the method of accounting used by the taxpayer. Any medical expense deduction will be reduced by the amount of any insurance reimbursement or other similar compensation. Only medical expenses in excess of 10 percent of adjusted gross income (7.5 percent of AGI for those 65 or over through 2016) are deductible. Code Sec. 213.

EXAMPLE 8.1

Jerome Jenkins, 35, has an adjusted gross income of $20,000 and pays for the following medical expenses during the year:

Medical insurance	$1,820
Medicines and drugs	175
Other medical expenses	500

The medical deduction is computed as follows:

Medicines and drugs	$175
Medical insurance	1,820
Other medical expenses	500
Total Medical Expenses	$2,495
Less 10% of $20,000 (adjusted gross income)	2,000
Total Medical Expense Deduction	$495

For medical expenses to be deductible, they must be for the medical care of the taxpayer, the taxpayer's spouse, or a dependent of the taxpayer. A child of divorced parents is treated as the dependent of both parents for purposes of the medical expense deduction. The gross income requirement is waived for purposes of determining who is a "dependent" with respect to the medical care deduction.

EXAMPLE 8.2

Joan Farley pays medical expenses for the care of her father. Joan also pays over half of the support of her father but is unable to claim her father as a dependent because he has $5,000 of income for the year. The income ceiling for dependents in 2015 is $4,000. Joan may include the medical expenses for the care of her father in her medical expense computation even though she can not claim her father as a dependent.

¶8015 MEDICAL CARE EXPENSES

The medical expense deduction is specifically limited to amounts spent for medical care. The term "medical care" is broadly defined to include amounts paid for the diagnosis, cure, mitigation, treatment, or prevention of disease. Accordingly, payments for the following are payments for medical care: hospital services, nursing services, medical, laboratory, surgical, dental and other diagnostic and healing services, X-rays, medicines, and drugs. Amounts paid for accident or health insurance are generally deductible as medical expenses. Further, expenses paid for "medical care" include those paid for transportation primarily for and essential to medical care, such as the expense of using an ambulance. Amounts expended for illegal operations or treatments are not deductible. An expenditure which is merely beneficial to the general health of an individual, such as an expenditure for a vacation or for health club fees, is also not deductible.

Payments for unnecessary cosmetic surgery (such as facelifts or cheek implants) whose purpose is solely to improve the patient's appearance do not qualify as a medical expense deduction for tax purposes. This rule does not apply to cosmetic surgery necessary to help correct a deformity arising from a congenital abnormality, or heal an injury arising from an accident or a disfiguring disease. Any employer reimbursements for unnecessary cosmetic surgery under a medical expense reimbursement plan must be included in the gross income of the employee in the year received.

EXAMPLE 8.3

In June 2015, Jane Martin undergoes a liposuction operation solely to improve her physical appearance. None of the expenses related to this operation would be deductible for tax purposes on her 2015 income tax return.

EXAMPLE 8.4

Should the costs of changing one's sex qualify as a medical deduction? After all, the change is just cosmetic and isn't necessary, is it? Interestingly, gender identity disorder is a condition recognized by the medical community, so a strong case can be made that a sex change operation is just a means of treating that condition. Although it initially disagreed, the IRS later decided to follow this decision. Action on Decision 2011-003, Nov. 4, 2011. A 2010 Tax Court case (*O'Donnabhain*, 134 TC No. 34, Dec. 58,122 (2010)) ruled that a sex change operation was deductible as a medical expense.

¶8025   CAPITAL EXPENDITURES

Capital expenditures for home improvements and additions which are constructed primarily for the medical care of an individual generally qualify for a medical expense deduction only to the extent that the cost of the improvement or addition exceeds any increase in the value of the affected property that is due to the improvement. The entire cost of additions or improvements that do not increase the value of the home is deductible as a medical expense. Medical expense deductions have been allowed for the costs of installing elevators in the homes of persons suffering from heart disease, air conditioning devices for persons suffering from allergies, and specially built swimming pools for persons suffering from polio.

EXAMPLE 8.5

Gary Greene is advised by a physician to install an elevator in his residence so that his wife, who is afflicted with heart disease, will not be required to climb stairs. If the cost of installing the elevator is $1,500 and the increase in the value of the residence is only $1,100, the difference of $400 is deductible as a medical expense. However, if the value of the residence is not increased by the addition, the entire cost of installing the elevator qualifies as a medical expense.

Specific types of capital expenditures incurred to accommodate a personal residence to the needs of a physically handicapped individual are fully deductible medical expenses since these types of expenditures do not increase the fair market value of the residence. Examples are construction of entrance ramps, widening of doorways, or installation of railings to allow use of wheelchairs,

Capital expenditures which are related only to the sick person and not related to permanent improvement or betterment of property are deductible if such expenditures otherwise qualify as expenditures for medical care. For example, expenditures for eye glasses, handicapped service animals, dentures, artificial limbs, wheel chairs, crutches, inclinators, or air conditioners (if detachable from the property and purchased only for the use of a sick person) are deductible.

¶8035   TRANSPORTATION AND LODGING EXPENSES

Transportation expenses incurred in order to obtain medical care are deductible. However, the transportation deduction does not include the cost of any meals while away from home receiving medical treatment unless the meals are provided as part of the in-patient care at a hospital or similar facility. If a doctor prescribes an operation or other medical care, and the taxpayer chooses for purely personal considerations to travel to another locality for the medical care, neither the cost of transportation nor the cost of meals and lodging is deductible. Instead of a deduction for actual expenses incurred, a standard mileage rate of $.23 per mile for 2015 is allowed in computing the cost of driving an automobile for medical purposes. Parking fees and tolls may be deducted in addition to the mileage rate deduction.

Lodging while away from home on trips that are primarily for and essential to medical care is deductible. This deduction is not allowed for amounts paid for lodging that is lavish or extravagant. No medical deduction is allowed for any amount of lodging expenses if there is any significant element of personal pleasure, recreation, or vacation in the travel away from home.

The amount of the deduction for lodging is subject to a limitation of $50 per night for each eligible person. The deduction is allowed not only for the patient but also for a person who must travel with the patient. This means that if a parent accompanies a dependent child on a trip away from home for medical treatment, the parent could deduct up to $100 per day for lodging expenses.

EXAMPLE 8.6 | Corola Combs travels out of state for special surgery for her daughter. She travels 400 miles round trip and incurs $12 in parking fees and tolls. Corola spends three nights in a hotel while her daughter is in the hospital. Her lodging expense totals $165, and she spends $90 eating out. Her meal expenses are not deductible. Her other qualifying medical expenses are:

Lodging limited to $150 ($50 per night × 3 nights)	$150
Mileage 400 miles × $.23 per mile	92
Parking fees and tolls	12
Qualifying medical expenses from trip	$254

¶8045 HOSPITAL AND OTHER INSTITUTIONAL CARE

The cost of in-patient hospital care (requiring an overnight stay), including the cost of meals and lodging, is deductible. The extent to which expenses for care in an institution other than a hospital (e.g., a nursing home, home for the aged, or therapeutic center for alcohol or drug addiction) qualify as a deduction for medical care is primarily a question of fact, and depends on the condition of the individual and the nature of the services received. If the availability of medical care in an institution is the principal reason for the patient's presence there, the entire cost of the care, including meals and lodging furnished incident to such care, is deductible. However, if an individual is placed in the institution primarily for personal or family reasons, then only that portion of the cost attributable to medical or nursing care (excluding meals and lodging) is deductible.

EXAMPLE 8.7 | Alexis Amberson is 80, totally disabled, and suffers from a chronic ailment. Her family places her in a nursing home equipped to provide medical and nursing care services. The nursing home expenses are $25,000 a year. Of this amount, $8,500 is directly attributable to medical and nursing care. Since Alexis is in need of intensive medical and nursing care and has been placed in the nursing home facility for this purpose, all $25,000 is deductible (subject to the 7.5 percent of AGI limitation). Had Alexis been placed in the nursing home primarily for personal or family considerations, only $8,500 would be deductible.

Although education ordinarily does not qualify as medical care, special schooling for a mentally or physically handicapped individual is deductible, if the resources of the institution for alleviating the individual's mental or physical handicap are the principal reason for the individual's presence there. In such a case the cost of attending the school includes the cost of meals and lodging, if supplied, and the cost of ordinary education that is incidental to the special services furnished by the school.

¶8055 MEDICINES AND DRUGS

Only amounts paid for insulin and prescription medicines or drugs are deductible as a medical expense. Pharmaceutical items acquired without a prescription (such as over-the-counter ibuprophen or allergy medicines) do not qualify even though they are used for a particular illness, disease, or medical condition. Cosmetics and toiletries are not considered medicines and drugs.

EXAMPLE 8.8 | Larry James, 28, had adjusted gross income of $22,000 in 2015. He paid a doctor $800 for medical expenses, a hospital $2,000, $200 for prescription drugs, and $150 for over-the-counter cold remedies and vitamins during 2015. His 2015 medical expense deduction is computed as follows:

Doctor	$800
Hospital	2,000
Medicine and drugs	200
Over-the-counter cold remedies and vitamins	0
Medical expenses	$3,000
Less: 10% of $22,000 (adjusted gross income)	2,200
Allowable medical expense deduction	$ 800

¶8065   MEDICAL INSURANCE PREMIUMS

A medical expense deduction is allowed for premiums paid for medical care insurance (including contact lens insurance), subject to the 10 (or 7.5) percent limitation. If amounts are payable under an insurance contract for other than medical care (such as indemnity for loss of income or, life, limb, or sight), no amount paid for the insurance is deductible unless the medical care charge is stated separately in the contract or furnished in a separate statement. Long-term health care insurance premiums are deductible, but in 2015, the maximum deduction for prepaid long-term care insurance premiums is $380 for a taxpayer age 40 or less to $4,750 for a taxpayer more than age 70.

The basic cost of Medicare insurance (Medicare Part A) is not deductible unless voluntarily paid by the taxpayer for coverage. However, the cost of extra Medicare (Medicare Part B) is deductible. Self-employed persons are allowed to deduct 100 percent of amounts paid for health insurance for herself, her spouse, her dependents, and her under-27-year-old children as a business expense (deductible for adjusted gross income). Code Sec. 162(l). See ¶6575 for a discussion of deductions for Medical Savings Accounts. In general, this deduction is reduced by any premium tax credits the taxpayer takes.

Under the Affordable Care Act's individual mandate, taxpayers without health insurance will pay a penalty of the higher of a flat penalty of $325 per person or 2% of income. "Income" for this purpose is generally adjusted gross income minus the standard deduction and personal exemption(s). For example, a single individual making $50,000 would have a $794 penalty for 2015. The penalty is not deductible.

Medical expenses are deductible only in the year paid. If medical expenses are reimbursed under a medical care insurance plan in the same year as paid, then the reimbursement merely reduces the amount that would otherwise be deductible. However, where reimbursement, from insurance or otherwise, for medical expenses is received in a year subsequent to a year in which a deduction was claimed, the reimbursement must be included in gross income in the year received to the extent attributable to deductions allowed in the prior year.

EXAMPLE 8.9

Morris Masters, 45, had adjusted gross income of $60,000 in 2015. He had a medical operation and, as a result, paid $5,000 in 2015 for hospitalization and $700 in doctors' bills. His transportation mileage for medical reasons totaled 200 miles. He also paid $640 for prescription medicines and drugs, $275 for contact lenses, and a $900 medical insurance premium in 2015. Under the medical insurance policy carried by the taxpayer, there is an allowance for the operation of only the first $1,000, which amount Morris received in 2015. His deduction for medical expenses is computed as follows:

Hospitalization (medical operation)	$5,000	
Less: Reimbursement from insurance company	1,000	$4,000
Premium on medical insurance policy		900
Doctors' bills		700
Prescription medicines and drugs		640
Contact lenses		275
Transportation for medical purposes (200 miles × $.23)		46
Total		$6,561
Less: 10% of $60,000 (adjusted gross income)		6,000
Total medical expenses deduction		$ 561

If Morris received the $1,000 reimbursement in 2016 rather than 2015, he would have a deduction of $1,561 ($561 + $1,000) in 2015 and income of $1,000 in 2016 (assuming he itemizes in 2015).

Taxes

¶8101   SUMMARY OF DEDUCTIBLE TAXES

The following taxes are deductible as itemized deductions (Code Sec. 164(a)):

1. State, local, or foreign real property taxes
2. State or local personal property taxes

3. State, local, or foreign income taxes
4. State and local general sales taxes (through 2014)

Other state, local, and foreign taxes not listed above are deductible only if they are trade or business expenses or are incurred in the production of income. The following discussion of taxes relates only to the deductibility of nonbusiness taxes by individuals.

¶8105 PROPERTY TAXES

Local, state, and foreign real property taxes are generally deductible only by the person upon whom they are imposed, and in the year in which they were paid or accrued. If they relate to nonbusiness real property, they are deductible as an itemized deduction.

A tax paid for local benefits such as street, sidewalk, and other similar improvements (also known as special assessments) is not deductible if imposed because of some direct benefit to the property against which the assessment is levied. Special assessments are not deductible, even though some incidental benefit may flow to the public welfare. Special assessments can, however, be added to the basis of the related property.

If real property is sold during the year, the real property tax deduction must be allocated between the buyer and the seller based on the number of days during the year that each party held the property. The seller is treated as paying the taxes up to, but not including, the date of sale. This allocation is required regardless of which party actually writes the check for the property tax or the method of accounting used by the taxpayers.

EXAMPLE 8.10	William Wasserman sold land to David Deere on April 1. Property taxes of $1,460 were paid by David on November 27 to cover the real property taxes for the entire calendar year. Assuming it is not a leap year, William is entitled to a $360 real property tax deduction ($1,460/365 = $4 per day × 90 days). David is entitled to a $1,100 real property tax deduction ($4 per day × 275 days).

A tenant-stockholder in a cooperative housing corporation may deduct amounts paid or accrued to the corporation to the extent that they represent the tenant-stockholder's proportional share of the real property taxes on the apartment building or houses and land on which situated. Similarly, a taxpayer who owns an apartment in a condominium apartment complex may deduct the taxes assessed on the taxpayer's interest in the property and paid by the taxpayer each year, provided the taxpayer itemizes deductions in filing a federal income tax return.

To be deductible, personal property taxes must be ad valorem (i.e., a tax that is based on the value of the personal property.) A tax which is based on criteria other than value does not qualify as ad valorem. For example, a motor vehicle tax based on weight, model year, and horsepower, or any of these characteristics, is not an ad valorem tax. However, a tax which is partly based on value and partly based on other criteria may qualify in part.

EXAMPLE 8.11	Gayla Gopher paid $135 for motor vehicle license plates. The license plate fee is based on a combination of value and weight of the automobile. If $75 of the $135 fee is based on the value of the automobile, then $75 is deductible as a tax.

Taxes imposed by some states on intangible personal property or the income therefrom are deductible.

¶8115 INCOME TAXES

State or city income taxes, including franchise taxes measured by net income, are deductible as itemized deductions by individuals. Prior to 2015, either state and local sales taxes or state and local income taxes can be deducted, but not both. State and local income taxes on interest income that is exempt from federal income tax are also deductible. However, state and local income taxes on other exempt income are not deductible.

Taxpayers may deduct state and local income taxes withheld from their salary. They may also deduct tax payments made on prior year income in the year they were actually withheld or paid.

EXAMPLE 8.12	During 2015, Carl Castor had $1,200 in state income taxes withheld from his salary. In addition, he paid an additional $325 in 2015 when he filed his 2014 state income tax return. Carl's state income tax deduction for 2015 is $1,525, the amount he actually paid during 2015.

Any estimated state tax payments made that are in fact not required to be made are not deductible. For example, if a taxpayer made an estimated state income tax payment but the estimate of the state tax liability for the year shows that the taxpayer will receive a refund of the full amount of the estimated payment, then the taxpayer was not required to make the payment and may not deduct it as an itemized deduction.

If a taxpayer receives a refund of state, local, or foreign income taxes, all or part of the refund may need to be included in income in the year received. The tax benefit rule requires the taxpayer to include a tax refund in gross income of the year received to the extent that a tax benefit resulted from the deduction of the item in the earlier year. This includes refunds resulting from taxes that were overwithheld, not determined correctly, or redetermined as a result of an amended return. A refund of state, local, or foreign taxes may not be used to reduce the amount of taxes paid during the year to lower the deduction. The taxes paid and the refund received must be reported separately.

EXAMPLE 8.13	Paul Plymouth, a single taxpayer, received a refund of $1,000 in 2016 from his 2015 state income tax return. Paul had total itemized deductions in 2015 of $6,900, including $2,500 for state income taxes. The amount to be included in gross income for 2016 is $600. The amount included is the lesser of the refund received ($1,000) or the excess itemized deductions taken in 2015 ($600). The $1,000 refund received in 2016 will not affect the itemized deduction for state income taxes in either 2016 or 2015.

Itemized deductions for 2015	$6,900
Less: Standard deduction for 2015	6,300
Excess itemized deductions for 2015	$600

For tax years through 2014, individual taxpayers are able to deduct the greater of state and local income taxes or state and local general sales taxes as an itemized deduction on their federal income tax returns. Code Sec. 164(b)(5). The amount to be deducted for state and local general sales taxes is either (1) the total of actual general sales taxes paid as substantiated by accumulated receipts, or (2) an amount from IRS-generated tables, plus the amount of general sales taxes from the purchase of a motor vehicle, boat, or motor home.

Interest

¶8201   REQUIREMENTS FOR DEDUCTION

Interest is the amount which one has contracted to pay for the use of borrowed money. For tax purposes the term has the usual ordinary, everyday meaning given to it in the business world. *Old Colony R.R. Co.,* 3 USTC ¶880, 284 U.S. 552, 52 S.Ct. 211 (1932). Interest incurred in a trade or business is deductible. However, as discussed in Chapter 6, interest incurred to purchase assets on which the income is tax exempt (such as state and municipal bonds) is not deductible.

It is not necessary that the parties to a transaction label a payment made for the use of money as interest for it to be treated as interest. The method of computation also does not control its deductibility, so long as the amount in question is an ascertainable sum paid for the use of borrowed money.

The timing of a deduction for interest expense depends on whether the taxpayer is on the cash basis or the accrual basis. Taxpayers on the cash basis will deduct interest expense when the payment of the interest is actually made. Deducting the amount of the interest from the original loan amount is not considered "payment" for this purpose. Accrual basis taxpayers, on the other hand, will deduct interest as it accrues. Prepaid interest ("points") is generally amortized over the life of the loan, but is currently deductible if paid in connection with a loan made to purchase the taxpayer's principal residence. (See ¶8265 for further information.)

EXAMPLE 8.14	On November 1 Ben borrows $10,000 to be used in his business. He actually receives $9,400, but will have to pay the full $10,000 back on April 30 of the next year. If he is a cash basis taxpayer, he will deduct the entire $600 of interest in the next year, when it is paid. If he is on the accrual basis, he would deduct $200 (2/6) this year and $400 (4/6) next year.

Interest deductions for tax purposes can be separated into six types: personal (consumer) interest, qualified residence interest, investment interest, trade or business interest, passive investment interest, and qualified education loan interest. Each of these six types of interest deductions is explained in the following sections.

¶8205 PERSONAL (CONSUMER) INTEREST

Generally, interest on personal loans is not deductible by individuals. The vast majority of nondeductible personal interest consists of interest on credit card debt, automobile loans, or student loans. Of course, if the credit card or automobile are used for business purposes then the related interest is business, not personal, interest, and is deductible. Similarly, under certain circumstances student loan interest is deductible (see below). Interest on tax deficiencies (even those arising from individual business income) is also personal interest, and it is therefore not deductible.

EXAMPLE 8.15	Sara Short incurs personal interest of $1,000 on an auto loan. Sara is not allowed an itemized deduction for the auto loan interest.

¶8210 QUALIFIED EDUCATION LOAN INTEREST

Taxpayers are allowed an interest deduction *for AGI* of up to $2,500 for interest paid on qualified education loans. Qualified education loans are loans incurred to pay expenses for undergraduate and graduate tuition, room and board, and related expenses. In 2015 the deduction is phased out for single taxpayers with AGI between $65,000 and $80,000 and married taxpayers filing joint returns with AGI between $130,000 and $160,000. The deduction will be allowed in figuring adjusted gross income.

¶8215 QUALIFIED RESIDENCE INTEREST

Taxpayers may deduct interest on loans secured by first or second homes, but the homes must be "qualified residences." A home is a qualified residence if it is the taxpayer's principal residence or if it is a second residence designated for this purpose that is used for personal purposes for more than the greater of 14 days or 10 percent of the number of days it is rented (such as a vacation home). Taxpayers having more than two residences can designate each year which residence is to be considered the second residence. If the second residence is not used by the taxpayer or rented at any time during the year, the taxpayer need not meet the requirements that the residence be used for personal (nonrental) purposes for more than 14 days. Code Sec. 163(h). For 2007 through 2014, "qualified residence interest" includes premiums for qualified mortgage insurance, which are otherwise nondeductible. Code Sec. 163(h)(3)(E)(i).

Qualified residence interest on acquisition indebtedness is deductible. Acquisition indebtedness is up to $1,000,000 of debt incurred to acquire, construct, or substantially improve any qualified residence and which is secured by the residence. If a residence is refinanced, the amount qualifying as acquisition indebtedness is limited to the amount of acquisition debt existing at the time of refinancing plus any of the amount of the new loan which is used to substantially improve the residence.

A taxpayer can also deduct the interest on a limited amount of home equity loans. The limit is the lesser of $100,000 or the equity (fair market value less acquisition indebtedness) in the home. "Fair market value" for this purpose is determined on the date the last debt was secured by the home, so a later decline in fair market value will not affect the deduction. No restrictions are placed on the use of the home equity loan funds other than the purchase of tax-free investments. (However, if the proceeds are not used for home improvement, the interest is not deductible for AMT purposes.) Interest on the debt equal to or under the above limits is fully deductible while interest attributable to debt over the limits is not deductible.

The IRS has taken the position that if the initial mortgage exceeds $1,000,000, up to $100,000 of the excess will qualify as home equity interest. Rev. Rul. 2010-25.

EXAMPLE 8.16

Shelly McGuire bought a house for $1,500,000 and paid $300,000 down on it. Her interest on the $1,200,000 initial mortgage was $72,000. The interest on $1,100,000 of her mortgage will be deductible, since $1,000,000 would be treated as acquisition indebtedness and $100,000 would qualify as a home equity loan. Her residence interest deduction will be limited to $1,100,000/$1,200,000 of $72,000, or $66,000.

TAX BLUNDER

Tim Johnson borrowed $20,000 on a car loan to finance the purchase of a new car. Tim also owns a home on which he has no mortgage. He did not consider a home equity loan when he purchased his car. The interest payments on his car do not qualify for an interest deduction on his tax return. Tim should have considered a home equity loan to finance the purchase of his car.

Taxpayers can turn nondeductible personal (consumer) interest into deductible qualified residence interest by taking out a home equity loan on their personal residence and using the proceeds to pay off personal loans, automobile loans, and credit card balances.

¶8225   INVESTMENT INTEREST

The deduction for investment interest is limited to the amount of net investment income. Investment interest in excess of this limitation is carried forward and treated as investment interest in the succeeding tax year. However, an investment interest carryover is allowed in a subsequent year only to the extent the taxpayer has net investment income in the later year.

Definition of Investment Interest

Interest that is subject to the investment interest limitation is defined as interest on debt incurred or continued to purchase or carry property held for investment. Property held for investment includes any property that produces income of the following types: interest, dividends, annuities, or royalties not derived in the ordinary course of a trade or business. The most common types of property held for investment are stocks, bonds, and raw land.

Investment income includes gross income from property held for investment such as dividends, interest, and royalties. Net short term gains are normally included in the definitiion of investment income, and net long term gains are not. However, a taxpayer has the option of giving up the long-term capital gain rate (0/15/20%) on the sale of long term capital assets in order to have all or a portion of the long-term capital gains included as net investment income, thereby increasing the allowable deductible investment interest expense. The taxpayers also have the option of giving up the preferential tax rate treatment for dividends in order to have the dividend income included as net investment income.

Net investment income is investment income net of investment expenses. Investment expenses are deductible expenses (other than interest) directly connected with the production of investment income, such as investment advisor fees.

EXAMPLE 8.17

Roberta Ramsey has $17,000 of investment interest expense and $4,000 of net investment income in 2015. Her investment interest deduction for 2015 is $4,000. The other $13,000 of investment interest she paid may be carried over to 2016 and deducted in that year to the extent that it, together with 2016 investment interest and other investment interest carryovers, does not exceed the investment interest limitation.

¶8235   TRADE OR BUSINESS INTEREST

Most interest payments incurred in a trade or business are fully deductible for tax purposes. Trade or business interest payments are deductible in computing adjusted gross income and are discussed in Chapter 6.

¶8245   PASSIVE INVESTMENT INTEREST

Passive investment interest is the interest incurred on money borrowed to invest in a passive activity. The amount of passive investment interest is subtracted from any gain or added to any loss from the passive activity. Losses from passive activities are subject to the passive loss limitation rules explained beginning at ¶7201.

¶8255   PAYMENTS FOR SERVICES

Payments for specific services which the lender performs in connection with the borrower's account are not deductible as interest. For example, interest does not include the separate charges made for investigation of the prospective borrower and the borrower's collateral, closing costs of the loan and the papers drawn in connection with the closing, or fees paid to a third party for servicing and collecting the particular loan. Rev. Rul. 69-188, 1969-1 CB 54.

¶8265   PREPAID INTEREST

Taxpayers on either the accrual or cash method of accounting are generally required to deduct prepaid interest over the time period during which the prepaid interest represents the cost of using the borrowed funds. Interest subtracted in advance from the proceeds of a loan is not considered paid until the loan payments are made.

EXAMPLE 8.18

> On October 1, 2015, Horace Holmes borrows $50,000 from the bank on a one-year, 10 percent loan. The bank subtracts the interest in advance and remits $45,000 to Horace. He pays the due amount of $50,000 on September 30, 2016. Horace has an interest expense deduction of $5,000 for 2016. He is not considered to have prepaid the interest in 2015. If he had received the full $50,000 from the bank and prepaid the $5,000 interest in 2015, $1,250 (3/12) would have been deductible in 2015 and $3,750 (9/12) would have been deductible in 2016.

"Points" are additional interest charges which are usually paid when a loan is closed and which are generally imposed by the lender in lieu of a higher interest rate. Where points are paid as compensation for the use of borrowed money, rather than as payment for the lender's services, the points substitute for a higher stated annual interest rate. These types of points are similar to a prepayment of interest, and are to be treated as paid over the term of the loan. An exception allows the current deduction of points paid in connection with a mortgage incurred in the purchase or improvement of the taxpayer's principal residence. This exception applies only if points are generally charged in the geographical area where the loan is made and to the extent of the number of points generally charged in that area for a home loan. Points paid on refinancing must be deducted ratably over the life of the loan. Any unamortized points are deductible when the loan is paid off.

¶8275   MORTGAGE INSURANCE PREMIUMS

Mortgage insurance premiums paid by a taxpayer in connection with acquisition indebtedness on a qualified residence are treated as qualified residence interest and are deductible as an itemized deduction through 2014. The allowable deduction is phased out ratably if the taxpayer's adjusted gross income exceeds $100,000 ($50,000 for a married taxpayer filing a separate return). In addition, the deduction only applies to mortgage insurance contracts issued after December 31, 2006.

Charitable Contributions

Contributions made to "qualified domestic organizations" by individuals and corporations are deductible as charitable contributions. Code Sec. 170. Any charitable contribution actually paid during the year is allowable as a deduction regardless of the method of accounting used by the taxpayer.

Ordinarily, a contribution is deemed made at the time delivery is made. The unconditional delivery or mailing of a check which subsequently clears in due course will constitute a contribution on the date of delivery or mailing. A "pledge" by a taxpayer to make a contribution is not deductible until it is actually paid.

EXAMPLE 8.19

> On December 1, 2015, Sherri Jones made a pledge to donate $1,200 to the City Museum. She mailed a check for $800 to the museum on December 30, 2015, and mailed another check for $400 on January 31, 2016. The museum did not receive the $800 check until January 5, 2016, and deposited it on January 6. The museum received and deposited the $400 check on February 3, 2016. Her pledge does not affect the timing or the deductibility of her contributions. She can deduct $800 in 2015, the year the $800 check was mailed (the time of "delivery"), and the other $400 is deductible in 2016.

¶8301   QUALIFIED ORGANIZATIONS

To qualify for the deduction, a contribution must be made to one of the following organizations:

1. The United States, a state, a possession of the United States, or any political subdivision of the foregoing
2. Corporation, trust, community chest, fund, or foundation that is created or organized in the United States and operated exclusively for religious, charitable, scientific, literary, or educational purposes
3. Veterans' organization
4. Domestic fraternal society
5. Nonprofit cemetery company

Generally, contributions made to foreign organizations are not deductible. No deduction is allowed for amounts paid to an organization which participates in any political campaign activities on behalf of or in opposition to any candidate for public office.

Gifts made to individuals generally are not deductible. For a contribution to be deductible, a donor cannot earmark it for the benefit of a specific individual.

EXAMPLE 8.20   Fred Fromm made donations to needy individuals. The payments were made by Fred from personal funds directly to the individuals after an investigation of their needs. There was no specific fund established or maintained by Fred or any other person for the purpose of distributing the money to the needy individuals. Fred is not allowed a charitable contribution deduction for his donations to the individuals.

TAX BLUNDER

Referring to the facts in Example 8.20, Fred should have made donations to qualified charitable organizations who help needy individuals instead of making the contribution directly to needy individuals. In this way, Fred would have preserved a charitable contribution deduction on his federal income tax return.

An organization must meet specific requirements in order to be exempt from taxation. Code Sec. 501. However, this does not necessarily mean that a contribution to that organization is deductible by the donor. The IRS publishes a list of organizations which have applied for and received rulings or determination letters holding contributions to them to be deductible. If an organization has not received a determination letter, it is not recognized as an organization to which contributions are deductible unless it is an organization described in (1), above.

Qualified charitable organizations are divided into two categories: public charities and private charities. Public charities include:

1. Churches or a convention or association of churches
2. Educational organizations which normally maintain a regular faculty, curriculum, and a regularly enrolled body of students
3. Hospitals and medical research organizations
4. Organizations supported by the government which are organized to administer property to or for the benefit of a college or university described in (2), above
5. Governmental units
6. A corporation, trust, or community chest, fund, or foundation that is created or organized in the United States and is organized and operated exclusively for religious, charitable, scientific, literary, or educational purposes
7. Certain types of private foundations

Private foundations are organizations which do not normally receive donations from the general public. There are two types of private foundations: operating and nonoperating. A private operating foundation is generally an organization with respect to which more than 50% of its assets are devoted directly to activities for which it is organized and operated and that distributes substantially all of its income for the conduct of its charitable purposes. Private operating foundations are treated as public charities.

Most private foundations fall into the nonoperating foundation classification. Private nonoperating foundations that distribute all of their contributions to public charities are also treated as public charities. Thus, a public charity is any qualified charity except for private nonoperating foundations that do not distribute all of their income to public charities. These private nonoperating foundations not contributing all of their income are classified as private charities.

¶8315 VALUATION OF CHARITABLE DONATIONS

If a charitable contribution is made in property, the amount of the contribution is normally the fair market value of the property at the time of the contribution. The fair market value is generally the price at which the property would change hands between a willing buyer and a willing seller, with both having a reasonable knowledge of relevant facts. No charitable deduction is allowed for the contribution of services.

Where the taxpayer receives some benefit in return for payment to a charitable organization, the deduction is reduced by the value of the benefit received. Where a charitable organization sponsors charity balls, bazaars, banquets, shows, or athletic events, there is a presumption that the price of admission is not a gift, and that the payment is for an item of value. The burden is on the taxpayer to show that the amount paid exceeds the fair market value of admission. The fact that the full payment or a portion of the payment made by the taxpayer is used by the organization exclusively for charitable purposes has no bearing upon the determination to be made as to the value of the admission or the amount qualifying as a contribution. The IRS says that a benefit is "insubstantial" and won't reduce the deduction if it is not more than the lesser of 2% of the payment or $105 (for 2015).

EXAMPLE 8.21

Members of a charitable organization sell candy to raise funds for the charity. The candy is purchased at $5 per box, normally sells for $8 a box, but is sold at $10 per box. The organization promotes the sale as a "tax-deductible donation." Only $2 per box qualifies as a charitable contribution. Other instances in which a deductible contribution could be claimed for the excess paid above fair market value would be (1) purchase of a ticket (from a charitable organization) to an artist's benefit performance and (2) purchase of an item at a benefit auction for more than its fair market value.

Taxpayers who make a payment to a college or university for the right to purchase tickets to an athletic event are entitled to deduct only 80 percent of the payment as a charitable deduction regardless of whether the tickets would have been available without making the payment.

The IRS has ruled that a taxpayer could deduct a portion of its donation to a state university's foundation for which the taxpayer received the right to purchase tickets for seating at university athletic events in a special skybox. The IRS concluded that the payment for the skybox lease was made to an educational institution for the right to purchase tickets and for the tickets themselves and, thus the taxpayer was allowed to deduct 80 percent of its payment under Code Sec. 170(l). TAM 200004001.

Unreimbursed expenditures made incident to the rendering of services to an organization may constitute a deductible contribution. These expenses include reasonable expenditures for meals and lodging while away from home in the course of performing donated services.

Automobile expenses incurred in travel or transportation to perform charitable services are deductible. A standard mileage rate of $.14 per mile (not indexed for inflation) or the actual expenses of operating the automobile may be used. Rev. Proc. 2004-64. Parking fees and tolls are added to either method of computation. General repairs or maintenance expenses, depreciation, insurance, or registration fees are not deductible. The costs of meals for the volunteers or the costs of child care for the volunteer's own children while the individual is performing services are not deductible.

TAX BLUNDER

John Adams does volunteer work for a number of charitable organizations. He uses his car in connection with his volunteer work but does not keep track of the miles driven while performing his charitable duties. Because he didn't keep track of his mileage, John has foregone a $.14 per mile charitable contribution deduction for all of the miles driven while performing his volunteer work.

¶8325 LIMITATIONS ON CHARITABLE CONTRIBUTIONS

An individual's charitable contribution deduction is subject to 20 percent, 30 percent, and 50 percent of AGI limitations. If a husband and wife file a joint return, the deduction for contributions is the aggregate of the contributions made by the spouses.

The limitation that applies generally depends on the type of property contributed and the type of charity (public or private) to which the contribution is made. Individuals are limited to a deduction of 50 percent of adjusted gross income for charitable contributions of cash and "ordinary income property" made to public charities (such as churches, Goodwill, etc.—see ¶8301). Contributions of appreciated capital gain property to public charities and contributions of cash and "ordinary income property" to private charities are limited to 30 percent of adjusted gross income. An individual may only deduct charitable contributions made to certain private charities to the extent the contributions do not exceed 20 percent of adjusted gross income. In addition, the total charitable contribution deduction is limited to 50 percent of adjusted gross income. For purposes of the charitable contribution deduction limitations, adjusted gross income is computed before any deduction for net operating loss carrybacks.

Ordinary Income Property

"Ordinary income property" means property that if sold at the time of contribution would trigger income other than long-term capital gains. For example, ordinary income property includes property held by the donor as inventory, depreciation recapture property, a work of art created by the donor, a manuscript prepared by the donor, letters and memorandums prepared by or for the donor, and capital assets held one year or less by the donor (short term capital gain property).

When ordinary income property is contributed, the amount of the deduction must be reduced by the amount that would have been recognized as ordinary income if the property had been sold by the donor at its fair market value at the time of the contribution. Essentially, the deduction for ordinary income property is limited to the basis of the property.

EXAMPLE 8.22   Donna Fairfield contributes equipment held as inventory to the Salvation Army. The equipment has a basis of $10,000 and a fair market value of $12,000. Her charitable deduction is limited to $10,000 ($12,000 fair market value – $2,000 ordinary income).

Capital Gain Property

Capital gain property is appreciated property where the sale would result in a long-term capital gain if the property were sold at fair market value at the time of the contribution. Section 1231 property (which is discussed in Chapter 12) is considered capital gain property for charitable contributions purposes. If the contributed property would have produced both ordinary income and long-term capital gain if sold, the fair market value (as used for computing the deduction) must be reduced by the amount which would have been ordinary income, typically the potential depreciation recapture on the property.

EXAMPLE 8.23   Brent Bates contributed an asset to a qualified charity. The asset has a fair market value of $1,000 and a basis to him of $400. If the sale would result in a $600 gain of which $250 would be classified as ordinary income and $350 as long-term capital gain, the asset is considered to be capital gain property. However, the charitable contribution deduction is limited to $750 ($1,000 FMV – $250 ordinary income element).

The charitable contribution deduction for capital gain property that is either (1) contributed to a private charity or (2) tangible personal property which has an "unrelated use" to the organization receiving it must be reduced by the property's unrecognized long-term capital gain. This reduced contribution amount is the basis of the property.

"Unrelated use" means a use which is unrelated to the purpose or function of the charitable organization. For example, if a painting contributed to an educational institution is used by the organization for educational purposes by being placed in its library for display and study by art students, its use is "related" to the educational purpose of the institution. However, if the painting is sold and the proceeds are used by the organization for educational purposes, the use of the property is unrelated.

¶8325

EXAMPLE 8.24	Lois Lacey contributes an antique lamp to a qualified charity. The lamp has a fair market value of $5,000 and a basis to her of $3,000. The charity intends to sell the lamp and use the proceeds for charitable purposes. Lois's charitable deduction is limited to $3,000.

Contributions of "qualified appreciated stock" to private charities are deductible at the full fair market value of the stock. "Qualified appreciated stock" is any stock of a corporation (1) for which market quotations are readily available on an established securities market, and (2) which is a long-term capital asset.

PLANNING POINTER	If the property to be contributed has not appreciated over the taxpayer's basis, the contribution is valued at fair market value. It is not wise to contribute property that would otherwise create a deductible loss if sold. The taxpayer should sell the property and donate the proceeds to the charitable organization.

Charitable Contribution Percentage Limits

As indicated previously, charitable contributions are subject to several limitations that are based on adjusted gross income. There are 50 percent, 30 percent, and 20 percent category limits that are determined by the type of property contributed and the type of charity receiving the donated property. In addition, there is an overall limit on total charitable contributions that is 50 percent of adjusted gross income.

A carryover of any unused charitable contributions is allowed for up to five years, even if the taxpayer does not itemize for the current year. Current charitable contributions are considered first and then carryforwards are considered on a first-in, first-out basis. Any carryovers will be subject to the same percentage limitations as when they were first originated.

50 Percent Limitation Category

The deduction for contributions of cash and ordinary income property made to public charities may not exceed 50 percent of an individual's adjusted gross income for the year. The deduction for the 50 percent category is the smaller of (1) the 50 percent category contribution amount or (2) 50 percent of adjusted gross income.

EXAMPLE 8.25	Beatrice Bold donates $10,000 to State University, a public charity. Her adjusted gross income for the year is $17,000. She would be limited to a charitable deduction of $8,500 ($17,000 × 50%). She would have a five-year carryover of $1,500, which would be subject to the 50% of AGI limitation in all future years.

30 Percent Limitation Category

The 30 percent limit category is comprised of two distinct 30 percent limits that must be kept separate. The 30 percent public category consists of contributions of capital gain property or appreciated Section 1231 (depreciable) property made to any public charitable organization. The 30 percent private category consists of contributions of cash or ordinary income property to private charities.

An individual may elect to reduce 30 percent capital gain property (contributed to a public charity) by the long-term capital gain and have the reduced contribution qualify for the 50 percent limitation category. This "reduced contribution election" applies to all contributions of 30 percent capital gain property made during the year or carried over to such year. The "reduced contribution election" is normally only tax advantageous to the taxpayer if the contributed property has appreciated only a small amount.

Neither capital assets reduced because of the "reduced contribution election" nor capital assets reduced because of "unrelated use" are considered 30 percent capital gain property, but instead are placed in the 50 percent limitation category.

EXAMPLE 8.26

Teri Rogers contributes $5,000 of common stock to the local homeless shelter, which is a public charitable organization. The stock has a basis to her of $4,800. Teri could now elect to reduce the 30 percent capital gain property by the $200 long-term capital gain on the property and classify the contribution as 50 percent limitation category property. If Teri has AGI of $10,000, a "reduced contribution election" would allow her to deduct a $4,800 charitable contribution deduction (with zero carryover) instead of a $3,000 charitable contribution deduction (with $2,000 carryover) with no election. If the basis of the stock to her was $3,400, a "reduced contribution election" would result in a deduction of $3,400 (with zero carryover) instead of a $3,000 deduction (with $2,000 carryover) with no election. Clearly, the tax advantage of the "reduced contribution election" is greater if the property has appreciated only a small amount.

20 Percent Limitation Category

An individual may deduct charitable contributions made during the year to any qualified charitable organization not considered to be a public charity (generally any "private charity"). Such contributions are limited to 20 percent of adjusted gross income. The 20 percent limitation generally applies to private charities and to certain other organizations, such as war veterans' organizations, domestic fraternal societies, and nonprofit cemeteries.

The deduction for capital gain property donated to a private charity must be reduced by the long-term capital gain inherent in the property. Donations of "qualified appreciated stock," however, are deductible at full fair market value.

EXAMPLE 8.27

Brandon Fryar has adjusted gross income for the year of $100,000. On February 1, 2015, he donates stock to a private charity. The stock has a fair market value of $25,000 and a basis to him of $10,000. He must reduce the fair market value by the long-term capital gain, leaving a charitable contribution deduction of $10,000. If the stock were qualified appreciated stock, his deduction in the current year would be $20,000. He would be allowed a deduction equal to the full fair market value but would only be able to deduct up to 20 percent of adjusted gross income this year. The other $5,000 would be carried over to the five subsequent years (subject to the 20% limitation in each year).

50 Percent Overall Limitation

There is an overall limitation placed on total deductions for all charitable contributions equal to 50 percent of adjusted gross income. This limitation is applied after the other limitations are computed. In applying the overall limitation, the 50 percent deduction, 30 percent public deduction, 30 percent private deduction, and 20 percent deduction must be taken, in that order.

Since the overall 50 percent limitation amount is the same as the specific 50 percent limitation amount, if the 50 percent contributions exceed the 50 percent limitation there will be no further deductions allowed from the other categories.

The 30 percent public deduction limit is determined by taking the smaller of (1) 30 percent of AGI or (2) 50 percent of AGI minus the 50 percent contributions.

The 30 percent private deduction limit is determined by taking the smaller of (1) 30 percent of AGI or (2) 50 percent of AGI minus all 50 percent contributions and minus the 30 percent public contributions. The 50 percent and 30 percent public *contribution* amounts are used in computing the limitations rather than the related *deduction* amounts.

The 20 percent deduction limit is determined by taking the smaller of (1) 20 percent of AGI or (2) 50 percent of AGI minus the 50 percent contributions, the 30 percent public contributions, and the 30 percent private contributions. (Further limitations on 20 percent contributions exist but are beyond the scope of this book. They can be found in Publication 526.)

EXAMPLE 8.28 | Darin Drum has adjusted gross income for the year of $100,000. On March 1, 2015, he makes two charitable contributions. He makes 30 percent public charity contributions in the amount of $42,000. He also contributes $23,000 in qualified appreciated stock to a private charity. His charitable contribution deduction for the year is limited to $38,000, computed as follows. His $42,000 30 percent public charity contribution is limited to $30,000 ($100,000 × 30%). His $23,000 contribution of qualified appreciated stock to a private charity is first limited to $20,000 ($100,000 × 20%) and further limited to $8,000 ($50,000 maximum charitable deduction under the 50 percent overall limitation minus the $42,000 30 percent contribution amount). His total deduction will therefore be $30,000 + $8,000 = $38,000. Next year Darin will have a $12,000 ($42,000 - $30,000) carryover subject to the 30 percent public limit and a $15,000 ($23,000 - $8,000) carryover subject to the 20 percent limit.

Steps In Determining Individual Charitable Contributions

Step 1. Determine the contribution amounts. The contribution amount is the fair market value reduced by any ordinary income and by the long-term capital gain deduction required because of unrelated use, reduced contribution election, or contribution to a private charity.

Step 2. Place all contributions into 50 percent, 30 percent public, 30 percent private, and 20 percent limitation categories.

Property Given	Contribution Amount	Limitation Category
Cash		
Public Charity	Cash	50%
Private Charity	Cash	30% Private
Ordinary Income Property		
Public Charity	Basis	50%
Private Charity	Basis	30% Private
Capital Gain Property		
Public Charity	FMV-OI	30% Public
Public Reduced Contribution Election	Basis	50%
Private Charity	Basis	20%
Appreciated Tangible Personal Property with Unrelated Use		
Public Charity	Basis	50%
Private Charity	Basis	20%
Qualified Appreciated Stock		
Public Charity	FMV	30% Public
Private Charity	FMV	20%

Step 3. Determine each percent limit amount based on the 50 percent, 30 percent public, 30 percent private, and 20 percent limits.

Step 4. Determine each percent deduction limit. Any difference between the contribution amount and the deduction allowed in each category is carried over for five years.

Step 5. Add the respective percent deduction amounts, as limited, to arrive at the total charitable contribution deduction for the year.

EXAMPLE 8.29   Grace Goodheart has $100,000 of adjusted gross income and made charitable contributions as follows: $13,000 cash to the Red Cross, $24,000 (fair market value) in stock to the Boy Scouts, $9,000 in cash to a private charity, and $23,000 in qualified appreciated stock to a private charity. The charitable contribution deduction is computed as follows:

Limitation Category	Contribution Amounts	AGI Limit Amounts	Remaining Overall Limit (50%)	Deductible Amounts	Carryover
50%	$13,000	$50,000	$50,000	$13,000	$0
30% Public	24,000	30,000	37,000	24,000	0
30% Private	9,000	30,000	13,000	9,000	0
20%	23,000	20,000	4,000	4,000	19,000
Total Charitable Deduction				$50,000	

There are no reductions to arrive at the contribution amounts above. The AGI limit amounts are AGI times the percent (50%, 30%, or 20%) that relates to the limitation category.

The deductible amounts are determined as follows:

1. The 50 percent deduction is the smaller of the $13,000 contribution or $50,000 ($100,000 × 50 percent).
2. The 30 percent public deduction is $24,000, the smaller of (1) the $24,000 contribution amount, (2) $30,000 ($100,000 AGI × 30 percent) or (3) $37,000 [$50,000 minus $13,000 (50% contributions)].
3. The 30 percent private deduction is $9,000 because it is the lesser of (1) the $9,000 contribution, (2) $30,000 (30% of $100,000 AGI) or (3) the $50,000 limit minus the 50 percent and 30 percent public contributions ($50,000 - $13,000 - $24,000 = $13,000).
4. The 20 percent limit deduction is $4,000, the lesser of (1) the $23,000 contribution amount, (2) $20,000 ($100,000 AGI × 20 percent), or (3) $4,000, the $50,000 (50% overall) limit minus the $13,000 50 percent contribution amount, the $24,000 30 percent public contribution amount, and the $9,000 30 percent private contribution amount.

After reducing the overall 50% limit for prior 50% and 30% contributions, there is only $4,000 of 50% limit left in which to deduct the 20% contributions.

¶8355   FILING AND SUBSTANTIATION REQUIREMENTS

The deduction for contributions is an itemized deduction and is therefore made on Schedule A of Form 1040. Cash contributions of less than $250 must be substantiated by a bank record (cancelled check, bank statement, credit card statement) or a written acknowledgment from the donee organization. Any charitable contribution of $250 or more must be substantiated by a contemporaneous written acknowledgment of the contribution from the donee organization. The written acknowledgment should include the amount of cash contributed and/or a description of the property contributed. The written acknowledgment must state whether the donee provides any goods or services in consideration for the contribution.

If the contribution is made in property other than money and is over $500, the taxpayer is required to state the kind of property contributed, the method used in determining the fair market value of the property at the time the contribution was made, and whether or not the amount of the contribution was reduced.

For contributed property for which the claimed value of one item or group of similar items exceeds $5,000, the taxpayer claiming the deduction must attach an appraisal of the donated property's fair market value to the income tax return. The appraisal must be obtained from a qualified appraiser. If the donee sells the property within two years (three years for related-use tangible personal property), the donee must furnish the IRS and the donor with a statement regarding the sale.

In regard to donations of automobiles to charities, if the claimed value of the donated motor vehicle, boat or plane exceeds $500 and the item is sold by the charity, the taxpayer is limited to a charitable donation equal to the gross proceeds from the sale.

Personal Casualty and Theft Losses

¶8501

CASUALTY LOSSES

This section discusses personal casualty and theft losses. Business casualty losses are discussed in Chapter 7. Personal casualty and theft losses are deductible as itemized deductions while business casualty and theft losses are deductible from gross income.

Criteria for Deduction

Any uninsured loss arising from fire, storm, shipwreck, or other casualty is allowable as a deduction in the year in which the loss is sustained. Code Sec. 165(c)(3). The IRS position is that the loss must be the result of sudden, unexpected, identifiable, and provable events of an unusual nature, such as an accident, mishap, or sudden invasion by a hostile agency, the cause of which was unknown, or was an unusual effect of a known cause, which occurred by chance and unexpectedly.

Loss through progressive deterioration of property through a steadily operating cause or a normal process is not deductible. The following have been found not to qualify as casualty losses: destruction of trees by disease or insects (*J.A. Appleman,* 64-2 USTC ¶9860, 338 F.2d 729 (CA-7 1964); *H.F. Burns,* 59-2 USTC ¶9514, 174 F.Supp. 203 (DC Ohio 1959), aff'd per curiam, 61-1 USTC ¶9127, 284 F.2d 436 (CA-6 1960); Rev. Rul. 57-599, 1957-2 CB 42); death of livestock; dry rot damage; gradual damage to pilings by storms, tides, and worms; various automobile breakdowns; accumulated water damage to basement walls; freeze and thaw road damage (*H. Stacy,* 29 TCM 542, Dec. 30,132(M), T.C. Memo. 1970-127); and damage from termites (*J.A. Austra,* 25 TCM 178, Dec. 27,837(M), T.C. Memo. 1966-28).

Determination of Amount of Loss

To determine the amount of deductible loss, the fair market value of the property immediately before and immediately after the casualty generally must be ascertained by competent appraisal. This appraisal must recognize the effects of any general market decline affecting undamaged as well as damaged property, which may have occurred simultaneously with the casualty, so that any deduction will be limited to the actual loss resulting from damage to the property.

Cleanup expenses are deductible as a part of the casualty loss. Costs of photographs and appraisal fees are not deductible as part of the casualty loss, but are deductible as an itemized expense in the determination of correct tax liability. Costs incurred to protect damaged property from future losses are not deductible as part of the casualty loss. Personal living expenses, such as temporary housing, rentals, medical care, lights, fuel, food and drink, or moving expenses are also not deductible as casualty losses.

The cost of repairs of the property damaged is acceptable as evidence of the loss of value. The taxpayer must show that (1) the repairs were necessary to restore the property to its condition immediately before the casualty, (2) the amount spent for such repairs was not excessive, (3) the repairs don't repair more than the damage suffered, and (4) the value of the property after the repairs doesn't, as a result of the repairs, exceed the value of the property immediately before the casualty.

A casualty loss occurs when an automobile owned by the taxpayer is damaged due to the faulty driving of the taxpayer or other person operating the automobile. However, an automobile accident will not qualify as a casualty loss if it is due to the willful act or willful negligence of the taxpayer or of one acting on the taxpayer's behalf. Damage resulting from the faulty driving of the operator of the vehicle with which the taxpayer collides is also eligible for the casualty deduction.

The amount of loss to be taken into account is the lesser of either (1) the excess of the fair market value of the property immediately before the casualty minus the fair market value of the property immediately after the casualty, or (2) the amount of the adjusted basis of the property.

Limitations on Losses

Each personal casualty loss must be reduced by $100. The $100 reduction is applied per event, not per item damaged in an event. Where the recognized casualty losses exceed the recognized casualty gains, the annual casualty deduction is limited to the net casualty loss in excess of 10 percent of adjusted gross income. If the recognized casualty losses exceed the recognized casualty gains after reductions, all gains and losses are ordinary. Where the recognized gains exceed the recognized losses, each gain or loss is treated as a capital gain or loss. The $100 and 10 percent of adjusted gross income reductions apply separately to each individual taxpayer who sustains a loss, even though the property damaged or destroyed is owned by two or more individuals. However, a husband and wife filing a joint return are treated as one individual taxpayer. Business casualty losses are not subject to either the $100 or the 10 percent of AGI reductions.

EXAMPLE 8.30	Roberta Reynolds has $60,000 of adjusted gross income, a casualty loss of $8,500, and a casualty gain of $12,000. The casualty loss of $8,500 is reduced by $100 to $8,400 and netted against the $12,000 gain. The 10 percent of AGI reduction does not apply since a gain results from the netting. The $12,000 casualty gain is treated as a capital gain and the $8,400 casualty loss is treated as capital loss.

EXAMPLE 8.31	Ken Garrett has $40,000 of adjusted gross income, a $9,000 casualty loss after the $100 reduction, and a $3,000 casualty gain. The casualty loss deduction is limited to $2,000. The casualty loss must be reduced by the casualty gain and then reduced by 10 percent of adjusted gross income ($9,000 – $3,000 – $4,000).

If a loss is sustained in respect of property used partially for business and partially for nonbusiness purposes, the 10 percent and $100 reductions apply only to that portion of the loss properly attributable to the nonbusiness use.

Casualty losses are deductible in the year incurred. However, no portion of the casualty loss can be taken until it can be determined with reasonable certainty whether or not a reimbursement for the loss will be received. If a portion of the loss is not covered by a claim for reimbursement, then that portion of the loss is deductible in the year in which the casualty occurs.

EXAMPLE 8.32	Robert Rayer's personal use property having a basis of $20,000 and a fair market value of $23,000 is completely destroyed by fire in 2015. Robert has an insurance claim for $8,000, which is settled in 2016. He had adjusted gross income of $17,000 in 2015. Robert's 2015 loss equals $10,200 ($20,000 – $8,000 – $100 – $1,700 (10 percent of adjusted gross income)). The loss is deductible in 2015, the year incurred, because the loss can be ascertained with reasonable accuracy.

A taxpayer is not permitted to deduct a casualty loss for damage to insured property unless a timely insurance claim is filed. This rule applies to the extent that any insurance policy provides for full or partial reimbursement of the loss. The portion of the loss not covered by insurance (for example, a deductible) is not subject to this rule.

EXAMPLE 8.33	Tom Tower's automobile was damaged when Tom struck a tree during a snow storm. The damage amounted to $2,300. Rather than notify his automobile insurer because of fear of an increase in the cost of his insurance or cancellation of his policy, Tom paid for the repair costs. Except for the amount of his insurance deductible, Tom may not deduct any casualty loss because he failed to file an insurance claim.

Losses from Federally Declared Disasters

In order to accelerate tax refunds to taxpayers that have sustained a disaster loss, a taxpayer who has sustained a disaster loss may elect to deduct the loss for the tax year immediately preceding the year in which the loss actually occurred. This special provision applies only to disasters occurring in an area determined by the President of the United States to warrant assistance by the federal government. In addition, in federally declared disaster areas, taxpayers will never have to recognize gain on the receipt of insurance proceeds for personal property contained in personal residences.

If an election is made, the disaster is deemed to have occurred in the tax year immediately preceding the year in which the disaster actually occurred, and the loss deemed to have been sustained in the preceding tax year. An election to claim the disaster deduction must be made by filing a return, an amended return, or a claim for refund clearly showing that the election has been made.

¶8525   THEFT LOSSES

Any loss arising from theft is generally deductible in the year the taxpayer discovers the loss. However, if there is a reasonable prospect of reimbursement of the loss, no portion of the loss is deductible until the year in which it can be ascertained with reasonable certainty whether or not a reimbursement for the loss will be received.

The deductible amount of a theft loss is determined in the same manner as a casualty loss. The fair market value of the property immediately after the theft is considered to be zero. Theft losses of nonbusiness personal property are limited by the same $100 and 10 percent of adjusted gross income reductions that apply to casualty losses.

Miscellaneous Itemized Deductions

Miscellaneous itemized deductions include the following items: employee business expenses, job-seeking expenses, education expenses, investment expenses, wagering losses, and tax counsel and return preparer fees. Most miscellaneous itemized deductions, with some exceptions, are grouped together on a tax return and are deductible to the extent that the total of all of the miscellaneous items exceeds 2 percent of the taxpayer's adjusted gross income. All of these miscellaneous itemized deductions are discussed in more detail in the following sections.

¶8601   EMPLOYEE BUSINESS EXPENSES

The tax treatment of employee business expenses depends on whether the expenses are categorized as reimbursed expenses or nonreimbursed expenses. Business expenses incurred by an employee under a reimbursement arrangement with an employer are normally not shown on the tax return. Unreimbursed business expenses are deductible as miscellaneous itemized deductions, limited to amounts in excess of 2 percent of the taxpayer's adjusted gross income.

¶8603   REIMBURSED EMPLOYEE EXPENSES

The tax treatment of reimbursed expenses of employees depends on whether or not the employee makes an adequate accounting to the employer for the expenses. An adequate accounting by an employee to an employer would normally include filing an expense report listing time, place, and nature of an expense along with any supporting documentary evidence. Reg. §1.162-17(b)(4). Also, the reimbursement arrangement must not allow the employee to keep any excess reimbursement.

If an employee makes an adequate accounting to the employer and reimbursement equals expenses, neither the reimbursement nor the expenses have to be shown on the employee's tax return. If an employee makes an adequate accounting to the employer and expenses exceed reimbursement and the employee desires to deduct the excess expenses, all employee expenses and all reimbursement must be listed on the employee's tax return, with the excess unreimbursed expenses being deductible as miscellaneous itemized deductions subject to the 2 percent nondeductible floor.

EXAMPLE 8.34

Mary Turner incurs the following employee expenses which she submits to her employer for reimbursement under an adequate accounting reimbursement plan.

Travel expenses	$1,100
Transportation expenses	300
Entertainment expenses	600
Total expenses	$2,000

If Mary receives $2,000 in reimbursement from her employer, neither the expenses nor the reimbursement would have to be shown on her return. If Mary receives $1,400 in reimbursement from her employer, she would have to show the $2,000 of expenses and the $1,400 of reimbursement on her return in order to claim the $600 of excess employee expenses as an itemized deduction. The $600 deduction would be allocated proportionately to each type of expense incurred ($600/$2,000 = 30%). The allocation would be $330 to travel, $90 to transportation, and $180 to entertainment expenses. The $180 deduction for entertainment expenses would be subject to a 50 percent limitation, which would then put the entertainment deduction at $90. The total of the $330 travel, the $90 transportation and the $90 entertainment deductions would be subject to the 2 percent of AGI floor on miscellaneous itemized deductions.

¶8603

If an employee does not make an adequate accounting to an employer, all employee expenses and any reimbursement would have to be listed on the employee's return. Reg. §1.162-17(b). Employee business expenses paid or incurred under "nonaccountable plans" are deductible by an employee only as miscellaneous itemized deductions subject to the 2 percent of AGI floor. "Nonaccountable plans" are arrangements that: (1) do not require the employee to substantiate the reimbursed expenses to the employer, or (2) permit the employee to retain amounts in excess of the substantiated expenses covered under the arrangement. Code Sec. 62(c); Temp. Reg. §1.62-1T(f).

¶8605   UNREIMBURSED EMPLOYEE EXPENSES

Unreimbursed employee expenses are allowed only as miscellaneous itemized deductions, and are only deductible to the extent they exceed 2 percent of adjusted gross income. Major categories of employee expenses, which, if unreimbursed, must be taken as itemized deductions subject to the 2 percent of AGI floor, include the following: transportation expenses, travel expenses, entertainment expenses, job-seeking expenses, and qualifying educational expenses.

Other allowable employee expenses (subject to the 2 percent of AGI limitation if the expenses are unreimbursed) include professional society dues, employment agency fees, cost of small tools and supplies needed on the job, subscriptions to professional journals, union dues, and work clothes and uniforms not suitable for everyday use. Transportation, travel, and entertainment expenses are discussed in Chapter 6. Job-seeking expenses, education expenses, and other miscellaneous itemized deductions are discussed in greater detail in the following sections of this chapter.

KEYSTONE PROBLEM

Ralph Unit incurs the following qualified employee (business) expenses:

Travel expenses (excluding meals)	$4,000
Meals	1,600
Transportation expenses	2,000
Entertainment expenses	2,400
Total expenses	$10,000

What amounts of the above employee (business) expenses are deductible for AGI on Ralph's tax return and what amounts are deductible from AGI as itemized deductions based on each of the following assumptions? (Treat each assumption independently from the other assumptions.)

Assumption 1: Ralph is self-employed.

Assumption 2: Ralph is a business executive and receives reimbursement of $8,000 from his employer for these expenses under an adequate accounting reimbursement plan.

¶8655   JOB-SEEKING EXPENSES

Job-seeking expenses incurred by an individual are deductible for tax purposes if the individual is employed in a particular trade or business and is looking for work in the same trade or business (e.g., a teacher looking for work as a teacher, an accountant looking for work as an accountant, etc.) Rev. Rul. 75-120, 1975-1 CB 55, clarified by Rev. Rul. 77-16, 1977-1 CB 37. Job-seeking expenses include travel and transportation expenses incurred while going to and from different job locations, expenses of preparing a resume, mailing expenses, and employment agency fees. If deductible, job-seeking expenses are deductible from AGI as miscellaneous itemized deductions subject to the 2 percent of AGI floor.

Job-seeking expenses are deductible by an individual looking for work in the same trade or business regardless of whether or not the individual is successful in finding a job. Job-seeking expenses are not deductible if the individual is looking for work in a new trade or business or if the expenses relate to the individual's first job. If an individual is unemployed when incurring the job seeking expenses, the expenses are deductible if the individual is looking for work in the same trade or business in which the individual was employed prior to unemployment.

EXAMPLE 8.35

> Larry Kemp, a high school business teacher in Michigan, is looking for a high school teaching position in another state. He incurs travel expenses, employment agency fees, and some other miscellaneous expenses in his search for a new position. Larry eventually finds a teaching position in Iowa. Larry's job-seeking expenses are deductible since he was looking for work in the same trade or business. Even if Larry had been unsuccessful in finding a new job, the expenses would have been deductible since he was looking for work in the same trade or business.
>
> If, instead, Larry was planning to leave the teaching profession and was looking for work as a public accountant, none of his job-seeking expenses would have been deductible since he was looking for work in a new trade or business. This is true regardless of whether Larry was successful or unsuccessful in finding a job as a public accountant.

If an individual combines job-seeking trips in the same trade or business with other personal activities, such as vacationing, the travel and transportation costs incurred on the trip are deductible only if the primary purpose of the trip was to seek new employment. Rev. Rul. 75-120, 1975-1 CB 55. If the purpose of the trip was primarily personal in nature, only the actual expenses incurred at the destination in seeking new employment are deductible for tax purposes.

¶8665   EDUCATION EXPENSES

Education expenses incurred by an individual taxpayer for continuing professional education and vocational education courses, professional development courses, and, in some instances, college degree programs are deductible for tax purposes if certain requirements are met. Education expenses are deductible by an individual taxpayer if incurred (1) to maintain or improve skills required in a present job or (2) to meet expressed requirements of an employer or applicable law to retain an employment position or rate of compensation. Reg. §1.162-5(a). However, even though either of these two requirements are met, education expenses are not deductible if they are personal expenditures. The two categories of nondeductible education expenses are those that (1) are required of the individual in order to meet the *minimum education* requirements for qualification in present employment, trade, or business or (2) qualify the individual for a *new trade or business.*

For tax years through 2014, taxpayers can claim an "above the line" deduction (a deduction for AGI for qualified education expenses. Code Sec. 222. The maximum deduction is $4,000. Single taxpayers with adjusted gross income below $65,000 ($130,000 for married filing jointly) can claim the deduction. Taxpayers whose adjusted gross income falls between $65,000 and $80,000 ($130,000 and $160,000 for joint filers) may deduct $2,000. Married individuals filing a separate return are not eligible for this deduction. The tuition deduction cannot be taken in the same year as an American Opportunity Tax Credit or Lifetime Learning Credit for the same student. See ¶9031.

Maintaining or Improving Skills

Education expenses incurred by an individual taxpayer to maintain or improve skills required in a present job such as a business executive taking a continuing education course in management techniques normally are deductible for tax purposes by the taxpayer. If education expenses incurred by an individual to maintain or improve existing skills also qualify the individual for a new trade or business, the education expenses are not deductible for tax purposes.

EXAMPLE 8.36

> Joan Mackey, a business executive, takes a three-day continuing professional education management course entitled "Advanced Management Techniques" which is relevant to her current management position. The $2,400 cost of the course is paid by Joan from her personal funds and is not reimbursed by her employer. The $2,400 payment is deductible on Joan's tax return as an education expense deduction. Joan is also attending law school at the present time and plans to get a law degree since knowledge of legal affairs will be of considerable help to her in her present management position. Joan is paying the cost of law school from her personal funds. The costs associated with attending law school are not deductible by Joan as education expenses since a law degree will qualify her for a new trade or business. It does not matter that knowledge of legal affairs will help Joan in her present management position.

Employer Requirements or Minimum Standards

Education expenses incurred by an individual taxpayer to meet expressed requirements of an employer or applicable law to retain an employment position or rate of compensation normally are deductible for tax purposes. If the education expenses are incurred, however, to meet minimum education standards for qualification in the individual taxpayer's existing trade or business, the expenses are not deductible.

EXAMPLE 8.37

The Trotwood School System normally requires that all school teachers have, as a minimum, a bachelor's degree in education before they can teach in the school system. An exception to this rule is made for Jane Prim, who is hired in her senior year of college. Education expenses incurred by Jane to finish her senior year of college are not deductible on her individual income tax return since they are incurred to meet minimum education standards for qualification in Jane's trade or business which is teaching.

One year after Jane receives her bachelor's degree in education, the Trotwood school board adopts a requirement that all teachers in the school system must have a master's degree in education within six years in order to continue to teach in the system. If Jane decides to pursue her master's degree in education, the education expenses related to the degree are deductible on Jane's individual income tax return since Jane would incur the expenses in attempting to meet expressed requirements of her employer to retain her employment position.

New Trade or Business

Normally, education expenses incurred by an individual taxpayer to obtain a bachelor's degree are not deductible since the degree either is needed to meet minimum education requirements for the job the college graduate takes after graduation or qualifies the graduate for a new trade or business. Education expenses incurred by an individual relating to a master's degree may or may not be deductible depending on whether the degree qualifies the recipient for a new trade or business. For such expenses to be deductible, the individual usually has to establish a connection between the courses taken and the taxpayer's present business position. If the master's degree qualifies the individual for a new trade or business, education expenses incurred while working on the degree are not deductible even if there is a connection between the courses taken and the person's present position. Education expenses incurred when working on professional degrees such as the M.D. degree and J.D. degree normally are not deductible by an individual since, in each instance, the degree qualifies the individual for a new trade or business.

A review of all surrounding facts should be made in deciding whether certain education expenditures have qualified an individual for a new trade or business. A change in duties such as an elementary school teacher taking courses to become a high school teacher is not considered to be a new trade or business. Reg. §1.162-5(b)(3). Education expenses related to bar exam review courses and CPA review courses have been considered to be nondeductible since they prepare an individual for a new trade or business. Rev. Rul. 69-292, 1969-1 CB 84.

Classification of Education Expenses

Deductible education expenses include tuition, books, other miscellaneous education expenses, and any related travel and transportation costs. Transportation costs include the costs of going from a work location to school for a night school student. If an individual taxpayer is self-employed, all deductible education expenses are deductible for AGI. If the taxpayer is an employee, all deductible education expenses (except for qualified higher education expenses) are deductible from AGI as miscellaneous itemized deductions, subject to the 2 percent floor. Reg. §1.162-6.

¶8675   WORK CLOTHES AND UNIFORMS

Taxpayers generally may not deduct the cost and upkeep of work clothing. Taxpayers may deduct the cost and upkeep of special equipment or work clothes only if they are required as a condition of employment and are not suitable for everyday use. Both conditions must be met to qualify such expenses as miscellaneous itemized deductions, subject to the 2 percent of AGI limitation.

The cost of uniforms that must be worn by ballplayers, fire fighters, police officers, letter carriers, nurses, jockeys, and civilian faculty members of a military school is deductible. Generally, the cost of uniforms of full-time active duty personnel in the armed forces is not deductible.

¶8680   **TAX COUNSEL AND RETURN PREPARER FEES**

Expenses paid or incurred by an individual in connection with the determination, collection, or refund of any tax are deductible. The deduction is allowed whether the taxing authority is federal, state, or municipal, and whether the tax is income, estate, gift, property, or any other tax. Thus, expenses paid or incurred by a taxpayer for tax counsel or expenses paid or incurred in connection with the preparation of returns or in connection with any proceedings involved in determining the extent of the tax liability or in contesting a tax liability are deductible as miscellaneous itemized deductions, subject to the 2 percent floor.

Investment Expenses

Deductions for investment expenses are allowed if the expenses are incurred for the production or collection of income or for the management, conservation, or maintenance of property held for the production of income. To be deductible, investment expenses must be ordinary and necessary, must be reasonable in amount, cannot be capital expenditures, cannot relate to the generation of tax-exempt income, and cannot frustrate public policy.

Most investment expenses are categorized as miscellaneous itemized deductions and are deductible by individuals only if the aggregate amount of miscellaneous itemized deductions exceeds 2 percent of the taxpayer's adjusted gross income. Code Sec. 67(a). One exception is deductions attributable to property held for the production of rents or royalties, which are deductible for adjusted gross income. Code Sec. 62(a)(4).

In this section the following investment expense deductions are reviewed: rent and royalty expenses and miscellaneous investment expenses.

¶8701   **RENT AND ROYALTY EXPENSES**

Rents and royalties are closely related for tax purposes. Rents generally involve payments for the use of land, buildings, and other tangible property whereas royalties usually involve payments for copyrights, patents, and oil, gas, or mineral property. Rental income and expenses are normally treated as related to investment property if only minimal services are provided to the tenants. "Minimal service" usually means that service is limited, for instance, to providing heat, light, and trash pickup. If additional services (such as maid services) are provided to tenants, rental income and expenses may have to be considered as business income and expenses. If royalty income and expenses are derived from royalty property where the taxpayer has an operating interest or if the taxpayer is self-employed and created the royalty property, such as a writer with a copyright on a book, royalty income and expenses are trade or business income and expenses instead of investment income and expenses.

All rent and royalty expenses are deductible for AGI. Code Sec. 62(a)(4). Normal rent and royalty expenses include depreciation, depletion, repairs and maintenance expenditures, insurance, interest, taxes, and other items. If one piece of property is part rental property and part personal property, expenses must be allocated between the investment portion of the property and the personal portion with only the investment portion of the expenses being deductible for tax purposes.

¶8745   **MISCELLANEOUS INVESTMENT EXPENSES**

Typical investment expenses which are deductible under Code Sec. 212 were mentioned previously in Chapter 6. These included safe deposit box rentals, rent and royalty expenses, investment counseling fees, subscriptions to investment-related journals, newspapers, and other publications, investment custodial fees, legal and accounting fees related to investments, investment interest expense subject to limitations previously discussed, investment-related clerical fees, and investment-related office rents. Expenses of attending conventions, seminars, or similar meetings for investment purposes, however, are not deductible for tax purposes.

Investment-related expenses allowed under Code Sec. 212 are deductible from adjusted gross income as miscellaneous itemized deductions, subject to the 2 percent of AGI limitation. Rent and royalty expenses, however, are an exception and are deductible for adjusted gross income.

Other Miscellaneous Expenses

A small group of miscellaneous expenses is not subject to the 2% of AGI floor. These expenses include gambling losses to the extent of gambling winnings, certain casualty and theft losses related to income-producing property, federal estate tax on income in respect of a decedent, and the unrecovered investment in an annuity at the taxpayer's death.

¶8775　WAGERING LOSSES

Losses sustained during the year on wagering transactions are allowed as an itemized deduction but only to the extent of the gains during the year from wagering. In the case of a husband and wife filing a joint return, the combined wagering losses of the spouses are allowed to the extent of the combined wagering gains. Code Sec. 165(d).

The Supreme Court has ruled that a professional gambler is entitled to deduct gambling losses as a trade or business expense. The fact that the taxpayer did not offer goods or services to others did not preclude characterization of the activities as a trade or business, rather, the appropriate "business" test was that the taxpayer must be involved in the activity with continuity and regularity and the taxpayer's primary purpose for engaging in the activity must be for income or profit. *R.P. Groetzinger,* 87-1 USTC ¶9191 480 U.S. 23, 107 S.Ct. 980 (1987), aff'g 85-2 USTC ¶9622, 771 F.2d 269 (CA-7 1985).

Thus, if gambling is conducted as a business, any wagering losses are deductible as business losses, but only to the extent of wagering gains. However, the deduction of a professional gambler's non-wagering business expenses, such as transportation, meals and lodging, are not limited by wagering gains. *Mayo,* 136 TC — No. 4, Dec. 58,524 (2011); Action on Decision 2011-006. Losses of nonprofessional gamblers are nonbusiness losses and are deductible (to the extent of gains) only if itemized on Schedule A of Form 1040. They are not subject to the 2 percent floor on miscellaneous itemized deductions.

¶8785　UNRECOVERED INVESTMENT IN ANNUITY

A taxpayer who contributes after-tax amounts to the cost of an annuity can exclude from income a part of each annuity payment received as a tax-free return of the cost of the annuity. If the taxpayer dies before the entire cost of the annuity is recovered tax-free, any unrecovered cost of the annuity can be deducted as a miscellaneous deduction on the taxpayer's final tax return, not subject to the 2 percent floor.

SUMMARY

- Personal expenditures are generally disallowed as deductions on the tax return. However, certain personal expenses, as listed in the Internal Revenue Code, are specifically allowed as itemized deductions. These deductions are taken on Schedule A of Form 1040. Itemized deductions are beneficial to a taxpayer only if the total of the itemized deductions exceeds the standard deduction.

- Only medical expenses actually paid during the year are allowed as an itemized deduction. The total of the allowable medical expenses must be reduced by 10 percent of adjusted gross income. Medical expenses must be for the medical care of the taxpayer, spouse, or a dependent of the taxpayer.

- State, local, and foreign property taxes, income taxes, and sales taxes (through 2014) make up the taxes category of itemized deductions. Federal income, estate, gift, and Social Security taxes imposed on the taxpayer are not deductible.

- Certain interest paid or accrued on indebtedness qualifies as a deduction in computing taxable income. Prepaid interest is not deductible when paid but must be allocated to the periods for which it represents the cost of borrowing funds. Interest expense incurred to purchase tax-exempt income-producing assets is not deductible.

- Charitable contributions must be made to qualified organizations in order to qualify for the deduction. Only contributions made during the year are deductible. There are limits imposed on charitable contributions equal to 50 percent, 30 percent, and 20 percent of adjusted gross income, depending on the type of property given and the charity to which it is given.

- Certain personal casualty and theft losses may qualify as itemized deductions. Generally, the loss is equal to the smaller of the reduction in fair market value or the basis of the asset, reduced by (1) insurance proceeds, (2) $100 for each casualty, and (3) 10 percent of adjusted gross income.

- Most miscellaneous itemized deductions are deductible only to the extent they exceed 2 percent of adjusted gross income. However, some miscellaneous itemized deductions (such as wagering losses) are not subject to the 2 percent floor.

QUESTIONS

1. What limits are imposed on the medical expense deduction?

2. When are capital expenditures incurred for medical reasons deductible?

3. When is the cost of transportation deductible as a medical expense?

4. Harry and Mary Holmes had the following health expenses. Which expenses are deductible as medical expenses?
   a. Nonprescription vitamins for Harry
   b. Trip to Florida for general health reasons
   c. Trip to Hawaii for specialized surgery only performed by one doctor located in Hawaii
   d. Crutch rental for period after surgery
   e. Cost of transportation to and from doctor

5. Ron and Judy Rupert have the following health expenses. Which expenses are deductible as medical expenses?
   a. Toothpaste and dental floss for cavity prevention
   b. Acupuncture treatments for Ron
   c. Medical insurance premiums
   d. Contact lenses for Judy
   e. Cosmetic surgery (liposuction operation) for Judy

6. What criteria must be met for personal property taxes to qualify as an itemized deduction?

7. When is a refund of a state or local income tax reported as income?

8. Which of the following taxes are deductible for federal income tax purposes as an itemized deduction?
   a. Ad valorem personal property tax
   b. FICA tax imposed on employees
   c. Federal gift tax
   d. Sales taxes imposed in 2014 on purchase of living room furniture

9. Which of the following taxes are deductible for federal income tax purposes as an itemized deduction?
   a. Federal income tax
   b. Federal gasoline tax
   c. State income tax
   d. Excise tax imposed on cigarettes

10. What items are included in "net investment income" for purposes of the investment interest limitation?

11. What special rules apply to prepaid interest?

12. Briefly describe the two major categories of qualified charitable organizations for tax purposes.

13. Distinguish between private operating foundations and private nonoperating foundations.

14. Dana Davenport donates eight hours of her time on a Saturday to help out a qualified charity. What is her charitable deduction?

15. If an asset is given to a charitable organization and the asset is sold, what is the effect on the charitable contribution deduction?

16. What happens to any unused charitable contributions?

17. When is the taxpayer required to attach an appraisal of a charitable contribution to his or her return?

18. What is the definition of a casualty loss?

19. When is a theft loss deductible?

20. In order for employee expenses to be deductible for tax purposes, what basic requirement(s) must be met?

21. What are nonaccountable employee reimbursement plans?

22. What conditions must be present before an individual taxpayer can deduct job seeking expenses? What types of expenditures are included in job seeking expenses for tax purposes?

23. Under what conditions would education expenses be deductible for tax purposes by an individual taxpayer?

PROBLEMS

24. Oliver Olms pays all of his father's medical expenses for the year, which total $8,800. Oliver also pays over half of his father's support but is unable to claim his father as a dependent because his father has $4,000 in gross income. Will Oliver be able to claim the $8,800 as a medical expense deduction on his individual income tax return?

25. You have a heart ailment. On the advice of your doctor, you install an elevator in your home so you will not have to climb the stairs. It costs $15,000 to install the elevator. The elevator has a 20-year life and increases the fair market value of your home by $3,000. What is the medical deduction for the elevator assuming the 10 percent limitation has been met?

26. Tom and Shannon Shores, both age 40, filed a joint return and paid the following medical expenses:

Hospital costs	$3,200
Doctor's bills	1,600
Medicine and drugs	800
Hospitalization insurance premiums	4,000

In addition, they incurred the following medical expenses for Tom's mother who is totally dependent upon and lives with Tom and Shannon:

Cosmetic surgery (face-lift operation)	$5,400
Doctor's bills	2,600
Medicines and drugs	1,000

They live 10 miles from the medical center and made 20 trips there for doctor office visits and hospital stays this year. Tom and Shannon's adjusted gross income is $85,000. What is Tom and Shannon's medical expense deduction for this year?

27. Assume the same facts as in Problem 26, except that the insurance company reimbursed Tom and Shannon $4,100 of their hospital and doctor's bills. Determine the medical expense deduction.

28. Blake sold a house to Miranda on July 1. Blake paid the entire calendar-year property taxes of $4,380 on June 1. How much will each of them be entitled to deduct for the year?

29. Carlos Diego paid the following expenses during 2015:

State sales tax	$600
Sales tax on purchase of automobile	800
License plate "tax" based on weight of vehicles	35
State income tax paid	6,000
Federal income tax paid	16,000

What is Carlos's tax expense deduction for 2015?

30. During the following years Adolpho T. (single) had (1) withheld, (2) paid (by check – presumably estimated tax payments or paid with the extension) and (3) received a refund of the following amounts for state income tax purposes:

	2015	2016
Withheld	$2,500	$3,000
Paid by check	$1,200	$1,400
Refund	$800	$1,600

The refunds were all of amounts "paid" (withheld and paid by check) in the prior year. Adolpho's total itemized deductions in 2015 were $8,000. What is Adolpho's state income tax deduction for each year, and his income from the refund in 2016?

31. On December 1, Raphael Renoir borrows $20,000 from the bank on a 15 percent, one-year business loan. Raphael prepays the interest of $3,000 at the time of the loan. What is the interest deduction allowed Raphael, assuming he is a cash basis, calendar year taxpayer? What would your answer be if, instead of prepaying the $3,000 interest, it was deducted from the loan proceeds?

32. In 2015, Sally Morris, a single taxpayer, pays $3,000 of interest on qualified student loans. Her AGI is $40,000. What is her qualified student loan interest deduction in 2015?

33. Assume the same facts as in Problem 32, except that Sally has AGI of $70,000. What is her qualified student loan interest deduction in 2015?

34. The interest paid on Josephine Young's personal residence for the year 2015 totals $4,800; the interest paid on her personal credit card is $80; the interest paid on a note to the National Bank (¾ of which was used to buy state and municipal bonds, the rest to buy stock) is $1,000. If she has interest income of $2,000, what is Josephine's total interest deduction for the year?

35. Mike and Sally Card file a joint return for the 2015 tax year. Their adjusted gross income is $65,000 and they incur the following interest expenses:

Qualified education loans	$3,500
Personal loan	1,000
Home mortgage loan	4,000
Loan used to purchase a variety of stocks, bonds, and securities	15,000

Investment income and related expenses amount to $7,000 and $500, respectively. What is Mike and Sally's interest deduction for the 2015 tax year?

36. Greg Grove pays $21,600 interest in 2015 on a home equity loan with an interest rate of 10 percent and an average balance of $216,000 during the year. His equity (fair market value minus acquisition debt) in his house is $150,000. How much of this interest is deductible on Greg's tax return for 2015?

37. Matilda Moore has $21,000 of investment interest expense and $7,000 of net investment income in 2015. How much of the investment interest expense is deductible for tax purposes in 2015?

38. On December 1 Bernie took out a 15-year loan for $300,000. He paid 2% in "points" in order to get the loan, or $6,000. This is essentially prepaid interest. If the loan is used to purchase his principal residence, what is the maximum he can deduct in the current year? If the loan is used to purchase a home he will use as a rental property, what is the maximum he can deduct?

39. Frank Freshman mailed a check for $200 on December 30, 2015, in part payment of a $350 pledge he made to State University on November 1. The University did not deposit the check until January 3, 2016. What is the amount of the charitable contribution deduction allowed Frank for 2015?

40. Mark Moody has adjusted gross income of $50,000 for the year. During the year, he gave his church $3,000 cash and land having a fair market value of $40,000 and a basis of $20,000. The land was held long-term. A contribution of $8,000 in cash was also made to a private charity. How much may be deducted as contributions if Mark does not elect to reduce the fair market value by the appreciation in value of the land donated? How much is the charitable contributions carryover?

41. Elmore Eisner made the following contributions during the current tax year:

Cash to United Way	$5,000
Land to Boy Scouts to be used as a summer camp:	
Cost	20,000
Fair market value	30,000
Painting to a 20 percent charity for permanent display in foundation's public gallery:	
Cost	5,000
Fair market value	7,000
Cash to individual needy families around town	3,000

a. Assuming Elmore's adjusted gross income is $80,000, what is his charitable contribution deduction for the year and carryover?

b. What is the charitable contribution and carryover if the cost and fair market value of the painting are $25,000 and $27,000, respectively?

42. In each of the following independent cases determine the amount of charitable contributions allowed the individual before consideration of any percentage limitations.

a. Charlie Chubbs contributed an item of inventory from his sole proprietorship to a public charity for its use. The fair market value of the asset was $800 and his basis was $600.

b. Durwood Dodson contributed some shares of common stock that he had held long-term to a private charity. The basis of the stock was $8,000 and it had a fair market value of $7,000.

c. Esther Ensign contributed tangible personal property that she had held long-term to a public charity. The asset had a fair market value of $10,000 and a basis of $6,000. The charity intended to sell the asset and use the proceeds for charitable purposes.

43. Ralph Reeves gave some stock that he owned to charity. The stock had a FMV of $40,000 and a basis of $32,000. His adjusted gross income is $100,000. Determine the allowed charitable contribution deduction and carryover under the following assumptions:

a. Given to a public charity, no election

b. Given to a public charity, elects the reduced contribution election

c. Given to private charity

d. Qualified appreciated stock given to private charity

44. Jackson Jumper has owned a beach house at Padre Island for the last 20 years. In 2015, while swimming in the surf at Padre one afternoon, someone stole his billfold (containing $150 cash), his wristwatch (cost $250; FMV $200) and, worst of all, his ice chest full of beer (cost = FMV = $75). As if that were not enough, later that day his beach house was completely destroyed by fire. His adjusted basis in the house was $200,000 but the FMV was $270,000 because of the resort areas developing around his property. The house was insured for only $170,000. What is Jackson's casualty and theft loss for the year assuming a $100,000 adjusted gross income?

45. Billy Pilgrim owned a car which he used two-thirds for business and one-third for personal use. The car had cost $18,000 and he had taken $6,000 depreciation on the business-use portion of the car. He was involved in a wreck for which repairs for the damage to the car amounted to $3,600. He had no insurance. What is Billy's casualty loss for the current tax year assuming a $15,000 adjusted gross income?

46. In 2015, Pablo Pacheco was involved in an auto collision which totally destroyed his new car. He sued the other driver for damages and his lawyer was confident of relief. The FMV of the car immediately before the accident was $24,000. In 2016, the other driver died penniless, but up to that date Pablo has received only $1,000 of the damage award. What is Pablo's casualty loss for each year, assuming his adjusted gross income each year is $50,000?

47. For 2015, Sam Simpson was involved in a collision while driving his automobile. The automobile, which originally cost $16,000 and was used solely for his personal use, had an appraised value of $7,200 for trade-in purposes just before the accident. After the collision, the car was traded in on a new car, but the trade-in value was only $1,300. Assuming that Sam has adjusted gross income of $30,000 and carried no collision insurance, what amount can he deduct as a net casualty loss for the year?

48. In 2015, Peter Carlson incurs the following qualified employee expenses, which he submits to his employer for reimbursement under an adequate accounting reimbursement plan.

Travel expenses	$2,400
Meal and entertainment expenses (100 percent of cost)	1,200
Total expenses	$3,600

How would these employee expenses and reimbursement be treated on Peter's individual tax return if he receives the following reimbursement from his employer?
   a. $3,000
   b. $3,600

49. Kathleen incurs $2,000 of travel expenses looking for a job. Her AGI is $11,000. How would she treat these expenses if she is a graduating student looking for her first job? What if she is an accountant looking for a different accounting position? What if she is in sales, but would like to find a job in information systems?

50. Kearney Kramer donated to his church stock which he had held for five months. The stock had a fair market value of $1,000 at the time of the gift, but had only cost Kearney $700. What is the amount deductible as a charitable contribution?
   a. $1,000
   b. $880
   c. $700
   d. $300
   e. None of the above

51. Which of the following unreimbursed employee expenses is deductible for adjusted gross income?
   a. Transportation expenses
   b. Union dues
   c. Travel expenses
   d. None of the above

52. If an employee does not make an adequate accounting to the employer and employer reimbursement of employee expenses exceeds the expenses, the employee business expenses are:
   a. Not shown on the employee's tax return
   b. Shown as miscellaneous itemized deductions subject to the 2 percent nondeductible floor
   c. Shown as miscellaneous itemized deductions not subject to the 2 percent nondeductible floor
   d. None of the above

53. If an employee makes an adequate accounting to the employer and employer reimbursement of employee expenses is less than the expenses, the excess expenses are:
   a. Not deductible on the employee's tax return
   b. Deductible as miscellaneous itemized deductions subject to the 2 percent nondeductible floor
   c. Deductible as miscellaneous itemized deductions not subject to the 2 percent nondeductible floor
   d. None of the above

54. **Comprehensive Problem.** Andy and Marcia Tufts, both age 35, are married with two dependent children and file a joint return. From the following information, compute their tax owed or refund due for 2015.

Andy's salary	$50,000
Federal income tax withheld	4,000
Marcia's salary	42,000
Federal income tax withheld	3,500
Andy's contribution to an IRA (assume IRA is deductible for AGI)	2,000
Dividends received from domestic corporations	950
Medical expenses for doctors and hospitals	8,200
Premiums for health insurance	2,600
Prescription drugs and medicines	800
Eyeglasses for one of the children	175
Interest on home mortgage	7,800
Interest on credit cards	300
Real property taxes on residence	2,300
State income taxes	2,800
Fee for preparation of tax returns	125
Union dues and subscriptions	480

55. **Comprehensive Problem.** Larry Johnson, 45 and single, has the following income and deductions in 2015. Using the tax rate schedules rather than the tax tables, compute Larry's tax owed or refund due for 2015. Assume dividends are not qualified.

Salary	$50,000
Interest income	3,200
Dividends	800
Medical Expenses	6,150
Property Taxes on Personal Residence	3,600
Interest on Home Mortgage	7,600
State and Local Income Taxes	2,400
State and Local Sales Taxes	2,000
Investment Interest Expense	5,000

In addition, Larry's car (value = $15,000, cost = $20,000) was stolen during the year, and the insurance reimbursement was only $7,000. He also had $2,000 of travel expenses related to his job that were not reimbursed and $3,000 of federal income tax withheld from his salary.

He elects to treat his dividends as net investment income, so they are not subject to the special long-term capital gains tax rates.

56. **Research Problem.** Mary Sage's daughter has a serious medical problem. Mary, 36, must take her daughter to a distant city to be treated. Mary and her daughter stay for seven days to receive treatment. Mary incurs $1,000 in transportation costs, $800 in motel costs, and $240 for meals. What amount is deductible as a medical expense deduction before the 10 percent limitation?

57. **Research Problem.** The following selected court cases have helped to shape the tax law in regard to travel expense deductions. Read the following cases and prepare a brief written abstract for each case.
   a. *Burns v. Gray,* 61-1 USTC ¶9294, 287 F.2d 698 (CA-6 1961).
   b. *R. Rosenspan,* 71-1 USTC ¶9241, 438 F.2d 905 (CA-2 1971), cert. denied, 404 U.S. 864, 92 S.Ct. 54.
   c. *H.A. Stidger,* 67-1 USTC ¶9309, 386 U.S. 287, 87 S.Ct. 1065 (1967).

Chapter

9

Tax Credits, Prepayments, and Alternative Minimum Tax

OBJECTIVES

After completing Chapter 9, you should be able to:

1. Understand tax credits, both nonrefundable and refundable.
2. Compute estimated tax payments.
3. Apply the alternative minimum tax rules to individual taxpayers.

OVERVIEW

After completing this chapter, a student should be able to distinguish between the various types of tax credits available to taxpayers and to determine which credits represent a reduction of the income tax, which credits represent a return of a taxpayer overpayment of other types of taxes, and which credits can be used in other years if not fully used in the present year. This chapter will also provide tax planning hints on avoiding the alternative minimum tax provisions.

Nonrefundable Tax Credits

¶9001   ## TYPES OF CREDITS

A tax credit is a direct reduction of the tax due. It differs from a deduction which is a reduction in income subject to tax. For this reason, a credit is more valuable than the same amount of deduction. For example, a tax credit of $100 saves $100 in tax; a deduction of $100 saves $25 of tax for a taxpayer in the 25 percent marginal tax bracket and $15 for a taxpayer in the 15 percent marginal tax bracket.

Credits are divided into two types: (1) nonrefundable and (2) refundable. In the case of nonrefundable credits, there have been no payments to the government and therefore a taxpayer cannot obtain a refund of a credit if the credit exceeds the gross tax. Nonrefundable credits cannot be used to offset the recapture of any other credit or to offset taxes other than the income tax.

With the exceptions of the credit for earned income and the child tax credit, refundable credits are prepayments. Refundable credits can be offset against the recapture of other credits and against other taxes.

The credits must be computed in the order in which they are presented to insure that any limitations are properly applied. The limitations are stated in terms of the gross tax reduced by previously computed credits.

¶9015   ## HOUSEHOLD AND DEPENDENT CARE CREDIT

A credit is allowed up to 35 percent of employment-related expenses for care of qualifying individuals. Job-related expenses are allowed up to $3,000 (maximum $1,050 credit) for one individual and up to $6,000 (maximum $2,100 credit) for two or more individuals. The credit is reduced by one percentage point for each $2,000 of adjusted gross income, or fraction thereof, above $15,000. Code Sec. 21(a)(2) and (c). The credit is not reduced below 20 percent. Thus, taxpayers with adjusted gross income of over $43,000 will have a credit of 20 percent.

Adjusted Gross Income		Applicable Percentage	Credit Limitation	
			One Person	Two or More Persons
$0 to	$15,000	35%	$1,050	$2,100
15,001 to	17,000	34	1,020	2,040
17,001 to	19,000	33	990	1,980
19,001 to	21,000	32	960	1,920
21,001 to	23,000	31	930	1,860
23,001 to	25,000	30	900	1,800
25,001 to	27,000	29	870	1,740
27,001 to	29,000	28	840	1,680
29,001 to	31,000	27	810	1,620
31,001 to	33,000	26	780	1,560
33,001 to	35,000	25	750	1,500
35,001 to	37,000	24	720	1,440
37,001 to	39,000	23	690	1,380
39,001 to	41,000	22	660	1,320
41,001 to	43,000	21	630	1,260
43,001 and above		20	600	1,200

Employment-related expenses are those expenses paid for household and personal care of qualifying individuals which are necessary for the taxpayer to be gainfully employed or in active search for gainful employment. Code Sec. 21(b)(2); Reg. §1.44A-1(c)(1). Gainful employment includes working for others, either full time or part time, or employment in one's own business or partnership. Volunteer work for a nominal salary does not constitute gainful employment.

If the taxpayer is not employed or actively seeking employment during any part of the year, expenses allocable to that part of the year are not considered for the credit. Thus, for example, a teacher who does not teach during the summer months could not use child care expenses incurred during the summer in computing the credit.

The maximum expenses eligible for the credit must be reduced by amounts excludable from income under an employer-provided dependent care assistance program. The name, address, and the taxpayer identification number of the person providing the dependent care must be shown on the return of the taxpayer receiving the credit.

A "qualifying individual" is a dependent under age 13; a dependent of the taxpayer who is physically or mentally incapable of caring for himself or herself and who has the same principal place of abode as the taxpayer for more than one-half of the year; or the spouse of the taxpayer, if the spouse is physically or mentally incapable of caring for himself or herself and who has the same principal place of abode as the taxpayer for more than one-half of the year. Code Sec. 21(b)(1). The uniform definition of dependent for the dependency exemption is used for the dependent care credit. An individual is not treated as having the same principal place of abode of the taxpayer if at any time during the year the relationship between the individual and the taxpayer is in violation of local law. Code Sec. 21(e)(1).

The credit is available to a divorced or separated parent who has custody of a child who is under age 13 or who is physically or mentally incapable of self-care, even though the parent may not be entitled to a dependency exemption under the terms of a divorce decree or settlement agreement. Code Sec. 21(e)(5). The child will not be a qualifying individual for the other parent.

Only employment-related expenses qualify for the credit. These include ordinary and necessary household services to maintain a home. Any taxes required to be paid for FICA and federal unemployment or similar state payroll taxes on wages paid to an individual for providing household and personal care that constitutes employment are considered to be employment-related expenses. Disabled dependent or spouse care expenses for services performed outside the taxpayer's home are includible only if the disabled spouse or disabled dependent regularly spent at least eight hours a day in the taxpayer's home. Child care expenses are not confined to services performed within the taxpayer's home and include those for household services, day care centers, nursery school, and kindergarten. Expenditures for services provided by a dependent care center not in compliance with state or local regulations are not eligible for this credit. Expenses incurred to send a dependent to an overnight camp may not be claimed. Code Sec. 21(b)(2). No credit is allowed for any amounts paid to an individual for which the taxpayer is allowed a personal exemption deduction or who is a child of the taxpayer and has not reached the age of 19 at the close of the tax year. Code Sec. 21(e)(6).

Employment-related expenses cannot exceed the earned income of a single taxpayer. In the case of married taxpayers, expenses are limited to the earned income of the spouse with the lower income. Code Sec. 21(d)(1).

EXAMPLE 9.1

> Bob and Linda are married taxpayers filing a joint return with two dependents. They incurred $7,200 of employment-related child care expenses. Linda worked part time and had earnings of $5,400. Bob had earnings of $40,000. Since Linda's income was less than the amount of the employment-related expenses, the credit was based on her earnings. Since their adjusted gross income exceeds $43,000, the credit is reduced to 20 percent. The credit would be $1,080 ($5,400 × 20%).

In case of married taxpayers where, for any month, one spouse is either a full-time student at an educational institution or incapable of self-care, that spouse will be considered to have earned income of $250 per month if there is one qualifying individual in the household, and $500 per month if there are two or more qualifying individuals. Code Sec. 21(d)(2). If both spouses are students or are incapable of self-care, this rule applies to only one spouse for any one month. The $250 and $500 figures are used only in computing the lower income of the two spouses and are not included in the income of the taxpayers.

Married couples must file a joint return to claim the credit. The taxpayer who (1) has not lived with the other spouse for over six months at the end of the year, (2) lives with a qualifying dependent, and (3) provides over one-half of the cost of maintaining the household will be considered as single for the purpose of this credit. Code Sec. 21(e)(2) and (4). The taxpayer will not have to take the other spouse's income into consideration or file a joint return. There is no carryover of any unused household and dependent care credit.

¶9025　ELDERLY AND DISABLED PERSONS CREDIT

An important tax benefit for the elderly is the retirement income credit. This provision was added in 1954 because of concern that persons receiving Social Security benefits were favored over persons receiving comparable forms of retirement income. In 1976, changes were made to eliminate what was viewed as discrimination against those who are required to support themselves by working in their later years. Beginning in 1984, the credit was expanded to include the permanently and totally disabled. This expansion of the credit for the elderly was coupled with the repeal of the disability income exclusion effective for years after 1983.

Individuals can receive a 15 percent credit to be applied against their tax on all types of income, including earned income. To qualify for the credit for the elderly, an individual must (1) have reached age 65 before the end of the tax year or (2) have retired on disability before the close of the tax year and must have been permanently and totally disabled when he or she retired. The maximum base amount against which the 15 percent credit can be claimed is $5,000 for a single person and married persons filing jointly where only one spouse qualifies. The maximum is $7,500 when both spouses are qualified individuals and file a joint return. The figure is $3,750 when a married individual files a separate return. Code Sec. 22(a)-(c).

Where a qualified individual has not attained age 65 before the end of the tax year, the maximum base amount cannot exceed that individual's disability income for the year. Married individuals must file a joint return to receive the credit unless the spouses lived apart for the entire year. Nonresident aliens are not eligible for the credit. Code Sec. 22(c), (e)(1), and (f).

The maximum base amount must be reduced by Social Security, railroad retirement benefits, or other exempt pension benefits. Code Sec. 22(c)(3). Social Security and railroad retirement benefits also may be partially taxed under Section 86. Any amounts included in gross income will not reduce the maximum base amount. No reduction is required for pension or annuity payments from a tax-qualified pension plan, even though the amounts may be excluded from gross income. The maximum base amount is also reduced by one-half of the amount of adjusted gross income above certain income levels: $10,000 for married persons filing jointly, $5,000 for married persons filing separately, and $7,500 for single persons. Code Sec. 22(d)(1). Thus, for a single person, the credit would no longer be available when adjusted gross income reaches $17,500 ($7,500 plus two times $5,000). For the joint return the credit would be available up to an income level of $20,000 if only one spouse qualifies and up to $25,000 if both spouses qualify. On a joint return, the reduction is based on amounts received by either spouse.

The amount of the credit cannot exceed the income tax due for the year. There are no provisions for carryovers of any unused credit. Thus, if the credit exceeds the tax due, any remaining credit is lost.

EXAMPLE 9.2	Larry is single over 65 and reports $11,900 of adjusted gross income. In addition, he received Social Security benefits of $1,500 for the year. His credit for the elderly will be computed as follows:		
	Maximum Base Amount		$5,000
	Less: Social Security	$1,500	
	1/2 (AGI in excess of $7,500)	2,200	3,700
	Balance available for credit		$1,300
	Credit allowed ($1,300 × 15%) based on compensation		$195
	Taxable income ($11,900 −$6,300−$1,550−$4,000 =$50)		
	Income tax due		$5
	Credit allowed		$5

¶9031　AMERICAN OPPORTUNITY TAX AND LIFETIME LEARNING CREDITS

Beginning in 1998, two new tax credits became available to low- and middle-income individuals for tuition expenses incurred by students pursing college or graduate degrees or vocational training.

The American Opportunity Tax Credit (formerly the HOPE Credit) provides a maximum nonrefundable tax credit of $2,500 per student for each of the first four years of post-secondary education. The $2,500 per year limitation is made up of 100 percent of the first $2,000 of qualified expenses plus 25 percent of next $2,000 of qualified expenses. The American Opportunity Tax Credit applies for the first four years of higher education. The credit is applicable to the taxpayer, spouse, and dependents. The student must be enrolled at least half time to qualify for the American Opportunity Tax credit. Qualified expenses include tuition, fees, books, and course materials. The American Opportunity Tax credit phases out for AGI between $80,000 and $90,000 for singles; and $160,000 and $180,000 on a joint return. Except for dependent taxpayers subject to the kiddie tax, 40% of the credit is refundable.

The Lifetime Learning Credit provides a maximum credit of $2,000 for 20 percent of qualified tuition expenses paid by the taxpayer for any year the American Opportunity Tax Credit is not claimed. The Lifetime Learning credit is 20 percent of the first $10,000 of qualified tuition, fees, and course materials paid for taxpayer, spouse, and/or dependent. It is figured on a per tax return basis. The credit applies for any number of years of higher education. The Lifetime Learning credit phases out for single taxpayers with income exceeding $55,000 and marrieds with income exceeding $110,000.

EXAMPLE 9.3	Joe and Sheila Ames have three children in college. Joni, a freshman, incurs $2,400 in tuition expenses during 2015. Mike, a junior, incurs $3,000 in tuition expenses. Sally, in graduate school, incurs $8,500 in tuition expenses. Joe and Sheila paid all of the tuition expenses, and their adjusted gross income does not exceed the limits. They will be allowed a credit on their 2015 tax return of $6,050. The American Opportunity Tax Credit applies to Joni and Mike and is limited to 100 percent of the first $2,000 of expenses and 25 percent of the next $2,000 for each of them. The Lifetime Learning Credit applies to Sally and is limited to 20 percent of the first $10,000 of expenses.

¶9032   CHILD TAX CREDIT

Taxpayers are allowed a credit for qualifying children under age 17. The credit is $1,000 per child for tax years after 2002. The credit phases out when modified adjusted gross income exceeds $75,000 for single taxpayers, $110,000 for married taxpayers filing a joint return, and $55,000 for married taxpayers filing separately. The credit is reduced by $50 for each $1,000, or fraction thereof, of modified adjusted gross income above the threshold levels. Modified adjusted gross income is determined without regard to the exclusions from gross income for foreign earned income and foreign housing costs and income of residents of Guam, American Samoa, the Northern Mariana Islands, and Puerto Rico.

The child tax credit generally uses the same relationships to define an eligible child as are used in the uniform definition of a child for purposes of the dependency exemption. This means that a qualifying child for purposes of the child credit includes the taxpayer's children and their descendants, as well as the taxpayer's siblings (including half-siblings and step-siblings) and their descendants. A qualifying child must share the same principal place of abode as the taxpayer, and must not provide more than one-half of his or her own support for the year. A taxpayer's child may also be the taxpayer's stepchild; a child legally adopted by the taxpayer or lawfully placed with the taxpayer for legal adoption by the taxpayer; or a foster child who has been placed with the taxpayer by an authorized placement agency or by a judgment, decree, or other order of any court of competent jurisdiction.

At least a portion of the child tax credit is refundable for all taxpayers with qualifying children, regardless of the amount of the taxpayer's regular tax or alternative minimum tax liability. The child tax credit is refundable to the extent of 15 percent of the taxpayer's earned income in excess of $3,000, up to the per child credit amount.

Taxpayers with three or more children may calculate the refundable portion of the credit using the excess of their Social Security taxes (i.e., the taxpayer's share of FICA taxes and the employee's share of self-employment taxes) over the earned income credit, instead of the 15 percent amount.

The nonrefundable child tax credit allowable must be reduced by the amount of this refundable child tax credit.

EXAMPLE 9.4

Arleta Kern is single and has two qualifying children. If Arleta has gross income of $21,250, she will have a child tax credit of $2,000. Her gross income will be reduced to zero by the standard deduction for head of household and three personal exemptions. The initial nonrefundable child tax credit of $2,000 ($1,000 × 2) is unavailable since there is no income tax liability. Arleta's refundable child tax credit is $2,738, which is 15 percent of her earned income over $3,000. However, the refundable credit is limited to $2,000. If Arleta has gross income of $26,250, she would have a tax of $500. The $500 would be reduced to zero by the first $500 of the nonrefundable credit, leaving a refundable credit of $1,500. Any tax liability must first be reduced by any dependent care credit, credit for the elderly, and education credits.

EXAMPLE 9.5

John and Barbara Hassen have three children. Their adjusted gross income would have to exceed $32,600 before they could qualify for the nonrefundable child tax credit. The standard deduction for a married couple plus five personal exemptions will reduce their taxable income to zero. They will not qualify for a nonrefundable child tax credit. They will qualify for a refundable child tax credit of $3,000 (($32,600 – $3,000) × .15 = $4,440 limited to $3,000 ($1,000 × 3)). If the entire $32,600 were subject to FICA taxes, the Hassens would have paid $2,494 in FICA taxes. Assuming they qualify for the maximum earned income credit, their earned income credit would be $4,353. Thus, until the FICA taxes exceed the earned income credit, the second method of computing the refundable child tax credit will create no refundable child tax credit. However, when using a $3,000 reduction, the 15 percent computation will always give a higher refundable credit than the excess of FICA taxes over the earned income credit.

¶9033 CREDIT FOR QUALIFIED RETIREMENT SAVINGS

A nonrefundable tax credit is allowed for elective contributions made by eligible taxpayers to a qualified retirement plan. The maximum annual contribution eligible for the credit is $2,000. The credit rate depends on the adjusted gross income of the taxpayer. Only joint returns with adjusted gross income of $61,000 or less, head of household returns of $45,750 or less, and single returns of $30,500 or less are eligible for the credit.

The credit is in addition to any deduction or exclusion that would otherwise apply with respect to the contributions. The credit is available to individuals who are 18 or over, other than individuals who are full-time students or claimed as a dependent on another taxpayer's return.

The credit rates based on adjusted gross income are as follows:

Adjusted Gross Income						Applicable percentage
Joint Return		Head of a household		All other cases		
Over	Not over	Over	Not over	Over	Not over	
$0	$36,500	$0	$27,375	$0	$18,250	50
36,500	39,500	27,375	29,625	18,250	19,750	20
39,500	61,000	29,625	45,750	19,750	30,500	10
61,000	—	45,750	—	30,500	—	0

¶9034 ADOPTION ASSISTANCE CREDIT

A nonrefundable tax credit of up to $13,400 of qualified adoption expenses per child has been provided for 2015. Qualified expenses include adoption fees, court costs, attorney fees, and other expenses related to the legal adoption of an eligible child. Also, employees are entitled to exclude from income up to $13,400 of adoption expenses per adopted child where such amounts are paid or incurred by their employers under a qualified adoption assistance program. In the case of a special needs child, $13,400 is allowed as an adoption credit and as an exclusion from income, regardless of whether the taxpayer has qualified adoption expenses. The credit and exclusion are phased out beginning at modified adjusted gross income levels between $201,010 and $241,010. No credit is allowed for any expenses reimbursed by the employer or by a federal, state, or local program.

Expenses may include the cost of construction, renovations, alterations, or purchases specifically required by the state to meet the needs of the child. The increase in basis of the property that would result from such an expenditure must be reduced by the amount of credit allowed. Expenses incurred in carrying out a surrogate parenting arrangement or in adopting a spouse's child do not qualify for the credit. The child must be under age 18 or incapable of self-care in order to qualify for the credit.

The credit is taken in the year of adoption and includes expenses incurred in previous years. The adoption credit for the special needs child is allowed for the tax year in which the adoption becomes final. A carryforward period of five years is allowed for any credit disallowed because of limitation based on tax liability. Code Sec. 23.

EXAMPLE 9.6	In 2015, a married couple incurs $12,000 in adoption expenses for a child. Their modified adjusted gross income is $205,010. They would be allowed a credit of $12,060 ($13,400 – (($205,010 – $201,010)/$40,000 × $13,400).

EXAMPLE 9.7	A married couple incurs $12,000 in adoption expenses for a child. The employer reimburses the couple for $8,000 of the expenses under a qualified adoption assistance program. The couple will be eligible for an adoption credit of $4,000 ($12,000 expenses incured minus $8,000 exclusion from employer plan). However, taxpayers should always choose the adoption credit for the first $13,400 of adoption expenses before using any exclusion.

¶9035   FOREIGN TAX CREDIT

Both individuals and corporations may claim a credit against the United States tax for certain income taxes of foreign countries and possessions of the United States. Code Sec. 27(a). The foreign tax credit is the method employed by the United States and many other economically developed countries to deal with the problem of double taxation that arises whenever two taxing jurisdictions have a reasonable claim to impose a tax on the same income.

For example, a United States citizen is subject to tax on his or her worldwide income simply because of his or her citizenship. But if he or she were employed in Canada, the Canadian government has at least an equal right to tax the income. To avoid the possibility that combined taxes may exceed 100 percent, the usual rule is that "home yields to source." Thus, the U.S. citizen would be required to include and pay tax to Canada. To avoid double taxation, a credit is allowed for the Canadian tax against the U.S. liability.

As an alternative to the credit, a deduction of foreign income taxes may be taken under Code Sec. 164. A credit against the tax ordinarily results in a greater tax benefit than a deduction from gross income. However, in a few instances the limitation on the allowable credit will cause the deduction to be of greater benefit. All foreign taxes must be treated the same way—they must all be deducted or all claimed as a credit. The credit does not apply to payment of royalties made in the guise of a tax, such as under an oil production sharing agreement made after 1977. Code Sec. 901(e).

The credit is equal to the lesser of the actual tax paid to the foreign country or a limitation. Taxpayers are required to compute the limitation on the amount of foreign tax that can be used to reduce U.S. tax under the overall limitation. A taxpayer totals the taxes paid to all foreign countries and possessions. This total is then subjected to a limitation computed by multiplying the U.S. tax liability by a fraction consisting of taxable income from foreign sources over the worldwide taxable income. Code Sec. 904(a). For individuals, worldwide taxable income is computed as adjusted gross income less total itemized deductions or standard deduction (personal exemptions are not deducted). Thus, the credit cannot exceed that proportion of the U.S. tax which U.S. taxable income from sources within that country bear to the entire U.S. taxable income for the same year.

EXAMPLE 9.8	Anco, a domestic corporation, had worldwide taxable income of $500,000 and a tentative U.S. tax liability of $170,000. From its operations in a foreign country, Anco had $100,000 of taxable income on which a $45,000 tax was imposed. Anco's foreign tax credit is limited to $34,000 (($100,000/$500,000) × $170,000 = $34,000). If the actual tax paid the foreign country was less than the computed limitation, the credit would be the actual tax paid.

EXAMPLE 9.9

> Allen Armstrong has worldwide taxable income (after the standard deduction) of $380,000 for 2015 and a tentative U.S. tax liability of $109,006. Included in his worldwide income was $100,000 taxable income from a foreign country on which a $38,000 tax was imposed. Allen's foreign tax credit is limited to $28,686 (($100,000/$380,000) × $109,006). The personal exemption is totally phased out.

Unused foreign taxes may be carried back one year and then forward ten years. The credit is first carried to the earliest year and then to the next earliest year. There is no carryover to the year the foreign tax is deducted.

After 1997, an individual with $300 or less ($600 on a joint return) of creditable foreign taxes is exempt from the foreign tax credit limitation. Taxpayers can take a credit for the full amount of the foreign taxes provided all of their gross foreign-source income is from interest and dividends and all of that income and the foreign tax paid on it is reported to them on Form 1099-INT or Form 1099-DIV (or substitute statement).

TAX BLUNDER

John Jones worked part of the year in a foreign country. He paid $20,000 in income taxes to the foreign country. On his tax return he took an itemized deduction for the income taxes paid. Unless the limitation reduced the credit significantly, it is very likely that taking a credit for the foreign income taxes paid will provide a much larger tax benefit to John than will an itemized deduction.

¶9042 RESIDENTIAL CREDITS

Individual taxpayers are allowed a residential energy property credit of up to $500 for nonbusiness energy property, such as residential exterior doors and windows, insulation, heat pumps, furnaces, central air conditioners, and water heaters. Code Sec. 25C. The credit applies to qualified energy efficiency improvements and qualified energy property placed in service in 2011 through 2013.

A credit is allowed individuals for solar and fuel cell equipment installed on a personal residence. The tax credit is available to help individual taxpayers pay for residential alternative energy equipment. Code Sec. 25D. The credit is 30 percent of the cost of eligible solar water heaters, solar electricity equipment (photovoltaics), and fuel cell plants. The credit is available for equipment placed in service during 2011 through 2014. The credits are expected to be renewed for 2015.

¶9045 GENERAL BUSINESS CREDIT

In order to provide a uniform limitation on the amounts of business credits that may be offset against tax liability and uniform rules for carrybacks and carryforwards, there are over 30 business credits that have been combined into a single credit called the general business credit. The amount of the current year business credit is the sum of those credits determined for the tax year. Some of the more important credits are listed:

1. Investment credit
2. Work opportunity credit
3. Alcohol fuels credit
4. Increasing research credit
5. Low-income housing credit
6. Disabled persons access credit
7. Renewable electricity production credit
8. Empowerment zone credit
9. Indian employment credit
10. Employer Social Security credit from employee tips
11. Orphan drug credit
12. New markets tax credit
13. Small employer pension plan startup cost credit
14. Employer-provided child care credit
15. New hire retention credit
16. Energy-efficient home credit
17. Energy-efficient applicances credit
18. Alternative motor vehicle credit

The ceiling limitations, carryover, and recapture provisions apply to the total of the general business credits.

Investment Credit

Taxpayers purchasing "qualified investments" are allowed a credit against the tax liability for a portion of the amount of their investment for the year the property is placed in service. Under Section 46(a) the investment credit is the sum of:

1. Rehabilitation credit
2. Energy credit

Rehabilitation Credit

A two-tier investment credit for qualified rehabilitated buildings makes up the rehabilitation credit. The credit is (1) 20 percent for rehabilitations of certified historic structures and (2) 10 percent for rehabilitations of other buildings originally placed in service before 1936. The 20 percent credit applies to both residential and nonresidential buildings and the 10 percent credit applies to nonresidential property. Code Sec. 47(a).

Certain expenditures do not qualify for the credit. The costs of acquiring a building or an interest in a building, such as a leasehold interest, are not considered as qualifying expenditures. The costs of facilities related to an existing building, such as a parking lot, also are not considered as qualifying expenditures. Expenditures incurred by a lessee do not qualify for the credit unless the remaining lease term on the date the rehabilitation is completed is at least as long as the applicable recovery period under the general depreciation rules (generally, 27.5 years for residential property and 39 years for nonresidential property). Straight-line depreciation must be used to qualify for the rehabilitation credit.

In addition, the cost of constructing a new building, or of completing a new building after it has been placed in service, will not qualify. Construction costs are considered to be for rehabilitation and not for new construction if (1) at least 50 percent of the existing external walls are retained as external walls, (2) at least 75 percent of existing external walls are retained as internal or external walls, and (3) at least 75 percent of the existing internal structure framework is retained in place. These tests do not apply to certified historic structures. Code Sec. 47(c).

The basis of a rehabilitated building must be reduced for the full rehabilitation credit.

Energy Credit

An energy credit is available for a taxpayer's investment in energy property. The eligible property and rates are shown in the table below.

Qualified fuel cell property	30%
Solar energy property	30%
Geothermal property	10%

The energy property must be depreciable property built or acquired by the taxpayer and must be either depreciable or amortizable. The energy property basis must be reduced by 50 percent of the credit taken. Code Sec. 48(a). The energy credit expired at the end of 2013. It is expected to be renewed.

Recapture of Credit

If qualified property is disposed of by sale or exchange, gift, or involuntary conversion before the close of the recapture period, the investment credit may be recaptured. For recovery property, the amount of increase in tax is determined by applying the recapture percentage to the amount of investment credit taken on the asset. Code Sec. 50.

If Property Ceases To Be Investment Credit Property Within	Recapture Percentage
First Year	100
Second Year	80
Third Year	60
Fourth Year	40
Fifth Year	20

EXAMPLE 9.10	Billingsly Corporation purchased qualified business energy investment property with a MACRS life of five years for $30,000. Billingsly claimed an investment credit of $3,000 ($30,000 × 10%). If Billingsly sold the asset after four years of useful service, 20 percent of the $3,000, or $600, would be the increase in tax due because of the recapture.

If property with a basis reduced is disposed of in a transaction that triggers the recapture of an investment credit, then the basis "immediately before the event resulting in such recapture" is increased by 50 or 100 percent of the recaptured amount. Code Sec. 50(c)(3). The basis adjustment will affect gain or loss on disposition of the asset and also depreciation recapture.

EXAMPLE 9.11	Jerome Jackson purchased five-year Section 38 depreciable property for $30,000. After holding the asset for more than four years, Jerome sells it. A 10 percent investment credit of $3,000 was taken in the year of purchase and the asset basis was reduced by 50 percent of the credit taken. On disposition, investment credit would be recaptured in the amount of $600. The basis of the asset would be increased by one-half of this amount, or $300, for purposes of determining gain or loss and depreciation recapture.

Any increase in income tax because of recapture is treated as income tax imposed on the taxpayer even though the taxpayer has no income tax liability, has a net operating loss for the year, or no income tax return is otherwise required for the year. The investment credit recapture is not reduced by other nonrefundable tax credits.

If the investment credit allowable has not been used as a tax reduction, but is reflected in an unused carryover, the recapture will result in an adjustment of the carryover.

In determining the actual useful life of qualified property, the property is treated as placed in service on the first day of the month in which the property is placed in service. If property ceases to be qualified property, the cessation is treated as occurring on the actual date of the disqualification (i.e., sale, transfer, retirement). When the cessation is for any reason other than the occurrence of an event of a specific date, the cessation is treated as occurring on the first day of the tax year.

EXAMPLE 9.12	Bare Corporation purchases energy equipment with a life of five years on June 15, 2010, for $12,000. On June 7, 2015, the equipment is sold. Even though the asset was held for less than five years, for investment credit purposes, the asset was held more than five years (considered placed in service June 1, 2010, and sold June 7, 2015). None of the investment credit taken will be recaptured.

Taxpayers using an averaging convention in computing depreciation for qualified property may use the assumed dates of additions and retirements in determining the actual useful life of the property. This election must be used consistently and may not result in a substantial distortion of investment credit.

The death of a taxpayer does not trigger investment tax credit recapture. Moreover, recapture does not apply to the transfer caused by death of a partner's interest in a partnership, a beneficiary's interest in an estate or trust, or a shareholder's shares of stock in an S corporation. The property is treated as if it had actually been held for the entire useful life.

EXAMPLE 9.13	Benjamin Burr purchased $9,000 worth of energy equipment for his sole proprietorship, taking a $900 investment tax credit. He died four years later, leaving the equipment to his daughter. There is no recapture of the credit and the daughter can dispose of the equipment immediately without recapture.

Recapture does not occur when property is transferred in a tax-free transfer by a corporation pursuant to a reorganization or a liquidation of a controlled subsidiary. Also, recapture does not occur when property is transferred in connection with a mere change in the form of carrying on a trade or business, provided that the taxpayer maintains a substantial interest in the business. Recapture will still occur if an early disposition occurs in a subsequent transaction that is not exempt.

PLANNING POINTER	Since recapture is affected by the holding period of the asset, care should be taken to dispose of an asset at the optimum time. Delaying the sale or disposition of property can reduce the amount of recapture.

TAX BLUNDER

Alvin Armend purchased energy equipment for $20,000 on June 1, 2010, taking the investment credit of $2,000. He sold the equipment on May 18, 2015. Since he sold the equipment before the five-year holding period, he must recapture $400 of the investment credit. Had Alvin held on to the asset for two more weeks he would have saved $400 in taxes.

At-Risk Limitations

The Economic Recovery Tax Act of 1981 contained an investment credit at-risk limitation which applies to businesses which are subject to loss limitations under Section 465. Generally, the taxpayer is allowed an investment credit for only that portion of an investment for which the taxpayer is at risk. A taxpayer is generally not at risk for nonrecourse debt. Where the taxpayer's at-risk amount increases, additional investment credit is allowed on the increase. If the taxpayer's at-risk amount decreases, the investment credit may be subject to recapture.

The investment credit at-risk rules do not apply to amounts borrowed for qualified energy property. In order to qualify under the exception, the taxpayer must have an investment in the property that is at risk in an amount that is at least 25 percent of the unadjusted basis of the property. In addition, any nonrecourse financing for the property must be a level payment loan. A level payment loan is a loan repaid in substantially equal installments including both principal and interest. Code Sec. 49.

Work Opportunity Credit

The work opportunity tax credit may be elected by employers who hire individuals for certain target groups suffering from unusually high unemployment. The credit is taken with respect to first-year wages paid to eligible individuals who begin work after September 30, 1997, and before January 1, 2015. It is expected that the Work Opportunity Credit will be renewed for 2015. The work opportunity credit equals 40 percent of the first $6,000 of wages for the first year of employment. The $6,000 limit is computed on each eligible employee for wages attributable to services rendered during the one-year period beginning with the day the individual begins work for the employer (maximum credit of $2,400 per employee). Code Sec. 51(a) and (b). The employee must complete a minimum of 120 hours of service for the credit to apply. If the employee completes at least 120 hours of service but less than 400 hours of service, the employer is entitled to a credit of 25 percent rather than the 40 percent.

EXAMPLE 9.14	Astabula Corp. hires Maxine Brown, a certified targeted group member, on December 1, 2014. The company pays $1,200 of wages to Maxine in December 2014 and $14,000 in 2015. The work opportunity credit for 2014 is $480 ($1,200 × 40%). The first $4,800 of wages paid in 2015 are also eligible for the credit of $1,920.

The Vow to Hire Heroes Act provides for an expanded Work Opportunity Credit (WOC) of up to $5,600 for employers that hire veterans who have been looking for employment for more than six months. Employers that hire veterans who have been unemployed for more than four weeks but less than six months are eligible for a maximum tax credit of $2,400. A $9,600 tax credit is available to employers that hire veterans with service-connected disabilities who have been looking for employment for more than six months. The credit applies for eligible veterans starting work after November 21, 2011, and before January 1, 2015. The credit is expected to be renewed. The credit is 40% of first-year wages. Tax exempt groups can take the credit as an offset against payroll taxes.

An employer's deduction for wages is reduced by the amount of the work opportunity credit. Also, wages taken into account in computing the work opportunity credit are not taken into account in computing any empowerment zone employment credit allowed by Code Sec. 1396.

The following individuals are members of targeted groups eligible for the work opportunity credit: (1) a qualified IV-A (Aid to Families with Dependent Children (AFDC)) recipient, (2) a qualified veteran, (3) a qualified ex-felon, (4) a designated community resident, (5) a vocational rehabilitation referral, (6) a qualified summer youth employee, (7) a qualified food stamp recipient, (8) a qualified SSI recipient, or (9) long-term family assistance recipients.

An employer must obtain certification from a state employment security agency that an individual is a member of a targeted group. An individual may not be treated as a member of a targeted group unless an employer either obtains written certification from the designated local agency on or before the day the individual begins work indicating that the individual is a member of a targeted group or completes a prescreening notice on or before the day employment is offered.

The work opportunity credit is elective with the taxpayer. If the credit is elected, the employer's deduction for wages is reduced by the amount of the tentative credit before application of the various limitations. Therefore, the employer has the option of taking the credit or the deduction.

EXAMPLE 9.15

Bertram Ross hired a qualified work opportunity credit employee. The employee begins work on March 2, 2014, and is paid $8,800 during the year. The work opportunity credit allowed is $2,400 ($6,000 maximum amount × 40%). The taxpayer's tax deduction for wages is $6,400 ($8,800 wages paid – $2,400 work opportunity credit).

For long-term family assistance recipients the amount of the credit for a tax year is 40 percent of the qualified first-year wages plus 50 percent of the qualified second-year wages. The credit applies only to the first $10,000 of wages in each year with respect to any individual. Thus, the maximum total credit per qualified employee is $9,000 for the two years.

EXAMPLE 9.16

Dewey Corporation hires Nina Alexis on June 5, 2013. Dewey pays Nina $7,000 in wages in 2013. Dewey Corporation can take a credit of $2,800 ($7,000 × 40%) in 2013. Dewey will also be eligible for a 40 percent credit on any wages paid Nina before June 5, 2014, but limited to $1,200 ($3,000 × 40%). The first $10,000 of wages paid Nina during the period of June 5, 2014, and June 4, 2015, will be eligible for a 50 percent credit.

Alcohol Fuels Credit

To foster the production of gasohol, an income tax credit for alcohol and alcohol blended rules applies to fuel sales and uses. There is a 60-cent-per-gallon credit for alcohol of at least 190 proof and a 40-cent-per-gallon credit for alcohol of at least 150 but less than 190 proof for persons producing alcohol fuels or using them in a trade or business. Further, the amount of the allowable tax credit must be reduced to the extent that the alcohol is used in gasohol and other alcohol fuels for which there is an excise tax exemption for fuel taxes. Code Sec. 40.

The alcohol fuels credit is claimed as one of the components of the general business credit. Thus, it is subject to the maximum tax liability rules and the carryback and carryforward rules.

Taxpayers may elect to have the alcohol fuels credit not apply for any tax year. The election may be made or revoked at any time before the three-year period beginning on the last date for filing a return for such tax year, without regard to extensions.

Research Credit

A tax credit is allowed for qualifying research and development expenditures paid or incurred after June 30, 1996, and before January 1, 2015. The credit is expected to be renewed for 2015. The research credit is equal to the sum of (1) 20 percent of the excess (if any) of the *qualified research expenses* for the tax year over the base amount and (2) 20 percent of the *basic research payments*. Code Sec. 41(a). Thus, the research activities credit has two components: an incremental credit and a basic research credit.

Incremental Research Activities Credit

The credit for increasing research activities applies only to research expenditures incurred in carrying on a trade or business in which a taxable entity is already engaged. Expenditures incurred, for example, in developing or improving a product, a formula, an invention, a plant process, or an experimental model are eligible for the credit. No credit is available for expenses relating to a potential trade or business. Thus, new businesses conducting research for future production that undertake research geared to the development of a new business activity may not claim the credit.

Qualified research expenses are the same as those costs eligible for a deduction under Code Sec. 174 (see ¶6435) other than expenses for foreign research, research in the social sciences, arts or humanities, or subsidized research. Credit-eligible research is limited to research undertaken to discover information that is

(1) technological in nature and (2) intended to be useful in the development of a new or improved business component. Further, the research must be elements of a process of experimentation for a functional purpose (i.e., it must relate to a new or improved function, performance, reliability, or quality). Qualified research expenses cover in-house expenses for the taxpayer's own research (wages for substantially engaging in or directly supervising or supporting research activities, supplies, and computer use charges) and 65 percent of amounts paid or incurred for qualified research done by a person other than an employee of the taxpayer. Prepaid contract research expenses are to be taken into account over the period in which the research is conducted.

Basic Research Credit

The second element of the research credit computation is 20 percent of the basic research payments. This is sometimes referred to as the university research credit because the credit is available to corporations for basic research to be performed by universities, colleges, and other qualified organizations (scientific research organizations, organizations promoting scientific research, and organizations that make basic research grants). The amount of basic research payments taken into account is the excess of such basic research expenditures over the qualified organization base period amount. Those expenses that do not exceed such base period amount are treated as contract research expenses and are subject to the 65-percent rule.

Any business deduction for qualified research expenses or basic research payments must be reduced by 100 percent of the research credit. An election permits a taxpayer to avoid reducing the deduction by electing to reduce the research credit by the product of (1) 50 percent of the credit and (2) the maximum corporate tax rate. The election is made for each tax year. It is irrevocable and must be made no later than the time for filing the taxpayer's return for the year of the election.

Low-Income Housing Credit

A nonrefundable income tax credit applies to newly constructed or substantially rehabilitated qualified low-income housing projects placed in service after 1986 and before 2015. It is expected to be renewed for 2015. The credit is claimed over a credit period which is the 10 tax years beginning with the tax year in which the building is placed in service. First-year credits must be prorated to reflect a partial year of qualification. If the credit is prorated, the balance of the first year's credit is available in the eleventh year. The basis for purposes of depreciation is not reduced by the amount of low-income credit claimed. Code Sec. 42(a).

The applicable credit rate is the appropriate percentage issued by the IRS for the month in which the building is placed in service. For newly constructed units or rehabilitation expenditures exceeding specified minimum amounts per low-income unit that are not federally subsidized, the credit rate is computed so that the present value of the 10 annual credit amounts at the beginning of the credit period equals 70 percent of the qualified basis of the low-income units. For qualified federally subsidized units the rate is such that the present value equals 30 percent.

The credit rate equal to the 30 percent present value also applies to the cost of acquisition of certain existing low-income units. The credit for acquisition cost may be claimed only if the property was placed in service more than 10 years before the acquisition and there is substantial rehabilitation. Rehabilitation expenditures during any 24-month period must constitute a qualified basis equaling the greater of $3,000 per low-income unit or 10 percent of the unadjusted basis of the building. Rehabilitation expenses for any building are treated as a separate new building. If such test is satisfied and the substantial rehabilitation expenditures are not federally subsidized, such expenditures are eligible for the credit determined under the 70 percent present value applicable credit rate. A 30 percent present value applicable credit rate would apply to the existing portion of such building.

| EXAMPLE 9.17 | Mildred Meridian incurs $100,000 in qualifying costs to rehabilitate low-income property on January 1, 2014. The expenditures are not federally subsidized. Assume that the applicable credit rate is 9 percent. Mildred is eligible for a $9,000 credit for each year from 2014 through 2023. |

The amount of the credit is the product of the applicable credit rate and the taxpayer's share of the qualified basis of the property allocable to the units occupied by low-income tenants. A separate calculation to compute the qualified basis must be made for property qualifying for each of the credits. Each qualified basis amount is equal to the total basis of the low-income property multiplied by the percentage of units occupied by tenants with the appropriate income level.

A low-income housing project qualifies for the credit if it is residential rental property, if the units are used on a nontransient basis, and if a minimum occupancy requirement is met. Hotels, dormitories, nursing homes, hospitals, life-care facilities, and retirement homes do not qualify for the credit. At least 20 percent of a project's units must be occupied by individuals having incomes of 50 percent or less of the area median income (adjusted for family size) or at least 40 percent of the units must be occupied by individuals having incomes of 60 percent or less of area median income (again adjusted for family size). The taxpayer must irrevocably elect which of the two requirements (the 20 percent or the 40 percent test) will apply to the project. The gross rent paid by families in units qualifying for the credit cannot exceed 30 percent of the income limitation applicable to the tenants, based on family size.

Qualified low-income housing projects must maintain their qualification for a minimum of 15 years from the beginning of the year in which the project first qualifies for the credit. If not, a portion of the credits must be recaptured with interest. The allowable credits are reduced to two-thirds per year prior to recapture in determining the recapture amount.

The credit receives special treatment under the passive activity loss limitations. Qualifying projects are considered "active real estate rentals" regardless of the form of ownership or the investor's actual participation in the operations. The "active" status covers only the credit and does not extend to any income or loss from the project. There is no phaseout of the credit benefits as adjusted gross income exceeds $100,000. The credit is subject to the general business credit limitation and is subject to the carryback and carryforward rules.

Disabled Persons Access Credit

A tax credit is available to an eligible small business for expenditures incurred to make the business accessible to disabled individuals. An eligible small business is defined as any person (including any predecessor) that either (1) had gross receipts for the preceding tax year that did not exceed $1 million or (2) had no more than 30 full-time employees during the preceding tax year. The amount of the credit is equal to 50 percent of the amount of the eligible access expenditures for that year that exceed $250 but that do not exceed $10,250. The amount of the credit must reduce the expenditures otherwise eligible for deduction or basis increase. Code Sec. 44.

EXAMPLE 9.18

Dana Corporation, an eligible small business, spends $8,750 to install ramps to its building to make the building accessible to handicapped individuals. Dana is allowed a credit of $4,250 (($8,750 – $250) × 50%). Only $4,500 is eligible for depreciation as the $8,750 expenditure must be reduced by the $4,250 credit.

A taxpayer may elect to currently deduct up to $15,000 annually of barrier removal expenses. Code Sec. 190. A deduction is not allowed to the extent that a credit is taken for these expenditures.

Renewable Electricity Production Credit

The renewable electricity production credit is an amount determined by the kilowatt hours of electricity produced by the taxpayer from qualified energy resources. The production must take place at a qualified facility during the 10-year period beginning on the date the facility was originally placed in service. The electricity production must be sold to an unrelated person during the year. Code Sec. 45.

Empowerment Zone Employment Credit

The general business credit includes an empowerment zone employment credit for employers. The credit is generally equal to 20 percent of the first $15,000 of wages paid during the year to each employee who is a resident of a designated empowerment zone and who performs substantially all employment services within the zone in a taxpayer's trade or business. Code Sec. 1396. The deduction that the employer would normally be allowed for wages is reduced by the amount of the empowerment zone credit claimed for the tax year. Several empowerment zones have been designated by the Secretary of Housing and Urban Development and the Secretary of Agriculture from urban and rural areas nominated by state and local governments.

Indian Employment Credit

The amount of the Indian employment credit is an amount equal to 20 percent of the excess of qualified wages paid or incurred during the year plus qualified employee health insurance costs paid or incurred over the sum of the qualified wages and qualified employee health insurance costs paid or incurred during the calendar year 1993. The credit is expected to be renewed for 2015. Code Sec. 45A. A qualified employee must be a member of an Indian tribe or the spouse of an enrolled member of an Indian tribe. Substantially all of the services performed must be performed within an Indian reservation. The principal place of abode of the employee while performing the services must be on or near the reservation in which the services are performed.

Employer Social Security Credit

A business credit is allowed to food and beverage establishments for the amount equal to the employer's Federal Insurance Contribution Act (FICA) obligation (7.65 percent) attributable to tips in excess of those treated as wages for purposes of satisfying the minimum wage provisions of the Fair Labor Standards Act. To prevent a double benefit, no deduction is allowed for any amount taken into account in determining the credit.

Orphan Drug Credit

The orphan drug tax credit is available for amounts paid or incurred after June 30, 1996. The credit is an amount equal to 50 percent of the qualified clinical testing expenses for the taxable year. Code Sec. 45C(a). Basically, the term "clinical testing" means any human clinical testing that is carried out under an exemption for a drug being tested for a rare disease.

New Markets Tax Credit

A tax credit was created in 2000 to spur investment in low-income or economically disadvantaged areas. The new markets tax credit is five percent of a qualified equity investment in a qualified community development entity (CDE). The five-percent rates for the first three allowance dates and increases to six percent for each of the four remaining dates. The allowance dates are the initial offering date and the first six anniversary dates of the initial offering date. The total credit is, therefore, 39 percent and is claimed over seven allowance dates.

A qualified equity investment is the cost of any stock in a corporation or any capital interest in a partnership that is a qualified CDE if:

1. The investment is acquired on the original issue date solely in exchange for cash,
2. Substantially all of the cash is used to make qualified low-income community investments, and
3. The investment is designated by the qualified CDE for new markets credit purposes.

If, during the seven years from the original issue date of the qualified equity investment, a recapture event occurs with respect to the investment, then the new markets tax credit must be recaptured. The recaptured credit will increase the tax for the year in an amount equal to the amount of credits claimed plus interest for the resulting underpayment. The interest will not be deductible, nor may any other credits be taken against the addition to tax caused by the credit recapture.

Credit for Plan Startup Costs of Small Employers

Small employers with no more than 100 employees will receive a tax credit for some of the costs of establishing new retirement plans. The credit equals 50 percent of the startup costs incurred to create or maintain a new employee retirement plan. The credit is limited to $500 in any tax year, and it may be claimed for qualified costs incurred in each of the three years beginning with the tax year in which the plan becomes effective. The employer must not have established or maintained a qualified employer plan during the three-tax-year period immediately preceding the first tax year in which the new plan is effective. Deductible expenses must be offset by the amount of the credit taken. At an employer's election, the credit may be claimed in the year immediately preceding the first year in which the new plan is effective.

Credit for Employer-Provided Child Care Expenses

A tax credit for child care expenses acts as an incentive for businesses to provide child care for their employees. The credit is equal to the sum of 25 percent of the qualified child care expenses plus 10 percent of the qualified child care resources and referral expenditures. The total credit amount claimed for any given tax year cannot exceed $150,000. Double benefit for child care expenses is prevented by a reduction in the basis of the qualified property for the expenses claimed as a credit and the barring of the use of the same expenses to claim any other deductions or credits. If an employer terminates its interest in providing child care, all or part of the claimed credit must be recaptured as an increase in tax.

Other Credits

Congress added a number of new credits during 2005 with the Energy Act and the Hurricane Relief Act.

A homebuilder's credit for new energy-efficient homes is available during 2006 through 2014. The credit is expected to be renewed for 2015. An eligible contractor may claim a tax credit of $1,000 or $2,000 for a qualified new energy-efficient home that a person acquires from the contractor during 2006 through 2014 for use as a residence during the tax year. An eligible contractor is a person who constructs a new energy-efficient home, or a manufacturer that produces a qualified new energy-efficient manufactured home. A $2,000 credit per dwelling is allowed where consumption of energy is at least 50 percent below that of a comparable dwelling unit sold for use as a residence. A $1,000 credit is allowed for a manufactured home that meets a 30 percent energy efficiency standard.

A new credit has been added for the manufacture of energy-efficient applicances, including only dishwashers, clothes washers, and refrigerators.

A series of new tax credits have been added by the Energy Act to encourage the development, manufacture, and use of alternative fuel motor vehicles. Taxpayers with qualified motor vehicles that are used in a trade or business and subject to depreciation will claim the alternative motor vehicle credit as a part of and subject to the rules of the general business credit. Individuals will claim the credit as a personal credit.

Limitation on General Business Credit

The general business credit may not exceed "net income tax" minus the greater of (1) the tentative minimum tax or (2) 25 percent of "net regular tax liability" above $25,000. Code Sec. 38(c). The term "net income tax" means the sum of the regular tax plus the alternative minimum tax and minus all other nonrefundable credits, except the credit for prior year minimum tax. "Net regular tax" is the regular tax liability reduced by such credits.

EXAMPLE 9.19	Lindy Corporation has purchases that entitle it to $62,000 in general business credits. Its tax liability before the deduction of the general business credit is $45,000. Except for the ceiling, Lindy's credit for the year would be $62,000. However, the ceiling on the credit yields a maximum credit of $40,000 ($45,000 – 25% × ($45,000 – $25,000)).

Where a husband and wife file separately, the $25,000 amount becomes $12,500. However, this reduction will not apply if the spouse of the taxpayer has no qualified investment for the tax year and no carryback or carryover to the tax year. The $25,000 is apportioned among component members of a controlled corporation. Each partner in a partnership takes the $25,000 figure into account separately, as do beneficiaries of estates and trusts and shareholders in S corporations.

Carryback and Carryforward of Unused Credits

When the general business credit exceeds the above limitation in any year, the excess or unused credit may be carried back for one year and forward for 20 years. The entire amount of the unused credit must be carried back and then forward to each of the 20 remaining carryover years in order. Credits carried over are used first and then credits earned currently; after that, any carryback credits are applied. Unused credits from two or more years are used up in the order they occurred—the oldest first. The credit for investment in the current year, plus any carryover credits, cannot exceed the general limitations in effect for that year.

The first-in, first-out method of general business credit carryover reduces the potential loss of general business credits from the expiration of credit carryovers, since the earliest years are used before the credit for the current year. Code Sec. 39.

Refundable Tax Credits

Since refundable credits generally represent payments that have been made to the government, fewer difficulties are encountered in carryback and carryover, recapture, limitations, and sequencing.

¶9105   WITHHOLDING OF TAX ON WAGES CREDIT

The tax deducted and withheld on wages is allowable as a credit against the tax. If the tax has actually been withheld, a credit or refund will be made even though the tax has not been paid to the government by the employer. However, the IRS may credit any overpayment against any outstanding tax, interest, or penalty owed by the taxpayer. Code Sec. 31(a).

¶9115   SOCIAL SECURITY TAX REFUNDS CREDIT

Where an employee receives wages from more than one employer during the year, amounts may be deducted and withheld as employee Social Security tax on amounts exceeding $118,500 for 2015. A special refund of the excess amount may be obtained only by claiming credit for the amount in the same manner as if such special refunds were an amount deducted and withheld as income tax at the source. The present rate is 6.2 percent on $118,500. The credit is computed separately for each spouse on a joint return. Code Sec. 31(b).

| EXAMPLE 9.20 | Lorence Larsen works for two different employers during 2015. He earned $58,000 from the first employer and $63,100 from the second. Each employer withheld Social Security taxes. Lorence is allowed a credit for the excess Social Security taxes paid in of $161.20 (($121,100 − $118,500) × 6.2%). |

Where an employer withholds Social Security taxes on more than the maximum amount, a credit may not be claimed for the excess. The employer should adjust the overcollection with the employee.

¶9125   EARNED INCOME CREDIT

A refundable tax credit is provided for low-income workers. The credit is based on "earned income," which is explained below. The earned income credit may be characterized as a form of negative income tax since the credit is refundable to the taxpayer even if no tax liability exists. This credit does not represent a refund of a previous payment made by the taxpayer.

Taxpayers entitled to exclude income under the foreign earned income exclusion are not allowed the credit. The earned income credit is reduced by any alternative minimum tax imposed for the tax year.

Basic Earned Income Credit

For 2015, the maximum credit is 34 percent of earned income up to $9,880, or a credit of $3,359 for one child. The maximum credit of $3,359 is reduced by an amount equal to 15.98 percent of the excess of the greater of the adjusted gross income or earned income over $18,110. Code Sec. 32. For two children, the credit percentage is 40 percent of earned income up to $13,870, with a maximum credit of $5,548 and a phaseout percentage of 21.06 percent. For three children, the credit is 45 percent of earned income up to $13,870, with a maximum credit of $6,242 and a phaseout of 21.06 percent.

Eligible taxpayers with no children may receive a credit of 7.65 percent of the first $6,580 of earned income, for a maximum of $503. The phaseout percentage is also 7.65 percent on income exceeding $8,240. The phaseout amounts are increased by $5,520 for married filing jointly.

The definition of a qualifying child for purposes of the earned income credit is generally the same as the uniform definition of a child contained in the dependency exemption rules. A qualifying child must be the taxpayer's son, daughter, step-son, step-daughter, brother, sister, stepbrother, stepsister, or a descendant of any such individual. An adopted child is treated as a child by blood if the child was legally adopted by the taxpayer, or was lawfully placed with the taxpayer for legal adoption by the taxpayer. A foster child is also treated as the taxpayer's child if the child was placed with the taxpayer by an authorized placement agency or by judgment, decree, or other order of any court of competent jurisdiction. A child providing more than one-half of his/her own support can still be a qualifying child for the earned income credit. The custodial parent qualifies for the earned income credit when the exemption is granted to the noncustodial parent. The child must have the same principal place of abode as the taxpayer for more than one-half of the tax year. The child must be under 19 (or under age 24 in the case of a full-time student) in order to be a qualifying child. No age limit applies to individuals who are totally and permanently disabled at any time during the tax year. Married individuals must file a joint return in order to receive the benefits of the credit.

Taxpayers without qualifying children must meet three requirements: (1) the individual has a principal residence in the United States for more than one-half of the taxable year, (2) the individual (or, if married, either the individual or the individual's spouse) is at least 25 years old and not more than 64 years old at the end of the taxable year, and (3) the individual cannot be claimed as a dependent for any taxable year beginning in the same calendar year as the taxable year for which the credit is claimed.

Earned income includes wages, salaries, tips, and employee compensation. In addition, net earnings from self-employment are included in earned income. Earned income is to be reduced by any loss in earnings from self-employment. Earned income is to be computed without regard to any community property laws which may otherwise be applicable. Pension and annuity income is not considered earned income for the purpose of the credit. Taxpayers may choose to include combat pay in earned income for purposes of computing the earned income credit.

The earned income credit is denied to individuals where the aggregate amount of disqualified income exceeds $3,400 for 2015. Disqualified income includes both taxable and nontaxable interest, dividends, net rental and royalty income, net capital gain income, and net passive income.

EXAMPLE 9.21

Malcolm Meyers maintains a household for himself and his 12-year-old son. For the year, he received $18,610 in wages and $300 in interest income. His earned income credit for the year is computed as follows:

Maximum credit: 34% of $18,610, limited to $3,359		$3,359.00
Reduction: Greater of AGI or earned income	$18,910	
Less phaseout amount	18,110	
Excess	$800	
15.98% of excess		127.84
Allowable earned income credit		$3,231.16

The credit is refundable. Thus, taxpayers with a credit exceeding their liability can claim the difference as a refund. Even if a return is not required because of an individual's low income, a return should be filed to obtain the credit.

EXAMPLE 9.22

Nancy Pearson maintains a household for herself and her dependent daughter. Nancy's only income is $7,000 from wages. Under the filing requirement rules, she is not required to file a return. However, to receive the $2,380 ($7,000 × 34%) earned income credit, a return must be filed.

¶9135 WITHHOLDING OF TAX AT SOURCE CREDIT

Taxpayers are allowed a credit for income taxes withheld on nonresident aliens, foreign corporations, and tax-free covenant bonds. Code Sec. 33.

¶9155 GASOLINE AND SPECIAL FUELS TAX CREDIT

Generally, the taxpayer can claim a credit for federal excise taxes on the nonhighway use of gasoline and special fuels. These include gasoline or special fuels used for farming purposes and special fuels used in local transit systems and for aviation purposes. Code Sec. 34.

Gasoline and lubricating oil must be used in a trade or business or in an income-producing activity. The credit for gasoline must be included in income where the cost of the product was deducted as a business expense.

¶9165 ESTIMATED TAX PAYMENTS CREDIT

A credit is permitted for quarterly estimated payments made by taxpayers. Individuals whose tax liability is not substantially covered by withholding may have to pay estimated taxes. All individuals must file a declaration of estimated tax for the year if the estimated tax, including self-employment tax, exceeds the tax to be withheld by $1,000 or more.

The estimated tax for the current year is computed by (1) estimating the taxpayer's gross income for the year, (2) subtracting estimated deductions and exemptions, and (3) computing the income tax on the balance. The estimated self-employment tax and alternative minimum tax are added to the resulting income tax. The tax to be withheld from wages during the year and other expected credits are subtracted. The result is the "estimated tax," and if it is less than $1,000 no estimated payments need be made.

Where estimated returns are required for the current tax year, they must be filed by April 15, June 15, September 15, and January 15 (following year). The taxpayer may elect to credit a preceding year's overpayment against the current year's estimated tax.

In filing a declaration of estimated tax, the taxpayer is required to take into account the then existing facts and circumstances, as well as those reasonably to be anticipated. In the absence of contrary indications, current employment, salary rate, and regularly paid dividends may be presumed to continue throughout the year. Amended or revised declarations may be made in any case in which the estimates differ from those reflected in the previous declaration.

No penalty is imposed for failure to file an estimated tax declaration, or for errors in the declaration, but there is a penalty for underpayment of estimated tax. The amount of the penalty is the amount of the underpayment times the underpayment interest rate for the period of the underpayment.

An "underpayment," for other than high-income individuals, is determined by adding the amount of income taxes paid and the excess Social Security credit and then subtracting the lesser of (1) 90 percent of the actual amount of tax due on the return or (2) the previous year's tax. The underpayment is computed as of each of the four quarterly filing dates. Thus, a taxpayer making uneven payments throughout the year could have an underpayment for some quarters and not others. The penalty applies despite any reasonable cause and is not deductible as an expense.

After 2002, high-income individuals must use 110 percent of the previous year's tax liability. A high-income individual is one who had more than $150,000 in adjusted gross income for the preceding year ($75,000 for married individuals filing separately).

An equal part of tax withheld from wages is considered as tax paid on each of the four quarterly filing dates, unless the taxpayer proves otherwise.

PLANNING POINTER	Generally, a taxpayer cannot avoid a penalty on underpayments in early quarters of the year by increasing estimated payments in the later quarters. However, if an employee realizes that he or she has underpaid for the earlier quarters, the employee could have a larger amount of income taxes withheld late in the year. Since any withholding is considered to be equally withheld throughout the year, the extra year-end withholding will increase the amount considered to have been paid in the earlier quarters and help lessen or eliminate any underpayment penalty.
KEYSTONE PROBLEM	There are two kinds of tax credits, nonrefundable and refundable, that basically must be taken in the proper order. Since some of the credits have no carryover provisions and are lost if not used in a particular year, what effect could an increase in a credit, such as the investment credit, have on the other credits?

Alternative Minimum Tax

¶9401   IMPOSITION OF TAX

The minimum tax is a special form of tax imposed on certain taxpayers in addition to the regular federal income tax. The objective of the tax is to recapture tax reductions resulting from the use of special tax relief or "tax shelter" provisions of the tax law.

"Alternative minimum taxable income" (AMTI) means the taxable income of the taxpayer for the year determined with adjustments and increased by tax preferences. Alternative minimum taxable income is reduced by an exemption amount to arrive at net alternative minimum taxable income which is then multiplied by a 26 or 28 percent alternative minimum tax rate. The first $185,400 of AMTI is taxed at 26 percent and AMTI in excess of $185,400 is taxed at 28 percent. However, dividends taxed at 15 percent and long-term capital gains taxed at 15 and 25 percent for regular tax purposes are also taxed at those rates in the alternative minimum tax computation. The foreign tax credit and the nonrefundable personal credits are the only nonrefundable credits allowed against the tax in arriving at the tentative minimum tax. The alternative minimum tax is the amount resulting after deducting the regular tax (reduced by all nonrefundable credits) from the tentative minimum tax. Code Sec. 55(b).

Alternative Minimum Tax Formula

	Taxable Income
+ or −	Adjustments to Taxable Income
+	Tax Preferences
=	Alternative Minimum Taxable Income (AMTI)
−	Exemption Amount
=	Net Alternative Minimum Taxable Income
×	26 or 28% Tax Rate
=	Tax
−	Alternative Minimum Tax Foreign Tax Credit
=	Tentative Minimum Tax (TMT)
−	Regular Tax for the Year
=	Alternative Minimum Tax (AMT)

The alternative minimum tax (AMT) requires additional recordkeeping and separate basis computations. The AMT adds substantial complexity to the tax system.

¶9415   ADJUSTMENTS TO TAXABLE INCOME

In determining AMTI, taxable income must be computed with the following adjustments. Code Sec. 56(a). Adjustments to taxable income can increase or decrease alternative minimum taxable income.

Depreciation

Taxpayers who, in calculating regular tax liability, depreciate real property under MACRS must use the alternative depreciation system in calculating AMTI. The real property alternative depreciation system calls for a 40-year straight line depreciation. The alternative depreciation system is not required for real property acquired after 1998.

Depreciation deductions for personal property and property which is not subject to straight-line depreciation must be recomputed under the 150 percent declining-balance method under the alternative depreciation system. Taxpayers must switch from the declining-balance method to the straight-line method in the first tax year that maximizes the deduction. Thus, the excess of AMT depreciation over MACRS depreciation in the later years of an asset can be used to offset the excess of accelerated depreciation over straight line in the early years of other assets.

EXAMPLE 9.23

A corporation purchases a $10,000 five-year machine for use in business in 2014. The depreciation methods for regular tax and alternative minimum tax purposes along with the adjustment are as follows:

Year	200% Declining Balance	150% Declining Balance		Adjustment
2014	$2,000	$1,500	+	$500
2015	3,200	2,550	+	650
2016	1,920	1,785	+	135
2017	1,152	1,666	–	514
2018	1,152	1,666	–	514
2019	576	833	–	257

In the first three years an amount must be added to taxable income, while a deduction is taken in the last three years.

Mining Exploration, Circulation, Research and Development Expenditures

Circulation expenditures of periodicals must be amortized ratably over three years. Mining exploration and development expenditures must be amortized ratably over 10 years. Research and experimentation expenditures must be amortized ratably over 10 years. For tax years after 1990, individuals who materially participate in an activity are not required to capitalize and amortize research and experimental expenditures generated by such activity that are otherwise allowed as a business expense deduction under Code Sec. 174(a).

The basis for gain or loss upon disposition is determined using the AMTI basis.

Pollution Control Facilities

For property placed in service after 1986, the five-year amortization method for depreciating pollution control facilities must be replaced by the alternative depreciation system. The adjusted basis used in AMTI calculations (but not for regular tax calculations) to determine the gain or loss on the sale of property for which depreciation has been adjusted must reflect the depreciation adjustment rather than the costs that were deductible in regular tax computations.

Long-Term Contracts

The percentage-of-completion method of accounting to determine gain or loss from long-term contracts must be substituted for any other method of accounting, such as the completed-contract method or the cash basis method, for both regular tax purposes and for AMT purposes. This change will directly affect those taxpayers who were using a form of completed-contract method of accounting for AMT purposes.

The adjustment is the excess of income from use of the percentage-of-completion method over the long-term contract method used on long-term contracts. For example, if the deferred income from a three-year contract is $750,000, no income is reported under the completed-contract method of reporting until the third year. Assuming the costs on the contract are incurred in equal proportions, $250,000 is included in AMTI for each of the three years.

Passive Farming Losses

No deduction is allowed for losses from any farming syndicate or any other farming activity in which the taxpayer does not materially participate. A loss from one farm activity may not be used to offset income from another farm activity. Disallowed losses are carried forward indefinitely and used for AMTI purposes to offset future income from the farming activity. Suspended losses are deductible when the activity is disposed of. Code Sec. 58(a).

Incentive Stock Options

An adjustment must be made to taxable income when incentive stock options are exercised. The excess (if any) of the stock's fair market value at the time of exercise over the amount paid by the employee for the stock is an adjustment that in figuring AMT taxable income is added to the taxable income shown on the tax return. This adjustment is made in the first year in which the rights in the stock are freely transferable or are not subject to a substantial risk of forfeiture.

EXAMPLE 9.24	Arthur Aster pays an exercise price of $15 to purchase stock having a fair market value of $20. The adjustment in the year of exercise is $5, and the stock has a basis of $15 for determining gain or loss for regular tax purposes and $20 for alternative minimum tax purposes. If, in a subsequent year, Arthur sells the stock for $45, the gain recognized is $30 for regular tax purposes and $25 for alternative minimum tax purposes.

Net Operating Losses

The net operating loss (NOL) must be calculated under special rules and cannot offset more than 100 percent of AMT income. The AMT rules generally require that the regular tax NOL must be adjusted for AMTI adjustments and tax preferences.

Gains and Losses on Sale or Exchange of Property

AMTI must be adjusted for any difference between gain or loss reported for the regular tax and that figured for the AMT. For AMT purposes, a property's basis is reduced only by the amount of depreciation allowed in computing AMTI. Therefore, the adjusted basis of the property may differ for regular and minimum tax purposes. The gain or loss for AMTI upon disposition of the asset is determined by the AMTI basis. Similar adjustments must be made to gains and losses on the sale of assets involving mining exploration and development costs, circulation expenditures, research and development expenditures, pollution control facilities, long-term contracts, and incentive stock options.

Personal Exemption

No deduction for personal exemptions may be claimed against alternative minimum taxable income. Code Sec. 56(b)(1)(E). Accordingly, the personal exemption taken in computing taxable income must be added back as an adjustment.

Itemized Deductions

The standard deduction is not allowed for the alternative minimum taxable income computation. Code Sec. 56(b). Only an individual's actual itemized deductions are allowed in computing AMTI and then only those itemized deductions not limited by the discussion below. In some situations it may be better to itemize even when the standard deduction is larger than the itemized deductions because only certain itemized deductions are added back for AMT purposes.

In computing taxable income, total itemized deductions for 2015 must be reduced for high income taxpayers by 3 percent of adjusted gross income exceeding $309,900 for married filing jointly, $284,050 for head of household, $258,250 for single, and $154,950 for married filing separately. This reduction does not apply to the alternative minimum tax. Consequently, itemized deductions included in the alternative minimum taxable income computation do not have to be reduced. The alternative minimum tax form reduces adjusted gross income by the disallowed itemized deduction.

Miscellaneous Itemized Deductions

No deduction is allowed for AMTI computation for any allowable miscellaneous itemized deductions except:

1. Wagering losses
2. Any deduction for impairment-related work expenses
3. The deduction for estate tax in case of income in respect of a decedent
4. Any deduction in connection with personal property used in a short sale
5. The deduction where a taxpayer restores substantial amount held under claim of right
6. The deduction where annuity payments cease before investment is recovered
7. The deduction for amortizable bond premium
8. The deduction in connection with cooperative housing corporations

Thus, the disallowed miscellaneous itemized deductions are added back to taxable income in arriving at AMTI.

Medical Expenses

Medical expenses are deductible for AMTI only to the extent that they exceed 10 percent of adjusted gross income. Thus, taxpayers over 65 using taxable income as the starting point must add back the smaller of 2.5 percent of adjusted gross income or the medical expense deduction taken for regular tax purposes.

Taxes

State, local, and foreign *real property* taxes, state and local *personal property* taxes, and state, local and foreign *income,* war profits, or excess profits taxes allowed as itemized deductions for regular tax purposes are not allowed in the AMTI computation. Thus, the only taxes deductible for AMTI purposes are the windfall profit tax (on oil removed before August 23, 1988) and the generation-skipping tax imposed on income distributions. A refund of state and local taxes paid, for which no alternative minimum tax deduction was allowed, is not included in alternative minimum taxable income.

Interest

The amount deductible for regular tax purposes for home mortgage interest may be greater than the permitted AMT deduction. For minimum tax purposes, upon refinancing a loan that gives rise to qualified housing interest, interest paid on the new loan is treated as qualified housing interest to the extent that (1) it so qualified under the prior loan, and (2) the amount of the loan was not increased. Thus, the home-equity loan exception to the regular tax rules does not apply to AMT.

| EXAMPLE 9.25 | Jane Juniper owes $80,000 on a mortgage on a principal residence purchased for $100,000 and with a current fair market value of $125,000. June takes out a second mortgage for $25,000. The interest on the additional $25,000 principal in excess of the prior $80,000 loan cannot be deducted for AMT purposes. |

¶9425   TAX PREFERENCE ITEMS

The following tax preferences must be added back to taxable income in arriving at alternative minimum taxable income. Code Sec. 57.

Depletion

The depletion preference is the excess of the percentage depletion deduction over the adjusted basis of the property at the end of the year. The preference applies to percentage depletion for all minerals, not just oil and gas.

Intangible Drilling Costs

The tax preference for intangible drilling costs on oil, gas, and geothermal wells is the amount by which the excess intangible drilling costs are greater than 65 percent of net income from the resource properties. Excess intangible drilling costs are the amount by which the intangible drilling deduction for regular tax purposes exceeds the amount which would have been allowable if the costs had been capitalized and amortized over 120 months.

Tax-Exempt Interest

A tax preference has been added for tax-exempt interest on private activity bonds issued after August 7, 1986. This preference does not apply to bonds issued for the benefit of tax-exempt charitable or educational institutions or to bonds issued for public purposes such as schools and municipally owned public utilities. Tax-exempt interest on private activity bonds issued in 2009 and 2010 is not an item of tax preference.

Accelerated Depreciation or Amortization

There is a tax preference for excess depreciation and amortization taken on certain properties acquired before 1987. (However, any properties acquired in 1986 that use the cost recovery rules are not subject to this tax preference.) Pre-1987 tax preference items include:

1. Depreciation on real property acquired before 1987 that is in excess of straight-line depreciation over the useful life
2. Amortization of certified pollution control facilities (the excess of 60-month amortization over depreciation otherwise allowable)

Exclusion for Gains on Sale of Certain Small Business Stock

An amount equal to 7 percent of the amount excluded from gross income under the provisions of Code Sec. 1202 which allow a taxpayer to exclude up to 50 percent of the gain on the sale of certain small business stock held more than five years is considered a tax preference for the alternative minimum tax. Thus, for taxpayers not exceeding the per-issuer limitation, 3.5 percent of the gain will be treated as an AMT preference.

¶9435   EXEMPTION AMOUNT

The allowable exemption amounts for 2015 are $83,400 for married persons filing joint returns and surviving spouses, $53,600 for single individuals, and $41,700 for married individuals filing separate returns or estates or trusts. The exemption amounts are reduced by 25 cents for each $1 by which alternative minimum taxable income exceeds $158,900 for married taxpayers filing jointly, $119,200 for single individuals, and $79,450 for married taxpayers filing separately. Code Sec. 55(d).

EXAMPLE 9.26   A married couple with AMTI of $300,000 is allowed an exemption amount of $48,125 ($83,400 – .25 × ($300,000 – $158,900)). If their AMTI were to exceed $492,500, there would be no deduction for the exemption amount.

The exemption phaseout level for married taxpayers filing separately has been made equal to the phaseout level for married taxpayers filing jointly. In the case of taxpayers filing separately whose AMTI exceeds $246,250, a special computation is necessary. The taxpayer must increase the AMT taxable income by 25 percent of the amount it exceeds $246,250. However, the increase cannot be more than $41,700.

The AMT exemption amount for minor children is limited to the greater of the child's earned income for the year plus $1,050 or the child's share of the unused parental minimum tax exemption (the excess of the Code Sec. 55(d) amount over the parent's AMTI) for tax years beginning in 1991.

¶9445   TAX CREDITS

Only the personal nonrefundable credits plus the foreign tax credit reduce AMT liability for noncorporate taxpayers. Thus, the general business credit is unavailable against the AMT for individuals even if it is allowable for regular tax purposes arising from qualified purchases or as a carryover. Taxpayers remaining in an AMT position for a number of years may lose allowable general business credits because the carryovers will have expired before they can be used. Even if the credits are used before expiring, the passage of time will erode the value of the credits. Code Sec. 59.

Individuals paying foreign taxes are permitted to use a portion of the specially calculated foreign tax credit against the tentative minimum tax. The foreign tax credit is allowed to the extent of the foreign tax on the taxpayer's foreign-source alternative minimum taxable income.

In computing the income tax on taxable income, the general business credit is taken only to the extent that it reduces the regular tax for the year to the tentative minimum tax. Thus, we cannot have a situation where the general business credit reduces the regular tax and then the alternative minimum tax is increased to offset the general business credit taken.

EXAMPLE 9.27	Matches Corporation has a regular tax before the general business credit of $50,000, general business credits of $22,000, and a tentative minimum tax of $40,000. Only $10,000 of the general business credit is taken, reducing the regular tax to $40,000. Since the regular tax is equal to the tentative minimum tax, no alternative minimum tax is imposed.

¶9455 CARRYOVER OF CREDIT

The alternative minimum tax paid in one year may be carried forward indefinitely as a credit against the regular tax liability. The credit may not be used, however, to offset any future minimum tax liability. A taxpayer is not allowed to take a credit larger than the amount necessary to reduce the regular tax to the amount of the tentative minimum tax. Code Sec. 53.

EXAMPLE 9.28	Andrew Ames has a tentative minimum tax of $100,000, a regular tax before the AMT credit of $120,000, and an AMT credit of $35,000 from previous years. Without the AMT credit, the taxpayer would have no alternative minimum tax because the regular tax exceeds the tentative minimum tax. Since the full AMT credit would reduce the regular tax below the tentative minimum tax, only $20,000 of the AMT credit carryforward may be used to reduce the regular tax.

The AMT credit for any tax year is the excess of the adjusted net minimum tax imposed for all tax years beginning after 1986 over the amount allowable as a credit in previous years. The adjusted net minimum tax is the amount of net minimum tax (alternative minimum tax) for a year reduced by the amount which would be the net minimum tax (alternative minimum tax) for that year if only certain adjustments and tax preferences were taken into account. The adjustments and tax preferences taken into account for this computation include:

1. The same itemized deduction adjustments discussed under the AMTI adjustments
2. The following tax preferences: depletion, tax-exempt interest, and gain exclusion allowed on small business stock.

The purpose of the minimum tax credit is to prevent the double taxation of deferral preferences and adjustments. These deferral preferences and adjustments are subject to the alternative minimum tax in a tax year earlier than the year they are subject to the regular tax. For example, accelerated depreciation taken in a year creates a tax adjustment or tax preference. This adjustment or preference may cause an additional tax because of the alternative minimum tax. In later years, taxable income will be higher because of the smaller depreciation deductions under accelerated depreciation, thus causing a higher income tax. Thus, the total depreciation deductions will not be received without the benefit of the alternative minimum tax credit. Therefore, the amount of the minimum tax credit to be carried forward is the excess of the AMT paid over the AMT that would be paid if AMTI included only "exclusion" preferences and adjustments (those items that result in a permanent reduction of regular tax liability).

TAX BLUNDER

Tommy Rose, who is subject to the alternative minimum tax, each year purchases some private activity bonds. The interest on these bonds will be free from income tax but will be taxed at 26 or 28 percent under the alternative minimum tax.

¶9475 ALTERNATIVE MINIMUM TAX PLANNING

Individuals subject to the alternative minimum tax generally benefit by accelerating income into an AMT year. Income recognized in an AMT year will generally be taxed at 26 or 28 percent rather than at the higher regular tax rate.

Ways to accelerate income into an AMT year include:

1. Taking capital gains before year-end
2. Receiving bonuses, commissions, and other income before year-end
3. Redeeming Treasury bills and U.S. savings bonds before year-end
4. Exchanging tax-exempt municipal bonds for taxable bonds paying a higher interest rate

Individuals may also benefit by delaying expenses until a regular tax year. Payment of allowed itemized deductions, such as charitable contributions, provides a tax benefit in an AMT of only 26 or 28 percent, while delaying the payment to a regular tax year may allow a deduction at greater than 28 percent. Any payment in an AMT year of an itemized deduction not allowed for AMT purposes, such as property taxes, will produce no tax savings, since reducing the regular tax merely increases the AMT by an equal amount.

Care must be taken not to accelerate too much income into an AMT year or to defer too many expenses into a regular tax year. Only accelerate receipt of income or defer expenses up to the point where the tax due under the tentative minimum tax equals the regular tax.

Taxpayers may be able to improve their AMT position by finding investments that produce passive income to offset passive tax-shelter losses. Since tax-shelter losses are not deductible for AMT purposes, the alternative minimum tax will not be increased to the extent that the passive income offset passive losses. Income-producing limited partnerships and rental properties generating passive income may be appropriate investments.

Interest on private-activity municipal bonds is a tax preference for the AMT. Thus, taxpayers holding private-activity municipal bonds in AMT years will find this income taxable. These taxpayers may be better off to trade these bonds for regular municipal bonds or higher paying taxable bonds.

EXAMPLE 9.29 Mark and Samantha Mandell, the parents of two children, had the following tax facts:

Income

Wages	$241,198
Business Income	89,500
1202 Capital Gain	50,000
Dividend Income	7,000
Interest Income	8,500

Expenses

1/2 Self-Employment Tax	1,198
Moving Expenses	10,000
Medical Expenses	42,000
Casualty Loss	39,100
Housing Interest	8,000
Investment Interest	28,000
Personal Interest	2,000
Charitable Contributions	27,000
Real Estate Taxes	10,500
Other Nonbusiness Deductions	23,000

Other Tax Preferences

Gain Exclusion on Small Business Stock	1,750
Private Purpose Municipal Bond Income	12,050
Excess of Accelerated Depreciation	20,000
General Business Credit	10,000

The computation of their income is as follows:

Gross Income

Wages	$241,198	
Business Income	89,500	
1202 Capital Gain	25,000	
Dividend Income	7,000	
Interest Income	8,500	
Total Gross Income		$371,198

Deductions from Gross Income

1/2 Self-Employment Tax	$ 1,198	
Moving Expenses	$10,000	
Adjusted Gross Income		$360,000

Itemized Deductions

Medical Expenses ($42,000 – 10% AGI)	$ 6,000	
Real Estate Taxes	10,500	
Housing Interest	8,000	
Investment Interest	8,500	
Personal Interest ($2,000 × 0%)	0	
Charitable Contributions	27,000	
Casualty Loss ($39,100 – $100 – 10% AGI)	3,000	
Other Itemized Deductions ($23,000 – 2% AGI)	15,800	
Less: 3% ($360,000 – $309,900)	– 1,503	
Total Itemized Deductions		– 77,279
Personal Exemptions ($4,000 × 4) × .6		– 9,600
Taxable Income		$273,103
Income Tax		$63,143
General Business Credit		0
Regular Tax for the Year		$63,143

EXAMPLE 9.29 CONTINUED

Alternative Minimum Tax Computation

Taxable Income		$273,103
Itemized Deduction Adjustment		– 1,503
Personal Exemptions ($4,000 × 4) × .6	$9,600	
Medical Expenses	0	
Real Estate Taxes	10,500	
Other Itemized Deductions	15,800	
Total Adjustments to Taxable Income		+ 35,900
Tax Preferences		
Gain Exclusion on Small Business Stock	$1,750	
Private Purpose Municipal Bond Income	12,050	
Excess Depreciation	20,000	
Total Tax Preferences		33,800
Alternative Minimum Taxable Income		$341,300
Alternative Minimum Tax Exemption		– 37,800
Net Alternative Minimum Taxable Income		$305,300
Tax Rate		× 26/28%
Tentative Alternative Minimum Tax		$80,362
Regular Tax for the Year		63,143
Alternative Minimum Tax		$17,219

The gain on the Code Sec. 1202 stock is reduced by 50 percent with 7 percent of the gain becoming a tax preference item.

The personal exemptions of $16,800 was reduced to $9,600 because of adjusted gross income. The adjusted gross income caused the itemized deductions to be reduced.

The 1202 capital gain is taxed at the 28 percent 1202 rate. The dividends are taxed at the 15 percent rate. These special rates are used for both the regular tax and AMT computations.

The investment interest expense is limited to the $8,500 investment income. The capital gains and dividend income are taxed at 15% dividend rate and thus are not investment income.

$55,093	Tax on $241,103 ($273,103 – $25,000 taxable Sec. 1202 gain – $7,000 dividends)
7,000	Tax on Sec. 1202 gain ($25,000 × 28%)
1,050	Tax on dividends ($7,000 × 15%)
$63,143	Income Tax

The alternative minimum tax computation begins with taxable income and adds back certain adjustments and tax preferences.

The itemized deduction reduction reduces taxable income.

The personal exemption is added back.

The medical expenses are reduced by an additional 2.5 percent of adjusted gross income only for taxpayers over 65.

Taxes are not allowed as an alternative minimum tax itemized deduction. Other itemized deductions are also not allowed in the alternative minimum tax computation.

The housing interest, charitable contributions, and casualty losses are not adjusted as they are allowed in AMT computation.

The alternative minimum tax exemption of $83,400 is reduced by $45,600 because the taxpayers' alternative minimum taxable income exceeds $158,900. The reduction is 25 percent of any excess over $158,900.

The taxpayers are unable to use the $10,000 general business credit because of the alternative minimum tax. They are able to carry the unused general business credit back one year and forward 20 years.

EXAMPLE 9.29 CONTINUED

The AMT credit carryforward is computed as follows:

Taxable Income		$273,103
Itemized Deduction Adjustment		– 1,503
Personal Exemptions	$9,600	
Medical Expenses ($360,000 × 2.5%)	0	
Real Estate Taxes	10,500	
Other Itemized Deductions	15,800	
Total Adjustments to Taxable Income		+ 35,900
Tax Preferences for AMT Credit		
Gain Exclusion on Small Business Stock	$1,750	
Private Purpose Municipal Bond Income	12,050	
Total Tax Preferences for AMT Credit		+ 13,800
AMTI for AMT Credit		$321,300
Alternative Minimum Tax Exemption		– 42,800
Net AMTI for AMT Credit		$278,500
Tax Rate		× 26/28%
Tentative AMT for Credit Purposes		$73,362
Regular Tax for the Year		– 63,143
Alternative Minimum Tax for AMT Credit		$10,219
Alternative Minimum Tax		$17,219
Alternative Minimum Tax for AMT Credit		– 10,219
Alternative Minimum Tax Credit		$7,000

The alternative minimum tax exemption is $42,800. Since AMTI exceeded $158,900, there was a $40,600 reduction in the exemption amount.

A comparison of the computation of the alternative minimum tax and the alternative minimum tax for AMT credit reveals two differences: (1) the $20,000 depreciation tax preference is not included in the AMT credit computation because it is not an exclusion item and (2) the alternative minimum tax exemption is $42,800 instead of $37,800. These two differences, $25,000, at a 28 percent rate results in a $7,000 alternative minimum tax credit.

SUMMARY

- A tax credit is a direct reduction in the tax due. A tax credit is more valuable than a deduction of the same amount.
- Credits are divided into two types: nonrefundable and refundable.
- In nonrefundable credits, there have been no payments to the government, so the taxpayer is not entitled to a refund even of the credit exceeds the gross tax. Nonrefundable credits must be taken in the proper order.
- Refundable credits allow the taxpayer to reduce the tax liability below zero. With the exception of the earned income credit and the child tax credit, the refundable credits represent a return of money paid into the government.
- The alternative minimum tax is a tax imposed in addition to the regular income tax to recapture the reductions resulting from the use of special tax relief provisions of the tax law. Certain adjustments and preferences are added back to taxable income and then an exemption amount is subtracted before applying the alternative minimum tax rates.

QUESTIONS

1. Explain the difference between a tax credit and a tax deduction. Which would help a 28 percent tax bracket taxpayer most, a $2,000 deduction or a $400 credit? A 15 percent tax bracket taxpayer?

2. Explain what is meant by the terms "refundable" and "nonrefundable" credits. How might these classifications affect the tax liability of a taxpayer?

3. Why is the household and dependent care credit sometimes only 20 percent and other times as high as 35 percent?

4. Can a taxpayer qualify for the household and dependent care credit if he or she is not employed?

5. Is the dependency exemption required for the household and dependent care credit?

6. What limits are placed on employment-related expenses for the household and dependent care credit?

7. Must married taxpayers file a joint return in all cases to qualify for the household and dependent care credit?

8. How does an individual qualify for the credit for the elderly?

9. What effect does the receipt of Social Security benefits have on the credit for the elderly?

10. What is the amount of the child tax credit for 2015?

11. What is the maximum child tax credit a taxpayer may receive for an 18-year-old full-time college student in 2015?

12. Can the child tax credit for taxpayers result in a refundable personal credit?

13. What expenses are eligible for the Hope Scholarship Credit?

14. How many years of post-secondary education expenses are eligible for the Hope tuition credit?

15. What expenses are eligible for the Lifetime Learning Credit?

16. What is the purpose of the foreign tax credit?

17. When would a taxpayer choose to itemize foreign taxes rather than take the foreign tax credit?

18. How are the various business credits reported on the tax return?

19. What buildings qualify for the rehabilitation credit?

20. How does the rehabilitation credit differ from the investment credit?

21. How does an investment credit affect the basis of an item purchased?

22. How will a premature disposal of investment credit property affect a taxpayer?

23. What happens to the basis of an asset that has a recapture of an investment credit?

24. Are taxpayers allowed a credit on the total expenditure for research?

25. What is the ceiling limitation for the general business credit?

26. When several years of general business credits are carried over to the present year which also has a general business credit, in what order are the credits taken?

27. What basic group of employees qualifies for the work opportunity credit?

28. Which nonrefundable credits if not used in the present year can be carried over to other years?

29. Is it possible for a taxpayer to have a credit for excess Social Security if the taxpayer worked for more than one employer and the total wages came to $38,000?

30. Describe the earned income credit.

31. Sara's only source of income was wages of $6,000. She and her daughter live with her parents. The daughter is claimed as a dependent by the father. Is Sara eligible for the earned income credit?

32. Discuss the declaration of estimated tax filing requirements of individuals.

33. If a taxpayer does not file estimated taxes and is underpaid for the year, what penalty may be imposed?

34. What is the purpose of the alternative minimum tax?

35. What is a tax preference item?

36. When is it possible to have a tax preference for the alternative minimum tax if the taxpayer is using straight-line depreciation?

37. List the itemized deductions that are not allowed in the computation of alternative minimum taxable income.

38. When is interest deductible as an itemized deduction for income tax purposes but not allowed as an itemized deduction for the alternative minimum tax.

39. What items create the alternative minimum tax credit?

PROBLEMS

40. Compute the child and dependent care credit in each of the following independent cases:
    a. Jack and Jill Jones are married and file a joint return. Jill worked full time earning $20,000, while Jack attended law school the entire year. They incurred $6,500 of child care expenses during the year for their two children, ages eight and six.
    b. Mary Morgan is a widow who worked full time the entire year earning $23,000. She incurred the following child care expenses for her six-year-old daughter in order to be employed during the year:

Kindergarten	$400
Babysitters	600
Private school (first grade)	600

    c. Bill and Debra Page are divorced and have one dependent child, Betty, age nine. Bill had custody of Betty for five months this year and claimed Betty as an exemption on his tax return. Debra had custody of Betty for the remainder of the year. Debra incurred $3,600 of employment-related expenses during the year, while Bill incurred $2,500 of employment-related expenses. Both were employed for the entire year and each earned $20,000 in wages this year.

41. Frank and Emma Browne are both over 65 and file a joint return. Emma received $800 from Social Security benefits and Frank received $1,200 from railroad retirement benefits. In addition to the benefits, they reported income of $18,000 from their antique shop.
    a. Compute Frank and Emma's tax credit for the elderly.
    b. Assume that only Emma was over 65 and compute the tax credit for the elderly.

42. A married couple with two children has $16,000 of earned income. There is no taxable income after deducting the standard deduction and personal exemptions. What is the amount of their child tax credit?

43. Fannie, a widow, lives in an apartment with her two minor children (ages 4 and 6) whom she supports. Fannie earns $35,000 during 2014. She uses the standard deduction. Calculate the amount, if any, of Fannie's earned income credit.

44. A married couple with two children has earned income of $29,700 with no withholding. Assume they have a taxable income of $100, they paid $2,272 in FICA taxes, and they will receive an earned income credit of $3,528. Their tax on $100 is $10. What is the amount of their income tax liability?

45. A married couple with three children has earned income of $15,000 and adjusted gross income of $50,000 with no withholding. Assume a standard deduction of $12,600 and personal exemptions of $20,000. Their tax on $17,400 is $1,740. They have no earned income credit. They paid $1,148 in FICA taxes. What is the amount of their income tax due?

46. Walt is single, age 67, and retired. His taxable income for 2014 is $1,320, and the tax on this amount is $132. Walt's tax credit for the elderly is $225. What is the amount of the credit for the elderly that Walt can claim on his tax return?

47. Philip and Susan Moyer have two children who are both in the first four years of college. They incur $4,500 in tuition expenses for each of the two children. What is the maximum amount of American Opportunity Tax Credit?

48. Cathy Thomas, a single mother, has modified AGI of $82,000. In 2015, her daughter begins work on her bachelors degree at an accredited institution. Cathy pays $6,000 in qualified tuition for the daughter's first semester. What is the amount of American Opportunity Tax Credit Cathy is allowed on her return?

49. Michael is divorced and the exemption for his daughter is claimed by his ex-wife. What is the amount of American Opportunity Tax Credit allowed Michael when he pays $2,500 in tuition for his daughter to attend her first year at an accredited four-year college?

50. What is the amount of Lifetime Learning Credit allowed a taxpayer assuming that he or she incurred $3,000 in tuition and fees and $8,000 in room and board for an eligible college student?

51. In 2015, Lenny Traveler had adjusted gross income of $26,300 from investments in the U.S., while earning $40,000 from foreign sources. Lenny's potential U.S. tax liability is $9,469, and he had to pay $9,000 in foreign income taxes. What amount can Lenny, a U.S. citizen, claim as a foreign tax credit?

52. ABC Corporation has international earnings of $500,000 and a U.S. tax liability of $170,000. From foreign operations ABC generated $120,000 of income on which a $55,000 tax was imposed. What is ABC's foreign tax credit and total tax liability?

53. Mark has a tentative general business credit of $120,000 for the current year. His net regular tax liability before the general business credit is $135,000, and his tentative minimum tax is $100,000. Compute Mark's allowable general business credit for the year.

54. Zap Industries had a tentative general business credit in 2015 of $60,000. Its tax liability in 2014 was $20,000. Its tax liability before the general business credit in 2015 is $50,000.
    a. What is Zap Industries' 2015 tax liability?
    b. Are there any effects on the tax liabilities of the previous year?
    c. If so, what are they?

55. Yoyo Corporation bought $42,000 worth of energy equipment in November 2010, taking an investment credit of $4,200. In March 2015, the firm sells the equipment for $30,000. What is the investment credit recapture?

56. Martha and Marty Mertens are married and file a joint return. Marty started his own business at the beginning of the current tax year and reported net income of $14,000 for the year. Martha worked full time as a waitress earning $8,000, excluding tips of $3,000. Marty and Martha maintained a home for their 11-year-old son. What is their earned income credit for 2015?

57. What is the adjustment that must be made to taxable income in computing alternative minimum taxable income for 2015, assuming that an individual purchased an office building on January 8 for $400,000?

58. What is the amount of tax preference for alternative minimum tax purposes assuming that an individual sells some qualified small business stock held more than five years at a $20,000 gain.

59. What is the allowable exemption for the alternative minimum tax assuming that a married couple has alternative minimum taxable income of $200,000?

60. Calculate the exemption amount for the following cases for 2015 for a single taxpayer, married taxpayer filing jointly, and a married taxpayer filing separately when AMT is $300,000.

61. Tamara and Tony Mapp, a married couple, report the following items for the year:

Taxable income	$80,000
AMT adjustments	30,000
Tax preferences	40,000
Regular tax liability	16,000

What is their alternative minimum tax for the year?

62. Donna, an unmarried individual who is age 66, has taxable income of $245,000. She has AMT positive adjustment of $68,000 and tax preferences of $6,000.
    a. What is Donna's AMT?
    b. What is the total amount of Donna's tax liability?

63. Alex and Alicia Andrews file a joint tax return. On the return they show Alex's salary of $110,000, interest income from corporate bonds of $3,000, dividends from domestic corporations of $1,000, and a net long-term capital gain of $60,000. They also had the following expenses for itemized deductions: $18,000 medical expenses, $8,000 home mortgage interest, $5,000 in consumer interest, $4,000 in deductible taxes, $2,000 charitable contributions, and $1,200 in miscellaneous deductions not subject to the 2 percent limitation. The Andrews claim five exemptions on their return. Determine their net alternative minimum taxable income.

64. What is the amount of AMT credit carryforward for 2015, assuming that an individual had an alternative minimum tax of $20,000 and an alternative minimum tax for AMT credit of $12,000?

65. Which of the following are tax adjustments or preference items for purposes of the alternative minimum tax?
    a. $20,000 net long-term capital gain over net short-term capital losses
    b. $3,000 net short-term capital gain
    c. $10,000 straight-line depreciation on building acquired in 1989
    d. $1,500 interest from City of Buffalo bonds

66. Which of the following qualify as "employment-related" expenses for the credit for child care?
    a. Nursery school fees
    b. Transportation to nursery school
    c. Housekeeper's salary
    d. Housekeeper's meals
    e. Gardener's salary

67. What is the amount of dependent care credit before any income tax limitation for a couple with two children where they spend $6,500 for dependent care and the husband earns $25,000 for the year and the wife earns $4,500?
    a. $1,755
    b. $1,215
    c. $90
    d. $0

68. Which of the following items is not an adjustment for the alternative minimum tax?
    a. Taxes
    b. Wagering losses
    c. Personal exemption
    d. Standard deduction

69. **Comprehensive Problem.** Determine the tax due, including the alternative minimum tax, for Patty Perkins, assuming she is single using the following tax information:

Adjusted Gross Income	$100,000
Itemized Deductions	20,000
Alternative Minimum Tax Itemized Deductions	12,000
Tax Preference Items	40,000
General Business Credit	17,000

70. **Comprehensive Problem.** From the following information determine the total 2015 tax due for Charlene and Dick Storm, assuming they file a joint return, have three dependents, and are not members of a qualified retirement plan.

Dick's Wages	$33,000
Charlene's Wages	41,000
Dick's Contribution to an IRA	2,000
Charlene's Contribution to an IRA	800
Charlene's Self-Employment Income	12,000
Tax Preference Items	40,000
General Business Credit	7,000
Housing Interest	8,000
Consumer Interest	2,000
Property Taxes	3,000

71. **Research Problem.** An asset is purchased on May 15, 2011, for $100,000. The full 10 percent investment credit of $10,000 is taken on the asset. On June 23, 2015, a Code Sec. 108 election is made to exclude gain arising from the discharge of business indebtedness in the amount of $7,000. What is the amount of investment credit recapture? See *Panhandle Eastern Pipe Line Co. & Affiliates,* 81-2 ustc ¶9496, 654 F.2d 35 (Ct Cls 1981).

Property Transactions: Determination of Basis and Gains and Losses

OBJECTIVES

After completing Chapter 10, you should be able to:

1. Understand the factors in determining realized and recognized gain or loss.
2. Determine the basis in various types of asset purchases and the allocation of basis.
3. Determine the basis of property acquired by gift and from a decedent.
4. Determine the basis in stock transactions, including stock dividends, stock rights, and wash sales.
5. Compute gains and losses in related party transactions and the income recognized in installment sales.

OVERVIEW

Chapters 10 through 12 contain discussions of topics related to the income tax consequences of property transactions including sale, exchange, or other disposition of property. By the end of the three chapters on property transactions, the student should gain familiarity with the following broad topics: (1) determination of basis; (2) realized gain or loss; (3) recognized gain or loss; (4) situations where gain or loss is not recognized or only partially recognized; and (5) classification of recognized gain or loss as ordinary or capital.

Chapters 10 and 11 discuss the first four broad topics while Chapter 12 focuses on the classification of recognized gain or loss as ordinary or capital. More specifically, Chapter 10 is concerned with the realization and recognition of gain or loss and with the determination of basis under varying circumstances including: an ordinary purchase, a bargain purchase, acquisition through gift, acquisition through inheritance, conversion of property from personal use to business use, nontaxable and taxable stock dividends and stock rights, and wash sales.

Factors in Determining Gain or Loss

¶10,001 **DEFINITION OF REALIZED GAIN OR LOSS**

Realized gain or loss is the difference between the amount realized (see ¶10,015) from the sale or other disposition of property and the adjusted basis (see ¶10,025) at the time of sale or disposition. If the amount realized exceeds the adjusted basis, there is a realized gain. On the other hand, if the adjusted basis exceeds the amount realized, there is a realized loss. Code Sec. 1001(a); Reg. §1.1001-1(a).

The term "other disposition" is interpreted broadly and includes transactions such as trade-ins, casualties, thefts, and condemnations. The term does not include a fluctuation in market value of an asset because the possibility for the taxpayer to gain or lose value of an asset still exists and no identifiable event has occurred to "fix" the gain or loss realized. Reg. §1.1001-1(c)(1).

EXAMPLE 10.1

Adam Acres sells property with an adjusted basis of $20,000 for $30,000 and has a realized gain of $10,000. If he had sold the property for $15,000, he would have had a $5,000 realized loss. If Adam exchanged Beach Corporation stock with an adjusted basis of $4,000 for Clark Corporation stock with a fair market value of $7,000, he has a realized gain of $3,000. If, however, Adam had Danville Corporation stock with an adjusted basis of $5,000 that has appreciated in value to $8,000, there is no realized gain because there is no sale or other disposition of the property.

The recovery of cost doctrine allows the taxpayer to recover the cost of property before being taxed on the sale proceeds. While owning the asset, the taxpayer may recover the cost through depreciation deductions, providing it is depreciable property. Basis is reduced for the depreciation deductions and at the time of sale or other disposition the remaining amount of cost is recovered through a comparison of the amount realized with the adjusted basis to determine whether there is a realized gain or loss.

¶10,015 **AMOUNT REALIZED**

The amount realized from the sale or other disposition of property is the sum of any money received plus the fair market value of other property received. It does not include any amount received from the purchaser as reimbursement for real property taxes which are treated as imposed on the purchaser, but it does include amounts representing real property taxes which are treated as imposed on the seller, if they are paid by the purchaser. Code Sec. 1001(b). The amount realized from a sale or other disposition of property also includes the amount of liabilities from which the transferor is relieved as a result of the sale or disposition. The amount realized is reduced by selling expenses.

EXAMPLE 10.2

Darlene Brown owns land worth $40,000 which is subject to a $16,000 mortgage. She sells it to Edward Greene who pays $24,000 cash and also assumes the mortgage. She incurs $2,000 selling expenses. Darlene's amount realized is $38,000 ($24,000 + $16,000 – $2,000).

The "fair market value" of the property is the price a willing buyer and a willing seller would reach after bargaining where neither party is acting under compulsion. Various sources can provide evidence of value. Stock exchange quotations generally provide evidence of the fair market value of stock except for unusually large blocks of stock. Sales of similar property on the open market are also evidence of value, and the opinion of appraisers or experts is generally given significant weight.

To summarize:

	Cash Received
+	Fair Market Value of Property and Services Received
+	Liabilities of Seller Assumed by Buyer
−	Selling Expenses
	Amount Realized

¶10,025   ADJUSTED BASIS

The concept of basis is important in federal income taxation. In effect, it measures the amount of the taxpayer's investment in the property, which the taxpayer is able to have returned without tax consequences. The taxpayer's original basis of property purchased is generally cost, but in some situations it may be fair market value, or a substituted basis. To figure the adjusted basis, the original cost or other basis is adjusted in various ways to reflect additions and reductions in investment.

The basis of property must be increased by capital expenditures and decreased by capital returns. These adjustments are made to all types of property for all events occurring after acquisition whether original basis is cost, fair market value, or a substituted basis. Code Secs. 1011 and 1016. Increases in basis have the effect of reducing the amount of gain realized or increasing the amount of realized loss as well as depreciation or cost recovery. Decreases in basis have the effect of increasing the amount of realized gain or decreasing the amount of loss and depreciation or cost recovery.

To summarize:

	Original Basis
+	Capital Expenditures
–	Capital Returns
	Adjusted Basis

Capital *expenditures* are costs chargeable to the capital account. Routine repair and maintenance expenses are not capital expenditures. However, improvements, betterments, acquisition costs, purchase commissions, and legal costs for defending title are all capital expenditures. Capital *returns* include depreciation, depletion, amortization, tax-free dividends, compensation or awards for involuntary conversions, deductible casualty losses, insurance reimbursements, and cash rebates received by a purchaser. Code Sec. 1016(a).

The basis reduction for ACRS or MACRS cost recovery, depreciation, amortization, or depletion is no less than that allowable under the law. If the taxpayer claimed a higher deduction than was allowable and that deduction was allowed for tax purposes (i.e., actually deducted on the taxpayer's return), the basis reduction is that higher allowed amount. If a taxpayer takes no depreciation, then the amount allowable is the amount allowable under the straight-line method. Code Sec. 1016; Reg. §1.1016-3(a)(2)(i). (Basis, of course, is not reduced for depreciation on assets where it is not allowable, such as on personal use assets as a residence or personal automobile.)

EXAMPLE 10.3	Judy Jergens purchased a business building in January 2002 for $390,000 to be depreciated straight-line over 39 years. She took depreciation of $10,000 a year from 2002 through 2012 and none for 2013 and 2014. She sold the asset on January 2, 2015, for $450,000 and reported a $170,000 gain ($450,000 – ($390,000 – $110,000)). She was incorrect, however, because she should have reduced the basis by the greater of the allowed or allowable depreciation, and $10,000 depreciation was also allowable for 2013 and 2014. Thus, her gain should have been $190,000 ($450,000 – ($390,000 – $130,000)).

Basis may also be reduced by the amortization of a premium on taxable bonds at the taxpayer's election, and a reduction in interest income in computing taxable income is then allowed. The basis is reduced because it is a recovery of the cost. If no election to amortize premium on taxable bonds is made, then the taxpayer recognizes a smaller capital gain or a larger capital loss upon ultimate sale or disposition. The premiums on tax-exempt bonds must be amortized for purposes of reducing basis, but no reduction in interest income in computing taxable income is allowable because the interest income is not included in taxable income. Reg. §1.171-1(b).

EXAMPLE 10.4	On January 2, 2015, Vernon Vaughn paid $1,200 for a $1,000 face value taxable bond which will mature on January 1, 2025, and he elects to amortize the premium. For 2015, he is allowed a $20 reduction in interest income, and the adjusted basis of the bond at December 31, 2015, is $1,180. If the bond is tax-exempt, the basis is reduced to $1,180, but no reduction in interest income is allowed in computing taxable income.

¶10,030   **HOLDING PERIOD**

Property has to be held for longer than one year to be long-term. Code. Sec. 1222. In figuring the holding period, the day the property was acquired is excluded, but the day it was disposed of is included. Holding period will be discussed in detail in Chapter 12.

¶10,035   **RECOGNITION AND NONRECOGNITION OF GAIN OR LOSS**

If a realized gain or loss is recognized, the gain is includible and the loss is deductible in determining taxable income. Thus, "recognition" means that the result of a particular transaction is considered to be taxable income or a deductible loss. Generally, recognition occurs at the time of sale or exchange.

There are certain situations where the realized gain or loss is not recognized. In the case of like-kind exchanges, part or all of the gain or loss may not be recognized. Also, in the case of involuntary conversions and sales of residences, part or all of the realized gain may not be recognized (Chapter 11).

There are also situations where a realized gain may be recognized, but realized losses are not recognized. For example, a sale of a personal-use asset, such as an automobile, results in gain recognition but not loss recognition. (An exception to the latter rule is that losses resulting from casualty and theft of personal-use assets are deductible, provided they exceed certain limits, but the condemnation loss on a personal-use asset is not deductible.) Similarly, sales between related taxpayers may result in gain recognition but no loss recognition. Code Sec. 267(a)(1).

Exhibit 1. Gain or Loss Summary

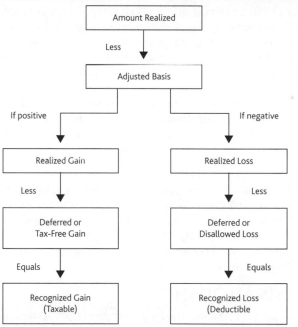

The following examples and Exhibit 1 illustrate the above rules.

EXAMPLE 10.5   Albert Austin sold for $14,000 stock with an adjusted basis of $10,000. His realized and recognized gain is $4,000. If he sells the stock for $7,000, his realized and recognized loss is $3,000.

EXAMPLE 10.6   Ellen Eagle trades in a business machine with an adjusted basis of $10,000 for another like-kind business machine with a fair market value of $15,000. Although she realizes a gain of $5,000, this gain is not recognized because of the like-kind provisions of Code Sec. 1031.

EXAMPLE 10.7	Patrick Power has land with an adjusted basis of $50,000 that was condemned, and the authorities gave him a $75,000 award. Although Patrick has a $25,000 realized gain, he does not have to recognize this gain if the land were replaced with land costing $75,000 or more.

EXAMPLE 10.8	Karen Kohl sells her personal use automobile that cost her $10,000 for $12,000. She has a $2,000 realized gain which must be recognized. If she sells it for $7,000, she has a $3,000 realized loss but none of it is recognized.

EXAMPLE 10.9	Joyce Johnson sells stock costing $8,000 to her brother, Fred, for $12,000. The $4,000 realized gain must be recognized by Joyce. If Joyce sells the stock to Fred for $5,000, the $3,000 realized loss is not recognized because the stock was sold to a related party.

Determination of Basis

Basis is important in computing (1) gain or loss on sale or disposition of property and (2) MACRS or depreciation deductions, cost depletion, and amortization.

¶10,101 COST

The original basis for property is its cost, except as otherwise provided in the law. The cost is the amount paid for such property in cash or other property. Code Sec. 1012; Reg. §1.1012-1(a). Basis includes acquisition costs such as commissions, legal fees, recording fees, sales taxes, as well as installation and delivery costs. The cost of property includes not only the amount of money or other property paid but also the amount of mortgage or liability incurred in connection with the purchase. It makes no difference whether the taxpayer assumes the liability or merely takes the property subject to the liability. When the property is disposed, any remaining amount of mortgage or liability of which the seller is relieved is treated as part of the amount realized. Real estate taxes are included as part of the property's basis if the buyer assumes the seller's obligation to pay them. In some cases, a taxpayer may elect to deduct certain expenditures (such as interest) currently or capitalize them. Code Sec. 266; Reg. §1.266-1(b).

EXAMPLE 10.10	Rodney Reeves purchased a new machine to be used in his business. He paid $20,000 in cash and signed a note payable in the amount of $40,000. In addition, he paid $3,000 in state sales tax, installation charges of $2,000, and delivery charges of $1,000. Rodney's cost basis of the machine is $66,000 ($20,000 + $40,000 + $3,000 + $2,000 + $1,000).

¶10,115 BASIS ALLOCATION

If a single transaction involves a number of properties, in order to establish their basis, the total cost must be allocated among the separate properties according to their relative fair market value. The basis that each property takes as a result of this allocation is the original unadjusted basis for tax purposes. This rule applies in determining basis for gain or loss and depreciation purposes. Reg. §§1.61-6(a) and 1.167(a)-5.

EXAMPLE 10.11	Cathy Camper purchases a tract of land for $2,500,000 with an office building on it. The contract does not specify the amount for each piece of property, so relative fair market value is used to allocate the basis. If the fair market value of the building is $1,800,000 and the fair market value of the land is $1,200,000, the building basis is $1,500,000 and the remaining $1,000,000 is allocated to the basis of the land.

Allocation is necessary for several reasons. Some of the property may be depreciable (buildings) and other property not depreciable (land). Different treatment may be necessary for the assets—such as Section 1231 assets compared to capital asset treatment. (See Chapter 12.) Or it may be that only some of the assets purchased are sold. If only one item is involved, allocation may be required because of different treatment such as in the case where part of the asset is used for business and part for personal use. Or the initial one asset may be sold in separate transactions, such as when a piece of land is divided into two parcels and sold. If a business is purchased, goodwill is assigned to the excess of the purchase price over the fair market value of the assets. Code Sec. 1060.

PLANNING POINTER	The purchaser will likely want an allocation to depreciable assets as high as possible so as to obtain larger depreciation in the future. From a seller's viewpoint, it may be preferable to have a larger amount allocated to nondepreciable assets, so as to get potentially more capital gain treatment (Chapter 12). Purchasers and sellers are required to specify the values of individual assets where multiple assets are acquired in a single transaction (Form 8594).

¶10,125 STOCK DIVIDENDS

Allocation of basis may also be necessary in the case of nontaxable stock dividends and nontaxable stock rights. For nontaxable stock dividends, the basis of the original stock is allocated to the old and new shares. Code Secs. 305(a) and 307; Reg. §§1.305-1–1.305-7. See ¶4401 for further discussion on the determination of whether or not stock dividends and stock rights are taxable. In the case of identical stock (common on common), the basis of the original common shares is allocated among the total number of shares owned. The holding period begins on the day following the date of the original acquisition. To be held long-term, an asset must be held more than one year. For a discussion of holding period, see ¶12,201–¶12,215.

If the stock is not identical (e.g., preferred shares received on common), then the basis of the common stock is allocated between the common and preferred stock according to the relative fair market value.

EXAMPLE 10.12	Curt Coleman owns 1,000 shares of Brockwood Corp. common stock and receives a nontaxable 20 percent common stock dividend. He paid $12,000 for the stock originally ($12 per share). His basis per share on both the old and new shares is $10 ($12,000/1,200).

EXAMPLE 10.13	Assume instead that Curt received a nontaxable preferred stock dividend of 100 shares of Brockwood Corp. preferred shares when the fair market value (FMV) of the preferred was $80 per share and the fair market value of the common was $16 per share. Then the basis of the preferred shares is $4,000 as follows:

$$\left[\frac{\text{FMV of Preferred Stock}}{\text{FMV of Preferred Stock} + \text{FMV of Common Stock}} \times \text{Basis of Common Stock} \right]$$

$$\left[\frac{\$8,000}{\$8,000 + \$16,000} \times \$12,000 \right]$$

and the basis of the common shares is $8,000 ($12,000 – $4,000).

In the case of taxable stock dividends, the amount of income is the stock's fair market value at the date of distribution. The basis of the new stock is its fair market value at the time of the receipt of the stock dividend and the basis of the old stock remains the same. The holding period of the new stock begins on the day following the date of the receipt of the stock dividend.

EXAMPLE 10.14	Jim Juniper owns 1,000 shares of Brown Corp. common stock with a basis of $5,000. He receives a 20 percent taxable stock dividend when the fair market value of each share of stock is $8. Jim reports $1,600 of income (200 shares at $8) and his basis for the new shares is $8 per share. The holding period of the new shares begins on the day following the date of receipt of the stock dividend. His basis in the old stock remains the same.

¶10,130 STOCK RIGHTS

If nontaxable stock rights are received, whether or not any part of the basis of the stock is allocated to the rights depends on the fair market value of the rights as compared with the fair market value of the stock. If the fair market value of the rights at the time of the distribution is less than 15 percent of the fair market value of the old stock at that time, the basis of such rights is zero unless the taxpayer elects to allocate. If the value is 15 percent or more, a basis must be allocated to the rights, but only if the rights are exercised or sold. The stock basis is allocated between the stock and the rights according to the relative fair market value at their distribution date.

If nontaxable rights are sold, the holding period begins on the day following the date the original stock was acquired. Code Sec. 1223(5); Reg. §1.1223-1(e). If the rights are exercised, the new stock's holding period starts on the day following the date of exercise. Reg. §1.1223-1(f).

EXAMPLE 10.15	On January 19, 2014, Florence Frost purchased 100 shares of Duke Corporation common stock for $88 per share. On July 22, 2015, she received 100 nontaxable rights to subscribe to 100 additional shares at $90 per share. The fair market value of each right was $10 and the fair market value of each share of stock is $100 on the date of issuance of the rights. Since the relative fair market value is less than 15 percent, Florence need not allocate any of her basis in the stock to the rights. Any proceeds from the sale of the rights are long-term capital gain and the basis of the new shares that may be purchased through exercise of the rights is the subscription price of $90.

EXAMPLE 10.16	If Florence in the preceding example elected to allocate part of the basis of the stock to the rights, she would allocate $800 to the 100 rights, or $8 per right as follows:

$$\left[\frac{\text{FMV of Rights}}{\text{FMV of Rights} + \text{FMV of Stock}} \times \text{Basis of Stock} \right]$$

$$\left[\frac{\$1,000}{\$10,000 + \$1,000} \times \$8,800 \right]$$

If one-half or 50 of the rights are sold for $1,000, there is $600 long-term capital gain ($1,000 − $400). If 50 rights are exercised, the basis of each share obtained through exercise of the rights is $98 ($90 + $8) and the holding period for the new shares begins on the day following the date of exercise of the rights.

Note: The property must be held more than 12 months to be long-term and to be eligible for the lowest capital gains rate (i.e., a maximum rate of 15 percent or 20 percent for those in the 39.6 percent tax bracket). Property is held short-term if it is held 12 months or less. (See Chapter 12 for more discussion.).

PLANNING POINTER

With the opportunity to elect to allocate part of the basis of the stock to the rights, the taxpayer has the opportunity to control income to a limited extent. In Example 10.16 above where Florence sold 50 rights for $1,000, she has either $1,000 long-term capital gain if she did not allocate any of the basis of the stock to the rights or $600 long-term capital gain if she did allocate basis to the rights. The latter might be preferable if she already had capital gains from other transactions. If, on the other hand, she had capital losses, she might prefer not to allocate basis to the rights so as to offset a larger $1,000 capital gain against her losses.

In the case of taxable stock rights, the amount of income and the basis of the rights constitute the fair market value of the rights at the date of distribution, and the holding period of the rights begins on the day following the date of distribution. If the rights are exercised, the basis of the new shares is the subscription price plus the basis of the rights, and the holding period of the new shares begins on the day following the date of exercise. The basis and holding period of the old stock remain the same.

EXAMPLE 10.17

Betty Blue owns 100 shares of King Corp. stock purchased in January 2013 for $1,300. On January 20, 2015, she receives 100 taxable stock rights valued at $300 with the right to purchase additional shares at $15. Betty reports $300 income as a result of receipt of the stock rights, which is also the basis of the rights. The holding period of the rights begins on January 21, 2015. On February 23, 2016, she exercises 50 rights and sells the remaining 50 rights for $4 each. The basis of each new share is $18 ($15 + $3) and the holding period begins on the day following the date of exercise. She has long-term capital gain of $50 (50 × ($4 − $3)) on the sale of the rights, and since the rights were held longer than 12 months the gain will be taxed at a maximum rate of 15 percent (assuming her taxable income is less than $413,200).

¶10,135 FAIR MARKET VALUE

If property is received in exchange for services, there is a taxable transaction. If property is acquired in a taxable exchange, the basis of the property received is generally its fair market value at the time of exchange. See ¶10,015 for definition of fair market value.

EXAMPLE 10.18

Wilbur Wilson gives up inventory with a basis of $2,000 in exchange for a machine with a fair market value of $3,000. He has a realized and recognized gain of $1,000. His basis in the machine is the fair market value of $3,000.

EXAMPLE 10.19

Diane Davis does accounting work for Wanda Wales, and, in exchange for the services rendered, she receives a ring with a fair market value of $500. Diane reports $500 of income and has a basis of $500 for the ring (i.e., the fair market value).

Other situations may require the use of fair market value as basis. If the price paid is a bargain purchase, then the basis of the property is its fair market value. Reg. §§1.61-2(d)(2)(i) and 1.301-1(j). For example, assume an employee pays only $4,000 for an asset purchased from his employer when the fair market value is $7,000. The employee reports $3,000 as income and has a basis in the asset of $7,000, its fair market value. On the other hand, if the price paid for property includes payments made for reasons other than the acquisition of the asset (such as making a capital contribution or helping out a family member), then the amount in excess of the fair market value is not included in the buyer's cost or basis.

¶10,145 PROPERTY ACQUIRED BY GIFT

A taxpayer's original basis for property acquired by gift is the same as the property's adjusted basis in the hands of the donor or the last preceding owner by whom it was not acquired by gift. If, however, the property's fair market value at the time of the gift is less than the adjusted basis to the donor, then the basis for determining *loss* is the fair market value at the time of the gift. Code Sec. 1015(a). A selling price of gift property between the basis for determining gain and a lesser fair market value will result in neither gain nor loss. If the property was depreciable property to the donor, the gain basis is used by the donee to calculate depreciation, cost recovery, or amortization. Reg. §1.167(g)-1.

The holding period of gift property begins on the day following the date the property was acquired by the donor. If, however, the fair market value of the property at the date of the gift was less than the donor's adjusted basis and the property is sold at a loss, the holding period begins on the day following the date of the gift. Code Sec. 1223(2); Reg. §1.1223-1(b).

EXAMPLE 10.20	On June 3, 2013, Mary Marvel buys stock for $25,000, and, on January 21, 2015, she gives the stock to her daughter Irene when its fair market value is $28,000.

1. If Irene sells the property for $32,000 on June 7, 2015, her gain is $7,000 ($32,000 – $25,000). The gain will be a long-term capital gain since Irene includes in her holding period the time the stock was held by Mary.
2. If Irene sells the property for $24,000, she will have a long-term capital loss of $1,000 ($24,000 – $25,000).

EXAMPLE 10.21	Assume that the fair market value of the stock in Example 10.20 on the date of the gift is $22,000 instead of $28,000.

1. If Irene sells the property for $20,000, the loss is $2,000 ($20,000 – $22,000) and it will be short-term capital loss since the holding period begins on the day following the date of the gift when fair market value is used as the basis.
2. If Irene sells the property for $23,000, she will have neither gain nor loss. In other words, in this example, any selling price between $22,000 and $25,000 results in no gain or loss.

PLANNING POINTER	Taxpayers should avoid making gifts of property that have a fair market value less than basis because neither the donor nor the donee is able to take a deduction for the unrealized loss that occurred between the original acquisition and the gift by the donor. The donee is not able to take the deduction for the unrealized loss because of the loss rules for gift property. A better alternative is for the donor to sell the property that has declined in value, take the loss deduction (assuming it is deductible), and then give the proceeds to the donee. If, however, there is the expectation that the donee will keep it until the value exceeds the adjusted basis in the hands of the donor, then the donor may still wish to consider giving property that has declined in value.

EXAMPLE 10.22	Allen Armstrong has 300 shares of Pierce Corporation stock that he purchased five years ago for $30,000. Allen would like to give the property to his son Michael, but the total fair market value is now only $20,000. If the gift is made and Michael sells the stock for $20,000, neither Allen nor Michael will be able to take advantage of the $10,000 loss deduction for the decline in value. Allen should sell the stock, take the loss deduction (subject to the capital loss rules), and then give the proceeds to Michael. If, however, Michael wants to keep the stock, and it is expected that the stock will increase in value to above the $30,000 basis for determining gain, Allen should feel free to give the stock to Michael.

Increase in Basis for Gift Taxes Paid

The basis of gift property may be increased if gift taxes were paid by the donor. If the property's fair market value at the date of the gift is greater than the donor's adjusted basis, then the donee's basis is increased by all or a portion of the gift tax paid by the donor.

For gifts made after December 31, 1976, the basis is increased by the portion of gift tax that is attributable to the net appreciation in value of the gift. Net appreciation in value is defined as the amount by which the fair market value of the gift exceeds the donor's adjusted basis immediately before the gift. Code Sec. 1015(d)(6). The amount of basis increase is as follows:

$$\frac{\text{Net appreciation}}{\text{Taxable amount of gift}} \times \text{Gift tax paid}$$

This adjustment plus the donor's adjusted basis becomes the basis for asset write-offs and for gain or loss determination.

EXAMPLE 10.23	In 2015, Todd Tromb gave property with an adjusted basis of $34,000 to Stephen Strom when the fair market value was $74,000. After the exclusion, gift taxes paid on the property were $7,500. Since the net appreciation is $40,000 and the taxable amount of the gift after the $14,000 gift tax exclusion is $60,000, two-thirds of the gift taxes, or $5,000, is added to $34,000 to obtain a $39,000 basis.

EXAMPLE 10.24	If the adjusted basis to Todd in Example 10.23 is $80,000, there is no appreciation and none of the $7,500 gift tax is added to determine the donee's basis. In this case, Stephen's gain basis is $80,000; his basis for determining loss is $74,000, the fair market value at the time of the gift.

If a gift consists of several items, then the taxpayer must allocate the gift tax paid with respect to each item. Also, a special allocation of gift taxes must be made where a taxpayer receives a gift of property from a donor who has made gifts to more than one person during the year the gift taxes were paid. Code Sec. 1015(d)(2).

For gifts made prior to 1977, the full amount of the gift tax is added to the donor's adjusted basis, but the basis may not be increased above the fair market value at the date of the gift. Code Sec. 1015(d)(1).

EXAMPLE 10.25	Assume that in 1976 Todd gave Stephen property with an adjusted basis of $50,000 when its fair market value was $60,000. Gift taxes paid on the property were $7,500. Then Stephen's basis is $57,500. If the fair market value was $55,000 at the time of gift, then the basis increase would have been limited to $55,000 since the addition of gift taxes paid cannot cause the donee's basis to go above the fair market value at the time of the gift.

PLANNING POINTER	The donor is able to avoid recognition of gain on any appreciated property by giving away the property. Assuming that the donee sells the property and that the donee is in a lower tax bracket, there could be benefits from making the gift. Also, since the basis of appreciated property would be increased for at least a portion of gift taxes paid, this would provide a "step-up" in basis. Even if the low tax bracket donee keeps the property for some time, there may be an advantage to making the gift.

¶10,175   PROPERTY ACQUIRED FROM DECEDENT

The general rule is that the basis of property acquired from a decedent is the fair market value of the property at the date of the decedent's death. Code Sec. 1014(a). This is often referred to as a "step-up" in basis since the fair market value of property of the decedent is generally more than the adjusted basis. The effect of this rule is that any appreciation while the decedent owned the property escapes income taxation. However, there could, of course, be a "step-down" in basis if the fair market value of the property at the date of the decedent's death were lower than the adjusted basis. In this case, the decline in value while the decedent owned the property is not recognized for income tax purposes.

EXAMPLE 10.26	If Sally Sparrow purchased land parcel A for $5,000 in 1975 and it appreciated in value to $100,000 by 2015, when she died, her daughter Jane, the heir, will have $100,000 as her basis in the land. Thus, the $95,000 increase in value is never subject to income taxation. If Sally owned land parcel B costing $50,000 in 2005 that declined in value to $30,000 by 2015, when she died, Jane would have $30,000 as the basis in land. Here, the $20,000 decline in value while Sally owned the land is not deductible for tax purposes. **Note:** The basis of the property is the same as the value placed on the property for estate tax purposes. There is no basis adjustment for any estate tax that may have been paid on the property. (Contrast this with the gift tax adjustment for the basis of gift property.)

Under the 2001 Act, the step-up in basis at death did not apply to decedents dying during 2010 and electing not to be subject to the estate tax. In general, the property passing out of an estate was subject to the gift tax rules governing basis. Code Sec. 1022(a). Basis was the lesser of the decedent's adjusted basis in the property or the fair market value of the property at the decedent's death. However, the decedent's spouse could receive $3 million of basis increase allocated to property that the spouse was to receive directly or in a qualifying marital trust. Code Sec. 1022(d)(4)(B)(iii). Also, an executor could allocate an aggregate basis increase of up to $1.3 million regardless of the beneficiary of the property. Code Sec. 1022(d)(4)(B)(i). Congress reinstated the step-up basis rules for 2011 and the step-up basis rules are used throughout the chapter.

PLANNING POINTER	As a general rule, appreciated property should be retained until death. Selling it causes gain to be recognized. Giving it away results in the donee taking the donor's low carryover basis. Conversely, property that has declined in value should be sold in order to take any available deductions for recognized losses.

EXAMPLE 10.27	Assuming the same facts as in the preceding example, if Sally had sold land parcel A, she would have recognized $95,000 gain. If she had given the property to Jane, Jane would use $5,000 as the carryover basis. If Sally had sold parcel B for $30,000, she would have had a loss of $20,000. Giving it to Jane would have been a poor choice since Jane would have taken as her basis the fair market value at the date of the gift if she sold it for less than $30,000 and none of the $20,000 decline in value would have been recognized by either party.

Alternate Valuation

If the executor elects for estate tax purposes to value the decedent's gross estate as of six months after death, the basis of the property is the fair market value at that time. Code Sec. 1014(a)(2). If the property is distributed before the alternate valuation date, the basis is the fair market value at the date of distribution or other disposition. The alternate valuation may be used only where the election will reduce both the value of the decedent's gross estate and the federal estate tax liability. Code Sec. 2032(a)(2) and (c).

EXAMPLE 10.28	Edward Eggard died during the year, and property he owned with an adjusted basis of $50,000 and a fair market value of $150,000 went to his beneficiary, Larry Larsen. The executor elected to value the property at the alternate valuation date when the value was $140,000. In this case, $140,000 is the basis to Larry even if the property is distributed later. If, however, the property was distributed three months after Edward's death when the fair market value was $145,000 and the executor chose the alternate valuation date, the basis to Larry is $145,000.

Exception

Where appreciated property was acquired by the decedent by gift during the one-year period before death and the property is acquired from the decedent by the original donor, the adjusted basis to the recipient is the adjusted basis in the hands of the decedent immediately before death. Code Sec. 1014(e).

EXAMPLE 10.29	Ken Kooms gave property to Wesley, his father, when the adjusted basis of the property was $5,000 and the fair market value was $75,000. Wesley died six months after the gift (when the property was valued at $80,000) and he left the property to Ken. Ken's basis in the property will be $5,000, the basis to Wesley at the time of his death. If Wesley had lived more than a year, then Ken's basis would have been the fair market value at the date of Wesley's death.

Survivor's Basis

For property that is jointly owned, the part of the property included in the estate of the decedent is considered to be acquired from the decedent by the survivor. In noncommunity property states, the survivor's basis in the part of the property included in the decedent's estate is the fair market value on the date of death (or alternate valuation date). The basis of the property not included in the decedent's estate is cost or other basis. Code Sec. 2040.

| EXAMPLE 10.30 | William and Nancy North live in a noncommunity property state and bought property jointly for $100,000. When William died, the total property value was $150,000 and $75,000 was included in his estate. Nancy's basis in the property after William's death is $125,000 (her $50,000 plus the $75,000 value of William's portion). |

Property which represents both the surviving spouse's share of community property and the decedent's share of community property will have a basis equal to its fair market value on the date of the decedent's death. Code Sec. 1014(b)(6).

| EXAMPLE 10.31 | Edwin and Dawn Durham live in a community property state and own community property acquired for $200,000. If Edwin dies when the fair market value is $500,000, one-half or $250,000 is included in Edwin's estate. If Dawn inherits Edwin's share of community property, the total basis of the property is $500,000 ($250,000, or Dawn's share of the community property, plus $250,000, the value of Edwin's property at the date of his death). |

Holding Period

The holding period of property acquired from a decedent is long-term. This is the case regardless of how long the beneficiary or decedent held the property and regardless of whether the property is disposed of at a gain or at a loss.

| EXAMPLE 10.32 | Norton Newbert purchases property on December 16, 2014, and dies on January 17, 2015. The property is distributed on February 17, 2015, to Perry Portman, who sells it on May 17, 2015. Even though Perry held the property only three months and the total time from acquisition by Norton to sale by Perry was only five months, the gain or loss will be deemed to be long-term. |

¶10,201 STOCK TRANSACTIONS

Identification of Shares

When a seller can identify the shares of stock sold or transferred, the basis is the basis of the stock so identified. Shares of stock are adequately identified if it can be shown that shares which were delivered to the buyer were from a lot acquired on a certain date or for a certain price. Reg. §1.1012-1(c)(2). If the shares of stock were purchased at different dates or at different prices and the lot from which the stock was sold or transferred cannot be adequately identified, the stock sold is charged against the earliest of the stock purchases (i.e., the FIFO rule). Reg. §1.1012-1(c)(1).

| EXAMPLE 10.33 | Violet Vernon acquires 100 shares of Wilson Corp. stock in 2012 at $15 a share and 200 shares of Wilson stock in 2013 at $25 a share. If she sells 200 shares in 2015 for $35 a share and can specifically identify the shares sold as those from the 2013 purchase, she has a $2,000 gain (($35 – $25) × 200). If she cannot specifically identify the shares, she must assume that 100 shares were from the 2012 purchase and the remaining 100 were from the 2013 purchase. Her gain in that case is $3,000 (($35 – $15) × 100) + (($35 – $25) × 100). |

| PLANNING POINTER | Specific identification of shares makes it easier to control income. If a lower income is desired, higher cost shares may be specifically identified as being sold. If, on the other hand, a higher income from sale of stock is preferable (perhaps because other income is low this year but expected to be high in future years), lower cost shares may be specifically identified as being sold. |

If stock is held by a broker or agent, an adequate identification is made if the taxpayer specifies to the broker the particular shares to be sold and within a reasonable time receives a written confirmation of the transfer instruction. If a single stock certificate represents stock from different lots, where such certificate is held by the taxpayer and where the taxpayer sells a part of the stock represented by such a certificate through a broker an adequate identification is made if the taxpayer specifies to the broker the particular shares to be sold and within a reasonable time receives a written confirmation of transfer instruction. Reg. §1.1012-1(c)(3).

Wash Sales

Wash sales occur when substantially identical stock is bought within 30 days before or after the sale. No deduction for losses is allowed on the sale of stock or securities if, within a period beginning 30 days before the date of the sale and ending 30 days after the date of sale, substantially identical stock or securities are acquired. Code Sec. 1091(a). Substantially identical stock or securities means the same in all important particulars such as earning power, interest rate, value of assets, preference, etc. Rev. Rul. 58-210, 1958-1 CB 523. Also, no deduction is allowed if the taxpayer has during that 61-day period entered into a contract or option to acquire substantially identical stock or securities. Reg. §1.1091-1(a).

The purpose of the wash sale rules is to prevent a tax avoidance scheme. Without the rules, taxpayers would be able to sell securities on which they could show a loss and then buy back substantially identical securities. With the wash sale rules, the realized loss is disallowed; however, the disallowed loss is not "lost" but is added to the basis of the newly acquired stock. Code Sec. 1091(d); Reg. §1.1091-2. In adding the disallowed loss to the cost of the new acquired stock, the taxpayer ultimately will be able to recover the cost of the new stock and the unrecovered cost of the old stock. The holding period of the new securities purchased in a wash sale includes the period the old securities were held. Code Sec. 1223(4).

EXAMPLE 10.34

Simon Sugarman has the following transactions:

September 12, 2014:	Purchases 100 shares of Winston Corp. stock for $20 a share.
February 24, 2015:	Sells 75 shares of stock purchased on September 12, 2014, for $14 per share.
March 7, 2015:	Purchases 50 shares of Winston Corp. stock for $15 per share.
November 17, 2015:	Sells the remaining 75 shares for $12 a share.

The results of the above transactions are as follows:

1. On the February 24, 2015 sale, the realized loss is $450, but $300 of it is disallowed and $150 is short-term loss (stock held less than 12 months). Only two-thirds of the realized loss is disallowed because only two-thirds (50 out of 75) is considered to be a wash sale (i.e., because 50 shares are later purchased on March 7).
2. The basis of the 50 shares acquired on March 7, 2015, is $1,050 ($750 + $300).
3. The loss realized on November 17, 2015, is $650, computed as follows:

Selling price		$900
Basis: $20 × 25 shares	$500	
March 7 stock	1,050	1,550
Loss		$(650)

It is considered long-term loss since the holding period of the stock acquired on March 7, 2015, includes the holding period from September 12, 2014, to February 24, 2015.

¶10,215   PERSONAL-USE PROPERTY CONVERSION

When property purchased for personal use is converted to business or income-producing use, the basis for determining loss is the lesser of (1) the fair market value of the property at the time of the conversion, or (2) the adjusted basis for loss at the time of the conversion. Reg. §1.165-9(b)(2). This rule is to prevent the taxpayer from converting a nondeductible personal loss into a deductible business loss. The basis for gain is the adjusted basis on the date of conversion. The basis for determining depreciation is the basis for determining loss. Reg. §1.167(g)-1. No gain or loss results on sale of converted personal-use property if the amount realized is between the basis for gain and the basis for loss.

EXAMPLE 10.35

Terry Trudman has a residence that had an adjusted basis of $150,000 but a fair market value of $100,000 at the time of conversion to rental property. The basis for determining loss is $100,000. The basis for determining gain is $150,000, the adjusted basis at the time of the conversion. If $10,000 depreciation (computed on the basis for determining loss) is taken between the time of conversion and sale, the results under the following assumptions are:

1. In a sale for $85,000, the loss is $5,000 or $85,000 – $90,000 ($100,000 –$10,000).
2. In a sale for $175,000, the gain is $35,000 or $175,000 – $140,000 ($150,000 – $10,000).
3. In a sale for $130,000, there is neither gain nor loss because by using the basis for gain one gets a loss of $10,000 ($130,000 – $140,000) and by using the basis for loss, one gets a gain of $40,000 ($130,000 – $90,000).

KEYSTONE PROBLEM

Determine what the initial basis of an asset would be in the following situations:

1. Purchase of asset
2. Bargain purchase
3. Lump-sum purchase of several assets
4. Property acquired by gift
5. Property acquired from a decedent
6. Property converted from personal use to business or income-producing use
7. Property acquired in a wash sale
8. Nontaxable stock dividends and stock rights

¶10,225   RELATED PARTIES

No loss deduction is allowed on sales or exchanges of property, directly or indirectly, between certain related parties. Without this provision, related taxpayers might enter transactions solely for the purpose of obtaining loss deductions and reducing their tax liabilities when the property still remained in the family. With the provision, the Internal Revenue Service does not have to be concerned about the reasonableness of the selling price. Any losses disallowed, however, may be used to offset the gain realized by the related purchaser on a later sale of the property. Code Sec. 267(a) and (d). This offset possibility is available only to the original transferee. The buyer's holding period includes only the time the buyer has held the property and does not include the period held by the seller. Reg. §1.267(d)-1(c)(3).

Related parties under Code Sec. 267(b) and (c) include the following:

1. Members of a family including brothers and sisters (including by the half blood), spouse, ancestors, and lineal descendants
2. A corporation where the taxpayer owns directly or indirectly more than 50 percent in value of the outstanding stock
3. Two corporations where more than 50 percent in value is owned, directly or indirectly, by the taxpayer if either corporation is a personal holding company or a foreign personal holding company during the taxable year
4. A grantor and a fiduciary of any trust
5. A taxpayer and an exempt organization controlled by the taxpayer

EXAMPLE 10.36

Norman Norseman owned stock costing $15,000 which he sold to his son Wayne for $12,000. Norman's $3,000 loss is disallowed. If Wayne later sells the stock for $17,000, he will have a gain of $2,000. His $5,000 realized gain is reduced by Norman's disallowed loss of $3,000. If Wayne sells the stock for $14,000, he does not recognize any gain. The $2,000 realized gain is wiped out by Norman's disallowed loss. If Wayne sells the stock for $10,000, he has a $2,000 recognized loss ($10,000 less $12,000). Norman's disallowed loss does not increase Wayne's loss, but can only reduce the amount of gain recognized. If the property sold was a personal use asset (rather than stock) and sold at $10,000, even the $2,000 loss would not be deductible by Wayne.

In case of a sale or exchange of property, directly or indirectly, between related taxpayers, any gain realized is ordinary income if the property is depreciable property in the hands of the transferee. Related parties for this purpose are (1) a taxpayer and an entity that is controlled by the taxpayer, and (2) a taxpayer and any trust of which such taxpayer is a beneficiary. Code Sec. 1239(a)-(c). This provision keeps a taxpayer, for example, from getting capital gain treatment on a sale of property to a controlled entity and the entity from then getting ordinary depreciation deductions on the amount paid for the property.

¶10,245   INSTALLMENT REPORTING

An installment sale is a disposition of property where at least one payment is to be received after the close of the taxable year in which the disposition occurs. The installment method allows gain to be spread over more than one year. The amount of income recognized is the proportion of the payments received in the year which the gross profit bears to the total contract price. Code Sec. 453(b) and (c). Installment reporting is discussed in more detail in Chapter 13.

EXAMPLE 10.37

On October 21, 2015, Brenda Brewster sells property with an adjusted basis of $30,000 for $100,000. The buyer pays Brenda $20,000 cash at the time of the sale transaction with the remaining $80,000 to be paid in five annual installments of $16,000 beginning in October 2016 with interest at 12 percent. During 2015, Brenda reports $14,000 ($20,000 × 70% gross profit rate), and in each of the following five years she would report $11,200 ($16,000 × 70% gross profit rate) in addition to the interest.

PLANNING POINTER

Installment reporting has advantages. The income is spread over a number of years and helps to keep income out of higher tax brackets. In the preceding example, the taxpayer reports income in six years instead of reporting all of the gain in the year of sale. In addition, because of the time value of money, there is the benefit that the taxpayer will be able to earn income on the taxes that do not have to be paid until future years.

TAX BLUNDERS

1. Harriet Harrison has investment property with an adjusted basis of $50,000 that has declined in value to $30,000 and she gives it to Jane Juniper. Needing cash, Jane sells the property a few months later for $31,000. Jane recognizes no gain or loss because the selling price is between the basis for determining gain ($50,000) and the basis for determining loss ($30,000). Harriet should have sold the property and then given the proceeds to Jane. Then Harriet could have had a $20,000 loss.

2. Paul Paget, age 85, has investment property that he has owned for 40 years with an adjusted basis of $20,000 that has appreciated to $400,000. He gives the property to his son, Tim, who will take $20,000 as his basis. Paul should have kept the property until his death so that Tim would be able to use a stepped-up basis of fair market value at the date of death. (Gift and estate tax considerations could alter the conclusions relating to this hypothetical situation.)

3. George Gainer, age 80, has rental property with an adjusted basis of $100,000 and a fair market value of $40,000. He has taxable income of $90,000. George has made a decision to keep the property because it has been in the family since he was a child. For best results, George should have sold the property and taken the loss deduction. If he gives it away, no one can take a deduction for the decline in value. If he keeps it until his death, the heir takes the fair market value at the date of death as the basis (a step-down in basis, assuming the fair market value remains around $40,000 until his death).

SUMMARY

- Realized gain or loss is the difference between the fair market value of the property received and the adjusted basis of property given up.
- Recognized gain or loss is the amount that appears on the tax return as an included income item or a deductible loss.
- The original basis for property acquired by purchase is its cost.
- Allocation of basis may be necessary in the case of nontaxable stock dividends and nontaxable stock rights.
- A taxpayer's original basis for property acquired by gift is generally the same as the property's adjusted basis in the hands of the donor.
- For inherited property, the general rule is that the basis of the property is the fair market value of the property at the date of the decedent's death.
- If a seller of stock wishes to identify the shares of stock sold, the basis is the basis of the stock so identified; otherwise, a taxpayer should use the FIFO rule.
- No loss deduction is allowed on sales or exchanges of property, directly or indirectly, between certain related parties.
- The installment method allows gain to be spread over more than one year.

QUESTIONS

1. Distinguish between realized gains and losses and recognized gains and losses.

2. How is the adjusted basis of property determined?

3. List three capital additions or expenditures and three capital returns or recoveries and discuss the treatment of each category for tax purposes.

4. Why is allocation of basis necessary?

5. Are gains and losses from the sale or exchange of personal use assets recognized for tax purposes?

6. When is fair market value of an asset used as the basis for an asset?

7. What is the basis and holding period of nontaxable stock dividends?

8. What is the basis and holding period of taxable stock dividends?

9. What is the basis and holding period of nontaxable stock rights?

10. What is the basis and holding period of taxable stock rights and the basis and holding period of the shares of stock if the rights are exercised?

11. What is the basis of gift property?

12. What adjustment, if any, must be made to the basis of property acquired by gift if the gift was made prior to 1977? After 1976?

13. What is the basis of an asset acquired from a decedent?

14. What is the alternate valuation of assets acquired from a decedent?

15. Distinguish the holding period of assets acquired by gift with that of assets acquired from a decedent.

16. How is basis computed when a sale of shares of stock occurs?

17. When is the sale or exchange of stock or securities considered a wash sale? How is any loss treated?

18. What is the basis of a personal use asset that is converted to business or income-producing use?

19. What are the special rules for gains or losses on sales to related parties?

20. What are the benefits of installment reporting?

PROBLEMS

21. Frank Fleming recently purchased some new equipment that he plans to use in his business. He paid $43,000 for the equipment. He also paid $2,500 in delivery and installation costs, $1,600 in legal fees, and $3,800 in sales taxes. What is Frank's basis in this equipment?

22. Martha McDonald purchased an office building in 1995 for $630,000. In 2015, she sells the building for $950,000. Over the years, she had replaced the windows and doors at a cost of $60,000, repainted the exterior at a cost of $15,000, and installed an elevator at a cost of $90,000. Martha had taken straight line depreciation on the building for 20 years, for a total of $400,000.
    a. What is Martha's basis in the building at the time of the sale?
    b. What is her realized gain?
    c. What is her recognized gain?

23. Albert Armstrong sells for $800,000 a business building, which he purchased 14 years ago for $570,000. During the 14 years of ownership, he painted the building at a cost of $7,500, installed an air conditioning system for $60,000, cleaned the carpeting for $3,000, repaired the fence for $5,000, installed permanent bookcases for $40,000, replaced the electrical wiring system at a cost of $150,000, and partitioned off some of the rooms at a cost of $50,000. Albert has taken straight-line depreciation on the building for a total of $420,000. What is his basis in the building at time of sale? What is his realized and recognized gain on the sale of the building?

24. Rex Redd purchased a business building on January 1, 2001, for $975,000 and used the straight-line depreciation over 39 years. He took $25,000 depreciation for 2001 through 2012 and none for 2013 and 2014. He sold the building on January 2, 2015. What is Rex's adjusted basis in the building on January 2, 2015?

25. On January 1, 2014, Rodney Rapp paid $110,000 for taxable bonds with a face value of $100,000 which mature on January 1, 2024. He sold them on December 31, 2015 for $104,000. What is Rodney's gain or loss? What if the bonds were tax exempt?

26. Lance Lang received 50 shares of $10 par value stock from Randy Rainey in return for performing legal services. The fair market value of the 50 shares was $750. What is Lance's basis in the stock and what amount, if any, is included in his taxable income?

27. Which of the following results in a recognized gain or loss?
    a. Sale of stock, which has an adjusted basis of $5,000, for $7,000.
    b. Sale of a personal auto with an adjusted basis of $10,000 for $12,000.
    c. Sale of a personal residence with an adjusted basis of $75,000 for $65,000.

28. Gail Gumm purchased a piece of land, a building, and two trucks for a lump sum of $630,000. On the date of purchase, the land had a fair market value of $125,000, the fair market value of the building was $500,000, one truck is valued at $25,000, and the other at $50,000. What is Gail's basis in the land, the building, and each truck?

29. Gordon Gladstone owns 120 shares of Jones Corp. common stock which he purchased on June 10, 2014, for $1,800. One year later, he received a 25 percent nontaxable common stock dividend. On December 16, 2015, he sold 85 shares at $20 a share. What is the basis of the shares sold and what is Gordon's gain upon sale?

30. On August 2, 2014, Henry Hughes paid $30,000 for 500 shares of Young Corp. common stock. On July 28, 2015, he received a nontaxable 20 percent common stock dividend. On December 23, 2015, he sold the 100 shares received in July for $4,400. What is the basis of the 100 shares sold? What is the gain or loss on the sale? Is it short-term or long-term?

31. Naomi owns 1,000 shares of Nordstrom Corp. common stock which she purchased for $40,000 and later receives a nontaxable preferred stock dividend of 200 shares of Nordstrom preferred stock when the FMV of the preferred was $75 per share and the FMV of the common was $60 per share. What is the basis of the common and preferred shares after the dividend?

32. Jamie owns 1,000 shares of Jasper Corp. common stock with a basis of $20,000. She receives a 10 percent taxable stock dividend when the FMV of each share of stock is $12. How much income does she have? What is the basis in the new shares? When does the holding period of the new shares begin? What is the basis in the old stock?

33. Whitney Wells owns 600 shares of Fargo Company stock. She purchased these shares in 2013 for $30 each. In 2015, she received 600 nontaxable stock rights to subscribe to 600 additional shares at $35/share. The fair market value of each right was $4 and the fair market value of each share of stock is $40. Assume that Whitney exercises 300 of the rights and sells the rest for $4,500.
    a. What is Whitney's basis in the old stock? What is the basis in the new stock?
    b. What is Whitney's basis in the old stock if the fair market value of each right was $8 instead of $4? What is the basis in the new stock?
    c. What is the amount of gain under the assumption in part (b) if Whitney sells the 300 rights for $4,500?

34. Kevin Klein owns 900 shares of Palmer Corp. stock which he purchased three years ago for $65 each. He receives one nontaxable right for each share of stock owned. The rights entitle Kevin to receive one share of stock for every three rights plus the payment of $50 per share. On the date of distribution, the market value of the stock was $75 and the market value of the rights was $12. If Kevin exercises 600 of the rights and sells the remaining rights for $3,000, what is his basis in the old stock, the rights, the newly purchased stock, and what is his gain or loss on the sale?

35. Brian owns 200 shares of Bell Corp. stock purchased in January 2013 for $2,400. On January 30, 2015, he receives 200 taxable stock rights valued at $5 with the right to purchase additional shares at $25.

    a. How much income does Brian have? What is the basis in the rights? When does the holding period of the rights begin?

    b. On February 20, 2016, Brian exercises 100 rights and sells the remaining 100 rights for $7 each. What is the basis of each new share? When does the holding period begin? How much and what kind of gain does he have on the sale of the rights?

36. Bradley Brownstone acquired depreciable gift property from Chester Craine. On the date of the gift, Chester's adjusted basis in the property was $17,000 and the fair market value was $12,000. What is Bradley's basis for purposes of determining a gain? For purposes of determining a loss?

37. Sarah Shore bought 500 shares of stock on October 22, 2014, for $30,000. On March 25, 2015, she gave half the shares to her sister Cindy when the fair market value of the shares was $55 per share. If Cindy sells the property for $14,000, what is her gain or loss?

38. Maria Mann gives Peggy property worth $15,000. Maria's basis in the property is $10,000.
    a. If Peggy sells the property for $17,000, what is her gain or loss on the sale?
    b. If Peggy sells the property for $5,500, what is her gain or loss?
    c. If the fair market value on the date of the gift is $7,500 and Peggy sells the property for $5,500, what is the gain or loss?
    d. If the fair market value is $7,500 and Peggy sells the property for $8,000, what is the gain or loss?

39. In 2015, Paula Pierce receives gift property with a fair market value of $94,000 (adjusted basis to the donor of $34,000). Assume the donor purchased the property in 2005 and paid gift tax of $12,000 on the transfer.
    a. What is Paula's basis for gain and loss?
    b. What is the holding period?

40. In February 2015, Judy Judd gave her son Steven a Mercedes for his graduation gift. The automobile had a basis of $54,000 to Judy but was worth $84,000 at the time of the gift. Judy paid $21,000 gift taxes on the gift. The taxable gift is $70,000 after the $14,000 exclusion. Assume that Steven used the car for business purposes.
    a. What is Steven's gain or loss if the automobile is sold in April 2015 for $86,000?
    b. What is the gain or loss recognized if the car is sold for $55,000?
    c. What is the gain or loss recognized if the fair market value at the time of the gift had been $45,000 instead of $84,000 and Steven sold the car for $86,000?
    d. What is the answer to (c) if the selling price is $44,000?
    e. What is the answer to (c) if the selling price is $47,000?

41. Marsha Moore gave property with an adjusted basis of $28,000 to Alfred when the fair market value of the property was $25,000. Gift taxes paid on the property were $3,000. What is Alfred's basis for gain? What is his basis for loss?

42. Callie Cooper purchased two pieces of property in 1985: Property Q cost $15,000 and Property R cost $30,000. In 2015, when Callie died, she left the property to her daughter, Christy. At that time Property Q had appreciated in value to $80,000 while Property R had declined in value, now worth only $10,000.
    a. What is Christy's basis in each piece of property?
    b. What are the tax consequences of the changes in value of the properties from the time of original purchase to the death of Callie?

43. Beverly Bergman purchased land for $30,000 in 2005. The land was valued at $180,000 on April 15, 2015, when Beverly died. Her son Jack inherited the land. Six months later, on October 15, 2015, the property was valued at $170,000.
    a. What is Jack's basis in the land?
    b. If the executor of Beverly's estate elected the alternate valuation date, what is Jack's basis?
    c. If the executor elected the alternate valuation date but distributed the property on July 21, 2015, what would be Jack's basis?
    d. If the executor elected the alternate valuation date but distributed the property on November 19, 2015, what would be Jack's basis?
    e. If Jack sells the property on December 22, 2015, will he have short-term or long-term gain or loss?

44. Evelyn Everest gave property to her mother Sharon when the adjusted basis of the property was $12,000 and the fair market value was $80,000. Sharon died eight months later when the property was valued at $85,000 and she left the property to Evelyn.
    a. What is Evelyn's basis?
    b. If Sharon had died more than a year after receiving the gift when the fair market value was $85,000, what would the basis have been to Evelyn?

45. Sam Spurr gave property to Robert Reddy when its fair market value was $70,000 and the adjusted basis was $50,000. Robert died two years later when the fair market value of the property was $75,000, and he left the property to Sam. What is Sam's basis in the property?

46. Brothers Andrew and Vincent Vaughn jointly acquired property for $200,000 with rights of survivorship, paying three-fourths and one-fourth, respectively. Andrew died; the property was valued at $300,000 and $225,000 was added to his estate. What is Vincent's basis in the property after Andrew's death?

47. On April 18, 2015, Jane Juniper purchased 30 shares of Bryan Corp. stock for $210, and on September 29, 2015, she purchased 90 additional shares for $900. On November 28, 2015, she sold 48 shares, which could not be specifically identified, for $576 and on December 8, 2015, she sold another 25 shares for $188. What is her recognized gain or loss?

48. Harold Haas owns 100 shares of Spartan Corp. common stock with an adjusted basis of $10,000. On July 28, 2015, he sold all 100 shares for $9,000. On August 18, 2015, he purchased 80 shares of Spartan common stock for $7,500 and 20 shares of Spartan preferred stock for $3,000. What is Harold's recognized gain or loss on the sale and what is his basis per share in the new stock?

49. Ashley Adams owns stock in C Corp costing $25,000. She sells the stock to her daughter, Brittany, for $18,000. Two years later, Brittany sells the stock for $27,000.
    a. What is Ashley's gain or loss on the transaction?
    b. What is Brittany's gain or loss on the transaction?
    c. What is Brittany's gain or loss if she sold the stock for $24,000?
    d. What is Brittany's gain or loss if she sold the stock for $16,000?

50. Brenda Brewster owned stock costing $12,000 which she sold to her daughter, Rita, for $8,000. Rita sold the stock later for $14,000.
    a. What is Brenda's gain or loss?
    b. What is Rita's gain or loss?
    c. If Rita had sold the stock for $10,000, how much gain or loss would she recognize?
    d. If Rita had sold the stock for $6,000, how much gain or loss would she recognize?

51. Emily Eagels owned stock with a basis of $50,000 which she sold to her sister, Janet, for $42,000. Three months later, Janet sold the stock through a broker for $52,000. What is the gain or loss to Emily? What is the gain or loss to Janet?

52. Sheryl Sugarman owned 60 percent of the outstanding stock of Octavian Corp. The corporation sold stock (cost $5,000) to her for $2,500. Sheryl sold the stock for $7,000. What is the corporation's allowed loss? What is Sheryl's gain?

53. On September 16, 2015, Donald Dunn sold for $80,000 property with an adjusted basis of $20,000. The buyer paid $20,000 down with the remaining $60,000 to be paid in four equal annual installments of $15,000 beginning in September 2016 with interest at 12 percent. How much income does Donald report in 2015 and the following four years? Ignore interest.

54. In 2015, Cathy Cummings, single, 66 years of age, and legally blind, had wages and net rental income (after depreciation) of $20,000 and received $500 in interest income. She had $9,000 of allowable itemized deductions. In addition, she had the following transactions during 2015:
    a. She sold stock for $2,800. She had inherited the stock from her father, who had an adjusted basis in the stock of $1,200. The fair market value at the date of his death was $1,800.
    b. During 2014, Cathy had purchased some Almond Corp. stock. On January 22, 2014, she paid $5 a share for 20 shares, and on May 13, 2014, she paid $8 a share for 10 shares. She sold 15 shares during 2015 for $10 a share. Those shares most recently purchased were identified as being sold.
    c. Cathy sold to her sister Janice stock in Bass Corp. for $800. She had an adjusted basis of $950 in this stock.
    d. Cathy built a new house in 2015 and converted her former residence into rental property. At the time of the conversion, the adjusted basis of the old house was $144,000 with a fair market value of $140,000. She sold the rental house for $141,000 in October 2015, four months after its conversion to rental property, and took depreciation of $1,000 for the four months.

    Compute Cathy's taxable income for 2015. Treat all income as ordinary income.

55. During 2015, Peter Patel sold a piece of land he had purchased for $40,000. The buyer paid cash of $50,000 and transferred to Peter a piece of farm equipment having a fair market value of $30,000. The buyer also assumed Peter's $10,000 loan on the land. Peter paid selling expenses of $5,000. What is Peter's recognized gain on this sale?
    a. $25,000
    b. $45,000
    c. $80,000
    d. $90,000

56. During 2005, John Johnson purchased 50 shares of common stock in Corporation DEF for $4,500. In 2011, DEF declared a stock dividend of 20 percent. The new stock received by John in the stock dividend was identical to the old stock. In 2015, DEF's stock split 3 for 1 at a time when the fair market value was $120 per share. What is John's basis in each of his shares of DEF's stock if both distributions were nontaxable?
    a. $120 per share
    b. $90 for 50 shares and zero for all additional shares
    c. $75 for 60 shares and $142.50 for 120 shares
    d. $25 per share

57. During 2015, Mary Maloney received a gift of property from her aunt. At the time of the gift, the property had a fair market value of $164,000, the taxable gift was $150,000, and the adjusted basis to her aunt was $104,000. Mary's aunt paid a gift tax on the property of $45,000. What is the amount of Mary's basis in the property?
    a. $104,000
    b. $122,000
    c. $150,000
    d. $164,000

58. Kenneth King inherited 100 shares of Corporation ABC stock from his father, who died on March 4, 2015. His father paid $17 per share for the stock on May 3, 1995. The fair market value of the stock on the date of death was $63 per share. On September 4, 2015, the fair market value of the stock was $55 per share. Kenneth sold the stock for $68 per share on December 5, 2015. The executor of the estate did not elect the alternate valuation date for valuing the father's estate. An estate tax return was filed. What was Kenneth's basis in the stock on the date of the sale?
    a. $1,700
    b. $4,600
    c. $5,500
    d. $6,300

59. **Comprehensive Problem (Tax Return Problem).** Kevin Korda, age 35, married Emily, age 30, during 2015. Kevin pays alimony of $1,000 a month and provides $7,200 a year in support for his son from a previous marriage. The son lives with Kevin's ex-wife, who provides $3,000 a year in support. During 2015, Kevin earned $45,000 and Emily earned $30,000 at her regular job and $8,000 in self-employment income from selling cleaning products out of her home. Kevin and Emily paid $3,800 state income taxes, $2,500 property taxes on their home, $2,300 charitable contributions, $4,400 interest on their home mortgage, and $3,000 medical expenses. In addition, they had the following transactions during 2015:
    a. Kevin sold for $34,000 property which he had received from his father. His father's basis in the property at the time of the gift was $35,000 and the fair market value was $30,000.
    b. Kevin sold his personal use automobile (adjusted basis of $25,000) for $15,000 and purchased a new car for $28,500.
    c. Emily received $300 in dividends from the 50 shares of $10 par Webster Corp. common stock which she owns. The stock has an adjusted basis of $1,400 to Emily and was purchased on April 28, 2015. On July 19, 2015, she also received 50 nontaxable stock rights with a fair market value of $5 when the fair market value of the stock was $30 per share. Five rights plus $20 entitle her to one share of common stock. On October 24, 2015, she exercised 30 of the rights and sold the other 20 for $100.

d. Kevin and Emily purchased 50 shares of Waverly Corp. stock for $35 a share on April 18, 2015. On May 19, 2015, they purchased 30 more shares for $45 each and on June 16, 2015, they purchased 20 shares for $50 each. On August 11, 2015, they sold 75 shares for $4,500.

Compute Kevin and Emily's taxable income. Treat any gain as ordinary income. Ignore the self-employment tax considerations.

60. **Comprehensive Problem (Tax Return Problem).** Carl Chubbs, age 64, earned $55,000 during 2015. His wife, Dawn, age 66, is blind. During 2015, Carl and Dawn received $1,000 in dividends. They sold their personal use automobile which they had owned for two years (adjusted basis of $18,500) for $19,000. They sold to their son 50 shares of Riverdale Corp. stock for $500. Their basis was $12 per share; fair market value was $20 per share. Carl and Dawn sold property Carl had inherited from his sister for $12,500. At the time of Carl's sister's death the basis of the property was $7,500 and the fair market value was $10,000; six months after death the fair market value was $9,000. The alternate valuation date was elected by the executor in valuation of the estate of Carl's sister. In addition, Carl and Dawn paid $8,500 interest on their home, made a cash contribution to their college alumni foundation in the amount of $5,000, paid state sales taxes of $500, paid state income taxes of $2,500, paid federal income taxes of $8,000, and had medical expenses of $800. Compute Carl and Dawn's taxable income. Treat all income as ordinary income.

61. **Research Problem.** Brian Bradley, a calendar year taxpayer, purchased 1,000 shares of Newton Corp. stock on October 23, 2014, for $15,000. He sold these shares on January 16, 2015, for $7,000. On each of the four days from January 19 through January 22, 2015, Brian purchased 500 shares of substantially identical stock for $3,000. What is the tax effect for Brian and what will be the basis of each of the four batches of new stock?

Chapter

11

Property Transactions: Nonrecognition of Gains and Losses

OBJECTIVES

After completing Chapter 11, you should be able to:

1. Describe the rules for exclusion of gain on the sale of a personal residence.
2. Discuss the nonrecognition of gain or loss in transactions involving like-kind exchanges and involuntary conversions.
3. Explain the holding period rules for property acquired in a nontaxable exchange.
4. Describe the mandatory rules for recognition and basis of new property and elective rules for nonrecognition and basis of new property in involuntary conversions.
5. Discuss other transactions in which gain or loss may be postponed or deferred, including exchange of property for stock or a partnership interest, exchanges of insurance policies, and exchange of stock in the same corporation by a shareholder.

OVERVIEW

As discussed in the previous chapter, a taxpayer has a realized gain when the fair market value of the property received is greater than the basis of the property given up. On the other hand, there is a realized loss when the fair market value of the property received is less than the basis of the property given up. The realized gain or loss upon a sale or other disposition of property is recognized unless there is a provision for nonrecognition.

This chapter deals with situations where there may be nonrecognition of gain or loss. Sometimes the gain or loss may be permanently excluded, meaning that the gain or loss will never be included in taxable income.

EXAMPLE 11.1	Mary Mertson, single, sold her personal residence for $275,000 so that she could move into a small apartment in a retirement home. Her basis in the residence was $60,000. Mary may exclude the $215,000 realized gain since single taxpayers may exclude up $250,000 of gain on a sale of a personal residence. This is a permanent exclusion.

At other times, however, nonrecognition is temporary in that there is deferral of recognition. This is because the basis of the replacement property will be adjusted to reflect the deferred gain or loss. A deferred or postponed gain is subtracted from the cost of the replacement property while a deferred or postponed loss is added to the cost to determine the basis of the new property.

EXAMPLE 11.2	Sam Sorges exchanged a business machine with an adjusted basis of $40,000 for another business machine with a fair market value of $90,000. The $50,000 realized gain is deferred because it is a like-kind exchange under Code Sec. 1031 and the basis of the new machine is $40,000 (fair market value of replacement property of $90,000 less deferred gain of $50,000). If the replacement property is sold for $95,000 shortly after the exchange, the recognized gain is $55,000. Thus, the original deferred gain of $50,000 and the $5,000 excess of the $95,000 over the $90,000 fair market value of the replacement property ultimately is recognized at the time of sale of the replacement property.

Deferral of gain or loss occurs in certain situations because the economic position of the taxpayer has not really changed in substance. Thus, the taxpayer, for example, by making an exchange of one business machine for another business machine is considered to have a continuation of the original investment. Another reason for nonrecognition of gain is that the transaction frequently results in no increase in resources to pay the tax. This reason is consistent with the wherewithal to pay concept, which recognizes that if a taxpayer lacks the resources coming from the transaction, he or she should not have to pay tax as a result of a transaction.

In this chapter, sales of residence, like-kind exchanges, and involuntary conversions will be discussed in detail, with less attention being devoted to exchanges of property for stock or partnership interests, exchanges of life insurance policies, exchanges of stock in the same corporation by a shareholder, exchanges of U.S. obligations, and reacquisition of real property.

Sale of a Personal Residence

The Taxpayer Relief Act of 1997 repealed Code Sec. 1034 (deferral of gain on sale of residence) and amended Sec. 121 (the once-in-a-lifetime exclusion of gain). Prior law under Code Sec. 1034 allowed taxpayers to defer the gain on the sale of a principal residence if a replacement residence was purchased within two years equal to or exceeding the adjusted selling price of the former residence. The current law under Code Sec. 121 is considerably more generous than the old law.

¶11,001 THE GENERAL RULES

For sales or exchanges of residences after May 6, 1997, married taxpayers may exclude up to $500,000 of gain upon the sale of their residence and single taxpayers may exclude up to $250,000 of their gain. Code Sec. 121(b)(1) and (2). Taxpayers must have owned and occupied the residence as their principal residence for two out of the last five years prior to the sale. Code Sec. 121(b)(3)(A). The exclusion applies to only one sale or exchange every two years. Code Sec. 121(b)(3)(B). For married taxpayers, the exclusion is allowed if (1) either spouse meets the ownership test, (2) both spouses meet the use test, and (3) neither spouse is ineligible for exclusion because of a sale or exchange of a residence within the last two years. Code Sec. 121(b)(2)(B), (C), and (D). Because this exclusion replaces the deferral of gain provision of Code Sec. 1034 and the one-time $125,000 exclusion for taxpayers age 55 or older, application of the exclusion does not result in a reduction of the basis of a replacement residence as was the case under prior law.

EXAMPLE 11.3

> Jack and Jill Jackson sold their residence that they had purchased for $175,000 in September 2005. During the time of their ownership, they made improvements totaling $25,000 and then sold the home in September 2015 for a selling price of $600,000. Their realized gain is $400,000 ($600,000 less $200,000). They can exclude the whole gain since it is less than $500,000.

Taxpayers may elect out of this exclusion provision for any sale or exchange. Code Sec. 121(f). Thus, for example, taxpayers who plan to sell within two years two properties that meet the exclusion eligibility requirements and who first sell the property with the lesser gain may choose to elect out of the exclusion to reserve its use for the second sale where the gain is larger.

The fact that the use of the provision is limited to once every two years does not prevent a husband and wife from filing a joint tax return and each excluding up to $250,000 of gain from the sale of each spouse's principal residence. The rule still applies as long as each spouse would have been eligible to exclude up to $250,000 of gain if the couple had filed separate returns. Further, if a single taxpayer eligible for the exclusion marries someone who has used the exclusion within two years before the marriage, that individual may still use the $250,000 exclusion.

The American Jobs Creation Act of 2004 does not allow an exclusion if the taxpayer sells a principal residence within five years of acquiring the property through a like-kind exchange. The law applies to sales after October 22, 2004.

EXAMPLE 11.4

> Suppose that Jack and Jill in Example 11.3 sold their residence for $800,000. Their realized gain is $600,000, but they can exclude $500,000 and will recognize $100,000. The $100,000 will be taxed at a maximum rate of 15 percent since they had held the residence more than 12 months. See Code Sec. 1(h)(1)(E) and Chapter 12. However, if Jack and Jill sold their residence for only $150,000, they have a realized loss of $50,000 that they will not be able to deduct.

¶11,005 PRINCIPAL RESIDENCE

In order to obtain exclusion of gain, the home must be the principal residence for two of the five years before the sale. A principal residence is the home in which the taxpayer lives. Whether or not a home is the taxpayer's principal residence depends upon all the facts and circumstances in each case. A principal residence can be a houseboat, a house trailer, or stock held by a tenant-stockholder in a cooperative housing corporation or a condominium. Reg. §1.1034-1(c)(3); Rev. Rul. 64-31, 1964-1 CB 300.

In December 2002, Regulations were issued clarifying some controversial areas relating to sale of residence. Taxpayers do not need to allocate gain between the business and residential use if the business use occurred within the same dwelling unit as the residential use. While they may exclude gain on the residence up to the allowed amount, they must pay tax at a maximum rate of 25 percent on any gain attributed to the total depreciation they took after May 6, 1997.

EXAMPLE 11.5	Rose Rambler bought a home in 2010 for $120,000 and used one-third of it as an office in her accounting practice. In 2015, she sells the home for $210,000 (realizing a gain of $90,000). Rose can exclude all of the gain except for the depreciation taken, which would be taxed at a maximum rate of 25 percent.

The Housing Assistance Tax Act of 2008 provides that gain from the sale of a principal residence that is allocable to periods of "nonqualified use" is not excluded from the taxpayer's income. Certain usage is not treated as nonqualified, including leaving the home vacant and temporary absences because of a change in employment, health, or unforeseen circumstances. The new rules apply to periods starting in 2009, but pre-2009 periods are grandfathered in and are considered qualified use. Gain is allocated to periods of nonqualified use based on the ratio of the aggregate periods of nonqualified use during the period the property was owned by the taxpayer to the total period of time the property was owned by the taxpayer. Thus, if a taxpayer bought a home on January 1, 2015, and rented it out until January 1, 2021, when the taxpayer moved into the home, then sold the home on January 1, 2023, the two-out-of-five year ownership and use requirements are met. However, six years out of the eight-year ownership period is nonqualified use, and therefore six eighths of the gain would not be eligible for exclusion.

¶11,015   SPECIAL PROVISIONS

Special provisions are included to consider other types of transactions or events or to take into consideration various types of taxpayers. In keeping with the main provisions of the law, the special provisions also often are more generous to particular taxpayers.

Proration of Exclusion

The $250,000 or $500,000 exclusion can still be prorated if the sale is due to a change in place of employment, a change in health, or unforeseen circumstances, even if a taxpayer does not meet the ownership, usage, or sale within two years requirement. The December 2002 Regulations clarified what could qualify as "unforeseen circumstances." The following must involve the taxpayer, spouse, co-owner, or a member of the taxpayer's household to qualify: death; divorce or legal separation; becoming eligible for unemployment compensation; a change in employment that leaves the taxpayer unable to pay the mortgage or reasonable basic living expenses; and multiple births resulting from the same pregnancy. Damage to the residence resulting from a natural or man-made disaster or an act or war or terrorism, and condemnation, seizure or other involuntary conversion of the property, and other circumstances at the discretion of the IRS Commissioner could also qualify as "unforeseen."

The amount of the exclusion is $250,000 or $500,000 multiplied by the portion that is the shorter of (1) the aggregate periods during which the ownership and use requirements were met during the five-year period ending on the date of the sale or (2) the period after the date of the most recent sale bears to two years. Code Sec. 121(c).

EXAMPLE 11.6	Wilbur and Wanda Windsor purchased a home in San Francisco for $300,000 on August 1, 2014. Wilbur obtains a job in Memphis, and on December 1, 2015, the Windsors sell their home in San Francisco for $750,000. The Windsors realized a $450,000 gain, but because they owned and resided in their home for less than two years (16 months), their exclusion is limited to $333,333 ($500,000 × 16 months divided by 24 months = $333,333), and they would have to recognize $116,667.

EXAMPLE 11.7

Assume that as a result of a job switch, Wilbur and Wanda, who purchased the San Francisco home (#2) on August 1, 2014, did not sell their prior residence (#1) until September 1, 2014. If they sell residence #2 for $750,000 on December 1, 2015, with a $450,000 realized gain, the time between the sale of residence #1 and the sale of residence #2 (9/1/14 to 12/1/15) is shorter than the ownership and use period (8/1/14 to 12/1/15) of residence #2. The proration is based on the shorter period of 15 months and the excluded gain is $312,500 ($500,000 × 15 months divided by 24 months = $312,500), and they would recognize $137,500.

Widowed Taxpayers

A widowed taxpayer's period of ownership of a residence includes the period the deceased spouse owned and used the property before death. Code Sec. 121(d)(2). The Mortgage Forgiveness Debt Relief Act of 2007 allows a surviving spouse to exclude from gross income up to $500,000 of the gain from the sale of a principal residence owned jointly with a deceased spouse if the sale occurs within two years of the death of the spouse and other ownership and use requirements have been met.

EXAMPLE 11.8

If Edwin Edwards dies, his spouse Elaine can sell the home they both occupied and be eligible for the exclusion during the two-year period following his death, provided the two-year ownership requirement was met prior to Ed's death. Elaine would be eligible for the $500,000 exclusion during the two years after his death, but would only be eligible for the $250,000 exclusion in subsequent years as a single taxpayer.

Divorced Taxpayers

In the case of a residence that is transferred to a taxpayer incident to a divorce, the time during which the taxpayer's spouse or former spouse owned the residence is added to the taxpayer's period of ownership. A taxpayer who owns a residence is considered to have used it as a principal residence while the taxpayer's spouse or former spouse is granted use of the residence under the terms of the divorce or separation instrument. Code Sec. 121(d)(3).

EXAMPLE 11.9

Rex and Robin Reed purchased a home for $150,000 on August 11, 2013. On March 26, 2014, they were divorced, and as part of the divorce agreement, the home was transferred to Robin, who sold the home on September 16, 2015, for $250,000. Robin can exclude the $100,000 gain since she owned and used the residence for more than two years.

EXAMPLE 11.10

Assume that in the preceding example, as part of the divorce agreement, Rex retained ownership of the residence but the use of the home was granted to Robin as long as Rex owns the residence. If Rex sells the residence on September 16, 2015, for $250,000, he can exclude the $100,000 gain since he can count the time that Robin used the residence as part of the divorce agreement.

PLANNING POINTER

If taxpayers are contemplating divorce and own a highly appreciated home (over $250,000 of appreciation), it may be preferable to sell the residence before the divorce. Prior to divorce, the full $500,000 exclusion applies, whereas after the divorce if only one of the taxpayers remains the owner, that spouse would be entitled to an exclusion of only $250,000.

Taxpayers should exercise caution in divorce planning. Traditionally, wives have received custody of the children and have often obtained ownership of the home. Now with the gain on the sale of residence eligible for a sizeable amount of exclusion, potential divorcees will need to consider this in their divorce agreement and in their negotiations. For some taxpayers, it may be preferable to sell the home prior to divorce to obtain the full $500,000 exclusion.

Incapacitated Taxpayers

If a taxpayer becomes physically or mentally incapable of self-care, the taxpayer is deemed to use a residence as a principal residence during the time in which the taxpayer owns the residence and resides in a care facility licensed by a State or political subdivision such as in a nursing home. The taxpayer must have owned and used the residence as a principal residence for a period of at least one year during the five years preceding the sale in order to use this provision. Code Sec. 121(d)(7).

EXAMPLE 11.11	Alice Adams purchased a residence for $150,000 on October 7, 2013. In November 2014 she became ill and was confined to a nursing home. On October 21, 2015, she sells her residence for $250,000. Alice can exclude the gain of $100,000 because she has used the residence at least one year during the preceding five years.

Involuntary Conversions

The exclusion is available in cases of involuntary conversion of a residence, such as destruction, theft, seizure, requisition, or condemnation of property, that are treated as a sale or exchange of a residence. Code Sec. 121(d)(5). The amount realized from the sale or exchange of property is reduced by the amount of gain excluded from gross income. If the basis of the property sold or exchanged was determined under the involuntary conversion rules of Code Sec. 1033(b), then the holding and use by the taxpayer of the converted property shall be treated as holding and use by the taxpayer of the property sold or exchanged.

EXAMPLE 11.12	Marvin and Mildred Matson purchased a residence on March 25, 2013, for $160,000. On September 3, 2015, a hurricane completely destroyed their home. The home was insured for its replacement value and homes in the Matsons' area had appreciated greatly. They received insurance proceeds of $460,000. The Matsons do not recognize any of the $300,000 realized gain on the involuntary conversion of their home by the hurricane because it is less than the $500,000 exclusion allowed under Code Sec. 121. If, however, the Matsons had received $725,000 of insurance proceeds (i.e., a realized gain of $565,000), the $725,000 would be reduced by the $500,000 gain excluded, leaving $225,000 of proceeds to be used when applying the gain deferral provision of Code Sec. 1033. In this case, a replacement residence would be required to defer the gain in excess of the exclusion. Thus, a replacement cost of $225,000 or more would be necessary to defer the remaining $65,000 of realized gain.

Co-ops

In the case of a tenant-stockholder of cooperative housing corporation (as defined in Code Sec. 216), the ownership requirement applies to the ownership of the stock of the corporation and the use requirement applies to the house or apartment that the taxpayer is entitled to occupy as a stockholder. Code Sec. 121(d)(4).

EXAMPLE 11.13	Carl Carlson is part owner of Red River Estates, a cooperative housing corporation that owns and manages a 15-unit complex. Carl may exclude gain on the sale of his interest if he owned the stock for at least two of the five years prior to the sale and if he occupied a unit in the complex for at least two of the five years prior to the sale.

PLANNING POINTER

Taxpayers should keep records of capital improvements since there always is the possibility that income might ultimately be recognized in the event they have extraordinarily large profits due to rapid appreciation and/or they keep their residence for a long period of time. If taxpayers personally make a number of capital improvements because they are skilled at making improvements or if they wish to claim a depreciation deduction for a home office or rental use of the residence, good records are also important. Further, if the residence is involved in a divorce settlement or tied up in an estate, accurate records could be critical.

Taxpayers who have large gains (over $500,000 for couples and over $250,000 for single taxpayers) may want to consider retaining the property the remainder of their lives, since the heirs will still get the step up in basis under Code Sec. 1014(a). Assume that Howard and Hilda Haley purchased a home in New York City for $200,000 in 1985 and are considering its sale in 2015. The expected selling price, however, is $2 million, which would require them to recognize gain of $1.3 million ($1,800,000 realized gain less excluded gain of $500,000). Even at a 20 percent maximum tax rate, this would still result in a tax of $260,000. Since the Haleys are in their seventies, they should consider retaining the property until their death since the appreciation will then not be taxed at all. The heirs will have a step-up in basis equal to the fair market value at the date of death. The value of the property, of course, will be included in the decedent's estate for estate tax purposes.

¶11,025   DEFINITIONS RELATED TO RESIDENCE

The following are the major terms encountered in sales of residences.

Amount realized is the selling price reduced by the selling expenses. The selling price includes not only the cash received but also the liability that might be assumed by the buyer. Reg. §1.1034-1(b)(4).

Adjusted basis of the residence is its cost and commissions, plus any capital improvements, less insurance reimbursements and deductible casualty losses, and less any nontaxable gain on the sale of the previous residence under prior law.

Gain realized is the excess, if any, of the amount realized over the adjusted basis of the residence.

Selling expenses include advertising costs, broker commissions, legal fees in connection with the sale, and "points" paid by the seller to obtain a mortgage for the buyer. Reg. §1.1034-1(b)(4); Rev. Rul. 68-650, 1968-2 CB 78.

Like-Kind Exchanges

¶11,201   DEFINITION

Exchanges involving like-kind property held for investment or business purposes can qualify for nonrecognition of gain or loss. The reason for nonrecognition is that the taxpayer is considered to be in the same economic position after the exchange has occurred and so is, in effect, continuing the old investment. Also, unless the taxpayer has received cash or other property, the taxpayer does not have the wherewithal to pay the tax on the realized gain as a result of the exchange transaction.

Section 1031(a) states that "no gain or loss shall be recognized on the exchange of property held for productive use in a trade or business or for investment if such property is exchanged solely for property of like kind which is to be held either for productive use in a trade or business or for investment." The word "solely" is important. If the property received also consists of other non-like-kind property or cash (known as "boot"), gain may be recognized. Code Sec. 1031(b). The nonrecognition rule for like-kind exchanges is mandatory—if one has a like-kind exchange, one must have nonrecognition of gain or loss.

EXAMPLE 11.14

Brad Burns exchanged an office building with an adjusted basis of $75,000 (fair market value $250,000) for another office building with a fair market value of $250,000. Although Brad has realized a gain of $175,000 ($250,000 fair market value received less the adjusted basis of $75,000), he does not recognize any gain under the Section 1031 like-kind exchange provision.

¶11,215   QUALIFYING PROPERTY

Property qualifying for like-kind exchange treatment must be held either for productive use in a trade or business or for investment. However, business property may be exchanged for investment property and vice versa. Property held for personal use does not qualify for nonrecognition but if held for both business and personal use, the business part qualifies. Certain properties are excluded from like-kind exchange treatment. Stock in trade or other property held primarily for sale, stock, bonds, notes, or other securities are not considered properties held for productive use in a trade or business or for investment. The transfer of partnership interests does not fall under the tax-free exchange provisions. Also, livestock of different sexes is not like-kind property. Code Sec. 1031(a) and (e); Reg. §1.1031(a)-1(a).

The words "like-kind" refer to the nature or character of the property and not to its grade or quality. Reg. §1.1031(a)-1(b). The exchange of real property for real property generally qualifies for like-kind exchange treatment. Examples include improved real estate for unimproved real estate, city real estate for a farm, and a lease of real property with 30 years or more to run for real estate. Like-kind treatment also applies to the exchange of personalty for personalty. However, not all exchanges of personalty used for investment or business purposes qualify for nonrecognition. The exchanged property must be of a like class. That is, the property must be within the same general "asset class" as indicated by Rev. Proc. 87-56, 1987-2 CB 674. Some of the business asset classes include:

1. Office furniture, fixtures, and equipment
2. Information systems such as computers and their peripheral equipment
3. Airplanes
4. Automobiles
5. Light general purpose trucks
6. Heavy general purpose trucks

Thus, an exchange of office equipment for a computer would not qualify as a like-kind exchange, nor would a business car for a light general purpose truck. Further, like-kind treatment does not apply to the exchange of realty for personalty. Thus, the exchange of a building (realty) for a machine (personalty) is not a like-kind exchange.

EXAMPLE 11.15

Eugene Eckbert made the following exchanges:

1. Office building for an apartment building
2. Apartment building for a personal residence
3. Land for an office building
4. Jewelry for a new personal automobile
5. Stock held as an investment for a business building
6. Inventory for a business automobile
7. Apartment building for a business truck

Only exchanges (1) and (3) qualify as like-kind exchanges. Exchange (2) is not a like-kind exchange because a personal residence is received; (4) involves personal use items; (5) involves stock; (6) has an exchange of inventory; and (7) involves an exchange of realty for personalty.

PLANNING POINTER	Taxpayers may prefer to avoid the nonrecognition rules. Since the rules are mandatory, taxpayers have to structure the transaction in such a way that the disposal of the old asset is a sale rather than a like-kind exchange. If a gain will be realized, taxpayers may prefer to sell the asset if they are in a low tax bracket in the year of sale, which would mean that the tax would be relatively low, especially if there were some opportunity for special capital gain treatment. In such a case, the basis of the newly purchased asset may be higher than the basis of the new asset if the transaction were a like-kind exchange. The high basis may be preferable especially if the taxpayer expected to be in higher tax brackets in future years.
	If a loss will be realized on disposal of an asset, it may be preferable to recognize it through a sale transaction rather than through a like-kind exchange. This could be especially important if the taxpayer were in a high bracket in the year of sale and in lower brackets in future years when the asset would be depreciated.
	There must be a genuine sale and purchase in order to avoid the Section 1031 nonrecognition rules. If the transaction involves a sale of an asset to one party and a purchase of another similar asset from the same party, the IRS could treat the two transactions as a like-kind exchange. Thus, it is advisable to have the sale and purchase be with different parties.

Trade-in of Property Used Partly for Business

Where there is an exchange of property used partly for business and partly for personal purposes, as in the case of trade-in of an automobile, only the gain or loss allocable to the business portion of the traded-in property affects the nonrecognition of gain or loss.

Commissions and Expenses

Brokerage commission expenses paid in connection with tax-free exchanges are applied in three different ways in determining the tax consequences that result from such exchanges. The Internal Revenue Service has ruled (1) that commission expenses can be deducted or offset in computing the amount of gain or loss that is realized in a like-kind exchange; (2) that commission expenses paid can be offset against cash payments received in determining the amount of gain that may be recognized in such exchanges; and (3) that commission expenses may also be included in the basis of the property received. Rev. Rul. 72-456, 1972-2 CB 468.

¶11,225   RECEIPT OF BOOT

As mentioned earlier, no gain or loss is recognized when like-kind property is exchanged. When property that is not like-kind (i.e., cash or other property, known as "boot") is received, then any realized gain is recognized to the extent of the boot received, but not to exceed realized gain. If there is a realized loss in a boot received situation, such loss is not recognized. Code Sec. 1031(b) and (c).

EXAMPLE 11.16	Kent Powers exchanged a business machine with an adjusted basis of $28,000 and a fair market value of $40,000 for a similar machine worth $35,000 and $5,000 cash. Kent's realized gain is $12,000 and because he received $5,000 cash, the recognized gain will be $5,000.

EXAMPLE 11.17	Assume the same facts as in Example 11.16, except that Kent's adjusted basis in his old machine was $36,000 instead of $28,000. The realized gain is $4,000 and the recognized gain is also $4,000 even though he received boot in the amount of $5,000. Recognized gain would not exceed the realized gain.

EXAMPLE 11.18	Assume the same facts as in Example 11.16, except that Kent's adjusted basis in the old machine was $44,000. He would have realized a loss of $4,000 which would not be recognized even though there was boot received.

¶11,235   GIVING BOOT

If boot is given, generally no gain or loss is recognized.

| EXAMPLE 11.19 | Greg exchanges a business machine with an adjusted basis of $12,000 and a fair market value of $18,000 for a similar machine with a fair market value of $26,000. He also gives $8,000 cash. Although Greg realizes $6,000 gain, he recognizes no gain. |

| EXAMPLE 11.20 | Assume the same facts as in Example 11.19, except that Greg's old machine had a basis of $28,000. He would have realized a loss of $10,000 which would not be recognized. |

If, however, the boot given is property that has a difference between its basis and fair market value, then gain or loss will be recognized on the boot given. Reg. §1.1031(d)-1(e). It is as if the boot property was sold separately from the like-kind property. Although this rule for recognition in a boot given situation is a special case, it can produce strange results. The taxpayer can have a recognized gain greater than realized gain or a realized gain and a recognized loss.

| EXAMPLE 11.21 | Becky Barrows exchanges real estate with a basis of $150,000 (fair market value of $165,000) for other real estate with a fair market value of $230,000. She also gives up shares of Ridgeway Corporation stock worth $65,000 with a basis of $30,000. Becky's realized gain is $50,000 ($230,000 – $150,000 – $30,000) and she must recognize a gain of $35,000 ($65,000 – $30,000). |

| EXAMPLE 11.22 | Assume the same facts as in Example 11.21, except that the fair market value of the Ridgeway Corporation stock was $95,000 and the fair market value of Becky's real estate is $135,000. Becky then has a realized gain of $50,000 but a recognized gain of $65,000 ($95,000 – $30,000). |

| EXAMPLE 11.23 | Assume the same facts as in Example 11.21, except that Becky's stock in Ridgeway Corporation had a fair market value of only $20,000 and the fair market value of Becky's real estate is $210,000. She then has a realized gain of $50,000 and a recognized loss of $10,000. |

¶11,245   ASSUMPTION OF LIABILITIES

If a liability is assumed by the transferee, such assumption is treated like boot received by the taxpayer-transferor. Code Sec. 1031(d). Accordingly, the transferor will recognize gain under the same rules as in a boot received situation outlined above. It is treated as if the transferor received cash and then paid off the liability.

| EXAMPLE 11.24 | Judy Murryhill exchanged a business machine with an adjusted basis of $20,000 and worth $38,000 for another machine worth $28,000. Judy still owed $10,000 on the machine and the liability was assumed by the transferee. Judy realized a gain of $18,000 and recognized a gain of $10,000 since the liability assumed by the transferee is like boot received. |

If the taxpayer as transferor also assumes a liability, then, in determining the amount of boot received, consideration given in the form of an assumption of liabilities by the transferor may be offset against consideration received in the form of an assumption of liabilities by the transferee. Reg. §1.1031(d)-2. The amount of boot given in the form of money or liabilities assumed by the transferor reduces the amount of liabilities treated as boot received.

EXAMPLE 11.25

Martin Merchant exchanges a farm with an adjusted basis of $100,000 and a fair market value of $170,000 for Richard Richmond's farm with a fair market value of $150,000. Martin's mortgage of $30,000 is assumed by Richard whose mortgage of $10,000 is assumed by Martin. Martin realizes a gain of $70,000, but since the mortgages can be offset, he recognizes only $20,000 gain ($30,000 − $10,000).

Fair market value of property received	$150,000
Plus: Mortgage assumed by transferee (Richard)	30,000
Less: Mortgage assumed by transferor (Martin)	10,000
Net consideration received	$170,000
Less: Adjusted basis	100,000
Gain realized	$70,000
Gain recognized	$20,000

EXAMPLE 11.26

Assume the same facts as in Example 11.25, except that Martin's farm had a fair market value of $140,000 and the mortgage assumed by him was $40,000. Martin has a realized gain of $40,000 but recognizes no gain since the mortgage assumed by Richard does not exceed that assumed by Martin.

Fair market value of property received	$150,000
Plus: Mortgage assumed by transferee (Richard)	30,000
Less: Mortgage assumed by transferor (Martin)	40,000
Net consideration received	$140,000
Less: Adjusted basis	100,000
Gain realized	$40,000
Gain recognized	$0

If the transferor assumes a liability in excess of the amount of liability assumed by the transferee, the excess does not reduce any cash received by the transferor in determining how much gain is recognized. Consideration given in the form of cash or a mortgage assumed by the transferor, however, is offset against consideration received in the form of an assumption of a mortgage by the transferee. Reg. §1.1031(d)-2.

EXAMPLE 11.27

Rose Rand exchanges an apartment building with an adjusted basis of $140,000 and a fair market value of $190,000 for Sylvia Simon's apartment building with a fair market value of $180,000 and cash of $45,000 from Sylvia. Rose's mortgage of $40,000 is assumed by Sylvia, whose mortgage of $75,000 is assumed by Rose. Rose realizes gain of $50,000, but recognizes a gain of $45,000, to the extent of the cash received. Only the mortgages can be offset; the cash received may not be offset against the excess mortgage assumed by Rose.

Fair market value of property received	$180,000
Plus: Cash	45,000
Mortgage assumed by transferee (Sylvia)	$40,000
Less: Mortgage assumed by transferor (Rose)	75,000
Net consideration received	$190,000
Less: Adjusted basis	140,000
Gain realized	$50,000
Gain recognized	$45,000

Exhibit 1. CALCULATION OF BASIS OF NEW PROPERTY IN LIKE-KIND EXCHANGE

Method 1

Method 1	General Rule	Boot Received			Boot Given			Liability Assumption		Offset Liabilities		Liability and Cash	
Adjusted basis of property given	$75,000	$28,000	$36,000	$44,000	$150,000	$150,000	$150,000	$20,000	$36,000	$100,000	$100,000	$140,000	$140,000
+ Boot Given					+30,000	+30,000	+30,000					+20,000	
+ Gain recognized		+5,000	+4,000		+35,000	+65,000		+10,000		+20,000		+45,000	+10,000
+ Liability assumed by transferor										+10,000	+40,000	+10,000	+75,000
− Boot received		−5,000	−5,000	−5,000									−45,000
− Loss recognized							−10,000						
− Liability assumed by transferee								−10,000		−30,000	−30,000	−40,000	−40,000
= Basis of acquired property	$75,000	$28,000	$35,000	$39,000	$215,000	$245,000*	$170,000**	$20,000	$36,000	$100,000	$110,000	$175,000	$140,000

Method 2

Method 2	General Rule	Boot Received			Boot Given			Liability Assumption		Offset Liabilities		Liability and Cash	
FMV received	$250,000	$35,000	$35,000	$35,000	$230,000	$230,000	$230,000	$28,000	$26,000	$150,000	$150,000	$180,000	$180,000
− Deferred gain	−175,000	−7,000			−15,000		−50,000	−8,000		−50,000	−40,000	−5,000	−40,000
+ Deferred loss				+4,000		+15,000*	−10,000**		+10,000				
= Basis of acquired property	$75,000	$28,000	$35,000	$39,000	$215,000	$245,000*	$170,000**	$20,000	$36,000	$100,000	$110,000	$175,000	$140,000

* This is a special situation where because of the difference between the fair market value and the basis of boot given, there was recognized gain of $65,000 and a realized gain of $50,000. The $15,000 excess of recognized gain over realized gain has to be added to the fair market value of the new property.

** This is a special situation where because of the difference between the fair market value and the basis of the boot given, there was a recognized loss of $10,000 and a realized gain of $50,000. The gain is deferred and subtracted from the fair market value of the new property as is the $10,000 recognized loss.

PLANNING POINTER	Relative to Example 11.27, before the transfer Sylvia should have paid off $30,000 of the mortgage with cash received by Rose as $15,000 and the mortgage assumed by Rose $45,000 (instead of $75,000). The realized gain would still have been $50,000, but the recognized gain would have been only $15,000.

EXAMPLE 11.28	Assume the same facts as in Example 11.27, except that Sylvia's mortgage assumed by Rose is $10,000 and the cash given by Rose is $20,000 (instead of Rose's receipt of cash from Sylvia). Rose's realized gain is $50,000 but her recognized gain is only $10,000. Both the mortgage assumed by Rose and the cash given by Rose may be offset against Rose's liability assumed by Sylvia.

Fair market value of property received		$180,000
Plus: Mortgage assumed by transferee (Sylvia)		$40,000
Less: Mortgage assumed by transferor (Rose)		10,000
Net consideration received		$210,000
Less: Adjusted basis	$140,000	
Cash	20,000	160,000
Gain realized		$50,000
Gain recognized		$10,000

¶11,255 BASIS OF ACQUIRED PROPERTY

There are two ways of figuring the basis of the newly acquired property in a like-kind exchange.

1. One method starts with the adjusted basis of the property given up (Code Sec. 1031(d)) as follows:

   Adjusted basis of the like-kind property given

   + Boot given
   + Gain recognized
   + Liability assumed by the transferor
   − Boot received
   − Loss recognized
   − Liability assumed by the transferee
   = Basis of the property acquired

2. The second method starts with the fair market value of the property received as follows:

   Fair market value of the like-kind property received

   − Deferred gain
   + Deferred loss
   = Basis of the acquired property

Exhibit 1 summarizes what the basis would be for each of the situations in the example at ¶11,201 and the examples at ¶11,225–¶11,245 under the two methods of figuring the basis of newly acquired property in a like-kind exchange.

¶11,265 HOLDING PERIOD

The holding period for property acquired in a nontaxable exchange includes the holding period of the property given in exchange if the property was a capital asset or property used in a taxpayer's trade or business. Code Sec. 1223(1); Reg. §1.1223-1(a). However, the holding period of property received as boot in a like-kind exchange transaction begins on the day following the date of its receipt. This holding period rule also applies to property acquired through an involuntary conversion under Code Sec. 1033 (see ¶11,301).

EXAMPLE 11.29	Linda Lane traded in a machine purchased in 2012 for another machine during 2015. The holding period of the new machine begins on the day following the date of the 2012 purchase. If, in addition, Linda received shares of stock as boot, the holding period of the stock begins on the day following the date of the receipt of the stock in 2015.

¶11,275   THREE-PARTY EXCHANGES

Sometimes a taxpayer is unable to find a party with whom to have a like-kind exchange because the party whose property the taxpayer seeks wants to sell for cash rather than trade. The three-party exchange is a device that is designed to solve this dilemma. If the taxpayer can find a purchaser who is willing to pay cash and arrange a triangular exchange, the taxpayer can effect a tax-free exchange and a cash sale can be obtained by the party who holds the desired property. Generally, a transaction will be a nontaxable exchange to the taxpayer if the taxpayer intends to and does exchange the property, and does not receive or have control over the cash flowing to the seller. There is a 45-day deadline on identifying the substitute like-kind property and a 180-day deadline on receipt of the exchange property after the taxpayer transfers the property relinquished in the exchange. Code Sec. 1031(a)(3).

An acceptable arrangement to the taxpayer can take different forms. In each of the following examples it is assumed that the taxpayer wishes to exchange business property for like-kind property owned by a taxpayer who wants to sell rather than have an exchange.

EXAMPLE 11.30	Alice Amber transfers her property to Betty Beryl, who transfers cash to Carla Crystal, who then transfers her property to Alice. For Alice, this would be considered to be a nontaxable exchange even though she transferred her property to someone other than the person from whom she received the property. Rev. Rul. 57-244, 1957-1 CB 247; *W.H. Haden Co.,* 48-1 ustc ¶9147, 165 F.2d 588 (CA-5 1948).

EXAMPLE 11.31	Alice and Carla exchange their properties and Betty then purchases Alice's former property from Carla. The courts have maintained that this transaction will qualify as an exchange for Alice even though IRS might attempt to argue that Carla would be acting as Alice's agent for a sale. *L.Q. Coupe,* 52 TC 394, CCH Dec. 29,610 (1969), Acq. 1970-2 CB XIX; *J.H. Baird Publishing Co.,* 39 TC 608, CCH Dec. 25,816 (1962), Acq. 1963-2 CB 4. It would be an exchange for Alice because she has received property in exchange for property without receiving or controlling cash.

EXAMPLE 11.32	Betty could purchase the property from Carla and then immediately exchange the property for the property owned by Alice. The transaction would be an exchange for Alice if it could be shown that Alice intended to make an exchange, and if Betty used her own funds to acquire Carla's property. Rev. Rul. 77-297, 1977-2 CB 304; *J. Alderson,* 63-2 ustc ¶9499, 317 F.2d 790 (CA-9 1963).

If arrangements more complicated than the above examples are made, there could potentially be difficulties in obtaining exchange treatment for the taxpayer. The regulations, however, allow for the use of an intermediary if the intermediary takes three steps: (1) acquires the seller's property; (2) acquires the replacement property; and (3) transfers the replacement property to the seller. Reg. §1.1031(a)-3(g)(4)(ii).

Involuntary Conversions

Gain may be deferred in an involuntary conversion through an election, providing the replacement occurs with qualified property within a specified time period and of a sufficient magnitude. An involuntary conversion occurs through a casualty, theft, or condemnation. The reason for possible deferral is to assist those who have sustained financial difficulties through one of the above events and because the taxpayer's economic position has not changed if replacement property is acquired. Also, the wherewithal to pay concept is another justification for this provision in that the taxpayer frequently does not have the financial resources to pay taxes on any realized gain.

¶11,301   DEFINITION OF AN INVOLUNTARY CONVERSION

An involuntary conversion is the compulsory or involuntary conversion of property resulting from "its destruction, in whole or in part, theft, seizure, or requisition or condemnation or threat or imminence thereof." Code Sec. 1033(a).

A condemnation generally occurs when a governmental body takes private property for public use and pays a reasonable price for it. A property transfer due to threat or imminence of condemnation also qualifies as an involuntary conversion. A news report that property is being considered for condemnation is not a threat or imminence. There must be confirmation that the property is going to be acquired for public purposes and the taxpayer has reasonable grounds to believe the property will be taken. Rev. Rul. 74-8, 1974-1 CB 200, modifying Rev. Rul. 63-221, 1963-2 CB 332. Sales to third parties (as opposed to the condemning authority) also qualify as involuntary if made under the threat or imminence of condemnation. Rev. Rul. 81-180, 1981-2 CB 161. The later sale of the property by the third party to the condemning authority also qualifies for involuntary conversion treatment if the proceeds are reinvested in qualified property even if the third party knew that the threat existed before he acquired the property. A "condemnation" does not include a notice that property will be condemned because it is unfit for human use. Rev. Rul. 57-314, 1957-2 CB 523.

| EXAMPLE 11.33 | Joseph Jordon, who owned a lot, learned that the City Council had just approved the condemnation of the lot for use as a city parking garage to be built in two or three years. Joseph decides to sell the property to Judy Garnet at a gain. The sale is an involuntary conversion and Joseph may elect deferral of the gain recognition. |

If livestock is destroyed by or sold or exchanged on account of disease or because of drought, such events are involuntary conversions. Also, if it is not feasible because of soil contamination or other environmental conditions to replace the livestock with other livestock, other farm property (including real property) qualifies as replacement property. Code Sec. 1033(d)-(f).

¶11,305   INVOLUNTARY CONVERSION RULES FOR PROPERTY DAMAGED IN DISASTER

For purposes of the nonrecognition-of-gain rule regarding involuntarily converted property that is replaced with similar property, any tangible property that is acquired and held for productive use in a business is treated as similar or related to business or investment property that was involuntarily converted as a result of a Presidentially declared disaster. Code Sec. 1033(h)(2).

This provision is intended to afford relief to businesses forced to suspend operations for a substantial time because of the property damage. If valuable markets and customers are lost during the suspension and the business fails, the owner may want to reinvest the capital in a new business venture.

| EXAMPLE 11.34 | Ena ran a small retail store on the beaches of Florida. The area was hit by a hurricane and her business was destroyed. The President declared the area a disaster area. Ena used the insurance proceeds from her business to purchase equipment to enter into a consulting business. Ena may elect not to recognize gain with respect to the involuntarily converted beach business. |

¶11,315   REPLACEMENT PROPERTY— MANDATORY RULES

There are two mandatory rules for recognition of gain or loss in case of an involuntary conversion.

1. If there is a direct conversion of property into other property similar or related in service or use instead of into a money award, no gain will be recognized. The basis of the replacement property is the same as the adjusted basis of the old property. Code Sec. 1033(a)(1) and (b).

| EXAMPLE 11.35 | Sandra Storm owned land which had an adjusted basis of $25,000. The land was condemned by the state and she received other land to replace her condemned property. The replacement land had a fair market value of $40,000. Sandra will recognize no gain and the basis in the new land is also $25,000. |

2. If there is a realized loss, the loss must be recognized (assuming the loss is allowed). The basis of the replacement property acquired is its cost.

EXAMPLE 11.36	Wade Wilson's factory building having an adjusted basis of $600,000 was destroyed by fire, and he received insurance proceeds in the amount of $500,000. He purchased another factory for $800,000. Wade recognizes his realized loss of $100,000, and the basis of the new factory is $800,000.

Losses realized from involuntary conversions of income-producing or business property are recognized. Casualty and theft losses of personal use assets are also recognized (subject to limits discussed in Chapter 8); however, condemnation losses of personal use assets are not recognized.

EXAMPLE 11.37	Sara Sheridan's personal residence with an adjusted basis of $80,000 is destroyed by fire and she receives insurance proceeds of $60,000. The $20,000 realized loss is recognized subject to the limitations for personal casualty loss deductions. If Sara's residence is condemned instead of destroyed by fire, the $20,000 realized loss is not recognized.

¶11,325   REPLACEMENT PROPERTY—ELECTIVE RULES

If the cost of the replacement property exceeds the proceeds or amount realized, the taxpayer may make an election to recognize none of the realized gain. The basis of the replacement property is the cost of the replacement property less deferred gain. Code Sec. 1033(a)(2) and (b). The holding period of the replacement property, if an election to defer gain is made, includes the holding period of the old converted property. Code Sec. 1223(1)(A).

EXAMPLE 11.38	Jim Johnson's office building with an adjusted basis of $175,000 is destroyed by fire, and he receives insurance proceeds of $250,000. He buys a replacement office building for $280,000. Jim realized a gain of $75,000, but he can make an election to recognize no gain since the replacement cost is greater than the insurance proceeds. The basis of the replacement property is $205,000 ($280,000 less $75,000 deferred gain) and the holding period of the replacement property begins with the holding period of the old property.

PLANNING POINTER	There may be times when it is better not to make the election for nonrecognition of gain. This may be the case if the taxpayer is in a relatively low tax bracket in the current year or because an expiring net operating loss carryover may be offset against the gain. Also, the election may not be desirable if the basis of the replacement asset would be a cost that would result in a higher basis than if the gain had not been recognized.

If the amount realized exceeds the cost of the replacement property, the taxpayer may make the election to recognize gain only to the extent of that excess. The basis of the replacement property is the cost of the replacement property less any deferred gain. Code Sec. 1033(a)(2) and (b).

EXAMPLE 11.39	Thomas Thompson owned land with an adjusted basis of $100,000 that was condemned by the state. He received an award of $140,000, and he purchased other land for $125,000. Thomas realizes gain of $40,000 and (assuming he makes the election to defer recognition) recognizes gain of $15,000, the extent to which the amount realized ($140,000) exceeds the cost of the replacement property ($125,000). His basis in the replacement land is $100,000 ($125,000 less $25,000 deferred gain).

If more than one property is bought, the basis is allocated among the properties according to their relative costs. Rev. Rul. 73-18, 1973-1 CB 368.

EXAMPLE 11.40

Assume the same facts as in the preceding example, except that the replacement property consisted of three parcels of land costing $60,000, $40,000, and $25,000. The basis of $100,000 would be allocated among the three parcels as follows:

$$\text{Parcel 1:} \quad \frac{\$60,000}{\$125,000} \quad \times \quad \$100,000 \quad = \quad \$48,000$$

$$\text{Parcel 2:} \quad \frac{\$40,000}{\$125,000} \quad \times \quad \$100,000 \quad = \quad \$32,000$$

$$\text{Parcel 3:} \quad \frac{\$25,000}{\$125,000} \quad \times \quad \$100,000 \quad = \quad \$20,000$$

The acquisition of involuntary conversion replacement property from related parties is not allowed. However, a de minimis exception applies if the realized gain on the involuntary conversion is $100,000 or less.

¶11,335 SEVERANCE DAMAGES

Severance damages may be paid to a taxpayer when part of the taxpayer's property is condemned and the value of the remaining property is decreased by the condemnation. Severance damages reduce the basis of the damaged property and any excess received above the basis of the property is recognized gain. Rev. Rul. 68-37, 1968-1 CB 359. An award received from a condemning authority may be considered as severance damages only where such designation has been stipulated by both contracting parties. When it is not clearly shown that the award includes a specific amount as severance damages, it is assumed that the proceeds were given in consideration of the property taken by the condemning authority (i.e., the condemnation award). Rev. Rul. 59-173, 1959-1 CB 201.

EXAMPLE 11.41

Margaret Moore receives severance damages of $100 per acre for 40 acres because of the decline in value resulting from an earlier condemnation of an adjacent parcel of Margaret's land. The $4,000 received in severance damages reduces the basis of the 40 acres of land. If the damages exceed the basis of the land, any excess is recognized gain.

¶11,345 QUALIFYING REPLACEMENT PROPERTY

With some exceptions, the rules for replacement property for involuntary conversions under Code Sec. 1033 are more strict than for like-kind exchanges under Code Sec. 1031. The Code provides that the replacement property in an involuntary conversion must be similar or related in service or use to the property converted. Code Sec. 1033(a)(1).

Functional-Use Test

It sometimes is difficult to determine just what qualifies as "similar or related in service or use"; however, two tests have generally been applied depending on whether the taxpayer is an owner-user or an owner-investor. If the taxpayer owned and used the property that was converted, the replacement property must be used in the same way as the converted property. This is known as the functional-use test. Rev. Rul. 64-237, 1964-2 CB 319.

EXAMPLE 11.42

Assume that the taxpayers make the following replacements as a result of a casualty:

1. Personal residence is replaced by a rental apartment house.
2. Manufacturing plant is replaced by a retail store.
3. Bowling alley is replaced with a billiard center. Rev. Rul. 76-319, 1976-2 CB 242.
4. Business car is replaced with a delivery truck.
5. Farm with one residence is replaced by a farm with two residences, one of which is leased. Rev. Rul. 54-569, 1954-2 CB 144.

The first four replacements do not meet the functional-use test and any gain realized would have to be recognized.

Taxpayer-Use Test

If the taxpayer is an owner-investor, the replacement property must have the same relationship of service or use to the taxpayer as the converted property had. This is known as the taxpayer-use test. Rev. Rul. 64-237, 1964-2 CB 319. The taxpayer decides this by determining (1) whether the properties are of similar service; (2) the nature of the business risks connected with the properties; and (3) what the properties demand in the way of management, service, and relations to tenants. IRS Publication No. 334, Tax Guide for Small Business.

EXAMPLE 11.43	Assume that the taxpayers make the following replacements as a result of a casualty:
	1. Rental manufacturing plant is replaced by a building rented out as a warehouse.
	2. Rental apartment house is replaced by a personal residence.
	The first replacement qualifies as replacement property, but the second replacement does not.

Exchanges of Stock

A taxpayer can also elect nonrecognition of gain in an involuntary conversion by purchasing 80 percent or more of the stock of a corporation owning similar property. The purchase of the stock qualifies as replacement property, and the gain would be recognized under Code Sec. 1033 to the extent the amount realized exceeds the cost of the stock. Code Sec. 1033(a)(2). The basis of the corporation's assets must be reduced by the amount which the taxpayer must reduce the basis of the stock.

¶11,355   CONDEMNATION OF REAL PROPERTY—SPECIAL RULE

A more liberal replacement rule applies for a condemnation of real property. If real property held for productive use in a trade or business or for investment purposes is involuntarily converted, property of a like kind qualifies as property similar or related in service or use.

EXAMPLE 11.44	Malcolm Moore's factory building was condemned. He purchases a rental apartment building, which qualifies as "like-kind," thus meeting the test for proper replacement property for condemnation of real property.

A taxpayer may elect to treat outdoor advertising displays as real property for purposes of the involuntary conversion rules providing the taxpayer has not elected to write off part of the cost under Code Sec. 179. Code Sec. 1033(g)(3)(A).

¶11,365   TIME LIMIT

The allowed period for replacement with qualified property begins on the earlier of the date of disposition of the converted property or the earliest date of the threat or imminence of the condemnation of the converted property. The taxpayer has until two years after the close of the first taxable year in which any part of the gain is realized from the involuntary conversion to replace with qualified property. For Presidentially declared disaster areas, the time limit for a principal residence is increased to four years. Code Sec. 1033(h)(1)(B). The taxpayer has three years after the close of the first taxable year in which gain is first realized in the case of condemnations of real property. Code Sec. 1033(a)(2)(B) and (g)(4).

EXAMPLE 11.45	Arthur King's office building (adjusted basis of $200,000) is destroyed by fire on October 18, 2014, and he receives insurance proceeds on January 22, 2015, in the amount of $350,000. Assuming Arthur is a calendar year taxpayer, he has until December 31, 2017, to replace the property. He has until two years after the end of the tax year in which gain is realized (realization occurred on January 22, 2015). The date the fire occurred was not the date from which to count.

EXAMPLE 11.46	If Arthur's office building had been condemned, he would have until December 31, 2018, to replace the property, which is three years after the end of the year in which the gain was first realized.

¶11,385   REPORTING REQUIREMENTS

If the taxpayer elects to defer gain in an involuntary conversion because of either replacement or intended replacement, the taxpayer should include supporting details in the return for the taxable year in which any of the gain is realized. If the taxpayer later finds that property will not be replaced at all or does not purchase new replacement property costing a sufficient amount, the taxpayer will have to file an amended return recomputing the tax liability for the year the election was made. If the taxpayer did not make an election when the property was involuntarily converted, and the replacement time period has not expired, the taxpayer can still file a claim for credit or refund. Reg. §1.1033(a)-2(c)(2).

EXAMPLE 11.47	In 2015, Jim Jacobs receives a $200,000 award for the condemnation of his office building that has a basis of $120,000. He elects to defer recognition of the $80,000 gain, expecting to pay at least $200,000 for the new building. In 2016, he purchases another office building for $175,000. Jim must file an amended return for 2015 and recognize the $25,000 gain ($200,000 award less $175,000 replacement cost).

KEYSTONE PROBLEM	Are there times when a taxpayer might prefer the following? 1. To have a sale rather than a like-kind exchange 2. To recognize the realized gain rather than make the nonrecognition of gain election in an involuntary conversion

PLANNING POINTER	It is often advisable to take advantage of the nonrecognition of gain provision for like-kind exchanges and involuntary conversions under Code Secs. 1031 and 1033. This is true even though the basis of the new assets will be reduced. The time value of money is relevant here in that the present value of current tax reductions will be greater than the present value of future reduced depreciation deductions.

¶11,395   DEPRECIATION RULES

Taxpayers who exchange modified accelerated cost recovery system (MACRS) property through either a Section 1031 like-kind exchange or a Section 1033 involuntary conversion, are required to treat the excess basis of the acquired MACRS property as newly purchased. The new asset will now be treated as two separate properties for depreciation purposes.

Generally, exchanged basis (carryover basis from the exchange property) is depreciated over the remaining recovery period of the relinquished MACRS property, using the same depreciation method and convention. This general rule applies if the replacement property has the same or shorter recovery period, or the same or more accelerated depreciation method, than the relinquished property. If the replacement property MACRS property has a longer recovery period, or less-accelerated depreciation method, the replacement property is treated as placed in service when the relinquished property was placed in service.

Excess basis, the additional basis in the replacement property over and above the amount of exchanged basis, will be placed in a separate asset with a new depreciation schedule.

Taxpayers may elect not to apply the new rules if the rules are too burdensome or depreciation components are too difficult to track. However, if a taxpayer elects not to apply the new rules, the taxpayer must treat the entire basis (both the exchanged and excess basis) of the replacement MACRS property as being placed in service by the acquiring taxpayer at the time of replacement.

Other Transactions Involving Nonrecognition

This focus of this chapter is on residence sales, like-kind exchanges, and involuntary conversions. Additional provisions resulting in nonrecognition of gain or loss are discussed only briefly.

¶11,401   CORPORATE AND PARTNERSHIP EXCHANGES

No gain or loss is recognized by shareholders if property is transferred to a controlled corporation by one or more persons in exchange for stock in the corporation. Code Sec. 351. Moreover, no gain or loss is recognized to a corporation upon the receipt of money or other property in exchange for the stock of such corporation. Code Sec. 1032. Similarly, no gain or loss is recognized to either a partnership or its partners when property is contributed to the partnership in exchange for a partnership interest. Code Sec. 721. These corporate and partnership provisions are examined more closely in other chapters.

¶11,405   STOCK-FOR-STOCK EXCHANGES

No gain or loss is recognized if common stock (in a corporation) is exchanged solely for common stock in the same corporation, or if preferred stock is exchanged solely for preferred stock in the same corporation. Nonrecognition applies even though voting stock is exchanged for nonvoting stock or nonvoting stock is exchanged for voting stock. Code Sec. 1036(a); Reg. §1.1036-1(a). This nonrecognition provision applies to an exchange between two individuals and to transactions between a stockholder and the corporation. This nonrecognition provision does not apply if stock is exchanged for bonds, or preferred stock is exchanged for common stock (or vice versa), or if common stock in one corporation is exchanged for common stock in another corporation. However, exercising the right to convert bonds into the obligor corporation's stock or converting preferred stock for common stock in the same corporation under a conversion privilege in the preferred stock is nontaxable. Rev. Rul. 72-265, 1972-1 CB 222.

¶11,415   INSURANCE CONTRACT EXCHANGES

No gain or loss is recognized on the exchange of the following:

1. Life insurance contract for a life insurance contract, endowment contract, or annuity contract
2. Endowment contract for another endowment contract providing for regular payments beginning at a date not later than the date payments would have begun under the contract exchanged, or for an annuity contract
3. Annuity contract for an annuity contract (Code Sec. 1035(a))

EXAMPLE 11.48	Michelle Millard exchanges a life insurance contract for an endowment contract. She recognizes no gain or loss on the exchange.

¶11,435   U.S. OBLIGATIONS EXCHANGES

No gain or loss is recognized upon the surrender of U.S. obligations to the United States if they were issued under chapter 31 (Public Debt) of Title 31 (Money and Finance) in exchange solely for other such obligations. Code Sec. 1037(a).

¶11,455   REACQUISITIONS OF REAL PROPERTY

Where a sale of real property gives rise to indebtedness to the seller which is secured by the real property sold and such property is repossessed by the seller to satisfy the purchase obligation, no loss is recognized on repossession. Gain is recognized only to the extent of the cash (or other property) received less the gain on the original sale already included in income. The amount of the gain is limited to the gain on the original sale less repossession costs and gain previously reported. Code Sec. 1038; Reg. §1.1038-1.

TAX BLUNDERS

1. Henry and Hillary Houseman purchased a home in September 2011 in Boom City for $75,000. Henry is an excellent carpenter and spent a great deal of time fixing up and renovating the home. The Housemans spent $150,000 on materials and capital improvements during 2012. Considerable new business came to Boom City so that the city grew rapidly over a three-year time period, and there was a heavy demand for housing. In 2015, the Housemans sold their home for $720,000. The Housemans maintained no records so they would have a $645,000 gain of which $500,000 would be excluded, leaving $145,000 to be recognized. If, however, they had maintained records of their improvements, they would have had a gain of $495,000, all of which could be excluded.

2. Gordon Gimbel had an office building that he wanted to dispose of but he could not decide whether to sell it or try to exchange it. His building had an adjusted basis of $50,000 and a fair market value of $150,000. He located another office building with an equivalent fair market value and made the exchange. Gordon is in a low tax bracket in the year of the exchange but, because of expansion of his business, he expects high income in future years.

    Gordon will recognize no gain in the year of the exchange and he will carry over the $50,000 low basis. Thus, when he has low income he has no gain from the exchange and he will have low depreciation deductions in high income years. It would probably have been preferable to sell the property, recognize the gain while he is in a low tax bracket and then buy another asset which would have a high basis and for which he would be able to take higher depreciation deductions in years in which he has high income.

3. Irene Wildwood had a rental building which she wanted to dispose of, but could not decide whether to sell it or try to exchange it. The building had a fair market value of $250,000 and a basis of $50,000. She decided to sell the building and purchased another apartment building in another part of the city for $275,000. Irene is in a high tax bracket this year, but expects to have significantly lower income in future years. Irene should have attempted, if at all possible, to have a like-kind exchange so that she would have had no income recognized in the current year when she is in a high tax bracket and then she would have a lower basis (and low depreciation) in the future years when she would be in a low tax bracket. With a sale, she has high income in the current year and a high basis in the new building on which high depreciation deductions will be taken in years when she has low income.

4. Lorraine Larsen has an office building in a declining neighborhood which has an adjusted basis of $500,000 and a fair market value of $300,000. She would like to dispose of the building but cannot decide whether to sell or exchange it. Lorraine is in a high tax bracket this year and expects to be in lower tax brackets in the future years. She ends up exchanging it for a building in another part of the city. It has a fair market value of $250,000, and she receives boot of $50,000. No loss is recognized even though she realized a $200,000 loss and she will have a high basis ($450,000) on which she will take high depreciation in low income years. Lorraine should have sold the old building so that she could have recognized the loss when she is in a high tax bracket. If she had bought a new building for comparable fair market value, she would have had a lower basis on which to take depreciation in the future years, when her income would be low anyway.

SUMMARY

■ Married taxpayers may exclude up to $500,000 of gain upon the sale of their residence and single taxpayers may exclude up to $250,000 of their gain.

■ No gain or loss is recognized on the exchange of property held for productive use in a trade or business or for investment if such property is exchanged solely for property of like kind that is held either for productive use in a trade or business or for investment.

■ In a like-kind exchange, when property that is not like-kind is received, then any realized gain is recognized to the extent of the boot received. If there is a realized loss in a boot received situation, such loss will not be recognized. If boot is given, generally no gain or loss is recognized. If a liability is assumed by the transferee, such assumption is treated like boot received by the taxpayer transferor.

■ There are two ways of determining the basis of the newly acquired property in a like-kind exchange.

■ There are two mandatory rules for recognition of gain or loss in the case of an involuntary conversion, relating to a direct conversion of property and a realized loss.

■ There are elective rules in involuntary conversions that allow the taxpayer to elect to recognize gain realized only to the extent that the proceeds exceed the cost of the replacement property.

QUESTIONS

1. Describe the current tax law for sale of residence.

2. Why might a taxpayer wish to elect out of the new exclusion on the sale of residence?

3. Is it possible to defer gain through the purchase of a new residence?

4. Why would the exclusion on sale of residence be prorated?

5. What special rules affect three types of taxpayers?

6. What residence-related matter did the Housing Assistance Tax Act of 2008 address?

7. Why are certain exchanges permitted to be nontaxable?

8. When might a taxpayer prefer a sale over a like-kind exchange that would result in nonrecognition of gain under Section 1031?

9. What are two acceptable methods of calculating the basis of new property acquired in a like-kind exchange?

10. What are four broad types of like-kind exchanges?

11. Define the following relative to like-kind exchanges:
    a. Boot
    b. Postponed gain or loss
    c. Gain or loss realized
    d. Gain or loss recognized

12. Discuss the tax consequences if a personal residence is involuntarily converted.

13. What are the broad types of involuntary conversions?

14. Explain the rules for nonrecognition of gain in an involuntary conversion.

15. What is necessary for a "threat or imminence of condemnation" to qualify property for involuntary conversion treatment?

16. What is the time limitation for replacing involuntarily converted property?

17. How are losses from involuntary conversions treated?

18. Explain the difference between the taxpayer-use test and the functional-use test, and give an example as to when each applies.

19. What exchanges of insurance policies, endowment contracts, or annuities qualify for nonrecognition?

20. How is adjusted basis of a residence computed?

PROBLEMS

21. Leonard and Linda Lindsay sold for $350,000 in October 2015 their residence that they had purchased in 2005 for $100,000. They made major capital improvements during their 10-year ownership totaling $30,000.
    a. What is their excluded gain? How much must they recognize?

    b. Suppose instead that the Lindsays sold their home for $700,000. They moved into a smaller home costing $200,000. What is their excluded gain? How much must they recognize?

    c. Assume instead that the Lindsays resided in a very depressed neighborhood and the home was sold for only $80,000. How much gain or loss is recognized?

22. John Johnson, single, sold his home that he had owned for 20 years for $650,000. He purchased it for $125,000 and made $50,000 of capital improvements on the home during his time of ownership.
    a. How much gain is excluded? How much is recognized?
    b. If John purchased another home for $425,000, how much is excluded and recognized?

23. Milton and Maxine Miller purchased a home in New York City for $350,000 on October 1, 2014. Milton obtained a job in Richmond, Virginia, and on December 1, 2015, the Millers sold their home in New York for $550,000.
    a. How much gain can the Millers exclude and how much is recognized?
    b. Assume that the Millers instead sold their home on December 1, 2015, for $750,000. How much gain can the Millers then exclude and how much is recognized?

24. Tina and Tom Talley purchased a home in 2000 for $450,000. Over the years, they made substantial improvements, totaling $100,000. In 2014, the couple was divorced. As part of the settlement, the house was transferred to Tina. In 2015, Tina sold the house for $850,000.
    a. What is Tina's realized gain on the transaction?
    b. What is her recognized gain?

25. Thomas and Tonya Taylor purchased a home for $125,000 on September 15, 2013. On October 8, 2014, they were divorced, and as part of the divorce agreement, the home was transferred to Thomas, who sold it on October 16, 2015, for $245,000.
    a. How much can Thomas exclude and how much is recognized?
    b. Assume instead that, as part of the divorce agreement, Tonya retained ownership of the residence but the use of the home was granted to Thomas as long as Tonya owns the residence. If Tonya sells the residence on October 16, 2015, for $245,000, how much can Tonya exclude?

26. Arnold Atkins purchased a residence for $160,000 on September 26, 2013. In October 2014 he became ill and was confined to a nursing home. On October 8, 2015, he sold the residence for $245,000. How much gain can Arnold exclude?

27. Oscar Olson, single, purchased a residence on February 19, 2013, for $170,000. On September 7, 2015, a tornado completely destroyed his home. The home was insured for its replacement value, and homes in Oscar's area had appreciated greatly. He received proceeds of $400,000.
    a. How much does Oscar exclude and recognize?
    b. If Oscar instead had received proceeds of $525,000, how much gain would be excluded and recognized? How much of a replacement residence would have to be purchased in order to exclude or defer all gain realized?

28. Carl Carter had purchased a residence on January 12, 2014, for $165,000 and then sold it on April 12, 2015, for $440,000 because of severe health problems.
    a. How much gain can Carl exclude and how much must he recognize?
    b. If Carl instead sold the home for $300,000, how much could Carl exclude and how much must he recognize?

29. Which of the following exchanges qualify as like-kind exchanges?
    a. Unimproved land for warehouse
    b. Factory for apartment building
    c. Computer for small building
    d. Inventory for business machine
    e. Computer for a printer

30. Lewis Lamont owns a yacht (personal use) that has a fair market value of $220,000 and an adjusted basis of $310,000. His AGI in the current year is $150,000. Calculate Lewis's realized and recognized gain or loss on the yacht if:
    a. Lewis sells the yacht for $220,000.
    b. Lewis exchanges the yacht for another worth $220,000.
    c. The yacht burns and is completely destroyed and Lewis receives insurance proceeds of $200,000.

31. Sheila Sprinkle transferred business property with a fair market value of $50,000 and an adjusted basis of $25,000 for business property worth $40,000 and $10,000 cash.
    a. What is Sheila's recognized and realized gain on the transaction and the basis in the new property?
    b. What is the answer to (a) if Sheila's adjusted basis in her old property was $45,000?
    c. What is the answer to (a) if Sheila's adjusted basis in her old property was $55,000?

32. Ben Bonn and Lester Lambert exchange business machines. Ben's adjusted basis in his property is $3,200, and the fair market value is $4,500. Lester's property has an adjusted basis of $1,700 and a fair market value of $2,000. Lester also gives Ben $2,500 cash. What is Ben's realized and recognized gain and basis in the new property? What is Lester's realized and recognized gain and basis in the new property?

33. Lily Landry and Emma Erickson exchange equipment in a like-kind exchange. Emma gives up equipment with a fair market value of $30,000 (adjusted basis $25,000) and Lily transfers equipment with a fair market value of $23,000 (adjusted basis $20,000) plus $7,000 in cash.
    a. What is Emma's realized and recognized gain or loss and basis in the new property?
    b. What is Lily's realized and recognized gain or loss and basis in the new property?

34. Betsy Banks owns a car which she uses exclusively for business. The car's fair market value is $22,000 and the adjusted basis is $25,000. Betsy exchanges the car for another car worth $28,000 to be used exclusively in business and gives $6,000 cash.
    a. What is her realized and recognized gain or loss and basis in the new car?
    b. How would your answers to (a) change if she used the car for personal use?

35. Wayne Wyatt exchanges land with an adjusted basis of $300,000 and a fair market value of $600,000 for Fred Forbes's office building, worth $500,000, and $100,000 cash. Fred had an adjusted basis of $350,000 in the building.
    a. What is Wayne's realized and recognized gain or loss and the basis in the office building?
    b. What is Fred's realized and recognized gain or loss and the basis in the land?
    c. Assume no cash was received by Wayne and the office building was worth $600,000. What is Wayne's realized and recognized gain or loss and the basis in the office building?

36. Joe Jenner exchanges property with an adjusted basis of $120,000 (fair market value $150,000) for property worth $200,000. As part of the exchange, he gave up stock in Riveris Corporation worth $50,000 with a basis of $30,000.
    a. What is Joe's recognized gain and basis in the new property?
    b. If the fair market value of the stock is $90,000 and the fair market value of Joe's property is $110,000, what is Joe's recognized gain and basis in the new property?
    c. If the fair market value of the stock is $20,000 and the fair market value of Joe's property is $180,000, what is Joe's recognized gain or loss and basis in the new property?

37. Susan Sundry exchanges her small office building (adjusted basis of $127,000 and fair market value of $154,000) for Tina Thompson's warehouse (adjusted basis of $112,000 and fair market value of $123,000). Tina assumes Susan's mortgage of $31,000. What is Susan's recognized gain on the exchange and her basis in the warehouse?

38. Allen Aubrey exchanges his factory (adjusted basis of $339,000 and fair market value of $525,000) for an apartment building with a fair market value of $360,000. He also receives $165,000 in cash. What is his realized and recognized gain or loss? Determine the basis of his apartment building using two different methods.

39. Charlotte Citron exchanged business machines with Darlene Darbey. Charlotte's machine had an adjusted basis of $10,500 and a fair market value of $9,000. Darlene's machine had an adjusted basis of $8,500 and a fair market value of $6,000 and Darlene gave Charlotte $3,000 cash. What is Charlotte's realized gain or loss, recognized gain or loss, and the basis of the new property? Answer the same questions for Darlene.

40. Debbie Davis and Elizabeth Engels exchanged like-kind property. Debbie had an adjusted basis of $12,000 in her property (fair market value is $15,000). Elizabeth's property had an adjusted basis of $9,000 and a fair market value of $10,500, and Elizabeth gave Debbie $4,500 in cash. Determine Debbie's and Elizabeth's realized gain or loss, recognized gain or loss, and the basis in their new property.

41. Bruce Baxter exchanges an office building worth $1,025,000 for a warehouse owned by Dan Denton. Bruce's adjusted basis in the office building is $750,000 and Dan's basis is $800,000. The fair market value of Dan's warehouse is $825,000. Bruce's office building is subject to a $200,000 mortgage which Dan assumes.
    a. What is Bruce's realized and recognized gain or loss and his basis in the warehouse?
    b. What is Dan's realized and recognized gain or loss and his basis in the office building?

42. Emmett Embers exchanges a business building with an adjusted basis of $207,000 and a fair market value of $300,000 for George Gunn's land (to be held as investment) with an adjusted basis of $165,000 and a fair market value of $390,000. Emmett assumes George's $90,000 mortgage on the land. Determine Emmett's and George's realized gain or loss, recognized gain or loss, and the basis in the new property.

43. Linda Loren transfers an apartment building with an adjusted basis of $150,000 and a fair market value of $240,000 for Carol Comb's apartment building (adjusted basis $140,000) with a fair market value of $200,000. Linda's mortgage of $60,000 is assumed by Carol whose mortgage of $20,000 is assumed by Linda. What is the realized and recognized gain or loss for Linda and Carol and what are their bases in their acquired buildings?

44. Peter Paterson transfers an apartment building with an adjusted basis of $160,000 and a fair market value of $235,000 for Charlie Claussen's apartment building (adjusted basis $120,000) with a fair market value of $220,000 and cash of $55,000 from Charlie. Peter's mortgage of $45,000 is assumed by Charlie whose mortgage of $85,000 is assumed by Peter. What is the realized and recognized gain or loss for Peter and Charlie and what are their bases in their acquired buildings?

45. Chad Carter exchanged land with an adjusted basis of $100,000 and a fair market value of $150,000 for Nash Nunn's land worth $140,000 (basis $120,000) and $15,000 cash. Chad's mortgage of $35,000 is assumed by Nash and Nash's mortgage of $40,000 is assumed by Chad.
    a. What is Chad's realized and recognized gain or loss and the basis in his new land?
    b. What is Nash's realized and recognized gain or loss and the basis in his new land?

46. Sidney Southern owned a restaurant which was condemned on November 20, 2014. On January 15, 2015, he received a condemnation award of $280,000. The adjusted basis of his restaurant was $120,000. He purchased another restaurant on March 17, 2015, for $300,000.
    a. What is Sidney's lowest recognized gain or loss? What is his basis in the restaurant?
    b. What would be the answer to (a) if the replacement cost was $240,000?
    c. What is the last possible date on which Sidney could have purchased qualified replacement property?
    d. What is the answer to (c) if the restaurant had been destroyed by fire instead of being condemned?

47. Gerald Gold's property is condemned by the local authorities. The property has an adjusted basis of $135,000 and a fair market value of $225,000. The local authorities replace Gerald's property with other property with a fair market value of $160,000. What is Gerald's realized gain, recognized gain, and the basis in the new property?

48. The government condemns and seizes Gary Greene's business property in order to widen the interstate. His adjusted basis in the property is $160,000. Gary receives $50,000 from the government.
    a. What is the amount of Gary's realized and recognized gain or loss in this transaction?
    b. What if the property is Gary's personal home?

49. Herbert Harrison's business property with an adjusted basis of $170,000 is condemned by the local authorities. He receives a $250,000 condemnation award.
    a. What is Herbert's realized and recognized gain or loss?
    b. What is Herbert's realized and recognized gain or loss if he purchases qualified replacement property for $220,000?

       What is Herbert's basis in the new property?

    c. What is Herbert's realized and recognized gain or loss if he purchases replacement property for $280,000?

       What is Herbert's basis in the new property?

    d. What is Herbert's realized and recognized gain or loss and the basis in the new property if the condemnation award is $150,000 and the replacement property costs $220,000?

50. Steven Seller owned and managed a clothing store that was destroyed by a hurricane. He received an insurance award of $200,000 for the store, which had an adjusted basis of $120,000. A year later he replaced the clothing store with another one for $225,000.
    a. What is Seller's realized and recognized gain or loss, and the basis of the replacement clothing store?
    b. What is Seller's realized and recognized gain or loss and the basis if he replaced the clothing store with a car repair shop which he managed?

51. John and Amy Turner, married filing jointly, are both 36 years of age. They have two sons and a daughter. John and Amy have earned income of $93,500 and $58,300 respectively, and their allowable itemized deductions are $14,400. They had the following transactions during 2015:
    a. On March 31, 2015, they sold their personal residence for $160,000. Their basis in the residence was $108,000. Six months later, they purchased a new residence for $130,000. They had incurred $6,000 of selling expenses.
    b. Amy exchanged land obtained before the marriage for an office building. She had a basis in the land, which was worth $100,000, of $50,000. The office building was worth $105,000.
    c. John sold property for $45,000. He had inherited the property from an aunt who had an adjusted basis of $10,000 in the property. The property was worth $30,000 at the time of the aunt's death.
    d. John and Amy sold stock which they had received as a wedding present. The donor had an adjusted basis of $8,000 in the stock. The stock was worth $12,000 at the time of the gift. John and Amy received $10,000 for the stock.

    Compute John and Amy's lowest taxable income. Treat all income as ordinary income.

52. Jim Loner, a self-employed individual, owned a truck driven exclusively for business use. The truck had an original cost of $32,000 and an adjusted basis on December 31, 2014, of $14,400. On January 2, 2015, he traded it in for a new truck costing $40,000 and was given a trade-in allowance of $8,000. The new truck will also be used exclusively for business purposes and will be depreciated with no salvage value. What is the basis of the new truck?
    a. $32,000
    b. $33,600
    c. $40,000
    d. $46,400

53. For purposes of determining like-kind property for nontaxable exchanges, which of the following items held for business or investment purposes are not like-kind property?
    a. Improved real estate for unimproved real estate
    b. Store building for farm buildings
    c. Machine for truck
    d. Dairy herd for farm acreage
    e. Tractor for combine

54. Which of the following statements is true regarding the exchange of like-kind property?
    a. If like-kind property is exchanged and money is paid, a taxable gain or deductible loss must be recognized by the payer of the cash.
    b. If like-kind and unlike property are given up, a taxable gain or deductible loss must be recognized only on the unlike property given up.
    c. The realized gain or loss in (a) (above) is recognized to the extent of the cash payment. The liability assumed does not limit the recognized gain.
    d. The gain or loss in (b) (above) is equal to the difference between the fair market value of the like-kind property and that property's adjusted basis.

55. Fred Frisby sells his personal residence for $178,000 (adjusted basis of $156,000) and within three months moves into a new residence he purchased for $250,000. What is his basis in the new residence?
    a. $250,000
    b. $228,000
    c. $178,000
    d. $156,000

56. Within a 30-day time period, Martha Meyer transfers her property to Michelle Mann, who transfers cash to William Woolsey, and William transfers his like-kind property to Martha. Which of the following statements is true?
    a. This constitutes a nontaxable exchange to Martha.
    b. The transaction will be taxable to all parties involved.
    c. The transaction is nontaxable to William and Martha.
    d. This exchange is a transaction that is taxable to Martha.

57. **Comprehensive Problem (Tax Return Problem).** Adam Armstrong, age 60 and single, earned $51,000 during 2015. He contributed $3,000 to the United Fund, paid $16,000 in federal income taxes, $2,750 in state income tax, $400 in state sales tax, and $2,300 in mortgage interest charges. Adam also had the following transactions:

   a. Sold for $50,000 stock that he had received as a gift which had an adjusted basis of $26,000 to the donor and a fair market value of $46,000 on the date of the gift and the taxable gift was $35,000. The donor had held the stock for two years and paid a gift tax of $14,000.

   b. Exchanged land held for five years as an investment for an apartment building and $25,000 cash. On the date of exchange, the land had an adjusted basis of $135,000. The apartment building had a fair market value of $335,000.

   c. An office building Adam owned was condemned by the state to make room for a state building. The building had an adjusted basis of $70,000 and a fair market value of $172,000. Adam received another building from the state and it had a fair market value of $150,000.

   d. Adam sold his personal residence for $145,000. He incurred $2,500 in selling expenses. The residence had an adjusted basis of $56,000. He moved into an apartment.

   Calculate Adam's lowest taxable income. Treat all income as ordinary income.

58. **Comprehensive Problem (Tax Return Problem).** Barry and Connie Rawles, husband and wife, are both age 34 and have two sons. Barry earned $51,000 and Connie earned $45,000 during 2015. Barry and Connie paid $3,200 state income taxes, $12,000 federal income taxes, $3,500 property taxes, $4,600 to First Presbyterian Church, $600 to needy families, $6,400 interest on their home mortgage, and $6,800 medical expenses. In addition, they had the following transactions:

   a. They sold their personal residence for $170,000. Their basis in the residence was $104,000. They incurred $7,000 in selling expenses. They purchased a new residence six months later for $220,000.

   b. Connie sold for $40,000 property she had inherited from her father in 2010. Her father's basis in the property was $15,000 and the fair market value on the date of death was $30,000.

   c. They sold for $6,000 business property which they had acquired as a gift in 2012. The basis to the donor was $7,500 and the fair market value on the date of the gift was $7,000.

   d. They exchanged 100 shares of Conway Corp. common stock, with a basis of $3,000, for 75 shares of Conway Corp. nonvoting common stock with a fair market value of $10,000.

   Determine Barry and Connie's lowest taxable income. Treat all income as ordinary income.

59. **Research Problem.** Carl Cushman, a college professor, age 58, purchased and moved into a house on August 1, 2013. He used the house continuously until September 1, 2014, on which date he went abroad for a one-year sabbatical leave. During part of the period of leave, the property was unoccupied and it was leased during the remainder of the period. On October 1, 2015, one month after returning from such leave, he sold the house. Can Carl use the exclusion for the sale of residence?

12

Property Transactions: Treatment of Capital and Section 1231 Assets

OBJECTIVES

After completing Chapter 12, you should be able to:

1. Discuss the special rules and limitations on transactions involving capital gains and losses.
2. Compute capital gains and losses for individuals and corporate taxpayers.
3. Define capital assets.
4. Describe the rules for holding periods, including special rules where property is stock or is acquired through involuntary conversions, exchanges, or gifts, or from decedents.
5. Describe the rules for reporting an individual taxpayer's capital gains and losses.
6. Define Section 1231 assets and describe the netting procedures.
7. Give the reasons for Section 1231, 1245, and 1250 as well as the definition and operations of the provisions.
8. Describe the nature of the recapture rules for Section 1245 and 1250 property.
9. Discuss the special recapture rules for gifts and inheritances, like-kind exchanges, involuntary conversions, charitable contributions, and installment sales.

OVERVIEW

The previous two chapters dealt with the determination of realized and recognized gain or loss and with basis as well as situations where there might be nonrecognition of gain or loss. Up to this point, recognized gains and losses have been treated as if they were ordinary gains and losses, which means they are includible or deductible in full respectively. This chapter focuses on transactions involving capital gains and losses which are subject to some special rules and limitations.

Some of the significant items excluded from the definition of capital asset are land and depreciable property used in a trade or business. These items, however, may receive capital gain treatment through Section 1231. This chapter examines the definition of Section 1231 assets and the netting procedures. Also included in the chapter is a discussion of the rules for recapture of depreciation under Sections 1245 and 1250. The recapture rules mean that some of the realized gain on disposition of certain Section 1231 assets may be recognized as ordinary income. In the Section 1250 asset area, the recapture rules vary with the type of property and, because they have undergone changes over the years, they are somewhat involved for the beginning tax student.

Special Rules and Limitations on Transactions

¶12,001   BACKGROUND

The Taxpayer Relief Act of 1997 significantly changed the taxation of capital gains. Prior to 1997, capital gains were divided into two categories: short-term capital gains and long-term capital gains. From 1991 until the 1997 changes, short-term capital gains ended up being taxed at ordinary income tax rates, which could be as high as 39.6 percent, while long-term capital gains were taxed at a maximum of 28 percent. To qualify as long-term capital gain or loss, a taxpayer must have held the capital asset for more than one year; if the asset was held one year or less, the capital gain or loss was short-term.

Congress wished to lower the maximum long-term capital gains tax rate to 20 percent in the 1997 Act. However, Congress did not wish to make the lower rate available to all long-term capital gains, and the 1997 rules divided long-term capital gains into three categories: long-term capital gains taxed at a maximum rate of 28 percent, long-term capital gains taxed at a maximum rate of 25 percent, and long-term capital gains taxed at a maximum rate of 20 percent.

To qualify for the 20 percent long-term capital gain tax rate, the capital asset had to be held for more than 12 months. For taxpayers in the 15 percent tax bracket, this long-term capital gains tax rate became 10 percent. Prior to the Taxpayer Relief Act of 1997, there was no special long-term capital gains tax rate available to the lower tax bracket taxpayers.

The 2003 Tax Act included a reduction in rates for long-term capital gains and qualified dividends to 15 percent for the four highest tax brackets and 5 percent for the two lower brackets. The lower rates apply to sales and dispositions of capital assets after May 5, 2003. The 15 percent rate on dividends applies to all qualified dividends received in 2003 and later years. For 2008 through 2012, the long-term capital gain and qualified dividend tax rate is 0 percent for taxpayers in the two lower tax brackets.

The American Taxpayer Relief Act of 2012 raised the top rate for capital gains and dividends to 20 percent effective in 2013. In 2015, that rate applies to the extent that a taxpayer's income exceeds the thresholds set for the 39.6 percent rate ($413,200 for single filers; $464,850 for joint filers and $439,000 for heads of households). All other taxpayers will continue to be allowed a capital gains and dividends tax at a maximum rate of 15 percent. A zero percent rate also will continue to apply to capital gains and dividends for those taxpayers in the 10 and 15 percent tax brackets.

EXAMPLE 12.1

In calculating the tax on net capital gain in 2015, the results are as follows under two assumptions, for taxpayers with married filing jointly status:

(1) assuming $500,000 net capital gains and $100,000 ordinary taxable income;
(2) assuming $420,000 ordinary income and $100,000 capital gains.

Given the $464,850 threshold for both the 39.6 percent ordinary income rate and the 20 percent maximum rate on capital gain set under the American Taxpayer Relief Act of 2012, the following rates would apply:

For (1), $100,000 ordinary income will be taxed under the regular income tax tables, up through the 25 percent marginal rate that starts at $74,900; $364,850 of the capital gain will be taxed at the 15 percent rate ($464,850 threshold less $100,000 ordinary income); and the remaining $135,150 capital gain is taxed at 20 percent.

For (2), $420,000 ordinary income will be taxed under the regular income tax tables, up through the 35 percent marginal rate that starts at $411,500; $44,850 of the capital gain will be taxed at the 15 percent rate ($464,850 threshold less $420,000 ordinary income); and the remaining $55,150 capital gain is taxed at 20 percent.

The 28 percent long-term capital gains tax rate applies to collectibles and Section 1202 gains. Generally, collectibles (as defined in Code Sec. 408(m)) include works of art, rugs, antiques, metal, gems, stamps, coins, and alcoholic beverages. However, certain newly minted gold and silver coins issued by the federal government and coins issued under state laws are subject to the 15 percent tax rate even though such coins generally qualify as "collectibles." Section 1202 stock is certain small business stock that meets very specific criteria. Gains on the disposition of Section 1202 stock held at least 5 years qualify for a 50 percent exclusion. Stock qualifying for the exclusion is included in the 28 percent long-term capital gains tax rate category.

The 25 percent long-term capital gains tax rate applies to what is referred to as "unrecaptured Section 1250 gain." Unrecaptured Section 1250 gain is the amount of the long-term capital gain that would be treated as ordinary income if a Section 1250 asset were classified as a Section 1245 asset. (See a later part of the chapter for a discussion of Section 1245 and 1250 assets, depreciation recapture, and the determination of the amount of "unrecaptured Section 1250 gain.") Under the old rules, the unrecaptured Section 1250 gain was taxed at a maximum tax rate of 28 percent. Congress did not wish for this amount to be taxed at the then new lower 20 percent tax rate.

Because of the potential benefit of long-term capital gains, the capital loss limitations, and the continuation of Section 1231 assets (as discussed at ¶12,601), the study of the tax structure applicable to capital gains continues to be of importance to the student. Indeed, a tax rate increase occurred in 1993, when the top ordinary rate increased to 39.6 percent, thereby creating a potential differential of 19.6 percent over the capital gain rate of 20 percent. Similarly, in 2015, the top ordinary rate of 39.6 percent exceeds the 20 percent capital gain rate by 19.6 percent.

¶12,025   CAPITAL ASSET DEFINITION

Capital assets are not actually defined in the Internal Revenue Code. Instead, Code Sec. 1221 defines a capital asset as any property held by the taxpayer *except:*

1. Stock in trade or other inventory property or property held by the taxpayer primarily for sale to customers in the ordinary course of a trade or business
2. Depreciable property used in a trade or business
3. Real property used in a trade or business
4. Copyright, literary, musical, or artistic composition, letter or memorandum, or similar property held by (1) a taxpayer whose personal efforts created such property, (2) a taxpayer for whom such property was prepared or produced, or (3) a taxpayer in whose hands the basis of the property is determined by reference to the basis of the property held by a taxpayer described in (1) or (2)
5. Accounts or notes receivable acquired in the ordinary course of a trade or business for services rendered or from the sale of property
6. U.S. government publications (1) received by the taxpayer from the government other than by purchase at the price at which they are offered for sale to the public, or (2) held by a taxpayer whose basis in such publications is determined by reference to a taxpayer described in (1)

As seen from the above definition, the Code defines a capital asset by listing the assets that are not capital assets. The major items excluded from capital assets are inventory and business fixed assets such as land, buildings, machinery, and equipment. Because these assets are excluded from capital assets, the conclusion might be drawn that they are subject to ordinary income treatment. This, however, is not the case. Depreciable property and land used in a trade or business receive special treatment. Under Code Sec. 1231, if the net result from sales of such properties is a gain, it may be subject to capital gain treatment and, if the net result is a loss, it is subject to ordinary loss treatment.

The primary capital assets are investment property such as stocks and bonds and personal-use assets such as a residence or personal automobile. Gains and losses from the sale of investment property are recognized as capital gains and losses. Gains from the sale or exchange of personal-use assets are capital gains, but losses from transactions in personal-use assets are never deductible, unless a casualty or theft is involved.

| EXAMPLE 12.2 | Caroline Collector sold at a loss some jewelry she used for two years. She is not able to deduct the loss, since jewelry is a personal-use asset. If she sold the jewelry at a gain, she would have a capital gain. If, on the other hand, Caroline held the jewelry as an investment in her safe deposit box and never wore the jewelry, any gain or loss would be a capital gain or loss. |

| PLANNING POINTER | The classification of an asset as capital or ordinary can be important. Not only is there potential special tax treatment for long-term capital gains and losses, but there may be advantages if capital gain property is given as a charitable contribution. In that case, the amount of the charitable contribution is the fair market value of the donated property which, if it were sold, would result in a long-term capital gain. If it is ordinary income property, the charitable contribution is limited to the basis of the property. |

Special Situations in Capital v. Ordinary Treatment

¶12,101   ## INVENTORY

Taxpayers may no longer avoid capital asset treatment by proving that property, which otherwise fits within the definition of a capital asset, was acquired for business rather than investment purposes. The U.S. Supreme Court has held that a taxpayer's motivation in purchasing an asset is irrelevant to a determination of whether the asset falls within the broad statutory definition of a "capital asset." *Arkansas Best Co.,* 88-1 USTC ¶9210, 485 U.S. 212, 108 S.Ct. 971 (1988), aff'g 86-2 USTC ¶9671, 800 F.2d 215 (CA-8 1986). Thus, losses incurred by a diversified holding company from the sale of bank stock that had been purchased in order to supply new capital to the financially troubled institution were capital in nature.

¶12,115   ## SALE OF A BUSINESS

When a business that has operated as a sole proprietorship is sold, the sale is not treated as the sale of one asset. Instead, it is treated as the sale of the individual assets of the business. *E.A. Watson,* 53-1 USTC ¶9391, 345 U.S. 544, 73 S.Ct. 848 (1953); *Williams v. McGowan,* 46-1 USTC ¶9120, 152 F.2d 570 (CA-2 1945); Rev. Rul. 55-79, 1955-1 CB 370. The proceeds received are allocated to the assets according to their relative fair market values. The gain or loss on some of the assets will be ordinary gain or loss and on other assets there will be capital gain or loss.

The sale of a partnership interest is the sale of a capital asset and results in capital gain or loss to the partners except that the part of the gain or loss that is related to unrealized receivables or substantially appreciated inventory items is treated as ordinary gain or loss. Code Secs. 741 and 751(a). The sale of corporate stock results in a capital gain or loss if the stock was a capital asset in the hands of the seller.

¶12,125   ## PATENTS

Certain transfers of patents may result in capital gain treatment. Code Sec. 1235. The reason for this provision is to encourage invention, although the same tax treatment is not available to authors and artists. In the latter cases, their works (writings and art) are specifically excluded from capital assets. However, a taxpayer can elect to treat the sale or exchange of a musical composition or copyright in musical works by the taxpayer's personal efforts as a sale of a capital asset.

If an inventor transfers (other than by gift, inheritance, or devise) property consisting of all substantial rights to a patent, or an undivided interest therein, the transfer is considered the sale or exchange of a capital asset held the requisite time period to meet the long-term holding period rules. This rule holds even if payments are payable periodically over a period ending when the purchaser's use of the patent ends or if payments are contingent on the productivity, use, or disposition of the property transferred. Code Sec. 1235(a).

EXAMPLE 12.3   Bennett Burrow, an inventor, sold his patent to Smith Corporation for a lump-sum payment of $100,000 plus $6 per unit sold. He had a zero basis in the patent. Bennett has a long-term capital gain of $100,000 and the $6 per unit royalty will also receive long-term capital gain treatment regardless of how long the patent was held.

"All substantial rights" means all rights which are of value at the time the rights to the patent are transferred. It does not include a grant of rights to a patent (1) which is limited geographically within the country of issuance; (2) which is limited in duration by the terms of the agreement to a period less than the remaining life of the patent; (3) which grants rights to the grantee in fields of use within trades or industries, which are less than all the valuable rights at the time of the grant; or (4) which grants to the grantee less than all the claims or inventions covered by the patent at the time of the grant. Reg. §1.1235-2(b).

| EXAMPLE 12.4 | Vance Vox sells patent rights to his invention, but the rights limit the use of the invention to the state of California. Vance's sale of patent rights does not qualify for capital gain treatment since the rights are limited within the United States. |

The transferor must be a holder which refers to the creator of the property or any individual who has purchased an interest in the property from such creator if such individual is neither the employer of the creator nor related to the creator. Code Sec. 1235(b).

¶12,135   FRANCHISES

A franchise includes an agreement which gives one of the parties (the transferee) the right to distribute, sell, or provide goods, services, or facilities, within a specified area. Rules are provided for the treatment to the transferee and transferor of a franchise, trademark, or trade name. Code Sec. 1253. Specifically, a transfer of a franchise, trademark, or trade name is not treated as a sale or exchange of a capital asset if the transferor retains any significant power, right, or continuing interest with respect to the property. Amounts received on account of a transfer, sale, or disposition which are contingent on the productivity, use, or disposition of the property are also not treated as a sale or disposition of a capital asset. Code Sec. 1253(a)-(c).

The term "significant power, right, or continuing interest" includes but is not limited to the following rights with respect to the transferred interest:

1. To disapprove any assignment of such an interest
2. To terminate the franchise at will
3. To prescribe the standards of quality of products
4. To require that the transferee sell or advertise only products or services of the transferor
5. To require the transferee to purchase substantially all supplies or equipment from the transferor
6. To require payments contingent on the productivity, use, or sale of the property (Code Sec. 1253(b)(2))

Since most franchises involve the transferor retaining at least some of these rights, the transferor is going to have ordinary income upon the transfer of a franchise.

Amounts paid by the transferee which are contingent on the productivity, use, or disposition of the property transferred are allowed as business deductions. Other payments are generally amortized over 15 years. Code Sec. 197(g).

| EXAMPLE 12.5 | Farmers Corporation grants Grace Gobbler a franchise to sell fried chicken for a period of 20 years with renewals. Farmers Corporation retains the powers and rights described above. Grace is required to pay $100,000 initially and then three percent of sales. The $100,000 payment and the percentage payments are ordinary income to Farmers. Grace may deduct the percentage payments as ordinary business expenses. The initial payment of $100,000 is amortized over 15 years beginning in the year the payment is made. |

| EXAMPLE 12.6 | Denny Doone, a transferee of a franchise, sells the franchise to a third party, transferring all significant powers and rights. Payments to Denny are not contingent. Any reportable gain will be capital gain to him. |

¶12,155   LEASE CANCELLATION PAYMENTS

Amounts received by a lessee (tenant) for the cancellation of a lease are considered as amounts received for the exchange of such lease or agreement. Code Sec. 1241. The type of gain or loss will depend on the character of the lease. A nondepreciable leasehold (for example, for a personal-use asset as a residence) is a capital asset. A depreciable lease used in a trade or business is either an ordinary asset or a Section 1231 asset. Amounts received by the landlord for canceling a lease are ordinary income. *W.M. Hort,* 41-1 USTC ¶9534, 313 U.S. 28, 61 S.Ct. 757 (1941).

EXAMPLE 12.7	Terry Thomson pays Lydia Lancer, the owner of his apartment, $500 in order to cancel his lease. Lydia treats the $500 as ordinary income.

EXAMPLE 12.8	Lydia pays Tony Terrace, a tenant of one of her apartments, $900 to cancel the lease. Tony would report $900 capital gain since the lease was a nondepreciable leasehold and thus a capital asset.

¶12,165   OPTIONS

Gain or loss from the sale or exchange of an option to buy or sell property or from failure to exercise such option is of the same character as the property to which the option relates. If loss is attributable to failure to exercise an option, the option is deemed to have been sold or exchanged on the day it expired. Code Sec. 1234(a).

EXAMPLE 12.9	Jerrold Jackson had an option on 1,000 shares of King Corporation stock. Although the stock increased in value, Jerrold did not purchase the stock. Instead, he sold the option at a gain. Jerrold would report a capital gain since the King Corporation stock would have been a capital asset to him if he had purchased it.

Holding Period

¶12,201   COMPUTATION OF HOLDING PERIOD

Holding period continues to be important in 2015 because of the reduced rate at which net capital gains are taxed and because the basic structure for capital gains and losses has been retained in the Code. Additionally, the definition of Section 1231 assets includes those assets used in a trade or business and held long-term. Gains and losses on these Section 1231 assets continue to be separately computed.

Property has to be held for longer than one year to be long-term. Code Sec. 1222. Note, as discussed in a later section, the tax advantages on the gain side occur when property is held greater than 12 months (where the maximum rate is generally 15 percent). In figuring the holding period, the day the property was acquired is excluded, but the day it was disposed of is included. Since the day after acquisition is the start of the holding period, this same date in each of the following months is the start of the new month. It does not matter how many days are in each month. Property acquired on the last day of the month must be held on or after the first day of the thirteenth succeeding month to be held long-term. Rev. Rul. 66-7, 1966-1 CB 188.

EXAMPLE 12.10	Cindy Crier purchased shares of stock on February 17, 2014. If she sells the stock on February 18, 2015, or later, she will have long-term capital gain or loss in the 15/20 percent basket. If she sells the stock on February 17, 2015, or earlier, she will have short-term capital gain or loss.

EXAMPLE 12.11	If Jack Jeffrey purchases shares of stock on January 31, 2014, and sells the stock on February 1, 2015, or later, he will have long-term capital gain or loss in the 15/20 percent basket. If he sells the stock on January 31, 2015, or earlier, he will have short-term capital gain or loss.

¶12,215   SPECIAL RULES FOR HOLDING PERIOD

The general rule is that the holding period runs from the day following the date of acquisition to the date of disposition, but there are special rules in certain circumstances.

Property Acquired Through Exchanges and Conversions

The holding period of property received in an exchange includes the holding period of the property given in the exchange if the basis of the acquired property has the same basis in whole or in part as the property exchanged. Code Sec. 1223(1). The property exchanged must be a capital asset or Section 1231 assets (i.e., property used in a trade or business). Property acquired as a result of an involuntary conversion is also considered an exchange for this purpose.

EXAMPLE 12.12	On July 9, 2015, George Grundy exchanged 100 shares of Jones Corporation Class A stock (bought on July 14, 2011, for $1,500) for Jones Corporation Class B stock in a nontaxable exchange. George sells the Class B shares on December 16, 2015, for $1,200. Since the holding period of the Class B shares began on July 15, 2011, and the basis is $1,500, George has a long-term capital loss of $300.

EXAMPLE 12.13	Kathy Krupp sold her office building on November 15 at a gain. She had purchased this building only four months earlier upon receiving insurance proceeds after a fire destroyed her old building, on which she had deferred all the realized gain and which she had owned for five years. Kathy's sale of her building on November 15 results in a long-term capital gain since she would have a holding period of five years, four months on the building. That is, she counts the five years she owned the former building in her holding period.

Property Acquired by a Gift and from a Decedent

The holding period of property acquired by gift includes the holding period of the donor if the basis of the property is the same in whole or in part as it had been in the hands of the donor. Code Sec. 1223(2); Reg. §1.1223-1(b). If at the date of the gift the property has a fair market value that is less than the donor's adjusted basis and the property is sold at a loss, the holding period begins on the day following the date of the gift.

EXAMPLE 12.14	On March 17, 2015, Justin Jaeger received shares of stock as a gift from his father, who had owned it for four years and who had an adjusted basis of $5,000 in the stock. The stock had a fair market value of $8,000. Justin sold the stock on June 17, 2015, for $9,000. Although Justin has owned it only three months, he has a $4,000 long-term capital gain since he includes the period that his father owned it.

EXAMPLE 12.15	Assume the facts in the preceding example, except that the fair market value at the date of the gift was $3,000 and he sold it for $2,500. Justin has a short-term capital loss of $500 since his holding period begins on the day following the date of the gift which means he held the stock three months.

Gains and losses from the sale or exchange of inherited property are treated as long-term (greater than 12 months and subject to the capital gains rates) regardless of how long the property was held. Code Sec. 1223(11).

EXAMPLE 12.16	On April 23, 2015, Alice Amberson inherited stock from her aunt, who had owned the stock for three months. On June 23, 2015, Alice sells the stock at a gain. Alice has long-term capital gain even though she owned the property only two months and even though the total ownership by Alice and her aunt was only five months.

Individual Taxpayers

¶12,301   DETERMINATION OF TAXABLE INCOME

An individual's capital gains and losses are reported on Form 8949 and carried to Schedule D. The process is not specifically described in the Code but is necessary under the definitions in Code Sec. 1222.

For sales and exchanges after 1998, it is necessary to hold assets more than 12 months in order for the lowest long-term capital gains rates to apply, in which case the maximum rate is 15 percent (0 percent for individuals in the 10 and 15 percent tax bracket) or 20 percent for those taxpayers in the 39.6% bracket. Further, the 15 and 20 percent (0 percent for 10 and 15 percent bracket taxpayers) rates applies only to adjusted net capital gains, which are net capital gains (i.e., the excess of net long-term capital gains over the net short-term capital losses) without regard to:

1. **Collectibles Gain.** Generally, collectibles (as defined in Sec. 408(m)) do not qualify for the lowest rates. Thus, stamps, antiques, gems, and most coins would still be taxed at the maximum rate of 28 percent. (Taxpayers will only be taxed at the maximum 28 percent rate if they are in the 28 percent or higher marginal tax bracket.) Certain newly minted gold and silver coins issued by the federal government and coins issued under state law, however, are subject to the lower capital gains rate, even though such coins generally qualify as "collectibles."

2. **Section 1202 Gains.** When a taxpayer sells or exchanges Sec. 1202 stock (i.e., certain small business stock) that the taxpayer has held for more than five years, 50 percent of the gain is excluded from the taxpayer's gross income. If the taxpayer qualifies for this 50 percent exclusion, any recognized gains from the sale or exchange of this stock would be taxed at the maximum rate of 28 percent. (Taxpayers will only be taxed at the maximum 28 percent rate if they are in the 28 percent or higher marginal tax bracket.)

3. **Unrecaptured Section 1250 Gain.** Unrecaptured Sec. 1250 gain is the amount of the long-term capital gain that would be treated as ordinary income if Sec. 1250(b)(1) included all depreciation with an applicable percentage of 100 percent, and only gains from Sec. 1250 property held for more than 12 months were taken into account. This gain is taxed at a maximum rate of 25 percent. (Taxpayers will only be taxed at the maximum 25 percent rate if they are in the 25 percent or higher marginal tax bracket.) See ¶12,815.

The steps for determining taxable income are as follows:

1. Group all gains or losses into four "baskets" and determine a net figure for each basket. The *short-term basket* contains short-term capital gains and losses and short-term capital loss carryovers. The *28 percent basket* contains collectibles gains and losses, Section 1202 gains, and long-term capital loss carryovers. The *25 percent basket* contains any Section 1250 gain (up to total depreciation taken but not to exceed the recognized gain) that exceeds the portion of gain recaptured at the taxpayer's ordinary marginal tax rate (see ¶12,801 to ¶12,935 to see how this is calculated). The *15/20 percent basket* contains long-term capital gains and losses, not included in the other brackets, and unrecaptured Section 1231 long-term gains.

2. A net loss from the 28% group is used
   a. To reduce gain from the 25% basket
   b. Then to reduce net gain from the 15/20% basket

3. A net loss from the 15/20% group is used
   a. To reduce gain from the 28% basket
   b. Then to reduce gain from the 25% basket

4. Net short-term capital losses are applied
   a. To reduce net long-term gains from the 28% basket
   b. Then to reduce gain from the 25% basket
   c. Finally to reduce net gain from the 15/20% basket

5. Net short-term capital gains are applied to reduce net losses from either the 15/20% or 28% baskets.

6. Any resulting net capital gain that is attributable to a particular rate basket is taxed at the basket's marginal tax rate.

7. Any excess loss is deductible up to $3,000 ($1,500 for married filing separately) as under prior law, and the remainder is carried over.

EXAMPLE 12.17 On May 26, 2015, Nancy Northfield sold for $4,000 shares of stock acquired on December 23, 2014, for $3,200. She has a short-term capital gain of $800. On July 22, 2015, she sold for $8,000 shares of stock purchased for $8,300 on March 21, 2015. She has a short-term capital loss of $300. Nancy's net short-term capital gain is $500. If these are the only capital transactions, the $500 is taxed at an ordinary rate up to 39.6 percent.

EXAMPLE 12.18	On June 16, 2015, John Jennings sold for $3,000 shares of stock he had acquired for $2,400 on January 24, 2015. He has a short-term capital gain of $600. On August 19, 2015, he sold for $7,000 shares of stock he purchased for $8,300 on April 15, 2015. He has a short-term capital loss of $1,300 on this sale. John's net short-term capital loss is $700. If these are the only capital transactions, John receives a $700 deduction.
EXAMPLE 12.19	On December 15, 2015, Nancy sold for $6,200 shares of stock she had acquired for $10,000 on November 18, 2014. She has a long-term capital loss of $3,800. On November 14, 2015, she sold for $14,000 shares of stock she had acquired for $12,000 on October 14, 2014. This is a $2,000 long-term capital gain. Nancy's net long-term capital loss is $1,800. If these are the only capital transactions, Nancy has a deductible loss of $1,800.
EXAMPLE 12.20	On November 10, 2015, John sold for $11,000 stock that he had acquired for $8,000 on October 14, 2014. He has a long-term capital gain of $3,000 on this transaction. On December 12, 2015, he sold for $6,000 stock he had acquired for $7,800 on November 11, 2014. He has a long-term capital loss of $1,800 on this transaction. John has a net long-term capital gain of $1,200. If these are the only capital transactions, John would be taxed at a maximum rate of 15/20 percent.
EXAMPLE 12.21	On December 2, 2015, Brian Boyd sold for $12,000 collectibles he had purchased on October 29, 2014, for $7,000. He also sold on the same day for $14,000 stock he had purchased on July 29, 2014, for $8,000. Brian is taxed at a maximum rate of 28 percent on the collectibles gain of $5,000 and at a maximum rate of 15/20 percent on the $6,000 gain.
EXAMPLE 12.22	If Nancy has the net short-term capital gain of $500 from Example 12.17 and the net long-term capital loss of $1,800 from Example 12.19, she has a net overall loss of $1,300, which is deductible.
EXAMPLE 12.23	If John has the net short-term capital loss of $700 in Example 12.18 and the net long-term capital gain of $1,200 in Example 12.20, John has an overall gain of $500 taxed at a maximum rate of 15/20 percent.
EXAMPLE 12.24	Edwin Edwards, a 33 percent bracket taxpayer, had three stock transactions that gave the following results during 2015: STCG $6,000, LTCG $8,000, collectibles gain $10,000. His overall net gain is $24,000, and he will be taxed at 15 percent on the $8,000, 28 percent on the $10,000, and 33 percent on the $6,000.
EXAMPLE 12.25	During 2015, Tim Turner had a net LTCG of $7,500 and a net STCL of $10,500. Tim's net overall loss is $3,000, and he may take a $3,000 deduction.
EXAMPLE 12.26	During 2015, Joan Janner had a net STCG of $5,000 and a net LTCL of $7,000. The net overall loss is $2,000 and Joan receives a deduction for $2,000.
EXAMPLE 12.27	Beth, a single 33 percent taxpayer, had 2015 capital gains and losses as follows: a short-term capital loss of $12,000 and a short-term capital gain of $5,000, a 28 percent collectibles gain of $4,000, $1,000 unrecaptured Section 1250 gain (losses are not possible here), and a 15 percent long-term capital gain of $1,000. Beth has an initial net short-term capital loss of $7,000. The $7,000 net loss is used to offset the $4,000 in the 28 percent basket, then the $1,000 in the 25% basket, and finally the $1,000 in the 15 percent basket. The remaining short-term loss is $1,000. This loss is deductible by Beth in 2015.

EXAMPLE 12.28	If Beth's figures were the same as in the previous example but she did not have the short-term capital loss of $12,000 then her short-term netting would result in a $5,000 net gain, since it is the only item in her short-term basket. The remaining nettings would all be net gains. Beth's $5,000 net short-term capital gain would be taxed at 33 percent, her net collectibles gain of $4,000 would be taxed at 28 percent, the $1,000 unrecaptured Section 1250 gain would be taxed at 25 percent, and her long-term capital gain of $1,000 would be taxed at 15 percent.

EXAMPLE 12.29	If Beth's figures from Example 12.28 were as follows: a short-term capital loss of $12,000 and a short-term capital gain of $5,000, a collectible gain of $4,000, $1,000 of unrecaptured Section 1250 gain, and a 15 percent long-term capital gain of $5,000. Beth has a net short-term capital loss of $7,000. The $7,000 net short-term capital loss is first used to offset the $4,000 in the 28 percent basket, then the $1,000 in the 25 percent basket, and finally the $5,000 in the 15 percent basket. This leaves $3,000 to be taxed at the 15 percent long-term capital gains rate.

¶12,315 CAPITAL LOSS CARRYOVERS

If the capital losses exceed the limits described above, the excess may be carried over indefinitely. The amounts carried over are offset against capital gains in the subsequent years. The carryforward losses will be treated as if they occurred in the subsequent years. For example, a capital loss is carried over to the following year and is offset against capital gains according to the regular steps for computation of net overall capital gain or loss. If the taxpayer has both short-term and long-term losses in total exceeding the limit allowed as a deduction, short-term losses are applied to the limit first even if they were incurred after the long-term losses. Any long-term carryovers are placed in the 28 percent basket in the following year.

EXAMPLE 12.30	Greg Grove has a net STCL of $2,000 and a net LTCL of $5,500 during 2015. The net STCL is used up first dollar for dollar to give a $2,000 deduction. Then the net LTCL is used up to get the remaining $1,000 deduction for a total $3,000 deduction. This leaves $4,500 LTCL to be carried over to 2016. In 2016, this $4,500 LTCL carryover is treated as if it were a LTCL incurred during 2016 and is placed in the 28 percent basket.

EXAMPLE 12.31	Michelle Martin has a net STCL of $4,000 and a net LTCL of $2,000 in 2015. The STCL is used up first for a $3,000 deduction and $1,000 STCL is carried over to 2016. The net LTCL of $2,000 is also carried over to 2016. In 2016, she has a STCG of $600 and a LTCG of $1,200. In 2016, the STCL carryover of $1,000 is offset against the STCG of $600 to get a net STCL of $400. The LTCL carryover of $2,000 is offset against the LTCG of $1,200 for a net LTCL of $800. For 2016, Michelle is allowed a deduction of $1,200 ($400 + $800).

¶12,401 CORPORATE TAXPAYERS DISTINGUISHED

The capital gain and loss treatment of corporate taxpayers differs from that of individual taxpayers in four ways.

1. The corporation is not allowed any special advantage for net capital gains (i.e., the excess of net LTCG over net STCL). Instead, corporate capital gains are taxed at regular corporate tax rates, with the maximum tax rate of 35 percent.
2. The corporation is not allowed a deduction in the current year for a net overall capital loss position. Capital losses for corporations are allowed only to the extent of the capital gains.
3. A net overall capital loss can still be used by a corporation. It is carried back three years and carried forward five years against capital gains.
4. Corporate carrybacks and carryovers are treated as short-term.

Special Provisions for Certain Investments

¶12,501 NONBUSINESS BAD DEBTS

Nonbusiness bad debts are debts that are not related to the taxpayer's trade or business. They are treated as a short-term capital loss in the year of worthlessness, regardless of how long they were outstanding. The debts must be completely worthless. Code Sec. 166(d)(1); Reg. §1.166-5(a)(2). However, a taxpayer has a totally worthless bad debt when none of what is still owed can be collected, even though the taxpayer may have collected some of the debt in the past. Only a bona fide debt qualifies for deduction as a bad debt. A bona fide debt is a debt that arises from a debtor-creditor relationship based on a valid and enforceable obligation to pay a sum of money. Reg. §1.166-1(c).

EXAMPLE 12.32   In 2013, Beth Burrow loaned $7,000 to her friend Nancy Newburg. In 2015, Nancy declared bankruptcy, with the result that the debt is totally worthless. Beth may deduct the $7,000 loss as a short-term capital loss. If she has no other capital gains or losses, she deducts $3,000 in 2015 and carries the remaining $4,000 to 2016.

PLANNING POINTER   Since nonbusiness bad debts result in short-term capital losses, the taxpayer is subject to the regular capital loss limitation of $3,000. Taxpayers should be cautious in making large nonbusiness loans that may become worthless (unless they have capital gains to offset the losses) since it might take a long time to receive the tax deduction given the limitation on the capital loss deduction in a particular year.

¶12,515 WORTHLESS SECURITIES

If a security that is a capital asset becomes worthless, the loss is a capital loss on the last day of the taxable year in which the security becomes worthless. Code Sec. 165(g)(1). Thus, worthless stock that may have been held short-term may result in a long-term capital loss.

EXAMPLE 12.33   Donna Drummond, a calendar-year taxpayer, purchased stock for $4,000 on May 31, 2014. On January 31, 2015, the stock became worthless. She is considered to have held the stock from May 31, 2014, to December 31, 2015 (more than 12 months). Donna has a long-term capital loss even though the stock was worthless after she held it only eight months.

¶12,525 SMALL BUSINESS STOCK

Individual taxpayers are allowed ordinary loss deductions for losses from the sale or exchange, or from worthlessness of certain small business stock (known as "Section 1244 stock"). Code Sec. 1244(a). The maximum deduction for any taxable year is limited to $50,000. Code Sec. 1244(b). On a joint return, the limit is $100,000 whether the stock is owned by one spouse or both spouses. Reg. §1.1244(b)-1. Any excess above these limits is capital loss. The ordinary loss deduction not used in the year sustained is treated as attributable to a trade or business and increases the net operating loss of the shareholder and becomes part of the shareholder's net operating loss carryback and carryover. Code Sec. 1244(d)(3).

The term "Section 1244 stock" refers to stock issued by a small business corporation for money or other property. Code Sec. 1244(c)(1). Section 1244 stock must not be convertible into other securities of the corporation. Reg. §1.1244(c)-1(b). A corporation is considered a small business corporation if the aggregate amount of money and other property received by the corporation for stock as a contribution to capital and as paid-in surplus does not exceed $1 million at the time of stock issuance. Code Sec. 1244(c)(3).

The amount of the "other property" is the adjusted basis to the corporation of such property reduced by any liability to which the property was subject or which was assumed by the corporation. In addition, for the period of five years ending before the loss the corporation must have derived more than 50 percent of its gross receipts from sources other than royalties, rents, dividends, interest, annuities, and sales or exchanges of stocks or securities. If the corporation has been in existence for less than five years, the relevant time period is the time it has been in existence. Special rules also apply for corporations where deductions exceed gross income. Code Sec. 1244(c)(1)-(3).

EXAMPLE 12.34	Elaine Eggelston, single, acquires 1,000 shares of Section 1244 stock in 2009 for $150,000 and sells all of it in 2015 for $80,000. She has a $50,000 ordinary loss and a $20,000 long-term capital loss. If she had been married and filed a joint return, she would have had a $70,000 ordinary loss. This assumes that the five-year, 50 percent test is met.

PLANNING POINTER	The taxpayer should consider selling stock in two or more taxable years in order to take advantage of the loss limits. Thus, in this example, if Elaine had sold 500 shares in 2015 for $40,000 and the other 500 shares for $40,000 in 2016, she would have had a $35,000 ordinary loss deduction in both years.

The allowance of an ordinary loss deduction on Section 1244 stock is permitted only to an individual who must be the original owner, or to an individual who is a partner in a partnership at the time of original acquisition. Code Sec. 1244(a); Reg. §1.1244(a)-1(b). The partner's share of the ordinary loss is the partner's share of the partnership's loss on sale of the stock. An individual acquiring stock from a shareholder by purchase, gift, or inheritance is not entitled to ordinary loss deductions under Section 1244.

If a shareholder receives Section 1244 stock as a result of contributing property that had a fair market value less than its adjusted basis immediately before the exchange, the basis of the stock is reduced to the fair market value of the property in computing the amount of the ordinary loss.

EXAMPLE 12.35	In 2009, Walter Winston, single, transfers property with an adjusted basis of $160,000 and a fair market value of $120,000 in exchange for 100 percent of the Section 1244 stock of Thompson Corporation. In 2015, he sells the stock for $85,000. Although he has a recognized loss of $75,000, Walter may recognize only $35,000 ordinary loss and the remaining $40,000 loss is long-term capital loss.

If a taxpayer makes additional contributions to capital after acquiring Section 1244 stock causing the basis in the stock to increase, a loss on the stock is treated as allocated partly to Section 1244 stock and partly to stock which is not Section 1244 stock. Code Sec. 1244(d)(1).

EXAMPLE 12.36	Joe Jamestown purchased Section 1244 stock costing $50,000 in 2008 and made an additional capital contribution in 2009 in the amount of $20,000. In 2015, Joe sells the stock for $28,000. Of the $42,000 loss, five-sevenths ($50,000/$70,000) or $30,000 is ordinary loss and the remaining $12,000 is a capital loss.

PLANNING POINTER	Instead of just making an additional capital contribution of $20,000, Joe should have received additional stock for his $20,000 investment. With the additional investment qualifying as Section 1244 stock, the entire $42,000 loss would be an ordinary loss.

¶12,530   GAINS ON SMALL BUSINESS STOCK

Noncorporate investors who were the original holders of qualified small business stock acquired after August 10, 1993, and who held it for at least five years were eligible to exclude 50 percent of the gain from the sale of the stock from their gross income. The American Recovery and Reinvestment Act of 2009 increased the exclusion to 75 percent for stock acquired after the date of enactment (February 17, 2009) and before January 1, 2011. The remaining portion of the gain would be taxed as long-term capital gain at a maximum rate of 28 percent. Taxpayers subject to the alternative minimum tax, however, would have to include 7 percent of the excluded gain as a tax preference item. The Small Business Jobs Act of 2010 raised the exclusion for stock purchased after September 27, 2010 and before January 1, 2011, to 100%. The excluded gain is not an AMT preference. The Tax Relief, Unemployment Insurance Reauthorization, and Job Creation Act of 2010 extended the provisions through 2011. The American Taxpayer Relief Act extended the provisions through 2013 and in 2014, the provision was extended through 2014. Code Sec. 1202. In 2015, the exclusion is 50%.

The exclusion is limited to $10 million of the gain from the sale of the stock by an investor in the same corporation or, if greater, 10 times the adjusted basis of the stock in the corporation that the investor sold during the year.

Other major requirements for the exclusion are:

1. The stock must be issued by a C corporation in exchange for money, property other than stock, or compensation for services rendered to the corporation.
2. The corporation must use at least 80 percent by value of its assets in the active conduct of one or more trades or businesses and can have no more than $50 million in gross assets when it issues the stock.
3. The corporation cannot engage in certain types of businesses, such as businesses that provide personal services (e.g., health, law, or accounting); banking, insurance, financing, leasing, or investing; the extraction or production of natural resources eligible for percentage depletion; farming; and the operation of hotels, motels, and restaurants.
4. Gain from the sale of stock of a DISC (or former DISC), regulated investment company, real estate investment trust, real estate mortgage investment conduit, cooperative, or corporation claiming the possessions tax credit does not qualify for the exclusion.

¶12,535   DEALERS IN SECURITIES

Generally, securities held by a dealer are ordinary assets because they are considered to be inventory. The gains or losses from sale of these securities are considered ordinary gains or losses. However, under special circumstances, it is possible for a dealer to classify securities as capital assets and receive capital gain or loss treatment on the sale or exchange.

Gain from the sale or exchange of a security is not considered as a capital gain unless the security was clearly identified in the dealer's records as a security held for investment before the close of the day on which it was acquired. Also, it may not be held by the dealer as primarily for sale to customers in the ordinary course of a trade or business at any time after the day of acquisition. Losses are not considered ordinary if the security was clearly identified in the dealer's records as a security held for investment. Code Sec. 1236(a) and (b).

For purposes of these rules, the term "security" means any share of stock in any corporation, note, bond, debenture, or evidence of indebtedness, or any evidence of an interest in or right to subscribe to or purchase any of the foregoing. "Floor specialists" have until the seventh business day after acquisition to make their identification. A floor specialist is a person who is a member of a national securities exchange, is registered as a specialist with the exchange, and meets the requirements for specialists established by the Securities and Exchange Commission. Code Sec. 1236(c) and (d).

EXAMPLE 12.37	Wilbur Washburn, a dealer in securities, purchases XYZ Corporation stock on January 14, 2015. On that date, he identifies the stock as assets held for investment. On November 21, 2015, he sells the stock. Any resulting gain or loss is capital gain or loss.

EXAMPLE 12.38	If Wilbur, in the preceding example, withdrew the stock from the investment account and held it as inventory, then the sale at a gain results in ordinary gain, but the sale at a loss results in a capital loss.

¶12,545   SUBDIVIDED REAL ESTATE

Taxpayers who sell developed real estate that has been subdivided can be considered to be dealers and may have to report gain as ordinary income. However, some relief is provided to investors in real estate. Code Sec. 1237. Any lot or parcel which is a part of a noncorporate taxpayer's or S corporation's real property is not considered to be held primarily for sale to customers solely because of subdivision activities. The property may not previously have been held primarily for sale to customers and no substantial improvements may have been made to the lots. Code Sec. 1237(a)(1) and (2).

Substantial means that the improvements have increased the value of a lot by more than 10 percent. Shopping centers, other commercial or residential buildings, and the installation of hard surface roads or utilities such as sewers, water, gas, or electric lines are considered substantial improvements. Surveying, filling, draining, leveling and clearing operations, and the construction of minimum all-weather access roads are not considered substantial improvements. Reg. §1.1237-1(c)(3) and (4). The lots also must have been held, except in case of inheritance, for a period of five years.

If the above conditions are met and the taxpayer has not sold more than five lots or parcels from a single tract through the end of the tax year, capital gain treatment results. If more than five lots or parcels are sold or exchanged, gain from any sale or exchange of any lot occurring in or after the taxable year in which the sixth lot or parcel is sold is recognized as ordinary income up to five percent of the selling price. The remaining gain is capital gain. Selling expenses first offset the amount taxed as ordinary income and then offset the capital gain. Code Sec. 1237(b)(1) and (2). Section 1237 does not apply to losses realized upon the sale of subdivided property. Reg. §1.1237-1(a)(4)(i).

EXAMPLE 12.39

Jerry Johnson, who meets all requirements of Code Sec. 1237, sells five lots during 2014 at a gain of $20,000. During 2015, he sells the sixth lot (basis $4,000) at a selling price of $15,000 and incurs $500 of selling expense. Jerry recognizes long-term capital gain of $20,000 in 2014. In 2015, he has $250 ordinary income and $10,250 capital gain computed as follows:

Selling price		$15,000
Less: Basis	$4,000	
Selling expenses	500	4,500
Gain on sale of lot		$10,500
5% of selling price	$750	
Less: Selling expense	500	
Amount reported as ordinary income		250
Capital gain		$10,250

If the selling expenses had been $750 or more, the total amount of gain would have been capital gain.

PLANNING POINTER

Taxpayers may wish to have investor status because there may be a significant difference in tax on the gain side. If there is a loss situation, however, the taxpayer will be better off by having dealer status so that the taxpayer's losses will be ordinary without limits, instead of capital losses with limits.

Section 1231 Assets and Procedure

¶12,601 **BACKGROUND**

Prior to 1938, business property was included as a capital asset. However, this meant that taxpayers selling such assets at a loss were subject to the capital loss limitations. This resulted in taxpayers' retaining their business property as long as possible rather than selling it. Therefore, in the Revenue Act of 1938, depreciable property used in a trade or business was excluded as a capital asset. Although this meant that there would not be a capital loss limitation, it also meant that gains would be ordinary income rather than the more favorable capital gains. In 1942, Congress responded by allowing taxpayers to treat net gains from the sale of business property as capital gains and net losses as ordinary losses.

¶12,615 **DEFINITION OF SECTION 1231 ASSETS**

Section 1231 assets include depreciable property and land used in a trade or business and held long-term. Code Sec. 1231(b). (Long-term means more than 12 months.) Such assets consist mainly of machinery and equipment, business cars and trucks, buildings, and land. They also include a number of items not specifically related to a trade or business:

1. Timber, coal, or domestic iron ore to which Code Sec. 631 applies
2. Livestock including:
   a. Cattle and horses held for draft, breeding, dairy, or sporting purposes for 24 months or more.
   b. Livestock (other than cattle, horses, and poultry) held for draft, breeding, dairy, or sporting purposes for 12 months or more.
3. Unharvested crops on land used in a trade or business and held long-term if the crop and the land are sold or exchanged at the same time and to the same person.
4. The involuntary conversion of business property and capital assets held long-term.

Note. Gains and losses from casualties and thefts are treated separately, as will be seen later.

Certain items are specifically excluded from the definition of Section 1231 assets:

1. Inventory on hand at the close of the tax year and property held primarily for sale to customers in the ordinary course of the trade or business.
2. A copyright, a literary, musical, or artistic composition, a letter, or memorandum, or similar property held by a taxpayer whose personal efforts created such property. A taxpayer can elect to treat the sale or exchange of a musical composition or copyright in musical works created by the taxpayer's personal efforts as a sale of a capital asset.
3. A publication of the United States government received from the government other than by purchase at the price offered for sale to the public.

It should be noted that to be Section 1231 property, property must be held more than 12 months (24 months or more for cattle and horses). If a business asset is held short-term, the income from sale will be ordinary. In the case of involuntary conversions resulting from a business casualty or theft, Section 1231 does not apply where recognized losses exceed the recognized gains from such conversions. In this case, the net casualty and theft loss is treated as ordinary loss. This is what is often referred to as the first netting (to be discussed later). Although capital assets that are involuntarily converted were included above as Section 1231 assets, for personal-use assets this provision applies only to condemnation gains since losses on condemnations of personal-use assets are not deductible. Personal-use casualty and theft gains and losses are not part of Section 1231, but are subject to a separate netting.

| EXAMPLE 12.40 | Maria Martina is an artist who owns an art gallery where she sells paintings she has painted. The building is a Section 1231 asset as is the furniture in the gallery. The paintings, however, are ordinary assets since they were created by her own personal efforts. |

¶12,645   COMPUTATIONAL PROCEDURES

In working with Section 1231 transactions, the taxpayer must take into account three steps after the determination of the realized gain or loss. The realized gain or loss, of course, is the difference between the fair market value of the property received and the adjusted basis of the property given up.

Step 1. Determine the amount of the gain to be recaptured as ordinary income. There is no recapture if there is a realized loss. The determination of the amount to be recaptured as ordinary income is more complicated under the law for Section 1250 property that is sold or exchanged and which has depreciation that has not been recaptured (see later section).

Step 2. Nonpersonal casualty or theft gains and losses from assets held more than 12 months must be netted (sometimes referred to as the first netting). Condemnation gains and losses do not enter into this netting. Casualty and theft gains and losses are the difference between (1) the insurance proceeds, if any, and (2) the adjusted basis of the property for complete destruction of business property (or the lesser of the adjusted basis or the sustained loss for partial destruction of business property).

   a. If the casualty or theft gains exceed the casualty or theft losses, then a further netting is made with the Section 1231 gains or losses (see Step 3) for the taxable year.
   b. If the casualty or theft losses exceed the casualty or theft gains, the casualty or theft gains and losses are separately treated as ordinary. The gains are ordinary income and the losses are deducted for adjusted gross income.

Note. With the special netting for casualty and theft gains and losses, especially for Section 1231 assets, such events will be given the same treatment as if the assets were disposed of through sale or exchange.

EXAMPLE 12.41	Betty Blue has a casualty gain of $5,000 resulting from an insurance recovery from an accident with her business car, and a fire loss after insurance recovery to her office building in the amount of $6,000. Betty has adjusted gross income of $35,000 before considering these items. After netting the above, Betty has a loss of $1,000, meaning that the casualty and theft gains and losses will be ordinary. The $5,000 is ordinary income and the $6,000 is an ordinary deduction for adjusted gross income. After considering the $5,000 income and the $6,000 deduction, Betty has final adjusted gross income of $34,000. (Examples 12.41 and 12.42 ignore recapture potential.)

EXAMPLE 12.42	If Betty's casualty gain from the accident of her business car in Example 12.41 was $10,000 instead of $5,000, she has a net gain of $4,000 ($10,000 – $6,000) which means that the $4,000 will be further netted with the Section 1231 gains or losses (in Step 3).

PLANNING POINTER	If the taxpayer has a business casualty loss and a business casualty gain (of approximately the same magnitude) in the same year, the taxpayer may wish to attempt to postpone recognition of the casualty gain under the involuntary conversion nonrecognition rules of Code Sec. 1033. In this way, the taxpayer can receive an ordinary deduction for the casualty loss. Otherwise the casualty loss and casualty gain cancel each other out.

Step 3. Section 1231 gains and losses and any net casualty gains from Step 2 (the first netting) are netted. Gains and losses from condemnations of business property held more than 12 months are included in this netting. For personal-use assets, condemnation gains are included; condemnation losses from personal-use assets are not deductible and thus are not considered.

a. If the gains exceed the losses, the excess of gains over losses is treated as ordinary income to the extent of Section 1231 net losses for the previous five years that have not been recaptured. Any remaining Section 1231 gain in excess of these prior losses is a long-term capital gain. Code Sec. 1231(a) and (c). If a portion of a taxpayer's net Section 1231 gain is recharacterized as ordinary income under Section 1231(c), that portion will consist first of any net Section 1231 gain in the 28 percent basket, then any Section 1231 gain in the 25 percent basket, and finally any net Section 1231 gain in the 15/20 percent basket.

b. If the losses exceed the gains, all the gains and losses are ordinary. The losses are deducted for adjusted gross income.

EXAMPLE 12.43	Bill Bradley had sales of assets held long-term with results as follows:

Office equipment loss	($20,000)
Office equipment gain (in addition to recapture)	$45,000

Bill has a net gain of $25,000 ($45,000 – $20,000) on his Section 1231 transactions assuming no prior years' Section 1231 net losses. His net gain of $25,000 will be treated as a long-term capital gain and can be used to offset other capital losses.

EXAMPLE 12.44	Anne Arkady has a Section 1231 net gain of $20,000 during 2015. In the past, the net Section 1231 transactions were as follows:

Year	Net Sec. 1231 Transactions
2014	($4,000)
2013	($8,000)
2012	$25,000
2011	($5,000)
2010	($1,000)

In 2012, Anne had $6,000 ordinary income and $19,000 long-term capital gain after recapturing the losses from 2010 and 2011. In 2015, Anne has ordinary income of $12,000 (recapture of the $8,000 2013 loss plus the $4,000 2014 loss) and long-term capital gain of $8,000 ($20,000 gain less $12,000 losses recaptured). If her 2015 net gain were $10,000 instead of $20,000, all of it would be ordinary and $2,000 of the 2014 net loss would remain to offset Section 1231 net gain in post-2015 years.

EXAMPLE 12.45	Carl Collins had sales of assets held long-term with results as follows:

Machinery gain (in addition to recapture)	$14,000
Factory building loss	($35,000)

Carl has a net loss of $21,000 ($35,000 – $14,000) on his Section 1231 transactions and each item will be treated as ordinary. The $21,000 net loss is an ordinary loss *for* adjusted gross income.

EXAMPLE 12.46	Assume that Betty Brewer had a $10,000 casualty gain, a $6,000 casualty loss, a Section 1231 gain of $9,500 on the sale of business equipment and a Section 1231 loss of $6,500 on the sale of a business truck. With the $4,000 gain ($10,000 casualty gain – $6,000 casualty loss) carried from the first netting, Betty has a net gain in the second netting of $7,000 ($4,000 + $9,500 – $6,500), which will be considered as a long-term capital gain assuming no prior years' Section 1231 net losses.

EXAMPLE 12.47	If Betty in Example 12.46 had only the Section 1231 loss of $6,500 (and no Section 1231 gain of $9,500) along with the net casualty gain of $4,000 ($10,000 casualty gain – $6,000 casualty loss) carried over from the first netting, she has a net loss of $2,500 on the second netting. All gains and losses are ordinary. Thus, Betty has the following:

Ordinary income from the casualty gain	$10,000
Ordinary loss deduction for adjusted gross income	(6,000)
Ordinary loss deduction for adjusted gross income	(6,500)
Net effect on adjusted gross income	($2,500)

If Betty had adjusted gross income of $15,000 without the transactions in these examples, she would have a final adjusted gross income of $12,500.

¶12,655   PERSONAL CASUALTY AND THEFT GAINS AND LOSSES

Personal-use casualty and theft gains and losses are separately netted and do not enter into the business casualty netting or the Section 1231 netting. If the gains exceed the losses, then all such gains and losses are treated as capital gains and losses. Personal-use casualty and theft losses are determined after the $100 per occurrence reduction. If the personal-use casualty and theft losses exceed the gains, the gains and losses are ordinary. Losses are deducted in full to the extent of gains. Losses in excess of gains are subject to the 10 percent adjusted gross income floor. Code Sec. 165(h).

EXAMPLE 12.48

Jim Jannings had the following gains and losses:

1. Gain from office equipment held four months	$500
2. Loss from theft of watch held two years (after $100 reduction)	($600)
3. Gain from insurance recovery on accident of business car owned three years in addition to recapture	$6,000
4. Loss from hurricane damage to office building owned five years (after insurance recovery)	($8,000)
5. Loss from sale of business equipment held more than one year	($5,000)
6. Gain from sale of warehouse held two years (in addition to recapture)	$8,000
7. Net LTCG	$6,000
8. Net STCL	($2,000)

Jim's adjusted gross income before the above transactions was $50,000. Ignoring recapture of depreciation (discussed at ¶12,701) and assuming no prior years' Section 1231 net losses, the tax treatment is as follows: Item (1) is an ordinary gain since the property was not held more than 12 months. Item (2) is a potential casualty deduction but does not enter the first netting because it is a personal theft. Items (3) and (4) are considered in the netting of casualty gains and losses, giving a net loss of $2,000 and making the items ordinary. This net loss is a deduction for adjusted gross income. Items (5) and (6) are considered in the Section 1231 netting, resulting in a net gain of $3,000. This will be treated as a long-term capital gain and will be combined with the Net LTCG of $6,000 to give $9,000. The overall net capital gain is $7,000 ($9,000 – $2,000), which would be taxed at a maximum rate of 15 percent.

Initial adjusted gross income	$50,000
Add: Item (1)	500
Less: Items (3) and (4)	(2,000)
Add: Items (5), (6), (7), and (8)	7,000
Adjusted gross income	$55,500

Since the personal casualty loss of $600 on the stolen watch (Item (2)) is less than $5,550 (10% of $55,500), there is no casualty or theft itemized deduction allowable for that item.

EXAMPLE 12.49

Assume the facts of Example 12.48, except that Item (2) was a fire damage loss to a personal residence of $10,000 after the $100 per occurrence reduction instead of the theft loss of the watch. Since the personal casualty loss of $10,000 is greater than $5,550 (10% of $55,500), there is an itemized deduction of $4,450 ($10,000 – $5,550) from adjusted gross income.

Depreciation Recapture—Section 1245

¶12,701 ## PURPOSE OF RULES

The purpose of Section 1245 is to prevent taxpayers from taking ordinary depreciation deductions and then receiving long-term capital gain treatment through Section 1231 at the time of sale of the property. The following example illustrates how the law worked *before* 1962.

EXAMPLE 12.50

Lloyd Lewis purchased equipment for $10,000 in January 1956 and took depreciation of $6,250 under the straight-line method through December 1960. On December 31, 1960, he sold the equipment with a basis of $3,750 for $9,000 resulting in a realized and recognized gain of $5,250, which was Section 1231 gain. Assuming that Lloyd had no other Section 1231 transactions, this gain would be treated as long-term capital gain. Thus, Lloyd was able to take $6,250 ordinary depreciation deductions while owning the equipment from 1956-1960 and then obtain long-term capital gain treatment at the time of sale. Long-term capital gains had significant tax advantages at that time.

Congress believed that this was too much of a benefit to taxpayers; therefore, in 1962, it enacted Section 1245 which significantly changed the effect of Section 1231 for many assets. The idea in Section 1245 is that there should be recapture of depreciation as ordinary income in realized gain situations. There is no recapture of depreciation, however, when losses are realized. Calculation of the recapture is necessary to determine how much of the realized gain is ordinary income and how much is Section 1231 gain.

¶12,715   DEFINITION OF SECTION 1245 PROPERTY

Section 1245 property is really a subcategory of depreciable Section 1231 property. Section 1245 property is personal property (in the legal sense—not personal-use property) which is subject to depreciation or amortization. Code Sec. 1245(a)(3). It includes:

1.   Property (not including a building or its structural components) if such property is tangible and was used as an integral part of specified business activities
2.   Amortizable property such as patents and leaseholds of Section 1245 property
3.   Single purpose agricultural or horticultural structures
4.   Storage facilities (not including a building or its structural components) used in connection with the distribution of petroleum or any primary product of petroleum
5.   Railroad gradings or tunnel bores (as defined in Code Sec. 168(e)(4))

Section 1245 property includes personal property such as machinery, equipment, cars, and trucks, all used in a trade or business. Depreciable property which is expensed under Section 179 is also Section 1245 property. Expenditures to remove architectural and transportation barriers to the handicapped which are deductible under Section 190 are Section 1245 property as are properties subject to accelerated amortization under Section 169 for pollution control facilities, and Section 188 for child care facilities. In addition, Section 1245 provisions apply to nonresidential real property if the recovery of cost is under the statutory percentage method of the accelerated cost recovery system (ACRS) rather than the straight-line method. Such property is technically not Section 1245 property, but it receives Section 1245 treatment on recapture.

EXAMPLE 12.51

Peter Paulson owns the following assets:

1.   Machinery used in his auto repair shop
2.   Truck used in his business
3.   Furniture in the office of the shop
4.   Furniture in his home
5.   Oil and inventory items used in his business

Items (1), (2), and (3) are Section 1245 assets. Item (4) consists of capital assets and item (5) consists of inventory or ordinary assets.

¶12,725   COMPUTATIONAL PROCEDURES

On the disposition of Section 1245 property, ordinary income is recognized to the extent of the total depreciation taken (including immediate expensing under Code Sec. 179), but not to exceed the recognized gain. Any excess recognized gain over the amount recaptured as ordinary income is treated as Section 1231 gain (in the second netting). In a casualty gain, any excess gain over the amount recaptured as ordinary income is a casualty gain. There is no recapture as ordinary income where there is a recognized loss. All the recognized loss on the sale or disposition of Section 1245 property (a subcategory of Section 1231 property) is treated as a Section 1231 loss.

EXAMPLE 12.52

Jack Jumper purchased business equipment for $20,000 on January 1, 2011, and took depreciation of $13,752 up to January 1, 2015, when he sold it for $11,248. Jack's adjusted basis is $6,248 and he has a realized and recognized gain of $5,000. He has recapture potential of $13,752, the amount of the depreciation taken, but he will recapture only $5,000 as ordinary income since the amount recaptured as ordinary income does not exceed the recognized gain.

EXAMPLE 12.53	Assume the facts of Example 12.52, except that the equipment was sold for $21,248 on January 1, 2015. Jack has realized and recognized gain of $15,000 ($21,248 – $6,248), of which $13,752 is recaptured as ordinary income and the remaining $1,248 is Section 1231 gain.

EXAMPLE 12.54	Assume the same facts as in Example 12.52, except that the equipment was sold for $2,000 on January 1, 2015. There is no recapture when there is a recognized loss, so the $4,248 is a Section 1231 loss.

¶12,735   DEPRECIATION METHODS

Prior to 1981, a number of methods of depreciation were available including both accelerated and straight-line methods. Useful lives were estimated and played an important part in depreciation, as did salvage value. For property placed in service after 1980, the accelerated cost recovery system (ACRS) applies and is required for most properties. Under this system, salvage value and useful lives are not important as they were formerly. ACRS was substantially modified by the Tax Reform Act of 1986. Most tangible property placed in service after 1986 must now be depreciated under the Modified Accelerated Cost Recovery System (MACRS). Under MACRS, different types of property are placed in specific categories. See Chapter 6, ¶6401, for further discussion on depreciation.

¶12,745   ACRS OR MACRS PROPERTY

The same general rule on Section 1245 recapture that applied to pre-ACRS property applies to ACRS or MACRS property. However, there is one difference. Although there are specific recapture rules under Section 1250 for real property, nonresidential real property purchased under ACRS receives Section 1245 recapture treatment if the accelerated method of cost recovery (depreciation) is used. (See ¶12,835.)

¶12,755   SUMMARY: SECTION 1245 RECAPTURE

1. Section 1245 property held long-term is a subcategory of depreciable Section 1231 property.
2. All gains or losses on property held short-term are recognized as ordinary income or loss since property held for that time period is not Section 1231 property.
3. The amount of recapture potential is the *total* depreciation taken after 1961. This will frequently mean that all the recognized gain on Section 1245 property is recognized as ordinary income since the total depreciation taken is usually higher than the recognized gain.
4. There is no recapture when losses are recognized on Section 1245 assets. Such losses are Section 1231 losses.
5. The recapture rules for Section 1245 property acquired before 1981 and under ACRS or MACRS are the same.
6. Although Section 1245 includes depreciable personal property, nonresidential real property can receive Section 1245 recapture treatment if the accelerated method is used under ACRS.

Depreciation Recapture—Section 1250

¶12,801   DEFINITION OF SECTION 1250 PROPERTY

Section 1250 property is depreciable real property that is not Section 1245 property. It, like Section 1245 property, is a subcategory of depreciable Section 1231 property. It consists mainly of buildings and their structural components as well as other depreciable real property. It also includes intangible real property such as leaseholds of land or Section 1250 property. Code Sec. 1250(c); Reg. §1.1250-1(e)(3).

EXAMPLE 12.55

Charles Cobb owns the following assets:

1. Office building
2. Apartment building containing 10 apartments rented to tenants
3. Personal residence

Items (1) and (2) are Section 1250 assets, but item (3) is a capital asset.

¶12,815   PURPOSE OF RULES

The purpose of Section 1250 is to prevent taxpayers from receiving the full benefits of accelerated depreciation and long-term capital gain treatment through Section 1231 at the time of sale of the property. Section 1250 was originally enacted in 1964 but has undergone several changes since that time. Therefore, it is important to keep track of the time periods involved as well as the types of property.

The recapture potential under Section 1250 differs from that under Section 1245 in at least one very important respect. Section 1250 deals with excess depreciation (the excess of accelerated depreciation over straight-line), whereas Section 1245 deals with total depreciation. Thus, the recapture potential under Section 1250 is less severe than that under Section 1245. Under Section 1250, the taxpayer has ordinary income to the extent of the lesser of (1) the gain recognized or (2) additional (excess) depreciation. Any gain not recaptured as ordinary income is Section 1231 gain. Recapture as ordinary income is not applicable to Section 1250 property disposed of at a recognized loss, just as with Section 1245 property; such losses are Section 1231 losses.

Additional depreciation for real property held more than one year is the excess of the amount of depreciation deducted over the amount of depreciation that would have been taken if straight-line depreciation had been used. Code Sec. 1250(a)(1) and (b)(1). The additional (or excess) depreciation has a specified percentage applied to it depending on the time period the property was held and the type of property held. If property is held for less than one year, the entire gain upon sale will be ordinary.

Under the Taxpayer Relief Act of 1997, unrecaptured Sec. 1250 gain is long-term capital gain taxed at a rate of 25 percent and is the amount of the long-term capital gain that would be treated as ordinary income if Section 1250(b)(1) included all depreciation taken with an applicable percentage of 100 percent. For property sold after July 28, 1998, only gain from Section 1250 property held for more than 12 months is taken into account. In less complex language, all or a portion of the recognized gain from the sale or exchange of depreciable real property is to be recaptured. This is determined by treating the property as if it were depreciable personal property (i.e., Section 1245 property) and is taxed at a maximum rate of 25 percent. The remaining gain would be Section 1231 gain and would be considered in the Section 1231 netting and ultimately taxed at a maximum rate of 15/20 percent, assuming that it was not offset by losses in the Section 1231 and capital nettings.

¶12,825   NONRESIDENTIAL REAL PROPERTY— PRE-1981 ACQUISITIONS

For property acquired before 1981, taxpayers could use various depreciation methods subject to limitations and were required to estimate useful lives and salvage values. Taxpayers who acquired the property prior to 1981 are required to continue using the old methods as long as that property is held. Basically, the most liberal depreciation methods available for various types of property were as follows:

New nonresidential real property	150% declining balance
Used nonresidential real property	Straight-line
New residential real property	200% declining balance
Used residential real property with an estimated useful life of at least 20 years	125% declining balance

For nonresidential real property, the recapture potential is 100 percent of the amount of the excess depreciation taken after December 31, 1969. Code Sec. 1250(a). The amount to be recaptured as ordinary income cannot exceed the recognized gain. If there is excess recognized gain above the amount recaptured as ordinary income as a result of the "excess depreciation" calculation, any unrecaptured depreciation will be taxed at the maximum rate of 25 percent. If there is then still any excess recognized gain, it is a 15/20 percent gain. If straight-line depreciation was used, the 1997 Act requires that there is recapture to the extent of total depreciation taken (taxed at the maximum rate of 25 percent) but not to exceed recognized gain.

EXAMPLE 12.56

Paul Prentice purchased an office building on January 1, 1975, for $400,000 and used the 150 percent declining balance depreciation method for the 40 years he owned the asset. The estimated useful life was 40 years with no salvage. On January 1, 2015, Paul sells the property for $500,000. His depreciation is as follows:

Year(s)	150% Declining Balance	Straight-Line Depreciation	Excess Depreciation
1975	$15,000	$10,000	$5,000
1976-2013	375,999	380,000	(4,001)
2014	9,001	10,000	(999)
	$400,000	$400,000	$ 0

Paul has a realized and recognized gain of $500,000 ($500,000 – $0 adjusted basis). He has $0 (($400,000 – $400,000) × 100%) recaptured as ordinary income, $400,000 is taxed at 25 percent, and the remaining $100,000 is taxed at a maximum of 15/20 percent.

EXAMPLE 12.57

If Paul in the preceding example had sold the property on January 1, 2015, for $8,000, none of the recognized gain of $8,000 ($8,000 – $0) would have been recaptured as ordinary income and there would have been $8,000 taxed at 25 percent, and none taxed at the 15/20 percent rate.

¶12,835   NONRESIDENTIAL REAL PROPERTY—ACRS

Under ACRS (1981–86 acquisitions), nonresidential real property may be depreciated using the prescribed (accelerated) method or the optional straight-line method. The taxpayer may select one of various recovery periods if the optional straight-line method is used. If the taxpayer uses the accelerated method, gain is treated as ordinary income to the extent of *total* depreciation taken. Code Sec. 1245(a). Thus, by using accelerated cost recovery or depreciation, the taxpayer is subject to the more severe recapture rules of Section 1245. With the 1997 Act, even if the optional straight-line depreciation method was used, there is a recapture of total depreciation (but not to exceed recognized gain), which is taxed at a maximum rate of 25 percent. Any excess recognized gain is 15/20 percent gain.

EXAMPLE 12.58

Mary Murphy purchased an office building on January 1, 1984, for $150,000. She used the statutory percentage (accelerated) method in computing cost recovery under ACRS. On January 1, 2015, she sold the building for $170,000. She took cost recovery allowances (depreciation) of $150,000, which gives her an adjusted basis of $0 and a realized and recognized gain of $170,000. She has $150,000 of ordinary income, and the remaining $20,000 is a 15/20 percent gain.

Because Mary used the accelerated method rather than the straight-line method, she must recapture as ordinary income to the extent of the *total* depreciation taken rather than the excess depreciation, as would have been the case for real nonresidential property acquired prior to 1981 or for real residential rental property both before 1981 and after 1980 (see ¶12,845).

EXAMPLE 12.59

If Mary in Example 12.58 had used the optional straight-line method over 15 years, she would have had depreciation each year of $10,000 ($150,000 divided by 15) or $150,000 total for the 15 years. In this case, Mary would have no recapture as ordinary income and the total recognized gain of $170,000 ($170,000 selling price less $0 adjusted basis ($150,000 – $150,000)) would consist of $150,000 unrecaptured Section 1250 gain subject to the 25 percent tax rate and $20,000 taxed at a maximum of 15/20 percent.

¶12,841   NONRESIDENTIAL REAL PROPERTY—MACRS

Nonresidential real property acquired after 1986 (and before May 13, 1993) is depreciated under a straight-line method over a 31.5-year period. For nonresidential real property placed in service on or after May 13, 1993, the recovery period is 39 years. Starting with the 1997 Act, dispositions of this type of property result in recapture to the extent of total depreciation taken (and taxed at a maximum rate of 25 percent), but not to exceed recognized gain. Any excess recognized gain is 15/20 percent gain.

EXAMPLE 12.60

On December 19, 2015, Jane Judd, a 35 percent bracket taxpayer, sold for $500,000 an office building she had acquired on January 4, 2010, for $390,000. During her time of ownership, she took straight-line depreciation over a 39-year time period, mid-month convention, in the amount of $59,166. She has a realized and recognized gain of $169,166 ($500,000 less adjusted basis of $330,834), of which $59,166 is Section 1231 gain, and which will be netted with other Section 1231 gains and losses. (If this is the only Section 1231 transaction for Jane, it would be taxed at a rate of 25 percent on $59,166 and at a maximum of 15/20 percent on $110,000.)

¶12,845   RESIDENTIAL REAL PROPERTY—PRE-1981 ACQUISITIONS

As with taxpayers who acquired personal or nonresidential real property prior to 1981, taxpayers who acquired residential rental real property prior to 1981 are required to continue using the old depreciation methods as long as that property is held.

For residential real property, the recapture potential is 100 percent of the amount of the excess depreciation taken after December 31, 1975. The 1970 through 1975 recapture potential percentage is 100 percent minus one percentage point for each full month the property was held over 100 months. Code Sec. 1250(a). In other words, the percentage for the 1970-1975 period is 200 minus the total number of months held. This is the only difference between the recapture rules of nonresidential real property and residential rental housing for property acquired prior to 1981.

Because of this difference, the following steps are necessary for recapture on residential rental housing:

1. Determine the excess depreciation for the period after 1975.
2. Multiply the lesser of the recognized gain or the excess depreciation in (1) by 100 percent.
3. Subtract the post-1975 excess depreciation from the recognized gain to get the "unabsorbed gain."
4. Determine the excess depreciation for the 1970-1975 time period.
5. Multiply the lesser of the unabsorbed gain in (3) or the excess depreciation in (4) by (200 less the total of months held, but not less than zero).
6. Add the amounts obtained from steps (2) and (5). This is the amount recaptured as ordinary income.
7. If there is excess recognized gain above the amount recaptured as ordinary income as a result of the "excess depreciation" calculation, any unrecaptured depreciation is taxed at the maximum rate of 25 percent under the Taxpayer Relief Act of 1997. The amount to be recaptured as ordinary income cannot, of course, exceed the recognized gain. Any excess of recognized gain over the amount recaptured as ordinary income in step (6) and over the amount recaptured subject to the 25 percent rate is subject to the 15/20 percent rate.

EXAMPLE 12.61

Assume the same facts as in Example 12.56 at ¶12,825, except that the building was residential rental housing and Paul used the 200 percent declining-balance method for the 40 years he owned the asset rather than the 150 percent declining-balance method. His depreciation is as follows:

Year(s)	200% Declining Balance	Straight-Line Depreciation	Excess Depreciation
1975	$20,000	$10,000	$10,000
1976-2013	372,835	380,000	(7,165)
2014	7,165	10,000	(2,835)
	$400,000	$400,000	$ 0

If Paul sells the building for $500,000, he has a realized and recognized gain of $500,000. This is the difference between the selling price of $500,000 and the adjusted basis of $0 ($400,000 – $400,000). Following the steps outlined above for residential rental housing, the following computations result:

1. The excess depreciation for the period 1976 through 2014 is $0 ($380,000 – $390,000).
2. Step (1) is less than the recognized gain, so $0 is multiplied by 100 percent.
3. The unabsorbed gain is $500,000 ($500,000 – $0).
4. The excess depreciation for 1975 is $10,000 ($20,000 – $10,000).
5. The lesser of (3) or (4) is $10,000, which is multiplied by zero percent (200 less 480 months held, but not less than zero percent) to give $0.
6. The total amount recaptured as ordinary income is $0 ($0 from Step (2) and $0 from Step (5)).
7. The remaining depreciation taken of $400,000 ($400,000 less $0 from Step (6)) is taxed at the maximum rate of 25 percent. The remaining gain of $100,000 is taxed at the 15/20 percent rate.

EXAMPLE 12.62

Assume the same facts as in Example 12.61, except that the selling price was $835 instead of $500,000. This would give a realized and recognized gain of $835 ($835 – $0). The unabsorbed gain in Step (3) is then $835 ($835 – $0) and it would then be $835 (the lesser of the unabsorbed gain in Step (3) or the excess depreciation in Step (4)) that would be multiplied by zero percent to give $0 (Step (5)). Then the amount recaptured as ordinary income is $0 (Step (6)) and the remaining $835 is taxed at the maximum rate of 25% (Step (7)).

¶12,855

RESIDENTIAL REAL PROPERTY—ACRS

The tax treatment of residential real property under ACRS (1981-86 acquisitions) is the same as that for such property acquired prior to 1981 (i.e., the post-1975 period). Gain is recaptured as ordinary income to the extent of 100 percent of excess depreciation, but not to exceed recognized gain. Excess depreciation is the excess of accelerated depreciation over the straight-line method over the relevant time period (15-year period for property placed in service before March 16, 1984). With the 1997 Act, even if the optional straight-line depreciation method was used, there is recapture of total depreciation (but not to exceed realized gain), which is taxed at a minimum rate of 25 percent. Any remaining recognized gain is then 15/20 percent gain.

EXAMPLE 12.63

Assume the same facts as in Example 12.58 at ¶12,835, except that Mary purchased an apartment building instead of an office building. Mary still has a realized and recognized gain of $170,000. This is the difference between the selling price of $170,000 and the adjusted basis of the building of $0 ($150,000 – $150,000). Since straight-line depreciation would have been $150,000 (15 × $10,000 per year ($150,000/15)), her excess depreciation to be recognized as ordinary income is $0. There is $150,000 that is taxed at the maximum rate of 25 percent and the remaining $20,000 is subject to 15 percent. This is less severe than the recapture for nonresidential real property in Example 12.60 at ¶12,841.

¶12,861   RESIDENTIAL REAL PROPERTY—MACRS

Residential real property acquired after 1986 is depreciated under a straight-line method over a 27.5-year period. With the 1997 Act, even if the optional straight-line depreciation method was used, there is recapture of total depreciation, which is taxed at a maximum rate of 25 percent, but not to exceed recognized gain. Any excess recognized gain after depreciation has been recaptured is subject to 15/20 percent.

EXAMPLE 12.64

On December 19, 2015, Jane Judd, a 33 percent bracket taxpayer, sold for $500,000 an apartment building she had acquired on January 4, 2010, for $275,000. During her time of ownership, she took straight-line depreciation over a 27.5-year time period, mid-month convention, in the amount of $59,166. She has a realized and recognized gain of $284,166 ($500,000 less adjusted basis of $215,834), of which $59,166 is taxed at the maximum rate of 25 percent, and the remaining $225,000 is taxed at a maximum rate of 15/20 percent.

¶12,865   LOW-INCOME HOUSING—PRE-1987 ACQUISITIONS

For periods after 1969, the applicable recapture percentage as ordinary income for low-income housing is 100 percent minus one percentage point for each full month the property was held over 100 months. Code Sec. 1250(a)(1)(B)(iii). (This is 200 – the total number of months held.) This rule applies for sale of federally assisted housing projects and low-income housing depreciated under Code Sec. 167(k). With the 1997 Act, the remaining depreciation taken is recaptured and taxed at a maximum rate of 25 percent, but not to exceed recognized gain. Any excess gain after depreciation has been recaptured is 15/20 percent gain.

EXAMPLE 12.65

On January 1, 1986, Fred Frombly purchased for $2 million an apartment building that qualified as low-income housing. On January 1, 2015, he sold the building for $2.1 million. Accelerated depreciation has been taken in the amount of $900,000. Straight-line depreciation would have been $600,000. Realized and recognized gain is $1 million ($2,100,000 – $1,100,000), of which $0 is ordinary income (0% (200 – 348 months) × $300,000 ($900,000 – $600,000)), $900,000 is taxed at a maximum rate of 25 percent, and the remaining $100,000 is taxed at a maximum of 15/20 percent.

¶12,875   SUMMARY: SECTION 1250 RECAPTURE

1. Section 1250 property held long-term is a sub-category of depreciable Section 1231 property.
2. Section 1250 property is real property, but if accelerated depreciation is used for nonresidential real property under ACRS, the recapture rules of Section 1245 apply.
3. All gains or losses on property held one year or less are recognized as ordinary income or loss since property so held is not Section 1231 property.
4. The amount of recapture potential as ordinary income is based on excess depreciation in Section 1250 rather than total depreciation as in Section 1245.
5. There is no recapture when losses are recognized on Section 1250 assets. Such losses are Section 1231 losses.
6. There are differences between types of real property—nonresidential, residential rental, and low-income housing.
7. There are differences in the recapture rules for property acquired before 1981, after 1980 but before 1987, and after 1986.
8. The Taxpayer Relief Act of 1997 requires any unrecaptured Section 1250 gain to be taxed at a maximum capital gains rate of 25 percent, although total recaptured depreciation is not to exceed recognized gain.

KEYSTONE PROBLEM

An asset was purchased on January 1, 1975, for $500,000. Depreciation taken on the asset up to the time of sale on January 1, 1987, was $480,000. The selling price was $300,000. Straight-line depreciation would have been $360,000. Depreciation taken during 1975 was $50,000.

1. How is the recognized gain treated for tax purposes for the following assets?
   a. Business machine
   b. Factory building
   c. Apartment building
2. How is the recognized gain treated if the acquisition date is January 1, 1986, the asset is depreciated under the same assumptions, but is fully depreciated when it is disposed of 29 years later on January 1, 2015?
   a. Factory building
   b. Apartment building

Recapture Rules in Other Events

There are special rules with respect to the recapture rules for different types of events.

¶12,901   GIFTS AND INHERITANCES

Gifts do not trigger recapture to the donor, but the recapture potential carries over to the donee. Code Secs. 1245(b)(1) and 1250(d)(1); Reg. §§1.1245-4(a) and 1.1250-3(a). Thus, when the donee disposes of the property, the donee must take into account the donor's depreciation deductions that are subject to recapture in addition to his or her own depreciation if it is depreciable property to the donee. If it is not depreciable property to the donee (e.g., personal-use property), the recapture potential from the donor still carries over.

EXAMPLE 12.66

Clara Cranberry gives a gift of Section 1245 property to her son David. The adjusted basis of the property at the time of the gift is $5,000 and the amount of recapture potential is $6,000. David takes $2,000 depreciation on the property before he sells it for $12,000. There is no recapture for Clara, the donor. The gain realized and recognized by David is $9,000 ($12,000 less $3,000 basis), of which $8,000 is recaptured as ordinary income ($6,000 recapture from Clara and $2,000 recapture from the time that David owned it). The remaining $1,000 is Section 1231 gain.

When property is transferred at death, both the decedent and the heir escape recapture. Code Secs. 1245(b)(2) and 1250(d)(2).

¶12,915   LIKE-KIND EXCHANGES AND INVOLUNTARY CONVERSIONS

Generally, a like-kind exchange does not result in income recognition under Section 1031. However, gain may be recognized if boot is received. Such gain is ordinary income if subject to recapture under Sections 1245 and 1250 and the 25 percent rate recapture under the 1997 Act.

EXAMPLE 12.67

Herbert Hughes has a machine (Section 1245 property) with an adjusted basis of $6,000 (fair market value of $10,000), originally costing $15,000 when purchased in 2009. In 2015, he exchanges it for another machine with a fair market value of $8,000 and receives cash of $2,000. Herbert's realized gain is $4,000 (amount realized of $10,000 ($8,000 + $2,000) less basis of $6,000). The recapture potential is $9,000, to the extent of the total depreciation taken, but since the recognized gain is $2,000 (to the extent of boot received), only $2,000 is recognized and it will be ordinary income. The remaining $7,000 recapture potential carries over to the new machine.

| EXAMPLE 12.68 | If Herbert in Example 12.67 had received a machine with a fair market value of $10,000 and no cash, he would still have a realized gain of $4,000, but he would have no recognition of gain because no boot was received. The total $9,000 recapture potential carries over to the new machine. |

In the case of involuntary conversions, the taxpayer has an election under Code Sec. 1033 to recognize gain only to the extent that the proceeds exceed the cost of the replacement property. The recognized gain is subject to ordinary income recapture and the 25 percent rate recapture under the 1997 Act. Code Secs. 1245(b)(4) and 1250(d)(4).

¶12,925 CHARITABLE CONTRIBUTIONS

If charitable contributions of Section 1245 or Section 1250 property are made, the contribution deduction is reduced by the amount of income recaptured as ordinary income if the property had been sold. Code Sec. 170(e)(1)(A).

| EXAMPLE 12.69 | In 2015, Mark Matches donated a small apartment building (acquired in 1986) to a qualified charity when the adjusted basis was $160,000 and the fair market value was $300,000. Mark had taken depreciation deductions in excess of straight line of $60,000. His charitable contribution deduction is $240,000 ($300,000 less the $60,000 recapture potential as ordinary income) subject to the limitations on charitable deductions for individuals in any given year. |

¶12,935 INSTALLMENT SALES

For installment sales of depreciated property, the full amount of any depreciation recapture as ordinary income is to be reported in the year of sale even if no payments are received in that year. Code Sec. 453(i). The remaining gain, if any, is Section 1231 gain.

| EXAMPLE 12.70 | In February 2015, Helen Humphrey sells equipment used in her business for $40,000 to be paid in five annual installments of $8,000 plus interest beginning in 2016. The equipment was acquired in 2010 for $30,000 and its adjusted basis was $12,000 at the time of the sale. The realized gain is $28,000 ($40,000 – $12,000) and a total of $18,000 is to be recaptured as ordinary income (i.e., the total depreciation taken) in 2015. The basis is increased by the amount recaptured to $30,000, and the remaining gross profit is then $10,000 resulting in a 25 percent gross profit rate. Of each annual payment of $8,000, $2,000 (25 percent of $8,000) is taxed at the 15/20 percent rate.

If a portion of the capital gain from an installment sale is 25 percent gain and a portion is 15/20 percent or 0 percent gain, the taxpayer is required to take the 25 percent gain into account before the 15/20 percent or 0 percent gain, as payments are received. |

COMPREHENSIVE EXAMPLE

Alan B. Arrow, single, age 40, had the following sales and casualty and theft items during 2015:

1. On January 1, he sold for $11,000 business equipment with an adjusted basis of $4,000. Alan had paid $10,000 for the equipment on January 1, 2011, and had taken $6,000 depreciation.
2. On January 1, he sold for $325,000 an apartment building with an adjusted basis of $175,000. He had paid $275,000 for the building on January 1, 2005, and had taken $100,000 straight-line depreciation.
3. On January 1, he sold for $3,000 a business car with an adjusted basis of $5,000 (cost $22,000 and depreciation taken of $17,000), and acquired on January 1, 2011.
4. Alan's Rolex watch that cost $4,000 in 2004 was stolen in July. The insurance company paid him $4,500.
5. A fire damaged his personal residence (owned three years) in Florida in the amount of $8,000 over his insurance coverage and the $100 per occurrence reduction.
6. A fire damaged Alan's warehouse (owned two years) in the amount of $10,000 above his insurance coverage.

(Assume that there are no prior years' Section 1231 net losses to recapture.)

Alan's adjusted gross income before considering the above items was $60,000. Item (1) results in a realized gain of $7,000 ($11,000 –$4,000) of which $6,000 is recaptured as ordinary income to the extent of total depreciation taken and the remaining $1,000 is Section 1231 gain. Item (2) results in a realized gain of $150,000 ($325,000 – $175,000) of which $100,000 is unrecaptured Section 1250 gain taxed at the top rate of 25 percent and the remaining $50,000 is Section 1231 gain. Item (3) results in a Section 1231 loss of $2,000 ($3,000 – $5,000). Item (4) is a personal theft gain of $500, Item (5) is a personal casualty loss of $8,000, and Item (6) is a business casualty loss of $10,000. The personal casualty and theft netting of Items (4) and (5) is a loss of $7,500, and the $7,500 is deducted as an itemized deduction only to the extent it exceeds 10 percent of adjusted gross income. The first netting of the business casualty and theft gains and losses is a loss of $10,000 (Item (6)) which means that the item will be ordinary.

There is $6,000 depreciation recaptured as ordinary income. The second netting of Section 1231 gains and losses yields a $149,000 gain ($1,000 gain + $50,000 gain – $2,000 loss + $100,000 Section 1250 gain). $100,000 is taxed at the 25 percent rate and $49,000 will be taxed at a maximum rate of 15 percent.

Alan's income would be computed as follows:

Initial adjusted gross income	$60,000
Ordinary income recapture	6,000
Unrecaptured Section 1250 gain (taxed at 25 percent rate)	100,000
Casualty loss on warehouse (ordinary)	(10,000)
Long-term capital gain	49,000
Adjusted gross income	$205,000

Alan does not get itemized deduction for the personal casualty loss, ($7,500 is less than 10% of $205,000). The $100,000 recaptured depreciation in item (2) is taxed at a maximum rate of 25 percent.

TAX BLUNDERS

1. Homer Holmes made a loan of $100,000 to his supplier, the Harris Company, because he was a friend of the major shareholder, George Harris, and because he wanted his supply of reasonably priced inventory to continue. Harris Company goes bankrupt and is unable to repay the loan. Because he was not in the business of making loans, Homer thought he was entitled only to a nonbusiness bad debt deduction, which would be treated as a short-term capital loss, and he treated it as such on his tax return. However, Homer could probably argue successfully that his loan was a business loan since it was made in order to assure a supply of inventory for his business.

2. Bruce Bradley, a 39.6 percent marginal bracket taxpayer, has a casualty loss on one of his office buildings held more than one year in the amount of $50,000 during 2015. He also incurred during 2015 a casualty gain on another office building held more than one year in the amount of $195,000 (including $140,000 unrecaptured Section 1250 gain taxed at 25 percent) which he chose to recognize. He replaced the latter building with another similar office building within a few months at a cost exceeding his proceeds from the insurance on his old building. Bruce has a casualty gain of $145,000 which will be carried over to the second netting. Assuming he has no Section 1231 gains and losses and no capital gains or losses, Bruce will have taxes on that in the amount of $35,750 (15 percent × $5,000 plus 25 percent × $140,000). Bruce should have elected to defer the casualty gain under the Section 1033 rules for nonrecognition of gain in an involuntary conversion. In that way, he could have taken a $50,000 ordinary loss deduction giving him a tax benefit or reduction of $19,800 (39.6 percent of $50,000).

SUMMARY

- The Code defines a capital asset by listing the assets that are not capital assets.
- There are short-term and long-term capital gains and losses that have to be considered.
- There are special rules for holding periods where property is acquired through involuntary conversions, exchanges, gifts, or from decedents.
- Working with capital gains and losses involves following a sequence of steps.
- Section 1231 assets include depreciable property and land used in a trade or business and held long-term, as well as several other items not specifically related to a trade or business.
- Working with Section 1231 transactions involves a sequence of steps, including the calculation of the amount of income to be recaptured as ordinary income, which depends on the type of property and the time period in which the property is acquired.
- There are special recapture rules for the disposal of property received through gifts, inheritances, and involuntary conversions, and for disposal through charitable contributions and installment sales.

QUESTIONS

1. How are capital assets defined?

2. When a sole proprietorship is sold, how is it treated for tax purposes?

3. What determines whether or not a transfer of a patent is considered to be a sale or exchange of a capital asset resulting in long-term capital gain treatment?

4. What determines whether or not a transfer of a franchise is to be considered as a sale or exchange of a capital asset?

5. How are lease cancellation payments treated by a lessee and a lessor?

6. When does the holding period begin for property acquired through the following transactions?
   a. Nontaxable exchange
   b. Involuntary conversion

7. How is the holding period determined for property acquired by a gift and from a decedent?

8. What potential advantage is there for a net overall capital gain situation?

9. How are net overall capital losses treated?

10. What happens to capital losses in excess of the allowed current year deduction?

11. How does the capital gain and loss treatment of corporate taxpayers differ from that of individuals?

12. How are nonbusiness bad debts treated?

13. What is the tax treatment of worthless securities?

14. What is Section 1244 stock? What are its advantages?

15. What special tax treatment is available for subdividers of real estate?

16. Why did Congress enact Section 1231?

17. What is included in Section 1231 property?

18. What is not included in Section 1231 property?

19. Describe what is meant by the "first netting."

20. Describe what is meant by the "second netting."

21. What was the purpose of enacting Section 1245?

22. What is Section 1245 property? What is the Section 1245 recapture rule?

23. What is Section 1250 property?

24. When is recapture on nonresidential real property governed by Section 1245 rules and when is it governed by Section 1250 recapture rules?

25. Describe the recapture provisions for both the donor and the donee when Section 1245 and Section 1250 property are given away.

26. What are the recapture rules in the event of death of the Section 1245 or Section 1250 property owner?

27. Is there recapture of depreciation when like-kind exchanges of Section 1245 and Section 1250 property occur? Explain.

28. What are the recapture rules when an involuntary conversion occurs with nonrecognition of some of the gain?

29. What effect does giving away property with recapture potential have upon a charitable contribution?

PROBLEMS

Note. In the problems below, assume there are no prior years' Section 1231 losses to recapture unless stated otherwise.

30. Which of the following is a capital asset? Explain.
    a.   Gold ring received as a gift
    b.   Personal automobile
    c.   Accounts receivable obtained in the ordinary course of business
    d.   Shares of stock in the Riviera Corporation
    e.   Building owned and used by the Riviera Corporation
    f.   Business cars and trucks owned and used by the Riviera Corporation
    g.   Home in Florida used for only four months during the winter
    h.   Copyright on a book written and owned by the author

31. Explain the difference between the following situations:
    a.   Lois sells a letter written to her by President Ronald Reagan in 1982 to a collector for $5,000.
    b.   Lois sells a signed copy of the book *To Kill a Mockingbird*, which she purchased in 1980 for $5 to a collector for $5,000.

32. Byron Bright, an inventor, sells the patent rights on his latest invention to Wilson Corporation. Wilson intends to manufacture and sell Byron's invention. Byron will receive $50 per unit Wilson sells plus a lump-sum payment of $500,000. What is the tax treatment of each type of payment for Byron? If Wilson Corporation is limited to producing and selling Byron's invention in the western section of the United States, what is the tax treatment of each type of payment?

33. Cathy Crafts grants Dan Deputy a franchise to sell cards and gifts. Dan pays Cathy a fee of $1,000 per month plus a percentage of the monthly profits. Dan must purchase his supplies from Cathy and Cathy retains the right to terminate Dan's franchise. What are the tax consequences of this arrangement to Cathy and Dan?

34. Jim Junction purchased a truck for business on November 17, 2014, for $40,000. On July 21, 2015, he exchanged the truck for another truck in a like-kind exchange. The new truck had a fair market value of $42,000. When does the holding period on the new truck begin and what is its basis?

35. Boyd Bayer acquired 100 shares of Evans Corporation stock for $3,000 on January 8, 2014. He gave the stock to his daughter Susan on January 8, 2015, when the fair market value was $2,400. On March 22, 2015, Susan sold the stock for $1,500. What is the nature and the amount of the gain or loss for Susan in 2015?

36. Alice Almond purchased Smith Corporation stock on February 23, 2014, and on November 15, 2014, she gave the stock to her son Dennis. She paid $10,000 for the stock and the value at the time of the gift was $12,000. On April 19, 2015, Dennis sold the stock for $13,000.
    a.   Does Dennis have short-term or long-term gain or loss and how much?
    b.   If the value of the stock at the time of the gift was $9,500, and Dennis sold it on April 19, 2015, for $8,000, does he have short-term or long-term gain or loss and how much?

37. Ed Elsewhere has the following capital gains and losses during 2015 as a result of sales of shares of stock. What is the net effect of the gains and losses on Ed's tax return in each of the following cases?

    a. STCG $1,500
        STCL   ($2,250)
        LTCG $5,500
        LTCL   ($2,500)
    b. STCG $6,000
        STCL   ($4,500)
        LTCG $0
        LTCL   ($750)
    c. LTCL   ($4,000)
        LTCG $8,500
        STCL   ($2,250)
        STCG $3,000
    d. LTCG $750
        LTCL   ($2,250)
        STCG $900
        STCL   ($800)
    e. LTCG $3,500
        LTCL   ($3,000)
        STCG $2,000
        STCL   ($6,500)
    f. LTCL   ($4,250)
        LTCG $250
        STCL   ($2,500)
        STCG $500

38. Ted Thomas, a single taxpayer with no dependents, has the following transactions in 2015:

AGI (before capital gains and losses)	$500,000
Long-term capital gain	18,000
Long-term capital loss	(4,000)
Short-term capital gain	6,000
Short-term capital loss	(8,000)

    a. What is Ted's net capital gain or loss?
    b. If your answer to (a) was a net capital gain, what is the maximum rate at which it would be taxed?
    c. If his AGI were $25,000, what is the maximum rate at which it would be taxed?

39. Gordon Grumps is married and files separately. During 2015, he had the following capital gains and losses:

STCL	($1,000)
STCG	1,900
STCL carryover from 2014	(200)
LTCG	600
LTCL	(10,000)

    Gordon's taxable income is $6,000. What is Gordon's capital loss deduction for 2015 and his carryover?

40. Bert Baker had $50,000 salary during 2015 and had the following capital gains and losses:

STCL carryover from 2014	($4,000)
STCL	(2,000)
STCG	1,000
LTCL carryover from 2014	(5,000)
LTCL	(3,000)
LTCG	6,000

    How should Bert treat the above on his 2015 tax return?

41. Cannon Corporation had a net long-term capital gain of $50,000 and a net short-term capital loss of $75,000 in 2015. What are the tax consequences to Cannon as a result of its capital transactions?

42. On April 22, 2015, Al Aikens, a calendar year taxpayer, purchased stock in Webster Corp. for $15,000. What is the nature of Al's loss if Webster Corp. files for bankruptcy and Al's stock becomes worthless on the following dates?
    a. December 20, 2015
    b. January 17, 2016
    c. September 19, 2016

43. Charlotte and Carl Conner purchased 1,000 shares of qualifying Sec. 1244 stock in 2011 for $125,000. In 2015, they sold the stock for $15,000.
    a. What is the amount of their loss?
    b. What is the tax treatment of the loss?

44. Compute the taxpayer's losses for the following situations.
    a. Arthur Angler, single, acquires 500 shares of Section 1244 stock in 2012 for $100,000 and sells all of it for $40,000 in 2015. How is the loss treated by Arthur?
    b. Assume in the preceding part that Arthur made an additional capital contribution of $50,000 in 2013 and then sold all of the stock for $90,000 in 2015. How is the loss treated by Arthur?

45. Shirley Swift transferred property with an adjusted basis of $24,000 and a fair market value of $18,000 to Alex Corporation in exchange for 100 shares of its Section 1244 stock. Three years later, in 2015, Shirley sold 50 shares of the stock for $7,200. What is the nature and the amount of gain or loss for Shirley?

46. Kirk Kelley, a single taxpayer, was engaged in the following transactions in 2015:
    ■ Kirk lent a friend $2,500; that person did not pay the loan when it was due and then declared bankruptcy. The loan was deemed totally uncollectible.
    ■ Kirk was notified on July 20, 2015 by his stock broker that some corporate bonds he owned have become worthless. He had purchased the bonds for $12,000 on August 22, 2014.
    ■ Kirk had a $40,000 loss on the disposition of Sec. 1244 stock purchased several years ago.
    a. What are the nature and amount of the losses on Kirk's transactions?
    b. What is his AGI for 2015 assuming gross income before the transactions was $700,000?

47. Terry Thompson, who meets all the requirements of Section 1237, sells five lots during 2014 at a gain of $30,000. During 2015, he sells the sixth lot (basis $5,000) at a selling price of $20,000 and incurs $300 in selling expenses. What is the nature of Terry's 2015 income from this transaction?

48. Which of the following are Section 1231 assets? Explain. Assume all the items have been held long-term.
    a. Machinery used in the business
    b. Personal home
    c. Factory building
    d. Land held as an investment
    e. Land used in a business
    f. Shares of stock in Jones Corporation
    g. Inventory
    h. Musical composition held by the composer

49. Andrew Graham had the following recognized gains and losses during 2015:

Personal use casualty loss (watch owned 2 years)	($ 400)
Section 1231 gain	$ 500
Section 1231 loss	($ 750)
Net LTCG	$3,000
Net STCL	($2,000)

What are the net tax consequences of these gains and losses to Andrew?

Andrew's adjusted gross income is $40,000 without considering the above items.

50. Barbara Bliss had the following recognized gains and losses during 2015:

Casualty items:

Business casualty gain (property held 5 months)	$100
Business casualty loss (property held 19 months)	($200)
Business casualty gain (property held 21 months)	$500
Section 1231 gain	$750
Section 1231 loss	($600)
LTCL	($4,000)
STCL	($250)

What are the net tax consequences of these gains and losses for Barbara?
Barbara's adjusted gross income is $30,000 without considering the above items.

51. Steven Stronghold had a Section 1231 net gain of $25,000 in 2015. His previous net Section 1231 items were $12,000 in 2008, ($8,000) in 2009, ($6,000) in 2010, ($3,000) in 2011, ($1,000) in 2012, ($4,000) in 2013, and ($1,000) in 2014.
    a. How is Steven's $25,000 net Section 1231 gain treated in 2015?
    b. If Steven's 2015 net Section 1231 gain was $12,000 instead of $25,000, how would it be treated?

52. Jackie Jaguar had a fur coat that cost $12,000 when purchased in 2005 and that was worth $14,000 when it was stolen on April 15, 2015. Her television, which cost $800 in 2009 and was worth $600, was also stolen. She received $10,000 from her insurance company for the theft of the two items. On July 20, 2015, her summer cottage with a basis of $50,000 and a fair market value of $62,000 was completely destroyed by a tornado. The insurance proceeds were $65,000. What gain or loss would Jackie recognize and how is it treated? Jackie's adjusted gross income for 2015 is $25,000.

53. What type of asset is each of the following?
    a. Machinery used in the taxpayer's business
    b. Personal-use automobile
    c. Business-use automobile
    d. Office furniture in taxpayer's business
    e. Furniture in the taxpayer's home
    f. Business inventory

54. Indicate whether the following items are Section 1245 or Section 1250 property or, if neither, indicate what type of property they are considered to be (e.g., capital asset, Section 1231 asset). (Remember that Section 1245 and Section 1250 properties are sub-categories of depreciable Section 1231 property.) Assume all the items have been held long-term.
    a. Equipment used in the business
    b. Personal automobile
    c. Truck used in the business
    d. Escalator used in the business
    e. Inventory
    f. Residential rental housing
    g. Nonresidential real property depreciated under the straight-line method
    h. Leasehold of Section 1245 property

55. In 2015, Dan Dunne sold a business machine for $75,000. He had purchased the machine in 2011 for $90,000, had depreciated it on the straight-line basis using a life of five years, and had taken a total of $63,000 depreciation.
    a. How should Dan treat the recognized gain or loss on the sale?
    b. How should Dan treat the gain or loss if he had used an accelerated depreciation method with a total of $71,100 taken in the four years?

56. In 2015, Emma Evans sold a piece of equipment from her business for $80,000. The equipment was purchased in 2011 for $72,000, had a useful life of five years, and was depreciated on a straight-line basis. A total of $50,400 depreciation was taken.
    a. How will the gain or loss on the sale be treated?
    b. How would Emma have treated the gain or loss if she had sold the property for $15,000?

57. Harold Hunch purchased Section 1250 commercial property on January 1, 1980, and sold it on January 1, 2015, at a gain of $250,000. Depreciation taken was $500,000; straight-line depreciation would have been $400,000.
    a. How should Harold treat the gain or loss?
    b. What would your answer have been in (a) if the property had been residential rental housing?

58. Determine the taxpayer's income and the treatment of the income.
    a. On January 1, 1975, Glen Gopher purchased an office building for his business for $1,000,000. He sold the building on January 1, 2015, for $1,250,000. Glen used the accelerated depreciation method over a 40-year life and his total depreciation deductions amounted to $1,000,000, of which $37,500 was depreciation taken before January 1, 1976. Straight-line depreciation would have been $25,000 a year. How much income does Glen recognize and how will it be treated?
    b. Assume the facts of (a), except that the building was an apartment building rented to tenants. How much income does Glen recognize and how will it be treated?

59. On January 1, 1985, Ivan Innkeeper purchased an office building for $900,000. He used the ACRS statutory (accelerated) depreciation method and took $900,000 depreciation before he sold the building for $950,000 on January 1, 2015. Straight-line depreciation would have been $900,000.
    a. How much income does Ivan recognize and how will it be treated?
    b. What would your answer be to (a) if he had used the optional straight-line method?

60. Assume the facts of the preceding problem except that the building was an apartment building.
    a. How much income does Ivan recognize and how will it be treated?
    b. What would your answer be to (a) if he had used the optional straight-line method?

61. Irene Irwin gave her son James a Section 1245 machine. The machine has an adjusted basis of $25,000 and Irene had taken $10,000 in depreciation. James used the machine for 15 months and took $5,000 in depreciation before selling the machine for $30,000. What is the amount of depreciation Irene must recapture as ordinary income? What is James's gain on the sale and how is it treated?

62. Karen Klaus has a machine (Section 1245 property) with an adjusted basis of $4,000 and a fair market value of $16,000. The machine originally cost $17,000 when purchased in 2011. In 2015, she exchanged it for another machine with a fair market value of $12,000 and received $4,000 cash.
    a. What are the tax consequences of the exchange for Karen?
    b. What would the tax consequences be if the new machine had a fair market value of $16,000 and no cash was received?

63. Larry Lyons donated a small office building to a qualified charity when the adjusted basis was $90,000 and the fair market value was $160,000. Larry had taken depreciation deductions in excess of straight-line depreciation of $50,000. What is Larry's charitable contribution before application of limits?

64. In March 2015, Mary Marionette sold equipment used in her business for $80,000, to be paid in eight annual installments of $10,000 plus interest beginning in 2016. The equipment was acquired in 2011 for $48,000, and its adjusted basis was $20,000 at the time of the sale. How is the income from this sale recognized and how will it be treated?

65. Ivan Investor sold a parcel of land during 2015 realizing a $50,000 gain. Ivan has used this parcel for a parking lot during the 120 months that he has owned the land. The amount and tax classification of the gain recognized by Ivan on this sale is:
    a. Ordinary income of $50,000
    b. A Section 1231 gain of $50,000
    c. A Section 1245 ordinary income item of $50,000
    d. A Section 1250 ordinary income item of $50,000

66. Mary Martin owns a custom curtain/ drapery business. In 2015, she purchased three new sewing machines and in a separate transaction, sold her three old machines for $6,000. She had bought the old machines for $5,000 and had properly claimed depreciation of $3,000. What is the amount and character of Mary's gain?
    a. $0 ordinary gain and $4,000 Section 1231 gain
    b. $2,000 ordinary gain and $4,000 Section 1231 gain
    c. $3,000 ordinary gain and $1,000 Section 1231 gain
    d. $4,000 ordinary gain and $0 Section 1231 gain

67. In 2015, Gordon Grant sold an office building for $180,000. He had purchased the building in 1986 for $150,000 and had properly deducted $100,000 of depreciation, which included $15,000 in additional (excess) depreciation. How will Gordon treat the gain on the sale of this office building?
    a. $15,000 ordinary income; $115,000 Section 1231 gain
    b. $30,000 ordinary income; $100,000 Section 1231 gain
    c. $100,000 ordinary income; $30,000 Section 1231 gain
    d. $0 ordinary income; $130,000 Section 1231 gain

68. Which of the following property is not Section 1231 property?
    a. Unharvested crop on land held for more than one year and used for farming
    b. Dairy cattle held more than two years
    c. Musical instruments in a music store
    d. Music store building

69. Section 1250 recapture provisions apply to all of the following except:
    a. Residential real property
    b. Government-financed housing
    c. Low-income housing
    d. ACRS nonresidential real property depreciated under the statutory (accelerated) method

70. **Comprehensive Problem.** Terry Trooper, a single taxpayer, had the following transactions during 2015:
    a. Sold 60 shares of Troy Corporation common stock on March 22, 2015, for $660. The stock was purchased on January 31, 2015, for $7 per share.
    b. Sold family gemstones held for three years for $10,000. The gemstones had a cost and basis of $7,800.
    c. Three-year note from his brother became worthless. The note was $750.
    d. Stock in Tyler Corporation became worthless on December 20, 2015, when the corporation filed for bankruptcy. The stock was purchased for $250 on June 30, 2015.
    e. Received $200 from a renter to cancel a lease held on rental property.

    What is Terry's taxable income if his only other income was salary, net rental income and interest totaling $40,000? He has itemized deductions of $7,000 and no dependents.

71. **Comprehensive Problem (Tax Return Problem).** Bill and Alice Savage, husband and wife and both age 42, have the following transactions during 2015:
    a. They sold their old residence on January 28, 2015, for $380,000. The basis of their old residence, purchased in 2005, was $70,000. The selling expenses were $20,000. On May 17, 2015, they purchased and moved into another residence costing $150,000.
    b. On April 28, 2015, they sold for $8,000 stock that Alice had received as a gift from her mother, who had purchased the stock for $10,000 in 2010. Her mother gave Alice the stock on November 15, 2014, when the fair market value was $9,400.
    c. On May 24, 2015, Bill sold for $21,000 stock inherited from his father. His father died on June 14, 2014, when the fair market value of the stock was $9,000. Bill's father paid $7,000 for the stock in 2008.
    d. On August 11, 2015, they sold a personal automobile for $8,000; basis of the automobile was $20,000 and it was purchased in 2012.
    c. They had a carryover and other stock transactions as follows:

LTCL carryover from 2014	($7,000)
STCG	$2,000
LTCG	$3,500

Bill had salary of $40,000 and Alice had salary of $28,000. They have no children. They paid state income taxes of $3,200, sales tax of $400, federal income taxes of $15,000, and property taxes of $1,800. In addition, they contributed $5,600 to their church and paid $4,000 interest on their home mortgage.

Compute Bill and Alice's taxable income for 2015.

72. **Comprehensive Problem.** Kate King had the following transactions or involuntary conversions during 2015:

   a. Her uninsured diamond ring that cost $3,500 in 2009 was stolen.

   b. Her vacation home purchased in 2009 for $70,000 was destroyed by a tornado. Insurance recovery was $85,000.

   c. Machinery purchased in 2011 for $12,000 with a basis at the time of sale of $3,000 was sold on January 1 for $13,000.

   d. A business car purchased in 2010 for $20,000 with a basis of $8,700 at the time of sale was sold on January 1 for $6,700.

   e. Land owned for six years was condemned by the state. The award was $100,000 and the land had cost $65,000. No replacement of the property was made.

   f. 100 shares of Atlas Corporation stock were sold for $8,000 on July 17. The stock was originally purchased in 2005 for $3,000.

   g. 200 shares of Brown Corporation stock were sold for $4,000 on April 19, 2015. The stock was originally purchased on December 23, 2014, for $10,000.

   Kate, single and age 34 with no dependents, has adjusted gross income of $44,000 and itemized deductions of $7,000 without considering the above items. What is her taxable income for 2015?

73. **Comprehensive Problem.** Mark Mullins had the following transactions or involuntary conversions during 2015:

   a. His diamond gemstones costing $4,000 in 2009 were sold for $5,000.

   b. His office building owned for four years was damaged by fire. The loss after insurance recovery was $12,000.

   c. Equipment purchased in 2010 for $18,000 with a basis at the time of sale of $6,000 was sold for $11,000 on January 1, 2015.

   d. An apartment building purchased on January 1, 1986, for $300,000 was sold for $124,000 on January 1, 2015. Mark took accelerated depreciation of $236,000. Straight-line depreciation would have been $200,000.

   e. Land used in his business for four years was condemned by the state. The award was $60,000. Cost of the land was $74,000. No replacement of the property was made.

   f. 200 shares of Carter Corporation stock were sold for $19,000 on August 25, 2015. The stock was originally purchased in 2010 for $15,000.

   g. 100 shares of Dalton Corporation stock were sold for $8,000 on July 23, 2015. The stock was originally purchased on February 10, 2015, for $2,000.

   Mark, single and age 42 with no dependents, has adjusted gross income of $56,000 and itemized deductions of $8,000 without considering the above items. What is Mark's taxable income for 2015?

74. **Research Problem.** In 2014, Allen Appleton sells his business to David, but he sells the claim against Fred that arose during the course of his business to George, who is not in a business. The claim becomes worthless in George's hands in 2015. Can George take a business loss for the bad debt since it originally arose in the course of a business?

75. **Research Problem.** Harlan Huston had a net Section 1231 gain in 2015 of $40,000. His net Section 1231 gains and losses were as follows:

Year	Net Sec. 1231 Gains/(Losses)
2014	($15,000)
2013	($6,000)
2012	($16,000)
2011	$5,000
2010	($20,000)

How is the $40,000 net Section 1231 gain treated by Harlan in 2015?

Chapter

13

Tax Accounting

OBJECTIVES

After completing Chapter 13, you should be able to:

1. List what are permissible tax years.
2. Explain the requirements for changing a tax year.
3. Identify the available accounting methods.
4. Understand the rules for accounting method changes.
5. Account for the capitalization of inventory costs.
6. Describe long-term contract reporting.
7. Define the installment method of accounting.

OVERVIEW

The first 12 chapters are presented primarily from the individual taxpayer's point of view (including self-employed taxpayers). This chapter provides a general discussion of the previous material as it applies to other entities and provides a discussion of accounting periods and accounting methods as they apply to all entities. Discussions of specific provisions as they apply to other entities (e.g., corporations, partnerships, etc.) are contained in subsequent chapters.

The term "financial accounting" refers to the reporting of the financial data of an enterprise through financial statements prepared in accordance with generally accepted accounting principles.

Income tax accounting, hereafter referred to as "tax accounting," is concerned with the reporting of financial data to satisfy the requirements of the Internal Revenue Code, the Regulations which interpret the Code, rulings by the IRS which further interpret the Code and Regulations, and the decisions of the courts on litigated issues.

Tax accounting is statutory. It is concerned with the determination of taxable income as the base to which tax rates are applied to establish the tax liability for a period, usually one year. Basically, taxable income or taxable loss is the net result of summarizing revenues, gains, expenses, and losses. This result is determined in considerable degree in accordance with accepted accounting principles and conventions. At every step in the process, however, there are differences, based on tax statutes and interpretations thereof, which distinguish taxable income from financial income. These differences are numerous and may prove substantial in amount.

The variations between taxable income and financial income are so great as to require specialization in taxation as distinguished from financial accounting. The two disciplines, however, are fundamentally related, and tax issues are usually resolved concurrently with the financial accounting issues.

The basic approach of the income tax is to impose a tax on the net result of financial transactions occurring during a fixed period of time called the tax year. The time for reporting income and deductions thus becomes of vital importance in determining taxable income. Therefore, the Internal Revenue Code provides that taxable income must be computed on the basis of the taxpayer's tax year and permissible method of accounting.

There are some differences between financial and tax accounting, differences that are attributable to a number of factors. Financial accounting is designed to reflect the income position of a profit-seeking taxpayer; the rules of tax accounting not only must have regard for this but also must reflect the need to raise revenue equitably. Further, the general thrust and purpose of the tax law, to prescribe detailed rules in the interest of certainty, is bound to create conflicts with tailor-made systems designed for particular taxpayers in many instances. Experience has indicated that certain tax rules are necessary in order to control tax avoidance. Thus, the Internal Revenue Service has been provided with Code Sec. 482, under which it may reallocate items of income, deduction, credit, or allowance in order to prevent tax avoidance when two or more organizations are controlled by the same interest. Further, if the taxpayer's method of accounting does not clearly reflect income, Code Sec. 446 authorizes the IRS to require the use of a method that will do so. Additionally, the Supreme Court has indicated that the use of generally accepted accounting principles (GAAP), which apply to financial accounting and are considered to be the "best" accounting practices, does not necessarily clearly reflect income and does not shift the burden of proof to the IRS to show otherwise. *Thor Power Tool Co.,* 79-1 USTC ¶9139, 439 U.S. 522 (1979).

Once the questions of what items are includible in gross income and what items are deductible in computing taxable income are answered, a second set of questions must be faced. These relate to when such qualifying items are to be utilized in that computation. In other words, in what tax year is an item of income actually to be included in gross income? In what tax year is a deduction to be subtracted from gross income?

The general answers to most of these "when" questions are furnished in terms of the method of accounting regularly employed by the taxpayer in his or her business and recordkeeping. That record, however, must "clearly reflect income." Various accounting methods are available in computing taxable income, but the significant effect of the selection of one method of reporting over another is that of timing. Total income and total deductions over the long run will generally be the same regardless of the method used. However, yearly determinations of taxable income may differ materially depending on the method selected.

Taxable Income and Tax Liability for Various Entities

¶13,001

RECAPITULATION OF TAXABLE INCOME AND TAX LIABILITY

Table 1 contains a general outline of the computation of taxable income for various entities. A comparison of each provides an indication of some similarities and differences. All entities subtract exclusions to determine gross income. However, the types of exclusions are different; some apply to all entities (e.g., the exclusion for municipal bond interest income), and some apply to particular entities (e.g., the exclusion for qualified fringe benefits, which applies to individuals). Additionally, Code Sec. 61 applies to all entities in computing gross income.

Each entity also is permitted to reduce gross income by qualified deductions. However, the type, classification, and computation of deductions can vary. Only individuals dichotomize their deductions into "for adjusted gross income" and "from adjusted gross income," the latter being deductions for personal expenses such as personal exemptions and itemized deductions that do not apply to other entities. Corporations have routine deductions and several "special" deductions such as the dividends-received deduction. This deduction applies only to corporations. Some items are not deductible by conduit entities (e.g., S corporations) but instead pass through to the owners, while some have different constraints. For example, the charitable contribution deduction is constrained by adjusted gross income for individuals, but is constrained by "modified" taxable income for corporations; yet both entities must go through the same general process of classifying the contributions as cash, ordinary income assets, and long-term capital assets.

To the extent that each entity (including self-employed taxpayers) has business activities, Code Sec. 162 applies to trade or business expenses, and the general criteria for a deduction apply (e.g., ordinary, necessary, reasonable, etc.). Code Sec. 212 applies to an entity's nonbusiness expenses and is most applicable to individuals. Similarly, the "hobby loss" rules of Code Sec. 183 apply to individuals and S corporations. Thus, while each entity is entitled to deductions in the computation of its taxable (or ordinary) income, the nature of these deductions can vary. In subsequent chapters, significant differences are explained further.

Table 1. COMPUTATION OF TAXABLE INCOME

Individuals

Income Broadly Conceived	XXXXX
Less: Exclusions	– XXX
Gross Income	XXXXX
Less: Deductions for Adjusted Gross Income	– XX
Adjusted Gross Income	XXXXX
Less: Deductions from Adjusted Gross Income	– XX
Taxable Income	XXXXX

C Corporations

Income Broadly Conceived	XXXXX
Less: Exclusions	– XXX
Gross Income	XXXXX
Less: Deductions	
Routine	– XX
Special	– XX
Taxable Income	XXXXX

S Corporations

Income Broadly Conceived	XXXXX
Less: Exclusions	– XXX
Gross Income	XXXXX
Less: Deductions	– XX
Ordinary Income	XXXXX

Partnerships

Income Broadly Conceived	XXXXX
Less: Exclusions	– XXX
Gross Income	XXXXX
Less: Deductions	– XX
Ordinary Income	XXXXX

Estates and Trusts

Income Broadly Conceived	XXXXX
Less: Exclusions	– XXX
Gross Income	XXXXX
Less: Deductions	– XX
Taxable Income	XXXXX

Table 2 contains a general outline of each entity's computation of net tax due or refund due. Pure conduits do not pay an income tax; rather, various components such as income, certain deductions, and credits pass through to the owners or beneficiaries. Those entities that do pay a tax utilize taxable income to determine gross tax liability, which is then reduced by the credits and prepayments to which they are entitled. However, the type and/or computation varies (e.g., only individuals are entitled to the earned income credit).

Table 2. NET TAX LIABILITY	
Individuals	
Gross Tax Liability	yyyyy
Less: Credits	– yy
Net Tax Liability	yyyyy
Less: Prepayments	– yy
Net Tax or Refund Due	yyyyy
C Corporations	
Gross Tax Liability	yyyyy
Less: Credits	– yy
Net Tax Liability	yyyyy
Less: Prepayments	– yy
Net Tax or Refund Due	yyyyy
Estates and Trusts (assuming not completely a conduit)	
Gross Tax Liability	yyyyy
Less: Credits	– yy
Net Tax Liability	yyyyy
Less: Prepayments	– yy
Net Tax or Refund Due	yyyyy

In summary, many of the concepts that you learned in the first 12 chapters apply to all entities. However, there are numerous and substantial differences that require additional explanation. The remainder of this chapter deals with accounting periods and accounting methods as they pertain to all entities, but the focus begins to shift to business entities. Subsequent chapters deal with the specific entities.

Accounting Periods

The basic approach of income taxation is to impose a tax on the net result of financial transactions occurring during a fixed period of time, otherwise called the "tax year." The time for reporting income and deductions is of vital importance in determining taxable income. Therefore, Code Sec. 441 requires that taxable income must be computed on the basis of the taxpayer's tax year. This annual accounting period may be either a calendar year or a fiscal year.

¶13,007

THE TAX YEAR

"Tax year" means the calendar year or the fiscal year on the basis of which the taxable income is computed. The tax year may not exceed 12 calendar months, except where a 52-53-week tax year is adopted. (No further mention of this option is made in this text because of the relative infrequency with which this taxable period is encountered in practice.) The term "calendar year" means a period of 12 months ending on December 31. A taxpayer who has not established a fiscal year must file a tax return on the basis of a calendar year.

A "fiscal year" is defined as a period of 12 months ending on the last day of any month other than December. A fiscal year will be recognized by the IRS only if it is established as the annual accounting period for the taxpayer and the taxpayer's books are kept on the same basis. Therefore, to establish and maintain a fiscal year as the tax year, the taxpayer must correlate accounting, financial, and business practices with the fiscal year used for tax returns.

The keeping of books does not require that the records be bound. Records that are sufficient to reflect income adequately and clearly on the basis of an annual accounting period are normally regarded as the keeping of books. Informal records consisting of check stubs, rent receipts, and dividend statements are not considered regular books of account.

When a return is required for a fractional part of a year, the "tax year" means the period for which such return is filed. This fractional period is referred to as a "short tax year." A short tax year is any period for which a return has been filed that contains less than 12 months. Frequently, the first or the final tax period of a particular tax entity is a short tax year. Additionally, when a tax year is changed, the period between the end of the old tax year and the beginning of the new tax year is a short tax year for which a return must be filed.

¶13,015   ELECTION OF THE TAX YEAR

Individuals

A new taxpayer may adopt any tax year without obtaining prior approval of the IRS in the first year. The first tax year must be adopted on or before the time for filing the initial return. An extension of the time for filing, however, does not extend the time for adoption of the tax year.

The establishment and maintenance of adequate books of account may not be delayed beyond the end of the first accounting period if the taxpayer selects a fiscal year. Informal records do not meet this requirement, even if they become part of a formal system of accounting after the close of the fiscal year. In such cases, calendar-year reporting is required and a fiscal-year accounting period cannot be elected. Also, taxpayers who do not have books (e.g., employees) must use the calendar year. Code Sec. 441.

Income Averaging for Farming and Fishing Businesses

The above rules regarding tax periods apply to farmers. However, Code Sec. 1301 allows individual farmers and fisherman to elect to use income averaging over a three-year period when determining tax liability. The irrevocable election applies to farm income or fishing income attributable to a farm or fishing business. The tax liability in any tax year is equal to the tax on the taxpayer's taxable income reduced by that year's elected farm or fishing income to be averaged over the three preceding years and increased by the tax due on the increase in taxable income of the three prior years due to the one-third farm or fishing income averaged over the three preceding years.

Sole Proprietors

Sole proprietors of a business must use the same period for business tax reporting purposes that they use for their personal books.

EXAMPLE 13.1	Evelyn Aldo establishes a tax year when she files her first return. She begins business in a later year as a sole proprietor. Evelyn must use the same tax year for the business unless permission from the IRS to change is obtained.

Partnerships

Except for partnerships that qualify under the business purpose exception, a partnership must use the same tax year as that of its partners who have a majority interest (an aggregate interest of greater than 50 percent) in partnership profits and capital. If partners owning a majority interest have different tax years, the partnership must adopt the same tax year as that of its principal partners. When neither condition is met, a partnership is required to adopt a year that results in the least aggregate deferral of income to the partners. Reg. §1.706-1. A principal partner is a partner having an interest of 5 percent or more in partnership profits or capital. Partnership income is considered to be earned by the partners on the last day of the partnership's tax year. The least aggregate deferral method requires the partnership to calculate the income that would be deferred by the partners based on the partners' tax years (and therefore the number of months from the partnership's tax year-end to the partner's tax year-end). The calculation is based on each partner's ownership percentage and tax year-end. For each possible year-end, each partner's ownership percentage is multiplied by the number of months the partner would defer income. The result for each partner is totaled, and the totals for all possible tax years are compared. The partnership tax year is the one with the smallest total. These tax year requirements are designed to reduce the partners' income deferral opportunities via tax year selection.

The partnership must adopt the tax year of its majority interest partner or partners if that interest has a common tax year on the first day of the partnership's existing tax year. Further, if a change in the tax year is required under this rule, no additional change is required in the next two years following the year of change.

EXAMPLE 13.2	A partnership is formed by an individual and a corporation, each owning a 50 percent interest. The individual has a calendar year as its tax year, and the corporation has a tax year that ends on August 31. The partnership must determine its tax year using the least aggregate deferral method because neither the majority interest rule nor the principal partnership rule applies. If the corporation owned more than a 50 percent interest in the partnership, the partnership would have to adopt a tax year ending on August 31.

EXAMPLE 13.3	A partnership is owned by numerous individuals and corporations. All of the individuals have calendar years and none of the individuals are principal partners. One corporation owns 45 percent and has a fiscal year ending on May 31. The other corporations have various other fiscal years and none are principal partners. If the individuals together own more than 50 percent of the partnership, the partnership must adopt the calendar year because the majority partners have a calendar year. If the individuals do not own more than 50 percent, the partnership must adopt a fiscal year ending on May 31 because the principal partners have a fiscal year ending May 31.

EXAMPLE 13.4

The BPT partnership has three owners, Barry, Pete, and Tom. Barry and Pete each own 30 percent, and Tom owns 40 percent. Their tax years end on March 31, September 30, and December 31, respectively. In this situation neither the majority interest nor the principal partner methods can be used to determine BPT's tax year; thus, the least aggregate deferral method must be used, and it is determined as follows.

Partnership		Partner	\multicolumn{6}{c	}{Possible Tax Year-Ends}
			\multicolumn{2}{c	}{3/31}	\multicolumn{2}{c	}{9/30}	\multicolumn{2}{c	}{12/31}
Partner	Interest	Tax Year	Months Deferred	Total	Months Deferred	Total	Months Deferred	Total
Barry	30%	3/31	0	0	6	1.8	3	0.9
Pete	30%	9/30	6	1.8	0	0	9	2.7
Tom	40%	12/31	9	3.6	3	1.2	0	0
				5.4		3.0		3.6

Note: Months deferred equals the months from the possible partnership tax year-end to the partner's tax year-end. Total equals the months deferred multiplied by the partner's ownership interest.

Thus, the BPT partnership must use a September 30 tax year-end because it has the lowest total amount (3.0) and, therefore, the least aggregate deferral.

In all other circumstances, the adoption of a tax year requires IRS approval of an application to be filed on or before the 15th day of the third calendar month following the short period. The application must establish a satisfactory business purpose. For example, a partnership's selection of a tax year to coincide with a natural business year would constitute a sufficient business purpose. Approval from the IRS can be received to adopt a fiscal year corresponding to the partnership's natural business year.

The natural business year can be established by the partnership showing that it received at least 25% of its gross receipts in the last two months ending on the proposed year's end and for the corresponding time period of each of its three preceding years.

a. Partnerships can use an expedited procedure under Rev. Proc. 2002-38, 2002-1 CB 1037, that does not require a user fee; otherwise a $2,700 user fee must accompany Form 1128.
b. Even though the 25% test is met, the IRS is not required to approve a change to the natural business year.
c. If the partnership has not existed long enough to meet the three-year period test, it cannot establish a natural business year. (Rev. Proc. 2002-39, 2002-1-CB 1046)

Application is made on Form 1128 (Application for Change in Accounting Period). This form may be modified to indicate that it is an application for adoption of a tax year.

A newly formed partnership must file with its first return one of the following:

1. A copy of the letter approving the adoption of a tax year that differs from the tax year of the majority partners or all of the principal partners.
2. A statement that the partnership tax year is the same as the tax year of the majority partners or all of its principal partners, or that all of its principal partners are concurrently changing to the tax year the partnership has adopted.

Corporations

Every newly organized corporation has the unrestricted right to select its annual accounting period. The election is signified by filing the first return on or before the statutory due date for filing. The tax year may either be the calendar year or a fiscal year. The tax year of a corporation may differ from that of the shareholders.

A corporation in existence during any portion of a tax year must file a return. If a corporation is not in existence throughout an entire accounting period, the corporation must file a return for that fractional part of a year during which it is in existence. A new corporation comes into existence on the date of its incorporation. This may cause problems for a corporation that is inactive for a period of time after incorporation. Unless the corporation files a return selecting a tax year during the initial period, the time period may pass for electing a tax year, and the corporation may be forced to file a calendar-year return. This will happen if the first tax year ends more than 12 months after incorporation.

Filing Form 7004 (Application for Automatic Extension of Time to File Certain Business Income Tax, Information, and Other Returns) with respect to a first return is an election to adopt the accounting period indicated on that form. The late filing of a taxpayer's initial return will not prevent adoption of a fiscal year, provided the taxpayer adopted a fiscal accounting period before the due date for filing its return, and its books and records reflect the adoption of this period. Rev. Rul. 68-125, 1968-1 CB 189.

S Corporations

The tax year of an S corporation is generally required to be a calendar year. However, a tax year other than a calendar year may be used if the S corporation can satisfy the IRS that there is a legitimate business purpose for such use. Code Sec. 1378(b).

Estates

An estate is a new taxpayer, and it may adopt any tax year without obtaining prior approval. The ability to select a fiscal period enables the executor to do two things: (1) control the number of months in the first and final returns of the estate, thereby controlling the amount of income taxable to the estate during this period, and (2) postpone the time of realization of income by the beneficiaries due to the timing of distributions.

Trusts

Trusts, other than charitable and tax-exempt trusts, must use the calendar year. Code Sec. 644.

Business Year

The intent of an entity to make its tax year coincide with its natural business year constitutes a valid business purpose. Where a business has a nonpeak and a peak period, the natural business year usually ends at, or soon after, the close of the peak period. A business with a steady monthly income does not have a natural business year.

A business purpose generally exists if, in the last two months of the selected tax year, a taxpayer receives at least 25 percent of its gross receipts and has done so for three consecutive 12-month periods. The following factors are ordinarily insufficient to establish a business purpose with respect to a particular fiscal tax year: (1) the use of a particular year for regulatory or financial accounting purposes; (2) the hiring patterns of a particular business; (3) the use of a particular year for administrative purposes, such as the promotion of staff and the compensation or retirement arrangements for staff, partners, or shareholders; and (4) the fact that a particular business involves the use of price lists, model years, or other items that change on an annual basis.

In order to use a fiscal tax year, a partnership or an S corporation must obtain the IRS's consent. A partnership or S corporation that received permission to use a fiscal year under Rev. Proc. 74-33, 1974-2 CB 489, can continue to use such year without seeking approval from the IRS.

Change of Accounting Periods

If a taxpayer wishes to change the annual accounting period and adopt a new tax year, with certain exceptions, prior approval must be obtained before using the new period for tax purposes. A change in accounting period usually is approved if there are substantial business reasons for the change. Code Sec. 442.

If a taxpayer's records are inadequate or there is an accounting period that does not meet the requirements for a fiscal year, the tax year must be the calendar year. In this instance, the adoption of a fiscal year is treated as a change in the annual accounting period and prior approval from the IRS is required.

A change in accounting period usually involves a short-period tax year. This period begins with the first day after the close of the former accounting period and ends at the close of the day preceding the beginning of the new accounting period.

EXAMPLE 13.5	Mita Corporation wishes to change its tax year from a calendar year to a tax year ending on May 31, 2016. Mita Corporation will have a short tax year for the period January 1 to May 31, 2016.

¶13,101   IRS PERMISSION OR CONSENT

In order to secure prior approval, the taxpayer must file an application on Form 1128 on or before the 15th day of the third calendar month following the end of the short year. Reg. §1.442-1(b). An application should show that there is a substantial business purpose for the change and that any tax cost to the IRS is insignificant. The IRS will respond to the taxpayer with Form 5654 (Notification of Action on Application for Change in Accounting Period). The form lists several conditions to be met by the taxpayer for final acceptance of the change. No change should be made until the request has been approved.

To prevent substantial distortion of income that may result from a change in tax period, an agreement between the taxpayer and the IRS is required. This agreement must provide the terms, conditions, and adjustments necessary to implement the change. The following examples of income distortion are given in Reg. §1.442-1(b):

1. Deferring a substantial portion of income, or shifting a substantial portion of deductions, from one year to another so as to reduce the tax liability
2. Causing a similar deferral in the case of a related taxpayer, such as a partner, a beneficiary, or a shareholder in an S corporation
3. Creating a short period in which there is either a net operating loss or, in the case of an S corporation, amounts treated as long-term capital gain

If approval is granted, the taxpayer must file an income tax return for the short period. There are special rules for computing the tax for a short year caused by a change in the accounting period. These are discussed later in the chapter.

¶13,115   EXCEPTIONS TO PERMISSION REQUIREMENTS

However, despite the prior approval requirements, there are some instances when a tax year may be changed without receiving advance approval.

Individuals

An individual whose income is derived solely from wages, salaries, interest, dividends, capital gains, pensions and annuities, or rents and royalties does not need prior approval for making a change from the fiscal year to the calendar year if Form 1128 is filed with the District Director on or before the last day of January following the close of the short period for which a return is required. A copy of the application is to be attached to the return filed for the short period. Unless a letter is received by the individual(s) from the District Director denying approval, it is assumed that the change has been approved.

Since a joint return may not be filed if a husband and wife have different tax years, Reg. §1.442-1(e) provides that a newly married individual may adopt the accounting period of the other spouse without prior approval. He or she must file a return for the short period required by the change on or before the 15th day of the fourth month following the end of the short period. If the due date for the short-period return occurs before the date of marriage, a joint return may not be filed until the second year ending after the date of marriage, and then only if a timely short-period return is filed for that year. The short-period return filed in the first or second tax year after the date of marriage must be accompanied by a statement that the accounting period is being changed according to Reg. §1.442-1(e).

EXAMPLE 13.6

Larry Raser and Donna Chilton marry on September 24, 2015. Donna is on a fiscal year ending June 30, and Larry is on a calendar year. Donna wishes to change to a calendar year in order to file a joint return with Larry. Donna may not change to a calendar year for 2015 since she would have to file a return for the short period from July 1 to December 31, 2014, by April 15, 2015. Since the date of marriage occurred after this due date, the return could not be filed under the special rule for newly married couples.

Donna, however, may change to the calendar year for 2016 by filing a return by April 15, 2016, for the short period from July 1 to December 31, 2015. If Donna files such a return, Larry and Donna may file a joint return for calendar-year 2016, which is Larry's second tax year ending after the date of marriage. Of course, Donna could request and receive permission to change to the calendar year before the marriage and thus be allowed to file a joint return for the calendar-year 2015.

Any other husband and wife wishing to change to the accounting period of the other spouse so that they may file a joint return must make proper application. Permission may be granted for this reason in appropriate cases, even though no substantial business purpose for requesting the change is established.

Partnerships, S Corporations, and Personal Service Corporations

All partnerships, S corporations, and personal service corporations generally must conform their tax years to the tax year of their owners, unless such entities can establish a business purpose for having a different year. An entity that must change its tax year to match that of its owner is required to file a return for the resulting short tax year.

An election is provided whereby a partnership, S corporation, or personal service corporation that is otherwise required to change its tax year may retain the tax year currently used by the entity. An election is also provided for such entities to adopt or change to tax years with limited deferral periods. The limited deferral period must be the lesser of the deferral period currently in use or three months.

S corporations and partnerships are required to make enhanced estimated tax payments for any tax year for which this special tax election is in effect. Willful failure to make the enhanced estimated tax payments results in the cancellation of the election by the entity.

Corporations

Rev. Proc. 2002-37, 2002-1 CB 1030, provides measures whereby a corporation (other than an S corporation) may change its annual accounting period without prior approval from the IRS. The automatic approval rules do not apply to a corporation:

1. That has changed its accounting period at any time within four calendar years ending with the calendar year in which the short period resulting from the changes begins;
2. Is a member of a partnership or a beneficiary of a trust or estate (although some exceptions may apply);
3. Is a shareholder in a foreign sales corporation (FSC) or interest charge domestic international sales corporation (IC-DISC) at the end of the short period resulting from the change (although some exceptions may apply);
4. Is an FSC or an IC-DISC (although an exception may apply);
5. Is a personal service corporation (Rev. Proc. 2002-38, 2002-1 CB 1037, contains procedures for certain automatic changes);
6. Is a controlled foreign corporation, a foreign personal holding company, or a passive foreign investment company or a shareholder in any of such entities (certain exceptions may apply);
7. Is a corporation which has in effect a Code Sec. 936 election (Puerto Rico and possession tax credit); or
8. Is a tax-exempt organization (certain procedures apply to tax-exempt organizations).

If the corporation has an NOL or capital loss (CL) in the short period resulting from the change then the NOL or CL may not be carried back but must be carried forward beginning with the first taxable year after the short period. However, the NOL or CL may be carried back if it is $50,000 or less or results from a short period of nine months or longer and is less than the NOL or CL for a full 12-month period beginning with the first day of the short period.

EXAMPLE 13.7

In 2015, Jeffco changed its accounting period from a September year end to a December year end. It had a $100,000 NOL for the three-month short period ending December 31, 2015. Jeffco cannot carry back the NOL. It must carry it forward to the new accounting period (calendar-year 2016).

If Jeffco's NOL had been $45,000 and its short period had started on April 1 and ended December 31, then it might be able to carry back the NOL. If its results from operations for September 1, 2015 – August 31, 2016, produce an NOL that is less than $45,000, then Jeffco may carry back the NOL.

A statement on behalf of the corporation must be filed on or before the time for filing the return for the short period. The statement must indicate that the corporation is changing its annual accounting period under Reg. §1.442-1(b) and must contain information indicating that all the above conditions have been met.

¶13,165   SHORT TAX YEARS

When a change in an accounting period is instituted, a separate return is filed for the short period beginning with the day following the close of the old tax year and ending with the day preceding the first day of the new tax year. The return is due from a corporation on the 15th day of the third month after the short period. Other taxpayers must file the return on or before the 15th day of the fourth month following the short period.

General Rule

The general rule calls for the tax to be computed for the short period by placing the short period's taxable income on an annual basis. This is accomplished by multiplying the modified taxable income by 12 and dividing the result by the number of months in the short period. The tax for the short period is the same as the tax computed on an annual basis. Without this provision, taxpayers would be able to avoid a large tax liability by having a portion of the income taxed for a shorter period. Tax preferences must be annualized to determine the applicability of the alternative minimum tax. Code Sec. 443(d).

A change in accounting period could result in tax savings due to the progressive tax rate structures. Some income would be "sheltered" by avoiding a higher tax rate. To prevent this from happening, the tax for the short period is based on annualized income. The procedures are as follows:

1. Annualize the short-period income

$$\text{Annualized income} = \text{Short-period income} \times \left[\frac{12}{\text{No. months in short period}} \right]$$

2. Determine the tax on the annualized income
3. Determine the short-period tax

$$\text{Short-period tax} = \text{Tax on annualized income} \times \left[\frac{\text{No. months in short period}}{12} \right]$$

EXAMPLE 13.8

Xeno Corporation files a return, because of a change in its accounting period, for the three-month short period ending June 30, 2015. It has taxable income of $20,000 during the short period. Its tax liability is computed as follows:

1.	Taxable Income Annualized ($20,000 × 12/3)	$80,000.00
2.	$50,000 × 15%	$7,500
	$25,000 × 25%	6,250
	$5,000 × 34%	1,700
	Tax on Annualized Income	15,450.00
3.	Tax for Short Period ($15,450 × 3/12)	$3,862.50

Individuals must use the tax rate schedules to compute their tax liabilities for the short period. Also, they cannot use the standard deduction; instead they must reflect the itemized deductions incurred in the short period. Personal exemptions must be prorated to the short period. Very few individuals change their accounting period.

Alternative Method

Because annualization of the short-period income may result in inequities to the taxpayer, there is an exception to the general rule which may result in less tax. Code Sec. 443(b)(2). The procedures are as follows:

1. Determine taxable income for the 12-month period beginning on the first day of the short period.
2. Determine the tax on the taxable income for this 12-month period.

3. $$\text{Short-period tax} \;=\; \text{Tax on 12-month period} \;\times\; \left[\frac{\text{Taxable income for short period}}{\text{Taxable income for 12-month period}}\right]$$

4. The short-period tax computed in Step 3 cannot be less than it would have been if it had been computed on short-period taxable income without placing it on an annualized basis.

EXAMPLE 13.9	Referring to Example 13.8, assume that Xeno's taxable income for the 12-month period beginning April 1, 2015, is $30,000. The tax on $30,000 is $4,500. The short-period tax would be $3,000 ($4,500 × $20,000/$30,000). This amount is not less than the tax on the short-period income without being annualized ($3,000 = ($20,000 × 15%)). The $3,000 short-period tax determined via the alternative method is compared to the short-period tax computed under the regular method ($3,862.50) and, if less, will be used. In this example, the alternative method produces a tax savings of $862.50 and Xeno Corporation would file a claim for a refund.

The short tax year which results from a change in accounting period is treated as a full tax year for other purposes of the tax rules such as carrybacks and carryforwards. Tax planners must be careful that the creation of a short tax year return does not reduce the benefits a taxpayer would obtain from loss and credit carrybacks and carryforwards which could otherwise be obtained without the short tax year.

¶13,175   ACCOUNTING PERIOD TAX PLANNING

A taxpayer should consider the various factors influencing the choice of accounting period and select the accounting period as soon as possible after beginning operations. The significant factor in selecting an accounting period is timing. Most frequently, total income and total deductions over the long run will generally be the same regardless of the period used. However, yearly determinations of taxable income may differ materially depending on the accounting period selected.

Business Factors

The choice of an annual accounting period depends on several business factors, such as a slack season when personnel are available, or a date when inventories and bank loans are low, which in turn presents a favorable balance sheet for credit purposes. Because income tax rates are on a graduated basis, the lowest taxes over a period of years will be achieved if income can be kept as level as possible over this period of time. Generally, this objective can be obtained if the expenses incurred in earning income are charged off in the same year the income is earned.

Natural Business Year

It is desirable that the accounting period chosen be in agreement with the natural business year. That is, the tax period should include both the income earned and the expenses incurred in generating that income. For example, if a business earns most of its income in the fall while most of the expenses are incurred or paid in the following spring, the calendar year should not be selected as the accounting period, since income would be perpetually distorted. Some advantages of closing a tax period at the end of the natural business year are: (1) inventories are at their lowest point and may be inspected and tabulated more quickly and valued more accurately, (2) receivables are at their minimum and bad debt adjustments can be determined more accurately, and (3) bank loans usually have been liquidated or reduced to their minimum for the tax period. Additionally, financial statements prepared at the end of a natural business year more accurately reflect the results of activities over one complete cycle of operations.

The accounting method adopted by the taxpayer may well be an important factor. Since income and expenses generally accrue before they are received or paid, it may be possible to close the accounting period earlier if the accrual method is used rather than the cash receipts and disbursements method, thereby reflecting a more accurate picture of the income for the period.

Special Circumstances

A corporate taxpayer can select its year based on the particular circumstances of the initial period, rather than any adherence to the concept of the natural business year. The objective is usually to defer tax. Accordingly, a corporation may close its first year at the time it reaches a taxable income of $75,000 and thus avoid the 34 percent rate. If the corporation is an S corporation, where income is passed through to its shareholders who report on the calendar year, adoption of a year ending on the last day of January or a subsequent month, instead of the preceding December 31, serves to defer taxation of the income to the shareholders. However, new S corporations are required to adopt a calendar year unless the taxpayer can show a business reason for electing a fiscal year.

Affiliated Groups

In the case where a new corporation is a subsidiary or a parent of an affiliated group, the accounting period selected should conform to that of the existing members of the group. The consolidated return regulations require that the tax year of all members of an affiliated group be the same as that of the common parent corporation. Accordingly, recognition of this possibility may avoid the trouble of changing the accounting period for the new corporation, the subsidiary, or the entire group, if the new corporation is the parent.

¶13,180   ## SPECIAL RULES—THE TAX YEAR

Among the most important tax principles supplementing or providing relief from the integrity of the taxable year are the following:

Carrybacks and Carryforwards. Net operating losses generally are carried back two years and forward 20, with an election to forego the carryback. Capital losses of corporations are carried back three years and forward five years. Charitable contributions in excess of annual limits are carried forward five years. Unused credits also are carried back and forward.

Installment Method. Certain taxpayers may defer tax payments until sales proceeds are collected.

Ten-Year Forward Averaging. A special averaging formula, independent of other income, is available for lump-sum distributions from qualified pension and profit-sharing plans for taxpayers born before 1936.

Mitigation Provisions. To prevent double taxation or double deductions, special rules are provided. Code Secs. 1311-1314.

Arrowsmith Doctrine. A judicially developed rule allows the character of an item in the current year to be determined by looking back to a related transaction in a prior year.

Claim-of-Right Doctrine. If a taxpayer must pay back an amount in the current year which was included in income in a previous year, a deduction in the current or previous year is permitted. Code Sec. 1341.

Tax Benefit Rule. If a taxpayer recovers an amount deducted in a previous year, then this amount is included in income in the year recovered to the extent a deduction was allowed in the previous year. Code Sec. 111.

Cost recovery. Capital expenditures may have to be written off over a number of years through amortization (intangibles), depletion (natural resources), or depreciation or cost recovery (tangibles). Upon disposition, previous write-offs may have to be taken into ordinary income, in full or in part ("recapture").

Accounting Methods

¶13,201   ## OVERALL METHODS

In computing taxable income, taxpayers for expediency purposes or out of ignorance frequently follow those general tax accounting procedures that are well publicized. Unfortunately, this often results in lost opportunities to improve cash flow and/or minimize tax liability.

In addition to selecting one general method of accounting, a taxpayer must select many specific accounting procedures and conventions to be utilized in implementing a single method of accounting. Once a taxpayer knows that a choice exists, the alternative most appropriate to the particular set of circumstances may then be selected. Each election may have a significant impact on the tax liability ultimately reported for any taxpayer.

Section 446 specifies that taxable income is to be computed in accordance with the accounting method regularly used in keeping books. A "method of accounting" includes not only the overall system of accounting of the taxpayer but also the accounting treatment of any item. No uniform method of accounting can be prescribed for all taxpayers. A taxpayer may adopt the forms and systems of accounting that are best suited to the taxpayer's purpose. Informal records are not sufficient; regular books of account are necessary.

A taxpayer whose sole source of income is wages need not keep formal books in order to have an accounting method. Tax returns or other records may be sufficient to establish the use of the method of accounting utilized in the preparation of the taxpayer's tax returns.

If the accounting method regularly used by the taxpayer in keeping books for tax purposes clearly reflects income, that method must be used in the annual return. However, no method of accounting will be regarded as clearly reflecting income unless all items of gross profit and deductions are treated with consistency from year to year.

Approved standard methods of accounting ordinarily will be regarded as clearly reflecting income. Where the method used by the taxpayer does not clearly reflect income, or if no method of accounting has been regularly used by the taxpayer, then the tax computation is to be made under a method that the IRS agrees will clearly reflect income. "Clearly reflects income" means that income should be reflected with as much accuracy as standard methods of accounting practice permit, not merely that the taxpayer's books should be kept fairly and honestly.

The two most commonly used overall methods that are specifically authorized are (1) the cash method and (2) the accrual method. Code Sec. 446. Other permissible methods of accounting for income and expenses are the long-term contract method and the crop method for farmers.

Special treatment is accorded various types of revenue (e.g., installment sales, prepaid subscription income, and obligations issued at a discount) and many types of expenses (e.g., bad debts, real estate taxes, redemption of trading stamps, and expenses whose benefits are received over a period of years). In addition, any combination of permissible methods may be authorized under the regulations.

Subject to the limitations on the cash method of accounting discussed below, a taxpayer filing a first return is allowed to adopt any permissible method of accounting in computing taxable income for the tax year covered by such return. These requirements are sufficiently flexible to permit every taxpayer a maximum opportunity to select the most favorable method of accounting. Except for an occasional refusal to authorize a change in accounting method, the statutory requirements have been interpreted rather liberally.

¶13,215   CASH METHOD

The vast majority of individuals and many businesses use the cash method, primarily because of its simplicity. It generally is used by taxpayers whose principal income is derived from the performance of a service. Unless other restrictions apply, the cash method must be used if the taxpayer keeps no regular books or has inadequate books for the accrual method. Income is recognized in the tax year when cash and/or cash equivalents are actually or constructively received. Expenses generally are deductible in the year paid unless they are attributable to more than one year.

Income may be received in the form of cash, a check, or cash equivalents. Reg. §1.446-1(a)(3). The fair market value of the property is the measure of income. Thus, if a taxpayer receives stock in return for the performance of a service, then the taxpayer's income is equal to the fair market value of the stock, regardless of accounting method. Similarly, the receipt of a negotiable promissory note produces taxable income in the year of receipt equal to the note's fair market value. Mere promises to pay, not represented by notes or secured, are not regarded as income when received. *A.M. Bedell*, 1 ustc ¶359, 30 F.2d 662 (CA-2 1929).

Income also may be received in other forms. A taxpayer may receive the right to use another's property; that is, the taxpayer does not receive the property outright but is allowed to use the property. In this situation the taxpayer recognizes income equal to the fair rental value of the property. Alternatively, a taxpayer may receive services from another taxpayer. Instead of receiving cash or property, the taxpayer enters into a bartering agreement whereby the form of payment is the rendering of services to the taxpayer. In this situation the taxpayer recognizes income equal to the fair market value of the services received. Finally, the form of income may be the discharge of indebtedness; the taxpayer does not receive cash directly but instead has debt forgiven. Depending on the circumstances, all, some or none of the forgiven debt may be included in income. Code Sec. 61. Thus, cash equivalents may take many different forms.

Cash or cash equivalents are income in the year actually or constructively received. Reg. §1.446-1(c)(1)(i). Income is constructively received in the tax year in which it is credited to the taxpayer's account, set apart for the taxpayer, or made available to the taxpayer to draw upon if the taxpayer's control of its receipt is not subject to substantial limitations or restrictions. Reg. §1.451-2(a). The payer must have the ability to pay, must set aside funds for payments, and must not place substantial restrictions on the taxpayer's ability to access the funds (or property). If these conditions are met, then the taxpayer cannot deliberately turn his or her back on income and thus select the year of reporting. *Hamilton National Bank of Chattanooga*, 29 BTA 63, Dec. 8240 (1933).

EXAMPLE 13.10	In 2015, Fry Company credits its employees with bonus stock, but the stock is not available to them until 2018. The employees have not constructively received the stock in 2015.

EXAMPLE 13.11	Sally James received a $700 dividend check from Astin Company on December 26, 2015. Sally did not cash the check until January 4, 2016. Sally must include the $700 in her gross income for 2015. If Astin Company had mailed the check on December 29, 2015, and it was not received until January 2016, then Sally would not include it in her gross income for 2015 because she has no constructive or actual receipt until 2016.

The deductibility of expenses does not coincide with the recognition of income under the cash method. There is no such thing as constructive payment. Expenses are recognized in the year they are paid. However, some expenditures (fixed assets, prepaid interest, prepaid rent) must be capitalized (treated as an asset) and recognized as an expense over the asset's life (e.g., depreciation).

An expense may be "paid" in cash or in property but not by the note of the taxpayer even if secured by collateral. Generally, unconditional delivery of a check has the same consequences as delivery of cash. Delivery means actual delivery of the check to the payee or an agent. However, one court has held that a check is considered delivered when it is put in the mail on the theory that the postal service is acting as the agent for both the sender and receiver. *Estate of E.B. Witt v. Fahs*, 56-1 USTC ¶9534, 160 F.Supp. 521 (DC Fla. 1956).

If a cash-basis taxpayer borrows funds with which to pay deductible expenses (as opposed to directly giving the creditor a note for repayment)—whether the funds are paid to the taxpayer first or directly to the creditor (subject to an understanding that the taxpayer will make repayment to the lender)—the payments are deductible in the year made, not in the later year when the taxpayer makes repayment to the person who advanced the funds to the taxpayer or paid the expenses on the taxpayer's behalf.

Rev. Proc. 2000-22, 2000 CB 1008, as modified by Rev. Procs. 2001-10, 2001-1 CB 272 and 2002-28, 2002-1 CB 815, allows taxpayers with inventories, whose average annual gross receipts (averaged over three years) do not exceed $1 million, to use the cash method of accounting. Inventories on hand must be accounted for under Reg. §1.162-3 as supplies that are not incidental. The taxpayer must not regularly use any method other than the cash method to ascertain income as reported to shareholders, partners, or other owners or beneficiaries.

Notice 2001-76 allows certain taxpayers (whose principal business activity is providing services or is custom manufacturing) with average gross receipts between $1 million and $10 million to use the cash method of accounting. However, manufacturing, wholesale trade, retail trade, mining activities, and information industries do not generally qualify.

¶13,225 LIMITATIONS ON USE OF CASH METHOD

Three types of taxpayers cannot use the cash method of accounting for tax purposes after 1986. (Code Sec. 448). These three types of taxpayers include:

1. C corporations
2. Partnerships which have a C corporation as a partner
3. Tax shelters

The prohibition on use of the cash method does not apply to farming and timber businesses, qualified personal service corporations, and entities with gross receipts of not more than $5 million. The $5 million exemption does not apply to any tax shelter. Individuals, partnerships that do not have a C corporation as a partner, and S corporations are not prohibited from using the cash method. Code Sec. 448.

A tax shelter is defined as: (1) any enterprise, other than a C corporation, for which, at any time, interests in such enterprise have been offered for sale in any offering required to be registered with any federal or state securities agency; (2) any partnership or other entity if more than 35 percent of the losses of such entity during the tax year are allocable to limited partners or limited partnerships; or (3) any partnership, investment plan, or other plan or arrangement the principal purpose of which is the avoidance of federal income tax. Reg. §1.448-1T(b).

Small businesses that can use or continue to use the cash method of accounting are those businesses with average annual gross receipts of $5 million or less over the past three years. The three-year period does not include the current tax year in which the determination is being made. The enterprise is required to change to the accrual method in the year following the year it fails to meet the small business test. A business may not change back to the cash method when its average receipts later fall below $5 million.

Average annual gross receipts are computed by dividing the sum of the gross receipts for so many of the previous three years as the taxpayer conducted business by the number of such tax years. The change to the accrual method must be made in the tax year following this three-year period. In those cases where the enterprise has not been in existence for the entire three-year period, the test will be based on the number of tax years the enterprise was in existence.

Gross receipts are computed by deducting sales returns and allowances from gross receipts. Gross receipts, as defined in the Form 1120 instructions, include gross receipts or sales from business operations with the exception of dividends, interest, gross rents, other income, and net gains and losses from sales of capital and business assets. Gross receipts for a short tax year of less than 12 months are annualized for purposes of the $5 million test. This annualization is computed by multiplying the gross receipts by 12 and dividing the result by the number of months in the short tax year. Code Sec. 448(c).

A qualified personal service corporation may use the cash method of accounting. A corporation is treated as a qualified service corporation only if it meets both a function test and an ownership test. The function test is met if substantially all of the corporation's activities involve the performance of services in the fields of health, law, engineering, architecture, accounting, actuarial science, performing arts, or consulting. The ownership test in general limits stock ownership in the corporation to certain types of persons. Specifically, this test requires that "substantially all" of the value of the corporation's stock must be owned by (1) current or retired employees, (2) the estates of current or retired employees, or (3) persons who acquired the stock by reason of the death of such employees within the prior 24 months. For purposes of applying the ownership test, community property laws are disregarded, and stock owned by an ESOP or a pension plan is considered to be owned by the beneficiaries of the plan. At least 95 percent of the value of the stock must be held directly or indirectly by the required individuals in order for the "substantially all" requirement to be met. Reg. §1.448-1T(e).

¶13,230   SPECIAL RULES—CASH METHOD

Among the most important tax rules interacting with the cash method of accounting are:

Exchanges of Property. In the absence of a nonrecognition provision, both parties recognize gain or loss even if no cash changes hands. The gain or loss equals value received less the adjusted basis of property relinquished. Code Sec. 1001.

Exchanges of Services. If a CPA renders accounting services to a dentist who settles the account with "free" dental services then each party has income equal to the fair market value of the service received.

Constructive Receipt. Actual receipt is not required. Thus, a paycheck is taxable on receipt even if not cashed until the next tax year and interest credited to a savings account is taxed immediately, even if not withdrawn until the next tax year.

Prepayments of Services. Generally, no deduction is allowed until services have been rendered, except for *de minimis* amounts.

Capital Expenditures. Cash and accrual method taxpayers alike must amortize, deplete, depreciate and cost recover assets with a life extending "substantially beyond" the current tax year. Reg. §1.461-1(a)(1).

Farmers. Farmers generally may use the cash method even if inventories are substantial. Reg. §1.471-6(a). Limitations are imposed on farming "tax shelters." Code Secs. 447, 448, and 464.

Checks. A deductible payment made by check is deductible in the year the check is mailed or delivered, even if not cashed until the next tax year.

¶13,235   ACCRUAL METHOD

In general, two tests (the all-events test and economic-performance test) must be met before income or an expense is recognized under the accrual method. Under the accrual method, income is reported when the right to receive income comes into being, that is, when all the events which determine the right to receive income have occurred and the amount can be determined with reasonable accuracy. Reg. §1.451-1(a). Deductions are taken in the year when the legal obligation to make payments comes into existence and all the events have occurred that determine the fact of the liability and the amount can be determined with reasonable accuracy, unless properly allocable to another year. Reg. §1.461-2. The all events test is not met until economic performance with respect to the item has occurred. Code Sec. 461(h).

If the liability arises because a service or property is provided to the taxpayer, then economic performance occurs when the other party provides such service, such property, or the use of such property. If the liability requires the taxpayer to provide a service or property, then economic performance occurs when said service or property is provided. However, Code Sec. 461(h)(3) provides an exception for recurring items if the all events test is met. In such situations the item is deductible during the year if economic performance occurs within eight and one-half months after the close of the tax year.

The accrual basis has not been allowed where the taxpayer has not kept any books or has kept inadequate ones. Also, the accrual method cannot be used where, due to the nature of the business, the amounts accrued—constituting the bulk of reported income—represent only a tentative estimate which cannot be verified from the records until subsequent years.

If the income has not been reduced to possession or constructively received, it becomes taxable under the accrual method when three circumstances are present: (1) there is an unconditional right to receive it, (2) the amount is determinable with reasonable accuracy, and (3) the amount is collectible.

Thus, in order that income be accruable, existence of the right to the income, subject to no contingencies, is the primary essential. If a taxpayer's right to receive is dependent upon future events, there is no accrual until those contingencies occur or lapse.

Second, it also is essential to first provide the general formula (or rules for determining the amount of the income) even if the precise amount has not been determined at this time. The taxpayer may make his or her own determination and accrue the amount so determined, even though the actual determination for payment purposes may show it to be in error or even though some portion of the money received by the taxpayer might have to be refunded in some future year.

The third and final condition is that the amount must be collectible. Even though notes or other receivables may not be marketable, they may be collectible. If the right to receive arises from a sale of real property, an accrual-basis seller should report such right at its fair market value. However, if the sale is of personal property, the full face value of the right must be reported as income.

| EXAMPLE 13.12 | Darryl Harris sells a building for $200,000, receiving $50,000 in cash and a $150,000 mortgage note due in five years with a 10 percent interest rate. The mortgage note has a $135,000 fair market value. The basis of the building is $95,000. Darryl will report a gain of $90,000 ($50,000 cash + $135,000 fair market value of the mortgage note = $185,000 selling price minus $95,000 basis). If the full $200,000 is collected, $15,000 will be reported as interest income. If the asset sold were personal property rather than the building, the selling price would be $200,000. |

Only if there is clear and convincing evidence that real doubt and uncertainty exist as to whether the amount due will ever be collected can there be postponement of reporting income. The possibility of default is not sufficient. The courts have held that year-end is the time to test collectibility on unpaid items. An event occurring subsequent to that time has no effect on the accountability.

An accrual-basis taxpayer need not accrue as income any portion of amounts billed for the performance of services which, on the basis of experience, it will not collect. However, the income must be accrued if the taxpayer charges any interest or penalty for failure to make timely payments in connection with the amount billed. The offering of a discount for early payment of an amount billed will require the reporting of income as long as the full amount of the bill is otherwise accrued as income and the discount for early payment treated as an adjustment to income in the year such payment is made.

The amount of billings that, on the basis of experience, will not be collected is equal to the total amount billed, multiplied by a fraction whose numerator is the total amount of such receivables that were billed and determined not to be collectible within the most recent five tax years of the taxpayer and whose denominator is the total of such amounts billed within the same five-year period. If the taxpayer has not been in existence for the prior five tax years, the portion of such five-year period that the taxpayer has been in existence is to be used.

EXAMPLE 13.13	Assume that an accrual-basis taxpayer has $150,000 of receivables that have been created during the most recent five tax years. Of the $150,000 of accounts receivable, $3,000 has been determined to be uncollectible. The amount, based on experience, which is not expected to be collected is equal to 2 percent ($3,000 divided by $150,000) of any receivables arising from the provision of services that are outstanding at the close of the tax year.

If a taxpayer is contesting a liability of a claimed amount, the deduction cannot be taken until the contest is settled by court decision, compromise, or otherwise. However, if the taxpayer pays the disputed amount or places it beyond its control (e.g., in an escrow account) then the taxpayer can claim a deduction when payment is made. Any difference between what was placed in escrow and the actual settlement amount is either deducted (if settlement was greater than escrow payment) or included in income (if settlement was less than escrow payment) in the year of settlement.

A taxpayer who has not recognized income on amounts not expected to be collected must recognize additional income in any tax year in which payments on amounts not recognized are received. If a receivable is determined to be partially or wholly uncollectible, no portion of the loss arising as a result of such determination that was not recognized as income at the time the receivable was created is allowed as a deduction.

The main disadvantage of the accrual method of accounting is a reduction in the taxpayer's control over the timing of both gross income and tax deductions. Under accrual accounting, a taxpayer may have to recognize income prior to the receipt of cash with which the taxpayer can pay the tax liability.

Prepaid Income and Expenses

The treatment of payments received in advance by an accrual-basis taxpayer for services to be rendered or goods to be delivered in a subsequent tax year has been the subject of litigation for many years. Generally, prepaid income has been held to be taxable in the year received. The treatment varies from financial accounting conventions consistently used by many accrual-method taxpayers in the treatment of payments received in one tax year for services to be performed by them in succeeding tax years. The Supreme Court has supported the IRS position that the deferral of prepayments under financial accounting rules does not clearly reflect taxable income because the seller has already received payment. See *American Automobile Assn.,* 61-2 USTC ¶9517, 367 U.S. 687 (1961). The contingent liability to refund part of the income received does not postpone income recognition.

A taxpayer is generally allowed a deduction in the tax year which is the proper tax year under the method of accounting used in computing taxable income. If, however, the taxpayer's method of accounting does not clearly reflect income, the computation of taxable income must be made under the method which, in the opinion of the IRS, clearly reflects income.

EXAMPLE 13.14	Smith Co. uses the cash basis of accounting. On July 1, 2015, Smith Co. prepaid insurance premiums for the next two years. The annual premium amount was $2,400. Smith Co. deducted $4,800 as insurance expense for 2015 since the cash was paid on July 1 of that year. Even though Smith Co. uses the cash basis of accounting, the IRS will conclude that the deduction does not create a clear reflection of income. It will require Smith Co. to recognize insurance expense over the life of the policy ($4,800/24 = $200 per month; $1,200 insurance expense in 2015).

Other areas that under certain circumstances and within certain limits that receive special treatment include:

(1) prepaid subscription income—the taxpayer may elect to recognize income over the subscription period;
(2) prepaid membership dues—the taxpayer may elect to recognize income ratably over the time period it is liable (if not more than 36 months);
(3) prepaid service income—if the taxpayer will perform the services by the close of the next tax year then it may elect to recognize income as earned over that time period;
(4) certain advanced payments for future sales of inventories—under very specific rules, the taxpayer may elect to defer income until properly earned;
(5) prepaid interest expense—the expense is deductible in the periods in which the use of money occurs (e.g., over the life of the debt); and
(6) bad debts—most taxpayers cannot use the reserve method of accounting for bad debts.

EXAMPLE 13.15	On November 1, 2015, a calendar-year, accrual-basis membership organization sells a two-year membership for $2,400 payable in advance. It elects to recognize income over the life of the membership; so it recognizes $200 ($2,400 × 2/24) in gross income in 2015, $1,200 ($2,400 × 12/24) in 2016 and $1,000 ($2,400 × 10/24) in 2017.

EXAMPLE 13.16	On October 1, 2015, Maria Juarez, a calendar-year, accrual-basis taxpayer who runs a dance school, receives a $1,200 payment for a one-year contract beginning on that date to provide 48 dance lessons. Ten lessons were provided in 2015 and 38 are provided in 2016. Maria elects to recognize income as earned; so she recognizes $250 ($1,200/48 × 10) in 2015 and $950 in 2016. Even if Maria only provided 25 lessons in 2016 she still would recognize $950 because the maximum deferral is to the next tax year.

TAX BLUNDER

Bob Mumper is an accrual-basis, calendar-year taxpayer who performs a service. In 2015, he received prepayments of $200,000 for services he will perform in 2016. Mumper is in the 39.6% tax bracket in 2015, and he is uncertain about future years' tax brackets. Mumper assumed that under the claim of right doctrine he had to include the $200,000 in gross income in 2015 and did so accordingly.

Mumper could have and should have used the prepaid service income method. This would have deferred income recognition until 2016, which would have reduced his tax liability by at least $79,200 (39.6% × $200,000) in 2015. Even if Mumper is in the 39.6% bracket in 2016, the time value of money would have worked in his favor and would have increased the present value of his after-tax cash flows.

¶13,240   ACCRUAL METHOD TAX PLANNING

Tax planning by accrual method taxpayers can affect the amount of taxable income being reported for the year. Listed below are various techniques that taxpayers may use to increase or decrease taxable income for the tax year.

Income may be *deferred* by the following techniques:

1. Delays in shipping goods sold (if shipping time is accrual time)
2. Shipping F.O.B. destination, delaying the title change (if title change is accrual point)
3. If allowed, switching from accrual to installment reporting
4. Sales and leasebacks at a loss (e.g., Section 1231 property)
5. Lease with option to buy or just sales of options
6. Using an independent escrow account beyond year end
7. Deferring December billings for services until January (if billing is accrual point)
8. Advanced payments may be structured as conditional prepayments or as loans.

Income may be *accelerated* by the following techniques:

1. The reverse of the above reduction techniques
2. The sale of installment notes
3. Sales and leasebacks of appreciated assets
4. Increased year-end orders through payment deferrals, next year discounts, and special promotions
5. Electing out of the installment method for casual sales.

Deductions may be *increased* by the following techniques:

1. Paying bonuses to officers and/or shareholder-employees
2. Prepaying nonrefundable commissions
3. Increasing deferred compensation contributions, such as to an ESOP or a Code Sec. 401(k) plan
4. Incurring expenses before the end of the year, such as charitable contributions, advertising, accelerating repairs, settling disputed amounts
5. Purchasing business equipment and autos at year-end. The depreciation deduction generally is the same as if the property were purchased at the beginning of the year (if the mid-quarter rules do not apply)
6. Making use of all travel and entertainment expenses.

Deductions generally will be decreased if the reverse of the above is done. If a deduction will be more beneficial next year then its incurrence should be deferred.

¶13,245　SEPARATE SOURCES OF INCOME

Where a taxpayer has two or more separate and distinct businesses, a different method may be used for each business, provided separate books and records are maintained clearly reflecting the income of each. But the taxpayer may not shift profits and losses between businesses through inventory adjustments, sales, purchases, or expenses. Reg. §1.446-1(d).

EXAMPLE 13.17　Olivia Lee operates a beauty shop and a record store as separate sole proprietorships. The income and deductions of the beauty shop can be accounted for under the cash method of accounting, while those of the record store must be under the accrual method of accounting because inventories are an income-producing factor (see ¶13,265).

In a situation where there are overlapping costs, expenditures on behalf of each activity are to be taken up in the books or tax return for that activity in accordance with the applicable method of accounting. As to any business for which separate records are maintained, the rule of consistency would continue to apply.

This principle has been extended to situations where the taxpayer uses one method for business income and another for personal income. The Regulations state that a taxpayer using one method of accounting in computing items of income and deductions for trade or business may compute other items of income and deductions not connected with the trade or business under a different method of accounting.

¶13,265　HYBRID METHODS

Many combinations of permissible accounting methods may be used. For example, the accrual method, which must be used for purchases and sales of inventory, may be combined with the cash method for other items of income and expense. But a taxpayer's choice is not unlimited. If the cash method is used for income, it must also be used for expenses. And if the accrual method is used for expenses, it must also be used for income.

The accrual method is required if inventories are an income-producing factor. Reg. §1.446-1(c)(2)(i). If this were not mandatory, a cash-basis taxpayer could very easily reduce reported net income by increasing stock of inventory and could increase reported net income by depleting normal inventory. The effect of this required adjustment is to change only the computation of the tax deduction for the cost of inventory sold from a strict cash basis to an accrual basis of accounting.

The fact that inventories are essential does not necessarily mean that an accrual method of accounting is needed on an overall basis, especially if the business is one in which inventories are comparatively small, with little change from year to year, and little of the business (purchase or sales) is done on a credit basis. In such cases, a taxpayer may keep books and prepare returns almost entirely on a cash basis, making adjustments only for the variations in opening and closing inventories.

¶13,275　TANGIBLE PROPERTY REGULATIONS

The regulations apply to costs incurred throughout the entire life cycle of the taxpayer's tangible property, from the time the taxpayer (1) first begins considering whether (and which) property to acquire, (2) through maintaining and improving the property during its operational life, and (3) finally to the treatment of the property's remaining basis when the taxpayer disposes of the property. The final regulations seek to provide guidance for each of these three phases of expenditures.

Section 263(a) generally requires the capitalization of amounts paid to acquire, produce, or improve tangible property. Section 162 allows a deduction for all the ordinary and necessary expenses paid or incurred during the taxable year in carrying on any trade or business, including the costs of certain supplies, repairs, and maintenance.

The regulations provide criteria for determining the unit of property, which is the first step for determining whether expenditures to improve tangible property must be capitalized or can be currently expensed.

Change of Accounting Methods

¶13,301   ## IRS PERMISSION OR CONSENT

While there is no prohibition against changing the method of accounting, Code Secs. 446 and 481 require that permission be obtained from the IRS before adopting the new method for income tax purposes. (Rev. Proc. 2008-52, 2008-2 CB 587, Rev. Proc. 2009-39, 2009-2 CB 371 and Rev. Proc. 2011-14, IRB 2011-4 provide instances whereby a taxpayer may obtain automatic consent to change the method of accounting.) The purpose of the prior consent provision is intended to promote consistency in accounting practices from year to year, thereby securing uniformity in the collection of the revenue, and to protect against a loss of revenue. The prior consent requirement applies even though the taxpayer's reporting method no longer conforms to the bookkeeping method.

Permission to change the method of tax accounting will not be granted unless the taxpayer and the IRS agree to the terms and conditions under which the change will be effected. Where two methods clearly reflect income, the IRS has considerable discretion in prescribing the conditions under which it will consent to a change from one to the other.

Change in Overall Plan or Material Items

A change of accounting method includes a change in the overall plan of accounting as well as a change in the treatment of any material item used in the plan. In most instances, a method of accounting is not established for an item unless there is a pattern of consistent treatment. Major changes in accounting method include:

1. Change to or from the cash-basis method
2. Change in the method of valuing inventory
3. Change from the accrual method to a long-term contract method or vice versa
4. Change involving the adoption, use, or discontinuance of any other specialized method of computing income, such as the crop method by farmers
5. Certain changes in computing depreciation or amortization
6. Change for which the Code or Regulations specifically require that the consent of the IRS be obtained (Reg. §1.446-1(e)).

A material item is any item that involves the timing of inclusion or deduction. According to the Tax Court, the term means a "material item of gross income or deductions," not "a material item of net income" or "a material difference in income" resulting from the computation under two different methods of accounting. *Connors, Inc.,* 71 TC 913, Dec. 35,900 (1979).

Correction of Mathematical Errors

A change in method does not include correction of mathematical and posting errors, or of errors in the computation of tax liability. For example, corrections of items that were deducted as interest or salary, but which are in fact payments of dividends, and of items that were deducted as business expenses, but which are personal expenses, are not changes in method. An adjustment to the useful life of a depreciable asset also is not an accounting method change. Although such adjustments may involve the question of the proper timing of a deduction, these items are traditionally corrected by adjustments in the current and future years.

Change in Underlying Facts

An accounting change does not include a change in treatment resulting from a change in underlying facts. On the other hand, a correction to require depreciation in lieu of a deduction for the cost of a class of depreciable assets which had been consistently treated as an expense in the year of purchase involves the question of the proper timing of an item and is to be treated as a change in method of accounting. Reg. §1.446-1(e).

IRS-Directed Changes

Although taxable income is to be computed according to a taxpayer's regular accounting method used in keeping the books, if that method does not clearly reflect income, then the IRS may prescribe a method which does.

The IRS's authority to require a taxpayer to adopt an overall or specific change in accounting method necessary to clearly reflect income does not justify an arbitrary requirement of change. If a taxpayer's accounting method clearly reflects income, the IRS may not determine income by another method which would also clearly reflect income. Presumably, this rule would also apply to the method of treating a particular item of income or expense, such as depreciation. A taxpayer may, of course, conform books or returns to a suggestion by an Internal Revenue agent, for convenience, to cooperate with the local office of the Internal Revenue Service and facilitate audits of returns, or to avoid the expense of an appeal or refund proceedings, but the taxpayer cannot be required to make the change.

The IRS can change an incorrect method, but the change must be to a correct method. If the IRS has directed a taxpayer to change the method of accounting and the taxpayer has complied, the IRS cannot later argue that the change was improper because the taxpayer had not obtained formal permission to make it. And where an unusual method of accruing expenses on construction contracts was proposed by the IRS and the taxpayer followed that method, the IRS was not allowed to object in later years that the method did not clearly reflect income.

The Fifth Circuit has held that, where a taxpayer changed the accounting method and not the basis of the tax returns, the IRS may not require the returns to be filed on the new basis if both methods clearly reflect income despite the Code requirement that the book method must be used in computing income. *J.C. Patchen*, 58-2 USTC ¶9733, 258 F.2d 544 (CA-5 1958).

Combination of Methods

A combination of acceptable methods of accounting will be permitted if such combination clearly reflects income and is consistently used. However, if the taxpayer uses a hybrid method that is not authorized by the Regulations, the IRS may make adjustments to conform to either the cash or accrual basis, whichever more closely resembles the taxpayer's method of keeping books. The burden is on the taxpayer to show errors in determining which method predominates for book purposes, or to show that the hybrid method is acceptable. The fact that a taxpayer has filed returns on a hybrid basis for a number of years, without objection, does not bar the IRS from requiring a change.

Cash to Accrual Method

Taxpayers desiring to change their overall method of accounting from the cash receipts and disbursements method of accounting to the accrual method may do so by filing a timely request with the National Office. If this condition is satisfied, the IRS's consent to the change is considered to have been granted.

Net operating losses and tax credit carryforwards can reduce the amounts of any positive adjustment. For purposes of determining estimated payments, adjustments are recognized as occurring ratably throughout the year.

Denial of Change

Refusal to consent to a change in accounting method is ordinarily within the IRS's administrative discretion and cannot be reversed unless the taxpayer can prove the IRS abused its discretion. The IRS is not required to permit a change of accounting method for tax purposes just because the taxpayer is ordered to change the accounting method by another administrative agency. The Tax Court stated "that a taxpayer may be required to account one way for one government agency and another way for a different government agency may well be a hardship, and we have no doubt it is, but we are certain that the remedy does not lie with us as a judicial byproduct of a tax determination." *National Airlines, Inc.*, 9 TC 159, Dec. 15,940 (1947).

¶13,325 ADJUSTMENT—VOLUNTARY/REQUIRED CHANGE

When a taxpayer computes taxable income under a different accounting method than that used in the preceding year, adjustments must be made in order to prevent items from being duplicated or entirely omitted. The general intent is that no item may be omitted and no item may be duplicated as a result of a change. These adjustments apply not only when the taxpayer voluntarily changes the accounting method with the consent of the IRS, but also when a change in method is required by the IRS.

The term "adjustments" is defined as the net amount of all adjustments, taking only the net dollar balance into account. The net amount of the adjustments would be the result of the consolidation of adjustments (both plus and minus) for the various accounts, such as inventory, accounts receivable, and accounts payable at the beginning of the tax year. In the case of a change in the treatment of a single material item, the amount of the adjustment is determined by the net dollar balance of that particular item. Reg. §1.481-1(c).

EXAMPLE 13.18

Jones Co. is on the calendar year and uses the cash method of accounting. Jones Co. changed to the accrual method in 2016. Net income for 2016 under the accrual method was $60,000, computed as follows:

Sales	$200,000
Cost of goods sold	120,000
Gross profit	$80,000
Expenses	20,000
Net income	$60,000

In December 2015, there was $10,000 inventory on hand. Also, accounts receivable and accounts payable were $6,000 and $4,000, respectively.

The $60,000 net income must be adjusted for amounts which would be duplicated or be omitted because of the change in accounting methods. The net adjustment is $12,000; therefore, adjusted net income for 2016 would be $72,000. The adjustments are as follows:

Positive adjustment for the ending inventory balance because this amount was deducted when acquired	$10,000
Positive adjustment for the ending accounts receivable because this amount has never been included in income	6,000
Negative adjustment for the ending accounts payable because this amount has never been deducted	(4,000)
Net adjustment	$12,000

Rev. Proc. 2008-52, provide a single adjustment period for positive and negative adjustments to replace the various adjustment periods that were available under Code Sec. 481 and related Regulations. In general, the adjustment period for taxpayer-initiated changes that result in a positive adjustment is four years of which the tax year is the first year. However, if the adjustment is less than $50,000, the taxpayer may elect a one-year adjustment period. Rev. Proc. 2015-13. If the taxpayer ceases business operations (e.g., the firm liquidates) prior to the end of the four-year period, then any remaining adjustment is taken into consideration in the year of cessation. The adjustment period is one year for negative adjustments. Finally, a positive adjustment due to a change initiated by the IRS generally is recognized over the four-year period as noted above. However, the IRS can require that it be recognized over a shorter time period. Under Rev. Proc. 2002-19, 2002-1 CB 696, a negative adjustment due to an IRS-initiated change can be recognized in the year of the change.

EXAMPLE 13.19

In Example 13.18, Jones Co. has two options regarding the $12,000 adjustment. It can spread the $12,000 over four years, increasing net income for 2016 to $63,000 and increasing net income by $3,000 in 2017, 2018, and 2019. Alternatively, since the adjustment is less than $25,000, Jones could elect to use a one-year adjustment period and add the $12,000 to its $60,000 in 2016. If Jones has losses from other activities or a net operating loss carryover, then it might want to select this option.

EXAMPLE 13.20

Harry Co. changed its method of accounting in 2015. The net adjustment due to the change was $44,000. Since this amount exceeds the less-than-$50,000 threshold, Harry Co. is not eligible to elect the one-year adjustment period. Thus, Harry Co. must use the four-year adjustment period, and one-fourth of the $44,000 will be included in income in 2015, 2016, 2017, and 2018.

If a taxpayer has claimed insufficient depreciation in prior years, the taxpayer may change his or her depreciation method to claim allowable depreciation. This is considered to be a change in accounting method, and the omitted depreciation from previous years is considered to be an adjustment which the taxpayer may elect to use the one-year adjustment period. The taxpayer is required to own the asset on the first day of the tax year in which the change of accounting method applies. Rev. Proc. 2008-52.

¶13,355   TIME AND FORM OF APPLICATION

A taxpayer wishing to change the method of accounting may file Form 3115 (Application for Changes in Accounting Methods) anytime before the due date (including extensions) of the tax return for the tax year for which the change is requested. Rev. Proc. 2008-52. However, if the taxpayer is under examination, more stringent rules apply.

The taxpayer should, to the extent applicable, furnish (1) all information requested on the form, disclosing in detail all classes of items which would be treated differently under the new method and showing all amounts which would be duplicated or omitted as a result of the proposed change, and (2) the computation of the adjustments to take into account such duplications and omissions. In addition, the IRS may require such other information as may be necessary in order to determine whether the proposed change will be permitted. The IRS charges a user fee for a change in accounting method. However, a number of different changes are automatic and do not involve a user fee.

It should also be stated in the application that the taxpayer proposes to take the adjustment into account over the appropriate period as required by the IRS in accordance with rules that have been discussed previously. Code Sec. 481; Rev. Proc. 84-74, 1984-2 CB 736; Rev. Proc. 2008-52. Permission will not be granted unless the taxpayer and the IRS agree to the terms, conditions, and adjustments under which the change will be effected.

There is no requirement that, once the IRS has approved the change, the taxpayer must use the new accounting method in filing returns thereafter. However, the IRS, in its letter granting the change of accounting method, states that if the taxpayer does not wish to make the change, the IRS should be advised within 30 days of the date of the letter. The taxpayer who decides not to change a method of accounting after the 30-day period is not precluded from keeping the present method in effect.

¶13,365   ACCOUNTING METHOD TAX PLANNING

Keeping income levels near average from year to year is a major tax saver. The desire to balance income stems from the graduated scale of tax rates. Two persons having the same total taxable income over a number of years may pay widely different taxes because of the progressive rate structure. A taxpayer should choose accounting methods and procedures that will stabilize taxable income over the years so as to produce minimum taxes. Of course, where there are greater ups and downs in taxable income at higher rates, the tax savings become greater as taxable income is leveled out. The cash-basis taxpayer may time the receipt of income either by accelerating it to boost an otherwise poor year or by postponing it so as not to overburden the current year. There is nothing in income tax law that requires a creditor to press or decline to press for payment of an obligation in a particular tax year.

Income from sales arises when title to the goods passes to the customer; that is, in the case of most regular sales, at the time of delivery to a common carrier. By withholding shipment until after the end of the accounting period, a taxpayer may keep the amount of sales for the year down and thereby reduce income. In other instances, the seller may defer income by shipping goods on approval or on consignment subject to acceptance or sale in the following year.

A taxpayer may also reduce taxable income by accelerating business expenses for replenishment of supplies that are not part of inventory, performance of repairs, advertising, or business trips. Remember, however, that only ordinary and necessary expenses are deductible.

For an individual who engages in investment activities in occasional "business" ventures, the cash basis of accounting may offer substantial tax advantages through its ability to control year-end expenditures and receipts. For a business activity, the accrual method of accounting may offer advantages by its tendency to level out income, thus avoiding high-bracket peak income periods. There is no rule that would preclude a taxpayer from using the cash basis for nonbusiness items and salary and the accrual method for business income.

The number of alternative accounting procedures and conventions is substantially greater than the number of alternative general methods of accounting. The Code authorizes a number of accounting procedures to determine the cost allocation available for depreciation. The cost-of-goods-sold determination can be made under any of several alternative inventory costing conventions. Each of these accounting conventions or procedures will yield a different taxable income for a given tax year.

TAX BLUNDER

Dean Chips operated a successful garage as a sole proprietorship on the cash basis. He obtained IRS permission to change to the accrual method, which resulted in a net increase in income under Code Sec. 481(a).

Pursuant to Code Sec. 481(c), he spread the adjustment over 10 years (the adjustment period used at that time—it now is four years), starting with the year of change. Two years later, he incorporated his business in a "tax-free" Code Sec. 351 transaction. The IRS argued that the remaining 70 percent of the adjustment was accelerated upon incorporation, resulting in taxable income to Dean immediately. The Ninth Circuit agreed with the IRS that Code Sec. 481 requires continuity of the *taxpayer,* rather than the *business. D.R. Shore,* 80-2 USTC ¶9759, 631 F.2d 524 (CA-9 1980); Rev. Rul. 77-264, 1977-1 CB 238. Furthermore, the exception under Code Sec. 381 does not apply to corporate *organization,* only to corporate *reorganization.* Thus, even if Dean was the sole shareholder and even though the incorporation did not result in gain, it did accelerate income (so much for tax-free incorporations).

¶13,375 TIMELINESS

Making an accounting election usually requires some overt act on the part of a taxpayer. Proper timing is critical to making a valid election. Failure to make a timely election precludes a consideration of procedural compliance since the election will not be effective. To this extent, then, timing should be deemed of paramount importance.

The Code contains many elections that pertain to newly organized businesses. Failure to make the election on a timely basis may result in higher immediate taxes.

Inventories

¶13,401 USE OF INVENTORIES

If inventories are an income-producing factor, not only must inventories be kept, but the taxpayer must use the accrual method of accounting for purchases and sales. Reg. §§1.446-1(a)(4)(i) and 1.471-1. The result is that a major deduction, cost of goods sold, is deferred until the inventory is sold. Because cost of goods sold equals opening inventory, plus inventory purchased or produced, less ending inventory, an incentive exists to value ending inventories as low as possible. A low valuation results in an immediate tax benefit through a higher cost of goods sold deduction. Although the benefit is theoretically a mere deferral, the deferral is of indefinite duration. Also, as inventories grow with the expansion of the business, more and more profits are deferred. The value of ending inventory is a function of (1) what costs are included and (2) the cost flow assumptions made. The details are discussed below.

¶13,415 VALUATION OF INVENTORY

An inventory is an itemized list, with valuations, of goods held for sale or consumption in a manufacturing or merchandising business. The inventory should include all finished or partly finished goods, and only those raw materials and supplies that have been acquired for sale or that will physically become a part of merchandise intended for sale. Goods in transit to which the taxpayer has title should be included in inventory, and goods on hand in which title has passed to the buyer should not be included in inventory. Reg. §1.471-1.

There are two fundamental requirements for valuation of inventory: (1) it must conform as nearly as possible to the best accounting practice in the trade or business and (2) it must clearly reflect income. Code Sec. 471. In determining whether income is clearly reflected, great weight is given to consistency in inventory practice. Reg. §1.471-2. Nevertheless, a legitimate accounting system will be disallowed where it distorts income.

Inventory may be valued at cost or lower-of-cost-or-market. Reg. §1.471-2. However, if the LIFO method (discussed later) is used, then the taxpayer cannot use lower-of-cost-or-market. Also, lower-of-cost-or-market must be applied to each item in inventory; a taxpayer cannot value the entire inventory at cost and at market and then select the lower amount.

¶13,425 COST METHODS

The cost of merchandise on hand at the beginning of the period (beginning inventory) is its inventory price as of the last day of the previous year. The cost of merchandise purchased is the invoice price, less trade discounts, plus incidental costs incurred to acquire the goods (such as transportation and other handling costs). Reg. §1.471-3. Additionally, the following indirect costs must be capitalized unless the taxpayer's average annual gross receipts for the preceding three taxable years do not exceed $10 million: storage and warehousing; purchasing; handling, processing, assembly, and repacking; and administrative costs. Code Sec. 263A(b).

The cost of merchandise produced by the taxpayer includes the cost of direct materials, direct labor, and indirect costs. Reg. §1.471-3. Manufacturers must use absorption costing (full costing) to value inventories; they cannot use direct costing or prime costing. Indirect costs that must be capitalized include repairs, maintenance, utilities, rent, and indirect labor and materials. Indirect costs do not include marketing expenses, advertising and selling expenses, and research and experimentation costs. Reg. §1.471-11. Additionally, Code Sec. 263A expanded the definition of includible costs by requiring most entities (especially manufacturers) to use the uniform capitalization (UNICAP) rules. This expanded list requires the capitalization of more items than does financial accounting.

¶13,435   UNIFORM CAPITALIZATION RULES

UNICAP generally applies to real or personal property produced by the taxpayer and real or personal property acquired by the taxpayer for resale. Code Sec. 263A(b). Costs to be capitalized include direct costs and an expanded list of indirect costs. Reg. §1.263A-1(b)(2). Under UNICAP, indirect costs include:

1. Factory repairs and maintenance; utilities; rent; depreciation, amortization, and depletion; small tools; and insurance;
2. Indirect labor and production supervisory labor; administrative costs; indirect materials and supplies; rework, scrap, and spoilage; storage and warehousing costs; purchasing costs; handling, processing, assembly, and repacking costs; and quality control and inspection costs;
3. Taxes (other than income taxes);
4. Deductible contributions to pension, profit-sharing, stock bonus, or annuity plans; and
5. Interest, but only for real property, long-lived property, or property requiring more than two years to produce (one year for property costing more than $1 million).

Costs not required to be capitalized include nonmanufacturing costs such as marketing, selling, advertising and distribution expenses, and research and experimentation costs.

Cost Allocation Procedures

After identifying all costs that are required to be capitalized (known as total additional Code Sec. 263A costs), the next step in costing inventory is to allocate these costs. The Regulations provide allocation methods for direct labor, direct materials, and indirect costs. The allocation method should result in the capitalization of all costs that directly benefit or are incurred because of production or resale activities. Reg. §1.263A-1(b)(3).

All direct labor costs must be capitalized. The costs should be associated with specific production activities and products, and allocated to them accordingly (using specific identification or tracing). All direct material costs also should be capitalized. These costs should be allocated to products using the taxpayer's method of accounting for inventories that contain the direct materials (e.g., FIFO, LIFO, specific identification). The above mentioned allocation methods are not mandatory; the taxpayer may use any other method which reasonably allocates such costs.

Indirect costs are allocated to activities and products using one of three methods: specific identification (in which the costs are specifically identified with activities or products that directly benefit from the costs), standard costing (in which the costs are allocated to products based upon established standards), or burden rates (in which the costs are allocated based on direct labor hours, direct labor costs, and similar expenses).

Simplified Retail Method

Taxpayers who acquire property for resale and are required to capitalize costs under Code Sec. 263A may elect to use the simplified retail method to allocate costs. Under this method, costs for off-site storage and warehousing; purchasing; and handling, processing, assembly, and repacking are fully capitalized. Determining the amount of mixed service costs (general and administrative costs) to be allocated requires two steps. First determine the amount of mixed service costs that are additional Code Sec. 263A costs, then allocate this amount to ending inventory.

The amount of mixed service costs included under Code Sec. 263A is determined by multiplying such costs by the ratio of

1. Total labor costs included in off-site, storage, purchasing, and handling cost, to
2. Total labor costs incurred in the taxpayer's business, excluding the labor included in the mixed service costs.

Once this amount is determined, then it is allocated to ending inventory by multiplying the amount in ending inventory that was purchased during the year by the ratio of

1. Total additional Code Sec. 263A costs, to
2. Taxpayer's total purchases during the year.

EXAMPLE 13.21	Kimby Co. uses the first-in, first-out (FIFO) method of accounting for its inventory. During the year it incurred $200,000 of storage costs, $300,000 of purchasing costs, $100,000 in handling and processing costs. The labor costs included in these amounts were $180,000. The company also incurred $250,000 of mixed service costs. Kimby Co.'s total labor costs, excluding amounts included in mixed service costs, were $2,000,000. Kimby's beginning inventory (excluding additional Code Sec. 263A costs) was $1,000,000. Total purchases during the year were $7,000,000 and ending inventory was $1,500,000 (excluding additional Code Sec. 263A costs). Since Kimby Co. uses the FIFO method, the full $1,500,000 of ending inventory is considered purchased during the year.

Kimby Co.'s ending inventory is $1,633,350, consisting of the original cost of $1,500,000, increased by capitalized additional Code Sec. 263A resale costs of $133,350. This is determined as follows. First, determine the amount of mixed service costs that are considered to be additional Code Sec. 263A costs using the labor ratios:

Labor ratio	=	$180,000/$2,000,000 = 9%
Mixed service costs considered additional Code 263A costs	=	9% × $250,000 = $22,500.

Next, determine total additional Code Sec. 263A and allocate this amount to ending inventory using the additional Code Sec. 263A costs to purchases ratio.

Costs to purchase ratio	=	$622,500/$7,000,000 = 8.89%
Additional Code Sec. 263A costs allocated to ending inventory	=	8.89% × $1,500,000 = $133,350.

Simplified Production Method

Taxpayers may elect to use the simplified production method to allocate capitalized costs for property produced. This method can only be used for property that is the taxpayer's stock in trade or includible in inventory, or for property held by the taxpayer primarily for sale to customers in the ordinary course of business. The method cannot be used for property acquired for resale and for property produced by the taxpayer for use in its business. Reg. §1.263A-1(b)(5). Under this method, additional Code Sec. 263A costs are allocated based on an absorption ratio and the allocation requires two steps. First, compute the absorption ratio. This is the ratio of

1. total additional Code Sec. 263A costs incurred during the year, to
2. total Code Sec. 471 costs incurred during the year.

(Code Sec. 471 costs are those costs that otherwise would be capitalized under absorption costing.) Once this ratio is determined, then the amount of additional Code Sec. 263A costs required to be capitalized is determined by multiplying the absorption ratio times the amount of Code Sec. 471 costs incurred during the year which, under the taxpayer's method of accounting for inventory (e.g., FIFO or LIFO), are included in the taxpayer's ending inventory.

If the taxpayer uses FIFO, then the absorption ratio is applied to the Code Sec. 471 costs included in ending inventory. However, if the taxpayer uses LIFO, then the absorption ratio is applied to the Code Sec. 471 costs included in this year's increase in inventory (the incremental layer).

EXAMPLE 13.22

Nifo Co. produces widgets. It began operations this year. It uses the FIFO method to account for its inventories. During the year it incurred $15,000,000 of Code Sec. 471 costs and $2,000,000 of additional Code Sec. 263A costs. Ending inventory consisted of $1,000,000 of Code Sec. 471 costs.

Nifo Co.'s ending inventory is $1,133,333, consisting of $1,000,000 of Code Sec. 471 costs, increased by capitalized additional Code Sec 263A costs of $133,333. This is determined as follows:

Absorption ratio	=	$2,000,000/$15,000,000 = 13.33%
Additional Code Sec. 263A costs allocated to ending inventory	=	13.33% × $1,000,000 = $133,333.

¶13,445   LOWER-OF-COST-OR-MARKET (LCM) METHOD

Unless the taxpayer is using LIFO, the ending inventory may be written down to a lower market value (e.g., replacement cost). Reg. §1.472-4. In addition, damaged or obsolete goods may be written down to realizable prices less costs of disposition. Reg. §1.471-2(c). The determination of lower cost or market must be applied to each *item* of inventory. Reg. §1.471-4(c).

EXAMPLE 13.23

A lumber dealer has three grades of lumber at the end of the tax year. They are valued as follows:

Grade	Cost	Market	LCM
1	$3,000	$5,000	$3,000
2	2,000	1,500	1,500
3	5,000	4,000	4,000
	$10,000	$10,500	$8,500

The ending inventory is $8,500, written *down* from $10,000, even though the inventory as a whole has *increased* in value.

¶13,453   VALUATION OF INVENTORY ITEMS

Taxpayers may use one of four cost flow assumptions to value their inventories: specific identification; first-in, first-out (FIFO); last-in, first-out (LIFO); or weighted average. The accounting method selected does not have to agree with the actual physical flow of goods. Specific identification usually is impractical because each item in inventory must be tracked very carefully. Generally, it is used for large items, such as appliances, which are more easily tracked. It is more convenient in many instances to use one of the other cost flow assumptions.

The FIFO method assumes that goods on hand in beginning inventory and the first goods purchased are the first goods sold to customers. Thus, ending inventory is valued at the price of most recent purchases. Cost of goods sold is based upon the cost of beginning inventory and the prices of goods purchased earlier in the year. Taxpayers using FIFO also may use the lower-of-cost-or-market method.

The LIFO method assumes that the goods most recently purchased are the first goods sold to customers. Thus, ending inventory is valued at beginning inventory amounts and at the price of goods acquired earlier in the year. Cost of goods sold is based upon the prices of the most recent purchases.

Taxpayers must receive IRS approval to use the LIFO method. Code Sec. 472. If the LIFO method is adopted in the taxpayer's first year of business or in the initial year that inventories are maintained, then advanced approval is not required. The method is adopted (approval received) by using it on that year's tax return. The taxpayer can change to the LIFO method by attaching Form 970 (Application to Use LIFO Inventory Method) with the tax year for the year of change. If LIFO is used for tax purposes then it also must be used for financial reporting purposes. LIFO produces a smaller taxable income when prices are rising, so there is an incentive (tax savings) to select this method. However, because of the conformity requirements for tax and financial reporting purposes, some firms do not select LIFO because it also produces a smaller net income on the financial statements. However, those taxpayers using LIFO are permitted to use other methods in the footnotes, appendices or supplements to the financial statements. Reg. §1.472-2(e)(3). Also, taxpayers using LIFO may not use the lower-of-cost-or-market method.

The weighted average method values ending inventory (and cost of goods sold) based on the weighted average price of all goods available for sale during the year. The value of ending inventory generally is between those amounts obtained under the FIFO and LIFO methods.

| **EXAMPLE 13.24** | James Co. sells desks. Inventory on January 1 consisted of 300 desks valued at $400 per desk ($120,000). It purchased 700 desks on April 3 at $425 per desk ($297,500) and 900 desks on September 3 at $500 per desk ($450,000). During the year it sold 1,500 desks at a total sales price of $1,050,000. Ending inventory, cost of goods sold and gross profit using FIFO, LIFO and weighted average are as follows: |

	FIFO	LIFO	Weighted Average
Sales	$1,050,000	$1,050,000	$1,050,000
Beginning inventory	$120,000	$120,000	$120,000
Purchases	747,500	747,500	747,500
Cost of goods available for sale	$867,500	$867,500	$867,500
Ending inventory			
FIFO (400 $500)	200,000		
LIFO (300 $400; 100 $425)		162,500	
Weighted average			
($867,500/1,900 = $457/unit)			
(400 $457)			182,800
Cost of goods sold	$667,500	$705,000	$684,700
Gross profit	$382,500	$345,000	$365,300

If a taxpayer changes his or her inventory method, an adjustment is needed to account for the differences at date of conversion. The change could be from LIFO to FIFO, FIFO to LIFO, lower-of-cost-or-market to LIFO, etc. In such a situation, the adjustment is spread over four years (unless the adjustment is less than $50,000, in which case the taxpayer may elect to use the one-year adjustment period).

KEYSTONE PROBLEM	Financial management has traditionally been opposed to adopting LIFO because it would result in reporting lower earnings in the financial statements to shareholders.
	1. Are they correct in the short run? Why?
	2. Are they correct in the long run? Why?

¶13,473   DOLLAR-VALUE LIFO METHOD

Instead of determining quantity increases of each item in the inventory and then pricing each item, as is required under regular LIFO, the dollar-value LIFO method may be used. The increase in LIFO value is determined by comparing the total dollar value of the beginning and ending inventories at base-year (first LIFO year) prices and then converting any dollar-value increase to current prices by means of an index. Taxpayers are allowed, under the dollar-value LIFO method, to determine base-year dollars through the use of government indexes. Code Sec. 472(f). The Regulations permit the use of several price index methods. Reg. §1.472-8. The "double extension method," the most frequently used, works as follows:

1. Determine opening inventory at base-year prices (the prices in effect when LIFO was adopted).
2. Determine ending inventory at base-year prices.
3. Compute the difference. The result is either an increase (increment) or a decrease (decrement).

4. Determine a price index to value the increment, if any. The index equals ending inventory at current prices/ending inventory at base-year prices.
5. Adjust the inventory "layers" for any increment or decrement. Every increment represents a new layer. Any decrement uses up the most recently added layer or layers first.

The following example is adapted from Reg. §1.472-8(e)(2)(v), Examples (1) and (2).

EXAMPLE 13.25

Skylark Inc. adopts LIFO in Year 1. Opening inventory was $14,000, which became the base period price. Ending inventory was $24,250 at actual prices, $20,000 at base-year prices. Thus, keeping prices constant, the increment was $6,000. The index was:

$$\frac{\$24,250}{\$20,000} = 1.2125$$

The increment is therefore $6,000 × 1.2125, or $7,275, and the ending inventory is $21,275, as opposed to $24,250 under FIFO, resulting in an increased cost of goods sold of $2,975. To summarize:

	1/1/Year 1	Index	12/31/Year 1
Opening inventory	$14,000	1.0	$14,000
Increment	6,000	1.2125	7,275
Ending LIFO inventory	$20,000		$21,275

If, at the end of Year 2, ending inventory was $18,000 at base period prices and $27,000 at current prices, there was a decrement with the following result:

	1/1/Year 1	Index	12/31/Year 2
1/1/Year 1 inventory	$14,000	1.0	$14,000
Remaining Year 1 increase	4,000	1.2125	4,850
LIFO inventory	$18,000		$18,850

At the end of Year 3, ending inventory was $25,000 at base period prices and $30,000 at current prices (30/25 = 1.2). The Year 3 year-end inventory consists of three "layers" as follows:

	1/1/Year 1	Index	12/31/Year 3
1/1/Year 1 inventory	$14,000	1.0	$14,000
Year 1 increase	4,000	1.2125	4,850
Year 3 increase	7,000	1.2	8,400
LIFO inventory	$25,000		$27,250

The computations above assume that only one "pool" was used. If substantially heterogeneous products exist, more than one pool must be used. Since each pool generates its own index and each pool may have numerous layers, the feasibility of dollar-value LIFO techniques depends on the availability of computers.

¶13,481   SIMPLIFIED DOLLAR-VALUE LIFO METHOD

Taxpayers may elect to use the simplified dollar-value LIFO method, but it then must be used to value all LIFO inventories. The simplified dollar-value LIFO method is designed to enable small businesses to use the LIFO method but avoid the extra costs and burden of maintaining records needed for the other LIFO methods. A taxpayer may elect the method for any year in which its average annual gross receipts for the preceding three years do not exceed $5 million. Code Sec. 474(c).

Using the method is relatively easy and straightforward. The taxpayer groups its inventory into pools for each major category in the applicable government price index provided by the Bureau of Labor Statistics (11 categories for retailers and 15 categories for all other taxpayers). Each pool then is separately adjusted using the appropriate government index. Retailers use the Consumer Price Index, and all other taxpayers use the Producer Price Index.

The taxpayer does not compute base period prices. Instead, the taxpayer uses year-end inventory values and determines an assumed base period value by applying the government price index. If the resulting base period value exceeds the opening inventory value at base period prices, then the increment is valued using the same index.

EXAMPLE 13.26

Susan Co. adopted the simplified dollar-value LIFO method. Inventory at actual prices in Year 1 and Year 2 was $200,000 and $300,000, respectively. The Consumer Price Index for Years 1 and 2 was 115 percent and 125 percent, respectively. Susan Co.'s ending inventory for Year 2 would be valued at $282,609, consisting of $200,000 from Year 1 plus the Year 2 increment of $82,609. The Year 2 increment is determined as follows:

Year 2 ending inventory at assumed base-year prices	=	$300,000 × 1.15/1.25 = $276,000
The increment at Year 1 base price	=	$276,000 – $200,000 = $76,000
The increment at Year 2 base price	=	$76,000 × 1.25/1.15 = $82,609

¶13,485 ESTIMATES OF INVENTORY SHRINKAGE

Code Sec. 471 permits a business to determine its year-end closing inventory by using estimates for shrinkage (e.g., loss due to theft). A year-end physical count is not necessary if the business: (1) normally takes a physical count of its inventories at each business location on a regular and consistent basis and (2) makes proper adjustments to its inventories and to its estimating methods to the extent its estimates differ from actual shrinkage.

Using this method results in a change in accounting method, but IRS permission is not required to make the change. Also, any adjustments to income due to this change are taken into account over a four-year period.

EXAMPLE 13.27

SQ Co., a calendar-year taxpayer, generally takes a physical count of inventory every three months. In 2015, it claimed a $30,000 deduction for inventory shrinkage based on an estimate of shrinkage on December 31, 2015. Since it takes a physical count on a regular basis, it is permitted to use an estimate for inventory shrinkage.

PLANNING POINTER

A widely-held view is that a major potential cost in changing from the "lower-of-cost-or-market" method of valuing inventories to LIFO is that opening inventory must be written back up to cost and the write-up taken into income. This adverse tax aspect may be avoided or may be nonexistent in the following situations:

No inventory on hand at the end of the year prior to the year of change was written down from cost.

The portion of the inventory written down may be (any of the following):

1.   Sold before year-end at a discount or disposed of as giveaways, prizes, or bonuses to customers
2.   Given to employees as deductible compensation
3.   Contributed to charity, resulting in nonrecognition of income as well as a deduction (prior to year-end)
4.   Abandoned (i.e., "dumped")

Thus, with proper tax planning, no income will have to be recognized.

TAX BLUNDER

Hind Co. uses the FIFO inventory method because this method reflects the true physical flow of inventory. Ending inventory under FIFO was $400,000 in 2015. Had Hind Co. used LIFO, ending inventory would have been $240,0000. Hind Co. has been in the 34% tax bracket and believes it will continue to be in the 34% tax bracket.

Actual physical flow of inventory is irrelevant for costing purposes. The cost flow used (assumed) is artificial and does not need to coincide with the actual physical flow. Had Hind Co. used LIFO, it would have increased cost of goods sold by $160,000, and taxable income would have decreased by $160,000, producing a tax savings of $54,400 (34% × $160,000). Again, given the time value of money, this would be preferable.

Long-Term Contracts

¶13,501   ALTERNATIVE ACCOUNTING METHODS

The term long-term contract means any contract for the manufacture, building, installation, or construction of property if such property is not completed within the taxable year into which the contract is entered. A contract for the manufacture of property will not be treated as a long-term contract unless it involves the manufacture of any unique item which is not normally included in finished goods inventory or requires more than 12 calendar months to complete. Code Sec. 460(f). A taxpayer generally has two alternatives to account for long-term contracts: the percentage-of-completion method (or modified percentage-of-completion method in some cases) and the completed-contract method (in limited circumstances). The accounting method selected must be used for all long-term contracts in the same trade or business. Reg. §1.451-3(a).

Under the percentage-of-completion method taxpayers report income under the contract annually based on estimated progress. The percentage of completion is determined by comparing allocated costs to the contract and direct costs incurred by the close of the year to the estimated total contract costs. Code Sec. 460(b). The total contract price is multiplied by the percentage to determine the amount of income reported in that year.

Under the percentage-of-completion method the taxpayer must use a look-back method in the year the contract is completed. This method requires the taxpayer to compare the actual completion level to the claimed level (to reflect the actual profit for each year of the contract) and to redetermine taxable income and tax liability accordingly. Interest is charged on any underpayment and is received for any overpayment. However, long-term contracts completed within two years of contract commencement are exempt from the look-back method if the gross contract price does not exceed the lesser of $1,000,000 or 1 percent of the taxpayer's average gross receipts for the last three years preceding the year in which the contract was entered. Code Sec. 460(b).

Code Sec. 460 permits taxpayers to elect not to apply the look-back method for long-term contracts completed during the year and in all subsequent years if the actual contract taxable income is within 10 percent of estimated taxable income under the percentage-of-completion method (using estimated contract price and costs).

EXAMPLE 13.28	Jones Co. enters into a three-year construction contract in 2015. Jones Co. estimated (reported) net income using the percentage-of-completion method was $100,000, $200,000, and $300,000 for 2015, 2016, and 2017 respectively. In 2017, when the contract is completed, Jones Co. determines that actual net income for each year was $108,000, $210,000, and $282,000, respectively, for the three years. Ten percent of $108,000 is $10,800, and 10% of $318,000 is $31,800. Since the $100,000 claimed in 2015 and the $300,000 cumulative income in 2016 ($200,000 in 2016 and $100,000 in 2015) are within the 10 percent range, Jones can elect not to apply the look-back method.

The modified percentage-of-completion method is available for contracts that are less than 10 percent complete at the end of the year. If this condition is met, then taxpayers may elect to defer reporting any income from the contract until at least 10 percent of the work is completed. Code Sec. 460(b)(5). In the year that 10 percent is completed, the taxpayer will report income on all the work completed in that year using the "regular" percentage-of-completion method described above. The rationale for this election is that it often is difficult to estimate the total costs of a long-term project at its beginning; the modified method gives the taxpayer some time and experience to provide a "better" estimate.

Under the completed-contract method taxpayers report no income until final completion of the contract, regardless of when the funds are collected. All costs are accumulated and recognized at completion. The use of this method provides substantial opportunity to defer income, and as such is severely restricted. Only small construction contractors and home construction contractors can use this method. Small contractors are those whose average gross receipts for the three preceding tax years do not exceed $10,000,000. Contracts of small construction must be expected to be completed within two years of the commencement date. Code Sec. 460(e).

Final completion of the contract is based on an analysis of all the facts and circumstances. However, a taxpayer may not delay completion of a contract for the principal purpose of deferring federal income taxes. Reg. §1.460-1(c)(3). Additionally, if the buyer reasonably disputes the work, then income or deduction with respect to said dispute is recognized in the year the dispute is resolved. If the amount reasonably in dispute is extensive and so affects the contract price that it is not possible to determine whether a gain or loss will result from the contract, then no gain or loss is recognized until the dispute is settled. Reg. §1.460-4(d)(4).

¶13,515   COMPARISON OF THE METHODS

The following, simplified example illustrates the difference between the percentage-of-completion and completed-contract methods:

EXAMPLE 13.29

In 2015, Building Construction Co. entered into a contract to build a small warehouse for $2,500,000. Total estimated costs to complete are $2,000,000, and the project is expected to be completed in 2016. Actual costs incurred in 2015 and 2016 were $800,000 and $900,000, respectively. Results for 2015 and 2016 are shown below.

Percentage-of-Completion Method	2015	2016
Gross Revenue	$1,000,000[a]	$1,500,000[b]
Actual Costs	(800,000)	(900,000)
Gross Profit Reported	$200,000	$600,000

    a. ($800,000/$2,000,000) × $2,500,000

    b. $2,500,000 – $1,000,000

Completed-Contract Method		
Gross Revenue	$0	$2,500,000
Actual Costs	0	(1,700,000)
Gross Profit Reported	$0	$800,000

¶13,535   CAPITALIZATION OF EXPENSES

All costs associated with the contract are capitalized and are deducted as profits are recognized. This principle applies to direct costs, such as material and direct labor costs, as well as to overhead, such as repairs and maintenance, utilities, rent, cost recovery, shipping costs, general and administrative expenses, scrap and spoilage costs, etc. Construction period interest must always be capitalized. The following expenses must be capitalized; they may not be expensed if the percentage-of-completion method is used:

1. Cost recovery of assets employed for work on specific contracts
2. Pension costs representing current service costs
3. General and administrative expenses relating to specific contracts
4. Research and development expenses with respect to specific contracts
5. Scrap and spoilage costs

In any event, bidding expenses, indirect research and development expenses, and marketing, advertising, and selling expenses may be deducted currently.

¶13,540   SPECIAL RULES

The Regulations provide guidance in those situations where a long-term contract is either being disputed in amount or is delayed beyond its scheduled date of completion.

Disputed Amounts

Generally, the disputed amount, if any, simply reduces gain or increases a loss in the year of completion. However, if the disputed amount is "substantial" then no gain or loss is recognized until the controversy is settled. Reg. §1.460-4(d)(4).

Unreasonable Delays

The completion of a contract may not be delayed (e.g., by deferring the formal acceptance of the project) for the principal purpose of tax postponement. Reg. §1.460-4(d)(4). Because of the time value of money, a deferral of the income from the last month of one year until the first month of the next year may be quite valuable, even with no change in the marginal tax rate.

Installment Sales

¶13,601   ## USE OF INSTALLMENT METHOD

An installment sale is a disposition of property where at least one payment is received after the close of the taxable year in which the disposition occurs. Code Sec. 453(b). Thus, there is no requirement for numerous payments over several years; one payment in a subsequent year would qualify as an installment sale. The installment method may be used by cash-basis taxpayers as a means to defer gain recognition or to spread gain recognition over several tax periods. The method may not be used if the property is disposed of at a loss. Additionally, the installment method only affects when the gain is recognized, it does not change the character of the gain (capital or ordinary). How this gain is taxed is determined by the applicable laws in the year the installment payment is received, not in the year of sale. The seller reports gains under the installment method on Form 6252 (Installment Sale Income).

Any depreciation recapture coming under Sections 1245 and 1250 must be taken into income in the year of sale. If a portion of the capital gain from an installment sale is 25 percent gain and a portion is 15 percent or 0 percent gain, the taxpayer is required to take the 25 percent gain into account before the 15 percent or 0 percent gain, as payments are received.

The installment method is not available to all taxpayers. It cannot be used: by dealers in real and personal property; for any sale of personal property under a revolving credit plan; for sales of depreciable property to a controlled entity (e.g., to a corporation in which the taxpayer owns directly and indirectly more than 50 percent of the value of the outstanding stock), unless the taxpayer can establish that tax avoidance was not a principal purpose of the disposition; and for sales of stock or securities which are traded on an established securities market (or to the extent provided in the regulations for property other than stock or securities regularly traded on an established market). Code Sec. 453.

Although nondealers may use the installment method, Code Sec. 453A imposes a special interest charge if the sale price of the real or personal property (other than personal-use and farm property) exceeds $150,000. This interest charge is on the tax liability deferred on the property sold. However, the interest charge only applies if the installment obligation is outstanding at year-end and if the face amount of all installment obligations which arose during the year and are outstanding at year end exceeds $5 million.

The taxpayer must use the installment method for tax purposes if the taxpayer disposes of property under an installment contract and the disposition qualifies for the installment method. However, the taxpayer may make an irrevocable election not to use the installment method. Code Sec. 453(d). In such a case, the gain would be recognized in the year of disposition. Finally, all depreciation recapture occurs in the year of sale, regardless of the fact that the taxpayer uses the installment method.

EXAMPLE 13.30

James Hoffman sold a truck in 2015 for $36,000. The truck's adjusted basis was $15,000 at the time of sale, and $9,000 had been claimed in depreciation. James collected $12,000 in 2015 and will receive $12,000 in 2016 and 2017. James uses the installment method for this sale.

Amount realized	$36,000
Adjusted basis	15,000
Realized gain	21,000
Code Sec. 1245 gain	$9,000
Gross profit percentage = 33.33% ($12,000/$36,000)	

In 2015, James will recognize a $9,000 Code Sec. 1245 gain and a $4,000 Code Sec. 1231 gain ($12,000 x 33.33%). James also will recognize a $4,000 Code Sec. 1231 gain ($12,000 x 33.33%) in 2016 and in 2017.

¶13,655 COMPUTATION OF GAIN

The installment method recognizes income as payments are received. There are several steps to follow.

Step 1.	Determine the gross profit from the sale. Gross profit equals the selling price minus the property's adjusted basis, selling expenses, and depreciation recapture (if any).
Step 2.	Determine the contract price. The contract price generally equals the amount the seller will receive. If there are no liabilities on the property which the buyer assumes, then contract price equals selling price. If there are liabilities on the property which the buyer assumes, then the contract price equals all payments to be received by the seller (i.e., the selling price reduced by the mortgage assumption). If the liabilities exceed the property's adjusted basis (increased by selling expenses for this comparison only), then such excess increases the contract price (it equals all payments to be received by the seller plus the excess). The contract price can never be less than the gross profit.
Step 3.	Compute the gross profit percentage (which can never be greater than 100 percent). Gross profit percentage = Gross profit/Contract price.
Step 4.	Determine the amount of gain to be recognized in the year of sale. Recognized gain = Payments received × Gross profit percentage.

EXAMPLE 13.31 Ann Rogers, 45 years old, sold property for $125,000. Her selling expenses were $5,000 and her basis was $40,000. She received $25,000 down and will receive $20,000 in each of the following five years. Ann's gross profit is $80,000 ($125,000 – ($5,000 + $40,000)). The contract price is $125,000, and the gross profit percentage is 64 percent ($80,000/$125,000). She will recognize a gain of $16,000 in the year of sale (64% × $25,000) and $12,800 in each of the following five years (64% × $20,000). Thus, total gain recognized over the six years is $80,000 ($16,000 + (5 × $12,800)). Ann also will recognize income for the interest she receives over this period.

EXAMPLE 13.32 Assume the same facts as in Example 13.31 except that the property was depreciable property subject to $15,000 of depreciation recapture under Code Sec. 1245. Ann's gross profit is $65,000 ($125,000 – ($5,000 + $40,000 + $15,000)). The contract price is still $125,000. The gross profit percentage is 52 percent ($65,000/$125,000). She will recognize a $13,000 gain in the year of sale (52% × $25,000) and $15,000 ordinary income from the depreciation recapture. In each of the following five years she will recognize a gain of $10,400 (52% × $20,000). Total gain recognized over the six years also is $80,000 ($13,000 + $15,000 + (5 × $10,400)). Ann also will recognize income for the interest she receives over this period.

EXAMPLE 13.33 Assume the same facts as in Example 13.31 except that there is a $5,000 mortgage on the property which the buyer assumes. Additionally, Ann will receive $20,000 in the year of sale and $20,000 in each of the following five years. In this case, Ann's gross profit is $80,000 ($125,000 – ($5,000 + $40,000)). The contract price is $120,000 ($125,000 – $5,000); Ann will receive $120,000 in cash payments from the buyer. The gross profit percentage is 66.67 percent ($80,000 ÷ $120,000). She will recognize a gain of $13,333 ($20,000 × 66.67%) in the year of sale and in each of the following five years. Total gain recognized over the six years is $80,000 ($13,333 × 6), allowing for a $2 roundoff. Ann also will recognize income for the interest she received over this period.

EXAMPLE 13.34 Assume the same facts as in Example 13.31 except the property is subject to a $50,000 mortgage which the buyer assumes. Additionally, Ann will receive $15,000 in the year of sale and $12,000 in each of the following five years. In this case the liability exceeds the adjusted basis by $5,000 ($50,000 – ($40,000 + $5,000 selling expenses)). Whenever the liability exceeds the adjusted basis (increased by selling expenses), the gross profit percentage is 100 percent. Also, the excess is treated as a payment in the year of sale. Thus, Ann recognizes a gain of $20,000 (100% × ($15,000 + $5,000)) in the year of sale and $12,000 (100% × $12,000) in each of the following five years. Total gain recognized over the six years is $80,000 ($20,000 + (5 × $12,000)). Ann also will recognize income for the interest she received over this period.

EXAMPLE 13.35	Sal Weintraub sold $20 million of nondealer real estate during the year under the installment method. At year-end $15 million is outstanding. Deferred gross profit on the outstanding obligations is $4 million. The maximum tax rate in effect during the year was 35 percent. Code Sec. 453A applies in this situation, and Sal must pay the special interest charge. Assume that the federal short-term interest rate in December was 8 percent. The interest due is $102,672, computed as follows:

1. Determine the portion of installment obligations outstanding at year-end in excess of $5 million and divide this by the total amount of installment obligations outstanding at year-end.

    ($15,000,000 – $5,000,000)   ÷ $15,000,000   =   66.67%

2. Determine the tax liability deferred on all installment obligations outstanding at year-end by multiplying the deferred gross profit on such obligations by the maximum tax rate in effect for the tax year.

    ($4,000,000 × 35%)   = $1,400,000

3. Determine the applicable interest rate, which is equal to the federal short-term interest rate for the last month of the tax year, increased by 3 percentage points.

    (8% + 3%)   =   11%

4. Determine the interest due (which is considered personal interest expense).

    (66.67% × $1,400,000 × 11%)   = $102,672

¶13,675   **ELECTING OUT OF INSTALLMENT REPORTING**

As noted earlier, a taxpayer may elect not to use the installment method. This election must be made by the due date (including extensions) for filing the tax return for the year of the installment sale. Reg. §15A.453-1(d)(3). However, there are potential drawbacks to such an election. For example, if a capital asset or a Section 1231 asset is sold at a gain on the installment plan and the seller elects not to use installment reporting, there are at least two obvious drawbacks:

1. The gain is accelerated and the tax is due in the year of sale before the proceeds are received.
2. If the value of the note is less than its face value, a cash-basis taxpayer will limit the capital gain and may convert the discount into ordinary income on collection if the collection of a note does not qualify as a "sale or exchange." (This problem does not affect accrual-method sellers since they accrue the face value.) Under Code Sec. 1271(a)(1) and (b)(1), retiring a debt instrument is a sale or exchange, unless issued by a natural person.

| EXAMPLE 13.36 | Rita Brown sells a painting held for five years as an investment. The painting was purchased for $5,000 and sold to Joe Smith for $15,000, $6,000 down and a $9,000 face value note worth $7,000 due in three years together with 10 percent interest. If she opts for installment reporting, her gross profit percentage is 66 2/3: |

$$\frac{(\$15,000 - \$5,000)}{\$15,000}$$

resulting in a capital gain of $4,000 in the year of sale and $6,000 upon collection of the note (plus interest).

If Rita elects *not* to use installment reporting, the result is as follows:

Year of Sale:

Amount realized	
Cash	$6,000
Fair market value of note	7,000
	$13,000
Less adjusted basis	5,000
Long-term capital gain	$8,000
Year of Collection:	
Collection of principal	$9,000
Less basis in note	7,000
Ordinary income	$2,000

Which action is preferable depends on Rita's tax bracket (and the rate applicable to her capital gain).

The Regulations are flexible enough to permit installment reporting even if the selling price and, therefore, gross profit percentage are unknown at the initial sale. Reg. §15A.453-1(c). Three main situations can be identified:

1. **Maximum selling price.** If payments are contingent, but subject to a ceiling, the ceiling is presumed to be the selling price. The gross profit percentage is initially based on this maximum and is subsequently modified as more facts become available.
2. **Given payment period.** Here the seller's basis is prorated over the term. The result may be gains in some years, losses in others.
3. **No maximum price, no given term.** Here the seller recovers basis over 15 years, which may also lead to gain or loss in any given year, presumably of the same character.

In view of this expansion of the scope of the installment reporting provisions, the cost recovery method (the "open transaction" approach) is likely to have even less applicability than before.

| PLANNING POINTER | The taxpayer's current and expected future tax rates should be carefully considered when deciding to use the installment method of reporting. If the taxpayer's future tax rates are expected to decline, then using the installment method could produce significant tax savings. Conversely, if the taxpayer expects to be in higher tax brackets in the future, then the installment method could result in significant increases in taxes. Remember, the time value of money also must be considered. |

EXAMPLE 13.37	Jennifer Lynn sold a short-term capital asset in 2015. She has no capital loss carryovers and sold no other capital assets during the year. She does not plan to sell any capital assets during the next four years. The amount realized from the sale was $40,000, and the property's adjusted basis was $20,000. Her realized and recognized gain is $20,000. Jennifer will receive $8,000 at the date of sale and $8,000 (plus interest) per year for the four years after the year of sale. The value of the note is equal to its face value. The gross profit percentage is 50 percent ($20,000/$40,000). If she uses the installment method of reporting, then she will recognize a $4,000 ($8,000 x 50%) short-term capital gain (plus interest income) in each of the five years. If she elects out of the installment method of reporting, then she will recognize a $20,000 short-term capital gain (which will be taxed as ordinary income since she has no other capital asset transactions) in 2015, plus interest income as received.

If Jennifer is in the 33 percent bracket in 2015 but expects to be in the 15 percent bracket in 2016 through 2019, then she would save $2,400 in taxes by using the installment method (ignoring the time value of money).

Tax on $20,000 if recognized in 2015 ($20,000 x 33%)		$6,600
Tax on $4,000 in 2015 ($4,000 x 33%)	$1,320	
Tax on $4,000 in 2016 through 2019 ($4,000 x 15% = $600 x 4)	2,400	3,720
Tax savings from using the installment method of reporting		$2,880

If Jennifer is in the 15 percent bracket in 2015 but expects to be in the 28 percent bracket in 2016 and 2017 and the 25 percent bracket in 2018 and 2019, then she would save $2,320 in taxes by electing out of the installment method (ignoring the time value of money).

Tax on $20,000 if recognized in 2015 ($20,000 x 15%)		$3,000
Tax on $4,000 in 2015 ($4,000 x 15%)	$600	
Tax on $4,000 in 2016 through 2017 ($4,000 x 28% = $1,120 x 2)	2,240	
Tax on $4,000 in 2018 and 2019 ($4,000 x 25% =$1,000 x 2)	2,000	4,840
Tax savings from electing out of the installment method of reporting		$1,840

¶13,685   DISPOSITIONS OF INSTALLMENT OBLIGATIONS

There are times when a taxpayer who sold property on the installment method needs or wants to dispose of the installment obligation prior to maturity. In this instance, the taxpayer must determine the obligation's adjusted basis and determine the gain or loss on the disposition. The adjusted basis of the installment obligation is equal to the face amount of the obligation in excess of the income that would have been reported if the obligation had been paid in full. To determine gain or loss, the adjusted basis is compared to the amount realized if the obligation is sold and to the obligation's fair market value if it is disposed of other than by sale. The character of the gain or loss is based upon the property which was sold under the installment method. Code Sec. 453B(a).

EXAMPLE 13.38	In 2015, Katherine Beales sold a piece of art for $50,000. She received $10,000 in 2015 and in 2016. She purchased the piece in 2005 for $8,000; thus, her gross profit was $42,000 and the contract price was $50,000. The gross profit percentage was 84 percent ($42,000/$50,000). In 2017, she sold the installment obligation for $28,000. Her basis in the obligation is $4,800 (unpaid balance of $30,000 minus amount of income reported if unpaid balance paid in full (84% × $30,000)). Thus, Katherine's gain on the sale of the installment obligations is $23,200 ($28,000 – $4,800). The gain is a long-term capital gain since the art piece was a long-term capital asset when it was sold in 2015. Katherine also will recognize income for the interest she received while the obligation was outstanding.

In addition to a sale, there are several other situations where a disposition of an installment obligation results in a recognized gain or loss, primarily to prevent income-shifting among taxpayers. In each of these, the fair market value of the obligation is used as the amount realized. Code Sec. 453B(a).

The following lead to income recognition at the time the installment obligation is transferred: gifts or forgiveness of payments, especially if the obligee and obligor are related; taxable exchanges; and corporate distributions. Additionally, gain recognition occurs on "second dispositions," whereby the taxpayer sells the property to a related party and within two years of the sale and before the taxpayer receives all payments with respect to such sale, the related party disposes of the property (i.e., the "second" disposition). At the time of the second disposition, the amount realized from the second distribution is treated as being received by the original taxpayer. Code Sec. 453(e).

Gain or loss is not recognized in the following situations: transfers to a controlled corporation under Code Sec. 351; transfers in certain corporate reorganizations and liquidations; certain transfers to and from partnerships; transfers upon the death of a taxpayer; transfers incident to a divorce; and transfers to a spouse.

EXAMPLE 13.39	Jack Moore purchased land in 2007 for $40,000. Jack sold the land to his daughter in 2014. The terms of the sale call for Jack to receive $20,000 in 2014 and $15,000 in 2015, 2016, 2017, and 2018, plus interest. The gross profit is $40,000, the contract price is $80,000 and the gross profit percentage is 50 percent. Jack received payments in 2014 and 2015, recognizing $10,000 and $7,500, plus interest, respectively, in 2014 and 2015. In 2016, Jack forgave the remaining payments. The forgiveness is a taxable disposition. Jack is considered to have received the remaining payments ($45,000) and his recognized gain in 2016 is $22,500 (50% × $45,000).

¶13,695   REPOSSESSIONS

The repossession of personal property sold under the installment method is a taxable event. Gain or loss is recognized equal to the difference between the fair market value of the property repossessed and the adjusted basis of the installment obligation. Any costs incurred during the repossession increase the adjusted basis of the installment obligation. The character of the gain or loss recognized is the same as the character of the gain or loss recognized on the original sale of the property. The basis of the repossessed property is its fair market value. Code Sec. 453B.

Loss is not recognized and no bad debt deduction is allowed on the repossession of real property. Gain is recognized to a limited extent. Code Sec. 1038 limits gain recognition to the lesser of (1) the cash and fair market value of property received from the buyer in excess of gain previously recognized by the holder of the installment obligation or (2) the gain not yet recognized by the holder of the installment obligation (deferred gross profit), reduced by the costs incurred during the repossession. The character of the gain is the same as that recognized under the original sale of the property. The basis of the repossessed real property is the adjusted basis of the installment obligation, increased by costs incurred during the repossession and by any gain recognized from the repossession.

EXAMPLE 13.40	John Wells sold a car in January 2015 for $20,000. He received $4,000 down and $16,000 was due in 2016. His basis in the car at the time of sale was $12,000. John made numerous attempts to collect the $16,000 and in December he repossessed the car. He incurred $700 in repossession costs and the car's fair market value at time of repossession was $15,000. In 2015, John reported a capital gain of $1,600 (40% × $4,000). The adjusted basis of the installment obligation at the time of repossession was $9,600 ($16,000 − (40% × $16,000)). To determine John's gain on the repossession, this basis is increased by the repossession costs. Thus, John recognizes a $4,700 capital gain in December 2016 ($15,000 − ($9,600 + $700)). John's basis in the repossessed car is $15,000, its fair market value.

EXAMPLE 13.41	Tom O'Brien sold land in January 2015 for $50,000. He received $20,000 down and $30,000 was due in January 2016. Tom acquired the land in 2008 for $10,000. The gross profit percentage is 80 percent. Tom recognized a $16,000 long-term capital gain in 2015. Tom was unable to collect the $30,000 and repossessed the land in October 2016, incurring $1,000 in the process. The land's fair market value in October 2016 was $52,000. Tom's recognized long-term gain is $4,000, equal to the lesser of $4,000 ($20,000 received − $16,000 gain previously recognized) or $23,000 ($24,000 gain not yet recognized − $1,000 repossession costs). His basis in the repossessed land is $11,000 (the basis of the installment obligation ($30,000 − (80% × $30,000)) plus the gain recognized on repossession ($4,000) plus the costs incurred to repossess ($1,000).

¶13,699   INTEREST ON DEFERRED PAYMENT SALES

A seller of capital assets historically had an incentive to charge little or no interest while inflating the selling price, thus converting ordinary interest income into capital gains or a reduced capital loss. Section 483 limits the taxpayer's opportunity to do so, but does not eliminate it altogether. Unless the seller charges at least a rate equal to the "applicable federal rate" the IRS will impute interest at such a rate compounded semiannually, resulting in additional interest income to the buyer and a lower selling price (and a lower gross profit), but also providing the buyer with higher interest deductions (and a lower basis). Interest will not be imputed to a sale where all the payments are due within six months. Additionally, there are several special rules, including:

1. Unlike installment reporting, Code Sec. 483 applies to sales at a loss.
2. No interest is imputed unless the selling price is in excess of $3,000.
3. Sales of patents where the selling price is contingent on the use, production, or disposition of such patents, and private annuity sales are excluded.
4. Only 6 percent interest need be charged for sales of up to $500,000 of real property to a family member, including siblings, spouses, an ancestor, or a lineal descendant.

EXAMPLE 13.42

Antoinette Clerici sold land in 2015 for $40,000. The adjusted basis of the property was $50,000. Antoinette received $12,000 in 2015 and will receive $28,000 in 2016. No interest was charged. Antoinette has a $10,000 loss and cannot use the installment method to report it. However, since it is a deferred contract she must charge interest; thus, the IRS will impute interest and reduce the selling price accordingly. This increases her loss, causes her to recognize interest income, reduces the buyer's basis in the land, and causes interest expense for the buyer which may or may not be deductible.

Since the statutory rate may be below the market rate for second mortgages and unsecured personal loans, some flexibility of designing a price/terms combination that is attractive for tax purposes still exists.

¶13,710   ADVANTAGES AND DISADVANTAGES OF INSTALLMENT METHOD

There are several advantages and disadvantages associated with the installment method of reporting.

Advantages of engaging installment sales and reporting profits when collections are made include:

1. Tax liabilities are deferred until the proceeds from the sales are available
2. Marginal tax rates may decline in future years
3. Interest income, to some extent, may be converted to capital gains by charging a lower interest rate and a higher price (but the imputed interest rules affect this)
4. Since the seller finances the purchase, sales are more easily made.

Disadvantages of installment sales include:

1. There is a default risk and potential collection costs
2. In periods of inflation there is a loss of purchasing power
3. Although taxes are deferred, so are collections. Because the after-tax proceeds are likely to far exceed the taxes payable, an installment sale is unlikely to be made merely for tax purposes
4. Marginal tax rates may increase during the collection years
5. Although the *holding period* in the year of sale determines whether the transaction is short-term or long-term, the *character* of the gain is determined in the year of collection. In one case, the taxpayer sold a capital asset but wound up with ordinary income, in part, in the years of collection. *Z. Klien,* 42 TC 1000, Dec. 26,947.
6. All depreciation recapture takes place in the year of sale.

Olga Lopez purchased some land years ago as an investment for $40,000. She owns it free and clear, wishes to sell it for its value of $100,000 and would like as much cash up front as possible while deferring the tax as long as possible. Any potential buyer would most likely wish to finance the acquisition. If Olga sells the land on the installment plan, her gross profit of 60 percent will apply to payments in the year of sale as well as to future collections. After competent tax advice, she did the following:

1. She borrowed $40,000 with the property as collateral. The receipt of the loan proceeds is tax free.
2. After a reasonable time, she sold the property for $100,000 by letting the buyer take over the $40,000 loan and taking back a second mortgage below the market rate.
3. Even though her gross profit is now 100 percent, she received $40,000 tax free and converted interest income and favorable terms into an additional long-term capital gain on a tax-deferred basis.

SUMMARY

- Taxable income must be computed on the basis of the taxpayer's tax year.
- The annual accounting period may be either a calendar year or a fiscal year.
- The tax year cannot exceed 12 months except where a 52-53-week tax year is adopted.
- A fiscal year is a period of 12 months ending on the last day of any month other than December or a 52-53-week annual accounting period.
- A fiscal year is permitted only if the taxpayer's books are kept on the same basis.
- Usually the taxpayer needs a business purpose for approval of a change in tax periods.
- Prior approval must be obtained before changing to a new tax year.
- A return required for a fractional part of the year (due to a change in accounting periods) is known as a short-period return.
- To obtain IRS approval to change accounting periods, Form 1128 must be filed on or before the 15th day of the second calendar month following the end of the short period.
- The taxpayer's method of accounting must "clearly reflect income."
- A taxpayer may change accounting methods voluntarily or may be required to change.
- To obtain IRS permission to change accounting methods, Form 3115 must be filed anytime during the year in which the change is desired.
- The taxpayer faced with a substantial tax due to a change of accounting methods generally has a four-year adjustment period.
- An understanding of accounting periods and methods is crucial to understanding the taxation of any entity.
- Many accounting methods used for financial accounting are similar to those used for tax accounting, but there are many differences too.
- Several inventory methods are available to the taxpayer: specific identification, FIFO, and LIFO, and variations thereto.
- Certain costs with respect to inventory must be capitalized.
- The percentage-of-completion method must be used for long-term contracts.
- The installment method of accounting is used when proceeds from the sale of certain property are received in a year other than the year of sale.
- A taxpayer may elect not to use the installment method.
- Accrual-basis taxpayers may not use the installment method.

QUESTIONS

1. How does financial accounting differ from tax accounting?

2. Jason is single and uses the calendar year for his tax year. He died on May 15, 2015. When is his final income tax return due?

3. If a taxpayer is on the fiscal year, what is the requirement regarding the taxpayer's books?

4. Pam recently married Henry. When she was single she used a calendar tax year. For a variety of reasons she is considering changing her tax year. When would she not need IRS permission to change her tax year?

5. Can a sole proprietor use a fiscal tax year for a business if the individual is on a calendar tax year?

6. What tax year options are available to a partnership?

7. Small Company wants to elect a tax year that follows its business cycle, which ends July 20. Is it permitted to do this?

8. If a corporation begins business on June 12, 2015, when may it close its first tax year?

9. What tax year options are available to an S corporation?

10. Must an estate use the calendar year only for its tax year?

11. What is the latest time that an application for a change in accounting period may be filed?

12. Big Co. changed its tax year at midyear. It must annualize its short year to determine its tax liability. What does annualizing a short year mean?

13. In which of the following cases must the taxpayer annualize its income for a period of less than 12 months?
    a. Alpha Corporation was formed on August 17 and decided to report on the calendar year.
    b. Beta Corporation was formed on March 8 and decided to use the fiscal year ending July 31.
    c. Gamma Corporation has been using a fiscal year ending April 30 and changed to a calendar year.
    d. Zeta Corporation, a calendar-year corporation, was liquidated on September 23.

14. What is the definition of "method of accounting"?

15. Code Sec. 446 requires the taxpayer's method of accounting clearly reflects income. What does "clearly reflects income" mean?

16. Name the two most commonly used overall methods of accounting.

17. Thomas is a sole proprietor who uses the cash method of accounting. As such, the constructive receipt rule applies to him. What is the purpose of the constructive receipt rule?

18. When considering the cash versus the accrual method of accounting:
    a. Is there any type of business that must be on the cash method?
    b. Is there any type of business that must be on the accrual method?
    c. What kind of business has a choice?

19. A cash-basis taxpayer generally is allowed a deduction upon payment of business expenses. May it deduct all payments when paid?

20. May the same taxpayer use several different methods of recognizing income simultaneously?

21. Can the IRS require Bill Inc. to change its method of accounting in all circumstances?

22. Generally, what additional indirect production costs incurred in the manufacture of inventory must be capitalized under the uniform capitalization rules that were not required to be capitalized under the full absorption method?

23. Rock Inc. is a manufacturer. It incurred numerous overhead costs this year. How should it treat the costs in determining its inventory?

24. Char Co.'s uses financial accounting practices/methods for tax purposes. Is this practice an automatic defense against a challenge by the IRS that some (all) such practices do not clearly reflect income?

25. Why should an individual not use an installment sale as opposed to a cash sale?

26. Spancer Co. is in the construction business. Can it use the completed contract method to account for its long-term contracts?

27. How are liabilities in excess of basis treated in an installment sale?

PROBLEMS

28 Which entities utilize deductions for adjusted gross income and deductions from adjusted gross income? Why do only these entities use said deductions?

29. A partnership is owned 62 percent by a corporation and 38 percent by an individual. The corporation has a fiscal year ending on September 30. The individual is a calendar-year taxpayer. What is the tax year of the partnership, assuming it does not qualify under the business purpose exception?

30. An S corporation wishes to adopt a fiscal year ending on August 31 because that is the end of its model year. Will the S corporation be given permission to adopt the fiscal year?

31. What are the accounting period options for the following businesses?
    a. C corporation starting business on March 11
    b. Sole proprietorship starting business on May 27 with a proprietor on the calendar-year basis and a natural business year ending January 31
    c. Partnership owned by three calendar-year individuals and a natural business year ending April 15
    d. S corporation with a natural business year ending March 31

32. A partnership has two equal calendar-year partners and is switching from a fiscal year ending on June 30 to a calendar year. If the partnership has $40,000 in net income resulting from the short period, how will each partner report the short period income?

33. Hal is single and in 2015 he obtained IRS permission to change from the calendar year to a fiscal year ended August 31, 2015. Hal earned $70,000 through August 31, 2015 and had $6,000 in itemized deductions during January 1 through August 31, 2015. What is Hal's gross tax liability for the short period?

34. The Light Record Corporation has been on the calendar year since its inception five years ago. It wishes to change to an April 30 natural business year. For 2015, the calendar year of proposed change, Light had a taxable income of $200,000, of which $50,000 was earned from January through April.
    a. What must Light Corporation do to obtain the change in period? When must it do it?
    b. What is the tax liability for the short year?

35. Lyle Inc. is a cash-basis, calendar-year taxpayer. In 2015, it changes to the accrual method of accounting. Its 2015 income computed under the accrual method is $75,000. The following information also is available:

	December 31, 2014	December 31, 2015
Accounts receivable	$27,000	$34,000
Accounts payable	17,000	13,500

What is Lyle's required adjustment to income for 2015 and how should Lyle report it?

36. X Corporation was formed and began operations on September 1, 2015. X Corporation expects to have taxable income of $25,000 each quarter of operations for the first two years. X Corporation is indifferent with respect to its accounting period. What would you suggest regarding initial selection of an accounting period?

37. Wagner Co. is a cash-basis, calendar-year taxpayer. On August 1, 2015, it paid an insurance premium of $4,800 for coverage from August 1, 2015 to July 31, 2016. What is the largest deduction Wagner Co. can take in 2015?

38. Assume the same facts as the problem above except the premium is for coverage from August 1, 2015 to July 31, 2017. What is the largest deduction Wagner Co. can take in 2015?

39. Jennifer uses the cash method. Which of the following transactions result in gross income in the current year?
   a. Car, worth $7,000, received as a consulting fee
   b. $500 of interest credited to his checking account, but not withdrawn
   c. Wages payable from a corporation with ample funds, in which he is a 12 percent shareholder, unpaid at year-end
   d. Stock, worth $20,000, for services rendered, fully vested if Jennifer still works for the corporation in three years
   e. $700 of dental services (bill cancelled upon Jennifer's estate planning advice to the dentist's mother-in-law)
   f. Sale of a used car for a note due in one year, face value $3,000, fair market value $2,500. No elections were made

40. Jen Company decided to change its method of accounting from the cash basis to the accrual basis in 2015 because sale of inventories had become a material income-producing item. Its taxable income for 2015 under the accrual basis was $250,000. It determined that the balances of accounts receivable, inventory, and accounts payable as of December 2014 were:

Accounts receivable	$18,000
Inventory	14,000
Accounts payable	11,000

   a. What is Jen Company's required adjustment due to the change in accounting methods?
   b. What can Jen Company do with the adjustment?

41. Berry Co. started business in 2014. Its ending inventory at actual prices was $150,000 at base-period prices. It uses the simplified dollar-value LIFO inventory method and the price index was 130% in 2014. Its ending inventory at actual prices in 2015 is $180,000 and the price index is 140%. What is Berry Co.'s 2015 ending inventory?

42. Ludlow Inc. started business in 2014. It uses the simplified dollar-value LIFO inventory method. Ending inventories at actual prices are as follows:

Year	Amount
2014	$200,000
2015	220,000
2016	210,000

The price index in 2014, 2015 and 2016 is 120%, 125%, and 130%, respectively. What are the dollar values of its ending inventory in 2015 and 2016?

43. Smith Inc. discovered it had made several math errors during 2015. It wants to correct the errors and is unsure as to whether this would qualify as a major change in accounting method requiring IRS approval. Advise Smith Inc.

44. Wash Company sells washing machines. On January 1, 2015, it had 20 units in inventory, valued at $400 per unit. During 2015, it sold 200 units at $700 per machine. Wash Company purchased 190 units during 2015 at a cost of $420 per unit. Determine Wash Company's gross profit under the FIFO and LIFO methods.

45. Mill Co., a calendar-year manufacturer, which uses the FIFO inventory method, previously allocated production costs to inventory by use of a burden rate based on the ratios of total indirect production costs incurred during the year compared to total direct labor costs during the year. Mill Co. incurred the following costs during the year:

Direct material	$500,000
Direct labor	1,500,000
Indirect costs inventoried under pre-1986 TRA law	1,500,000
Additional costs inventoried under Code Sec. 263A	750,000
Ending Inventory prior to the capitalization of additional Code Sec. 263A costs	700,000

Mill Co. had an inventory turnover rate of five times.

Compute the total amount of additional Code Sec. 263A costs to capitalize for FIFO inventory under the simplified production method.

46. Sugarcane Company incurs handling costs totaling $15 million and purchasing costs of $4 million. Inventoriable general and administrative costs related to handling and purchasing totals $1 million. Purchases for the year are $100 million. Sugarcane Company uses FIFO. Its purchases in ending inventory total $40 million. Compute the total resale costs to be capitalized to ending inventory using the simplified resale method.

47. X Company has four inventory items at year end. Inventory information (based on FIFO) is as follows:

Item	Cost	Market
1	$6,000	$8,000
2	3,000	2,400
3	10,000	9,000
4	4,000	7,000

Determine X Company's ending inventory using the lower-of-cost-or-market method.

48. Sam Co. sells a product whose cost (and sales price) has risen continually. This has produced increases in Sam Co.'s gross receipts and Sam Co. would like to use an inventory method that would minimize its tax liability. Would you recommend specific identification, FIFO, or LIFO? Why?

49. Falzone Inc. uses the dollar-value LIFO method to account for its inventory. Inventory on January 1, 2015, was $30,000 at base-year prices. Inventory on December 31, 2015, was $63,000 at actual prices and $50,000 at base-year prices. Determine Falzone's ending inventory using dollar-value LIFO.

50. Mar Co. is a construction company. In 2015, it entered into a two-year contract to construct a building for $3,000,000. It estimated that actual costs will be $2,500,000. Actual costs in 2015 are $1,500,000. In 2016, actual costs are $800,000. What income does Mar Co. report in 2015 and 2016 under the completed contract and percentage-of-completion methods?

51. Steve sold for $200,000 his undivided one-third interest in an apartment building in which he had a $30,000 adjusted basis. The buyer put $40,000 down, assumed Steve's share of the mortgage, and signed an installment obligation with a face value of $120,000. $20,000 of the principal was paid at the end of the year of sale. Compute the following:
    a. Contract price
    b. Gross profit and gross profit percentage
    c. Payment in year of sale
    d. Gain in the year of sale

52. Do either of the transactions below qualify for installment reporting? If not, why not?
    a. Credit sales of dealer inventory
    b. Credit sales of property not held as inventory

53. $20 million of nondealer real estate obligations arose in and are outstanding at the end of calendar-year 2015. Deferred gross profit on such installment obligations equals $5 million. Assume that the highest tax rate applicable in 2015 is 28 percent and the interest rate for December 2015 is 7 percent. Compute the amount of interest to be paid for 2015 on the amount of deferred gross profit, assuming the property was used in a trade or business.

54. Brice sells a piece of raw land with a basis of $10,000 which he has owned for years as an investment. What are the tax consequences to Brice, a cash-basis taxpayer, for the following consideration received:
    a. Cash of $30,000
    b. Motel worth $50,000, subject to $20,000 of liabilities
    c. Installment note due in one year without interest with a face value of $30,000 and a fair market value of $27,000
    d. Same as (c), but Brice elects out of installment reporting

55. Joe England sold equipment on May 10, 2014 for $100,000. He bought the equipment on November 7, 2012 for $140,000, and accumulated depreciation at the date of sale was $60,000. Joe collected $50,000 in 2014 and will collect $50,000 in 2015. Joe used the installment method for the sale. What is Joe's recognized gain in 2014 and 2015?

56. Assume the same facts as the problem above except the selling price is $180,000 and Joe will collect $90,000 in 2014 and 2015.
    a. What is Joe's recognized gain in 2014 and 2015?
    b. Go to irs.gov and print the most-recent form 6252. Complete form 6252 for 2014's income tax filing purposes.

57. Adjustments due to a change in accounting method do not include which of the following:
    a. Taken into account in the year of change
    b. Spread over four years starting with the year of change
    c. Spread over four years starting in the year of change only if a negative adjustment
    d. None of the above

58. In 2015, Bob will sell land that he bought in 2005 for $50,000 to Tom. The selling price is $250,000. Tom has given Bob two options for the sale. Under option 1, Bob would receive the $250,000 at the date of sale. Under option 2, Bob would receive $125,000 at sale date and $125,000 one year later (in 2016). Tom also would pay Bob $8,750 interest in 2016 (at the time he pays the remaining $125,000 to Bob). Bob's overall tax rate is 35% and the land is a capital asset to Bob. Bob uses a 5% after-tax discount rate for all his investment decisions. Which option should Bob take?
    a. Option 1
    b. Option 2
    c. Neither, Bob is indifferent

59. Jessica sold an apartment building, in which she had a $400,000 adjusted basis, for $1,100,000. The buyer paid $150,000 down, assumed Jessica's mortgage, and signed an installment obligation with a face value of $500,000. $50,000 of principal was paid at the end of the year of sale. Jessica's contract price, gross profit percentage, and payment in the year of sale are:
    a. $550,000, 100 percent, and $200,000
    b. $700,000, 100 percent, and $200,000
    c. $700,000, 100 percent, and $250,000
    d. $1,100,000, 60 percent, and $200,000

60. In 2015, Chris sold a painting to Bernie for $40,000. Chris received $10,000 in 2015 and will receive $30,000 in 2016. Chris's bought the painting in 2011 for $15,000. Bernie did not pay Chris $30,000 when it was due, and after numerous attempts to collect (and $1,000 in expenses), Chris repossessed the paining in 2016. The painting was worth $45,000 when repossessed.

What is Chris's recognized gain in 2015?
a. $25,000
b. $10,000
c. $6,250

What are the results of the repossession to Chris?
a. $45,000 LTCG; basis = $45,000
b. $33,750 LTCG; basis = $45,000
c. $33,750 LTCG; basis = $44,000
d. $32,750 LTCG; basis = $45,000

61. Which of the following is not considered "constructive receipt" of income?
a. X was informed its check for services rendered was available on December 20, 2015, but it waited until January 21, 2016, to pick up the check.
b. Earned income of X was received by its agent on December 30, 2015, but not received by X until January 6, 2016.
c. X received a check on December 30, 2015, for services rendered, but was unable to make a deposit until January 3, 2016.
d. A payment on the sale of real property was placed in an escrow account on December 20, 2015, but not received by X until January 13, 2016, when the transaction closed.

62. Xeno Corporation purchased supplies from Kimbo Company in 2015. The total invoice was for $20,000, but Xeno claimed that only one-half of the order was received and paid only $10,000 in 2015. Both parties honestly disputed the bill and Xeno refused to pay the contested amount. They went to court and a judgment requiring Xeno to pay an additional $5,000 was issued in 2016. How should Xeno report this expense?
a. $10,000 in 2015 and $5,000 in 2016
b. $15,000 in 2015
c. $15,000 in 2016
d. $20,000 in 2015 and $5,000 of income in 2016
e. None of the above

63. Bevin Inc. uses the FIFO method for valuing inventory. Its inventory purchases in 2015 totaled $5,000,000 and its ending inventory on December 31, 2015 is $2,000,000 (before the Code Sec. 263A cost allocation). It incurred the following costs in 2015:

Item	Amount
Storage	$190,000
Purchasing	200,000
Handling	80,000
Labor costs for the above items	150,000
Mixed services	220,000

Total labor costs excluding amounts in the mixed service costs are $4,000,000. What is the value of Bevin Inc.'s ending inventory?
a. $2,470,000
b. $2,191,300
c. $2,008,250
d. $2,000,000

64. X uses the LIFO method in computing its inventory. It had 1,000 units on hand at the end of 2016. Based on the following information, what is the value of its ending inventory on December 31, 2016?

    Beginning inventory: 500 units with a per-unit cost of $2.00 and a per-unit market value of $3.00

    Purchases: September 25, 2016, 1,500 units with a per-unit cost of $3.00 and a per-unit market value of $3.00. November 12, 2016, 1,000 units with a per-unit cost of $4.00 and a per-unit value of $4.00.
    a. $2,500
    b. $3,000
    c. $4,000
    d. $5,000

65. Y uses the FIFO method in computing its inventory. On January 1, 2016, its beginning inventory of 3,500 units consisted of the following:

    1,000 purchased April 10, 2015, at $1.00 per unit
    2,000 purchased June 23, 2015, at $2.00 per unit
    500 purchase July 11, 2015, at $3.00 per unit

    During 2016, Y purchased the following units:

    3,000 purchased September 1, 2016, at $4.00 per unit
    1,000 purchased December 16, 2016, at $5.00 per unit

    During 2016, it sold 2,300 units. What is the value of its ending inventory?
    a. $13,300
    b. $15,300
    c. $19,900
    d. $22,900
    e. None of the above

66. Richard sold a rare automobile he had held as an investment in 2014. Richard purchased the automobile in 1989; its adjusted basis at the time of the sale was $70,000, and the selling price was $250,000. Richard received $50,000 in 2014 and was to receive $50,000 per year plus interest in each of the four succeeding years. On January 5, 2016, Richard sold the installment obligation (he did not receive an installment payment in 2015) for $145,000. Richard's gain on the sale of the installment obligation in 2016 is:
    a. $42,000
    b. $72,000
    c. $103,000
    d. $108,000
    e. $150,000

67. John sold a painting in February 2015 for $40,000. He received $10,000 in February and was to receive $15,000 in 2016 and 2017, plus interest. He purchased the painting in 2005 for $15,000, and its basis at time of sale was $15,000. The buyer defaulted on the obligation on January 1, 2016, and John repossessed the painting. He incurred no costs to repossess the painting, and its fair market value at repossession date was $39,000. John's recognized gain on the repossession is:
    a. $6,250
    b. $11,250
    c. $25,000
    d. $27,750
    e. $39,000

68. John's basis in the painting in problem 67 is:
    a. $0
    b. $25,000
    c. $30,000
    d. $39,000
    e. $42,250

69. **Comprehensive Problem.** Bill is a cash-basis, calendar-year taxpayer. Which of the following December items result in gross income or deductions for the current year?
    a. Check received for December rent, $700, not deposited until January 4
    b. Check for $1,100 to pay Bill's state income taxes mailed December 28, cashed January 7
    c. Cash received in the amount of $500 for services to be rendered the following year
    d. Interest of $800 credited to his savings account, added to Bill's account balance
    e. Check received for January rent, $700, deposited on January 9
    f. Charitable contribution of $300, charged on Bill's MasterCard
    g. Bills totaling $2,000 sent for services rendered during the year, uncollected as of year-end

70. **Comprehensive Problem.** Do any of the transactions below qualify for installment reporting? If not, why not?
    a. Sale of property in December, with payment received in full the following January at a gain
    b. Sale of property at a loss, payments to be received in equal annual installments over seven years
    c. Exchange of like-kind investment property where the transfer took place in two different years
    d. Sale in one year at a gain, 90 percent of the proceeds received immediately, the remaining 10 percent in year two
    e. Sale of securities at a gain, the proceeds being 13 percent a year of current fair market value to be received over the life of the seller
    f. Sale of stock with zero basis for 10 percent of the gross life of the gross sales of a business for 11 years

71. **Research Problem.** A manufacturer of pollution control facilities reported its profits on the completed-contract method. To value its raw materials and work in process, the taxpayer used the LIFO method, thus "having it both ways" (i.e., deferring profits and maximizing the cost of goods sold). The IRS claimed that the two methods are mutually exclusive and that the costs of materials, labor, supplies, etc. are to be treated as deferred expenditures, deductible only when the contracts are completed. Is the IRS correct? (See *Peninsular Steel Products & Equipment Co., Inc.,* 78 TC 1029, Dec. 39,113 (1982).)

72. **Research Problem.** John Smythe has a margin account with Investit Investment Company. The stocks and bonds in the account earned dividends and interest of $10,000 in 2015. The $10,000 was paid directly to the margin account and used for reinvestment purposes only. Smythe received a substitute Form 1099-DIV which indicated the composition of the $10,000. However, Smythe did not report the $10,000 as income in 2015. He reported it as income in 2016 when he closed the margin account. The IRS has indicated that Smythe must include the $10,000 in 2015, and in addition to taxes has assessed interest and penalties. Smythe seeks your advice. (See, for example, *A.L. Christoffersen,* 84-2 USTC ¶9990, 749 F.2d 513 (CA-8 1984).)

14

Deferred Compensation and Education Savings Plans

OBJECTIVES

After completing Chapter 14, you should be able to:

1. Identify the key differences between qualified and nonqualified deferred compensation plans.
2. Explain the hurdles that must be cleared in order to achieve tax deferral status for qualified deferred compensation plans.
3. Explain the specific rules governing the timing and amount of distributions from qualified deferred compensation plans.
4. Explain how contributions to qualified deferred compensation plans are taxed.
5. Explain how distributions from qualified deferred compensation plans are taxed.
6. Identify the basic types of qualified deferred compensation plans that employers can sponsor and describe their features.
7. Identify the deferred compensation plans available to self-employed taxpayers and describe their features.
8. Distinguish between traditional and Roth IRAs and explain how they operate and are taxed.
9. Understand how nonqualified deferred compensation plans are set up to achieve tax advantages similar to those offered by qualified deferred compensation plans.
10. Identify vehicles available for educational savings and describe their features.

OVERVIEW

Investing For The Future: The Grocery Store Analogy.

An analogy can be drawn between grocery shopping and investing for future consumption.
Identifying The "Goods" To Buy. The starting point might be to select the "goods/investments" to buy such as the sample listed in the table below:

	Fruit:	Vegetables:	Cereal:	Coffee:	Soup:	Bread:
Identify the Food to Buy →	Apples, Oranges, etc,	Carrots, Celery, etc.	Fiber, Frosted, etc.	Freeze-dried, Instant, etc.	Vegetable, Tomato, etc.	Rye, Wheat, etc.

	Stocks:	Treasury Securities:	Corporate Bonds:	Real Estate:	Commodities:	Highly Liquid Cash Equivalents:
Identify the Investments to Buy → (this is a mere glimpse into the thousands of possibilities)	S&P 500, Russell 3000, Industry-specific (e.g., consumer staples, utilities), Geographic-specific (e.g., Pacific rim, Latin America), Risk specific (e.g., aggressive growth stocks, "blue chips"), Dividend specific (e.g., high yield stocks) Market-size specific (e.g., emerging markets), etc.	T-Bills, T-Notes, T-Bonds, I-Bonds, EE- Bonds, TIPS etc.	Risk Specific, Term Specific, etc.	Equity REITS, Mortgage REITS, Hybrid REITS	Foreign Currencies, Natural Resources, Industrial Metals Precious Metals, Grains, etc.	Interest-Bearing Time Deposits, Interest-Bearing Demand Deposits, etc.

Selecting The "Store." Once the goods/investments are identified, a specific "store" might be selected. Any brokerage company, bank, mutual fund management company, savings and loan association, or insurance company that is IRS-approved may be selected. Code Sec. 408(a) & (b). A short list of possible "stores" (grocers & financial institutions) is shown below.

Select the grocery store →	Kroger	Whole Foods	Costco	Farmers Market	Wal-Mart	7-Eleven
Select the financial institution →	Fidelity	Bank of America	Vanguard	1st Federal S&L	E-Trade	Prudential

Choosing The Best "Store-Shelf Packaging." When buying the "goods" identified above, the manner in which the goods are "packaged" is often an important consideration. Investment "packaging" alternatives include *mutual funds, exchange-traded funds (ETFs), money market funds, bank certificates of deposit (bank CDs), savings accounts* and *annuity contracts.* Mutual funds and ETFs are "bundles" of targeted investments such as publicly-traded stocks, corporate bonds, treasury securities, commodities and Real Estate Investment Trusts (REITs). A sample of "packaging" types is shown below:

Choose the Type of Food Packaging →	Cans	Plastic wrappers	Cartons	Jugs	Jars	Rubber bands
Choose the Type of Investment "Packaging" →	Mutual Funds	Exchange-Traded Funds	Money Market Funds	Bank Certificates of Deposit	Savings Accounts	Annuity Contracts

Choosing The Best "Check-Out Carrier." The manner in which the food packages will be carried to the car may be another important consideration. The cashier at a check-out line might ask, "Paper or plastic?" For example, corn purchased at, say, Krogers, whether packaged in pressurized cans, frozen boxes or banded bundles, might be carried out in *paper bags, plastic bags* or *boxes.* Similarly, investments such as S&P 500 stocks, purchased at, say, Schwab, whether "packaged" in mutual funds or ETFs, might be carried in *tax-deferred, tax-free* or *taxable* accounts:

Choose the Best "Check-Out Carrier" →	Paper			Plastic	Box
	Tax Deferred Accounts			Tax-Free Accounts	Taxable Accounts
Choose the Best Investment "Carrier" →	**Employer-Sponsored Plans:**	**Educational Savings Plans:**			
	401(k) plan, 403(b) plan, Employee stock ownership plan (ESOP), Solo 401(k) plan (for self-employed taxpayers or single-employee entities) Keogh plan, Simplified employee pension (SEP) IRA, Savings incentive match plan ("SIMPLE") Nonqualified employer-sponsored plans	529 Plans Coverdell Savings Account	Traditional IRA	Roth IRA Roth 401(k) Roth 403(b)	Any account maintained at a financial institution that generates interest income, dividend income and/or capital gains that are currently taxable

Buying The "Goods." Both grocery store purchases and direct contributions into retirement or educational plans for the purpose of investment purchases must be made in U.S. dollars (using cash, check, credit card or debit card).

The focus of this chapter is directed mainly toward the advantages of *tax-deferred* and *tax-free* accounts and the rules for holding investments in these two broad types of "investment carriers." Qualified and nonqualified retirement plans for employees and the self-employed are discussed, as well as individual retirement accounts (IRAs), including Roth IRAs. While education savings plans are not forms of deferred compensation, they are treated in this chapter of the book because they also enjoy tax deferral on the earnings from the contributions.

Employer-Sponsored Deferred Compensation Plans: "Qualified" and "Nonqualified"

¶14,001   ## QUALIFIED EMPLOYER-SPONSORED PLANS

Qualified deferred compensation plans (QPs) are employer-sponsored plans that satisfy certain requirements in order to qualify for special tax benefits.

Qualifying Requirements

An employer-sponsored qualified plan must satisfy the following types of requirements:

1. *Nondiscrimination.* The plan cannot discriminate in favor of highly compensated employees. Code Sec. 401(a)(4).
2. *Distribution rules.* Distributions made too soon may be subject to a 10 percent penalty. If made too late and/or too little in amount, a 50 percent penalty may be imposed on the recipient.
3. *Limitation on annual employee compensation.* For most employer-sponsored retirement plans in which employer and employee contributions are based on percentages of compensation, such compensation amount is limited to $265,000 in 2015. Code Sec. 401(a)(17).
4. *Limitation on annual contributions.* Specified limits may apply to how much employees and employers can contribute to defined contribution plans. Code Sec. 415.
5. *Limitation on annual benefits.* Specified limits may apply to the amount of annual retirement benefits paid out of defined benefit plans. Code Sec. 412.
6. *Independence of trustee.* For most employer-sponsored retirement plans, retirement funds must be held in a trust managed by an independent trustee. *Exceptions include Keogh plans for self-employed taxpayers.*
7. *Participation and coverage.* Employees meeting certain minimum age and service requirements must be eligible to participate in an employer-sponsored retirement plan. In addition, the plan must generally cover at least 70 percent of eligible employees on a nondiscriminatory basis. Code Sec. 410.

8. *Written and continuous plan.* The plan must be in writing and constitute a continuous program.
9. *Vesting.* An employee's nonforfeitable right to receive future benefits must take effect within a prescribed time frame. Code Sec. 411.
10. *Exclusive benefit of employees.* The plan must be created and operated for the exclusive benefit of the employee/participants and isolated from potential misfortunes of the employer.

Most of these requirements were enacted in 1974 with the passage of the Employee Retirement Income Security Act (ERISA) which overhauled the rules governing QPs. The ERISA requirements governing QPs such as 401(k) plans, 403(b) annuity contracts, and Keogh plans are complex and detailed. However, easier-to-administer QPs became available after 1974. For example, the Revenue Act of 1978 added Simplified Employee Pension Plans (SEP IRAs), the Small Business Job Protection Act of 1996 added the Savings Incentive Match Plan for Employees (SIMPLE IRAs), and the Economic Growth and Tax Relief Reconciliation Act of 2001 added the solo 401(k) effective January 1, 2002, and the Roth 401(k) effective January 1, 2006.

Tax Benefits of Qualified Plans

The tax law encourages QPs by providing several tax benefits including the following:

1. *Contributions may be tax deferred.* Taxation of contribution amounts are generally postponed until they are distributed to participants.
2. *Deductions are immediately available to employers.* Corporate employers, self-employed taxpayers, or individuals (for IRAs) may deduct contributions even though income tax is deferred. For all plans except IRA's, the contribution may create an NOL.
3. *Income may be tax deferred.* Interest, dividends, and other income can accumulate tax free until benefits are paid. (With Roth 401(k) plans, accumulated income can be tax-free forever.)
4. *Future payouts may be subject to lower tax rates.* Tax benefits are typically paid out after retirement when the employee's effective tax rate is often lower.
5. *Payroll tax exemption may apply.* Employer contributions (but not employee contributions) are exempt from FICA and FUTA taxes when paid in and paid out of a QP.
6. *Portability option may be available.* Generally, transfers between QPs and from QPs to traditional IRAs are tax-free, thereby permitting extended tax deferral.
7. *Credit to employers for startup costs may be available.* Small employers may be entitled to receive a credit for some of the costs of establishing new QPs (see Chapter 9 ¶9045).
8. *Credit to employees for contributions to a QP may be available.* Low to middle income employees may be entitled to receive a saver's credit for elective contributions to a QP (see Chapter 9 ¶9033).

Nontax Benefits of Qualified Plans

Most QPs also have the following nontax features:

1. *Bankruptcy protection.* Plan assets are protected from the employer, employer creditors, and employee creditors. *(O.J. Simpson receives $25,000 monthly from his pension plan despite losing a $36 million judgment to the Goldman family.)*
2. *Employment incentive.* QPs can be used to attract and retain employees;
3. *Loan option available to employees.* Participants may be permitted to borrow up to $50,000 from their QPs.

¶14,015　NONQUALIFIED EMPLOYER-SPONSORED PLANS

Nonqualified Employer-Sponsored Plans (NPs) may be useful as part of an employee compensation package designed to provide executives and middle management employees with special incentives in excess of those allowed under the QP rules. According to the ERISA Industry Committee, approximately 92 percent of Fortune 1000 companies maintain NPs. Some of the more common types of NPs discussed in this chapter are listed below.

- Rabbi Trusts,
- Employee stock purchase plans,
- Incentive stock options,
- Nonqualified stock options,
- Restricted stock,
- Variable annuity contracts,
- Informal short-term arrangements.

NPs share the same fundamental goal as QPs: the deferral of tax. However, certain features of NPs are generally regarded as favorable or unfavorable as they relate to QPs.

Favorable Features of Nonqualifed Plans

Nonqualified plans have the following favorable features:

- *More flexibility in choosing who participates.* NPs are not subject to the same minimum coverage and nondiscrimination requirements as QPs. Therefore, an NP can be designed to cover a limited group of employees.
- *Unlimited benefits.* An NP can provide benefits in excess of those permitted under QP limits.

Unfavorable Features of Nonqualifed Plans

Nonqualified plans have the following unfavorable features:

- *Limited deferral of NP benefits.* For most NPs, tax deferral on employee compensation can be achieved only under either of two conditions: (1) the employer's obligation to pay the benefits remains merely an unfunded and unsecured promise to pay; or (2) the employer's obligation is funded or secured but the employee must bear a substantial risk of losing amounts contributed to the plan.
- *No immediate tax deduction.* An employer is not entitled to a tax deduction until such time as the benefits are actually paid to the employee. As previously explained, employer contributions into most QPs are currently deductible by the employer.
- *Payroll tax on employer contributions.* Unlike QPs, for NPs, employer contributions are generally subject to Social Security and Medicare taxes when services are performed or, if later, when a person's right to receive the compensation no longer is subject to a substantial risk of forfeiture. Code Sec. 3121(v).

Basic Types of Employer-Sponsored Qualified Retirement Plans

¶14,101   DEFINED CONTRIBUTION PLANS

One of the two basic types of employer-sponsored qualified retirement plans is a defined contribution plan.

With a "defined contribution plan," an individual account is established for each participant, and contributions are made to the account. Contributions may be made by employers and/or employees. Typically, an employer will contribute a specified percentage of an employee's compensation (up to a specified amount) and/or permit an employee to contribute a specified percentage of the employee's compensation (up to a specified amount).

No specific amount of retirement benefits is promised. Instead, the amount of benefits that a participant receives will depend upon the amount contributed to the participant's account and the amount of income, expenses, gains, losses, and any forfeitures of accounts of other participants that are allocated to the participant's account. Code Sec. 414(i).

Amounts contributed to an employee's account are invested on the employee's behalf. Unlike a defined benefit plan, investment risk is borne by plan participants, not the employer. If plan assets are invested poorly, the plan participant's retirement benefits will be reduced. Employers are not required to make up for any poor investment performance.

The basic types of defined contribution plans are:

1. Profit-sharing plans.
2. Money purchase pension plans.
3. Stock bonus plans.
4. Employee stock ownership plans (ESOPs).
5. 401(k) plans.
6. Savings incentive match plans for employees (SIMPLE plans).
7. Simplified employee pension (SEP) plans.
8. Qualified annuity plans [403(a) plans], which also may be structured as defined benefit plans.
9. 403(b) plans (tax-sheltered annuity plans).

¶14,110   DEFINED BENEFIT PLANS

The second of the two basic types of employer-sponsored qualified retirement plans is a defined benefit plan (also referred to as a "pension plan"). The Code defines a "defined benefit plan" as any plan that is not a defined contribution plan. Code Sec. 414(j).

For a "defined benefit plan" to be a qualified retirement plan, it must be established and maintained by an employer primarily to provide systematically for the payment of definitely determinable benefits to its employees over a period of years, usually for life, after retirement. Retirement benefits generally are measured by, and based on, such factors as years of service and compensation received by the employees. The determination of the amount of retirement benefits and contributions to provide such benefits cannot be dependent on an employer's profits. Reg. §1.401(a)-1(b)(1). Whenever the amount of any benefit is to be determined on the basis of actuarial assumptions, those assumptions must be specified in the plan in a way that precludes employer discretion. Code Sec. 401(a)(25).

EXAMPLE 14.1	Delta Corporation has a defined benefit plan providing that a retired employee will receive 1% of his or her average salary for the last three years of employment for every year of service with the employer. Kelly Scollard retired after 20 years of service. Her average salary for the last three years of her employment was $50,000. Kelly's retirement benefit will be $10,000 (20 × 1% × $50,000 = $10,000) per year.

How much money an employer must contribute to a plan is calculated actuarially. The amount of money that an employer must contribute each year depends on assumptions made about how much money will be needed to fund the plan's obligations to plan participants and the rate of return that can be earned on amounts contributed to the plan. Investment risk is borne by the employer, not the plan participants. If the return on a plan's investments is less than projected, the employer will have to make up the difference.

Exhibit 1. COMPARISON OF DEFINED CONTRIBUTION & DEFINED BENEFIT PLANS

	Defined Contribution Plans (DCPs)	Defined Benefit Plans (DBPs)
Contributions	(a) Fixed percentages; or (b) Flat dollar amounts.	Determined actuarially based on defined benefits.
Contribution Limit	Lesser of: (1) = $53,000 in 2015, or (2) = 100% employee's gross compensation (25% for profit sharing, money purchase, or stock bonus plans). (Note: This limit applies to the aggregate of employer and employee contributions, as well as forfeitures allocated to the employee's account.)	N/A
Benefits	The final benefits depend upon investment performance of the trust account. Upon retirement, an employee is entitled to the account balance, either as a lump-sum or an annuity.	The final benefit is a fixed and pre-determinable lump-sum or annuity.
Benefit Limit	N/A	Lesser of: = $210,000 in 2015 = Average salary for highest 3 years of employment (Adjustments based on age, years' participation or years' employment may be required.)
Forfeitures	Increase employee benefits, or Reduce future contributions by employer.	Must reduce future contributions by employer. (Forfeitures cannot increase employee benefits.)
Ideal Employee Targets	More favorable for younger employees since, over a longer period of time, higher benefits may result.	More favorable for older employees at the time the plan is adopted since it is possible to fund higher benefits over a shorter period.
Complexity	Less than DBPs	Require greater reporting requirements and more actuarial and administrative costs. (This explains why (a) it is impractical for many small businesses and (b) there has been a massive shift away from DBPs over the past decade.)

¶14,115 PROFIT-SHARING PLANS

A profit sharing plan is a defined contribution plan that provides for employee participation in the company's profits. Contributions are paid from the employer's current or accumulated profits to a trustee and are commingled in a single trust fund. Separate trust accounts are maintained for each participant. Payments are distributable after certain events, such as: layoffs, illness, number of years' employment, or age. A profit sharing plan may include a 401(k) plan (discussed in ¶14,401).

Meaning of "Profit-sharing"

Employer contributions may depend on profits; however, the term "profit sharing" is a misnomer. An employer may make contributions even though it has no profits, and it may make no contributions even though it has profits. However, merely making a single or occasional contribution out of profits does not establish a profit-sharing plan. Contributions to a plan must be substantial and recurring. Code Sec. 401(a)(27); Reg. §1.401-1(b).

Aggregate Annual Limit on Employee/Employer Contributions

The maximum annual contribution to an account may not exceed the lesser of:

1. $53,000 in 2015; or
2. 25% gross compensation *[not the 100% limit available for 401(k) plans]*.

Forfeitures Applied

An employee, whose employment has been terminated before a statutory vesting period, may forfeit all or a portion of employer contributions made on their behalf. Employers can elect to apply the amounts forfeited toward increased benefits or reduced employer contributions in the future. These rules are similar to the rules governing defined contribution plans. However, with defined benefit plans, forfeitures cannot be used to increase employee benefits; rather, they must reduce future contributions by the employer.

Ideal Participant

For *younger* employees profit-sharing plans may be more favorable than defined benefit pension plans because:

- over a longer period, higher benefits may result,
- forfeitures may be allocated to remaining plan participants, and
- higher benefits may result over a longer period of time, due to the forfeitures.

¶14,120 STOCK BONUS PLANS

A stock bonus plan is another form of defined contribution plan that must generally follow the same rules as a profit-sharing plan except that distributed benefits usually are in the form of employer's stock. Reg. §1.401-1(b)(1)(iii). If stock is distributed, the tax on its appreciation is deferred until its taxable sale. As with profit sharing plans, there must be a definite predetermined formula for allocating contributions among participants, but no formula for determining the amount of overall contributions is required. Reg. §1.401-1(b)(1)(iii). Also, the aggregate annual limit on employee/employer contributions is the same as for profit sharing plans.

Advantages of Stock Bonus Plans

Some employers favor stock bonus plans for the following reasons:

1. No cash flow drain on the corporation since it usually contributes its own stock rather than cash. The stock is either (a) unissued stock or (b) treasury stock (stock purchased by the corporation on the open market).
2. The corporation may deduct the market value of the stock, with no gain or loss recognized by the employer on the excess market value over cost.
3. If employer contributions consist of stock, the tax on its appreciation is deferred until its taxable sale. Distributable fractional shares may be paid in cash which is taxable upon distribution.

¶14,125   EMPLOYEE STOCK OWNERSHIP PLANS (ESOPS)

An ESOP is a stock bonus trust that is tax exempt under Code Sec. 401(a). Technically, it is a defined contribution plan that is either:

- A qualified stock bonus plan; or,
- A stock bonus and money purchase plan.

An ESOP must invest primarily in employer securities.

Distinction Between ESOPs and Stock Bonus Plans

Unlike stock bonus plans, ESOPs are used as financing vehicles by employers. In fact, the ESOP is the only form of qualified employer-sponsored plan which is permitted to borrow funds to acquire employer stock. The ESOP trust borrows funds to purchase employer stock. The loan is secured by the stock and typically guaranteed by the employer. The loan is repaid through annual *employer* contributions and the stock is then assigned to employee participants. The participants are entitled to the full value of their accounts after retirement.

How ESOPs Work

The following example illustrates how a typical ESOP works:

1. An employer sets up an independent trust to manage the ESOP.
2. The employer issues stock valued at, say, $1 million and sells it to the ESOP for a $1 million demand note.
3. The ESOP borrows $1 million from a bank, pledging stock as collateral. The employer guarantees the bank loan.
4. The ESOP pays off the employer demand note with the bank loan proceeds. *At this point, the employer has received $1 million in tax-free cash and the ESOP owns $1 million of stock, offset by the bank loan.*
5. The employer makes tax-deductible contributions to the ESOP that are used to pay down the bank loan plus interest. *If the employer's taxable income before the deduction was less than the contribution amount, an NOL results, which may be carried back 2 years and carried forward 20 years. Thus, if up to $1 million taxable income had been reported for the two immediately preceding years, an immediate refund of up to $350,000 (35%) would be possible.*
6. The ESOP pays off the bank loan.
7. The ESOP now owns the stock free and clear for the exclusive benefit of the employees.

Aggregate Annual Limit on Employee/Employer Contributions

The maximum annual contribution to an ESOP account may not exceed the lesser of:

1. = $53,000 in 2015; or
2. = 100% gross compensation *(not the 25% limit available for stock bonus plans).*

¶14,130   MONEY PURCHASE PENSION PLANS

A money purchase plan is a defined contribution qualified plan under which the employer must make definitely determinable contributions to the account of each participant in the plan each year.

Determination of Employer Contributions

Under a money purchase plan, the employer must make yearly contributions using a definitely determinable formula. Thus, unlike a profit-sharing plan, an employer's annual contributions are fixed and not based on profits. Reg. §1.401-1(b)(1)(i). For example, under a money purchase plan, the plan may require that the employer contribute five percent of each participating employee's wages, regardless of whether the employer shows a profit for the year.

Determination of Benefits Payable

In general, the benefits payable under a money purchase plan, like any other defined contribution plan, are based on the account balance of the employee at the time the benefit payments are to begin. The account balance equals the amount of employer contributions and forfeitures, if any, that are allocated to the employer's account, employee contributions, plus the net earnings received by the fund holder.

Qualified Plan Requirements

¶14,201 ## SOURCES OF LEGISLATIVE AUTHORITY

In order to be "qualified," a plan must meet several complex and detailed requirements. More than 30 provisions are listed under Code Sec. 401(a), many of which lead into the more detailed provisions from Code Sec. 401 through Code Sec. 418E. The chart below serves as a guide to some of the more significant sections of the Code relating to qualified plans that are covered in this chapter.

Major Code Secs. Dealing with Qualified Plans:	
Code Sec.	Area of Coverage
401	Requirements for Qualification
402, 403, 72	Taxation of the Beneficiary
404	Employer's Deduction for Contributions
410	Participation Requirements
411	Vesting Requirements
412	Funding Requirements
413	Collectively Bargained & Multiemployer Plans
414	Definitions and Special Rules
415	Contribution and Benefit Limitations
416	Special Rules for Top-Heavy Plans
417	Survivor Annuity Requirements
418	Special Rules for Multiemployer Plans
501	Tax Exemption of the Trust
4971-5	Penalty Provisions
6057-8	Registration and Information Requirements

¶14,205 ## NONDISCRIMINATION REQUIREMENTS

Contributions and benefits provided under a qualified deferred compensation plan must not discriminate in favor of highly compensated employees. Code Sec. 401(a)(4).

An employee is a "highly compensated employee" if the employee satisfies either of the following tests (Code Sec. 414(q)):

1. The employee was a five-percent owner at any time during the year or the preceding year. If the employer is a corporation, a five-percent owner is any person who owns (or is considered as owning under the constructive ownership rules of Code Sec. 318) more than five percent of the outstanding stock of the corporation or stock possessing more than five percent of the total combined voting power of all of the corporation's stock. If the employer is not a corporation, a five-percent owner is any person who owns more than five percent of the capital or profits interest in the employer.
2. For the preceding year, the employee had compensation in excess of $120,000 (for 2015). At the employer's election, the employee also may be required to be among the top 20 percent of employees in compensation for that preceding year.

EXAMPLE 14.2

Audrey Jackson's annual compensation at Art Classics, Inc. was $160,000, but she was not among the top 20 percent of employees in terms of compensation. Even though Audrey is relatively highly paid, she may, at her employer's election, be excluded from the group of highly compensated employees.

For a plan to satisfy the nondiscrimination requirements, it must satisfy each of the following requirements (Reg. §1.401(a)(4)-1(b)):

1. Either the contributions or benefits provided under the plan must be nondiscriminatory in amount. It need not be shown that both the contributions and benefits provided are nondiscriminatory in amount.

2. All benefits, rights, and features provided under the plan must be available in a nondiscriminatory manner.
3. The timing of plan amendments must not have the effect of discriminating significantly in favor of highly compensated employees.

A plan will not be considered discriminatory merely because the contributions or benefits of, or on behalf of, the employees under the plan bear a uniform relationship to the compensation of the employees.

EXAMPLE 14.3	AJR Inc.'s qualified plan provides for the allocation of employer contributions based upon a flat rate of four percent of each employee's compensation. Nathaniel and Micaela's annual compensation is equal to $20,000 and $200,000, respectively. The plan would not be discriminatory even though Micaela's trust account would receive an $8,000 employer contribution (4% × $200,000) while Nathaniel's would receive only $800 (4% × $20,000).

Moreover, a qualified plan will not be considered discriminatory merely because the plan takes the employer's share of the Social Security tax or employer-derived Social Security benefits into account in determining its contribution or benefits formula. Such an arrangement is called social security integration.

¶14,215   LIMITATIONS ON CONTRIBUTIONS TO A DEFINED CONTRIBUTION PLAN

The annual additions to a defined contribution plan cannot exceed the lesser of the following amounts (Code Secs. 401(a)(16), 415(a), and (c)):

1. $53,000 (for 2015); or
2. 100 percent of the participant's compensation (earned income in the case of a self-employed individual). The annual compensation of each employee taken into account under the plan for any year may not exceed $265,000 (for 2015).

EXAMPLE 14.4	Bert Richards participates in his employer's qualified retirement plan, which provides a 10 percent employer contribution formula. Bert's annual compensation is equal to $1,060,000. The employer may contribute only 2.5 percent of this compensation into Bert's retirement plan account due to the $265,000 annual compensation limit [2.5% = (10% × $265,000) ÷ $1,060,000].

The "annual addition" is the sum for any year of the following amounts:

1. Employer contributions.
2. Employee contributions. Employee contributions do not include rollover contributions or employee contributions to a simplified employee pension that are excludable from gross income.
3. Forfeitures.

A participant's compensation includes any elective deferrals and any amount not included in the participant's income by reason of Code Secs. 125 (salary reduction contributions made to a cafeteria plan), 132(f)(4) (qualified transportation fringe benefits), or 457 (elective contributions to a deferred compensation plan of a state or local government or tax-exempt organization). In the case of a tax-deferred annuity plan, the term "participant's compensation" is the amount of compensation received from the employer that is includible in gross income (determined without regard to the foreign earned income exclusion or foreign housing cost exclusion or deduction), plus any elective deferrals and any amount not included in the participant's income by reason of Code Secs. 125, 132(f)(4), or 457, but not including any amount contributed by the employer for an annuity contract.

A self-employed individual's earned income is the individual's net earnings from self-employment with respect to a trade or business offering the plan and is reduced by the deduction for one-half of self-employment taxes and the deduction allowed for contributions to a qualified retirement plan on behalf of the self-employed individual.

For purposes of applying the limitations, all defined contribution plans of an employer are treated as one defined contribution plan. Code Sec. 415(f).

Elective Deferrals

There are special limits for elective deferrals. "Elective deferrals" include the sum of the following amounts (Code Sec. 402(g)):

1. Any employer contributions to a 401(k) plan.
2. Any employer contributions to a simplified employee pension (SEP).
3. Any salary reduction contributions to a 403(b) plan.
4. Any elective employer contributions to a SIMPLE plan.

The annual limit on elective deferrals to plans other than SIMPLE plans is $18,000 for 2015. The limit for subsequent years will be adjusted for inflation. The annual limit on elective deferrals to a SIMPLE plan is $12,500 for 2015 and will be adjusted for inflation in subsequent years. If permitted by a plan, a participant who is age 50 or older at the end of a calendar year may make catch-up contributions. The limit on catch-up contributions is $6,000 in 2015. In the case of a SIMPLE plan, the limit on catch-up contributions is $3,000 in 2015. The $6,000 and $3,000 dollar limits on catch-up contributions will be adjusted for inflation after 2015. Code Sec. 414(v).

Matching contributions made on behalf of a self-employed individual will not be treated as elective employer contributions to a 401(k) plan.

¶14,225 LIMITATIONS ON BENEFITS PROVIDED BY A DEFINED BENEFIT PLAN

The annual benefit provided by a defined benefit plan with respect to a participant cannot exceed the lesser of the following amounts (Code Secs. 401(a)(16), 415(a), and (b)):

1. $210,000 (for 2015). If the benefit under the plan begins before age 62, the dollar limitation is reduced so that it equals an annual benefit equivalent to a $210,000 annual benefit beginning at age 62. If the benefit begins after age 65, the dollar limitation is increased so that it equals an annual benefit equivalent to a $210,000 annual benefit beginning at age 65. In the case of an employee who has fewer than 10 years of participation in the plan, the limitation is $210,000 multiplied by a fraction whose numerator is the number of years (or part thereof) of participation in the plan and whose denominator is 10.
2. 100 percent of the participant's average compensation for the participant's high three years.

A participant's "high three years" is the period of consecutive calendar years (not more than three) during which the participant both was an active participant in the plan and had the greatest aggregate compensation from his or her employer. The annual compensation of each employee taken into account under the plan for any year may not exceed $265,000 (for 2015). A self-employed individual's "compensation" is the individual's earned income, which is the individual's net earnings from self-employment with respect to the business offering the plan, reduced by the deduction for one-half of self-employment taxes and the deduction allowed for contributions to a qualified retirement plan on behalf of the self-employed individual.

"Annual benefit" means a benefit payable annually in the form of a straight life annuity under a plan to which employees do not contribute and under which no rollover contributions are made. If the benefit under the plan is payable in a different form or if employees contribute or make rollover contributions to the plan, whether the limitation on benefits has been satisfied is determined by adjusting the benefit so that it is equivalent to a straight life annuity under a plan to which employees do not contribute and no rollover contributions are made.

For purposes of applying the limitations, all defined benefit plans of an employer are treated as one defined benefit plan. The 100 percent of the participant's average compensation limitation is applied separately with respect to each defined benefit plan, but the high three years of compensation taken into account is the period of consecutive calendar years (not more than three) during which the individual had the greatest aggregate compensation from the employer. Code Sec. 415(f).

¶14,235 REQUIRED MINIMUM DISTRIBUTION RULES

Code Sec. 401 contains provisions which relate to the commencement of the payment of benefits and the minimum amounts and timing of distributions.

Commencement of Benefit Payments

The plan must provide that, unless the participant elects otherwise, payments of benefits will begin no later than the 60th day after the close of the plan year in which the latest of three events occurs (Code Sec. 401(a)(14)):

1. the participant attains age 65 or, if earlier, the normal retirement date specified under the plan,
2. the 10th anniversary of the year in which the participant commenced participation in the plan occurs, or
3. the participant terminates service with the employer.

EXAMPLE 14.5
In Year 1, Nick Dudley marked his 10th anniversary year of participation in his employer's 401(k) calendar-year plan. In Year 2, Nick attained age 65. In Year 3, Nick terminated his employment. Unless Nick elects otherwise, benefit payments to Nick must commence no later than March 1, Year 4.

The regulations also provide that a plan may permit a participant to delay the commencement of his benefit payments to a date later than the above dates. The plan must require that the election be in writing and specify the date on which the payment of the benefits shall commence. Reg. §1.401(a)-14(b). However, there are limits on the extent to which such deferrals may be made. (See the discussion of required minimum distributions below.)

Early Retirement Option

Many qualified retirement plans provide for an early retirement option. In order to qualify for early retirement, participants must usually reach a certain age and have a certain number of years of service, for example, age 55 and 20 years of service. In such a plan, if a participant satisfies the service requirements for early retirement benefits, but separates from service prior to reaching the early retirement age, the plan must provide that the participant will be ineligible to receive the early retirement benefit until the attainment of the required age. Code Sec. 401(a)(14). The minimum age that must be attained in order to qualify for the early retirement option is 55. Code Sec. 72(t)(2)(A)(v). The early retirement option is not available to 5-percent owners (taxpayers owning five percent or more of the business at any time during the five plan years preceding the current plan year). Code Sec. 72(m)(5).

Mandatory Cash-outs

A qualified plan may pay out the balance of a participant's account without the participant's consent if the present value of the benefit does not exceed $5,000. Code Sec. 411(a)(11)(A). This eases the administrative burden and cost of maintaining relatively small amounts. If the present value of the benefit exceeds $1,000, and the participant does not elect otherwise, a mandatory distribution must be transferred directly to an IRA established by the plan for the benefit of the participant. Code Sec. 401(a)(31)(B), Notice 2005-5.

Required Minimum Distribution Deadlines

Code Sec. 401(a)(9) contains provisions that govern the commencement and longevity of benefit payments to a participant and to the participant beneficiary after the death of the participant. Failure to meet the minimum distributions required under this section can result in a 50 percent penalty assessment on the shortfall under Code Sec. 4974. However, "after-tax" balances are not subject to this 50 percent penalty. (The concepts "after-tax" and "before-tax" amounts are explained at ¶14,301.) The minimum distribution rules apply to qualified employer-sponsored plans (except to the extent of any Roth 401(k) amounts), certain nonqualified employer-sponsored plans (e.g., governmental 457(b) plans), and traditional Individual Retirement Accounts (IRAs).

Required Beginning Date for "Before-death" Distributions

The "required beginning date" generally is April 1 of the calendar year following the later of (1) the calendar year in which the employee attains age 70 ½ or (2) the calendar year in which the employee retires.

Special Timing Rule for Owners of Traditional IRAs

For owners of traditional IRAs, the required beginning date is April 1 of the calendar year following the calendar year in which the employee attains age 70 ½. Code Sec. 401(a)(9)(C)(ii).

EXAMPLE 14.6
Dick Ragan, age 70, works full-time at Mary's Luggage and Gifts where he participates in a qualified employer-sponsored plan. He also owns a traditional IRA. Dick would be able to delay distributions from his employer-sponsored plan until after he retires. However, distributions from the traditional IRA must begin no later than April 1 following the year he attains age 70 ½.

EXAMPLE 14.7

Doc Reeves and Kitty Pitts attain age 70 in Year 1. Doc's birthday is February 14 and Kitty's is September 18. Each owns separate traditional IRAs. The deadline for their required minimum distributions (RMDs) is shown in the table below.

	Doc	Kitty
Birthday:	Feb. 14, Yr. 1	Sep. 18, Yr. 1
Part of year when age 70 is attained:	1st half, Yr. 1	2nd half, Yr. 1
Year when age 70½ is attained:	Yr. 1 (Aug. 14, Yr. 1)	Yr. 2 (Mar. 18, Yr. 2)
Deadline for 1st RMD:	April 1, Yr. 2	April 1, Yr. 3
Deadline for 2nd RMD:	December 31, Yr. 2	December 31, Yr. 3
Deadline for 3rd RMD:	December 31, Yr. 3	December 31, Yr. 4

(Subsequent RMDs are due by December 31 of subsequent years.)

Special Timing Rule for More Than Five-percent Owners

In the case of an employee who is a five-percent owner with respect to the plan year ending in the calendar year in which the employee attains age 70½, the "required beginning date" is April 1 of the calendar year following the calendar year in which the employee attains age 70½. As with traditional IRA owners, distributions for a five-percent owner cannot be delayed until after the employee retires. If an employee's employer is a corporation, a "five-percent owner" is any person who owns (or is considered as owning under the constructive ownership rules of Code Sec. 318) more than five percent of the outstanding stock of the corporation or stock possessing more than five percent of the total combined voting power of all stock of the corporation. If the employer is not a corporation, a "five-percent owner" is any person who owns more than five percent of the capital or profits interest in the employer.

Meaning of "Year of Retirement"

The required minimum distribution (RMD) rules do not provide a statutory definition for "year of retirement." The Internal Revenue Manual states that a qualified plan "[must] have procedures in place, if not plan language, for determining the date when an employee has retired." IRM 4.72.14.3.7.2-4 (05-04-2001). For many plans, the year of retirement begins when the taxpayer is no longer a full-time employee or voluntarily decides to withdraw from active participation in the employer-sponsored retirement plan. However, an employee is not considered to have separated from service if the employee continues to perform substantial similar services for the employer in the capacity of an independent contractor or if an individual continues in the same job for a new employer in a merger or consolidation, in which the old employer disappears as a legal entity. *Reinhardt*, 85 TC 511, Dec. 42,413 (1985) and Rev. Rul. 72-440, 1972-2 CB 225.

PLANNING POINTER

Even if an unretired taxpayer age 70½ or older were able to avoid the required minimum distribution (RMD) rules for the taxpayer's employer retirement plan (due to continued employment), the taxpayer would still be subject to the RMD rules for all pre-tax IRAs and employer-sponsored plans (e.g., 401(k)s, 403(b)s, 457(b)s, etc.) that are not affiliated with the current employer. These RMDs can be avoided by completing a timely tax-free rollover of the other plan balances into the current employer's plan [if the plan accepts such rollovers; there is no requirement that it does so. Code Sec. 408(d)(3)(ii)]. This way, the employer's current plan protects the amounts previously carried by the other plans from the RMD rules.

Although pre-tax qualified plan balances generally can be rolled over into qualified employer-sponsored plans, no rollover is permitted for amounts required to be distributed because the taxpayer has reached age 70½. Code Sec. 408(d)(3)(E).

Required Beginning Date for "After-death" Distributions

If a participant/owner of a qualified employer-sponsored plan or IRA dies, the balance of the account can be rolled over to the qualified plan or IRA of a surviving spouse and treated as if the spouse were the participant/owner. If not rolled over to the spouse's account, distributions to the surviving spouse do not need to begin until the date the deceased participant/owner would have attained age 70½. Code Sec. 401(a)(9)(B)(iv).

An IRA inherited by a nonspouse beneficiary may not be rolled over. Code Sec. 408(d)(3)(C). However, a direct trustee-to-trustee transfer can be made by a nonspouse beneficiary from an employer-sponsored plan of a deceased participant/owner into an IRA. The following treatment applies to such transfers:

- The transfer is treated as a tax-free rollover.
- The transferee IRA is treated as an inherited account titled in the name of the deceased participant but payable to the beneficiary; thus, the assets once transferred may not be further rolled over.
- The amount rolled into a transferee IRA must be distributed to the designated nonspouse beneficiary at least as rapidly as under the distribution method used before the participant/owner died. If the participant/owner dies before required minimum distributions have begun, the entire rolled-over interest must (1) be distributed within five years after the participant/owner's death, or (2) begin by the end of the year following the participant/owner's death and be paid out over the beneficiary's life or life expectancy. Code Sec. 401(a)(9)(B).

A nonspouse beneficiary who does not elect to make a qualified rollover into an inherited IRA is subject to the same five-year-or-lifetime distribution rule that applies to qualified rollovers into inherited IRAs (see above).

PLANNING POINTER	The main benefit of the rollover rule for non-spouse beneficiaries relates to plans that require such persons to receive only the lump sum distributions (whether shortly after the participant's death or within the five-year rule). The non-spouse beneficiary rollover could enable a beneficiary under a lump-sum-only plan to reduce taxes by taking several IRA payments spread over the five years following the participant's death, or to defer taxes for as long as possible by arranging for immediate installment distributions from the IRA over the beneficiary's life or life expectancy.

TAX BLUNDER

If a check is issued directly by the trustee of a deceased participant/owner's plan to the non-spouse beneficiary, the entire amount of the distribution will be immediately taxable, even though the entire amount may be redirected to an "inherited" IRA within 60 days (the time limit for completing a qualified indirect rollover—see ¶14,345). A similar result will occur if a trustee-to-trustee transfer is made to a transferee IRA titled in the name of the non-spouse beneficiary instead of the name of the deceased participant. The transferee IRA should be titled in a manner similar to the following: "Betty Participant, deceased, IRA f/b/o Wilma Participant (beneficiary)."

Required Minimum Distribution Amounts

The RMD amount for a year is generally equal to the participant's *accrued benefit* (for defined benefit plans) or *account balance* (for defined contribution plans) as of the end of the prior year, divided by the appropriate distribution period. Reg. §1.401(a)(9)-5, Q&A-1; Reg. §1.401(a)(9)-6, Q&A-1.

Before-death Distributions

If RMDs begin while the participant is alive, the distribution period used in determining the RMD amount is generally determined from the Uniform Lifetime Table (see below). The Uniform Lifetime Table provides the joint life expectancy of a participant and a hypothetical beneficiary whose age would be exactly ten years younger than the participant's. This table is used for all calculations, regardless of the designated beneficiary (if any), with one exception—if the sole designated beneficiary is the participant's spouse and the spouse is more than ten years younger than the participant, the applicable distribution period is determined from the Joint and Last Survivor Table at Reg. §1.401(a)(9)-9. With this table the joint life expectancies of the participant and the younger spouse are based on their actual ages. For purposes of calculating a required minimum distribution, marital status is determined as of January 1 of each year. In either case, the required minimum distribution is redetermined annually based on age at year end. Prop. Reg. §1.401(a)(9)-5, Q&A-4.

Exhibit 2. CALCULATING RMDS USING THE UNIFORM LIFETIME TABLE

Minimum amount of first distribution = (a) ÷ (b), where:

(a) = Accrued benefit or account balance as of December 31 of the year preceding the year in which the taxpayer attains the age of 70 ½, or retires, if applicable.

(b) = Hypothetical joint life expectancy provided in the Uniform Lifetime table below, that is based on:

(i) the taxpayer's age on December 31 of the year in which the taxpayer attains the age of 70 ½, (or retires, if applicable,) and

(ii) a hypothetical beneficiary whose age is exactly ten years younger than the taxpayer's.

Minimum amount of subsequent distributions = (c) ÷ (d), where:

[c] = Accrued benefit or account balance as of December 31 of the year preceding the year in which a distribution must be made (e.g., use the balance as of December 31, Year 1 if a second distribution is due by December 31, Year 2).

(d) = Redetermined joint life expectancy provided in the Uniform Lifetime table below.

EXAMPLE 14.8

Earl and Betty maintain traditional IRAs. Each reaches age 70 in Year 1—Earl on April 10 and Betty on November 2. Earl's first RMD deadline will be April 1, Year 2 while Betty's will occur on April 1, Year 3 (as previously discussed). In order to compute the first RMD amounts, the joint life expectancy of each individual (and a hypothetical beneficiary 10 years younger) must be determined from the Uniform Lifetime Table. The age on December 31 of the year in which age 70 ½ is attained must be used—age 70 for Earl (as of December 31, Year 1) and age 71 for Betty (as of December 31, Year 2). The hypothetical joint life expectancies used in computing subsequent RMD amounts must be redetermined as of December 31 of each subsequent year.

Uniform Lifetime Table
Age of IRA Owner / Distribution Period

Age	Life Exp.	Age	Life Exp.	Age	Life Exp.	Age	Life Exp.	Age	Life Exp.
70	27.4	80	18.7	90	11.4	100	6.3	110	3.1
71	26.5	81	17.9	91	10.8	101	5.9	111	2.9
72	25.6	82	17.1	92	10.2	102	5.5	112	2.6
73	24.7	83	16.3	93	9.6	103	5.2	113	2.4
74	23.8	84	15.5	94	9.1	104	4.9	114	2.1
75	22.9	85	14.8	95	8.6	105	4.5	115	1.9
76	22.0	86	14.1	96	8.1	106	4.2	(or older)	
77	21.2	87	13.4	97	7.6	107	3.9		
78	20.3	88	12.7	98	7.1	108	3.7		
79	19.5	89	12.0	99	6.7	109	3.4		

EXAMPLE 14.9

Roger Jennings is the owner of a traditional IRA. Roger will attain age 75 in the current year. The before-tax account balance as of the end of the prior year was $100,000. The distribution period for someone who will attain age 75 in the current is 22.9. Therefore, the minimum amount that Roger must withdraw from the IRA by the end of the current year is $4,367 ($100,000 ÷ 22.9 = $4,367).

Computing the 2nd RMD Amount

If the first RMD amount had been received between January 1 and April 1 of the year following the year the taxpayer became 70 ½, it must be subtracted from the prior year account balance (at (c) in Exhibit 2 above) in order to compute the second RMD amount.

EXAMPLE 14.10   Eve's traditional IRA account balances for five years are shown below:

Date	Account Balance
December 31, Year 1	$274,000
December 31, Year 2	$296,200
December 31, Year 3	$320,000
December 31, Year 4	$345,800
December 31, Year 5	$340,500

Eve becomes age 70 on June 1, Year 2, and retires at the end of Year 3. Since Eve's plan is not employer-sponsored, the retirement date is irrelevant in determining her RMD. The initial RMD (deadline and amount) is based on the year in which she becomes 70 ½ (Year 2). The deadlines and amounts associated with the first four RMDs are shown below.

Computation of RMD Deadlines and Amounts

No.	RMD Date	Relevant Acct. Bal. Date (12/31)	Relevant Age on Dec. 31 of:	(refer to the Uniform Lifetime Table above)	RMD Amount
1st	4/1, Yr 3	Yr 1	Yr 2: 70	$274,000 ÷ 27.4	$10,000
2nd	12/31, Yr 3	Yr 2	Yr 3: 71	[$296,200 – $10,000] ÷ 26.5	$10,800
3rd	12/31, Yr 4	Yr 3	Yr 4: 72	$320,000 ÷ 25.6	$12,500
4th	12/31, Yr 5	Yr 4	Yr 5: 73	$345,800 ÷ 24.7	$14,000

EXAMPLE 14.11   Refer to the preceding example above. If, instead of maintaining a traditional IRA, Eve maintained an employer-sponsored account such as a 401(k) plan, the retirement date is relevant in determining her RMD. If she is not a "five-percent owner," the required RMD dates and amounts would be as shown below.

Computation of RMD Deadlines and Amounts

No.	RMD Date	Relevant Acct. Bal. Date (12/31)	Relevant Age on Dec. 31 of:	(refer to the Uniform Lifetime Table above)	RMD Amount
1st	4/1, Yr 3	Yr 1	71	$296,200 ÷ 26.5	$11,177
2nd	12/31, Yr 3	Yr 2	72	[$320,000 – $11,177] ÷ 25.6	$12,063
3rd	12/31, Yr 4	Yr 3	73	$345,800 ÷ 24.7	$14,000
4th	12/31, Yr 5	Yr 4	74	$340,500 ÷ 23.8	$14,307

For the third and subsequent distributions, if the participant receives more than the minimum RMD amount, the participant will not receive credit for such excess in determining the RMD amount in a future year.

If an IRA owner has more than one traditional IRA, the RMD must be determined separately with respect to each traditional IRA. However, the RMD can be taken from any or all of the traditional IRAs. Amounts required to be distributed cannot be rolled over into another traditional IRA or into an employer-sponsored plan.

After-death Distributions: Death Before RMDs Begin

If the qualified plan participant died before the distributions began, and an individual (other than the participant's surviving spouse) is designated as the beneficiary of the account, the RMD for a year after the year of the decedent-owner's death is determined by dividing the account balance at the end of the preceding calendar year by a figure calculated by determining the beneficiary's life expectancy (determined from the following Single Life Table) as of the beneficiary's birthday in the year following the year of the participant's death and reducing that figure by one for each year since the year following the participant's death.

If the sole designated beneficiary is the decedent's surviving spouse and the surviving spouse has not elected to treat the qualified plan account as his or her own, no distribution has to be made to the surviving spouse until the year in which the decedent would have reached age 70 ½. Once required minimum distributions have to be made, they are calculated by dividing the account balance at the end of the preceding calendar year by the surviving spouse's life expectancy (determined using the following Single Life Table) as of the surviving spouse's birthday during the year distributions must be made. A surviving spouse's life expectancy is redetermined each year (not merely reduced by one each year).

If the designated beneficiary is not an individual, the entire account balance must be distributed by the end of the fifth year following the year of the participant's death. No distribution is required for any year before the end of that fifth year.

Single Life Table—Age Life Expectancy

Age	Life Exp.	Age	Life Exp.	Age	Life Exp.	Age	Life Exp.	Age	Life Exp.
0	82.4	25	58.2	50	34.2	75	13.4	100	2.9
1	81.6	26	57.2	51	33.3	76	12.7	101	2.7
2	80.6	27	56.2	52	32.3	77	12.1	102	2.5
3	79.7	28	55.3	53	31.4	78	11.4	103	2.3
4	78.7	29	54.3	54	30.5	79	10.8	104	2.1
5	77.7	30	53.3	55	29.6	80	10.2	105	1.9
6	76.7	31	52.4	56	28.7	81	9.7	106	1.7
7	75.8	32	51.4	57	27.9	82	9.1	107	1.5
8	74.8	33	50.4	58	27.0	83	8.6	108	1.4
9	73.8	34	49.4	59	26.1	84	8.1	109	1.2
10	72.8	35	48.5	60	25.2	85	7.6	110	1.1
11	71.8	36	47.5	61	24.4	86	7.1	111	1.0
12	70.8	37	46.5	62	23.5	87	6.7	(or older)	
13	69.9	38	45.6	63	22.7	88	6.3		
14	68.9	39	44.6	64	21.8	89	5.9		
15	67.9	40	43.6	65	21.0	90	5.5		
16	66.9	41	42.7	66	20.2	91	5.2		
17	66.0	42	41.7	67	19.4	92	4.9		
18	65.0	43	40.7	68	18.6	93	4.6		
19	64.0	44	39.8	69	17.8	94	4.3		
20	63.0	45	38.8	70	17.0	95	4.1		
21	62.1	46	37.9	71	16.3	96	3.8		
22	61.1	47	37.0	72	15.5	97	3.6		
23	60.1	48	36.0	73	14.8	98	3.4		
24	59.1	49	35.1	74	14.1	99	3.1		

EXAMPLE 14.12

Lawson Coop's mother died in Year 1. Lawson Coop, who will attain age 53 in Year 2, was designated as the sole beneficiary of his mother's traditional IRA. If the account balance at the end of Year 1 was $100,000, the minimum required distribution for Year 2 is calculated by dividing $100,000 by Lawson's life expectancy as of his birthday in Year 2 (31.4 years): $100,000 ÷ 31.4 = $3,185. If the account balance at the end of Year 2 again is $100,000, the minimum required distribution for Year 3 is calculated by dividing $100,000 by Lawson's life expectancy for the previous year (31.4 years) and subtracting one (31.4 -1.0 = 30.4): $100,000 ÷ 30.4 = $3,289.

After-death Distributions: Death On or After RMDs Begin

If the qualified plan participant died on or after the required beginning date and an individual has been designated as the beneficiary of the plan account, the required minimum distribution for a year after the year of the participant's death is determined by dividing the account balance at the end of the preceding calendar year by a figure calculated by determining the beneficiary's life expectancy (determined from the Single Life Table) as of the beneficiary's birthday in the year following the year of the participant's death and reducing that figure by one for each year since the year following the participant's death.

If the designated beneficiary is the deceased participant's surviving spouse and the surviving spouse has not elected to treat the plan account as his or her own, the amount of the minimum required distribution for a year is calculated by dividing the account balance at the end of the preceding calendar year by the surviving spouse's life expectancy (determined from the Single Life Table) as of the surviving spouse's birthday during the year distributions must be made.

If the designated beneficiary is not an individual, the amount of a required minimum distribution for a year is calculated by dividing the account balance at the end of the preceding year by the life expectancy (determined using the Single Life Table) for the participant as of the participant's birthday in the year of death and subtracting one for each year since the year of the participant's death.

Designated Beneficiary

If more than one individual has been designated as a beneficiary of a traditional IRA, the beneficiary with the shortest life expectancy is treated as the designated beneficiary. A trust cannot be a designated beneficiary. However, the beneficiaries of a trust will be treated as having been designated as beneficiaries if the following requirements are satisfied:

1. The trust is a valid trust under state law (or would be except that there is no trust principal).
2. The trust is irrevocable or will, by its terms, become irrevocable when the owner dies.
3. The trust beneficiaries are identifiable from the trust instrument.
4. The IRA trustee, custodian, or issuer has been given a copy of the trust agreement or a list of the trust beneficiaries.

Penalty for Not Making Required Minimum Distributions

If a minimum required distribution is not made, a 50 percent excise tax has to be paid on the amount not distributed as required. Code Sec. 4974(a). The penalty is reported on Form 5329 Additional Taxes on Qualified Plans (Including IRAs) and Other Tax Favored Accounts. If the individual believes the tax should not apply due to reasonable error, the tax should be paid and a letter of explanation attached to Form 5329. If the IRS waives the tax, it will issue a refund.

¶14,245   EARLY WITHDRAWAL RESTRICTIONS

If a taxable distribution is made before an employee attains age 59 ½, a 10-percent additional tax will be imposed on amounts distributed unless one of the exceptions applies. Code Sec. 72(t).

No additional tax will be imposed under the following circumstances:

1. **Distributions after the employee's death.** The distribution is made to a beneficiary or the employee's estate after the employee's death.
2. **Distributions on account of disability.** The distribution is attributable to the employee's being disabled. An employee is considered to be disabled if the employee is unable to engage in any substantial gainful activity by reason of any medically determinable physical or mental impairment that can be expected to result in death or to be of long-continued and indefinite duration.
3. **Substantially equal periodic payments.** The distribution is part of a series of substantially equal periodic payments (not less frequently than annually) made for the life (or life expectancies) of the employee or the joint lives (or joint life expectancies) of the employee and his or her designated beneficiary.
4. **Separation from service.** The distribution is made to an employee after separation from service after attainment of age 55. This early retirement exception does not apply to a distribution from a traditional IRA. Code Sec. 72(t)(3)(A).
5. **Dividends on employer securities.** The distribution consists of dividends paid with respect to employer securities.
6. **Levy.** The distribution is made on account of a levy on the qualified retirement plan.
7. **Medical expenses.** To the extent that the distribution does not exceed the amount of medical expenses allowable as a deduction for the year to the employee (determined without regard to whether the employee itemizes deductions for the tax year).
8. **Alternate payees.** Distributions to an alternate payee pursuant to a qualified domestic relations order (discussed in ¶14,345).
9. **Military call-up reservists.** Distributions to individuals called to active duty for a period in excess of 179 days.

Additional Exceptions for IRAs

In addition to the general exceptions listed above, the following exceptions apply to premature taxable distributions from IRAs:

1. **Medical insurance premiums.** Early distributions from a *traditional IRA*, as well as a *SEP* or *SIMPLE IRA*, are not subject to the 10 percent penalty if applied toward medical insurance of the individual, spouse, or dependents (without regard to the 10 percent of adjusted gross income medical expense limitation). In order to qualify, the individual must have received federal or state unemployment compensation for at least 12 weeks, and the distribution must have been made in the year such unemployment compensation had been received or the following year.

2. **Education expenses.** Early distributions from *traditional IRAs* to cover "qualified higher education expenses" may not be subject to the 10 percent penalty. In order to avoid the penalty, the expenses must have been incurred by the individual, the individual's spouse or child, or a grandchild of the individual or individual's spouse. Qualified expenses include tuition at a post-secondary educational institution, books, fees, supplies, and equipment. Code Sec. 72(t)(2)(E). Such expenses are reduced by amounts excluded from gross income that are used for education.

3. **"First-Time" Homebuyer Expenses.** Premature withdrawals from *traditional IRAs*, and *Roth IRAs* may not be subject to the 10 percent penalty if used to pay up to $10,000 (lifetime limit) of first-time homebuyer expenses. The funds must be used within 120 days of distribution to acquire, construct, or reconstruct a home that is the principal residence of taxpayer, spouse, child, grandchild or ancestor of taxpayer or spouse. "Acquisition costs" include any usual or reasonable settlement, financing, or other closing costs.

   An individual is a "first-time homebuyer" if the individual (and, if married, the individual's spouse) had no present ownership interest in a principal residence during the two-year period ending on the date that the principal residence was acquired. Thus, as long as the taxpayer (and spouse, if married) had not owned a home in the two years immediately preceding the closing date (not contract date), distributions can be made from an IRA to help pay for the "new" home even though it may not actually be the taxpayer's first home. Code Sec. 72(t)(2)(F).

TAX BLUNDER

Don and Sharon Bacek, both in their late 40's, sell their house after occupying it for 20 years and rent a flat. After three years in the flat, they decide to return to home ownership. They find a house to purchase, however, in order to complete the transaction, they need $10,000 for a down payment. Their only sources of funds are Sharon's traditional IRA and Don's employer-sponsored retirement account. If the funds are withdrawn from Sharon's traditional IRA, they will not be subject to the penalty, provided the funds are applied toward the purchase of the new house within 120 days of the closing date. If, on the other hand, the funds are withdrawn from Don's employer-sponsored account, they will be subject to the 10 percent early withdrawal penalty, even though they are applied toward the new home purchase within the 120-day statutory period.

SIMPLE Plan Penalty

For employees who withdraw any amount from a SIMPLE plan during the first two years of participation, the 10 percent penalty is increased to 25 percent. Code Sec. 72(t)(6).

¶14,255 PARTICIPATION REQUIREMENTS

For a trust (or annuity contract or custodial account) to constitute a qualified trust under Code Sec. 401(a), the plan of which it is a part may impose certain age and service requirements on employees as a condition for participating in the plan. Code Secs. 401(a)(3), 410(a). These requirements must be satisfied on at least one day in each quarter of the tax year. Code Sec. 401(a)(6).

Minimum Age and Service Requirements

As a general rule, a plan may not require, as a condition of participation in the plan, that an employee complete a period of service with the employer extending beyond the date on which the employee completes one year of service or, if later, the date on which the employee attains age 21. However, two years of service may be required as a prerequisite for participation in a plan if plan participants have a nonforfeitable right to 100 percent of their accrued benefit after no more than two years of service. If a plan maintained exclusively for employees of a tax-exempt educational institution provides that each participant with at least one year of service has a nonforfeitable right to 100 percent of his or her accrued benefit under the plan at the time that the benefit accrues, the plan may require as a condition of participation that the employee attain age 26. Code Sec. 410(a)(1).

A "year of service" means a 12-month period during which the employee has no fewer than 1,000 hours of service. For a maritime industry, 125 days of service is treated as 1,000 hours of service. Code Sec. 410(a)(3).

Maximum Age Requirement

A trust cannot be a qualified trust if the plan of which it is a part excludes from participation (on the basis of age) employees who have attained a specified age. Code Sec. 410(a)(2).

Time Participation Must Commence

A trust cannot be a qualified trust unless the plan of which it is a part provides that any employee who has satisfied the minimum age and service requirements and otherwise is entitled to participate in the plan will commence participation no later than the earlier of the first day of the first plan year beginning after the date on which the employee satisfies such requirements or six months after the date on which the employee satisfies such requirements, unless the employee separates from service before participation otherwise would commence. Code Sec. 410(a)(4).

¶14,265   COVERAGE REQUIREMENTS

For a trust (or annuity contract or custodial account) to be a qualified trust, the plan of which it is a part must satisfy one of the following tests (Code Secs. 401(a)(3) and 410(b)):

1. Percentage test. It benefits at least 70 percent of employees who are not highly compensated.
2. Ratio test. The percentage of employees who are not highly compensated employees that are benefited is at least 70 percent of the percentage of highly compensated employees who benefit under the plan.
3. Average benefit percentage test. The plan benefits a class of employees found by the IRS not to be discriminatory in favor of highly compensated employees and the average benefit percentage for employees who are not highly compensated employees is at least 70 percent of the average benefit percentage for highly compensated employees.

The coverage requirements must be satisfied on at least one day each quarter during the tax year. Code Sec. 401(a)(6). "Highly compensated employee" is defined by Code Sec. 414(q), discussed in ¶14,205.

EXAMPLE 14.13	For a plan year, Plan A benefits 40% of the employer's non-highly compensated employees and 60% of the employer's highly compensated employees. Plan A fails to satisfy the ratio test because the ratio between the percentage of non-highly compensated employees covered under the plan (40%) divided by the percentage of highly compensated employees covered by the plan (60%), 40% / 60% = 66.67%, is not 70% or more.

EXAMPLE 14.14	Koala Kola, Inc. has 550 employees, including 50 who are highly compensated. To satisfy the percentage test, 350 (70% × 500 = 350) of the non-highly compensated employees have to be covered. To satisfy the ratio test, if 50% of the highly compensated employees (50% × 50 = 25) are covered, 70% of 50%, or 35% of the non-highly compensated employees have to be covered (35% × 500 = 175).

Certain employees are excluded for purposes of determining whether the coverage requirements have been satisfied:

1. Employees who are included in a unit of employees covered by a collective bargaining agreement if there is evidence that retirement benefits were the subject of good faith bargaining.
2. Nonresident alien employees who receive no earned income from the employer that is U.S.-source income.
3. Employees who do not satisfy minimum age and service requirements prescribed by the plan as a condition of participation.

An employer may elect to designate two or more trusts, one or more trusts and one or more annuity plans, or two or more annuity plans as part of one plan for purposes of determining whether the coverage requirements have been satisfied. Such trusts or annuity plans also will be treated as one plan for purposes of applying the nondiscrimination requirements.

If an employer is treated as operating separate lines of business for a year, the employer may apply the coverage requirements separately with respect to employees in each separate line of business. Code Sec. 410(b)(5). An employer will be treated as operating separate lines of business during a year if the following requirements are satisfied (Code Sec. 414(r)):

1. The employer has bona fide business reasons for operating separate lines of business.
2. Each line of business has at least 50 employees, not including employees who have completed six or fewer months of service, employees who normally work fewer than 17 ½ hours per week, employees who normally work during no more than six months during any year, employees who have not attained age 21, and employees covered by a collective bargaining agreement.
3. The employer notifies the IRS that the lines of business are being treated as separate.
4. The lines of business meet guidelines prescribed by the IRS, or the employer receives a determination from the IRS that the lines of business may be treated as separate. This requirement does not apply to a line of business if the percentage of employees performing services for the line of business that are highly compensated employees is not less than 50 percent of, and not more than twice, the percentage that highly compensated employees are of all employees of the employer.

EXAMPLE 14.15	Picard Corporation is a domestic corporation that manufactures and sells consumer food and beverages and provides data-processing services to private businesses. Picard Corporation may treat its consumer food and beverages business and its data-processing services business as separate lines of businesses.

EXAMPLE 14.16	The Firm operates a law practice. Its employees include lawyers, paralegals, and legal assistants, all of whom work together to provide services to The Firm's clients. It would be unreasonable for The Firm to treat the services of its lawyers, paralegals, and legal assistants as separate lines of business.

¶14,275 VESTING REQUIREMENTS

"Vesting" refers to the process by which an employee's right to receive benefits provided by a qualified retirement plan becomes nonforfeitable. For a trust that is part of a retirement plan to be a qualified trust, the plan must give participants certain nonforfeitable rights to amounts contributed to the plan and earnings on those contributions. Code Secs. 401(a)(7), 411. These rights are the minimum rights that an employer must give an employee. Employers may give employees a faster vesting schedule.

If an employee leaves an employer before his or her right to benefits provided by the plan becomes nonforfeitable, the employee will forfeit the nonvested portion of his or her benefits.

Employee Contributions

Employees must have a nonforfeitable right to the accrued benefit derived from their own contributions (i.e., elective deferrals) to a qualified retirement plan. Code Sec. 411(a)(1). In the case of a defined contribution plan, "accrued benefit" means the balance in the employee's account. In the case of a defined benefit plan, "accrued benefit" means the employee's accrued benefit determined under the plan, expressed in the form of an annual benefit commencing at normal retirement age. Code Sec. 411(a)(7). "Normal retirement age" is the time a plan participant attains normal retirement age under the plan or, if earlier, the later of the time a plan participant attains age 65 or the fifth anniversary of the time a plan participant commenced participation in the plan. Code Sec. 411(a)(8).

Employer Contributions

Employees must have a nonforfeitable right to their accrued benefit derived from employer contributions to a defined contribution plan under either of the following vesting schedules (Code Sec. 411(a)(2)(B)):

1. **Three-Year ("Cliff") Vesting.** A plan satisfies three-year vesting if an employee has a nonforfeitable right to 100 percent of the employee's accrued benefit derived from employer contributions after the employee has completed at least three years of service.

2. **Two-to-Six-Year ("Graded") Vesting.** A plan satisfies two-to-six-year vesting if an employee has a nonforfeitable right to the percentage of the employee's accrued benefit derived from employer contributions determined from the following table:

Years of Service	Nonforfeitable Percentage
2	20
3	40
4	60
5	80
6 or more	100

Accrued benefits derived from employer contributions to a defined benefit plan using cliff vesting must vest with the participant after five years of service. If a defined benefit plan uses graded vesting, accrued benefits derived from all employer contributions must vest with the participant at the rate of 20 percent per year, beginning with the third year of service. Code Sec. 411(a)(2)(A).

In computing the years of an employee's service for purposes of determining the nonforfeitable percentage, all of an employee's years of service with an employer must be taken into account except for the following (Code Sec. 411(a)(4)):

1. Years of service before age 18.
2. Years of service during a period for which the employee declined to contribute to a plan requiring employee contributions.
3. Years of service with an employer during any period for which the employer did not maintain a qualified deferred compensation plan.
4. Years of service before any one-year break in service, until the employee has completed a year of service after his or her return to work.

A "year of service" means a calendar year, plan year, or other 12-consecutive-month period designated by the plan during which the participant completed 1,000 hours of service. Code Sec. 411(a)(5). A "one-year break in service" is a calendar year, plan year, or other 12-consecutive-month period designated by the plan during which the participant did not complete more than 500 hours of service. Code Sec. 411(a)(6).

¶14,285   "EXCLUSIVE BENEFIT OF THE EMPLOYEE" REQUIREMENT

General Investment Requirements

No specific limitations are provided in Code Sec. 401(a) with respect to investments that may be made by the trustees of a qualified trust. Reg. §1.401-1(b)(5). However, Rev. Rul. 69-494 (1969-2 CB 88) provides general requirements that must be met:

1. **Cost of plan assets.** The cost of fund assets must not exceed their market value at the time of purchase.
2. **Liquidity.** The plan must maintain sufficient liquidity to permit distributions.
3. **Return.** The plan must provide a fair return commensurate with market yield.
4. **Safeguards.** Prudent safeguards and diversification must be met.

With regard to *employee contributions* and elective deferrals invested in employer securities, an individual must be allowed to elect to direct the plan to divest employer securities into other investment options. Code Sec. 401(a)(35)(B). An individual who is a participant in the plan with at least three years of service or is a beneficiary of such a participant must be able to elect to divest the portion of the account invested in employer securities that is attributable to *employer contributions* in other investment options. Code Sec. 401(a)(35)(C).

TAX BLUNDER

Despite the collapses of General Motors and Lehman Brothers, which highlighted the dangers of investing in the stock of an employer, company stock still constitutes too large a portion of most 401(k) balances, experts say. In plans that offer company stock, about one in four employees have half or more of their total 401(k) balance invested in it, according to Hewitt Associates, a human resources outsourcing and consulting firm.

Prohibited Transactions

A qualified trust instrument must make it impossible, before the satisfaction of *all* liabilities to employees and their beneficiaries, for any portion of the trust income or principal to be used for, or diverted to, purposes other than for the exclusive benefit of the employer's employees or their beneficiaries. This provision must be specifically written into the trust instrument. Reg. §1.401-2.

To ensure that the plan is solely for the exclusive benefit of employees and not for the employer, Code Sec. 4975(c) specifies certain "prohibited transactions" which restrict the dealings between the plan and certain "disqualified persons." Prohibited transactions generally include acquisition by the plan of employer securities and other property owned by the employer and the lending of money by the plan to the employer.

Assignment and Alienation Prohibited

Arrangements by a qualified plan which provide for the payment to the employer of plan benefits which would otherwise be due to the participant are prohibited. Also, except for qualified domestic relations orders (see below), arrangements whereby a party acquires a right or interest enforceable against the plan in any part of a plan benefit payment which is due to the participant or beneficiaries are prohibited. Code Sec. 401(a)(13).

Qualified Domestic Relations Order

A domestic relations order generally is a judgment or court order awarding child support, alimony payments, or marital property rights to a spouse, former spouse, child, or other dependent of a participant pursuant to state domestic relations law. Code Sec. 414(p)(1)(B). In general, a plan must prohibit the assignment and alienation of a right to benefits by a domestic relations order, unless it is a "qualified domestic relations order (QDRO)." To be a QDRO, a domestic relations order must create or recognize the existence of the right of an alternate payee (spouse, former spouse, child or other dependent) to receive all or a portion of the benefits payable with respect to a participant under the plan. Code Sec. 414(p)(1)(A).

If an alternate payee of a plan participant receives a distribution under a qualified domestic relations order, the alternate payee will be taxed on the distribution unless the alternate payee makes an eligible rollover contribution (discussed later in the chapter). Code Sec. 402(e).

Tax Consequences to Employer and Employee

¶14,301   ## CONTRIBUTIONS AND DISTRIBUTIONS: BASIC TERMINOLOGY

Lump-sum v. Partial Distributions

A lump-sum distribution is a distribution of a participant's entire interest in a qualified plan within a single tax year. Any distribution of an amount constituting less than an entire interest is a partial distribution.

A participant other than a self-employed taxpayer, may qualify for a lump-sum distribution if any of the following events occurs:

- the participant's death,
- separation from the service of the employer, or
- attainment of age 59 ½.

In the case of a self-employed person, the distribution must be made because of the individual's death, disability, or attainment of age 59 ½. Code Sec. 402(e)(4)(D)(i). Unlike common law employees, self-employed persons cannot qualify for a lump-sum distribution on account of separation from service.

"Before-tax" v. "After-tax Contributions

Grasping the distinction between "before-tax" and "after-tax" contributions is essential to understanding the contribution and distribution rules governing qualified deferred compensation plans. If contributions made to qualified plans such as traditional IRAs or 401(k) plans are *deductible*, then the subsequent withdrawal of these contributions is *taxable*.

If an account balance includes *nondeductible* (i.e., after-tax) *contributions*, the owner would have a *cost basis* in the account. An individual's cost basis in distributions received from a retirement account is the sum of all nondeductible contributions minus prior distributions of nondeductible contributions (if any). Notice 87-16. The recovery of this cost basis is never recognized as taxable income.

The rules governing the deductibility of contributions are explained later in this chapter. For now, it's important to understand why deductible contributions are "before-tax" and why nondeductible contributions are "after-tax." This distinction is illustrated in Example 14.17 below.

EXAMPLE 14.17

Jonathan Ruppel earns a $100,000 salary and contributes $10,000 into a qualified retirement account. He makes no additional contributions and the account has no accumulated income. Years later, Jonathan receives a $10,000 distribution representing the original contribution amount. Assuming a 30 percent tax rate, if the original contribution had been deductible, a $3,000 federal income tax would be imposed on the distribution amount. If, on the other hand, the original contribution had not been deductible, the distribution amount would be tax-free. The relationship between deductibility and taxability is illustrated in Exhibit 3 below.

Exhibit 3. TAX EFFECT FROM BEFORE- AND AFTER-TAX CONTRIBUTIONS

Formula:	Description:	If the contribution is before tax:	If the contribution is after tax:
(a) = Given	Contribution amount	$10,000	$10,000
(b) = "Yes" or "No"	Deductible? (The rules for qualifying for a deduction are explained later in this chapter.)	Assume Yes	Assume No
(c) = Given	Gross income	$100,000	$100,000
(d) = (a) if (b) ="yes"	Deduction	(10,000)	0
(e) = (c) – (d)	Taxable income (ignoring other deductions)	90,000	100,000
(f) = Given	Tax rate	30%	30%
(g) = (e) × (f)	Tax	27,000	30,000
(h) = (d) × (f)	Immediate tax savings from the $10,000 deduction	3,000	0
(i) = (d) × tax rate in effect in the year of dist'n	Estimated future taxes payable when the $10,000 is subsequently distributed	3.000 (assuming a 30% future tax rate; however, if the future tax rate is lower (or higher), the tax burden will be less (more) than $3,000)	0
(j) = (a) [if (b) ="yes"] (j) = (a) ÷ [1 – (f)] [if (b) ="no"]	Gross income needed to fund the $10,000 contribution	10,000 (Same as the contribution amount. This explains why the contribution is "before-tax".)	14,286 (To fund a $10,000 contribution, the taxpayer needs to earn at least $14,286, which, taxed at 30%, would result in $10,000 cash after-tax. This explains why the nondeductible contribution is considered to be "after-tax." Proof: 70% × $14,286 = $10,000)

Any portion of a distribution representing accumulated income is taxable unless the plan from which the distribution is made is a Roth IRA or a Roth 401(k). These plans are discussed later in this chapter.

¶14,305 CONTRIBUTIONS AND DEDUCTIONS—GENERAL RULES

Contributions to a qualified retirement plan on behalf of an employee are excluded from the employee's gross income. Code Sec. 402. Elective deferrals also are excluded from an employee's gross income. However, elective deferrals are subject to Social Security, Medicare, and federal unemployment (FUTA) taxes.

Employers are entitled to a current deduction for contributions made to a qualified retirement plan even though the contributions are not currently includible in their employees' gross income. Code Sec. 404. The amount that an employer may deduct depends on the type of plan:

1. **Defined benefit plans.** The deduction is based on actuarial assumptions and computations.
2. **Defined contribution plans.** 25 percent of the compensation paid or accrued to eligible employees participating in such plans may be deducted. For purposes of applying this limit, the maximum compensation .that can be taken into account for each employee is $265,000 (for 2015). Elective deferrals are included in compensation but not subject to the limit.

If an employer contributes to both a defined contribution plan and a defined benefit plan and at least one employee is covered by both plans, the employer's deduction cannot exceed the greater of the following amounts:

1. 25 percent of the compensation paid or accrued during the year to eligible employees participating in the plans.
2. The employer's contributions to defined benefit plans, but only to the extent that the amount of contributions does not exceed the amount of employer contributions necessary to satisfy the minimum funding standard.

Deduction Limit for Self-Employed Individuals

The deduction limit for self-employed individuals is based on the individual's net earnings from self-employment (reduced by half of the individual's self-employment tax). The maximum percentage of those earnings that can be deducted is determined by dividing the plan contribution rate by that rate plus 1.0. For example, a plan that deducts 25 percent of the compensation of plan participants may not deduct more than 20 percent [0.25/(1.0 + 0.25) = .20] of the owner's net earnings from self-employment (reduced by half of the owner's self-employment tax).

Year for Which Contributions May Be Deducted

Employers may deduct contributions for the tax year with or within which the calendar year for which the contributions were made. Contributions can be deducted for a tax year if they are made by the due date (including extensions) for filing a federal income tax return for that year.

Penalty Tax on Excess Contributions

A 10-percent penalty tax is imposed on nondeductible contributions to a qualified employer plan that exceed statutory limits. "Qualified employer plan" includes a qualified pension, stock bonus, or profit-sharing plan, a 403(a) plan, a SEP, or a SIMPLE plan. Code Sec. 4972.

¶14,315   EARNINGS ON CONTRIBUTIONS

The value of a deferred compensation plan for its participants is that earnings on contributions accumulate tax-free. Greater financial benefits are possible if contributions can be made with pre-tax money instead of after-tax money.

The following examples illustrate how employees can benefit from deferred compensation plans. Note that the benefits of a deferred compensation plan increase the greater the rate of return that can be earned, the higher a taxpayer's marginal tax rate when contributions are made, and the greater the difference between the taxpayer's marginal tax rate when contributions are made and the taxpayer's marginal tax rate when funds are withdrawn.

EXAMPLE 14.18	Catherine Bell's marginal tax rate is 28%. Her employer gives her a choice between contributing her $2,000 annual bonus to a deferred compensation plan earning a 6% rate of return or taking that $2,000, paying the tax due (28% × $2,000 = $560) and investing the remaining $1,440 in certificates of deposit paying a 6% rate of interest (4.32% after taxes). After 20 years, Catherine will accumulate $77,985.45 in the deferred compensation plan. After the same number of years, she will accumulate $46,247.72 in her certificates of deposit. If Catherine's marginal tax still is 28% when she withdraws the $77,985.45 after 20 years, she will be left with $56,149.52 ($77,985.45 − (28% × $77,985.45)), $9,801.80 more than she would have had if she had not contributed her bonus to the deferred compensation plan.

EXAMPLE 14.19	Same facts as in the previous example but Catherine's marginal tax rate is 15% at the time she withdraws money from the deferred compensation plan. After paying taxes on the $77,985.45 accumulated in the deferred compensation plan, she will have $77,985.45 − (15% × $77,985.45) = $66,287.63 ($20,039.91 more than if she had taken the $2,000, paid tax on it, and invested the remainder in certificates of deposit).

EXAMPLE 14.20	Same facts as in the previous example but the rate of return Catherine can earn on amounts contributed to the deferred compensation plan or certificate of deposit is 8% (5.76% after taxes). After 20 years, Catherine will accumulate $98,845.84 in the deferred compensation plan and $54,598.29 in certificates of deposit. After paying taxes on the $98,845.84, Catherine will have $98,845.84 – (15% × $98,845.84) = $84,018.96 ($29,420.67 more than if she had taken the $2,000, paid tax on it, and invested the remainder in certificates of deposit).

EXAMPLE 14.21	Same facts as in the previous example but Catherine's marginal rate of return at the time she makes contributions is 35% (her marginal tax rate at the time she makes withdrawals remains 15%). After 20 years, Catherine still will accumulate $98,845.84 in the deferred compensation plan. However, because her marginal tax rate is 35%, she will have $1,300 after taxes ($2,000 – (35% × $2,000)) to invest in certificates of deposit, and her after-tax return will be 5.2%. After 20 years, Catherine will have $46,188.74 in her certificates of deposit ($37,830.22 less than what she would have had if she contributed the money to the deferred compensation plan).

¶14,325   PARTIAL DISTRIBUTIONS—COMPUTING TAX LIABILITY

The three possible forms of partial distribution (defined at ¶14,301) include:

1. distributions made *before* an annuity starting date;
2. annuities;
3. nonannuity distributions made *on or after* the starting date of an annuity (if any).

The rules for each form of distribution are explained below.

Distributions Made Before an Annuity Starting Date

If a distribution is made before an annuity starting date (if any), it is treated in much the same way as an annuity distribution. Code Sec. 72(e)(2)(B). That is, the amount of income that is excluded from income is equal to:

(a) × [(b) ÷ (c)], where

(a) = the distribution amount
(b) = the individual's cost basis in the distribution (explained above) and
(c) = the value of the nonforfeitable portion of the taxpayer's total account balance.

EXAMPLE 14.22	Nora Lyons, age 60 and retired, receives a $10,000 partial distribution from her 401(k) plan. The plan does not pay out an annuity. Immediately before the distribution, her account balance is $100,000, including $25,000 in nondeductible contributions. Nora will exclude $2,500 from gross income ($10,000 × [$25,000 ÷ $100,000]).

The amounts at (b) and (c) above are to be determined as of the date of distribution. Alternatively, the amount at (b) may be determined as of December 31 of the calendar year immediately preceding the calendar year of the distribution and the amount at (c) may be determined as of the last valuation date in the calendar year preceding the calendar year of the distribution if such date is used on a reasonable and consistent basis in determining the cost basis and value for all nonannuity distributions under the plan.

Distributions That Are Annuities

If the annuity option is available, a qualified plan must allow married parties to choose between a joint and survivorship ("J&S") annuity and a single life ("SL") annuity. A J&S annuity stops being paid when both spouses are deceased. It is designed to provide the surviving spouse with some financial security. However, the amount of this annuity is lower, since it is based on the combined life expectancy of both spouses jointly, which, actuarially, is longer than that of either spouse.

A SL annuity, on the other hand, stops being paid when the employee dies. A surviving spouse therefore receives no benefits after the death of the participating spouse. However, the amount of a SL annuity is larger than a J&S annuity, since it's based only on the employee's life expectancy. With most plans, an employee's spouse must provide written consent for the single life annuity election. Code Sec. 401(a)(11). Annuity payments are taxed using the Sec. 72 exclusion ratio (explained at ¶5,125).

Nonannuity Distributions Made On or After an Annuity Starting Date

A nonannuity distribution made on or after an annuity starting date is generally included in full in gross income. Code Sec. 72(e)(2)(A).

EXAMPLE 14.23	Molly Darden has been receiving a $100 monthly annuity from her qualified plan account over several years. At the end of the current year, her account balance is $100,000, including a $25,000 cost basis. In order to satisfy a personal obligation, she withdraws an extra $10,000 from her account in the current year. If the withdrawal does not affect the amount of her subsequent annuity payments, the entire $10,000 is taxable in the current year. Since the distribution occurred on or after the annuity starting date, the Sec. 72 annuity rules do not apply.

¶14,335 LUMP-SUM DISTRIBUTIONS—COMPUTING TAX LIABILITY

The entire amount of a lump-sum distribution may not be taxable. To determine the taxable portion of the lump-sum distribution, the amount that is includible in gross income may be reduced by five items as follows:

1. After-tax contributions by the participant;
2. Any premiums paid by the plan to furnish the participant with life insurance protection, if the plan trustee has a right to retain any of the proceeds of the life insurance contract [Reg. §1.72-16(b)(6)];
3. Any portion of a lump-sum distribution that is used to repay loans from the plan if such loans had been included in the participant's gross income when received [Code Sec. 72(p)(1)(A)];
4. The current actuarial value of any annuity contract that was included in the lump-sum distribution; (i.e., the value is taxable as the beneficiary receives the annuity payments over time) [Reg. §1.402(a)-1(a)(2)]; and,
5. The net unrealized appreciation in any securities that were distributed as a part of the lump-sum distribution [Code Sec. 402(e)(4)(B)].

If a participant or beneficiary elects to exclude the net unrealized appreciation from gross income upon distribution of the securities, tax is deferred until the securities are sold or exchanged. However, the cost or other basis of the employer securities is included in the taxable portion of the distribution. Code Sec. 402(e)(4)(B).

Lump-sum distributions to individuals born before January 2, 1936 may be subject to favorable ten-year averaging. The rules are complex and intentionally omitted from this text.

¶14,345 ROLLOVERS

Direct Rollovers

Any amount transferred between eligible retirement plans in a direct trustee-to-trustee transfer is not includible in gross income for the tax year of the transfer. Code Sec. 402(e)(6). Such direct rollovers are not subject to the 20 percent mandatory income tax withholding that applies to indirect rollovers.

Indirect Rollovers

If any portion of the balance to the credit of an employee in a qualified employer-sponsored retirement plan is paid to the employee in an eligible rollover distribution and the distributee transfers any portion of the property received in the distribution to an eligible retirement plan within 60 days following receipt, the amount distributed will not be included in the employee's gross income for the tax year in which it was paid. Code Sec. 402(c). However, such indirect rollovers are subject to 20 percent mandatory income tax withholding.

The IRS may waive the 60-day rule for tax-free rollovers in hardship cases and in cases where taxpayers make good faith efforts to comply with the rule but fail through no fault of their own. Mitigating events include: casualty, disaster, hospitalization, incarceration, death, disability, restrictions imposed by a foreign government, and error by the financial institution. Rev. Proc. 2003-16.

Eligible Retirement Plans

The benefits accrued under a retirement plan are *portable* if they can be rolled over to another retirement plan without losing tax-advantaged status. An "eligible retirement plan" includes (Code Sec. 402(c)(8)(B)):

1. A qualified trust such as a 401(k) plan.
2. A 403(a) plan.
3. A 403(b) plan.
4. A governmental 457(b) plan.
5. A traditional IRA.

Refer to Exhibit 4 for a chart on the portability of common retirement plans.

Election by alternate payee under a QDRO

If the spouse or former spouse of a plan participant receives a distribution as the alternate payee under a qualified domestic relations order, the alternate payee will be taxed on the distribution unless the alternate payee makes an eligible rollover contribution. Code Sec. 402(e).

Ineligible rollovers

An "ineligible rollover" is any distribution of all or any portion of the balance to the credit of an employee in a qualified retirement plan that is:

1. one of a series of substantially equal periodic payments (not less frequently than annually) made for the life expectancy of the employee or the joint life expectancies of the employee and the employee's designated beneficiary or for a specified period of 10 years or more;
2. required to be made from the trust under the required minimum distribution rules—see ¶14,235; or,
3. made on account of the employee's hardship.

Prohibited Rollovers

A qualified plan is under no obligation to accept rollovers. It may limit the circumstances under which it will accept rollovers or limit the type of assets it will accept. Reg. §1.401(a)(31)-1, Q&A 13. A taxpayer should make appropriate inquiries before initiating a rollover from a qualified plan account.

PLANNING POINTER

Qualified plan participants who terminate their employment may wish to roll the funds from their account into another qualified account for any of the following reasons:

1. The pension fund of a distressed company may be in jeopardy.
2. The former employer may merge or become acquired by another company. As a result, the plan may undergo unfavorable changes to the provisions.
3. The participant may qualify for and benefit from a conversion to a Roth IRA.
4. With a rollover to any IRA, the taxpayer can select the investment company and control when, where, and how the money is invested.
5. The employer-sponsored plan fees may be higher than the fees associated with the rollover account.
6. A participant in more than one qualified plan may wish to consolidate the funds in order to minimize the risk of misplacing or losing track of the money.
7. If retirement funds are left in a qualified employer-sponsored plan and the participant marries, the consent of the new spouse will be needed if the participant decides to name anyone other than the new spouse as the beneficiary. A rollover into an IRA account enables the taxpayer to retain the flexibility to name any beneficiary, e.g. a child from a former marriage.
8. A rollover IRA may provide a terminated employee greater access to the funds. For example, the employer may allow terminated employees to withdraw only a portion of the funds or it may prohibit their borrowing from the plan. With a rollover to an IRA, a small part or all of the funds may be withdrawn without penalty for qualified distributions such as education expenses, first-time homebuyer expenses (up to $10,000), and medical expenses.
9. Some companies require large portions of the employees' profit sharing and 401(k) funds to be invested in company stock. By rolling these funds into another qualified plan, the taxpayer may achieve greater diversification and reduced investment risk.

Some reasons why terminated employees may prefer not to rollover funds from a qualified plan may include the following:

1. If a significant portion of the plan consists of company stock, significant tax advantages such as long-term capital gains treatment may be lost with a rollover.
2. If the taxpayer terminated employment with an outstanding plan loan, the loan cannot be rolled over, rather, it must be paid back into the plan. A loan not paid off may be treated as a taxable distribution.
3. The specific type of investments within the plan may not be found outside of the plan. If these investments are highly attractive, the individual may wish to leave them alone.
4. If the qualified plan is a SIMPLE plan established less than two years ago, a rollover (or any other distribution) occurring during the first two years, will result in a 25 percent penalty. However, a trustee-to-trustee rollover to another SIMPLE plan within the two-year period will not be subject the penalty.

TAX BLUNDER

If a qualified plan participant arranges an indirect rollover into another eligible plan account, the participant would lose the earning power of 20% of the rollover amount for a period of time because the plan's trustee is required to withhold 20 percent of the rollover amount. If the participant fails to transfer 100 percent of the rollover amount into another eligible plan account within 60 days following receipt, the shortfall will be subject to a 10 percent penalty plus regular income tax.

Exhibit 4. PORTABILITY CHART

ELIGIBLE ROLLOVER TO RECIPIENT PLAN? (Yes v. No)

TO:	401(k)	Roth 401(k)/ 403(b)	403(b) Plan	Gov't. 457(b)	Keogh Plan	SEP IRA	SIMPLE IRA	Trad'l IRA	Roth IRA
FROM:									
401(k) – Other Than Roth 401(k)	Y[d]	N	Y[c]	Y[c]	Y[d]	Y	N	Y	Y
403(b) – Other Than Roth 403(b)	Y	N	Y	Y	Y	Y	N	Y	Y
Roth 401(k)/ 403(b) by Direct Rollover	N	Y	N	N	N	N	N	N	Y
Governmental 457(b)	Y	N	Y	Y	Y	Y	N	Y	Y
Keogh	Y[d]	N	Y[c]	Y[c]	Y[d]	Y	N	Y	Y
SEP IRA	Y[a]	N	Y[a]	Y[a]	Y[a]	Y	N	Y	Y
SIMPLE IRA [b]	Y	N	Y	Y	Y	Y	Y	Y	Y
Traditional IRA	Y[a]	N	Y[a]	Y[a]	Y[a]	Y	N	Y	Y
Roth IRA	N	N	N	N	N	N	N	N	Y

Superscript Notes:
[a] Only pretax amounts from a traditional IRA or SEP IRA may be rolled to these plans.
[b] Rollovers from SIMPLE IRAs are prohibited until after 2 years of participation.
[c] Pretax amounts only.
[d] After-tax amounts may be received only by direct transfer or direct rollover.

¶14,355   LOANS

General Rules

As a general rule, any amount received as a loan from a qualified employer plan will be treated as a taxable distribution. Any pledge or assignment of a portion of an interest in a qualified employer plan also will be treated as a taxable distribution. Code Sec. 72(p).

An exception is made under Code Sec. 72(p)(2) and (4) for loans from most qualified employer plans (excluding IRAs) and nonqualified governmental 457(b) plans that satisfy the following requirements:

1. The amount of the loan, when added to the outstanding balance of all other loans made from the plan, does not exceed the lesser of (1) $50,000, reduced by the excess (if any) of the highest outstanding balance of loans from the plan during the one-year period ending on the day before the date on which the loan was made over the outstanding balance of loans from the plan on the date on which the loan was made, or (2) the greater of one-half of the employee's nonforfeitable accrued benefit under the plan or $10,000.
2. The terms of the loan must require that the loan be repaid within five years (unless the loan is used to acquire a participant's principal residence).
3. Required repayments must be substantially equal in amount and payable not less frequently than quarterly.

Owner-employees

Self-employed taxpayers who are owner-employees (which include sole proprietors and more-than-ten-percent partners) are eligible to borrow against a qualified retirement plan that is not an IRA. Code Sec. 4975(f)(6)(B)(iii).

Common Retirement Plans For Large Businesses

The most common types of qualified employer-sponsored retirement plans offered by businesses with more than 100 employees include:

- 401(k) plans (at ¶14,401),
- Roth 401(k) supplemental plans (at ¶14,405),
- 403(a) annuity contracts (at ¶14,415),
- 403(b) tax sheltered annuities (at ¶14,425),
- 457(b) state and local governmental and nongovernmental plans (at ¶14,435), and
- Retirement plans for federal and postal employees (at ¶14,445).

This section provides a summary and a comparison of the most important features of these plans.

¶14,401 401(k) PLANS

A 401(k) plan is a defined contribution plan that provides a cash or deferred arrangement (CODA) within a qualified profit-sharing, stock bonus, or pre-ERISA (i.e., established before 1974) money purchase plan. The 401(k) plan has become the dominant retirement vehicle for many Americans. More than 95% of U.S. companies offer a Sec. 401(k) plan, compared to only 36% in 1984. More than 75% of the employees of these firms participate in the Sec. 401(k) plan. The main reason for the popularity of Sec. 401(k) plans is that, unlike other qualified retirements plans, a 401(k) plan participant can elect either to receive current cash compensation or have the employer contribute like amounts on a pre-tax basis to the qualified plan. The arrangement typically contains a salary reduction agreement under which employer contributions are made only if the participant elects to reduce the amount of compensation or not to take a pay increase.

Three types of contributions may be made to 401(k) CODA plans:

1. Nonelective employer contributions which are essentially treated the same way for tax purposes as employer contributions to other qualified plans (i.e., they are excludable to the participant);
2. Elective deferral contributions made by employees under a salary reduction plan. They are also excludable for income tax purposes when contributed but are subject to social security tax (FICA) and federal unemployment tax (FUTA) under Code Secs. 3121(v)(1) and 3306(r)(1).
3. Employer matching contributions equal to the amount or a certain percentage of the employees' elective contributions.

Limit on Employee Elective Deferral Contributions

Employee elective contributions are regular-tax deferred. The amount may not exceed the lesser of:

- **Percentage limit:** 100% of compensation; or
- **Amount limit:** $18,000 in 2015, indexed for inflation.

The employee elective deferral limitation is subject to the following rules:

- **Reduction in $18,000 limit.** The maximum employee annual elective contribution limit is reduced dollar-for-dollar by additional salary reduction contributions to 403(b) plans, and to other Sec. 401(k) plans (but not to governmental 457(b) plans).
- **Age 50+ catch-up contributions.** Any plan participant who is at least or will become age 50 before the end of the year can make additional elective deferral contributions of $6,000 in 2015. The age 50+ catch-up contribution does not count towards the maximum total contribution limit of $53,000.

Aggregate Limit on Employer and Employee Contributions

An aggregate limit applies to the employer contributions made on behalf of a participating employee. This sum may not exceed the lesser of:

1. **Percentage Limit** = 100% of compensation; or
2. **Amount Limit** = $53,000 in 2015, indexed for inflation. Code Sec. 415(c)(1).

EXAMPLE 14.24	Connor Corbett participates in his employer's 401(k) plan. Under the plan, employees may elect to reduce their salary by a certain percentage and have it paid into the plan's trust. In 2015, Connor elects to defer $18,000 as a CODA contribution from his $200,000 salary. The plan provides that the employer will match the employee contribution up to 5.0 percent of compensation ($10,000). Under the general definition of compensation, the employer and employee contributions are within the Code Sec. 415(c) limit. See recap below.

(a) = Given	Compensation before reduction	200,000
(b) = Given	Employee elective deferral contribution	18,000
(c) = Given	Employer matching contribution	10,000
(d) = (b) + (c)	Total employer/employee contributions	28,000
(e) = lesser of (a) or $18,000	Employee contribution limit in 2015	18,000
(f) = the lesser of: [100% × (a)] or $53,000	Aggregate contribution limit in 2015	53,000

Compensation, as defined in Code Sec. 414(s), includes any amount deferred under a cash or deferred arrangement (CODA). These include elective deferrals under Code Secs. 125 cafeteria plans and 132(f)(4) qualified transportation fringe benefit plans (see chapter 5), Code Secs. 403(b) tax shelter annuity plans (see ¶14,425), 457(b) governmental plans (see ¶14,435), and 402(h) SEPs (see ¶14,535).

Employer and employee contributions are not subject to regular tax until the distribution year. Employee contributions are subject to FICA and FUTA tax in the contribution year while employer contributions are permanently exempt from FICA and FUTA tax.

EXAMPLE 14.25	Referring to the preceding example, the tax consequences to Connor Corbett are summarized below.

Amount. of salary subject to employee FICA:	$200,000 *(i.e., elective employee contributions, but not employer contributions, are subject to FICA tax.)*
Amount of salary currently subject to federal income tax:	$182,000 *($200,000 – $18,000)*
Amount of income currently not subject to federal income tax:	$28,000 *($18,000 employee contribution + $10,000 employer contribution)*

If Connor Corbett's plan had been a 403(b) or a governmental 457(b) plan, the tax consequences would have been the same. These plan types are discussed later in this chapter.

The employer deduction limit is equal to 25% of the compensation paid to all plan participants during that year. Code Sec. 404(a)(3)(A)(v)(I).

Excess Contribution Penalties

Employee elective contributions in excess of the maximum limit are included in the employee's income and may be subject to a 10 percent penalty. The employee must withdraw the excess contribution from the plan before April 15 of the following tax year along with any attributable income. If the excess contribution remains in the plan past the April 15 deadline, it will be taxable a second time when distributed. Reg. §1.402(g)-1(e)(8)(iii). The 10 percent penalty may be imposed on the employer for failing to return the excess funds to the employee within 2 ½ months following the plan year in which the excess contributions arose.

EXAMPLE 14.26

In January, Year 1, an employee makes an elective deferral contribution into a 401(k) plan. The contribution exceeds the statutory limit by $2,000. Explain the tax consequences with and without a timely return of the $2,000 excess contribution to the employee. Assume that the 401(k) plan year-end is June 30.

Tax Consequences	With a Timely Return	Without a Timely Return
Employee deadline	April 15, Yr. 2	(deadline not met)
Employer deadline	September 15, Yr. 1	(deadline not met)
Employee's taxable portion of the elective deferral contribution:	$2,000 in the contribution year (taxed only once)	$4,000: $2,000 in the contribution year and $2,000 in the distribution year (double taxed).
Employer penalty:	$0	$200 (10% × $2,000)

¶14,405   ROTH 401(k) PLANS

Annual Contribution Limits

A 401(k) (or a 403(b)) plan may be amended to incorporate a qualified Roth contribution program. Under such a program, participants can elect to have all or a portion of their regular elective deferrals treated as Roth contributions. Catch-up contributions may also be made as Roth contributions. For participants under age 50, the maximum contribution amount is $18,000 in 2015 ($24,000 for participants age 50 or older). Unlike regular elective deferrals, Roth contributions are included in the participant's current income; however, as explained below, qualified distributions from a designated Roth account are not included in income. Code. Sec. 402(A).

Qualified Distributions

A qualified Roth 401(k) distribution must meet essentially the same criteria as one from a Roth IRA account (see ¶14,635). The portion of a distribution consisting of direct or rollover contributions is never included in a participant's income since such contributions were funded by after-tax earnings. The earnings portion of a distribution is not included in the distributee's income if the qualifying criteria have been met.

Qualified Rollovers

Qualified distributions from a Roth 401(k) account may be rolled over to either (a) another designated Roth 401(k) for the participant (if the new plan allows for rollovers), or (b) the participant's Roth IRA only to the extent permitted under Code Sec. 402(c). Such rollovers are not taken into account for purposes of the annual limits on elective deferrals. Code Sec. 402(A)(c)(3).

Plan Requirements

Because qualified distributions are not included in an employee's income, the plan must establish and maintain a separate "designated Roth account" for designated Roth contributions and attributed earnings for each employee. Failure to maintain this separate account and recordkeeping will disqualify the program. An employer may not offer a Roth 401(k)-only plan. If a 401(k) (or 403(b)) plan is offered, pre-tax elective deferrals must also be permitted.

Ideal Participants

One major advantage of a qualifed Roth contribution program is that it allows 401(k) (or 403(b)) plan participants to avoid income tax entirely on the earnings associated with designated Roth contributions. This feature may be especially advantageous to younger, lower-paid participants who have a longer retirement horizon and for whom the benefit of tax-free distribution will significantly outweigh the tax cost. Another major advantage is that the Roth 401(k) program permits contributions that are substantially greater than the Roth IRA contribution limits. In addition, income limitations are not applicable to contributions made to a qualified Roth 401(k) program. These features may be particularly appealing to higher-paid executives who do not qualify for Roth IRA contributions because their income exceeds a statutory limitation.

¶14,415   ## QUALIFIED ANNUITY (403(a)) PLANS

A "403(a) plan" is a qualified annuity plan that pays retirement benefits under an annuity contract usually issued by an insurance company. It may be structured as a defined benefit plan or as a defined contribution plan.

With a 403(a) plan, an employer purchases retirement annuity contracts for its employees as part of a plan to provide them with retirement benefits. The annuity contracts may be purchased as the employer's contribution to its employee's retirement benefits (pursuant to a defined contribution plan), or the annuity contracts may be purchased to fund the employer's obligation to furnish a stated retirement benefit (pursuant to a defined benefit plan). Code Secs. 403(a) and 404(a)(2).

Qualifying Requirements

An annuity contract will be treated as a qualified trust under Code Sec. 401 if it would constitute a qualified trust except for the fact that it is not a trust. Code Sec. 401(f). To qualify as a qualified trust, the annuity contract and qualified annuity plan must satisfy the same requirements that must be satisfied by trusts that form a part of a pension, profit-sharing, or stock bonus plan.

If the annuity contract qualifies as a qualified trust, contributions and distributions will be taxed the same as contributions to and distributions from a qualified trust.

¶14,425   ## TAX-SHELTERED ANNUITY (403(b)) PLANS

A tax-sheltered annuity ("TSA") plan (also referred to as a "403(b)" plan), is a defined contribution plan in which an employer establishes an individual custodial account for each employee in the form of an annuity contract or mutual funds. Employers eligible to offer these plans include Code Sec. 501(c)(3) educational, religious, charitable or scientific non-profit institutions (such as private schools, colleges and universities, churches, hospitals, museums, research institutes, and foundations), public schools, and organizations other than Code Sec. 501(c)(3) institutions that employ a minister. 403(b) plans are also available for self-employed ministers.

Contribution Types

The following types of contributions may be made to a 403(b) account:

1. Elective deferrals by employees under a salary reduction agreement.
2. Nonelective contributions by the employer. Nonelective contributions include matching contributions, discretionary contributions, and mandatory contributions.
3. After-tax contributions by employees.

Contributions are directed to a financial institution approved by the employer. Before-tax contributions and account earnings remain tax-deferred until withdrawn, usually on or after retirement. When withdrawn, these amounts are taxable as ordinary income.

Employee Elective Deferral Contribution Limits

The limits imposed on employee elective deferral contributions are similar to the 401(k) plan limits previously discussed. For example, the contribution amount may not exceed the lesser of:

1. 100% of compensation; or
2. $18,000 in 2015, indexed for inflation.

As with 401(k) plans, elective employee contributions are not exempt from social security and federal unemployment taxes, the $18,000 employee elective deferral limit must be reduced by employee contributions to certain other plans, and the same "age 50+" catch-up contributions are available to 403(b) plan participants.

A plan participant who has completed at least 15 years of service with a public school system, hospital, home health service agency, health and welfare service agency, or church, may be eligible to make additional elective deferrals. The maximum allowable additional contribution for a particular year is the lesser of (a), (b), or (c), where,

(a) = $3,000;
(b) = $15,000 minus any catch-up contributions made in prior years;
(c) = the excess of $5,000 multiplied by the number of years of service over total elective deferrals made for prior years. Code Sec. 402(g)(7).

Participants are permitted to contribute under both the *age 50+* catch-up provision and the *15+ service years* catch-up provision. These catch-up contributions do not count towards the maximum total contribution limit of $53,000.

"Includible compensation" for an employee's most recent year of service is the amount of taxable compensation (not including foreign earned income or the foreign housing cost exclusion or deduction) received from the employer for the most recent period (ending no later than the close of the tax year) that may be counted as one year of service and that precedes the tax year by no more than five years. "Includible compensation" includes elective deferrals, employer contributions made on an employee's behalf that are excludable from gross income, and amounts not included in gross income by reason of Code Secs. 125 (salary reduction contributions made to a cafeteria plan), 132(f)(4)(qualified transportation fringe benefits), or 457 (elective contributions to a deferred compensation plan of a state or local government or tax-exempt organization).

Aggregate Limit on Employer and Employee Contributions

The aggregate limit imposed on aggregate employer and employee contributions is similar to the 401(k) plan limits previously discussed. For example, the aggregate contribution amount may not exceed the lesser of:

1. 100% of compensation; or
2. $53,000 in 2015, indexed for inflation.

Rules pertaining to compensation and taxable income are similar to the rules for 401(k) plans. For example, compensation, as defined in Code Sec. 414(s), includes any amount deferred under a cash or deferred arrangement (CODA) Also, the rules of taxation are similar under both plans: (a) employer contributions are permanently exempt from social security tax and federal unemployment tax; (b) regular tax is imposed in the distribution year, not the contribution year.

Qualifying Criteria

An employee's rights to benefits under an annuity contract must be nonforfeitable (except for failure to pay future premiums). If the plan (other than a plan offered by a church) offers a salary reduction agreement, it must satisfy the same types of nondiscrimination and minimum coverage requirements imposed on qualified pension, profit-sharing, and bonus plans.

Distribution Requirements

Distributions generally may not be made from a 403(b) account until the employee reaches age 59 ½, has a severance from employment, dies, becomes disabled, or, in the case of salary reduction contributions, encounters financial hardship.

Distribution requirements are similar to those imposed by Code Sec. 401(a)(9) and (31) on qualified pension, profit-sharing, and stock bonus plans (including the incidental death benefit requirement). Amounts distributed are taxed under the rules relating to annuities. Amounts included in gross income are treated as ordinary income even though they are attributable to capital gains.

EXAMPLE 14.27

Kelly, age 53, participates in GSU's 403(b) plan. Her employment at GSU began on January 1, 1996, thus, she had accumulated 19 years of service prior to 2015. Her annual salary is $50,000 in 2015 and her elective deferrals in prior years amounted to $78,000. Kelly's only prior year catch-up contribution had been a $1,000 *age 50+ catch-up contribution* in 2014. Kelly's 2015 elective deferral contributions are limited to $27,000. Had she completed less than 15 years of service, the limit would have been $24,000. See computations below.

Type of Limits:	Formula:	Years of Service:	
		19 Years	**Less than 15 Years**
Limit on regular elective deferral contributions	The lesser of: (1) = $50,000 (i.e., 100% of compensation); or (2) = $18,000 (the statutory limit).	$18,000	$18,000
Limit on "age 50+" catch-up contribution	$6,000 is the statutory limit for 2015	6,000	6,000
Limit on "15-year +" catch-up contribution If Kelly has completed 15 or more years of service, this limit is the least of (a), (b), or (c), where, (a) = $3,000; (b) = $14,000, i.e., the $15,000 maximum lifetime limit – $1,000 catch-up contributions made in prior years; (c) = $17,000, or [$5,000 statutory amount × 19 years of service] - $78,000, the total elective deferrals made in prior years.		3,000	0
Total limit on 2015 elective deferral contributions		$27,000	$24,000

EXAMPLE 14.28

Continuing from the preceding example above, if Kelly makes the maximum elective deferral contribution allowable ($27,000 with 19 years of service; $24,000 with less than 15 years), the maximum amount that GSU can contribute on her behalf would be $23,000 and $26,000, respectively. See computations below.

With 19 Years of Service: $23,000
The lesser of:
(1) = $23,000, (100% of compensation – the $27,000 elective deferral amount); or
(2) = $35,000, the $53,000 statutory limit – the $18,000 regular employee contribution (at Example 14.27 above).
  (Note that $18,000 is subtracted, not $27,000, because the catch-up contributions do not count towards the maximum statutory limit of $53,000.)

With < 15 Years of Service: $26,000
The lesser of:
(1) = $26,000 (100% of compensation – the $24,000 elective deferral amount); or
(2) = $35,000, i.e., $53,000 statutory limit – $18,000 employee contribution (computed above).
  (Again, $18,000 was subtracted, not $24,000, because the catch-up contributions do not count towards the maximum statutory limit of $53,000.)

¶14,435   SECTION 457(b) DEFERRED COMPENSATION PLANS

The 457(b) plan is a tax deferred arrangement available to employees of state and local governmental entities and certain tax-exempt organizations. It is often used as a supplement to a qualified plan such as a 403(b) plan. Participants can include: *local and state government workers, firefighters, police personnel, public and private school teachers, private and state-run hospital workers, labor union employees, employees of trade associations and private clubs,* and *independent contractors.* Although technically a nonqualified plan, the 457(b) plan is discussed in the qualified plan section of this chapter rather than the nonqualified section because it is subject to many of the same rules governing qualified plans. For example, governmental 457(b) plans must follow the same rules that apply to 401(k) and 403(b) plans with regard to:

1. employee elective deferral contributions,
2. age 50+ catch-up contributions,
3. minimum distribution rules,
4. rollover distributions and portability,

5. distributions under divorce decrees,
6. loans,
7. the requirement that amounts deferred be held for the exclusive benefit of plan participants and their beneficiaries. and
8. savings tax credits.

An advantage of 457(b) plans over qualified plans is that participants may sever their employment and receive distributions at any age without incurring a 10 percent early withdrawal penalty. Amounts received are subject only to regular income tax under Code Sec. 457(a)(1). A disadvantage is that, unlike most qualified plans, 457(b) plans cannot accept after-tax deferrals.

Two types of 457(b) plans exist: governmental and nongovernmental. Public schools are considered governmental. Members of 501(c)(3) organizations (e.g., charitable foundations, private schools, museums and hospitals, and unions) are considered nongovernmental.

Minimum Distribution Requirements

Both governmental and nongovernmental 457(b) plans must meet certain minimum distribution requirements under Code Sec. 457(d). In general, a 457(b) plan participant cannot receive a distribution from the plan earlier than:

1. the calendar year in which a participant attains age 70 ½ (if still actively employed),
2. the participant severs employment due to death, termination, or retirement, or
3. the participant is faced with an unforeseeable emergency

An unforeseen emergency includes any of the following:

    a. severe financial hardship to the participant or the participant's dependent resulting from a sudden and unexpected illness or accident
    b. loss of the participant's property due to casualty
    c. other similar extraordinary and unforeseeable circumstances arising as a result of events beyond the control of the participant

The circumstances that make up an unforeseen emergency vary depending on the facts of each case. The general rule of thumb is that if you can foresee the expense, you cannot get a 457(b) plan distribution for it. Distributions for unforeseen emergencies also cannot be made if the hardship can be reversed:

    a. through insurance or similar reimbursement or compensation
    b. through liquidating the participant's own assets, provided liquidation does not itself cause severe financial hardship
    c. by stopping deferrals to the 457 plan.

Examples of extraordinary and unforeseeable circumstances include the imminent foreclosure of, or eviction from, a primary residence or the need to pay for medical or funeral expenses. However, educational expenses are not unforeseen, so are not included.

Tax aspects that are unique to governmental and nongovernmental 457(b) plans are discussed below.

Governmental 457(b) Plans

Governmental 457(b) plans have become increasingly popular in recent years due to an expanded deferral advantage and portability.

Expanded Deferral Feature

The maximum deferral limit for employee elective contributions to 457(b) plans is not reduced by employee elective deferral contributions made to a 401(k) or 403(b) plans. Therefore, a participant covered by a governmental 457(b) plan coupled with a 401(k) or 403(b) plan may defer the maximum $18,000 for 2015 into *each* plan for a total $36,000 in deferrals ($48,000 if age 50 or older, given the $6,000 catch-up provision for each plan).

EXAMPLE 14.29	Mrs. Pruneda, age 52, earns a $55,000 salary teaching in a local public high school. Since her husband's income is substantial, she can afford to defer the maximum amount of her salary for tax purposes. Her employer offers its employees both a 403(b) plan and a 457(b) plan, and she participates in both. The maximum amount of employee deferral contributions that Mrs. Pruneda can elect in 2015 is $48,000 (for each plan, $18,000 regular deferral contributions plus $6,000 *age 50*+ catch-up contributions).

Portability

Distributions from governmental 457(b) plans are eligible to roll over to or from other plans (401(k), 403(b), or other governmental 457(b) plans, SEP IRAs, SIMPLE IRAs, and traditional IRAs) without losing tax-deferred status.

EXAMPLE 14.30	Continuing from the previous example, assume Mrs. Pruneda decides to leave public teaching in order to begin a consulting job with a private company offering a 401(k) plan. She would be permitted to roll over her 403(b) and 457(b) funds (contributions plus income) into the 401(k) plan account. Alternatively, she could roll over the funds into an IRA account.

PLANNING POINTER	Although the rollover provisions for governmental 457(b) plans offer substantial flexibility, the rules do not require qualified plans or another governmental 457(b) plan to accept rollovers. (A rollover to an IRA, though, is always an available option.)

Employee Elective Deferral Contribution Limits

Employee elective contributions are regular-tax deferred. The deferral contribution amount may not exceed the lesser of:

1. **Percentage Limit:** Up to 100% of *gross* compensation; or
2. **Amount Limit:** $18,000 in 2015, indexed for inflation.

As with 401(k) and 403(b) plans, gross compensation under a governmental 457(b) plan is the combination of employee salary and benefits. The formula above also represents the aggregate limit on employer and employee contributions (in contrast to 401(k) and 403(b) plans for which the aggregate employer and employee contribution limit is the lesser of (1) 100 percent of net compensation or (2) $53,000 in 2015).

EXAMPLE 14.31	Melissa Clayton, age 18, earns a $12,000 salary as a part-time helper at the city zoo's arachnid center. Melissa participates in her employer's 457(b) plan. Since she lives with her parents, she can afford to defer the maximum amount of her salary for tax purposes. The maximum deferral amount that Melissa can contribute in 2015 is $12,000 (the lesser of $12,000 gross compensation or the $18,000 statutory limit).

Although elective employee contributions are regular-tax deferred, they may still subject to employer and employee social security tax if the governmental employer has entered into an agreement with the Social Security Administration to cover its employees under FICA. Federal unemployment taxes do not apply to compensation deferred under governmental 457(b) plans, since employees of state and local governments are not subject to federal unemployment taxes under Code Sec. 3306(c)(7).

EXAMPLE 14.32	In the previous example, none of Melissa Clayton's $12,000 salary would be subject to federal income tax or federal unemployment tax. However the entire amount may be subject to social security tax if the city government had arranged with the Social Security Administration to cover its employees under FICA.

The maximum employee annual elective contribution limit is reduced dollar-for-dollar by additional salary reduction contributions to other 457(b) plans but not by contributions to 401(k) and 403(b) plans.

EXAMPLE 14.33	During the first half of 2015, Barney worked as jail keeper for the city of Raleigh and contributed $10,000 into his 457(b) plan account. Later in the year, he left the Raleigh job and began working as deputy sheriff for the town of Mayberry. If Mayberry also offered a 457(b) plan, Barney would be permitted to contribute only a maximum $8,000 into the Mayberry 457(b) plan account ($18,000 statutory limit reduced by the $10,000 previously contributed into Raleigh's 457(b) plan). If Mayberry had provided a 403(b) plan instead of a 457(b) plan, Barney would have been permitted to contribute a maximum $18,000 into his 403(b) plan account at Mayberry, even though he had already contributed $10,000 into Raleigh's 457(b) plan.

Final Three-year Catch-up Contributions

Governmental 457(b) plan participants who have not contributed the maximum amounts in prior years can make additional elective deferral contributions in 2015 during the 3 years prior to "normal" retirement age (as defined by the plan). The additional amount that can be deferred is the lesser of:

1. $18,000 (i.e., the regular elective deferral limit in 2015); or
2. That portion of the regular elective deferral limit that has not been used in prior years.

Participants who choose to take advantage of the *final three year* catch-up provision cannot also take advantage of the *age 50* + catch-up provision. If, in prior years, an employee was eligible to participate in both a 457(b) plan and a 403(b) plan and elected to contribute the maximum amount allowed only to the 403(b) account, the employee is not entitled to make *final 3-year* catch-up contributions, even though no contributions had been previously made to the 457(b) plan.

EXAMPLE 14.34	Professor Krank, age 63, participates in Ansley State University's 457(b) plan. The normal retirement age at ASU is 65. Krank's annual salary is $160,000 in 2015. In earlier years, he had underutilized his allowable elective deferrals by a total amount of $12,000. If Krank elects to make the *final 3-year* catch-up contribution, the maximum amount of elective deferral contributions for 2015 will be limited to $30,000 If instead, he elects to make the *age 50+* catch-up contribution, the limit will be $24,000. See computations below.

Comparison of Catch-Up Contribution Elections		Catch-Up Contribution Elected:	
		Final 3-Year	**Age 50+**
Limit on regular elective deferral contributions	The lesser of: (1) = $160,000 (i.e., 100% of compensation); or (2) = $18,000 (the statutory limit).	$18,000	$18,000
Limit on "age 50+" catch-up contribution	$6,000 is the statutory limit for 2015. However, this catch-up amount is not permitted if the taxpayer elects to make a "final 3-year catch-up" contribution. (See below.)	(Not permitted if a final 3-year catch-up contribution is made)	6,000
Limit on "final 3-year catch-up" contribution	The lesser of: (1) = $18,000 (i.e., an amt. equal to the regular elective deferral limit of $18,000 in 2015); or (2) = $12,000 (i.e., the portion of the regular elective deferral limit that had not been used in prior years—from the facts above).	12,000	(Not permitted if an age 50+ catch-up contribution is made)
Maximum amount of elective deferral contributions in 2015.		$30,000	$24,000

Protection from Creditors

Section 1448 of the Small Business Jobs Protection Act of 1996 (SBJPA) added Sec. 457(g) of the Code, which requires that 457(b) plan maintained by state or local government employers hold all plan assets and income in trust, or in custodial accounts or annuity contracts (described in Code Sec. 401(f)), for the exclusive benefit of their participants and beneficiaries. This provision provides governmental 457(b) plan participants the same protection from employers and employer creditors afforded participants in qualified plans.

Participation and Coverage

There are no specific coverage requirements for Section 457(b) plans. For a governmental employer, the plan can be offered to all employees or to any group of employees—even a single employee. Individuals who perform services for the employer are eligible to participate. Code Sec. 457(b)(1). This includes employees as well as independent contractors. The plan document should spell out the specific rules for participation. Each participant has a segregated account and can direct the account balance into any approved investment option.

Rollovers

Rollovers to and from governmental 457(b) plans will generally follow the restrictions and guidelines for rollovers from IRAs and qualified plans such as 401(k)s. and 403(b)s. For example, a direct trustee-to-trustee rollover can be made to avoid a 20 percent withholding tax being taken out. Also, an indirect rollover must be completed within 60 days. If 457(b) plan proceeds are rolled over to an IRA, the amount will be subject to the one-year waiting period for successive IRA rollovers.

PLANNING POINTER	Rollovers, like other distributions, are reported on IRS Form 1099-R by the plan trustee or custodian. That is how the IRS identifies a taxpayer who receives a distribution from a retirement plan and does not roll it over as required.

TAX BLUNDER

As stated above, 457(b) plan participants may sever their employment and receive distributions at any age without incurring a 10 percent early withdrawal penalty. However, if governmental employees roll over 457(b) funds into a 403(b), 401(k), IRA or any other plan [other than a 457(b) plan], this benefit will be lost and the 10 percent penalty will apply if premature distributions are later received. Conversely, if funds from a qualified plan such as a 403(b) are rolled over into a governmental 457(b) plan, the 10% early withdrawal penalty cannot be avoided. For these reasons, plan providers or sponsors must account for the rollover funds separately.

Nongovernmental 457(b) Plans

Timing of Taxation on Deferral Amounts

The rules governing the timing of taxation on deferral amounts differ between governmental and nongovernmental 457(b) plans. State and local government employees need not include in gross income amounts of deferred compensation until such amounts are paid. The fact that such amounts may have been funded at an earlier date for the exclusive benefit of the employees is irrelevant. Code Sec. 457(a)(1)(A). However, employees of nongovernmental 501(c)(3) tax-exempt organizations must report ordinary income in the year the amounts are first made available to them under the terms of the plan, even if the amounts have not yet been distributed to them. Code Sec. 457(a)(1)(B); Reg. §1.457-7(c)(1). In general, amounts are considered to be made available (and, thus, are includible in the gross income of the participant) at the earliest date, on or after severance from employment, on which the plan allows distributions to commence. Reg. §1.457-7(c)(2)(i).

EXAMPLE 14.35	Jennifer Otwell's employment with the Zueta Foundation, a Sec. 501(c)(3) tax exempt organization, is terminated effective October 15, Year 1. During her employment with the foundation, she had accumulated $100,000 deferred compensation in her 457(b) account. This amount is paid to her on January 31, Year 2. The terms of the 457(b) plan state that *"distributions of amounts deferred are to commence on the date that is two months after the effective date on which a participant has a severance from employment."* Therefore, the $100,000 is considered to be made available (and, thus, includible in Jennifer's gross income), on December 15, Year 1, two months after the October 15 severance date, even though she does not actually receive payment until January 31, Year 2. If Jennifer's employer had been a state or local government, the $100,000 would not have been includible in gross income until January 31, Year 2, the date the funds had been paid to her.

TAX BLUNDER

Since the timing of taxation is determined largely on the date on which the nongovernmental 457(b) plan allows distributions to commence, an employee may inadvertently and prematurely have to pay tax on a deferral, even if a distribution is not made, because of an error in the way the 457(b) plan is set up.

Participation and Coverage

Nongovernmental 457(b) plans are generally structured as unfunded nonqualified deferred compensation plans covering only a select group of management or highly compensated employees (a "top-hat" plan). Providing such limited coverage is *necessary* in order for a nongovernmental plan to be eligible for tax deferral under Code Sec. 457(b). The reason for this unusual requirement centers on incompatible funding requirements under the Employee Retirement Income Security Act ("ERISA") and Code Sec. 457(a)(1)(B). A top-hat plan is not subject to the participation, vesting, funding, and fiduciary responsibility requirements of ERISA. (ERISA secs. 201(2), 301(a)(3), 401(a)(1), and 4021(b)(6)) By avoiding ERISA's funding requirements, current compensation need not be funded into a trust or an annuity contract for the exclusive benefit of employees in order to achieve a tax deferral advantage. Such funding would be incompatible with Code Sec. 457(a)(1)(B) which requires inclusion in a participant's gross income in the year such amounts are first made available to participants under the terms of a 457(b) plan, even if merely payable and not yet paid. Moreover, Code Sec. 457(b)(6) requires that an eligible deferred compensation plan must provide that all amounts of compensation deferred under the plan and all income attributable to such amounts should remain unfunded with respect to the participant's interest: *"[Deferred amounts] shall remain (until made available to the participant or other beneficiary) solely the property and rights of the employer ... subject only to the claims of the employer's general creditors."* Thus, by providing coverage only to a top-hat group, a tax exempt organization's 457(b) plan is able remain unqualified and unfunded, and therefore eligible for tax deferral.

TAX BLUNDER

A Sec. 501(c)(3) tax exempt organization that wishes to establish an unfunded nonqualified deferred compensation plans under Code Sec. 457(b) should *not* make it available to all of its employees. Allowing such broad coverage would place the plan in the undesirable position of having to comply with the funding requirements under section 403(c)(1) of ERISA. Such funding would render the 457(b) plan ineligible for tax deferral.

PLANNING POINTER

Employees who participate in a tax-exempt organization's 457(b) deferred compensation plan run the risk that their employer may not have sufficient funds to meet future payout obligations. The lack of security that such a plan offers (with plan assets being available to the employer's creditors) may deter a prudent investor from utilizing a nongovernmental 457(b) as a vehicle for saving any significant amount toward retirement.

Prohibited Rollovers

Unlike government 457(b) plans, tax-exempt organizations are not allowed to hold assets in trust for employees. Therefore, employees of tax-exempt organizations are unable to rollover 457(b) funds to or from other plans. A tax-exempt organization on the other hand, is permitted to move its own 457(b) funds from one nongovernmental 457(b) plan to another if the other plan accepts such transfers. However, such funds may not be rolled into an IRA or another type of employer-sponsored retirement plan.

Exhibit 5. COMMON RETIREMENT PLANS FOR LARGE EMPLOYERS—ELIGIBLE EMPLOYERS

Characteristics:	401(k)	403(b) ("Tax Sheltered Annuity" Plan)	457(b) (Governmental)	457(b) (Nongovernmental)
Description of Eligible Employers:	Taxable entities	Tax-exempt organizations that are: (a) charitable, (b) educational, (c) religious, or (d) scientific Public school systems	State and local governments	Tax-exempt organizations that are: (a) charitable, (b) educational, (c) religious, or (d) scientific
Examples of eligible employers:				
For-profit employer formed as a C or S corporation, partnership, LLC, or proprietorship	Yes	No	No	No
Federal government (refer to a discussion later in the chapter)	No	No	No	No
State and local governments	No	No (unless it's an educational institution)	Yes	No
Schools (K to university level)	No (unless it's a for-profit business)	Yes for both governmental (state & local) or 501(c)(3) tax exempt organizations	Yes for governmental (state & local) employers	Yes for 501(c)(3) organizations
Hospitals	No (unless it's a for-profit business)	Yes for 501(c)(3) organizations	Yes for governmental (state & local) employers	Yes for 501(c)(3) organizations
Museums that are tax-exempt	No	Yes for 501(c)(3) organizations	Yes for governmental (state & local) employers	Yes for 501(c)(3) organizations
Libraries that are tax-exempt	No	Yes for 501(c)(3) organizations	Yes for governmental (state & local) employers	Yes for 501(c)(3) organizations
Private research foundations	No	Yes	No	Yes
Labor unions	No	Yes	No	Yes
Private clubs	No	Yes	No	Yes

Exhibit 6. COMMON RETIREMENT PLANS FOR LARGE EMPLOYERS—BASIC FEATURES

Features:	401(k)	403(b) ("Tax Sheltered Annuity" Plan)	457(b) (Governmental)	457(b) (Nongovernmental)
Plan type	Qualified	Qualified	Nonqualified	Nonqualified
Able to discriminate?	No	No	Yes	Yes
Loans up to $50,000 OK?	Yes	Yes	Yes	No
Subject to 10% penalty on premature withdrawals?	Yes	Yes	No (unless the distribution consists of an amount previously rolled over from another type of plan)	No
Subject to 50% penalty on late RMDs?	Yes	Yes	Yes	No
Subject to $5,000 mandatory cash-out rules?	Yes	Yes	Yes	No
Portable with other employer-sponsored plans and IRAs?	Yes	Yes	Yes	No
Subject to statutory vesting rules for employer contributions?	Yes	Yes	No	No
Must be for exclusive benefit of employees?	Yes	Yes for retirement income accounts; No for annuity contracts and custodial accounts.	Yes	No
Protection from creditors of employer?	Yes	Yes	Yes	No

Exhibit 7. COMMON RETIREMENT PLANS FOR LARGE EMPLOYERS—CONTRIBUTION LIMITS

Limits:	401(k)	403(b) ("Tax Sheltered Annuity" Plan)	457(b) (Governmental)	457(b) Non-governmental
Are employee elective deferral contributions allowed? ("GC" is defined below)	Yes, limited to the lesser of: (1) = 18,000; (2) = 100% GC + $6,000 if age 50+	Yes, limited to the lesser of: (1) = 18,000; (2) = 100% GC + $6,000 if age 50+ + $3,000 (max.) if completed 15 years of service	Yes, limited to the lesser of: (1) = 18,000; (2) = 100% GC + $6,000 if age 50+ OR + $18,000 (max.) if within 3 years of retirement	Yes, limited to the lesser of: (1) = 18,000; (2) = 100% GC + $18,000 (max.) if within 3 years of retirement (The 50 + catch-up contribution is not permitted.)
Aggregate Limit on Employer and Employee Contributions	Lesser of: (1) = $53,000 or (2) = 100% GC plus catch-up contributions	Lesser of: (1) = $53,000 or (2) = 100% GC plus catch-up contributions	Same as employee elective deferral contribution limit above.	Same as employee elective deferral contribution limit above.
Are contributions subject to FICA or FUTA?	No for employer contributions; Yes for employee contributions.	Same as 401(k)	Same as 401(k)	Yes
Are employee supplemental after-tax contributions allowed?	Yes if written into the plan	Same as 401(k)	No	No

"GC:" Gross compensation is equal to the employee's salary plus any qualified benefits such as medical insurance premiums under a cafeteria plan.

¶14,445   RETIREMENT PLANS FOR FEDERAL AND POSTAL EMPLOYEES

Federal Employees' Retirement System

Qualified Employees

The Federal Employees' Retirement System (FERS) provides retirement benefits for federal or postal employees who first were employed by the federal government on or after January 1, 1984, and those employers hired before 1984 who elected to change from Civil Service Retirement System (CSRS) coverage (explained below) to FERS coverage. Federal employees covered by FERS are required to pay Social Security taxes and are entitled to receive Social Security benefits based on their compensation from the federal government.

Description of Plan

The FERS Basic Annuity is a *defined benefit program*. This means that the benefits received from a FERS annuity are based on the employee's years of service and salary, rather than on the amount of contributions and earnings. Most contributions to this annuity program are made by the federal agency employer on the employee's behalf. In addition, employee contributions are mandatory and the amount contributed is defined by law. The plan is administered by the U.S. Office of Personnel.

Civil Service Retirement System

Qualified employees

The Civil Service Retirement System (CSRS) provides retirement benefits for federal or postal employees who were employed by the federal government before 1984 and have not opted to be covered by FERS. Federal employees covered by CSRS do not have to pay Social Security taxes and are not entitled to receive any Social Security benefits based on their compensation from the federal government.

Description of Plan

Like the FERS Basic Annuity plan, the CSRS annuity plan is a defined benefit program. Benefits distributed under this plan are defined according to years of service and salary while contributions are adjusted periodically to support the level of defined benefits. In general, the formula used to compute the CSRS annuity is more favorable to participants than the formula used to compute the FERS annuity. Like FERS plan, the CSRS plan is administered by the U.S. Office of Personnel.

Thrift Savings Plans

Qualified employees

Participants covered under FERS or CSRS, as well as non-participating uniformed service personnel (both active duty and ready reserve status) may, at their option, participate in a thrift savings plans (TSP). TSP participants can be full- or part-time employees.

Description of Plan

The TSP is a *defined contribution plan* that offers participants the same type of tax savings and tax benefits as offered by 401(k) plans in the private sector. The income available at retirement will depend on how much has been contributed to the account and the earnings of those contributions. Unlike employee contributions under FERS and CSRS annuity plans, employee contributions to TSPs are voluntary and separate from FERS and CSRS contributions. The TSP is administered by the Federal Retirement Thrift Investment Board, an independent government agency, comprising five members appointed by the President, and an executive director.

TSP Investment Choices

There are six investment funds available to TSP participants:

1. G Fund (investments in short-term, non-marketable U.S Treasury securities;
2. C Fund (large-capitalization, i.e., $5 billion or higher, of U.S. stock)
3. F Fund (a bond index fund consisting of a mix of government and corporate bonds);
4. S Fund (small capitalization, i.e., $150 to $500 million, and mid-capitalization, i.e., $500 million to $500 billion, U.S. stocks);
5. I Fund (mostly large-capitalization foreign stocks).

6. L Fund (investment mix among the G, C, F, S, and I Funds, using professionally determined investment allocations that are tailored to different time horizons).

All participants may elect to invest any portion of their current account balances or future contributions in any or all of the funds. All participants also may make interfund transfers. An interfund transfer is the movement of all or some of the money in a participant's account among the funds.

Limit on TSP Employee Contributions

As previously discussed, the formula used to compute the FERS Basic Annuity is not as favorable to participants as the formula used to compute the CSRS annuity. Thus, for FERS employees, the TSP is an *integral part* of their retirement package, along with their FERS Basic Annuity and Social Security. For CSRS employees, the TSP is a *supplement* to their CSRS annuity and Social Security. The TSP limits for FERS and CSRS participants are covered below.

TSP Limits for FERS Participants

FERS participants can contribute up to 100% of basic pay (not to exceed a $18,000 statutory limit in 2015) to a TSP account as soon as they become a Federal employee. Participants who are age 50 or over at the end of the year generally can make $6,000 catch-up contributions to the plan in 2015. Once they are eligible, they will receive:

- agency automatic contributions *(equal to 1% of salary, beginning in the last month of the second open season after the hiring date);*
- agency matching contributions *(Generally, an agency will match each employee contributions up to 3% of pay, and will contribute $0.50 for each additional dollar of employee contributions up to 2% of pay. This also begins in the last month of the second open season after the hiring date);*
- immediate vesting in agency matching contributions and vesting—generally in 3 years—in agency automatic (1%) contributions.

Newly hired employees can sign up to contribute to the TSP as soon as they are hired. Their contributions will begin no later than the first full pay period after their employer-agency accepts their election. If they do not make an election within this 60-day period, they must wait until an "open season" to do so. The two open seasons are April 15 through June 30 and October 15 through December 31. Generally, elections are made effective during the last month of the open season.

TSP Limits for CSRS Participants

CSRS participants can contribute up to 100% of their basic pay each pay period (not to exceed an annual limit of $18,000 in 2015) to a TSP account. Contributions can be made as soon as the employee is hired. CSRS participants do not receive agency contributions.

Other Features of TSPs

TSPs offer the following features to all participants:

- **Rollovers.** Ability to transfer tax-deferred funds into the TSP from a traditional IRA or other eligible employer plan.
- **Portability.** Once a participant separates from Federal service, the participant's TSP account balance is eligible to be transferred to most qualified employer-sponsored retirement account, traditional IRAs, and governmental 457(b) accounts while preserving its tax-deferred status.
- **Catch-up contributions.** Participants who are or will become age 50 in 2015 are entitled to make "50+ catch-up" elective deferral contributions. The annual limit for 2015 is $6,000.
- **Early withdrawals.** In-service withdrawals for financial hardship or after reaching age 59½ are permitted.

Common Retirement Plans For Small Businesses

The most common types of qualified employer-sponsored retirement plans among incorporated employers and self-employed persons with not more than 100 employees include:

- Solo (or "individual") 401(k) plans (at ¶14,515),
- Keogh plans (at ¶14,525),

¶14,445

- Simplified Employer Plans ("SEPs") (at ¶14,535), and
- Savings Incentive Match Plan for Employees ("SIMPLEs") (at ¶14,545).

The following sections provide a summary and a comparison of some of the most important features of these plans.

¶14,501   PLANS FOR SMALL BUSINESSES—BASIC CONCEPTS

Classification of Plans

No distinction is generally made between pension, profit-sharing, and other retirement plans (e.g., a 401(k) plan or SEP IRA) established by corporations and those established by individual proprietors and partnerships. In the past, the terms "Keogh Plan," or "H.R. 10 Plan" were used to distinguish a retirement plan established by a self-employed individual from a plan established by a corporation or other entity. However, retirement plans for self-employed persons are now generally referred to by the name that is used for the particular type of plan (e.g., solo 401(k), SEP IRA, or SIMPLE IRA). Keogh plans include money purchase plans and profit-sharing plans. See ¶14,525.

Most retirement plans covering self-employed persons are defined contribution plans. There are basically two types: profit-sharing plans and money purchase pension plans. Typically, contributions to a profit-sharing plan are made out of profits, although there is no requirement that a qualified profit-sharing plan contain a definite predetermined formula for determining the amount of profits to be shared. Rev. Rul. 56-366, 1956-2 CB 976.

In a money purchase pension plan, contributions are not based on profits. Reg. §1.401-1(b)(1)(i). Typically, contributions to a money purchase pension plan are expressed as a percentage of compensation and must be made regardless of whether or not the enterprise has profits. If a plan provides that contributions on behalf of participants are a fixed percentage of compensation and defines the compensation of a self-employed person as his earned income, the plan apparently will be classified as a money purchase pension plan, even though no contributions will be made on behalf of self-employed participants in a year when the enterprise has no profits. Reg. §1.401-11(b)(1).

Comparison of Plan Features

In choosing the right qualified plan for a small business, the plan features should be carefully considered to insure that owner objectives will be met. Ten important considerations are discussed below.

1. *Self as trustee.* With a solo 401(k) plan or a Keogh plan, a taxpayer may achieve maximum investment flexibility by electing to serve as trustee and manage the trust funds. This election is not available for SEP or SIMPLE IRAs.
2. *Legal entity.* Keogh and SEP IRA plans are available only to self-employed taxpayers (e.g., proprietors, partners, and members of LLCs) as well as their employees. Shareholders in C and S corporations are viewed as common-law employees rather than self-employed taxpayers. Thus, C and S corporations are not eligible to establish Keogh or SEP IRA plans.
3. *Multiple employees.* A business with more than one full-time employee (other than the taxpayer's spouse) is not eligible to maintain a solo 401(k) plan. If a sole owner-employee participating in a solo 401(k) plan hires one or more full-time employee (other than a spouse) at any time during the year, the solo 401(k) plan must revert to a corporate-styled traditional 401(k) plan with potentially cumbersome reporting requirements.
4. *IRS reporting requirements.* Taxpayers with SEP or SIMPLE IRA plans are not required to file annual reports with the IRS (except for W-2 reporting). Taxpayers with solo 401(k) plans and Keogh plans may be required to file annual IRS reports, depending on the size of the plan assets. If a solo 401(k) or a Keogh plan does not provide benefits to anyone except the owner and owner's spouse, or in the case of a partnership, one or more partners and their spouses, and total plan assets are $250,000 or less, there are no IRS reporting requirements. However, once the amount of plan assets rises above $250,000, Form 5500-EZ must be filed by the last day of the 7th month after the plan year ends (July 31 for calendar-year plans). If any plan benefits are provided by an insurance company or insurance service, or, in the case of solo 401(k) plans, if the plan has more than one participant (other than the taxpayer's spouse), Form 5500 and appropriate schedules are required by the same deadline.
5. *Statutory deadlines.* The SEP IRA offers the most flexibility with respect to deadlines. The deadline for establishing a SEP IRA and making a contribution for the current year is the automatic six-month

extension due date for the taxpayer's return (October 15 of the following year in the case of an individual taxpayer). The SIMPLE IRA plan must be established by October 1 of the current year. However, once established, contributions for the current year can be made as late as October 15 of the following year (the six-month extension due date of an individual taxpayer's return). Solo 401(k) plans and Keogh plans must be established, and contributions must be made, no later than December 31 of the current year. (Some institutions may require earlier cutoff dates.) The deadline for deemed employee elective deferral contributions under a solo 401(k) is October 15 of the following year (the six-month extension due date of an individual taxpayer's return).

6. *Vesting.* Another unique feature of a Keogh plan is that accrued employee benefits from employer contributions generally are subject to the regular vesting rules of Code Sec. 411 (previously discussed at ¶14,265). From an employer perspective, this feature may be viewed favorably because it may discourage unexpected terminations by employee-participants. Accrued employee benefits under SEP or SIMPLE plans must be free of vesting requirements and nonforfeitable at all times.

7. *Plan loans.* A taxpayer participating in a solo 401(k) or Keogh is permitted to borrow against the plan, subject to the limits described at ¶14,355. Taxpayers participating in any form of IRA (e.g., SEP, SIMPLE, traditional, or Roth), are prohibited from borrowing against the plan.

8. *Participation requirements.* Participation requirements warrant a discussion by plan.

   ▪ **Solo 401(k).** The solo 401(k) plan may be adopted only by businesses whose only eligible persons to participate in the plan are the business owner and spouse. If the business has non-owner employees who are eligible to participate in the plan, the business is not eligible to adopt the solo 401(k) plan. However, a business with non-owner employees may still be eligible to adopt a solo 401(k) only if the non-owner employees are not eligible to participate in the plan. The determination of whether other employees are eligible depends on the eligibility requirements stated in the plan. However, the requirements must remain within the following limitations for employees who:
     a. attained age 21, or
     b. have worked 1,000 hours in any 12-consecutive-month period.
       When determining the eligibility requirements for a solo 401(k) plan, the plan may exclude from participation employees who are non-resident aliens and/or those who receive benefits under a collective bargaining agreement.

   ▪ **Keogh.** A Keogh plan cannot exclude any employee from participation on account of age or years of service, except for the exclusion of employees who:
     a. are under age 21, or
     b. have less than one "year of service," i.e., less than 1,000 hours in any 12-consecutive-month period. (However, a plan that provides for 100 percent vesting after no more than two years of service may require a two-year period of service for eligibility to participate.)

   ▪ **SEP.** The SEP participation rules are most favorable from an employer perspective because they permit stricter employee-eligibility requirements than Keogh or SIMPLE plans. Under a SEP arrangement, the employer is required to contribute to the IRA of each employee who:
     a. has attained the age of 21,
     b. has performed services for the employer during at least three out of the immediately preceding five calendar years, and
     c. has received at least a specified dollar amount of compensation ($600 in 2015) from the employer for the year. Code Sec. 408(k)(2).

   ▪ **SIMPLE.** For SIMPLE IRA plans, there are no age limits. All employees who received at least $5,000 in compensation from the employer during any two preceding calendar years and who are reasonably expected to receive $5,000 in compensation during the current year must be eligible to participate. SIMPLE 401(k) plans on the other hand, generally follow the same participation requirements as traditional 401(k) plans. (The 401(k) requirements also apply to Keogh plans—see above).
       Less restrictive participation requirements may be imposed than the statutory limits described above. Notice 98-4, 1998-1 CB 269, Q&As C-1 and C-2; Code Sec. 408(p)(4).

9. *Rollovers.* The rollover rules governing SIMPLE IRA plans are the most restrictive among qualified plans. A SIMPLE IRA account is not permitted to receive rollover funds from another qualified account unless the originating account is also a qualified SIMPLE IRA account. An employee is permitted to execute a SIMPLE-to-SIMPLE rollover at any time after inception of the employee's participation

in the plan. Code Sec. 408(d)(3)(G). However, rollovers from SIMPLE IRAs into SEP or traditional IRAs are permitted after two years from the inception of the employee's participation. See ¶14,345 for a general discussion of rollovers to and from other qualified plans.

10. *Contribution and deduction limits.* At different levels of employee compensation ("net SEI" in the case of owner-employees as defined below) different plans may produce the largest contribution and deduction for the owner-employee. Specific formulas for the solo 401(k), Keogh plan, SEP IRA and SIMPLE IRA are explained later in this chapter.

EXAMPLE 14.36	J. P. Zack, Inc. is a calendar year corporation. A few years ago, the corporation established a SEP for its eligible employees. In order to be eligible for a current-year deduction, contributions to the separate SEP IRAs of each employee must generally be made by the due date of the corporate tax return (i.e., March 15, of the following year). However, if it has requested a six-month filing extension, the contributions may be made up to September 15 of the following year. If the employer had been a proprietor, the deadline for contributions would have been April 15 of the following year, or October 15 of that year if an automatic six-month extension had been filed. The same deadlines would apply to a Keogh or SIMPLE plan.

PLANNING POINTER	1. Taxpayers participating in a SEP, SIMPLE, or traditional IRA cannot borrow from the IRA. However, for SEP and traditional IRAs (but not SIMPLE IRAs), the account funds can be rolled into a qualified employer-sponsored plan (e.g., a solo 401(k) or a Keogh plan) that is not an IRA and then borrowed. 2. Loans from SIMPLE 401(k) (unlike SIMPLE IRAs) are permitted. An employer may wish to establish a SIMPLE 401(k) rather than a SIMPLE IRA in order to include loans as a feature of the plan. For employees who need to tap into their retirement assets when they are ineligible to receive distributions from the plan, loans can be an attractive plan feature.

Taxation—Exposure and Timing

Employer and employee contributions generally are subject to the same rules that govern retirement plans for large, multiemployee employers. Employer contributions are permanently exempt from FICA and FUTA tax under Code Secs. 3121(v)(1) and 3306(r)(1); however, employee elective deferral contributions (to solo 401(k) and SIMPLE plans, for example) are subject to FICA and FUTA taxes in the contribution year. In most cases, employer contributions and employee elective deferral contributions (if eligible) are tax-deferred in the contribution year and taxable in the distribution year.

General Limits on Contributions, Deductions, and Benefits

Defined Contribution Plan Limits on Additions

For 2015, the *total additions* to a defined contribution plan cannot be more than the *lesser* of: (1) 100% of the participant's compensation (compensation is limited to a maximum of $265,000 in 2015) or (2) $53,000. Code Sec. 415(c)(1). The term "total additions" includes employer contributions, employee contributions, and forfeitures. Code Sec. 415(c)(2). Forfeitures under a profit-sharing plan, arising as a result of severance of employment of participants whose interests have not vested in full, may not revert to the employer upon termination of the plan. For self-employed taxpayers with employees, forfeiture allocations from other participants' accounts may not revert to the employer under any circumstances. Reg. §1.401(k)-11(b)(3).

Defined Contribution Plan Limits on Deductions

For 2015, an employer's *deduction* for its contributions to a defined contribution plan may not exceed the *lesser* of: (1) 25% of the participant's compensation ($265,000 is the maximum compensation that may be considered in 2015) or (2) $53,000. Code Sec. 402(h) and Code Sec. 404(j)(1)(B). Any unused deduction can be carried over and deducted (subject to the percentage limitation for the carryover year) in later years.

Defined Benefit Plan Limits on Benefits and Deductions

For 2015, the annual benefit from a defined benefit plan may not exceed the *lesser* of $210,000 or 100% of the participant's average compensation for the highest three consecutive years. Code Sec. 415(b)(1)(A). The deduction for contributions to a defined benefit plan must be based upon the computations of an actuary.

Concepts Related To Plans For Self-Employed Persons

The following definitions relate specifically to plans established by an unincorporated trade or business, i.e., a sole proprietorship or a partnership. These definitions are all found in Code Sec. 401(c).

"Employer"

In the qualified plan provisions, when reference is made to the term "employer," a sole proprietor is treated as the proprietor's own employer (thus, the proprietor serves two roles: that of *employer* and of *employee*). However, a partnership is considered to be the employer of each partner. Code Sec. 401(c)(4). As a result, while sole proprietors may establish their own retirement plans, only a partnership may establish a retirement plan for its partners.

Owner-employee

If a qualified retirement plan provides contributions for an owner-employee, contributions on behalf of the owner-employee may be made only with respect to earned income of the owner-employee that is derived from the trade or business with respect to which the plan is established. Code Sec. 401(a)(10)(A), (D). An "owner-employee" is any of the following (Code Sec. 401(c)(3)):

1. An employee who owns the entire interest in an unincorporated trade or business (i.e., a sole proprietor).
2. In the case of a partnership, a partner who owns more than 10 percent of either the capital interest or profits interest in the partnership. (Note that all owner-employees are also self-employed individuals. However, the reverse is not true, since a five-percent partner would be considered a self-employed individual, but not an owner-employee.

Computing the Contribution and Deduction Amounts

Contributions and deductions for a self-employed participant covered by a qualified plan are subject to the same basic rules that apply to participants who are common law employees (see 401(k) plan contribution limits at ¶14,401). However, special computations pertaining to the earned income of the self-employed individual must be made in order to determine the contribution and deduction amounts.

As a starting point, references to "compensation," in the case of a proprietor or partner, are to the "earned income" of that person from the business for which the plan is established. "Earned income" is defined as net earnings from self-employment ("net SEI"). Code Sec. 401(c)(2)(A).

In determining the amount of net SEI upon which contributions and deductions are based, the net profit from a business activity (Schedule C in the case of a proprietorship) is reduced by the following two adjustments:

1. The deduction from gross income that is allowed under Code Sec. 164(f) for 50% of the self-employment tax paid by the self-employed participant. Code Sec. 401(c)(2)(A)(vi). After this adjustment, but before the second adjustment below, the resulting amount is gross self-employment income ("gross SEI").
2. The deduction allowed for contributions made on behalf of the self-employed participant. Code Sec. 401(c)(2)(A)(v). When the entire contribution is deductible, the amount of the deduction is determined by multiplying a converted plan contribution rate by gross SEI. The plan rate is converted by dividing the *nominal plan rate* by the *integer one, plus that rate*.

EXAMPLE 14.37 If a self-employed taxpayer's plan calls for a contribution rate equal to 10 percent of the participant's compensation, the converted contribution rate is 9.0909% (determined by dividing 10% by 1.10).

EXAMPLE 14.38

Continuing from the example above, a self-employed participant who reports a Form 1040, Schedule C net profit of $100,000 and pays $10,000 self-employment tax for the same year, will be permitted a contribution (and deduction) in the amount of $8,636. (Refer to the calculation and proof below.)

(a) = Given	Schedule C net profit	100,000
(b) = ½ × $10,000	½ SE tax	5,000
(c) = (a) − (b)	Gross SEI	95,000
(d) − 10% ÷ 1.10	Converted plan rate	9.0909%
(e) = (c) × (d)	Contribution & deduction	8,636
(f) = (c) − (e)	Net SEI	86,364
(g) = plan rate × (f)	Proof ($86,364 × 10%)	8,636

The short-cut formula above is a practical necessity. Otherwise, computing the contribution and deduction amount by multiplying a nominal plan rate times net SEI, would pose an algebraic dilemma: net SEI would have to be known in order to compute the deduction amount; and, conversely, the deduction amount would have to be known in order to compute net SEI.

"Contribution" Not a Business Expense

A deduction for a contribution to a qualified plan for the benefit of a self-employed individual is not a business expense of that individual. *D.L. Gale*, 91-2 USTC ¶50,356. Therefore, it cannot be used in calculating self-employment tax. Also, it is limited to income and cannot create or increase an NOL. Code Sec. 172(d)(4)(D).

For self-employed taxpayers (proprietors and partners), a deduction is reported as an adjustment to gross income on page 1 of Form 1040 rather than on Schedule C of Form 1040 (for proprietorships) or on page 1 of Form 1065 (for partnerships). A partnership's deduction for contributions on behalf of a partner must be allocated solely to that partner. Reg. §1.404(e)-1A(f). It cannot be allocated among all of the partners pursuant to a partnership agreement.

Distributions

A self-employed taxpayer or a beneficiary will qualify for a lump-sum distribution (discussed ¶14,301) only on account of death, disability, or attainment of age 59½. A common-law employee or a beneficiary on the other hand, will qualify for a lump-sum distribution prior to age 59½ only on account of death or separation from service. A common-law employee's disability is treated as separation from service.

¶14,515   SOLO 401(k) PLANS

The Solo 401(k) plan is referred to by various other names including: uni-401(k), one-man 401(k), mini-401(k), self-employed 401(k), and individual 401(k) plans. Since 2002, the Economic Growth and Tax Relief Reconciliation Act of 2001 has permitted any business that employs only the owner—including C corporations, S corporations, single member LLCs, partnerships, and sole proprietorships—to participate in this plan. The employment of an owner's spouse is also permitted.

In general, the same rules that apply to traditional 401(k) plans established by multiemployee entities apply to solo 401(k) plans. Reg. §1.401(k)-1(a)(6)(i). Employer and employee contributions into the plan and income generated from these contributions are tax-deferred until the year(s) retirement benefits are received. Also, participants in Solo 401(k), unlike participants in SEP or SIMPLE IRAs, may be eligible to borrow against the plan under the same rules that apply to traditional 401(k) plans (see ¶14,355).

Solo 401(k) Plan for the Self-Employed

The self-employed taxpayer can contribute and deduct both "deemed employer" and "deemed employee" contributions (subject to the general limit for additions to defined contributions plans explained at ¶14,501).

TAX BLUNDER

Taxpayers should consider their long-term business horizons before establishing a solo 401(k) plan. Once a solo 401(k) has been established, if one or more full-time employees are hired (other than the taxpayer's spouse), the employer must revert to a traditional 401(k) and may be required to perform certain non-discrimination and top-heavy testing to ensure that the plan operates in compliance with regulatory requirements. Generally, such testing is done by professionals who specialize in that area and can be quite costly. If employees elect not to make a deferral contribution, the employer may not be eligible to contribute into the plan. If the expanded rules are violated, the IRS could disqualify the plan, forcing the employer to pay taxes and penalties on the tax-deferred amounts that had accumulated in the account.

Limit on Employee Elective Deferral Contributions

Employee contributions ("deemed employee" contributions if self-employed) are regular-tax deferred. The contribution amount may not exceed the lesser of:

1. **Amount Limit:** $18,000 in 2015; or
2. **Percentage Limit:** Up to 100% of compensation for employees (or 100% of gross SEI for proprietors and partners).

Aggregate Limit on Employer and Employee Contributions

The amount of employer contributions ("deemed employer" contributions if self-employed) may not exceed the lesser of:

1. **Amount Limit:** $53,000 in 2015; or
2. **Percentage Limit:** Up to 25% of compensation for employees (or 20% of gross SEI for proprietors and partners).

"Gross SEI" and "net SEI" are explained in the preceding section.

EXAMPLE 14.39

Ethan Robinson, age 45, is planning to start a new business through a proprietorship and is considering establishing a solo 401(k). He would like to know the maximum amount of contributions and deductions he could expect based on gross SEI projections of $5,000, $50,000, and $500,000. (Refer to computations below.)

Gross SEI Projections	Limit on Deemed Employee Contribution	Limit on Deemed Employer Contributions	Aggregate Limit on Contributions & Deductions
(a) = Sched. C Net Profit Less ½ Self-Employment Tax Deduction	(b) = Lesser of: • $18,000 or • 100% × (a)	(c) = Lesser of: • $53,000 or • 20% × (a)	(d) = Least of: • (a) or • [(b) + (c)] or • $53,000
$5,000	$5,000	$1,000	$5,000 (the gross SEI amount at "(a)")
$50,000	$18,000	$10,000	$28,000
$500,000	$18,000	$53,000	$53,000

Reduction in $18,000 Limit

The maximum employee or "deemed employee" annual elective contribution limit is reduced dollar-for-dollar by contributions to other Solo 401(k) plans but not by contributions to regular 401(k) or other multiemployee qualified retirement plans. Thus, an employee participating in an employer's 401(k) plan, who also owns a separate business (i.e., "moonlights"), may make the maximum contributions to both the corporate 401(k) plan and a solo 401(k) plan. However, the aggregate $18,000 limit would apply if a self-employed taxpayer had more than one business, with each business offering a separate Solo 401(k) plan.

Age 50+ Catch-up Contributions

Any plan participant who is at least or will become age 50 before the end of the year can make additional elective deferral contributions of $6,000 in 2015. The age 50+ catch-up contribution does not count toward the $53,000 aggregate limit on employer and employee contributions.

¶14,525   KEOGH PLANS

Keogh plans were established in 1983 to create parity between self-employed taxpayers and corporate employees with regard to deferred compensation benefits. There are three basic forms of Keogh plans:

1. **Money purchase pensions plan.** A Keogh can be set up as a money purchase pension plan in which contributions are mandatory each year at a predetermined percentage and not based on profits. This type of plan may be best suited for businesses that have stable income and can assure the ability to make the same contribution percentage each year.

2. **Unpaired profit-sharing plan.** Alternatively, the Keogh plan can be an unpaired profit-sharing plan in which business profits are shared with employees. The profit sharing does not need to provide a definite formula for computing profits to be shared. The contribution rates can vary from year to year or can be skipped all together. However, the plan must be maintained with the intention of making regular contributions, and such contributions must be "systematic and substantial." This type of plan may be suitable for businesses where income fluctuates year to year.

3. **Paired profit-sharing plan.** A third alternative, the paired profit-sharing plan, is a profit-sharing Keogh plan that is paired with a fixed money purchase arrangement. The money purchase arrangement often involves a mutual fund, funded by the employer, to supplement the basic plan. Often, the employee can pick among several mutual funds. In this paired situation, employer contributions are based on two formulas, one tied in to profits, and the other, a fixed percentage similar to a money purchase pension. The contribution limitation is spread between the profit-sharing Keogh and the money purchase pension (see below). The paired plan may be best suited for an employer who wants a low mandatory contribution percentage as well as discretion over making larger contributions.

Contribution Limits

For money purchase pension plans and paired profit sharing plans, the amount of employer contributions ("deemed employer" contributions if self-employed) may not exceed the lesser of:

1. **Amount Limit:** $53,000 in 2015; or
2. **Percentage Limit:** 100% of compensation for employees (or 100% of net SEI for proprietors and partners).

Most money purchase and paired profit Keogh plans provide a nominal plan rate that does not exceed 25% of employee compensation, due to the 25% deduction limitation discussed below under "deduction limits."

For unpaired single profit-sharing plans, the amount of employer contributions ("deemed employer" if self-employed) may not exceed the lesser of:

1. **Amount Limit:** $53,000 in 2015; or
2. **Percentage Limit:** 25% of compensation for employees (or 20% of gross SEI for proprietors and partners).

(See ¶14,501 for an explanation of "gross SEI" and "net SEI.")

The 50+ catch-up contribution feature available under most qualified plans is not available to Keogh participants.

Deduction Limits

Deduction limit for all Keogh plans are the lesser of:

1. Contribution amount based on actual plan rate; or
2. 25% of compensation paid or accrued on behalf of employees (or 20% of gross SEI for contributions made by, and on behalf of, proprietors and partners who are owner-employees—defined at ¶14,501).

EXAMPLE 14.40

Will Feldman, age 46, a sole proprietor with no employees, is considering establishing for himself a pension Keogh or a paired or unpaired profit-sharing Keogh. He would like to know the maximum amount of contributions and deductions he should anticipate based on gross SEI projections of $5,000, $50,000, and $500,000. Referring to the table below, at any level of gross SEI, the deduction amounts for the three types of Keoghs will always be the same. However, the pension and paired Keogh plans will provide the largest contributions at gross SEI levels below $265,000 (proof: the $53,000 statutory limit divided by the 20 percent statutory rate equivalent for contributions). At or above $265,000, the contribution limits are the same.

Gross SEI Projections	Pension and Paired Keoghs Limits		Single Profit-Sharing Keogh Limits	
(a) = Sched. C Net Profit Less ½ Self-Employment Tax Deduction	Contribution Lesser of • $53k or • 100% net SEI	Deduction Lesser of • $53k or • 20% gross SEI	Contribution Lesser of • $53k or • 25% net SEI	Deduction Lesser of • $53k or • 20% gross SEI
$5,000	$4,000 (net SEI is equal to $5,000 gross SEI minus $1,000 deduction)	$1,000	$1,000	$1,000
$50,000	$40,000 (net SEI is equal to $50,000 gross SEI minus $10,000 deduction)	$10,000	$10,000	$10,000
$265,000	$53,000	$53,000	$53,000	$53,000
$500,000	$53,000	$53,000	$53,000	$53,000

PLANNING POINTER

A Keogh plan may take the form of one of several funding vehicles, including mutual funds, annuities, real estate shares, certificates of deposit, debt instruments, commodities, securities and personal properties. The plan may be either self-managed or managed by a financial institution. Most Keogh plans are defined contribution plans since they are easier to maintain than defined benefit plans.

EXAMPLE 14.41

Hank Spearman reports the following information from his proprietorship for the year:

Gross Income = $300,000
Business Deductions = $192,000
Self-Employment tax = $16,000

Hank maintains a Keogh plan with a 30 percent nominal contribution rate (as applied to net SEI—discussed at ¶14,501). If the plan is a pension (or paired) Keogh, Hank will be able to contribute $24,000 into the plan and claim a $24,000 deduction on his return. If the plan is a profit-sharing Keogh, Hank will be able to contribute and deduct $24,000 and $20,000, respectively. The deduction can be claimed on Hank's current return even if the contributions are made as late as October 15 of the following year (the six-month extension due date of an individual taxpayer's return).

Formula:	Description:	Pension/ Paired Keogh	Profit- Sharing Keogh
(a)	Gross Income	300,000	300,000
(b)	Business Deductions	192,000	192,000
(c)	SET Deduction: SET × ½ = $16,000 × ½ = $8m	8,000	8,000
(d) = (a) – (b) – (c)	Gross SEI (i.e., SEI before the Keogh deduction)	100,000	100,000
(e) = $265,000	Statutory limit on compensation [Sec. 401(a)(17)]	265,000	265,000
(f) = Lesser of (d) or (e)	Allowable income amount for deduction formula	100,000	100,000
(g) = (f) × [plan rate ÷ (1 + rate)]	Deduction limit—based on 30% nominal plan rate for contributions	23,077	23,077
(h) = (f) × [25% ÷ (1.25)]	Deduction limit—based on 25% statutory rate	20,000	20,000
(i) = Lesser of (g) or (h)	Deduction allowed	20,000	20,000
(j) = (d) – (i)	Net SEI (i.e., gross SEI minus Keogh deduction)	80,000	80,000
(k) = Lesser of: [(e) – (i)][or (j)]	Allowable income amount for contribution formula	80,000	80,000
(l) = (k) × plan rate	Contribution limit—based on nominal plan rate	24,000	24,000
(m) = (k) × 100% (for pension plans) (m) = (k) × 25% (for profit-sharing plans)	Contribution limit—based on statutory rate of 100% (pension plan) or 25% (profit-sharing plan)	80,000	20,000
(n) = $53,000	Contribution limit—based on statutory amount	53,000	53,000
(o) = Lesser of (l), (m), or (n)	Maximum allowable contribution	24,000	20,000

¶14,535

SIMPLIFIED EMPLOYEE PENSION (SEP) PLANS

A simplified employee pension (SEP) is a written arrangement that allows an employer to make deductible contributions to a traditional IRA (a SEP IRA) set up for employees to receive such contributions. Generally, distributions from SEP IRAs are subject to the withdrawal and tax rules that apply to traditional IRAs (see ¶14,625). Code Sec. 402(h)(3) and Code Sec. 408(d).

Adopting the Plan

SEP IRAs are simpler to adopt than most other plans. An employer need only fill out the one-page IRS Form 5305-SEP by the extension due date of the employer return. The form is not filed with the IRS but is distributed to each participant. The only report containing the amount of employer contributions that the employer must file with the IRS is the employee's W-2 form.

Contribution and Deduction Limits

Contribution and deduction limits for all SEP IRAs are the lesser of:

1. $53,000; or
2. 25% of compensation paid or accrued on behalf of employees (or 20% of gross SEI for contributions made by, and on behalf of, proprietors and partners).

EXAMPLE 14.42

Peggy Warner, a sole proprietor, is considering establishing a SEP IRA for herself. She would like to know the maximum contribution and deduction limits available to her, based on gross SEI projections of $5,000, $50,000, and $500,000. (Refer to computations below.)

Gross SEI Projections: Schedule C Net Profit Less ½ SE Taxes Actually Paid for the Year	Statutory Contribution & Deduction Limits: The lesser of: (1) $53,000 or (2) 20% gross SEI
$5,000	$1,000
$50,000	$10,000
$500,000	$53,000

EXAMPLE 14.43

CKS partnership maintains three separate SEP accounts for each of its eligible employees, Ashley, Kathy and Mary. If the annual compensation of each employee is $5,000, $50,000, and $500,000, respectively, the maximum contribution and deduction limits available to CKS will be $1,250, $12,500, and $53,000, as shown below.

Employees	Annual Compensation	Statutory Contribution & Deduction Limits: The lesser of: (1) $53,000 or (2) 25% compensation
Ashley	$5,000	$1,250
Kathy	$50,000	$12,500
Mary	$500,000	$53,000

Age 50+ Catch-up Contributions

As with a solo 401(k) participant, a SEP IRA participant who has attained age 50 before the end of the plan year can make elective deferral contributions of $6,000 in 2015. (See ¶14,501 for a discussion of the tax treatment for elective deferral contributions.) The age 50+ catch-up contribution does not count towards the statutory contribution limit of $53,000 for these plans.

EXAMPLE 14.44

Referring to the preceding example above, if Mary had attained age 50 by the end of the year, she would be permitted to make a $6,000 elective deferral contribution to her SEP account. The total contributions to her SEP account for the year would be $59,000, i.e., $53,000 employer deductible contributions plus $6,000 employee deferral contributions.

No Minimum Contribution Requirements

Employers with SEPs are not subject to minimum contribution requirements. This feature compares favorably with Keogh and SIMPLE plans, which have annual minimum contribution requirements from 1 to 3 percent of employee gross compensation annually, depending on the plan type.

Deemed IRA

A SEP IRA cannot offer CODAs (cash or deferred arrangements) to employees as can Solo 401(k) and SIMPLE plans. However, it may allow employees to make voluntary contributions to a separate account in lieu of contributing to a traditional IRA or a Roth IRA. Code Sec. 408(q). The aggregate limit on contributions to a traditional IRA, a Roth IRA, and a deemed IRA (employee contributions) is $5,500 ($6,500 if age 50 or over (see ¶14,601).

Salary Reduction SEPs (SARSEPs)

In plan years beginning before 1997, an employer could establish a salary reduction (cash or deferred) arrangement as part of a SEP. Such an arrangement—commonly known as a SARSEP —may not be established in plan years beginning after 1996. However, SARSEPs established before 1997 may continue to operate, subject to the same conditions and requirements that have always applied (Sec. 1421(c) of P.L. 104-188).

¶14,545   SIMPLE PLANS

Employers with 100 or fewer employees may establish a Savings Incentive Match Plan for Employees ("SIMPLE" plan). LLCs, partnerships, sole proprietorships, and C or S corporations may be eligible to establish SIMPLE plans. Also, 501(c) tax-exempt organizations and state and local governmental entities may also be eligible.

The plan can be in the form of a 401(k) plan or an IRA. The SIMPLE 401(K) participation rules are more favorable from an employer perspective because they provide stricter employee-eligibility requirements than SIMPLE IRAs (see ¶14,501). Under either form of plan, the employer must contribute a matching contribution to the account of each eligible employee on whose behalf elective contributions were made for the plan year. Code Sec. 408(p)(2)(A)(iii). These contributions must be 100 percent nonforfeitable at all times. Neither form of SIMPLE is subject to discrimination testing.

Adopting the Plan

To adopt a SIMPLE IRA an employer need fill out only the two-page IRS Form 5305-SIMPLE (employer selects the financial institution) or 5304-SIMPLE (employer permits employees to select their own financial institution) by October 1 of the employer's current tax year. The form is not filed with the IRS but is distributed to each participant. The SIMPLE IRA trustee must file Form 5498 annually with the IRS. This form contains employer and employee contribution amounts and the fair market value of the account at year-end.

Generally, an employer must permit an employee to select the financial institution for the SIMPLE to which the employer will make all contributions on behalf of the employee. If an eligible employee who is entitled to a contribution under a SIMPLE is unwilling or unable to establish a SIMPLE account with any financial institution prior to the date on which the contribution is required to be made, an employer may execute the necessary documents to establish the SIMPLE account with a financial institution selected by the employer.

Cash or Deferred Arrangement (CODA)

Both types of SIMPLE plans, the *401(k)* type and the *IRA* type, are cash or deferred arrangements in which employees (or "deemed employees" described in ¶14,501) may elect to either:

1. be taxed on all of their compensation and receive it, net of withholdings, in the form of cash,
2. defer all or a portion of their salary (up to $12,500, or $15,500 if age 50 or older) by directing their employer to contribute it into the SIMPLE plan. The amounts contributed by employee-participants is tax deferred.

Limit on Employee Elective Deferral Contributions

Employee contributions ("deemed employee" contributions if self-employed) are regular-tax deferred. For both SIMPLE 401(k) and SIMPLE IRA plans, the contribution amount may not exceed the lesser of:

1. **Amount Limit:** $12,500 in 2015; or
2. **Percentage Limit:** Up to 100% of compensation for employees (or 100% of gross SEI for proprietors and partners).

Limit on Employer Contributions

The amount of employer contributions ("deemed employer" contributions if self-employed) may not exceed the lesser of:

1. **Amount Limit:** $12,500 in 2015; or
2. **Percentage Limit:** Up to 3% of compensation for employees (or 3% of gross SEI for proprietors and partners).

Statutory Compensation Limit

For SIMPLE 401(k) plans, *all* employer contributions are subject to the statutory compensation limit under Sec. 401(a)(17) ($265,000 in 2015). For SIMPLE IRAs, only *non-elective* employer contributions are subject to this limit.

EXAMPLE 14.45	An eligible employee with $100,000 compensation in 2015 could elect to have up to 100% of that compensation, subject to the $12,500 limitation, contributed to a SIMPLE 401(k) or IRA plan on a pre-tax basis. If the nominal plan rate for employee contributions were, say, 2%, then the contribution amount would be $2,000; if 5%, then $5,000; if 15% then $12,500 (given the $12,500 limitation); if 100%, then still $12,500. The employee contribution, while regular tax-deferred, is nevertheless subject to FICA and FUTA tax.

EXAMPLE 14.46	Eugenia Hobbs earns a $300,000 salary and participates in DT Inc.'s SIMPLE IRA. The plan provides for a 100 percent nominal rate for elective employee contributions. Eugenia could contribute $12,500 into her SIMPLE IRA account (i.e., the lesser of $12,500, the statutory limit or 100% × $300,000). DT's matching contribution could be as much as $9,000 (i.e., the lesser of $12,500, or 3% × $300,000). If the plan had been a SIMPLE 401(k), DT's matching contribution could be as much as $7,950 instead of $9,000 because, under a SIMPLE 401(k) plan, employer contributions are subject to the statutory compensation limit discussed above (i.e., $7,950 is equal to the lesser of $12,500, or 3% × $265,000).

EXAMPLE 14.47	Same facts as in the preceding example except that the plan provides for a 2 percent nominal rate for elective employee contributions. Eugenia's contribution would be limited to $6,000 (i.e., the lesser of $12,500 or 2% × $300,000). The employer's matching contribution to the SIMPLE IRA could be as much as $6,000 (the lesser of the $6,000 employee contribution or 3% × $300,000).

Computing Gross SEI

"Gross SEI" and "net SEI" are explained at ¶14,501. For SIMPLE plans, gross SEI refers to (a) – (b) – (c) where

(a) = self-employed taxpayer's gross income from the business;
(b) = business deductions; and
(c) = [(a) – (b)] × 0.9235.

For Keogh and SEP IRAs, gross SEI is determined under a similar formula except that "(c)" is equal to ½ the self-employment taxes *actually* paid.)

EXAMPLE 14.48	Richard Fenner maintains a SIMPLE IRA and reports $500,000 Schedule C net earnings. The nominal plan rate for "deemed employee" contributions is 100%, (which is limited to the $12,500 statutory amount). Richard may contribute and deduct up to $25,000 into his SIMPLE IRA account. On his tax return, he will report a $25,000 deduction on Form 1040 p. 1. *[Computations: $25,000 = $12,500 "deemed employee" limit + $12,000 "deemed employer" limit. The $12,500 deemed employer limit is based on the following computation: 3% × ($500,000 × 0.9235) = $13,853, limited to the $12,500 statutory limit for employer contributions.]*

EXAMPLE 14.49	Same facts as in the preceding example, except that Richard reports Schedule C net earnings of $12,500 instead of $500,000. He may contribute and deduct a total of $12,846. [Computations: $12,846 = $12,500 "deemed employee" limit, + $346 "deemed employer" limit. The $346 deemed employer limit is based on the following computation: 3% × (12,500 × 0.9235) = $346].

Age 50+ Catch-up Contributions

Any plan participant who is at least or will become age 50 before the end of the year can make additional elective deferral contributions of $3,000 in 2015. The age 50+ catch-up contribution does not count towards the statutory contribution limit of $12,500 for these plans.

Reducing Matching Contributions

For the SIMPLE IRA, an employer who elects to make matching contributions may choose to reduce the amount to one that is less than 3 percent but not less than 1 percent for two out of every five years. This option is not available for the SIMPLE 401(k).

Alternative Employer "Nonelective" Contributions

As an alternative to making matching contributions under a SIMPLE 401(k) or SIMPLE IRA plan on behalf of all participating employees, an employer may make "nonelective" nonmatching contributions on behalf of all eligible employees, regardless of whether they participate in the plan. (The term "non-elective" may seem to be somewhat misleading since the employer can "elect" this alternative. The label, "nonelective" refers to the fact that employers who make this election *must* contribute on behalf of all eligible employees, even those who choose not to participate in the SIMPLE plan.) Employer nonelective contributions are limited to the lesser of:

1. 2% of every eligible employee's compensation (subject to a $265,000 statutory compensation limit under Code Sec. 401(a)(17) for both SIMPLE 401(k) and SIMPLE IRA plans), or
2. $12,500 (effectively limited to $5,300, given that the $265,000 compensation limit applies to alternative employer nonelective contributions).

EXAMPLE 14.50   ABC has ten employees, each receiving a $300,000 salary. Although all ten employees are eligible to participate in ABC's SIMPLE IRA plan, only seven choose to do so. Each of these seven participants contributes the maximum amount of $12,500 into the plan. If ABC's contributions are "matching," then ABC could contribute as much as $9,000 (i.e., 3% × $300,000) on behalf of each *participating* employee. The employer contributions would total $63,000, (i.e., 7 × $9,000). If ABC's contributions are "nonelective," then ABC could contribute a maximum $5,300 (i.e., 2% × $265,000, the statutory income limitation amount) on behalf of each *eligible* employee. The employer contributions could total no more than $53,000 (i.e., 10 × $5,300).

Deemed IRA

A SIMPLE IRA may allow employees to make voluntary contributions to a separate account in lieu of contributing to a traditional IRA. Code Sec. 408(q). The aggregate limit on contributions to a traditional IRA, a Roth IRA, and a deemed IRA (i.e., employee contributions that are not CODA contributions) is $5,500 ($6,500 if age 50 or over (see ¶14,601).

Penalty for Premature Distributions

Generally, distributions received by a participant before attaining age 59 ½ are subject to a ten-percent penalty tax in addition to the regular income tax (see ¶14,235). However, for SIMPLE IRA plans, a penalty of 25 percent (rather than 10 percent) is applicable during the two-year period beginning on the date the participant first participated in the SIMPLE IRA plan. Code Sec. 72(t)(6).

PLANNING POINTER   Because 100 percent of earnings can be contributed to a SIMPLE, SIMPLEs are well suited to employed individuals with side businesses who want to contribute as much of their self-employment earnings as possible toward retirement. However, if a taxpayer participates in a 401(k) plan as an employee, and a SIMPLE as a self-employed person, the sum of the SIMPLE and 401(k) deferrals cannot exceed the statutory limit ($18,000 in 2015). If the taxpayer is already making an employee elective deferral contribution of $18,000 into a 401(k) plan, then the taxpayer should consider either a Keogh (see ¶14,525) or a SEP (see ¶14,535) rather than a SIMPLE, in order to achieve maximum deferral.

Exhibit 8. COMMON RETIREMENT PLANS FOR SMALL BUSINESSES—BASIC FEATURES

Features	Solo 401(k)	Keogh	SEP	SIMPLE
Form of plan:	401(k)	Pension, profit-sharing, or both	IRA	IRA or 401(k)
Self as trustee OK?	Yes	Yes	No	No
Permitted legal entity type:	LLC Partnership Sole proprietorship C or S corporation	LLC Partnership Sole proprietorship	LLC Partnership Sole proprietorship	LLC Partnership Sole proprietorship C or S corporation
Limit on number of employees:	Must not exceed 1 owner-employee (except for spouse)	No limit	No limit	Must not exceed 100 employees
Annual filing requirements:	Annual IRS Form 5500-EZ or Form 5500 once balance exceeds $250,000 (by last day of 7th month after year-end)	Annual IRS Form 5500-EZ or Form 5500 once balance exceeds $100,000, or $250,000 for a one-participant plan (by last day of 7th month after year-end)	None (although certain W-2 reporting is required)	None (although certain W-2 reporting is required)
Statutory establishment deadline (financial institutions may set earlier deadlines):	By December 31 of the current year	By December 31 of the current year	By extension due date of employer return	By October 1 of current year
Statutory contribution deadline:	Employee: By Dec. 31 of current year Employer: By extension due date	By extension due date of employer return	By extension due date of employer return	By extension due date of employer return
Vesting requirements:	None (since no employee other than spouse may be employed)	Regular vesting rules (e.g., 3-yr. cliff or 6-yr. graded) apply	None (Employer contributions are always nonforfeitable)	None (Employer contributions are always nonforfeitable)
Plan loans ok?	Yes, up to $50,000	Yes, up to $50,000	No	No
Participation requirements:	Only owner-employee (and spouse) may participate	Each employee: age 21 or over & with 1 year of service (2 years with 2-year vesting)	Each employee: age 21 or over who performed services in current year and in 3 out of past 5 years who earned at least $550 for current year	SIMPLE IRA: Each employee: Any age limit Earn at least $5k for any past 2 years and be expected to do so in current year SIMPLE 401(k): (same as Keogh)
Rollovers permitted?	Yes	Yes	Yes	Yes, but rules are very restrictive for SIMPLE IRAs

Exhibit 9. COMMON RETIREMENT PLANS FOR SMALL BUSINESSES—CONTRIBUTION AND DEDUCTION LIMITS

Features	Solo 401(k)	Keogh	SEP	SIMPLE
Contribution limits for employees (or "deemed employees") (see "Terms" below):	Lesser of: (1) = 18,000; (2) = 100% GC or gross SEI	N/A	N/A	Lesser of: (1) = 100% GC (or gross SEI), or (2) = $12,500
Contribution limits for employers (or "deemed employers")	(See aggregate contribution limit below.)	(See aggregate contribution limit below.)	(See aggregate contribution limit below.)	Elective contributions: Lesser of (a) or (b): (a) = Employee (or "deemed" employee) contributions (from above), or (b) = 3% GC (or gross SEI) for each participating employee Nonelective contributions: 2% GC for each eligible employee
Aggregate contribution limit for employers and employees	Lesser of: (1) = $53,000 or (2) = 25% GC (or 20% *gross* SEI)	Lesser of: (1) = $53,000 or (2) = 100% GC or *net* SEI (25% for single- profit sharing plans)	Lesser of: (1) = $53,000 or (2) = 25% GC (or 20% *gross* SEI)	(Separate employee and employer limits apply—see above)
$265,000 (of GC or net SEI) limit in contribution formula?	Yes	Yes	Yes	For SIMPLE 401(k)s: Yes For SIMPLE IRAs: No, except for nonelective contributions
Age 50+ catch-up contributions:	Yes, $6,000 for 2015. *(This is in addition to the $53,000 aggregate limit.)*	No	Yes, $6,000 for 2015. *(This is in addition to the $53,000 maximum limit.)*	Yes, $3,000 for 2015
Minimum contribution limits	None	1% to 3%, depending on the form of Keogh	None	The 3% employer contribution percentage shown above may be reduced to 1% in any 2 out of 5 years.
Deduction limit for owner-employees	Same as aggregate contribution limit (see above)	Lesser of: (1) = $53,000 or (2) = 25% GC or *net* SEI	Same as aggregate contribution limit (see above)	For corporate employers: Same as employer limit above. For owner-employees: Sum of the separate contribution limits for deemed employees and deemed employers

Terms:
"GC" means gross compensation, i.e., salary paid or accrued to employees.
"Gross SEI" refers to (a) – (b) – (c) where
    (a) = self-employed taxpayer's gross income from the business;
    (b) = business deductions;
    (c) = ½ × self-employment tax actually paid (for Keoghs and SEP IRAs); or, [(a) – (b)] × .9235 (for solo 401(k)s & SIMPLE IRAs).
"Net SEI" is equal to gross SEI – the actual retirement plan deduction.

¶14,555   ## "DB/K" PLANS

Beginning in 2010, the 2006 Pension Protection Act allows small employers to offer employees a combined defined benefit and 401(k) plan (a "DB/K" plan). The DB/K plan is designed to repair a perceived flaw in the current retirement system. The 401(k), originally conceived as a supplement to employer paid pensions, has become the primary source of retirement income for most taxpayers. For many 401(k) participants, distributions received after retirement, even if managed well, may be inadequate. To mitigate this dilemma, Congress has established the DB/K plan for small employers. For purposes of the DB/K rules, a "small employer" is a business employing an average of at least two but not more than 500 employees on business days during the preceding calendar year and who employs at least two employees on the first day of the plan year. Code Sec. 414(x)(2)(A).

The DB/K plan combines two components:

- Defined benefit in the form of a small guaranteed income stream; and
- a 401(k) defined contribution savings plan.

Each component is subject to separate provisions of the Code and ERISA as if each were not part of the DB/K plan.

Defined Benefit ("DB") Component. The DB component must consist of either (1) a defined payout design or (2) a defined cash balance design.

1. **Defined payout design.** The defined payout must be equal to one percent of final average pay for each year of the employee's service, up to 20 years. Final average pay is based on a period of not more than 5 consecutive years during which a participant has the greatest aggregate compensation. Code Sec. 414(x)(2)(B)(i) and (ii).

2. **Cash balance design.** The cash balance design provides participants a pay credit for each plan year of not less than a certain percentage of compensation. The percentage of compensation is determined based on the participant's age. If the participant is age 30 or less, then the percentage is two percent; if over age 30 but less than age 40, four percent; if age 40 or over but less than age 50, six percent; and if the participant is age 50 or over, the percentage is eight percent. Code Sec. 414(x)(2)(B)(iii). The DB component must provide the required benefit to each participant, regardless of whether the participant makes elective deferrals to the plan. Code Sec. 414(x)(2)(B)(iv). These benefits are fully vested after 3 years of service. Code Sec. 414(x)(2)(D).

401(k) Defined Contribution ("K") Component. Under the "K" component, certain automatic enrollment and matching contribution requirements must be met with respect to employee and employer contributions:

1. **Employee Contributions.** The K component must provide for a 4%-of-pay automatic enrollment of employees. However, an employee may specifically opt out or lower the 4% contribution level. Code Sec. 414(x)(2)(C) and (5)(A).

2. **Employer Contributions.** An employer must match at least 50% of employee 401(k) contributions (i.e., a maximum required match of 2% of pay). Code Sec. 414(x)(2)(C)(i)(II).

PLANNING POINTER

The market for DB/K plans is significant. About 99.7% of the 5.8 million companies in the United States employ fewer than 500 employees, according to the 2010 Economic Census published by the U.S. Census Bureau in Washington. Companies with high profit margins or those flush with cash are more likely to undertake the significant funding commitment, particularly in hard-to-staff fields, or where worker poaching is widespread (e.g., professional firms, such as CPA, medical, engineering and law firms and small manufacturing firms).

KEYSTONE PROBLEM

Joanie Jones, age 49, has recently started a consulting business in the form of a sole proprietorship. Currently, the business has no full-time employees and generates $5,000 gross self-employment income. Joanie anticipates that her gross self-employment income will increase to $100,000 within the next two years and eventually level off at $300,000. She seeks your advice on selecting a qualified retirement plan that meets her primary objective. Each objective listed below should be viewed independently and treated as Joanie's primary objective.

1. To achieve the largest contribution and deduction amounts available by law.
2. To have the ability to continue with the same type of plan in the event the business becomes incorporated.
3. To have the freedom to manage the plan's investment funds.
4. To be able to impose vesting restrictions on employer contributions in the event full-time employees are later hired.
5. To have the flexibility to vary contributions from year to year or even to skip a year altogether.
6. To be permitted to establish the plan and make contributions after the current tax year has ended and still be able to claim deductions retroactively on the current-year tax return.
7. To have the flexibility to allow voluntary employee salary deferral contributions in the event employees are later hired.
8. To minimize the cost and effort associated with setting up and maintaining the plan.
9. To have the ability to roll account funds into a Roth IRA.
10. To be permitted to make age 50+ catch-up contributions.

Personal Retirement Plans for Working Individuals

Individuals with taxable compensation who either are not covered by a qualified employer-sponsored plan (such as a 401(k) plan) or who desire to provide for additional retirement income may choose between two tax-favored arrangements to meet their retirement planning needs: the traditional individual retirement account (IRA) and the Roth IRA. A review and comparison of these arrangements is provided in the sections that follow.

¶14,601   COMMON RULES FOR TRADITIONAL AND ROTH IRAS

The rules governing traditional and Roth IRAs are the same with respect to:

- contribution limits,
- minimum compensation requirements,
- investment alternatives,
- establishment and funding deadlines,
- spousal IRAs,
- saver's credit for IRA contributions, and,
- tax treatment for IRA losses.

These rules are explained below. The rules that are specific for each type of IRA are covered at ¶14,625 (traditional IRAs) and ¶14,635 (Roth IRAs).

Annual Dollar Limit

In 2015, contributions to a traditional or Roth IRA are subject to an annual dollar limit that generally is the lesser of:

1. $5,500 per individual ($11,000 if married); or
2. 100% of the compensation of the taxpayer's (and taxpayer's spouse if married) taxable compensation.

For individuals who are age 50 or older at the end of the year, the annual dollar limit is increased by $1,000 in 2015. Code Sec. 219(b). Contributions to a Roth IRA may be subject to income phase-out rules (see ¶14,635).

If an individual has more than one IRA, the annual dollar limit applies to the total amount of contributions made by the individual to all of the traditional, Roth, and "deemed" (see ¶14,535 and ¶14,545) IRAs. If an individual contributes less than the annual dollar limit, the individual cannot make up the difference in subsequent years.

Brokers' commissions paid by an IRA owner on transactions involving IRA assets count toward the annual dollar limit on contributions. However, trust administration fees paid by an IRA owner are not subject to the annual contribution limit. Rev. Rul. 86-142, 1986-2 CB 60.

The rules for deducting contributions to traditional IRAs are discussed at ¶14,625. The income phase-out rules specific to Roth IRAs are explained at ¶14,635.

Minimum Compensation Requirements

Individuals with qualified compensation may establish and contribute money to a traditional or Roth IRA to provide retirement income or to supplement employer-provided retirement income. Code Sec. 408. Qualified compensation includes taxable salary, wages, professional fees, net earnings from self-employment (including an active partner's distributive share of income from a service partnership) and any alimony included in gross income. Qualified compensation does not include the following amounts (Code Secs. 219(f) and 401(c)(2)):

1. Any amount received as a pension or annuity.
2. Any amount received as deferred compensation.
3. Interest.
4. Dividend income.
5. Income from a partnership if services that are a material income-producing factor are not provided
6. Unemployment compensation.

EXAMPLE 14.51

Nancy does not work, but during the current year, she receives $40,000 in taxable alimony from her ex-husband. Nancy has sufficient qualified compensation to contribute to an IRA for the current year.

EXAMPLE 14.52

Bobby was laid off from his job and has not been able to find work. During the current year, he received $6,000 in unemployment compensation and $50,000 from the proceeds of stock held for investment (resulting in a $30,000 gain). Bobby cannot contribute to an IRA in the current year since he has no qualified compensation for the year.

Investment Alternatives

A traditional IRA or a Roth IRA may be established at any time with a bank, savings and loan association, brokerage company, mutual fund, insurance company, or other IRS-approved institution. Code Sec. 408(a), (b). Contributions, other than rollover contributions, must be made in cash. With a self-directed IRA, an IRS-approved custodian agrees to allow the taxpayer to exercise greater control over investment decisions. Self-directed IRAs can be invested in real estate (including single-family homes, urban loft developments, and farms), mortgage notes, options on real estate, private placements, investment partnerships, and operating businesses. However, the assets must be purchased by the custodian (as directed by the taxpayer) in an arm's-length transaction. Under Sec. 4975(c)(1), the asset is not permitted to be titled in the taxpayer's name. Also, under Sec. 4975(e)(2), the taxpayer cannot have owned the property, live in the property, or be involved in the investment of the asset. This stipulation also applies to the taxpayer's spouse, parents, children, fiduciaries, business associates, and persons providing services to the plan. In order for the plan to be truly self-directed, the custodian handling cash transferred in and out of the IRA cannot give the taxpayer advice about investments. Thus, it is often advisable for the taxpayer to seek investment advice from an outside professional experienced in the type of investment held in the self-directed IRA.

TAX BLUNDER

Taxpayers should exercise caution when choosing investments for a traditional IRA account. The taxable amount of an IRA distribution is subject to ordinary income treatment regardless of the nature of the investment. Thus, capital assets that are normally subject to tax-favored treatment, e.g., stocks or tax-exempt municipal bonds, are treated as ordinary income property upon distribution.

Establishment and Funding Deadlines

Individuals may establish a traditional or Roth IRA and make contributions for a year at any time during that year or by the due date (not including the six-month automatic extension) for filing their income tax return for that year. Code Sec. 219(f)(3). A contribution may be made for a year by the due date even though the contribution is made after a tax return is filed for the year (so long as the contribution is made on or before the due date for the return). Rev. Rul. 84-18, 1984-1 CB 88.

EXAMPLE 14.53　　Kate Marani is eligible to make a deductible contribution to a traditional IRA in the current year but does not have sufficient money to make a contribution. However, if she could make a $1,500 contribution, she would be eligible for an income tax refund of $1,500. If Kate files her tax return after January 1 of the following year, and claims a $1,500 deduction for a contribution to a traditional IRA, she can use her $1,500 tax refund to make the contribution by the April 15 filing deadline.

Spousal IRAs

An individual ("contributing spouse") may establish and make contributions to a traditional or Roth IRA on behalf of a spouse with little or no income ("contributee spouse"). Code Sec. 219(c).

To be eligible to establish and fund a spousal IRA, a contributee spouse must satisfy the following requirements:

1. A joint income tax return must be filed for the tax year.
2. The amount of the contributee spouse's taxable compensation must be less than the taxable compensation of the contributing spouse.

Each year, a contributing spouse can fund a spousal IRA up to $5,500 in 2015, (plus a catch-up contribution of up to $1,000 in 2015 if the spouse is age 50 or older) by the end of the year. However, the amount contributed cannot exceed the sum of the following (Code Sec. 219(c)):

1. The contributing spouse's taxable compensation.
2. The taxable income of the contributee spouse, reduced by the amount of any deductible and nondeductible contributions made on behalf of the contributee spouse to a traditional or Roth IRA.

EXAMPLE 14.54　　Conor and Sara Adelaide file a joint income tax return for 2015 and report a modified adjusted gross income of $65,000. Sara is 37, and Conor is 36. All of the income is earned by Conor. Sara stays at home and cares for their three children. Conor may contribute to a traditional IRA, a Roth IRA, or both, subject to an aggregate limit of $5,500. He also may also contribute up to $5,500 to either or both types of IRAs on behalf of Sara. Sara may not make any contributions on her own behalf because she has no taxable compensation.

Saver's Credit for Contributions

Individuals who have attained age 18 as of the close of the tax year are allowed an income tax credit equal to the applicable percentage of so much of their contributions to a traditional or Roth IRA (plus other qualified retirement savings contributions) that do not exceed $2,000. See ¶9033 for a further discussion of this credit.

Tax Treatment for IRA Losses

For traditional and Roth IRAs, loss recognition is permitted only if:

1. all of the amounts in all of the taxpayer's traditional IRAs *or* Roth IRAs have been distributed, and,
2. total distributions are less than the unrecovered basis.

The loss rule applies separately to each type of IRA. Thus, to claim a loss on a traditional IRA, all the traditional IRAs (but not Roth IRAs) owned by the individual have to be liquidated; and to report a loss on a Roth IRA, all the Roth IRAs (but not traditional IRAs) have to be liquidated.

The unrecovered basis is the portion of the account balance consisting of nondeductible contributions. Deductible traditional IRA contributions are not part of unrecovered basis because they have a zero basis (i.e., the compensation amount needed to contribute to a traditional IRA, minus an equal amount claimed as an IRA deduction).

Traditional and Roth IRA losses are reported on Schedule A as miscellaneous itemized deductions, subject to the 2%-of-adjusted-gross-income limit.

¶14,625 SPECIFIC RULES FOR TRADITIONAL IRAS

The rules that are common to both traditional and Roth IRAs are covered in the previous section (at ¶14,601). The rules that are specific for traditional IRAs are explained in this section.

Eligible Individual

Any individual with taxable compensation (described at ¶14,601) may be eligible to contribute to a traditional IRA. In the taxable year an individual turns 70 ½, no further contributions to a traditional IRA can be made by that individual. Secs. 219(d)(1) and 408(o). However, the individual may establish a new traditional IRA and fund it with funds transferred from another traditional IRA or employer-sponsored qualified retirement plan.

EXAMPLE 14.55	On November 8, Year 1, Baxter will turn 70. Since Baxter will turn 70 ½ on May 8, Year 2, he can continue to contribute to a traditional IRA through Year 1, provided he has compensation in those years, but not in Year 2.

EXAMPLE 14.56	Margaret will turn 70 on April 2, Year 1. Since Margaret will turn 70 ½ in Year 1, i.e., on October 2, Year 1, she can no longer contribute to a traditional IRA beginning on January 1, Year 1.

Deduction Limit

Individuals may deduct the full amount of their contributions to a traditional IRA (subject to the annual dollar limit discussed at ¶14,601) unless they or their spouse are active participants in a pension, profit-sharing, or stock bonus plan that is a qualified retirement plan, a Section 403(a) annuity plan, a tax-deferred Section 403(b) annuity plan, an SEP, a SIMPLE plan, or a plan established for its employees by the United States, any state or political subdivision of a state, or any agency or instrumentality of any of the foregoing. Code Sec. 219(g). No deduction is allowed for amounts transferred from another traditional IRA or employer-sponsored qualified retirement plan. Code Sec. 219(d)(2). The deduction is an above-the-line deduction. Code Sec. 62(a)(7).

Deduction Limit for Nonparticipants

If *neither* taxpayer nor taxpayer's spouse (if married) participates in a qualified employer-sponsored retirement plan, then each individual's traditional IRA contribution is fully deductible (within the limits discussed at ¶14,601), regardless of AGI.

EXAMPLE 14.57	Mr. and Mrs. Harralson's 2015 joint MAGI exceeds $1 million. Neither spouse participates in an employer-sponsored qualified retirement plan. If each spouse contributes $5,500 into separate traditional IRAs, they may report an $11,000 IRA deduction on their 2015 joint return. The MAGI phase-out rules do not apply if neither spouse participates in an employer-sponsored retirement plan.

Deduction Limit for Active Participants

If a taxpayer is an active participant in an employer-sponsored qualified retirement plan, the general limit for traditional IRA deductions is phased out proportionately according to the MAGI figures listed at Exhibit 10.

Exhibit 10. PHASE-OUT RANGES FOR TRADITIONAL IRA DEDUCTIONS OF ACTIVE PARTICIPANTS IN 2015		
Filing Status:	**Beginning MAGI Amount:**	**Ending MAGI Amount:**
Single and head of household	$61,000	$71,000
Married filing jointly	$98,000	$118,000
Married filing separately	0	$10,000

An individual's modified adjusted gross income (MAGI) is the individual's adjusted gross income, including any Social Security and tier 1 Railroad Retirement Act benefits that have to be included in gross income and applying the passive loss limitations. Modified adjusted gross income also includes interest from U.S. savings bonds used to pay college expenses, employer-provided adoption assistance, interest paid on education loans, foreign earned income, the foreign housing cost exclusion or deduction, the deduction for qualified tuition and related expenses, and contributions to traditional IRAs.

The amount of the reduction is determined by multiplying the annual limitation by a fraction whose numerator is the excess of the taxpayer's modified adjusted gross income for the year over the applicable dollar amount and whose denominator is $10,000 ($20,000 if the taxpayer is a qualifying widow(er) or the taxpayer is married and filing a joint return, unless the taxpayer is not an active participant but his or her spouse is). The annual dollar limitation cannot be reduced below $200 until the amount of the reduction exceeds the annual limitation. Any reduction that is not a multiple of $10 is rounded to the next lowest $10.

The IRS Form W-2 that an individual receives from an employer will indicate whether the individual is an active participant in an employer's retirement plan. If an individual and the individual's spouse is an active participant, the deductible amount may be reduced (but not below zero). The amount of the reduction depends on the individual's tax filing status and modified adjusted gross income. Although the amount of deductible contributions that an individual can make to a traditional IRA may be reduced, the nondeductible amount nevertheless can be contributed to a traditional IRA as a nondeductible contribution. IRS Form 8606, Nondeductible IRAs, must be filed with the contributor's tax return for the year a nondeductible contribution is made.

EXAMPLE 14.58	Mr. & Mrs. Smith, both age 25, report $108,000 joint MAGI in 2015. Each spouse is an active participant in a qualified employer-sponsored retirement plan. If each spouse contributes $5,500 into separate traditional IRAs ($11,000 total), they may report only a $5,500 deduction ($2,750 attributable to each spouse) on their 2015 joint return. The deductible amount must be phased out because (a) each spouse is an active participant and (b) joint MAGI is within the $98,000-to-$118,000 phase-out range for active participants. The $2,750 deductible amount attributable to each spouse is computed as follows: $2,750 deduction = $5,500 contribution – $5,500 × [($108,000 – $98,000) ÷ ($118,000 – $98,000)]

Deduction Limit for Non-Active Spouses of Active Participants

If the spouse of an active participant does not participate in an employer plan, the $5,500 ($6,500 if age 50 or older) maximum traditional IRA deduction attributable to the non-participating spouse (but not the active-participant spouse), is phased out at MAGI levels between *$183,000 and $193,000*, jointly computed. Code Sec. 219(g)(7). This range is favorable relative to the *$98,000-to-$118,000* phase-out range that applies to active-participant spouses.

EXAMPLE 14.59	Referring to the preceding example above, if Mr. Smith had not been an active participant in a qualified employer-sponsored plan, the deduction attributable to him would have been the same as his $5,500 contribution since the Smiths' $108,000 joint MAGI did not exceed the $183,000 MAGI phase-out threshold for nonparticipants.

EXAMPLE 14.60	Mr. & Mrs. Jones, both in their 40's, report $190,000 joint MAGI for 2015. Only Mrs. Jones was an active participant in a qualified employer-sponsored retirement plan. Each may contribute $5,500 into a traditional IRA, regardless of MAGI or active participation in a qualified employer plan. However, only a $1,650 deduction attributable to Mr. Jones may be reported on the joint return since (a) Mr. Jones is a nonparticipant and (b) joint MAGI is within the $183,000-to-$193,000 MAGI phase-out range for nonparticipants. The $1,650 deductible amount attributable to Mr. Jones is computed as follows: $1,650 deduction = $5,500 contribution – $5,500 × [($190,000 – $183,000) ÷ ($193,000 – $183,000)]

PLANNING POINTER	Any income generated from a nondeductible contribution to a traditional IRA is tax deferred. However, a better avenue may be to contribute a nondeductible amount into a Roth IRA where the income generally accumulates tax-free.

¶14,625

Borrowing to Fund a Traditional IRA

The money needed to fund a traditional IRA may be borrowed without disallowance of the interest deduction. The interest deduction however, cannot exceed net investment income. (See ¶8,680 for a discussion on investment expense limitations).

Taxation of Distributions

If a distribution is made to the IRA owner or a beneficiary and no nondeductible contributions were made to the traditional IRA, the entire amount received by the IRA owner or beneficiary has to be included in the recipient's gross income (unless the amount received is rolled over into another traditional IRA or employer-sponsored qualified retirement plan that can accept rollover contributions). The amount of the distribution has to be included in gross income as ordinary income even though earnings consisted, in part, of capital gains. Code Sec. 408(d).

If nondeductible contributions were made to the traditional IRA, the beneficiary has basis in the IRA, and distributions are treated as partly taxable and partly as a return of capital under the rules (Code Sec. 72) for taxing annuities.

When applying these annuity rules, Code Secs. 408(d)(1) and (2) require:

1. all traditional IRAs of an individual (including SEPs described at ¶14,535 and SIMPLEs described at ¶14,545) to be treated as one contract;
2. all distributions during the individual's tax year to be treated as one distribution; and
3. the value of the contract, income on the contract, and investment in the contract to be calculated (after adding back distributions made during the year) as of the close of the calendar year in which the taxable year begins.

EXAMPLE 14.61

Ted Ransopher, age 60, maintains separate IRA accounts at three banks, Tau, Alpha, and Chi. For each bank, the type of IRA, form of investment, and annual return is shown below.

Investment Information:	Tau Bank	Alpha Bank	Chi Bank
Type of IRA	Traditional	Traditional	SEP
Type of investment	Mutual Fund	CD	CD
Annual Return	0%	6%	6%
	(underperforming)		

Ted's tax accountant reports the following IRA information pertaining to each bank as of year-end (after adding basic distributions made during the year):

Year-End IRA Information:	Tau Bank Amount	%	Alpha Bank Amount	%	Chi Bank Amount	%
After-tax contributions	600,000	100%	0	0%	0	0%
Before-tax contributions	0	0%	100,000	50%	100,000	50%
Income accumulation	0	0%	100,000	50%	100,000	50%
Balance	$600,000	100%	$200,000	100%	$200,000	100%

During the current year, Ted withdrew $100,000 from the under-performing IRA account at Tau Bank. Even though the $600,000 adjusted account balance at Tau Bank consisted entirely of after-tax contributions, only 60 percent of the withdrawal ($60,000) is tax-free while 40 percent ($40,000) is taxable. The reason: in determining how much of the $100,000 distribution tax-free, the IRA balances at all three banks must be combined and viewed as one account. The analysis is shown below.

Tau, Alpha, and Chi Bank Accounts Viewed as One Account:

Components of Account Balance	Three Banks Combined	%
After-tax amounts:		
Nondeductible contributions	600,000	60%
Before-tax amounts		
Deductible contributions	200,000	20%
Income accumulation	200,000	20%
Total before-tax amounts	400,000	40%
IRA account balance	$1,000,000	100%

Required Minimum Distributions (RMDs)

The owner of a traditional IRA must withdraw at least a minimum amount of assets from the traditional IRA each year starting April 1 of the year following the year the owner attains age 70 ½. If the required minimum distribution is not made, a 50 percent excise tax has to be paid on the amount not distributed as required. Code Sec. 4974(a). The penalty is calculated using IRS Form 5329, Additional Taxes on Qualified Plans (Including IRAs) and Other Tax-Favored Accounts. These rules are similar to the rules governing qualified employer-sponsored plans and governmental 457(b) plans (see ¶14,235).

If an individual maintaining more than one traditional IRA in a calendar year is required to receive a minimum distribution, the RMD amount from each IRA must be computed separately and the separate amounts totaled. The total amount may be withdrawn from one or more of the IRAs in any amount the individual chooses. Reg. §1.408-8, Q&A-9.

Rollovers of IRA Assets

Assets in a traditional IRA may be transferred to or from another IRA, a qualified employer-sponsored plan, or a governmental 457(b) plan. The rules that apply to rollovers are explained at ¶14,345.

Death of IRA Owner

How the required minimum distributions are calculated after the death of an IRA owner depends on who is the designated beneficiary of the traditional IRA and whether the IRA owner died before or after the required beginning date. The rules governing after-death distributions are covered at ¶14,235.

Penalty for Premature Distributions

A non-qualified distribution prior to age 59 ½ is fully taxable and subject to a 10% nondeductible penalty. A premature distribution of the full account balance may be deemed to occur if the participant borrows from the IRA or pledges it as loan collateral. However, a *60-day* grace period is allowed if treated as a rollover from or to another qualified retirement plan. These rules are explained at ¶14,235.

¶14,635   RULES SPECIFIC FOR ROTH IRAS

This section addresses the rules that apply only to Roth IRAs. The rules that are common to both traditional and Roth IRAs were previously explained at ¶14,601.

Comparison of Features Between Traditional and Roth IRAs

The differences between a traditional IRA and a Roth IRA include the following:

- Individuals may contribute to a Roth IRA without age restrictions. Individuals may contribute to a traditional IRA until the year in which they attain the age of 70 ½.
- Contributions to a Roth IRA are never tax deductible; contributions to a traditional IRA may be tax deductible.
- Earnings from a Roth IRA may be exempt from income tax. Earnings from a traditional IRA are taxed when withdrawn.
- The owner of a Roth IRA has penalty-free access to direct contributions and to nontaxable rollover contributions (but not to taxable rollover contributions and accumulated earnings), at anytime.
- AGI restrictions affect the amount of Roth IRA contributions; different AGI restrictions affect the amount of traditional IRA deductions.
  See Exhibit 13 for a side-by-side comparison of the major features of these two plans.

Contribution Limits

The annual dollar limit on Roth contributions, explained at ¶14,601, is reduced to the extent that an individual's modified adjusted gross income exceeds the applicable dollar amount. The amount of the reduction is determined by multiplying the annual dollar limit by a fraction whose numerator is the excess of the taxpayer's modified adjusted gross income for the year over the applicable dollar amount and whose denominator is $15,000 ($10,000 if the taxpayer is filing a joint return or is married but filing a separate return or is a qualifying widow(er)). The annual dollar limit cannot be reduced below $200 until the amount of the reduction exceeds the annual limitation. Any reduction that is not a multiple of $10 is rounded to the next lowest $10.

An individual's modified adjusted gross income (MAGI) is the same term that is used in applying the phase-out rules for traditional IRA deductions (see ¶14,625).

The table at Exhibit 11 summarizes the limits on the amount that can be contributed to a Roth IRA for 2015.

Exhibit 11. PHASE-OUT RANGES FOR ROTH IRA CONTRIBUTIONS IN 2015		
Filing Status:	**Beginning MAGI Amount:**	**Ending MAGI Amount:**
Single and head of household	$116,000	$131,000
Married filing jointly	$183,000	$193,000
Married filing separately	0	$10,000

EXAMPLE 14.62

Conor Finn, age 25, files as a single individual. In 2015, he reports MAGI in the amount of $119,750, all from a salary. He has not yet made any traditional, Roth, or deemed IRA contributions for the year. Conor is eligible to contribute up to $4,125 to a Roth IRA. $4,125 is the least of (a), (b) or (c), where,

(a) = $4,125, i.e., $5,500 annual dollar limit – $1,375 phase-out amount, where the $1,375 phase-out amount = $5,500 × [($119,750 – $116,000) ÷ ($131,000 – $116,000)];

(b) = $5,500, i.e., $5,500 annual dollar limit – $0 previous IRA contributions for 2015; and

(c) = $119,750, i.e., $119,750 qualified compensation – $0 previous IRA contributions for 2015.

EXAMPLE 14.63

Referring to the preceding example, assume that Conor has already contributed $3,000 to a traditional IRA in 2015. Conor is eligible to contribute up to $2,500 to a Roth IRA in 2015. The amount represents the least of (a), (b) or (c), where,

(a) = $4,125, i.e., $5,500 annual dollar limit – $1,375 phase-out amount, (as computed Example 14.62);

(b) = $2,500, i.e., $5,500 annual dollar limit – $3,000 previous traditional IRA contribution for 2015; and

(c) = $116,750, i.e., $119,750 earned income – $3,000 previous traditional IRA contribution for 2015.

EXAMPLE 14.64

Joe Ragner, age 25, lives with his parents and files as a single individual. In 2015, he reports AGI in the amount of $5,000, which consists of: (1) $2,000 self-employment income after the deduction for ½ self-employment taxes, and (2) $3,000 taxable unemployment compensation. Joe has not yet made any IRA contributions for the year. Joe could contribute up to $2,000 to a Roth IRA. This contribution limit is the least of (a), (b), or (c), where,

(a) = $5,500, i.e., $5,500 annual dollar limit – $0 phase-out amount;

(b) = $5,500, i.e., $5,500 annual dollar limit – $0 previous IRA contributions for 2015; and

(c) = $2,000, i.e., $2,000 qualified compensation – $0 previous IRA contributions for 2015.

The $3,000 taxable unemployment income does not qualify as compensation for purposes of determining the annual dollar limit.

Conversion of a Traditional, SEP or SIMPLE IRA to a Roth IRA

Individuals and married couples filing jointly may be able to convert amounts in a traditional IRA (or in a SEP or SIMPLE IRA treated as a "deemed" traditional IRA—see ¶14,535 and ¶14,545) into a Roth IRA by directing the trustee to transfer the amounts from the traditional IRA to a Roth IRA or by withdrawing the amounts from the traditional IRA and redepositing the amounts in a Roth IRA as a qualified rollover contribution. There is a "qualified rollover contribution" if an amount received is paid into a Roth IRA no later than 60 days after the date on which the amount was received. Unlike the rule for indirect transfers between traditional IRAs, there is no one-year waiting period between rollover contributions.

Beginning in 2010, the modified AGI and filing status requirements for converting a traditional IRA to a Roth IRA are permanently eliminated. Taxpayers making rollovers in 2011 and thereafter must recognize the entire amount of the taxable distribution amount as income in the tax year the distribution takes place. Amounts transferred are not subject to the 10% early-withdrawal penalty; however, the "pre-tax" portion of the transferred amount (i.e., accumulated earnings plus deductible contributions) must be included in the taxpayer's gross income.

EXAMPLE 14.65

Cindy Ragan maintains a traditional IRA that was created with deductible contributions. Her account balance as of March 4 is $60,000, consisting of (1) $10,000 deductible contributions, (2) $20,000 after-tax contributions, and (3) $30,000 accumulated earnings. If Cindy decides to rollover her $60,000 traditional IRA balance into a Roth IRA on this date, she must include $40,000 in gross income for the year.

PLANNING POINTER

1. A taxpayer who wishes to convert a traditional IRA into a Roth IRA should consider the advantages associated with staggering partial rollovers over more than one year. A full conversion within one year may force the taxpayer into a higher tax bracket (a "bunching" effect). An increase from, say, the 33% bracket to the 35% bracket may not be consequential. However, an increase from, say, the 15% bracket to the 25% or higher bracket could create a severe tax burden for the taxpayer. Another advantage associated with staggered rollovers is that a taxpayer may have cash available to pay tax on a partial conversion but not enough to pay tax on a full conversion.
2. If a traditional IRA contains different types of assets, the taxpayer may indicate which ones to move. For example, if a traditional IRA is split between two mutual funds, the taxpayer may choose to move one fund or the other to the Roth IRA, or move part of each.

Roth-to-Traditional IRA Reconversions

A taxpayer may wish to "undo" a traditional-to-Roth IRA conversion. The two most common reasons for reconversions are (a) *market-driven motivation,* and (b) the need for *corrective action.*

Market-driven Motivation

A taxpayer would be motivated to reconvert a Roth IRA back to a traditional IRA if the taxable amount transferred to a Roth declined in value. Without the reconversion, the taxpayer might have to pay taxes on income that had disappeared in a market decline.

EXAMPLE 14.66 Will Feldman maintains a $100,000 taxable balance in his traditional IRA. In February of the current year, he converts the $100,000 balance into a Roth IRA. Several months later, the Roth IRA loses 40% of its value. Without a reconversion, Will would have to pay ordinary income tax on $100,000 by April 15 of the following year, even though only $60,000 of that amount remained in his Roth IRA account.

Corrective Action

If, after a direct contribution to a Roth IRA, the taxpayer determined that MAGI (as defined at ¶14,625) for the year exceeded the income limit for direct Roth contributions ($116,000-$131,000 range for single filers; $183,000-$193,000 range for joint filers), a corrective reconversion would be necessary. Otherwise the Roth earnings since inception would be subject to income taxes and penalties.

Reconversion Deadline

The deadline for "undoing" a traditional-to-Roth IRA conversion depends on whether the taxpayer's motivation for reconversion is *market-driven* or *corrective.* If market driven, the reconversion can be made as late as October 15 of the year following the conversion year, provided the automatic six-month extension has been timely filed.

Corrective reconversions can also be made as late as October 15 of the year following a traditional-to-Roth conversion year. However, unlike the deadline for market-driven conversions, filing an automatic six-month extension is not required to meet this deadline. However, a timely return must have been filed for the conversion tax year and an amended return must be filed to reflect the reconversion.

EXAMPLE 14.67 In January of the current year, Sally made a $5,500 contribution to a Roth IRA. Sally was certain her MAGI would be low enough to enable her to qualify for a full $5,500 Roth IRA contribution. However, later in the year, her employer gave her a very large and unexpected bonus, which caused her MAGI to exceed the allowed limit for any Roth IRA contribution. Her Roth IRA, because of some wise investments, had grown to $12,000 during the year. If Sally transfers the $5,500 from the Roth IRA back into her personal checking account, the entire pre-tax portion of her Roth IRA balance, $6,500, will be subject to taxation and the 10-percent early withdrawal penalty. Sally can avoid this unfavorable result by transferring the entire balance of the Roth IRA to a traditional IRA. Sally has until October 15 of the following year to make the corrective reconversion. This favorable treatment is subject to three requirements: 1. a timely return filed for the original conversion year; 2. a reconversion transfer made by October 15 of the year following the conversion year; and 3. an amended return to reflect the reconversion.

Rollover to a Roth IRA After a Reconversion

Individuals who have completed a Roth-to-traditional IRA reconversion may later wish to make a new rollover back to a Roth IRA. The earliest allowable date for such a rollover is the later of:

1. January 1, Year 2 (the beginning of the year following the year in which the amount was originally converted to the Roth IRA).
2. The end of the 30-day period following the reconversion date.

EXAMPLE 14.68   Frannie Fickle maintains a traditional IRA. In May, Year 1, she converts the traditional IRA into a Roth IRA. However, on August 19, Year 1, she decides to reconvert the Roth IRA back to the traditional IRA. If Frannie later wants to make a new rollover back to a Roth IRA, the earliest possible date that she can make a new traditional-to-Roth IRA rollover is January 1, Year 2, i.e., the later of:

1. January 1, Year 2 (the beginning of the year following the year in which the amount was reconverted to a traditional IRA);
2. September 19, Year 1 (the end of the 30-day period following the day on which she had completed a Roth-to-traditional IRA reconversion).

If Frannie makes an untimely rollover before January 1, Year 2, the before-tax portion of the rollover contribution (plus any income subsequently earned from the entire rollover amount) will be subject to a 10% early-withdrawal penalty in addition to ordinary income tax.

Roth Distributions

Code Sec. 408A(d)(4) imposes strict aggregation rules for multiple Roth IRA accounts and ordering rules for distributions of Roth contributions, conversions, and earnings for tax purposes. These rules are discussed below.

Aggregation Rules for Multiple Roth IRAs

In order to determine the tax effect of a Roth distribution, Roth IRAs, whether or not maintained in separate accounts, will be considered a single Roth IRA. (Code Sec. 408A(d)(4)(A). The rules for aggregating multiple Roth IRA accounts must follow the rules under Code Sec. 408(d)(2) for combining multiple traditional IRAs (see ¶14,625).

Ordering Rules for Distributions

Once the Roth IRA accounts have been aggregated (if necessary), the ordering rules require the Roth IRA holder to treat any amounts distributed as coming from the following sources in the order listed (Code Sec. 408(A)(d)(4)(B)):

1. Direct contributions (e.g., payments by check) to Roth IRA accounts are deemed to be withdrawn first;
2. Then, the taxable amount of rollover contributions, on a first-in-first-out basis;
3. Next, the nontaxable amount of rollover contributions, on a first-in-first-out basis;
4. Finally, earnings from the Roth IRA are treated as withdrawn.

Tax Consequences

In determining the taxability of Roth IRA distributions, it is first necessary to determine if the distribution is a qualified distribution or a non-qualified distribution. *Qualified* Roth distributions are not subject to income tax or the additional 10 percent penalty. *Nonqualified* Roth distributions are taxable only to the extent of the earnings portion of the Roth IRA included in the distribution. A 10 percent penalty is imposed on nonqualified distributions only to the extent of *taxable rollover contributions* and *accumulated earnings*. Nonqualified distributions consisting of *direct contributions* or *nontaxable rollover contributions* are not subject to the 10 percent penalty.

Qualified Distributions

A payment or distribution is a "qualified distribution" if two tests have been satisfied:

1. **Five-year holding period.** A qualified distribution must be made after the five-tax-year period beginning with the first tax year for which the individual made a contribution to a Roth IRA (or the individual's spouse made a contribution to a Roth IRA) established for that individual. (Code Sec. 408A(d)(2)(B). The date of a five-year holding period begins on January 1 of the contribution year. For *direct contributions*, once the five-year holding period requirement has been satisfied for the initial contribution, this requirement is deemed to be satisfied for all subsequent direct contributions, even if made into different Roth IRAs. For *rollover contributions*, a separate five-year holding period applies to each rollover.

2. **Qualifying event.** Code Sec. 408A(d)(A) identifies a qualifying event as a distribution made
   a. on or after the date on which the individual attains age 59½;
   b. to a beneficiary (or to the individual's estate) on or after the individual's death;
   c. because the individual is disabled (an individual is considered to be disabled if he or she is unable to engage in any substantial gainful activity by reason of any medically determinable physical or mental impairment that can be expected to result in death or to be of long-continued and indefinite duration); or
   d. for a "first home" purchase, not to exceed $10,000 (lifetime aggregate limit). (See ¶14,635 for a further discussion of this qualifying event.)

Nonqualified Distributions

A distribution that is not a qualified distribution (and neither is contributed to another Roth IRA in a qualified rollover contribution nor constitutes a corrective distribution) is includible in the owner's gross income to the extent that the amount of the distribution, when added to the amount of all prior distributions from the owner's Roth IRAs (whether or not they were qualified distributions) and reduced by the amount of those prior distributions previously includible in gross income, exceeds the owner's contributions to all of the owner's Roth IRAs. Any amount distributed as a corrective distribution (described earlier) is treated as if it never had been contributed. Reg. §1.408A-6, Q&A-4.

Returns of taxable rollover contributions that were not held in the IRA account for five years and taxable earnings are subject to the 10 percent early distribution penalty. Reg. §1.408A-6, Q&A-5. Determining the 10 percent penalty requires knowledge of extensive information, including the amount of the distribution, basis in contributions, basis in conversions, years in which conversions were made, and the amount of earnings. This requires diligent tracking of amounts contributed, amounts converted, and amounts previously distributed.

The tax consequences associated with qualified and nonqualified Roth distributions are summarized at Exhibit 12.

Exhibit 12. APPLYING THE TWO QUALIFYING TESTS TO ROTH DISTRIBUTIONS

	Ordering of Roth IRA Sources			
Tests:	1st Direct Contributions	2nd Taxable Portion of Rollover Contributions	3rd Nontaxable Portion of Rollover Contribution	4th Accumulated Earnings
(1) Has the five-year holding period requirement been met?				
If yes: →	Penalty-free	Penalty-free	Penalty-free	Penalty-free only if (2) below is also met
If no: →	Penalty-free	10% Penalty	Penalty-free	10% Penalty
(2) Has the age 59 ½, death, disability, or 1st time home buying requirement been met?				
If yes: →	Tax-free	Tax-free	Tax-free	Tax-free
If no: →	Tax-free	Tax-free	Tax-free	Taxable

For direct contributions, once the five-year holding period requirement has been satisfied for the initial contribution, this requirement is deemed to be satisfied for all subsequent direct contributions, even if made into different Roth IRAs.

EXAMPLE 14.69 John-Paul, age 30, begins making direct contributions to a Roth IRA in Year 1. He contributes $2,000 per year from Year 1 to Year 7, resulting in a $14,000 Roth direct contribution basis. If, in Year 8, John-Paul takes a Roth distribution of $14,000 or less, none of the distribution would be subject to income tax (since it represents a return of basis), and none of the distribution would be subject to the 10 percent early distribution penalty. *Note: If John-Paul had taken a distribution in excess of $14,000, the amount distributed in excess of $14,000 (i.e., accumulated earnings) would have been subject to both income tax and the 10% early distribution penalty.*

PLANNING POINTER	An individual who would not reach age 59 ½ (or satisfy any other qualifying event) in five years can nonetheless convert a traditional IRA or employer-provided account (e.g., 401(k)) to a Roth IRA, and receive a distribution of the rollover contribution after five years, without being subject to the 10 percent penalty. In contrast, the same distribution from a traditional IRA or employer-provided account would be subject to the 10 percent penalty.

EXAMPLE 14.70	Conor, age 25, rolled over a $14,000 deductible traditional IRA to a Roth IRA in Year 1. Thus the entire rollover amount was taxed in Year 1, creating a $14,000 Roth rollover contribution basis. Conor made no additional contributions to the Roth IRA, and did not convert any other amounts. If, in Year 6, Conor takes a Roth distribution of $14,000 or less, none of the distribution would be subject to income tax (since it represents a return of basis), and none of the distribution would be subject to the 10 percent early distribution penalty (since separate 5-year holding period requirements had been met for each of the five rollover contributions). *Note: If Conor had taken the distribution from a traditional IRA instead of a Roth IRA, the entire distribution would have been subject to the 10% early distribution penalty since he had not reached age 59 ½ on the distribution date (or satisfied any other qualifying events).*

After-death Distributions

The minimum distribution and incidental death benefit rules that apply to traditional IRAs do not apply to Roth IRAs prior to the owner's death. Code Secs. 401(a)(9) and 408A. Thus, no distributions from a Roth IRA have to be made after the owner turns 70 ½. However, after the death of the owner of a Roth IRA, the minimum required distribution rules applicable to traditional IRAs following the owner's death apply to Roth IRAs. These rules are covered at ¶14,235.

Reporting Roth IRA Distributions

Distributions from Roth IRAs are reported on Part III of Form 8606 (Nondeductible IRAs). If the 10% early distribution tax applies, it is reported on Form 5329 (Additional Taxes on Qualified Plans (Including IRAs) and Other Tax-Favored Accounts).

Exhibit 13. Personal Retirement Plans for Working Individuals

Features:	Traditional IRA	Roth IRA
Ideal Investor Time Frame	Shorter time horizon	Longer time horizon
Age of Contributor	Must not be 70 ½ or older	No age restrictions
Minimum Compensation Requirement?	Yes	Yes
Establishment Deadline	By filing due date (April 15 of following year)	Same deadline
Contribution Deadline	By filing due date (April 15 of following year)	Same deadline
Maximum Contribution Amount	$5,500 ($6,500 if age 50+) aggregate limit for traditional IRAs, deemed IRAs (SEP or SIMPLE), and Roth IRAs	Same limit
Contribution Phase-Out (MAGI Limits)	None	MFJ: $183,000 – 193,000 Single: $116,000 – $131,000
Deduction Phase-Out (MAGI Limits)	For active participants: MFJ: $98,000 – $118,000 Single: $61,000 – $71,000 For nonparticipant spouses of active participants: $183,000 – $193,000 For nonparticipants (including married taxpayers who are both nonparticipants): Contributions are fully deductible	Never deductible
IRA Earnings	Taxed when withdrawn	Tax exempt if conditions are met
Penalty for Early Withdrawals	10%	10%
Penalty for Late Withdrawals	50% (distributions to begin no later than April 1 after the year in which the participant becomes age 70½)	None (no minimum distribution rules apply while participant is living)

Nonqualified Deferred Compensation Plans

The most common types of nonqualified deferred compensation plans include:

- Rabbi Trusts (at ¶14,705),
- Employee stock purchase plans (at ¶14,715),
- Incentive stock options (at ¶14,725),
- Nonqualified stock options (at ¶14,735),
- Restricted stock plans (at ¶14,745),
- Variable annuity contracts (at ¶14,755),
- Informal, short-term arrangements (at ¶14,765).

General concepts common to nonqualified plans and features associated with specific plans are explained in the sections that follow.

¶14,701 NONQUALIFIED PLANS—BASIC CONCEPTS

Common Characteristics

Nonqualified deferred compensation arrangements provide employees or independent contractors with future compensation for work performed currently. Being "nonqualified" means these plans need not meet the rules for funding, distributions, vesting, nondiscrimination, and other criteria imposed on qualified plans (discussed at ¶14,201 to ¶14,285). However, under a nonqualified plan, an employer generally is not entitled to deduct contributions paid for the benefit of an employee (or independent contractor) until the beneficiary reports taxable compensation from the contributions.

Tax Effect to Employees

Compensation payable in the future (deferred events) is not taxed currently if:

- the plan is neither funded nor secured by a negotiable and freely transferable promissory note (i.e., the *economic benefit doctrine*—see ¶4101—is not met if the employee relies on the employer's mere promise to pay); or
- the employee's right to compensation amounts is subject to a substantial risk of forfeiture (i.e., the *constructive receipt doctrine*—see ¶4125— is not met if the employee lacks complete dominion and control over the amounts earned).

The courts have ruled that substantial risk of forfeiture does not mean the likelihood of a forfeiture-triggering event, rather, the likelihood of forfeiture once a triggering event occurs. For example, in *Robinson*, 86-2 USTC ¶ 9790 (1st Cir. 1986), an employee received restricted stock options that carried a risk of forfeiture one year beyond the exercise date. The triggering event that would cause forfeiture, a sale by the employee of the stock within one year of the exercise date, was highly improbable. Nevertheless, the court allowed deferral until one year later, when the restriction was lifted. It reasoned that, despite the improbability of the employee selling the stock during the one-year period, forfeiture was highly likely if this improbable event had occurred.

EXAMPLE 14.71   Ernie Larkins, age 22, is to receive a $1 million bonus in year 1, for signing a professional football contract. Realizing that his quarterbacking days may be numbered, he wishes to defer the bonus for 10 years, beginning in the year he attains age 32. The employer offers to establish an escrow account in which the $1 million would be transferred to an escrow agent. The escrow agent, at her sole discretion, would invest the funds in securities, which may act as a hedge against inflation. After ten years, the bonus becomes payable in equal amounts over years 11 through 20. With this arrangement the $1 million bonus would be taxable in full in year 1 since it would be both funded and nonforfeitable. The employer would be entitled to a $1 million deduction in year 1.

EXAMPLE 14.72	Referring to the preceding example above, Ernie's bonus could be structured in one of two ways to achieve tax deferral:
	
	1. Avoiding the economic benefits doctrine. If the employer gives a mere promise to pay the $1 million plus accrued interest beginning in year 11 through 20, rather than actually funding an escrow account, the bonus would be tax deferred. This arrangement may be appropriate with a financially secure employer.
	2. Avoiding the constructive receipts doctrine. Had there been a substantial risk of forfeiture (i.e., payment conditioned upon performance, attendance, gate receipts, etc.), the $1 million signing bonus could have been tax deferred until the earlier of:
	  a. The date the risk of forfeiture disappears, or
	  b. The dates of receipt, i.e., years 11 through 20.

Conditioning a substantial risk of forfeiture upon the achievement of specific performance by an employee may not be appealing, particularly when the employee is a professional athlete whose success or failure depends in part upon a team effort. However, as explained at ¶14,705, the Rabbi Trust has become a popular devise for creating the requisite substantial risk of forfeiture without future payment being conditioned upon the employee's performance.

Applicability of Payroll Taxes

Nonqualified deferred compensation is part of the taxable wage base for both FICA and FUTA tax purposes. Under Code Secs. 3121(v) and 3306(r), amounts deferred under a "nonqualified deferred compensation plan" are included as wages for FICA and FUTA tax purposes in the later of:

1. the year in which the services are performed; or
2. the year in which there is no substantial risk of forfeiture of the amounts.

The amount included in the wage base generally is the principal amount credited to the employee for the period plus any income attributable to that amount through the date the amount is taken into account for FICA and FUTA tax purposes. Reg. §31.3121(v)(2)-1(c).

Special Requirements For Nonqualified Retirement Plans

If a nonqualified deferred compensation plan fails to meet the funding and distribution requirements under Code Sec. 409A, all compensation deferred under the plan for the tax year and all preceding tax years will be includible in gross income for the tax year to the extent it is not subject to a substantial risk of forfeiture and not previously included in gross income. The amount of tax will be increased by 20 percent of the amount of compensation required to be included in gross income. Code Sec. 409A(a)(1)(B).

Funding Requirements

Assets held in trust for purposes of paying deferred compensation should not be located or transferred outside the United States. The fair market value of such offshore property, whether or not available to satisfy the claims of an employer's creditors, will be included in the gross income of plan participants at the time the property becomes transferable or not subject to a substantial risk of forfeiture. Code Sec. 409A(b)(1).

Distribution Requirements

A nonqualified deferred compensation plan must provide that compensation deferred under the plan may not be distributed earlier than (Code Sec. 409A(a)(2)):

1. Separation from service. In the case of a key employee, a distribution may not be made earlier than six months after the date of separation from service (or, if earlier, the employee's death).
2. The date the participant becomes disabled.
3. The participant's death.
4. A specified time (or pursuant to a fixed schedule) specified under the plan at the date the compensation is deferred.
5. A change in ownership or effective control of the corporation or in the ownership of a substantial portion of the assets of the corporation.
6. The occurrence of an unforeseeable emergency. An "unforeseeable emergency" is a severe financial hardship to the participant resulting from an illness or accident of the participant, the participant's spouse, or a dependent of the participant, loss of the participant's property due to casualty, or

other similar extraordinary and unforeseeable circumstances arising as a result of events beyond the participant's control.

Acceleration of Benefits

A nonqualified deferred compensation plan may not permit the acceleration of the time or schedule of any payment under the plan. Code Sec. 409A(a)(3).

¶14,705 RABBI TRUSTS

A Rabbi Trust is an arrangement under which the employer places assets into an irrevocable trust to secure the payment of promised deferred compensation to selected employees. Rabbi Trusts have four common characteristics:

1. **Unsecured promise.** Employees earn compensation currently and receives an unsecured promise from the employer to pay at a future date.
2. **Employer creditors.** Trust assets are subject to claims of employer creditors, not employee creditors; employees must have no vested ownership rights (similar to beneficiaries of grantor trusts).
3. **Non-employee trustee.** No employee/beneficiary may serve as trustee.
4. **Trustee powers.** The trustee has full investment discretion.

Tax Effect on Employee

Employees may defer employer contributions to a Rabbi Trust for either of two reasons:

1. The *economic benefit doctrine* does not apply because the contributions are not unconditionally and irrevocably for the employees' benefit. This lack of immediate benefit to employees is the result of the trust's exposure to employer assets.
2. The *constructive receipt doctrine* does not apply because the employee cannot receive the deferred compensation until some future time such as the termination of employment or retirement.

Tax Effect on Employer

Employer contributions to the plan are not deductible until the year in which the employee reports taxable compensation. However, income earned by the trust is taxable to the employer if it is subject to the same restriction as the contributed amounts. If, on the other hand, employees have unrestricted access to the income earned by the trust, it is taxable to the employees, even if unpaid. The character of income earned depends on the character of the assets.

Origin of Rabbi Trust

The Rabbi Trust dates back to 1980, when IRS issued a favorable ruling on a trust funded by a congregation for the benefit of a rabbi. Trustees managed and invested the trust funds; income was distributed to the rabbi quarterly; and upon the rabbi's death, disability or retirement, the trust fund, including accumulated income, would be disbursed to the rabbi or his beneficiaries. During its existence, the trust's assets were available to the creditors of the grantors, but not those of the rabbi. IRS ruled that unpaid contributions provided no economic benefit to the rabbi since they were subject to the claims of the grantor's creditors. IRS also ruled that the constructive receipt doctrine should not apply because the employee could not receive the deferred compensation until some future time. *The IRS has issued guidance setting forth model Rabbi Trust provisions.* Rev. Proc. 92-64, 1992-2 C.B. 422, *modified in part by* Notice 2000-56, 2000-2 C.B. 393.

¶14,715 EMPLOYEE STOCK PURCHASE PLANS

Many large companies offer employee stock purchase plans (ESPPs) that allow employees to buy employer stock at a discount. These plans are offered as an employment incentive, giving employees an opportunity to share in the growth potential of the company's stock (and, by implication, encouraging employees to work productively in order to achieve this growth potential). Generally employee-participants make after-tax contributions to a stock purchase fund for a certain period of time, usually six months, through payroll deductions. No employee may purchase more than $25,000 in fair market value of stock in any year and the employee-grantee must not own more than 5% of the company's stock immediately before the grant date. Regs. §1.423-2(d) and (i). At designated points in the year, the employer uses the accumulated funds to purchase stock for the employees. The discounted price is known as the offering (grant) price. The employer maintains the stock in the employee's name until the employee decides to sell it.

Look-back Provision

An ESPP may include a "look-back provision," in which the employee purchase price is retroactively determined by comparing:

1. the market price of a share of stock as of the offering date (i.e., as of the beginning date of the period during which an employee's right to purchase stock is outstanding) with
2. the market price of a share of stock on the exercise date (i.e., on a pre-determined date upon which stock is bought for all participants, usually at the end of an offering period).

Under an ESPP, an employer may allow the employee a stock purchase discount up to a statutory limit of 15 percent, applied to the lower of the two prices above. Reg. §1.423-2(g)(1).

Tax Effect on Employee

Generally, an employer's purchase of stock for employees under an ESPP does not trigger taxation to the employee. However, once the employee sells the stock, the purchase discount is generally considered additional compensation to the employee, and is subject to ordinary rates. Depending on when the right to purchase the stock was initially granted (the grant or offering date), and how long the employee held the stock, any profit in excess of the compensation amount, may be treated as a long-term capital gain. The portion of the gain that constitutes ordinary compensation depends on whether the sale of stock is a "qualifying disposition" under Code Sec. 423 or a "disqualifying disposition".

Qualifying Disposition

A qualified disposition is one that satisfies a "one-two" holding period rule: the employee must hold onto the stock for at least (1) one year after the purchase date, and (2) two years after the beginning of the offering period. If this condition is met, the gain at sale is divided into taxable ordinary income and taxable capital gains. Taxable compensation is defined as the lesser of (a) the spread between the fair market value at the time of sale and the purchase price or (b) the discount at the beginning of the offering period (or possibly the end of the offering period under a look-back provision in which the stock value has declined). The portion that is taxable as compensation is subject to FICA and FUTA taxation as well. The taxable capital gain (or loss) is simply that part of the gain at sale not treated as compensation. The formula for computing compensation and capital gain in a qualifying disposition is provided in the solution to Example 14.73 below.

EXAMPLE 14.73

Consider an ESPP with a 10% discount, a look-back provision, and a 6-month offering period. Assume Avery Cobb is paid $90,000 annually and contributes 5% of gross pay to purchase stock, or $4,500. The share price is $50 on the first day of the offering period and $200 on the last day of the offering period. With the discount and look-back, Avery gets to purchase stock at a per share price of $45, which is equal to 90 percent of the lesser of (a) the offering price ($50) or (b) the purchase price ($200). The total number of shares purchased with the $4,500 contributed is thus 100 ($4,500 ÷ $45). Assume first that Avery holds the shares 18 months for a qualified disposition. If the price per share at disposition is $250, the total gain per share is $250 - $45 = $155. The discount at the start of offering period was $5 per share ($50 × 10%). This is less than the $155 per share total gain on sale, so $5 per share is taxed as compensation and is subject to FICA and FUTA taxes; the remainder, $150 per share, is taxed as a long-term capital gain. The corporation gets a deduction for the amount reported as compensation. See per share computations below.

Formula	Description	Per Share Amt.
(a) = Given	Grant price (FMV at beginning of offering period)	$50
(b) = Given	Purchase price (FMV at end of offering period)	$200
(c) = Given	Sale price (upon disposition of stock)	$250
(d) = Given	Employee purchase discount percentage	10%
(e) = (d) × [the lesser of (a) or (b)]	Employee purchase discount amount: 10% × $50 = $5	$5
(f) = [the lesser of (a) or (b)] – (e)	Actual cost to employee: $50 – $5 = $45	$45
(g) = the lesser of: (c) – (f); (a) × (d)	Ordinary income = the lesser of: $250 – $45 = $205; $50 × 10% = $5	$5
(h) = (f) + (g)	Tax basis for computing capital gain: $45 + $5 = $50	$50
(i) = (c) – (h)	Capital gain: $250 – $50 = $200	$200

Disqualifying Disposition

Participants in an ESPP may not meet the holding requirements of the 1-2 rule and, therefore, trigger a *disqualifying* disposition. The spread between the fair market value on the purchase date and the actual cost to the employee is treated as cash compensation and is taxed *in the calendar year in which the disposition occurs*. The difference between the sale price and fair market value at purchase is taxed as a capital gain (or loss) at the appropriate capital gains rate depending upon how long the stock was held. The most common disqualifying disposition is to buy company stock and sell it immediately after purchase, known as a "same-day sale." For disqualifying dispositions, the spread between the fair market value on the purchase date and the actual employee cost is treated as cash compensation and is taxed *in the calendar year in which the purchase occurs*. The difference between the sale price and the fair market value at purchase is taxed as a capital gain (loss) at the appropriate capital gains rate depending upon how long the stock was held.

| EXAMPLE 14.74 | Referring to the preceding example, assume that the shares were disposed of immediately after purchase in a same-day sale. The sale would be a disqualifying disposition for either of two reasons: Avery would have sold the stock (1) within one year or less from the exercise (purchase) date and (2) less than two years after the offering (grant) date. In this case, the disposition is $200 per share and the gain per share is $200 - $45 = $155, all of which is taxed as ordinary income and is subject to FICA and FUTA taxes. Because the shares were sold in a disqualifying disposition, the employer gets a corporate tax deduction for the compensation amount of $155 per share. The employer's statutory FICA and FUTA taxes on the $155 per share ordinary income are deductible as well. The formula for disqualifying dispositions is provided in the computations below. |

Formula	Description	Per Share Amt.
(a) = Given	Grant price (FMV at beginning of offering period)	$50
(b) = Given	Purchase price (FMV at end of offering period)	$200
(c) = Given	Sale price (upon disposition of stock)	$200
(d) = Given	Employee purchase discount %	10%
(e) = (d) × [the lesser of (a) or (b)]	Employee purchase discount amount: 10% × $50 = $5	$5
(f) = [the lesser of (a) or (b)] − (e)	Actual cost to employee: $50 − $5 = $45	$45
(g) = (b) − (f)	Ord. income: $200 − $45 = $155	$155
(h) = (f) + (g)	Tax basis for computing capital gain: $45 + $155 = $200	$200
(i) = (c) − (h)	Capital gain: $200 − $200 = $0	$0

¶14,725 INCENTIVE STOCK OPTIONS (ISOS)

Tax Effect on Employees with ISOs

An ISO is a right granted by an employer corporation that allows an employee to purchase the employer's stock at a fixed price for a stated period of time. The employee thus benefits from the potential appreciation in the value of the underlying stock from the grant date to the exercise date of the option. ISOs have become very popular in recent years because of the favorable tax treatment afforded employees under Code Sec. 422. ISOs do not trigger ordinary income at the grant date or the exercise date. Instead, all of the potential income is treated as capital gain and is not recognized until the ultimate disposition of the stock by the employee.

Qualifying Dispositions

Holding Period Requirements

ISOs must satisfy a "one-two-three" holding period rule: the employee must hold onto the stock for at least *one* year after the exercise date and *two* years after the grant date. In addition, the exercise date must not occur more than *three* months after "employee" status has terminated. Code Sec. 422(a).

Other Qualifying Conditions

The option must also meet all of the following requirements under Code Sec. 422(b) in order to qualify for special tax treatment:

1. The plan must be approved by shareholders within 12 months of adoption;
2. The grant date must be within 10 years of plan adoption;
3. The exercisable date must be within 10 years of the grant date;
4. The option price must not be less than the fair market value at grant date;
5. The option must be nontransferable to third parties (except in death);
6. The employee-grantee must not own more than 10% of the company's stock immediately before grant date.

EXAMPLE 14.75	ABC Corp. grants George Willingham 1,000 ISOs on January 1, Year 1 (the "grant" date). On this date, the stock's fair market value is $10 per share and each ISO entitles the holder to buy one share of ABC stock for $10 (the exercise price). George can exercise the ISO after one year of employment but not more than 10 years after the grant date and not more than three months after the effective severance date in the event his employment is terminated. George exercises the ISOs on December 31, Year 2 (the "exercise" date) when the stock is worth $200 per share. He sells the stock on January 1, Year 4 (the "sale" date) for $250 per share. Neither the granting nor exercising of the stock will have regular tax consequences to George in a qualifying disposition (but see discussion on AMT below). In the year of sale, George will report a $240 per share long-term capital gain. ABC is not allowed any deduction in connection with the ISOs, since no ordinary income was recognized by George. See per share computations below.

Key Dates	Qualifying Disposition
Jan. 1, Year 1 (ISO is granted.)	No ordinary income (OI); ISO's tax basis = $0 per ISO ISO tax basis = $0 cost + $0 ordinary income
Dec. 31, Year 2 (ISO is exercised.)	No ordinary income (OI); stock basis = $10 per share Stock basis = $10 cost + $0 ordinary income
Jan. 1, Year 4 (Stock is sold.)	$240 per share long-term capital gain (LTCG) $240 LTCG = $250 sale price – $10 stock basis The holding period begins on January 1, Year 3, the day after the exercise date; therefore, the holding period is long-term.

Disqualifying Dispositions

If the employee fails to satisfy any part of the "one-two-three" rule above, the gain, up to the spread at the exercise date, will be treated as compensation income. Any excess will be treated as capital gain. Thus, an early disposition disqualifies the ISO and treats the transaction as if it were a nonqualified ISO, with the exception of the date of income recognition. The example below illustrates the effects of a disqualifying disposition.

EXAMPLE 14.76	Referring to the foregoing example, suppose that George Willingham sold his shares on June 30, Year 3. Because the stock was not held for one year from the exercise date, December 31, Year 3, George made a disqualifying disposition of the stock. As before, George will recognize no income on the grant date or on the exercise date. On June 30, Year 3 (the sale date) however, George will recognize $190 per share in ordinary income ($200 - $10) and $50 per share short-term capital gain ($250 - $200). The holding period of a disqualified ISO begins on the day after the exercise date; thus, George's holding period is short-term (from January 1, Year 3, the day after the exercise date, to June 30, Year 3, the sale date). ABC is allowed a corresponding deduction of $190 per share for its tax year which includes December 31, Year 3, George's year-end.

Key Dates	Disqualifying Disposition
Jan. 1, Year 1 (ISO is granted.)	No ordinary income (OI); ISO's tax basis = $0 per ISO ISO tax basis = $0 cost + $0 ordinary income
December 31, Year 2 (ISO is exercised.)	No tax effect; stock basis = $10 per share Stock basis = $10 cost + $0 ordinary income
June 30, Year 3 (Stock is sold.)	(a) $190 per share ordinary income (OI) $190 OI = $200 exercise price – $10 stock basis (b) $50 per share short-term capital gain (STCG) $50 STCG = $250 sale price – $200 FMV at exercise date The holding period begins on January 1, Year 3, the day after the exercise date; therefore, the holding period is short-term.

Alternative Minimum Tax

For alternative minimum tax (AMT) purposes, the spread between the ISO exercise price and the fair market value of the stock on the exercise date (or on the date a substantial risk of forfeiture has been lifted) is treated as a tax prefernce for AMT. The stock's AMT basis is increased by the income recognized. The disposition of the stock triggers a negative AMT adjustment, since the AMT basis includes the tax preference income.

¶14,735   NONQUALIFIED STOCK OPTIONS (NSOs)

Tax Effect on Employees with NSOs

Nonqualified stock options (NSOs) are currently the most popular method of stock acquisition plans. These options are sometimes labeled, "nonstatutory options," because they are not described anywhere in the Code. Thus, they are not afforded any favorable tax treatment; rather, they are taxed under Code Sec. 83(a).

NSO Taxation Upon Grant Date

A nonqualified stock option is taxed when it is granted if the NSO has a "readily ascertainable fair market value" at the grant date. Reg. §1.83-1(a) and Reg. §1.83-7(a). If an NSO has a readily ascertainable fair market value, the employee must recognize compensation in the amount of that fair market value in the year the NSO is granted. Reg. §1.83-1(a). If the employee paid for the NSO, he recognizes the value of the NSO minus its cost. The employee is not taxed again when he exercises the NSO and buys corporate stock. However, the employee is taxed when he sells the stock. The employee's basis in the stock is the fair market value of the NSO on which he paid taxes, plus the amount he paid for the stock. Capital gain or loss is recognized when the stock is sold.

An NSO that is not actively traded on an established market may still have a readily ascertainable fair market value only if all of the following requirements are met:

1. the option must be transferable,
2. the option must be exercisable immediately and in full when it is granted,
3. there can be no condition or restriction on the option that would have a significant effect on its fair market value, and
4. the fair market value of the option privilege must be readily ascertainable.

Because these requirements are seldom satisfied, most nonqualified options that are not traded on an established market do not have a readily ascertainable fair market value.

NSO Taxation upon Exercise Date

If the nonqualified option does not have a readily ascertainable fair market value, it is the exercise of the option, and not the grant, that triggers the taxable event. Reg. §1.83-7(a). When the employee exercises the NSO, the employee recognizes compensation in the amount of the fair market value of the stock purchased minus any amount paid for the stock. Later, when the employee sells the stock, any gain or loss recognized is treated as capital gain or loss. The employee's holding period of the stock begins the day after the NSO was exercised.

Holding Period

The holding period of stock acquired through an NSO begins on the date after the option is granted or exercised, depending on which event triggers compensation. If an NSO has a readily ascertainable fair market value (triggering compensation recognition at the grant date), the holding period of the stock begins on the day after the grant date. If the NSO has no readily ascertainable value and compensation is not recognized until the NSO is exercised, the holding period of the stock begins on the day after the exercise date.

Lapse of NSOs

When an employee allows an NSO with a readily ascertainable fair market value to lapse, the employee's capital loss is determined by the employee's basis in the NSO (i.e., the value of the NSO that was taxed). Code Sec. 1234(a)(2). The NSO is treated as if it were sold or exchanged on the date that it lapsed. Reg. §1.1234-1(b).

Tax Effect on Employer

An employer may deduct the value of an NSO as a business expense for the tax year in which the option is included in the gross income of the employee. When the NSO has a readily ascertainable value, the employer is allowed the deduction for the year in which the option is granted. When the NSO does not have a readily ascertainable value, the employer is allowed the deduction for the year in which the option is exercised. The employer's deduction equals the amount of compensation recognized by the employee. When the employer and the employee have different tax years, the employer claims the deduction in the tax year in which or with which the employee's tax year ends. Code Sec. 83(h).

EXAMPLE 14.77	XYZ Corp. grants Wesley Bloeme 1,000 NSOs on January 1, Year 1 (the "grant" date). Each NSO grants the holder the right to buy 1 share of XYZ stock for $10. Wesley can exercise the NSO after one year of employment. The NSO's readily ascertainable fair market value on the grant date is $50 per share. (Note that with NSOs, the exercise price may be below the market value of the stock since the Code Sec. 422(b)(4) pricing rules do not apply as they do for incentive stock options.) Wesley exercises the NSO on December 31, Year 2 (the "exercise" date) when the stock is worth $200 per share. He sells the stock on January 1, Year 4 (the "sale" date) for $250 per share. Wesley must recognize $50 per share compensation on the grant date and XYZ is allowed a corresponding deduction of $50 per share for its tax year which includes December 31, Year 1, Wesley's year-end. Wesley must also report a $190 per share long-term capital gain in the year of sale. See per share computations below.

Key Dates	Readily Ascertainable Value at Grant Date
Jan. 1, Year 1 (NSO is granted.)	Compensation (OI) = $50 per share $50 OI = $50 NSO market value − $0 cost] NSO tax basis = $50 per NSO $50 NSO tax basis = $0 cost + $50 OI
Dec. 31, Year 2 (NSO is exercised.)	No compensation (OI); stock basis = $60 $60 stock basis = $10 cost + $0 OI + $50 NSO basis
Jan. 1, Year 4 (Stock is sold.)	$190 per share long-term capital gain (LTCG) $190 LTCG = $250 selling price − $60 stock basis The holding period begins on January 2, Year 1, the day after grant date; therefore, the holding period is long-term.

EXAMPLE 14.78	Referring to the foregoing example, suppose that the XYZ NSO had no readily ascertainable value on the grant date. Wesley recognizes no compensation on the grant date. He recognizes $190 per share of ordinary compensation income on December 31, Year 2, when he exercises the NSO. XYZ will be allowed a deduction of the same $190 per share for its taxable year which contains December 31, Year 2, Wesley's year-end. Wesley will also recognize a $50 per share long-term gain upon the sale of the stock on January 1, Year 4, since his holding period was more than twelve months (January 1, Year 3 – January 1, Year 4.

Key Dates	No Readily Ascertainable Value at Grant Date
Jan. 1, Year 1 (NSO is granted.)	No compensation (OI); NSO tax basis = $0 per NSO NSO tax basis = $0 cost + $0 ordinary income
Dec. 31, Year 2 (NSO is exercised.)	Compensation (OI) = $190 per share $190 OI = $200 stock value − $10 cost] Stock basis = $200 per share $200 stock basis = $10 cost + $190 OI
Jan. 1, Year 4 (Stock is sold.)	$50 per share long-term capital gain (LTCG) $50 LTCG = $250 selling price − $200 stock basis The holding period begins on January 1, Year 3, the day after exercise date; therefore, the holding period is long-term.

¶14,745   RESTRICTED STOCK PLANS

Under a restricted stock program, an employee is awarded stock that is subject to certain restrictions of transferability and to a substantial risk of forfeiture for a specific period of time. The stock may be provided under outright grants at no cost to the employee or through some nominal purchase arrangement. The employee's ownership rights are typically made contingent on continued employment with the company for a certain period. These restrictions generally expire over a period of time (either ratably or nonratably) or at retirement. In the event the shares are forfeited (for example, because the employee terminates employment before the specified period of time has expired), employers normally will provide a repurchase price equal to the original cost paid by the employee.

Tax Effect on Employees

Restricted stock is not afforded any favorable tax treatment; rather it is taxed under Code Sec. 83(a). Under this provision, the excess of the fair market value of the property over the price paid (if any) by the employee is included in income when the property recipient's rights in the property become transferable or no longer subject to a substantial risk of forfeiture. Thus, under the normal rules, an employee would recognize ordinary income upon the expiration of the restrictions. The employee's basis in the stock is equal to the amount paid for the property, plus any amount included in gross income. Reg. §1.83-4(b). The holding period for the stock begins just after the date the restrictions expire. Reg. §1.83-4(a).

Taxation under a Code Sec. 83(b) Election

Code Sec. 83(b) permits the person providing services to elect to recognize compensation from the restricted property in the year in which the services are performed instead of waiting until the time the person's rights to the property become substantially vested. If the election is made, the service performer must recognize, as compensation, the fair market value of the property at the time of the transfer minus the amount paid for the property. The election can be made even if the amount paid equals the fair market value of the property at the time of the transfer. Reg. §1.83-2(a). The amount included in income is added to the taxpayer's basis in the property. Thus, any appreciation in value of the property after that time receives favorable capital gain treatment if the property had been held for a long-term period. The election must be made within 30 days of receipt of the restricted property. Rev. Proc. 2012-29.

The employer is generally entitled to a deduction equal to the amount of compensation income that the service performer includes in income as compensation in the year in which the income is recognized. Code Sec. 83(h).

EXAMPLE 14.79	CTK Corp. transfers one hundred shares of its common stock to Matt Andres, an executive of CTK on January 1, Year 1. On the date of the transfer, the stock has a market value of $50 per share. Matt's cost of the shares is discounted to $10 per share. The stock is intended as a bonus for Matt's work for the year, but is issued with the restriction that if Matt leaves CKS's employment within the next two years, he must return the shares to the corporation. On December 31, Year 2, when the restrictions expire, the stock is trading publicly at $200 per share. On January 1, Year 4, Matt sells the stock for $250 per share. Matt will recognize $40 per share compensation in Year 1 under the special Code Sec. 83(b) election, or he may postpone recognizing any compensation until the expiration of the restriction in Year 2. However, his recognized compensation would be $150 per share more. One of the principal advantages of the Code Sec. 83(b) election is the conversion of what would be compensation into a more favorable capital gain. For example, if Matt had sold the stock at its market value on the date of the lapse of the restrictions, December 31, Year 2, the entire gain of $190 would have been taxed as compensation without the election. With the election, he would have converted $150 per share of compensation into long-term capital gain. Since the tax rate on compensation can be substantially higher than the long-term capital gain rate, the Code Sec. 83(b) may be advantageous, despite accelerating the recognition of a portion of the income. See per share computations below.

Dates:	Without Sec. 83(b) Election	With Sec. 83(b) Election
Jan. 1, Yr. 1 (Stock is issued.)	No compensation (OI) Stock basis = $10 per share Stock basis = $10 cost + $0 OI	Compensation (OI) = $40 per share $40 OI = $50 stock value − $10 stock cost] Stock basis = $50 per share $50 stock basis = $10 cost + $40 OI
Dec. 31, Yr. 2 (Restriction is lifted.)	Compensation (OI) = $190 per share $190 OI = $200 stock value − $10 stock cost] Stock basis = $200 per share $200 stock basis = $10 cost + $190 OI	No compensation (OI) Stock basis = $50 per share (Unchanged from above)
Jan. 1, Yr. 4 (Stock is sold.)	$50 per share long-term capital gain (LTCG) $50 LTCG = $250 selling price − $200 stock basis The holding period begins on January 1, Year 3, the day after the restriction is lifted; therefore, the holding period is long-term.	$200 per share long-term capital gain (LTCG) $200 LTCG = $250 selling price − $50 stock basis The holding period begins on January 2, Year 1, the day after the stock is issued; therefore, the holding period is long-term.

¶14,755   VARIABLE ANNUITY CONTRACTS

A variable annuity contract is a nonqualified deferred compensation arrangement between any investor (or employer on behalf of an employee) and an insurance company, under which the insurer agrees to make periodic payments to the individual, beginning either immediately or at some future date. Variable annuity contracts are purchased by making either a single purchase payment or a series of purchase payments. The investment options for a variable annuity are typically mutual funds that invest in stocks, bonds, money market instruments, or some combination of the three.

Variable annuity contracts differ from mutual funds in three ways:

1. **Tax Deferral.** The investor pays no taxes on the income and investment gains from the annuity until the money is withdrawn. The investor may also transfer money from one investment fund to another within a variable annuity without paying tax at the time of the transfer. This is referred to as a *Sec. 1035 tax-deferred exchange.*
2. **Periodic Payments.** Variable annuities let the investor receive periodic payments for the rest of the investor's life (or the life of the investor's spouse or any other person designated as beneficiary). This feature offers protection against the possibility that, after retiring, the investor will outlive the assets.
3. **Death Benefit.** If the investor dies before the insurer has started making payments, the investor's beneficiary is guaranteed to receive a specific amount—typically at a minimum, the amount of the investor's purchase payments. The beneficiary benefits from this feature if, at the time of the investor's death, the account value has fallen below the guaranteed amount.

A variable annuity has two phases: an *accumulation phase*, and a *payout phase*.

Accumulation Phase

During the accumulation phase, the investor makes purchase payments, which can be allocated to a number of investment options. For example, 40% of the payments could be designated to a bond fund, 40% to a U.S. stock fund, and 20% to an international stock fund. The money allocated to each mutual investment fund will increase or decrease over time, depending on fund performance. In addition, variable annuity contracts often allow the investor to allocate part of the purchase payments to a fixed account. A fixed account, unlike a mutual fund, pays a fixed rate of interest. The insurance company may reset this interest rate periodically, but it will usually provide a guaranteed minimum (e.g., 2% per year).

Payout Phase

At the beginning of the payout phase, the investor may recover purchase payments plus investment income and gains (if any) as a lump-sum payment, or the investor may choose to receive them as a stream of payments at regular intervals (generally monthly). If the investor chooses to receive a stream of payments, the investor may have a number of choices of how long the payments will last. Under most annuity contracts, the investor can choose to have the annuity payments last for a set period (such as 20 years) or for an indefinite period (such as the investor's lifetime or the lifetime of a spouse or other beneficiary). During the payout phase, the annuity contract may permit the investor to choose between receiving fixed payments or payments that vary based on the performance of the mutual fund investment options. The amount of each periodic payment will depend, in part, on the time period that is selected for receiving payments. In addition, some annuity contracts are structured as *immediate annuities*, which means that there is no accumulation phase and the investor will start receiving annuity payments just after purchasing the annuity.

Typical Costs Associated with a Variable Annuity Contract

An investor will pay several charges when investing in a variable annuity. These charges will reduce the account value and the investment return. Often, they include the following:

1. **Surrender charges.** If the investor withdraws money for a variable annuity within a certain period after a purchase payment (typically within six to eight years), the insurance company usually will assess a "surrender" charge, which is a type of sales charge. This charge is used to pay the investor's financial professional a commission for selling the variable annuity. Generally, the surrender charge is a percentage of the amount withdrawn, and declines gradually over a period of several years, known as the "*surrender period.*"
2. **Mortality and expense risk charge.** This charge is equal to a certain percentage of account value, typically in the range of 1.25% per year. This charge compensates the insurance company for insurance risks it assumes under the annuity contract. Profit from the mortality and expense risk charge

is sometimes used to pay the insurer's cost of selling the variable annuity, such as a commission paid to the financial professional for selling the variable annuity contract to the investor.

3. **Administrative fees.** The insurer may deduct charges to cover record-keeping and other administrative expenses. This may be charged as a flat account maintenance fee (perhaps $25 or $30 per year) or as a percentage of the account value (typically in the range of 0.15% per year).

4. **Underlying fund expenses.** The investor will also pay the fees and expenses imposed by those mutual funds that are the underlying investment options for the variable annuity contract.

Some insurers offer special optional features that have extra charges. These include the following:

1. **Stepped-up death benefit.** The feature allows the minimum death benefit to be based on a greater amount than purchase payments minus withdrawals. Its purpose is to "lock-in" investment performance and prevent a later decline in account value from eroding the amount the investor leaves to heirs.

2. **Guaranteed minimum income benefit.** This feature guarantees a particular minimum level of annuity payments, even if the account value does not have enough money (perhaps because of investment losses) to support the level of payments.

3. **Long-term care insurance.** This feature pays for home health care or nursing home care if the investor becomes seriously ill.

Variable annuity contracts typically have a "free look" period of ten or more days, during which the investor can terminate the contract without paying any surrender charges and get back the purchase payments (which may be adjusted to reflect charges and the performance of the investment during that time).

¶14,765 SHORT-TERM INFORMAL ARRANGEMENTS

Accrual basis corporations often receive services from cash basis taxpayers in a current year and pay in the subsequent year. Sec. 404(a)(5) treats this as a type of nonqualified deferred compensation plan. The cash basis taxpayers may be employees as well as independent contractors.

Reg. §1.404(b)-1T, Q & A-2(b)(1) provides for a "bright line" presumption that payments to service providers made more than 2½ months after the close of an accrual basis taxpayer's year are part of a deferred compensation arrangement. This results in the payment being not deductible until includible in the income of the service provider. The disallowance of the deduction applies without regard to other relationships between the parties. For example, the disallowance will apply to salaries accrued to certain non-controlling shareholders of C corporations, other employees and independent contractors. Cash method service providers recognize ordinary income in the year of receipt. Code Sec. 404(a)(11).

EXAMPLE 14.80

ABC Corp. is an accrual method taxpayer that follows a calendar tax year. In Year 1, John Fennster, a cash method taxpayer, provides ABC with accounting services valued at $100,000. ABC pays John $25,000 on March 15, Year 2, the filing due date of its corporate return. On the following day, ABC pays John the remaining balance of $75,000. ABC is permitted to deduct $25,000 in Year 1 because this payment was made within 2½ months after the close of ABC's tax year. However, the $75,000 amount paid more than 2 ½ months after the close of the tax year is not deductible until Year 2.

The timing rules are more restrictive between related parties as defined under Code Sec. 267(b). Payment by accrual method payors to cash method related parties must be made in the same year as the services are rendered in order to permit the payor a current year deduction. A payment even one day after the close of the accrual year precludes a current deduction. However, the deduction becomes merely deferred, not lost.

Related parties include family members, an S corporation and any of its shareholders, a partnership and any of its partners (with respect to non "guaranteed payments"), and a C corporation and any of its shareholders controlling more than 50 percent in the value of the entity.

KEYSTONE PROBLEM

Lindsey Romula, age 22, is to receive a $1,000,000 bonus in year 1 for signing a professional sports contract. Lindsey wants to defer payment of this bonus for at least 10 years. How can a nonqualified deferred compensation arrangement be structured to avoid immediate taxation?

Education Savings Vehicles

¶14,801   ## COVERDELL EDUCATION SAVINGS ACCOUNTS

A Coverdell education savings account ("Coverdell ESA") is a tax-favored vehicle that can be used to pay the qualified education expenses for the elementary, secondary, and college education of a designated beneficiary. Contributions to a Coverdell ESA are not deductible, but earnings on contributions grow tax-free and are not taxed if used to pay qualified education expenses. Code Sec. 530.

Establishing a Coverdell ESA

A Coverdell ESA is a trust or custodial account created or organized in the United States for a designated beneficiary who is under age 18 (or a special-needs beneficiary). It may be opened at any bank or other IRS-approved entity that offers Coverdell ESAs. A special-needs beneficiary is an individual who, due to a physical, mental, or emotional condition (including a learning disability), requires additional time to complete his or her education.

Qualified Education Expenses

"Qualified education expenses" means "qualified higher education expenses" and "qualified elementary and secondary expenses." The term also includes contributions to a 529 plan on behalf of the designated beneficiary.

"Qualified higher education expenses" means tuition, fees, books, supplies, and equipment required to attend college and expenses for special-needs services incurred in connection with the enrollment or attendance of a designated beneficiary who has special needs. "Qualified higher education expenses" includes room and board for students attending college at least half-time.

"Qualified elementary and secondary education expenses" means expenses for tuition, fees, academic tutoring, special-needs services in the case of a special-needs beneficiary, books, supplies, and other equipment that are incurred in connection with the enrollment or attendance of the designated beneficiary as an elementary or secondary school student at a public, private, or religious school. "Qualified elementary and secondary education expenses" also includes expenses for room and board, uniforms, transportation, and supplementary items and services (including extended day programs) that are required or provided by a public, private, or religious school in connection with enrollment or attendance and expenses for the purchase of any computer technology or equipment or Internet access and related services, if such technology, equipment, or services are to be used by the designated beneficiary and the designated beneficiary's family during any of the years that the beneficiary is in school. Expenses for computer software designed for sports, games, or hobbies cannot be "qualified elementary and secondary education expenses" unless the software is predominantly educational in nature.

Contributions

Contributions may be made to a Coverdell ESA by any individual (including the designated beneficiary) whose modified adjusted gross income for the year is less than $110,000 ($220,000 if the individual is married and filing a joint income tax return or a qualifying widow(er)). Contributions also can be made by organizations, such as corporations and trusts, regardless of income. Contributions to a Coverdell ESA must be in cash and may not be made after the designated beneficiary attains age 18 (unless the designated beneficiary has special needs).

The maximum amount that may be contributed each tax year to all Coverdell ESAs for the benefit of a particular designated beneficiary is $2,000. This limit applies to contributions by all persons for the benefit of a particular designated beneficiary.

EXAMPLE 14.81   Michael Crocket, his parents, and his wife's parents all want to contribute to a Coverdell ESA for Michael's daughter, Rosie. If Michael contributes $800 to a Coverdell ESA for Rosie's benefit, the most that the others can contribute for that year is $1,200.

The amount that an individual may contribute for a tax year has to be reduced if the contributor's modified adjusted gross income exceeds $95,000 ($190,000 if the taxpayer is married and filing a joint return or a qualifying widow(er)). The amount of the reduction is determined by multiplying $2,000 by a fraction whose numerator is the difference between the individual's modified adjusted gross income and $95,000 ($190,000 if the taxpayer is married and filing a joint return or a qualifying widow(er)) and whose denominator is $15,000 ($30,000 if the individual is married and filing a joint return or a qualifying widow(er)).

EXAMPLE 14.82	Rufus Lynch would like to make a contribution to a Coverdell ESA that he established for his son, Steven. In the current year, Rufus's modified adjusted gross income is $104,000. Rufus is unmarried. The maximum amount that he can contribute to the Coverdell ESA is $800 [$2,000 – ($2,000 × [($104,000 – $95,000)/$15,000]) = $2,000 – ($2,000 × 0.60) = $2,000 – $1,200 = $800].

A taxpayer's "modified adjusted gross income" is the taxpayer's adjusted gross income increased by the following amounts:

1. Any foreign earned income excluded from gross income under Code Sec. 911.
2. Any foreign housing costs excluded or deducted from gross income under Code Sec. 911.
3. Income excluded from gross income under Code Sec. 931 because it was derived by a bona fide resident of American Samoa from sources within, or effectively connected with the conduct of a trade or business within, American Samoa.
4. Income excluded from gross income under Code Sec. 933 because it was derived by a bona fide resident of Puerto Rico from sources within Puerto Rico.

If excess contributions are made to a Coverdell ESA for a particular designated beneficiary, the beneficiary must pay a six percent penalty tax on the excess contributions. Excess contributions are the sum of the following amounts (Code Sec. 4973):

1. Contributions to a designated beneficiary's Coverdell ESAs for the year that exceed $2,000 (or, if less, the total of each contributor's limit for the year).
2. Excess contributions for the preceding year, reduced by distributions (other than those rolled over) during the year and the contribution limit for the current year minus the amount contributed for the current year.

No excise tax has to be paid on excess contributions made for one year if the contributions, plus any earnings on the contributions, are distributed before the first day of the sixth month of the following tax year.

A contribution for a tax year may be made at any time during the year and up to the due date (not including extensions) for filing a federal tax return for that year. Contributions are eligible for the gift tax annual exclusion.

Rollovers and Other Transfers

Assets in a Coverdell ESA may be rolled over tax-free from one Coverdell ESA to another Coverdell ESA if the amount withdrawn is deposited into the second Coverdell ESA within 60 days after the distribution and the second Coverdell ESA benefits the same designated beneficiary or a member of that beneficiary's family who has not attained age 30. Members of a beneficiary's family include the beneficiary's spouse, a son or daughter of the beneficiary or a descendant of either, a stepson or stepdaughter, a brother, sister, stepbrother or stepsister, the father or mother of the beneficiary or an ancestor of either, a stepfather or stepmother, a niece or nephew, an uncle or aunt, a son-in-law, daughter-in-law, father-in-law, mother-in-law, brother-in-law or sister-in-law, the spouse of any of the foregoing, or any first cousin of the beneficiary. A rollover contribution may be made only once every 12 months.

If an individual's interest in a Coverdell ESA is transferred to the individual's spouse or former spouse under a decree of divorce or separate maintenance or a written instrument incident to such a decree, the transfer will not be treated as a taxable distribution. Following the transfer, the spouse or former spouse can treat the Coverdell ESA as his or her own.

Change in Designated Beneficiary

Any change in the beneficiary of a Coverdell ESA will not be treated as a taxable distribution if the new beneficiary is a member of the family of the old beneficiary and has not attained age 30 as of the time of the change.

Distributions

The designated beneficiary of a Coverdell ESA may take a distribution at any time. No amount distributed from a Coverdell ESA has to be included in the beneficiary's gross income if it does not exceed the designated beneficiary's adjusted qualified education expenses for the year. A beneficiary's adjusted qualified education expenses are the beneficiary's qualified education expenses reduced by tax-free educational assistance, such as tax-free scholarships and fellowships, veterans' educational assistance, Pell grants, employer-provided educational assistance, and any other nontaxable payments (other than gifts or inheritances) received as educational assistance.

If the amount of a beneficiary's distributions for a year exceeds the beneficiary's adjusted qualified education expenses, the amount that has to be included in the beneficiary's gross income is calculated as follows:

1. Multiply the amount distributed by a fraction whose numerator is the amount of contributions not distributed at the end of the prior year plus the total contributions made during the year and whose denominator is the value of the account at the end of the current year plus the amount distributed during the year. This is the basis portion of the distribution.
2. Subtract the amount determined in (1) from the total amount of distributions made during the current year. This is the amount of earnings included in the distributions.
3. Multiply the amount of earnings calculated in (2) by a fraction whose numerator is the adjusted qualified education expenses paid during the current year and whose denominator is the total amount distributed during the current year. This is the amount of tax-free earnings.
4. Subtract the amount determined in (3) from the amount determined in (2). This is the amount of earnings that has to be included in the beneficiary's gross income.

If a beneficiary receives a taxable distribution, the beneficiary generally has to pay a 10-percent additional tax on the amount included in the beneficiary's gross income. However, the additional tax will not apply to distributions paid to a beneficiary (or to the estate of the designated beneficiary) on or after the death of the designated beneficiary, made because the designated beneficiary is disabled, included in gross income because the designated beneficiary received a tax-free scholarship or fellowship, veterans' educational assistance, employer-provided educational assistance, or any other nontaxable payments (other than gifts or inheritances) received as educational assistance, included in gross income only because qualified education expenses were taken into account in determining a Hope or lifetime learning credit, made on account of attendance at a U.S. military academy, or constituting a timely distribution of excess contributions.

Any balance to the credit of a designated beneficiary on the date on which the beneficiary attains age 30 must be distributed within 30 days after that date to the designated beneficiary, unless the designated beneficiary has special needs. If the designated beneficiary dies before attaining age 30, any balance to the credit of the designated beneficiary must be distributed within 30 days after the date of the designated beneficiary's death.

Coordination with Hope and Lifetime Learning Credits

The Hope or lifetime learning credit can be claimed in the same year that a beneficiary takes a tax-free distribution from a Coverdell ESA. However, the same expenses cannot be used for both benefits. A beneficiary must reduce adjusted qualified education expenses by any expenses taken into account in determining a Hope or lifetime learning credit.

¶14,815   529 PLANS

A "529 plan" is a tax-favored plan that permits persons to prepay a designated beneficiary's qualified higher education expenses at a discount ("prepaid tuition plan") or contribute money to an account that earns money that is tax-free if used to pay a student's qualified higher education expenses ("college savings plan"). Such plans are sometimes collectively referred to as "qualified tuition plans." Code Sec. 529.

A wide variety of such plans are offered. For a summary of such plans and links to more details, see www.savingforcollege.com.

Prepaid Tuition Plan

A prepaid tuition plan, which may be offered by a state or college, permits persons to purchase tuition credits or certificates at a discount on behalf of a designated beneficiary. The credits or certificates entitle the designated beneficiary to the waiver or payment of the designated beneficiary's qualified higher education expenses.

College Savings Plan

A college savings plan, which may be established only by a state, permits persons to make contributions to an account established to pay the qualified higher education expenses of the designated beneficiary of the account.

Qualified Higher Education Expenses

"Qualified higher education expenses" means tuition, fees, books, supplies, and small equipment such as calculators and microscopes required for the enrollment or attendance of a designated beneficiary at a college. "Qualified higher education expenses" includes room and board for a student attending college at least half-time. The American Recovery and Reinvestment Act of 2009 allows 529 plan beneficiaries to use tax-free distributions to pay for computers and computer technology such as internet access. Expenses for special-needs services incurred in connection with enrollment or attendance of a special-needs beneficiary are "qualified higher education expenses." A special-needs beneficiary is an individual who, due to a physical, mental, or emotional condition (including a learning disability) requires additional time to complete his or her education.

Contributions

Only cash may be contributed to a 529 plan, and no deduction is allowed for contributions. The amount that may be contributed to a 529 plan on behalf of a beneficiary cannot exceed the amount needed to pay the beneficiary's qualified higher education expenses. There are no income restrictions on who can contribute to a 529 plan.

Contributions can be made to a 529 plan and Coverdell ESA for the same beneficiary. Contributions are eligible for the gift tax annual exclusion.

Rollovers and Other Transfers

No tax has to be paid when assets from one 529 plan are withdrawn and deposited in a second 529 plan for the benefit of the same beneficiary or for the benefit of a member of the beneficiary's family if the rollover is completed within 60 days after the date of the distribution. Members of a beneficiary's family include the beneficiary's spouse, a son or daughter of the beneficiary or a descendant of either, a stepson or stepdaughter, a brother, sister, stepbrother or stepsister, the father or mother of the beneficiary or an ancestor of either, a stepfather or stepmother, a niece or nephew, an uncle or aunt, a son-in-law, daughter-in-law, father-in-law, mother-in-law, brother-in-law or sister-in-law, the spouse of any of the foregoing, or any first cousin of the beneficiary. A rollover may be made only once every 12 months.

Change in Designated Beneficiary

Any change in the beneficiary of a 529 plan will not be treated as a taxable distribution if the new beneficiary is a member of the family of the old beneficiary.

Distributions

No tax has to be paid on a distribution from a 529 plan unless the amount distributed exceeds the beneficiary's adjusted qualified education expenses. A beneficiary's adjusted qualified education expenses are the beneficiary's qualified education expenses reduced by tax-free educational assistance, such as tax-free scholarships and fellowships, veterans' educational assistance, Pell grants, employer-provided educational assistance, and any other nontaxable payments (other than gifts or inheritances) received as educational assistance.

If the amount of a beneficiary's distributions for a year exceeds the beneficiary's adjusted qualified education expenses, the amount that has to be included in the beneficiary's gross income is calculated as follows:

1. Multiply the total distributed earnings shown in Box 2 of IRS Form 1099-Q, Payments From Qualified Education Programs (Under Sections 529 and 530), by a fraction whose numerator is the adjusted qualified education expenses paid during the year and whose denominator is the total amount distributed during the year.
2. Subtract the amount determined in (1) from the total distributed earnings. This is the amount that the beneficiary must include in his or her gross income.

If a beneficiary receives a taxable distribution, the beneficiary generally has to pay a 10-percent additional tax on the amount included in the beneficiary's gross income. However, the additional tax will not apply to distributions paid to a beneficiary (or to the estate of the designated beneficiary) on or after the death of the designated beneficiary, made because the designated beneficiary is disabled, included in gross income because the designated beneficiary received a tax-free scholarship or fellowship, veterans' educational assistance, employer-provided educational assistance, or any other nontaxable payments (other than gifts or inheritances) received as educational assistance, included in gross income only because qualified education expenses were taken into account in determining a Hope or lifetime learning credit, made on account of attendance at a U.S. military academy, or constituting a timely distribution of excess contributions.

Coordination with Hope and Lifetime Learning Credits

A Hope or lifetime learning credit may be claimed for the same year that a beneficiary takes a tax-free distribution from a 529 plan. However, the same expenses cannot be used to qualify for both benefits.

Exhibit 14. SAVINGS PLANS FOR EDUCATION

Item	Coverdell ESA	529 Prepaid Tuition Plan	529 Savings Plan
Purpose:	Tax-exempt accumulation of income to pay for the qualified kindergarten through postsecondary education expenses of a beneficiary under age 30.	Tax-exempt accumulation of income to pay for the qualified postsecondary education expenses of a beneficiary at any age.	Tax-exempt accumulation of income to pay for the qualified postsecondary education expenses of a beneficiary at any age.
Age Restrictions:	For qualified contributions: the beneficiary must not be over age 18 at the end of the contribution year. For qualified distributions: the beneficiary must not be more than age 30 at the end of the distribution year.	None	None
Establishment Deadline:	By December 31 of current year.	Depends on the plan	Depends on the plan
Contribution Deadline:	By filing due date (April 15 of following year).	Depends on the plan	Depends on the plan
Maximum Contribution Amount:	$2,000 per beneficiary (not per contributor) per year	Determined by each state	Determined by each state
Contribution Phase-Out (MAGI Limits):	MFJ: $190k- $220k Other: $95k - $110k	None	None
Control of the Account:	In most states, account assets become property of the beneficiary at age 18.	In most states, control of the account will always remain with the contributor.	In most states, control of the account will always remain with the contributor.
Assignability to Other Relatives:	Immediate family of beneficiary, including cousins, step-relatives, and in-laws	Same as CESA	Same as CESA
Earnings:	Tax exempt if conditions are met.	Same as CESA	Same as CESA
Penalty for Non-Qualified Withdrawals:	Earnings are taxed as ordinary income to contributor, plus a 10% penalty.	Same as CESA	Same as CESA
Effect on Financial Aid Calculation:	Considered to be an asset of the beneficiary, which means a large portion of the assets will be considered in the financial aid calculation.	Considered to be the student's resource and thus reduces financial aid dollar-for-dollar.	Assets are considered to be property of the account owner, which—unless the owner is also the beneficiary—means only a small portion of the assets will be considered in the financial aid calculation.

SUMMARY

- A qualified employer-sponsored deferred compensation plan is a plan providing for retirement benefits that satisfies strict requirements of the Code and the Employee Retirement Income Security Act of 1974 (ERISA).

- Qualified plan requirements include nondiscrimination in favor of highly-compensated employees, limitations on contributions to a defined contributions plan, limitations on benefits provided by a defined benefit plan, required minimum distributions, early withdrawal restrictions, participation requirements, coverage requirements, vesting requirements, and the "exclusive benefit of employee" requirement.

- The two basic types of qualified employer-sponsored deferred compensation plans are defined contribution plans (such as profit-sharing plans, ESOPs, money purchase pension plans, and 401(k) plans) and defined benefit plans (such as pension plans).

- Employees generally are not taxed on contributions made to a qualified employer-sponsored retirement plan until they are withdrawn and may be entitled to a saver's credit for contributions. Earnings on contributions accumulate tax-deferred until they are withdrawn.

- Employers are entitled to a current deduction for contributions made to a qualified retirement plan and may claim a credit for a portion of their startup costs.

- Common retirement plans for large businesses (more than 100 employees) include 401(k) plans, supplemental Roth 401(k) plans, qualified annuity (403(a)) plans, tax-sheltered annuity (403(b)) plans, and governmental and nongovernmental 457(b) plans. Federal and postal employers generally provide a basic annuity plan (Federal Employees' Retirement System or Civil Service Retirement System) that may be supplemented with a thrift savings plan.

- Common retirement plans for small business (100 or fewer employees) include the Solo (Individual) 401(k), Keogh plan, Simplified Employee Pension (SEP) plan, and Savings Incentive Match Plan for Employees (SIMPLE).

- Individuals with taxable compensation may accumulate money for their retirement by making contributions to a traditional or Roth IRA. Contributions to a traditional IRA may be deducted unless the contributor's modified adjusted gross income exceeds a specified amount. However, deductible contributions and earnings on all contributions are taxed when withdrawn from the traditional IRA. Contributions to a Roth IRA cannot be deducted, but earnings on contributions may be withdrawn tax-free on or after age 59½.

- Nonqualified retirement plans are used to benefit key employees because they do not have to satisfy the same nondiscrimination, participation, and coverage requirements imposed on qualified retirement plans. If properly structured, contributions are not taxed to employees until withdrawn. An employer is not entitled to a deduction for contributions until they are included in the employee's gross income.

- Common nonqualified deferred compensation plans include Rabbi Trusts, Employee Stock Purchase Plans (ESPPs), Incentive Stock Options (ISOs), Nonqualified Stock Options (NSOs), restricted stock plans, variable annuity contracts, and short-term informal arrangements.

- Contributions can be made to a Coverdell ESA to accumulate funds on a tax-favored basis to pay for elementary, secondary, and college education expenses. Contributions may be made only if the contributor's modified adjusted gross income is less than $110,000 ($220,000 if the individual files a joint income tax return).

- 529 prepaid tuition and college savings plans can be used by any person, regardless of income, to accumulate funds for college on a tax-favored basis.

QUESTIONS

1. What are the major requirements of qualified employer-sponsored plans?

2. What are the tax advantages associated with a qualified employer-sponsored plan?

3. What are the major nontax advantages associated with qualified employer-sponsored plans?

4. What are the major similarities and differences between qualified plans and nonqualified plans?

5. Explain the difference between a defined contribution plan and a defined benefit plan.

6. What options are available to a qualified plan's trustee after a participant severs employment?

7. In Year 1, Will Gensler attained age 65. In year 3, Will terminated his employment. In year 5, Will marked his 10th anniversary year of participation in his employer's 401(k) calendar-year plan. What is the latest date on which benefit payments to Will must commence?

8. When are plan participants required to begin withdrawing taxable distributions from their qualified retirement accounts?

9. What penalty is imposed on taxpayers who fail to make a required minimum distribution?

10. How early can amounts be distributed from a qualified plan penalty-free?

11. Define the term "vesting" and identify the two vesting methods that are available to employer-sponsored qualified plans.

12. What is a lump-sum distribution and how is the taxable portion of a lump-sum distribution determined?

13. What distinguishes a direct rollover from an indirect rollover?

14. What is a Section 401(k) plan?

15. What is a Roth 401(k) plan and what are its advantages?

16. What is a Section 457(b) plan?

17. What retirement options are available to federal and postal employees?

18. What are the most common types of qualified plans for small businesses?

19. Explain how the features listed below affect the choice of a qualified plan for a small business.
    a. Investment flexibility.
    b. Eligible legal entities.
    c. Permitted number of employees.
    d. Minimal IRS reporting requirements.
    e. Flexible IRS deadlines.
    f. Optional vesting.
    g. Plan loans.
    h. Discretion regarding employee participation.
    i. Rollover eligibility.
    j. Allowable contribution and deduction amounts.

20. How much may be contributed annually to a defined contribution Keogh plan?

21. What is the penalty for early withdrawals from SIMPLE?

22. Explain the rationale for the DB/K plan, the types of companies likely to adopt the plan and the main features of the plan.

23. What rules do traditional IRAs and Roth IRAs have in common?

24. How much may be contributed to an IRA on an annual basis?

25. Under what circumstances is loss recognition for traditional or Roth IRAs permitted?

26. What are the major differences between a traditional IRA and a Roth IRA?

27. Under what circumstances can employees defer compensation under a nonqualified plan?

28. Explain when payroll taxes are applied to deferred compensation under a nonqualified plan.

29. What is a Rabbi Trust?

30. What is a variable annuity contract?

31. What is a Coverdell Education Savings Account?

32. What is a 529 plan?

PROBLEMS

33. Alta Corporation has a defined benefit plan providing that a retired employee will receive 2% of average salary for the last three years of employment for every year of service with the employer. Sara Payne retired after 25 years of service. Her average salary for the last three years of her employment was $100,000. What will be the amount of Sara's annual retirement benefit?

34. AJR Inc.'s qualified plan provides for the allocation of employer contributions based upon a flat rate of four percent of each employee's compensation. Nathaniel's annual compensation is equal to $20,000 and his trust account receives $800 (4% × $20,000). Micaela's annual compensation is equal to $200,000 and her trust account receives an $8,000 employer contribution (4% × $200,000). Is the plan discriminatory?

35. Tom Couch participates in his employer's qualified retirement plan, which provides a 10 percent employer contribution formula. Tom's annual compensation is equal to $1,325,000. What employer contribution rate can be applied to Tom's compensation?

36. Fred and Ginger attain age 70 in Year 1. Fred's birthday is June 30 and Ginger's is July 1. Each owns separate traditional IRAs. What is the deadline for Fred and Ginger's first required minimum distribution payment?

37. Bob Carnick is the owner of a traditional IRA. Bob will attain age 76 in the current year. The before-tax account balance as of the end of the prior year was $1,000,000. What is the minimum amount that Bob must withdraw from the IRA by the end of the current year?

38. Thomas Andrews' mother died in Year 1. Thomas, who will attain age 27 in Year 2, was designated as the sole beneficiary of his mother's traditional IRA. If the account balance at the end of Year 1 was $1,000,000, and Thomas elected to receive a lifetime annuity, what will be the deadline and amount of the first required minimum distribution?

39. Peppy Pop Inc. has 1,000 employees, including 100 who are highly compensated. If Peppy Pop wishes to establish a qualified plan, what coverage requirements must be met in order to satisfy the
    (a) percentage test?
    (b) ratio test?

40. Float's Toyboats, Inc., has 60 employees, all of whom are covered by the company's defined benefit pension plan. Fifteen employees are highly compensated. In the current year, contributions are actually made on behalf of all highly compensated employees, but only on behalf of 30 of the rest. Is it possible for the above plan to be qualified?

41. Kathy Runde, age 66 and retired, receives a $20,000 partial distribution from her 401(k) plan. The plan does not pay out an annuity. Immediately before the distribution, her account balance is $50,000, including $10,000 in nondeductible contributions. How much of the $20,000 distribution must Kathy include in gross income?

42. Bonnie Sparks has been receiving a $200 monthly annuity from her qualified plan account over several years. At the end of the current year, her account balance is $50,000, including a $10,000 cost basis. In order to satisfy a personal obligation, she withdraws an extra $20,000 from her account in the current year. The withdrawal does not affect the amount of her subsequent annuity payments. How much of the $20,000 distribution must Bonnie include in gross income?

43. Nanette McPhee receives $100,000 as a lump-sum distribution from a noncontributory, qualified pension plan upon early retirement to start a child care business. If, after receiving the distribution, Nanette decides not to start the business, is she permitted to roll over the distribution to a traditional IRA?

44. Harrison Bernhardt participates in his employer's 401(k) plan. Under the plan, employees may elect to reduce their salary by a certain percentage and have it paid into the plan's trust. In the current year, Harrison elects to defer $15,000 as a cash or deferred arrangement (CODA) contribution from his $80,000 salary. The plan provides that the employer will match the employee contribution up to 5 percent of compensation ($4,000).

    a. What amount is subject to employee FICA tax?

    b. What amount is subject to federal income tax?

    c. What amount is currently not subject to federal income tax?

    d. How would the tax consequences be different if Harrison's plan had been a 403(b) or 457(b) governmental plan?

45. During the 1st half of 2015, Mrs. Snerdley, age 52, earns a $50,000 salary at MacroHard, Inc and participates in her employer's 401(k) plan. During the 2nd half of the year, Mrs. Snerdley earns a $30,000 salary teaching in the local middle school. She participates in her new employer's 403(b) and 457(b) plans. What is the maximum deferral contribution amount that Mrs. Snerdley can elect for all three plans in 2015?

46. Viva Yeboah's 401(k) plan provides a supplemental Roth 401(k) arrangement. If Viva's compensation is $500,000, will she be eligible to contribute to a Roth 401(k) account?

47. Answer the following questions about IRAs:

    a. What is the maximum amount that may be contributed annually to the separate IRA of a nonworking spouse?

    b. Is it possible to contribute the maximum annual amount to an IRA by making just one deposit every other year?

    c. What are the tax consequences of transferring an IRA to the spouse as a divorce property settlement?

    d. When is it possible to fund a million dollar balance in a newly established IRA?

48. Assuming adequate security and interest, how much may the qualified plan participant borrow from the plan in the following independent cases:

    a. The account balance is $100,000 and the participant is 60 percent vested.

    b. The account balance is $150,000 and the participant is fully vested.

    c. Same as (b), but the participant is an owner-employee and the plan is a Keogh plan.

    d. The plan is a SEP IRA with a $12,000 account balance.

    e. Assuming a loan is made, when must it be repaid?

49. During 2015, Alec Meachin earned a net profit of $80,000 from his sole proprietorship (as reported on Schedule C). He paid $10,000 self-employment taxes during the year. What is the maximum contribution and deduction amount available to Alec if he maintains a

    a. Solo 401(k) plan?

    b. SEP IRA?

50. **Comprehensive Problem.** Spencer Strank reports the following items of income for the current year on a joint return:

Employee salary	$23,000
Interest income	2,000
Net income from consulting	20,000
Self-employment tax paid	2,800

He is a participant in his employer's qualified defined contribution retirement plan and has a nonworking spouse.

    a. How much, if anything, may Spencer deduct if he contributes the maximum amount on behalf of himself and his wife to a traditional IRA?

    b. Same as (a), but AGI is $114,000.

    c. What are the maximum contribution and deduction amounts available to Spencer if he maintains a solo 401(k) plan?

    d. What are the maximum contribution and deduction amounts available to Spencer if he maintains a money purchase Keogh plan?

    e. What are the maximum contribution and deduction amounts available to Spencer if he maintains a SEP IRA?

    f. What are the maximum contribution and deduction amounts available to Spencer if he maintains a SIMPLE 401(k)?

51. Norman Stonewell reports a salary of $60,000 this year on a joint return. He also reports $8,000 in royalty income from two books he wrote. Norman is age 48, and his wife Betty is 50.
    a. Is Norman eligible to maintain both a traditional IRA and a Keogh plan?
    b. If Betty is a nonworking spouse, what is the maximum traditional IRA contribution allowable?
    c. When must the traditional IRA accounts be opened and the contribution made?
    d. What are the maximum contribution and deduction amounts available to Norman if he maintains a profit-sharing Keogh plan?
    e. When must the Keogh plan be opened and the contribution made?

52. In 2015, Hunter and Monda (both under age 50) had compensation income of $1,000,000 and $200,000, respectively. Adjusted gross income on their joint return was $1,200,000, and neither taxpayer was a participant in a qualified retirement plan. How much may each contribute to a traditional IRA account and deduct from taxable income?

53. Jasper Fern, age 62, works full time and maintains two traditional IRA accounts. On March 23 of the current year, he withdraws $6,500 from one of his IRA accounts. The account is funded only with $6,500 nondeductible contributions. Its balance is $2,333 immediately after the withdrawal and $2,525 at year-end. The other IRA account is funded only with deductible contributions. Its balance is $40,177 as of March 23, and $43,500 balance as of December 31, the same year. What portion of Jasper's distribution constitutes gross income?

54. Abraham is single, age 48, has no employer-sponsored plan, and has a MAGI of $122,000 for 2015. What is the maximum contribution that he may make to a Roth IRA?

55. During the period Years 1 through 3, Martha made direct contributions to her Roth IRA totaling $10,000. By the end of Year 7, the IRA balance, including earnings, had grown to $30,000. At the beginning of Year 8, before Martha turned 59 1/2, she withdrew $25,000 from her Roth IRA to buy a new car. What is the tax result for Martha?

56. David Mitchell participates in his employer's employee stock purchase plan (ESSP). The plan provides for a 20% stock purchase discount, a look-back provision, and a 6-month offering period. Avery is paid $500,000 annually and he contributes 10% of gross pay ($50,000) to purchase stock during the offering period. The share price is $10 on the first day of the offering period and $20 on the last day of the offering period. What are the tax consequences if Avery sells the stock for $30 per share in a qualified disposition?

57. Orange Computer Inc. grants Steve Werks 10,000 incentive stock options (ISOs) on January 1, Year 1 (the "grant" date). On this date, the stock's fair market value is $100 per share and each ISO entitles the holder to buy one share of Orange stock for $100 (the exercise price). Steve exercises the ISOs on December 31, Year 5 (the "exercise" date) when the stock is worth $300 per share. What are the tax consequences if, in Year 7, Steve sells the stock in a qualifying disposition for $500 per share?

58. Moonbacks Inc. grants Howard Schmidt 10,000 NSOs on January 1, Year 1 (the "grant" date). Each NSO grants the holder the right to buy 1 share of Moonbacks stock for $100 over the next 10 years. The NSO's readily ascertainable fair market value on the grant date is $100 per share. Howard exercises the NSOs on December 31, Year 5 (the "exercise" date) when the stock is worth $300 per share. What are the tax consequences if, in Year 7, Howard sells the stock for $500 per share?

59. Referring to the foregoing example, if Moonbacks' NSOs had no readily ascertainable value on the grant date, how would the tax consequences be different for Howard?

60. Gaggle Corp. transfers 10,000 shares of its common stock to Larry Pagget on January 1, Year 1. The shares are issued at no cost to Larry. On the date of the transfer, the stock has a market value of $100 per share. The stock is intended as a bonus for Larry's work for the year, but is subject to a substantial risk of forfeiture. On December 31, Year 5, the restrictions expire when the stock is valued at $300 per share. What are the tax consequences to Larry if, in Year 7, he sells the stock for $500 per share?

61. Referring to the foregoing example, if Larry Pagget elects to report ordinary income in Year 1 under Section 83(b), how will his tax consequences be different?

62. ACC is an accrual method corporation that reports income in a calendar tax year. In Year 1, John Cash, a cash method taxpayer, entertains ACC employees at a December holiday party for a $60,000 fee. ACC pays John $40,000 on March 15, Year 2, the filing due date of its corporate return. On the following day, ACC pays John the remaining balance of $20,000. What are the tax consequences to ACC?

63. **Research Problem.** Locate a copy of IRS Publication 590 either on the Internet or in a tax or government documents library. Prepare a chart comparing distributions from various individual retirement arrangements.

Chapter

15

Tax Planning for Individuals

OBJECTIVES

After completing Chapter 15, you should be able to:

1. Know the general principles of tax planning.
2. Discuss the tax treatment of the self-employed taxpayer versus the employee.
3. Explain family tax planning, including income shifting, planning for college, and divorce planning.
4. Discuss asset planning, including considerations of leasing versus buying, sale versus exchange, involuntary conversion elections, residence and vacation homes, and capital and Section 1231 assets.
5. Understand planning for various deductions and the basics of retirement planning.

OVERVIEW

There are many ways in which taxpayers, by careful planning, can reduce their tax liabilities. Students need to be familiar with some of the tax planning opportunities in order to effectively use their tax knowledge and advise future clients. They also need to be aware of the pitfalls that can cost taxpayers additional taxes.

This chapter points out some of the tax planning opportunities and pitfalls. The chapter begins with some general principles of tax planning and then proceeds to more specific tax planning advice.

General Principles of Tax Planning

Chapters 1 and 2 mentioned that tax avoidance and tax planning are reasonable and legitimate pursuits of taxpaying entities. The opportunities for effective tax planning are significantly greater when the possible tax results are considered before transactions have been completed instead of after they have been completed. Tax planning can take various forms: avoiding the recognition of income, deferring income recognition, or accelerating deductions. It may involve the transfer of assets to other family members, controlling deductions in such a way as to minimize after-tax costs, or making proper decisions regarding investments.

¶15,001   AVOIDING INCOME RECOGNITION

Some taxpayers have a tendency to want to obtain as much gross income as possible. It may be wise, however, to avoid the recognition of some gross income if it will result in a higher net benefit after taxes. For example, a taxpayer may be able to avoid gross income by borrowing money.

EXAMPLE 15.1

> Andrew Anderson needs $100,000 for a business he is starting. Although he has a piece of land with a basis of $20,000 which could be sold for $100,000, he would then be taxed on the gain of $80,000. He decides instead to borrow the $100,000 by mortgaging the land. Andrew thus has avoided the gain on the sale of the land but has been able to obtain financing for his business, and the interest on his debt will be deductible.

Many of the exclusions that were discussed in Chapter 5 can be used effectively to avoid the recognition of income. Investments in many types of municipal bonds in 2015 continue to be attractive investments to taxpayers with the top marginal tax rate of 39.6 percent.

Employees can gain by receiving certain fringe benefits that are nontaxable. An employee can perhaps arrange to receive such nontaxable benefits as health insurance coverage, group-term life insurance, employer discounts, educational assistance, or other fringe benefits in lieu of an equivalent amount of taxable salary.

EXAMPLE 15.2

> Joyce Judson has two job offers: (1) an offer for $30,000 with fringe benefits valued at $5,000 consisting of group health insurance coverage, group-term life insurance, employer discounts, and educational assistance, and (2) an offer for $35,000 with none of the above benefits. All other job factors being equal, Joyce should choose the first offer since she would not be taxed on the $5,000 of fringe benefits.

Taxpayers can take advantage of the exclusion available to those who have owned and used their home as a principal residence two years out of the five-year period ending on the date of sale.

¶15,015   DEFERRAL OR ACCELERATION OF INCOME

If one can defer recognition of income until a later period, one can avoid payment of tax until the later period and thereby continue to use the money for a longer period of time.

Investors in Series EE bonds may elect to defer the interest recognition until the date of maturity of the bonds. An additional benefit is provided for Series EE bondholders who use the bonds to finance their higher educational needs or those of family members (see ¶15,201 for further discussion). In addition, several of the transactions discussed in Chapter 11 are examples of deferring or postponing income. With the like-kind exchange rules for nonrecognition of gain (or loss) under Section 1031, the taxpayer postpones the gain (or loss) recognition. There might, however, be some recognition, and the taxpayer needs to know how to avoid recognition of gain (e.g., through the avoidance of receipt of boot). Also, the election not to recognize gain in an involuntary conversion under Section 1033 can be beneficial. Other methods of deferring income include postponing the sale of investments at a profit to a future year, an especially beneficial approach if the tax rates in the succeeding year(s) are lower. Also, a taxpayer may be able to participate in deferred compensation arrangements. Income recognition can also be deferred by selling property on the installment method.

Taxpayers may wish to accelerate income into an earlier year if they believe that in later years they would have higher income or if they expect tax rates to rise. They might then decide to sell investments with gains early. Investors in Series EE bonds could recognize the interest as it accrues.

¶15,025   **ACCELERATION OR DEFERRAL OF DEDUCTIONS**

A taxpayer may wish to accelerate deductions into the current year. This can be especially beneficial if the taxpayer's tax rates will be declining next year. A taxpayer can take a number of steps to accelerate deductions:

1. Pay two years of charitable contributions at once, making both this year's and next year's contributions this year.
2. Take losses on investments this year.
3. Prepay state or local income taxes, especially where the taxing authority has an estimated tax system.
4. Incur certain controllable medical expenses this year.
5. Take advantage of the Section 179 expensing election on qualified property.
6. Pay all margin interest that has accrued during the tax year.

Taxpayers may wish to postpone deductions into a later year if they believe that in later years they would have higher income or if they expect tax rates to rise. They could pay this year's charitable contributions early next year, making both this year's and next year's contributions next year. They could decide to sell investments with losses next year, defer state or local income taxes, or incur controllable medical expenses next year.

¶15,035   **ITEMIZED OR THE STANDARD DEDUCTION**

In Chapter 3, it was pointed out that taxpayers may deduct from adjusted gross income either the standard deduction or the total of itemized deductions, whichever is higher. On an inflation-adjusted basis and to adjust for the marriage penalty, the standard deductions for 2015 are as follows:

Married persons filing jointly and surviving spouses	$12,600
Heads of households	9,250
Single individuals	6,300
Married individuals filing separately	6,300

An elderly or blind individual is allowed an additional deduction amount of $1,250 ($2,500 if both elderly and blind) if married (whether or not filing a separate return) or a surviving spouse and $1,550 if single or a head of household ($3,100 if both blind and elderly).

There are a few planning items individuals should be aware of regarding the standard deduction. If a taxpayer's itemized deductions are generally just a little above or a little below the standard deduction, a tax planning device to consider is to attempt to load as many itemized deductions in one year as possible so that itemized deductions will be significantly higher than the standard deduction. This would be followed in the next year by incurrence of itemized deductions which are less than the standard deduction. One is able to control charitable contributions, property taxes, some medical expenses, and possibly mortgage interest and miscellaneous deductions.

EXAMPLE 15.3   Edward Grey, single, has about $7,000 a year on the average in itemized deductions. He is able to control $5,000 of these deductions through charitable giving. Edward should then move to 2015 the additional $5,000 charitable contributions that would have been given in 2016 to get total itemized deductions of $12,000 in 2015. In 2016, his itemized deductions will be only $2,000, but he will have a standard deduction of $6,300 (adjusted for inflation). Thus, by moving the 2016 deductions to 2015, he has total deductions of $18,300 ($12,000 itemized in 2015 plus $6,300 standard deduction in 2016) instead of $14,000 (i.e., $7,000 in itemized deductions each year).

If a married couple files separately, they are required to either both itemize or both use the standard deduction. They should determine which status is more beneficial from a combined standpoint. Assume Jim and Mary Greene have itemized deductions of $6,500 and $2,500, respectively. If Jim itemizes, then Mary would be required to itemize, giving them total itemized deductions of only $9,000. However, they would each receive $6,300, for a total of $12,600, if they both elected to use the standard deduction.

Another planning consideration relative to the standard deduction is to effectively increase one's standard deduction by transferring assets resulting in $1,050 of unearned income to one's child or other tax dependent(s). A tax dependent is allowed a standard deduction of $1,050 against which unearned income can be offset. Unfortunately, the tax dependent cannot also claim a personal exemption which, if it were possible, would have further increased the amount of sheltered unearned income.

Taxpayers may want to consider reorganizing their financial affairs because all unearned income over a $1,050 floor for a child under age 18 is taxed at the parents' top marginal rate (the "kiddie tax"). In addition, if a child is 18 at year end and does not have earned income that exceeds half of his or her support, the kiddie tax applies if the child has unearned income above the threshold for the year and has positive income after subtracting any deductions. Further, if a child is 19 to 23 and a full-time student during at least 5 months of the year and does not have income that exceeds half of his or her support, the kiddie tax applies if the child has unearned income above the threshold for the year and positive taxable income after subtracting any deductions. The kiddie tax applies after the $1,050 standard deduction is taken into consideration. Therefore, the parents' top marginal rate for unearned income of a child under age 18 would essentially apply to the child's unearned income over $2,100 ($1,050 floor, taxed at the child's rate + $1,050 standard deduction).

EXAMPLE 15.4	Bill and Cathy Monroe transfer assets that produce interest income of $1,150 to their son Dean, age 7. This way Dean will be taxed on $100 at his tax rate. If assets producing more than $2,100 in unearned income were transferred to Dean, he would be taxed at Bill and Cathy's top marginal rate on the income in excess of $2,100.

Self-Employed v. Employee Tax Planning

There are a number of factors that can make the tax situation of the self-employed person more favorable than that of the employee. Though not feasible in many situations, an individual may wish to try to qualify as a self-employed individual. Some individuals may prefer to go into business for themselves rather than work as employees.

¶15,101　HEALTH INSURANCE PLANS

Self-employed persons may take 100 percent of the cost of their family's health insurance as a deduction for adjusted gross income. This provision also applies to partners in a partnership and S corporation shareholders who own more than 2 percent of the stock in the corporation. This is in contrast to the health insurance costs of an employee who may deduct (as an itemized deduction) medical costs only to the extent that they exceed 10 percent of adjusted gross income (7.5 percent for those age 65 or older). The self-employed individual must not be eligible to participate in the health insurance plan of an employer or in the plan of a spouse. The deduction is not allowed to the extent that it exceeds the adjusted earned income for the trade or business activity to which the plan providing for health insurance is established. Also, the deduction reduces self-employment income for purposes of the self-employment tax.

¶15,115　TRADE OR BUSINESS EXPENSES

The self-employed person takes travel and transportation expenses on Schedule C as a deduction for adjusted gross income and not as a miscellaneous itemized deduction subject to the 2 percent floor as in the case of an employee. Similarly, for business meals and entertainment, 50 percent of the costs would be deductible on Schedule C for a self-employed individual, but 50 percent of such unreimbursed expenses would be deductible as miscellaneous itemized deductions subject to the 2 percent floor for the employee.

Self-employed individuals are able to take interest on the purchase of business automobiles as Schedule C expenses, whereas employees must consider interest on the business use of cars as consumer interest, which is not deductible. Also, employees are at a disadvantage in the depreciation of certain employer-provided property, such as a computer, where the requirement for deduction is that the computer be for the convenience of the employer and that it be required as a condition of employment.

Family Tax Planning

¶15,201　INCOME-SHIFTING

During the last few years many of the devices for spreading income among taxpayers have been curtailed or eliminated. At first blush, it would seem that much of the incentive for spreading income among taxpayers is gone since the 39 percentage point spread between the highest and lowest tax brackets in 1986 (50 percent to 11 percent) is reduced to 29.6 percent in 2015 (39.6 percent to 10 percent). However, with the demise of many tax saving opportunities, the relative advantage of income shifting may be emphasized.

The motivation for parents to gift income-producing property to their children in order to take advantage of the child's standard deduction, personal exemption, and lower tax bracket has been reduced due to the disallowance of a personal exemption if an individual filing a return is claimed as a dependent on another return. The standard deduction on a dependent filer's return is limited to the greater of $1,050 or earned income plus $350, and there is the provision that all unearned income in excess of $2,100 ($1,050 standard deduction + $1,050 unearned income allowed to be taxed at the child's rate) will be taxed at the parents' top marginal rate. Given the constraints of the above provisions, a taxpayer can still eliminate tax on $1,050 of unearned income through gifting property to a child due to the $1,050 standard deduction still allowed the child. If the child is age 24 or over or age 19-23 and not a student, the parents could achieve a lower tax rate for unearned income up to the cut-off amount for taxable income provided in the rate tables assuming the child has no other income source. If the child is not subject to the kiddie tax, only $1,050 of unearned income could be taxed at the child's rate, but the $1,050 at a lower rate will result in some savings.

EXAMPLE 15.5	Nancy and Richard Kern have two children, Cherie and Bruce. Cherie is 15 years old and Bruce is 20 years old and not a student. Nancy and Richard predict they will be in the 28 percent bracket (they anticipate their taxable income will be between $170,000 and $180,000) for 2015 and would like to shift some anticipated unearned income to Cherie and Bruce. By shifting $2,100 of unearned income to Cherie, Nancy and Richard will achieve a tax savings of $483 ($588 – $105), as computed below. Assume that Nancy and Richard could give investments generating up to $30,000 of income.

	Cherie's Return	Nancy & Richard's Return
Unearned income	$2,100	$2,100
Standard deduction	1,050	—
Personal exemption	0	—
Taxable income	$1,050	$2,100
Tax rate	10%	28%
Tax liability	$105	$588

It would not be advantageous for Mr. and Mrs. Kern to shift additional unearned income to Cherie due to the tax provision which imposes the highest marginal tax rate of the parents, 28 percent, to any unearned income exceeding $2,100 reported on Cherie's return.

For 2015, Nancy and Richard can achieve a tax savings of $4,245 ($7,812 – $3,567) by gifting investments generating $27,900 of unearned income ($30,000 – $2,100) to Bruce, as computed below:

	Bruce's Return	Nancy & Richard's Return
Unearned income	$27,900	$27,900
Standard deduction	1,050	—
Personal exemption	0	—
Taxable income	$26,850	$27,900
Tax rate		28%
Tax on $9,225 @ 10%	$ 923	
Excess of $17,625 @ 15%	2,644	
Tax liability	$ 3,567	$ 7,812

A much larger amount can be shifted to Bruce because he is 20 and not a student and not subject to taxation at his parents' tax rate. Actually, unearned income up to $90,750 could be transferred to Bruce with tax savings since his top marginal rate of 25 percent would be less than his parents' top rate of 28 percent (assuming the Kerns had the ability to give gifts generating that much income).

For purposes of this example, it has been assumed that the taxation of unearned income for Nancy and Richard is considered after all other income is taken into effect. Therefore, no standard deduction or personal exemption is taken into account for comparative purposes because it is assumed that such amounts are already utilized to offset earned income, and the tax rate considered is Richard's top marginal rate.

Even in cases where unearned income from property in the child's name will be taxed at the parents' rate, it still may be beneficial for the property to be in the child's name. This may come about in instances where the property would generate a tax preference for alternative minimum tax purposes if held in the parents' names. Another possibility is retaining a trust for a minor child (even though most of the income tax advantages have been eliminated or decreased) due to possible estate tax savings achieved through perpetuating the trust.

Government Bonds

Taxpayers should look for tax-deferred investments as vehicles for a child subject to the kiddie tax. For example, if a child is given a Series EE U.S. savings bond which matures after the child is no longer subject to the kiddie tax, the child can opt to defer the reporting of income until the maturity date of the bond. At the time of the maturity date, income will be taxed at the child's generally lower tax bracket since the child is no longer subject to the kiddie tax. If a child already owns such bonds and has been reporting accrued income on an annual basis, the child must continue to do so unless an election is made to defer the interest by filing Form 3115, Application for Change in Accounting Method, with the child's tax return. Specific details for making this change are provided in Rev. Proc. 89-46, 1990-2 CB 597.

In addition, there is a tax exemption for the accrued interest of Series EE U.S. Savings Bonds that are purchased after 1989 and are used to finance the higher education needs of the taxpayer and the taxpayer's family. Specifically, such accrued interest may be excluded from gross income if the amount received at the time of redemption (i.e., both principal and interest) does not exceed the higher education expenses incurred by the taxpayer for that year. The exclusion is not available to married individuals who file separately.

EXAMPLE 15.6	During the tax year, Jerry Jergens redeems Series EE bonds, receiving a return of principal of $12,000 and accrued interest of $8,000. If his higher education expenses are $20,000 or more for the year, then the entire $8,000 of interest is excludable from gross income. If, however, his educational expenses are only $15,000, then only $6,000 is excludable from income, calculated on a pro rata basis ($8,000 × $15,000/$20,000 = $6,000).

In addition, this exclusion treatment is subject to disallowance if a modified computation of the taxpayer's adjusted gross income exceeds a specified level. For 2015, this amount is $115,750 for married taxpayers filing jointly, and $77,200 for those who file as single taxpayers or heads of households, with the exclusion fully phased out once adjusted gross income equals or exceeds $145,750 and $92,200, respectively. Married individuals filing separately are not eligible for this exclusion.

The taxpayer must also keep in mind that the amount of higher education expenses taken into account for the purpose of computing the exclusion of interest on Series EE U.S. savings bonds redeemed is reduced by the amount of such expenses that are taken into account in computing the American Opportunity Tax Credit or the Lifetime Learning Credit.

EXAMPLE 15.7	Assuming that Jerry in the preceding example filed a return as a married taxpayer filing jointly, had educational expenses of $15,000, and had modified adjusted gross income of $123,250 in the example above, $4,500 of the $6,000 in accrued interest income is excluded because adjusted gross income exceeded the threshold amount of $115,750 by $7,500 and this is 25 percent of the phaseout range of $30,000 (i.e., the difference between $115,750 and $145,750). Consequently, 25 percent of the $6,000 is *included* in income, and 75 percent (i.e., $4,500 of a total of $6,000) remains excluded from income reporting.

Municipal Bonds

Deep discount municipal bonds serve as another debt instrument which may save taxes if gifted to a child. Again, one can buy bonds which will mature after the child is no longer subject to the kiddie tax. The interest will retain a tax-free status and the discount will be taxable at the child's rate when the bond is redeemed at maturity. However, one could amortize the discount over the life of the bond, which would be advantageous taxwise.

Stock and Land

Growth stock may prove to be the best investment in the hands of dependents. The dividend income to be reported on an annual basis will be minimal. The potential capital gains due to appreciation in the investment can be deferred for tax purposes until after the child is no longer subject to the kiddie tax, at which time the appreciation will be taxed at the child's lower tax bracket. Raw land is another appreciation investment which can be sold to achieve a lower tax rate after the child is no longer subject to the kiddie tax.

Life Insurance

Cash value life insurance policies have the advantage of accumulating income tax free on the investment portion of the fund. In addition, loans from cash value life insurance policies can often be achieved tax free.

Employment in Family Business

Of all the shifting options, the one with perhaps the potentially greatest tax savings impact may be for unincorporated businesses to employ family members. The family members employed must perform a bona fide service for the company and must not be paid more than a reasonable amount for the service they performed. Taxpayers considering this option for children as employees should investigate the child labor laws within their state.

One advantage is that the child is entitled to a standard deduction up to the amount of earned income plus $350. If earned income exceeds the standard deduction allowed, an additional $5,500 of income sheltering could be achieved by establishing an IRA in the name of the child. In addition, if a couple does not qualify for deductible IRA contributions, they still can achieve some advantage even if their IRA contributions are nondeductible (see the IRA section of this chapter).

If a medical reimbursement plan, which compensates employees for uninsured medical expenses, is established by the company for which the spouse and/or children work, the family will receive reimbursement for the out-of-pocket costs of medical expenses and the company can deduct some of the insurance premiums and other costs associated with the medical reimbursement plan. For tax purposes, this is a more advantageous method of handling family medical expenses which otherwise would be limited by the 10 percent floor on medical deductions for individuals (if under age 65).

Intrafamily Loans

Though not as direct as the aforementioned opportunities, an intrafamily loan may result in tax savings. The Internal Revenue Code allows interest-free or below-market loans of up to $10,000 before interest is imputed. The use of intrafamily loans is an effective means of shifting income from a high-bracket taxpayer (the parent) to the low-bracket taxpayer (the child who is no longer subject to the kiddie tax). Upon receipt of the funds, the borrower can invest them in income-producing assets. Although the borrower must pay taxes on the income produced by the assets, the loan results in an overall lower tax liability within the family unit because the income is shifted away from the high-bracket taxpayer and taxed at lower rates.

¶15,225   COLLEGE PLANNING

Many of the vehicles previously used by middle and upper income taxpayers for financing educational costs have been eliminated or restricted (i.e., the *Clifford* and other trust arrangements, the custodial account for gifts to children no longer subject to the kiddie tax, intrafamily loans, installment sales, and sale/leasebacks). Following are some possible techniques still available to these taxpayers.

Custodial Accounts and Nongrantor Trusts

Although a child subject to the kiddie tax is taxed at the parents' marginal rate for unearned income over $2,100, an older child is not taxed at the parents' marginal rate. Establishing a custodial account to finance educational costs for a child who is no longer subject to the kiddie tax may prove to be advantageous since the child will pay income tax at a rate of 10 and 15 percent for income (up to $37,450 over the $1,050 standard deduction) versus a possible 39.6 percent rate to be paid by the parent in 2015. Another possible trust alternative is nongrantor trusts, such as Section 2503(c) trusts in which the proceeds of the trust are distributed to the beneficiary once the beneficiary reaches age 21. Accrued income under such a trust arrangement is taxed to the beneficiary at a rate of 15 percent for the first $2,500 of trust income, 25 percent for the trust income between $2,500 and $5,900, 28 percent between $5,900 and $9,050, 33 percent between $9,050 and $12,300, and 39.6 percent over $12,300 income. The child beneficiary is not eligible for a personal exemption due to the child's being claimed as a dependent on the parents' return. However, the child is allowed a $1,050 standard deduction.

Compensation for Services

Children can take part in saving for their education by earning income. A child can benefit from a standard deduction of $6,300 in 2015 to shelter earned income. Though the child's earning capacity is generally limited, it may be more advantageous for a grandparent or parent to pay a child (up to the standard deduction allowed) for performing domestic services such as baby-sitting or house cleaning than to put that money into a trust account. In a trust account, the 1,050th dollar is taxed, whereas if earned, the 6,300th dollar would be taxed in 2015. Of course, the compensation for the services must be reasonable and, unfortunately, the payer of the charge for domestic services does not receive a tax deduction for the payment.

It is, however, possible for the parent/grandparent to receive a deduction for services performed by a child if the child is employed by a business owned by the parent/grandparent either solely or through a partnership. In the instance of business employment, the parent/grandparent should determine whether employment taxes will be incurred for the child.

Individual Retirement Accounts

If a child has earned income in excess of the standard deduction allowed, an IRA may prove to be an advantageous method of saving for college. The benefits of tax deferral and high yields may surpass the costs of early withdrawal penalties, especially if the IRA is opened early in the child's life. See ¶15,701 for opportunities under an education IRA.

Universal Life Policies

The purchase of single premium universal life policies by the parent serves as a method by which to defer the tax on the child's college fund since the earnings on the investment portion of the policy are not currently taxable. A single premium deferred annuity may serve as a similar option since earnings on the investment portion are also deferred. Payout should begin with the commencement of the child's college career. The premature withdrawal penalty associated with annuities can be avoided if the payments occur over the annuitant's life expectancy. If annuity funds are not needed for educational purposes, the taxpayer may want to consider delaying payout and continuing the deferral of taxes on annuity earnings.

Campus Rental Property Purchases

If the child has already reached or is close to reaching college age, one alternative available to parents (particularly if the child is attending college in another city) is to purchase rental property and compensate the child for management or other services performed in relation to the rental property. The child is thus provided with nontaxable accommodations and a portion of the child's income is shielded through the standard deduction. The parents have the advantage of deductions and possibly income associated with the rental property. If the parents prefer a loss situation, losses of $25,000 (subject to a phaseout for high-income taxpayers) are allowed if the owners of the property are involved in actively managing the rental property.

Qualified Tuition Programs

Code Sec. 529 provides for tax-exempt status to qualified tuition programs (QTPs) established by a state under which persons may (1) purchase tuition credits or certificates on behalf of a beneficiary entitling the beneficiary to a waiver or payment of qualified education expenses, or (2) contribute to an account established exclusively for the purpose of meeting qualified higher education expenses of the beneficiary.

Qualified higher education expenses are tuition, fees, books, supplies, and equipment required for enrollment or attendance at an eligible educational institution, as well as room and board expenses for students who attend an eligible educational institution at least half-time.

EXAMPLE 15.8   Over the years, John Jones paid $40,000 into a QTP in connection with the future education of his daughter, Jennifer. By the time Jennifer attends college, the annual tuition had increased to $15,000 a year and the tuition is considered paid by the QTP. During each of the years that Jennifer uses the tuition prepayment, she has no gross income.

American Opportunity Credit and Lifetime Learning Credit

The American Opportunity Credit provides a maximum nonrefundable tax credit of $2,500 per student for each of the student's first four years of post-secondary education expenses. Specifically, the American Opportunity Credit allows taxpayers a 100 percent credit for the first $2,000 of tuition expenses per eligible student and a 25 percent credit for the second $2,000 paid. The credit can be claimed for four tax years for the taxpayer, spouse, and dependents and qualified expenses include tuition, fees, and course materials. The American Opportunity Credit phases out when the taxpayer's modified AGI is between $80,000 and $90,000 for singles, and $160,000 and $180,000 for joint filers.

The Lifetime Learning Credit allows a 20 percent credit per taxpayer for up to $10,000 per year of qualified tuition expenses and fees paid with respect to one or more students. Unlike the American Opportunity Credit, the Lifetime Learning Credit does not vary with the number of students in the household; is available for an unlimited number of years; is available for undergraduate, graduate, or professional degree expenses; and may be claimed for any course at an eligible institution that helps an individual acquire or improve their job skills.

The allowable amount of Lifetime Learning Credit is phased out for joint filers with modified AGI between $110,000 and $130,000 and for single filers with modified AGI between $55,000 and $65,000. The credits are only available to married taxpayers who file jointly. The Lifetime Learning Credit is not allowed in any tax year in which the American Opportunity Credit is claimed with respect to the same student's tuition.

¶15,255   DIVORCE SETTLEMENTS

Initially, it appears that recent tax acts have not substantially affected divorce settlements because no major changes to the taxation of divorce settlements were addressed. Alimony is still taxable income to the recipient and a tax deduction for the payer. Child support is still nontaxable to the recipient and nondeductible by the payer. The recipient of property in a property transfer receives a cost basis the same as that of the transferring spouse at the time of the transfer. However, marginal tax rates, the reduction in tax shelters, and an increase in the amount of dependency exemptions may have an effect on divorce settlements.

Front-Loading Provisions

Minor changes have been made relating to front loading of alimony payments (payments which are concentrated in the early years of divorce rather than level payments made over many years). The Internal Revenue Code regards as alimony, divorce settlement payments which are paid in level annual installments over a minimum period of years and which will terminate at the death of the former spouse receiving the payments. If the former spouse receives an amount in excess of the level payment amount, the excess payment is regarded as alimony for tax purposes if the excess payment is a de minimis amount.

The number of years for which payment is required in order to be classified as alimony payments is three years and the de minimis amount is $15,000. If the payment exceeds the de minimis amount, then recapture occurs in the third post-separation year. Thus, it is now easier for a high-income former spouse to make settlement payments which are classified as alimony payments and the payer is able to achieve higher deductions in years when they are most advantageous.

Basically, the second-year payment can be $15,000 greater than the third-year payment and the first-year payment can be $7,500 greater than the second-year payment. Effectively, the first-year payment can exceed the third-year payment by $22,500. Therefore, if desired, the payer can achieve an additional $22,500 of deductions over the level payment amount if this proves to be beneficial for tax purposes for the first three tax years after divorce.

Timing is also very important in regard to maximizing deductions. Even if a taxpayer is required to make settlement payments within a year and a half of the divorce, the taxpayer can take advantage of the three-year minimum period condition because this provision can be accomplished within one year and two days.

EXAMPLE 15.9   Joe and Jane Monroe signed their final decree of divorce in November 2015. According to the settlement, Joe must pay Jane $165,000 within the next year and a half. With careful planning of payments, Joe can achieve tax deductions for the entire $165,000. The three-year requirement is determined on a calendar year basis. So, Joe can make one payment in December of 2015, one in January of 2016, and one in January of 2017 and still comply with the three-year rule. To achieve maximum deductions and not be subject to the recapture provisions, Joe should make payments as follows: $65,000 in year one, $57,500 in year two, and $42,500 in year three. Each of these payments would be deductible and no recapture would be required. The payments listed comply with the guidelines regarding recapture which allow the second-year payment to exceed the third-year payment by $15,000 and the first-year payment to exceed the second-year payment by $7,500.

Termination of Payments

Other minor changes regarding divorce settlements are that it is no longer required that divorce settlements state that payments will terminate upon the death of the payee if state law already mandates that payments terminate upon the death of the payee, and the agreements need not specify a minimum three-year term. Also, the rules regarding qualified domestic relations orders have been changed to make it easier for designated former spouse recipients to receive distributions from their ex-spouses' benefit plans.

Personal and Dependency Exemptions

Taxpayers will want to take a closer look at exemptions. The amount of each personal and dependency exemption is $4,000 in 2015. With the loss or curtailment of tax shelters, bargaining to gain a tax exemption may be worth increasing the child support payment for the payer. In determining who is to receive the dependency deduction, taxpayers should take into account the relative marginal tax bracket of divorced spouses.

EXAMPLE 15.10

Jack and Karen Johnson completed divorce proceedings in 2015. Jack and Karen have one child, Jill, who is 10 years old and under the custody of Karen. Jack predicts his AGI will be around $220,000 for 2015. Karen predicts her income will be approximately $30,000 for 2015. Karen agrees to give Jack the dependency exemption for 2015 in exchange for some property she will receive in the settlement. Jack will benefit from the dependency exemption for his 2015 return. Jack's tax advantage gained through this exemption will be $1,320 (33 percent tax rate × $4,000 exemption allowed). In comparison, Karen's tax advantage would be only $600 (15 percent tax rate × $4,000 exemption allowed).

Since the allocation of dependency exemptions can be determined on a year-by-year basis, Jack and Karen should review the tax implications of the exemption each year.

To further complicate the dependency issue, personal exemptions are denied to individuals listed as dependents on returns other than their own and the parents' tax rate is imposed on a child subject to the kiddie tax for unearned income over $2,100. In regard to the standard deduction for individuals for whom a dependency exemption is allowable to another taxpayer, such an individual's standard deduction may not exceed the greater of $1,050 or the amount of earned income plus $350. One also should keep in mind that the child tax credit goes to the parent claiming the exemption.

Alimony Payments

Taxpayers should keep in mind that alimony is considered earned income for individual retirement account purposes; rules concerning IRAs have undergone changes which consider alimony received as earned income. Further, there are phase-outs for individual retirement accounts. Taxpayers facing divorce should consider that the cost of tax advice sought on income, estate, or gift tax matters related to a divorce is tax deductible. However, the cost of tax advice related to divorce is subject to the 2 percent of AGI floor for miscellaneous and employee business expenses. In order to be deductible, the fees for tax advice must be separately allocated by a firm providing a package of services to the taxpayer (either through a preliminary agreement or in the firm's invoice) or the taxpayer must have sought services from a firm which strictly engages in tax practice.

Fixed and Other Assets Tax Planning

¶15,401   ## EXPENSING ELECTION

Taxpayers with small businesses may want to consider taking advantage of the Section 179 expensing election. Taxpayers are able to expense up to $25,000 for 2015 if the total investment in tangible personal property is $200,000 or less. For every dollar of investment exceeding $200,000, the $25,000 ceiling is reduced by $1. The amount eligible to be expensed is limited to the taxable income from any active trade or business. In deciding whether to take advantage of the Section 179 expensing election, taxpayers must consider their tax bracket and later recapture of tax benefits at the time of sale. Also, taxpayers may prefer not to invest in excess of $200,000 in tangible personal property for the year in order to avoid the phase out of the expensing election. See Chapter 6 for limited expensing of some real property. Prior to 2015, taxpayers were allowed to expense up to $500,000 under Section 179. It is expected that Congress will extend the provisions for 2015.

¶15,411   LEASING v. BUYING

There are arguments on both sides of the issue of buying versus leasing, and taxpayers should carefully analyze their personal situation to determine which alternative is more advantageous.

Since employees are not allowed a personal interest deduction, taxpayers may be led to believe that it is advisable to lease certain assets used for business purposes, such as a car or a computer. However, the business share of the leasing costs is deductible as a miscellaneous deduction for the employee only to the extent that it exceeds the 2 percent of AGI floor. Furthermore, taxpayers who are homeowners may be allowed an interest deduction if they purchase the assets and if they fund the purchase of their autos or computers through home-equity loans.

¶15,425   LIKE-KIND EXCHANGES

By falling under the Code Sec. 1031 rules for nonrecognition of gain in like-kind exchanges, taxpayers are able to avoid some or all of the taxation that would occur if the asset were sold instead of exchanged. Even if there is some recognition, with long-term capital gains taxed at 15, 20, 25, or 28 percent, for taxpayers in the 25, 28, 33, 35, or 39.6 percent tax bracket, there is a potentially large difference between capital gains rates and ordinary rates.

EXAMPLE 15.11

Brad Greene has a choice of selling his apartment building (held more than 12 months) for $600,000 with an adjusted basis of $120,000 depreciated under the straight-line method or exchanging it for another apartment building with a fair market value of $600,000. If he sells, he has a $480,000 Section 1231 gain. If this is the only transaction Brad has and if this occurs in 2015, he will be taxed at rates of 15 and 25 percent. If, on the other hand, he decides to make the exchange, there will be no recognized gain and the basis of the asset will be the carryover basis of $120,000. It is true that the basis of the new building will be lower in the case of an exchange than if there was a purchase of a new building for $600,000. The new asset is depreciated over the remaining life of the old asset. For sales of depreciable real property, unrecaptured Section 1250 gain is taxed at a maximum rate of 25 percent even if straight-line depreciation was taken.

There is a major exception for this provision. If property received in a like-kind exchange between related parties is dis posed of before a date that is two years after the date of the last transfer in the exchange, any gain or loss that was not recognized on the original exchange must be recognized as of the date that the property is disposed.

¶15,435   RESIDENCE SALE

Taxpayers who avoid recognition on the sale of a residence save taxes up to the rate of 15 or 20 percent in 2015. Married taxpayers may exclude up to $500,000 ($250,000 for single taxpayers) of realized gain on the sale of a residence. The exclusion is available only once every two years. It may be advantageous for a taxpayer to rent the former residence while seeking a buyer. If a taxpayer otherwise qualifies for exclusion of the gain recognized on the sale of the former home, rental of the residence while it is held out for sale will not disqualify a taxpayer from use of the exclusion provisions. Keep in mind that the rental can only be a maximum of 3 years; otherwise the taxpayer will not meet the 2 out of 5 year rule.

Exclusion of gain on the sale of the residence is now allowed (up to the above limits) for any of the residence sale attributed to a home office. However, if depreciation was taken on a home office after May 6, 1997, it is recaptured at a maximum rate of 25 percent.

Remodeling and Home Improvements

Remodeling and home improvements can lead to tax savings. Home improvements can increase a home's cost basis for tax purposes. A stepped-up basis is especially important where mortgage interest deductions are limited to the purchase price of a first and second residence plus improvements (up to an aggregate limit of $1,000,000). If the mortgage on a house is increased for the purpose of home improvements, the mortgage limit may be increased to reflect the planned improvements. Also, with capital gains generally being taxed at no more than 15 or 20 percent in 2015, taxpayers will want to have the highest basis possible for their residence when sold, especially if there has been substantial appreciation with the residence that causes realized gain to be above the maximum exclusion.

Taxpayers can easily overlook many costs capitalizable as home improvement expenditures. The IRS guidelines state that improvements add to value, prolong useful life of the home, or adapt a home to new uses. Alternatively, repairs are concerned with home maintenance and do not add to the value of a home. Whether an expenditure is appropriately classified as a home improvement or a repair is determined by the fact situation at hand and taxpayers should use the guidelines as set forth by the IRS. Taxpayers should save invoices and contracts associated with home improvement costs. Cancelled checks are merely supporting documents.

EXAMPLE 15.12   At various times during 2015, Lynn and Eddie Embers completed many household projects. They have lived in their current home for five years. Among the projects taken on by Lynn and Eddie were: the addition of a study, the replacement of a wire fence with a wooden fence, the repainting of their bedroom, and plumbing repairs. The addition of the study will add to the value of the house and is clearly a home improvement expenditure. The repainting of the bedroom will not add to the value of the house and would be considered a repair. The plumbing and the fencing are not as clear-cut, however. If the plumbing and fencing merely resulted in replacing or fixing rather than upgrading, then they would be considered repairs, but since the fencing seems to be an upgrade of quality (wood replacing wire), it would seem that the fencing would qualify as a home improvement. Further details would be required to properly categorize the plumbing work.

EXAMPLE 15.13   Using the facts of the above example, with the exception that Lynn and Eddie had just purchased the home, they could argue that the above projects were taken on to restore a run-down house and all such repairs added value to their purchase price. If successful, the costs of the projects would be considered home improvement costs.

EXAMPLE 15.14   Using the facts of the above example, if Eddie and Lynn can group all the projects listed as part of an extensive remodeling or restoration undertaking, then entire costs associated with all the projects listed would be considered improvement expenditures. Hence, "repair costs" would be reclassified into improvement costs. That is, the repainting, plumbing, and fencing would be considered improvement expenditures.

Passive Activity Losses

Property taxes paid on all residences are tax deductible. Secondary homes with a rental and personal use provide a tax advantage if they are not rented out for more than 14 days a year because rental income is then not taxed. Passive activity losses may offset only passive income with one exception. The exception to the passive income offset rule allows $25,000 of passive losses to offset ordinary income provided the taxpayer is an "active" participant in the management or maintenance of the rental real estate. To be classified as an "active" participant, a taxpayer must arrange for services to be provided or must participate in management decision making in a significant and genuine sense. Active participation does not require continuous or substantial involvement in the operations of the rental property.

EXAMPLE 15.15   Johnny Greystone has adjusted gross income of $50,000 in 2015. He has a gulf view condominium in Florida which he rented out for most of 2015 and used for personal purposes for less than 14 days. Johnny engages a rental agent to rent the condo, but he has set the rental period to be no less than 10 days per occupancy. Believing that the real estate agent had the best "feel" for the going rental rates, Johnny left the rental rate up to the agent, but did stipulate that he did not want the condo rented for less than $80 per night as a cheaper rent might attract undesirables. Johnny approves the servicing of all repairs recommended to him by the real estate agent and gives a dollar limitation on costs incurred for most repairs, though he gives the agent power to engage the businesses she feels will properly perform the services. Though Johnny uses the agent on a regular basis and the agent does have the power to make substantial decisions regarding the rental of the condo, Johnny may still be classified as an "active" participant since he participates in the management decisions of rate and term setting and approves repair expenditures.

There is a problem for taxpayers with adjusted gross incomes of $100,000 or more; the $25,000 advantage is phased out for taxpayers within the adjusted gross income range of $100,000 to $150,000 and is eliminated for taxpayers with adjusted gross incomes over $150,000.

If a taxpayer is denied the $25,000 exception or if the taxpayer had passive losses exceeding the $25,000 exception, passive losses are not lost but can be carried over to future years. If the property is sold before the passive losses are fully utilized, the taxpayer may deduct unused passive losses at the time the property is sold.

Even if the taxpayer is allowed the $25,000 loss or a portion thereof, the loss is disallowed for alternative minimum tax purposes. Also, the depreciation deductions allowed for alternative minimum tax purposes are not as generous.

¶15,445   INVOLUNTARY CONVERSIONS

Taxpayers will also want to consider election of nonrecognition of gain with respect to involuntary conversions under Section 1033. This election remains an important consideration to avoid recognition of gain, which can be taxed up to 15, 20, or 25 percent.

EXAMPLE 15.16	Gloria Maine has a realized gain on a condemnation of a commercial building in the amount of $500,000 (proceeds of $800,000 with an adjusted basis of $300,000). She replaces the building with another that costs $800,000 and elects nonrecognition of gain. Her basis in the new building will be $300,000. If she had recognized the $500,000 gain, she would have had a basis of $800,000 in the new building. The replacement asset is depreciated over the remaining life of the old asset.

¶15,465   SECTION 1231 ASSETS

In Chapter 12, the Section 1231 rules were discussed. Section 1231(c) provides that, if Section 1231 gains exceed Section 1231 losses, the excess is treated as ordinary income to the extent the net Section 1231(c) losses in the previous five years have not been recaptured under Section 1231(c). Any excess gain is treated as long-term capital gain.

This rule has a tax planning implication. If there are no preceding Section 1231 loss years, the taxpayer should try to take gains first to preclude the recapture that results if losses are taken prior to gains. If gains are taken in early years and losses in later years, this would allow full ordinary loss treatment for the taxpayer. If, however, Section 1231 losses are taken first followed by Section 1231 gains, the years in which gains occurred would result in recapture as ordinary income.

Deduction Tax Planning

The tax structure has adjustments to income taken into account for adjusted gross income and from adjusted gross income. The significance in characterization as a deduction for or from AGI is that deductions for AGI reduce gross income on a dollar for dollar basis whereas deductions from AGI serve as an added deduction to arrive at taxable income only to the extent they exceed the standard deduction. Furthermore, certain deductions from AGI are subject to a floor based on a given percentage of AGI.

Most unreimbursed employee business deductions are deductions from AGI. These include employee travel expenses, transportation expenses, and business expenses of outside salespersons.

¶15,501   ITEMIZED DEDUCTIONS—TWO-TIER SYSTEM

There are two levels of itemized deductions. The first level or tier includes deductions that are not subject to any deduction floor. Property taxes and state income taxes are deductible in this manner. The second tier of itemized deductions includes deductions that are deductible only to the extent they exceed a fixed percentage of AGI. For example, medical expenses must exceed 10 percent of AGI (if under age 65), casualty losses must exceed 10 percent of AGI, and miscellaneous itemized deductions, such as unreimbursed employee expenses, must exceed 2 percent of AGI.

Given the 2 percent of AGI floor for miscellaneous deductions and the standard deduction level, itemized deductions need to be significantly higher than in the past in order to result in additional tax savings. If an individual is to gain any tax advantage or to maximize the tax advantage through itemized deductions, all potential deductions should be considered. The checklist in the following section serves as a reminder of many of the often forgotten, yet still available, itemized deductions which an individual may want to consider in tax planning.

EXAMPLE 15.17	Doug Renard, a single employee, has charitable contributions of $5,000, unreimbursed meals and entertainment expenses of $1,000, and travel and transportation expenses of $2,000. His adjusted gross income is $45,000. Doug's itemized deductions are $6,600, computed as follows:

Charitable contributions		$5,000
Meals and entertainment (50% of $1,000)	$500	
Travel and transportation	2,000	
	$2,500	
Less: 2% of AGI ($45,000 × .02)	900	1,600
Total itemized deductions		$6,600

Thus, of the $8,000 expenses incurred, Doug is allowed itemized deductions of only $6,600.

PLANNING POINTER	It may be worthwhile for taxpayers to incur eligible miscellaneous expenses in a year in which adjusted gross income is relatively low because that will allow a larger amount of deductions to exceed the 2 percent floor.

EXAMPLE 15.18	Assume Roger Short's adjusted gross income averages around $50,000, except that in 2015 his adjusted gross income is $20,000. He should pay as many miscellaneous expenses as possible in 2015 because he will be able to deduct those expenses to the extent they exceed $400 (2 percent of $20,000). Otherwise, assuming he incurs the miscellaneous expenses in 2016 with adjusted gross income of $50,000, his miscellaneous deductions would be allowed only to the extent they exceed $1,000 (2 percent of $50,000).

Assuming relatively stable adjusted gross income, taxpayers should attempt to incur eligible miscellaneous expenses in alternate years, especially if their miscellaneous deductions are fairly close to the two percent floor level.

EXAMPLE 15.19	Assume Beth's adjusted gross income generally is around $20,000 and that her miscellaneous deductions average about $400 per year. She is receiving little, if any, use from her miscellaneous deduction expenditures. However, by accelerating $300 of next year's expenses into this year, she can have a $300 miscellaneous deduction this year ($300 + $400 − $400 (2% of $20,000)) and $0 deduction next year ($100 − $400 (2% of $20,000)).

Some taxpayers might be able to include some miscellaneous expenses as Schedule C deductions not subject to the 2 percent floor. An employee who has a related type of business in addition to employee activities and who incurs the type of expenditures that could be related to either activity could include some of these expenses as Schedule C deductions. Some possible examples of such expenditures include educational expenses, professional dues, subscriptions to professional periodicals, technical books and tools, and professional meeting expenses.

¶15,515   CHECKLIST OF ITEMIZED DEDUCTIONS

TIER 1. Itemized Deductions Separately Listed on Schedule A

1. State and local income taxes
2. Property taxes
3. Mortgage interest (limited to two residences)
4. Investment interest on property held for investment (does not include passive activities) (limited to investment income)

Itemized Deductions Allowable as Other Miscellaneous Deductions on Schedule A

1. Gambling losses to the extent of gambling winnings
2. Federal estate tax on income in respect of decedent
3. Amortizable bond premiums for taxable bonds purchased before October 23, 1986
4. Repayment of amounts under a claim of right if more than $3,000
5. Unrecovered investment in an annuity
6. Impairment related work expenses of handicapped persons

TIER 2. Itemized Deductions Subject to a Fixed Percentage Limitation of AGI

1. Medical expenses (reduced by 10 percent of AGI) (7.5 percent if 65 or older)
2. Charitable contributions (subject to 50, 30, and 20 percent of AGI)
3. Casualty and theft losses (reduced by 10 percent of AGI)

Itemized Deductions Subject to 2 Percent of AGI Limitation

Employee Expenses (unreimbursed under employer plans)

1. Dues to professional societies
2. Employment-related education expenses
3. Malpractice insurance premiums
4. Job-hunting expenses, including resumé preparation costs
5. Home office expenses
6. Subscriptions to professional publications
7. Work clothes and uniforms
8. Union dues and fees
9. Business/entertainment expenses (50 percent limit on deductible business meals and entertainment)
10. Travel and transportation expenses
11. Technical books and tools
12. Safety clothes and equipment
13. Bonds required for employment
14. Laboratory breakage fees paid by researchers
15. Job-related legal fees such as a discrimination suit
16. Teacher's cost of a substitute teacher
17. Employer-required physical exams
18. Outside salesperson's expenses

Production of Income Expenses

1. Legal and accounting fees
2. Custodial fees related to income-producing property
3. IRA custodian fees
4. Collection of interest or dividends fees
5. Hobby expense up to hobby income
6. Investment counsel fees
7. Safe deposit box rentals (used to store non-tax-exempt securities)
8. Telephone, postage, office supplies, clerical help, statistical services, office rental, and publications related to investment activities
9. Tax services, periodicals, return preparation manuals, telephone, office supply, postage, and similar items related to the determination, collection, or refund of tax
10. Appraisal fees for casualty losses or charitable contributions

¶15,525   MEDICAL EXPENSES

The floor for medical expense deductions is 10 percent of AGI (7.5 percent if 65 for older), thereby making it difficult for taxpayers to obtain deductions for medical expenses. However, taxpayers may have a tax advantage in that certain capital expenditures incurred to modify their homes to assist a handicapped household member may be deductible as medical expenses if the fair market value of the home does not increase (Publication 502). Under present law, generally the deduction is limited to the excess of the amount expended over the increase in the value of the home. However, the increase in the home's value attributed to certain capital improvements is deemed to be zero in the case of handicapped individuals where the fair market value of the home does not increase.

EXAMPLE 15.20

Tony Mayberry's wife, Terri, age 55, is confined to a wheelchair as a result of an auto accident that occurred in 2010. Tony decided to make some structural changes to his home in 2015 in order to accommodate Terri's condition. Tony intends to construct entrance ramps, widen doorways and hallways for easier access with the wheelchair, add support bars to the bathrooms, lower kitchen cabinets, and adjust electrical outlets and fixtures at a total cost of $20,000. Assume that these expenditures do not increase the value of the home. The cost of all of the above will be deductible to the extent the total cost exceeds 10 percent of AGI. Assuming no other medical expenses, if Tony and Terri have an AGI of $50,000, they will be able to deduct $15,000 or the costs in excess of $5,000 ($50,000 × 10%).

In looking at medical deductions for future planning, as always, taxpayers should try to incur and pay for medical expenses in years in which they exceed the medical deduction floor and should itemize their deductions. In 2015, there is a 10 percent of AGI floor for taxpayers under 65 years (there is also a 10 percent floor for purposes of the alternative minimum tax) and, historically, this floor has been increased rather than decreased. (Prior to 2015, the regular tax floor for medical expenses increased from 3 percent to 5 percent to 7.5 percent to 10 percent.) Therefore, taxpayers need to be aware of the effect of the AGI floor when planning for elective medical treatment and capital expenditure outlay for medical purposes.

¶15,535   STATE AND LOCAL TAXES

State and local income taxes and property taxes are deductible. There may be some opportunity to prepay such taxes, especially when the taxing authority has an estimated tax system.

For sales taxes, there is a possible planning opportunity for individuals who can characterize a purchase as qualified business or investment property. Sales tax can be added to the basis of investment or business property for depreciation purposes.

For 2014, individual taxpayers could elect to deduct the greater of state and local income taxes or state and local general sales taxes as an itemized deduction on their federal income tax returns. The amount to be deducted for state and local general sales taxes is either (1) the total of actual general sales taxes paid as substantiated by accumulated receipts, or (2) an amount from IRS-generated tables plus, if any, the amount of general sales taxes paid in the purchase of a motor vehicle, boat, or other items prescribed by the IRS. The provision may be extended for 2015.

¶15,545   CHARITABLE CONTRIBUTIONS

The appeal of charitable contributions is directly affected by the taxpayer's marginal tax rate. The higher a taxpayer's marginal tax rate, the greater the incentive to make charitable contributions because the after-tax cost of the contribution is less than it would be at a lower marginal rate. Generally, individuals presently have a lower marginal tax rate, so there may be less incentive to make charitable contributions.

EXAMPLE 15.21

Jane Meyer, single, files an itemized return for tax year 2015. She is in the 28 percent tax bracket and has itemized deductions in excess of the standard deduction even without the inclusion of her $1,000 charitable deduction. The after-tax cost of the contribution would be $720 in 2015 due to a marginal tax rate of 28 percent.

The value of charitable contributions should by no means be discounted because of the possible reduction of tax advantages. Although itemized deductions have been greatly curtailed, charitable deductions are among the remaining items which can be fully included in itemization. Hence, though affected by the reduction in tax rates, charitable contributions still provide a good tax deduction and taxpayers should consider this if they intend to itemize. Taxpayers may deduct the full fair market value of appreciated capital gain property donated to a public charity, subject to the percentage-of-AGI limitations, without having to report the increase in value as income.

Charity volunteers who donate services while away from home are allowed a deduction for travel if they can prove that the charitable services performed during the trip were significant, and that they were required to engage in service activities for a significant portion of the trip. If a taxpayer incurs costs for third-party charity participants, the costs are allowable deductions.

EXAMPLE 15.22

Kimberly Keynote is a talented member of her church choir. Kim's church is sponsoring a benefit show to raise money for earthquake victims, and Kim was asked to participate as a back-up singer for one of the featured acts. Kim spent three days participating in the show in a neighboring state. During these three days, Kim spent most of her time studying the music, rehearsing, and performing. Kim donated clothing and food to an organization assisting the earthquake victims. Kim thoroughly enjoyed the trip and the exposure she gained.

Enjoyment of the trip does not prevent Kim from getting a deduction for her travel costs. Since Kim's participation is deemed substantial, her travel costs as well as the cost of food and clothing she donated are deductible.

¶15,547   CHARITABLE GIFTING

A charitable gifting program can provide tremendous benefits for a taxpayer because contributions, if they are properly planned, can be made at a time that is best for the donor. A taxpayer should ensure that all gifts generate the highest possible deduction and that the deduction is fully usable in the year of the gift. There are many different forms of giving available to individuals to facilitate their meeting these criteria.

The most common form of charitable contribution is a gift of cash or property to a public charity. However, other forms of gifting may provide greater tax or financial benefits. For example, a gift of appreciated property may provide greater tax benefits than a gift of cash.

EXAMPLE 15.23

For the last several years, Joe Joiner has given $5,000 cash to the church which he attends. Joe owns 100 shares of stock in XYZ Inc. that he purchased in 2005 for $2,000. The stock is currently worth $5,000. Joe could generate additional tax savings this year by contributing the appreciated securities to the church instead of the $5,000 cash. In either circumstance, his charitable contribution deduction will be $5,000. However, if Joe contributes the property in 2015, he will avoid paying tax on the $3,000 of appreciation in the securities, a savings of $450 (15 percent of $3,000) if he is in the 25 percent or higher tax bracket. Furthermore, Joe could repurchase the stock in XYZ with the $5,000 cash he has should he so choose.

Another advantageous method of gifting, especially for taxpayers who need the use of the income that the gift would provide if they kept it, is deferred gifting. For example, an individual could gift bonds that are owned to a public charity, but retain the right to use the interest income from the bonds until death. In that case, the taxpayer would receive a current deduction for the present value of the bonds given to the charity. In order to qualify for the deduction, the gift must be in the form of a charitable remainder annuity trust, a charitable remainder unitrust, a pooled income fund, or a future interest in a personal residence.

Another form of gifting is through the use of a charitable lead trust. In this situation, an individual can gift the income stream to be generated by an investment for a period of time but retain ownership of the underlying property. For example, an individual may transfer certain bonds to a trust, and specify that 100 percent of the interest earned by the bonds over the next five years will be given to a specified charity. After five years, the property will revert back to the taxpayer. The advantage of a lead trust is that the taxpayer receives a charitable deduction for the present value of the gift in the year the lead trust is established, even though the interest will actually be paid to the charity over the next five years. This form of gifting may be especially prudent if the individual's marginal tax rate may be declining in the future. Note, however, that the taxpayer will be taxed on the interest earned by the bonds for the life of the trust as the interest is earned.

The main point to remember about charitable remainder and lead trusts is that if they are properly structured, they provide a current charitable contribution deduction while allowing the donor to retain more of the benefits than if a complete gift had been made.

A final form of gifting that should be considered are contributions to a private foundation. Because private foundations are subject to many rules and restrictions, they are usually only used by individuals who wish to make substantial contributions. Their advantage is that they allow the taxpayer to make eligible contributions to purposes that usually are not undertaken by typical public charities. The disadvantage is that contributions to a private foundation are subject to the 30 percent of AGI contribution limitation.

¶15,555   PERSONAL INTEREST

The characterization of interest is an important tax planning consideration. In previous years an itemized deduction was allowed individual taxpayers for personal interest. In exemplifying what is considered personal debt, Congress has included personal use auto loans, credit card interest, and interest on tax deficiencies in general. No amount has been allowed as a deduction for 1991 and thereafter.

Taxpayers should try to pay off consumer loans; however, recharacterization may be a better alternative than acceleration. Given the rules on the deductibility of mortgage interest (discussed at ¶15,565), taxpayers may want to recharacterize their personal interest as qualified residence interest to achieve a full deduction for interest payments. For 2015, individuals are allowed to deduct up to $2,500 interest paid during the tax year on any qualified education loan to arrive at adjusted gross income subject to adjusted gross income phase-outs. (See ¶8210.)

¶15,565   QUALIFIED RESIDENCE INTEREST

Interest on debt secured by a mortgage on up to two residences is deductible. The deductible interest is limited to aggregate borrowings used to finance the taxpayer's purchase price plus the cost of improvements to the property (limited to $1 million) if the loans are newly incurred on or after October 13, 1987. Otherwise, for home mortgage indebtedness incurred prior to this date, the $1 million limit does not apply, allowing for 100 percent deductibility of such interest as home mortgage interest expense. In addition to the treatment of "acquisition indebtedness" as described above, a homeowner may fully deduct interest on home equity loans incurred on or after October 13, 1987 (typically, second mortgages secured by the real property), on up to $100,000 of loan proceeds, regardless of the manner in which such loan proceeds are actually spent. Again, this interest is fully deductible (with no ceiling limit imposed) if the home equity or second mortgage loan was obtained prior to October 13, 1987.

Home equity interest is not deductible for AMT purposes. The following example is provided to put these limitations into perspective.

| EXAMPLE 15.24 | Richard and Patti Steele purchased a new home in 2015 for $350,000, borrowing $250,000 to finance its acquisition. Later in the year, they borrow an additional $40,000 as a home equity loan, using the proceeds to pay off all outstanding personal debt obligations (such as their outstanding car loans). The interest expense on both loans is fully deductible as home mortgage interest expense, as the amounts borrowed are under both thresholds (i.e., $1,000,000 and $100,000, respectively). Keep in mind that a loan is limited to the fair market value of the home. |

From the above example, it is quite obvious that a strong incentive now exists to refinance existing consumer debt obligations into "home equity" indebtedness secured by a principal or second residence of the taxpayer. This will lead to full interest expense deductibility for an indefinite period of time in the future.

The second residence, which may be a cooperative apartment, must be used by the taxpayer the greater of 14 days or 10 percent of the rental period. The taxpayer may designate the second residence each year; naturally, the taxpayer would want to designate as the second residence that which has the highest mortgage interest payments. If a taxpayer owns a vacation home which is rented out, the taxpayer should compare the effects of classifying that home as a second residence rather than as rental property. In light of the passive loss rules and the extension of the depreciation period for real property, the mortgage interest deduction and property tax deductions allowed for a second residence may exceed the deductions allowed through rental property classification given the present limitations.

¶15,575   INVESTMENT INTEREST

Investment interest can be deducted only against net investment income. Investment interest is any allowable interest (not consumer or home mortgage interest) incurred to purchase or maintain property held for investment (including portfolio investments and nonpassive trade or business activities in which the taxpayer does not materially participate).

¶15,585   BUSINESS MEALS AND ENTERTAINMENT

Generally, deductions for business meals and entertainment are limited to 50 percent of their face value and, for employees, are subject to the 2 percent of AGI floor after application of the 50 percent disallowance rule. Furthermore, the 50 percent restriction is applied after a "lavish" or "extravagant" expenditure reduction has been made.

Business meals must meet the same "directly related to" or "associated with" test that entertainment expenses must currently meet. A discussion related to a taxpayer's investments is not sufficient, nor is a meal for public relations purposes (i.e., to "touch base" with business associates). Another limitation imposed is that the business meal is deductible only for the taxpayer or a representative, the taxpayer's business guest(s), and their spouses. Even if a taxpayer does not meet the "business meal" standard, a deduction for the event may be allowed. In the alternative, the taxpayer may claim the expense as a business gift but is limited to a $25 deduction per donee per year.

For tax planning purposes, some exceptions exist to the 50 percent rule as to business meals and entertainment expenses. If there is an adequate accounting and reimbursements equal expenses, neither the reimbursement nor the expenses have to be shown on the tax return. However, the reimburser is limited to the 50 percent deduction for the reimbursed expenses paid to the recipient. Reimbursed expenses are 100 percent deductible by the reimburser if the amount reimbursed is included as compensation to the recipient.

It is not necessary that the recipient be an employee, but only that the full value of the business meal or entertainment benefit is taken into account for tax purposes. In tax planning, employees and others who incur business meal and entertainment expenses on behalf of someone else should try to establish a reimbursement arrangement so as not to be subjected to the 50 percent of cost and 2 percent of AGI floor limits. A reimbursement arrangement is especially desirable if the employee or outsider is a highly compensated individual where the 2 percent floor represents a substantial amount or if the taxpayer is otherwise a nonitemizer.

EXAMPLE 15.25

Eddie Marsh is an outside salesperson for Printing Partners. Eddie conducts most of his business deals over meals or other forms of entertainment and has incurred $4,000 of expenses for 2015. Eddie's commission income plus AGI for 2015 is $40,000.

If Eddie's employer has a reimbursement policy, Eddie will not be "out-of-pocket" any portion of the expense and Printing Partners will be allowed a $2,000 (50% × $4,000) business expense deduction.

If Printing Partners does not have a reimbursement arrangement and Eddie is a nonitemizer, he would be out-of-pocket $4,000. If Eddie itemizes, his business expense deduction will be computed as follows:

Entertainment expenses ($4,000 × 50%)	$2,000
Less: ($40,000 × 2%)	800
Business expense deduction	$1,200

Eddie's nondeductible costs would be $2,800 ($4,000 – $1,200).

If Eddie were a 50 percent owner of Printing Partners, it might be more advantageous for the company to have a $2,000 deduction versus Eddie's $1,200 deduction depending upon the individual and corporate tax rates involved.

Transportation to or from the business meal or entertainment site is not subject to the 50 percent limit. This exception could be easily overlooked since everything else associated with the business meal (including gratuities and taxes) is subject to the 50 percent limitation.

EXAMPLE 15.26

Lynn Baker, a lawyer and an employee, has kept an excellent diary of all of her business meals and entertainment expenditures. Lynn is not participating in any reimbursement plans. In 2015, she incurred $9,000 in meals and entertainment expenses, $500 in cab fares, and $1,000 in taxes and gratuities and her AGI is $176,800. Assuming Lynn itemizes, her allowable business meal and entertainment deduction is $1,964. Lynn also has charitable contributions and deductible taxes of $12,000.

Meals and entertainment	$9,000
Taxes and gratuities	1,000
Total expenditures subject to the 50% limit	$10,000
	× .50
50% amount deductible	$5,000
100% expenditures	500
Total deductible expenses	$5,500
Less: 2% floor	3,536
Total allowable deduction, meals and entertainment	$1,964
Total itemized deductions	$13,964

Another expense not subject to the 50 percent limitation is the cost of samples and promotional activities. A full deduction is allowed if these items are made available to the general public. This exception could provide a tax benefit for outside salespersons.

Tickets for charitable sports events can escape the 50 percent limitation rule. The event must benefit a tax-exempt organization, the entire net proceeds must be distributed to charity, and charity volunteers must perform substantially all of the work. Sports tickets for charitable events may be a favorable perk for business associates since the taxpayer's deduction includes the entire ticket package: cost-event seating and related services, meals which are included as part of the event, parking, and the use of entertainment areas. Unfortunately for fans of high school and college sporting events, the cost of tickets to these events is not excluded because the referees and coaches are paid employees of the event. But charity golfing event costs are deductible even if participating golfers are eligible for prizes.

The remaining exceptions apply more to companies than to individuals, but should be mentioned because owners of businesses may be able to take advantage of them. Fringe benefits which are deemed "de minimis fringes" or subsidized eating facilities are fully deductible by the provider. This includes the cost of traditional retirement gifts for length of service. Finally, recreational or social activities paid for by an employer are deductible in full by the employer.

¶15,595 BUSINESS AND EDUCATIONAL TRAVEL

Employees may also want to arrange a reimbursement agreement with employers for travel and transportation expenditures since they too are subject to the 2 percent of AGI floor. Travel expenses, however, are not subject to the 50 percent limitation.

The meal expenses incurred while the taxpayer is in travel status are deductible (subject to the 50 percent limitation) regardless of whether the meal is "directly related to" or "associated with" the taxpayer's trade or business provided the taxpayer eats alone or with "non-business connected persons." If the taxpayer dines with "business connected persons," the "directly related to" or "associated with" rule applies. This should serve as a rule of caution for taxpayers who are attending a convention. If dining with other conventioneers, the taxpayer may have to prove business purpose.

EXAMPLE 15.27

Cindy Bane is away from home for a trade convention. Cindy's air fare of $150 and hotel accommodations of $300 are fully reimbursed by her employer. Cindy entertains business associates for two days, incurring a cost of $100 to discuss personal vacations. Cindy dines alone on the third day incurring a cost of $50. Cindy's intra-city transportation cost and gratuities totaled $120. Cindy's other miscellaneous itemized deductions totaled $600 and her AGI was $25,000. What is Cindy's deduction from AGI for the above expenses?

The reimbursed expenses of $450 (i.e., $150 + $300) are "above the line" deductions. $100 meal expenses are disallowed since the meals were with business associates, but not incurred in the active conduct of a trade or business. (Cindy may be better off taking a per diem allowance.)

Meals remaining ($50 × 50%)	$25
Other travel expenses	120
Other miscellaneous deductions	600
	$745
Less: 2% of AGI limit	– 500
Net deduction	$245

The deduction for luxury water travel used for business transportation is limited to twice the U.S. government per diem rate. In contrast, business gatherings on cruise ships are not subject to this per diem limit. The $2,000 deduction allowed for certain cruise conventions remains available. If a taxpayer chooses water transportation for business purposes, even when subject to the per diem restrictions, the taxpayer should opt for an expense package which does not separately state meal and entertainment costs. If the cost of meals and entertainment is not distinguished from other costs, the 50 percent rule is suspended. Conversely, if the cost of meals and entertainment is separately stated, then the 50 percent rule would apply prior to application of the per diem restriction.

In investigating possible seminar opportunities, taxpayers should ascertain that they can establish a link between their purpose in attending the seminar and their trade or business. The costs of attending seminars with a purpose associated with the individual's passive or investment income sources are not deductible. This means that the cost of attending seminars for the purpose of improving investment income or increasing one's investment knowledge is not deductible.

Similarly, regarding education, the taxpayer must prove that the travel expenses were for educational purposes only. The taxpayer may be able to overcome this hurdle if the taxpayer can establish a specific need for the travel, transforming the travel costs into business expenses related to education. To explain the case in point, travel to expand one's cultural enrichment for an education subject is not allowed, but traveling to utilize research or educational facilities available only in the place of travel is allowed.

EXAMPLE 15.28

Lance Coons, an economics professor, journeys to Russia to obtain a "general feel" for the country's economic system, which is a topic covered in two of his courses. Lance's travel costs are not deductible. If he needs to do library research for a proposed article and Russia has the only library facilities to conduct this research, his travel costs are deductible, provided his nontravel research costs are also deductible.

¶15,601   HOBBY LOSSES

The profit test for hobby losses is such so that an activity must now show a profit in three out of five consecutive years, to escape presumption as a hobby. Hobby loss deductions are limited to hobby gross income. There remains an exception for horse breeding, training, showing, or racing, which must show a profit in two out of seven consecutive years for the activity to be deemed operated for profit.

A rebuttable presumption is created that an activity was not engaged in as a hobby (thus permitting the taxpayer to avoid the restrictions on the deduction of hobby losses) if profit resulted from the activity. A taxpayer may elect to delay a determination as to whether the presumption applies until the close of the fourth (or sixth) taxable year after the taxable year in which the taxpayer first engages in the activity. A taxpayer is required to execute a waiver of the statute of limitations in order to make the election.

As a tax planning device, in proving business motive, it is very significant that the taxpayer be able to demonstrate a businesslike manner of conducting the activity. Proper accounting records, arm's-length transactions, and essential legal documents are among the elements which exemplify a businesslike manner.

¶15,605   HOME OFFICE EXPENSES

To curtail abuses in business deductions for home office expenses, rules have been adopted that severely restrict the allowance of such deductions for many taxpayers. Home office expenses are deductible only if a portion of the home (or separate structure) is used exclusively on a regular basis as (1) the principal place of the taxpayer's business, (2) a meeting place for dealing with patients, clients, or customers, or (3) a separate structure not attached to the dwelling unit, in connection with the taxpayers trade or business. The Taxpayer Relief Act of 1997 expanded the definition of "principal place of business." After 1998, a home office qualifies as a taxpayer's principal place of business under the Act if the office is used by the taxpayer to conduct administrative or management activities of the taxpayer's trade or business and if there is no other fixed location of the trade or business where the taxpayer conducts substantial administrative or management activities of the trade or business.

The home office deduction is limited to gross income from the activity, reduced by expenses that are deductible without regard to business use (such as home mortgage interest) and all other deductible expenses attributable to the activity but not allocable to the use of the unit itself. Deductions not allowable because of the gross income limitation may be carried forward for deduction in a succeeding year. There is an optional deduction for home office limited to $1,500, based on $5 per square foot for up to 300 square feet. See Chapter 7.

Employees are subject to additional restrictive rules. In order for an employee to qualify for the home office deduction, the employee must meet the requirements stated above, and the exclusive use of the home office must be for the convenience of the employer. However, regardless of whether or not an employee meets the requirements, an employee is denied a home office deduction for any portion of the home rented or leased to the employer (except for expenses such as home mortgage interest and real property taxes that are deductible absent business use). Additionally, any unreimbursed expenses of an employee (including home office expenses) must be taken as a miscellaneous itemized deduction subject to the 2 percent of AGI floor.

The rule which disallows the home office deduction for an employer/lessee arrangement also applies to independent contractors. Independent contractors are treated as employees of those for whom they perform services and likewise are not able to deduct home office expenses where the independent contractor leases part of a home to the other contracting party. Again, deductions that are allowed regardless of the home office characterization, such as home mortgage interest or real property taxes, are deductible.

The gross income limitation for home office deductions has been further modified to include a reference to rental activity of the home. Deductions for the business use of a dwelling unit that the taxpayer also used as a home are limited to the amount of gross income received from the trade or business activity that is conducted in the home and from the amount of income generated from rental activity of the home. This amount is further reduced by (1) those deductions allowed for expenses that are deductible without regard to the business use of the residence, and (2) those deductions that are allocable to the trade or business (or rental activity) in which such use occurs but that are not allocable to such use.

In view of the many severe restrictions, taxpayers must tread carefully if they are planning on being allowed deductions for home office expenses. "Exclusively" means just that: Use of the business portion of a home by the taxpayer or members of the family for purposes unrelated to business will result in the disallowance of business expense deductions. Nevertheless, a taxpayer can have a principal place of business for each separate trade or business. However, with respect to personal investment activities, the IRS follows the rule that such activities are not eligible for home office deductions. This deduction is available only to those who are considered traders in their activities.

Taxpayers may exclude the gain on the sale of a residence attributed to home office usage (up to the $250,000 of $500,000 limit). However, if depreciation was taken on a home office after May 6, 1997, it is recaptured at a maximum rate of 25 percent. (See ¶7351 for an optional method of claiming a home office deduction.)

Retirement Planning

In regard to formal retirement plans sponsored by employers, the rules governing qualified plan requirements and plan distributions have been made more stringent. The changes may cause a gradual shift in the responsibility of retirement planning from the employer to the individual due to the potential increase in the cost and administration of plans in compliance with "qualified" plan provisions. With its objective of filtering the benefits of qualified retirement plans to rank-and-file employees, Congress has adopted modifications which could motivate some employers to decrease plan coverage.

Among the changes which may serve to increase the cost of qualified plans are more rapid vesting schedules, increased integrated benefit levels, stricter coverage requirements, and antidiscrimination rules. Such potential indirect consequences accentuate the motivation for taxpayers to maximize opportunities available for tax-free accumulation of retirement funds.

¶15,701   INDIVIDUAL RETIREMENT ACCOUNTS (IRAS)

Regular IRA

In 2015, the IRA deduction is not allowed for individuals who are active participants in a qualified retirement plan where their AGI exceeds $71,000 for a single return and $118,000 for a joint return. The deduction is phased out for individuals whose AGI exceeds $61,000 for a single return and $98,000 for a joint return. The taxpayer's deduction amount is reduced proportionately according to the ratio of "excess AGI" to the $10,000 phaseout range for singles and $20,000 phaseout range for joint filers (rounded to the next lowest multiple of 10). Therefore, for single filers whose income level allows them to deduct the maximum $5,500 contribution (under age 50), the $5,500 deduction is reduced $550 ($275 for joint filers) for each $1,000 by which the individual's AGI exceeds the $61,000 ceiling ($98,000 for joint filers). In addition, a $1,000 catch-up contribution is available to taxpayers age 50 and over, increasing the annual, per-taxpayer amount to $6,500.

EXAMPLE 15.29   Sam Saver, single, age 40, with adjusted gross income of $65,000 for 2015 is eligible to invest in a deductible IRA. His contributions deduction is reduced by $2,000 ($500 × 4 thousands of dollars of AGI over $61,000) to $3,500.

Even if a taxpayer is precluded from making a deductible contribution, the taxpayer may make a nondeductible contribution. Although the taxpayer does not receive an IRA deduction, the taxpayer is able to defer the interest earned on the IRA until the funds are distributed. The nondeductible contributions are subject to the same limits as deductible contributions, the lesser of $5,500 or 100 percent of compensation, or designated nondeductible contributions.

Homemakers may take a full $5,500 deduction ($6,500 if age 50 or older) for a contribution to an IRA, regardless of whether their spouse is covered under a retirement plan at work. The maximum deductible contribution for an individual who is not an active participant, but whose spouse is, will be phased out between $183,000 and $193,000 of AGI.

Whether a taxpayer should make nondeductible IRA contributions hinges on the yield of the IRA investment, and whether greater after-tax return could be achieved outside of the IRA. As a long-term investment, the return on IRAs may prevail over the return on many alternative investments since the earnings base portion of the IRA is not reduced by yearly income taxes. Furthermore, IRAs may provide a means by which to shelter gain on high yield investments previously subject to the capital gains exclusion.

However, before opting for a higher yielding IRA, taxpayers will want to consider whether they want to subject retirement funds to a possible increase in risk. Upper income taxpayers who may have a relatively high tolerance for risk may still be attracted to the deferred earnings potential for IRAs since they lost many tax shelters under tax reform. Individuals choosing IRAs as a means of deferring income should realize that nondeductible IRAs will not usually prove to be a good short- to intermediate-term investment for the taxpayer who faces a 10 percent penalty on early withdrawals.

Coverdell Education Savings Accounts

Education savings accounts allow a taxpayer to contribute up to $2,000 per beneficiary (child) per year to save for education expenses. Although contributions are not deductible, earnings on contributions to an education savings account will be distributed tax free provided they are used to pay for the beneficiary's qualified education expenses. The $2,000 annual contribution limit is phased out for joint filers with modified AGI between $190,000 and $220,000 and for single filers with modified AGI between $95,000 and $110,000.

Distributions from education savings accounts are only excludable from gross income to the extent that they do not exceed the beneficiary's qualified higher education expenses during the year in which the distribution is made. A beneficiary may attend an eligible education institution on a full-time, half-time, or less than half-time basis; however, room and board expenses only qualify as higher education expenses if the beneficiary is enrolled on at least a half-time basis. Distributions are deemed to be paid from both contributions and earnings on a pro rata share basis. If aggregate distributions do not exceed qualified expenses for the year, all of the distributions will be free of tax. If aggregate distributions exceed qualified expenses, a portion of the earnings will be included in gross income.

After the beneficiary attains the age of 18, no contributions may be accepted by the education savings account. Also, when the beneficiary reaches the age of 30, any remaining balance in the education savings account must be distributed and the earnings portion of the distribution will be included in the beneficiary's gross income and are subject to a 10 percent early withdrawal penalty. However, the amount may be rolled over into another education savings account for the benefit of another member of the beneficiary's family. The types of expenses that may be paid with tax-free earnings from the education savings account include elementary and secondary education expenses.

Roth IRA

Nondeductible contributions can be made to a type of tax-favored IRA known as the Roth IRA. The buildup of earnings within the account may be tax free depending on how and when withdrawals are made. The maximum yearly contribution that can be made by an individual to all IRAs (deductible, nondeductible, and Roth) is $5,500 ($6,500 for taxpayers age 50 and over), not counting rollover distributions. However, unlike regular, deductible and nondeductible IRAs, taxpayers may continue to make contributions to a Roth IRA even after attaining the age of 70½. The maximum yearly contribution limitation of $5,500 for Roth IRAs is phased out for single taxpayers with AGI between $116,000 and $131,000 and for joint filers with AGI between $183,000 and $193,000.

Qualified distributions from a Roth IRA are not taxable and are not subjected to the 10 percent early withdrawal penalty. In order to qualify, a distribution may not be made before the end of the five-tax-year period beginning with the first tax year for which the individual made a contribution to the Roth IRA. In addition, a distribution must be made on or after the individual attains the age of 59 ½, must be made to a beneficiary on or after the taxpayer's death, must be attributable to the individual being disabled, or must be used to pay for "qualified first-time homebuyer expenses." All nonqualified distributions are made from contributions in the account first. Only when distributions exceed total contributions will they be attributable to earnings and be includable in gross income.

An ordinary IRA may be converted into a Roth IRA. Any earnings from the ordinary IRA are included in gross income for the year in which the distribution is made. In the case of a rollover conversion to a Roth IRA, the 10 percent early withdrawal tax does not apply. Taxpayers may find that the Roth IRA is a better retirement vehicle than a regular IRA because earnings on the Roth IRA are tax free, rather than tax deferred.

¶15,715   SECTION 401(k) PLANS

Although elective employee contributions are limited, taxpayers should still utilize Section 401(k) plans to the extent possible since they are one of the few remaining means of tax deferral on before-tax dollars and the associated return on the investment. Elective contributions do not have the same magnitude of savings potential due to a reduction in the tax rates, but as previously mentioned, with a potential increase in the responsibility on individuals for retirement planning, use of Section 401(k) plans may become increasingly important.

Participation in a Section 401(k) plan may prevent a taxpayer from receiving an IRA contribution deduction (though the taxpayer may make nondeductible contributions and defer gains earned on the contribution), but since the IRA limit is only $5,500, the Section 401(k) plan may prove to be more beneficial. In addition, the Section 401(k) plan contributions are excluded from current income in their entirety.

The Roth 401(k) arrangement allows a nondeductible contribution for employees up to $18,000 (an additional $6,000 for individuals age 50 or more). The employer may match these contributions with a total combined limit of $53,000 in 2015 and this match goes into a regular 401(k) plan. Later distributions, however, are not taxed.

¶15,725   RETIREMENT PLAN DISTRIBUTIONS

The 10 percent premature withdrawal penalty for distributions to a taxpayer prior to attaining age 59 ½ covers qualified plan withdrawals and distributions as well as IRA account distributions. However, there are a number of exceptions which allow a taxpayer to escape the early withdrawal penalty for withdrawals made from qualified retirement plans and may make emergencies or a desired early retirement easier to manage financially. These exceptions include military call up, amounts to pay qualified higher education expenses, withdrawals made for the reason of hardship, level annuity payments for life after separation from service, early retirement for a taxpayer 55 years or older, withdrawals for payment of medical expenses, distributions to beneficiaries after the account owner's death, withdrawals for first-time homebuying (a lifetime limit of $10,000), and some employee stock option plan distributions. The hardship withdrawal, early retirement, and employee stock option plan exceptions are not applicable to IRA distributions.

Qualified plan distributions must begin no later than April 1 of the year following the year in which the participant turns age 70 ½, regardless of whether the participant is still employed. Failure to comply with this rule will result in a 50 percent penalty on the difference between the required (if greater) and actual distributed amount. A possible means by which a taxpayer can reduce the required distribution amount is to use contingent beneficiaries and annual readjustment of distributions based on life expectancy which extend the period for which payout of plan benefits is expected.

The five-year averaging rule for lump-sum distributions is not available after 1999, and the 10-year averaging rule is available only to participants who were age 50 prior to 1986.

SUMMARY

- Taxpayers may do tax planning in the form of avoiding income recognition and deferral or acceleration of income or expenses.

- Self-employed individuals often have tax advantages over the employee.

- Family tax planning can involve some income shifting, college planning, and divorce planning.

- Taxpayers can do tax planning related to fixed assets, leasing versus buying, sale versus like-kind exchanges, involuntary conversion elections, residences and vacation homes, and capital and Section 1231 assets.

- Itemized deductions take various forms: some are not subject to any deduction floor; some are allowed only to the extent that they exceed a fixed percentage of AGI; and some are limited for high-income taxpayers.

- Planning can be done with respect to many deductions, such as charitable giving, residence interest, business and educational expenses, and home office expenses.

- Proper retirement planning can be very helpful to taxpayers.

QUESTIONS

1. How may a taxpayer avoid recognition of income?

2. How might a taxpayer postpone or delay the recognition of income?

3. How might a taxpayer accelerate deductions?

4. In general, what tax planning steps should an individual take to maximize the standard deduction or itemized deductions?

5. What are some tax advantages that a self-employed individual has over an employee?

6. How might one possibly reduce the tax disadvantages for taxpayers who would like to transfer assets to children under age 14?

7. How might a taxpayer best provide for the future college education of his or her children, given the present tax environment?

8. What are the major tax factors to be considered by divorced taxpayers?

9. Are there advantages to leasing rather than buying assets?

10. Why could tax planning for like-kind exchanges, sale of residences, and involuntary conversions be important in 2015?

11. Which employee expenses are deductions from adjusted gross income?

12. What are some tax planning pointers that should be considered given the three-tier structure for itemized deductions?

13. Although personal interest deductions have been phased out, how can taxpayers possibly obtain interest deductions on what might appear to be personal debt?

14. What tax disadvantages are there for an employee's business meals and entertainment deductions?

15. When can an employee obtain an IRA deduction? What are factors that might determine whether an employee should invest in an IRA?

16. Joyce and Peter have an adjusted gross income of $80,000 and have on average about $14,000 in itemized deductions. Their charitable contributions average $8,000 per year. What tax planning can Joyce and Peter do?

17. How can donating appreciated stock to a charitable organization, rather than giving cash, be beneficial to a taxpayer?

18. What are the basic guidelines for making a Roth IRA contribution?

19. What factors should be considered in rolling over previously contributed retirement account funds into a Roth IRA?

20. What is the Coverdell Education Savings Account?

PROBLEMS

21. Jean and Larry wish to transfer assets to their 8-year-old son and to their 24-year-old daughter. What step(s) could they take to minimize the taxes to the family overall?

22. Mary transfers assets that yield interest income of $2,200 each year to her daughter, Missy, age 12. How will the interest be taxed to Missy?

23. Mr. and Mrs. Champagne shift unearned income of $27,000 in the beginning of 2015 to their son Morris, age 24. Their top marginal tax rate is 28 percent since they have taxable income of $180,000 a year. How much will the Champagnes save by transferring income to Morris?

24. Ron redeems Series EE U.S. Savings Bonds in 2015 for a total amount of $16,000 (i.e., $10,000 in principal and $6,000 in interest). What portion of the interest is excluded from income, given that his educational expenditures totaled only $12,000 in 2015, he is married and files a joint return, and has adjusted gross income (computed on a modified basis) of $123,250 for that year?

25. Alice and Bill are getting divorced in 2015. Alice would like to receive $150,000 as early as possible. Bill would like to obtain the deduction for the payment, but has some liquidity problems, so would like at least until February 2017 to complete the payment. How could payments be made in order for them to be deductible by Bill without his being penalized for front-loading the payments?

26. Jane, single, has an apartment building with a fair market value of $800,000 and an adjusted basis of $200,000, depreciated under the straight-line method. She would like either to exchange this building for another one or to sell this building and buy another building. What factors should Jane consider in making her decision assuming she is in the highest tax bracket and would make the sale or exchange in 2015?

27. Steven, an accountant who works for ABC Company, generally has adjusted gross income of about $40,000, except that in 2015 his adjusted gross income is $20,000. His charitable contributions average $1,500 a year and his miscellaneous employee expenses average $900 a year, of which $400 is controllable (i.e., can be incurred in other years). What should Steven do to maximize his deductions in 2015?

28. Andrew, an employee, has the following expenses during 2015:

Moving expenses	$5,000
State and local income and property taxes	2,000
Gambling losses to the extent of gambling winnings	300

How much of these items would be included in Andrew's itemized deductions?

29. The Harrisons wish to purchase a home for $200,000. The bank extends a mortgage to the Harrisons in the amount of $150,000. Subsequent to the acquisition, the Harrisons borrow an additional $125,000, $100,000 of which is used to make improvements to the property and $25,000 of which is used to purchase a new car. How much of the combined interest expense is tax deductible and for what reasons?

30. Bob bought a residence for $150,000. He financed 65 percent of the purchase and made $15,000 worth of improvements with additional second mortgage financing. He has paid $2,000 towards the principal balance of the first loan. How much more may Bob borrow in "acquisition indebtedness" and still qualify for the residential interest deduction?

31. Linda is an outside salesperson for XYZ Company. On the average, she spends $6,000 for meals or other forms of entertainment in connection with her business. Her adjusted gross income is $60,000. What alternatives should Linda and/or her employer consider?

32. Matt, single, age 35, has an adjusted gross income of $62,000. He is a participant in a qualified retirement plan, but is eligible to invest in a deductible IRA. What is the amount of his allowable IRA deduction for 2015?

33. Cheri and Rick, age 45, have an adjusted gross income of $104,000 and are both active participants in qualified retirement plans. What is the amount of their allowable IRA deductions for 2015?

34. Which of the following expenses is a deduction for adjusted gross income?
    a. Travel and transportation expenses of an employee (prior to reimbursement)
    b. Moving expenses
    c. Charitable contributions
    d. Mortgage interest
    e. None of the above

35. Which of the following expenses is a deduction from adjusted gross income and not subject to the 2 percent floor?
    a. Employee travel and transportation expenses
    b. Employee dues to professional societies
    c. Legal and accounting fees paid for tax advice
    d. Charitable contributions
    e. None of the above

36. Which of the following expenses is subject to the 2 percent floor?
    a. Casualty and theft losses
    b. Medical expenses
    c. Employee meals and entertainment
    d. Gambling losses to the extent of gambling income
    e. None of the above

37. The Section 179 expensing election for a taxpayer who invests $210,000 in tangible personal property in 2015 is:
    a. $15,000
    b. $25,000
    c. $490,000
    d. $500,000
    e. $210,000

38. Which of the following education credits were made available by the Taxpayer Relief Act of 1997?
    a. The Continuing Education Credit
    b. The Hope Scholarship Credit
    c. The Lifetime Learning Credit
    d. Only (b) and (c)
    e. All of the above

39. **Comprehensive Problem.** Gail and Ron, both age 50, have two boys, ages 24 and 16, and adjusted gross income of $226,800 in 2015. Consider each of the following parts independently.
    a. Gail and Ron would like to transfer to their children assets that would best reduce the family's overall tax liability. They have assets earning $20,000 that could be transferred and they are not concerned about giving each child an equal amount. Any inequity to one child would be made up to him later. What should they do? Assume allowable standard deductions and that they will have adjusted gross income of about $225,000 in 2016.
    b. Gail, a Spanish teacher in college, would like to go to Spain to do research on Spanish literature. A library in Madrid is the only place she can get the information. Cost of the travel is as follows:

Airfare	$1,000
Lodging in Madrid	800
Meals in Madrid	500
Meals in the rest of Spain	300
Lodging in the rest of Spain	400

How much of the expenses can be deducted?
    c. Gail and Ron's itemized deductions consist of:

Mortgage interest	$6,000
Personal interest	1,000
State income tax	7,400
State sales tax	1,000
Miscellaneous expenses	2,800

How much of each of the expenses would be deductible?

40. **Research Problem.** Could assets be given by John and Mary to their grandchildren, Susan and Tom, ages five and six, so as to avoid having the unearned income taxed at Susan and Tom's parents' tax rate?

Chapter
16

Partnerships, Corporations, and S Corporations

OBJECTIVES

After completing Chapter 16, you should be able to:

1. Identify problems in the choice of form of entity.
2. Recognize the characteristics of a partnership.
3. Determine the characteristics of a corporation, Subchapter C type.
4. Determine the characteristics of a corporation, Subchapter S type.
5. Determine when entity income is taxable to the owners.

OVERVIEW

The decisions in selecting the form of an entity involve weighing the elements of risk as well as the division of rewards.

The simplest and most common form of multiple ownership of a business is the partnership. Deceptively easy to form, it is extremely flexible in its operation and its recognition of divisions of labor and capital contribution. Susceptible to tax avoidance, limitations are placed upon transactions between partners and the partnership, the choice of tax years, division of items of income, deductions, and credits.

Limitation of liability and fringe benefits are often the impetus for using the corporate form. However, since creditors are going to require owners to guarantee debt of thinly capitalized corporations, the liability limitation may be nonexistent. Limitations are placed on the fringe benefits of owners of partnerships and corporations. Complex rules govern transfers to and distributions from the corporation. The problem of multiple taxation of the same income and the problems of disassociation through redemption of interest or liquidation of the entity are complicated and involved.

The S corporation, now treated for the most part in a manner very similar to a partnership, provides for closely held business groups an intermediate choice between the partnership and the type C corporation.

Choice of Business Organization

¶16,001   ## GENERAL CONSIDERATIONS

Any person embarking upon a business enterprise must initially decide upon which business form may best be used to accomplish the business's objectives. If the entrepreneur has ample resources, both in talent and finances, the choice may be to "go it alone."

On the other hand, if financing or talent must be attracted from others, then a partnership or a corporation may be the logical choice. In addition, in attracting others into the enterprise, the exposure to loss is diluted. As had been emphasized in commercial law, each general partner is either jointly or jointly and severally liable for the liabilities of the partnership.

¶16,005   ## LIMITATION OF LIABILITY

If limitation of liability is an essential element, the corporate form offers the most promise. But from a practical point of view, the limited liability touted for corporate operations is often more apparent than real. For example, on commencing business in the corporate form, in many instances the owner will be the principal person. Any acts on behalf of the corporation will be done by the owner. If the owner is negligent in performance, he or she will be personally liable for any resulting injury. True, insurance will indemnify the owner against liabilities arising from the wrongful acts of others employed by the corporation. But, in most instances, no matter what business form is chosen, insurance to indemnify against such eventualities is a necessity.

The hope of personal liability protection for the debts of the corporation is often a forlorn wish. A corporation devoid of substantial assets (as most beginning corporations are) will be unable to obtain credit without the personal guarantee of the owner. Thus, if the corporation is unable to service its debts, the owner must answer on the guarantee. Of course, if the corporation has ample resources to establish its own credit rating, the owners may be insulated from personal liability.

Characteristics of a Partnership

¶16,101   ## ORGANIZING A PARTNERSHIP

In general, when parties organize a partnership, they are merely converting personal assets or investment assets into business assets, or they are changing the form in which they have been conducting business (i.e., from a sole proprietorship to the partnership form). While gain or loss will likely be *realized* on the exchange of these assets for an interest in the partnership, the transaction generates no wherewithal to pay tax, and no taxable gain or loss is *recognized*.

¶16,109   ## ORGANIZATION EXPENSE & START-UP COSTS

Often there is much preplanning prior to the commencement of a partnership. The costs incurred incident to its creation which are chargeable to its capital account have a theoretical life equal to that of the partnership. The partnership may elect to take a deduction for the year in which the partnership begins business an amount equal to the lesser of the amount of organizational expenditures or $5,000 reduced by the amount organizational expenditures exceed $50,000. The remainder of the organizational expenditures are deductible ratably over the 180-month period beginning with the month in which the partnership begins business. Code Sec. 709(b)(1). If this election is not made, no deduction is permitted for these organizational expenses.

The qualifying expenses include legal fees in drafting the partnership agreement, accounting fees for establishing records, expenses of planning meetings for the organizers, and any organizational fees which might be charged by state or local authorities.

The expenses are limited to those incurred within a reasonable time prior to the commencement of the partnership's business and incurred prior to the filing date (without extensions) for the partnership's first income tax return. The filing date is the 15th day of the fourth month after the end of the partnership's tax year. Cash basis partnerships may include in organization costs only those costs actually paid prior to the end of the partnership's first tax year.

Closely associated with organization expenses are the costs of investigating and starting up the operation (e.g., the cost of site selection, of market surveys and of training personnel, advertising, etc.). Again, in theory these costs should be spread over the period of benefit, and they should not be currently expensed. The partnership may elect to deduct the lesser of the amount of start-up expenditures with respect to the trade or business or $5,000 reduced by the amount by which such start-up expenditures exceed $50,000. These amounts were raised to $10,000 and $60,000 for 2010 only. The remainder of such start-up expenditures are allowed as a deduction ratably over the 180-month period beginning with the month in which the active trade or business begins. Code Sec. 195.

¶16,115   PARTNER'S BASIS IN THE PARTNERSHIP

There is no recognition of the gain or loss on the transfer of property to the partnership. In general, the basis for the partner's interest in the partnership is the basis for the property transferred, and that basis is subsequently increased by:

1. The basis of any additional contributions made by the partner to the partnership
2. The partner's share of any partnership ordinary income
3. The partner's share of long-term and short-term capital gains recognized by the partnership
4. The partner's share of net Section 1231 gains recognized by the partnership
5. The partner's share of tax-exempt income of the partnership
6. Dividends and interest reportable by the partner as portfolio income
7. The partner's share of any other partnership item of income required, or agreed, to be reported separately by the partner
8. The partner's share of any increase in partnership liabilities

The partner's basis is decreased (but not below zero) by:

1. The basis of any partnership property distributed to the partner, to the extent of the partner's basis in the partnership interest
2. The partner's share of any partnership ordinary loss
3. The partner's share of long-term and short-term capital losses recognized by the partnership
4. The partner's share of net Section 1231 losses recognized by the partnership
5. The partner's share of nondeductible items paid or accrued by the partnership
6. The partner's share of partnership charitable contributions
7. The partner's share of taxes paid or accrued to foreign countries or U.S. possessions
8. The partner's share of any other partnership item of loss or deduction required, or agreed, to be reported separately by the partner
9. The partner's share of any decrease in partnership liabilities

Some of these adjustments are discussed in more detail below.

¶16,120   PARTNERSHIP INCOME AND DEDUCTIONS

In a sense, the partnership's "ordinary income or loss" is the composite of the items of income and deductions which are not required to be reported separately by the individual partners. A partnership in the business of selling goods reports its income from its business operations (i.e., sales, cost of goods sold, selling, and administrative expenses).

Because some items of income and expense may or do receive special treatment on the individual income tax returns of the partners, they are required to be reported separately. Each partner must be notified of the share of the ordinary income or loss of the partnership's trade or business activities and the share of the following items:

- Net income/loss from rental real estate activities
- Net income/loss from other rental activities

- Portfolio income, including:

  - Interest income
  - Dividend income
  - Royalty income
  - Net short-term capital gains/losses

- Net long-term capital gains/losses
- Guaranteed payments
- Casualty gain/losses
- Section 1231 gain/loses (excluding casualties)

■ Each partner must also have separately stated the following items of deduction:

- Charitable contributions
- Expensing of cost recovery property under Section 179
- Expenses of producing portfolio income
- Deductions to be reported as an itemized deduction by the partner
- Premature withdrawal penalties imposed on savings
- Retirement payments made for partners

In addition, the separate reporting includes each partner's share of self-employment income, preference items, investment interest, foreign taxes, and the various credits and their recapture. Also, if the partners have agreed to a division of any item in a manner different from the general determination of the partnership income or loss, that item must be separately reported. The above items are put on Schedule K, which is part of the partnership return, Form 1065.

¶16,125   REPORTING REQUIREMENTS

Partnership Form 1065 is accompanied by a separate Schedule K-1 for each partner where there are listed (1) each partner's share of the partnership's ordinary income; (2) the partner's "guaranteed payments" (i.e., salary or interest on capital investment that the partnership has agreed to pay whether or not profits exist); and (3) all of the items mentioned above that require separate treatment on the individual partner's personal income tax return.

As will be discussed later, because of inequities resulting from a difference in bases of property contributed to the partnership and its fair market value at contribution, the partners are required to make "special allocation" of items which ordinarily would be included in partnership ordinary income. Their exclusion from partnership ordinary income requires their separate reporting.

Tax Year of the Partnership

Generally, new and existing partnerships are required to elect the "majority interest tax year" of their partners (i.e., the same tax year of partners who have a common tax year and together own a majority interest in the partnership's capital and profits). If there is no majority interest tax year, then the partnership must elect that year used by the principal partners (i.e., the year of those partners owning 5 percent or more interest in either the profits or capital of the partnership). If the principal partners do not have the same tax year, then the partnership must use the year which gives the least aggregate deferral of income to its partners.

EXAMPLE 16.1

Bob and Tony begin the BT partnership. BT is a limited partnership. Bob and Tony are BT's general partners, and there are 20 limited partners who contribute substantial amounts of capital to the partnership. Bob and Tony each have a 20 percent interest in the partnership's capital and profits. Each of the limited partners has a 3 percent interest. Bob and Tony have very successful sole proprietorships, and each has a fiscal tax year which runs from October 1 through September 30. Half of the limited partners have a calendar tax year, and half have a fiscal tax year which runs from July 1 through June 30. The BT partnership must adopt a fiscal year which runs from October 1 through September 30 as its tax year. The reason is that there are no partners who in the aggregate own a majority interest in the partnership and have a common tax year, but the principal partners (Bob and Tony) have a common tax year which must be adopted by the BT partnership.

A partnership also is permitted to choose a tax year other than the required tax year as determined under the above rules. However, the year chosen must end within no more than three months of when the required tax year would end. For example, the BT partnership in the above example could elect to have a fiscal tax year which ends on June 30, July 31, or August 31. If the partnership elects a year other than the required tax year, it must pay a toll charge. The toll charge is effectively a prepaid deposit of the tax which the partners eventually will have to pay on the amount of deferred income.

The above rules notwithstanding, if a partnership can justify a tax year with a business purpose, the IRS will allow the partnership to use the "business purpose" tax year. An example of a business purpose is when the partnership's tax year conforms to a natural business year, that is the end of a peak period of operations which is followed by a relative lull in operations. The IRS specifies that a "natural business year" occurs when 25 percent of the partnership's gross receipts are collected during the last two months of a 12-month period, and this gross receipts pattern occurs over three consecutive years.

Partner's Distributive Share of Income/Loss

A partner's distributive share of partnership income and loss items must be reported for the tax year with which or in which the partnership year ends. Code Sec. 706(a). It is irrelevant that the partner has not actually received the particular item from the partnership. The rule of inclusion applies whether the partnership is on the accrual or cash basis; it applies to the partner if the item is reported by the partnership.

EXAMPLE 16.2   Jim Smith, a 50 percent partner, is entitled under the partnership agreement to receive $1,000 per month as salary and 50 percent of the profits of the partnership after consideration of his salary. The partnership uses the accrual method of reporting its income; Jim, the cash receipts method. Both report on the calendar year. During the current year, the partnership agrees to pay Jim a salary of $12,000. It pays Jim his salary for the month of January but does not pay him for the remaining eleven months, although it accrues the remaining $11,000 as a liability. In addition, Jim's share of the partnership profits totals $18,000 for the year, but because the partnership is short of cash, none of this is paid to Jim either. Nevertheless, for the current year, Jim will report income of $30,000 from the partnership.

Closing the Partnership Year

As a general rule the partnership tax year continues until the partnership terminates. Code Sec. 706(c). A termination will not occur merely upon the sale of a partnership interest by a partner, or upon the retirement or the death of a partner. The tax year will end with respect to the partner who sells or exchanges an entire partnership interest. However, the tax year does not end with respect to the partnership unless the sale of 50 percent or more of the total interest in the partnership's capital and profits takes place within a 12-month period.

EXAMPLE 16.3   Kyle, Bob, Fred, and Joe are equal partners in the VB partnership, formed January 1, 1998, which partnership reports on the calendar year. On September 1, 2014, Kyle sells his 25 percent interest to Jack. The partnership 2014 tax year closes on September 1st but only with respect to Kyle. On July 1, 2015, Bob sells his 25 percent interest to Howard. The partnership 2015 tax year closes on July 1 with respect to Bob. Even though Fred, Joe, Jack and Howard continue the partnership, the tax year of VB also ends on July 1, 2015.

The partnership year will terminate when there is no partner carrying on the business as a partnership. On retirement, if the partner continues to share in the profits of the partnership after retirement, the partnership continues until the retired partner is paid out for an interest. Upon the death of a partner, even in a two-member partnership, the partnership year will not end upon the death of the partner, but will continue to its normal year-end. The partnership may continue after death for later years if the deceased partner has a successor in interest who continues to share in the partnership profits. The partners may by agreement provide that the partnership year will end upon the death of a partner.

¶16,133   RELATED PARTIES

The provision which matches the deduction of an expense and its inclusion in income of a related person applies in the partnership situation when the transaction is between the partnership and any partner who owns any interest in the partnership capital or income. Code Sec. 267(b) and (e). This treatment should be contrasted with the treatment (discussed below) for the disallowance of losses on sales between the partner and the partnership.

When the partnership is controlled by a partner it is tempting for that partner to use the partnership as a tax foil and plan transactions which, while having a tax impact, have little economic impact when the partner and the controlled partnership are viewed as an integrated economic entity. To prevent this type of artificial tax planning, restrictions are imposed upon the recognition of losses and the character of gain to be recognized in certain sales or exchanges of property between persons and controlled partnerships.

Losses Not Recognized

No loss will be recognized in a sale or exchange between a person and a partnership in which the person owns, directly or indirectly, more than a 50 percent interest in the partnership capital or profits. Code Sec. 707(b)(1). The restriction applies whether the sale is by the partnership to the person or by the person to the partnership. The loss, though disallowed, is recouped by the transferee before the recognition of a subsequent gain.

EXAMPLE 16.4	Archie Jones, who owns 60 percent of the capital of Acme Partnership, sells the latter land, with an adjusted basis of $15,000, for its fair market value of $10,000. The basis of the land to the partnership is its cost, $10,000, and the $5,000 loss to Archie is not recognized. If the partnership subsequently sells the land for $8,000, the partnership will recognize a loss of $2,000. The partnership would recognize no gain unless the sales price exceeds $15,000, its cost plus the loss not recognized upon the sale to the partnership by Archie.

EXAMPLE 16.5	The facts are the same as in Example 16.4, except Archie's married daughter is the owner and seller of the land. The results are the same, since Archie's daughter is considered to indirectly own Archie's 60 percent interest in Acme Partnership.

Conversion of Capital Gain to Ordinary Income

The general rule states that cost is the basis for assets acquired and that depreciation, or cost recovery, is based upon that basis. In the absence of a restriction a partner could acquire depreciable real property, for example, depreciate it fully using the straight-line method, sell the property to the partnership, have the latter depreciate its full cost, again using the straight-line method, and resell the property back to the original partner, who would repeat the process. The effect of all this is the repetitive write-off of the cost basis of this asset, achieving a deduction against ordinary income, with a recoupment of this write-off at capital gains rates.

This "double benefit" is prevented where there is the possibility for clear abuse, limiting the restriction to transactions between a partnership and a person who owns, directly or indirectly, more than a 50 percent interest in partnership capital or profits. It is further limited by inquiring into the use of the acquired asset by the purchaser. If the asset in the hands of the purchaser is other than a capital asset, as defined in Section 1221, the entire recognized gain on the sale or exchange is ordinary income. Code Sec. 707(b)(2).

EXAMPLE 16.6	Mark Baker, who owns a 60 percent interest in the Bakro Partnership, sells to Bakro an unimproved parcel of realty which Baker had held as an investment. Baker recognizes a gain of $20,000, the excess of the sales price over his basis. Code Sec. 707(b)(2) classifies the entire $20,000 as ordinary income to Baker if Bakro either holds the realty for sale to customers in the ordinary course of its trade or business (inventory, not a capital asset) or builds its plant upon the site (Section 1231 asset, not a capital asset).

PLANNING POINTER	The purpose of the sale in the above example was to obtain a step-up in basis upon the sale of the property to the partnership, but as shown this resulted in ordinary income to the selling partner. If the property were converted to inventory by the partnership, all additional gains will also be ordinary income. If the individual had selected a corporation as an investment entity, the sale of the property to the controlled corporation would have resulted in a step-up in basis and the profit would be classified as a capital gain. (Section 1239 imposes ordinary income on such a sale only when the property sold is, in the hands of the transferee, of a character subject to depreciation.) Also, if the property which Baker sold in the above example were subject to depreciation by the partnership, even though it might be used as a capital asset by the partnership and escape Code Sec. 707(b)(2), Code Sec. 1239 would cause Baker to recognize ordinary income.

¶16,141   CONTRIBUTIONS TO THE PARTNERSHIP

Property Contributions

As a general rule, partners who transfer property to a partnership are merely changing the form in which they conduct their business and while gain or loss may be realized, none is recognized. Code Sec. 721. The contributing partner takes as the basis for the interest in the partnership the basis for the property contributed to the partnership. Code Sec. 722. The partnership takes as its basis for the contributed assets the basis those assets had to the contributing partner. Code Sec. 723. The holding period of the transferred property tacks on to the property acquired. Code Sec. 1223. If the assets transferred are ordinary income assets (i.e., neither capital assets nor Section 1231 assets), the holding period for the partner's partnership interest commences with the date of their transfer.

While the general rule is that the character of an asset is determined by the purpose for which it is held by the taxpayer, there are three exceptions. Those exceptions are: (1) in the case of certain inventory items, the ordinary income character of the asset in the hands of the partner carries over to the partnership for a five-year period, (2) the ordinary income character of certain unrealized trade or business receivables also carries over to the partnership for an indefinite period, and (3) a similar five-year rule applies to contributed capital assets which have a "built-in" loss—the difference between the adjusted basis and the fair market value at the time of contribution. The character of the built-in loss is preserved for five years.

EXAMPLE 16.7	Mr. Apple contributes inventory items to his partnership in exchange for an interest in the partnership. Although the partnership may hold these assets as investments and not for sale to customers in the ordinary course of business, if they are sold within five years of their contribution, the entire gain or loss is ordinary income or loss.

EXAMPLE 16.8	Same as in Example 16.7, except Mr. Apple contributes accounts receivable which were earned in his cash basis sole proprietorship prior to their contribution. Whenever they are collected or disposed of, the entire proceeds are ordinary income.

EXAMPLE 16.9	Same as in Example 16.7, except Mr. Apple contributes a capital asset with an adjusted basis to him of $20,000 and a fair market value at that time of $15,000. In the hands of the partnership, the property is held for sale to customers in the ordinary course of the partnership business and is sold for $12,000 within five years of its receipt by the partnership. The partnership has a capital loss of $5,000 ($20,000 – $15,000) and an ordinary loss of $3,000 ($12,000 sales price – $15,000 cost of goods sold).

Contribution of Services

When an incoming partner does not contribute property, but receives an interest in the partnership capital in payment for services rendered to the partnership, the transaction results in a taxable transaction for both the partnership and the incoming partner. The incoming partner is credited with an interest in the partnership (and its underlying assets) as compensation. The measure of the partner's ordinary income is the fair market value of the partnership interest with which the partner is credited. The partnership has income or loss by comparing the amount of the partnership obligation with the basis of the partnership assets attributed to the incoming partner.

EXAMPLE 16.10	The Arnold, Beatrice, Carol partnership holds assets with a fair market value of $48,000 and an adjusted basis of $30,000. Damon is admitted to a one-fourth partnership capital interest in payment of $12,000 due him for services rendered the partnership. Damon has ordinary income of $12,000. The partnership paid a liability of $12,000 by allocating to Damon $7,500 of partnership asset basis. Thus, the partnership recognizes a gain of $4,500 ($12,000 – $7,500).

The partnership has satisfied a claim for compensation, and it is entitled to a deduction. The nature of the expenditure determines whether it is currently deductible (salary for operations) or it must be capitalized (architectural services for a building).

PLANNING POINTER	The partnership and the service partner could defer the recognition of income/gain by imposing substantial risks of forfeiture upon the incoming partner's interest. For example, the partnership could give an employee an interest in the partnership but make that interest contingent upon the completion of two years of additional service. The recognition of the income/deduction would occur when the substantial risks pass.

¶16,149   DEBTS

Cost Basis Determination

When determining cost basis, generally there is no concern with the timing of the payment or the means by which the cost obligation of an asset was satisfied.

EXAMPLE 16.11	Land costing $100,000 has the same basis to the acquirer whether the consideration was $100,000 cash paid at the time of acquisition or whether the purchase was on credit with the entire acquisition price evidenced by a promissory note, payable over several years in the future.

Acquisition debt must be a part of the basis of an acquired asset, particularly if the asset is depreciable. Otherwise, the deduction for the cost recovery of the asset depends upon the payment of its purchase price and does not comport to the useful life (accounting concept of benefit) or to the cost recovery period.

Debt Assumed or Property Taken Subject to Debt

Every general partner is ultimately liable for unpaid partnership debts. Under the "marshalling of assets" rule, partnership debts are payable first from partnership assets. As the liability imposed on the partners arises after the exhaustion of partnership assets, the shares of the partners' liabilities are allocated, as a general rule, based on the partners' economic risk of loss (e.g., loss-sharing ratios). Accordingly, as to an unsatisfied obligation, it is of little significance whether the debt is secured or is unsecured. It is of significance whether property is taken by the partnership merely subject to an outstanding liability as opposed to the partnership's taking property and assuming the related liability. The essential difference is that where there is an assumed liability, the entire debt is reflected in the basis of the partners' interests; however, where the property is merely taken subject to an outstanding debt, the liability reflected in the basis is limited to the fair market value of the property. Code Sec. 752(c).

EXAMPLE 16.12	The Phillips Partnership purchased certain property, paying $10,000 cash and assuming a liability of $70,000 encumbering that property. The basis of the partners' interest in Phillips Partnership is increased by $70,000.

EXAMPLE 16.13	Assume the above property was purchased for $1,000 cash, Phillips Partnership took the property subject to (but not assuming) a liability of $70,000 encumbering that property, but the fair market value of the property was only $60,000. The basis of the partners' interest in Phillips Partnership is increased by $60,000.

¶16,157   PARTNERSHIP LIABILITIES—CONTRIBUTED PROPERTY

When a partner contributes property to a partnership, and the property is encumbered by a liability which is assumed by the partnership, the contributing partner effectively is relieved from part of the risk of the liability to the extent it is assumed by the other partners. To the extent of the relief, the contributing partner is deemed to receive a cash distribution from the partnership. The basis of the contributing partner's partnership interest is reduced by the deemed cash distribution. Thus, when a partner contributes encumbered property, the contributing partner's basis for the partnership interest is increased by the basis of the property transferred, and it is decreased for the part of the liability assumed by the partnership's other partners. At the same time, the other partners increase the basis of their partnership interests for the part of the liability which they assume. The reason for the basis increase is that the other partners are deemed to contribute the cash to the partnership which the contributing partner is deemed to have received.

EXAMPLE 16.14

Charles, for a 25 percent interest in the Apex Partnership, a former three-member partnership, contributes to the partnership land with a fair market value of $100,000, a basis to him of $50,000, encumbered by a mortgage of $50,000, a debt he incurred after his purchase of the land. Charles has held the land for three years. Charles's basis for his interest in the partnership is $12,500. This is the amount of his basis in the transferred property, $50,000, less that portion of the $50,000 debt, $37,500, which is now the obligation of his partners. Each of the other three partners would have a basis increase of $12,500. The basis of the property to the partnership is $50,000.

However, the basis of a partner's interest cannot be reduced below zero. Thus, as the allocation of the liability to the other partners is treated as a distribution of money and that "money" exceeds the basis of the property to the contributing partner, the excess is treated as proceeds—and thus gain—from the sale or exchange of the partnership interest.

EXAMPLE 16.15

Suppose in Example 16.14 that the mortgage on the property had been $80,000 and Charles transferred it to the partnership for a 25 percent interest worth $20,000. Charles is deemed to have received money equal to $60,000, the amount now allocated to his three partners, and each of the other partners has a partnership basis increase of $20,000. The basis of the property to the partnership is $50,000. This is the basis to Charles of the property prior to the transfer. The gain, $10,000 (excess of "money" received $60,000 over his basis $50,000), recognized by Charles on the transfer is considered a gain arising from the sale of his partnership interest, not from the sale of the land. As Charles' holding period for the land "tacks" on to the holding period of his partnership interest, he has received a long-term capital gain. Charles' basis for his partnership interest is zero.

¶16,165   BASIS ALLOCATIONS BY PARTNERS

When one partner contributes property with a value different from its basis, there appears to be a question of equity between the partners. If there has been precontribution appreciation in the value of the contributed property, because the property will take the partner's basis, this appreciation, as well as any future appreciation, is taxed to the partners when it is recognized. The tax burden of this precontribution appreciation is placed on the contributing partner. Code Sec. 704(c).

EXAMPLE 16.16

Mary Lewis and Jan March form an equal two-member partnership. Mary contributes $10,000 cash; Jan contributes inventory items with a basis to her of $1,000 but a fair market value of $10,000. Jan will be credited with $1,000 in her capital account. The partnership will have a $1,000 basis in the inventory. When the partnership sells the inventory for $12,000, the partnership will have recognized ordinary income of $11,000. Code Sec. 704(c) requires that Jan be responsible for any precontribution appreciation so that upon the sale, Jan reports $10,000 of the gain ($9,000 precontribution appreciation and one-half of the $2,000 post-contribution profit). Mary reports the remaining $1,000 gain. As a result, the partnership will have assets of $22,000, which is the sum of each partner's interest, $11,000, each having contributed $10,000 in value and each having been taxed on $1,000 of partnership profit. To reflect this arrangement on the partnership return, the $2,000 is included in partnership ordinary income; the $9,000 is separately reportable by Jan.

Where depreciable property has a fair market value greater than its basis, when contributed, the problem is more complex. Since the cost (basis) to be recovered is less than the amount which would have been recoverable had the property been purchased at fair market value, an allocation of the cost recovery must be made to the noncontributing partners. Code Sec. 704(c).

EXAMPLE 16.17   Assume that Jan in Example 16.16 above had contributed seven-year property which had been depreciated using the straight-line method; at the time of the contribution the property had a remaining life of five years, an adjusted basis of $5,000, and a fair market value of $10,000. Assume further that the partnership, continuing the straight-line method, deducted $1,000 in each of the years following the contribution. The entire $1,000 each year would be allocated to Mary.

In Example 16.17, notice that since Mary effectively purchases one-half of the economic depreciation in the property, or $5,000, and the basis of the property equals at least that much, there is no inequity to Mary because of the special precontribution rule. An inequity does arise, however, when the basis of the contributed property does not at least equal the economic depreciation which the other partner(s) has purchased.

EXAMPLE 16.18   Assume that in Example 16.17 the basis of the property is $4,000. If straight-line depreciation is used over five more years, the maximum tax depreciation deduction to which the partnership is entitled each year is $800, even though Mary has "purchased" $1,000 with her $10,000 cash contribution. The entire $800 of annual depreciation must be allocated to Mary. The partnership may wish to make special allocations of other partnership deductions, or partnership cash flow, to Mary to account for her "lost" depreciation deductions.

PLANNING POINTER   An equitable adjustment in situations similar to that described above is to have the contributor of the appreciated property make an initial cash contribution equal to the present value of the other party's lost tax benefits.

In addition to differences between tax basis and fair market values at the time of contribution of property by partners, there may be other reasons for special allocations of certain items of income, gain, loss, deduction, etc., among the partners. These allocations must have an economic effect, and the economic effect itself must be substantial when compared with the tax effect of the allocation. This means that any allocation of deduction must be accompanied by a cost to the partner to whom it is allocated; that is, it must affect the partner's capital account, and liquidations must be based upon capital account balances. Also, generally any partner with a deficit balance in the capital account when the partnership is liquidated must restore the amount of the deficit to the partnership. Transitory allocations such as allocating all deductions to one partner for a period of time with offsetting deductions to the other partner at a later period will not pass muster.

¶16,171   ADMISSION OF A NEW PARTNER

When a new partner is admitted into an ongoing partnership, the contribution made will rarely match the tax basis of the share of the partnership assets which will be attributed to the incoming partner. There will inevitably be appreciation or depreciation in value of the partnership assets which will be reflected in the amount of the incoming partner's contribution. An agreement to allocate items of income, deductions, etc., will be honored if such allocation has substantial economic effect as discussed above.

In addition, unless the new partner is admitted at the beginning of the partnership tax year, there will be items of income, gains, deductions, losses and credits that the partnership incurred during the tax year prior to the new partner's admission. There can be no retroactive allocation to the new partner of items incurred by the partnership prior to the new partner's admission. Further, "allocable cash basis items" for this purpose generally are reflected under the accrual method even though the partnership reports on the cash basis. Code Sec. 706(d).

EXAMPLE 16.19   Mary Brown invests $100,000 cash for a one-fourth capital and income interest in the Apex Company, a cash basis, calendar year partnership, making her capital contribution on December 1. On December 31, the partnership pays interest and principal on an outstanding debt which requires one annual payment at year-end. Mary may have allocated to her only 1/4 × 1/12 of the interest deduction.

¶16,175   PARTNERSHIP DISTRIBUTIONS

The interest of a partner in a partnership bears a close analogy to an investment by a stockholder in a corporation, and for the most part the interests are treated comparably. Neither interest is excluded from the definition of a capital asset in Code Sec. 1221, but, to avoid assignment of income problems, the partnership interest is sometimes also treated as a partial interest in certain underlying assets of the partnership. The problem is particularly acute where there are disproportionate distributions to the partners or a sale of a partnership interest when the underlying assets are comprised of ordinary income items which have not been reflected in the partnership's income. Section 751 identifies two classes of such items: (1) "unrealized receivables," contract rights which have not been recognized in income, most often accounts receivable of cash basis partnerships, as well as certain recapture items, for example the depreciation recapture in Section 1245 property, and (2) "substantially appreciated inventory items," primarily items held for sale which have a fair market value greatly in excess of their bases.

Distributions Not in Liquidation

If a partnership makes a distribution of property to a partner, not in liquidation of the partnership interest, the partner does not recognize any gain unless the property distributed includes money and certain marketable securities that are in excess of the basis in the partnership interest. No loss is recognized. Code Sec. 731.

Partner's Basis in Distributed Property

When property is distributed to a partner, obviously cash has as its basis its face amount, and the partner must reduce the basis in the partnership interest by the amount of cash received. If the cash distributed exceeds the partner's basis immediately before the distribution, the partnership basis is reduced to zero and the partner has a gain, usually capital gain, for the amount that would have created a negative basis.

When unrealized receivables and inventory are distributed, the distributee partner takes the basis the partnership had in such assets to the extent that the reallocation of basis does not reduce the basis of the partnership interest below zero.

Distributions of marketable securities to a partner are treated as cash for purposes of measuring gain. The amount of cash considered received is the fair market value of the marketable securities less the partner's share of the gain on the marketable securities. The partner recognizes gain to the extent of the partner's share of the gain on the marketable securities and the basis of the marketable securities to the partner is fair market value.

EXAMPLE 16.20	John receives $10,000 in marketable securities in a distribution from the partnership. The partnership has a basis in the marketable securities of $8,000. John's share of profit and losses is 25 percent. John will be considered to have received cash in the amount of $9,500 ($10,000 fair market value less his $500 share of the gain). John will report a $500 gain from the distribution and the marketable securities will have a $10,000 basis to him. John also may have to report gain if the $9,500 "cash" disbursement exceeds his basis in the partnership immediately before the distribution.

If other assets are distributed in a distribution not in liquidation of the partner's entire interest, their basis is their carryover basis from the partnership to the extent of the remaining basis of the partner's interest after the reductions for cash, unrealized receivables, and inventory. The basis for the partnership interest is the remaining balance, if any, after these reallocations.

EXAMPLE 16.21

In each of the three independent cases below assume David received a nonliquidating distribution of cash and property with partnership basis and fair market value as set forth:

	Case #1	Case #2	Case #3
Partner's basis in his partnership interest	$12,000	$12,000	$12,000
Distribution—Cash	11,000	11,000	11,000
Tentative remaining basis	$1,000	$1,000	$1,000
Distribution—Property			
Property basis to partnership	500	3,000	8,000
Fair market value	3,000	8,000	3,000
Basis of property to partner	$500	$1,000	$1,000
Basis of partnership interest	$500	$0	$0

If a distribution consists of cash and other property, the basis of the partnership interest first is reduced by the amount of the cash. Had David received $14,000 in cash in the distributions above, he would have recognized a gain of $2,000, and the other property distributed as well as his partnership interest would have bases of zero.

EXAMPLE 16.22

The Stephens partnership makes a distribution to Paul, an equal partner, consisting of the following property: cash, $4,000; inventory, $6,000 basis to the partnership, and $7,000 fair market value; land #1, $15,000 basis to the partnership, and $20,000 fair market value; and land #2, $5,000 basis to the partnership, and $6,000 fair market value. Paul has a $12,000 basis in his partnership interest before the distribution. Paul first reduces the basis of his partnership interest by the $4,000 cash, and has no gain on the distribution. Next, he reduces the basis of his partnership interest by the $6,000 basis of the inventory to the partnership. Paul takes the $6,000 carryover basis for the inventory. The remaining $2,000 basis in his partnership interest must be allocated to land #1 and land #2. The $2,000 is allocated to the two pieces of land according to their relative bases to the partnership. So, land #1 is allocated a $1,500 basis ($2,000 × ($15,000 / ($15,000 + $5,000))), and land #2 is allocated the remaining $500 basis of Paul's interest in the Stephens partnership. After the distribution, Paul has a zero basis in his partnership interest.

Distributions in Complete Liquidation

When a distribution is made in complete liquidation of a partner's interest, the same gain rule applies: gain is recognized only upon the receipt of cash and certain marketable securities in excess of the partner's basis in the partnership interest. Loss is generally recognized only where the distribution is in complete liquidation of the partner's interest in the partnership and that distribution is composed only of cash, unrealized receivables, and inventory, and then only to the extent that the sum of the amount of cash and the basis to the partnership of the unrealized receivables and inventory is less than the partner's basis for the partnership interest.

EXAMPLE 16.23

Partner George Sitwell has a basis in his partnership interest of $20,000. In complete liquidation of that interest, he receives only cash in the amount of $25,000. George will recognize a capital gain of $5,000.

EXAMPLE 16.24

If George in Example 16.23, above, in complete liquidation of his partnership interest receives $12,000 in cash and unrealized receivables and inventory with a basis to the partnership of $3,000 and a fair market value of $9,000, George will reduce his basis by the $12,000 cash and by the basis that the distributed unrealized receivables and inventory had to the partnership, $3,000. George's basis for the unrealized receivables and inventory is $3,000, the basis to the partnership, and he will recognize a capital loss of $5,000 ($20,000 – ($12,000 + $3,000)).

Distributions of Other Property in Complete Liquidation

If in addition to cash and unrealized receivables and inventory there is distributed other property, that other property has as its basis the remaining unreallocated basis of the partnership interest, regardless of the fair market value of the property.

EXAMPLE 16.25	If in Example 16.24, above, there had been distributed to George the $12,000 in cash, the unrealized receivables and inventory with a basis of $3,000 (fair market value of $9,000), and a parcel of real estate with a basis to the partnership of $1,000 (fair market value $500), there would be no recognized loss. The unrealized receivables and inventory would retain their $3,000 basis, and the land would have a basis to George of $5,000.

EXAMPLE 16.26	Same as in Example 16.25, above, except the land had a basis to the partnership of $10,000 and a fair market value of $15,000. Neither gain nor loss would be recognized and the land would still have a basis to George of $5,000.

Observe that in Example 16.25, the basis of the land to George, the $5,000 remaining basis in his partnership interest, is $4,000 more than the partnership's $1,000 pre-distribution basis in it. Also, observe that in Example 16.26, the basis of the land to George, again $5,000, is $5,000 less than the partnership's $10,000 pre-distribution basis in it. If the partnership has a special election in effect, it reduces the basis of similar partnership properties by the $4,000 increased basis which George takes in the land distributed in Example 16.25, and it increases the basis of similar partnership properties by the $5,000 of "lost" partnership basis for the land distributed in Example 16.26. Code Secs. 734, 751, and 755.

When the receivables are collected or the inventory items are sold by the distributee, he or she will report as ordinary income the excess of the proceeds over the basis of those assets.

Disproportionate Distributions or Sale of Partnership Interest When There Are Section 751 Assets

When a partner receives in a distribution less than that partner's share of the Section 751 assets, the partner is deemed to have sold the excess of the proportionate share over the amount received, and ordinary income will be recognized by the partner. When the partner receives more than that partner's share of Section 751 assets, the partnership recognizes gain on the excess distribution. A like treatment is provided for on the sale of a partner's share of the Section 751 assets when there is a sale by a partner of the interest in the partnership. Ordinary income is recognized to the extent of the gain attributable to the sale of the Section 751 assets. The balance of the gain is capital gain.

EXAMPLE 16.27	Frank, a one-third partner in Preston Partnership, receives in complete liquidation of his interest $10,000 cash and two of three parcels of real estate held by the partnership for investment, basis of each to the partnership, $3,000, fair market value each, $10,000. The balance sheet of the Preston Partnership immediately before the distribution was as follows:

Assets		Basis	FMV	Equities	
Cash		$30,000	$30,000	Liabilities	$0
				Frank Cap.	13,000
				George Cap.	13,000
Accts. Receivable		0	30,000	Harry Cap.	13,000
Invest. Realty		9,000	30,000		
		$39,000	$90,000		$39,000

Frank has a realized gain on his distribution of $17,000, the $30,000 value he receives over his basis in the partnership ($13,000). He receives his proportionate share of the cash, $10,000, but he receives two-thirds of the investment realty, surrendering to the partnership his one-third of the unrealized receivables. Frank will recognize ordinary income of $10,000. He is deemed to have sold his one-third share of the receivables, basis zero, for $10,000 value in the partnership realty. His basis in the realty is $13,000, his one-third of the partnership's basis of $9,000 plus his "purchase price" for the balance, $10,000.

¶16,181 SALE OR EXCHANGE OF PARTNERSHIP INTEREST

When a partnership interest is sold to another, most often the consideration received is not the same as the basis sold. Thus, the acquiring partner receives a fractional part of the bases of the partnership's underlying assets, though the acquiring partner may have paid more or less than their basis. The same is true when a partnership interest is purchased at retirement.

¶16,187 ESTIMATED INCOME TAX

Notwithstanding the rule that a partner recognizes the distributive share of partnership income, loss, etc., in the taxable year within which or with which the partnership year ends, the current year's distributive share from the partnership must be reflected in the partner's quarterly estimates of individual income tax as it is earned by the partnership under its method of accounting. For a calendar year partnership and calendar year partners, the estimated partnership income is included through the usual report dates, the last day of the months of March, May, August, and December. Reg. §1.6654-2(d)(2).

¶16,195 FAMILY PARTNERSHIPS

Generally, for a family partnership to be recognized for tax purposes, an inquiry is made into the nature of the force generating the income. Reg. §1.704-1(e)(3). If capital is a major income-producing factor, earnings of a partnership can be allocated, in part, based on the capital contributions. It is irrelevant that the capital of a child may have been derived from a gift from a parent-partner. However, in a capital intensive family partnership, equitable recognition must be given to the efforts contributed by each partner before there is a division of profits based upon capital.

If the partnership is a service partnership, with little need of capital, recognition must be given to the services rendered by the partners. In the absence of "significant" or "vital" services rendered, the child will not be recognized as a partner, and the income of the partnership will be allocated to those partners who do render the services for the partnership.

Characteristics of a Corporation

¶16,215 CORPORATE FORMATION

There is no tax problem when a corporation is formed and all parties receive stock in return for their cash investments. The basis of the stock in the hands of the stockholders is its cost. However, as the corporation is a new entity, separate from its stockholders, if a party exchanges property, other than cash, for stock in the transferee corporation, any gain realized may be recognized. Yet, if the formation of the corporation is a mere change in the form of doing business, or the stockholders of the corporation are merely increasing their investment in the corporation, neither gain nor loss is recognized. To receive this tax-free treatment it is necessary that the transferors of the property receive only stock of the corporation and they are in control (own 80 percent or more of the voting power and 80 percent or more of each class of the other stock of the corporation) immediately after the exchange. Code Sec. 351.

TAX BLUNDER

Mary Martin is in the 35 percent tax bracket. She transfers property with an adjusted basis of $40,000 and a fair market value of $25,000 to Alpha Corporation in a transaction that qualifies under Code Sec. 351. Mary will not recognize a loss on the transfer. Mary should not have transferred the property to the corporation. She would have been better off selling the property to the corporation (assuming the related party loss rules of Code Sec. 267 do not apply) and recognizing the $15,000 loss. She also could have sold the asset to an unrelated party and contributed the cash to the corporation.

The stock takes the basis the transferred property had to the transferors, less money and the fair market value of "boot" received, plus any gain recognized by the transferors. Code Sec. 358. The property in the hands of the corporation has the same basis as it had in the hands of the transferors increased by the gain recognized by them. Code Sec. 362. The holding period of the transferor for the property transferred tacks to the holding period for the corporation. Code Sec. 1223. The holding period to the transferor for the stock received in exchange depends upon the nature of the asset transferred. Stock received in exchange for capital assets or Section 1231 assets will tack the period of time the transferor held the asset. Stock received for "ordinary income" assets has its holding period commence upon issuance of the stock by the corporation.

Notwithstanding the general rule for nonrecognition of gain, a transferor recognizes gain if in addition to stock the transferor receives "boot" (i.e., any other property). Gain recognized is the lesser of the gain realized or the fair market value of the boot received. In no case is loss recognized.

EXAMPLE 16.28

Peggy, Nancy, Opal, and Ruth decide to form a corporation and respectively they transfer the following assets and receive in return the stated instruments and cash from the transferee corporation.

		TRANSFERRED			RECEIVED	
		Basis	FMV	Stock	Securities	Other
Peggy:	Land	$20,000	$30,000	$30,000		
Nancy:	Inventory	$18,000	$28,000	$10,000	$18,000	
Opal:	Equipment	$15,000	$25,000	$5,000	$12,000	Cash $8,000
Ruth:	Machinery	$30,000	$20,000	$5,000	$5,000	Cash $10,000

Peggy, Nancy, and Opal realize a gain of $10,000 each. Nancy recognized gain of $10,000 of the boot she received, the securities worth $18,000. Opal receives boot of $20,000 ($12,000 securities and $8,000 cash) but her recognized gain is limited to her realized gain of $10,000. Ruth does not recognize her loss. The bases of the assets to the corporation are: Land, $20,000; Inventory, $28,000; Equipment, $25,000; and Machinery, $30,000. The incorporators have as their bases for their investments in the corporation the following:

Peggy: Stock, $20,000—Her basis for the land.

Nancy: Stock, $10,000—Her basis in the inventory ($18,000) less boot received ($18,000) plus gain recognized ($10,000). Securities, $18,000—Their fair market value.

Opal: Stock, $5,000—Her basis in the equipment ($15,000) less boot received ($20,000) plus gain recognized ($10,000). Securities, $12,000—Their fair market value.

Ruth: Stock, $15,000—Her basis in the machinery ($30,000) less boot received ($15,000) plus gain recognized ($0). Securities, $5,000—Their fair market value.

Generally, when a party receives stock in exchange for services that the party has rendered or will render to the corporation, the party is not treated as a transferor of property. The stock is not counted in the determination of control after the transfer, and the receipt of stock is taxable as compensation.

Any liability transferred to the corporation is treated as the receipt of cash by the transferor and reduces the basis of the transferor's stock by the amount of the liability. If a party transfers properties to the controlled corporation subject to liabilities which in their aggregate exceed the adjusted bases of the transferred properties, the excess liabilities are treated as gain. Where gain is recognized, the stock received has a basis of zero to the property transferor. Where tax avoidance is a motive, the realized gain may be recognized to the extent of the transferred liabilities, not merely their excess over adjusted bases of transferred assets. A nonstockholder who transfers property and receives only securities in exchange has merely made a sale.

EXAMPLE 16.29 John Abrams transfers the following property to his newly formed corporation and receives in exchange only stock of the corporation.

	Case #1	Case #2	Case #3
Property, basis to John	$10,000	$10,000	$10,000
Property, fair market value	20,000	20,000	20,000
Liability of John assumed by corporation	8,000	15,000	
With tax avoidance motive			15,000
Fair market value of stock received	$12,000	$5,000	$5,000
Gain realized by John	$10,000	$10,000	$10,000
Gain recognized by John	$0	$5,000	$10,000
Basis for John's stock	$2,000	$0	$5,000

In Case #1, John's realized gain results from the excess of fair market value ($20,000) over basis ($10,000). Since he received no boot, no gain is recognized. His basis for the stock is the contributed property basis ($10,000) less the liability assumed by the corporation ($8,000).

In Case #2, John's realized gain is the same $10,000. He has a recognized gain because the liability assumed by the corporation ($15,000) exceeds the basis of the property contributed ($10,000). The basis of the stock received is $0 ($10,000 basis of property contributed minus $15,000 liability given up plus $5,000 gain recognized).

In Case #3, John has the same realized gain of $10,000. He must recognize the entire $10,000 gain because the $15,000 liability assumed by the corporation is considered boot because of the tax avoidance motive.

The transfer of property with liabilities in excess of basis can generate a recognized gain even in excess of the amount of gain realized.

EXAMPLE 16.30 Sol Moser transfers to his wholly owned corporation an asset with a basis to him of $10, a fair market value of $25, but subject to a liability of $30. As the corporation would not accept this uneconomic transfer without additional contribution, Sol also contributes his promissory note to pay the corporation an additional $5. Sol has a realized gain of $15, the net amount of liabilities he is relieved of, $25 ($30 – $5) over his basis $10 (asset $10, note $0). His recognized gain is $20 (excess of liability ($30) over basis of property transferred ($10)).

If taxpayers who transfer liabilities exceeding the basis of assets to controlled corporations are willing to undertake genuine personal liability for the excess, gain need not be recognized. This was the case where a taxpayer (a sole proprietor) transferred to a controlled corporation liabilities that included an accounting entry representing a personal debt not evidenced by a promissory note. The liability to the corporation was real, continuing, and indirectly enforceable by the corporation's creditors. The note was deemed to have a basis equal to its face amount. Therefore, the liabilities did not exceed the basis of assets and no recognition of gain was necessary. *S. Lessinger,* 89-1 USTC ¶9254, 872 F.2d 519 (CA-2 1989).

KEYSTONE PROBLEM

Archie, Sam, Tom, Willie, Zeb, and Jerry decide to form a corporation, making the following transfers and receiving the designated consideration from their newly formed corporation.

| | | TRANSFERRED PROPERTY | | | RECEIVED | | |
		Basis	FMV	Liabilities	Stock	Security	Other
Archie:	Cash	$60,000	$60,000		$60,000		
Sam:	Cash	20,000	20,000		20,000		
	Property A	10,000	30,000	$10,000		$20,000	
Tom:	Property B	40,000	60,000	20,000	10,000	10,000	$20,000
Willie:	Property C	50,000	40,000		20,000	20,000	
Zeb:	Property D	20,000	30,000		30,000		
Jerry:	Personal Services	0	20,000		20,000		

What gain or loss does each of the transferors realize on the incorporation? What do they recognize? What is the basis to them of the stock, security, or other property each receives? What is the basis to the corporation for the assets transferred?

¶16,225 CORPORATE INCOME, DEDUCTIONS, AND CREDITS

The corporate income tax is reported on Form 1120. A casual perusal will reveal the similarity of the first page of the partnership return Form 1065 discussed above. In general, the same rules governing income, deductions, and credits apply with respect to corporate determinations. Corporations may not deduct items peculiar to individuals, such as medical expenses (unless they are paid as a part of a compensation package), nor are they entitled to a personal exemption. However, there are some items unique to the corporate form which will be discussed below.

Organization Expenses

In theory, the cost of organizing a corporation represents a benefit which will be enjoyed so long as the corporation is in existence, and, as most corporate lives extend into perpetuity, these costs should never be written off until the corporation ceases to exist. However, the corporation is allowed a deduction for the year in which the corporation begins business in an amount equal to the lesser of the amount of organizational expenditures or $5,000 reduced by the amount organizational expenditures exceed $50,000. The remainder of the organizational expenditures are dedutible ratably over the 180-month period beginning with the month in which the corporation begins business. Code Sec. 248. The corporation makes this election by attaching a statement indicating such to the tax return for its first tax year.

These costs include legal fees in the drafting of the corporate charter, by-laws, and organizational minutes, the expense of the meeting of the incorporators, accounting fees for establishing an accounting system, and incorporation fees paid to the state. To qualify as organization costs they must be "incurred" before the end of the taxable year in which the corporation begins business. It makes no difference if the corporation reports on the cash or the accrual basis or whether the expenses are actually paid in the year incurred. Costs incurred in the issuance of the stock certificates, their printing costs, underwriting costs, etc., are not considered organization costs. They are capital costs and are not amortizable.

In addition to the election to amortize organization costs, a corporation may elect to deduct the lessser of the amount of start-up expenditures with respect to the trade or business or $5,000 reduced by the amount by which such start-up expenditures exceed $50,000. The remainder of such start-up expenditures are allowed as a deduction ratably over the 180-month period beginning with the month in which the active trade or business begins. Code Sec. 195. Business start-up costs include pre-operational advertising, employee training costs, and other pre-operational expenditures.

Dividends Received Deduction

One of the deductions peculiar to corporations is the dividends received deduction (DRD). Because the earnings of a corporation do not accrue to a shareholder until they are distributed in the form of a dividend, where there exist several tiers of stock ownership, the same income passing up the corporate ladder is taxed several times before it finally is paid to an individual owner. Where the corporations involved are parents and subsidiaries filing a consolidated income tax return, the intercompany dividends are eliminated. However, there are many reasons why affiliated corporations that are eligible to file consolidated returns choose not to do so. To minimize the multiple taxation of the same income, there is allowed a dividends received deduction. Code Sec. 243. For domestic corporations which qualify as "affiliated" but do not file a consolidated income tax return, there is a 100 percent dividends received deduction. For corporate stockholders holding 20 percent or more of the voting power and value of the distributing corporation's stock, there is an 80 percent dividends received deduction, and for those corporate shareholders which hold less than 20 percent of the voting power and value of the distributing corporation's stock, there is a 70 percent dividends received deduction.

The 80 (70) percent dividends received deduction is subject to a limitation. The deduction is the lesser of 80 (70) percent of domestic dividends received or 80 (70) percent of the taxable income of the corporation without considering the dividends received deduction. However, if in applying the 80 (70) percent deduction to the dividends received that computation results in a net operating loss, the 80 (70) percent of taxable income test is not applied. A very small change in taxable income can theoretically result in a substantial change in taxable income.

EXAMPLE 16.31

Assume the Major Corporation has the following ordinary income, exclusive of dividend income and the indicated dividend income from minority interests in domestic corporations:

	Case #1	Case #2	Case #3
Ordinary income (loss)	$200,000	$(200,000)	$(200,001)
Domestic dividends	1,000,000	1,000,000	1,000,000
Taxable Income w/o DRD	$1,200,000	$800,000	$799,999
Test #1: 80% Div. recd.	800,000	800,000	800,000
Tentative income (NOL)	$400,000	$0	$(1)
Test #2: 80% of Taxable income w/o DRD if less than dividends and if no NOL results	$—	$640,000	$—
Div. recd. deduction	800,000	640,000	800,000
Taxable income (NOL)	$400,000	$160,000	$(1)

If in the above example, the corporate shareholder held less than 20 percent of the stock of the distributing company and the loss from operations had been $300,000 in Case #2 and the loss from operations had been $300,001 in Case #3, the results would be similar. Case #2 would have taxable income of $210,000 (using a $490,000 DRD, or 70 percent of $700,000), while Case #3 would have an NOL of ($1) with a $700,000 DRD, or 70 percent of $1,000,000.

If Corporation X holds 20 percent or more of the stock in Corporation A and it also holds less than 20 percent of the stock in Corporation B, Corporation X will compute its dividends received deduction in two steps. First, it will compute the DRD for the dividends of Corporation B, eliminating from taxable income for this purpose the dividends from Corporation A. Second, Corporation X will compute the DRD for the dividends of Corporation A, including 100 percent of the dividends from Corporation A in taxable income. The two dividends received deductions are then aggregated as a single deduction.

EXAMPLE 16.32	Corporate shareholder has the following income.	
	Operations (net loss)	$(10,000)
	Dividends from 20 percent or more corporations	100,000
	Dividends from less than 20 percent corporations	100,000
	Taxable income	$190,000
	Less: Dividends from 20 percent or more corporations	100,000
	Modified taxable income	$90,000
	DRD from less than 20 percent corporations	
	The lesser of $70,000 (70% × $100,000) or $63,000 (70% × $90,000)	63,000
	Taxable income from above	$190,000
	Less: DRD (lesser of $80,000 (80% × $100,000)) or $152,000 ($190,000 × 80%)	$80,000
	DRD (70% × $90,000)	63,000 143,000
	Taxable income	$47,000

A practice developed where a corporation would purchase the stock of another corporation shortly before the ex-dividend date. When the dividend was received, the dividend received deduction would be taken, and then shortly thereafter the stock would be sold. As its value would be diminished by the dividend payment, the sale of the stock would generate a short-term capital loss. The interplay of the dividends received deduction and the reduced sales price would generate a tax loss when there was, in fact, an economic gain. This loophole was closed by a rule which provides that no dividends received deduction may be taken if the stock is held by the corporate shareholder for 45 days or less. Code Sec. 246(c).

EXAMPLE 16.33	On June 10, Progress Corporation purchases 1,000 shares (less than 20 percent) of Domestic Corporation for $125,000. Domestic Corporation had declared on June 1 a $20 per share dividend, payable on June 30 to shareholders of record June 20. Progress Corporation received the $20,000 dividend and then sold the Domestic Corporation stock on July 1 for $105,000. Progress Corporation will report dividend income of $20,000, no dividends received deduction, and a short-term capital loss of $20,000.

Capital Gains and Losses

Unlike an individual, the corporation may not deduct a capital loss against ordinary income. Capital losses may offset only capital gains. Also, unlike individuals, corporations carry capital losses back three years and are limited in their carry forwards to five years. The capital loss of a corporation carried to another year is always treated in that year as a short-term capital loss.

EXAMPLE 16.34	Milburn Corporation is a calendar-year corporation. For its 2015 tax year, Milburn has a net short-term capital gain of $30,000 and a net long-term capital loss of $90,000. Milburn is able to use $30,000 of the loss to offset the $30,000 of capital gain, leaving a $60,000 unused capital loss, which is treated as a short-term capital loss. Assume that in 2012 Milburn Corporation had $80,000 of net short-term capital gain and $50,000 of net long-term capital gain. The $60,000 of short-term capital loss carryback first is applied to the 2012 net short-term capital gain, leaving $20,000 of net short-term capital gain and $50,000 of net long-term capital gain for 2012. Milburn files an amended return to recover any amount for taxes overpaid in 2012 because of the carryback.

Under the tax rate schedules currently in effect, it makes no difference whether the gain is treated as short-term or long-term since both types of gain are taxed at the same rate. However, if there is a re-establishment of a preferential rate for long-term gains, the nature of the loss carryover again will be extremely important.

Transactions with Corporation's Own Stock and Securities

A corporation generally recognizes neither gain nor loss in transactions involving its own stock. Authorized but previously unissued stock or treasury stock issued for property will cause no gain or loss recognition to the corporation. Code Sec. 1032. On the other hand, if a corporation purchases its stock and pays for it with appreciated property, the corporation reports a gain upon this "sale or exchange" of the appreciated property. A corporation may also incur income upon the distribution of property when the fair market value of the property is greater than its adjusted basis. If an item is expensed, its basis is reduced to zero. If that item possesses any value when it is distributed to the shareholders, the distribution is treated as a sale of the item for its fair market value.

EXAMPLE 16.35	Corporation Yak has neither accumulated nor current earnings and profits at the end of its tax year at which time it distributes to its sole shareholder the following property:

	Capital Asset	Supplies Expensed
Fair Market Value	$10,000	$5,000
Basis to Corporation Yak	2,000	0

Corporation Yak has taxable income comprised of $8,000 capital gain and $5,000 ordinary income.

Although a corporation recognizes neither gain nor loss upon the issuance of its own securities, if it acquires its outstanding securities at a discount, it realizes income. This income may be deferred by insolvent or bankrupt taxpayers.

¶16,235 CHARITABLE CONTRIBUTIONS

In general, a corporation may deduct contributions made to the same charities as those selected by individuals, except gifts do not qualify for deduction if made to certain fraternal societies or to organizations for use outside of the United States.

Timing of the Deduction

Generally, in order to be deductible, the charitable contribution must actually be made in the tax year for which it is claimed, but an accrual method corporate taxpayer may deduct a charitable contribution in the year it is accrued by action of its board of directors, provided the contribution is actually paid to the charity within two and one-half months of the close of the corporate tax year.

Percentage Limitation and Carryforward

The charitable deduction is limited to 10 percent of the corporation's taxable income for the year, computed before the charitable deduction, the dividends received deduction, and the carryback of a capital loss or the carryback of a net operating loss. Any excess contribution is carried forward for no more than five years. The excess which is carried forward cannot be deducted to the extent it increases a net operating loss carryover in the carryover period.

EXAMPLE 16.36	Donor Corporation has book income for the year of $200,000, which includes a charitable contribution deduction of $30,000, and domestic dividend income of $21,250 from more than 20 percent owned corporations. It also has a $5,000 net operating loss carryforward from the previous year.

Book income	$200,000
Plus: Charitable contribution	30,000
Contribution base	$230,000
Less:	
Charitable contribution (10 percent base)	– 23,000
Dividends received deduction (80% of $21,250)	– 17,000
NOL carryforward	– 5,000
Taxable Income	$185,000

Donor has a charitable contribution deduction of $23,000 and a $7,000 charitable contribution carryover for a maximum of five years.

Ordinary Income Property

As with individual taxpayers, the corporation's charitable deduction for ordinary income property is limited to the basis of that property. A corporation may donate certain inventory to public charities, or operating foundations, for the elderly, infants, or the needy and claim a deduction for an amount equal to its basis plus one-half of its normal gross profit for those items. However, the gross profit add-on cannot increase the amount of the deduction to a sum greater than twice the basis of the inventory property.

¶16,241   CORPORATE DISTRIBUTIONS

Corporate Income Payable to Shareholders

Sometimes with small, closely held corporations, there might be a confusion of corporate and shareholder income, and related items. The substance of such transactions for closely held corporations must be closely examined to determine the proper treatment of the transaction.

For example, income due to the corporation may be paid directly to the shareholder. The earnings of a corporation do not accrue to its shareholders until distributed in the form of a dividend. So, were a corporation's income paid directly to the shareholder, there might be an attempt to have the income taxed only once (i.e., just to the shareholder). Such transactions likely would be recast by the IRS as income to the corporation first, and then a dividend distribution from the corporation to the shareholder, for which there is no corporate deduction.

As another example, consider if the shareholder pays personal obligations out of the corporation's funds (i.e., by using the corporation's checkbook). This transaction possibly could be recast in one of two ways. One interpretation is that there is compensation to the shareholder, deductible by the corporation, in the amount of the personal obligation. Another interpretation is that there is a corporate dividend to the shareholder in the amount of the obligation. Under this interpretation, the dividend is not deductible by the corporation.

The corporation is an entity separate and apart from its shareholders. Attempts by shareholders to commingle corporate and personal transactions are resisted by the IRS. The separateness of the corporation will be emphasized, and the substance of transactions should prevail over the form.

Cash Distributions

When a corporation makes a distribution to its stockholders with respect to its stock, the recipient reports dividend income to the extent of earnings and profits (E&P) of the current year. Any excess is also treated as a dividend to the extent of earnings and profits accumulated by the corporation in years prior to the current year. Any excess distribution is a return of the stockholder's basis. When the stockholder's basis for the stock is reduced to zero, any further distributions are treated as proceeds from the sale of the stockholder's stock, resulting in long-term or short-term capital gain, depending upon the stockholder's holding period of the stock at the time of the distribution. Current earnings and profits are deemed distributed pro rata for the current year; accumulated earnings and profits are deemed distributed on a FIFO basis.

EXAMPLE 16.37

Betty Bowes was the sole stockholder of Cable Corp. Her basis for the stock she acquired in 2011 was $1,000. As of January 1, 2015, Cable Corp. had accumulated earnings and profits of $6,000. For 2015, it had current earnings and profits of $5,000. Betty sold all of her stock to Ann on July 31, 2015, for $2,400. Cable Corp. made four distributions of $4,000 to its shareholders, March 31, June 30, September 30, and December 31, 2015. The distributions are classified as follows:

		March 31	June 30	Sept. 30	Dec. 31
Dividend to Betty:	Current E&P	$1,250	$1,250		
	Accum. E&P	2,750	2,750		
Dividend to Ann:	Current E&P			$1,250	$1,250
	Accum. E&P			500	
	Return of Ann's Capital			2,250	150
	Ann's S-T Capital Gain				2,600

Thus, Betty, in addition to her long-term capital gain on the sale of her stock of $1,400, has dividend income of $8,000. Ann reports dividend income of $3,000, a return of her $2,400 basis, and a short-term capital gain of $2,600. Ann's basis in her stock in Cable Corp. is zero, and Cable Corp. has no remaining earnings and profits.

EXAMPLE 16.38	Jeremiah Baker is the sole shareholder of Yahoo Corporation. He has a basis for his stock of $15,000. As of January 1, 2015, Yahoo had accumulated earnings and profits of $35,000. During 2015, it has a loss which generates negative current earnings and profits of $40,000. On July 1, 2015, Yahoo made a cash distribution to Baker of $18,000. Absent a showing to the contrary, the 2015 deficit is deemed to be incurred ratably over the year. Hence, as of July 1, 2015, available earnings and profits were $15,000 ($35,000 – ($40,000/2)). Thus, Baker has a taxable dividend of $15,000 and a return of capital of $3,000. The basis for his stock is $12,000.

PLANNING POINTER	If a corporation has an accumulated deficit in its earnings and profits and begins making current earnings, the delay of the payment of a dividend beyond the end of the first profitable year accompanied by a doubling of the dividend in the following year can result in a partially tax-free distribution of what would otherwise be a fully taxable dividend out of current earnings and profits.

Property Distributions Received

When a noncash property distribution is made by a corporation, the measure of the distribution is its fair market value upon distribution. That amount is dividend income, a return of capital, capital gain, or a combination of these, depending upon the earnings and profits of the distributing corporation and the basis of the stock to the recipient. The property basis to the recipient is its fair market value. Code Sec. 301.

Of course, if the property is subject to a liability, the amount of the distribution is reduced by the amount of the liability. However, the basis to the recipient of the property would include the liability to its full amount, if the liability is assumed by the recipient. If the recipient merely takes the property subject to the liability and the value of the property is less than the amount of the liability, the basis of the property will not exceed its fair market value.

Gain upon Property Distributions

A corporation must recognize gain upon the distribution of appreciated property. Code Sec. 311. It will not recognize a loss upon the distribution of property which has declined in value. The earnings and profits of the distributing corporation reflect the treatment accorded the recipients. With appreciated property, earnings and profits are increased by the gain recognized, and earnings and profits are then reduced by the fair market value of the property. Where there is a distribution and no gain is recognized, earnings and profits are reduced by the adjusted basis (for E&P purposes) of the property distributed. Code Sec. 312.

Where there are liabilities to which the distributed property is subject, or liabilities which the shareholder assumes with the distribution, the distribution to the shareholder is reduced by such liabilities as is the charge against the distributing corporation's earnings and profits.

EXAMPLE 16.39	Hornby Corporation distributes an investment asset to its sole shareholder. At the time of the distribution, the property has a basis to Hornby of $17,000, and a fair market value of $31,000. The investment asset is subject to a $12,000 liability, and the property is distributed subject to the liability. Hornby Corporation recognizes a $14,000 capital gain. Hornby increases its earnings and profits by the $14,000 gain, and it reduces its earnings and profits by $19,000 ($31,000 fair market value – $12,000 liability). The shareholder reports a $19,000 dividend, and takes a $31,000 basis in the investment asset.

Stock Dividends

In general, a stockholder recognizes no income upon the receipt of the stock of the issuing corporation distributed with respect to the stockholdings. Code Sec. 305. The stockholder's investment is merely represented by more shares. Accountants should notice that the distinction between stock dividends and stock splits (the 20-25 percent rule) is ignored for tax purposes. The earnings and profits of a corporation are unaffected by either such distribution.

A stock dividend is taxable to the shareholder if any shareholder has the option of taking cash (other than to avoid fractional shares) in lieu of the stock distribution. It is irrelevant that no stockholder elected to actually take the cash. A dividend distribution is taxable where some common stockholders receive preferred stock and other common stockholders receive common stock, and a distribution is also taxable if it results in the receipt of property by some stockholders and an increase in the proportionate interests of other shareholders in the assets or earnings and profits of the corporation.

A distribution of preferred stock to common stockholders where there was no preferred stock previously outstanding is tax free. The stock is referred to as Section 306 stock. Code Sec. 306. It is likely that the subsequent sale of that preferred stock may result in ordinary income to the seller. This will occur if, at the time the preferred stock was distributed, cash had been distributed instead and the cash distribution would have resulted in a taxable dividend.

"Informal" Dividends

Unlike local law, there is no need in tax law for a dividend to be paid pro rata to all stockholders. Often, "constructive" dividends are found where the stockholder-employee pays himself or herself an excessively large salary or sells or rents assets to the corporation at an unreasonably high price. Another instance is where the stockholder-employee (or someone else because of the stockholder's position) is able to make a bargain purchase, paying less than fair market value for goods or services of the corporation.

¶16,245   REGULAR RATES AND GRADUATED SCALE

Corporate taxable income is taxed under the following graduated rate structure:

Taxable Income	Rate
$0 to $50,000	15%
$50,001 to $75,000	25%
$75,001 to $100,000	34%
$100,001 to $335,000	39%
$335,001 to $10,000,000	34%
$10,000,001 to $15,000,000	35%
$15,000,001 to $18,333,333	38%
Over $18,333,333	35%

To discourage corporations from taking advantage of the lower brackets, certain affiliated corporations must share the lower brackets. Code Sec. 1563.

Corporations with over $100,000 in taxable income are subject to a 5 percent tax on such excess between $100,000 and $335,000. The maximum additional tax is $11,250 (($335,000 – $100,000) × 5%). This figure represents the savings from being in a tax bracket below 34 percent on the first $75,000. At $335,001 of taxable income, the result is the equivalent of a "flat tax" of 34 percent. The 34 percent "flat tax" is imposed on corporations whose taxable income ranges from $335,001 to $10,000,000. At $10,000,001 the tax rate increases to 35 percent. Corporations with over $15,000,000 in taxable income are subject to a 3 percent tax on the excess between $15,000,000 and $18,333,333. The maximum additional tax is $100,000 (($18,333,333 – $15,000,000) × 3%). This figure represents the savings from being in the 34 percent bracket on the first $10,000,000. At $18,333,333 of taxable income, the result is the equivalent of a "flat tax" of 35 percent. These tax rates are shown in the above tax rate schedule.

EXAMPLE 16.40   Pelzer Corporation has $180,000 of taxable income. Pelzer's federal income tax liability is $53,450, calculated as follows: (15% × $50,000) + (25% × $25,000) + (34% × ($25,000)) + (39% × ($180,000 – $100,000)).

As the marginal corporate tax rate on income over $75,000 (34%) almost equals the highest marginal rate for individuals (39.6%), the corporate form, at least in terms of rates, ceases to be as attractive a tax shelter.

Corporate capital gains are taxed at regular corporate income tax rates, with the maximum tax on corporate capital gains at 35 percent. While the capital gains themselves will not be taxed at greater than 35 percent, that income is included in determining whether income other than capital gains is subject to the 5 percent surcharge. Capital losses are still deductible only against capital gains. All of the classification provisions are left in the Internal Revenue Code in the likely event that the marginal tax on ordinary income will once again exceed the rate deemed appropriate for gain on long-term investments and the special treatment of capital gains will be reinstated.

¶16,250   PERSONAL SERVICE CORPORATIONS

Personal service corporations are those which are engaged in performing services in the fields of health, law, engineering, architecture, accounting, actuarial science, performing arts, and consulting, and substantially all of whose stock is owned by employees performing those types of services for the corporation.

Personal service corporations are excepted from the general corporate requirement that necessitates use of the accrual method of accounting. Also, they are eligible to retain their fiscal years or to elect limited deferral of income by electing a fiscal year for tax reporting as provided for partnerships, as discussed at ¶16,125.

These corporations are not permitted to use the graduated rates; their entire taxable income is taxed at the maximum corporate rate of 35 percent. Thus, there is an incentive for the corporation to zero out its taxable income by paying salaries and other deductible expenses. However, this tactic is limited. While the personal service corporation does not have to make any "required payments" for its fiscal year privilege, there are minimum distribution requirements in the deferral period. If those requirements are not met, the corporation is limited in the deductions it can take for payments to employees who are more than 10 percent owners on any day during the tax year.

¶16,255   CORPORATE ALTERNATIVE MINIMUM TAX

Corporations are subject to an alternative minimum tax (AMT) that is equal to the excess of the tentative minimum tax for the tax year over the regular tax for the tax year. Corporations with average gross receipts of $5,000,000 or less for the three previous years are not liable for the alternative minimum tax. Essentially, the corporation pays the higher of its regular tax or its tentative minimum tax. In addition to the foreign tax credit, which can be taken by all taxpayers, corporations reduce their regular tax, for purposes of calculating the AMT, by their possession tax credit. The calculation of the corporation's alternative minimum taxable income (AMTI) (to which the 20 percent alternative minimum tax rate is applied) is done by making adjustments to the following items of the corporation's regular taxable income for the year before any net operating loss deductions have been taken.

1. Depreciation on pre-1987 acquisitions and post-1986 acquisitions using MACRS depreciation
2. Mining and exploration and development costs
3. Long-term contracts
4. Net operating losses
5. Pollution control facilities
6. Installment sales
7. Circulation expenditures
8. Capital construction funds
9. Farming losses

See Chapter 9 for a discussion of AMT adjustments.

In all of the above cases, the deduction (or income inclusion) required under the AMT rules is substituted for the regular tax deduction (or income inclusion). The difference between the deduction (or inclusion) is reflected through an adjustment (it could be negative or positive) to regular taxable income to compute AMTI.

EXAMPLE 16.41   A corporation's 2015 regular taxable income is $135,000. Included in its regular taxable income are the following two items: (1) a MACRS depreciation deduction of $15,000 for property acquired in 2010, and (2) $12,000 of income from a $100,000 installment sale made in 2015. Assume that the special AMT rules permit a depreciation deduction of $19,000 for the property acquired in 2010. Also, the rules do not permit the installment method, and so all $100,000 from the sale is required to be included for AMT purposes. The depreciation adjustment would require that regular taxable income be reduced by $4,000 to compute AMTI. The installment sale adjustment would require that regular taxable income be increased by $88,000.

Following the application of the preceding adjustments, the corporation's regular taxable income must be increased by the following tax preferences:

1.   Percentage depletion
2.   Intangible drilling costs
3.   Bad debt reserves of financial institutions
4.   Private activity bonds tax-exempt interest
5.   Accelerated depreciation and amortization on certain pre-1987 property

Following the increase of the regular taxable income by tax preferences, the corporation is entitled to a special energy deduction for tax years beginning after 1990, provided the corporation is not a member of an integrated oil company. The deduction is based upon a specified portion of various oil and gas related tax preference items which has the effect of reducing AMTI for increases from the depletion preference, the intangible drilling cost preference, and (in the case of corporate taxpayers) the adjusted current earnings adjustment treatment accorded depletion and intangible drilling costs.

After the above adjustments are made to arrive at tentative AMTI, the adjusted current earnings (ACE) of the corporation must be determined. Different depreciation rates and lives are used for ACE than for either regular income tax computation, the AMT, or earnings and profits. Some of the other adjustments to determine ACE are intangible drilling costs, circulation and organization expenses, LIFO inventory adjustments, and depletion.

Tentative AMTI is subtracted from ACE and 75 percent of the difference becomes the ACE adjustment which is added to tentative AMTI. From this balance there is deducted an exemption of $40,000 (reduced by 25 percent of the excess of AMTI over $150,000). The resulting net AMTI is taxed at a rate of 20 percent to provide the tentative minimum tax. From this tentative minimum tax is subtracted the regular corporate tax liability. Any excess is payable as the AMT.

¶16,265   MINIMUM TAX COMPUTATION

The following is a simplified illustration of a computation of the AMT.

EXAMPLE 16.42   The New Corporation has taxable income as shown. The corporation has $100,000 of interest from municipal "nonessential function" bonds (private activity bonds) issued after September 1, 1986, and it incurred a $10,000 expense in connection with that exempt income. Excess depreciation with respect to cost recovery property placed in service prior to 1987 resulted in a preference of $30,000. Depreciation computed under the alternative method for post-1986 property amounted to $130,000. The applicable state income tax rate is 6 percent.

	ACE	Regular	AMT
Gross Sales	$1,500,000	$1,500,000	$1,500,000
Cost of Sales	900,000	900,000	900,000
Gross Margin	$600,000	$600,000	$600,000
Tax-Exempt Interest	110,000		110,000
Nondeductible Cost	(10,000)		(10,000)
Domestic Dividends	300,000	300,000	300,000
80 percent DRD	(240,000)	(240,000)	(240,000)
Depr. Pre-87 Property	(100,000)		
ACRS		(170,000)	(170,000)
Preference			30,000
Depr. Post-86 Property	(120,000)		
MACRS		(135,000)	
Alternate Method			(130,000)
Other Expenses	(300,000)	(300,000)	(300,000)
Net Adjustments	(360,000)	(545,000)	(410,000)
Income Before Tax	$240,000	$55,000	$190,000
State Income Tax	28,000	28,000	28,000
Income Before U.S. Tax	$212,000	$27,000	$162,000
Tentative AMTI	162,000		
Total ACE	$50,000		
Percentage	×.75		
Excess ACE	$37,500		$37,500
AMTI			$199,500
Exemption ($40,000 − .25 ($199,500 − $150,000))			27,625
Net AMTI			$171,875
AMT Rate			×.20
Tentative Minimum Tax			$34,375
Regular Tax ($27,000 × .15)			$4,050
AMT Due			$30,325

¶16,275   PENALTY TAXES

Accumulated Earnings Tax

A corporation which is "availed of" for the purpose of unreasonably accumulating earnings, not paying sufficient dividends to its stockholders, or retaining earnings beyond its reasonable needs may be subject to a tax on its accumulated taxable income at a rate of 15 percent after 2003. Code Sec. 531. This penalty tax is in addition to the regular (or minimum) tax the corporation will pay; however, the corporation will be permitted a deduction for its regular income tax and for its long-term capital gains in computing accumulated taxable income. The accumulated earnings tax (AET) can be avoided by the corporation's paying out earnings as a dividend during the taxable year, having the stockholders consent to be taxed as if they had received a dividend on the last day of the corporate year, or paying a dividend within two and one-half months of the close of the taxable year of the corporation.

Instead of establishing reasonable business needs for accumulating earnings, the corporation may claim a credit of up to $250,000 for a nonservice corporation, $150,000 for a service corporation. This credit is applied first against accumulated earnings and profits of prior years and is not a new credit for each year. Earnings and profits is a measure of the corporation's economic capacity to pay dividends. Code Sec. 312.

EXAMPLE 16.43	Assume a corporation had accumulated earnings and profits (for purposes of the AET) at the end of the previous year of $100,000, that it paid no dividends for the current year, and had earnings and profits for the current year of another $200,000. If it were a nonservice corporation, it would have $50,000 subject to the penalty tax for the current year.

The AET applies to all corporations, regardless of their size and the number of their stockholders. Code Sec. 532(c). However, the prohibited purpose envisaged by the statute is the intent to avoid income tax on the shareholder level by withholding the payment of dividends. In view of the pressure exerted by stockholders of publicly held corporations for the payment of dividends, it is difficult to imagine the penalty tax being imposed upon a large, widely held corporation.

Personal Holding Company Tax

The personal holding company (PHC) tax is another penalty tax. Code Sec. 541. It, however, is a burden peculiar to closely held corporations. The computation of the "undistributed personal holding income" subject to the tax is not radically different from the computation of accumulated taxable income. Again, a deduction is allowed for regular income tax paid or accrued, and the tax does not apply to long-term capital gains. Code Sec. 545. The rate of this tax is a flat 15 percent after 2003 and, again, it is in addition to the regular tax.

The purpose of this tax also is to force the payment of earnings to the shareholders in the form of dividends. Thus, a deduction against taxable income is permitted for dividends paid during the taxable year, consent dividends (constructively paid at the end of the corporate year), post-end-of-year dividends, and deficiency dividends. The post-end-of-year dividends must be paid within two and one-half months after the close of the taxable year (same as with the accumulated earnings tax), but this deduction is limited to such dividends as do not exceed 20 percent of the amount of the dividends which were paid during the year in question. "Deficiency dividends" are those paid by the taxpayer corporation after the IRS has assessed a deficiency for this tax.

Two tests must be satisfied before a corporation is subject to the PHC tax. During the last half of its taxable year, on at least one day, more than 50 percent of its outstanding stock must be owned, directly or indirectly, by five or fewer persons. Extensive ownership attribution rules are applied. If the ownership test is met, then a personal holding company income (PHCI) test is applied. The "ordinary gross income" of the corporation is determined. In general, this is the corporation's gross income exclusive of capital gains and Section 1231 gains treated as long-term capital gains. From this ordinary gross income there are permitted a limited number of specific deductions against certain types of income (i.e., there are permitted against ordinary gross income from rents only the deductions for interest, taxes, depreciation, and rental of equipment (there is no attempt to determine net profit from rents, for example)). This resulting amount is designated "adjusted ordinary gross income."

If PHCI is at least 60 percent of the adjusted ordinary gross income of the corporation, the corporation is potentially subject to the PHC tax. Personal holding company income is generally passive income (i.e., interest, dividends, royalties, etc.). However, rents, mineral royalties, copyrights, and certain shareholder source income can be included in the determination of PHC income if minimum dividend payments have not been made by the corporation.

If the adjusted rental income is less than 50 percent of the adjusted ordinary gross income, rents are included in PHCI. Adjusted rental income will not be included in PHCI if two tests are met. The adjusted rental income must equal or exceed 50 percent of adjusted ordinary gross income. If this test is met, then such PHCI (other than rents) included in ordinary gross income is totaled. This sum is reduced by 10 percent of PHCI ordinary gross income. If the company paid or is deemed to have paid dividends to its stockholders at least equal to the remainder, the rents are not included in PHCI.

| EXAMPLE 16.44 | This example illustrates the computations necessary to determine (1) whether the corporation is a personal holding company and (2) whether the corporation is subject to the penalty tax. |

	Ord. Gross Income	Adj. Ord. Gross Income
Gross Margin from Sale of Goods	$5,000	$5,000
Dividend Income	4,000	4,000
Interest Income	5,000	5,000
Rents	25,000	13,000*
Totals	$39,000	$27,000

* Gross rents reduced by the statutory deductions permitted (taxes, interest,depreciation, and rental of equipment (i.e., adjusted rents)).

Rents being less than 50 percent of adjusted ordinary gross income, they are PHCI. Therefore, PHCI is $22,000 (Dividends of $4,000 + Interest of $5,000 + Rents of $13,000), and since 22/27 is more than 60 percent of AOGI, the company is a PHC.

If adjusted rents had been $15,000 so that AOGI would be $29,000, rents still would be PHCI unless the corporation had paid out so much of its other PHCI ($9,000) as exceeds 10 percent of its ordinary gross income ($3,900). Thus, unless the corporation paid out dividends amounting to more than $5,100, rents would be PHCI and the corporation would be subject to the penalty tax.

| PLANNING POINTER | Even in the absence of the payment of dividends, the statute permits every $10 of ordinary gross income to shelter $1 of investment income from PHCI classification. Thus, a corporation with $900,000 of gross rental income could have $100,000 dividend income and still avoid the penalty tax even if it paid no dividends to its shareholders. |

The one favorable aspect of the AET and the PHC penalty taxes is that a corporation cannot be subject to both for the same year. The AET will not be applied to a personal holding company or a corporation exempt from tax. Banks, lending companies, life insurance companies, surety companies, and corporations exempt from income tax are excluded from the PHC tax.

¶16,285 CORPORATE LIQUIDATIONS

In general, gain or loss is recognized by the corporation upon the distribution of property to its shareholders in a complete liquidation. Code Sec. 336. The corporation's earnings and profits are usually eliminated along with the corporation's basis (adjusted for gain recognized on the distribution) in any property distributed in the liquidation. Section 331 provides that a shareholder treat the property received in liquidation of a corporation as proceeds obtained from the sale of stock. As to the mechanics, the shareholder's gain or loss is determined by deducting the adjusted basis of this stock from the fair market value of the liquidating distributions. A capital gain or loss is recognized immediately. The shareholders pick up a fair market value basis in any property distributed. Code Sec. 334(a).

Where certain requirements are met, no gain or loss is recognized by a parent corporation upon the receipt of assets in the complete liquidation of a controlled subsidiary. Further, the parent can retain the tax attributes of the subsidiary. This provision allows a group to eliminate unwanted subsidiaries and to avoid any tax which might otherwise occur if the subsidiary's assets have appreciated in value. Minority stockholders determine gain or loss without regard to this special provision.

S Corporations

¶16,301 TAX TREATMENT

A corporation created under state law and in all other respects the same as a "regular" corporation may, if it qualifies, elect to be governed by Subchapter S of the Internal Revenue Code. Such corporation is designated as an "S corporation." Code Sec. 1361, *et seq.*

An S corporation is treated much the same as a partnership (i.e., its items of income, deductions, loss, credits, and tax preferences retain their character and are passed through to the shareholders, whether or not there are any actual distributions). The items are passed through to the shareholders on a per-share, per-day basis.

Generally, an S corporation does not pay federal income taxes. However, there are four instances when an S corporation may have income tax liability. The potential tax liability facing an S corporation represents a significant difference from the partnership, which never has to pay federal income taxes. If a former C corporation elects to be treated as an S corporation, and it has realized gain in its assets at the time of the election, this gain subsequently may be taxed. Also, if an S corporation has excess passive investment income, it may have to pay tax on some of that income. These taxes are covered at ¶16,345.

There are two other instances when an S corporation may have to pay Federal income taxes. If a corporation elects to be treated as an S corporation, and the corporation formerly had used the LIFO method to value its inventories, it must pay income tax on the difference between the LIFO and FIFO inventory valuation amounts at the time of the election. The tax on the difference is paid through four equal annual installments. Code Sec. 1363. Also, if the corporation is subject to any general business credit recapture, the S corporation is subject to paying the recapture if it materializes after the S election is made. Code Sec. 1371.

It should be recalled that S corporation status is for federal income tax purposes, and a state may treat the S corporation as any other corporation, subjecting it to regular corporate income tax treatment. An information return, Form 1120S, is required of an S corporation.

¶16,315   S CORPORATION ELECTION

Requirements for Filing

An eligible corporation may elect S corporation status. All of its shareholders must consent to that election. To be eligible there can be no more than 100 shareholders; there can be no corporate shareholder; there can be only one class of stock (but the same class may have different voting privileges); shareholders may be individuals, estates, and certain trusts; and no shareholder may be a nonresident alien.

All members of a family will be treated as one shareholder for purposes of the rules limiting the number of permissible shareholders in an S corporation. The term "members of a family" includes the common ancestor and all lineal descendants of the common ancestor, plus spouses (or former spouses) of these individuals. The common ancestor cannot be more than six generations removed from the youngest generation of shareholders at the time the S election is made. A spouse or former spouse will be treated as being of the same generation as the individual to which he or she is or was married.

TAX BLUNDER

Fred Smyth uses funds in his self-directed individual retirement account to purchase shares in an S corporation. The corporation would no longer be an eligible S corporation as it has an ineligible shareholder. Fred should have purchased the shares with his own funds.

Time for Filing

A corporation elects to be treated as an S corporation by filing Form 2553. All shareholders on the day the election is made must consent to it. If the election is made before the fifteenth day of the third month of the corporation's taxable year, it is effective for the current year, provided (1) the corporation satisfied all the requirements above, and (2) all those who were shareholders during the pre-election period consent to the election. If a new corporation's first taxable year is a short taxable year, and the corporation wants to make the election to be an S corporation, it has two months and fifteen days from the beginning of its first taxable year to make a valid election for that year.

| EXAMPLE 16.45 | Gray Corporation, a new corporation, begins its first taxable year on August 21, 2015. Because it cannot establish a business purpose for a taxable year other than a calendar year (see ¶16,325 below), its first taxable year will run from August 21, 2015, through December 31, 2015. Gray Corporation has until November 4, 2015, to make an effective election to be an S Corporation for its first taxable year. |

If the election is made after the fifteenth day of the third month of the current taxable year, it is not effective until the first day of the next taxable year. The consenting shareholders who make the election before the fifteenth day of the third month of the current taxable year may specify that the election is not to be effective until the first day of the subsequent taxable year. Once the election is made, new shareholders do not have to consent for the continuation of the election, for it will continue until the corporation no longer satisfies the requirements of being an S corporation, or until the shareholders owning more than 50 percent of the voting stock of the corporation vote to revoke the election.

¶16,325   TAXABLE YEAR

The election of a tax year by an S corporation does not conform with the election by a C corporation (complete freedom). The S corporation must use the calendar year unless it can obtain permission from the IRS to use a fiscal year. Permission may be granted upon a showing of a genuine business purpose such as a natural business year. See ¶16,125.

The "required payments" and other rules applicable to partnerships discussed at ¶16,125 also apply to S corporations.

¶16,335   TERMINATION OF ELECTION

An election can be revoked by a vote of stockholders who hold more than one-half of the corporation's shares. Code Sec. 1362. If the revocation is made prior to the 15th day of the third month of the corporate year, it is effective for the entire corporate year, but the shareholders can specify that the revocation take effect after the date of the vote. An election is terminated if the corporation no longer is eligible for the election (i.e., has 101 shareholders, a nonresident alien stockholder, two classes of stock, etc.).

If a corporation is a "C corporation" (i.e., it has operated as a "regular" corporation prior to electing S corporation status and it has accumulated earnings and profits at the time of the election), accumulated earnings must be distributed or the S corporation election may be terminated. Termination occurs if such a corporation has more than 25 percent of its gross receipts from passive investment income for each of three consecutive years and it has any such pre-S corporation earnings and profits at the end of each of those three years. Termination is effective the first day of the year following such third consecutive year.

When the election is terminated (or revoked) during a taxable year, the corporation files two returns for the one year. An S corporation return, Form 1120S, is filed for the part of the year prior to the termination of the election, and a C corporation return, Form 1120, is filed for the balance of the year. Code Sec. 1362(e). The time period ends on the same day the tax year would have ended had there been no termination, and only one year is counted for purposes of carryovers. The S return is due at the same time as the C return. The allocation of income, etc., between the S corporation and the C corporation portions of the year is prorated on the basis of days unless all the shareholders consent to reflect the items in the respective short tax periods on the basis of when they are actually earned or incurred. The tax on the C corporate year is computed on an annualized basis.

¶16,345   TAX ON S CORPORATION INCOME

If a C corporation elects S corporation status and there exists at the time of the election a "built-in gain," upon the disposition of those assets by the S corporation within 5 years of the election, that gain is taxed at the maximum corporate rate (35 percent). The tax will be imposed on the lesser of the amount of the recognized built-in gain for the year or the corporate income computed as if the entity were a C corporation. NOLs and business credits from C corporation years may be used to reduce this tax. Code Sec. 1374.

| EXAMPLE 16.46 | Cantrell Corporation has been a regular C corporation for 10 years. Effective January 1, 2015, Cantrell elects to be an S corporation. Assume that it uses the calendar year. At the time of the election, the basis of Cantrell's assets totals $150,000, and the fair market value is $185,000. One of Cantrell's assets is accounts receivable, which has a zero basis, and a face and fair market value of $15,000. The accounts receivable are collected in 2015. Cantrell's 2015 taxable income is $90,000. Cantrell Corporation must pay built-in gains tax in 2015. It pays $5,250 ($15,000 × 35%) of federal income tax due to the collection of the accounts receivable. |

The S corporation may be subject to an income tax on its excess passive investment income. This tax applies to a corporation which has C corporation earnings and profits and passive investment income which is more than 25 percent of the corporation's gross receipts. This tax is not imposed upon a corporation which has been an S corporation from its inception or a previous C corporation which has reported under the S corporation election but has distributed its pre-S corporation earnings and profits.

The tax rate is the maximum corporate rate of 35 percent. The 35 percent rate is multiplied by the tax base, excess net passive income, which is as follows: net passive income (passive investment income less costs of its production) multiplied by a fraction the numerator of which is the passive income of the S corporation reduced by 25 percent of the gross receipts of the corporation and the denominator of which is the passive income of the corporation for the year. Excess net passive income may not exceed the corporation's taxable income for the year. Code Sec. 1375.

EXAMPLE 16.47

Androx Corporation, founded in 2001, operated as a C corporation until 2010, at which time it elected S corporation status. It had and continues to have earnings and profits accumulated as a C corporation. For its tax year ending December 31, 2015, Androx Corporation had gross receipts of $100,000. It had taxable income of $15,000 and passive income of $40,000 and could demonstrate the cost of $5,000 in producing that passive income. Androx's excess net passive income for 2015 is:

$$(\$40{,}000 - \$5{,}000) \quad \times \quad \frac{\$40{,}000 - (.25 \times \$100{,}000)}{\$40{,}000} \quad = \quad \$13{,}125$$

The tax is .35 of the lesser of $13,125 or the corporation's taxable income, $15,000 (i.e., .35 × $13,125 = $4,593.75).

¶16,355   ALLOCATION OF INCOME, DEDUCTIONS, AND CREDITS

The S corporation files a Schedule K-1 for each shareholder. Upon that schedule are reported essentially the same items as are reported by a partnership for its partners (i.e., separately reported items and the "nonseparately" computed income or loss). See ¶16,125. Code Sec. 1366(a)(1). The shareholder takes the separately reported items into account for the tax year within which the corporate year ends. Allocations are generally made on the basis of stock ownership on a per-day, per share basis.

If a shareholder should die during an S corporation year, the shareholder's final return, like a partner in a partnership, reports pro rata income from the S corporation to the date of death. For example, assume an entity had $100,000 taxable income for the year. A 20 percent owner died at midyear. The deceased owner would include $10,000 ($100,000 × 20% × ½ year) on the owner's last income tax return.

Following the partnership analogy, the S corporation is treated as a conduit, with the income and deduction items retaining the same character in the hands of the shareholder as they had in the hands of the S corporation. Code Sec. 1366(b).

When an S corporation is subject to a tax because of built-in gain or excessive passive investment income, the income taxed is reduced by the tax applied. Thus, if the S corporation is subject to a passive investment income tax, the pass-through passive investment income is reduced by that tax.

The adjustments to the shareholder's basis are also analogous to the adjustments made to a partner. Code Secs. 705 and 1367(a). However, the shareholder does not increase or decrease the basis of stock because of the corporation's liabilities to nonshareholders, as a partner does in a partnership.

Where a calendar year S corporation, reporting on the accrual basis, owes an expense item to a shareholder, reporting on the cash basis, the S corporation is treated as on the cash basis with respect to that item and cannot deduct it until it is paid. Thus, the related parties reflect the same item in the same year. Code Sec. 267(b) and (e).

¶16,365   TREATMENT OF LOSSES

Losses are passed through currently to the shareholders on a per-share, per-day basis. Unlike for a partnership, the shareholders may deduct passed through losses only to the extent of their basis in their stock and their basis in the amount of corporate debt owed directly to them. Recall from above that debts owed by the corporation to others do not enter into the computation of a shareholder's basis. Since these losses pass through to the stockholders, the corporation has neither a loss carryback nor a loss carryforward.

Losses passed through first reduce the basis of the stockholder's stock, then the basis of debt owed to the stockholder by the corporation. Future earnings replenish the basis of the debt first and then are applied to increase the basis of the stock. Code Sec. 1367.

EXAMPLE 16.48   Oscar Trevon had a basis for his 40 percent stock investment in S corporation of $20,000, and he had loaned the corporation an additional $50,000. In 2014, the S corporation incurred a loss of $100,000, of which $40,000 passed through to Oscar, permitting him to deduct $40,000. His basis to his stock was reduced to zero; his basis to his note receivable, to $30,000. In 2015, S corporation generated taxable income of $60,000. Oscar reports $24,000 as his share. His basis to his note receivable is reinstated to $50,000; his stock to $4,000.

¶16,375   TREATMENT OF DISTRIBUTIONS

There are two separate sets of rules which apply to distributions which S corporations make to shareholders. The rules differ depending on whether the S corporation has earnings and profits. The earnings and profits could be from years when the corporation was a regular C corporation.

If the S corporation has no earnings and profits, the distribution is tax free up to the shareholder's basis in the S corporation stock. Amounts distributed beyond the basis cause long- or short-term capital gain, depending on the shareholder's holding period for the stock. Code Sec. 1368(b).

If the S corporation has earnings and profits, there are several tiers through which the distribution must pass. Generally the distribution is tax free up to the amount of the S corporation's accumulated adjustments account. If the shareholder's basis in the corporation's stock is less than the amount of the accumulated adjustments account, the difference is capital gain. Any remaining distribution (if it is in cash) is tax free to the extent of previously taxed income if the corporation was an S corporation before 1983. Next, the distribution is a dividend to the extent of the corporation's earnings and profits. The balance of the distribution, if any, is tax free up to the shareholder's remaining basis in the stock, and then causes capital gain. Code Sec. 1368(c).

For an S corporation which has earnings and profits only from years when it was a C corporation, there is a special election the corporation can make which permits distributions first to come out of earnings and profits. An S corporation would consider making this election to eliminate the possibility of incurring the tax for excess passive investment income (¶16,345), or to eliminate the risk of losing the election to be an S corporation because of too much passive investment income (¶16,335).

When an S corporation distributes appreciated property to a shareholder, as the appreciation has not been reflected in anyone's income, the corporation is deemed to have sold the asset to the stockholder at its fair market value. Thus, the corporation, upon distributing an appreciated capital asset, must report the gain, is subjected to a tax if the gain is built-in gain, and the gain, net of the tax, is passed through to the stockholder.

¶16,385   ACCUMULATED ADJUSTMENTS ACCOUNT

The accumulated adjustments account (AAA) is an important measuring rod in assessing the taxability of distributions from an S corporation which has earnings and profits. The account is an S corporation account (i.e., it is maintained by the S corporation). Code Sec. 1368(e). The rules for computing it are very similar to the rules for determining the shareholder's basis in the S corporation stock.

The AAA is increased for the corporation's separately reported items of income and gain and "nonseparately" computed income. It is decreased for separately reported items of deduction and loss and "nonseparately" computed loss. The AAA is reduced for nondividend distributions. The AAA is not adjusted for tax-exempt income and related expenses. This is a difference from the rules for maintaining the basis of the shareholder's stock, in that the shareholder increases the basis of the S corporation stock for the shareholder's part of tax-exempt income. Any federal taxes paid for the period the corporation was a regular C corporation do not affect the AAA.

TAX BLUNDER

Kathleen has a regular corporation in which she does not materially participate. She decides to convert the corporation to an S corporation. The corporation has $40,000 of investment income and an operating loss of $40,000 for the year. Kathleen's only other income is wages of $75,000. She has no other investment income or expenses and no other passive investments. The $40,000 of investment income from the S corporation is passed through and included in Kathleen's gross income. The $40,000 operating loss is also passed through but is not deductible by Kathleen since it deductible only against passive income. If Kathleen had not converted the corporation to an S corporation, she would have been able to offset the $40,000 net operating loss with the $40,000 of investment income, she would have incurred no corporate income tax, and she would not have to include the $40,000 investment income on her personal return.

SUMMARY

- The choice of the form of doing business depends upon the degree of reward and the risk the entrepreneur is individually willing to assume.
- Partnerships never pay federal income tax, while C corporations are taxed as separate entities. The S corporation may have to pay federal income taxes in some instances.
- Partnerships are the easiest to form, and the income, gains, deductions, and credits flow through to the partners, retaining their same identity.
- Items that are specially treated on the partner level must be reported separately from the ordinary income or loss of the partnership.
- The basis of a partner's interest in a partnership is affected by most economic events that cause the recognition of income or expense by the partnership, whether or not the event causes the recognition of those items for purposes of taxation.
- Partnerships are required to use the same tax year as those partners holding a majority interest in the partnership.
- The partnership year closes for a partner whenever that partner disposes of his or her partnership interest.
- The tax year of a partnership ends only when the partnership is terminated. Termination will happen when no partner continues the business of the partnership or when, within a 12-month period, there is a sale of 50 percent or more of the partnership interest.
- Generally, a partner can engage in transactions with the partnership just like nonpartners. However, losses between related taxpayers are disallowed, and sometimes gains must be reported as ordinary income.
- Gain will be recognized by partners when distributions exceed the partner's basis. Loss will be recognized only if the distribution is in complete termination of the partner's interest and the partner receives only money, accounts receivable, or inventory that is less than the partner's basis for the partnership interest.
- The sale of a partnership interest is a capital gain except for the portion of the gain that represents the sale of Section 751 assets.
- Neither gain nor loss is recognized by transferors of property to a corporation solely in exchange for stock of the transferee corporation if immediately after the transfer the transferors are in control of the corporation.
- If property other than stock is received in the transfer to a corporation, that property is "boot" and the gain realized is taxed to the extent of the boot received.
- The requirements for electing S corporation treatment include the number of shareholders, their domicile, and the class of stock. Generally, no corporations can be a shareholder.
- Corporations may be subject to the alternative minimum tax, the personal holding company tax, and the accumulated earnings tax.
- The S corporation election will be terminated if the S corporation ceases to qualify for the election or if the shareholders who own the majority of the corporation's stock vote to revoke the election.
- The S corporation may be subjected to tax on the corporate level when it disposes of built-in gain property, when it has excessive passive income, when the C corporation switching to S status is using LIFO inventory, and when there is general business recapture from a previous C corporation purchase.

QUESTIONS

1. Kenny and Leonard each own 50 percent of the outstanding common stock of Corporation Right and Corporation Wrong, both involved in the printing business. They often disagreed on management decisions and were pleased when Martin suggested to them that the three of them join in a joint venture to which Kenny and Leonard would each contribute their stock in Corporation Right and Corporation Wrong and Martin, their accountant, would equal their contribution in cash. It was agreed that the stock of each corporation had a value of $250,000, so Martin contributed cash of $250,000. Within weeks it became apparent that the venture would not function, so the partnership was dissolved and wound up with Kenny receiving all of the stock of Corporation Right, Leonard receiving all of the stock of Corporation Wrong, and Martin receiving his $250,000 in cash. Discuss the tax implications of the above.

2. The Baker partnership was formed and began business November 1, 2015. It incurred the following costs: legal fees from drafting partnership agreement, $4,000; accounting fees for establishing financial records, $3,000; recording fees payable to local government, $500; and expenses of organizational meeting, $1,500. The partnership is reporting on the accrual method and adopted the calendar year. It actually paid all of the above costs, except the accounting fee, on January 3, 2016. It is expected that the partnership will last 12 years, and the treasurer proposes to write off 2/144 × $9,000 for 2015. Discuss.

3. Partner Johnson owns a 4 percent interest in the Magma Partnership, an accrual basis, calendar year concern. On January 1, 2015, Johnson, a cash basis taxpayer, loaned the partnership $20,000 at 9 percent annual interest. Magma reported 2015 ordinary partnership income of $12,000 for financial purposes. Johnson was not paid his interest until February 3, 2016. Discuss the tax treatment for the partnership and the partner.

4. Jones and Bones formed the JB general partnership with separate contributions of $100,000 cash. JB purchased a capital asset from Jones at its fair market value of $100,000, paying $25,000 cash and assuming the outstanding $75,000 mortgage. The asset had been purchased by Jones two years prior for $40,000. Shortly after its acquisition, the partnership refinanced the capital asset, borrowing $90,000 and retiring the $75,000 obligation. Discuss the bases of the partners' interests in the partnership.

5. Assume in the above example that Jones, instead of selling the asset to the partnership, contributed it and received for his $25,000 equity an increase in his interest from 50 percent to 60 percent in the partnership's profits and losses. Discuss the bases of the partners' interests in the partnership.

6. Henry has been a dealer in real estate for some time. One particular parcel of land that he purchased several years ago for $100,000 has been difficult to sell as one parcel. Deciding that he would develop it for housing sites, he withdrew the land from his listing of properties for sale. He plans to form a partnership with a super salesman friend, Marvin, who will act as sales manager for the project and who is willing to invest $20,000 cash. Henry will invest $90,000 in cash. As the land is easily worth $400,000, the partnership will purchase the property from Henry at that price, paying $100,000 down and $250,000 from the proceeds of a first mortgage secured by the property and guaranteed by Henry and Marvin. The balance of the purchase price is evidenced by a purchase money mortgage note of $50,000 issued by the new partnership.
   a. State how much gain Henry will realize and recognize upon the transfer of the property to the partnership and how that gain will be classified.
   b. What will be the basis of the property to the partnership?

7. If a partnership makes a pro rata distribution of one half of its assets to each of its partners and those distributed assets consist of only

unrealized receivables and land held by the partnership as investment, no gain or loss will be reported by the partners upon the distribution even though the basis of the assets and their fair market values greatly exceed the basis of the partners in their partnership interests. Discuss.

8. Partner Rachael owned a 25 percent interest in the Manual Partnership, a cash basis taxpayer. In the current year, she received a current distribution of $18,750 from her partnership, reducing her interest to 20 percent. Prior to the distribution, her basis for the interest was $25,000, and the books of the partnership revealed the following:

	Basis	FMV
Cash	$50,000	$50,000
Accounts Receivable	0	40,000
Inventory	40,000	42,000
Operating Assets	110,000	168,000
	$200,000	$300,000

What is the tax treatment if the distribution made is $16,750 cash and $2,000 accounts receivable?

9. George, Sr. is a financial consultant operating as a sole proprietor. George, Jr. is commencing his senior year toward completing his undergraduate education in business school, majoring in finance. George, Jr. worked with his father during the last summer, and George, Sr. was so pleased that he offered his son a part interest in the firm. George, Sr. will invest all of his operating assets, valued at $40,000, and acquire an 80 percent interest in the firm's capital and profits. George, Jr. will invest $10,000, will render services upon demand, and will receive a 20 percent interest in the firm's capital and profits. As George, Jr. has no funds of his own, his father is giving him the $10,000 to invest. Discuss the validity of the partnership.

10. Is it true that when a person incorporates a sole proprietorship, the person, in effect, converts what was, at least in part, ordinary income assets in the person's hands into a capital asset investment? Explain.

11. In spite of a corporation's paying income tax on its income and the shareholder's paying tax when that income is extracted from the corporation, the corporate form may validly be classified as a tax shelter. Discuss.

12. If a taxpayer owns property with a great growth but little income potential, the taxpayer is generally better advised to hold that property as an individual investor or to transfer it to a controlled corporation, let it appreciate in value, and then sell the stock. Discuss.

13. Discuss briefly two situations where stockholders will be held taxable on the receipt of additional shares from their corporation paid to them with respect to their ownership of stock in that corporation.

14. Why is it significant to determine the degree of ownership a corporate shareholder holds in the stock of a corporation declaring a dividend?

15. Why would a professional person wish to incorporate a practice into a corporation?

16. Distinguish among the rules for taxable years for a partnership, a C corporation, and an S corporation.

17. Both the accumulated earnings tax and the personal holding company tax are penalty taxes. What is the primary purpose of the provisions?

18. S corporation shareholders may consent to have the corporation elect to have distributions of cash made to them treated as taxable dividends even though the shareholders have paid taxes on that amount of income earned, which they are entitled to treat as tax free. Why would they make such an election?

19. Under what circumstances does an S corporation pay federal income tax?

20. An S corporation is essentially a corporation treated for federal income tax purposes as if it were a partnership. Discuss.

PROBLEMS

22. The Urequa Partnership was formed and began business July 1, 2015. In the process of its formation, the partners spent the following sums during 2015. Determine the maximum amount they can deduct in 2015.
    a. $5,000 in legal fees paid for drafting a partnership agreement.
    b. $3,000 in accounting fees paid for setting up a bookkeeping system.
    c. $11,000 in start-up costs, training employees prior to the opening of the business in the proper operation of partnership equipment.

23. Alice, Betty, and Carol were all independently operating beauticians. They formed an equal partnership with Alice investing $10,000 cash, Betty contributing her equipment with an adjusted basis of $5,000, fair market value of $10,000, and Carol contributing her accounts receivable, face amount and value of $10,000, basis to Carol of zero. For bookkeeping purposes each has her capital account credited for $10,000.
    a. What is the basis each woman has for her partnership interest?
    b. What basis does the partnership take for the contributed assets?

24. Assume that the partnership in Problem 23 has no net income or loss for its first year—it breaks exactly even—except for the write-off of the equipment (using a five-year life and straight-line method) and the collection of the receivables.
    a. What income does the partnership report for the year?
    b. What income will each of the partners report for the year?
    c. What is each partner's basis at the end of the first year?

21. In terms of the effects on both the entity and the distributee, describe the tax consequences of a cash distribution from a partnership, a regular C corporation, and an S corporation.

25. Which of the following will be reported separately by the partners and not as an item included in the partnership's ordinary income?
    a. Net short-term capital gain of $1,000 comprised of: long-term capital gains of $5,000; long-term capital losses of $8,000 and short-term capital losses of $2,000; short-term capital gains of $6,000.
    b. Net gains from sale of Section 1231 assets, $10,000 comprised of: $14,000 gains from such sales and $4,000 losses from such sales.
    c. Charitable contributions of $1,000.
    d. Dividends from Queens Distributing Co. Ltd., London, England, of $1,200.
    e. Dividends from General Motors Inc. Detroit, Michigan of $5,000.
    f. Interest on General Obligation Bonds of State of New York of $6,000.

26. A partnership earned $12,000 each month during its fiscal year ending June 30, 2015. There were four equal partners: Peter, Paul, Mary, and Quincy. Peter sold his interest to Robert on January 31, 2015. Paul died on March 31, 2015, and his interest passed to his estate as his successor in interest which elected a January 31 fiscal year.

    Determine the amount of the partnership income each of the parties will report for calendar year 2015.

27. Brown and White are equal partners in the B&W Partnership. Brown is much more active, so the partners agreed to pay him a salary of $1,000 per month. White invested $100,000 cash while Brown invested only $10,000. Accordingly, the partnership agreement provides for 10 percent interest to each payable on his capital account balance. Any remaining profits or losses are to be shared equally. On January 1 of the current year, White loaned the partnership $40,000 and the partnership issued a demand note bearing 10 percent interest. Both the partnership and Brown and White report on the calendar year, the partnership on the accrual, and the partners on the cash basis. The partnership earned $60,000 before consideration of "salaries," interest on the capital account balances, and interest on White's demand loan. No payments were made by the partnership to the partners with respect to any of these items during the year.
    a. Compute partnership ordinary income.
    b. Compute the income items to be reported by Brown and White on their tax returns for the current year.

28. Dallas, Frank, and George are partners. Dallas owns 60 percent and Frank and George each own 20 percent of the partnership capital and profits. On January 1, Dallas sold for $8,000 (its fair market value), to the partnership, a parcel of land for which he had paid $12,000 and which he had held as an investment for eight months prior to the sale. The partnership held the land primarily for sale to customers for five months and finally sold it to Frank on June 1 for $10,000, its then fair market value.
    a. How much and what kind of loss, if any, did Dallas recognize on the sale to the partnership?
    b. What was the basis of the property to the partnership?
    c. What was the holding period of the property for the partnership at the time of its sale to Frank?
    d. How much gain or loss, if any, did the partnership recognize upon the sale to Frank?
    e. What was the character of the gain or loss *realized* by both Dallas and the partnership?

    f. Would your answer to (e) above be different if the partnership also held the property as an investment and not for sale to customers in the ordinary course of its business and the sale to Frank was for $14,000?

29. Irving and Jacob are partners in the IJ partnership, Irving owning 60 percent interest and Jacob 40 percent, and they share profits and losses according to the same percentages. At the beginning of 2015, their capital account balances were respectively $20,000 and $40,000. During 2015, the partnership suffered a loss of $50,000, and the partnership was forced to borrow approximately $30,000 to tide it over this slump. What difference does it make whether the partnership borrows the money in 2015 or 2016?

30. Martha and Mary are equal partners of the M&M partnership. Mary's basis for her partnership interest is only $2,000. Not in complete liquidation of her interest, she receives $1,000 cash and real property (an investment asset) with a basis to the partnership of $4,000 and a fair market value of $8,000.
    a. What gain will Mary realize upon the distribution?
    b. What gain will Mary recognize upon the distribution?
    c. What will be the basis of the land to her?
    d. What will be the basis of her partnership interest after the distribution?
    e. Assuming the distribution is in complete liquidation of her partnership interest, what will be the basis of the land to her?

31. Able Corporation, Bobby Baker, the Wham-Bam partnership, and the Happy Hollow Trust decide to form a new corporation, and they respectively transfer the following properties and receive the designated consideration from the newly formed corporation:

Properties		
A	=	Able Corp. Cash
B	=	Bobby Baker Land
W	=	Wham-Bam Marketable Securities
H	=	H-H Trust Building

	Transferred Basis	FMV	Received Stock	Securities	Other Property
A	$100,000	$100,000	$100,000		
B	40,000	100,000	30,000	$70,000	
W	80,000	100,000	80,000	10,000	Cash $10,000
H	110,000	100,000	20,000		Cash 80,000

a. Determine the gain/loss realized by each transferor.
b. Determine the gain/loss recognized by each transferor.
c. Determine the basis of the stock or securities received by each transferor.
d. Determine the basis of the property to the transferee corporation.

32. Roger Corporation has a book profit of $80,000, comprised of dividend income Roger Corporation received from domestic corporations of $120,000 and a loss from its operations of $40,000, which included a charitable contribution of $20,000 to the Red Cross.
a. Compute the charitable contribution deduction.
b. Compute the corporation's dividends received deduction, assuming that the dividends were received from domestic corporations the stock of which was 20 percent owned by Roger Corporation.
c. Same requirement as in (b), above, except assume Roger Corporation owned only 15 percent of the stock of the domestic corporations from which it received the dividends.
d. What carrybacks or carryovers will the corporation have?

33. On January 1, 2015, Whimpy Corporation had accumulated earnings and profits of $20,000. During the year, it made quarterly distributions of $30,000 to its stockholders, March 31, June 30, September 30, and December 31. For 2015, its current earnings and profits were $72,000. Sarah Winn had owned 100 percent of Whimpy since its organization when she invested $10,000, but she sold all her stock to her daughter Susan on December 1, 2015, for $200,000.
a. Determine the taxable status of the distributions to Sarah.
b. Determine the taxable status of the distributions to Susan.

34. Stainback Corporation, a calendar year taxpayer, had 10 equal shareholders until December 30, 2015, at which time five of the shareholders sold their shares to the then majority shareholder. During 2015, Stainback had gross income from real estate commissions earned of $9,000, dividends from domestic corporations of $6,000, interest on installment obligations of $8,000, and long-term capital gains of $40,000. It paid no dividends during 2015. Its retained earnings as of January 1, 2015, were $180,000.
a. Is the corporation a personal holding company?
b. Would your answer to (a) have been different if, in addition to the above, Stainback had rental income of $10,000?

35. Damion Corporation begins its first tax year on June 23, 2015. What is the latest date that Damion may apply for S corporation status to qualify as of the beginning of operations?

36. Alpha Corporation began business at the beginning of the year. On February 15, George sold his stock to Danny. Alpha files for S corporation status on March 10, but George refuses to consent to the election. Will S corporation status be granted?

37. What is the built-in gains tax on an S corporation, assuming the exceptions do not apply and the corporation has taxable income of $100,000, including a built-in gain of $60,000?

38. Hammerhead Corporation has been in existence for several years. It elected to be an S corporation on January 1, 2015, at which time the aggregate fair market value of its assets was $1,500,000 and the aggregate adjusted basis of those assets was $1,000,000. During 2015, Hammerhead Corporation recognized built-in gains of $400,000. However, during 2015 had Hammerhead Corporation been a C corporation its taxable income would have been only $300,000. What is Hammerhead Corporation's income tax liability for 2015?

39. What is the passive investment income tax on an S corporation that has gross receipts of $200,000, passive investment income of $80,000, and expenses of $10,000 directly connected to the production of the passive income?

40. Rollo Corporation was organized in 2002. Rollo operated as a regular C corporation until 2015, when it elected to be an S corporation for federal income tax purposes. Its S election was effective January 1, 2015, and Rollo is a calendar year corporation. Rollo Corporation has substantial earnings and profits from its years as a C corporation. For 2015, Rollo has the following income and deductions: $40,000 of income from its business operations, $20,000 of taxable interest, $25,000 of taxable dividends, $35,000 of deductions related to the income from its business operations, and $2,000 of deductions related to the taxable interest.
    a. Rollo Corporation is subject to the income tax for excess passive investment income in 2015. Why?
    b. Compute the tax which Rollo Corporation must pay in 2015 because of excess passive investment income.

41. Awkward Corporation, a calendar year S corporation since its organization 10 years ago, issued its previously authorized but unissued preferred stock on November 1 of the current year. The corporation's records show that its earnings for the year were ratable over the months, averaging $20,000 each month.
    a. What is the effect of the issuance of the preferred stock?
    b. Is Awkward liable for any income tax for the current year?
    c. If so, compute the amount of the income tax.

42. Ziad Corporation, and S corporation, distributes land held as an investment to its sole shareholder. The land was purchased for $17,000 and has a fair market value of $28,000 on the date of distribution. What are the tax implications of this distribution?

43. Delta Corporation, an S corporation, has $30,000 of taxable income before charitable contributions. The corporation has $5,000 in charitable contributions for the year. What is Delta's charitable contribution deduction?

44. An S corporation is on the accrual basis and the sole shareholder is on the cash basis. For the pay period ending December 27, 2015, the shareholder earns a salary of $400. He is paid on January 3, 2016. What is the amount allowable as a deduction for 2015?

45. Alpha Corporation, a calendar year S corporation, has no accumulated earnings and profits at the end of the year. An individual shareholder receives a cash distribution of $10,000 during the year. How will this distribution be recognized, assuming the shareholder has an $8,200 basis in his stock?

46. Beatle and Bailey share profits and losses equally in B&B partnership. On January 1, Beatle had a basis in the partnership of $22,000 and Bailey had a basis of $6,000. The partnership had a taxable income of $20,000 for the year and made a cash distribution of $18,000 to each of them on September 1. Select the correct answer.
    a. Beatle's includible income from B&B is $10,000.
    b. Beatle's basis in B&B at the end of the year is $14,000.
    c. Bailey's includible income from B&B is $12,000.
    d. Bailey's basis in B&B at the end of the year is $0.
    e. All of the above.

47. Which of the following is true:
    a. An S corporation may issue voting preferred and voting common stock.
    b. An S corporation may have as many as 160 different shareholders so long as they are 80 married couples.
    c. An S corporation which was never a C corporation will never pay a passive investment income tax.
    d. An S corporation which has its election terminated during the year will have to file two income tax returns on each of which it must annualize its income for the part year.
    e. None of the above.

48. Subaroo Inc. an S corporation, distributed to Misband, its sole shareholder, investment land which it had acquired two years ago for $10,000. At the time of the distribution, the property had a fair market value of $14,000. Aside from this transaction, Subaroo had income from its operations of $10,000. Misband's basis in his stock is $12,000. Misband will have:
    a. Ordinary income of $10,000; long-term capital gain of $2,000
    b. Ordinary income of $10,000; long-term capital gain of $4,000
    c. Ordinary income of $10,000; long-term capital gain of $12,000
    d. Ordinary income of $24,000
    e. None of the above

49. Acme Corporation, a calendar year S corporation, has $100,000 of Accumulated Earnings and Profits. Larry, the sole shareholder, has adjusted basis of $80,000 in stock basis with a $20,000 in Accumulated Adjustments Account. Determine the tax aspects if a $50,000 distribution is made to Larry.

50. From the previous problem determine the remaining balance in the Accumulated Earnings and Profits and the Accumulated Adjustments Account.

51. **Comprehensive Problem.** Jane and Henry formed an equal partnership as financial advisors in 2012, each contributing $10,000 cash. The following transactions have transpired:

Transactions	
1.	Partnership ordinary income (exclusive of items below)
2.	"Salary" to Jane
3.	Long-term capital gains
4.	Long-term capital losses
5.	Municipal bond interest
6.	Life insurance premiums—Manager
7.	Life insurance cash surrender value increments
8.	Life insurance proceeds—Manager died
	Total actual payments to partners:
9a.	Jane—Cash
9b.	Jane—Investment property
	Basis to partnership $10,000, FMV $20,000
9c.	Henry—Cash

	2012	2013	2014	2015 1st ½	2015 2nd ½
1.	$(2,000)	$(13,000)	$4,000	$2,000	$4,000
2.	5,000	5,000	5,000	2,500	
3.			6,000		
4.				(20,000)	
5.	1,000	1,500	2,000	3,000	4,000
6.	500	500	500	500	
7.		50	100	150	
8.				50,000	
9a.	1,000	0	0	2,000	
9b.				20,000	
9c.					5,000

On July 1, 2015, Jane sold her entire partnership interest for $30,000. The partnership has no Section 751 property. What gain/loss did Jane have upon her sale?

52. **Comprehensive Problem.** On December 31 of the current year, Corporation Xerces had accumulated earnings and profits of $90,000 and taxable income for the year and current earnings and profits of $20,000, when it decided to make a distribution to its two 50 percent shareholders, Corporation Riton and James J. Rouge. Corporation Xerces owned an investment parcel of land with a basis of $150,000 and a fair market value of $300,000. On December 31, Xerces borrowed $200,000 from Bank, placed a mortgage on the investment parcel of land, and distributed the land to Corporation Riton. At the same time, Xerces made a cash distribution to Rouge of $100,000. Discuss the tax consequences to all parties.

53. **Research Problem.** On January 17, 2015, Arnold contributed $50,000 cash to the Arnold-Parker partnership for a one-half interest in its capital and profits. Parker contributed property with a basis to him of $50,000 and a fair market value of $100,000. On March 13, 2015, the partnership transferred $50,000 cash to Parker. On March 17, 2015, the partnership borrowed $80,000 from a bank in order to finance the partnership business. While the note was secured by the property Arnold contributed to the partnership, the bank agreed to look only to the partnership asset for collateral, that is, if the partnership was unable to service the loan, the bank would seek recovery solely from the sales proceeds of the property. Arnold and Parker had no personal liability on the loan. Assuming Parker's basis for his partnership interest is at least $50,000 before the $50,000 cash distribution to him, has he made a tax-free contribution of property and received a tax-free distribution, or has he sold the property to the partnership in a taxable transaction? Discuss the tax results to Parker after referring to the following Reg. §§1.721-1, 1.731-1, and 1.707-3. Are the tax results different if the partnership transfers the $50,000 cash to Parker on March 13, 2017?

17

Federal Estate Tax, Federal Gift Tax, and Generation-Skipping Transfer Tax

OBJECTIVES

After completing Chapter 17, you should be able to:

1. Recognize legal terms used in connection with wills, trusts, and estates, as well as partial interests in property, such as life estates, remainders, and reversions.
2. Understand the elements in the estate tax formula—gross estate, allowable deductions, adjusted taxable gifts, and available tax credits.
3. Determine the tax aspects of transferred property, in particular inclusion of the property in the gross estate due to the grantor's retention of an interest, such as a life estate, a reversion, or a power to revoke.
4. Discuss the special tax aspects of jointly held property, life insurance, annuities, and gifts within three years of death.
5. Understand the valuation of assets at both the date of death and the alternate valuation date.
6. Calculate the taxation of involuntary deductions, such as funeral and administration expenses and debts, and deductions under testator's control, notably the marital and charitable deductions.
7. Determine the interplay between the gift and estate tax, the two being two sides of the same coin.
8. Describe the nature of the gift tax, the gift tax formula, and transactions subject to the gift tax.
9. Identify present-interest gifts, the marital and charitable deductions, and the applicable credit amount.
10. Explain the generation-skipping transfer tax, how and when it applies, and its relationship to gift and estate taxes.

OVERVIEW

In this chapter, estate, gift, and generation-skipping transfer taxes are surveyed. All three taxes may be viewed as aspects of one comprehensive excise tax on gratuitous transfers of property by individuals to anyone, be it during life or at death. In fact, all three taxes are computed using the same multipurpose tax table.

The estate tax is a wealth transfer tax, a tax on the transfer of property at death, not on the property itself. The estate tax base equals the gross estate, consisting of all property in which the decedent had an interest, less debts and expenses and marital and charitable bequests plus taxable lifetime gifts made after 1976. For 2015, up to $5.43 million is tax free; the rest is subject to tax at rates up to 40 percent. A tax credit is allowed for gift taxes paid and for state and foreign estate taxes. The gift tax discussed in this chapter is but one part of the same overall unified wealth transfer tax system.

Special, unique rules determine the inclusion in the gross estate of life insurance, annuities, jointly held properties, and property subject to powers of appointment. These concepts are largely unrelated to the income tax treatment and require special study. Valuation problems and income tax basis aspects of estates are also discussed in this chapter.

The gross estate may include properties previously transferred in which the decedent retained an interest or power, such as a life income interest, a reversion, or a power to revoke or appoint, as well as properties passing by operation of law, such as jointly held property and life insurance payable to a named beneficiary. A comprehensive list of legal property terms is provided to increase the understanding of estate administration and the law of property.

Gross gifts generally include all gratuitous transfers. Taxable gifts are computed after exclusions and deductions, notably the marital and charitable deductions.

The applicable credit amount may defer any tax until death, but gift taxes are payable when the tax on cumulative lifetime gifts exceeds it. Cumulative taxable gifts are included in the estate tax base, with a credit for gift taxes paid. The applicable credit amount is available to the estate since its only effect during life is to defer the actual payment of gift taxes until death, within limits.

The generation-skipping transfer tax is levied on individuals with a power or an interest in a generation-skipping trust and is a toll charge on skipping a generation.

Impact of Economic Growth and Tax Relief Reconciliation Act of 2001, Tax Relief Act of 2010, and American Taxpayer Relief Act of 2012

The 2001 Act made extensive changes to the estate and gift tax rules. However, the most dramatic alteration is the repeal of estate and generation-skipping transfer (GST) taxes, but this change was effective in 2010. The 2010 Tax Relief Act reinstates the estate and generation-skipping taxes for 2011. On the other hand, most changes, including lower tax rates, increased exemptions, and the replacement of the state death tax credit with a deduction are effective for earlier years. A summary of the major changes incorporating the **2010 Act**, and the **2012 Act** is shown in Table 1 below.

Calendar Year	Estate Tax Exemption	GST Tax Exemption	Gift Tax Exemption	Highest Tax Rates	State Death Tax Credit Limitation
2001	$675,000	$1,060,000	$675,000	55%	Unlimited
2002	$1 million	$1,100,000	$1 million	50%	75%
2003	$1 million	$1,120,000	$1 million	49%	50%
2004	$1.5 million	$1.5 million	$1 million	48%	25%
2005	$1.5 million	$1.5 million	$1 million	47%	N/A (Credit repealed; deduction allowed)
2006	$2 million	$2 million	$1 million	46%	Deduction only
2007	$2 million	$2 million	$1 million	45%	Deduction only
2008	$2 million	$2 million	$1 million	45%	Deduction only
2009	$3.5 million	$3.5 million	$1 million	45%	Deduction only
2010	Repealed carryover basis	Repealed carryover basis	$1 million	Top individual rate under the Act	Deduction only
2011	Reinstated [35%] rate and $5 million	Reinstated [35%] rate and $5 million	$5 million	35%	Deduction only
2012	$5.12 million	$5.12 million	$5.12 million	35%	Deduction only
2013	$5.25 million	$5.25 million	$5.25 million	40%	Deduction only
2014	$5.34 million	$5.34 million	$5.34 million	40%	Deduction only
2015	$5.43 million	$5.43 million	$5.43 million	40%	Deduction only

Table 1. SUMMARY OF MAJOR CHANGES MADE BY THE ECONOMIC GROWTH AND TAX RELIEF RECONCILIATION ACT OF 2001, THE TAX RELIEF ACT OF 2010, AND AMERICAN TAXPAYER RELIEF ACT OF 2012 AFFECTING ESTATE, GST, AND GIFT TAXES

Assessment of the 2010 Tax Relief Act

ESTATE TAXES

The law provided for a maximum tax rate of 35% and an exemption of $5 million for 2011. Also, this exemption is adjusted for inflation beginning in 2012 at $5.12 million.

In 2010, carryover basis was required to be used with a limited increase in basis of $1.3 million coupled with a basis increase of $3 million to a surviving spouse. However, the **Act** gives estates of decedents dying after December 31, 2009 and before January 1, 2011 the option to elect to apply the 2011 rules and receive a stepped-up basis.

The 2010 Tax Relief Act provides for "portability" between spouses of the unused estate tax exemption amount. Specially, portability would be available to the estate of decedents dying after December 31, 2010 and before 2013.

Example: Sam Williams dies in 2012 with a taxable estate of $4.12 million. An election is made on Sam's estate tax return for Sam's wife, Bertha, to use Sam's unused applicable exemption of $1 million; as a result, Bertha receives a total exemption of $6.12 million.

GENERATION SKIPPING TAX

The generation skipping tax is reinstated at the maximum estate tax rate of 35% and an exemption of $5 million beginning in 2011 and $5.12 million in 2012.

GIFT TAXES

For gifts made after December 31, 2009 and before January 1, 2011, the gift tax is computed using a rate schedule having a top rate of 35% and an applicable exemption of $1 million. For gift made after December 31, 2010, the gift tax is reunified with the estate tax for a top tax rate of 35% and an applicable exemption of $5 million in 2011 and $5.12 million in 2012.

ASSESSMENT OF AMERICAN TAXPAYER RELIEF ACT OF 2012

The American Taxpayer Relief Act permanently provides for a maximum federal estate, gift, and GST tax rate of 40 percent with an annually inflation-adjusted $5 million exclusion for estates, gifts, and GST transfers after December 31, 2012. As a result, in 2015, the exclusion is $5,430,000.

Also, the **American Taxpayer Relief Act** makes permanent **portability** between spouses. Consider the following illustration under the new law.

> **Example:** Sam Williams dies in 2015 with a taxable estate of $4.43 million. An election is made on Sam's estate tax return for Sam's wife, Bertha, to utilize Sam's unused exemption of $1 million; accordingly, Bertha receives a total exemption of $6.43 million.

The new unified rate schedule is reproduced below in Table 2.

Table 2. Unified Tax Rate Schedule 2013 under American Taxpayer Relief Act of 2012			
(A)	**(B)**	**(C)**	**(D)**
Amount subject to tax equal to or more than-	Amount subject to tax less than-	Tax on amount in column (A)	Rate of tax on excess over amount in column (A) Percent
.....	$10,000	.....	18
$10,000	20,000	$1,800	20
20,000	40,000	3,800	22
40,000	60,000	8,200	24
60,000	80,000	13,000	26
80,000	100,000	18,200	28
100,000	150,000	28,800	30
150,000	250,000	38,800	32
250,000	500,000	70,800	34
500,000	750,000	155,800	37
750,000	1,000,000	248,300	39
1,000,000		345,800	40

Legal Terms Common To Estates and Trusts

Administrator. Similar to an executor. The manager of an estate of a person who dies intestate or where the named executor fails to act as executor.

Bequest. A disposition of personal property by will; a legacy.

Conservator. A guardian; a protector; a preserver. The term conservator is usually used to designate the guardian of an incompetent person.

Devise. A disposition of land or real estate by will.

Devisee. The person to whom land or other real property is devised or given by will.

Donor. One who makes a gift. One who creates a trust.

Estate Tax. A tax levied on the *transfer* of property from a decedent.

Executor. A person appointed by a will to carry out the testator's direction and to dispose of property according to the will. The one who manages an estate. (Female=executrix).

Grantor. The person making a grant. One who creates a trust.

Guardian. One who has the care and management of the person (guardian of the person) or of the estate (guardian of the estate) or both, or of an individual during minority or incompetency.

Guardian ad litem. A guardian (usually an attorney) appointed by the court to protect and defend a minor's or incompetent's interest in the estate.

Heir. One who would receive the decedent's estate under the laws of descent and distribution where the decedent did not leave a will.

Inheritance tax. A tax levied on the receipt of property from a decedent.

Insurance trust. An agreement between the insured and a trustee whereby the proceeds of the life insurance will be payable directly to the trustee, who will hold the proceeds for investment and distribution according to the trust agreement.

Insured. The person who is insured under the life insurance policy in question.

Inter vivos trust. A trust created during the lifetime of the person setting up the trust. A testamentary trust is one set up under the will of the decedent.

Intestate. One not having a will; a person who dies without a will is said to die intestate.

Intestate laws. Statutes ("laws of intestate succession") that provide descent of estates of persons who die intestate (without a will).

Joint tenancy. Where property is held in the names of two or more persons with the title passing from the first joint tenant to die to the other joint tenant (or joint tenants) upon death.

Legacy. A disposition of personal property by will.

Legatee. The recipient of personal property by will.

Per capita. This term is used frequently in the area of the descent and distribution of a decedent's property. In effect, it means that the property should be divided equally among a group designated by the trust instrument or the will. In other words, if the decedent left two surviving children and a third child who predeceased the decedent but left two children (grandchildren of the decedent) and if the per capita method is applied, each person would receive 25 percent.

Per stirpes. This term is used frequently in the area of the descent and distribution of a decedent's property. It denotes that method of dividing an estate where a class or group of distributees takes the share to which their deceased representative would have been entitled had the deceased lived. In other words, they take according to their right of representing such deceased ancestor, and not as so many individuals. For example: If a decedent passed away leaving two surviving and one child who predeceased the decedent but left two children (the decedent's grandchildren), the two grandchildren would take the share of their deceased representative, namely, their parent. Therefore, the two grandchildren would share their parent's 1/3 and each would receive 1/6 of the total estate. The two surviving children of the deceased would each receive 1/3.

Power of appointment. A power or authority conferred by a trust or will upon another person to select or nominate the person or persons who are to receive and enjoy the property of the estate or trust or the income therefrom at a specific time.

Probate. A local law process for admitting the decedent's will, if any, and distributing the decedent's property pursuant to it or according to the laws governing the intestate's assets.

Remainderman. One who is entitled to the remainder of an estate after a particular life estate, which has been carved out of the overall estate, has expired.

Residuary clause. That provision in a will that disposes of that which remains after satisfying all debts, administration expenses, legacies, and devises.

Residuary estate. That portion of the estate that remains after the payment of debts, expenses of administration, legacies and devises. It consists of that part of the estate that has not been legally disposed of by the will prior to carrying out the residuary clause of said will.

Settlor. One who creates a trust.

Share on renunciation. When a surviving spouse renounces the will of a spouse, the surviving spouse is usually entitled to a one-third interest in all personal and real property if the decedent left a descendant. If the decedent did not leave a descendant, the surviving spouse is usually entitled to one-half of real and personal property in the estate (net of debts).

Surviving spouse's award (widow's award). The special allowance (usually money) given to the surviving spouse to cover the cost of support during the administration of the estate, which is usually limited to nine months.

Tenancy by the entirety. Generally speaking, this is a joint tenancy between husband and wife. A tenancy by the entirety cannot be terminated except by the joint action of the husband and wife during their lives. In the case of a joint tenancy, however, it may be terminated by either tenant merely by conveying the interest to another party.

Tenancy in common. Title is held by two or more persons, each owning a fractional interest in the undivided property. Upon the death of one tenant in common, the interest does not pass to the surviving tenant in common but becomes part of the probate estate and is distributed according to the deceased tenant's will.

Testamentary trust. A trust that is set up under the will of the decedent. Conversely, an inter vivos trust is one set up during the lifetime of the person setting up the trust.

Testamentary trustee. One who is appointed trustee to carry out a trust created by a will.

Testate. One having a will; a person who dies with a will is said to die testate.

Testator. One who makes or has made a will; one who dies leaving a will. (Female=testatrix).

Totten trust. A trust created by the deposit of a person's own money in his or her own name as trustee for another person. This is considered a revocable trust at the will of the trustee until the depositor dies or otherwise completes the gift during lifetime.

Trust. A fiduciary relationship with respect to property whereby the property is held by one party (called trustee) for the benefit of another party (called beneficiary). A trust is usually set up and governed by a written document.

Trust estate. Usually refers to the corpus or property of the trust.

Trustee. That person who is responsible for administering a trust agreement according to its terms. This party holds legal title to all the property in the trust for the benefit of the beneficiaries.

Computation and Payment of Estate Tax

¶17,001   ## ESTATE TAX COMPUTATION—SUMMARY

Here is a capsule version of the federal estate tax return filed on Form 706 (United States Estate (and Generation-Skipping Transfer) Tax Return):

Step 1.	Compile the *gross estate*, consisting of all property in which the decedent had an interest.
Step 2.	Subtract debts, funeral, and administration expenses. (The result is the *adjusted gross estate*.)
Step 3.	Subtract property passing to the surviving spouse (*the marital deduction*) and charitable transfers.
Step 4.	The result is the *taxable estate*.
Step 5.	Add *adjusted taxable gifts* (gifts, less exclusions and deductions) made after 1976.
Step 6.	The result is the estate tax base.
Step 7.	Find the *tentative estate tax* from the tax table. Code Sec. 2001. (See Table in the Appendix.)
Step 8.	Subtract gift taxes payable on gifts includible in the estate tax base.
Step 9.	Subtract the *applicable credit amount*.
Step 10.	If a tax is still payable, subtract other possible credits, such as the state tax credit, the credit for prior transfers, and the foreign tax credit.
Step 11.	The tax payable, if any, is due with the estate tax return.

For a graphic description of the estate tax elements, see Table 3.

Table 3. ESTATE TAX COMPUTATION

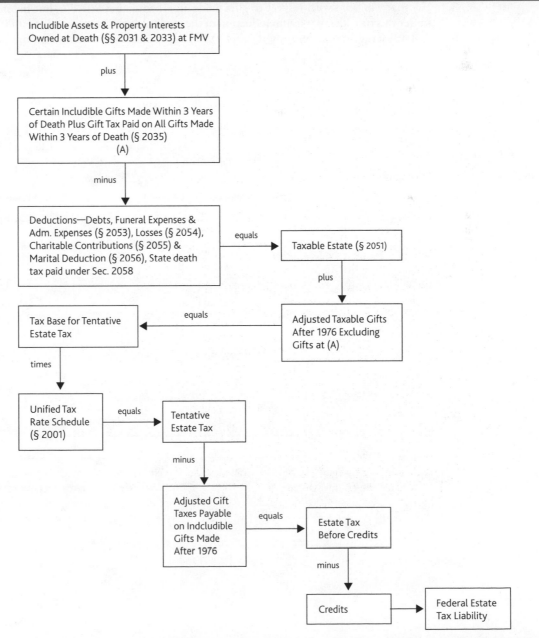

¶17,009   APPLICABLE CREDIT AMOUNT

An applicable credit amount is allowed against estate and gift taxes. Code Secs. 2010 and 2505. The applicable credit amount is a credit that is equal to the amount the government wishes to exclude from gift and estate taxation. This credit was first introduced as the "unified credit" in the Tax Reform Act of 1976. The credit eliminates the first portion of the gift and estate tax rate schedule. The amount eliminated has increased over the years since it was first introduced. The excluded amount is called the "applicable exclusion amount," and the unified credit was renamed the "applicable credit amount" by the Taxpayer Relief Act of 1997.

The applicable credit amount for estates of decedents dying after 1986 and prior to 1998 was $192,800. Any part of the credit used to offset gift taxes is still available to offset estate taxes. This is because adjusted taxable gifts are included in the estate tax base. Further, although the applicable credit amount applies for both estate and gift taxes, the computation of the credit for gift tax purposes is governed by special rules.

The applicable credit amount is subtracted from the taxpayer's estate and gift tax liability. However, the amount of the applicable credit amount available at death is not reduced, even if any portion of the credit is used to offset gift taxes on lifetime transfers. Further, the amount of the applicable credit amount is reduced by 20 percent of any portion of the $30,000 specific gift tax exemption allowable under pre-1977 law that was used with respect to gifts made after September 8, 1976, but before January 1, 1977. Thus, under this rule, the maximum reduction of the applicable credit amount is $6,000 (20 percent of $30,000).

For estates of decedents dying after 1981, the applicable credit amount has been phased in as follows:

	Unified Credit	Exemption Equivalent
1982	$62,800	$225,000
1983	79,300	275,000
1984	96,300	325,000
1985	121,800	400,000
1986	155,800	500,000
1987–1997	192,800	600,000

	Applicable Unified Credit Amount	Applicable Exclusion Amount
1998	$202,050	$625,000
1999	211,300	650,000
2000–2001	220,550	675,000
2002–2003	345,800	1,000,000
2004–2005	555,800	1,500,000
2006–2008	780,800	2,000,000
2009	1,455,800	3,500,000
2010	1,455,800	3,500,000
2011	1,730,800	5,000,000
2012	1,772,800	5,120,000
2013	2,045,800	5,250,000
2014	2,081,800	5,340,000
2015	2,117,800	5,430,000

EXAMPLE 17.1   In 2015, Kathy Kelly gives away $1 million and dies broke several years later. Due to the applicable credit amount, no gift tax was due. The $1 million gift, assuming no exclusions or deductions, is an adjusted taxable gift and becomes her estate tax base. As in the case of the gift, the transfer tax amounts to $345,000 but is offset by the applicable credit amount. Thus, the same applicable credit amount serves a dual function, both during life and in the estate.

¶17,015 UNIFIED RATE SCHEDULE

A single unified transfer tax applies to estate and gift taxes effective for the estates of decedents dying and gifts made after 1976. The rates are progressive on the basis of cumulative lifetime and at-death transfers.

For the estates of decedents dying after 1988, gift and estate tax rates presently applicable to U.S. citizens are applicable to the estates of nonresident aliens. Where permitted by treaty, the estate of a nonresident alien is allowed the applicable credit amount available to a U.S. citizen multiplied by a proportion of the total gross estate situated in the United States. In other cases, an applicable credit amount of $14,000 is allowed.

¶17,025 PAYMENT OF TAX AND RETURNS

The estate tax return filing requirements are geared to the exemption so that a return is required if the gross estate exceeds the exemption equivalent of the applicable credit amount. Code Sec. 6018(a)(1) and (3). For 2015, the applicable credit amount is $2,117,800, which represents an exemption equivalent of $5.43 million. Thus, for estates of decedents dying currently, an executor must file a return if a gross estate exceeds $5.43 million, reduced by the decedent's adjusted taxable gifts made after 1976 and the reduction in the decedent's applicable credit amount because of taxable gifts made after September 8, 1976, and before January 1, 1977.

EXAMPLE 17.2	John Tripper died in 2015. If his gross estate exceeds $5.43 million, a return is due, even if no estate tax may be due. His estate tax return reveals the following:

Gross estate	$5,530,000
Deductions	100,000
Taxable estate	$5,430,000
Tentative tax	$2,117,800
Less: Applicable credit amount	2,117,800
Tax payable	$0

Thus, it may be worthwhile to note that for 2015 estates of decedents owning $5.43 million or less are not subject to estate taxes and need not even file a return. As a result, the estate tax is applicable to a very small percentage of total estates, perhaps less than one percent. Because of the marital deduction, the estate tax, even when applicable, is often deferred for the lifetime of the surviving spouse.

In those cases where applicable, the estate tax must be paid at the time the return is filed. Code Sec. 6161. The estate tax return, Form 706, is due nine months after death when required, together with the tax, if applicable. Code Sec. 6075(a). However, the executor of an estate can obtain an extension of time for the payment of the estate tax for a period not to exceed 12 months from the date fixed for payment of the estate tax. Code Sec. 6161(a). This extension will be granted whenever there is reasonable cause to do so. The executor (or administrator) is generally liable for the payment of the estate tax. Code Sec. 2002. If there is no executor or administrator, persons in actual or constructive possession of any of the property in the decedent's estate are required to pay the tax.

If more than 35 percent of a decedent's adjusted gross estate consists of an interest in a farm or other closely held business (sole proprietorship, a partnership interest, or stock in a closely held corporation), an executor may elect, on a timely filed estate tax return, to defer all payment of tax for five years (paying interest only) and thereafter pay the tax in equal installments over the next 10 years. Code Sec. 6166. The maximum deferral period, however, is 14 rather than 15 years because the due date for the last payment of interest coincides with the due date for the first installment of tax. Interest is payable at a special two percent rate on the estate tax attributable to the first $1 million (indexed, $1,470,000 for 2015) of qualifying property. However, the interest rate on the remaining deferred amount is reduced to 45 percent of the rate charged for underpayment of taxes, and the estate tax deduction is eliminated for interest paid on these installments. Code Sec. 6601(j). A disposition of more than half the qualifying property will accelerate the tax, as may a default. Code Sec. 6166(g).

¶17,035   CREDITS AGAINST TAX

Foreign Death Taxes

A foreign death tax credit is provided for United States citizens and residents. The credit applies to property that is subject to both federal and foreign death taxes in order to prevent double taxation. Taxes paid to possessions of the United States are regarded as foreign death taxes. Code Sec. 2014. The foreign estate tax credit allowed against the estate tax is, however, limited by apportionment. Only taxes attributable to property taxed in both countries may be allowed as a credit. In addition, the credit cannot exceed the portion of United States taxes attributed to such property.

Death Taxes on Prior Transfers

A credit is allowed against the estate tax for all or a part of the estate tax paid with respect to the transfer of property to the present decedent by a prior decedent who died within 10 years before, or within two years after, the present decedent's death. Reg. §20.2013-1. This credit can never be larger than it would be if the present decedent had not received the property. Since the purpose of this provision is to prevent the diminution of an estate by the imposition of successive taxes on the same property within a brief period, no credit is available for any gift tax that may have been paid with respect to the transfer of property to the decedent.

EXAMPLE 17.3	Sam Spade died in 2009 leaving his entire estate to his son, Adam. Two years later Adam dies. In computing Adam's estate tax, a credit is allowed on Adam's estate tax return for the assets included in Adam's estate that were inherited from Sam. The credit is the lower of the estate tax paid by Sam or the marginal estate tax that Adam is assessed on the inherited assets. The credit is reduced by the length of time between Sam's death and Adam's death:

KEYSTONE PROBLEM	The applicable credit amount of $2,117,800 is available to estates of decedents who die in 2015. It has been referred to as the "exemption equivalent" of $5.43 million. Considering both small and large estates, is a credit of $2,117,800 really equivalent to an exemption of $5.43 million?

Gross Estate

¶17,101   PROPERTY INCLUDIBLE IN GROSS ESTATE

The gross estate of a decedent includes "the value of all property to the extent of the interest therein of the decedent at the time of death." Code Sec. 2033. This is a catch-all provision, serving the same purpose as Code Sec. 61 does for income tax purposes. The *gross* estate may be far in excess of the *probate* estate since the gross estate includes jointly held property and insurance payable to a named beneficiary although passing outside the will. No property is excluded, however small, be it real or personal, tangible or intangible, U.S. or foreign. Since the tax is levied on the *transfer* of property, not the property itself, even tax-free municipal bonds are included in the tax base. Citizens and nonresident aliens are subject to the U.S. estate tax on U.S. property. Code Sec. 2103(a). Most property owned outright by the decedent in his or her own name presents no problems as to inclusion. Property held merely as a fiduciary (e.g., as trustee), however, is *not* included.

Over the years, special rules have been designed to deal with *unique properties,* such as life insurance and pensions; *split interests,* such as life estates, remainders, and reversions; and *special situations,* such as powers of appointment and other retained powers. These problem areas, among others, are discussed below. In addition, any asset may present valuation problems.

Conservation Easement

¶17,105 CODE SECTION 2031(c) EXCLUSION

The enactment of Code Sec. 2031(c) by the Taxpayer Relief Act of 1997 (P.L. 105-34) has now made conservation easements more attractive. Specifically, Section 2031(c) provides another tax advantage by allowing a reduction in estate taxes for property that is encumbered with a conservation easement. The highlights of the new provision are as follows.

1. An additional estate tax deduction is provided for property containing an easement that was placed on the property before death.
2. If a conservation easement is placed on the property after death and on or before the due date (including extensions) for the estate tax return, a deduction will be allowed to the estate as long as no income tax charitable deduction is allowed to any person with respect to the easement.
3. If all requirements are met, then an estate will be able to generate tax savings of up to $200,000 ($500,000 × .40) in 2015.

In general, under Code Sec. 2031(c), when the executor makes the election, the amount excluded from the estate will be the lesser of:

A. "the applicable percentage of the value of land subject to a qualified conservation easement, reduced by the amount of any deduction under Section 2055(f) with respect to such land;" or
B. the exclusion limitation.

The applicable percentage means that the excluded amount is 40% of the FMV of the property that is encumbered with an easement if the easement reduces the value of the property by 30% or more. However, this value cannot exceed the maximum exclusion for the year at issue. Specifically, the amount that may be excluded for the gross estate is limited as follows: $100,000 in 1998; $200,000 in 1999; $300,000 in 2000; $400,000 in 2001, and $500,000 in 2002 or thereafter. If the easement does not reduce the value of the property by at least 30%, then the applicable percentage will be reduced below 40% by two percentage points for each percentage point by which the value of the conservation easement is less than 30% of the value of the property (Code Sec. 2031(c)(2)).

EXAMPLE 17.4

Jack Ames died owning land, on the Chesapeake Bay in Accomack County Virginia, subject to a qualified conservation easement. He did not retain any development rights in the property. The fair market value of the real property on the date of his death was $1 million without the conservation easement and $800,000 with the easement. Since the value of the conservation easement is $200,000, or 20% of the value of the real property without the easement, then the applicable percentage for the estate is 20% (40% reduced by twice the difference between 30% and 20%). Consequently, the exclusion amount is $160,000 (20% of $800,000).

¶17,109 PRESENT AND FUTURE INTERESTS IN PROPERTY

Anyone who owns property outright, whether personal or real, can divide up this ownership. The ways in which this can be done and the identification of these interests are crucial to the understanding of estate and gift taxes. *Life estates, remainders,* and *reversions* are such property interests and can best be illustrated through examples.

Case 1

The grantor (G) transfers (the income interest in) property to A for life. A has a *life estate;* A is a *life tenant.* A can sell the interest to B, but B still has a life estate for the life of A. G has a *reversion* because the property will revert back to G or G's heirs when A dies.

> **Estate tax consequences.** Nothing will be taxed in A's estate because the only interest A owned, the life estate (the income interest), is extinguished upon A's death. But the whole property will be included in G's estate, less the actuarially determined value of A's life estate if A survives G.

Case 2

G transfers the property to A, but retains the income and/or possession of it for life. Here G retains a life estate and A receives a *remainder.*

Estate tax consequences. G never gave up the present enjoyment of the property; therefore, the full value of it will be included in G's estate. A's estate will also be taxed. If G outlives A, the remainder will be taxed; if not, A dies owning the property outright.

Case 3

G transfers the property to A for life, then to B. A has a life estate; B has a vested remainder. G has divested all interests. Even if B predeceases A, B's heirs will receive ownership.

Estate tax consequences. Nothing is included in G's estate, but B owns either the remainder or the property, depending on whether or not B predeceases A. Note the following:

1. All transfers of property, even partial, are subject to gift tax.
2. All adjusted taxable gifts are included in the estate tax computation even if not part of the gross estate.

Case 4

G transfers the property to A for life, and if B survives A, then to B. A has a life estate and B has a contingent remainder because B must survive A to take anything. In addition, G has a reversion because G or G's heirs will receive the property if B predeceases A.

Estate tax consequences. A's estate is unaffected. B's estate has nothing if B predeceases A. If B survives A, B's estate will include the full value of the property. G's estate has nothing if B survives A prior to G's death. G's estate will include the property, less A's life estate if G predeceases A and B, but multiplied by the probability that B will predecease A.

Case 5

G transfers the property to A for life, then to B if B survives A, otherwise to C. A has a life estate, B has a contingent remainder, and C has an *executory interest,* a remainder of sorts.

Estate tax consequences. G can never get anything back, so G's gross estate includes nothing. A's estate is unaffected. B's estate will include the property if B survives A, otherwise nothing. C's estate problem is more complex:

1. If A predeceases B, nothing will be included.
2. If C predeceases A and B, there is still a possibility that B will predecease A. Therefore, the property will be included in C's estate, times the probability of this happening, but the value is reduced by A's life estate.

The above transactions are generally done for family members in trust (e.g., life estate to wife, remainder to children). Annuities, term interests, life estates, reversions, and remainders are valued actuarially, using unisex Treasury tables. The tables use an interest rate equal to 120 percent of the applicable federal midterm rate compounded annually (rounded to the nearest two-tenths of one percent), adjusted monthly. Code Sec. 7520.

¶17,117   GIFTS WITHIN THREE YEARS OF DEATH

The general rule is that outright gifts made prior to death are *not* brought back into the gross estate, even if made on the deathbed. Code Sec. 2035(a). However, the taxable portion of the gift is added to the estate tax base as an "adjusted taxable gift." There are several exceptions for gifts made within three years of death.

Any gift tax paid by the decedent or the decedent's estate within three years of death is includible in the gross estate. Code Sec. 2035(b). If the gift tax is to be paid by the estate, an offsetting debt deduction is allowed. Also, a gift tax credit is allowed since the adjusted taxable gift is included in the estate tax base.

Gifts made at any time with strings attached are includible if the strings were broken within the three-year period and they would have been includible if no action had been taken. Code Sec. 2035(a)(2). This affects the following transactions:

1. Giving up a retained life estate that would otherwise have resulted in inclusion under Code Sec. 2036.
2. Giving up a reversion that otherwise would have brought the property back under Code Sec. 2037.
3. Giving up a power to revoke a transfer that would have resulted in inclusion under Code Sec. 2038.
4. Giving up an incident of ownership in a life insurance policy that would have led to the proceeds being includible in the gross estate or transferring the policy itself.

With respect to the estates of decedents dying after August 5, 1997, the value of property transferred to a donee from a decedent's revocable trust (within three years of the decedent's death) and the value of property in such a trust (with respect to which the decedent's power to revoke is relinquished during the three years before death) is not includible in the decedent's gross estate. Transfers from a revocable trust are treated as if made directly by the decedent for purposes of Code Sec. 2035 and Code Sec. 2038. Accordingly, an annual exclusion gift from a revocable trust is not included in the decedent's gross estate.

For purposes of qualifying for special estate tax benefits dependent on the amount of the adjusted gross estate and solely for testing purposes, *all* gifts within three years of death are brought back, except gifts of present interests of $14,000 or less per donee for 2015 (the exclusion is indexed annually for inflation). Code Sec. 2035(c)(3). Examples of items qualifying for special estate tax benefits include qualifying for death tax redemptions (Code Sec. 303), special use valuation for farms and closely held businesses (Code Sec. 2032A), and installment payments of the estate tax (Code Sec. 6166).

Gifts of Life Insurance

The general rule that outright gifts made prior to death are not includible in the donor's gross estate does not apply to transfers of life insurance policies on the life of the decedent made within three years of death. Code Sec. 2035(c)(3). The following situations are possible:

1. If the transfer took place *more than* three years before death and the insured did *not* pay the premiums the last three years of life, no amount is includible in the gross estate.
2. If the situation is the same as under (1), except that the insured paid the premiums within three years of death, the premiums are includible in the gross estate.
3. If the policy was transferred *within* three years of death *and* the premiums were paid by the insured, the proceeds, but not the premiums, are includible in the gross estate.
4. If the situation is the same as (3), except that some of the last three years' premiums were paid by someone other than the insured, only the proceeds allocable to the premiums paid by the insured are includible.

EXAMPLE 17.5   Ten years before his death, John Hunter purchased a $100,000 term insurance policy. Two years before his death, he irrevocably transferred the policy and all incidents of ownership to a trust which paid the last two years' premiums. John's gross estate includes $80,000 of proceeds since John paid 80 percent of the premiums.

Even if the proceeds are not includible in the gross estate, the adjusted taxable gift is includible in the estate tax base. The value of an unmatured policy, however, is next to zero for a term policy and close to the cash surrender value for ordinary life policies (the "interpolated terminal reserve," i.e., the replacement value).

¶17,125   RETAINED LIFE ESTATES

Under the provisions of Code Sec. 2036, a decedent's gross estate includes the value of any interest in property transferred by the decedent prior to death (whether in trust or otherwise) for less than full or adequate and full consideration, if the decedent retained for life, or for any period that does not, in fact, end before death:

1. The use, possession, right to the income, or other enjoyment of the transferred property; or
2. The right, either alone or in conjunction with any person, to designate the person who may possess or enjoy the property, or the related income. Code Sec. 2036; Reg. §20.2036-1(a).

The use, possession, right to the income, or other enjoyment of the property is considered retained by the decedent to the extent that it is to be utilized to discharge a legal obligation of the decedent. A legal obligation includes one to support a dependent during the decedent's lifetime. Reg. §20.2036-1(b)(2). The right to designate includes a "reserved power" to designate the person or persons to receive the income, or to possess or enjoy nonincome-producing property during the decedent's life.

The most common example of transfers includible in the gross estate through the operation of Code Sec. 2036 is a transfer by trust, with a retained life estate. This may be illustrated as follows.

EXAMPLE 17.6	Bart Henderson transfers income-producing property into trust for his son, but retains the income from the property for his lifetime. Upon Bart's death, the total fair market value of the property will be included in his gross estate under Code Sec. 2036. (Incidentally, the transfer by Bart would be subject to federal gift taxes. The amount of the gross gift would be the fair market value of the property at the date of the gift, less the portion assignable to the value of the retained life estate.)

An illustration of reserving "the use or possession" of transferred property is an implied agreement or understanding between the transferor and the recipients. In many family situations, a father or mother may give the parents' residence to a son or daughter but continue to live there for life. As a result, the house will be fully includible in the parents' gross estate. Of course, legal title to the property is irrelevant in warding off the inclusion scenario. Naturally, if the parent (transferor) occupied only one-third of the house, then only that portion would be included in the gross estate. Also, it is significant to note that the decedent must be the transferor of the life estate in order for the property to be includible in the estate.

EXAMPLE 17.7	Jack Goodwin transfers income-producing property into trust for his son, Charlie, but retains a life estate for his wife, Ellen. The trust indenture provides that if Ellen predeceases Jack, the life estate will revert to Jack. If Jack predeceases Ellen, then the life estate enjoyed by Ellen would not be includible in Jack's gross estate under Code Sec. 2036. If Ellen predeceases Jack, none of the property will be included in Ellen's estate. Although Ellen held a life estate at the time of her death, she is not the transferor of the property. Therefore, Code Sec. 2036 is not operative.

Family Partnerships

A family partnership is a typical device to shift income and appreciation to other family members and is specifically sanctioned. Code Sec. 704(e). The grantor-partner should be careful not to run afoul of the retained life estate problem by retaining too much control. If the grantor retains a power to control income distributions after the transfer, the rule could apply. The exercise of traditional managerial powers by the grantor should not invoke the rule. Thus, the scope of powers customary in recognized business relationships should not be exceeded. Here are some key factors the IRS looks at:

1. Was the partnership created for business purposes or principally to carry out a desired estate plan?
2. Did the other partners contribute any capital?
3. Did the grantor-partner have the power to accumulate or distribute income?
4. What percentage of profits was in fact distributed to the grantor-partner?

Buy/sell agreements serve a business purpose and should not be a negative factor.

Family Transfers

Set out below are examples of lifetime transfers of property in the setting of family transfers and the tax consequences for each situation.

1. H transfers property to his wife (W) for life, then to himself for life, remainder to his children. Even if H predeceases W, the property (less W's outstanding life estate) is included in his estate.
2. G transfers securities to his wife for life, then to his son, but the trustee has discretion to distribute the income to G in whole or in part. Whether or not the trustee does so, Code Sec. 2036 has no application since the *decedent* retained no interest or right.
3. G makes a transfer in trust but retains the right to use the income for support of his minor children. If he dies before the youngest child reaches majority, he dies with a retained life estate, otherwise not.
4. G makes a transfer to A for life, then to B, retaining the right to designate C as income beneficiary, but only with A's consent. Even though G's power is illusory (i.e., G can exercise his power to substitute C for A only with the consent of A, the adverse party), G still has a retained life estate.

5. G transfers property to his son for life, leaving the remainder to his grandson. G has not retained a life estate and neither has his son since the son is not the transferor. (The son's death, however, causes a taxable termination and may be subject to the generation-skipping tax, discussed later in this chapter.)

6. Upon H's death, W, his widow, has the right to receive $200,000 of life insurance. However, she instructs the insurance company to pay her the interest only for life, then to pay the proceeds to her grandchildren in equal shares. Upon W's death, Code Sec. 2036 applies.

7. G transfers property to his brother, T, for life, then to T's children. T, in return, transfers property to G for life, then to G's children. Technically, neither party retained a life estate. However, the economic effect is the same as if they both did. The *reciprocal trust* doctrine creates a retained life estate in both. *J.P. Grace Est.,* 69-1 USTC ¶12,609, 395 U.S. 316, 89 S.Ct. 1730 (1969). If the trusts are of unequal value, only the smallest value is deemed to be reciprocal.

8. G has a retained life estate in a $1 million trust. At the age of 85, when the fair market value of his interest is $50,000, G sells it to his grandson and dies. Literally, Code Sec. 2036 does not apply since G did not die with a retained life interest.

    Furthermore, even if he died the next day, there is no gift in contemplation of death because the consideration was adequate. Nevertheless, $950,000 may be included in G's estate if the transaction is viewed as involving the property which otherwise would have been included. *C. Allen,* 61-2 USTC ¶12,032, 293 F.2d 916 (CA-10 1961).

¶17,133   REVERSIONS

Code Sec. 2037 also addresses the inclusion in the gross estate of the value of lifetime transfers by the decedent. This section refers to transfers "in trust or otherwise" except for an "adequate and full consideration," as does Code Sec. 2036. However, there are three conditions that must be satisfied for Code Sec. 2037 to become operative.

1. Possession or enjoyment of the property can be obtained, through ownership of such interest, only by surviving the decedent;
2. The decedent had retained a reversionary interest in the property at the time of the transfer; and
3. The value of the reversionary interest immediately before the decedent's death exceeded five percent of the value of the entire property.

The condition of survivorship cited in 1 above means that the subject property is not included in the decedent's gross estate if, immediately before the decedent's death, possession or enjoyment of the property could be obtained by a beneficiary either by surviving the decedent, or through another event such as the expiration of a term of years. The reversionary interest referred to in 2 above is, in effect, a remainder interest retained by the original transferor. The term "reversionary interest" does not include rights to income only, such as the right to receive the income from a trust after the death of another person. Reg. §20.2037-1(c)(2). To determine whether the decedent retained a reversionary interest in the property valued in excess of five percent, as referred to in 3 above, the value of the reversionary interest is compared to the value of the property transferred. This valuation does not include interests therein that are not dependent upon survivorship of the decedent. Application of the Code Sec. 2037 provisions discussed above are presented in the following examples.

EXAMPLE 17.8

John Henry transferred property into trust, giving his wife, Donna, a life estate and the remainder interest to John's then-surviving children. In the event there were no surviving children, the remainder would go to John or his estate. Each beneficiary can possess or enjoy the property without surviving John. Therefore, no part of the property is includible in John's gross estate under Code Sec. 2037, regardless of the value of John's reversionary interest.

EXAMPLE 17.9	John Henry transferred property into trust retaining a life estate, with the remainder interest to his surviving children. In the event there were no surviving children, the remainder would go to his brother or to his brother's estate. The decedent did not retain a reversionary interest. Therefore, no part of the property is includible in the decedent's gross estate under Code Sec. 2037, even though possession or enjoyment of the property could be obtained by the children only if they survived John Henry.

EXAMPLE 17.10	A transferred property into trust giving a life estate to B with the remainder to C if A predeceases B. However, if B predeceases A, the remainder would go to A. If, in fact, A predeceases B, the value of A's reversionary interest immediately before death is compared with the value of the trust corpus, without deduction for the value of B's outstanding life estate, in applying the five percent rule. Conceivably, a fractional remainder interest could be retained by the decedent. Referring to the above situation, if A had retained a reversionary interest in only one-half of the trust corpus, the value of the reversionary interest would be compared with the value of one-half of the trust corpus, without deduction for any part of the value of B's outstanding life estate.

In applying Code Sec. 2037, the value of the decedent's reversionary interest is computed in accordance with the Special Use Valuation Method.

¶17,141   REVOCABLE TRANSFERS

As did Code Secs. 2036 and 2037, Code Sec. 2038 also relates to the inclusion in the gross estate of the value of lifetime transfers by the decedent. This section also refers to transfers "in trust or otherwise" except for an "adequate and full consideration," as do Code Secs. 2036 and 2037. Under Code Sec. 2038, however, the value of property interests transferred by the decedent are includible in the gross estate if the enjoyment of the property transferred was subject, at the date of the decedent's death, to any power of the decedent to alter, amend, revoke, or terminate the transfer. Reg. §20.2038-1(a).

It is immaterial in what capacity the power was exercisable by the decedent or by another person, or persons, in conjunction with the decedent. Also, the time of exercise and the source of the power are of no importance. If the decedent transferred property by trust during life and was named as trustee with the power to revoke the trusts, the entire property would be includible in the gross estate under the operation of Code Sec. 2038. Likewise, if the decedent created a trust during life, named another person as trustee, but reserved the power to be named as a replacement trustee, Code Sec. 2038 would apply.

In order to preclude inclusion of the transferred property in the gross estate under Code Sec. 2038, the power to alter, amend, revoke, or terminate a trust must be held at all times "solely by a person other than the decedent." Further, the decedent must not have reserved any right to assume these powers. The amount includible in the gross estate under Code Sec. 2038 is "only" that portion of the property transferred that is subject, at death, to the "decedent's" power to alter, amend, revoke, or terminate. Reg. §20.2038-1(a)(3).

A revocable lifetime trust is the typical tool employed by the decedent to provide flexibility for changing personal and economic conditions. With respect to the estates of decedents dying after August 5, 1997, the value of property transferred to a donee from a decedent's revocable trust (within three years of the decedent's death) and the value of property in such a trust (with respect to which the decedent's power to revoke is relinquished during the three years before death) is not includible in the decedent's gross estate. Transfers from a revocable trust are treated as if made directly by the decedent for purposes of Code Sec. 2035 and Code Sec. 2038. Accordingly, an annual exclusion gift from a revocable trust is not included in the decedent's gross estate.

It should be obvious at this juncture that there may be considerable overlap between Code Secs. 2036, 2037, and 2038. A previous lifetime transfer by the decedent may subject the property to inclusion in the gross estate under one or more of these sections. Of course, the property is included only once, but perhaps for one or more reasons.

¶17,149   ANNUITIES

Commercial Annuities

By far, most annuities are of the commercial kind and are issued by insurance companies. Commercial annuities are valued on the basis of comparable sales. In other words, the issuer is asked: How much would a 60-year-old person have to pay to receive $3,000 a year for life? The answer is the value.

Most commercial annuities, including retirement annuities, can be divided into four groups:

1. *Straight-life annuities,* which are simply paid for the life of one person.
2. *Joint and survivor annuities,* whereby payments are made, typically to a married couple, as long as at least one of them lives.
3. *Self and survivor annuities,* whereby payments continue to be made to a beneficiary after the death of the buyer.
4. *Minimum guarantee annuities,* whereby a refund feature provides for a lump-sum payment, unless the annuitant survives a minimum period of time.

To qualify as an annuity, it is immaterial whether the payments are periodic or sporadic, equal or unequal, conditional or unconditional.

A straight-life annuity will never result in estate taxation, but once a survivor feature exists, the present value of the payments due after death will be included in the estate *if the decedent or an employer contributed to the purchase price.* This is similar to the tracing rule that applies to unmarried joint tenants (see below) and also applies to both private and commercial annuities. Code Sec. 2039(b).

EXAMPLE 17.11	H paid $500,000 to an insurance company for a joint and survivorship annuity, whereby $3,000 a month would be paid as long as he and/or his wife, W, survive. If H dies first, the full present value of W's expected payments, based on actuarial tables, will be included in his estate. If W dies first, nothing will be included in her estate.
EXAMPLE 17.12	Same as Example 17.11, except H and W pay half each. Whenever the first one dies, one-half of the full present value of the survivor's expected payments based on actuarial tables will be included in the deceased's estate.
EXAMPLE 17.13	Same as Example 17.12 except that H and W each buy separate annuities for $250,000. Since neither one contributed to the other's annuity, nothing is included in either estate.

Private Annuities

Private annuities are usually employed when there is an "estate planning sale" by an older person (the annuitant) to a younger family member (the obligor). If the annuity is simply paid to the annuitant for life with no survivor feature, nothing will be includible in the annuitant's estate since nothing passes from the decedent. Should the annuity continue to the surviving spouse or other beneficiary, the estate will include the present value of the future payments, based on the survivor's life expectancy times the fractional consideration paid by the decedent. Code Sec. 2039(b).

EXAMPLE 17.14	Several years ago, G and W sold their securities to their child for a private annuity of $5,000 a year for as long as both live, plus $3,000 a year for the life of the survivor. G had put up 80 percent of the purchase price of the securities and died first. Based on W's age at G's death, assume that according to the IRS tables prescribed under Code Sec. 7520, one dollar a year for life is worth $10.5376. As a result, G's estate will include $25,290 ($3,000 × 10.5376 × .80).
PLANNING POINTER	New proposed regulations have been issued that will tax gain on the exchange of highly appreciated property for the issuance of annuity contracts (effective date is April 18, 2007 for estate and succession planning).

Pension and Profit-Sharing Plans

No estate exclusion is allowed regardless of how annuity payments are made, even if there is a named beneficiary. Code Sec. 2039(a) and (b). Even IRAs and Keogh plans are fully includible. (All or part of a retirement annuity in "pay status" before 1985, however, may be excluded.)

¶17,157   CO-OWNERSHIPS OF PROPERTY

Tenancies in Common

Since there is no survivorship feature in a tenancy in common, the decedent's undivided interest in the property is included in the decedent's gross estate (and in the decedent's probate estate). Thus, if the decedent owned a 23 percent interest in a tract of land, 23 percent of its value is includible in the decedent's estate.

Joint Tenancies and Tenancies by the Entirety

Married Joint Tenants

If the decedent owned property as a joint tenant with a spouse with right of survivorship, including a tenancy by the entirety, a "qualified joint tenancy" exists. One-half of its value is included in the estate of the first spouse to die without regard to who paid for it. The surviving spouse becomes the sole owner by operation of law resulting in full inclusion in the surviving spouse's estate.

Unmarried Joint Tenants

Any two or more individuals may be joint tenants (e.g., parent and child, siblings, and unmarried couples). When the first joint tenant dies, the *full* value of the property is included in the estate, unless and to the extent the surviving joint tenant can show contributions in money toward the purchase price. Code Sec. 2040(a).

EXAMPLE 17.15	Fernanda and her daughter Fern own, as joint tenants, a condominium apartment, which Fernanda paid for. If Fernanda dies first, the full value is included in her estate, but if Fern predeceases her mother, *nothing* is includible in Fern's estate. If Fernanda contributed X percent of the original cost, X percent of the *value* at the time of her death would be includible in her estate if Fern survived her. If the surviving joint tenant receives the property subject to an unpaid mortgage, the mortgage balance counts as an original contribution to the extent the owner is personally liable. Rev. Rul. 79-302, 1979-2 CB 328.

Community Property

There are only 10 community property states (Alaska, Arizona, California, Idaho, Louisiana, Nevada, New Mexico, Texas, Washington, and Wisconsin). In these states, property acquired by married persons is community property, and such property retains its character once established even after a change of domicile. One-half of the value of community property owned by a husband and wife is includible in the gross estate of the first spouse to die. Community property is like an equal tenancy in common between spouses enforced by state law. That is, one-half of the community interest goes into the estate of the first to die. However, unlike joint tenancies with the right of survivorship between husbands and wives in common law states, both halves of community property receive a step-up in basis to fair market value. Code Sec. 1014(b)(6).

¶17,165   POWERS OF APPOINTMENT

If property is transferred in trust by gift or inheritance, a beneficiary may use and enjoy that property to a great extent *without that property being includible in the estate*. The beneficiary may have all the following rights and powers. Code Sec. 2041(b)(1) and (2).

1. The right to receive all the income from the property for life (i.e., a life estate).
2. The power to draw funds from the trust (invade corpus), as long as it is subject to an *ascertainable standard* relating to the beneficiary's health, education, support, or maintenance.
3. The power to withdraw the greater of five percent of the value of the trust property or, $5,000, each year.
4. The power to appoint all or part of the property to anyone the beneficiary wishes during life or by will, except to oneself, the estate, or the creditors of either.
5. The right to be the trustee of the trust.

None of the above will subject the property to estate tax in the beneficiary's estate, but there may be generation-skipping transfer tax consequences.

Definitions

If the decedent had transferred property as a gift and retained certain powers of control, they can be extremely limited and still cause the property to be included under the retained life estate, reversion, or revocable transfer rules discussed above. Once the decedent as a beneficiary simply has been given a power by someone else over property the beneficiary never owned, the power must be a *general power of appointment* to cause inclusion. The expression "general power" does not have to be stated as such.

Appointee. The person in whose favor the power is exercised.

Donee of the power. The person who has the right to appoint the property, let the power lapse, or release it.

Donor of the power. The grantor and transferor of the property subject to the power.

Taker in default. The person who winds up with the property if the power is released or lapses. This person will often be the remainderman.

General v. Special Powers

For the decedent to be deemed to have a general power of appointment, the decedent must have had the power to appoint the property to oneself, the estate, or the creditors of either by will and/or during life. Code Sec. 2041(b)(1) and (2).

The following are *not* general powers:

1. The power to appoint the property to anyone in the world, such as a child or grandchild, except to oneself, the estate, or the creditors of either.
2. The power to appoint the property to anyone, including oneself, but only with the consent of the grantor or an adverse party, such as the remainderman or an income beneficiary whose interest would be extinguished in the process.
3. The power to make use of capital up to five percent of value or $5,000, whichever is greater, once a year on a noncumulative basis.
4. The power to make use of capital for the beneficiary's health, education, support, or maintenance, but not for emergencies, welfare, or happiness.

Powers that fall short of general powers are called *special* or *limited* powers.

Once a general power exists, the release, lapse, or exercise of it during life creates a taxable gift. Code Sec. 2514. If the decedent exercises a general power in a will or lets it lapse or releases it, the property is includible in the decedent's estate.

If the donee of the power exercises it, but retains a life estate, reversion, or the power to alter, amend, or revoke, the property will be included in the donee's estate under Code Secs. 2035-2038.

General powers granted before October 22, 1942, lead to estate inclusion only if exercised, by will or during life. But a post-October 21, 1942, power is taxable whether it lapses, is released, or is exercised.

EXAMPLE 17.16	Max Mertens transfers property in trust to his son for life. The son has the power to give the property to any or all of his children *and* has the right to use whatever he needs for his own support. The property will not be included in the son's estate. If the son's power is worded as a power to consume for his happiness, welfare, and the like, chances are the power will be considered general for lack of an ascertainable standard.
EXAMPLE 17.17	B left property in trust to A for life, then to B. C has the power to appoint the property to himself. The property is includible in C's estate.
EXAMPLE 17.18	Same as Example 17.17, but C needs A's consent. Since A is the income beneficiary, A is an adverse party, and C does *not* have a general power. Therefore, none of the property would be includible in C's estate.

EXAMPLE 17.19	Same as Example 17.17, but C needs B's consent. As a remainderman, B is also an adverse party and there are no estate tax consequences to C.

EXAMPLE 17.20	G left property in trust to his wife, W, for life, then to his son, S. W has the power to appoint the property to anyone in the world but only with the consent of her daughter. Since the daughter is a permissible appointee, only one-half of the property would be includible in W's estate.

EXAMPLE 17.21	Same as Example 17.20, except that W needs the consent of both her daughters. Only one-third would be includible in W's estate.

EXAMPLE 17.22	A received a general power of appointment over a trust fund. A exercised one-half in favor of himself and the other half in favor of his grandson. Upon A's death, his estate includes one-half of the property itself to the extent he still has it. The one-half exercised in favor of his grandson is subject to gift tax.

TAX BLUNDER

The decedent was also both the trustee and the beneficiary of a trust that granted him the power to invade the trust for "proper support, maintenance, welfare, health and general happiness in the manner to which he was accustomed." Of course, the offending term is "general happiness." The estate argued that the term "happiness" was limited to support items, but the court disagreed. The court reasoned that if they were to resolve a conflict between the income and the remainder beneficiary, they would not take a "grudging and narrow interpretation." They concluded that there are several things, such as travel, that fall within the ambit of general happiness, which are not considered as necessary for health, education, support or maintenance. *Estate of Little*, 87 TC 599.

Note: Travel can be part of an ascertainable standard if the travel is part of an educational program or if it is part of the beneficiary's accustomed lifestyle.

¶17,173   LIFE INSURANCE

The proceeds of life insurance on the life of the decedent are includible in the decedent's gross estate under three sets of circumstances. Code Sec. 2042.

First, if the proceeds are payable to the decedent's estate, they are clearly includible in the gross estate. This could happen by choice, e.g., the estate is named as a beneficiary, or it could occur inadvertently, e.g., the named beneficiary predeceased the insured and no provision was made for a secondary beneficiary. Also, if the proceeds are payable to a trustee who is obligated to use the proceeds for the benefit of the estate, such as to pay debts and taxes, the proceeds are deemed payable to the estate. If the trustee has discretion as to whether the proceeds are to be used for the benefit of the estate, they are includible to the extent so used.

Second, if the decedent possessed at least one incident of ownership in the policy, the life insurance proceeds are includible in the gross estate. This means either that the decedent owned the policy until death or transferred the policy, but retained the right to:

1. Change the beneficiary
2. Borrow on the policy
3. Use it as collateral for a loan
4. Cancel the policy
5. Veto any of the above or retained a reversionary interest in excess of five percent

Third, if the policy was transferred irrevocably within three years of the insured's death, the proceeds are includible in the gross estate.

The standard procedure employed to completely transfer all incidents of ownership is to assign the policy to an irrevocable insurance trust. Note that the power to exercise any incident of ownership in conjunction with any other party, or the power to veto any incident of ownership, is still an incident of ownership resulting in estate inclusion. Since life insurance is a unique asset in that it can increase dramatically in value from one instant to the next, it makes sense to relinquish all incidents of ownership and make it payable to a named beneficiary. The transfer must take place more than three years prior to death to accomplish the estate exclusion. Code Sec. 2035(a)(2).

EXAMPLE 17.23	Mark Martin purchased flight insurance at the airport, handed the policy over to his son, embarked, and died one-half hour later in a plane crash. Since Mark possessed an incident of ownership in the policy, even though no opportunity existed for exercise, the full proceeds would nevertheless be included in his gross estate. *M.L. Noel Est.,* 65-1 USTC ¶12,311, 380 U.S. 678, 85 S.Ct. 1238 (1965). *Thus,* it is the *existence* of the *incident* that matters.

The rules under Code Sec. 2042 apply only to insurance on the life of the decedent. If the decedent owned "spouse insurance" or any policy on the life of another when the decedent died, only its *value,* not the proceeds, is includible in the decedent's gross estate under Code Sec. 2033. The value is the amount for which the individual insurance company would sell an identical policy at the time of death on a paid-up basis (i.e., the replacement cost, known as the "interpolated terminal reserve").

PLANNING POINTER	Here is a technique that can have favorable income, gift, and estate tax consequences: grantor transfers a life insurance policy on the grantor's own life to an irrevocable trust, whereupon the trust borrows to pay the premiums. The tax consequences are: **Gift tax.** No gift tax is incurred if the cash value does not exceed available exclusions. If the cash value is high, the grantor may borrow against the policy and transfer it subject to the loan. **Income tax.** If the trust income may be used to pay the premiums on the policy, the trust is a grantor trust and any available deductions belong to the grantor. Code Sec. 677(a)(3). **Estate tax.** If all incidents of ownership in the policy are transferred more than three years prior to the grantor's death, the proceeds are excluded from the insured's gross estate. Because of all these tax advantages, such a grantor-insurance trust is known in the profession as the "supertrust."

¶17,175   PART-SALE, PART-GIFT TRANSFERS

Sometimes a transfer is part sale and part gift. Whenever a transfer is for less than fair value (i.e., not a bona fide sale), the property is includible at full value in the estate, less consideration paid. Code Sec. 2043.

EXAMPLE 17.24	G transferred property to one of his sons, S, keeping a life estate for himself. When it is explained to him that the full value of the property will be included in his estate because of a retained life interest, he gets an idea. He sells his life interest to his other son for $5,000. Nevertheless, the full value of the property is included in his estate, less $5,000, assuming he dies within three years. Note that he did not sell the property itself, merely the life estate. This result follows even if the $5,000 was all the *life estate* was worth, which is all G had. The purpose of the rule is to avoid deathbed transfers of a retained life estate, powers of appointment, or a reversion. Otherwise, sales for a modest sum could remove sizeable amounts from the estate.

Valuation of Gross Estate

¶17,181   GENERAL PRINCIPLES

Valuing the gross estate is the paramount estate tax problem since the value determines the amount that will be subject to estate tax and, as a result, the estate's liquidity needs. The executor will value all property included in the gross estate either at its fair market value at the decedent's date of death or the alternate valuation date. Code Secs. 2031 and 2032.

Fair Market Value

In general, fair market value of property includible in a decedent's estate is the price at which it would change hands between a willing buyer and a willing seller, both having reasonable knowledge of relevant facts. Reg. §20.2031-1(b). Despite the brevity of the rule, valuation controversies make up a large share of audit and litigation issues.

If an item is generally available to the public in a particular market, the fair market value of the property is the price obtainable on the market in which it is most commonly sold to the public. If the item of property is generally obtainable by the public on the retail market, fair market value of the item is the price at which that item or a comparable one will sell at retail in a particular geographic market. Reg. §20.2031-1(b).

EXAMPLE 17.25	The fair market value of decedent Ginger Graham's car (property generally obtained by the public on the retail market) is the price at which a car of the same make, model, age, and condition could be purchased by members of the public. Fair market value would not be the price that a used-car dealer would pay for Ginger's car.

Alternate Valuation Date

Whenever the executor chooses the alternate valuation method, all property is valued six months after death or on the date of disposition if this date occurs first. Code Sec. 2032(a). It should be noted that whichever valuation date is selected, the election is all inclusive. That is, each asset included in the gross estate must be valued as of the elected date. Consequently, the executor may not value some items at date of death and others at the alternate date.

EXAMPLE 17.26	John Henry's gross estate consists of the following assets:

	FMV at Date of Death	FMV at Alternate Date
1,000 shares of Ed's Barbecue	$700,000	$690,000
House	480,000	470,000
Farm	600,000	590,000
Georgia Power bonds	300,000	298,000
Total	$2,080,000	$2,048,000

If the executor elects the date of death value, then the estate is valued at $2,080,000, and if the alternate valuation date is selected, the estate's value is $2,048,000. Note that no mixing of values is permissible.

The election to use the alternate valuation date must reduce the value of the decedent's gross estate and the sum of the decedent's estate tax and generation-skipping transfer tax liabilities. Code Sec. 2032(c). Even property that was transferred some time before death, but which is included in the gross estate because of the retention of certain rights or for other reasons, is valued as of the date of death or six months after death.

Basis of Property

Most properties receive a basis for income tax purposes equal to the estate tax value, be it the date of death value, the value on the alternate valuation date, or the special use value. Code Sec. 1014(a). The decedent's basis is irrelevant, and a step-up or a step-down may result. An instant long-term holding period is also given by statute. Code Sec. 1223(11). The fair market value basis rule applies without regard to whether estate or inheritance taxes are paid or whether an estate tax return is due.

Under the 2001 Act, the step-up in basis at death will not apply to decedents dying during 2010 that elected not to have the estate tax apply. In general, the property passing out of an estate will be subject to the gift tax rules governing basis. Code Sec. 1022(a). Basis will be the lesser of the decedent's adjusted basis in the property or the fair market value of the property at the decedent's death. However, the decedent's spouse may receive $3 million of basis increase allocated to property that the spouse is to receive directly or in a qualifying marital trust. Code Sec. 1022(d)(4)(B)(iii). Also, an executor may allocate an aggregate basis increase of up to $1.3 million regardless of the beneficiary of the property. Code Sec. 1022(d)(4)(B)(i). However, Congress did reinstate step-up basis for 2010 as an option.

¶17,185 SPECIFIC PROPERTIES

Even though all property included in the gross estate is valued as of the same date—that is, the date of death or the alternate valuation date—special problems arise in valuing particular types of property. For this reason, special rules apply in valuing the various kinds of property or interests in property that might be included in the gross estate and these are treated in the following paragraphs.

Real Estate

The valuation of real estate is not set out in the Regulations pursuant to any formula or other precise mechanism. Reg. §20.2031-1(b). Since each piece of real estate is unique, it is not surprising for the Regulations to take this approach. However, the following methods can be used to establish the estate tax value of real estate: expert testimony, comparable sales, market assessments, recent mortgages, capitalization of earnings, and reproduction costs.

Household and Personal Effects

Household and personal effects must be valued at the price that a willing buyer would pay a willing seller for such goods. Reg. §20.2031-6(a). If the household and personal effects exceed a total value of $3,000, then there must be an appraisal and an itemized list of the jewelry, furs, silverware, paintings, antiques, oriental rugs, stamps, coin collection, and books attached to the return.

Life Insurance

The value of life insurance for estate tax purposes will be either the proceeds of the policy or its replacement value. That is, where insurance is taxed to the estate of the insured because the insurance becomes due and payable on death, then the estate tax value will be the proceeds of the policy. On the other hand, life insurance may be taxed in the estate of a person other than the insured. When this happens, the policy has not matured. As a result, the estate tax value is the replacement cost and not its face value. Reg. §20.2031-8.

Life Estates, Remainder Interests, Term Certain Interests, and Reversionary Interests

Because an individual may have an interest less than the entire fee simple ownership in property, special IRS tables must be used to value these life estates, remainders, term certain interests, and reversions. Code Sec. 7520. This actuarial valuation system requires that the interest rate to be used in valuing limited interests be updated using an interest rate derived from the federal midterm rate for the month in which the valuation is required. The method prescribes that the interest rate will be at 120 percent of the applicable federal midterm rate (AFR) compounded annually (rounded to the nearest two-tenths of one percent).

Mutual Funds

Mutual fund shares can be sold back only to the issuer and by shareholders at a fixed price under federal laws governing mutual funds. This fixed price is called the redemption or bid price and is based on the net values of the assets held by the fund on a given date. Because of this fact, the U.S. Supreme Court has ruled that mutual fund shares owned by decedents must be valued for estate tax purposes by using the redemption or bid price at the date of death or on the alternate valuation date. *D.B. Cartwright*, 73-1 USTC ¶12,926, 411 U.S. 546, 93 S.Ct. 1713 (1973); Reg. §20.2031-8(b).

¶17,187 LISTED SECURITIES

Stocks and bonds owned by a decedent are includible in the gross estate and are valued for estate tax purposes on the date of death, or on a date six months after death if the estate representative so elects. Code Sec. 2033. When the valuation is made as of six months after death, if any of the securities have been distributed in the interval, the value on the date of distribution will control. Reg. §20.2032-1(c)(2). Similarly, the valuation date, in the case of a sale during the six-month period after death, is the date of sale.

The estate tax value of stocks and bonds is the fair market value per share or bond on the applicable valuation date. In the case of listed stocks and bonds, if there were actual sales of the securities on a stock exchange or in an over-the-counter market on the valuation date, then the mean between the highest and lowest quoted selling prices on that date is taken as the fair market value per share or bond. Reg. §20.2031-2(b).

EXAMPLE 17.27
John Hughes died on September 1, 2015, and he owned 1,000 shares of IBM stock that was traded on the New York Stock Exchange. IBM traded at a high of $116 and a low of $114 on September 1. As a result, Mr. Hughes's estate tax return will reflect a value for the IBM stock of $115 per share (average of $116 and $114) and a total value of the stock of $115,000.

If there were no actual sales on the valuation date, but there were sales on trading dates within a reasonable period both before and after the valuation date, the fair market value is derived by taking (1) the mean between the highest and lowest sales on the nearest trading date before and (2) the mean between the highest and lowest sales on the nearest trading date after the valuation date, and taking a weighted average of these two means. However, it should be noted that the average is weighted inversely by the respective number of trading days separating the selling dates and the date of death. Reg. §§20.2031-2(b) and 25.2512-2(b).

EXAMPLE 17.28
Sam Lett died on November 5, 2015, and owned 1,000 shares of Zebra Corporation stock, which is traded on an over-the-counter market. On November 5 there were no sales of Zebra stock. The sales of Zebra stock nearest the valuation date of November 5 took place two trading days before (November 3) and three trading days after (November 10). On November 3, 2015, the mean sales price was $50, and on November 10, 2015, the mean sales price was $40. As a result, the date of death value is as follows: $((3 \times \$50) + (2 \times \$40))/5 = \$46$.

In certain instances, securities may be actively traded on the date of death, but that is not the value that will be utilized for estate tax purposes. Specifically, the taxpayer may own a large block of securities, and the valuer must consider the depressing effect that the sale of such a large number of shares would have on the market. This situation is referred to as "blockage" and requires that the price per share be lowered to reflect the effect of marketing such a large block of securities. Reg. §§20.2031-2(e) and 25.2512-2(e); Rev. Rul. 59-60, 1959-1 CB 237.

¶17,191 CLOSELY HELD STOCK

One of the most vexing problems in the area of estate taxation is how to value the stock of a closely held corporation. The valuation of close corporation stock differs from that of listed and active corporate stock that passes freely on the market and has its value reflected on the stock exchange or over-the-counter listings. Closely held stock rarely finds its way to the market place and its value at any particular time is determined only by reference to various factors. Numerous courts, professional journals, and government publications have discussed this valuation question. Despite this wealth of information, few areas of taxation are as unresolved and misunderstood as the valuation of closely held stock. And, since there are several million closely held corporations in the United States, valuation represents an area of critical concern confronting taxing authorities and practitioners.

Obviously, a sale of stock occurring within a reasonable time of the valuation date can provide a good indication of the stock's value. Reg. §20.2031-2. However, the fair market value of a particular item of property is not to be determined by a forced sale price. Nor is the fair market value to be determined by the sale price of the item in a market other than that in which such item is most commonly sold to the public. Reg. §20.2031-1(b). If there is no sale (as is the usual case with closely held stock), an independent expert appraiser should be consulted.

In the case of corporate stock and securities that are not listed on an exchange and whose value thus cannot be determined on the basis of sales or bid and asked prices, the value must be determined by taking into consideration, in addition to other factors, the value of stock or securities of corporations engaged in the same or a similar line of business that are listed on an exchange. Code Sec. 2031(b). Thus, in the absence of an active market, consideration may be given in the case of bonds to such factors as the soundness of the security, the interest yield, and the date of maturity. In the case of stocks, consideration may be given to the company's net worth, prospective earning power, dividend-paying capacity, and other relevant factors, including a fair appraisal of the tangible and intangible business assets (including goodwill) as of the appropriate valuation date and the demonstrated earnings capacity of the business. Reg. §§20.2031-2(f), 20.2031-3, and 20.2031-6(b).

The IRS emphasizes the following factors to be considered as valuation guides in addition to all available financial data. Rev. Rul. 59-60, 1959-1 CB 237.

1. The nature of the business and the history of the enterprise from its inception.
2. The economic outlook in general and the condition and outlook of the specific industry in particular.
3. The book value of the stock and the financial condition of the business.
4. The earning capacity of the company.
5. The dividend-paying capacity.
6. Whether or not the enterprise has goodwill or other intangible value.
7. Sales of the stock and the size of the block of stock to be valued.
8. The market price of stock of corporations engaged in the same or a similar line of business having their stocks actively traded in a free and open market, either on an exchange or over the counter.

¶17,193   BUY-SELL AGREEMENTS

In a buy-sell agreement one business owner (partner or shareholder) is obligated to sell an interest on death, retirement, or disability to the owners (cross-purchase agreement) or to the business (redemption agreement). Such agreements may be used to ease the problems of liquidity and estate valuation. Buy-sell agreements have at least three advantages. First, if the buy-sell agreement is legally binding on both parties and fair when made, the price (fixed or based on a formula) is also helpful in establishing value for estate, gift, and income tax purposes, limiting the estate tax value. The agreement must not be merely an option or right of first refusal. Second, a guaranteed price will provide the estate with instant liquidity, rather than an unmarketable ownership interest. Third, an orderly continuity of business ownership is provided. Buy-sell agreements are often funded by insurance policies.

EXAMPLE 17.29   Paul Jones and Mary Wells are equal shareholders in Quincy Corporation. When either party dies, retires, or becomes totally disabled, the other shareholder is to purchase the shares, thus becoming the sole shareholder. This is an example of a cross-purchase agreement. It should be noted that the purchasing shareholder's basis in the stock is increased by the purchase price. If the corporation is the buyer, the remaining shareholder still becomes the sole owner of the business, but there will be no basis increase.

¶17,195   SPECIAL USE VALUATION FOR FARMLAND AND CLOSELY HELD BUSINESS REALTY

When a person dies, property generally passes to that person's heirs at its fair market value as of the date of death. Code Sec. 1014(a)(1). Alternately, the executor or executrix of the estate may elect to value such property at its fair market value on a date six months after the death of the decedent (or the date of distribution to beneficiaries, if sooner). Code Sec. 2032(a)(2). This election is permissible only if it will result in a lower value for the gross estate and a lower estate tax liability. Code Sec. 2032(c).

Even with the relief provided under the alternative valuation date option, many estates holding farmland and closely held businesses have been burdened with substantial estate tax liabilities. A major factor was the requirement that such property is valued at its "highest or best" use rather than at its current use. This requirement often resulted in sale of the family farm or business to raise cash to pay the estate taxes.

Congress enacted legislation providing for special use valuation, under Code Sec. 2032A, for real property used in farms and closely-held businesses. The intent of the legislation was to lessen the estate tax burden by permitting such property to be valued at its current use, rather than its highest and best use. A related goal was to encourage heirs to continue operating family farms or closely held businesses.

Real property included in the estate of the decedent may qualify for special use valuation if:

1. The decedent was a resident of the United States at the time of death.
2. The property is qualified real property.
3. The executor elects special use valuation on the estate tax return.
4. A written recapture agreement is filed with the estate tax return. Code Sec. 2032A(a)(1).

The aggregate decrease in value of the qualifying property may not exceed $1,100,000 for 2015. Code Sec. 2032A(a)(2) and Rev. Proc. 2014-61.

EXAMPLE 17.30   Pat McMullen dies in 2015 and his estate elects special use valuation with respect to his farm under Sec. 2032A. The estate would be entitled to a maximum reduction in estate value of $1,100,000.

Qualification Requirements

"Qualified real property" is property located in the United States. It must be acquired from, or pass from, the decedent to a qualified heir of the decedent. The property must also have been used, on the date of the decedent's death, for qualified use by the decedent or a member of the decedent's family. Code Sec. 2032A(b)(1).

The adjusted value of the qualified real or personal property used in farming or another business must make up 50 percent or more of the adjusted value of the gross estate of the decedent. Furthermore, 25 percent or more of the adjusted value of the gross estate must consist of qualified real property. Code Sec. 2032A(b)(1)(A) and (B). For purposes of the 50 percent test, personal property used in farming or another business is taken into account even though personal property does not qualify for special use valuation. The adjusted value of the property is its fair market value (FMV) for estate tax purposes (without considering its special use value), reduced by mortgages and other indebtedness on the property. Code Secs. 2032A(b)(3) and 2053(a)(4).

Qualified Heir

The term "qualified heir" refers to a member of the decedent's family who acquired the real property from the decedent or to whom the property has passed. If a qualified heir disposes of any interest in qualified real property to any member of his or her family, that person becomes the qualified heir of the property. Code Sec. 2032A(e)(1).

The term "member of the family" means an individual's spouse, ancestors, and lineal descendants. Also included are lineal descendants of the spouse, parents of the individual or of the spouse, and the spouse of any lineal descendant. A legally adopted child of a person is treated as that person's child by blood. Code Sec. 2032A(e)(2).

Qualified Use

The qualified use requirement is met if the property is used as a farm for farming purposes, or in a trade or business other than farming. Code Sec. 2032A(b)(2). The property must have been used for the qualified use for at least five of the eight years ending on the date of the decedent's death. Also, the decedent, or a member of the decedent's family, must have materially participated in the operation of the farm or business during the required period of time. Code Sec. 2032A(b)(1)(C).

EXAMPLE 17.31

Rachel Pitt died leaving a gross estate valued at $6.2 million to her daughter. The estate included the family farm, which was valued at $3.2 million. The value of the farm consisted of machinery and other personal property with a fair market value of $400,000 and real property with a highest and best use value of $1,000,000. At the time of Rachel's death, the real property was subject to a $40,000 mortgage on which she was personally liable. Rachel materially participated in the operation of the farm for the last 20 years prior to her death. The computation of the 50 percent and 25 percent tests are as follows:

Calculation of Adjusted Estate:

Gross estate (fair market value)	$6,200,000	
Secured debts	40,000	
Adjusted estate		$6,160,000

Calculation of Adjusted Value of Real Property:

Real property (fair market value)	$3,200,000	
Secured debts	40,000	
Adjusted value of real property		$3,160,000

Calculation of Adjusted Value of Real Property and Personal Property Used for Farming:

Personal property (fair market value)	$400,000	
Secured debts	0	
Adjusted value of personal property		$400,000
Adjusted value of real property		3,160,000
Adjusted value of real and personal property		$3,560,000

Computation of 50% Test:

$$\frac{3,560,000}{6,160,000} = 58\%$$

Computation of 25% Test:

$$\frac{3,160,000}{6,160,000} = 51\%$$

Under the above circumstances, the requirements of both tests have been fulfilled. The 50 percent test is met because the $3,560,000 adjusted value of the qualifying use real and personal property, which is determined by subtracting the $40,000 mortgage from the $3,600,000 fair market value of such property, is at least 50 percent of the $4,560,000 adjusted value of the gross estate, determined by subtracting the $40,000 mortgage from the $4,600,000 fair market value of the gross estate. The 25 percent test is also met. The $3,160,000 adjusted value of the real property, which is determined by subtracting the $40,000 mortgage from the $3,200,000 fair market value of the real property, is at least 25 percent of the adjusted estate. Consequently, rather than valuing the farm real property at $3,200,000, the property will be valued based on its actual use as a farm. However, it must be remembered that the value cannot be reduced by an amount greater than $1,100,000 for 2015.

The term "farm" includes stock, dairy, poultry, fruit, fur-bearing animal, and truck farms; plantations; ranches; nurseries; ranges; greenhouses or other similar structures used primarily for the raising of agricultural or horticultural commodities; and orchards and woodlands. Code Sec. 2032A(e)(4).

"Farming purposes" means cultivating the soil or raising or harvesting any agricultural or horticultural commodity, including the raising, shearing, feeding, caring for, training, and management of animals, on a farm. Also included in farming is:

1. The handling, drying, packing, grading, or storing on a farm of any agricultural or horticultural commodity in its unmanufactured state.
2. The planting, cultivating, caring for, or cutting of trees.
3. The preparation of trees for market. Code Sec. 2032A(e).

Valuation Methods

There are two different methods of arriving at a special use value for qualified real property in an estate. They are the farm value method and the multiple-factor method, and they must be used exclusively. That is, if any property is to be valued under the farm value method, all farm property eligible for special use valuation must be valued accordingly. The same is true for the multiple-factor approach, which often produces a valuation considerably higher than the farm method. Obviously, the farm value method should be used if at all possible.

Farm Value Method

The special use value of a farm is determined under the farm value method as follows:

1. The average annual gross cash rental or average annual net-share rental for comparable land used for farming purposes in the locality of such farm minus
2. The average annual state and local real estate taxes for such comparable land, divided by
3. The average annual effective interest rate for all new Farm Credit Bank loans in the district. Code Sec. 2032A(e)(7).

This may be expressed mathematically as follows:

$$\text{Special Use Value} = \frac{\substack{\text{Average Annual Gross Cash} \\ \text{Rental for Comparable Land} \\ \text{in Locality Used for Farming}} - \substack{\text{Average Real Estate Taxes} \\ \text{in the Locality for the} \\ \text{Comparable Land}}}{\substack{\text{Average Annual Effective Interest Rate for All New Farm Credit} \\ \text{Bank Loans in the District}}}$$

EXAMPLE 17.32

Abigail MacDonald wishes to use the farm value method to determine the special use value of a qualified 300-acre farm. MacDonald knows that the fair market value of the land is $2,500 per acre and that the cash-rental value of comparable property is $100 per acre. She also has ascertained that state and local tax on comparable property is $19 per acre and that the average annual effective interest rate established by the Farm Credit Bank for new loans in the district is 9 percent. MacDonald uses the above formula as follows:

(1) MacDonald determines the special use value of one acre of farmland:

$$\frac{\$100 - \$19}{.09} = \$900$$

(2) Jones determines the special use value of the entire 300-acre farm:

$$300 \times \$900 = \$270,000$$

The computation of each average annual amount is to be based on the five most recent calendar years ending before the date of the decedent's death.

Multiple-Factor Method

The special use valuation of qualifying nonfarm real property and of qualifying farm real property where the farm value method is not used must be determined by applying the following factors:

1. The capitalization of income that the property can be expected to yield for farming or closely held business purposes over a reasonable period of time under prudent management.
2. The capitalization of the fair rental value of the land for farmland or closely held business purposes.
3. Assessed land values in a state that provides a differential or use value assessment law for farmland or closely held business.
4. Comparable sales of other farm or closely held business land in the same geographical area far enough removed from a metropolitan or resort area so that nonagricultural use is not a significant factor in the sales price.
5. Any other factor that fairly values the farm or closely held business value of the property. Code Sec. 2032A(e)(8)(A)-(E).

Naturally, the multiple-factor method is very subjective. Questions about acceptable capitalization rates, fair rental values, and how to weight factors can produce taxpayer and IRS controversies. The multiple-factor method does not have the safe-harbor technique of the farm value method.

Electing Special Use Valuation

The estate must elect special use valuation for the qualifying property on the initial estate tax return. Once made, the election is irrevocable, and the following information must be provided in the election notice pursuant to Reg. §20.2032A-8(a)(3):

1. The name and taxpayer identification number of the decedent as they appear on the estate tax return.
2. The relevant qualified use of the property to be specially valued.
3. A listing of the real property to be specially valued.
4. The fair market value of the real property to be specially valued, and its value based on its qualified use (both values are determined taking into account outstanding mortgages or other debt to which the property is subject).
5. The adjusted value of all real property that is used in a qualified use and that passes from the decedent to a qualified heir and the adjusted value of all real property to be specially valued.
6. Items of personal property, including their adjusted value, listed on the estate tax return that pass from the decedent to a qualified heir and are used in a qualified use.
7. The adjusted value of the gross estate (as defined in Code Sec. 2032A(b)(3)(A)).
8. The method used to determine the special value based on use.
9. Copies of written appraisals of the fair market value of the real property.
10. A statement that the decedent and/or a member of the decedent's family has owned all specially valued real property for at least five of the eight years immediately preceding the date of the decedent's death.
11. A statement listing periods during the eight-year period preceding the date of the decedent's death during which the decedent or a member of his or her family did not own the property, use it in a qualified use, or materially participate in the operation of the farm or other business (within the meaning of Code Sec. 2032A(e)(6)).
12. The name, address, taxpayer identification number, and relationship to the decedent of each person taking an interest in each item of specially valued property. The value of the property interests, based on both fair market value and qualified use, passing to each of these individuals is also required.
13. Affidavits identifying the material participant or participants and describing their activities constituting material participation.
14. A legal description of the specially valued property.

The special use valuation agreement must be executed by all parties who have an interest in the property being valued. Code Sec. 2032A(d)(2).

Recapture

The Code refers to the recapture tax as an additional estate tax. Code Sec. 2032A(c)(1). It is imposed if the qualified heir disposes of any interest in the specially valued property (other than to another qualified heir) or ceases to use it for a qualified use within 10 years after the decedent's death. However, a two-year grace period is permitted immediately following the date of the decedent's death. Code Sec. 2032A(c)(7). During this period, failure to begin the qualified use of the property will not cause recapture. The 10-year recapture period is extended by a period equal to the actual time between the date of decedent's death and the date the qualified heir commences to use the property in the qualified use. Like-kind exchanges under Code Sec. 1031 and involuntary conversions under Code Sec. 1033 will not cause recapture if the replacement property is used for the same qualified use as the original qualified property. If the original election was not to treat timber as a crop, disposition or severance of standing timber does trigger recapture. Moreover, recapture refers to the tax difference between what the estate tax liability was and what it would have been but for the special use valuation.

Deductions from the Gross Estate

¶17,201

EXPENSES, DEBTS, AND LOSSES

All deductions are subtracted from the gross estate. The marital and charitable deductions are unique and are discussed separately below. The main "expense" deductions are funeral and administration expenses, debts (including unpaid taxes and interest), and casualty losses.

Funeral Expenses

Funeral expenses are never deductible for income tax purposes. However, they are deductible from the gross estate to the extent allowable under local law even if they go beyond "necessary." The expenses may be incurred in the U.S. or abroad. Reg. §20.2053-1(a)(1).

Administration Expenses

Administration expenses, such as fees paid to the executor, lawyer, accountant, and appraisers, and certain interest expenses must meet two tests to be deductible:

1. The expenses must be "allowable by the law of the jurisdiction."
2. The expenses must be "actually and necessarily incurred in the administration of the decedent's estate; that is, in the collection of assets, payment of debts, and distribution of property to the persons entitled to it." Reg. §20.2053-3(a).

Thus, the expenses must be allowable and necessary. Expenses incurred for the convenience of a beneficiary are disallowed, e.g., selling expenses when a house could have been deeded to a beneficiary rather than sold.

Debts

All enforceable claims against the estate are deductible if paid. This includes accrued interest up to the date of death and unpaid taxes of all kinds, such as income, property, and gift taxes, but not the estate tax itself. Reg. §20.2053-6. The property tax is deductible to the extent the real property is includible in the gross estate. Nonrecourse debts and mortgages are deductible only to the extent of estate tax value. Liabilities must have been incurred for full consideration to avoid collusion between family members, e.g., IOUs given as presents to friends and relatives are *not* deductible even if enforceable and paid.

EXAMPLE 17.33	When Gertrude London died, she owed unpaid federal, state, and local income taxes, gift taxes on deathbed gifts, and property taxes on her home. In addition, substantial estate taxes were due, as well as excise taxes on excess retirement accumulation. Except for the estate taxes, all of the other unpaid taxes are deductible as debts of the estate, be they federal, state, or local.

Claims Against the Estate

Probate Estate Assets

Expenses and debts relating to assets subject to claims are deductible regardless of how late they are paid. A deduction is allowed prior to payment as long as the amount "is ascertainable, with reasonable certainty, and will be paid." However, the sum of the deductions may not exceed the estate value of the probate estate unless paid by the due date of the estate tax return. Code Sec. 2053(c)(1) and (2); Reg. §20.2053-1(b)(3).

Nonprobate Assets

Deductions that relate to nonprobate assets (i.e., assets included in the gross estate solely for tax purposes) are allowable as long as they are paid within the statute of limitations (i.e., within three years after the due date of the return). There is no limitation as to amount, and estimates may be used. If actual expenses differ from the estimated deduction used, an amended estate tax return must be filed.

Casualty Losses

Losses from sudden casualties, such as fire, flood, shipwreck, or theft, are deductible if sustained by the estate. Code Sec. 2054. If sustained prior to death, they are deductible on the decedent's final Form 1040 and, if sustained after distribution, they are deductible by the beneficiary. Unlike the income tax treatment, the casualty deduction is not limited by a percentage or dollar floor, and the deduction is based on the estate tax value. As is the case for income tax purposes, any loss must be reduced to the extent compensated for by insurance or otherwise. If alternate valuation is used and a casualty loss has been incurred, no deduction is allowed if the reduced value is reported as the estate value.

Allocation of Deductions on Returns

Administration expenses and casualty losses may be deducted either on Form 1041, the fiduciary income tax return of the estate or trust, *or* on Form 706, the estate tax return. The decision may be made on an item-by-item basis or an allocation may be made for individual items. Reg. §1.642(g)-2.

Theoretically, expenses should be shifted until the marginal estate tax rate equals that of the income tax. Due to the increased applicable credit amount and the unlimited marital deduction, the trend is toward using administration expenses and losses as income tax deductions, thus reducing "distributable net income" (DNI). Section 265, which bars income tax deductions for expenses incurred to purchase or carry tax-exempt municipal bonds, does not apply to the estate deduction.

The decision as to where to deduct will have ripple effects on the charitable and marital deductions, and on the trust income beneficiaries and remaindermen, and may affect the applicability of death tax redemptions, installment payments of estate tax, and special use valuation.

¶17,217   MARITAL DEDUCTION

The marital deduction is available in computing the taxable estate of a citizen or resident of the United States. It is allowed where any part of a deceased person's estate passes or has passed to the surviving spouse. The property so passing is deductible in computing the taxable estate to the extent that it is includible in the gross estate. Code Sec. 2056.

The marital deduction is not available for estates of nonresident noncitizens unless the individual was a resident of a country that had entered into a treaty with the United States permitting the deduction. However, although property passing to a surviving spouse who is not a U.S. citizen is generally ineligible for the estate tax marital deduction, the marital deduction will be allowed for estate and gift tax purposes with respect to a nonresident alien whose spouse is a U.S. citizen.

There is no monetary ceiling on the estate tax marital deduction. Thus, unlimited amounts of property, except for certain terminable interests (such as life estates, terms for years, annuities, etc.), can be transferred between spouses free of estate taxes.

Passing of Property to Surviving Spouse

The person receiving the decedent's property for which a marital deduction is claimed must qualify as a surviving spouse at the date of the decedent's death. A legal separation that has not terminated the marriage at the time of death does not change the status of the surviving spouse. If an interest in property passes from the decedent to a person who was a spouse but is not married to the decedent at the time of death, the interest is not considered as passing to the surviving spouse.

For purposes of the marital deduction, an interest in property is considered as *passing* from the decedent to a spouse only if the surviving spouse can receive or has received the property interest in the following circumstances:

1. Heir, devisee, or legatee
2. Surviving joint tenant
3. Beneficiary of life insurance
4. Certain gifts within three years of death
5. Widow's support allowance during probate
6. Election against the will (the statutory share in lieu of dower)
7. Beneficiary of a lapse, release, or exercise of a general power of appointment, etc. (Code Sec. 2056(c))

Disclaimers by other beneficiaries will often lead to additional amounts passing to the surviving spouse. Only the net value of the property after deducting any encumbrance thereon qualifies.

Terminable Interests

To qualify for the marital deduction, it is not sufficient that property passes to the surviving spouse. The interest must also be nonterminable. A "terminable" interest is one that meets three requirements:

1. It may lapse, expire, or terminate with the passage of time or upon the happening or nonhappening of a contingency. However, the bequest may be conditional on survival for up to six months.
2. An interest passes or has passed by gift to a third party.
3. Such third party may possess or enjoy any part of the property after the surviving spouse's interest terminates.

Property interests meeting these tests, and therefore failing to qualify for the marital deduction, include term interests, life estates, and certain annuities. The rules make it more likely that the property does not escape estate taxation in both estates. Code Sec. 2056(b)(1) and (3).

EXAMPLE 17.34	G dies, leaving his wife, W, the income from property for life, whereupon the property itself passes to the grandchildren. The life interest does *not* qualify for the marital deduction.

EXAMPLE 17.35	G leaves the property to his mother for life, then to W. The remainder does qualify for the deduction.

EXAMPLE 17.36	G leaves real estate to W and son as tenants in common. W's interest is deductible, since even if W dies before the son, her individual half passes from her by will or the laws of intestate succession.

EXAMPLE 17.37	G dies, leaving W a life interest in his stock portfolio, but it goes to his children should she remarry. If she does not remarry, she can will the stocks to anyone. No marital deduction is available, due to the condition.

EXAMPLE 17.38	G purchased a joint and survivorship annuity providing for monthly payments to G for life, and then to W should she survive. Upon G's death, the value of W's annuity is included in his estate and a marital deduction is allowed. Although W's interest expires upon her death, G left her all he had and no other person may possess or enjoy the property after W's death. Code Sec. 2056(b)(6).

Minimum Required Interest of Surviving Spouse

The spouse does not have to be given outright ownership of property to qualify for the marital deduction. A life interest plus a general power of appointment will suffice, or specifically:

1. The surviving spouse must be entitled to all income from the property for life to be paid at least annually.
2. The surviving spouse must have a general power of appointment over the whole property to be exercised alone and in all events. Such power can be exercisable either during life and/or by will. The holder of a general power is treated as the owner of the property so that the gift or estate tax cannot be avoided. Code Sec. 2056(b)(5).

The marital bequest is a function of taxes, propensity to consume, love and affection, degree of confidence in the spouse, their relative ages and health, their respective wealth, number of children, and so on.

Qualified Terminable Interest Property (QTIP)

An election exists to convert a terminable interest, a life estate, into nonterminable property eligible for the marital deduction for either gift or estate tax purposes. Code Secs. 2056(b)(7) and 2523(f). The election is made by the donor for lifetime transfers and by the executor for testamentary transfers. To qualify as "qualified terminable interest property," known in the trade as a QTIP trust, two main requirements must be met:

1. *All* income must be distributed at least annually to the donee spouse (the trust must be *simple*).
2. No one can have a power to appoint any portion of the principal or income to anyone other than the spouse during the spouse's lifetime.

The result of the election is that the marital deduction is allowed to the donor or the donor's estate for the full market value of the property in the trust, regardless of to whom the remainder goes (e.g., the children, charity, etc.). This benefit carries a price tag; the full value at the death of the spouse is included in the gross estate (or is subject to gift tax if any portion of the spouse's interest is disposed of earlier). Code Secs. 2044 and 2519.

EXAMPLE 17.39

When Frederick died, he left $1 million in trust to his wife, Cynthia, all income (except capital gains) to be distributed to her annually for her life, the remainder to the local state university. If his executor did not make the QTIP election, no marital deduction is allowed, but the trust is not subject to transfer taxes in Cynthia's estate. If the QTIP election is made:

1. Frederick's estate receives a $1 million marital deduction, but no charitable deduction.
2. If, on Cynthia's death, there is $2 million in the trust, the full value is includible in her estate, but an offsetting charitable deduction is available.

The QTIP election is perhaps most useful when a wealthy individual wishes to provide for a second spouse for life, but wishes to ensure that the children from the previous marriage will receive the principal. It should be noted that the spouse may be granted any number of powers over the principal. The income interest is merely a minimum. Also, a surviving spouse never has to accept an income interest, but may insist on a statutory share, typically one-third of the net probate estate.

For the estates of decedents dying after August 5, 1997, Code Sec. 2056(b)(7)(C) clarifies that a nonparticipant spouse's survivorship interest in a participant spouse's qualified plan, IRA, or SEP that is attributable to community property laws may qualify for qualified terminable interest property treatment if the nonparticipant spouse predeceases the participant spouse.

¶17,225 CHARITABLE CONTRIBUTIONS

The income tax aspects of charitable gifts are outside the scope of this discussion. In comparison, the estate tax rules are more liberal because:

1. The estate tax value of *all* charitable gifts included in the gross estate is deductible in full without percentage limitations.
2. Whether the testator wills property to a private foundation or a public charity, 100 percent of the value is deductible for estate tax purposes. (The income tax deduction is often limited to basis and to 30 or 50 percent of adjusted gross income.)
3. Charitable contributions made before death do double duty. They are deductible for income tax purposes. They are not includible in the gross estate.

The combined tax savings may approach 90 percent of the value gifted.

Charitable Remainder Trusts

A donor may wish to make a charitable contribution now, but:

1. The donor may be unwilling to give up current income and/or control.
2. The donor may want a spouse and/or children to enjoy the property after the donor's death.
3. The donor may wish to obtain a current income tax deduction as well as an estate tax deduction.

The solution is a gift of a *remainder* to charity. A life estate plus a remainder equals 100 percent of the property. Thus, a gift of a remainder constitutes a transfer of property subject to the retention of the life estate. In other words, there is a *present* gift, but of a *future* interest.

If the transfer is done right, the donor receives a current deduction for the value of the remainder. The deduction equals the value of the property, less the present value of the interest retained, based on mortality tables. Upon the donor's death, the full value is included because of the retained life estate, but the full value is then subtracted out as a charitable deduction.

The retained interest can take several forms: (1) term of years (e.g., 20 years, the maximum), (2) life estate for the life of the donor, (3) life estate for the joint lives of the donor and spouse, or (4) one or more life estates for the life or lives of any other person (e.g., the donor's parents or children).

There are three types of eligible charitable remainder trusts: (1) pooled income funds, (2) charitable remainder annuity trusts, and (3) charitable remainder unitrusts. Code Sec. 2055(e)(2)(A).

Pooled Income Funds

The principal difference between a pooled income fund and a charitable remainder unitrust or annuity trust is that the donor or other beneficiary of a pooled income fund is entitled only to the income actually earned by the fund, rather than to a fixed amount of fixed percentage of its value. Code Sec. 642(c)(5). Pooled income funds can be described as follows:

1. Many donors irrevocably transfer remainder interests for the use of charity, retaining a life interest for one or more beneficiaries.
2. The properties are "pooled" (i.e., commingled).
3. No tax-exempt bonds are allowed.
4. The fund is managed by the charitable organization itself, and no grantor or beneficiary can be a trustee.
5. The trust fund owns only properties transferred under (1).
6. Each beneficiary receives a share of the income earned by the trust.

For purposes of determining the amount of any charitable contribution allowable by reason of a transfer of property to a pooled fund, the value of the income interest is determined using the highest rate of return earned by the fund for any of the three taxable years immediately preceding the taxable year of the fund in which the transfer is made and the applicable mortality table (or six percent per year in the case of a fund in existence less than three taxable years).

Charitable Remainder Annuity Trusts (CRATs)

A charitable remainder annuity trust is a trust from which a specified sum or percentage (not less than five percent of the initial fair market value of all the assets actually placed in trust) is to be paid annually to one or more named individuals as income beneficiaries. For transfers in trust occurring after June 18, 1997, the annual payout cannot exceed 50 percent of the initial fair market value of the trust's assets. For transfers in trust occurring after July 28, 1997, the value of the remainder interest must be a least 10 percent of the initial fair market value of all property placed in the trust. (However, under a special rule, the minimum 10 percent rule will not apply to transfers in trust under the terms of a will or other testamentary instrument executed on or before July 28, 1997, if the decedent (1) dies before January 1, 2000, without having republished the will or amending it by codicil or otherwise or (2) was on July 28, 1997, under a mental disability to change the disposition of the property and did not regain competency before dying.) Each one of these beneficiaries must be living at the creation of the trust and payments to them must terminate not later than 20 years after creation or at their deaths. When payments terminate, the remainder goes to the charitable organization. Code Sec. 664.

EXAMPLE 17.40	Clive Barker died, leaving $100,000 in trust. If his surviving spouse, Anna, were to receive $6,000 a year for 15 years ($90,000), with the remainder to go to charity, this would be a charitable remainder annuity trust.

The beneficiary is taxed under the trust conduit rules (i.e., the beneficiary has ordinary income, capital gains, tax-free income, and return of capital) as the case may be. The trustee will furnish information on the tax status of the receipts.

Charitable Remainder Unitrusts (CRUTs)

A charitable remainder unitrust is similar to an annuity trust, except that, rather than receiving a fixed amount each year, the beneficiaries receive a fixed percentage, not less than five percent (for the beneficiaries as a group) of the net fair market value of the assets valued annually. Thus, the amount received will fluctuate from year to year.

In the case of charitable remainder unitrusts, the annual payout cannot exceed 50 percent of the fair market value of the trust assets determined annually. Also, the 10 percent rule applies with respect to each contribution of property to the trust (note that additional deductible gifts may be made to a charitable remainder unitrust under Reg. §1.664-3(b)).

EXAMPLE 17.41	Decedent left $100,000 in trust for his children for life, with the remainder going to charity. The remainder does *not* qualify for a charitable deduction unless the trust is a unitrust or an annuity trust.

| EXAMPLE 17.42 | Decedent left $100,000 in trust for his son for life with a minimum guarantee of five percent of the value of corpus per year, with the remainder going to charity. A deduction is available for the remainder since the trust is a charitable remainder unitrust. |

| EXAMPLE 17.43 | Same as Example 17.42, except that the son has the power to invade corpus for his "welfare." No deduction is allowed since the son may easily deplete the principal, cutting off the charitable interest. |

| EXAMPLE 17.44 | Same as Example 17.43, except that the son dies after three months. A deduction is permitted the grantor's estate because the charity receives the full $100,000. The son's estate includes the property since he had a general power of appointment, but an offsetting charitable deduction is allowed in his estate as well. Code Sec. 2055(a) and (b). |

According to the Senate Committee Report, trusts failing to meet the requirements of the 50 percent test will be treated as complex trusts rather than charitable remainder trusts, and, as a result, all of their income will be taxed to the beneficiaries of the trust. However, there are several special provisions designed to provide relief for trusts that fail to meet the 10 percent test.

| PLANNING POINTER | Here is a planning device for the dying and the aged: If a taxable estate is likely to exist and the individual's income tax bracket is high, prepay all charitable bequests mentioned in the will. The estate will not include them, and this has the same effect as a deduction, even if made on the deathbed. In addition, an income tax deduction (subject to some limitations) will result. If the income and estate tax brackets are 40 and 40 percent respectively, 80 percent of the value of the property can be saved in taxes.

In fact, if taxation is the only consideration, a lifetime charitable transfer is always preferable to a testamentary bequest. |

A charitable contributions deduction is allowed for the fair market value of a charitable remainder interest in an annuity trust *or* a unitrust. The fair market value of the remainder interest of a charitable remainder annuity trust is the net fair market value of the property placed in trust less the present value of the annuity as computed by using special IRS valuation tables prescribed under Code Sec. 7520. Two actuarial factors are generally used in determining present value—a mortality component and an interest rate component. The mortality component is based on the life expectancy of a designated individual (or individuals). The interest rate component represents an assumed rate of return. The interest rate component of the IRS valuation tables is based on a rate that is 120 percent of the applicable federal midterm rate (AFR) compounded annually (rounded to the nearest two-tenths of one percent), adjusted monthly. Valuation of any interest for term of years or life, any annuity, or any remainder or reversionary interest as of May 1, 1989, requires the use of these IRS tables. The AFR is announced by the IRS monthly in a news release and published in a revenue ruling.

¶17,230 STATE DEATH TAXES

For estates of decedents dying after 2004, a deduction is allowed for death taxes paid to any state or the District of Columbia, in respect of property included in the gross estate of the decedent. Code Sec. 2058, added by P.L. 107-16. For years prior to 2005, state death taxes were creditable against the federal state tax (subject to limitations). Code Sec. 2011.

¶17,255 DISCLAIMERS

No one has to accept an unwanted gift or bequest. A qualified disclaimer within nine months leads to the property being treated as if it were never transferred. Sometimes substantial savings can result from a disclaimer. Following are some examples:

1. If the surviving spouse is left property, he or she may wish to disclaim part of the property. This could save estate taxes in the estate and the disclaimed portion would pass directly to the other beneficiaries, typically children or grandchildren. The disclaimer should be made only if the surviving spouse would not consume the excess for living expenses in any event.

EXAMPLE 17.45   John Jamieson leaves his entire estate of $6.43 million to his spouse who has no assets. There is no estate tax because of the marital deduction. However, when his wife dies, the $6.43 million will be included in her estate and the excess above $5.43 million will be taxed. If the wife were to disclaim $1 million, there would still be no tax to John's estate and his wife would only include $5.43 million in her estate upon death. There will be no estate tax on her death, saving $400,000 in estate taxes.

2. A third party, such as a child, may wish to disclaim a bequest to favor the surviving parent so as to increase the marital deduction and save estate taxes immediately. The disclaimer may also be prompted by a concern for the parent's financial needs and the hope that the property will eventually pass to the child anyway, either through a systematic gift program or by will.
3. A beneficiary may be financially secure and disclaim to benefit the residuary legatee without any gift tax liability.
4. If someone is given a general power of appointment and does not intend to exercise it, it makes sense for the donee to disclaim it to avoid estate tax in the donee's own estate if the donee dies possessing the power.
5. Someone receiving an income interest may wish to disclaim it to favor a lower tax bracket family member.
6. If a disclaimed interest will go to charity and the charity is one of the beneficiary's favorites, the beneficiary may disclaim the interest and reduce estate taxes. But the estate tax savings must be compared with the income tax savings resulting from acceptance plus contribution.

To qualify:

1. The disclaimer must be made in writing.
2. The disclaimer must be made within nine months of the initial transfer, including the creation of a joint tenancy, or nine months after the beneficiary reaches age 21.
3. The disclaimer must be irrevocable and unqualified.
4. The disclaimant must not have accepted the bequest or any benefits from it initially.
5. The disclaimant cannot direct to whom the disclaimed property will pass. Code Secs. 2046 and 2518.

EXAMPLE 17.46   Many years before he died, William Stone purchased numerous securities and put them in a joint tenancy with his wife, Wilma. As soon as William died, Wilma disclaimed the one-half undivided interest in the securities (William's half) that she acquired upon William's death. Since the disclaimer was made more than nine months after the initial transfer (the creation of the joint tenancy), it is too late to be a "qualified" disclaimer. Thus, the property is still treated as if transferred to Wilma upon William's death. In addition, Wilma has made a gift for gift tax purposes to the new recipient if the disclaimer is effective to make a transfer to the residuary legatee or devisee.

TAX BLUNDER

Oscar purchased a $250,000 life insurance policy on his own life. To save estate taxes in his estate, he transferred all rights in the policy to Sylvia, his wife. Many years later, Sylvia predeceased him, leaving him "everything she owned." Since this included the policy, Oscar was back to square one. Older, but wiser, he transferred the policy to an irrevocable trust with his children and grandchildren as beneficiaries. However, Oscar died two years later and the full proceeds of $250,000 were added to his gross estate. Also, no marital deduction was available, leading to a sizable estate tax. The proceeds of the insurance were not available to pay the tax, being held in trust with income to the children and a remainder to the grandchildren.

The above problem could have been easily avoided by using an insurance trust initially, bypassing both Sylvia's and Oscar's estates.

Federal Gift Tax

¶17,301

DEFINITION OF TRANSFERS BY GIFT

A federal gift tax is imposed on the right to transfer property from one person to another for less than full and adequate consideration. The transferor is called the donor and the transferee the donee. Any gift tax due as a result of a taxable gift is a liability of the donor. Code Sec. 2502(c). In the event the donor fails to pay the tax when it is due, the donee can be held liable for the tax to the extent of the value of the property received. Code Sec. 6324(b). The gift tax is an excise tax on the transfer, and is not a tax on the subject of the gift. Transfers by gift are defined in Reg. §25.2511-1(a) as follows:

> The gift tax applies to a transfer by way of gift whether the transfer is in trust or otherwise, whether the gift is direct or indirect, and whether the property is real or personal, tangible or intangible. For example, a taxable transfer may be effected by the creation of a trust, the forgiving of a debt, the assignment of a judgment, the assignment of the benefits of an insurance policy, or the transfer of cash, certificates of deposit, or federal, state, or municipal bonds.

In accordance with the above definition, all transactions whereby property or property rights or interests are gratuitously passed or conferred upon another constitute a transfer subject to the gift tax, regardless of the method or device employed to effect the transfer. The gift tax is imposed on the transfer of property, not on the performance of services. Code Sec. 2501(a)(1). Accordingly, a person who renders services for another without being compensated has not made a gift subject to the gift tax.

Time of Gift

A gift is complete as to property in which the donor has ceased to have dominion and control and has no power to change disposition of the property for the donor's own benefit or for the benefit of another, as previously cited. Reg. §25.2511-2(b). The effective date occurs at the time the donor can no longer revoke the gift, or revert the beneficial title to the property to the donor, or change the interest of the designated beneficiaries. Rev. Rul. 67-396, 1967-2 CB 351. Several examples of completed transfers are listed below:

1. The donor completes a legal check or note which constitutes a promise to pay. The gift is not complete until a check or note is paid or negotiated for value to a third person. Rev. Rul. 67-396.
2. The donor delivers a stock certificate, properly endorsed, either to the donee or to the donee's agent; the gift is complete for federal gift tax purposes on the date of delivery. Reg. §25.2511-2(h). If, however, the donor delivers a stock certificate, properly endorsed, to either his broker or the issuing corporation with directions for transfer to a donee, the gift is not complete until the stock is transferred on the corporation's books. Rev. Rul. 54-135, 1954-1 CB 205.
3. The donor transfers property, in trust, to himself as trustee for the benefit of specific named beneficiaries. The donor has made a complete gift at the time of delivery if he has retained fiduciary powers only. Reg. §25.2511-2(g).
4. The donor delivers his interest in a U.S. Savings Bond (Series E) to the registered co-owner. The gift is not complete until the bond is reissued in the donee co-owner's name alone. *E.G. Chandler*, 73-1 USTC ¶12,902, 410 U.S. 257, 93 S.Ct. 880 (1973).

¶17,315

BASIS OF PROPERTY TRANSFERRED BY GIFT

Generally, the income tax basis of property transferred by a gift is the same as the basis in the hands of the transferor. In certain instances, however, the basis of property acquired by gift may depend on whether the donee sells the property for a gain or loss and when the gift was made.

1. If the gift was made prior to 1921, the donee's basis for gain or loss is the fair market value of the property on the date of the gift. Code Sec. 1015(c).
2. If the gift was made after 1920 and prior to 1977, the donee's basis for gain is the donor's adjusted basis plus any gift tax paid on the transfer (but not to exceed fair market value on date of the gift). The basis for loss is the lower of the basis for gain or the fair market value of the property on the date of the gift. Code Sec. 1015(a) and (d)(1).

3. If the gift was made after 1976, the donee's basis for gain is the donor's adjusted basis plus only the gift tax attributable to the appreciation of the property to the point of the gift (but not to exceed the fair market value of the property on the date of the gift). Under Code Sec. 2503(b), to determine the amount of gift tax on the appreciation to be added to the donor's basis, the fair market value of the gift is reduced by the donor's basis and divided by the fair market value of the gift reduced by the annual exclusion. The basis for loss is the lower of the basis for gain or the fair market value of the property on the date of the gift. Code Sec. 1015(a) and (d)(6).

How to Apply the Basis Rules

The above rules are illustrated in the following examples:

EXAMPLE 17.47	In 1920, A transferred realty by a gift to create an irrevocable inter vivos trust. The property cost A $10,000 and was worth $25,000 on the date of the gift. The income tax basis to the trust for gain or loss is $25,000.

EXAMPLE 17.48	In 1975, B transferred realty by a gift to create an irrevocable inter vivos trust. The stock cost B $15,000 and had a fair market value of $60,000 on the date of the gift. B paid a gift tax of $8,000 on the transfer. As a result the trust's basis for gain or loss is $23,000 ($15,000 (B's basis) + $8,000 (gift tax paid by B)). The trust does not have a different basis for loss since the fair market value of the property on the date of the gift (i.e., $60,000) is not lower than the basis for gain (i.e., $23,000).

EXAMPLE 17.49	Assume the same facts as in Example 17.48, except that the gift occurred in 2015 (instead of 1975). The trust's income tax basis for gain is $22,826, determined as follows:

B's adjusted basis on the date of the gift	$15,000
Gift tax attributable to the $45,000 appreciation (($45,000/$46,000) × $8,000)	7,826
Trust's income tax basis for gain	$22,826

The trust's basis for loss would be $22,826, based on the same reasoning set forth in Example 17.46.

The effect of the rule provided in the Tax Reform Act of 1976 (as illustrated in Example 17.47) is to deny the donee (the trust) any increase in basis for gift tax attributable to the donor's adjusted basis. Incidentally, unless property with a fair market value of less than the donor's basis is expected to appreciate above the donor's basis prior to sale by the donee (the trust), it should not be used as gift property. In this case, to maximize the tax benefits, the donor should sell the property, recognize the tax loss, and transfer the proceeds by gift to the trust.

¶17,325   PRESENT v. FUTURE INTERESTS

An unrestricted right to the immediate use, possession, or enjoyment of property or the related income from the property (such as a life estate or term certain) is a present interest in the property. Reg. §25.2503-3(b). A future interest may be defined as one which will come into being (i.e., the use, possession, or enjoyment) at some future date. As defined in the Regulations:

Future interests is a legal term, and includes reversions, remainder, and other interests or estates, whether vested or contingent, and whether or not supported by a particular interest or estate, which are limited to commence in use, possession, or enjoyment at some future date or time. The term has no reference to such contractual rights as exist in a bond, note, (though bearing no interest until maturity), or in a policy of life insurance, the obligations of which are to be discharged by payments in the future. But a future interest or interests in such contractual obligations may be created by the limitations contained in a trust to other instrument to transfer used in effecting a gift. Reg. §25.2503-3(a).

Consider carefully the following illustrations of present versus future interests.

EXAMPLE 17.50	During the year, Ed O'Brien makes an outright cash gift of $10,000 to Dana Flanigan. This gift qualifies as a present interest.

EXAMPLE 17.51	During the year, Ed transfers property in a trust with a life estate to Dana with income to be paid annually. The trust provides that upon Dana's death the remainder interest goes to Sara Flanigan. Ed has made two gifts: one to Dana of a life estate and one to Sara of a remainder interest. The life estate is a present interest, and the remainder is a future interest.

EXAMPLE 17.52	Assume the same facts as in Example 17.51 except that the income from the trust does not have to be paid annually to Dana. At the trustee's discretion the income may be accumulated and added to the corpus. In this case the life estate does not qualify as a present interest. The mere possibility of the trustee accumulating the income renders the life estate a future interest. Reg. §25.2503-3(c).

Concerning Example 17.51, if the life estate beneficiary's right to current income is contingent on obtaining the permission of a third party other than the trustee (including other beneficiaries), the life estate interest is deemed to be a future interest. *J. W. Blasdel,* 58 TC 1014, Dec. 31,548 (1972), aff'd, 73-1 USTC ¶12,929, 478 F.2d 226 (CA-5 1973).

Notable Exceptions

There are some exceptions to the present versus future interest rules as set forth in this section. For example, the gift of a note, or bond, that yields no interest until maturity is a gift of a present interest, although the maturity and benefits are in the future. The same would be true for the gift of a life insurance policy or other similar contract right. T.D. 7238, 1973-1 CB 544. A major exception to the general rule relates to gifts to minors utilizing various vehicles so that the gifts will be deemed to be present interests. Excellent examples are *Crummey* trusts and gifts to minors, each of which is discussed below.

Crummey Trusts

A gift of the right to demand a portion of a trust corpus is a gift of a present interest, Rev. Rul. 80-261, 1980-2 CB 219, as long as the donee-beneficiary is aware of his or her right to make the demand. Rev. Rul. 81-7, 1981-1 CB 474. Typically, the beneficiary of such a trust (known as a *Crummey* trust, *D.C. Crummey* 68-2 USTC ¶12,541, 397 F.2d 82 (CA-9 1968)) is given the right to demand an amount of corpus equal to the annual gift tax exclusion. Because donors might not want the beneficiaries to be able to withdraw trust corpus up to the $10,000, $11,000, $12,000, $13,000, and $14,000 annual exclusions available after 1981, the Economic Recovery Tax Act of 1981 provided a special transitional rule to limit the power to the old $3,000 exclusion in certain instances.

Gifts to Minors

No part of a transfer for the benefit of a minor will be considered future interest (which would not qualify for the annual exclusion) if the terms of the transfer meet the following conditions:

1. Both the property and its income may be expended by, or for the benefit of, the minor donee prior to the donee attaining the age of 21. To the extent not so expended, it will pass to the donee at that time.
2. In the event of the donee's death prior to reaching 21 years of age, the property and the income not expended will pass to the donee's estate or to persons appointed by the donee under the exercise of a general power of appointment.

A gift to a minor under a trust that confers on its beneficiary upon reaching age 21 the right to compel immediate distribution of the corpus by written notice to the trustee that is either (a) a continuing right or permits the trust to remain on its own terms or (b) a right for a limited period that, if not exercised, will permit the trust to continue on its own terms is not a gift of a future interest and qualifies for the annual gift tax exclusion under condition (1), above. Rev. Rul. 74-43, 1974-1 CB 285.

Contributions to Qualified State Tuition Programs

Any contribution to a qualified tuition program (QTP) is handled as a completed gift of a present interest from the donor to the donee at the time of the contribution. As a result, the $14,000 annual exclusion ($10,000 indexed) or $28,000 for split giving would apply to contributions to qualified state tuition programs. A donor that makes a contribution in excess of the annual exclusion may treat the gift as if it were made ratably over five years. Code Sec. 529(c)(2)(B). However, a gift tax return is required for a contribution exceeding the annual gift exclusion.

Exclusions

¶17,341   GENERAL CONSIDERATIONS

Annual Exclusion

For 2015, the first $14,000 given to any person during a calendar year is excluded in computing taxable gifts, if the gift constitutes a "present interest" in the gifted property. The exclusion for gifts is indexed annually for inflation.

A distinction must be made between a present and future interest to assure the availability of the annual donee exclusion. The ostensible reason for denying the annual exclusion for gifts of future interests was the difficulty associated with the determining the number of eventual donees and the value of their respective gifts. H.R. Rep. No. 708, 72d Cong., 1st Sess. 29 (1932), reprinted in 1939-1 CB (Part 2) 457, 478; S. Rep. No. 665, 72d Cong., 1st Sess. 41 (1932), reprinted in 1939-1 CB (Part 2) 496, 526.

Unlimited Donee Opportunities

There is no limit on the number of donees. The donor can claim a $14,000 annual exclusion for each present interest. Only the first $14,000 ($28,000 if splitting is elected as discussed in the next section of this chapter) given to each donee may be excluded. If the donor's gifts of present interests to each donee during a calendar year do not exceed $14,000, the gifts do not have to be reported on a gift tax return. Code Sec. 6019(a). Gifts exempted from taxation under the $14,000 annual donee exclusion are not included in the tax base for the purposes of computing estate taxes. Only adjusted taxable gifts are includible in the computation, and adjusted taxable gifts are limited to taxable gifts.

Gift-Splitting

A donor's spouse may consent to treatment as the donor of one-half of any taxable gift made to a third person. Such a consent to "gift-split" allows a married couple to use two annual per-donee exclusions and two unified credits with respect to a single gift.

EXAMPLE 17.53

> In 2015, John Smith gives $5,444,000 in cash to his daughter. He gets one $14,000 annual exclusion, and so he makes a $5.43 million taxable gift. He uses up his previously unused applicable credit amount and owes no gift tax. However, if Sara Smith (John's wife) consents to gift-split, John and Sara will get two $14,000 annual exclusions, or $28,000, and can use two applicable credit amounts.

A donor can gift-split only if he or she is a United States person (a citizen or a resident alien) and is married to a United States person at the time the gift is made. Individuals are married for gift-splitting purposes, only if they are married at the time the gift is made.

EXAMPLE 17.54

> H makes a taxable gift to his son, S, on January 1, 2015. On February 17, 2015, his divorce from W is final. H and W may gift-split as long as neither remarry during the calendar year. Code Sec. 2513(a)(1).

Both the donor and the donor's spouse must consent to gift-split. The consent applies to all gifts either spouse makes during the calendar year in which they make the consent. Code Sec. 2513(a)(2). The consent does not apply, however, to any taxable gifts made by either spouse when they were not married to each other or when they were not both U.S. citizens or resident aliens. Reg. §25.2513-1(b).

The consent to split gifts applies to all gifts made during the calendar year by either spouse individually and by both spouses jointly. For example, Henry and Velma Holt consent to gift-split on a gift Velma made in January 2015. This consent also applies to any gifts Henry or Velma made during 2015 alone or jointly. Reg. §25.2513-1(b)(5).

In summary, gift-splitting has the following advantages:

1. Two annual exclusions are available instead of one.
2. Any gap between the sizes of the spouses' estates can be narrowed because only one-half of the gifts will come back as "adjusted taxable gifts" in the estate tax return of the contributing spouse.
3. The noncontributing spouse may be in a lower gift tax bracket or have an unused applicable credit amount. Because two sets of applicable credit amounts are available, no gift tax may be presently payable.

Unlimited Educational and Medical Expense Exclusion

An unlimited gift tax exclusion is available for amounts paid on behalf of a donee directly to an educational organization, provided that such amounts constitute tuition payments. In addition, amounts paid to health care providers for medical services on behalf of a donee qualify for an unlimited exclusion under this section. The exclusions for qualifying educational expenses and medical expenses are available without regard to the relationship between the donor and the donee and are available in addition to the annual exclusion Code Sec. 2503(e).

Qualifying medical expenses, for the purposes of this exclusion, are defined by reference to Code Sec. 213 (an income tax provision). The exclusion is not available to the extent the amounts paid are reimbursed by insurance.

¶17,345   MARITAL DEDUCTION

Beginning in 1982, a donor is allowed an unlimited marital deduction for lifetime gifts of separate and/or community property to his or her spouse. Code Sec. 2523(a). But the gift tax marital deduction is not permitted for a gift of a life estate or other terminable interest. An exception to the terminable interest rule for the gift tax marital deduction is qualified terminable interest property (QTIP). Code Sec. 2523(c).

QTIP Provisions

As previously mentioned, the QTIP provisions are an exception to the terminable interest rule. Pursuant to Code Sec. 2523(e), a property interest, whether or not in trust, qualifies for the marital deduction when the following requirements are adhered to:

1. The donee spouse is entitled for life to all of the income from the property interest.
2. Such income is payable annually or at more frequent intervals.
3. The donee spouse has the power, exercisable in favor of the donee or the donee's estate, to appoint the property interest.
4. Such power is exercisable by the donee spouse alone and (whether exercisable by will or during life) is exercisable in all events.
5. No part of the property interest is subject to a power in any other person to appoint any part to any person other than the surviving spouse.

Also, to have a qualifying terminable interest under Code Sec. 2523(e), the donee spouse must be entitled to receive all the income from the property at least annually. Furthermore, no person may be able to appoint the property during the spouse's lifetime to anyone other than the spouse. When the QTIP election is made by the donor, there will not be any gift tax at that juncture. However, when the donee spouse disposes of his or her QTIP interest, either during his or her lifetime or at death, the property will be subject to gift or estate tax.

EXAMPLE 17.55

> In 2015, Tony Owens creates a trust which is funded with $500,000 of Georgia Power bonds. Pursuant to the trust instrument, Donna Owens is to receive the income from the trust on an annual basis for her life. Upon Donna's death, the principal of the trust is to pass to their children. If Tony elects QTIP treatment, the interest passing to Donna will qualify for the marital deduction. The election is made on the gift tax return (Form 709, United States Gift (and Generation-Skipping Transfer) Tax Return) filed for the calendar year in which the donor transferred the interest. It should be noted that the fair market value of the QTIP property will be included in the gross estate of Donna when she dies.

Alien Spouses

An alien spouse of a U.S. citizen is generally not eligible for the unlimited gift tax marital deduction. However, the first $147,000 (for 2015) of gifts per year to an alien spouse will not be taxed. Code Sec. 2523(i). Also, it should be emphasized that the $147,000 annual exclusion for transfers by gift to a non-citizen spouse is only allowed for transfers that would meet the marital deduction test if the donee were a U.S. citizen. Therefore, a gift in trust would have to meet the exceptions to the terminable interest rule in order to qualify for the annual exclusion.

Divorce and Separation

Transfers to a spouse pursuant to a written agreement in connection with divorce are free of gift tax if the transfers are for the transferee's marital or property rights or for child support. Code Sec. 2516. This provision goes beyond the marital deduction since it covers terminable transfers and transfers after the parties are no longer married.

This special provision has no application to prenuptial agreements. When the parties transfer property pursuant to an agreement signed prior to marriage, the marital deduction is available under the general rule. Generally, divorce settlements are not treated as sales for income tax purposes, but are tax free. Code Sec. 1041.

¶17,355   CHARITABLE DEDUCTION

In the case of a donor who was a resident or a citizen of the United States at the time the gifts were made, there is an allowable charitable deduction for gifts included in the "total amount of gifts" made by the donor during the calendar year to or for the use of:

1. The United States, any State, Territory, or any political subdivision thereof, or the District of Columbia, for exclusively public purposes.
2. Any corporation, trust, community chest, fund or foundation organized and operated exclusively for religious, charitable, scientific, literary, or educational purposes, including the encouragement of art and the prevention of cruelty to children and animals, if no part of the net earnings of the organization inures to the benefit of any private shareholder or individual, if no substantial part of its activities is engaging in propaganda, or otherwise attempting to influence legislation, and if it does not participate in, or intervene in (including the publishing or distributing of statements), any political campaign on behalf of any candidate for public office.
3. A fraternal society, order, or association, operating under the lodge system, provided the gifts are to be used by the society, order, or association exclusively for one or more of the purposes set forth in subparagraph (2) of this paragraph.
4. Any post or organization of war veterans or auxiliary unit or society thereof, if organized in the United States or any of its possessions, and if no part of its net earnings inures to the benefit of any private shareholder or individual. Reg. §25.2522(a)-1(a).

The charitable deduction is not limited to gifts for use within the United States, or to gifts to or for the use of domestic corporations, trusts, community chests, funds, or foundations, or fraternal societies, orders, or associations operating under the lodge system.

Nonresident aliens are allowed a charitable deduction for gifts that relate primarily to domestic charities and for gifts to be used in the United States. Code Sec. 2522(b).

A donor who makes a gift to charity in excess of the annual gift tax exclusion is not required to file a gift tax return if the entire value of the donated property qualifies for a gift tax charitable deduction. This treatment extends to contributions of qualified conservation easements under Code Sec. 2522(d). The amount of the charitable deduction will first be reduced by the annual exclusion (if the interest is a present interest) and the remainder will be deducted as a charitable deduction. Also, charitable deductions are allowed for split interests when they qualify as annuity trusts, unitrusts, or pooled income funds.

EXAMPLE 17.56	On March 4, 2015, John Agor transferred Home Depot stock with a basis of $10,000 and market value of $30,000 to Louisiana Tech University. John had held the stock for two years at the time of the transfer. The full $30,000 is allowed to be taken on the gift tax return, but for income tax purposes, the deduction is limited to 30 percent of AGI subject to a five-year carryover. There is no taxable gift, computed as follows:

Gross gift		$30,000
Less: Annual exclusion	$14,000	
Charitable deduction	16,000	30,000
Taxable gift		$0

¶17,365 VALUATION OF GIFTS

Valuing gross gifts is the major gift tax problem since the value determines the amount that will be subject to gift tax. The gift tax regulations differ in no substantial respect from the corresponding estate tax regulations. All property is valued at fair market value at the time the gift is considered completed. Fair market value of property is the price at which such property would change hands between a willing buyer and a willing seller, neither being under any compulsion to buy or to sell, and both having reasonable knowledge of relevant facts.

Most of the concepts discussed earlier in this chapter concerning estate tax are also applicable to gift taxes. However, there is no alternative valuation date for gift tax as there is for estate taxes. Also, the special valuation methods are only available to estates.

¶17,375 NONTAXABLE TRANSFERS

Gratuitous transfers *not* subject to gift tax include:

1. Transfers to political organizations (Code Sec. 2501(a)(5)), but any appreciation is gross income to the donor (Code Sec. 84).
2. Transfers made for a business purpose (e.g., contributions to the capital of a corporation or partnership).
3. Revocable transfers, including the creation of revocable trusts, joint bank and brokerage accounts, and joint U.S. savings bonds.
4. Bargain purchases, if in arm's-length transactions.
5. Donation of services.
6. Support payments within the standard of living of the family. (Note: the support obligation to a child generally ceases on age 18 or earlier emancipation.)
7. Qualified disclaimers (in writing, within nine months). Code Sec. 2518.
8. Employment-related "gifts," such as a year-end bonus, but these are gross income items.

EXAMPLE 17.57	Two months before his death, Marvin Rose donated $5 million to a political campaign for mayor, an office sought by his best friend as candidate. The donation is not a gift for gift tax purposes. Furthermore, since there is no gift, there can be no adjusted taxable gift. Thus, the $5 million permanently escapes both gift and estate taxes. (However, no charitable deduction is allowed.)

¶17,385 CO-OWNERSHIPS OF PROPERTY

As a general rule, if property is purchased by co-tenants, any disproportional contribution results in a gift from the high to the low contributor.

EXAMPLE 17.58	Mother and daughter purchase a building as equal joint tenants for $200,000. If the daughter pays only $40,000, $60,000 is received by gift since this is her "discount" on her half. If the building is financed so that only $40,000 is put down, $8,000 by the daughter, only $12,000 is a gift. As the mother pays off the mortgage, additional gifts are made to the extent of principal payments, but they would not exceed the annual exclusion.

Revocable joint tenancies do not result in a gift until one joint tenant withdraws in excess of the contribution. Examples include joint bank accounts and U.S. savings bonds.

¶17,395   POWERS OF APPOINTMENT

General powers of appointment were discussed earlier in this chapter. If someone possesses a general power of appointment and the power is exercised, released, or simply lapses during the holder's lifetime, there is a gift. Code Sec. 2514. Special powers are not taxable.

EXAMPLE 17.59	G transfers property in trust to his wife, W, for life. W is also given the power to appoint the property to anyone in the world by gift or will. If W exercises the power in favor of anyone except herself, even an unrelated party, a taxable gift results.
EXAMPLE 17.60	Same as Example 17.59, except W has the power to appoint the property to anyone *except* herself, her estate, or the creditors of either. She exercises the power in favor of her children and grandchildren. There is no gift.
EXAMPLE 17.61	Same facts as Example 17.59, except that W needs G's consent to exercise the power. No gift tax will result because the power is reduced to a special power when the creator's consent is needed.
EXAMPLE 17.62	Same facts as Example 17.59, except that W needs G's consent to exercise the power. No gift tax will result be G transfers property to W for life, the remainder to his children. W can appoint the property to anyone, but only with the consent of the children. An exercise of power is not taxable because the consent of an adverse party is required. ause the power is reduced to a special power when the creator's consent is needed.
EXAMPLE 17.63	G transfers an insurance policy on his life to W. If their child is the beneficiary, W has completed a gift of the proceeds to such child when G dies. At that time, W's powers over the policy lapses.

Powers limited to an ascertainable standard (e.g., for the health, education, maintenance, and support of the powerholder) and powers to appoint up to $5,000 or five percent of the property (whichever is greater) each year are only special powers. Code Sec. 2514(c)(1) and (3).

¶17,405   LIABILITY FOR TAX

The gift tax is levied on the gratuitous transfer of property during life. It may not be intuitively obvious, but an individual who gives away property may have to pay an excise tax for the privilege. Thus, the gift tax is payable by *the donor* as a toll charge for the fact that the property transferred will not be subject to estate taxes (in most cases). Small gifts are disregarded and marital and charitable deductions are available. If the gift tax remains unpaid, the donee is liable to the extent of the value of the gifted property. Code Sec. 6324(b). U.S. residents and citizens are liable for gift taxes on worldwide transfers, while nonresident aliens are liable only for taxes on transfers of U.S. property, such as U.S. real estate. Code Secs. 2501(a)(1) and 2511(a).

Only individuals are subject to gift tax. The identity of the transferee is irrelevant; it could be an individual, estate, trust, or corporation, U.S. or foreign.

EXAMPLE 17.64

Richard O'Hara, U.S. citizen, sends $50,000 to the Irish government. Even though the donee is a foreign government the transfer reduces Richard's estate and is subject to gift tax, he being a U.S. citizen or resident. (No charitable contribution deduction is available for donations to foreign entities, either.)

The donor may gift the property subject to the condition that the donee pays the gift tax ("a net gift"). This has several consequences:

1. Since the donee assumes the donor's liability, the transaction becomes a part-sale part-gift, so that if the tax is in excess of the donor's basis, the donor must recognize gain.
2. The gift is reduced so that the gift tax is payable on the value of the property less the gift tax, requiring computations.
3. The donor is still primarily liable to the IRS for the tax; the donee simply owes the donor the amount of the tax.

EXAMPLE 17.65

Gustav Mueller gives away securities to his daughter, Agnes, worth $148,000, on the condition that she pays the gift tax. If the $14,000 exclusion is applicable and Gustav is in the 40 percent gift tax bracket, the gift tax is not $53,600, as it would have been if Gustav paid the gift tax. The gift tax would be $32,160 since the taxable gift of $134,000 is reduced by the donee's obligation to pay $53,600 in gift tax. Since the actual gift is only $80,400 ($148,000 – $14,000-$53,600), the gift tax is 40 percent of that, or $32,160.

Tax Return

The gift tax return, Form 709, is an annual return due April 15 under the following three circumstances. (Note: After August 5, 1997, a donor who makes a gift in excess of the annual gift tax exclusion is not required to file a gift tax return if the entire value of the donated property qualifies for a gift tax charitable deduction. Also, after 1998, the annual exclusion for gifts is indexed annually for inflation.)

1. Donor made at least one gift of a present interest in excess of $14,000 to one or more donees.
2. Donor made any gift at all of a future interest (i.e., a remainder).
3. Donor and spouse wish to elect gift-splitting, thus doubling available exclusions and credits. Code Secs. 6019(a) and 6075(b).

Gross gifts, less exclusions and deductions, are "adjusted taxable gifts." Because of the applicable credit amount ($2,117,800 in 2015), no gift tax may be due with the return. However, the *return* is still due and adjusted taxable gifts are brought back into the gross estate with a credit for gift taxes paid, if any. Note that the applicable credit amount is never "used up" for estate tax purposes and has but *one* effect during life: to defer the transfer tax until after the donor's death. (Some *states* also levy gift taxes.)

¶17,415   GIFT TAX COMPUTATION—SUMMARY

The gift tax complements the estate tax by taxing transfers depleting the estate.

Step 1.	Return required by April 15 following the calendar year in which taxable gifts were made.
Step 2.	List all gifts made during the calendar year, except gifts of nonterminable interests to spouse.
Step 3.	Husband and wife may elect to treat all gifts to third parties as made one-half by each (i.e., gift-splitting).
Step 4.	Exclude for each donee the lesser of $14,000 or amount of gifts of present interests.
Step 5.	Deduct gifts to charities in excess of exclusion.
Step 6.	Result is taxable gifts for period (A).
Step 7.	Add (A) to total lifetime prior taxable gifts (B) to get new lifetime total (C).
Step 8.	Compute from the tables the tentative tax on (C).
Step 9.	Compute from the tables the tentative tax on (B).
Step 10.	Difference is tax imposed on gifts for period.
Step 11.	Reduce tax by applicable credit amount of $2,117,800 (for 2015) or by the amount of credit previously allowable and 20 percent of the amount of the specific exemption claimed for gifts made after September 8, 1976, and before January 1, 1977 (prior law).

Generation-Skipping Transfer (GST) Tax

¶17,501   ## NATURE AND PURPOSE OF TAX

In 1976, Congress passed the original "generation-skipping transfer tax." The purpose was to supplement the federal gift and estate tax system to assure that the transfer of wealth from one generation to the next would bear substantially the same transfer tax burden, whether the transfer was outright to each succeeding generation or in trust, where it would skip a generation for federal estate tax purposes.

Prior to the 1976 legislation, a common planning device was the generation-skipping trust, which would pay income to one's child for the child's life and then distribute the trust property to his or her grandchildren at the child's death. If properly structured, there would be no federal estate tax payable at the child's death, even though the child had received the economic benefits of the trust for life. The 1976 legislation changed this and imposed a generation-skipping transfer tax on the trust at the child's death in an amount similar to what the federal estate tax would have been if the child had owned the trust property outright.

The present law, created by the Tax Reform Act of 1986, is based to a large extent on the prior law, but is described by the House Ways and Means Committee as a "simplified tax." In reality, the 1986 Act was a disappointment to those who had hoped for simplification, and the current generation-skipping rules certainly remain very complex. Although the 1986 law created an entire class of potentially taxable transfers, many additional planning opportunities are still available.

Under the 2001 Act, the generation-skipping tax was repealed for 2010. Beginning in 2011, the generation-skipping transfer exemption will equal the applicable exclusion amount. Refer to Table 1 for amounts. Code Sec. 2631(c).

¶17,515   ## OVERVIEW

The current generation-skipping transfer rules became effective under Sec. 1433(a) of the 1986 Act on October 22, 1986. The provisions also apply to all existing revocable trusts, current wills (assuming the person did not die before December 31, 1986) and inter vivos transfers made after September 25, 1985. However, a trust that was irrevocable on September 25, 1985, is exempt under Act Sec. 1433(b)(2)(A), except for transfers to the trust after that date.

The generation-skipping transfer tax is imposed on property transferred to what Code Sec. 2613(a) defines as a "skip person." A skip person is an individual or entity that is assigned to a generation that is two or more generations below that of the transferor. For example, one's grandchild would be considered a skip person. So would a partnership or corporation in which a grandchild had an interest (entity generation assignments are made based on the relationship of the person having a beneficial interest in the entity to the transferor).

Generation assignment is based on the lineal relationship of family members. A spouse is assigned to the transferor's generation, regardless of age. Code Sec. 2651(c)(1). For nonlineal descendants, generation assignment is determined by the ages of the individuals involved in relation to the age of the transferor.

A person born 12½ years or less after the transfer is assigned to the same generation as the transferor. There is a new generation for each additional 25 years thereafter from the transferor's birthdate. Code Sec. 2651(d). Thus, a person who is more than 37½ years younger than the transferor will be treated as a grandchild.

¶17,525   ## TAXABLE EVENTS

Under the law, three events will give rise to a generation-skipping transfer tax: a taxable termination, a taxable distribution, and a direct skip.

Taxable Termination

A taxable termination is defined as the termination of a nonskip person's interest in property held in trust, after which only a skip person has an interest in the trust property. Code Sec. 2612(a)(1). In general, a person has an interest in the trust if he or she obtains a *present* right to receive principal or income from the trust. Code Sec. 2652(c)(1).

| **EXAMPLE 17.66** | A father creates a trust for the benefit of his son, with the remainder passing to his grandson. Upon the death of the son, a taxable termination occurs. Had the trust been for the benefit of his wife, with the remainder going to the son, the death of the wife would not have resulted in a taxable transfer because a nonskip person maintained the interest in the trust. |

There are certain exclusions that keep a termination from being labeled a "*taxable* termination." A transfer to a person one generation below the transferor that is subject to federal estate or gift taxation is not a taxable termination, nor is a termination that is a transfer which qualifies for the Code Sec. 2503(e) medical or tuition exclusion. Code Sec. 2611(b)(1) and (2).

Taxable Distribution

A taxable distribution is a distribution from a trust to a skip person. Code Sec. 2612(b). The 1986 Tax Act repealed the exemption for income distributions so that now both corpus and income payments may fall into the category of a taxable distribution. The addition of this provision is one of the more significant changes made by the law and has profound ramifications for discretionary trusts.

| **EXAMPLE 17.67** | A trust is established which provides for the discretionary payment of income and corpus to the transferor's child and grandchild. In the first year, each beneficiary receives $25,000 of the trust's income. The income payment to the grandchild is a taxable distribution. |

The burden of this taxable distribution is eased somewhat by an income tax deduction allowed under Code Sec. 164(a)(5) to the distributee for any generation-skipping transfer tax paid on income distributions.

Direct Skip

The potential taxation of a direct skip is arguably the most important change made by the 1986 tax law in the generation-skipping area. Under prior law, transfers to a skip person (e.g., a grandchild) that circumvented the use of a trust were not taxable transfers. However, the current law dictates that a transfer of an interest in property to a skip person qualifies as a generation-skipping transfer if it is subject to federal estate or gift tax. Code Sec. 2612(c)(1).

| **EXAMPLE 17.68** | A wealthy grandparent transfers $1 million directly to his granddaughter. This transaction is a generation-skipping transfer. |

Special rules are applicable when the transfer is to a grandchild whose parent is deceased. The child of a predeceased child is not considered a skip person to which generation-skipping transfer would apply because this grandchild of the transferor is treated as if he were the transferor's child. Code Sec. 2612(c)(2). For terminations, distributions, and transfers occurring after December 31, 1997, the predeceased parent exception to the generation-skipping transfer tax is expanded to include collateral heirs, provided that the transferor had no living lineal descendants at the time of the transfer. (The exception is also expanded to taxable terminations and distributions.)

| **EXAMPLE 17.69** | A grandparent transfers $100,000 to his grandchild, whose father (the son of the grandparent) had passed away one year earlier. The grandchild is deemed to be in the child's generation, and thus is treated as a nonskip person. Accordingly, the transfer is not a direct skip. |

¶17,535   EXEMPTIONS FROM TAX

For purposes of determining the taxable amount of a generation-skipping transfer, the following exemptions from the tax are provided:

General Exemption

An exemption of $5,430,000 for 2015 is provided for each person making generation-skipping transfers ($10.86 million if gift-splitting is elected by the transferor's spouse). Code Sec. 2631. The exemption can be allocated by a transferor to property transferred at any time, but once it is made, it is irrevocable. Code Sec. 2631.

Annual Gift Tax Exclusion

The annual $14,000 gift tax exclusion per donee for gifts of present interests is also available when computing the generation-skipping transfer tax on such gifts.

Unused Exemption

Any unused generation-skipping transfer tax exemption is first allocated to inter vivos direct skips, then to testamentary direct skips, and finally to generation-skipping trusts from which taxable transfers may be made after death. Code Sec. 2632.

Incompetency Exemption

The generation-skipping transfer tax applies to transfers under a trust to the extent that the trust consists of property included in the gross estate of an incompetent decedent or to transfers that are direct skips that occur by reason of the death of the incompetent decedent after August 3, 1990. Under prior law there was an exclusion for incompetent decedents' property.

¶17,545   RATE OF TAX

All generation-skipping transfers are subject to tax at a flat rate equal to the product of the maximum estate and gift tax rate (i.e., 40 percent) and the "inclusion ratio" with respect to the transfer.

Inclusion Ratio

The inclusion ratio is the excess (if any) of one over the "applicable fraction" determined for the trust from which such a transfer is made or, in the case of a direct skip, the applicable fraction determined for such a skip. Stated differently, 1 − (applicable fraction) = inclusion ratio.

Applicable Fraction

The applicable fraction is determined as follows: the numerator is the amount of the GST exemption allocated to the trust or property transferred in the direct skip. Its denominator is the value of the property transferred to the trust (or involved in the direct skip) reduced by the sum of any federal or state death tax attributable to the property that was recovered from the trust and any charitable deduction allowed under Code Sec. 2055 or 2522.

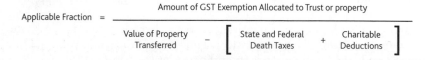

$$\text{Applicable Fraction} = \frac{\text{Amount of GST Exemption Allocated to Trust or property}}{\text{Value of Property Transferred} - \left[\text{State and Federal Death Taxes} + \text{Charitable Deductions}\right]}$$

The effect of using the inclusion ratio is to exempt the appreciation allocable to the GST exemption from the GST tax when ultimately imposed. Code Secs. 2641 and 2642.

EXAMPLE 17.70	Grandpa transfers $4 million in trust for his daughter for life, remainder to Grandson, and allocates $1 million of his $5.43 million exemption to the transfer. At the time the daughter dies, the trust fund is worth $8 million. Assuming there are no estate/death taxes and charitable deductions, the calculation of the generation-skipping transfer tax would be as follows: 1. Determination of the applicable fraction: ($1 million exemption divided by $4 million in property equals an applicable fraction of .25). 2. Determination of the inclusion ratio: Subtract the applicable fraction from 1. Thus, the inclusion ratio is 1 minus .25, or .75. The generation-skipping tax rate is the product of the inclusion ratio—in this case .75—and the maximum federal estate tax rate at the time of the transfer (i.e., 40 percent). Thus, the rate of tax on this transfer is .30 percent. The GST tax is $2,400,000 ($8 million × .30 percent).

¶17,555   TAX COMPUTATIONS

In general, the method of computing the tax base of the generation-skipping transfer tax parallels the method applicable to the most closely analogous transfer subject to estate and gift tax. The method of computing the taxable amount depends on whether a taxable distribution, a taxable termination, or a direct skip is involved. Unless otherwise directed by a trust instrument specifically referring to the generation-skipping transfer tax, the tax imposed on a generation-skipping transfer is to be charged to the property being transferred.

Taxable Distributions

In the case of a taxable distribution, the amount subject to the generation-skipping transfer tax is the amount received by the transferee, reduced by any expenses included in connection with the determination, collection, or refund of the generation-skipping transfer tax. The transferee pays the tax on the taxable distribution. If the trustee pays any amount of the tax, the trustee is treated as having made an additional taxable distribution of that amount.

Note that all of the examples that follow assume that exemptions are exhausted and that the tax rate is 40 percent in 2015.

EXAMPLE 17.71	A taxable distribution of $1 million is made to Grandson in 2015. Grandson must pay $400,000 in GST taxes, retaining $600,000.

Taxable Terminations

In the case of a taxable termination, the amount subject to tax is the value of the property in which the interest terminates. A deduction is allowed for expenses, indebtedness, and taxes attributable to the property with respect to which the termination has occurred. The trustee pays any tax due on a taxable termination.

EXAMPLE 17.72	Upon termination of a trust, $1 million remains in the trust and is subject to the GST tax. The trustee pays the tax of $400,000 in 2014 (40 percent × $1 million), remitting $600,000 in 2015 to the skip person, Grandson.

Direct Skips

In the case of a testamentary direct skip, the amount subject to tax is the value of the property received by the transferee. The person making the transfer pays the tax liability incurred from a direct skip.

EXAMPLE 17.73	Grandpa had a residual estate of $2,333,333 before taxes in 2015. He had already used up his $5.43 million estate exemption and his $5.43 million GST exemption. He left $1,000,000 to his grandson. After estate taxes, $1,400,000 remained. The GST tax is levied on the amount received by the distributee in a direct skip. Thus, $1,000,000 is distributed to Grandson and the trustee or executor pays a GST tax of $400,000 in 2015.

In the case of an inter vivos direct skip, the amount subject to the GST tax is the value of the property received by the transferee. In addition, the gift tax is computed on the combined value of the gift and the generation-skipping transfer tax.

EXAMPLE 17.74	Grandpa made a gift of $1 million to Grandson in 2015. The GST tax is $400,000. For gift tax purposes, a gift of $1.40 million was made. Thus, a gift tax of $560,000 is payable as well. Note, however, that it took only $1,960,000 to transfer $1 million to the Grandson, as opposed to $2,333,333 in a testamentary transfer to get the Grandson, $1 million.

¶17,565   PAYMENT OF TAX

The GST tax is paid by the transferor or trustee except that the distributee pays the tax on taxable distributions. The GST tax return is due by the 15th day of the fourth month after the taxable year of the person who pays the tax and during which the transfer takes place, except in the case of a direct skip, other than from a trust, where the return is due at the same time the estate or gift tax return is due with respect to the transfer. Code Secs. 2603 and 2662.

¶17,575   CREDITS AND DEDUCTIONS

If a generation-skipping transfer (other than a direct skip) occurs at the same time as, and as a result of, the death of an individual, a credit against the generation-skipping transfer tax paid to any state is permitted. However, the credit is limited to five percent of the amount of federal generation-skipping transfer tax imposed on the transfer. Expenses, debts, and taxes are deductible under the same principles as those used for estate tax purposes. Code Secs. 2604 and 2622(b).

TAX BLUNDER

Olive Harus had given her son a power of attorney seven years prior to becoming incompetent to handle her own affairs. Olive remained incompetent for nine years until death. The son's power of attorney was silent as to gifts. During the period of incompetency, the son used his power of attorney to make gifts of cash and real estate to the taxpayer's heirs. Under Virginia law, at the time of the gifts, a power of attorney did not enable the holder of the power to have gifting powers. Even though the purpose of these gifts was to reduce the estate's size by taking advantage of annual $10,000 gift tax exclusions, the IRS determined that the gifts were voidable under state law. Since the son was not legally authorized to make gifts of his mother's property, the gifts were includible in the mother's gross estate under Code Sec. 2038 as incomplete gifts. *O.D. Casey Est.,* CA-4, 91-2 USTC ¶60,091, 948 F.2d 895. The practitioner should always review the instrument creating the power of attorney and state law to ascertain gifting powers under a power of attorney authorization.

SUMMARY

- The federal estate, gift, and generation-skipping taxes are transfer taxes either at death or during life.

- The estate and gift transfer taxes are unified and subject to the same rate schedule. On the other hand, the generation-skipping tax is a flat tax at the highest estate tax rate (currently 40%).

- To understand the estate tax, one should start with the estate tax formula as depicted in Table 2. The formula begins with the gross estate less allowable deductions which yields the taxable estate. At this point, all taxable gifts after 1976 are added, and the tentative estate tax is determined. From the tentative estate tax, gift taxes payable on includible gifts after 1976 are subtracted, and, lastly, the estate tax credits are subtracted yielding the estate tax liability.

- The federal estate tax return (Form 706) must be filed within nine months of death, and the property on the return must be valued at date of death or the alternate valuation date (generally six months after death).

- The federal gift tax return (Form 709) is due April 15 following the year of the gift.

- Gifts of a present interest qualify for an annual exclusion of $14,000 per donee. However, a married couple may gift-split and thereby give $28,000 to a donee.

- The applicable credit amount for 2015 allows an estate of $5.43 million in value to not be subject to tax or a required filing. Also, an individual could give a present interest of $5,444,000 ($14,000 annual exclusion plus the $5.43 million exemption amount) in 2015 and not be subject to tax.

QUESTIONS

1. Distinguish between an estate tax and an inheritance tax.

2. What is the estate tax base?

3. What is the applicable credit amount?

4. Why is the gross estate different from the probate estate?

5. Greta Cook died in 2015. Her gross estate was $5,580,000, administration expenses were $60,000, and adjusted taxable gifts were $20,000. Compute the estate tax liability.

6. Why are certain gift taxes includible in the gross estate?

7. Why may the 50 percent "qualified joint tenancy" rule have adverse income tax effects?

8. What are the interests in, and powers over, property that may be given to a donee without estate tax consequences to the donee's estate?

9. Distinguish between a mere testamentary power to appoint property to the creditors of one's estate and a power to appoint property to anyone in the world, except oneself, one's estate, or the creditors of either.

10. Which transfers of life insurance policies prior to death are includible in the transferor's gross estate?

11. Which expenses may be deducted for income tax purposes or for estate tax purposes by election?

12. What are the requirements for a marital deduction?

13. What types of property passing to a spouse are considered terminable interests that would not qualify for the marital deduction?

14. Is it possible that a transfer made to a future spouse may later qualify for the estate tax marital deduction?

15. What is a QTIP trust, and what is the "price paid" for its use?

16. What are the main differences between the income tax and the estate tax charitable deduction?

17. What are the main differences between a unitrust and an annuity trust?

18. What are the tax advantages of a disclaimer?

19. What is the significance of a disclaimant reaching age 21?

20. Which transfers are subject to the gift tax?

21. What is a net gift?

22. What are the advantages of gift-splitting?

23. Why must the donor disclose his income tax basis in gifted property on the gift tax return?

24. What is a direct skip?

PROBLEMS

25. If Doria Oliva dies this year (2015), what estate tax is payable if the facts are:

Adjusted gross estate	$5,800,000
Adjusted taxable gifts after 1976	100,000
Gift tax paid	6,000

26. Melinda transferred $500,000 to an irrevocable, inter vivos trust, leaving the income to Elmo, her husband, for his life, and the remainder to their daughter, Ingrid, if she survives her mother. What are the estate tax consequences to Melinda's estate if:
    a. Melinda predeceased Elmo and Ingrid.
    b. Ingrid predeceased Melinda.
    c. Melinda survived Elmo, but predeceased Ingrid.

27. Janet Smith transferred, in trust, $500,000 of Georgia Power Bonds to her younger sister, Bertha Jones. These bonds pay interest quarterly, and Janet reserved the income for her life. Janet was age 60 at the time of the gift. Assume the remainder interest is 0.25509.
    a. What is the value of Janet's gift?
    b. Does the annual exclusion apply?

28. In each of the following cases, determine the amount includible in David's gross estate:
    a. An account balance of $200,000 in an IRA that the beneficiary immediately withdrew.
    b. A commercial annuity with a present value of $60,000, payable to David's wife, Selma, who contributed 40 percent of the purchase price.
    c. A qualified pension annuity with a present value of $180,000, one-third of which is attributable to David's own contributions, payable to Selma.
    d. A lump-sum distribution from a qualified profit-sharing plan of $30,000, payable to David's son, Kyle, who used five-year averaging.

29. Martha and Ludwig own their home in equal shares. Ludwig purchased the home with funds inherited from his grandfather, but Martha died first, leaving her half to Ludwig.

    What is includible in Martha's estate, and what is Ludwig's basis in the home if:
    a. They were married and owned the home as:
       1. Tenants in common
       2. Joint tenants
       3. Tenants by the entirety
       4. Community property
    b. They were brother and sister and owned the house as:
       1. Tenants in common
       2. Joint tenants

30. Identify the following property interests, powers, and events:
    a. Gus buys a piece of land with his brother, Jack. Gus's interest is 60 percent; Jack's is 40 percent.
    b. Bruce died, leaving his wife, Nancy, "30 percent of his adjusted gross estate, free and clear, in cash."
    c. Henry purchased a home "together with my wife, Ann, as co-owners with the right of survivorship."
    d. George transfers $10 million in trust to his wife, Wanda, for life, then to his son, Luke, for life, then to his daughter, Adele, if she survives Wanda, her mother. Adele also has the power to invade corpus to the extent needed to support her in her accustomed life style.
    e. Wendy owns half of all income and assets acquired by Harold during their marriage.
    f. Grandpa Jones died, still living rent free on a portion of the farm he deeded to Jack, his grandson, 11 years earlier.

31. Evelyn gave a Flymore sailplane to her husband who is an enthusiast of this sport for their wedding anniversary. Purchase cost was $37,000. She used her own funds from a separate checking account.
    a. What is the value of the gift?
    b. Does the gift have to be reported?
    c. What is the limit on a gift between spouses?

32. John and Janet Smith (husband and wife) purchased 1,000 shares of ABC Company common stock (NYSE) for $56,000 and immediately had it titled in the names of "Hugh and Donna Smith as joint tenants with rights of survivorship" (son and daughter-in-law). Assume gift-splitting in 2015.
    a. How much is the gift?
    b. What is the total of John's exclusions?
    c. What is the total of Janet's annual exclusions?

33. Joseph Grant's will provided that $1 million was to be placed in trust for his son, Steven, for life, with a remainder to Steven's children per stirpes.

    What are the estate tax consequences to Steven's estate if the trust instrument provides the following:
    a. All trust income must be distributed to Steven quarterly.
    b. Steven is to be trustee.
    c. Steven may appoint the trust property to anyone he chooses during life and by will, except to himself, his estate, or the creditors of either.
    d. Steven may invade corpus to whatever extent necessary for his support and maintenance in his accustomed mode of living, as well as for his health and education.
    e. Steven may withdraw from the principal the greater of $5,000 or five percent of the trust each year on a noncumulative basis.
    f. Is any transfer tax possible upon Steven's death?

34. In which of the following cases will the insurance proceeds be includible in Bertram's estate?
    a. Bertram purchased the policy on his life 11 years ago and transferred all rights to it to Donna, his daughter, five years before he died.
    b. Same as (a), but the transfer took place two years before Bertram's death.
    c. Two years before he died, Bertram talked his wife into buying a policy on his life. The only available funds during the marriage came from Bertram's salary.
    d. Unknown to Bertram, because Donna was concerned about his health, she bought a term policy on his life seven months before he died.

35. On June 28, 1994, Bart Richards married Martha Joiner in Atlanta, Georgia. Because Bart was so happy that Martha became his wife, he purchased a home in Atlanta for $500,000 out of his own separate funds. He immediately titled the home in their joint names with right of survivorship. Bart died on June 28, 2015. The house was worth $800,000 on Bart's date of death. The executor elects to value the home at the date of death. What value will be placed on Bart's joint interest in his estate tax return?

36. Assume the same facts as in Problem 35. What is Martha's income tax basis in the house?

37. Assume the same facts as in Problem 35, except that Bart and Martha resided in Dallas, Texas. What is Martha's income tax basis in the house?

38. Kermit Ames died on January 15, 2015. The fair market value of his house was $150,000 on his date of death. On July 15, 2015, the house was worth $130,000. Assume the alternate valuation date is selected by the executor. What value is used by the executor in the estate tax return?

39. Assume the same facts as in Problem 38, except that the executor sold the house on May 2, 2015, for $138,000. What value is used by the executor in the estate tax return?

40. Assume the same facts as in Problem 38. What is the due date of the estate tax return?

41. Tom Parks died on March 15, 2015. The values of Tom's assets on March 15 and September 15, 2015, are as indicated below:

Asset	VALUES	
	Mar. 15	Sept. 15
Land	$5,400,000	$5,350,000
Stocks	300,000	300,000
Bonds	400,000	350,000

The marginal federal estate tax bracket applicable to Tom's estate is 40 percent for property over $5.43 million. All of Tom's property, which consists of the above capital assets, will go to his children, Ted and Jason. Neither Ted nor Jason is a dealer in real estate. Should the executor elect alternate valuation under Code Sec. 2032? In deciding whether to elect the alternate valuation date, calculate both the estate tax consequences and the income tax consequences for the parties involved.

42. Mr. John Henderson died on February 17, 2015. For each of the following items indicate the amount to be included in John's gross estate. Unless stated to the contrary, assume that the items are valued as of John's death.
    a. John owned a 2004 Lincoln Town Car. At his date of death, the car's retail price was $11,750, and its wholesale price was $10,150.
    b. Same as (a), except that the executor sold the car on April 17, 2015, for $11,000 to a buyer who saw it advertised on the home shopping network on a local TV station.
    c. John owned 1,000 shares of I.B.M. On February 17, 2015, the stock sold at a high of 100 and low of 98. It closed at 99 1/4.

43. Which of the following items are deductible to the estate?
    a. Property taxes accrued at death on decedent's home, held in a qualified joint tenancy.
    b. Interest accrued during estate administration on decedent's debts for which he was personally liable.
    c. Administration expenses in excess of value of property subject to claims, if paid one year after death.
    d. Same as (c), except that the property was not subject to claims.
    e. Estimated accountants' fees to be paid when practicable.
    f. Decedent's medical expenses paid 11 months after death.

44. Because John was so happy that Dana had agreed to become his fiancee, on February 2, 2015, he gave Dana's mother, Ethel, $15,000 in cash.
    a. Does this gift qualify for gift-splitting?
    b. Does this gift qualify for gift-splitting if John and Dana marry by December 31, 2015?

45. Mortimer Piper transferred $5 million in trust to his wife, Mona, for life, then to their children in equal shares. After Mortimer died, Mona sold her income interest, then died 17 years later.
    a. What are the transfer tax consequences to Mortimer, his estate, Mona, and her estate if a QTIP election is made?
    b. Same as (a), but without a QTIP election?

46. When Harry died, he left his surviving wife, Clare, the following:
    a. A remainder in a summer house, with a life estate left to his mother.
    b. A life estate and a general power of appointment in closely held stock, which, in the last 17 years, paid no dividends.
    c. An insurance policy on her own life.
    d. An annuity payable from a qualified, noncontributory pension plan.
    e. A patent with three years to run.
    f. Income from a mutual fund for life, with a remainder to their two daughters.

    Which of the above bequests qualify for the marital deduction?

47. In 2015, Mr. Colburn created a trust for the benefit of his five adult children and transferred $300,000 to it. The trustee may decide how much income to pay to each child each year. The trust will terminate at the end of 40 years, and the assets will be divided equally among the children or their estates. Does Mr. Colburn receive a gift tax exclusion of $70,000? Explain.

48. John Henry Harris was left a 1962 Impala convertible by his uncle, Billy Bob Harris. After receiving the car, John determined that five cars in his family were too many. As a result, he disclaimed the property with direction that the car go to his brother, Lee Roy Harris. Is this a valid disclaimer for estate tax purposes?

49. Stanley Rosen's cumulative lifetime taxable gifts amount to $250,000. The following year, he gives his favorite nephew $164,000 to open a liquor store.
    a. What is the taxable gift?
    b. What is the tax on the gift (prior to credits)?
    c. What is the gift tax payable?

50. The $14,000 exclusion would be available in which of the following transfers?
    a. Revocable transfer in trust to W for life, then to S.
    b. Irrevocable transfer in trust to W for life, then to S.
    c. Irrevocable transfer of a life insurance policy to a trust with two income beneficiaries.
    d. Transfer in trust to A and/or B for life, then to L, and the grantor makes the distribution decisions.
    e. Same as (d), but the independent trustee makes the distribution decisions.
    f. Nonbusiness transfer to a corporation owned 50 percent by the donor's three children.
    g. Transfer in trust to a minor, all income to be accumulated.

51. In the following independent cases explain whether the exclusion, the marital deduction, the charitable deduction, and gift-splitting are available.
    a. To mother for life, then to spouse
    b. To spouse for life, then to child
    c. To charity for five years, then to spouse
    d. To spouse for life, then to charity
    e. To child A and/or child B for life, then to grandchild

52. During the year your client, Big Jim Smith, gave $9,000 to 70 different donees. Has Big Jim made any taxable gifts during the year?

53. Isaac Binder purchased 1,000 shares of Deep-Freeze Inc. five years ago for $15,000. Two years before he died, he gave his son, Edward, 500 shares worth $6,000. He died during a bull market and willed Edward the other 500 shares, then worth $12,000.
    a. What is Edward's basis for gain or loss in the stock received by inter vivos gift?
    b. What is Edward's basis in the testamentary gift?
    c. What is Edward's holding period in the two blocks of stock?

54. John Henry paid $60,000 in 2015 in medical bills to a doctor and a hospital for his invalid father. Has John Henry made any taxable gifts in 2015?

55. Under the annuity rules, all the following are includible in the decedent's estate, except:
    a. A lump-sum distribution from a qualified profit-sharing plan to a named beneficiary who waived forward averaging.
    b. A commercial joint and survivorship annuity payable to the decedent and the spouse where the spouse furnished the purchase price.
    c. The first $100,000 of an individual retirement account payable to the decedent's grandchildren.
    d. One-half of a joint and survivorship annuity payable to the decedent and the spouse. The latter's aunt had purchased the annuity for them as a golden anniversary gift.

56. As a rule, general powers of appointment are taxable, while special powers are not. The following powers are all special powers, except:
   a. The power to appoint property to any person or entity in the world except to the oneself, the estate, or creditors.
   b. The power to invade corpus to the extent necessary to maintain one's present mode of living (which includes $1 million a year for servants, trips, jewelry, and a yacht).
   c. The power to appoint the property to the holder's children and to anyone else, but with the remainderman's consent.
   d. The mere testamentary power to appoint the property to the creditors of the holder's estate.

57. During the current year, Dana makes the following cash gifts: $5,000 to her daughter, $9,000 to her brother, and $16,000 to a business partner. Does Dana need to file a gift tax return?

58. Which one of the following is not a deduction from the gross estate of a decedent?
   a. Unpaid income taxes on income received by the decedent during life.
   b. Interest payable on a loan incurred to pay estate taxes.
   c. Selling expenses for selling estate property if these sales are necessary to settle the estate.
   d. Interest payable after a decedent's death attributable to an installment obligation incurred by decedent.
   e. Casualty loss (uninsured) incurred during settlement of the estate.

59. In the typical gift situation, the donor pays the gift tax. When a "net gift" is made, however, the donee promises the donor to pay any gift tax due. The following statements relating to net gifts are all false, except:
   a. The donor may realize a gain or loss on the transfer.
   b. The donor becomes secondarily liable for the gift tax.
   c. The donee's basis will not include an adjustment for the gift tax paid by the donee.
   d. The amount of the gift is reduced by gift taxes actually paid by the donee, but not by any reduction in the donor's unified credit.

60. Hugh Colburn's financially destitute brother, Big Al, has a daughter named Violet. Hugh offers to pay for Violet's college education. In 2015, Hugh pays Columbia University's annual tuition of $50,000 and he also gives Violet an annual allotment of $16,000. Determine Hugh's taxable gifts for 2015.

61. The generation-skipping transfer tax supplements the estate and gift taxes. The following statements about this tax are all true, except:
   a. The generation-skipping trust is liable for any transfer tax due, but the distributee has transferee liability.
   b. A generation-skipping trust must have at least two beneficiaries in different generations below that of the grantor.
   c. The same top marginal tax rate applies to estate, gift, and generation-skipping transfer taxes.
   d. A person cannot be a beneficiary if the person has no present interest in the trust.

62. **Comprehensive Problem.** During 2015, Dale Davison made the following gifts:
   a. $30,000 to the political action group to re-elect Sam Nunn for the U.S. Senate.
   b. $25,000 to Scientific Atlanta Corporation (because he believed in their research objectives). Dale was not a shareholder in Scientific Atlanta Corp.
   c. $22,000 to Mount Paran Church of God.
   d. $100,000 was put in a joint tenants account. The joint tenants were Dale and his brother Sam.
   e. $45,000 was paid to Vassar University in tuition for his daughter Sara.
   f. $100,000 was placed in trust for his son, Ralph, for life, then the remainder will go to the Southern Methodist Foundation. Ralph's life estate is valued at $40,000.
   g. A gift of real estate (basis of $60,000 and fair market value of $310,000 to his sister, Karen).
   h. A gift of a life insurance policy on Dale's life to Sara (the beneficiary). The policy was worth $8,000 but had a face value of $50,000.

   What are Dale's taxable gifts for the year?

63. **Comprehensive Problem**. When Howard Foth died in the current year, in addition to his $4.7 million of certificates of deposit and investment property worth $200,000, the following facts were disclosed by the executor:

    a. In 1979, Howard Foth decided to see what kind of fiduciary the Bank of Georgia would be for his assets. However, he did not want to establish an irrevocable trust because the fiduciary might not perform up to expectations and he might need the property later for his own retirement needs. Consequently, Howard established a revocable trust funded at $300,000, but the fair market value at death was $700,000.

    b. In 1989, Howard made a taxable gift of $90,000 to his daughter, Bertha. Due to the unified credit, Howard did not incur any gift tax.

    c. In 1987, Howard purchased a paid-up life insurance policy with a face value of $300,000 payable at death to the executor of the estate to use against any estate taxes that might be due.

    d. In 1975, Howard's mother had left him a general power of appointment over a trust valued at $215,000. This power was subject to the standard of comfort.

    e. Funeral expenses were $30,000, and administration expenses of $70,000 are considered necessary for Howard's estate.

    f. Howard left his wife, Bella, $600,000 outright in certificates of deposit.

    g. The executor paid $40,000 in state death taxes to the state of Georgia.

    Compute the net estate tax payable.

64. **Comprehensive Problem**. Dave L. Jones, a calendar-year taxpayer using the cash method of accounting, was scared to death on Halloween night, October 31, 2015. Under the terms of the will, Dave devised and bequeathed all of the property he owned to his wife, Hildegard, except for a cash gift of $100,000 to the School of Accountancy at Louisiana Tech University, a condominium in Cancun, Mexico, to his beloved son, Billy Bob, a condominium in West Palm Beach, Florida, to Lee Ray Brown, and a $20,000 cash gift to Peggy Sue Elmore (who befriended him late in life).

A review of the executor's files and discussions with Mr. Jones's attorney reveal the following facts:

a. Mr. Jones's assets at (1) date of death and (2) six months later are as follows:

	Fair Market Value	
Real Estate	**10/31/15**	**4/30/16**
Personal residence	$ 500,000	$ 500,000
Cancun condominium	3,500,000	3,450,000
West Palm Beach condominium	3,000,000	3,525,000
Stocks and Bonds		
Ford Motor Co. bonds, 60 10% bonds, face value, $1,000 each. Interest payable semiannually on July 1 and January 1	72,000	75,000
Interest accrued on Ford Motor Co. bonds from July 1, 2015, to October 31, 2015	2,000	2,000
Littleton Telephone Co., common stock, 1,000 shares traded over the counter $10 per share on October 31, 2015, and $20 on April 30, 2016	10,000	20,000
West Lumber Co., traded NYSE, 5,000 shares common stock $100 per share on October 31, 2015, and $50 per share on April 30, 2016	500,000	250,000
Cash		
Checking Account No. 23-000, First National Bank of Greenville	15,000	15,000
Money Market Savings Account No. 1-23456, Beaver Run Savings & Loan	275,000	275,000
Life Insurance		
Policy No. 1 provided for $100,000 payable to wife with no incidents of ownership	100,000	100,000
Policy No. 2 provided for $100,000 to wife, listed as owner under state law, but Dave retained the power to change the beneficiary	100,000	100,000
Other Assets		
1959 White Cadillac El Dorado Convertible, red interior with bobbing dog in rear window	20,000	20,000
Civil war memorabilia	10,000	10,000
5 carat diamond ring, blue-white perfect	50,000	50,000
Miscellaneous personal effects (clothing and shoes)	6,800	6,800
Miscellaneous household goods (dishes, pots and pans, plants, silverware, and tools)	5,000	5,000
Furniture	25,000	25,000
Oriental rugs	18,000	18,000

b. On November 7, 1976, Mr. Jones, pursuant to the legal firm's suggestion of utilizing the annual exclusion and the specific exemption, gave $33,000 to his son Billy Bob. (Note that a $6,000 adjustment to the unified credit is required because of this transaction.)

c. Mr. Jones has made annual gifts of the exact annual exclusion amount to his son and each of his grandchildren each year (including 2015) since 1977. Other than these gifts and the one above, he made no gifts during his life.

d. Dividends of $2 per share were declared on the West Lumber Co. stock on October 1, 2015, but were not paid until November 15, 2015. Assume Mr. Jones was alive on the date of record.

e. Interest of $6,500 accrued on the savings account at date of death.

f. Fees:

Funeral expenses	$12,000
Attorney's fees	30,000
Accounting fees	30,000
Executor's fees	40,000
Appraisal fees	2,300

g. Mortgage on personal residence, United Financial Mortgage Corp., 10 percent, $50,000.

h. Debts:

Accrued property taxes on personal residence	$2,000
Accrued property taxes on West Palm Beach condo	3,000

i. Taxes:

North Carolina Inheritance Tax	$45,000
Mexico Estate Tax	12,000

j. A proviso in the will provided that the marital deduction for property passing to the wife shall not be reduced for death taxes, foreign death taxes, and funeral and administrative expenses.

k. The executor has decided to take all administrative expenses on the estate return.

l. Assume the executor elected to value the assets in the gross estate at their date of death values.

Required: Compute the net estate tax payable (note that the amount paid to Mexico is the amount of the foreign tax credit).

65. **Comprehensive Problem.** Mr. B died in 2015 at the age of 72. In his will, Mr. B made several bequests to the members of his family. The executor of B's estate wants to know which of the following bequests constitute generation-skipping transfers.

a. A testamentary trust to pay the income among Mr. B's four sons in such shares as the trustee determines. The trust agreement provides that, upon the death of the first son to die, one-fourth of the trust shall be paid to his descendants *per stirpes.*

b. A trust under which the trustee may distribute income among Mr. B's descendants or apply the income for the benefit of any one of them. The trustee decides to pay the college tuition and medical school tuition for Mr. B's grandchildren.

c. Mr. B's bequeathal of the ABC Widget Company to his son, M. M decides to disclaim the property in compliance with Code Sec. 2518 because the company would interfere with his acting career. As a result, the ABC Company passes to M's son.

d. A trust to be created under which the trustee may distribute income or corpus to any of Mr. B's children or his remote descendants. The trustee makes several distributions to Mr. B's grandchildren because they really loved their grandfather.

66. **Comprehensive Problem.** Assume that the farm property shown below has been physically farmed by the decedent for the last thirty years. He willed it to his favorite son, who will continue to farm it.

   a. In each of the independent cases, indicate whether or not special use valuation is available. The values shown for the farm assets are their fair market values as computed under the highest and best use concept.

   b. Assume in each of the cases that the real estate consists of 1,000 acres, the average gross cash rent is $30 per acre, and the average real estate taxes are $5 per acre. Further assume that 10 percent is the average annual effective interest rate charged by the Farm Credit Bank. At what amount would the parcels be valued per Section 2032A for 2015?

   c. Refer to case 1. Five years after the farmer's death, his son sold the entire farm realty to a land speculator for $2,000,000. Assume that the farmer-decedent was not survived by a spouse and died in 2015. What are the tax consequences five years after the farmer's death? Who pays the tax cost? Use only the unified credit in your calculations.

   d. Same as part c, except that the sale occurs twelve years after the farmer's death.

	CASES		
	(1)	(2)	(3)
Bonds	2,000,000	1,800,000	2,000,000
Stocks	200,000	400,000	300,000
Farm real estate	3,000,000	750,000	2,900,000
Farm equipment	600,000	2,550,000	300,000
	5,800,000	5,500,000	5,500,000
Mortgage against farm realty	(50,000)	(80,000)	(20,000)
Accounting fees	(25,000)	(30,000)	(25,000)
Appraisers' fees	(25,000)	(40,000)	(25,000)
Adjusted gross estate & Taxable estate	$5,700,000	$5,350,000	$5,430,000

67. **Research Problem.** On May 20, 1978, decedent's husband, Hugh P. Hughes, executed a will which contained the following paragraph:

   Third: I give, devise and bequeath the 300-acre farm which I own near Macon, Georgia, to my wife, Bertha O. Hughes, for and during the term of her natural life with remainder to my children, Vince Hughes, Hedy Henderson, and Chester Hughes, in equal shares. However, with the right reserved to my wife in case of necessity, that she may sell the land if that need arises. But it is my wish that the land be preserved for the benefit of my three children.

   Hugh P. Hughes died on April 15, 1999, and decedent, Bertha O. Hughes, died on June 2, 2015. At the time of Bertha's death, the farm was worth $4 million.

   Is the farm excluded from Bertha's estate?

   In your answer, address the power of appointment of issue, and read the case of *Bette J. Berg,* 81-2 USTC ¶13,428 (DC Minn 1981).

68. **Research Problem.** John and Mary Larsson purchased a joint and survivorship annuity from the Life and Death Insurance Co. John paid for the annuity and died 11 years later, at which time Mary's survivorship interest had a value of $50,000. Mary was killed in a car crash four months later, having collected $2,000 since her husband's death.

   a. Must the date of death value be used, even though it is known that the asset is worthless prior to the due date of the return?

   b. Does it make a difference that the alternate valuation date is elected? (See *Estate of John A. Hance,* 18 TC 499, Dec. 19,025 (1952), Acq. 1953-1 CB 4, and Code Sec. 2039(a) and (b).)

69. **Research Problem.** Greene Corporation, a closely held corporation, is owned by Al Manx with 6,000 shares, Bob Barnes with 2,500 shares, and Cora Crowley with 1,500 shares. In the current year, Cora passed away. As a result of Cora's death, the executor contacts you about valuing Cora's closely held stock. In your analysis, you discover that Greene Corporation has average earnings over the representative period of $80 per share. Also, over the same period, it has paid $20 of dividends per share. The book value of Greene Corporation is $50 per share. Since the stock is not very marketable and Cora had a minority interest, you have concluded that a discount of 25 percent is appropriate for lack of marketability and minority interest.

    Required: Value Cora's closely held stock interest for estate tax purposes. In your research, review the case of *Central Trust Co. v. U.S.,* 62-2 USTC ¶12,092, 305 F.2d 393 (Ct Cl 1962) for the applicable weights to be assigned to the valuation factors of earnings, dividends, and book value.

70. **Research Problem.** In 2015, Bert Richards transferred a $100,000 savings account to his wife in trust. The terms of the trust are that income is to be distributed annually to his wife, Mary Beth, the remainder to his two children, Oscar and Bertha, in equal shares or to their estate. The value of Mary Beth's income interest is $50,000.
    a. Is this a taxable gift to Mary Beth? (See Code Sec. 2523(b)(1) and (e).)
    b. Have taxable gifts been made for Oscar and Bertha?
    c. How many annual exclusions are available? (See Code Sec. 2503(b).)

71. **Gift Tax Return Problem.** Based on the facts summarized below, use two gift Tax Forms 709 to complete the appropriate gift tax returns for Mr. and Mrs. Smith for calendar year 2014 for which each is required to file. They want to keep any gift tax liability as low as possible as a family group for the current and future years. "NYSE" means the stock is traded on the New York Stock Exchange.

John F. Smith
a. 6/29/14: John and Janet purchased $30,000 of MNO Company common stock (NYSE) and immediately had it recorded in their joint names as "John and Janet as joint tenants, with right of survivorship." John furnished $10,000 from his separate funds and Janet furnished $20,000 from her separate funds.
b. 7/10/14: Transferred 200 shares of XYZ Company common stock (NYSE) to son James. Fair market value was $30,000. It was purchased 5/1/74 for $9,000. It was previously registered in John's name only.
c. 8/1/14: Purchased 1,000 shares of ABC Company common stock (NYSE) for $52,000 and immediately had it titled in the names of "Joseph and Barbara Smith, as joint tenants with right of survivorship" (son and daughter-in-law).
d. 9/14/14: Deposited $15,000 as a birthday gift in savings account of nephew Richard Osco, account titled in Richard's mother's name as custodian under his state's Uniform gifts to Minor Act.
e. Taxable gifts made in prior years: In 1970, gave away 1,000 shares of DEF Company common stock (closely held company). Fair market value at date of gift was $93,000. John inherited these from his father who died 3/31/60 when they were worth $29,000. John claimed one exclusion, used his lifetime (specific) exemption, and paid $7,125 in gift tax (no marital gift splitting elected).

Janet B. Smith

a. 4/30/14: Gave a Flymore sailplane to her husband, who is an enthusiast of this sport, for their wedding anniversary. Purchase cost was $37,000. She used her own funds from a separate checking account.

b. 6/29/14: See John's Item A.

c. 7/15/14: Gave check for $20,000 made payable to "William and Barbara Zuck" (son-in-law and daughter).

d. 2/10/14: Janet transferred, in trust, $500,000 of Georgia Power Bonds to her younger sister, Bertha Jones. These bonds pay interest quarterly, and Janet reserved the income for her life. Janet was age 60 at the time of the gift. Assume the remainder interest is .25509.

e. Taxable gifts made in prior years: On 12/1/76, gave away 250 shares of STU Company common stock (NYSE). Fair market value date of gift was $32,000. Janet received these as a gift from her uncle in 1960. The fair market value then was $40,000. Uncle paid no gift tax. He had purchased them in 1955 for $36,000. Janet claimed one exclusion and used her lifetime (specific) exemption to avoid paying any gift tax (no marital gift splitting elected).

COMPREHENSIVE PROBLEM

Facts

Esther and Simon Ames, ages 51 and 50, respectively, have been married for 30 years and have lived in Texas where she was employed as a vice president of advertising of Eighth-note, Inc., a Texas corporation engaged in the manufacture and sale of musical instruments. However, last year there was a takeover of the corporation, and Esther lost her job. She received $250,000 in separation payments in 2014, twice her annual salary. She decided that she wanted to own her own business.

Her third cousin, Billy Ray, approached her. He wanted to know if Esther knew anyone who was interested in buying his small but profitable business located in Virginia. After some negotiations, Esther decided that she was interested and bought all the stock of Burglar Beware Lock Company.

Burglar Beware has a narrow but profitable field of business in selling heavy-duty locks for fences at junkyards, police compounds, and lots at hardware stores. Its balance sheet is attached at the end of this section. Last year, it earned $150,000 on sales of $1,000,000, including a $125,000 per annum salary for Esther. Its liabilities are comparatively small, and its net worth is about $800,000.

Burglar Beware has health insurance policies but no disability insurance coverage for its workers. It also has no pension plan. Of Burglar Beware's 12 employees, only Esther and her son, Bob, would be regarded as managers. There is really no middle management. Burglar Beware has no record of dividend payments and elected S corporation status in December of 1986.

Simon is a skilled and experienced college professor. When they moved from Texas to Virginia, he determined that he would look for a teaching position. He found a post at a salary of $40,000 per year plus hospital and major medical insurance benefits. He expects a pension of 50 percent of salary (plus Social Security) at age 67. He has in his own name approximately $40,000 in bank accounts.

When Esther and Simon moved to Virginia, they sold their Dallas home in September 2015; for $500,000 (which cost them $125,000). Currently they are renting an apartment, but are looking for a new home. They are interested in the tax ramifications of this move and spend a good deal of their time on weekends going out with realtors on the Eastern Shore of Virginia.

Esther has a $25,000 ordinary life insurance policy on her life that she has held for some time and that currently has a cash value of $15,000. She acquired the life insurance policy while in Texas. She also has $10,000 of National Service Life Insurance and a term policy of $25,000 not convertible to ordinary life for another five years. Both of these policies were acquired before marriage. She and Simon are in good health. There is no group insurance program at Burglars Beware and Esther thinks it should be considered. Esther would also like to know about a pension plan. She has heard about a simplified employee pension plan and wants your opinion on it (See Chapter 24).

Simon and Esther have two children. The elder, Bob, is a college graduate and left a job with a major insurance company to join Burglar Beware primarily as a salesman. He is 26 years old and has worked with his mother at Burglar Beware for the last six months. He also has some distinct ideas with respect to a new hydraulic lock for which he hopes he can obtain a license from the patent owner. He believes this lock could permit Burglar Beware to double its gross sales in four years. Bob is divorced and has no current plans for remarriage.

Esther and Simon's younger child, Lucille, age 23, graduated from college last May. She is a substitute teacher and is looking for a permanent job. While living with her parents, she is dating a local farmer.

Esther has regularly contributed $2,000 per year to an IRA that currently has a value of about $18,000, including accumulated earnings. Simon has a similar IRA, but his has appreciated only to $12,000.

Esther and Simon have in their joint names listed stocks valued at $70,000, with a basis of approximately $30,000. Esther also has in her own name Series H Savings Bonds worth approximately $13,000. She paid approximately $5,000 for these bonds.

Esther (an only child) has a mother, Winona, age 80, who also lives in Virginia. She owns a home with a value of approximately $480,000 and a portfolio of listed stocks, mostly inherited from her husband, valued at $250,000. The home was worth $300,000 at her husband's death and had been jointly owned since 1957. She has a trust from her husband, who died in 1998, which will not be included in her estate because she has all of the income and only a limited power of appointment currently valued at $200,000. But Winona has been diagnosed as having a terminal malignancy. The doctors estimate that she has about three years to live.

Simon has very few relatives, but he does have an uncle. Uncle Harry is age 90 and lives nearby. He worked for a number of years and currently lives on a pension, Social Security, and interest. He lives in a small home that he owns outright. The home is worth about $80,000, but he has no other substantial assets except $5,000 in the bank. Simon's concern is that Uncle Harry is now becoming forgetful and less and less able to take care of himself. Simon believes he would never consent to going into a nursing home and could not afford it in any event. Simon feels a moral obligation to take in Uncle Harry to live with their family. Uncle Harry has one other relative, a nephew who lives in Idaho and whom he seldom sees.

Burglar Beware, Inc.
Balance Sheet
September 30, 2015

Assets

Cash			$100,000
Inventory			402,000
Equipment, furniture and fixtures		$140,000	
Less: Reserve for depreciation		(15,000)	
Net			$125,000
Automobile		$16,000	
Less: Accumulated depreciation		(8,000)	
Net			$8,000
Land		$150,000	
Building	$185,000		
Less: Accumulated Depreciation	30,000	155,000	$305,000
Total			$940,000

Liabilities & Owners' Equity

Accounts payable			$140,000
Capital Stock			$800,000
Total			$940,000

Suggested Items for Group Discussion Only:

1. Statement of objectives
2. Review of facts
3. Retirement planning
4. Disability planning
5. Community property status
6. Buy-sell agreements
7. AB trust setup
8. Sale of home and diversification of investments
9. Planning recommendations for Hugh's mother
10. Planning recommendations for Donna's uncle
11. Special use valuation
12. Paying estate tax in installments

Chapter

18

Income Taxation of Trusts and Estates

OBJECTIVES

After completing Chapter 18, you should be able to:

1. Understand the intricacies and planning opportunities in a decedent's final federal income tax return.
2. Determine when 1041 returns for an estate or trust are required and how they are prepared.
3. Depict the duties and responsibilities of a fiduciary in the preparation of a federal income tax return for an estate or trust.
4. Achieve an understanding of fiduciary accounting income and distributable net income.
5. Recognize how beneficiaries are taxed on distributions from estates or trusts.
6. Calculate the alternative minimum tax for estates and trusts.
7. Identify the impact of special tax rules affecting only estates and trusts.
8. Depict tax planning strategies for estates, trusts, and beneficiaries.

OVERVIEW

What happens to a taxpayer's taxpaying responsibilities when the taxpayer dies? Is the taxpayer relieved of future tax obligations? What date does the estate take over as a tax-paying entity? What happens when property is placed in a trust by a parent for the benefit of a child? Who is the taxpayer: the parent, the child, or the trust? What happens if an estate or trust distributes income to a beneficiary? Are there federal income tax implications? Answers to these questions and to many other related questions are discussed in this chapter.

The chapter deals first with the taxation aspects of estates, focusing on a decedent's final federal income tax return and how the return might differ from a regular return if the decedent was still living. The term decedent refers to a person who is deceased.

Next, the chapter discusses the federal income tax return of an estate. An estate comes into existence on the date of a decedent's death and continues in existence until all of the decedent's property is distributed to heirs (beneficiaries) and the estate is dissolved by law.

The second part of the chapter reviews the federal income tax return of a trust. A trust is a legal entity set up to hold property. A trustee administers the property according to the dictates of a trust agreement.

Intertwined in the discussion of estate and trust income tax returns is a discussion of the duties and responsibilities of fiduciaries. A fiduciary is a person such as an administrator, trustee, or executor who has been given a special confidence and responsibility to manage property in a trust or estate according to some legal agreement (will or trust agreement) and in the best interests of the beneficiaries of the trust or estate.

Next, the tax scheme of estates, trusts, and beneficiaries are discussed in this chapter. It is possible that some of the income earned by a trust or estate will not be taxable to the trust or estate but, instead, will be picked up as income on the income tax return of a beneficiary. In some instances, a decedent's income might also be required to be reported as income on the income tax return of a beneficiary.

Also, the chapter highlights tax planning techniques that have proven useful in regard to a decedent's final return, estate and trust income tax returns, and the tax status of beneficiaries. Also discussed are the tax planning options available in return preparation of the decedent's final Form 1040, the estate or trust Form 1041 (U.S. Fiduciary Income Tax Return), and the estate's Form 706 (United States Estate (and Generation-Skipping Transfer) Tax Return).

Taxation of Estates

¶18,001 DECEDENT'S FINAL INCOME TAX RETURN

In the year a person dies (decedent), a federal income tax return is due for the period from the beginning of the decedent's tax year up to the date of death. Reg. §1.6012-3(b)(1). Death does not speed up the due date of the return. The tax return is due on the regular due date as if the decedent had continued to live for the entire tax year. Reg. §1.6072-1(b). An illustration of due dates for a decedent's final return is provided below.

EXAMPLE 18.1	A calendar-year taxpayer died on February 18, 2015. A tax return for the calendar year 2014 must be filed on or before April 15, 2015, and the tax return for the fractional part of 2015, that is, January 1 to February 18, 2015, must be filed on or before April 15, 2016.

If the decedent's gross income is below the required filing level, then no return need be filed. A return should be filed, however, if it would result in the refund of tax previously paid in or withheld. Code Sec. 6012(a)(1). Death does not change the filing status of the decedent. A joint return can still be filed with a surviving spouse if it is advantageous for tax purposes to do so. Income of the surviving spouse is included on the tax return for the entire tax year, but income of the decedent is included only up to the date of death. However, a joint return that includes a decedent may not be filed if the surviving spouse remarries before the end of the tax year in which the decedent dies or if the surviving spouse files a return for only part of the tax year because of a change in accounting period.

A fiduciary (executor or administrator of an estate) who has the responsibility of concluding the decedent's affairs has the responsibility of filing and signing the decedent's final return. If there is no executor or administrator of the decedent's estate and a joint return is to be filed, the surviving spouse can sign and file the return and indicate the date of the decedent's death on the return. A fiduciary, if appointed at a later date, has the power to change the decedent's filing status from married filing a joint return to married filing separately if there is a justifiable reason. Code Sec. 6013(a); Reg. §1.6013-1(d).

¶18,015 INCOME AND DEDUCTIONS ON FINAL RETURN

The method of accounting used by the decedent while alive determines what income and deductions are recognized on the decedent's final return. If the decedent was on the accrual basis of accounting for tax purposes, then only income accrued up to the date of death is included on the final return. Deductions that accrued up to the date of death are also shown on the final return. Income or deductions accruable only because of death are not included on the final return. Code Sec. 451(b); Reg. §1.451-1(b).

EXAMPLE 18.2	Sam Lett, a businessman, keeps his records on the accrual basis of accounting. Sam dies on September 30, 2015. Income earned by Sam through September 30, 2015, is included on his final return.

If the decedent was on the cash basis of accounting, as are most individuals, only income actually or constructively received up to the date of death is included on the final return. Income earned by a cash-basis decedent but not received prior to death is not included on the decedent's final return. Instead, the income is included on the income tax return of the estate or beneficiary who is entitled to the payment and actually receives it (income in respect of the decedent, which is discussed later).

EXAMPLE 18.3	Dave Jones, a cash-basis taxpayer who is an accountant and works for a local CPA firm, receives his salary payment on the fifteenth of the month for work completed the prior month. Dave dies on December 8. The December 15 salary payment for work completed in November is not included on his final return. The income is taxable to the estate or beneficiary who is entitled to the payment and actually receives it.

All valid tax deductible expenses paid by a cash-basis decedent before death can be deducted on a final return. Valid tax deductible expenses, which are not paid by the date of death, are normally deductible by the estate or the beneficiary who has the responsibility of discharging the obligation. Reg. §1.691(b)-1.

There is an exception to this rule for medical expenses incurred for a decedent's medical care and paid by the estate. The decedent's medical expenses paid by the estate are treated as paid at the time they are incurred and deducted on the return for the year incurred as long as they are paid within one year of the decedent's death. Code Sec. 213(c); Reg. §1.213-1(d). The purpose of this exception is that significant medical expenses might be incurred by a decedent just prior to death and, without the exception, not be deductible on any tax return. Also, if medical expenses of the decedent are paid by a surviving spouse, they are deductible in the year paid. Rev. Rul. 57-310, 1957-2 CB 206. Additionally, medical expenses paid by the executor within one year of the decedent's death may be taken either as a deduction on the estate tax return (Form 706) or the decedent's return for the year incurred (Form 1040). Moreover, it should be taken into consideration in this planning analysis that if the entire medical expense deduction is taken on the decedent's final return, the deduction is subject to the statutory limitation of 7.5 or 10 percent while the limitation is not applicable if the entire deduction is taken on the estate tax return (Form 706).

EXAMPLE 18.4	Medical expenses associated with the final illness of the decedent were $10,000. These expenses were paid by the estate within one year of the decedent's death. On the decedent's final return these expenses will exceed the statutory limitation by $9,000. Assume the marginal tax rate on the decedent's final return is 39.6 percent and the marginal tax rate on the decedent's estate tax return is 40 percent for 2015.

PLANNING POINTER	Deduction of the entire allowable medical expense on the final return will produce a tax savings of $3,564 ($9,000 × 39.6 percent), while deduction of the entire allowable expense on the estate tax return will produce a tax savings of $4,000 ($10,000 × 40 percent).

The decedent taxpayer is entitled to a full standard deduction on a final income tax return regardless of date of death. The standard deduction does not have to be reduced because the decedent did not live for a full 12-month period. Also, the additional amounts to the standard deduction because of blindness or old age are allowed in full regardless of the date of death during the tax year. The same is true for personal exemptions on the final return. That is, the decedent is allowed full personal exemptions on the final return, regardless of date of death.

Income in Respect of the Decedent

If the decedent was entitled to receive income at the date of death but the income was not properly includible on the decedent's final return, normally because the decedent was on the cash basis of accounting, this income is considered to be income in respect of the decedent (IRD). Income in respect of the decedent is included on the income tax return of the estate or beneficiary who is entitled to the payment and actually receives it. Code Sec. 691(a); Reg. §1.691(a)-2. Income in respect of the decedent includes but is not limited to the following items: (1) accrued income of a cash-basis decedent that was not included on the decedent's final return, (2) interest on U.S. savings bonds that has accrued but has not been reported by a cash-basis decedent, (3) dividends on stock declared before the decedent's death but payable after the date of death, (4) interest on savings accounts for cash-basis taxpayers from the last interest payment date up to the date of death, and (5) income that arises solely by reason of death of the decedent. Rev. Rul. 79-340, 1979-2 CB 320. The following examples help to clarify the above items of income in respect of the decedent.

EXAMPLE 18.5	Susan Lewis, a cash-basis taxpayer, dies on November 18. Susan normally receives a paycheck at the end of the month for a full month's work. The paycheck received on November 30 covering the period November 1 to November 18 is income in respect of the decedent and is includible as income by the party receiving it.

EXAMPLE 18.6	Bob Burl purchased U.S. savings bonds in 1986 and still held the bonds at the date of his death. Bob had not previously recognized any interest income on the bonds. The unreported interest income on the bonds is income in respect of the decedent. The estate or beneficiary that receives the bonds can elect to report all prior unreported interest income on its tax return or wait until the bonds mature or are disposed of and report the interest income at that time. If desired, an election can be made by a fiduciary to have the unreported interest income up to the date of the decedent's death included on the decedent's final income tax return. Rev. Rul. 68-145, 1968-1 CB 203. Naturally, this election can be quite valuable if the decedent's income in the final tax year is nominal.
EXAMPLE 18.7	Joan Furrow owned 1,000 shares of Sonic Corporation stock at the date of her death. Sonic declared a dividend on its common stock on November 5 with a record date on November 15 and payment date on November 30. Joan died on November 18. Since she was alive on the date of record but deceased by date of payment, the dividend payment is IRD to the successor in interest. The same result is achieved for either cash-basis or accrual-basis taxpayer.
EXAMPLE 18.8	Patrick Ralls, a cash-basis taxpayer, has a savings account at a local bank that pays and credits interest to accounts on a quarterly basis. Patrick dies on December 12. Interest income from October 1 to December 12, when credited to the account on December 31, is income in respect of the decedent to the estate or beneficiary holding the property at December 31.
EXAMPLE 18.9	Helen Troy, who dies on January 12, has an agreement with her employer that a payment of $20,000 will be made to her estate or designated beneficiary upon Helen's death in lieu of claims to future bonuses, sales commissions, etc. This payment, which arises solely by reason of death of the decedent, is income in respect of the decedent when received by the estate or beneficiary.

The character of income in respect of the decedent is the same to the estate or beneficiary reporting the income as it would have been to the decedent if the decedent had continued to live and report the income on the tax return. Code Sec. 691(a)(3); Reg. §1.691(a)-3.

If an estate or beneficiary includes income in respect of the decedent as income on a tax return, the estate or beneficiary is entitled to an itemized deduction for any federal estate tax paid because the income was also included on the decedent's federal estate tax return. Code Sec. 691(c). This itemized deduction is not subject to the two percent floor that applies to miscellaneous itemized deductions.

Deductions in Respect of the Decedent (DRD)

If a decedent incurred tax deductible expenses before death that were not deductible on the decedent's final return because they were not paid and the decedent was on the cash basis, these expenses are deductible in the year paid by either the estate or the beneficiary. If the estate pays the expenses, they are deductible by the estate in the tax year paid. If a beneficiary has an obligation to pay an expense and pays it, the expense is a proper deduction on the tax return of the beneficiary in the year of payment. Reg. §1.691(b)-1. Also, it is important to note that items are deductible twice. That is, on both the Form 706 return and the Form 1041 return.

Business losses or capital losses incurred by a decedent prior to death end with the decedent's final return. The losses cannot be carried over to years subsequent to the final return. Business losses on the decedent's final return, however, are eligible for the net operating loss carryback and can be carried back to tax returns of prior years. Rev. Rul. 74-175, 1974-1 CB 52. In a community property state only 50 percent of the business or capital losses are nondeductible.

¶18,025   FEDERAL INCOME TAX CONCERNS OF AN ESTATE

The estate of a decedent is a separate taxable entity that comes into existence automatically at the death of an individual. The decedent's tax year ends on the date of death so that the tax year of the estate commences on the following day. Reg. §1.443-1(a)(2). An estate is a separate taxable entity for federal income tax purposes and retains this status until the final distribution of assets held in the estate of the beneficiaries.

The duration of an estate is the period actually required by the fiduciary to perform the ordinary duties of administration (i.e., collection of assets and the payment of debts, taxes, legacies and bequests). Because the estate is a taxable entity separate from the beneficiaries, the fiduciary may attempt to prolong its existence in order to take advantage of the lower tax bracket. That is, whenever beneficiaries of an estate are in higher tax brackets than the estate, substantial tax savings can be achieved by accumulating the estate's income in one year.

¶18,035   FIDUCIARY RESPONSIBILITIES

A fiduciary is a person such as an administrator, trustee, or executor who has been given a special confidence and responsibility to manage property in a trust or estate according to some legal agreement (will, trust agreement) and in the best interests of the beneficiaries of the trust or estate. The main responsibility of a fiduciary of an estate is to wind up the affairs of the decedent, specifically to gather the decedent's assets together, to pay claims against the assets, and to distribute the balance of the assets to the beneficiaries of the estate. A fiduciary of an estate is called an executor if named in the decedent's will, or an administrator if named by a court to settle the decedent's affairs. In some instances, a personal representative of the decedent may assume some fiduciary responsibilities with regard to an estate although not named as an executor or appointed as an administrator.

Payment of Decedent's Tax Liabilities

Included among the duties and responsibilities of a fiduciary of an estate (hereafter referred to as executor) is the responsibility to file any required tax returns and pay any tax liabilities of the decedent or the decedent's estate. Although the executor is required to file tax returns and pay taxes due, the executor ordinarily is not personally liable for the tax payments. The tax payments are made from the assets of the estate. Code Sec. 6903; Reg. §301.6903-1. If, however, the executor is negligent in handling claims against the estate and taxes are not paid, the liability for payment of the taxes extends to the executor. Reg. §1.641(b)-2.

An executor can obtain protection from personal liability for a decedent's taxes by filing Form 4810 (Request for Prompt Assessment) with the IRS after all tax returns have been filed. The request will reduce the normal three-year period within which the IRS must audit a return to eighteen months from the time the request is filed. Code Sec. 6501(d).

PLANNING POINTER   Filing of the request by the executor results in a shorter period for determining the final liability of the estate and can speed up the distribution of estate assets to the beneficiaries. Filing of the request also lessens the chance of an executor inadvertently distributing estate assets to beneficiaries that should have been used to pay the estate's tax liabilities.

¶18,045   ESTATE FEDERAL INCOME TAX RETURN

Each estate that has gross income of $600 or more during a tax year must file an estate income tax return. The appropriate IRS form for the return is Form 1041 (U.S. Fiduciary Income Tax Return). If one or more beneficiaries of an estate are nonresident aliens, a Form 1041 must be filed even if gross income is below $600. Code Sec. 6012(a); Reg. §1.6012-3.

Filing Period

Form 1041 must be filed on or before the fifteenth day of the fourth month following the close of the tax year of the estate. The executor is free to choose the end of an estate's first tax year. The executor is free to choose the same tax year as the decedent or any other year-end. The estate's first income tax return can cover a period less than 12 months. Once an executor chooses an estate's tax year-end on the first tax return, however, all subsequent returns must use the same year-end unless permission is received from the IRS for a change in accounting period.

Exemption

An estate is entitled to a $600 personal exemption on each income tax return except the final income tax return when no personal exemption is allowed. Code Sec. 642(b); Reg. §1.642(b)-1. An executor should carefully consider the choice of an estate's first tax year-end. Careful planning of the estate's tax year-end can result in maximum tax advantage.

EXAMPLE 18.10 The estate of James Johnson was in existence for the period February 1, 2015, through December 31, 2015. The executor chose an estate tax year-end of December 31, 2015. The first return of the estate was also the final return and no $600 exemption was allowed. In order to maximize tax advantage, the executor, in this case, could have chosen an estate tax year-end for the first return of any month-end from February 28, 2015, through November 30, 2015. A $600 personal exemption would then have been available on the first return. The estate's final income tax return would have covered the period from the end of the first return through December 31, 2015. Careful planning of the estate's tax year-end in the second case would have resulted in $600 of the estate's income being free from taxation. A disadvantage of the second case, however, is that two estate income tax returns need to be filed instead of one income tax return as in the first case. On the other hand, the advantage of filing two estate income tax returns instead of one is that the estate income is spread over two returns, thereby possibly lowering the effective marginal tax rate on the income.

Accounting Method

An executor is also free to choose an accounting method (cash or accrual) for an estate on the first income tax return. Subsequent income tax returns must use the same accounting method unless permission is received from the IRS to make a change. An executor should consider very carefully the initial choice of accounting method for an estate since later IRS permission to change the method of accounting may be difficult to obtain.

Estimated Tax

Normally, an executor of an estate is not required to pay estimated taxes. Instead, the full amount of tax liability is due with the tax return. If an estate stays in existence for more than two taxable years, however, it must start to pay estimated tax payments in the third year.

Extension of Time to File Return

An extension of time to file a Form 1041 may be granted to an executor for a justifiable reason. An extension of time to file a return, if granted, does not extend the time for payment of the tax. The tax liability must still be estimated and payments made by the regular due dates.

Tax Rates for Estates

Regular income tax rates for federal estate income tax returns are shown in the Appendix. In addition to regular income tax rates, an estate may also be subject to the alternative minimum tax that was discussed previously in individual income taxes. If the alternative minimum tax computation results in a larger tax due than the regular tax computation, the difference is added to the estate's income tax liability.

Taxation of Trusts

¶18,209 ## NATURE OF TRUSTS

A trust is a legal entity created to hold property. A trustee administers the property according to the dictates of a trust agreement. For income tax purposes, a trust is a separate taxable entity which, like an estate, is entitled to a deduction for income distributions to beneficiaries. The income distributions, in turn, are subject to taxation on the beneficiaries' income tax returns.

Creation of Trusts

As noted earlier, an estate is created automatically. On the other hand, a trust must be specifically created. There are many legal or tax definitions of trusts. That is, trusts may be inter vivos or testamentary, simple or complex. Also, there are trusts that are formed for a specific function, such as alimony trusts, insurance trusts, or charitable trusts. A breakdown of the common working trust terminology follows.

Inter Vivos Trust

An inter vivos trust is a trust created during the lifetime of the grantor.

Testamentary Trust

A testamentary trust is a trust created by the will of a decedent.

Simple Trust

Pursuant to the terms of its governing instrument, a simple trust must: (1) distribute all of its state law income currently, (2) have no charitable beneficiary, and (3) make no distribution from corpus. Code Sec. 651(a)(1) and (2); Reg. §1.651(a)-1.

Complex Trust

A complex trust is a trust that is not a simple trust. The term includes trusts with a charitable beneficiary and trusts that distribute corpus or accumulated income.

Categories of Beneficiaries

Beneficiaries of trusts are divided into two categories: income beneficiaries and remainder beneficiaries. An income beneficiary has an interest in the income of the trust. A remainder beneficiary has an interest in the trust property after an income interest expires. It is possible for one person to be both an income beneficiary and a remainder beneficiary.

EXAMPLE 18.11	John Burlington establishes a trust to provide income to care for his aged mother. Upon death of the mother, the trust agreement provides that the trust corpus will be distributed to James Burlington, John's son. In this trust, John Burlington is the grantor, the aged mother is an income beneficiary, and James Burlington is a remainder beneficiary.

Tax and Nontax Reasons for Creating Trusts

There are a number of tax and nontax reasons an individual might consider creating a trust. Nontax reasons for creating a trust include the following:

1. A trust can be created to protect and conserve property and to provide competent investment management for beneficiaries such as children who are not yet competent to handle their own affairs.
2. A trust can be created to protect and conserve property and to provide competent investment management for beneficiaries who are not interested or inclined to manage the property themselves.
3. A grantor can create a trust and give explicit instructions in a trust agreement as to how the trust property is to be invested and managed. The grantor thereby can have some control over the management of the trust property even though deceased.

EXAMPLE 18.12	John Creek creates a trust and names his aged grandmother as the income beneficiary of the trust for her remaining lifetime. The purpose of the trust is to provide the grandmother with a means of support for the rest of her life. The trustee has the responsibility to manage the affairs of the trust in the best interests of the grandmother according to the dictates of the trust agreement.

Tax reasons for creating a trust include the following:

1. By creating a properly constituted trust for tax purposes, a grantor has created a new tax entity. A separate tax return is prepared for the new tax entity and a new tax rate schedule is used in computing the tax due on the trust income. Trust income is subject to taxation starting at the bottom of a new tax rate schedule. Two taxpayers now exist, the grantor and the trust, and, considering the progressive nature of the federal income tax system, overall income may be subject to a lower effective tax rate.
2. By creating a properly constituted trust for tax purposes, a grantor can effectively shift income from the grantor's tax return to the income tax return of a beneficiary who may be in a lower income tax bracket, thereby lowering the overall effective income tax rate on the income of a family unit.

In some instances, a trust can be created that qualifies as a separate legal entity but that is not a properly constituted trust for federal income tax purposes. The income from a trust of this type is taxable to the grantor instead of to the trust or beneficiaries. For qualification as a properly constituted trust for tax purposes, effective control of the property placed in trust must be relinquished by the grantor. Trusts that do not qualify for recognition as trusts for federal income tax purposes are called grantor trusts.

TAX BLUNDER

A couple had established the trust to operate their farming business and to hold family personal assets. Although they had signed a closing agreement for two prior tax years agreeing that (1) the trust was their alter ego, (2) all assets held in the name of the trust were actually their assets, and (3) all of their income, expenses, deductions and credits would be reported on their individual returns for the years at issue and all subsequent years, they continued to use the trust with fraudulent intent. The taxpayers failed to establish any reasonable cause for their failure to file the returns, and the addition to tax under Code Sec. 6651(a) was sustained.

Additionally, the government established by clear and convincing evidence that the taxpayers understated their federal income tax for two consecutive years with the intent to commit fraud and that the husband failed to file his returns for three other years with the same intent. Therefore, the husband was liable for the Code Sec. 6651(f) addition to tax, and both taxpayers were liable for the fraud penalty under Code Sec. 6663. *J. M. Smoll*, 92 TCM 84.

¶18,215   TRUST FEDERAL INCOME TAX RETURN

Each trust that has gross income of $600 or more during a tax year must file a federal income tax return. The appropriate form for the return is Form 1041 (U.S. Fiduciary Income Tax Return). If one or more beneficiaries of a trust are nonresident aliens or if the trust has taxable income, an income tax return must be filed even if gross income is below $600. Code Sec. 6012(a).

Filing Period

A trust income tax return must be filed on or before the fifteenth day of the fourth month following the close of the tax year of the trust. All trusts, with some minor exceptions, must report income on a calendar-year basis.

Exemption

A simple trust is entitled to a $300 personal-exemption deduction while a complex trust is entitled to a $100 personal-exemption deduction. A full personal exemption can be taken on the first income tax return of a trust even if it covers a period of less than twelve months. No personal exemption is allowed on the final return of a trust.

Accounting Method

A trustee is free to choose an accounting method (cash or accrual) for a trust on the first income tax return. Subsequent income tax returns must use the same accounting method unless permission is received from the IRS to make a change.

PLANNING POINTER   A trustee should consider very carefully the initial choice of accounting method for a trust since later IRS permission to change the method of accounting may be difficult to obtain.

Estimated Tax

A trustee of a trust is required to pay estimated taxes. An extension of time to file a return may be granted to a trustee for a justifiable reason.

Extension of Time to File Return

An extension of time to file a return, if granted, does not extend the time for payment of the tax. The tax liability must still be estimated and payments made by the regular due date.

Tax Rates for Trusts

Regular tax rates for trust income tax returns are shown in the Appendix. In addition to regular income taxes, a trust may also be subject to the alternative minimum tax. If the alternative minimum tax computation results in a larger tax due than the regular tax computation, the difference is added to the trust's income tax liability.

Federal Income Taxation Scheme—Estates and Trusts

¶18,301　## DISTRIBUTABLE NET INCOME (DNI) SYSTEM

Because an estate or trust is a tax-paying entity, double taxation would be imposed if the income previously taxed to the fiduciary was again taxed when distributed to beneficiaries. In order to avoid double taxation, a system was needed to measure the amount and character of income distributed to beneficiaries or retained by an estate or trust. As a result, the concept of distributable net income (DNI) was brought into the Internal Revenue Code.

DNI Concept

In order to make the conduit principle work, a device was required to measure the *amount* of income distributed to beneficiaries or retained by the estate. Also, a measure was needed to determine the *character* of amounts distributed to beneficiaries or retained by the estate or trust. Furthermore, a true conduit approach must identify the items of estate income that are given special treatment elsewhere in the Code, such as capital gains and interest on municipal bonds, and must keep these items separate as they pass out to the estate's or trust's beneficiaries.

An analytical method or technique was required to measure the amount of income distributed and determine the character of amounts distributed. Such a method is supplied in the concept of distributable net income. DNI has three basic functions:

1. It limits the amount of the distribution deduction of the estate and trust.
2. It limits the amount on which beneficiaries can be taxed.
3. It is used to determine the character of amounts retained by an estate or trust and the character of amounts distributed to the beneficiaries. Reg. §1.643(a)-0.

Thus, DNI has been termed the yardstick or measuring rod to be employed in determining, on one hand, the maximum deduction for distributions which may be allowed to the estate or trust and for gauging, on the other hand, the extent to which beneficiaries may be taxable on the distributions.

DNI—Modification of Taxable Income

In order to serve as a measure of the maximum deduction to be allowed to trusts or estates for distributions to beneficiaries (and conversely to determine the amounts includible in the beneficiaries' gross income), taxable income must be modified in several important respects. Code Sec. 643(a) sets out the modifications to taxable income and labels this modified income "distributable net income." DNI is defined as the taxable income of the estate or trust computed with six modifications. (At this juncture, it should be noted that the taxable income of an estate or trust is generally the same as taxable income of an individual, with several exceptions. That is, the main component parts of taxable income are gross income, deductions, charitable contributions, income distribution deduction, and the personal exemption.) The modifications to taxable income for DNI are as follows:

1. No deduction is allowed for amounts distributed or distributable to beneficiaries.
2. No deduction is allowed for personal exemptions—$600 for estates, $300 for simple trusts, and $100 for complex trusts.
3. Gains from the sale or exchange of capital assets are excluded to the extent that they are allocated to corpus and are not paid, credited, or required to be distributed to any beneficiary, or paid or set aside for charities. Capital losses are excluded except to the extent that such losses are taken into account in determining the amount of capital gain to be paid, credited, or required to be distributed to any beneficiary during the taxable year.
4. With respect only to simple trusts, extraordinary dividends and taxable stock dividends are excluded if properly allocated by the trustee in good faith to corpus.
5. Interest that is fully tax-exempt (less nondeductible disbursements allocated to such interest) is included.
6. In the case of foreign trusts, income from sources without the U.S. (less nondeductible disbursements allocable to such income) is included.

¶18,325   DNI COMPUTATIONS—SIMPLE TRUSTS

The rules applicable to a trust required to distribute all of its income currently and to its beneficiaries (that is, a simple trust falling under Code Secs. 651 and 652) may be illustrated in the following manner. Reg. §1.652(c)-4.

EXAMPLE 18.13

Pursuant to the terms of a simple trust all of the income is to be distributed equally to beneficiaries X and Y and capital gains are to be allocated to corpus. The trust and both beneficiaries file returns on the calendar-year basis. No provision is made for depreciation in the governing instrument. Therefore, it will follow income. During the taxable year, the trust had the following items of income and expenses:

Rents	$25,000
Dividends of domestic corporations	50,000
Tax-exempt interest on municipal bonds	25,000
Long-term capital gains	15,000
Taxes and expenses directly attributable to rents	5,000
Trustee's commissions allocable to income account	2,600
Trustee's commissions allocable to principal account	1,300
Depreciation	5,000

Step 1—State Law Income. The state law income (also, called trust accounting income) of the trust for fiduciary accounting purposes is $92,400, computed as follows:

Rents		$25,000
Dividends		50,000
Tax-exempt interest		25,000
		$100,000
Deductions:		
Expenses directly attributable to rent income	$5,000	
Trustee's commissions allocable to income account	2,600	7,600
State law income computed under Code Sec. 643(b)		$92,400

One-half ($46,200) of the income of $92,400 is currently distributable to each beneficiary.

Step 2—Code Sec. 643(a) Ceiling. The distributable net income (income ceiling) of the trust computed under Code Sec. 643(a) is $91,100 determined as follows (cents are disregarded in the computation):

Rents		$25,000
Dividends		50,000
Tax-exempt interest	$25,000	
Less: Expenses allocable thereto ($25,000/$100,000 × $3,900)	975	24,025
Total		$99,025
Deductions:		
Expenses directly attributable to rental income	$5,000	
Trustee's commissions ($3,900 – $975 allocable to tax-exempt interest)	2,925	7,925
Distributable net income as the income ceiling		$91,100

In computing the distributable net income of $91,100, the taxable income of the trust was computed with the following modifications. No deductions were allowed for distributions to the beneficiaries and for a personal exemption of the trust. Code Sec. 643(a)(1) and (2). Capital gains were excluded. Code Sec. 643(a)(3). The tax-exempt interest was included. Code Sec. 643(a)(5).

<table>
<tr><td rowspan="1">EXAMPLE 18.13
CONTINUED</td><td></td></tr>
</table>

EXAMPLE 18.13 CONTINUED

Step 3—Code Sec. 651(a) Ceiling. The deduction ceiling allowable to the trust under Sec. Code 651(a) for distributions to the beneficiaries is $67,075 computed as follows:

Distributable net income computed under Code Sec. 643(a)	$91,100
Less: Tax-exempt interest as adjusted	24,025
Distributable net income (deduction ceiling) as determined under Code Sec. 651(b)	$67,075

Since the amount of the income ($92,400) required to be distributed currently by the trust exceeds the distributable net income ($67,075) as computed under Code Sec. 651(b), the deduction allowable under Code Sec. 651(a) is limited to the distributable net income of $67,075.

Step 4—Trust's Income. The taxable income of the trust is $14,700 computed as follows:

Rents		$25,000
Dividends		50,000
Long-term capital gains		15,000
Gross income		$90,000
Deductions: Rental expenses	$5,000	
Trustee's commissions	2,925	
Distributions to beneficiaries	67,075	
Personal exemption for a simple trust	300	75,300
Taxable income		$14,700

The trust is not allowed a deduction for the portion ($975) of the trustee's commissions allocable to tax-exempt interest in computing its taxable income.

Also, it should be noted that a simple trust which is allocating capital gains to corpus can perform a supplemental calculation to check its taxable income. For example, in the above calculation the trust's taxable income was $14,700; this could have been figured as follows:

Capital gains	$15,000
Less: Personal exemption	300
Taxable income	$14,700

Step 5—Inclusion and Characterization to Beneficiaries. In determining the character of the amounts includible in the gross income of X and Y, it is assumed that the trustee elects to allocate to rents the expenses not directly attributable to a specific item of income, other than the portion ($975) of such expenses allocated to tax-exempt interest.

The allocation of expenses among the items of income, as required by Sec. 652(b), is shown below:

	Rents	Dividends	Tax-exempt Interest	Total
Income for trust accounting purposes	$25,000	$50,000	$25,000	$100,000
Less:				
Rental expenses	5,000	0	0	5,000
Trustee's commissions	2,925	0	975	3,900
Total deductions	7,925	0	975	8,900
Character of amounts in the hands of the beneficiaries	$17,075	$50,000	$24,025	$91,100

Inasmuch as the income of the trust is to be distributed equally to X and Y, each is deemed to have received one-half of each item of income: that is, rents of $8,537.50, dividends of $25,000; and tax-exempt interest of $12,012.50. The dividends of $25,000 allocated to each beneficiary are to be aggregated with the beneficiary's other dividends.

Additionally, each beneficiary is allowed a deduction of $2,500 for depreciation of rental property attributable to the portion (one-half) of the income of the trust distributed to each beneficiary. If depreciation had been a charge against income and consequently required a reserve, then it should have appeared at Step 1 reducing state law or trust accounting income, Step 2 reducing DNI as an income ceiling, Step 4 as a deduction to the trust in computing its taxable income, and at Step 5 as a reduction to rental income. Note, of course, that the beneficiaries are responsible for only $91,100 of DNI while, in fact, $92,400 has been distributed to them.

¶18,331 DEPRECIATION AND DEPLETION DEDUCTIONS

Either an estate or trust may be entitled to depreciation and depletion deductions if it holds qualified property.

Rules for Estates

Even though an estate may be allowed a depreciation or depletion deduction, it must be recognized that this is a residual claim to these deductions. For an estate, the allowable deduction for depreciation and/or depletion must be apportioned between the estate and the heirs, legatees, and devisees on the basis of income of the estate which is allocable to each. Reg. §§1.167(h)-1(c) and 1.611-1(c)(5).

Rules for Trusts

Trusts are permitted greater flexibility than estates in receiving depreciation and depletion deductions. For instance, if property is held in trust, the depreciation or depletion deductions are to be apportioned between the income beneficiaries and the trust on the basis of the trust income allocable to each. However, if the governing instrument (or local law) requires or permits the trustee to maintain a reserve for depreciation in any amounts, then the deduction is first allocated to the trust to the extent that income is set aside for a depreciation reserve. Any part of the deduction in excess of this amount set aside for the reserve is apportioned between the income beneficiaries and the trust on the basis of the trust income allocable to each. Reg. §§1.167(h)-1(b) and 1.611-1(c)(4).

EXAMPLE 18.14

Melford Brock creates a trust, with his son, Bob, and his daughter, Nina, as income beneficiaries, by the transfer of income producing depreciable property. Pursuant to the terms of the trust instrument, the income from the trust is to be distributed annually on a 70 percent basis to Bob and 30 percent to Nina. Additionally, the trustee is permitted to set aside income as a depreciation reserve. In the current year, depreciation on the trust property amounts to $10,000, and the trustee allocates $5,000 of trust income as a depreciation reserve. As a result, the trust can claim $5,000 as a depreciation deduction, Bob can claim $3,500 ($10,000 – $5,000 × 70%)) and Nina can claim $1,500 ($10,000 – $5,000 × 30%)).

¶18,345 DNI COMPUTATIONS—COMPLEX TRUSTS AND ESTATES

In the case of a simple trust, the basic issue was the allocation of income between the trust and the beneficiaries. However, the problem of allocation among the beneficiaries will become more prominent with the complex trust and estate. Even though the complex trust and estate are taxed in substantially the same manner as a simple trust, nonetheless, some complications arise from the tier system and charitable contributions.

Tier System

There is a two-tier system of priorities (affecting DNI) that characterize the amounts distributed to beneficiaries as either income or corpus. This system provides: (1) *first tier*—income required to be distributed currently including annuity payments out of income, and (2) *second tier*—all other amounts properly paid, credited, or required to be distributed. Code Secs. 662(a)(1) and (2). This includes (a) current income that the trustee was not required to distribute; (b) accumulated income; and (c) corpus.

As a result of the system's hierarchy, the first tier has a priority on using up DNI. If the first-tier payments do not exhaust the ceiling amount of DNI, then any balance of DNI will affect the taxability of all other distributions that fall into the second tier.

EXAMPLE 18.15

In 2015, a trust is required to pay $20,000 out of income each year to Fred. Also, the trustee in his discretion may distribute to Joe an amount for his well being. This year the trust pays Joe $15,000. The DNI of the trust is $30,000. Thus, the tier system allocates $20,000 taxable income to Fred as a first-tier beneficiary, and $10,000 taxable income to Joe as a second-tier beneficiary. The other $5,000 distributed to Joe would be a tax-free return of corpus.

First-Tier Distributions in Excess of DNI

Whenever the amount of income required to be distributed currently to all beneficiaries (first tier) exceeds DNI, the amount includible in the beneficiary's gross income is computed as follows. Reg. §1.662(a)-2.

$$\frac{\text{Amount of income required to be distributed currently to first-tier beneficiary}}{\text{Amount of income required to be distributed currently to all first-tier beneficiaries}} \times \begin{array}{c}\text{Distributable net income} \\ \text{(computed without} \\ \text{deduction for charitable} \\ \text{contributions)}\end{array} = \begin{array}{c}\text{Amount beneficiary includes} \\ \text{in gross income}\end{array}$$

EXAMPLE 18.16   A trust has $50,000 of DNI in the current year. The trustee is required by the instrument to distribute $30,000 each year to both the wife and daughter of the deceased. By utilizing the above formula, the wife and daughter would each have $25,000 from DNI and $5,000 from corpus ($30,000/$60,000 × $50,000 = $25,000).

First- and Second-Tier Distributions in Excess of DNI

In the event that first-tier distributions do not exhaust DNI, then beneficiaries may be taxed as second-tier distributions. Furthermore, if both first- and second-tier distributions exceed DNI, then another allocation formula is necessary to determine the amount that a beneficiary will be taxed on. This formula is as follows (Reg. §1.662(a)-3):

$$\frac{\text{Second-tier distributions to the beneficiary}}{\text{Second-tier distributions to all beneficiaries}} \times \begin{array}{c}\text{Distributable net income} \\ \text{(less first-tier distributions} \\ \text{and charitable contributions)}\end{array} = \begin{array}{c}\text{Beneficiary's share of} \\ \text{distributable net income}\end{array}$$

EXAMPLE 18.17   A trust has $60,000 of DNI in 2015. The fiduciary is required to distribute $40,000 each year to Mary, the surviving spouse. However, at the fiduciary's discretion, amounts may be distributed to Bob and Donna, the son and daughter of the deceased, based on their health and education needs.

During the current year, the trustee distributed $40,000 to Mary, $20,000 to Bob, and $20,000 to Donna. The beneficiaries' taxable amounts are computed as follows:

Step 1—DNI	$60,000
Less: First tier	40,000
Available for second tier	$20,000
Step 2—$20,000/$40,000 × $20,000	$10,000

Thus, Mary is taxed on $40,000, and Bob and Donna are taxed on $10,000 each. However, the other $10,000 is tax free to Bob and Donna.

Planning for Types of Distributed Income

The character of distributed income in the hands of the estate or trust is the same as its character in the hands of the beneficiaries. Tax-exempt income to the estate or trust is also tax-exempt income to the beneficiaries when distributed. Capital gains and losses and ordinary income items to the estate or trust retain the same character when distributed to the beneficiaries. If a decedent's will directs that certain types of estate income be distributed to certain beneficiaries (e.g., "My son receives tax-exempt income, my daughter receives taxable income, etc."), the dictates of the will are followed in determining the taxability of estate income distributions to the beneficiaries. Code Secs. 652(b) and 662(b). If a will does not direct that income be distributed in specified ways, then all the beneficiaries share in the different types of income in proportion to the total estate income.

EXAMPLE 18.18	The executor of an estate distributes $10,000 of estate income to two beneficiaries. The distributed income consists of $6,000 of tax-exempt interest and $4,000 of taxable income. One beneficiary is entitled to 75 percent of the income; the other beneficiary is entitled to 25 percent of the income. The decedent's will does not specify the type of income to be distributed to either beneficiary. Accordingly, the 75 percent beneficiary is assumed to have received 75 percent of both types of income ($4,500 tax-exempt interest and $3,000 taxable income) while the 25 percent beneficiary is assumed to have received 25 percent of both types of income ($1,500 tax-exempt interest and $1,000 taxable income).

PLANNING POINTER	In drafting a will or trust instrument consideration should be given to the possible tax advantages of directing distributions of certain types of income to specified beneficiaries based on the character of the income. Thus, directing distributions of tax-exempt income to high tax bracket beneficiaries while directing distributions of taxable income to low tax bracket beneficiaries could result in an overall tax advantage to a family unit.

¶18,357 CHARITABLE CONTRIBUTIONS—COMPLEX TRUSTS AND ESTATES

Charitable contributions are deductible on an estate or complex trust income tax return and are not limited to a percentage of income as applicable to individuals. The instrument must indicate, however, that contributions are payable out of income before a charitable contribution can be taken. If a trust makes a charitable contribution, it is, by definition, a complex trust since simple trusts are required to distribute all income currently and cannot set aside any amount for charitable contributions. Any charitable contribution made out of tax-exempt income is not deductible on a trust or estate income tax return. If a trust or estate has both taxable and tax-exempt income and there is no designation in the will or trust agreement regarding which income was used for the contribution, the contribution is assumed to have come from all classes of income in relative proportion to the size of the contribution.

TAX BLUNDER

Taxpayers have found that whether amounts will be allowed to be claimed as charitable contributions by an estate or trust under Code Sec. 642(c) depends upon the wording of the will or trust instrument. In this respect, the courts have been strict in interpreting an intent to pay or set aside income for charitable contributions.

The taxpayer, an estate, was not allowed to deduct undistributed corporate income as a charitable contribution. Specifically, the income in question never really vested in the residuary estate so it was not permanently set aside or properly designated to be used for charitable purposes. *S. W. Richardson Foundation*, CA-5, 70-2 ustc ¶9483, 430 F.2d 710; *Riggs National Bank of Washington, D.C.*, 65-2 ustc ¶9728, 173 CtCls 479. Always check the governing instrument to see if an estate or trust is permitted to make charitable contributions.

EXAMPLE 18.19	A charitable contribution of $10,000 is made by a trust to Middleburg University. The trust agreement does not designate the specific income that should be used for the contribution. The trust has $20,000 of taxable income and $30,000 of tax-exempt income. A charitable contribution of $4,000 ($10,000 × $20,000/$50,000) is considered to have come from taxable income. The remaining charitable contribution of $6,000 ($10,000 × $30,000/$50,000) is considered to have come from tax-exempt income and is not deductible.

PLANNING POINTER	In structuring a trust agreement, consideration should be given to indicating that planned charitable contributions come from specific types of taxable income, thereby increasing the size of the charitable contribution deduction allowable to the estate or trust on the Form 1041 Income tax return.

The computational rules of charitable deductions may be exemplified by the following fact situation. Reg. §1.662(c)-4.

EXAMPLE 18.20	Under the terms of a testamentary trust, one-half of the trust income is to be distributed currently to W, the decedent's wife, for life. The remaining trust income may, in the trustee's discretion, either be paid to D, the grantor's daughter, paid to designated charities, or accumulated. The trust is to terminate at the death of W and the principal will then be payable to D.

No provision is made in the trust instrument or under local law with respect to depreciation of rental property. Therefore, depreciation will follow income. Capital gains are allocable to corpus under the applicable local law. The trust and both beneficiaries file returns on the calendar-year basis.

The records of the fiduciary show the following items of income and deduction for the taxable year:

Rents	$50,000
Dividends of domestic corporations	50,000
Tax-exempt interest	20,000
Taxable interest	10,000
Capital gains (long-term)	20,000
Depreciation of rental property	10,000
Expenses attributable to rental income	15,400
Trustee's commissions allocable to income account	2,800
Trustee's commissions allocable to principal account	1,100

Step 1—State Law Income. The state law income of the trust for fiduciary accounting purposes is $111,800, computed as follows:

Rents		$50,000
Dividends		50,000
Tax-exempt interest		20,000
Taxable interest		10,000
Total		$130,000

Deductions:		
Rental expenses	$15,400	
Trustee's commissions allocable to income account	2,800	18,200
Income as computed under Code Sec. 643(b)		$111,800

(Note that depreciation and long-term capital gain are not included.)

The trustee distributed one-half of the state law income ($55,900) to W and, in his discretion, makes a contribution of one-quarter ($27,950) to charity X and distributes the remaining one-quarter ($27,950) to D. The total of the distributions to beneficiaries is $83,850, consisting of (1) income required to be distributed currently to W of $55,900 and (2) other amounts properly paid or credited to D of $27,950.

Step 2—Code Sec. 643(a) Ceiling. The distributable net income of the trust as computed under Code Sec. 643(a) is $82,750, determined as follows:

Rents			$50,000
Dividends			50,000
Taxable interest			10,000
Tax-exempt interest		$20,000	
Less: Trustee's commissions allocable to tax-exempt interest ($20,000/$130,000 of $3,900)	$600		
Charitable contributions allocable to tax-exempt interest ($20,000/$130,000 of $27,950)	4,300	4,900	15,100
Total			$125,100

EXAMPLE 18.20 CONTINUED

Deductions:		
Rental expenses	$15,400	
Trustee's commissions	3,300	
($3,900 – $600 allocated to tax-exempt interest)		
Charitable deduction	23,650	42,350
($27,950 – $4,300 attributable to tax-exempt interest)		
Distributable net income		$82,750

In computing the distributable net income of $82,750, the taxable income of the trust was computed with the following modifications. No deductions were allowed for distributions to beneficiaries and for the personal exemption of the trust. Code Sec. 643(a)(1) and (2). Capital gains were excluded. Code Sec. 643(a)(3). The tax-exempt interest (as adjusted for expenses and charitable contributions) was included. Code Sec. 643(a)(5).

Step 3—Code Sec. 661(a) Ceiling. The distributable net income of $82,750, as determined under Code Sec. 643(a), is less than the sum of the amounts distributed to W and D of $83,850. Therefore, the deduction allowable to the trust under Code Sec. 661(a) is such distributable net income as modified under Code Sec. 661(c) to exclude therefrom the items of income not included in gross income of the trust. The following computation shows the effects:

Distributable net income	$82,750
Less: Tax-exempt interest (as adjusted for expenses and the charitable contributions)	15,100
Deduction allowable under Code Sec. 661(a)	$67,650

Step 4—Trust's Income. The taxable income of the trust is $19,900, determined as follows:

Rent Income		$ 50,000
Dividends		50,000
Taxable interest		10,000
Capital gains		20,000
Gross income		$130,000
Deductions:		
Rental expenses	$15,400	
Trustee's commissions	3,300	
Charitable contributions	23,650	
Distributions to beneficiaries	67,650	
Personal exemption	100	$110,100
Taxable Income		$19,900

Step 5—Inclusion and Characterization to Beneficiaries. For the purpose of determining the character of the amounts deductible under Code Secs. 642(c) and 661(a), the trustee elected to offset the trustee's commissions (other than the portion required to be allocated to tax-exempt interest) against the rental income. The determination of the character of the amounts deemed distributed to beneficiaries and contributed to charity is made as follows:

Character of Amounts Distributed to Beneficiaries and Contributed to Charity Under Code Sec. 661(a)

	Rents	Taxable Dividends	Tax-Exempt Interest	Taxable Interest	Total
Trust income	$50,000	$50,000	$20,000	$10,000	$130,000
Less:					
Charitable contributions	10,750	10,750	4,300	2,150	27,950
Rental expenses	15,400				15,400
Trustee's commissions	3,300		600		3,900
Total deductions	$29,450	$10,750	$4,900	$2,150	$47,250
Amounts distributable to beneficiaries	$20,550	$39,250	$15,100	$7,850	$82,750

EXAMPLE 18.20 CONTINUED

The character of the charitable contribution is determined by multiplying the total charitable contribution ($27,950) by a fraction consisting of each item of trust income, respectively, over the total trust income, except that no part of the dividends excluded from gross income is deemed included in the charitable contribution. For example, the charitable contribution is deemed to consist of rents of $10,750 ($50,000/$130,000 × $27,950).

Because the wife is a first-tier beneficiary and DNI is $82,750, the whole $55,900 is fully includible in her income. Thus, the character of the $55,900 is determined as follows:

$$\frac{\text{Total each class}}{\text{Total DNI}} \times \text{Includible amount}$$

					K-1 Amounts
Rents	$\dfrac{\$20,550}{\$82,750}$	×	$55,900	=	$13,882
Dividends	$\dfrac{\$39,250}{\$82,750}$	×	$55,900	=	26,515
Taxable interest	$\dfrac{\$7,850}{\$82,750}$	×	$55,900	=	5,303
Tax-exempt interest	$\dfrac{\$15,100}{\$82,750}$	×	$55,900	=	10,200
Total					$55,900

Additionally, she may deduct a share of the depreciation deduction proportionate to the trust income allocable to her; that is, one-half of the total depreciation deduction, or $5,000.

Since the sum of the amount of income required to be distributed currently to W ($55,900) and the other amounts properly paid, credited, or required to be distributed to D ($27,950) exceeds the distributable net income ($82,750) of the trust as determined under Code Sec. 643(a), D is deemed to have received $26,850 ($82,750 – $55,900) for income tax purposes. The character of the amounts deemed distributed to her is determined as follows:

					K-1 Amounts
Rents	$\dfrac{\$20,550}{\$82,750}$	×	$26,850	=	$6,668
Dividends	$\dfrac{\$39,250}{\$82,750}$	×	$26,850	=	12,735
Taxable interest	$\dfrac{\$7,850}{\$82,750}$	×	$26,850	=	2,547
Tax-exempt interest	$\dfrac{\$15,100}{\$82,750}$	×	$26,850	=	4,900
Total					$26,850

Also, D may deduct a share of the depreciation deduction proportionate to the trust income allocable to her; that is, one-fourth of the total depreciation deduction, or $2,500.

PLANNING POINTER

If no provision is made in the trust instrument with respect to depreciation, the depreciation deduction may be allocated to the amount distributed to the designated charity, and, as a result, be nondeductible by the trust or beneficiaries. Thus, tax planners would be well-advised to make sure that depreciation does not follow income. This can be easily accomplished by a trust because the trust instrument can create a reserve for depreciation and depletion deductions to the remainder beneficiaries and avoid any wastage problem.

¶18,365 TAX RETURN SPECIAL RULES

Tax Return Schedules

A fiduciary is required to file a Schedule K-1, Form 1041, trust or estate income tax return, for each beneficiary who receives an income distribution during the trust's or estate's tax year. Schedule K-1 gives information applicable to beneficiaries on how trust or estate income distributions affect their individual income tax returns. The fiduciary should furnish a copy of Schedule K-1 to each beneficiary who received a distribution during the year from an estate or trust. Beneficiaries of an estate or trust must file their returns in a manner consistent with the manner reported on the trust or estate's return or must file a notice of inconsistent treatment with the Secretary of the Treasury that identifies the inconsistent items.

Tax Credits

With some exceptions, estates and trusts are allowed the same tax credits as individual taxpayers. Tax credits of an estate or trust are allocated between the fiduciary and beneficiaries based on the amount of income distributed in relation to total state law income. Estates or trusts are not allowed to take the credit for the elderly or the earned income credit. Code Sec. 642(a) and (b).

Miscellaneous Deductions

The two percent floor imposed on miscellaneous itemized deductions for individuals also applies to estates and trusts with some exceptions. The two percent floor does not apply to the income distribution deductions.

Administration Fees

Reasonable expenditures for administering the estate, including executor fees, are deductible; but if these expenditures are deducted on the estate's estate tax return (Form 706), they cannot also be deducted on the estate's income tax return (Form 1041). If the executor of the estate claims administrative expenses as an income tax deduction, a waiver of right to an estate tax deduction must be filed with the income tax return. Code Sec. 642(g); Reg. §1.642(g)-1.

TAX BLUNDER

The Rudkin testamentary trust was established in 1967. The trustee engaged Warfield Associates, Inc., to provide investment management services for the trust. During the tax year 2000, Warfield Associates was paid $22,241 for its services. A Form 1041, U.S. Income Tax Return for Estates and Trusts, for 2000 was filed by the trust in which it reported that it had $624,816 in total income. The Form 1041 also reported a deduction of $22,241 on the line in the form for "other deductions not subject to the 2 percent floor." The trust reported that as investment management fees. The IRS issued a deficiency notice in the amount of $4,448 for 2000, disallowing in full the deduction of $22,241 in investment fees. Instead, the IRS allowed a deduction subject to the 2 percent floor.

In the instant case, the Tax Court sided with the positions taken by both the Federal and Fourth Circuits. *Rudkin Testamentary Trust*, 124 TC 304 (2005). Also, the Supreme Court on January 16, 2008 affirmed the Tax Court decision in *Rudkin*, 2008-1 USTC ¶50,132.

Caveat: Advisory fees paid by a trust are deductible only to the extent that they exceed 2 percent of the trust's adjusted gross income.

PLANNING POINTER

> The executor of the estate has to make an appropriate decision as to where the administrative expenses deduction has the greatest tax advantage to the estate, on the income tax return or on the estate tax return.

¶18,371 ALTERNATIVE MINIMUM TAX

For estates and trusts, the alternative minimum tax (AMT) may apply as an addition to the regular tax for a taxable year. That is, the alternative minimum taxable income (AMTI) of the entity and any beneficiary is determined by applying Subchapter J with modifications. Code Sec. 59(c). Specifically, these modifications are termed adjustments and preferences. Common adjustments to the AMTI are miscellaneous itemized deductions, state and local income taxes, real property taxes, accelerated depreciation for property placed in service after 1986, and passive activity losses. In addition to the adjustments, preferences will also affect the AMTI. Common preferences are tax-exempt interest from private activity bonds, depletion in excess of basis, accelerated depreciation of property placed in service before 1987, and intangible drilling costs.

After calculating the alternative minimum taxable income, there still remains one final adjustment. That is, the Code provides an exemption of $23,800 for estates and trusts. Code Sec. 55(d)(1)(C)(ii). The exemption will be reduced by 25 cents per $1.00 of AMTI exceeding $79,450. Estates and trusts are subject to a two-tiered graduated rate schedule. That is, a 26 percent rate applies for the first $185,400 of AMTI in excess of the exemption amount and 28 percent for the balance of AMTI.

EXAMPLE 18.21

The income tax return of John Henry's estate showed no regular tax liability. However, the estate did generate AMTI of $20,000. The use of the exemption will prevent the AMT from generating a tax liability.

EXAMPLE 18.22

Assume that John Henry's fiduciary return shows AMTI of $102,850. Because the AMTI exceeds $79,450, the exemption is reduced to $17,950 ($23,800 – (($102,850 – $79,450) × .25)).

The estate or trust must pay the higher of the tentative minimum tax or the regular tax. The following illustration describes in detail an application of the AMT.

EXAMPLE 18.23

In 2015, the John Henry estate had rental income of $200,000 and $40,000 of bonus income related to the deceased, John Henry. The estate had a MACRS depreciation deduction of $24,000, while depreciation for AMT purposes was $12,000. The trust incurred fiduciary fees of $18,000 and state fiduciary income taxes of $25,000. Also, the estate had a Code Sec. 691(c) trust tax deduction of $7,000. The fiduciary distributed $28,000 to the income beneficiary, Vivian Elmore, in 2015. For 2015, the trust's federal tax liability is calculated as follows:

	Regular Tax	AMT
Rental income	$200,000	$200,000
Bonus IRD	40,000	40,000
Depreciation	(24,000)	(12,000)
Fiduciary fees	(18,000)	(18,000)
State income tax	(25,000)	0
Code Sec. 691(c) trust tax deduction	(7,000)	(7,000)
Income distribution	(28,000)	(28,000)
Tax exemption	(600)	0
Regular taxable income	$137,400	
AMTI		$175,000
AMT exemption: $23,800 – ($175,000 – $79,450) × .25)		0
Taxable amount	$137,400	$175,000
Income tax liability	$ 52,719	
Tentative Minimum Tax		$45,500

The estate must pay $52,719 in taxes, which is the greater of the regular tax or the tentative minimum tax.

¶18,373   GIFTS, LEGACIES, AND BEQUESTS

In general, any distribution to a beneficiary by an estate or trust is treated as made out of income to the extent that the trust or estate has distributable net income. However, if amounts are properly paid or credited as gifts or bequests under the terms of the governing instrument and thus fall within the protection of Code Sec. 663(a), the distribution will not be taxed as a distribution under Code Sec. 661(a) or 662(a). That is, the amount will not be deductible by the trust nor will it be includible by the recipient. Such amounts will be received tax free under the gift exemption of Code Sec. 102.

Prior to the 1954 Code, the executor or trustee could designate the source of distribution as principal and thereby immunize the distribution. But, under the distributable net income approach adopted in the 1954 Code and continued in the 1986 Code, the distribution is taxed as income up to the extent of distributable net income regardless of the trustee's or executor's designation.

EXAMPLE 18.24

Assume that a will left equal one-third shares to a husband and two children. The estate contains $1,800,000 in securities and a house. In the first year, the estate has income of $240,000 and makes a partial distribution of the house, worth $360,000, to the widower. Under these facts, the widower has taxable income of $240,000, and, as a consequence, he is bearing a substantially disproportionate tax burden in relation to the other heirs.

Lump-Sum or Installment Payouts

In order to alleviate the inordinate tax problem (as illustrated above), that an ordinary estate distribution of corpus could cause, the Code embodies exemptions for specific legacies. The Code provision is based on the standard gift exclusion reasoning that distinguishes between gifts of corpus and gifts of income. It is, of course, traditional to say that a gift of corpus should be nontaxable to the recipient. However, this concept was redefined to require, in addition, that the gift be specific and practically lump-sum in payout (only three installments are permitted). Code Sec. 663(a).

Sixty-Five Day Rule

A fiduciary of a complex trust may elect to treat any amount or portion thereof that is properly paid or credited to a beneficiary within the first 65 days following the close of the taxable year as an amount that was properly paid or credited on the last day of that taxable year. Code Sec. 663(b). A decedent's estate may elect to treat distributions made within 65 days after the close of its tax year as if they were made on the last day of the tax year. Thus, the same income tax rule applicable to trusts is now applicable to estates.

Under the 65-day rule, distributions cannot exceed the greater of the trust accounting income for the year of election, or the trust's distributable net income for the year. Also, the limitation is reduced by distributions in the election year except those amounts for which the election was claimed in the prior tax year. Reg. §1.663(b)-1(a)(2)(i).

Separate Share Rule

Solely for the purposes of determining the amount of DNI of a trust that is allocable to a particular beneficiary, substantially separate shares of different beneficiaries in the trust are treated as separate trusts. Code Sec. 663(c). The separate share rule is a very beneficial exception to the normal taxing rules of a trust. That is, when determining the amount taxable to beneficiaries, allocation by tiers may work an injustice when a trust is administered in substantially separate shares. Consider carefully the following illustration.

EXAMPLE 18.25

Assume that a trust has two beneficiaries, Bob and Sally, and DNI of $50,000. The trustee makes a mandatory distribution of one-half this amount, or $25,000 to Bob. The trustee accumulates the other $25,000, for future distribution to Sally. Also, the fiduciary made a discretionary distribution of $20,000 from corpus to Bob. Under the tier system, Bob would be taxed on the entire $45,000 of DNI. Is this result reasonable or equitable? That is, Bob's tax is measured, in part, by $20,000 of income that can only go to Sally and will never be available for Bob.

In order to alleviate the tax problem depicted in the example above, the separate share rule was brought into the Internal Revenue Code. Therefore, in the above example, only $25,000 of DNI would be allocated to Bob and the rest would stay with the trust (Sally's share). However, the separate share rule is only allowed when the fiduciary has no discretion to allocate between beneficiaries. With respect to decedents dying after August 5, 1997, if under a decedent's will and applicable state law, separate economic interests are created in one beneficiary or class of beneficiaries that are not affected by economic interests accruing to other beneficiaries or classes of beneficiaries, the separate share rule will apply to the decedent's estate. According to the House Committee Report, application of the separate share rule to an estate is not elective (such treatment is mandatory if separate shares exist).

¶18,381 PROPERTY DISTRIBUTIONS

In-kind distributions require, at the fiduciary's election, either recognition of gain or a carryover basis. Code Sec. 643(e). The beneficiary's basis in property received in an in-kind distribution is the adjusted basis of the property in the hands of the estate or trust, increased by any gain and decreased by any loss recognized on the distribution. If no election is made, no gain or loss is recognized, but the amount deductible by the fiduciary and taken into income by the beneficiary as a distribution of DNI is limited to the lesser of the basis or the fair market value of the property. Code Sec. 643(e)(2). As a result, the beneficiary receives a carryover basis.

EXAMPLE 18.26 A trust distributes an asset with a fair market value of $20,000 and a basis of $14,000. That year it has $20,000 of DNI. Under the old rules, the distributee would have $20,000 of ordinary income and a basis of $20,000 in the asset. Under the present rules, the distribution would carry out only $14,000 of ordinary income to the beneficiary, leaving $6,000 of ordinary income to be taxed to the fiduciary, and the beneficiary would only receive a basis of $14,000.

When the fiduciary elects, the estate or trust may treat gain property as if it were sold to the distributee at its fair market value. Code Sec. 643(e)(3)(A)(iii). Nevertheless, a loss may not be recognized by a trust because recognition of losses on sales between a trust and its beneficiary are disallowed. Code Sec. 267(b)(6). An estate and a beneficiary of an estate are treated as related persons for purposes of the disallowance of a loss on the sale of an asset to a related person under Code Sec. 267 and the disallowance of capital gain treatment on the sale of depreciable property to a related person under Code Sec. 1239.

¶18,387 TERMINATION OF ESTATE OR TRUST

The termination of an estate or trust is marked by the end of the period of administration by the fiduciary and the distribution of assets to beneficiaries. At this juncture, even an insolvent estate or trust can pass out valuable tax attributes to beneficiaries. That is, in the year of termination, net operating losses, capital losses, and excess deductions of an estate or trust may be utilized by beneficiaries on their own tax returns.

PLANNING POINTER It should be noted that net operating losses and capital losses that flow out to the beneficiaries may be carried forward by beneficiaries when they are not used in the year of receipt. However, excess deductions may only be used in the year of receipt with no carryforward. Also, excess deductions are subject to the two percent of AGI floor. As a result, it is important to plan for the year of termination in order to have enough AGI to absorb the deductions.

KEYSTONE PROBLEM

Jason Argonaut died on October 16, 2015. His widow, Rita, is a personal friend of yours and knows that you are taking a college taxation course. She is seeking tax advice on the tax problems associated with Jason's death. In the past, Jason and Rita filed a joint return on the cash basis of accounting with a calendar year-end. Jason left a will and a substantial estate. Rita and Jason had no children, and Rita is the sole beneficiary of the estate. Rita has listed the following tax concerns about which she is seeking advice from you and another friend, Robert, a lawyer, who has been named executor of the estate. Rita has a substantial current yearly income of her own and is very concerned about high rates of taxation. What tax advice would you give Rita on the following questions?

1. Jason received a paycheck on October 21, 2015, covering the work period September 16–October 16, 2015. The executor of the estate cashed the check and the proceeds are currently in the estate. How will this income be recognized for tax purposes?
2. What filing status will Rita use when preparing her 2015 income tax return? What about personal exemptions, standard deduction, tax forms, etc.?
3. Rita received a dividend check on October 31, 2015, made out in Jason's name on stock he held in his own name. The dividend had been declared on September 11, 2015 to be paid on October 30, 2015 to shareholders of record on September 30, 2015. How will this dividend income be recognized for tax purposes?
4. It is anticipated that the estate will receive significant amounts of income. Who will pay tax on this income? What are some tax planning ideas that can be used by the estate to lessen the overall income tax burden on the estate and, ultimately, on Rita, the only beneficiary of the estate?

Taxation of Trusts—Special Rules

As stated previously, the scheme of federal income taxation of a trust is to have trust income taxed once, either directly to the trust or to trust beneficiaries who have received distributions from the trust. This scheme of income taxation for trusts is simple in theory but, in practice, has resulted in the development of some tax avoidance techniques involving multiple trusts, grantor trusts, and accumulation distributions. These tax avoidance techniques, along with tax legislation and IRS regulations adopted to counteract them, are discussed in this section.

¶18,503

MULTIPLE TRUSTS

A person may create more than one trust for the same or different beneficiaries. If the multiple trusts are recognized as valid for tax purposes, each trust is allowed a separate personal exemption and is taxed on its separate income. Whether multiple trusts have been created is a question of grantor intent as determined from the trust agreement. Tax avoidance motives could enter into the establishment of multiple trusts. Instead of having one trust taxed on a specified amount of income, why not create 10 trusts and have one-tenth of the income taxed to each trust? The obvious tax advantages of having 10 trusts would be 10 personal exemptions plus each trust starting over at the bottom of the tax rate schedule with its income and thereby mitigating the effects of a progressive tax system. However, multiple trusts are treated as a single trust for tax purposes if the trusts have the same grantor and similar beneficiaries, if there is no independent purpose for each trust, and if avoidance of the progressive rate of income tax or the alternative minimum tax appears to be the main reason why the multiple trusts were created. Code Sec. 643(e).

¶18,525

GRANTOR TRUSTS

In some instances, a trust can be created that qualifies as a separate legal entity but that is not a properly constituted trust for federal income tax purposes. The income from a trust of this type is taxable to the grantor instead of to the trust or beneficiaries. For qualification as a properly constituted trust for tax purposes, control of the property placed in trust must be relinquished by the grantor. Trusts that do not qualify for recognition as trusts for federal income tax purposes are called grantor trusts. A trust is usually classified as a grantor trust if the grantor or grantor's spouse owns an interest in the trust at any time or has certain proscribed powers over the trust.

Reversionary Interest

The grantor is taxed on the income from property placed in trust if it reasonably is expected that the trust property will revert to the grantor or grantor's spouse at anytime. This rule does not apply if the trust assets revert to the grantor or grantor's spouse only after the death of an income beneficiary of the trust who is a lineal descendant of the grantor or the grantor retains less than a five percent reversionary interest in the trust corpus.

Revocable Trust

If a grantor creates a trust and retains the right to revoke the trust, the trust income is taxable to the grantor. Code Sec. 676(a).

Income for Benefit of Grantor

If, at the discretion of the grantor, trust income can be distributed to the grantor or held for future distribution to the grantor, the trust income is taxable to the grantor. Code Sec. 677.

Beneficial Enjoyment

If, in certain instances, the grantor has the power to control the beneficial enjoyment of the trust income, the trust income is taxable to the grantor. Power to control beneficial enjoyment includes the power to change beneficiaries. Code Sec. 674(b).

Administrative Powers

If the grantor has administrative control over the trust property that can be exercised to the grantor's benefit, the trust income is taxable to the grantor. Code Sec. 675. Administrative control that could work to the grantor's benefit includes the right to borrow the trust property at a below-market interest rate.

TAX BLUNDER

In response to a summons by the IRS for records of a trust, the trustee, U.S. Bank, was ordered to have a representative appear before the court and produce records of the transactions of the Northwest Enterprise Trust. Springer, the "Executive Trustee," filed a motion to quash the summons. The IRS moved to dismiss the petition because Springer, as a non-lawyer, would not be legally empowered to pursue the action as trustee on behalf of the trust. Springer filed no response. The court ruled that, except for extraordinary occasions, corporations and other unincorporated associations must appear in court through an attorney. *Springer*, 83 AFTR 2d 99-541.

Caveat: A non-attorney may appear on his or her own behalf, but only an attorney may represent a corporation or **trust**.

SUMMARY

- Estates come into being automatically at the death of the taxpayer. The executor or administrator distributes the assets and satisfies the liabilities of the decedent either pursuant to the will or via the state's intestate succession statutes.

- Trusts must be specifically created either during the grantor's life (inter vivos) or at death (testamentary). Trusts are classified for tax purposes as either simple (distributes all trust accounting income) or complex (does not have to distribute all of its trust accounting income).

- Estate and trusts can either act as conduits or retain the income and be taxed on it.

- Estate and trusts are governed (1) by either the will or trust instrument and (2) by state law in its operations.

- To understand fiduciary taxation, an appreciation of state law income and distributable net income is required.

- Estates and trusts are subject to the alternative minimum tax (AMT) and are faced with numerous preferences and adjustments. However, estates and trusts are allowed a $23,800 exemption from the AMT.

QUESTIONS

1. On what date is a decedent's final income tax return due?

2. What income is included on a final income tax return for a cash-basis decedent? How would your answer change if the decedent was on the accrual basis of accounting?

3. What is "income in respect of the decedent"? On whose return is "income in respect of the decedent" recognized?

4. What are "expenses in respect of the decedent"? On whose return are "expenses in respect of the decedent" deducted?

5. Unreported interest income on U.S. government bonds owned by a decedent at the date of death can be handled in various ways for tax purposes. List and discuss the various ways.

6. What are the duties and responsibilities of an executor of an estate in regard to the income tax returns required by an estate?

7. Do all estates have to file federal estate income tax returns? If not, what are the requirements for filing estate income tax returns?

8. What requirements exist for determining the first tax year-end of an estate for income tax purposes?

9. When is a federal estate income tax return due? What options are available to an estate executor in paying the estate's income tax liability?

10. What exemption amounts are allowed to an estate, simple trust, and complex trust?

11. What is the difference between an inter vivos trust and a testamentary trust?

12. Define the following terms:
    a. Reversionary interest
    b. Income beneficiary
    c. Remainder beneficiary
    d. Simple trust
    e. Complex trust

13. List and discuss two nontax reasons why an individual might consider creating a trust.

14. When is a trust required to file a federal income tax return? What tax form is used for a trust's federal income tax return?

15. Why is it important for the trustee of a trust to carefully consider the choice of an accounting method for a trust?

16. Will a trust be entitled to deduct the full value of all charitable contributions made by the trust in all situations on the trust's federal income tax return?

17. What tax benefits are embodied in specific legacies and bequests?

18. What three functions does distributable net income serve in fiduciary taxation?

19. What problem does the separate share rule alleviate?

20. Beneficiaries of estates and complex trusts are subject to the tier system of taxation. Explain what is meant by a first- and second-tier beneficiary.

21. When depreciation follows income of an estate or complex trust, explain the situation where wastage could occur.

22. In relation to trust distributions to beneficiaries, explain the 65-day rule.

23. What is a Schedule K-1? When is a trustee of a trust required to file a Schedule K-1 with the trust's federal income tax return?

24. Explain when loss carryovers can be taken from a trust's federal income tax return and be used on the trust beneficiaries' individual income tax returns.

25. Explain some tax avoidance techniques that could arise in regard to multiple trusts.

PROBLEMS

26. Hershel Barker was the president and majority shareholder in Bulldog Inc. He was a cash-basis taxpayer who reported his income on a calendar-year basis. On March 1, 2015, Hershel was killed in a skiing accident. The estate has elected to report its income on a calendar-year basis.

    Required: Give the tax consequences for the parties involved in the following situations:
    a. Dividends of $10,000 had been declared by Bulldog Inc. on February 3, 2015, payable March 4, 2015, to shareholders of record on February 17, 2015. Hershel's executor received the dividends.
    b. What if the record date was March 10, 2015?

27. The trust instrument requires the trustee to distribute $40,000 annually to Carl Smith, the grantor's son. Any residual income may be distributed or accumulated for Bob Jones, Sam Smith, Earl Litt, and Carl Smith in the trustee's discretion. In the current year, the trust has distributable net income of $100,000 in domestic dividends. The trustee distributes $40,000 of income to Carl Smith. Next, he distributes $30,000 to Bob Jones, $20,000 each to Sam Smith and Earl Litt, and an additional $15,000 to Carl Smith. The trust does not have any undistributed net income from previous years.

    Required: How much of the distributions are taxable income to Carl Smith, Bob Jones, Sam Smith, and Earl Litt?

28. John Jefferson dies on November 10, 2015. John is on the cash basis of accounting for tax purposes. On November 29, 2015, a $4,000 paycheck covering the period November 1–November 8, 2015, is mailed to John's home. Who recognizes this paycheck as income? Would your answer to this question change if John was on the accrual basis of accounting at the date of his death?

29. Jane Jaffe dies on October 12, 2015. On the date of death, Jane has a bank account that pays interest on a quarterly basis. On December 31, 2015, $3,000 of interest income is credited to the bank account.
    a. If Jane was on the cash basis of accounting at the date of her death, is any of the income included on Jane's final income tax return?
    b. Would your answer to (a) change if Jane was on the accrual basis of accounting at the date of her death?
    c. If Jane does not recognize all of the interest income on her final income tax return in (a) and (b), who does recognize the interest income?

30. Richard Johnson held $50,000 of U.S. government savings bonds on the date of his death, December 11, 2015. The bonds mature in 2016. Unreported interest income on these bonds at the date of Richard's death amounted to $14,700. It is anticipated that Richard will be in the 28 percent marginal income tax bracket on his final income tax return. The one beneficiary to Richard's estate is expected to have a 15 percent marginal tax bracket in 2015 and a 28 percent marginal tax bracket in 2016. List and discuss some tax planning options that are available to the executor of Richard's estate and to the beneficiary of Richard's estate in regard to the recognition as income of the unreported interest income on the U.S. Government bonds.

31. An estate receives the following items of income and has the following deductions during the tax year 2015:

Income	
Dividends	$5,000
Taxable interest	5,000
Tax-exempt interest	5,000
Total income	$15,000
Deduction	
Fiduciary fee	$2,000

    The estate files an income tax return for the calendar year 2015. No distributions were made during the year to beneficiaries. Based on these facts, what is the 2015 federal income tax liability of the estate?

32. Refer to the facts in Problem 31. If a $10,000 distribution of income was made to a beneficiary during the 2015 tax year, what is the 2015 federal income tax liability of the estate? Assume that the decedent's will does not specify that the distribution is to be paid out of any specific type of income.

33. Refer to the facts in Problem 32. How much of the $10,000 income distribution will be taxable to the beneficiary?

34. Mr. Hughes died in 2015. Pursuant to his will a testamentary trust was established. The trust instrument requires that 60 percent of the trust income be distributed currently to his wife Donna, for her life and 40 percent of the trust income be distributed to his daughter, Holly, for her life. Also, the trustee is permitted to set aside income as a depreciation reserve. In the current year, depreciation on the trust property amounts to $30,000, and the trustee allocates $10,000 of trust income as a depreciation reserve.
    a. What is the amount of the depreciation deduction allowed to the trust?
    b. What is the amount of the depreciation deduction allowed to Donna?
    c. What is the amount of the depreciation deduction allowed to Holly?

35. In 2015, a trust has $2,000 of trust accounting income and $1,600 of distributable net income. The trust properly pays $1,100 to John Smith, a beneficiary, on February 3, 2015, which the trustee elects to treat under Code Sec. 663(b) (65-day rule) as paid on December 31, 2014. The trust also properly pays to John Smith $1,200 on August 1, 2015, and $900 on January 21, 2016. For 2015, how much may be elected under the 65-day rule as properly paid or credited on the last day of 2015?

36. John Henderson's will provides for the creation of a trust for the benefit of Holly Jones. Under the specific terms, the trust is required to distribute to Holly $50,000 cash and 1,000 shares of IBM stock when she reaches 25 years of age, $60,000 cash and 1,200 shares of Xerox when she reaches 30 years of age, $30,000 cash and 2,000 shares of General Motors stock when she reaches 35 years of age, and $100,000 cash and 500 shares of DuPont stock when she reaches 40 years of age. Which if any of these items qualify for exclusion as a specific legacy or bequest?

37. The trustee of the Astro trust makes a $15,000 charitable contribution to PennOhio University. The trust agreement is silent as to the specific type of income that should be used to pay the contribution. The trust had $15,000 of taxable income and $10,000 of tax-exempt income during the year.

    How much of the $15,000 charitable contribution is deductible on the trust's federal income tax return?

38. The trustee of the James trust makes a $30,000 charitable contribution to the United Way. The trust had $20,000 of taxable income and $30,000 of tax-exempt income during the year. The trust agreement states that all charitable contributions, to the extent possible, should be paid out of taxable income. How much of the $30,000 charitable contribution is deductible on the trust's federal income tax return?

39. A trustee distributes $10,000 of income to each of nine beneficiaries of the trust. The trust had $40,000 of tax-exempt interest income during the year and $80,000 of taxable income. The trust agreement does not specify the type of income to be distributed to any beneficiary.
    a. How much of the $10,000 distribution to each beneficiary is taxable income to each beneficiary?
    b. Would your answer to (a) change if the trust agreement specifies that tax-exempt income should be distributed to beneficiaries 1-4 and taxable income should be distributed to beneficiaries 5-9?

40. The trustee of the Peterson trust is required by the trust agreement to distribute $5,000 yearly to Peter Peterson, $4,000 yearly to John Peterson, and $3,000 yearly to Sally Peterson. The trustee has the authority per the trust agreement to make additional distributions to the beneficiaries at his discretion. During 2015, the trustee actually distributes $10,000 to Peter, $15,000 to John, and $20,000 to Sally. The trust has DNI of $30,000 in 2015.

What is the taxable amount of the distributions to Peter, John, and Sally?

41. An estate with distributable net income of $100,000 distributes the following assets to a beneficiary in December of 2015:

	Basis to Estate	Value at Date of Distribution
Cash	$40,000	$40,000
General Motors Stock	90,000	140,000
Real Estate	100,000	250,000
Mucho Taco Stock	70,000	50,000
	$300,000	$480,000

a. What is the beneficiary's basis in the distributed assets?
b. What would be the beneficiary's basis in the distributed assets if the election is made by the fiduciary under Code Sec. 643(e)(3)?

42. John and Ralph, two brothers who are over the age of 21, are beneficiaries of a trust created in 1982 by their father, Jim. At that time, Jim transferred securities and an apartment building to a corporate trustee. All of the income is to be distributed annually to John and Ralph for 40 years. Depreciation follows income, and at the end of 40 years, the trust will terminate and the corpus will be distributed to John and Ralph. During 2015, the trust has the following items of income and expense.

Rental income	$50,000
Taxable interest	40,000
Tax-exempt interest	30,000
Long-term capital gain (allocable to corpus)	15,000
Expenses attributable to rent	20,000
Trustee's commission (allocable to income)	4,000
Trustee's commission (allocable to principal)	1,000
Depreciation	8,000

Required:
a. Compute state law income.
b. Compute DNI as an income ceiling.
c. Compute DNI as a deduction ceiling.
d. Compute the trust's taxable income.
e. Compute DNI as a qualitative yardstick.

43. Which of the following items affects the charitable deduction of an estate or complex trust?
    a. Rental income
    b. Dividends
    c. Interest
    d. Tax-exempt interest

44. Which of the following deductions does not affect trust accounting income?
    a. Rental expenses
    b. Trustee's commissions allocable to income
    c. Interest expense
    d. Taxes
    e. Trustee's commissions allocable to corpus

45. Which of the following items does not normally enter into the computation of distributable net income?
    a. Charitable deduction
    b. Capital gains
    c. Trustee's commissions
    d. Rental income

46. An estate with depreciable property may not do one of the following:
    a. Pay income to first-tier beneficiaries
    b. Pay income to second-tier beneficiaries
    c. Distribute capital losses on termination
    d. Set up a reserve for depreciation

47. A trust can have the following taxable year-end:
    a. September 30
    b. June 30
    c. December 31
    d. March 31

48. John Doe had earned commissions on life insurance sold prior to his death. The commissions of $20,000 were to be paid in five annual installments. The executor of his estate collected the first installment of $4,000 and distributed the right to the remaining installments to his son, a beneficiary of the estate. How will the remaining four installments be reported for income tax purposes?

49. John Henry died on May 1, 2015. When does his final 1040 have to be filed?

50. In problem 49, when does the estate's taxable year begin?

51. In problem 49, when does the estate's taxable year end?

52. John and Mary Hughes file their income tax return on a calendar year basis. John dies on May 15, 2015. Mary remarries on July 4, 2015. Can Mary file a joint return with John for the taxable year 2015?

53. **Comprehensive Problem.** Thomas Able, a cash method, calendar-year taxpayer, died December 1, 2015. He is survived by his spouse, Nan. Tom was age 65 at the time of his death and Nan is age 66. They have no dependents, and Nan is the sole beneficiary of Tom's estate. Nan has been blind from cataracts since taking a tax course at Louisiana Tech University in 1983. The executor of the estate is the First Wachovia Corp., Winston-Salem, North Carolina. Nan and the executor elected to file a joint return for 2015. During 2015, the following cash receipts, disbursements, and expenses were recorded by the Ables and the estate of Tom Able:
    a. Cash dividends of $25,000 from Safflower Oil Corporation were received on November 28, 2015. These dividends were declared on November 3, 2015, and payable to shareholders of record on November 14, 2015. Tom Able was the stockholder in Safflower Oil Corporation.
    b. Tom was an executive in the Kane & Able Trucking Company in Winston-Salem, North Carolina, and for the two months preceding his death, Tom was not paid his monthly salary of $5,000 because of a moratorium on wages. On January 5, 2016, the trucking company paid the $10,000 to the executor of the Tom Able Estate. Tom had received all his other monthly salary payments at the end of each month.
    c. Interest of $1,800 was credited to Tom and Nan's savings accounts on August 1, 2015.
    d. Real estate taxes of $1,000 were paid by the estate on December 31, 2015, for the calendar year.
    e. Medical expenses of $5,700 related to Tom's last illness were paid by his estate on January 20, 2016. The executor has elected not to deduct these medical expenses on the estate tax return. Health insurance premiums of $500 were paid by Tom during 2015.
    f. A bonus of $4,500 from the Kane & Able Trucking Company was paid to Tom's estate on January 16, 2016.
    g. Charitable contributions of $1,200 were paid to the Ventura County Humane Society by Tom during 2015.
    h. Interest on the Ables' home mortgage amounted to $1,600 in 2015.

i. On May 29, 2015, Tom received $25,000 in life insurance proceeds paid by reason of the death of his mother.

j. Tom has always attended Saturday night cockfights. During 2015, he won $500 and lost $800.

k. On June 9, 2015, Tom submitted his entry in a Fairview Books Publishing Company contest. On August 1, 2015, it was announced that Tom had won $3,000 cash and a year's worth of free computer research time worth $900. Tom accepted the $3,000 but refused the computer research time because he had heard the system was difficult to use.

l. Nan and Tom sold stock that they had purchased on December 27, 2014, at $1,000 for $1,200 on June 24, 2015.

m. Tom also owned a farm that produced total annual revenue of $1,000 and expenses of $100 for utilities, $200 for fertilizer and lime, $100 for miscellaneous expenses, $100 for repairs and maintenance, and depreciation expense of $200 in 2015 prior to Tom's death. The farm has been idle since Tom's death.

n. Tom and Nan kept meticulous records verifying the $1,500 they paid in sales tax in 2015.

o. Federal and state income taxes of $9,900 and $2,000, respectively, were withheld from Tom's salary in 2015.

p. Tom and Nan had a $500 balance due on their 2014 North Carolina return that was paid on April 12, 2015.

Required: Compute the amount of taxable income that will go on the decedent's final return.

54. **Comprehensive Problem.** In 2015, Cabell Mapp passed away in Belle Haven, Virginia. Pursuant to his will, a testamentary trust was established. The trust instrument requires that $10,000 a year be paid to the University of Virginia. The balance of the income may, in the trustee's discretion, be accumulated or distributed to Sarah Mapp. Expenses are allocable against income and the trust instrument requires a reserve for depreciation. During the taxable year, the trustee contributes $10,000 to the University of Virginia, and in his discretion distributes $15,000 of income to Sarah Mapp. The trust has the following items of income and expenses for the taxable year.

Dividends	$10,000
Interest	10,000
Fully tax-exempt interest	10,000
Rents	20,000
Rental expenses	2,000
Depreciation of rental property	3,000
Trustee's commissions	5,000

a. Determine trust accounting income.
b. Determine DNI as an income ceiling.
c. Determine DNI as a deduction ceiling.
d. Determine the trust taxable income.
e. Determine DNI as a qualitative yardstick.
f. Determine Sarah Mapp's Schedule K-1 amounts.
g. Has any wastage occurred in connection with the charitable deduction? Could this wastage have been prevented?

55. Comprehensive Problem (Estate Tax Return Problem).

FACTS

Howard Hayes was killed in a freak barbecuing accident at a local eatery called P.K.'s Barbecue Shack on October 28, 2013, in Wilson, North Carolina. He was survived by his wife, Helen (age 56), and two children, Isaac (34) and Heidi (32). Howard's will provided that Helen would receive one half of the residuary estate and the balance of the residue would be divided equally between the children. The will provided that any direct obligations be paid out of the principal of the residuary estate.

The post-mortem tax plan instituted by the executor requires payment of commissions in the year of termination of the estate (no deductions for commissions on this return). All expenses are first allocable to farm income and, if farm income is exhausted, then to other ordinary income. Unattached or floating deductions will all be allocated against income on a pro rata basis. At the time of Mr. Hayes' death, he owned a small farm. In 2014, fertilizer expenses totaled $5,000, seed costs were $2,500, and proceeds from the sale of crops were $68,000.

At the time of his death, Howard wanted $10,000 to be paid out of estate income to East Carolina University. The executor, after ascertaining the status of this obligation, paid the pledge on December 10, 2014.

The executor elected to report income on a calendar-year basis. The following information pertains to 2014 income:

Farm Income	$68,000
Domestic Dividends	30,000
Interest from CD	10,000
Real Estate Taxes (related to the farm)	2,000
Other Farm Expenses: Insurance	2,000
Repairs & Maintenance	4,000
Filing Fees (Clerk of Superior Court)	600
Depreciation on Farm Building (straight line)	3,000

The executor was instructed via the will to distribute income during the period of administration as follows:

Helen:	One-half of State Law Income
Isaac:	One-eighth of State Law Income
Heidi:	One-eighth of State Law Income

Reidsville Bank & Trust Co., N.A., was named executor of Howard Hayes' estate and their trust department is responsible for preparing all of the 1041 returns. The address is 1454 Scales Street, Reidsville, NC 27390. The estate's identification number is 56-1053613; the return is filed on April 5, 2015; and the officer signing the return is Tom Phillips.

The following items are required:
(1) State Law Income under Code Sec. 643(b)
(2) DNI as an income ceiling
(3) DNI as a deduction ceiling
(4) Estate's taxable income
(5) DNI as a qualitative yard stick
(6) K-1 allocations
(7) U.S. Fiduciary Income Tax Return (Form 1041)
(8) Form 4562
(9) Schedule F
(10) Schedule K-1 for Helen Hayes
(11) Schedule K-1 for Isaac Hayes
(12) Schedule K-1 for Heidi Hayes

56. **Research Problem.** When a trust terminates, there are, in most instances, terminating commissions that are charged by the fiduciary. These commissions may generate excess deductions that can be passed out to beneficiaries as itemized deductions subject to the two percent of adjusted gross income rule. Nonetheless, the allocation of such expenses with respect to character of the income has spawned litigation as to the proper allocation base.

Read the following cases and prepare a brief written summary of the allowable allocation method for terminating commissions.
   a. *C.L. Whittemore, Jr. v. U.S.,* 67-2 USTC ¶9670, 383 F.2d 824 (CA-8 1967).
   b. *A.J. Fabens,* 75-2 USTC ¶9572, 519 F.2d 1310 (CA-1 1975).

57. **Research Problem.** The following court cases have helped to clarify the rightful recipient of depreciation of property held by an estate or trust.

Read the following judicial decisions and prepare a brief written summary for each case.
   a. *Sue Carol,* 30 BTA 443, Dec. 8520 (1934), Acq. XIII-2 CB 4.
   b. *R.J. Dusek,* 67-1 USTC ¶9418, 376 F.2d 410 (CA-10 1967).
   c. *W.H. Lamkin, Executor,* 76-2 USTC ¶9485, 533 F.2d 303 (CA-5 1976).

Appendix

Tax Rate Schedules For 2015

From 1993 through 2000, income has been taxed at the following rates: 15 percent, 28 percent, 31 percent, 36 percent, and 39.6 percent. For 2001 a 10 percent rate was added and the rates above 15 percent were reduced one-half of one percent. The rates above 15 percent were reduced another one-half percent for 2002. For 2004 through 2012, the rates above 15 percent were lowered to 25, 28, 33 and 35 percent. The American Taxpayer Relief Act of 2012 changed the rates again. For 2013 and later, the rates are 15, 25, 28, 33, 35, and 39.6 percent.

The tax rate schedules are subject to an inflation adjustment based on methods prescribed by the Internal Revenue Code. The income ranges and the applicable dollar amounts are adjusted to reflect increases in the Consumer Price Index (CPI). The CPI increase applicable to 2015 is provided by the Bureau of Labor Statistics, and the schedules below and on the following page reflect this adjustment.

Tax Rate Schedule X below is to be used by single individuals or by married persons treated as unmarried that have taxable incomes of $100,000 or more.

Single Individuals—Schedule X

Taxable Income		Pay	+	% on Excess	of the amount over
Over	But Not Over				
$0	$9,225	$0.00		10%	$0
9,225	37,450	922.50		15	9,225
37,450	90,750	5,156.25		25	37,450
90,750	189,300	18,481.25		28	90,750
189,300	411,500	46,075.25		33	189,300
411,500	413,200	119,401.25		35	411,500
413,200	—	119,996.25		39.6	413,200

Tax Rate Schedule Y-1 below is to be used by married taxpayers filing jointly and by surviving spouses that have taxable incomes of $100,000 or more.

Married Individuals, Joint Returns and Surviving Spouses—Schedule Y-1

Taxable Income		Pay	+	% on Excess	of the amount over
Over	But Not Over				
$0	$18,450	$0.00		10%	$0
18,450	74,900	1,845.00		15	18,450
74,900	151,200	10,312.50		25	74,900
151,200	230,450	29,387.50		28	151,200
230,450	411,500	51,577.50		33	230,450
411,500	464,850	111,324.00		35	411,500
464,850	—	129,996.50		39.6	464,850

Tax Rate Schedule Y-2 below is to be used by married taxpayers filing separately and by the bankruptcy estate of an individual debtor that have taxable incomes of $100,000 or more.

Married Individuals, Separate Returns—Schedule Y-2

Taxable Income					
Over	But Not Over	Pay	+	% on Excess	of the amount over
$0	$9,225	$0.00		10%	$0
9,225	37,450	922.50		15	9,225
37,450	75,600	5,156.25		25	37,450
75,600	115,225	14,693.75		28	75,600
115,225	205,750	25,788.75		33	115,225
205,750	232,425	55,662.00		35	205,750
232,425	—	64,998.25		39.6	232,425

Tax Rate Schedule Z below is to be used by individuals who qualify as heads of households that have taxable incomes of $100,000 or more.

Heads of Households—Schedule Z

Taxable Income					
Over	But Not Over	Pay	+	% on Excess	of the amount over
$0	$13,150	$0.00		10%	$0
13,150	50,200	1,315.00		15	13,150
50,200	129,600	6,872.50		25	50,200
129,600	209,850	26,722.50		28	129,600
209,850	411,500	49,192.50		33	209,850
411,500	439,000	115,737.00		35	411,500
439,000	—	125,362.00		39.6	439,000

Tax Rate Schedule for Estates and Trusts. The American Taxpayer Relief Act of 2012 changed the rates again. For 2013 and later, the rates are 15, 25, 28, 33, 35, and 39.6 percent.

Estates and Trusts

Taxable Income					
Over	But Not Over	Pay	+	% on Excess	of the amount over
$0	$2,500	$0.00		15%	$0
2,500	5,900	375.00		25	2,500
5,900	9,050	1,225.00		28	5,900
9,050	12,300	2,107.00		33	9,050
12,300	—	3,179.50		39.6	12,300

Tax Rate Schedule for Corporations. A graduated rate structure is employed in computing the income tax liability of corporate taxpayers. The 5 percent additional tax rate that applies to phase out the benefits of the graduated rates is incorporated in the rate schedule. The phaseout occurs between $100,000 and $335,000 of taxable income by means of an increase in the maximum 34 percent rate to 39 percent.

Corporations

Taxable Income					
Over	But Not Over	Pay	+	% on Excess	of the amount over
$0	$ 50,000	$0		15%	$0
50,000	75,000	7,500		25	50,000
75,000	100,000	13,750		34	75,000
100,000	335,000	22,250		39	100,000
335,000	10,000,000	113,900		34	335,000
10,000,000	15,000,000	3,400,000		35	10,000,000
15,000,000	18,333,333	5,150,000		38	15,000,000
18,333,333	—	6,416,667		35	18,333,333

Tax Table

2014 Tax Table

See the instructions for line 44 to see if you must use the Tax Table below to figure your tax.

Example. Mr. and Mrs. Brown are filing a joint return. Their taxable income on Form 1040, line 43, is $25,300. First, they find the $25,300-25,350 taxable income line. Next, they find the column for married filing jointly and read down the column. The amount shown where the taxable income line and filing status column meet is $2,891. This is the tax amount they should enter on Form 1040, line 44.

Sample Table

At Least	But Less Than	Single	Married filing jointly*	Married filing separately	Head of a household
			Your tax is—		
25,200	25,250	3,330	2,876	3,330	3,136
25,250	25,300	3,338	2,884	3,338	3,144
25,300	25,350	3,345	(2,891)	3,345	3,151
25,350	25,400	3,353	2,899	3,353	3,159

If line 43 (taxable income) is— At least	But less than	Single	Married filing jointly *	Married filing separately	Head of a household
			Your tax is—		
0	5	0	0	0	0
5	15	1	1	1	1
15	25	2	2	2	2
25	50	4	4	4	4
50	75	6	6	6	6
75	100	9	9	9	9
100	125	11	11	11	11
125	150	14	14	14	14
150	175	16	16	16	16
175	200	19	19	19	19
200	225	21	21	21	21
225	250	24	24	24	24
250	275	26	26	26	26
275	300	29	29	29	29
300	325	31	31	31	31
325	350	34	34	34	34
350	375	36	36	36	36
375	400	39	39	39	39
400	425	41	41	41	41
425	450	44	44	44	44
450	475	46	46	46	46
475	500	49	49	49	49
500	525	51	51	51	51
525	550	54	54	54	54
550	575	56	56	56	56
575	600	59	59	59	59
600	625	61	61	61	61
625	650	64	64	64	64
650	675	66	66	66	66
675	700	69	69	69	69
700	725	71	71	71	71
725	750	74	74	74	74
750	775	76	76	76	76
775	800	79	79	79	79
800	825	81	81	81	81
825	850	84	84	84	84
850	875	86	86	86	86
875	900	89	89	89	89
900	925	91	91	91	91
925	950	94	94	94	94
950	975	96	96	96	96
975	1,000	99	99	99	99

1,000

If line 43 (taxable income) is— At least	But less than	Single	Married filing jointly *	Married filing separately	Head of a household
			Your tax is—		
1,000	1,025	101	101	101	101
1,025	1,050	104	104	104	104
1,050	1,075	106	106	106	106
1,075	1,100	109	109	109	109
1,100	1,125	111	111	111	111
1,125	1,150	114	114	114	114
1,150	1,175	116	116	116	116
1,175	1,200	119	119	119	119
1,200	1,225	121	121	121	121
1,225	1,250	124	124	124	124
1,250	1,275	126	126	126	126
1,275	1,300	129	129	129	129
1,300	1,325	131	131	131	131
1,325	1,350	134	134	134	134
1,350	1,375	136	136	136	136
1,375	1,400	139	139	139	139
1,400	1,425	141	141	141	141
1,425	1,450	144	144	144	144
1,450	1,475	146	146	146	146
1,475	1,500	149	149	149	149
1,500	1,525	151	151	151	151
1,525	1,550	154	154	154	154
1,550	1,575	156	156	156	156
1,575	1,600	159	159	159	159
1,600	1,625	161	161	161	161
1,625	1,650	164	164	164	164
1,650	1,675	166	166	166	166
1,675	1,700	169	169	169	169
1,700	1,725	171	171	171	171
1,725	1,750	174	174	174	174
1,750	1,775	176	176	176	176
1,775	1,800	179	179	179	179
1,800	1,825	181	181	181	181
1,825	1,850	184	184	184	184
1,850	1,875	186	186	186	186
1,875	1,900	189	189	189	189
1,900	1,925	191	191	191	191
1,925	1,950	194	194	194	194
1,950	1,975	196	196	196	196
1,975	2,000	199	199	199	199

2,000

If line 43 (taxable income) is— At least	But less than	Single	Married filing jointly *	Married filing separately	Head of a household
			Your tax is—		
2,000	2,025	201	201	201	201
2,025	2,050	204	204	204	204
2,050	2,075	206	206	206	206
2,075	2,100	209	209	209	209
2,100	2,125	211	211	211	211
2,125	2,150	214	214	214	214
2,150	2,175	216	216	216	216
2,175	2,200	219	219	219	219
2,200	2,225	221	221	221	221
2,225	2,250	224	224	224	224
2,250	2,275	226	226	226	226
2,275	2,300	229	229	229	229
2,300	2,325	231	231	231	231
2,325	2,350	234	234	234	234
2,350	2,375	236	236	236	236
2,375	2,400	239	239	239	239
2,400	2,425	241	241	241	241
2,425	2,450	244	244	244	244
2,450	2,475	246	246	246	246
2,475	2,500	249	249	249	249
2,500	2,525	251	251	251	251
2,525	2,550	254	254	254	254
2,550	2,575	256	256	256	256
2,575	2,600	259	259	259	259
2,600	2,625	261	261	261	261
2,625	2,650	264	264	264	264
2,650	2,675	266	266	266	266
2,675	2,700	269	269	269	269
2,700	2,725	271	271	271	271
2,725	2,750	274	274	274	274
2,750	2,775	276	276	276	276
2,775	2,800	279	279	279	279
2,800	2,825	281	281	281	281
2,825	2,850	284	284	284	284
2,850	2,875	286	286	286	286
2,875	2,900	289	289	289	289
2,900	2,925	291	291	291	291
2,925	2,950	294	294	294	294
2,950	2,975	296	296	296	296
2,975	3,000	299	299	299	299

(Continued)

* This column must also be used by a qualifying widow(er).

2014 Tax Table — *Continued*

If line 43 (taxable income) is— At least	But less than	Single	Married filing jointly *	Married filing separately	Head of a household
3,000					
3,000	3,050	303	303	303	303
3,050	3,100	308	308	308	308
3,100	3,150	313	313	313	313
3,150	3,200	318	318	318	318
3,200	3,250	323	323	323	323
3,250	3,300	328	328	328	328
3,300	3,350	333	333	333	333
3,350	3,400	338	338	338	338
3,400	3,450	343	343	343	343
3,450	3,500	348	348	348	348
3,500	3,550	353	353	353	353
3,550	3,600	358	358	358	358
3,600	3,650	363	363	363	363
3,650	3,700	368	368	368	368
3,700	3,750	373	373	373	373
3,750	3,800	378	378	378	378
3,800	3,850	383	383	383	383
3,850	3,900	388	388	388	388
3,900	3,950	393	393	393	393
3,950	4,000	398	398	398	398
4,000					
4,000	4,050	403	403	403	403
4,050	4,100	408	408	408	408
4,100	4,150	413	413	413	413
4,150	4,200	418	418	418	418
4,200	4,250	423	423	423	423
4,250	4,300	428	428	428	428
4,300	4,350	433	433	433	433
4,350	4,400	438	438	438	438
4,400	4,450	443	443	443	443
4,450	4,500	448	448	448	448
4,500	4,550	453	453	453	453
4,550	4,600	458	458	458	458
4,600	4,650	463	463	463	463
4,650	4,700	468	468	468	468
4,700	4,750	473	473	473	473
4,750	4,800	478	478	478	478
4,800	4,850	483	483	483	483
4,850	4,900	488	488	488	488
4,900	4,950	493	493	493	493
4,950	5,000	498	498	498	498
5,000					
5,000	5,050	503	503	503	503
5,050	5,100	508	508	508	508
5,100	5,150	513	513	513	513
5,150	5,200	518	518	518	518
5,200	5,250	523	523	523	523
5,250	5,300	528	528	528	528
5,300	5,350	533	533	533	533
5,350	5,400	538	538	538	538
5,400	5,450	543	543	543	543
5,450	5,500	548	548	548	548
5,500	5,550	553	553	553	553
5,550	5,600	558	558	558	558
5,600	5,650	563	563	563	563
5,650	5,700	568	568	568	568
5,700	5,750	573	570	573	573
5,750	5,800	578	578	578	578
5,800	5,850	583	583	583	583
5,850	5,900	588	588	588	588
5,900	5,950	593	593	593	593
5,950	6,000	598	598	598	598

If line 43 (taxable income) is— At least	But less than	Single	Married filing jointly *	Married filing separately	Head of a household
6,000					
6,000	6,050	603	603	603	603
6,050	6,100	608	608	608	608
6,100	6,150	613	613	613	613
6,150	6,200	618	618	618	618
6,200	6,250	623	623	623	623
6,250	6,300	628	628	628	628
6,300	6,350	633	633	633	633
6,350	6,400	638	638	638	638
6,400	6,450	643	643	643	643
6,450	6,500	648	648	648	648
6,500	6,550	653	653	653	653
6,550	6,600	658	658	658	658
6,600	6,650	663	663	663	663
6,650	6,700	668	668	668	668
6,700	6,750	673	673	673	673
6,750	6,800	678	678	678	678
6,800	6,850	683	683	683	683
6,850	6,900	688	688	688	688
6,900	6,950	693	693	693	693
6,950	7,000	698	698	698	698
7,000					
7,000	7,050	703	703	703	703
7,050	7,100	708	708	708	708
7,100	7,150	713	713	713	713
7,150	7,200	718	718	718	718
7,200	7,250	723	723	723	723
7,250	7,300	728	728	728	728
7,300	7,350	733	733	733	733
7,350	7,400	738	738	738	738
7,400	7,450	743	743	743	743
7,450	7,500	748	748	748	748
7,500	7,550	753	753	753	753
7,550	7,600	758	758	758	758
7,600	7,650	763	763	763	763
7,650	7,700	766	768	768	768
7,700	7,750	773	773	773	773
7,750	7,800	778	778	778	778
7,800	7,850	783	783	783	783
7,850	7,900	788	788	788	788
7,900	7,950	793	793	793	793
7,950	8,000	798	798	798	798
8,000					
8,000	8,050	803	803	803	803
8,050	8,100	808	808	808	808
8,100	8,150	813	813	813	813
8,150	8,200	818	818	818	818
8,200	8,250	823	823	823	823
8,250	8,300	828	828	828	828
8,300	8,350	833	833	833	833
8,350	8,400	838	838	838	838
8,400	8,450	843	843	843	843
8,450	8,500	848	848	848	848
8,500	8,550	853	853	853	853
8,550	8,600	858	858	858	858
8,600	8,650	863	863	863	863
8,650	8,700	868	868	868	868
8,700	8,750	873	873	873	873
8,750	8,800	878	878	878	878
8,800	8,850	883	883	883	883
8,850	8,900	888	888	888	888
8,900	8,950	893	893	893	893
8,950	9,000	898	898	898	898

If line 43 (taxable income) is— At least	But less than	Single	Married filing jointly *	Married filing separately	Head of a household
9,000					
9,000	9,050	903	903	903	903
9,050	9,100	908	908	908	908
9,100	9,150	915	913	915	913
9,150	9,200	923	918	923	918
9,200	9,250	930	923	930	923
9,250	9,300	938	928	938	928
9,300	9,350	945	933	945	933
9,350	9,400	953	938	953	938
9,400	9,450	960	943	960	943
9,450	9,500	968	948	968	948
9,500	9,550	975	953	975	953
9,550	9,600	983	958	983	958
9,600	9,650	990	963	990	963
9,650	9,700	998	968	998	968
9,700	9,750	1,005	973	1,005	973
9,750	9,800	1,013	978	1,013	978
9,800	9,850	1,020	983	1,020	983
9,850	9,900	1,028	988	1,028	988
9,900	9,950	1,035	993	1,035	993
9,950	10,000	1,043	998	1,043	998
10,000					
10,000	10,050	1,050	1,003	1,050	1,003
10,050	10,100	1,058	1,008	1,058	1,008
10,100	10,150	1,065	1,013	1,065	1,013
10,150	10,200	1,073	1,018	1,073	1,018
10,200	10,250	1,080	1,023	1,080	1,023
10,250	10,300	1,088	1,028	1,088	1,028
10,300	10,350	1,095	1,033	1,095	1,033
10,350	10,400	1,103	1,038	1,103	1,038
10,400	10,450	1,110	1,043	1,110	1,043
10,450	10,500	1,118	1,048	1,118	1,048
10,500	10,550	1,125	1,053	1,125	1,053
10,550	10,600	1,133	1,058	1,133	1,058
10,600	10,650	1,140	1,063	1,140	1,063
10,650	10,700	1,148	1,068	1,148	1,068
10,700	10,750	1,155	1,073	1,155	1,073
10,750	10,800	1,163	1,078	1,163	1,078
10,800	10,850	1,170	1,083	1,170	1,083
10,850	10,900	1,178	1,088	1,178	1,088
10,900	10,950	1,185	1,093	1,185	1,093
10,950	11,000	1,193	1,098	1,193	1,098
11,000					
11,000	11,050	1,200	1,103	1,200	1,103
11,050	11,100	1,208	1,108	1,208	1,108
11,100	11,150	1,215	1,113	1,215	1,113
11,150	11,200	1,223	1,118	1,223	1,118
11,200	11,250	1,230	1,123	1,230	1,123
11,250	11,300	1,238	1,128	1,238	1,128
11,300	11,350	1,245	1,133	1,245	1,133
11,350	11,400	1,253	1,138	1,253	1,138
11,400	11,450	1,260	1,143	1,260	1,143
11,450	11,500	1,268	1,148	1,268	1,148
11,500	11,550	1,275	1,153	1,275	1,153
11,550	11,600	1,283	1,158	1,283	1,158
11,600	11,650	1,290	1,163	1,290	1,163
11,650	11,700	1,298	1,168	1,298	1,168
11,700	11,750	1,305	1,173	1,305	1,173
11,750	11,800	1,313	1,178	1,313	1,178
11,800	11,850	1,320	1,183	1,320	1,183
11,850	11,900	1,328	1,188	1,328	1,188
11,900	11,950	1,335	1,193	1,335	1,193
11,950	12,000	1,343	1,198	1,343	1,198

(Continued)

* This column must also be used by a qualifying widow(er).

Need more information or forms? Visit IRS.gov.

2014 Tax Table — *Continued*

12,000

At least	But less than	Single	Married filing jointly *	Married filing separately	Head of a household
12,000	12,050	1,350	1,203	1,350	1,203
12,050	12,100	1,358	1,208	1,358	1,208
12,100	12,150	1,365	1,213	1,365	1,213
12,150	12,200	1,373	1,218	1,373	1,218
12,200	12,250	1,380	1,223	1,380	1,223
12,250	12,300	1,388	1,228	1,388	1,228
12,300	12,350	1,395	1,233	1,395	1,233
12,350	12,400	1,403	1,238	1,403	1,238
12,400	12,450	1,410	1,243	1,410	1,243
12,450	12,500	1,418	1,248	1,418	1,248
12,500	12,550	1,425	1,253	1,425	1,253
12,550	12,600	1,433	1,258	1,433	1,258
12,600	12,650	1,440	1,263	1,440	1,263
12,650	12,700	1,448	1,268	1,448	1,268
12,700	12,750	1,455	1,273	1,455	1,273
12,750	12,800	1,463	1,278	1,463	1,278
12,800	12,850	1,470	1,283	1,470	1,283
12,850	12,900	1,478	1,288	1,478	1,288
12,900	12,950	1,485	1,293	1,485	1,293
12,950	13,000	1,493	1,298	1,493	1,299

13,000

At least	But less than	Single	Married filing jointly *	Married filing separately	Head of a household
13,000	13,050	1,500	1,303	1,500	1,306
13,050	13,100	1,508	1,308	1,508	1,314
13,100	13,150	1,515	1,313	1,515	1,321
13,150	13,200	1,523	1,318	1,523	1,329
13,200	13,250	1,530	1,323	1,530	1,336
13,250	13,300	1,538	1,328	1,538	1,344
13,300	13,350	1,545	1,333	1,545	1,351
13,350	13,400	1,553	1,338	1,553	1,359
13,400	13,450	1,560	1,343	1,560	1,366
13,450	13,500	1,568	1,348	1,568	1,374
13,500	13,550	1,575	1,353	1,575	1,381
13,550	13,600	1,583	1,358	1,583	1,389
13,600	13,650	1,590	1,363	1,590	1,396
13,650	13,700	1,598	1,368	1,598	1,404
13,700	13,750	1,605	1,373	1,605	1,411
13,750	13,800	1,613	1,378	1,613	1,419
13,800	13,850	1,620	1,383	1,620	1,426
13,850	13,900	1,628	1,388	1,628	1,434
13,900	13,950	1,635	1,393	1,635	1,441
13,950	14,000	1,643	1,398	1,643	1,449

14,000

At least	But less than	Single	Married filing jointly *	Married filing separately	Head of a household
14,000	14,050	1,650	1,403	1,650	1,456
14,050	14,100	1,658	1,408	1,658	1,464
14,100	14,150	1,665	1,413	1,665	1,471
14,150	14,200	1,673	1,418	1,673	1,479
14,200	14,250	1,680	1,423	1,680	1,486
14,250	14,300	1,688	1,428	1,688	1,494
14,300	14,350	1,695	1,433	1,695	1,501
14,350	14,400	1,703	1,438	1,703	1,509
14,400	14,450	1,710	1,443	1,710	1,516
14,450	14,500	1,718	1,448	1,718	1,524
14,500	14,550	1,725	1,453	1,725	1,531
14,550	14,600	1,733	1,458	1,733	1,539
14,600	14,650	1,740	1,463	1,740	1,546
14,650	14,700	1,748	1,468	1,748	1,554
14,700	14,750	1,755	1,473	1,755	1,561
14,750	14,800	1,763	1,478	1,763	1,569
14,800	14,850	1,770	1,483	1,770	1,576
14,850	14,900	1,778	1,488	1,778	1,584
14,900	14,950	1,785	1,493	1,785	1,591
14,950	15,000	1,793	1,498	1,793	1,599

15,000

At least	But less than	Single	Married filing jointly *	Married filing separately	Head of a household
15,000	15,050	1,800	1,503	1,800	1,606
15,050	15,100	1,808	1,508	1,808	1,614
15,100	15,150	1,815	1,513	1,815	1,621
15,150	15,200	1,823	1,518	1,823	1,629
15,200	15,250	1,830	1,523	1,830	1,636
15,250	15,300	1,838	1,528	1,838	1,644
15,300	15,350	1,845	1,533	1,845	1,651
15,350	15,400	1,853	1,538	1,853	1,659
15,400	15,450	1,860	1,543	1,860	1,666
15,450	15,500	1,868	1,548	1,868	1,674
15,500	15,550	1,875	1,553	1,875	1,681
15,550	15,600	1,883	1,558	1,883	1,689
15,600	15,650	1,890	1,563	1,890	1,696
15,650	15,700	1,898	1,568	1,898	1,704
15,700	15,750	1,905	1,573	1,905	1,711
15,750	15,800	1,913	1,578	1,913	1,719
15,800	15,850	1,920	1,583	1,920	1,726
15,850	15,900	1,928	1,588	1,928	1,734
15,900	15,950	1,935	1,593	1,935	1,741
15,950	16,000	1,943	1,598	1,943	1,749

16,000

At least	But less than	Single	Married filing jointly *	Married filing separately	Head of a household
16,000	16,050	1,950	1,603	1,950	1,756
16,050	16,100	1,958	1,608	1,958	1,764
16,100	16,150	1,965	1,613	1,965	1,771
16,150	16,200	1,973	1,618	1,973	1,779
16,200	16,250	1,980	1,623	1,980	1,786
16,250	16,300	1,988	1,628	1,988	1,794
16,300	16,350	1,995	1,633	1,995	1,801
16,350	16,400	2,003	1,638	2,003	1,809
16,400	16,450	2,010	1,643	2,010	1,816
16,450	16,500	2,018	1,648	2,018	1,824
16,500	16,550	2,025	1,653	2,025	1,831
16,550	16,600	2,033	1,658	2,033	1,839
16,600	16,650	2,040	1,663	2,040	1,846
16,650	16,700	2,048	1,668	2,048	1,854
16,700	16,750	2,055	1,673	2,055	1,861
16,750	16,800	2,063	1,678	2,063	1,869
16,800	16,850	2,070	1,683	2,070	1,876
16,850	16,900	2,078	1,688	2,078	1,884
16,900	16,950	2,085	1,693	2,085	1,891
16,950	17,000	2,093	1,698	2,093	1,899

17,000

At least	But less than	Single	Married filing jointly *	Married filing separately	Head of a household
17,000	17,050	2,100	1,703	2,100	1,906
17,050	17,100	2,108	1,708	2,108	1,914
17,100	17,150	2,115	1,713	2,115	1,921
17,150	17,200	2,123	1,718	2,123	1,929
17,200	17,250	2,130	1,723	2,130	1,936
17,250	17,300	2,138	1,728	2,138	1,944
17,300	17,350	2,145	1,733	2,145	1,951
17,350	17,400	2,153	1,738	2,153	1,959
17,400	17,450	2,160	1,743	2,160	1,966
17,450	17,500	2,168	1,748	2,168	1,974
17,500	17,550	2,175	1,753	2,175	1,981
17,550	17,600	2,183	1,758	2,183	1,989
17,600	17,650	2,190	1,763	2,190	1,996
17,650	17,700	2,198	1,768	2,198	2,004
17,700	17,750	2,205	1,773	2,205	2,011
17,750	17,800	2,213	1,778	2,213	2,019
17,800	17,850	2,220	1,783	2,220	2,026
17,850	17,900	2,228	1,788	2,228	2,034
17,900	17,950	2,235	1,793	2,235	2,041
17,950	18,000	2,243	1,798	2,243	2,049

18,000

At least	But less than	Single	Married filing jointly *	Married filing separately	Head of a household
18,000	18,050	2,250	1,803	2,250	2,056
18,050	18,100	2,258	1,808	2,258	2,064
18,100	18,150	2,265	1,813	2,265	2,071
18,150	18,200	2,273	1,819	2,273	2,079
18,200	18,250	2,280	1,826	2,280	2,086
18,250	18,300	2,288	1,834	2,288	2,094
18,300	18,350	2,295	1,841	2,295	2,101
18,350	18,400	2,303	1,849	2,303	2,109
18,400	18,450	2,310	1,856	2,310	2,116
18,450	18,500	2,318	1,864	2,318	2,124
18,500	18,550	2,325	1,871	2,325	2,131
18,550	18,600	2,333	1,879	2,333	2,139
18,600	18,650	2,340	1,886	2,340	2,146
18,650	18,700	2,348	1,894	2,348	2,154
18,700	18,750	2,355	1,901	2,355	2,161
18,750	18,800	2,363	1,909	2,363	2,169
18,800	18,850	2,370	1,916	2,370	2,176
18,850	18,900	2,378	1,924	2,378	2,184
18,900	18,950	2,385	1,931	2,385	2,191
18,950	19,000	2,393	1,939	2,393	2,199

19,000

At least	But less than	Single	Married filing jointly *	Married filing separately	Head of a household
19,000	19,050	2,400	1,946	2,400	2,206
19,050	19,100	2,408	1,954	2,408	2,214
19,100	19,150	2,415	1,961	2,415	2,221
19,150	19,200	2,423	1,969	2,423	2,229
19,200	19,250	2,430	1,976	2,430	2,236
19,250	19,300	2,438	1,984	2,438	2,244
19,300	19,350	2,445	1,991	2,445	2,251
19,350	19,400	2,453	1,999	2,453	2,259
19,400	19,450	2,460	2,006	2,460	2,266
19,450	19,500	2,468	2,014	2,468	2,274
19,500	19,550	2,475	2,021	2,475	2,281
19,550	19,600	2,483	2,029	2,483	2,289
19,600	19,650	2,490	2,036	2,490	2,296
19,650	19,700	2,498	2,044	2,498	2,304
19,700	19,750	2,505	2,051	2,505	2,311
19,750	19,800	2,513	2,059	2,513	2,319
19,800	19,850	2,520	2,066	2,520	2,326
19,850	19,900	2,528	2,074	2,528	2,334
19,900	19,950	2,535	2,081	2,535	2,341
19,950	20,000	2,543	2,089	2,543	2,349

20,000

At least	But less than	Single	Married filing jointly *	Married filing separately	Head of a household
20,000	20,050	2,550	2,096	2,550	2,356
20,050	20,100	2,558	2,104	2,558	2,364
20,100	20,150	2,565	2,111	2,565	2,371
20,150	20,200	2,573	2,119	2,573	2,379
20,200	20,250	2,580	2,126	2,580	2,386
20,250	20,300	2,588	2,134	2,588	2,394
20,300	20,350	2,595	2,141	2,595	2,401
20,350	20,400	2,603	2,149	2,603	2,409
20,400	20,450	2,610	2,156	2,610	2,416
20,450	20,500	2,618	2,164	2,618	2,424
20,500	20,550	2,625	2,171	2,625	2,431
20,550	20,600	2,633	2,179	2,633	2,439
20,600	20,650	2,640	2,186	2,640	2,446
20,650	20,700	2,648	2,194	2,648	2,454
20,700	20,750	2,655	2,201	2,655	2,461
20,750	20,800	2,663	2,209	2,663	2,469
20,800	20,850	2,670	2,216	2,670	2,476
20,850	20,900	2,678	2,224	2,678	2,484
20,900	20,950	2,685	2,231	2,685	2,491
20,950	21,000	2,693	2,239	2,693	2,499

(Continued)

* This column must also be used by a qualifying widow(er).

Need more information or forms? Visit IRS.gov.

2014 Tax Table — Continued

Column headers for all sections:

If line 43 (taxable income) is—		And you are—			
At least	But less than	Single	Married filing jointly *	Married filing separately	Head of a household
		Your tax is—			

21,000

At least	But less than	Single	MFJ *	MFS	HoH
21,000	21,050	2,700	2,246	2,700	2,506
21,050	21,100	2,708	2,254	2,708	2,514
21,100	21,150	2,715	2,261	2,715	2,521
21,150	21,200	2,723	2,269	2,723	2,529
21,200	21,250	2,730	2,276	2,730	2,536
21,250	21,300	2,738	2,284	2,738	2,544
21,300	21,350	2,745	2,291	2,745	2,551
21,350	21,400	2,753	2,299	2,753	2,559
21,400	21,450	2,760	2,306	2,760	2,566
21,450	21,500	2,768	2,314	2,768	2,574
21,500	21,550	2,775	2,321	2,775	2,581
21,550	21,600	2,783	2,329	2,783	2,589
21,600	21,650	2,790	2,336	2,790	2,596
21,650	21,700	2,798	2,344	2,798	2,604
21,700	21,750	2,805	2,351	2,805	2,611
21,750	21,800	2,813	2,359	2,813	2,619
21,800	21,850	2,820	2,366	2,820	2,626
21,850	21,900	2,828	2,374	2,828	2,634
21,900	21,950	2,835	2,381	2,835	2,641
21,950	22,000	2,843	2,389	2,843	2,649

22,000

At least	But less than	Single	MFJ *	MFS	HoH
22,000	22,050	2,850	2,396	2,850	2,656
22,050	22,100	2,858	2,404	2,858	2,664
22,100	22,150	2,865	2,411	2,865	2,671
22,150	22,200	2,873	2,419	2,873	2,679
22,200	22,250	2,880	2,426	2,880	2,686
22,250	22,300	2,888	2,434	2,888	2,694
22,300	22,350	2,895	2,441	2,895	2,701
22,350	22,400	2,903	2,449	2,903	2,709
22,400	22,450	2,910	2,456	2,910	2,716
22,450	22,500	2,918	2,464	2,918	2,724
22,500	22,550	2,925	2,471	2,925	2,731
22,550	22,600	2,933	2,479	2,933	2,739
22,600	22,650	2,940	2,486	2,940	2,746
22,650	22,700	2,948	2,494	2,948	2,754
22,700	22,750	2,955	2,501	2,955	2,761
22,750	22,800	2,963	2,509	2,963	2,769
22,800	22,850	2,970	2,516	2,970	2,776
22,850	22,900	2,978	2,524	2,978	2,784
22,900	22,950	2,985	2,531	2,985	2,791
22,950	23,000	2,993	2,539	2,993	2,799

23,000

At least	But less than	Single	MFJ *	MFS	HoH
23,000	23,050	3,000	2,546	3,000	2,806
23,050	23,100	3,008	2,554	3,008	2,814
23,100	23,150	3,015	2,561	3,015	2,821
23,150	23,200	3,023	2,569	3,023	2,829
23,200	23,250	3,030	2,576	3,030	2,836
23,250	23,300	3,038	2,584	3,038	2,844
23,300	23,350	3,045	2,591	3,045	2,851
23,350	23,400	3,053	2,599	3,053	2,859
23,400	23,450	3,060	2,606	3,060	2,866
23,450	23,500	3,068	2,614	3,068	2,874
23,500	23,550	3,075	2,621	3,075	2,881
23,550	23,600	3,083	2,629	3,083	2,889
23,600	23,650	3,090	2,636	3,090	2,896
23,650	23,700	3,098	2,644	3,098	2,904
23,700	23,750	3,105	2,651	3,105	2,911
23,750	23,800	3,113	2,659	3,113	2,919
23,800	23,850	3,120	2,666	3,120	2,926
23,850	23,900	3,128	2,674	3,128	2,934
23,900	23,950	3,135	2,681	3,135	2,941
23,950	24,000	3,143	2,689	3,143	2,949

24,000

At least	But less than	Single	MFJ *	MFS	HoH
24,000	24,050	3,150	2,696	3,150	2,956
24,050	24,100	3,158	2,704	3,158	2,964
24,100	24,150	3,165	2,711	3,165	2,971
24,150	24,200	3,173	2,719	3,173	2,979
24,200	24,250	3,180	2,726	3,180	2,986
24,250	24,300	3,188	2,734	3,188	2,994
24,300	24,350	3,195	2,741	3,195	3,001
24,350	24,400	3,203	2,749	3,203	3,009
24,400	24,450	3,210	2,756	3,210	3,016
24,450	24,500	3,218	2,764	3,218	3,024
24,500	24,550	3,225	2,771	3,225	3,031
24,550	24,600	3,233	2,779	3,233	3,039
24,600	24,650	3,240	2,786	3,240	3,046
24,650	24,700	3,248	2,794	3,248	3,054
24,700	24,750	3,255	2,801	3,255	3,061
24,750	24,800	3,263	2,809	3,263	3,069
24,800	24,850	3,270	2,816	3,270	3,076
24,850	24,900	3,278	2,824	3,278	3,084
24,900	24,950	3,285	2,831	3,285	3,091
24,950	25,000	3,293	2,839	3,293	3,099

25,000

At least	But less than	Single	MFJ *	MFS	HoH
25,000	25,050	3,300	2,846	3,300	3,106
25,050	25,100	3,308	2,854	3,308	3,114
25,100	25,150	3,315	2,861	3,315	3,121
25,150	25,200	3,323	2,869	3,323	3,129
25,200	25,250	3,330	2,876	3,330	3,136
25,250	25,300	3,338	2,884	3,338	3,144
25,300	25,350	3,345	2,891	3,345	3,151
25,350	25,400	3,353	2,899	3,353	3,159
25,400	25,450	3,360	2,906	3,360	3,166
25,450	25,500	3,368	2,914	3,368	3,174
25,500	25,550	3,375	2,921	3,375	3,181
25,550	25,600	3,383	2,929	3,383	3,189
25,600	25,650	3,390	2,936	3,390	3,196
25,650	25,700	3,398	2,944	3,398	3,204
25,700	25,750	3,405	2,951	3,405	3,211
25,750	25,800	3,413	2,959	3,413	3,219
25,800	25,850	3,420	2,966	3,420	3,226
25,850	25,900	3,428	2,974	3,428	3,234
25,900	25,950	3,435	2,981	3,435	3,241
25,950	26,000	3,443	2,989	3,443	3,249

26,000

At least	But less than	Single	MFJ *	MFS	HoH
26,000	26,050	3,450	2,996	3,450	3,256
26,050	26,100	3,458	3,004	3,458	3,264
26,100	26,150	3,465	3,011	3,465	3,271
26,150	26,200	3,473	3,019	3,473	3,279
26,200	26,250	3,480	3,026	3,480	3,286
26,250	26,300	3,488	3,034	3,488	3,294
26,300	26,350	3,495	3,041	3,495	3,301
26,350	26,400	3,503	3,049	3,503	3,309
26,400	26,450	3,510	3,056	3,510	3,316
26,450	26,500	3,518	3,064	3,518	3,324
26,500	26,550	3,525	3,071	3,525	3,331
26,550	26,600	3,533	3,079	3,533	3,339
26,600	26,650	3,540	3,086	3,540	3,346
26,650	26,700	3,548	3,094	3,548	3,354
26,700	26,750	3,555	3,101	3,555	3,361
26,750	26,800	3,563	3,109	3,563	3,369
26,800	26,850	3,570	3,116	3,570	3,376
26,850	26,900	3,578	3,124	3,578	3,384
26,900	26,950	3,585	3,131	3,585	3,391
26,950	27,000	3,593	3,139	3,593	3,399

27,000

At least	But less than	Single	MFJ *	MFS	HoH
27,000	27,050	3,600	3,146	3,600	3,406
27,050	27,100	3,608	3,154	3,608	3,414
27,100	27,150	3,615	3,161	3,615	3,421
27,150	27,200	3,623	3,169	3,623	3,429
27,200	27,250	3,630	3,176	3,630	3,436
27,250	27,300	3,638	3,184	3,638	3,444
27,300	27,350	3,645	3,191	3,645	3,451
27,350	27,400	3,653	3,199	3,653	3,459
27,400	27,450	3,660	3,206	3,660	3,466
27,450	27,500	3,668	3,214	3,668	3,474
27,500	27,550	3,675	3,221	3,675	3,481
27,550	27,600	3,683	3,229	3,683	3,489
27,600	27,650	3,690	3,236	3,690	3,496
27,650	27,700	3,698	3,244	3,698	3,504
27,700	27,750	3,705	3,251	3,705	3,511
27,750	27,800	3,713	3,259	3,713	3,519
27,800	27,850	3,720	3,266	3,720	3,526
27,850	27,900	3,728	3,274	3,728	3,534
27,900	27,950	3,735	3,281	3,735	3,541
27,950	28,000	3,743	3,289	3,743	3,549

28,000

At least	But less than	Single	MFJ *	MFS	HoH
28,000	28,050	3,750	3,296	3,750	3,556
28,050	28,100	3,758	3,304	3,758	3,564
28,100	28,150	3,765	3,311	3,765	3,571
28,150	28,200	3,773	3,319	3,773	3,579
28,200	28,250	3,780	3,326	3,780	3,586
28,250	28,300	3,788	3,334	3,788	3,594
28,300	28,350	3,795	3,341	3,795	3,601
28,350	28,400	3,803	3,349	3,803	3,609
28,400	28,450	3,810	3,356	3,810	3,616
28,450	28,500	3,818	3,364	3,818	3,624
28,500	28,550	3,825	3,371	3,825	3,631
28,550	28,600	3,833	3,379	3,833	3,639
28,600	28,650	3,840	3,386	3,840	3,646
28,650	28,700	3,848	3,394	3,848	3,654
28,700	28,750	3,855	3,401	3,855	3,661
28,750	28,800	3,863	3,409	3,863	3,669
28,800	28,850	3,870	3,416	3,870	3,676
28,850	28,900	3,878	3,424	3,878	3,684
28,900	28,950	3,885	3,431	3,885	3,691
28,950	29,000	3,893	3,439	3,893	3,699

29,000

At least	But less than	Single	MFJ *	MFS	HoH
29,000	29,050	3,900	3,446	3,900	3,706
29,050	29,100	3,908	3,454	3,908	3,714
29,100	29,150	3,915	3,461	3,915	3,721
29,150	29,200	3,923	3,469	3,923	3,729
29,200	29,250	3,930	3,476	3,930	3,736
29,250	29,300	3,938	3,484	3,938	3,744
29,300	29,350	3,945	3,491	3,945	3,751
29,350	29,400	3,953	3,499	3,953	3,759
29,400	29,450	3,960	3,506	3,960	3,766
29,450	29,500	3,968	3,514	3,968	3,774
29,500	29,550	3,975	3,521	3,975	3,781
29,550	29,600	3,983	3,529	3,983	3,789
29,600	29,650	3,990	3,536	3,990	3,796
29,650	29,700	3,998	3,544	3,998	3,804
29,700	29,750	4,005	3,551	4,005	3,811
29,750	29,800	4,013	3,559	4,013	3,819
29,800	29,850	4,020	3,566	4,020	3,826
29,850	29,900	4,028	3,574	4,028	3,834
29,900	29,950	4,035	3,581	4,035	3,841
29,950	30,000	4,043	3,589	4,043	3,849

* This column must also be used by a qualifying widow(er).

(Continued)

Need more information or forms? Visit IRS.gov.

2014 Tax Table — *Continued*

If line 43 (taxable income) is—		And you are—			
At least	But less than	Single	Married filing jointly *	Married filing separately	Head of a household
		Your tax is—			

30,000

At least	But less than	Single	MFJ *	MFS	HoH
30,000	30,050	4,050	3,596	4,050	3,856
30,050	30,100	4,058	3,604	4,058	3,864
30,100	30,150	4,065	3,611	4,065	3,871
30,150	30,200	4,073	3,619	4,073	3,879
30,200	30,250	4,080	3,626	4,080	3,886
30,250	30,300	4,088	3,634	4,088	3,894
30,300	30,350	4,095	3,641	4,095	3,901
30,350	30,400	4,103	3,649	4,103	3,909
30,400	30,450	4,110	3,656	4,110	3,916
30,450	30,500	4,118	3,664	4,118	3,924
30,500	30,550	4,125	3,671	4,125	3,931
30,550	30,600	4,133	3,679	4,133	3,939
30,600	30,650	4,140	3,686	4,140	3,946
30,650	30,700	4,148	3,694	4,148	3,954
30,700	30,750	4,155	3,701	4,155	3,961
30,750	30,800	4,163	3,709	4,163	3,969
30,800	30,850	4,170	3,716	4,170	3,976
30,850	30,900	4,178	3,724	4,178	3,984
30,900	30,950	4,185	3,731	4,185	3,991
30,950	31,000	4,193	3,739	4,193	3,999

31,000

At least	But less than	Single	MFJ *	MFS	HoH
31,000	31,050	4,200	3,746	4,200	4,006
31,050	31,100	4,208	3,754	4,208	4,014
31,100	31,150	4,215	3,761	4,215	4,021
31,150	31,200	4,223	3,769	4,223	4,029
31,200	31,250	4,230	3,776	4,230	4,036
31,250	31,300	4,238	3,784	4,238	4,044
31,300	31,350	4,245	3,791	4,245	4,051
31,350	31,400	4,253	3,799	4,253	4,059
31,400	31,450	4,260	3,806	4,260	4,066
31,450	31,500	4,268	3,814	4,268	4,074
31,500	31,550	4,275	3,821	4,275	4,081
31,550	31,600	4,283	3,829	4,283	4,089
31,600	31,650	4,290	3,836	4,290	4,096
31,650	31,700	4,298	3,844	4,298	4,104
31,700	31,750	4,305	3,851	4,305	4,111
31,750	31,800	4,313	3,859	4,313	4,119
31,800	31,850	4,320	3,866	4,320	4,126
31,850	31,900	4,328	3,874	4,328	4,134
31,900	31,950	4,335	3,881	4,335	4,141
31,950	32,000	4,343	3,889	4,343	4,149

32,000

At least	But less than	Single	MFJ *	MFS	HoH
32,000	32,050	4,350	3,896	4,350	4,156
32,050	32,100	4,358	3,904	4,358	4,164
32,100	32,150	4,365	3,911	4,365	4,171
32,150	32,200	4,373	3,919	4,373	4,179
32,200	32,250	4,380	3,926	4,380	4,186
32,250	32,300	4,388	3,934	4,388	4,194
32,300	32,350	4,395	3,941	4,395	4,201
32,350	32,400	4,403	3,949	4,403	4,209
32,400	32,450	4,410	3,956	4,410	4,216
32,450	32,500	4,418	3,964	4,418	4,224
32,500	32,550	4,425	3,971	4,425	4,231
32,550	32,600	4,433	3,979	4,433	4,239
32,600	32,650	4,440	3,986	4,440	4,246
32,650	32,700	4,448	3,994	4,448	4,254
32,700	32,750	4,455	4,001	4,455	4,261
32,750	32,800	4,463	4,009	4,463	4,269
32,800	32,850	4,470	4,016	4,470	4,276
32,850	32,900	4,478	4,024	4,478	4,284
32,900	32,950	4,485	4,031	4,485	4,291
32,950	33,000	4,493	4,039	4,493	4,299

33,000

At least	But less than	Single	MFJ *	MFS	HoH
33,000	33,050	4,500	4,046	4,500	4,306
33,050	33,100	4,508	4,054	4,508	4,314
33,100	33,150	4,515	4,061	4,515	4,321
33,150	33,200	4,523	4,069	4,523	4,329
33,200	33,250	4,530	4,076	4,530	4,336
33,250	33,300	4,538	4,084	4,538	4,344
33,300	33,350	4,545	4,091	4,545	4,351
33,350	33,400	4,553	4,099	4,553	4,359
33,400	33,450	4,560	4,106	4,560	4,366
33,450	33,500	4,568	4,114	4,568	4,374
33,500	33,550	4,575	4,121	4,575	4,381
33,550	33,600	4,583	4,129	4,583	4,389
33,600	33,650	4,590	4,136	4,590	4,396
33,650	33,700	4,598	4,144	4,598	4,404
33,700	33,750	4,605	4,151	4,605	4,411
33,750	33,800	4,613	4,159	4,613	4,419
33,800	33,850	4,620	4,166	4,620	4,426
33,850	33,900	4,628	4,174	4,628	4,434
33,900	33,950	4,635	4,181	4,635	4,441
33,950	34,000	4,643	4,189	4,643	4,449

34,000

At least	But less than	Single	MFJ *	MFS	HoH
34,000	34,050	4,650	4,196	4,650	4,456
34,050	34,100	4,658	4,204	4,658	4,464
34,100	34,150	4,665	4,211	4,665	4,471
34,150	34,200	4,673	4,219	4,673	4,479
34,200	34,250	4,680	4,226	4,680	4,486
34,250	34,300	4,688	4,234	4,688	4,494
34,300	34,350	4,695	4,241	4,695	4,501
34,350	34,400	4,703	4,249	4,703	4,509
34,400	34,450	4,710	4,256	4,710	4,516
34,450	34,500	4,718	4,264	4,718	4,524
34,500	34,550	4,725	4,271	4,725	4,531
34,550	34,600	4,733	4,279	4,733	4,539
34,600	34,650	4,740	4,286	4,740	4,546
34,650	34,700	4,748	4,294	4,748	4,554
34,700	34,750	4,755	4,301	4,755	4,561
34,750	34,800	4,763	4,309	4,763	4,569
34,800	34,850	4,770	4,316	4,770	4,576
34,850	34,900	4,778	4,324	4,778	4,584
34,900	34,950	4,785	4,331	4,785	4,591
34,950	35,000	4,793	4,339	4,793	4,599

35,000

At least	But less than	Single	MFJ *	MFS	HoH
35,000	35,050	4,800	4,346	4,800	4,606
35,050	35,100	4,808	4,354	4,808	4,614
35,100	35,150	4,815	4,361	4,815	4,621
35,150	35,200	4,823	4,369	4,823	4,629
35,200	35,250	4,830	4,376	4,830	4,636
35,250	35,300	4,838	4,384	4,838	4,644
35,300	35,350	4,845	4,391	4,845	4,651
35,350	35,400	4,853	4,399	4,853	4,659
35,400	35,450	4,860	4,406	4,860	4,666
35,450	35,500	4,868	4,414	4,868	4,674
35,500	35,550	4,875	4,421	4,875	4,681
35,550	35,600	4,883	4,429	4,883	4,689
35,600	35,650	4,890	4,436	4,890	4,696
35,650	35,700	4,898	4,444	4,898	4,704
35,700	35,750	4,905	4,451	4,905	4,711
35,750	35,800	4,913	4,459	4,913	4,719
35,800	35,850	4,920	4,466	4,920	4,726
35,850	35,900	4,928	4,474	4,928	4,734
35,900	35,950	4,935	4,481	4,935	4,741
35,950	36,000	4,943	4,489	4,943	4,749

36,000

At least	But less than	Single	MFJ *	MFS	HoH
36,000	36,050	4,950	4,496	4,950	4,756
36,050	36,100	4,958	4,504	4,958	4,764
36,100	36,150	4,965	4,511	4,965	4,771
36,150	36,200	4,973	4,519	4,973	4,779
36,200	36,250	4,980	4,526	4,980	4,786
36,250	36,300	4,988	4,534	4,988	4,794
36,300	36,350	4,995	4,541	4,995	4,801
36,350	36,400	5,003	4,549	5,003	4,809
36,400	36,450	5,010	4,556	5,010	4,816
36,450	36,500	5,018	4,564	5,018	4,824
36,500	36,550	5,025	4,571	5,025	4,831
36,550	36,600	5,033	4,579	5,033	4,839
36,600	36,650	5,040	4,586	5,040	4,846
36,650	36,700	5,048	4,594	5,048	4,854
36,700	36,750	5,055	4,601	5,055	4,861
36,750	36,800	5,063	4,609	5,063	4,869
36,800	36,850	5,070	4,616	5,070	4,876
36,850	36,900	5,078	4,624	5,078	4,884
36,900	36,950	5,088	4,631	5,088	4,891
36,950	37,000	5,100	4,639	5,100	4,899

37,000

At least	But less than	Single	MFJ *	MFS	HoH
37,000	37,050	5,113	4,646	5,113	4,906
37,050	37,100	5,125	4,654	5,125	4,914
37,100	37,150	5,138	4,661	5,138	4,921
37,150	37,200	5,150	4,669	5,150	4,929
37,200	37,250	5,163	4,676	5,163	4,936
37,250	37,300	5,175	4,684	5,175	4,944
37,300	37,350	5,188	4,691	5,188	4,951
37,350	37,400	5,200	4,699	5,200	4,959
37,400	37,450	5,213	4,706	5,213	4,966
37,450	37,500	5,225	4,714	5,225	4,974
37,500	37,550	5,238	4,721	5,238	4,981
37,550	37,600	5,250	4,729	5,250	4,989
37,600	37,650	5,263	4,736	5,263	4,996
37,650	37,700	5,275	4,744	5,275	5,004
37,700	37,750	5,288	4,751	5,288	5,011
37,750	37,800	5,300	4,759	5,300	5,019
37,800	37,850	5,313	4,766	5,313	5,026
37,850	37,900	5,325	4,774	5,325	5,034
37,900	37,950	5,338	4,781	5,338	5,041
37,950	38,000	5,350	4,789	5,350	5,049

38,000

At least	But less than	Single	MFJ *	MFS	HoH
38,000	38,050	5,363	4,796	5,363	5,056
38,050	38,100	5,375	4,804	5,375	5,064
38,100	38,150	5,388	4,811	5,388	5,071
38,150	38,200	5,400	4,819	5,400	5,079
38,200	38,250	5,413	4,826	5,413	5,086
38,250	38,300	5,425	4,834	5,425	5,094
38,300	38,350	5,438	4,841	5,438	5,101
38,350	38,400	5,450	4,849	5,450	5,109
38,400	38,450	5,463	4,856	5,463	5,116
38,450	38,500	5,475	4,864	5,475	5,124
38,500	38,550	5,488	4,871	5,488	5,131
38,550	38,600	5,500	4,879	5,500	5,139
38,600	38,650	5,513	4,886	5,513	5,146
38,650	38,700	5,525	4,894	5,525	5,154
38,700	38,750	5,538	4,901	5,538	5,161
38,750	38,800	5,550	4,909	5,550	5,169
38,800	38,850	5,563	4,916	5,563	5,176
38,850	38,900	5,575	4,924	5,575	5,184
38,900	38,950	5,588	4,931	5,588	5,191
38,950	39,000	5,600	4,939	5,600	5,199

* This column must also be used by a qualifying widow(er).

(Continued)

Need more information or forms? Visit IRS.gov.

- 80 -

2014 Tax Table — *Continued*

39,000

If line 43 (taxable income) is—		And you are—			
At least	But less than	Single	Married filing jointly *	Married filing separately	Head of a household
		Your tax is—			
39,000	39,050	5,613	4,946	5,613	5,206
39,050	39,100	5,625	4,954	5,625	5,214
39,100	39,150	5,638	4,961	5,638	5,221
39,150	39,200	5,650	4,969	5,650	5,229
39,200	39,250	5,663	4,976	5,663	5,236
39,250	39,300	5,675	4,984	5,675	5,244
39,300	39,350	5,688	4,991	5,688	5,251
39,350	39,400	5,700	4,999	5,700	5,259
39,400	39,450	5,713	5,006	5,713	5,266
39,450	39,500	5,725	5,014	5,725	5,274
39,500	39,550	5,738	5,021	5,738	5,281
39,550	39,600	5,750	5,029	5,750	5,289
39,600	39,650	5,763	5,036	5,763	5,296
39,650	39,700	5,775	5,044	5,775	5,304
39,700	39,750	5,788	5,051	5,788	5,311
39,750	39,800	5,800	5,059	5,800	5,319
39,800	39,850	5,813	5,066	5,813	5,326
39,850	39,900	5,825	5,074	5,825	5,334
39,900	39,950	5,838	5,081	5,838	5,341
39,950	40,000	5,850	5,089	5,850	5,349

40,000

At least	But less than	Single	Married filing jointly *	Married filing separately	Head of a household
40,000	40,050	5,863	5,096	5,863	5,356
40,050	40,100	5,875	5,104	5,875	5,364
40,100	40,150	5,888	5,111	5,888	5,371
40,150	40,200	5,900	5,119	5,900	5,379
40,200	40,250	5,913	5,126	5,913	5,386
40,250	40,300	5,925	5,134	5,925	5,394
40,300	40,350	5,938	5,141	5,938	5,401
40,350	40,400	5,950	5,149	5,950	5,409
40,400	40,450	5,963	5,156	5,963	5,416
40,450	40,500	5,975	5,164	5,975	5,424
40,500	40,550	5,988	5,171	5,988	5,431
40,550	40,600	6,000	5,179	6,000	5,439
40,600	40,650	6,013	5,186	6,013	5,446
40,650	40,700	6,025	5,194	6,025	5,454
40,700	40,750	6,038	5,201	6,038	5,461
40,750	40,800	6,050	5,209	6,050	5,469
40,800	40,850	6,063	5,216	6,063	5,476
40,850	40,900	6,075	5,224	6,075	5,484
40,900	40,950	6,088	5,231	6,088	5,491
40,950	41,000	6,100	5,239	6,100	5,499

41,000

At least	But less than	Single	Married filing jointly *	Married filing separately	Head of a household
41,000	41,050	6,113	5,246	6,113	5,506
41,050	41,100	6,125	5,254	6,125	5,514
41,100	41,150	6,138	5,261	6,138	5,521
41,150	41,200	6,150	5,269	6,150	5,529
41,200	41,250	6,163	5,276	6,163	5,536
41,250	41,300	6,175	5,284	6,175	5,544
41,300	41,350	6,188	5,291	6,188	5,551
41,350	41,400	6,200	5,299	6,200	5,559
41,400	41,450	6,213	5,306	6,213	5,566
41,450	41,500	6,225	5,314	6,225	5,574
41,500	41,550	6,238	5,321	6,238	5,581
41,550	41,600	6,250	5,329	6,250	5,589
41,600	41,650	6,263	5,336	6,263	5,596
41,650	41,700	6,275	5,344	6,275	5,604
41,700	41,750	6,288	5,351	6,288	5,611
41,750	41,800	6,300	5,359	6,300	5,619
41,800	41,850	6,313	5,366	6,313	5,626
41,850	41,900	6,325	5,374	6,325	5,634
41,900	41,950	6,338	5,381	6,338	5,641
41,950	42,000	6,350	5,389	6,350	5,649

42,000

If line 43 (taxable income) is—		And you are—			
At least	But less than	Single	Married filing jointly *	Married filing separately	Head of a household
		Your tax is—			
42,000	42,050	6,363	5,396	6,363	5,656
42,050	42,100	6,375	5,404	6,375	5,664
42,100	42,150	6,388	5,411	6,388	5,671
42,150	42,200	6,400	5,419	6,400	5,679
42,200	42,250	6,413	5,426	6,413	5,686
42,250	42,300	6,425	5,434	6,425	5,694
42,300	42,350	6,438	5,441	6,438	5,701
42,350	42,400	6,450	5,449	6,450	5,709
42,400	42,450	6,463	5,456	6,463	5,716
42,450	42,500	6,475	5,464	6,475	5,724
42,500	42,550	6,488	5,471	6,488	5,731
42,550	42,600	6,500	5,479	6,500	5,739
42,600	42,650	6,513	5,486	6,513	5,746
42,650	42,700	6,525	5,494	6,525	5,754
42,700	42,750	6,538	5,501	6,538	5,761
42,750	42,800	6,550	5,509	6,550	5,769
42,800	42,850	6,563	5,516	6,563	5,776
42,850	42,900	6,575	5,524	6,575	5,784
42,900	42,950	6,588	5,531	6,588	5,791
42,950	43,000	6,600	5,539	6,600	5,799

43,000

At least	But less than	Single	Married filing jointly *	Married filing separately	Head of a household
43,000	43,050	6,613	5,546	6,613	5,806
43,050	43,100	6,625	5,554	6,625	5,814
43,100	43,150	6,638	5,561	6,638	5,821
43,150	43,200	6,650	5,569	6,650	5,829
43,200	43,250	6,663	5,576	6,663	5,836
43,250	43,300	6,675	5,584	6,675	5,844
43,300	43,350	6,688	5,591	6,688	5,851
43,350	43,400	6,700	5,599	6,700	5,859
43,400	43,450	6,713	5,606	6,713	5,866
43,450	43,500	6,725	5,614	6,725	5,874
43,500	43,550	6,738	5,621	6,738	5,881
43,550	43,600	6,750	5,629	6,750	5,889
43,600	43,650	6,763	5,636	6,763	5,896
43,650	43,700	6,775	5,644	6,775	5,904
43,700	43,750	6,788	5,651	6,788	5,911
43,750	43,800	6,800	5,659	6,800	5,919
43,800	43,850	6,813	5,666	6,813	5,926
43,850	43,900	6,825	5,674	6,825	5,934
43,900	43,950	6,838	5,681	6,838	5,941
43,950	44,000	6,850	5,689	6,850	5,949

44,000

At least	But less than	Single	Married filing jointly *	Married filing separately	Head of a household
44,000	44,050	6,863	5,696	6,863	5,956
44,050	44,100	6,875	5,704	6,875	5,964
44,100	44,150	6,888	5,711	6,888	5,971
44,150	44,200	6,900	5,719	6,900	5,979
44,200	44,250	6,913	5,726	6,913	5,986
44,250	44,300	6,925	5,734	6,925	5,994
44,300	44,350	6,938	5,741	6,938	6,001
44,350	44,400	6,950	5,749	6,950	6,009
44,400	44,450	6,963	5,756	6,963	6,016
44,450	44,500	6,975	5,764	6,975	6,024
44,500	44,550	6,988	5,771	6,988	6,031
44,550	44,600	7,000	5,779	7,000	6,039
44,600	44,650	7,013	5,786	7,013	6,046
44,650	44,700	7,025	5,794	7,025	6,054
44,700	44,750	7,038	5,801	7,038	6,061
44,750	44,800	7,050	5,809	7,050	6,069
44,800	44,850	7,063	5,816	7,063	6,076
44,850	44,900	7,075	5,824	7,075	6,084
44,900	44,950	7,088	5,831	7,088	6,091
44,950	45,000	7,100	5,839	7,100	6,099

45,000

If line 43 (taxable income) is—		And you are—			
At least	But less than	Single	Married filing jointly *	Married filing separately	Head of a household
		Your tax is—			
45,000	45,050	7,113	5,846	7,113	6,106
45,050	45,100	7,125	5,854	7,125	6,114
45,100	45,150	7,138	5,861	7,138	6,121
45,150	45,200	7,150	5,869	7,150	6,129
45,200	45,250	7,163	5,876	7,163	6,136
45,250	45,300	7,175	5,884	7,175	6,144
45,300	45,350	7,188	5,891	7,188	6,151
45,350	45,400	7,200	5,899	7,200	6,159
45,400	45,450	7,213	5,906	7,213	6,166
45,450	45,500	7,225	5,914	7,225	6,174
45,500	45,550	7,238	5,921	7,238	6,181
45,550	45,600	7,250	5,929	7,250	6,189
45,600	45,650	7,263	5,936	7,263	6,196
45,650	45,700	7,275	5,944	7,275	6,204
45,700	45,750	7,288	5,951	7,288	6,211
45,750	45,800	7,300	5,959	7,300	6,219
45,800	45,850	7,313	5,966	7,313	6,226
45,850	45,900	7,325	5,974	7,325	6,234
45,900	45,950	7,338	5,981	7,338	6,241
45,950	46,000	7,350	5,989	7,350	6,249

46,000

At least	But less than	Single	Married filing jointly *	Married filing separately	Head of a household
46,000	46,050	7,363	5,996	7,363	6,256
46,050	46,100	7,375	6,004	7,375	6,264
46,100	46,150	7,388	6,011	7,388	6,271
46,150	46,200	7,400	6,019	7,400	6,279
46,200	46,250	7,413	6,026	7,413	6,286
46,250	46,300	7,425	6,034	7,425	6,294
46,300	46,350	7,438	6,041	7,438	6,301
46,350	46,400	7,450	6,049	7,450	6,309
46,400	46,450	7,463	6,056	7,463	6,316
46,450	46,500	7,475	6,064	7,475	6,324
46,500	46,550	7,488	6,071	7,488	6,331
46,550	46,600	7,500	6,079	7,500	6,339
46,600	46,650	7,513	6,086	7,513	6,346
46,650	46,700	7,525	6,094	7,525	6,354
46,700	46,750	7,538	6,101	7,538	6,361
46,750	46,800	7,550	6,109	7,550	6,369
46,800	46,850	7,563	6,116	7,563	6,376
46,850	46,900	7,575	6,124	7,575	6,384
46,900	46,950	7,588	6,131	7,588	6,391
46,950	47,000	7,600	6,139	7,600	6,399

47,000

At least	But less than	Single	Married filing jointly *	Married filing separately	Head of a household
47,000	47,050	7,613	6,146	7,613	6,406
47,050	47,100	7,625	6,154	7,625	6,414
47,100	47,150	7,638	6,161	7,638	6,421
47,150	47,200	7,650	6,169	7,650	6,429
47,200	47,250	7,663	6,176	7,663	6,436
47,250	47,300	7,675	6,184	7,675	6,444
47,300	47,350	7,688	6,191	7,688	6,451
47,350	47,400	7,700	6,199	7,700	6,459
47,400	47,450	7,713	6,206	7,713	6,466
47,450	47,500	7,725	6,214	7,725	6,474
47,500	47,550	7,738	6,221	7,738	6,481
47,550	47,600	7,750	6,229	7,750	6,489
47,600	47,650	7,763	6,236	7,763	6,496
47,650	47,700	7,775	6,244	7,775	6,504
47,700	47,750	7,788	6,251	7,788	6,511
47,750	47,800	7,800	6,259	7,800	6,519
47,800	47,850	7,813	6,266	7,813	6,526
47,850	47,900	7,825	6,274	7,825	6,534
47,900	47,950	7,838	6,281	7,838	6,541
47,950	48,000	7,850	6,289	7,850	6,549

* This column must also be used by a qualifying widow(er).

(Continued)

Need more information or forms? Visit IRS.gov.

2014 Tax Table — *Continued*

If line 43 (taxable income) is—		And you are—				Your tax is—
At least	But less than	Single	Married filing jointly *	Married filing separately	Head of a household	

48,000

At least	But less than	Single	MFJ*	MFS	HoH
48,000	48,050	7,863	6,296	7,863	6,556
48,050	48,100	7,875	6,304	7,875	6,564
48,100	48,150	7,888	6,311	7,888	6,571
48,150	48,200	7,900	6,319	7,900	6,579
48,200	48,250	7,913	6,326	7,913	6,586
48,250	48,300	7,925	6,334	7,925	6,594
48,300	48,350	7,938	6,341	7,938	6,601
48,350	48,400	7,950	6,349	7,950	6,609
48,400	48,450	7,963	6,356	7,963	6,616
48,450	48,500	7,975	6,364	7,975	6,624
48,500	48,550	7,988	6,371	7,988	6,631
48,550	48,600	8,000	6,379	8,000	6,639
48,600	48,650	8,013	6,386	8,013	6,646
48,650	48,700	8,025	6,394	8,025	6,654
48,700	48,750	8,038	6,401	8,038	6,661
48,750	48,800	8,050	6,409	8,050	6,669
48,800	48,850	8,063	6,416	8,063	6,676
48,850	48,900	8,075	6,424	8,075	6,684
48,900	48,950	8,088	6,431	8,088	6,691
48,950	49,000	8,100	6,439	8,100	6,699

49,000

At least	But less than	Single	MFJ*	MFS	HoH
49,000	49,050	8,113	6,446	8,113	6,706
49,050	49,100	8,125	6,454	8,125	6,714
49,100	49,150	8,138	6,461	8,138	6,721
49,150	49,200	8,150	6,469	8,150	6,729
49,200	49,250	8,163	6,476	8,163	6,736
49,250	49,300	8,175	6,484	8,175	6,744
49,300	49,350	8,188	6,491	8,188	6,751
49,350	49,400	8,200	6,499	8,200	6,759
49,400	49,450	8,213	6,506	8,213	6,769
49,450	49,500	8,225	6,514	8,225	6,781
49,500	49,550	8,238	6,521	8,238	6,794
49,550	49,600	8,250	6,529	8,250	6,806
49,600	49,650	8,263	6,536	8,263	6,819
49,650	49,700	8,275	6,544	8,275	6,831
49,700	49,750	8,288	6,551	8,288	6,844
49,750	49,800	8,300	6,559	8,300	6,856
49,800	49,850	8,313	6,566	8,313	6,869
49,850	49,900	8,325	6,574	8,325	6,881
49,900	49,950	8,338	6,581	8,338	6,894
49,950	50,000	8,350	6,589	8,350	6,906

50,000

At least	But less than	Single	MFJ*	MFS	HoH
50,000	50,050	8,363	6,596	8,363	6,919
50,050	50,100	8,375	6,604	8,375	6,931
50,100	50,150	8,388	6,611	8,388	6,944
50,150	50,200	8,400	6,619	8,400	6,956
50,200	50,250	8,413	6,626	8,413	6,969
50,250	50,300	8,425	6,634	8,425	6,981
50,300	50,350	8,438	6,641	8,438	6,994
50,350	50,400	8,450	6,649	8,450	7,006
50,400	50,450	8,463	6,656	8,463	7,019
50,450	50,500	8,475	6,664	8,475	7,031
50,500	50,550	8,488	6,671	8,488	7,044
50,550	50,600	8,500	6,679	8,500	7,056
50,600	50,650	8,513	6,686	8,513	7,069
50,650	50,700	8,525	6,694	8,525	7,081
50,700	50,750	8,538	6,701	8,538	7,094
50,750	50,800	8,550	6,709	8,550	7,106
50,800	50,850	8,563	6,716	8,563	7,119
50,850	50,900	8,575	6,724	8,575	7,131
50,900	50,950	8,588	6,731	8,588	7,144
50,950	51,000	8,600	6,739	8,600	7,156

51,000

At least	But less than	Single	MFJ*	MFS	HoH
51,000	51,050	8,613	6,746	8,613	7,169
51,050	51,100	8,625	6,754	8,625	7,181
51,100	51,150	8,638	6,761	8,638	7,194
51,150	51,200	8,650	6,769	8,650	7,206
51,200	51,250	8,663	6,776	8,663	7,219
51,250	51,300	8,675	6,784	8,675	7,231
51,300	51,350	8,688	6,791	8,688	7,244
51,350	51,400	8,700	6,799	8,700	7,256
51,400	51,450	8,713	6,806	8,713	7,269
51,450	51,500	8,725	6,814	8,725	7,281
51,500	51,550	8,738	6,821	8,738	7,294
51,550	51,600	8,750	6,829	8,750	7,306
51,600	51,650	8,763	6,836	8,763	7,319
51,650	51,700	8,775	6,844	8,775	7,331
51,700	51,750	8,788	6,851	8,788	7,344
51,750	51,800	8,800	6,859	8,800	7,356
51,800	51,850	8,813	6,866	8,813	7,369
51,850	51,900	8,825	6,874	8,825	7,381
51,900	51,950	8,838	6,881	8,838	7,394
51,950	52,000	8,850	6,889	8,850	7,406

52,000

At least	But less than	Single	MFJ*	MFS	HoH
52,000	52,050	8,863	6,896	8,863	7,419
52,050	52,100	8,875	6,904	8,875	7,431
52,100	52,150	8,888	6,911	8,888	7,444
52,150	52,200	8,900	6,919	8,900	7,456
52,200	52,250	8,913	6,926	8,913	7,469
52,250	52,300	8,925	6,934	8,925	7,481
52,300	52,350	8,938	6,941	8,938	7,494
52,350	52,400	8,950	6,949	8,950	7,506
52,400	52,450	8,963	6,956	8,963	7,519
52,450	52,500	8,975	6,964	8,975	7,531
52,500	52,550	8,988	6,971	8,988	7,544
52,550	52,600	9,000	6,979	9,000	7,556
52,600	52,650	9,013	6,986	9,013	7,569
52,650	52,700	9,025	6,994	9,025	7,581
52,700	52,750	9,038	7,001	9,038	7,594
52,750	52,800	9,050	7,009	9,050	7,606
52,800	52,850	9,063	7,016	9,063	7,619
52,850	52,900	9,075	7,024	9,075	7,631
52,900	52,950	9,088	7,031	9,088	7,644
52,950	53,000	9,100	7,039	9,100	7,656

53,000

At least	But less than	Single	MFJ*	MFS	HoH
53,000	53,050	9,113	7,046	9,113	7,669
53,050	53,100	9,125	7,054	9,125	7,681
53,100	53,150	9,138	7,061	9,138	7,694
53,150	53,200	9,150	7,069	9,150	7,706
53,200	53,250	9,163	7,076	9,163	7,719
53,250	53,300	9,175	7,084	9,175	7,731
53,300	53,350	9,188	7,091	9,188	7,744
53,350	53,400	9,200	7,099	9,200	7,756
53,400	53,450	9,213	7,106	9,213	7,769
53,450	53,500	9,225	7,114	9,225	7,781
53,500	53,550	9,238	7,121	9,238	7,794
53,550	53,600	9,250	7,129	9,250	7,806
53,600	53,650	9,263	7,136	9,263	7,819
53,650	53,700	9,275	7,144	9,275	7,831
53,700	53,750	9,288	7,151	9,288	7,844
53,750	53,800	9,300	7,159	9,300	7,856
53,800	53,850	9,313	7,166	9,313	7,869
53,850	53,900	9,325	7,174	9,325	7,881
53,900	53,950	9,338	7,181	9,338	7,894
53,950	54,000	9,350	7,189	9,350	7,906

54,000

At least	But less than	Single	MFJ*	MFS	HoH
54,000	54,050	9,363	7,196	9,363	7,919
54,050	54,100	9,375	7,204	9,375	7,931
54,100	54,150	9,388	7,211	9,388	7,944
54,150	54,200	9,400	7,219	9,400	7,956
54,200	54,250	9,413	7,226	9,413	7,969
54,250	54,300	9,425	7,234	9,425	7,981
54,300	54,350	9,438	7,241	9,438	7,994
54,350	54,400	9,450	7,249	9,450	8,006
54,400	54,450	9,463	7,256	9,463	8,019
54,450	54,500	9,475	7,264	9,475	8,031
54,500	54,550	9,488	7,271	9,488	8,044
54,550	54,600	9,500	7,279	9,500	8,056
54,600	54,650	9,513	7,286	9,513	8,069
54,650	54,700	9,525	7,294	9,525	8,081
54,700	54,750	9,538	7,301	9,538	8,094
54,750	54,800	9,550	7,309	9,550	8,106
54,800	54,850	9,563	7,316	9,563	8,119
54,850	54,900	9,575	7,324	9,575	8,131
54,900	54,950	9,588	7,331	9,588	8,144
54,950	55,000	9,600	7,339	9,600	8,156

55,000

At least	But less than	Single	MFJ*	MFS	HoH
55,000	55,050	9,613	7,346	9,613	8,169
55,050	55,100	9,625	7,354	9,625	8,181
55,100	55,150	9,638	7,361	9,638	8,194
55,150	55,200	9,650	7,369	9,650	8,206
55,200	55,250	9,663	7,376	9,663	8,219
55,250	55,300	9,675	7,384	9,675	8,231
55,300	55,350	9,688	7,391	9,688	8,244
55,350	55,400	9,700	7,399	9,700	8,256
55,400	55,450	9,713	7,406	9,713	8,269
55,450	55,500	9,725	7,414	9,725	8,281
55,500	55,550	9,738	7,421	9,738	8,294
55,550	55,600	9,750	7,429	9,750	8,306
55,600	55,650	9,763	7,436	9,763	8,319
55,650	55,700	9,775	7,444	9,775	8,331
55,700	55,750	9,788	7,451	9,788	8,344
55,750	55,800	9,800	7,459	9,800	8,356
55,800	55,850	9,813	7,466	9,813	8,369
55,850	55,900	9,825	7,474	9,825	8,381
55,900	55,950	9,838	7,481	9,838	8,394
55,950	56,000	9,850	7,489	9,850	8,406

56,000

At least	But less than	Single	MFJ*	MFS	HoH
56,000	56,050	9,863	7,496	9,863	8,419
56,050	56,100	9,875	7,504	9,875	8,431
56,100	56,150	9,888	7,511	9,888	8,444
56,150	56,200	9,900	7,519	9,900	8,456
56,200	56,250	9,913	7,526	9,913	8,469
56,250	56,300	9,925	7,534	9,925	8,481
56,300	56,350	9,938	7,541	9,938	8,494
56,350	56,400	9,950	7,549	9,950	8,506
56,400	56,450	9,963	7,556	9,963	8,519
56,450	56,500	9,975	7,564	9,975	8,531
56,500	56,550	9,988	7,571	9,988	8,544
56,550	56,600	10,000	7,579	10,000	8,556
56,600	56,650	10,013	7,586	10,013	8,569
56,650	56,700	10,025	7,594	10,025	8,581
56,700	56,750	10,038	7,601	10,038	8,594
56,750	56,800	10,050	7,609	10,050	8,606
56,800	56,850	10,063	7,616	10,063	8,619
56,850	56,900	10,075	7,624	10,075	8,631
56,900	56,950	10,088	7,631	10,088	8,644
56,950	57,000	10,100	7,639	10,100	8,656

(Continued)

* This column must also be used by a qualifying widow(er).

2014 Tax Table — *Continued*

57,000

If line 43 (taxable income) is—		And you are—			
At least	But less than	Single	Married filing jointly *	Married filing separately	Head of a household
		Your tax is—			
57,000	57,050	10,113	7,646	10,113	8,669
57,050	57,100	10,125	7,654	10,125	8,681
57,100	57,150	10,138	7,661	10,138	8,694
57,150	57,200	10,150	7,669	10,150	8,706
57,200	57,250	10,163	7,676	10,163	8,719
57,250	57,300	10,175	7,684	10,175	8,731
57,300	57,350	10,188	7,691	10,188	8,744
57,350	57,400	10,200	7,699	10,200	8,756
57,400	57,450	10,213	7,706	10,213	8,769
57,450	57,500	10,225	7,714	10,225	8,781
57,500	57,550	10,238	7,721	10,238	8,794
57,550	57,600	10,250	7,729	10,250	8,806
57,600	57,650	10,263	7,736	10,263	8,819
57,650	57,700	10,275	7,744	10,275	8,831
57,700	57,750	10,288	7,751	10,288	8,844
57,750	57,800	10,300	7,759	10,300	8,856
57,800	57,850	10,313	7,766	10,313	8,869
57,850	57,900	10,325	7,774	10,325	8,881
57,900	57,950	10,338	7,781	10,338	8,894
57,950	58,000	10,350	7,789	10,350	8,906

58,000

At least	But less than	Single	Married filing jointly *	Married filing separately	Head of a household
58,000	58,050	10,363	7,796	10,363	8,919
58,050	58,100	10,375	7,804	10,375	8,931
58,100	58,150	10,388	7,811	10,388	8,944
58,150	58,200	10,400	7,819	10,400	8,956
58,200	58,250	10,413	7,826	10,413	8,969
58,250	58,300	10,425	7,834	10,425	8,981
58,300	58,350	10,438	7,841	10,438	8,994
58,350	58,400	10,450	7,849	10,450	9,006
58,400	58,450	10,463	7,856	10,463	9,019
58,450	58,500	10,475	7,864	10,475	9,031
58,500	58,550	10,488	7,871	10,488	9,044
58,550	58,600	10,500	7,879	10,500	9,056
58,600	58,650	10,513	7,886	10,513	9,069
58,650	58,700	10,525	7,894	10,525	9,081
58,700	58,750	10,538	7,901	10,538	9,094
58,750	58,800	10,550	7,909	10,550	9,106
58,800	58,850	10,563	7,916	10,563	9,119
58,850	58,900	10,575	7,924	10,575	9,131
58,900	58,950	10,588	7,931	10,588	9,144
58,950	59,000	10,600	7,939	10,600	9,156

59,000

At least	But less than	Single	Married filing jointly *	Married filing separately	Head of a household
59,000	59,050	10,613	7,946	10,613	9,169
59,050	59,100	10,625	7,954	10,625	9,181
59,100	59,150	10,638	7,961	10,638	9,194
59,150	59,200	10,650	7,969	10,650	9,206
59,200	59,250	10,663	7,976	10,663	9,219
59,250	59,300	10,675	7,984	10,675	9,231
59,300	59,350	10,688	7,991	10,688	9,244
59,350	59,400	10,700	7,999	10,700	9,256
59,400	59,450	10,713	8,006	10,713	9,269
59,450	59,500	10,725	8,014	10,725	9,281
59,500	59,550	10,738	8,021	10,738	9,294
59,550	59,600	10,750	8,029	10,750	9,306
59,600	59,650	10,763	8,036	10,763	9,319
59,650	59,700	10,775	8,044	10,775	9,331
59,700	59,750	10,788	8,051	10,788	9,344
59,750	59,800	10,800	8,059	10,800	9,356
59,800	59,850	10,813	8,066	10,813	9,369
59,850	59,900	10,825	8,074	10,825	9,381
59,900	59,950	10,838	8,081	10,838	9,394
59,950	60,000	10,850	8,089	10,850	9,406

60,000

If line 43 (taxable income) is—		And you are—			
At least	But less than	Single	Married filing jointly *	Married filing separately	Head of a household
		Your tax is—			
60,000	60,050	10,863	8,096	10,863	9,419
60,050	60,100	10,875	8,104	10,875	9,431
60,100	60,150	10,888	8,111	10,888	9,444
60,150	60,200	10,900	8,119	10,900	9,456
60,200	60,250	10,913	8,126	10,913	9,469
60,250	60,300	10,925	8,134	10,925	9,481
60,300	60,350	10,938	8,141	10,938	9,494
60,350	60,400	10,950	8,149	10,950	9,506
60,400	60,450	10,963	8,156	10,963	9,519
60,450	60,500	10,975	8,164	10,975	9,531
60,500	60,550	10,988	8,171	10,988	9,544
60,550	60,600	11,000	8,179	11,000	9,556
60,600	60,650	11,013	8,186	11,013	9,569
60,650	60,700	11,025	8,194	11,025	9,581
60,700	60,750	11,038	8,201	11,038	9,594
60,750	60,800	11,050	8,209	11,050	9,606
60,800	60,850	11,063	8,216	11,063	9,619
60,850	60,900	11,075	8,224	11,075	9,631
60,900	60,950	11,088	8,231	11,088	9,644
60,950	61,000	11,100	8,239	11,100	9,656

61,000

At least	But less than	Single	Married filing jointly *	Married filing separately	Head of a household
61,000	61,050	11,113	8,246	11,113	9,669
61,050	61,100	11,125	8,254	11,125	9,681
61,100	61,150	11,138	8,261	11,138	9,694
61,150	61,200	11,150	8,269	11,150	9,706
61,200	61,250	11,163	8,276	11,163	9,719
61,250	61,300	11,175	8,284	11,175	9,731
61,300	61,350	11,188	8,291	11,188	9,744
61,350	61,400	11,200	8,299	11,200	9,756
61,400	61,450	11,213	8,306	11,213	9,769
61,450	61,500	11,225	8,314	11,225	9,781
61,500	61,550	11,238	8,321	11,238	9,794
61,550	61,600	11,250	8,329	11,250	9,806
61,600	61,650	11,263	8,336	11,263	9,819
61,650	61,700	11,275	8,344	11,275	9,831
61,700	61,750	11,288	8,351	11,288	9,844
61,750	61,800	11,300	8,359	11,300	9,856
61,800	61,850	11,313	8,366	11,313	9,869
61,850	61,900	11,325	8,374	11,325	9,881
61,900	61,950	11,338	8,381	11,338	9,894
61,950	62,000	11,350	8,389	11,350	9,906

62,000

At least	But less than	Single	Married filing jointly *	Married filing separately	Head of a household
62,000	62,050	11,363	8,396	11,363	9,919
62,050	62,100	11,375	8,404	11,375	9,931
62,100	62,150	11,388	8,411	11,388	9,944
62,150	62,200	11,400	8,419	11,400	9,956
62,200	62,250	11,413	8,426	11,413	9,969
62,250	62,300	11,425	8,434	11,425	9,981
62,300	62,350	11,438	8,441	11,438	9,994
62,350	62,400	11,450	8,449	11,450	10,006
62,400	62,450	11,463	8,456	11,463	10,019
62,450	62,500	11,475	8,464	11,475	10,031
62,500	62,550	11,488	8,471	11,488	10,044
62,550	62,600	11,500	8,479	11,500	10,056
62,600	62,650	11,513	8,486	11,513	10,069
62,650	62,700	11,525	8,494	11,525	10,081
62,700	62,750	11,538	8,501	11,538	10,094
62,750	62,800	11,550	8,509	11,550	10,106
62,800	62,850	11,563	8,516	11,563	10,119
62,850	62,900	11,575	8,524	11,575	10,131
62,900	62,950	11,588	8,531	11,588	10,144
62,950	63,000	11,600	8,539	11,600	10,156

63,000

If line 43 (taxable income) is—		And you are—			
At least	But less than	Single	Married filing jointly *	Married filing separately	Head of a household
		Your tax is—			
63,000	63,050	11,613	8,546	11,613	10,169
63,050	63,100	11,625	8,554	11,625	10,181
63,100	63,150	11,638	8,561	11,638	10,194
63,150	63,200	11,650	8,569	11,650	10,206
63,200	63,250	11,663	8,576	11,663	10,219
63,250	63,300	11,675	8,584	11,675	10,231
63,300	63,350	11,688	8,591	11,688	10,244
63,350	63,400	11,700	8,599	11,700	10,256
63,400	63,450	11,713	8,606	11,713	10,269
63,450	63,500	11,725	8,614	11,725	10,281
63,500	63,550	11,738	8,621	11,738	10,294
63,550	63,600	11,750	8,629	11,750	10,306
63,600	63,650	11,763	8,636	11,763	10,319
63,650	63,700	11,775	8,644	11,775	10,331
63,700	63,750	11,788	8,651	11,788	10,344
63,750	63,800	11,800	8,659	11,800	10,356
63,800	63,850	11,813	8,666	11,813	10,369
63,850	63,900	11,825	8,674	11,825	10,381
63,900	63,950	11,838	8,681	11,838	10,394
63,950	64,000	11,850	8,689	11,850	10,406

64,000

At least	But less than	Single	Married filing jointly *	Married filing separately	Head of a household
64,000	64,050	11,863	8,696	11,863	10,419
64,050	64,100	11,875	8,704	11,875	10,431
64,100	64,150	11,888	8,711	11,888	10,444
64,150	64,200	11,900	8,719	11,900	10,456
64,200	64,250	11,913	8,726	11,913	10,469
64,250	64,300	11,925	8,734	11,925	10,481
64,300	64,350	11,938	8,741	11,938	10,494
64,350	64,400	11,950	8,749	11,950	10,506
64,400	64,450	11,963	8,756	11,963	10,519
64,450	64,500	11,975	8,764	11,975	10,531
64,500	64,550	11,988	8,771	11,988	10,544
64,550	64,600	12,000	8,779	12,000	10,556
64,600	64,650	12,013	8,786	12,013	10,569
64,650	64,700	12,025	8,794	12,025	10,581
64,700	64,750	12,038	8,801	12,038	10,594
64,750	64,800	12,050	8,809	12,050	10,606
64,800	64,850	12,063	8,816	12,063	10,619
64,850	64,900	12,075	8,824	12,075	10,631
64,900	64,950	12,088	8,831	12,088	10,644
64,950	65,000	12,100	8,839	12,100	10,656

65,000

At least	But less than	Single	Married filing jointly *	Married filing separately	Head of a household
65,000	65,050	12,113	8,846	12,113	10,669
65,050	65,100	12,125	8,854	12,125	10,681
65,100	65,150	12,138	8,861	12,138	10,694
65,150	65,200	12,150	8,869	12,150	10,706
65,200	65,250	12,163	8,876	12,163	10,719
65,250	65,300	12,175	8,884	12,175	10,731
65,300	65,350	12,188	8,891	12,188	10,744
65,350	65,400	12,200	8,899	12,200	10,756
65,400	65,450	12,213	8,906	12,213	10,769
65,450	65,500	12,225	8,914	12,225	10,781
65,500	65,550	12,238	8,921	12,238	10,794
65,550	65,600	12,250	8,929	12,250	10,806
65,600	65,650	12,263	8,936	12,263	10,819
65,650	65,700	12,275	8,944	12,275	10,831
65,700	65,750	12,288	8,951	12,288	10,844
65,750	65,800	12,300	8,959	12,300	10,856
65,800	65,850	12,313	8,966	12,313	10,869
65,850	65,900	12,325	8,974	12,325	10,881
65,900	65,950	12,338	8,981	12,338	10,894
65,950	66,000	12,350	8,989	12,350	10,906

(Continued)

* This column must also be used by a qualifying widow(er).

Need more information or forms? Visit IRS.gov.

2014 Tax Table — Continued

If line 43 (taxable income) is—	And you are—

66,000 / 67,000 / 68,000

At least	But less than	Single	Married filing jointly *	Married filing separately	Head of a household
				Your tax is—	
66,000					
66,000	66,050	12,363	8,996	12,363	10,919
66,050	66,100	12,375	9,004	12,375	10,931
66,100	66,150	12,388	9,011	12,388	10,944
66,150	66,200	12,400	9,019	12,400	10,956
66,200	66,250	12,413	9,026	12,413	10,969
66,250	66,300	12,425	9,034	12,425	10,981
66,300	66,350	12,438	9,041	12,438	10,994
66,350	66,400	12,450	9,049	12,450	11,006
66,400	66,450	12,463	9,056	12,463	11,019
66,450	66,500	12,475	9,064	12,475	11,031
66,500	66,550	12,488	9,071	12,488	11,044
66,550	66,600	12,500	9,079	12,500	11,056
66,600	66,650	12,513	9,086	12,513	11,069
66,650	66,700	12,525	9,094	12,525	11,081
66,700	66,750	12,538	9,101	12,538	11,094
66,750	66,800	12,550	9,109	12,550	11,106
66,800	66,850	12,563	9,116	12,563	11,119
66,850	66,900	12,575	9,124	12,575	11,131
66,900	66,950	12,588	9,131	12,588	11,144
66,950	67,000	12,600	9,139	12,600	11,156
67,000					
67,000	67,050	12,613	9,146	12,613	11,169
67,050	67,100	12,625	9,154	12,625	11,181
67,100	67,150	12,638	9,161	12,638	11,194
67,150	67,200	12,650	9,169	12,650	11,206
67,200	67,250	12,663	9,176	12,663	11,219
67,250	67,300	12,675	9,184	12,675	11,231
67,300	67,350	12,688	9,191	12,688	11,244
67,350	67,400	12,700	9,199	12,700	11,256
67,400	67,450	12,713	9,206	12,713	11,269
67,450	67,500	12,725	9,214	12,725	11,281
67,500	67,550	12,738	9,221	12,738	11,294
67,550	67,600	12,750	9,229	12,750	11,306
67,600	67,650	12,763	9,236	12,763	11,319
67,650	67,700	12,775	9,244	12,775	11,331
67,700	67,750	12,788	9,251	12,788	11,344
67,750	67,800	12,800	9,259	12,800	11,356
67,800	67,850	12,813	9,266	12,813	11,369
67,850	67,900	12,825	9,274	12,825	11,381
67,900	67,950	12,838	9,281	12,838	11,394
67,950	68,000	12,850	9,289	12,850	11,406
68,000					
68,000	68,050	12,863	9,296	12,863	11,419
68,050	68,100	12,875	9,304	12,875	11,431
68,100	68,150	12,888	9,311	12,888	11,444
68,150	68,200	12,900	9,319	12,900	11,456
68,200	68,250	12,913	9,326	12,913	11,469
68,250	68,300	12,925	9,334	12,925	11,481
68,300	68,350	12,938	9,341	12,938	11,494
68,350	68,400	12,950	9,349	12,950	11,506
68,400	68,450	12,963	9,356	12,963	11,519
68,450	68,500	12,975	9,364	12,975	11,531
68,500	68,550	12,988	9,371	12,988	11,544
68,550	68,600	13,000	9,379	13,000	11,556
68,600	68,650	13,013	9,386	13,013	11,569
68,650	68,700	13,025	9,394	13,025	11,581
68,700	68,750	13,038	9,401	13,038	11,594
68,750	68,800	13,050	9,409	13,050	11,606
68,800	68,850	13,063	9,416	13,063	11,619
68,850	68,900	13,075	9,424	13,075	11,631
68,900	68,950	13,088	9,431	13,088	11,644
68,950	69,000	13,100	9,439	13,100	11,656

69,000 / 70,000 / 71,000

At least	But less than	Single	Married filing jointly *	Married filing separately	Head of a household
				Your tax is—	
69,000					
69,000	69,050	13,113	9,446	13,113	11,669
69,050	69,100	13,125	9,454	13,125	11,681
69,100	69,150	13,138	9,461	13,138	11,694
69,150	69,200	13,150	9,469	13,150	11,706
69,200	69,250	13,163	9,476	13,163	11,719
69,250	69,300	13,175	9,484	13,175	11,731
69,300	69,350	13,188	9,491	13,188	11,744
69,350	69,400	13,200	9,499	13,200	11,756
69,400	69,450	13,213	9,506	13,213	11,769
69,450	69,500	13,225	9,514	13,225	11,781
69,500	69,550	13,238	9,521	13,238	11,794
69,550	69,600	13,250	9,529	13,250	11,806
69,600	69,650	13,263	9,536	13,263	11,819
69,650	69,700	13,275	9,544	13,275	11,831
69,700	69,750	13,288	9,551	13,288	11,844
69,750	69,800	13,300	9,559	13,300	11,856
69,800	69,850	13,313	9,566	13,313	11,869
69,850	69,900	13,325	9,574	13,325	11,881
69,900	69,950	13,338	9,581	13,338	11,894
69,950	70,000	13,350	9,589	13,350	11,906
70,000					
70,000	70,050	13,363	9,596	13,363	11,919
70,050	70,100	13,375	9,604	13,375	11,931
70,100	70,150	13,388	9,611	13,388	11,944
70,150	70,200	13,400	9,619	13,400	11,956
70,200	70,250	13,413	9,626	13,413	11,969
70,250	70,300	13,425	9,634	13,425	11,981
70,300	70,350	13,438	9,641	13,438	11,994
70,350	70,400	13,450	9,649	13,450	12,006
70,400	70,450	13,463	9,656	13,463	12,019
70,450	70,500	13,475	9,664	13,475	12,031
70,500	70,550	13,488	9,671	13,488	12,044
70,550	70,600	13,500	9,679	13,500	12,056
70,600	70,650	13,513	9,686	13,513	12,069
70,650	70,700	13,525	9,694	13,525	12,081
70,700	70,750	13,538	9,701	13,538	12,094
70,750	70,800	13,550	9,709	13,550	12,106
70,800	70,850	13,563	9,716	13,563	12,119
70,850	70,900	13,575	9,724	13,575	12,131
70,900	70,950	13,588	9,731	13,588	12,144
70,950	71,000	13,600	9,739	13,600	12,156
71,000					
71,000	71,050	13,613	9,746	13,613	12,169
71,050	71,100	13,625	9,754	13,625	12,181
71,100	71,150	13,638	9,761	13,638	12,194
71,150	71,200	13,650	9,769	13,650	12,206
71,200	71,250	13,663	9,776	13,663	12,219
71,250	71,300	13,675	9,784	13,675	12,231
71,300	71,350	13,688	9,791	13,688	12,244
71,350	71,400	13,700	9,799	13,700	12,256
71,400	71,450	13,713	9,806	13,713	12,269
71,450	71,500	13,725	9,814	13,725	12,281
71,500	71,550	13,738	9,821	13,738	12,294
71,550	71,600	13,750	9,829	13,750	12,306
71,600	71,650	13,763	9,836	13,763	12,319
71,650	71,700	13,775	9,844	13,775	12,331
71,700	71,750	13,788	9,851	13,788	12,344
71,750	71,800	13,800	9,859	13,800	12,356
71,800	71,850	13,813	9,866	13,813	12,369
71,850	71,900	13,825	9,874	13,825	12,381
71,900	71,950	13,838	9,881	13,838	12,394
71,950	72,000	13,850	9,889	13,850	12,406

72,000 / 73,000 / 74,000

At least	But less than	Single	Married filing jointly *	Married filing separately	Head of a household
				Your tax is—	
72,000					
72,000	72,050	13,863	9,896	13,863	12,419
72,050	72,100	13,875	9,904	13,875	12,431
72,100	72,150	13,888	9,911	13,888	12,444
72,150	72,200	13,900	9,919	13,900	12,456
72,200	72,250	13,913	9,926	13,913	12,469
72,250	72,300	13,925	9,934	13,925	12,481
72,300	72,350	13,938	9,941	13,938	12,494
72,350	72,400	13,950	9,949	13,950	12,506
72,400	72,450	13,963	9,956	13,963	12,519
72,450	72,500	13,975	9,964	13,975	12,531
72,500	72,550	13,988	9,971	13,988	12,544
72,550	72,600	14,000	9,979	14,000	12,556
72,600	72,650	14,013	9,986	14,013	12,569
72,650	72,700	14,025	9,994	14,025	12,581
72,700	72,750	14,038	10,001	14,038	12,594
72,750	72,800	14,050	10,009	14,050	12,606
72,800	72,850	14,063	10,016	14,063	12,619
72,850	72,900	14,075	10,024	14,075	12,631
72,900	72,950	14,088	10,031	14,088	12,644
72,950	73,000	14,100	10,039	14,100	12,656
73,000					
73,000	73,050	14,113	10,046	14,113	12,669
73,050	73,100	14,125	10,054	14,125	12,681
73,100	73,150	14,138	10,061	14,138	12,694
73,150	73,200	14,150	10,069	14,150	12,706
73,200	73,250	14,163	10,076	14,163	12,719
73,250	73,300	14,175	10,084	14,175	12,731
73,300	73,350	14,188	10,091	14,188	12,744
73,350	73,400	14,200	10,099	14,200	12,756
73,400	73,450	14,213	10,106	14,213	12,769
73,450	73,500	14,225	10,114	14,225	12,781
73,500	73,550	14,238	10,121	14,238	12,794
73,550	73,600	14,250	10,129	14,250	12,806
73,600	73,650	14,263	10,136	14,263	12,819
73,650	73,700	14,275	10,144	14,275	12,831
73,700	73,750	14,288	10,151	14,288	12,844
73,750	73,800	14,300	10,159	14,300	12,856
73,800	73,850	14,313	10,169	14,313	12,869
73,850	73,900	14,325	10,181	14,325	12,881
73,900	73,950	14,338	10,194	14,338	12,894
73,950	74,000	14,350	10,206	14,350	12,906
74,000					
74,000	74,050	14,363	10,219	14,363	12,919
74,050	74,100	14,375	10,231	14,375	12,931
74,100	74,150	14,388	10,244	14,388	12,944
74,150	74,200	14,400	10,256	14,400	12,956
74,200	74,250	14,413	10,269	14,413	12,969
74,250	74,300	14,425	10,281	14,425	12,981
74,300	74,350	14,438	10,294	14,438	12,994
74,350	74,400	14,450	10,306	14,450	13,006
74,400	74,450	14,463	10,319	14,463	13,019
74,450	74,500	14,475	10,331	14,477	13,031
74,500	74,550	14,488	10,344	14,491	13,044
74,550	74,600	14,500	10,356	14,505	13,056
74,600	74,650	14,513	10,369	14,519	13,069
74,650	74,700	14,525	10,381	14,533	13,081
74,700	74,750	14,538	10,394	14,547	13,094
74,750	74,800	14,550	10,406	14,561	13,106
74,800	74,850	14,563	10,419	14,575	13,119
74,850	74,900	14,575	10,431	14,589	13,131
74,900	74,950	14,588	10,444	14,603	13,144
74,950	75,000	14,600	10,456	14,617	13,156

* This column must also be used by a qualifying widow(er).

(Continued)

2014 Tax Table — *Continued*

75,000

At least	But less than	Single	Married filing jointly *	Married filing separately	Head of a household
75,000	75,050	14,613	10,469	14,631	13,169
75,050	75,100	14,625	10,481	14,645	13,181
75,100	75,150	14,638	10,494	14,659	13,194
75,150	75,200	14,650	10,506	14,673	13,206
75,200	75,250	14,663	10,519	14,687	13,219
75,250	75,300	14,675	10,531	14,701	13,231
75,300	75,350	14,688	10,544	14,715	13,244
75,350	75,400	14,700	10,556	14,729	13,256
75,400	75,450	14,713	10,569	14,743	13,269
75,450	75,500	14,725	10,581	14,757	13,281
75,500	75,550	14,738	10,594	14,771	13,294
75,550	75,600	14,750	10,606	14,785	13,306
75,600	75,650	14,763	10,619	14,799	13,319
75,650	75,700	14,775	10,631	14,813	13,331
75,700	75,750	14,788	10,644	14,827	13,344
75,750	75,800	14,800	10,656	14,841	13,356
75,800	75,850	14,813	10,669	14,855	13,369
75,850	75,900	14,825	10,681	14,869	13,381
75,900	75,950	14,838	10,694	14,883	13,394
75,950	76,000	14,850	10,706	14,897	13,406

76,000

At least	But less than	Single	Married filing jointly *	Married filing separately	Head of a household
76,000	76,050	14,863	10,719	14,911	13,419
76,050	76,100	14,875	10,731	14,925	13,431
76,100	76,150	14,888	10,744	14,939	13,444
76,150	76,200	14,900	10,756	14,953	13,456
76,200	76,250	14,913	10,769	14,967	13,469
76,250	76,300	14,925	10,781	14,981	13,481
76,300	76,350	14,938	10,794	14,995	13,494
76,350	76,400	14,950	10,806	15,009	13,506
76,400	76,450	14,963	10,819	15,023	13,519
76,450	76,500	14,975	10,831	15,037	13,531
76,500	76,550	14,988	10,844	15,051	13,544
76,550	76,600	15,000	10,856	15,065	13,556
76,600	76,650	15,013	10,869	15,079	13,569
76,650	76,700	15,025	10,881	15,093	13,581
76,700	76,750	15,033	10,894	15,107	13,594
76,750	76,800	15,050	10,906	15,121	13,606
76,800	76,850	15,063	10,919	15,135	13,619
76,850	76,900	15,075	10,931	15,149	13,631
76,900	76,950	15,088	10,944	15,163	13,644
76,950	77,000	15,100	10,956	15,177	13,656

77,000

At least	But less than	Single	Married filing jointly *	Married filing separately	Head of a household
77,000	77,050	15,113	10,969	15,191	13,669
77,050	77,100	15,125	10,981	15,205	13,681
77,100	77,150	15,138	10,994	15,219	13,694
77,150	77,200	15,150	11,006	15,233	13,706
77,200	77,250	15,163	11,019	15,247	13,719
77,250	77,300	15,175	11,031	15,261	13,731
77,300	77,350	15,188	11,044	15,275	13,744
77,350	77,400	15,200	11,056	15,289	13,756
77,400	77,450	15,213	11,069	15,303	13,769
77,450	77,500	15,225	11,081	15,317	13,781
77,500	77,550	15,238	11,094	15,331	13,794
77,550	77,600	15,250	11,106	15,345	13,806
77,600	77,650	15,263	11,119	15,359	13,819
77,650	77,700	15,275	11,131	15,373	13,831
77,700	77,750	15,288	11,144	15,387	13,844
77,750	77,800	15,300	11,156	15,401	13,856
77,800	77,850	15,313	11,169	15,415	13,869
77,850	77,900	15,325	11,181	15,429	13,881
77,900	77,950	15,338	11,194	15,443	13,894
77,950	78,000	15,350	11,206	15,457	13,906

78,000

At least	But less than	Single	Married filing jointly *	Married filing separately	Head of a household
78,000	78,050	15,363	11,219	15,471	13,919
78,050	78,100	15,375	11,231	15,485	13,931
78,100	78,150	15,388	11,244	15,499	13,944
78,150	78,200	15,400	11,256	15,513	13,956
78,200	78,250	15,413	11,269	15,527	13,969
78,250	78,300	15,425	11,281	15,541	13,981
78,300	78,350	15,438	11,294	15,555	13,994
78,350	78,400	15,450	11,306	15,569	14,006
78,400	78,450	15,463	11,319	15,583	14,019
78,450	78,500	15,475	11,331	15,597	14,031
78,500	78,550	15,488	11,344	15,611	14,044
78,550	78,600	15,500	11,356	15,625	14,056
78,600	78,650	15,513	11,369	15,639	14,069
78,650	78,700	15,525	11,381	15,653	14,081
78,700	78,750	15,538	11,394	15,667	14,094
78,750	78,800	15,550	11,406	15,681	14,106
78,800	78,850	15,563	11,419	15,695	14,119
78,850	78,900	15,575	11,431	15,709	14,131
78,900	78,950	15,588	11,444	15,723	14,144
78,950	79,000	15,600	11,456	15,737	14,156

79,000

At least	But less than	Single	Married filing jointly *	Married filing separately	Head of a household
79,000	79,050	15,613	11,469	15,751	14,169
79,050	79,100	15,625	11,481	15,765	14,181
79,100	79,150	15,638	11,494	15,779	14,194
79,150	79,200	15,650	11,506	15,793	14,206
79,200	79,250	15,663	11,519	15,807	14,219
79,250	79,300	15,675	11,531	15,821	14,231
79,300	79,350	15,688	11,544	15,835	14,244
79,350	79,400	15,700	11,556	15,849	14,256
79,400	79,450	15,713	11,569	15,863	14,269
79,450	79,500	15,725	11,581	15,877	14,281
79,500	79,550	15,738	11,594	15,891	14,294
79,550	79,600	15,750	11,606	15,905	14,306
79,600	79,650	15,763	11,619	15,919	14,319
79,650	79,700	15,775	11,631	15,933	14,331
79,700	79,750	15,788	11,644	15,947	14,344
79,750	79,800	15,800	11,656	15,961	14,356
79,800	79,850	15,813	11,669	15,975	14,369
79,850	79,900	15,825	11,681	15,989	14,381
79,900	79,950	15,838	11,694	16,003	14,394
79,950	80,000	15,850	11,706	16,017	14,406

80,000

At least	But less than	Single	Married filing jointly *	Married filing separately	Head of a household
80,000	80,050	15,863	11,719	16,031	14,419
80,050	80,100	15,875	11,731	16,045	14,431
80,100	80,150	15,888	11,744	16,059	14,444
80,150	80,200	15,900	11,756	16,073	14,456
80,200	80,250	15,913	11,769	16,087	14,469
80,250	80,300	15,925	11,781	16,101	14,481
80,300	80,350	15,938	11,794	16,115	14,494
80,350	80,400	15,950	11,806	16,129	14,506
80,400	80,450	15,963	11,819	16,143	14,519
80,450	80,500	15,975	11,831	16,157	14,531
80,500	80,550	15,988	11,844	16,171	14,544
80,550	80,600	16,000	11,856	16,185	14,556
80,600	80,650	16,013	11,869	16,199	14,569
80,650	80,700	16,025	11,881	16,213	14,581
80,700	80,750	16,038	11,894	16,227	14,594
80,750	80,800	16,050	11,906	16,241	14,606
80,800	80,850	16,063	11,919	16,255	14,619
80,850	80,900	16,075	11,931	16,269	14,631
80,900	80,950	16,088	11,944	16,283	14,644
80,950	81,000	16,100	11,956	16,297	14,656

81,000

At least	But less than	Single	Married filing jointly *	Married filing separately	Head of a household
81,000	81,050	16,113	11,969	16,311	14,669
81,050	81,100	16,125	11,981	16,325	14,681
81,100	81,150	16,138	11,994	16,339	14,694
81,150	81,200	16,150	12,006	16,353	14,706
81,200	81,250	16,163	12,019	16,367	14,719
81,250	81,300	16,175	12,031	16,381	14,731
81,300	81,350	16,188	12,044	16,395	14,744
81,350	81,400	16,200	12,056	16,409	14,756
81,400	81,450	16,213	12,069	16,423	14,769
81,450	81,500	16,225	12,081	16,437	14,781
81,500	81,550	16,238	12,094	16,451	14,794
81,550	81,600	16,250	12,106	16,465	14,806
81,600	81,650	16,263	12,119	16,479	14,819
81,650	81,700	16,275	12,131	16,493	14,831
81,700	81,750	16,288	12,144	16,507	14,844
81,750	81,800	16,300	12,156	16,521	14,856
81,800	81,850	16,313	12,169	16,535	14,869
81,850	81,900	16,325	12,181	16,549	14,881
81,900	81,950	16,338	12,194	16,563	14,894
81,950	82,000	16,350	12,206	16,577	14,906

82,000

At least	But less than	Single	Married filing jointly *	Married filing separately	Head of a household
82,000	82,050	16,363	12,219	16,591	14,919
82,050	82,100	16,375	12,231	16,605	14,931
82,100	82,150	16,388	12,244	16,619	14,944
82,150	82,200	16,400	12,256	16,633	14,956
82,200	82,250	16,413	12,269	16,647	14,969
82,250	82,300	16,425	12,281	16,661	14,981
82,300	82,350	16,438	12,294	16,675	14,994
82,350	82,400	16,450	12,306	16,689	15,006
82,400	82,450	16,463	12,319	16,703	15,019
82,450	82,500	16,475	12,331	16,717	15,031
82,500	82,550	16,488	12,344	16,731	15,044
82,550	82,600	16,500	12,356	16,745	15,056
82,600	82,650	16,513	12,369	16,759	15,069
82,650	82,700	16,525	12,381	16,773	15,081
82,700	82,750	16,538	12,394	16,787	15,094
82,750	82,800	16,550	12,406	16,801	15,106
82,800	82,850	16,563	12,419	16,815	15,119
82,850	82,900	16,575	12,431	16,829	15,131
82,900	82,950	16,588	12,444	16,843	15,144
82,950	83,000	16,600	12,456	16,857	15,156

83,000

At least	But less than	Single	Married filing jointly *	Married filing separately	Head of a household
83,000	83,050	16,613	12,469	16,871	15,169
83,050	83,100	16,625	12,481	16,885	15,181
83,100	83,150	16,638	12,494	16,899	15,194
83,150	83,200	16,650	12,506	16,913	15,206
83,200	83,250	16,663	12,519	16,927	15,219
83,250	83,300	16,675	12,531	16,941	15,231
83,300	83,350	16,688	12,544	16,955	15,244
83,350	83,400	16,700	12,556	16,969	15,256
83,400	83,450	16,713	12,569	16,983	15,269
83,450	83,500	16,725	12,581	16,997	15,281
83,500	83,550	16,738	12,594	17,011	15,294
83,550	83,600	16,750	12,606	17,025	15,306
83,600	83,650	16,763	12,619	17,039	15,319
83,650	83,700	16,775	12,631	17,053	15,331
83,700	83,750	16,788	12,644	17,067	15,344
83,750	83,800	16,800	12,656	17,081	15,356
83,800	83,850	16,813	12,669	17,095	15,369
83,850	83,900	16,825	12,681	17,109	15,381
83,900	83,950	16,838	12,694	17,123	15,394
83,950	84,000	16,850	12,706	17,137	15,406

* This column must also be used by a qualifying widow(er).

(Continued)

Need more information or forms? Visit IRS.gov.

2014 Tax Table — *Continued*

If line 43 (taxable income) is—		And you are—			
At least	But less than	Single	Married filing jointly *	Married filing separately	Head of a household
		Your tax is—			

84,000

At least	But less than	Single	Married filing jointly *	Married filing separately	Head of a household
84,000	84,050	16,863	12,719	17,151	15,419
84,050	84,100	16,875	12,731	17,165	15,431
84,100	84,150	16,888	12,744	17,179	15,444
84,150	84,200	16,900	12,756	17,193	15,456
84,200	84,250	16,913	12,769	17,207	15,469
84,250	84,300	16,925	12,781	17,221	15,481
84,300	84,350	16,938	12,794	17,235	15,494
84,350	84,400	16,950	12,806	17,249	15,506
84,400	84,450	16,963	12,819	17,263	15,519
84,450	84,500	16,975	12,831	17,277	15,531
84,500	84,550	16,988	12,844	17,291	15,544
84,550	84,600	17,000	12,856	17,305	15,556
84,600	84,650	17,013	12,869	17,319	15,569
84,650	84,700	17,025	12,881	17,333	15,581
84,700	84,750	17,038	12,894	17,347	15,594
84,750	84,800	17,050	12,906	17,361	15,606
84,800	84,850	17,063	12,919	17,375	15,619
84,850	84,900	17,075	12,931	17,389	15,631
84,900	84,950	17,088	12,944	17,403	15,644
84,950	85,000	17,100	12,956	17,417	15,656

85,000

At least	But less than	Single	Married filing jointly *	Married filing separately	Head of a household
85,000	85,050	17,113	12,969	17,431	15,669
85,050	85,100	17,125	12,981	17,445	15,681
85,100	85,150	17,138	12,994	17,459	15,694
85,150	85,200	17,150	13,006	17,473	15,706
85,200	85,250	17,163	13,019	17,487	15,719
85,250	85,300	17,175	13,031	17,501	15,731
85,300	85,350	17,188	13,044	17,515	15,744
85,350	85,400	17,200	13,056	17,529	15,756
85,400	85,450	17,213	13,069	17,543	15,769
85,450	85,500	17,225	13,081	17,557	15,781
85,500	85,550	17,238	13,094	17,571	15,794
85,550	85,600	17,250	13,106	17,585	15,806
85,600	85,650	17,263	13,119	17,599	15,819
85,650	85,700	17,275	13,131	17,613	15,831
85,700	85,750	17,288	13,144	17,627	15,844
85,750	85,800	17,300	13,156	17,641	15,856
85,800	85,850	17,313	13,169	17,655	15,869
85,850	85,900	17,325	13,181	17,669	15,881
85,900	85,950	17,338	13,194	17,683	15,894
85,950	86,000	17,350	13,206	17,697	15,906

86,000

At least	But less than	Single	Married filing jointly *	Married filing separately	Head of a household
86,000	86,050	17,363	13,219	17,711	15,919
86,050	86,100	17,375	13,231	17,725	15,931
86,100	86,150	17,388	13,244	17,739	15,944
86,150	86,200	17,400	13,256	17,753	15,956
86,200	86,250	17,413	13,269	17,767	15,969
86,250	86,300	17,425	13,281	17,781	15,981
86,300	86,350	17,438	13,294	17,795	15,994
86,350	86,400	17,450	13,306	17,809	16,006
86,400	86,450	17,463	13,319	17,823	16,019
86,450	86,500	17,475	13,331	17,837	16,031
86,500	86,550	17,488	13,344	17,851	16,044
86,550	86,600	17,500	13,356	17,865	16,056
86,600	86,650	17,513	13,369	17,879	16,069
86,650	86,700	17,525	13,381	17,893	16,081
86,700	86,750	17,538	13,394	17,907	16,094
86,750	86,800	17,550	13,406	17,921	16,106
86,800	86,850	17,563	13,419	17,935	16,119
86,850	86,900	17,575	13,431	17,949	16,131
86,900	86,950	17,588	13,444	17,963	16,144
86,950	87,000	17,600	13,456	17,977	16,156

87,000

At least	But less than	Single	Married filing jointly *	Married filing separately	Head of a household
87,000	87,050	17,613	13,469	17,991	16,169
87,050	87,100	17,625	13,481	18,005	16,181
87,100	87,150	17,638	13,494	18,019	16,194
87,150	87,200	17,650	13,506	18,033	16,206
87,200	87,250	17,663	13,519	18,047	16,219
87,250	87,300	17,675	13,531	18,061	16,231
87,300	87,350	17,688	13,544	18,075	16,244
87,350	87,400	17,700	13,556	18,089	16,256
87,400	87,450	17,713	13,569	18,103	16,269
87,450	87,500	17,725	13,581	18,117	16,281
87,500	87,550	17,738	13,594	18,131	16,294
87,550	87,600	17,750	13,606	18,145	16,306
87,600	87,650	17,763	13,619	18,159	16,319
87,650	87,700	17,775	13,631	18,173	16,331
87,700	87,750	17,788	13,644	18,187	16,344
87,750	87,800	17,800	13,656	18,201	16,356
87,800	87,850	17,813	13,669	18,215	16,369
87,850	87,900	17,825	13,681	18,229	16,381
87,900	87,950	17,838	13,694	18,243	16,394
87,950	88,000	17,850	13,706	18,257	16,406

88,000

At least	But less than	Single	Married filing jointly *	Married filing separately	Head of a household
88,000	88,050	17,863	13,719	18,271	16,419
88,050	88,100	17,875	13,731	18,285	16,431
88,100	88,150	17,888	13,744	18,299	16,444
88,150	88,200	17,900	13,756	18,313	16,456
88,200	88,250	17,913	13,769	18,327	16,469
88,250	88,300	17,925	13,781	18,341	16,481
88,300	88,350	17,938	13,794	18,355	16,494
88,350	88,400	17,950	13,806	18,369	16,506
88,400	88,450	17,963	13,819	18,383	16,519
88,450	88,500	17,975	13,831	18,397	16,531
88,500	88,550	17,988	13,844	18,411	16,544
88,550	88,600	18,000	13,856	18,425	16,556
88,600	88,650	18,013	13,869	18,439	16,569
88,650	88,700	18,025	13,881	18,453	16,581
88,700	88,750	18,038	13,894	18,467	16,594
88,750	88,800	18,050	13,906	18,481	16,606
88,800	88,850	18,063	13,919	18,495	16,619
88,850	88,900	18,075	13,931	18,509	16,631
88,900	88,950	18,088	13,944	18,523	16,644
88,950	89,000	18,100	13,956	18,537	16,656

89,000

At least	But less than	Single	Married filing jointly *	Married filing separately	Head of a household
89,000	89,050	18,113	13,969	18,551	16,669
89,050	89,100	18,125	13,981	18,565	16,681
89,100	89,150	18,138	13,994	18,579	16,694
89,150	89,200	18,150	14,006	18,593	16,706
89,200	89,250	18,163	14,019	18,607	16,719
89,250	89,300	18,175	14,031	18,621	16,731
89,300	89,350	18,188	14,044	18,635	16,744
89,350	89,400	18,201	14,056	18,649	16,756
89,400	89,450	18,215	14,069	18,663	16,769
89,450	89,500	18,229	14,081	18,677	16,781
89,500	89,550	18,243	14,094	18,691	16,794
89,550	89,600	18,257	14,106	18,705	16,806
89,600	89,650	18,271	14,119	18,719	16,819
89,650	89,700	18,285	14,131	18,733	16,831
89,700	89,750	18,299	14,144	18,747	16,844
89,750	89,800	18,313	14,156	18,761	16,856
89,800	89,850	18,327	14,169	18,775	16,869
89,850	89,900	18,341	14,181	18,789	16,881
89,900	89,950	18,355	14,194	18,803	16,894
89,950	90,000	18,369	14,206	18,817	16,906

90,000

At least	But less than	Single	Married filing jointly *	Married filing separately	Head of a household
90,000	90,050	18,383	14,219	18,831	16,919
90,050	90,100	18,397	14,231	18,845	16,931
90,100	90,150	18,411	14,244	18,859	16,944
90,150	90,200	18,425	14,256	18,873	16,956
90,200	90,250	18,439	14,269	18,887	16,969
90,250	90,300	18,453	14,281	18,901	16,981
90,300	90,350	18,467	14,294	18,915	16,994
90,350	90,400	18,481	14,306	18,929	17,006
90,400	90,450	18,495	14,319	18,943	17,019
90,450	90,500	18,509	14,331	18,957	17,031
90,500	90,550	18,523	14,344	18,971	17,044
90,550	90,600	18,537	14,356	18,985	17,056
90,600	90,650	18,551	14,369	18,999	17,069
90,650	90,700	18,565	14,381	19,013	17,081
90,700	90,750	18,579	14,394	19,027	17,094
90,750	90,800	18,593	14,406	19,041	17,106
90,800	90,850	18,607	14,419	19,055	17,119
90,850	90,900	18,621	14,431	19,069	17,131
90,900	90,950	18,635	14,444	19,083	17,144
90,950	91,000	18,649	14,456	19,097	17,156

91,000

At least	But less than	Single	Married filing jointly *	Married filing separately	Head of a household
91,000	91,050	18,663	14,469	19,111	17,169
91,050	91,100	18,677	14,481	19,125	17,181
91,100	91,150	18,691	14,494	19,139	17,194
91,150	91,200	18,705	14,506	19,153	17,206
91,200	91,250	18,719	14,519	19,167	17,219
91,250	91,300	18,733	14,531	19,181	17,231
91,300	91,350	18,747	14,544	19,195	17,244
91,350	91,400	18,761	14,556	19,209	17,256
91,400	91,450	18,775	14,569	19,223	17,269
91,450	91,500	18,789	14,581	19,237	17,281
91,500	91,550	18,803	14,594	19,251	17,294
91,550	91,600	18,817	14,606	19,265	17,306
91,600	91,650	18,831	14,619	19,279	17,319
91,650	91,700	18,845	14,631	19,293	17,331
91,700	91,750	18,859	14,644	19,307	17,344
91,750	91,800	18,873	14,656	19,321	17,356
91,800	91,850	18,887	14,669	19,335	17,369
91,850	91,900	18,901	14,681	19,349	17,381
91,900	91,950	18,915	14,694	19,363	17,394
91,950	92,000	18,929	14,706	19,377	17,406

92,000

At least	But less than	Single	Married filing jointly *	Married filing separately	Head of a household
92,000	92,050	18,943	14,719	19,391	17,419
92,050	92,100	18,957	14,731	19,405	17,431
92,100	92,150	18,971	14,744	19,419	17,444
92,150	92,200	18,985	14,756	19,433	17,456
92,200	92,250	18,999	14,769	19,447	17,469
92,250	92,300	19,013	14,781	19,461	17,481
92,300	92,350	19,027	14,794	19,475	17,494
92,350	92,400	19,041	14,806	19,489	17,506
92,400	92,450	19,055	14,819	19,503	17,519
92,450	92,500	19,069	14,831	19,517	17,531
92,500	92,550	19,083	14,844	19,531	17,544
92,550	92,600	19,097	14,856	19,545	17,556
92,600	92,650	19,111	14,869	19,559	17,569
92,650	92,700	19,125	14,881	19,573	17,581
92,700	92,750	19,139	14,894	19,587	17,594
92,750	92,800	19,153	14,906	19,601	17,606
92,800	92,850	19,167	14,919	19,615	17,619
92,850	92,900	19,181	14,931	19,629	17,631
92,900	92,950	19,195	14,944	19,643	17,644
92,950	93,000	19,209	14,956	19,657	17,656

(Continued)

* This column must also be used by a qualifying widow(er).

Need more information or forms? Visit IRS.gov.

2014 Tax Table — *Continued*

93,000

If line 43 (taxable income) is—		And you are—			
At least	But less than	Single	Married filing jointly *	Married filing separately	Head of a household
		Your tax is—			
93,000	93,050	19,223	14,969	19,671	17,669
93,050	93,100	19,237	14,981	19,685	17,681
93,100	93,150	19,251	14,994	19,699	17,694
93,150	93,200	19,265	15,006	19,713	17,706
93,200	93,250	19,279	15,019	19,727	17,719
93,250	93,300	19,293	15,031	19,741	17,731
93,300	93,350	19,307	15,044	19,755	17,744
93,350	93,400	19,321	15,056	19,769	17,756
93,400	93,450	19,335	15,069	19,783	17,769
93,450	93,500	19,349	15,081	19,797	17,781
93,500	93,550	19,363	15,094	19,811	17,794
93,550	93,600	19,377	15,106	19,825	17,806
93,600	93,650	19,391	15,119	19,839	17,819
93,650	93,700	19,405	15,131	19,853	17,831
93,700	93,750	19,419	15,144	19,867	17,844
93,750	93,800	19,433	15,156	19,881	17,856
93,800	93,850	19,447	15,169	19,895	17,869
93,850	93,900	19,461	15,181	19,909	17,881
93,900	93,950	19,475	15,194	19,923	17,894
93,950	94,000	19,489	15,206	19,937	17,906

94,000

At least	But less than	Single	Married filing jointly *	Married filing separately	Head of a household
94,000	94,050	19,503	15,219	19,951	17,919
94,050	94,100	19,517	15,231	19,965	17,931
94,100	94,150	19,531	15,244	19,979	17,944
94,150	94,200	19,545	15,256	19,993	17,956
94,200	94,250	19,559	15,269	20,007	17,969
94,250	94,300	19,573	15,281	20,021	17,981
94,300	94,350	19,587	15,294	20,035	17,994
94,350	94,400	19,601	15,306	20,049	18,006
94,400	94,450	19,615	15,319	20,063	18,019
94,450	94,500	19,629	15,331	20,077	18,031
94,500	94,550	19,643	15,344	20,091	18,044
94,550	94,600	19,657	15,356	20,105	18,056
94,600	94,650	19,671	15,369	20,119	18,069
94,650	94,700	19,685	15,381	20,133	18,081
94,700	94,750	19,699	15,394	20,147	18,094
94,750	94,800	19,713	15,406	20,161	18,106
94,800	94,850	19,727	15,419	20,175	18,119
94,850	94,900	19,741	15,431	20,189	18,131
94,900	94,950	19,755	15,444	20,203	18,144
94,950	95,000	19,769	15,456	20,217	18,156

95,000

At least	But less than	Single	Married filing jointly *	Married filing separately	Head of a household
95,000	95,050	19,783	15,469	20,231	18,169
95,050	95,100	19,797	15,481	20,245	18,181
95,100	95,150	19,811	15,494	20,259	18,194
95,150	95,200	19,825	15,506	20,273	18,206
95,200	95,250	19,839	15,519	20,287	18,219
95,250	95,300	19,853	15,531	20,301	18,231
95,300	95,350	19,867	15,544	20,315	18,244
95,350	95,400	19,881	15,556	20,329	18,256
95,400	95,450	19,895	15,569	20,343	18,269
95,450	95,500	19,909	15,581	20,357	18,281
95,500	95,550	19,923	15,594	20,371	18,294
95,550	95,600	19,937	15,606	20,385	18,306
95,600	95,650	19,951	15,619	20,399	18,319
95,650	95,700	19,965	15,631	20,413	18,331
95,700	95,750	19,979	15,644	20,427	18,344
95,750	95,800	19,993	15,656	20,441	18,356
95,800	95,850	20,007	15,669	20,455	18,369
95,850	95,900	20,021	15,681	20,469	18,381
95,900	95,950	20,035	15,694	20,483	18,394
95,950	96,000	20,049	15,706	20,497	18,406

96,000

If line 43 (taxable income) is—		And you are—			
At least	But less than	Single	Married filing jointly *	Married filing separately	Head of a household
		Your tax is—			
96,000	96,050	20,063	15,719	20,511	18,419
96,050	96,100	20,077	15,731	20,525	18,431
96,100	96,150	20,091	15,744	20,539	18,444
96,150	96,200	20,105	15,756	20,553	18,456
96,200	96,250	20,119	15,769	20,567	18,469
96,250	96,300	20,133	15,781	20,581	18,481
96,300	96,350	20,147	15,794	20,595	18,494
96,350	96,400	20,161	15,806	20,609	18,506
96,400	96,450	20,175	15,819	20,623	18,519
96,450	96,500	20,189	15,831	20,637	18,531
96,500	96,550	20,203	15,844	20,651	18,544
96,550	96,600	20,217	15,856	20,665	18,556
96,600	96,650	20,231	15,869	20,679	18,569
96,650	96,700	20,245	15,881	20,693	18,581
96,700	96,750	20,259	15,894	20,707	18,594
96,750	96,800	20,273	15,906	20,721	18,606
96,800	96,850	20,287	15,919	20,735	18,619
96,850	96,900	20,301	15,931	20,749	18,631
96,900	96,950	20,315	15,944	20,763	18,644
96,950	97,000	20,329	15,956	20,777	18,656

97,000

At least	But less than	Single	Married filing jointly *	Married filing separately	Head of a household
97,000	97,050	20,343	15,969	20,791	18,669
97,050	97,100	20,357	15,981	20,805	18,681
97,100	97,150	20,371	15,994	20,819	18,694
97,150	97,200	20,385	16,006	20,833	18,706
97,200	97,250	20,399	16,019	20,847	18,719
97,250	97,300	20,413	16,031	20,861	18,731
97,300	97,350	20,427	16,044	20,875	18,744
97,350	97,400	20,441	16,056	20,889	18,756
97,400	97,450	20,455	16,069	20,903	18,769
97,450	97,500	20,469	16,081	20,917	18,781
97,500	97,550	20,483	16,094	20,931	18,794
97,550	97,600	20,497	16,106	20,945	18,806
97,600	97,650	20,511	16,119	20,959	18,819
97,650	97,700	20,525	16,131	20,973	18,831
97,700	97,750	20,539	16,144	20,987	18,844
97,750	97,800	20,553	16,156	21,001	18,856
97,800	97,850	20,567	16,169	21,015	18,869
97,850	97,900	20,581	16,181	21,029	18,881
97,900	97,950	20,595	16,194	21,043	18,894
97,950	98,000	20,609	16,206	21,057	18,906

98,000

At least	But less than	Single	Married filing jointly *	Married filing separately	Head of a household
98,000	98,050	20,623	16,219	21,071	18,919
98,050	98,100	20,637	16,231	21,085	18,931
98,100	98,150	20,651	16,244	21,099	18,944
98,150	98,200	20,665	16,256	21,113	18,956
98,200	98,250	20,679	16,269	21,127	18,969
98,250	98,300	20,693	16,281	21,141	18,981
98,300	98,350	20,707	16,294	21,155	18,994
98,350	98,400	20,721	16,306	21,169	19,006
98,400	98,450	20,735	16,319	21,183	19,019
98,450	98,500	20,749	16,331	21,197	19,031
98,500	98,550	20,763	16,344	21,211	19,044
98,550	98,600	20,777	16,356	21,225	19,056
98,600	98,650	20,791	16,369	21,239	19,069
98,650	98,700	20,805	16,381	21,253	19,081
98,700	98,750	20,819	16,394	21,267	19,094
98,750	98,800	20,833	16,406	21,281	19,106
98,800	98,850	20,847	16,419	21,295	19,119
98,850	98,900	20,861	16,431	21,309	19,131
98,900	98,950	20,875	16,444	21,323	19,144
98,950	99,000	20,889	16,456	21,337	19,156

99,000

If line 43 (taxable income) is—		And you are—			
At least	But less than	Single	Married filing jointly *	Married filing separately	Head of a household
		Your tax is—			
99,000	99,050	20,903	16,469	21,351	19,169
99,050	99,100	20,917	16,481	21,365	19,181
99,100	99,150	20,931	16,494	21,379	19,194
99,150	99,200	20,945	16,506	21,393	19,206
99,200	99,250	20,959	16,519	21,407	19,219
99,250	99,300	20,973	16,531	21,421	19,231
99,300	99,350	20,987	16,544	21,435	19,244
99,350	99,400	21,001	16,556	21,449	19,256
99,400	99,450	21,015	16,569	21,463	19,269
99,450	99,500	21,029	16,581	21,477	19,281
99,500	99,550	21,043	16,594	21,491	19,294
99,550	99,600	21,057	16,606	21,505	19,306
99,600	99,650	21,071	16,619	21,519	19,319
99,650	99,700	21,085	16,631	21,533	19,331
99,700	99,750	21,099	16,644	21,547	19,344
99,750	99,800	21,113	16,656	21,561	19,356
99,800	99,850	21,127	16,669	21,575	19,369
99,850	99,900	21,141	16,681	21,589	19,381
99,900	99,950	21,155	16,694	21,603	19,394
99,950	100,000	21,169	16,706	21,617	19,406

$100,000
or over
use the Tax
Computation
Worksheet

* This column must also be used by a qualifying widow(er).

Need more information or forms? Visit IRS.gov.

Glossary of Tax Terms

This tax dictionary defines the words and phrases most commonly used in talking about federal taxes. The language of federal taxation is the language of law, accounting, and business. Many of the terms have precise, technical meanings, as compared with their meanings in everyday use. The definitions in this glossary are, of course, only adaptations of the full meanings prescribed by the law, regulations, and rulings, that are discussed in the explanatory text. Refer to this glossary for an introduction to the language of federal taxation.

A

Accelerated Cost Recovery System (ACRS)

This system of recovering the cost of capital expenditures through periodic depreciation deductions (allowances) is mandatory for most depreciable tangible property placed in service after 1980 and before 1987. These costs are recovered over specified recovery periods by means of statutory percentages that do not require the computation of a useful life. An alternative straight-line allowance may be elected over one of several alternate statutory recovery periods.

Assets placed in service after 1986 must generally be depreciated using a Modified Accelerated Cost Recovery System (MACRS). MACRS generally results in lower depreciation deductions than ACRS because many assets are assigned a longer recovery period. Assets are depreciated using prescribed recovery methods and conventions. The MACRS deduction, however, may be computed by using optional tables, which have ACRS style percentages.

Accounting method

A taxpayer's accounting method is the basis of accounting by which records are kept. Usually, either the *cash* basis or the *accrual* basis is used. Special methods of reporting income, such as the installment basis, are variations of these two methods.

Accounting period

An accounting period is the 12-month period on the basis of which the taxpayer's records are kept. If no books are kept or if no other period is specified, the accounting period is the calendar year. If the books are kept on the basis of a 12-month period ending with a month other than December, the accounting period is a *fiscal* year. A special 52-53-week accounting period is also recognized for income tax purposes.

Accrual basis of accounting

The *accrual* basis is distinguished from the *cash* basis. On the accrual basis, income is accounted for as and when it is earned, whether or not it has been collected. Expenses are deducted when they are incurred, whether or not paid in the same period. In determining when the expenses of an accrual-basis taxpayer are incurred, the all-events test is applied. This test provides that the expenses are deductible in the year in which all of the events have occurred that determine the fact of liability where the amount of the liability can be determined with reasonable accuracy. Generally, all of the events that establish liability for an amount, for the purpose of determining whether such amount has been incurred, are treated as not occurring any earlier than the time that economic performance occurs.

Accumulated adjustments account (AAA)

The accumulated adjustments account consists of post-1982 accumulated gross income less deductible expenses and prior distributions allocable to the account of an S corporation.

Accumulated earnings tax

This additional tax is imposed on a corporation that permits its earnings to accumulate, instead of being distributed, in order to avoid payment of tax on dividends by individual stockholders. Generally, a corporation may accumulate up to $250,000 (only $150,000 for some personal service companies) over the years without risk of incurring this special tax. The applicable amount, plus whatever additional amount is necessary to be retained for the reasonable needs of the business, is allowed as a credit against taxable income. Only the remainder of undistributed income is subject to the accumulated earnings tax.

Adjusted basis

The basis for gain or loss and the basis for depreciation, etc. are explained below under *Basis*. After such a basis is determined, it must be adjusted (a) for capital items that increase it and (b) for deductions that decrease it, such as depreciation, depletion, etc.

Adjusted gross income

Adjusted gross income is gross income reduced by trade or business expenses of individual taxpayers, expenses for property held for production of rents or royalties, and certain loss adjustments. The amount of the adjusted gross income affects the extent to which medical expenses, nonbusiness casualty and theft losses, and charitable contributions may be deducted.

Administrator

Like an executor, the administrator manages the estate of a person who dies intestate or whose named executor fails to act.

Affiliated corporate groups—See Controlled corporate groups

Age 65 and older standard deduction

A taxpayer who has attained the age of 65 before the close of the tax year is allowed an additional standard deduction amount of $1,250 in 2015 if married; $1,550 in 2015 if unmarried.

Alimony

In a legal sense, alimony is support payment made after divorce or legal separation. In some respects, the income tax law definition is broader. It includes payments made under a decree of divorce or separate maintenance, under a decree for support if a wife is separated from her husband, or under a written separation agreement executed by the husband and wife if the wife is separated from her husband and they file separate returns. Alimony payments that meet certain tests are deductible by the payer and are income to the recipient.

All-events test—See Accrual basis of accounting

Alternative minimum tax

Alternative minimum tax rules have been devised to ensure that at least a minimum amount of income tax is paid by corporate and high-income noncorporate taxpayers (including estates and trusts) who reap large tax savings by making use of certain tax deductions and exemptions. A taxpayer's AMT for a tax year is the excess of the tentative minimum tax over the regular tax and must be paid in addition to year-end tax liability. The tentative minimum tax is determined by multiplying the excess of a taxpayer's alternative minimum taxable income over an exemption amount by 26 percent for adjusted gross income up to $185,400 and 28 percent for AGI in excess of $185,400 (20 percent for corporate taxpayers), and then reducing the product by the taxpayer's alternative minimum tax foreign tax credit. AMTI is computed by taking taxable income (including unrelated business taxable income, real estate investment trust taxable income, life insurance company taxable income, or any other income base used to calculate regular tax liability), adding or subtracting special adjustments, and adding tax preference items.

Amortization

The commonly known dictionary meaning of the word *amortization* differs from its income tax application. The principal dictionary meaning is the building up of a fund, through periodic payments, for the purpose of paying off an obligation when it becomes due in thefuture, such as a mortgage. But usually in income tax parlance, amortization means the writing off of an amount over a definite period (such as amortizing a bond premium or discount over the life of the bonds), similar to the depreciation write-off on depreciable property.

Amount realized

The term *amount realized* is given a special meaning in finding gain or loss on a sale or exchange of property. The realized gain or loss is the difference between the amount realized and the *adjusted basis* of the asset. The amount realized is the sum of the money and the fair market value of other property received.

Annualizing

Annualizing is a procedure whereby a taxpayer estimates from the income received during a portion of a year what the income for the entire year will be if income continues to be received at the same rate. This process is used in computing the tax on short-period returns and also for avoiding the penalty for underpayment of estimated taxes.

Annuity

An *annuity* is a periodic payment, whether for a period certain or for one or more lives. Under the general rule for taxing an annuity, the taxpayer's investment in the contract is usually divided by the number of payments expected, and that portion of each payment is nontaxable. The remainder of each payment is taxable as received. The Internal Revenue Service provides tables for computing tax-free portions of annuity receipts.

Assessment of tax

The Commissioner of Internal Revenue places the amount of unpaid tax on a list for collection, in effect a charge against the taxpayer on the books of the government. Before any additional tax may be assessed, the Commissioner must send a notice of deficiency and cannot assess the tax before allowing the taxpayer to file a petition with the Tax Court.

Assignment of income doctrine

The principle that income is taxed to the individual who earned it, even if the right to the income has been transferred to another prior to recognition.

Association

An *association* is a body of persons who unite for some special business or purpose, the body itself being invested with some, but not full, corporate rights and powers. For income tax purposes, an association is taxed in the same manner as a corporation.

B

Bad debt

Whether or not it relates to a business transaction, a bad debt can be deducted in the year in which it becomes uncollectible. If a business debt is partially uncollectible, a portion may be charged off. A nonbusiness bad debt is treated in the same way as a short-term capital loss. A debt that arises from the performance of services or the selling of goods by a cash-basis taxpayer may not be deducted if the income from the services or the profit from the sale has not previously been reported as income. However, a bad debt that arises from the lending of money is deductible, subject to the above-mentioned limitation on a nonbusiness bad debt.

Basis

The term *basis,* for income tax purposes, is used mainly in connection with determining the amount of gain or loss on a sale of property or in computing depreciation. It represents the cost of the property to the taxpayer, actually or constructively, but it has a broader meaning than the term *cost.* The *basis* (adjusted) of property is deducted from the *amount realized* to determine the realized gain or loss on its sale. If the property was acquired by the taxpayer through a purchase, the basis is its cost, except in special circumstances such as in the conversion of the property from personal to rental or other business purposes, in which case the basis for loss and for *depreciation* may be different from the basis for *gain.* If the property was acquired as gift property, inherited property, property received in an exchange, etc., then special rules for finding basis apply.

Bequest

A *bequest* is a gift by will of personal property. The law provides a special basis for finding gain or loss or depreciation in the case of property acquired by bequest. The basis is then the value of the property at the date of the testator's death. If a bequest is of money to be paid at intervals, then to the extent that it is paid out of income from property, it is taxable income to the recipient.

Blind and elderly deduction

An additional standard deduction amount of $1,250 is allowed for an elderly or blind individual who is married or who is a surviving spouse. An additional $1,550 is allowed for a single individual or for a head of household who is elderly or blind. Thus, a married couple, each of whom is both elderly and blind, receives an extra $5,000 ($1,250 × 4) standard deduction.

Boot

Boot is a term that is sometimes used to describe the other property received in an exchange which, but for such other property, would be nontaxable. Partial gain may be recognized from the receipt of such boot, not to exceed the fair market value of the boot. Such boot or other property consists of money or property other than stock or securities (or other than like property in like-kind exchanges) which may be received tax free.

Business purpose

When a transaction occurs it must be grounded in a business purpose other than tax avoidance. Tax avoidance is not a proper motive for being in business. The concept of business purpose was originally set forth in *Gregory v. Helvering*, 35-1 USTC ¶9043, 293 U.S. 465, 55 S.Ct. 266 (1935). In this case, the Supreme Court ruled that a transaction aiming at tax-free status had no business purpose. Further, the Court stated that merely transferring assets from one corporation to another under a plan which can be associated with neither firm was invalid. This was merely a series of legal transactions that when viewed by the Court in its entirety had no business purpose.

C

Cafeteria plan

A *cafeteria plan* is a separate written benefit plan maintained by an employer for the benefit of its employees, under which all participants are employees and each participant has the opportunity to select particular benefits. The participant may choose from among two or more benefits consisting of cash and qualified benefits.

Calendar year

A *calendar year* is a period of 12 months beginning January 1 and ending December 31. It is the most widely used accounting period. It must be used by a taxpayer who does not keep a regular set of books on a different accounting period.

Capital asset

The term *capital asset* in income tax law generally means all business and nonbusiness assets with the following exceptions: inventory, depreciable personal and real property, certain works created through personal efforts, business accounts and notes receivable, and certain U.S. publications.

Capital expenditure

A capital expenditure is one that is made for assets of a more or less permanent nature—those with a useful life of more than one year. Such an expenditure may not be deducted in the year made, even though made in connection with a trade or business. In other words, it is capitalized. But if the assets are wasting assets they may, in proper cases, be the subject of a depreciation deduction. Uniform capitalization rules require capitalization of certain costs and expenditures.

Capital gains

Capital gains are gains from the sale or exchange of a *capital asset* as that term is defined above. The excess of capital gains over capital losses is called capital gain net income. If a capital asset has been held for more than the requisite holding period at the time of sale, the gain is a long-term capital gain. Corporations must treat capital gains as ordinary income.

Capital losses

Capital losses are losses from the sale or exchange of a capital asset. The excess of capital losses over capital gains is called net capital loss. A corporation may deduct a capital loss of any taxable year in that year only to the extent of capital gain. The excess of losses may be carried back three years and carried forward five years, but only as an offset against capital gains of such later years. If there are no such capital gains, the deduction is lost. In the case of an individual, short-term and long-term capital losses are combined for purposes of offsetting up to $3,000 of ordinary income annually. Excess losses may be carried forward indefinitely.

Capitalization—See Capital expenditure

Carryback and carryover

Income tax carrybacks include the net operating loss carryback, the capital loss carryback (for corporations only), the foreign tax credit carryback, and the general business credit carryback. The first two are applied against income and the last two are credits against tax.

Carrying charge

This accounting term denotes an expense for idle or nonproductive property that is incurred for the purpose of *carrying* the property. The income tax law permits a taxpayer to capitalize instead of deducting currently as an expense taxes and interest chargeable to unimproved and unproductive real property. Also, a taxpayer can capitalize otherwise deductible expenses incurred during the period of construction or improvement of real property, and taxes and interest directly related to machinery and equipment purchased, up to the date they are put to productive use. In addition, if the finance or service charge on an installment purchase of personal property is separately stated but the actual interest charge cannot be ascertained, such a charge is referred to as a carrying charge. And a portion of the charge is deductible as interest under a special formula.

Cash basis

The cash basis is one of the two principal recognized methods of accounting. It must be used by all taxpayers who do not keep books. It is elective as to all other taxpayers (except corporations, certain partnerships, and tax-exempt trusts); however, it may not be used if inventories are necessary in order to reflect income. On the cash basis, income is reported only as it is received, in money or other property having a fair market value, and expenses are deductible only in the year they are paid.

Casualty loss

Although deduction for a loss generally is confined to a loss connected with a trade or business or a transaction entered into for profit, the law also allows deduction of a casualty loss for all types of assets, including personal assets such as a home, jewelry, clothing, etc. Theft, although not strictly a casualty, is in the same category for income tax deduction purposes. Personal casualty losses are deductible only to the extent that each such loss exceeds $100 per occurrence in 2015 and that the aggregate excess is greater than 10 percent of adjusted gross income.

Child-care expense—See Dependent care expense

Claim for refund

A claim for refund must be made by a taxpayer entitled to get back part or all of the tax paid. The claim may be made on the tax return or, in the case of individual or corporate income taxes, may be made on Form 1040X or 1120X. In other cases, refund claims should be made on amended returns or Form 843.

Claim of right

The term *claim of right* is used in the Code in connection with money or other property received as income which the recipient holds under a claim of right, but which the recipient is required to restore in whole or in part to the payer in a later year because it develops that the recipient did not have an unrestricted right to such property. If the amount restored exceeds $3,000, Code Sec. 1341 provides some relief, by means of a tax limitation in the year of restoration, from the requirement that the restored amount must be deducted in the year of restoration and may not reduce the income of the prior year. The *right* to the money or other property means a just and legal claim to hold, use, or enjoy it, or to convey or donate it.

Community property

Community property is property owned by husband and wife in community, each sharing equally in the income therefrom. The concept of ownership of property by a husband and wife in community is of Spanish origin, adopted from early Spanish law by nine western and southern states—Alaska, California, Nevada, New Mexico, Arizona, Idaho, Washington, Louisiana, and Texas—as well as Wisconsin.

Complex trust

A complex trust is one which permits accumulation of current income, provides for charitable contributions, or distributes principal during the taxable year. For tax purposes, it is to be distinguished from a *simple trust*.

Conduits

Some entities are not tax paying. They pass through their income (loss) to owners (beneficiaries). A partnership is an example of a conduit. Partnerships do not pay taxes; they merely report the partnership's taxable income or losses. The income (loss) flows directly to the partners. However, partnerships do compute partnership taxable income. Other types of conduits are grantor trusts and S corporations.

Consent dividend

A *consent dividend* is not a dividend actually paid by a corporation. It is merely represented by signed consents by a stockholder to be taxed as if the stockholder has really received the amount of the distribution stated in the consent. It is used in order to avoid the imposition of the accumulated earnings tax and the personal holding company tax in cases where this tax might otherwise be imposed and the company does not wish to make an actual distribution.

Consolidated return

Affiliated corporations may file one consolidated return, eliminating intercompany transactions, instead of filing separate returns.

Constructive ownership of stock

In determining the percentage of stock ownership of a stockholder in a corporation, in order to find whether the stockholder controls the corporation or to make other tests of ownership, the Code in several instances provides that the stockholder will be constructively regarded as the owner of shares of stock held by certain other persons. For example, the rule is applied in disallowing a loss on sales between certain related persons.

Constructive-receipt doctrine

A taxpayer on the cash basis is taxed on income only as it is *received*. However, if the income was unreservedly subject to the taxpayer's demand and the taxpayer could have received it but chose not to do so, it is regarded as having been *constructively received* and is taxable. Interest on a bank deposit is a good example.

Contribution to capital

A contribution to capital denotes the money or other property contributed to a corporation by either a stockholder or a nonstockholder. Where a stockholder advances money to a corporation, the tax question on insolvency of the corporation is whether the money was advanced as a loan or as a capital contribution. If it is a capital contribution, the stockholder may not deduct a nonbusiness bad debt. Where a nonstockholder makes a contribution to a corporation, such as payments by a city to a manufacturer for moving its factory to the city, the contribution is not income to the corporation. The basis of property so contributed (or property purchased with money contributions) is zero. If money is contributed and no property is purchased with it, the basis of the corporation's assets is reduced.

Contributions

Contributions usually means gifts made to charitable organizations. A contribution is deductible by both individuals and corporations, to a limited extent. In some cases, the word *contributions* is used in the Code in a different sense, but in those cases the meaning is apparent from the context. (*Contribution to capital*, above, is a case in point.)

Controlled corporate groups

Controlled groups of corporations basically fall into two classifications: parent-subsidiary controlled groups and brother-sister controlled groups. A parent-subsidiary controlled group is one in which one or more chains of corporations are connected through stock ownership with a common parent corporation. At least 80 percent of the voting power or stock value of each corporation in the group other than the parent is owned by one or more corporations in the group, and the common parent owns at least 80 percent of the voting power or stock value of one of the other corporations in the group. A brother-sister controlled group is a controlled group in which at least 80 percent of the voting power or stock value of two or more corporations is owned by the same five or fewer persons (individuals, estates, or trusts) and these persons own more than 50 percent of the voting power or stock value of each corporation.

A controlled group of corporations should be distinguished from an affiliated group of corporations, a term related to elections to file a consolidated return and to take a 100 percent dividends-received credit. An *affiliated group* is formed when at least 80 percent of the total combined voting power of all classes of stock and at least 80 percent of each class of nonvoting stock of each corporation in the group are owned by one or more other corporations in the group. Thus, a parent-subsidiary group is not an *affiliated* group unless at least 80 percent of the nonvoting stock of each corporation in the group is owned by another corporation in the group. A brother-sister controlled group can never qualify as an *affiliated* group since the voting power or stock value of two or more corporations is owned by a noncorporate entity.

Corporation

For income tax purposes, the word *corporation* has a broader meaning than its customary one. It includes an association, joint stock company, and insurance company. All are taxed as if they were corporations, although insurance companies are subject to special rules and are taxed at special rates.

Cost

Cost is the purchase price paid for property, or the value at which it is taken into income (as in the case of services paid for in property). It is the amount most often applied against the amount realized from the sale of property in determining the profit or loss. It is also the figure most often used in determining the depreciation deduction. However, in special circumstances, where property is not acquired by purchase, there may be a special basis for a finding of gain or loss or depreciation.

Cost depletion—See Depletion

Cost or market, whichever is lower

This phrase is used only in reference to inventory valuations. Most taxpayers prefer to use *cost or market, whichever is lower,* as a basis for valuing their inventories since this method affords an opportunity to take advantage of a drop in the market so that profits can be reduced accordingly before disposition of the goods. If *cost* only is used, a drop in the market cannot affect the income until the merchandise is sold. Either method ((a) cost, or (b) cost or market, whichever is lower) is acceptable, but either one, once adopted, must be followed unless a permission to change is obtained.

Credits against tax

A credit against the tax, or a tax credit, is an amount that is subtracted from the income tax liability of a taxpayer in a given taxable year. The tax credit differs from a deduction in that the credit is subtracted from the tax itself, resulting in a dollar-for-dollar reduction in the tax liability; the deduction is subtracted from either gross income or adjusted gross income, resulting in a reduction in the amount of income subject to tax. A nonrefundable credit is one that cannot be refunded to the extent that it exceeds the income tax of the current year (e.g., the investment credit). A refundable credit can be refunded to the extent that it exceeds tax liability (e.g., the earned income credit).

Credits or refunds

Where tax is overpaid for any year, it ordinarily will be refunded by the IRS if the taxpayer owes no tax for any other year. If the taxpayer does owe a tax, the overpayment is credited against the tax that is due the government, and any balance is refunded. Credits and refunds may be allowed only within specified periods if, within such periods, a claim for refund or credit is filed. See *Claim for refund.*

D

Dealer

A dealer, as referred to in income tax law, is one who sells to customers in the ordinary course of a trade or business. Examples are securities and real estate dealers and other dealers regularly selling on the installment plan.

Death benefit

The Code uses the phrase *death benefit* to exclude from gross income life insurance proceeds payable by reason of death.

Declining-balance method

Declining balance is the name for a method of depreciation under the general rules. An agreed-upon uniform rate is applied, not to the original cost or other basis of an asset but to its depreciating balance. Thus, the amount to which the uniform rate is applied *declines* every year. For this reason, the rate must be higher than the straight-line rate. The Code permits using a rate of up to 200 percent of the straight-line rate.

Deductions from gross income

Deductions from gross income are, as the name indicates, amounts representing expenditures or amounts of such personal exemptions for which deduction is allowed from the amount of gross income reported. They are to be distinguished from *exclusions* from gross income, which are not taken into income at all. Deductions are taken from gross income to arrive at adjusted gross income. See also *Taxable income* and *Adjusted gross income.*

Deficiency

A *deficiency* is the amount by which the actual tax (as it should have been computed) exceeds the amount shown on the return, if any, plus any amounts previously assessed as a deficiency and minus any rebates. See also *Assessment of tax.*

Dependent

A dependent is one of certain specified relatives for whom the taxpayer provides over half of the support for the calendar year. Nonrelatives living as members of the taxpayer's household are also treated as dependents if the support test is met. For each dependent, the taxpayer is allowed a deduction of $4,000 for 2015.

Dependent-care expense

A credit against tax is allowed for employment-related expenses paid by an individual to enable him or her to be gainfully employed. Taxpayers with adjusted gross incomes of $15,000 or less are allowed a credit equal to 35 percent of employment-related expenses. For taxpayers with adjusted gross incomes of over $15,000 through $43,000, the credit is reduced by one percentage point for each $2,000 of adjusted gross income, or fraction thereof, above $15,000. For taxpayers with adjusted gross incomes of over $43,000, the credit is 20 percent of employment-related expenses. The maximum amount of employment-related expenses to which the credit can apply is $3,000 if one child or dependent is involved and $6,000 if two or more are involved.

Depletion

The decrease in natural resources (minerals, coal, timber, etc.) due to their extraction from the source of supply and disposition by sale or otherwise is called depletion. The Code provides allowances for the exhaustion of such assets. There are two methods of computing depletion. One is known as cost depletion, which is the writing off of that part of the cost or other basis of the deposits which the number of units extracted in that year bears to the total estimated number of recoverable units. The other method, called percentage depletion, permits deduction of a specified percentage of the gross income from the property. In each year, the method that results in the greater deduction is to be used.

Depreciation

Depreciation is a decline in value or price. For income tax purposes, it is a deduction to reflect the gradual wasting away of an asset due to the passage of time or the use to which the asset is put, or a combination of both. The Code permits deduction of a reasonable allowance for this exhaustion of property used in a trade or business, including rental property, measured by certain criteria, such as useful life. The Accelerated Cost Recovery System (ACRS) and Modified ACRS (MACRS) are generally referred to as systems of depreciation that provide for recovery of cost over statutory periods that are shorter than the useful life of the property.

Devise

A devise is a gift of real property by will. In the income tax law, the term is used mainly in connection with determining the basis of property so acquired. Basis of property acquired by devise is the value at the date of death of the decedent, or at the alternate valuation date if elected for estate tax purposes. A devise is excluded from gross income for federal income tax purposes.

Disability income exclusion—See Tax credit for the elderly

Dissolution of corporation

The dissolution of a corporation follows its liquidation. It is the technical termination of a corporation's existence by surrender or forfeiture of its charter. A corporation remains liable for the filing of income tax returns as long as it is in existence and until its dissolution, even though it is not doing business.

Distributable net income

To the extent that an estate or trust has distributable net income, every distribution to a beneficiary except lump-sum payments of bequests, devises, or inheritances is taxable income. The distributable net income of an estate or trust is the same as its taxable income, with certain specified modifications.

Distribution by corporation

As used in the income tax law, the term *distribution by corporation* refers to any amounts paid by a corporation to its shareholders, or any property distributed to them, other than for value received in goods or services. It is a broader term than *dividend,* defined below, for a distribution may be a dividend and, therefore, taxable income, or it may be an offset against the stockholder's cost or other basis of the stock.

Dividend

A distribution by corporation, defined above, may be either a dividend or a return of capital invested. If it is a dividend, it is taxed as gross income. A dividend is any distribution by a corporation out of its accumulated earnings and profits or out of earnings and profits of the taxable year as of the close of the year (without diminution by reason of distributions during the year).

Dividends-received deduction

A corporation receives a 70 percent or 80 percent deduction—with limitations—for dividends it receives, unless it is an affiliated corporation which does not, or cannot, file a consolidated return. Such a corporation may elect a 100 percent dividends-received deduction.

Domestic corporation

For tax purposes, a corporation created or organized in the United States or under the laws of the United States or any state.

E

Earned income

Earned income, which is usually defined with reference to the self-employment income rules, generally means wages, salaries, tips, professional fees, and other amounts received as compensation for personal services rendered. This term is often used to distinguish unearned income, which includes interest and dividends. The term is sometimes more specifically defined, e.g., for purposes of the foreign income exclusion and for determining self-employment income. In addition to foreign income and self-employment income, the term is relevant to determining income tax liability of minors, IRA contributions, and credits for low-income and elderly or permanently disabled taxpayers.

Earnings and profits (E&P)

Accumulated earnings and profits, as well as earnings and profits of the current taxable year, measure the amount of a distribution by a corporation to its shareholders which represents a dividend. The earnings and profits of a distributing corporation are not the same as net income or taxable income. They include nontaxable as well as taxable income but do not include realized gains or losses which are not recognized for income tax purposes.

Elderly taxpayers—See Blind and elderly deduction and Tax credit for the elderly

Employee

For income tax purposes, an employee is distinguishable from an independent contractor. This is important, for the withholding of income taxes on wages applies only to an employee. Also, employee status will affect the manner and extent of allowance of some deductions. The regulations state that an employee is one who is subject to the will and control of the employer not only as to what is to be done but as to how it is to be done.

Employee stock option

An employee stock option is an option granted to an employee to purchase the employer's stock. Employee stock options to which special income tax treatment is accorded are known as statutory options. Incentive stock options and employee stock purchase plan options are the only two kinds of statutory options that may still be created and exercised.

Employee Stock Ownership Plan (ESOP)

An ESOP is a qualified stock bonus plan designed to invest primarily in qualifying employer securities.

Entity

Generally, for tax purposes there are four types of entities: individuals, corporations, trusts, and estates. Each entity determines its own tax and files its own tax return. Each tax entity has its specific rules to follow for the determination of taxable income. Basically the concept of "entity" answers the question "Who is the taxpayer?" Note that partnerships were not in the list of entities. For tax purposes partnerships are not tax-paying entities. The income (loss) flows directly to the partners.

Estate

The meaning of this word in the income tax law is much narrower than its general meaning, which, broadly speaking, is an interest in property. For federal tax purposes, it has two specific meanings. The gross estate of a decedent consists of the assets, both probate and nonprobate, of the decedent for estate tax purposes. Taxable estate is the gross estate less deductions and exemptions. In its most widely used sense, for income tax purposes, an estate is a taxpayer. It is the executorship or administration of a decedent's estate, subject to a court having probate jurisdiction by a fiduciary, and is treated as a separate taxpayer. For income tax purposes, although clearly distinguishable, an estate is generally subject to the same Code provisions in determining taxable income as a trust. Each is allowed deductions for distributions to beneficiaries, such deductions representing gross income in the hands of the beneficiaries. Income accumulated that is neither distributed nor distributable during the taxable year is taxable to the estate, after offsetting against it all allowable deductions.

Estimated tax

Individual taxpayers must pay estimated taxes on as many as four payment dates unless estimated tax is not expected to exceed $1,000. A corporation deposits its estimated tax in advance on as many as four payment dates (April 15, June 15, September 15, and December 15 for calendar-year corporations). Trusts and estates must make quarterly estimated tax payments in the same manner as individuals, except that an estate is exempt from making such payments during its first two taxable years.

Excess net passive income—See Passive investment income

Executor

An executor is a person appointed via a will to carry out the testator's directions and to dispose of property according to a will. The executor manages an estate. (Feminine form: executrix.)

Exemption

An exemption is a reduction in net income allowed on account of status or dependency. Thus, in arriving at the tax base, or the figure at which the tax rates are applied, net income is reduced by the amount of personal and dependency exemptions. Individuals, estates and trusts are allowed exemptions. Every estate is allowed an exemption of $600. A trust is allowed an exemption of $100 or $300, depending on the type of trust. Except for dependents, every individual taxpayer is allowed at least one exemption of $4,000 in 2015 (adjusted for inflation). On a joint return, the two (or more) exemptions of both the husband and wife are allowed. One spouse is allowed the exemption (or exemptions) of the other on a separate return if the other has no gross income and is not the dependent of another person. Exemptions also are allowable for dependents of the taxpayer.

Expenses

Expenses, for federal income tax purposes, are divisible into three general classes: (1) trade or business expenses, (2) nonbusiness expenses incurred in connection with the production of income, for management, conservation, or maintenance of property held for production of income, or in connection with the determination, collection, or refund of any tax, and (3) personal, family, or living expenses. Only expenses in the first two categories are deductible.

Expenses in the third category are not deductible, except in a few unusual cases (medical expenses, charitable contributions, etc.) where they are specifically allowed by law.

F

Fair market value

The fair market value of property is that amount which would induce a willing seller to sell and a willing buyer to buy the property. Market quotations are an acceptable measure of value, except where the quantity of property involved is so great that its sale would affect the market quotations before the sale is finished. Unlisted stocks sometimes are valued on the basis of the corporate assets, including goodwill, whether or not they are entered on the books. Real estate is valued on the basis of net earnings, location, etc., and this value is best proved by an expert appraisal.

Fiduciary

This term usually denotes the executor or administrator of the estate of a decedent or the trustee of a trust. Since an estate or trust is a taxpayer, the fiduciary is charged with the responsibility of filing a return for the estate or trust. The term also includes a guardian, conservator, or receiver. See also *Estate.*

Filing of return

Filing a return consists of filling it out and mailing or hand-delivering it, generally, to the appropriate IRS location. The time for filing an income tax return is specifically stated in the law, and penalties may be imposed for late filing.

First-in, first-out rule

This rule is generally applied to otherwise unidentifiable stocks where a number of shares of the same kind of stock have been bought at different times and different prices. If they cannot otherwise be identified, those which were purchased first are regarded as having been sold first in determining the cost price to be applied against the selling price for the purpose of determining any gain or loss on the sale. The term is also applied to inventory items where the LIFO method (see *Last-in, first-out rule,* below) is not used. As so used, the first-in, first-out rule is also referred to as the FIFO method.

Fiscal year

A fiscal year, for income tax purposes, is a period of 12 months, ending on the last day of a month other than December, or the special 52-53-week period. It is thus distinguished from a calendar year, which always ends on December 31. It is a recognized accounting period for income tax purposes.

Foreign corporation

A foreign corporation is one which is not organized under the laws of one of the states or territories or of the United States. Taxation of a foreign corporation depends on whether or not its income is *effectively connected* with a U.S. trade or business. Special rules apply to United States shareholders of certain controlled foreign corporations.

Foreign tax credit or deduction

If a United States citizen or resident or a domestic corporation incurs or pays income taxes to a foreign country, an election may be made to deduct such taxes in determining taxable income or to take them as a credit against United States tax. The election must be made as to all foreign taxes incurred or paid in the taxable year. Generally, the credit will be limited to the percentage of the total tax against which the credit is being taken that the taxable income from foreign countries is of the total taxable income. Special rules apply to a U.S. shareholder of a controlled foreign corporation or a shareholder in a foreign investment company.

G

General business credit

The general business credit consists of the investment tax credit (the sum of the rehabilitation investment credit, the energy investment credit, and the reforestation investment credit), the work opportunity credit, the welfare-to-work credit, the alcohol fuels credit, the research credit, the low-income housing credit, the disabled access credit, the enhanced oil recovery credit, and five other credits.

Gift

A gift has been defined as a valid transfer of property from one to another without consideration or compensation. For income tax purposes, the words *gift* and *contribution* usually have separate meanings, the latter word being used in connection with contributions to charitable, religious, etc. organizations, whereas the word *gift* refers to transfers of money or property to private individuals, needy persons, friends, relatives, etc. The recipient of a gift is not required to include it in gross income. The donor is not entitled to deduct it (except for a business gift to a customer of $25 or less per donee per year).

Grantor trust

A grantor trust is one in which the grantor retains control over the income or principal, or both, to such an extent that the grantor is regarded as being substantially the owner of the trust property and of the income. The grantor is taxable on this trust income. The law contains specific tests to find whether the grantor is the substantial owner of the trust property.

Gross estate

Gross estate is an estate tax term. It means a decedent's entire property which is subject to the estate tax, that is, prior to any deductions.

Gross income

Gross income, for income tax purposes, refers to all income which is taxable. The law enumerates specific items of income which are not to be included in gross income and, therefore, are nontaxable. With these exceptions, all income is includible in gross income.

H

Head of household

Head of household has a specific meaning in the income tax law. By means of a special tax rate table, a head of a household receives a tax advantage over a single individual but less than that afforded a husband and wife who file a joint return. Generally, a head of a household is an unmarried individual who is not a *surviving spouse* and who maintains as a home a household which is the principal place of abode of at least one child or grandchild or any other relative (except a cousin).

Holding period

The holding period of property is the length of time that property has been held by a taxpayer or the length of time the taxpayer is treated for income tax purposes as having held it. The term is most important for income tax purposes as it relates to capital gains transactions. Whether a capital gain or loss is long- or short-term depends on whether the asset sold or exchanged has been held by the taxpayer for more than 12 months.

I

Imputed interest

Taxpayers cannot sell property under a deferred payment contract in which no interest or unrealistically low interest is charged and realize all capital gains or increased capital gains on the sale. Unstated or imputed interest is taxable to the seller as ordinary interest income.

Incentive stock option

The incentive stock option is a statutory employee stock option. No income tax consequences result from the grant or exercise of such an option, and, if holding and other requirements are met, gain on eventual sale of the employer's stock will be long-term capital gain.

Income

Income, in its broad sense, is the gain derived from capital, labor, or both. It is distinguishable from the capital itself. Ordinarily, for income tax purposes, the word *income* is not used alone. It is used in conjunction with such descriptive terms as *gross income, taxable income,* and *adjusted gross income,* all of which are defined herein.

Income effectively connected

All income from U.S. sources which is *effectively connected* with the conduct of a trade or business in the United States is taxed to nonresident aliens and foreign corporations at the same rates as apply to U.S. citizens and domestic corporations. Investment and other fixed or determinable periodical income (interest, dividends, rents, wages, etc.) of a nonresident alien is taxed at a flat 30 percent rate, whether or not the recipient engages in a trade or business in the United States, so long as such income is not effectively connected with a trade or business in the United States. Income is considered effectively connected if it is derived from assets used in, or held for use in, the United States, and if the activities of the U.S. business are a material factor in the realization of the income.

Income-shifting

Income-shifting is the transfer of income from one family member to another who is subject to a lower tax rate or the selection of a form of business that decreases the tax liability for its owners.

Individual Retirement Account (IRA)

Any individual may contribute 100 percent of earned income, up to $5,500 a year, to an IRA ($11,000 on a joint return, i.e. $5,500 per spouse). Taxpayers over age 50 are allowed to contribute an additional $1,000. The contributions are deductible from gross income, except for individuals who participate in a qualified deferred compensation plan with AGI over a certain level ($61,000 in 2015, and for joint filers, $98,000 in 2015. The investment grows tax-deferred, but all withdrawals constitute gross income. A 10 percent penalty on gross income is levied on pre-age 59½ withdrawals, except on account of disability, death, first-time home purchases (up to $10,000), insurance premiums for the unemployed, deductible medical expenses, as well as withdrawals in the shape of annuities. Withdrawals must start with respect to the year the participant reaches age 70½. An IRA may receive tax-deferred rollovers from other qualified plans, including other IRAs. Distributions from IRAs are not subject to withholding.

The Roth IRA began in 1998. Nondeductible contributions to a Roth IRA can be made by individuals with AGI up to $116,000 ($183,000 on a joint return). The income is *never* taxed if the account is more than five years old *and* the participant is deceased, disabled, or over 59½ years old. The overall annual limit is $5,500 ($6,500 for taxpayers over age 50) per individual for *all* contributions to *all* IRAs (except education IRAs), deductible or not in 2015. No age limit exists for establishing, making contributions to, or accumulating funds in a Roth IRA. The 10 percent penalty provisions are the same as for a regular IRA, but the contributions may be withdrawn first, at any time, for any purpose, without tax or penalty consequences.

Inheritance

As distinguished from a bequest or devise, an inheritance is property acquired through laws of descent and distribution from a person who dies without leaving a will. Property so acquired takes as its basis, for gain or loss on later disposition or for depreciation, the fair market value of the property at the date of death of the decedent from whom it is acquired. An inheritance of property does not give rise to taxable income, but the *income* from an inheritance does. And if the inheritance is of income from property, such income is taxable.

Installment method

The installment method of reporting income allows the profit on an installment sale to be taxed over the period that payments are received. The amount taxed in any year is equal to the payments received times the gross profit ratio (the total gross profit divided by the total contract price). However, the entire amount of any gain recaptured under Code Sec. 1245 or 1250 is reported in the year of sale regardless of whether any payment is received in that first year. Use of the installment method is mandatory unless the taxpayer elects not to report on the installment method.

Inter vivos trust

An inter vivos trust is a trust created during the lifetime of the person setting up the trust. A testamentary trust is one set up under the will of the decedent.

Intestate

One not having a will; a person who dies without a will is said to die intestate.

Inventory

An inventory is a detailed list of articles of property. In the true accounting sense, and for income tax purposes, it refers only to a list of articles comprising stock in trade—articles held for sale to customers in the regular course of a trade or business. The cost of goods sold during the year is determined by adding to the inventory at the beginning of the year the purchases made during the year and subtracting from this sum the inventory at the close of the year.

Involuntary conversion

An involuntary conversion of property results when property is destroyed in whole or in part, stolen, seized, requisitioned or condemned (or where there is a threat or imminence of requisition or condemnation) and, as a result, the property is converted into money or other similar property, through insurance proceeds, condemnation awards, etc. The law has special provisions on involuntary conversion only where the conversion results in gain—that is, where the amount recovered exceeds the cost or other basis of the property converted. The law permits the nonrecognition of gain on such an involuntary conversion.

Itemized deductions

Itemized deductions are certain expenses of a personal nature that are specifically allowed as deductions. Included in this group are: moving expenses, medical expenses, state and local income taxes, property taxes, mortgage interest, charitable contributions, personal casualty losses, and miscellaneous employee expenses.

J

Joint return—See Surviving spouse

Joint tenancy

Where property is held in the names of two or more persons with the title passing from the first joint tenant to die to the other joint tenant (or joint tenants) upon death.

Joint venture

A joint venture is an enterprise participated in by associates acting together, there being a community of interests and each associate having a right to participate in its control or management. For income tax purposes, a joint venture is treated in all respects as a partnership, not taxable in its own capacity, but regarded as a taxpayer for the purpose of computing its taxable income, which is distributable among the associates in the proportions agreed upon. Such distributive shares are reported by the associates on their individual income tax returns.

K

Keogh plan—See Self-employed individual's retirement plan

Key employee

Long a term of general application, especially in regard to insurance, *key employee* now has a statutory definition for purposes of the rules that apply to *top-heavy* plans. For these purposes, *key employee* includes an officer of the employer earning more than a specified amount, any one of the 10 employees owning the largest interests in the employer, a 5 percent owner of the employer, or a 1 percent owner who is paid more than $180,000 per year. See also *Top-heavy plan*.

L

Last-in, first-out rule

LIFO is the popular abbreviation for the *last-in, first-out* rule for identifying items in an inventory to determine their cost. By this method, goods remaining on hand at the close of the taxable year are treated as being, first, those included in the opening inventory to the extent thereof, and, second, those acquired during the taxable year.

Legacy

A disposition of personal property by will.

Lien for taxes

The U.S. Treasury Department, as part of its tax collection machinery, has a legal claim to the property of a taxpayer whose taxes are delinquent or overdue. Assessment of tax, demand, and refusal or neglect to pay control the creation and the effective date of the lien. Sometimes the lien will attach to property in the possession of a third-person transferee or fiduciary. Sometimes a creditor or other nontaxpayer, as well as the government, may assert a claim to the same property. The question of priorities must then be settled.

Limitations—See Statute of limitations

Liquidation of corporation

Complete liquidation of a corporation is the winding up of its affairs by the settling of its accounts, the paying of all debts, the collecting of assets and the turning of the remainder over to the shareholders in exchange for their stock. Complete liquidation precedes dissolution of the corporation and is not entirely synonymous with it. See *Dissolution of corporation*. A partial liquidation is a calling in of a part of the stock, with or without cessation of a part of the corporate activities. Special rules apply to the sale by a corporation of its assets as a step in liquidation, and to the treatment of liquidation distributions received by the shareholders.

Long-term capital gain and loss

Long-term capital gains and losses are gains and losses on the sale or exchange of capital assets that have been held for more than 12 months. A net long-term capital gain or loss is the excess of gains over losses, or vice versa. An excess of net long-term capital gains over net short-term capital losses is taxed as ordinary income to corporations.

M

Merger

A statutory merger (that is, one effected under the laws of the state) is a reorganization for income tax purposes, upon which no gain or loss is recognized under the conditions specified in the Code. A merger is the union of two or more corporations into one, the others giving up their existence and transferring all of their properties and liabilities to the one continuing corporation. It is distinguishable from a consolidation, which is the transfer of two or more corporations into a new corporation, the transferring corporations giving up their existence.

Minimum tax—See Alternative minimum tax

Minority interest

Stock ownership of 20 percent or less in a corporation which is at least 80 percent owned by another corporation.

Modified Accelerated Cost Recovery System (MACRS)—
See Accelerated Cost Recovery System (ACRS)

Multiple support agreement

If two or more persons who would otherwise be entitled to an exemption for a dependent together furnish more than one-half of a dependent's support, anyone who furnishes more than 10 percent of the support is entitled to the exemption if all the others who furnish more than 10 percent of the support file written declarations that they will not claim an exemption for the individual supported for that taxable year.

N

Negligence

For income tax purposes, there is a penalty of 5 percent of the underpayment if any part of an underpayment of tax is due to negligence or intentional disregard of rules and Regulations, but without intent to defraud. Negligence is a lack of the reasonable care and caution expected of a prudent person.

Net operating loss (NOL)

A net operating loss is limited substantially to a net loss incurred in the operation of a trade or business, although a casualty loss or a loss from a sale of a business asset is included within its scope. A net operating loss may be carried back two years against the income of those two years to the earliest year first. Any unused portion of such loss may be carried forward past the taxable year for 20 years.

Net passive income—See Passive investment income

Nonrefundable credits

Nonrefundable credits are allowed as an offset against tax liability. Since no payment has been made to the government, the taxpayer cannot receive a refund if the credit exceeds the tax liability.

Nonresident alien

A nonresident alien, for income tax purposes, is an individual who is not a citizen or resident of the United States. Taxation depends on whether U.S. source income is effectively connected with the conduct of a U.S. trade or business. See also *Income effectively connected.*

O

Obsolescence—See Depreciation

Organizational expenses

Organizational expenses are the costs of organizing a corporation before it begins active business. The Code permits amortization of these expenses over a period to be chosen by the taxpayer, but not less than 60 months. Such charging off is elective with the taxpayer. Organizational expenses for this purpose do not include expenses of issuing or selling stock or reorganization expenses unless they are incident to the creation of a *new* corporation.

Overpayment of tax

An overpayment of tax is a payment or a total of payments in excess of the amount determined to be the correct amount of tax for the taxable year. The Code provides that the term includes that part of the amount of the payment of any internal revenue tax which is assessed or collected after the expiration of the limitation period properly applicable to such assessment or collection.

P

Paid-in surplus

Paid-in surplus is an accounting term. It represents amounts paid in to a corporation by its shareholders, not in payment for their stock, but, after their stock has been fully paid for, as additional working capital for the corporation. Such paid-in surplus is not taxable income to the corporation. Nor is it deductible by the shareholder. It becomes an additional cost of the shareholder's stock. If the paid-in surplus consists of property other than money, its basis in the hands of the corporation is the same as it was in the hands of the shareholder.

Parent corporation

A corporation which owns a required percentage of another corporation (subsidiary). Every group of affiliated corporations which files a consolidated return must have a common parent corporation.

Partnership

A partnership does not pay taxes. It is a conduit for nontaxable income, dividend income, partially taxable interest, ordinary income, and the capital gains and losses shares to be taken into the income of the individual partners. For income tax purposes, the term *partnership* is more comprehensive than when taken in its ordinary meaning. It includes a syndicate, group, pool and joint venture, as well as an ordinary partnership, in which two or more persons join their money and/or their skills in carrying on as co-owners a business for profit. If the organization of a limited partnership is more in the nature of an association than a partnership, it is deemed to be an association taxable as a corporation.

Passive activity losses

Losses arising from a passive activity are not deductible, except against income from a passive activity. The unused portion of the loss, however, is not lost but is suspended (i.e., carried over) until offset by passive income in a future tax year or until the entire activity is disposed of in a fully taxable transaction.

Passive investment income

Gross receipts derived from royalties, rents, dividends, interest, annuities, and sales or exchanges of stock or securities of an S corporation.

Net passive investment income. Passive investment income of an S corporation reduced by the allowable deductions directly connected with the production of such income.

Excess net passive income. Portion of net passive investment income for the tax year of an S corporation multiplied by a fraction comprised of (1) the amount by which the total net passive investment income for the tax year exceeds 25 percent of the gross receipts for the tax year, divided by (2) the total gross passive investment income for the tax year.

Pay-as-you-go tax system

The U.S. tax system is often referred to as a pay-as-you-go tax system. Much of the federal government's tax collections come from withholdings and estimated taxes. The various types of taxpayers pay tax throughout the year, not just at year-end. The United States has been on a pay-as-you-go system since 1943.

Penalties

The Code contains two types of additions to the tax—interest and penalties. Interest paid may be deductible; a penalty is not. A penalty usually is distinguishable from interest in that it is imposed at a flat rate without regard to lapse of time.

Pension

A *pension,* if received from a former employer for past services, is taxable; if it is received under Social Security laws, it may be partially taxable. It is exempt to a limited extent when received for injuries or sickness. If it is in the nature of an annuity, it is subject to the rules for annuities.

Pension plan

Pension plan is both a generic term applied to various types of plans designed to provide retirement income and a specific term used to distinguish a particular type of qualified plan from a stock bonus or profit-sharing plan. Qualified plans are accorded a wide range of special tax treatment.

Percentage depletion—See Depletion

Personal exemption—See Exemption

Personal holding company

A personal holding company is a close corporation organized to hold corporate stocks and bonds and other investment assets, including personal service contracts, and employed to retain the income for distribution at such time as is most advantageous to the individual stockholder from a tax viewpoint.

The Code prescribes percentages of certain types of gross income and of stock ownership by five or fewer individuals that will turn an ordinary corporation into a personal holding company. If it falls within this classification, a corporation must pay, in addition to the regular income tax on a corporation, a tax at the rate of 15 percent on its *undistributed* personal holding company income.

Q

Qualified Subchapter S Trust (QSST)

A qualified Subchapter S Trust is a trust with single income beneficiary eligible to be an S corporation shareholder.

R

Real estate investment trust

A qualifying real estate investment trust is one which has at least 100 beneficial owners and which distributes at least 95 percent of its income. The income from the distribution is taxed *only once,* and *only* to the beneficiaries. The trust may not be a personal holding company; it must elect to be treated as a real estate investment trust; and it may not hold property primarily for sale to customers.

Realized v. recognized gain or loss

A gain or loss is realized when a transaction is completed. However, not all realized gains and losses are taxed (recognized). A recognized gain or loss occurs when a taxpayer is obligated to pay tax on a completed transaction.

Recapitalization

A recapitalization is an internal reorganization—that is, a rearrangement of the capital structure of a corporation by changing the kind of stock or the number of shares outstanding or by issuing stock instead of bonds, or vice versa. As distinguished from most other types of reorganization, a recapitalization involves only one corporation and is usually accomplished by the surrender by shareholders or bondholders of their securities for stocks or securities of a different type.

Redemption

Redemption is a buying back, a repurchase. A redemption of stock is its repurchase from the stockholder by the corporation which issued it (whether or not it had originally been issued to the stockholder from whom it is repurchased). A bona fide redemption of stock is treated as a sale or exchange of the stock, and, in the case of a taxpayer other than a dealer in securities, gain or loss on the redemption is a capital gain or loss.

Refund of tax—See Credits or refunds

Regulations

The Commissioner publishes interpretations of the law in the form of Regulations. They do not have the force and effect of law; however, in those cases in which the law on a particular subject calls for rules on that subject to be expounded through Regulations, the courts afford them great weight. Provisions of the Regulations on a particular subject are disapproved by the courts in some rare instances, and in a few cases the weight of authority has resulted in the Commissioner's amending them.

Related taxpayers

The Code does not allow a loss, except in the case of a distribution in liquidation of a corporation, from the sale or exchange of property between related persons. A similar rule bars a deduction for expenses and interest incurred in transactions between related persons when the payer is on the accrual-basis method of accounting and the payee is on the cash-basis method. The following parties are considered related persons for purposes of these rules: (1) members of the same immediate family, except for transfers between spouses or incident to divorce; (2) an individual and a corporation in which the individual owns more than 50 percent of the outstanding stock (directly or indirectly); (3) two members of a controlled corporate group; (4) a trust fiduciary and a corporation of which more than 50 percent of the outstanding stock is owned by the trust or the grantor of the trust; (5) a grantor and fiduciary of any trust; (6) a fiduciary of one trust and a fiduciary of another trust if the same person is the grantor of both trusts; (7) a fiduciary of a trust and any beneficiary of such trust; (8) a fiduciary of a trust and a beneficiary of another trust if the same person is the grantor of the trusts; (9) a person and an exempt charitable organization controlled by that person; (10) a corporation and a partnership if the same person owns more than 50 percent of the outstanding stock in the corporation and more than 50 percent of the interest in the partnership; (11) two S corporations if the same person owns more than 50 percent of the outstanding stock of each corporation; or (12) an S corporation and a C corporation if the same person owns more than 50 percent of the outstanding stock of each corporation.

Reorganization

A *reorganization* occurs when a business undergoes a new capital arrangement, with or without new administration. If only one corporation is involved, it is a *recapitalization.* In income tax law, the term applies only to corporations. The Code contains provisions for nonrecognition of gain or loss on exchanges made in pursuance of a reorganization and the shareholders of the corporations involved exchange their shares or receive distributions without surrender of their shares. The provisions of the Code must be strictly complied with in order for such exchanges or distributions to be nontaxable.

Repairs

Repairs are expenditures made to keep property in good condition, but not basically intended to appreciably prolong the life or increase the value of the property. If the property is business or income-producing property, the amount of ordinary and necessary repairs is deductible.

Replacements

Replacements are expenditures for making good or whole a portion of property which has deteriorated through use or been destroyed through accident. Although deduction for the gradual deterioration or the destruction is allowable, subject to the limitations in the Code, a replacement is a capital expenditure to be distinguished from repairs.

Residual estate

That portion of the estate which remains after the payment of debts, expenses of administration, legacies and devises. It consists of that part of the estate which has not been legally disposed of by the will prior to the carrying out of the residuary clause of said will.

Retirement income credit—See Tax credit for the elderly

S

S corporation

An S corporation, as distinguished from a C corporation (the treatment of whose distributions is governed by Subchapter C), is a small business corporation that meets various requirements and has validly elected not to be taxed at the corporate level. Items of income or loss are passed through to shareholders in much the same manner that such items are passed through to the partner of a partnership.

Section 306 stock

Section 306 is designed to prevent preferred stock *bail-outs* where preferred stock (Section 306 stock) is issued as a dividend and either sold or redeemed in an attempt to realize capital gains. Section 306 accomplishes this by taxing the gain on sale or receipts from redemption as ordinary income to the extent of the corporation's accumulated earnings and profits.

Section 1231 dispositions

If, during the taxable year, the recognized gains on sales or exchanges of property used in the trade or business, plus the recognized gains from the compulsory or involuntary conversion of property used in the trade or business or of capital assets held long-term into other property or money, exceed the recognized losses from such sales, exchanges, and conversions, then such gains and losses are treated as capital gains and losses. If such gains do not exceed such losses, then the gains and losses are treated as ordinary gains and losses. However, to the extent that any Section 1231 gain contains gain from the disposition of Section 1245 or Section 1250 property (see below), such gain will be recaptured as ordinary income to the extent of certain depreciation deductions taken.

Section 1244 stock—See Small business stock

Section 1245 property

Section 1245 property includes depreciable personal property and other depreciable property (other than buildings or their structural components) used in manufacturing, production, or extraction or used in furnishing transportation, communications, electrical energy, gas, water, or sewage disposal services. When Section 1245 property is disposed of, any gain is treated as ordinary income to the extent of depreciation deducted. Thus, although Section 1245 property may also be a Section 1231 asset, Section 1231 gain will be realized on the disposition only to the extent that the gain realized exceeds the post-1961 depreciation. Single-purpose agricultural and horticultural structures and storage facilities used in connection with the distribution of petroleum and its primary products that are placed in service after 1980 are included in the Section 1245 property category. Such property placed in service before 1981 is Section 1250 property. A gain on the sale or disposition of Section 1245 property is taxed as ordinary income to the extent of the depreciation deductions allowed.

Section 1250 property

Section 1250 property is property that is depreciable or recoverable but is not subject to the recapture rule under Code Sec. 1245. This includes all intangible real property (such as leases of land, buildings and their structural components, including elevators and escalators placed in service after 1986) and all other tangible real property except property which is used as an integral part of manufacturing, production or extraction or used in furnishing transportation, communications, electrical energy, gas, water or sewage disposal services, or research or storage facilities used in connection with these activities.

Self-employed individual's retirement plan

Self-employed individual's retirement plans—or, as they are more commonly called, H.R. 10 plans or Keogh plans—are qualified retirement plans that must meet certain special requirements because they benefit owner-employees. The annual limit for a participant in a defined contribution plan for 2015 is the lesser of $53,000 or 100 percent of compensation. With respect to a participant in a defined benefit plan, the maximum benefit is the lesser of $210,000 for 2015 (indexed each year) or average compensation for the participant's three years of highest compensation.

Self-employment income

The Social Security provisions cover self-employed persons so that they are eligible for benefits upon retirement at the same age and in the same manner as wage earners. The combined rate of tax on self-employment income is 15.3 percent for 2015. The rate consists of a 12.4 percent component for old-age, survivors, and disability insurance (OASDI) and a 2.9 percent component for hospital insurance (medicare). For 2015, the maximum self-employment income subject to the OASDI component of the tax rate (12.4 percent) is $118,500; there is no cap on earnings subject to the medicare hospital insurance tax. If net earnings are less than $400, no self-employment tax is payable. Also, self-employed individuals may deduct one-half of the employee's share of the taxes for income tax purposes or, instead of this business expense deduction, they may reduce self-employment income by an amount equal to the product of their net earnings multiplied by one-half of the employer's share for the year. For 2015, this is 7.65 percent of the net earnings from self-employment. The Patient Protection and Affordable Care Act of 2010 imposes several new provisions effective January 1, 2013. The provisions include: 0.9 percent additional medicare tax on wages and self-employment income that exceeds $200,000 for individuals, $250,000 for married couples filing jointly, and $125,000 for married couples filing separate returns.

Short sale

A short sale, as applied to securities, is an agreement to transfer stock that the seller does not own or whose stock certificates are not in the seller's control but must be borrowed to cover the transaction. The borrowed stock must be replaced within a specified time through purchase on the market and transferred to the lender of the borrowed stock. For income tax purposes, there is no gain or loss on the transaction until the short sale is covered by purchase and transfer. Special rules apply for determining whether gain or loss on a short sale is a long-term or short-term capital gain or loss.

Short-term capital gain—See Holding period

Simple trust

A simple trust is one for which the trust instrument requires that all income be distributed currently, with no authority to make charitable contributions. Also, the trust is a simple trust only for a year in which it distributes current income and makes no other distributions to beneficiaries. A simple trust is entitled to a $300 deduction in lieu of a personal exemption. For a year in which the trust does not meet these requirements, it is a *complex trust.*

Small business corporation

A *small business corporation* is defined in the Code for two separate purposes. For the two definitions, see *S corporation* and *Small business stock.*

Small business investment company

A *small business investment company* is a term which, for federal income tax purposes, is restricted to a company operating under the Small Business Investment Act of 1958, that is, a company authorized by that Act to provide equity capital to small business concerns through the purchase of convertible debentures. These companies and their investors are given special income tax advantages, such as a 100 percent dividends-received credit and ordinary loss deductions for the worthlessness of stock or securities held by the investment company or stock issued by the company.

Small business stock

To encourage the flow of new funds into small business, Congress created a stock classification with a special tax treatment. This is Section 1244 stock. Under Code Sec. 1244, an original individual investor can treat a loss on small business corporation stock as an ordinary loss—up to $50,000 on a single return or $100,000 on a joint return. Because the Code Sec. 1244 loss is considered in any net operating loss computation, the carryback and carryover rules apply. To qualify under Code Sec. 1244, the stock must be common stock in a domestic small business corporation.

Spin-off

A *spin-off* is a distribution by a corporation of stock or securities in another corporation controlled by it (through at least 80 percent stock ownership) without the surrender of any shares by the shareholders. It is a type of corporate separation. The distribution need not be in reorganization. However, the law contains definite rules requiring that the controlled corporation must have been actively engaged in a trade or business and must continue to be so engaged after the distribution. Furthermore, the trade or business must have been conducted (but not necessarily by the controlled corporation) for at least five years prior to the distribution. The distribution will not be taxable to the shareholders if the distributing corporation distributes at least 80 percent of the outstanding stock of the controlled corporation.

Split-off

A *split-off* is a type of corporate separation, not necessarily in reorganization, whereby a parent corporation distributes to its shareholders stock in a corporation which it controls, under the same conditions as in a *spin-off,* except that the shareholders surrender a part of their stock in the parent corporation for the stock in the controlled corporation. As under the conditions described under *spin-off,* no gain is recognized to the shareholders from the exchange of their shares.

Split-up

A *split-up* occurs where a corporation transfers its assets to two or more corporations in exchange for their stock or securities and then completely liquidates by distributing the stock in the new corporations to its stockholders or security holders in exchange for its own stock. The same nonrecognition treatment applies as in the case of a *spin-off* or a *split-off.*

Standard deduction

Taxpayers receive the benefit of a minimum amount of itemized deductions called the standard deduction. The standard deduction is a fixed amount that is used to simplify the computation of the tax liability. It is also designed to eliminate lower-income individuals from the tax rolls. All taxpayers subtract from adjusted gross income the larger of their itemized deductions or the standard deduction. The standard deduction is based on the filing status of the taxpayer and is made up of the basic standard deduction plus any additional standard deduction. The standard deduction amounts are adjusted annually for inflation.

An additional standard deduction is allowed aged or blind taxpayers. For 2015, the additional standard deduction is $1,250 for an aged or blind individual who is married or is a surviving spouse; the additional standard deduction is $1,550 for a single individual or for a head of household who is aged or blind. Taxpayers receive an additional standard deduction for being both aged and blind. Thus, a married couple, both aged and blind, receives an additional standard deduction of $5,000 ($1,250 × 4).

Statute of limitations

A statute of limitations sets out the period within which actions may be brought upon claims or within which rights may be enforced. The limitations periods of greatest importance for tax purposes are the three-year period in which a tax deficiency may be assessed (subject to modifications and extensions) and the three-year period in which a taxpayer may claim a refund (also subject to modifications).

Stepped-up basis

A *stepped-up* basis is a higher basis (see *Basis*) than an asset had in the hands of a previous owner. Under present law, this is accomplished through a transfer on which the gain is taxable or through acquisitions (not subject to the carryover basis rules) from a decedent.

Stock bonus plan

A stock bonus plan is established and maintained to provide benefits similar to those of a profit-sharing plan, but the contributions are not necessarily dependent upon profits and the benefits are distributable in the stock of the employer. A stock bonus plan is often referred to as an employee stock ownership plan (ESOP) or an employee stock ownership trust.

Stock option—See Employee stock option

Straight-line depreciation

Straight-line depreciation is the method of writing off the cost or other basis of depreciable assets in equal annual amounts over the estimated useful life of the assets.

Straight-line MACRS election

A taxpayer may elect, under MACRS, to claim straight-line MACRS deductions instead of the regular MACRS allowance. The recovery periods under the straight-line election include the regular recovery period and longer recovery periods. The straight-line MACRS deductions are computed in much the same manner as the deductions under the general rules, except that salvage value is not taken into account.

Subchapter S corporation—See S corporation

Subsidiary—See Parent corporation

Substance v. form

Individuals should arrange their financial transactions in a manner that will minimize their tax liability. If a transaction is all it purports to be and not merely a transaction to avoid taxes, then it is valid. If the transaction is solely to avoid taxes and there is no business purpose to the transaction, then it is invalid. The fact that a taxpayer uses one form of transaction rather than another to minimize taxes does not invalidate the transaction. A good example of when substance v. form is a significant issue is in the area of leases. Payments under a lease are tax deductible. Payments under a purchase agreement are not tax deductible. Therefore, it is of utmost importance to determine the true "substance" of this type of transaction. Questions to be asked might include: Do any equity rights transfer to the lessee at the end of the lease period? May the lessee buy the property at a nominal purchase price? With a lease transaction it is immaterial that the parties refer to the transaction as a lease. The true substance of the transaction controls over the form.

Substituted basis

The basis for gain or loss on sale or for depreciation (see *Basis*) of property may, under certain conditions, be determined by reference to the basis of a prior owner of the property (as in the case of a gift) or by reference to the basis of other property (as in the case of a tax-free exchange). Both are defined in the Code as a substituted basis, although the former is sometimes referred to as a *transferred basis*.

Sum-of-the-years-digits method

The *sum-of-the-years-digits* method of deducting depreciation is a variation of the declining-balance method. Under this method, the successive numbers representing the life of the asset by years (one, two, three, and four, for example, if the asset has a life of four years) are added together $(1 + 2 + 3 + 4 = 10)$, and the first year's depreciation fraction is determined by using as the numerator the number of years of remaining life of the asset and as the denominator the sum of the digits. (Thus, if the life is four years, 4/10 of the cost of the asset would be written off in the first year.) Salvage value reduces the basis under the sum-of-the-years-digits method. Like the declining-balance method, it has the effect of writing off the larger part of the cost in the earlier years when the most depreciation on a new asset is actually sustained.

Surviving spouse

Surviving spouses are entitled to the income-splitting benefits of filing a joint return on the death of one spouse. The joint return is made for the regular tax year of the survivor and the short period of the decedent. Use of joint return rates is also allowed to an unmarried widow or widower who maintains a home as a household for a dependent child. This benefit is limited to the first two tax years following the year in which the decedent spouse died.

T

Tax benefit rule

A recovery is includible in income only to the extent that the deduction reduced tax in any prior year by any amount. Therefore, where a deduction reduced taxable income but did not reduce tax, the recovery amount is excludable from income. This rule applies to both corporate and noncorporate taxpayers.

Tax Court

The United States Tax Court is a legislative court under Article I, Section 8, Clause 9 of the Constitution. Its principal function is to review deficiencies assessed by the Commissioner for income, estate, gift, or certain excise taxes. Hearings are held in principal cities throughout the country.

Tax credit for the elderly

The tax credit for the elderly and the permanently and totally disabled replaced the old retirement income credit. One set of rules for credit purposes applies to individuals who are age 65 or older. Another set of rules applies to federal, state, and local government retirees who are under age 65 and to permanently disabled individuals.

Tax credit stock ownership plan—See Employee Stock Ownership Plan (ESOP)

Tax shelter

Basically, tax shelters are investments that provide investors with the possibility of reducing their current income taxes through methods sanctioned by the tax law, thereby *sheltering* current income from tax. Although tax shelters offer an investor the opportunity to invest in many different kinds of assets and, thus, offer a wide range of potential benefits to their investors, the following basic aims are common to the vast majority of tax shelters: (1) maximizing the tax incentives available to the investors; (2) reducing current income tax liability and deferring taxation on any income or gain from the investment until some future tax year; and (3) permitting investors to use borrowed money to finance their original investments (leveraging). Some tax shelters satisfy all three aims, while others satisfy one or two; some rely heavily on their ability to satisfy only one of the aims.

In recent years, Congress has enacted specific Code provisions aimed at restricting the tax benefits of certain tax shelters that permit high-income taxpayers to reduce or avoid tax. Further, the IRS has been vigilant in its examination of returns of taxpayers that indicate participation in a possibly abusive tax shelter.

Taxable income

Taxable income for a corporation is gross income minus all deductions allowable, including special deductions such as the one for dividends received. Taxable income for individuals who itemize deductions is equal to adjusted gross income minus personal exemptions, minus the greater of the itemized deductions or the standard deduction amount. For nonitemizers, taxable income is adjusted gross income minus personal exemptions minus the standard deduction.

Taxable year

Taxable year means the calendar year or a fiscal year ending during such calendar year upon the basis of which the taxable income is computed. In the case of a return made for a fractional part of a year, *taxable year* is the period for which such return is made.

Tenancy by the entirety

Generally speaking, this is a joint tenancy between husband and wife. A tenancy by the entirety cannot be terminated except by the joint action of the husband and wife during their lives. This is in contrast to a joint tenancy, which either party may terminate merely by conveying the interest to another party.

Tenancy in common

A form of ownership where title is held by two or more persons with each owning a fractional interest in the undivided property. Upon the death of one tenant in common, the interest will not pass to the surviving tenant in common but will become part of the deceased tenant's probate estate and will be distributed according to such tenant's will.

Testamentary trust

A trust which is set up under the will of the decedent. Conversely, an inter vivos trust is one set up during the lifetime of the person setting up the trust.

Testator

One who makes or has made a will; one who dies leaving a will. (Feminine form: testatrix.)

Top-heavy plan

Top-heavy plan refers to a qualified plan that must meet additional requirements because key employees' aggregate accumulated benefits or aggregate accounts exceed 60 percent of all such accumulated benefits or accounts in the plan.

Totten trust

A trust created by the deposit of a person's own money in his or her own name as trustee for another person. This is considered a revocable trust at the will of the trustee until the depositor dies or otherwise completes the gift during his or her lifetime.

Trade or business

A trade or business consists of any activity that occupies the time, attention, and labor of individuals for the purpose of earning a livelihood or making a profit. It includes the rendering of services to others as an employee for compensation, the carrying on of a profession, and every business occupation carried on for subsistence or profit and into which the elements of bargain and sale, barter, exchange, or traffic enter.

Transaction entered into for profit

A broad meaning is accorded the phrase *transaction entered into for profit,* losses from which are deductible. It includes the acquisition of any income-producing property or investment property, as distinguished from property for one's personal use or enjoyment. The acquisition may be by gift or inheritance if the property is investment or income-producing property. In some cases, the term can include a transaction entered into simply to avoid or cut down a loss on another transaction.

Transferee liability

If a taxpayer transfers assets to another at a time when the taxpayer is liable for outstanding income, estate, or gift taxes (whether or not determined) and the remaining assets after the transfer are insufficient to pay such taxes, the person who received the assets is liable for the taxes to the extent of the value of the assets received. If there are two or more transferees, each one is so liable.

Travel expenses

Travel expenses are deductible in determining adjusted gross income in the case of an individual involved in a trade or business or in a transaction entered into for profit. Travel expenses include transportation costs and the amount spent for meals and lodging *while away from home* in the pursuit of a trade or business. However, the 2 percent of adjusted gross income floor applies to unreimbursed travel expenses of employees and the 50 percent limitation applies to meal and entertainment expenses without regard to whether the taxpayer is traveling.

Trust

A fiduciary relationship with respect to property whereby the property is held by one party (the trustee) for the benefit of another party (the beneficiary). A trust is usually set up and governed by a written document.

W

Wash sale

In the language of the stock exchange, a wash sale is the simultaneous or almost simultaneous purchase and sale of the same stock. For income tax purposes, a sale of stock or securities at a loss cannot result in deduction of the loss if substantially identical stocks or securities are purchased within a 61-day period beginning 30 days before the date of the sale and ending 30 days after the sale. The acquisition or reacquisition of such stock or securities has no effect on sales at a gain.

Wherewithal to pay

The concept that the taxpayer should be taxed on a transaction when he or she has the means to pay the tax. For example, a taxpayer owns property that is increasing in value. The IRS does not tax the increased value until the taxpayer sells the property. At the time of sale, the taxpayer has the wherewithal to pay.

Withholding allowance

Since the graduated withholding system could cause taxpayers who have large itemized deductions to be seriously overwithheld, these taxpayers are permitted to claim extra exemptions which are called *withholding allowances.*

Withholding of tax at source

An employer is required to withhold income taxes from the wages of employees. The tax to be withheld is computed under the percentage method or by use of wage-bracket tables. There is also withholding of tax at source in the case of nonresident aliens receiving fixed or determinable annual or periodic income from United States sources.

Finding Lists

References are to paragraph (¶) numbers

Internal Revenue Code Sections, Regulations, Revenue Procedures and Revenue Rulings are to paragraph (¶) numbers.

Internal Revenue Code Sections

1(h)(1)(E) 11,001	51(a) 9045
21(a)(2) 9015	51(b) 9045
21(b)(1) 9015	53 9455
21(b)(2) 9015	55(b) 9401
21(c) 9015	55(d) 9435
21(d)(1) 9015	55(d)(1)(C)(ii) 18,371
21(d)(2) 9015	56(a) 9401
21(e)(1) 9015	56(b) 9415
21(e)(2) 9015	56(b)(1)(E) 9415
21(e)(4) 9015	56(b)(3) 4615
21(e)(5) 9015	57 9425
21(e)(6) 9015	58(a) 9415
22(a)-(c) 9025	59 9445
22(c) 9025	59(c) 18,371
22(c)(3) 9025	61 .... 13,001; 13,215; 17,101
22(d)(1) 9025	61(a) 4015; 4101; 4655
22(e)(1) 9025	61(a)(11) 5255
22(f) 9025	61(a)(12) 4485
23 9034	62 .... 6115; 6601
25C 9042	62(a) 6560
25D 9042	62(a)(1) 6601
27(a) 9035	62(a)(4) 6301; 8680; 8701
31(a) 9105	62(a)(7) 14,625
31(b) 9115	62(a)(13) 4331
32 9125	62(c) 8603
33 9135	66 4215
34 9155	71-90 4301
38(c) 9045	71 4451
39 9045	71(b)(1)(B) 4451
40 9045	72 .... 14,625; 15,225
41(a) 9045	72(a) 5125
42(a) 9045	72(c)(3) 5125
43 9045	72(e)(2)(A) 14,325
44 9045	72(e)(2)(B) 5015; 14,325
45 9045	72(m)(5) 14,235
45A 9045	72(p) 14,355
45C(a) 9045	72(p)(1)(A) 14,335
46(a) 9045	72(p)(2) 14,355
47(a) 9045	72(p)(4) 14,355
47(c) 9045	72(t) 14,245
48(a) 9045	72(t)(2)(A)(v) 14,235
49 9045	72(t)(2)(E) 14,245
49(a)(1)(D)(iv) 7125	72(t)(2)(F) 14,245
50 9045	72(t)(3)(A) 14,245
50(c)(3) 9045	72(t)(6) 14,245; 14,545

References are to paragraph (¶) numbers

74(b) 4335
79 5115
83 .... 4601; 4655
83(a) 4601; 14,745
83(a)(1) 4601
83(b) 4601; 14,735
83(c) 4601
83(h) 4601; 14,735; 14,745
84 17,375
101-139 .... 4301; 5255
101(a)(1) 5015
102 18,373
102(a) 4325; 4485; 5001
102(b) 4325
102(c) 4325
103(a) 5075
103(c) 5075
104(a) 5145
105 5101
105(b) 5155
105(c) 5155
106 5155
108(a) 4485
108(a)(3) 4485
108(b)(2) 4485
108(b)(3)(A) 4485
108(b)(3)(B) 4485
108(b)(5) 4485
108(e)(5) 4485
108(e)(6) 4485
108(f) 4485
111 13,180
117 5195
117(d) 5215
117(d)(5) 5215
119(a)(1) 5185
119(a)(2) 5185
119(d) 5185
121 11,015
121(b)(1) 11,001
121(b)(2) 11,001
121(b)(2)(B) 11,001
121(b)(2)(C) 11,001
121(b)(2)(D) 11,001
121(b)(3)(A) 11,001
121(b)(3)(B) 11,001
121(c) 11,015
121(d)(2) 11,015
121(d)(3) 11,015
121(d)(4) 11,015
121(d)(5) 11,015
121(d)(7) 11,015

121(f) 11,001
125 .... 5195; 14,215; 14,401
125(e) 5195
127 .... 5195; 5201
129 5235
129(e)(9) 5235
132 .... 5101; 5195; 5201
132(j) 5101
132(f)(4) 14,205; 14,401; 14,425
132(h)(8) 5101
134 5255
135 5075
141(e) 5075
148 5075
149 5075
152(e) 4451
162 .... 2147; 2225; 6001; 6115; 6201;
                6205; 6215; 6245; 6535; 6601;
                6725; 6735; 7261; 13,001; 13,275
162(a) 6201; 6235
162(a)(2) 6545
162(c) 6735
162(e) 6745
162(e)(2) 6745
162(f) 6735
162(g) 6735
162(l) 8065
162(l)(6) 6575
163 7345
163(d) 6315
163(h) 8215
163(h)(3)(E)(i) 8215
164 .... 6795; 7345; 9035
164(a) 8101
164(a)(5) 17,525
164(b)(5) 8115
164(d) 6245
164(f) 14,501
165 .... 2147; 6401
165(c) 7301
165(c)(3) 8501
165(d) 8775
165(g)(1) 12,515
165(h) 2147; 12,655
166(d)(1) 12,501
166(d)(1)(B) 6245
167 6795
167(k) 12,865
168 6795
168(c) 6801
168(d)(3) 6801
168(e) 6801

References are to paragraph (¶) numbers

168(e)(2)(A)	6815
168(e)(4)	12,715
168(e)(7)	6815
168(e)(8)	6815
168(k)(3)	6815
168(k)(3)(B)	6815
169	6795; 6865; 12,715
170	8275
170(b)	7331
170(e)(1)(A)	12,925
170(l)	8315
172	7331
172(b)(1)(G)	7331
172(b)(1)(J)	7331
172(c)	7331
172(d)(4)(D)	14,501
172(i)	7331
174	7261; 9045
174(a)	6875; 7261; 9415
174(c)	6875
178	6795
179	1151; 6805; 6825; 6835; 6845; 6855; 11,355; 12,715; 12,725; 15,025; 15,401; 16,120
179(b)(5)	6845
179(d)(1)	6855
179(d)(2)	6855
183	6715; 7345; 13,001
185	6795
188	6795; 12,715
190	9045; 12,715
195	6505; 16,109; 16,225
195(c)(1)	6505
197	6865
197(g)	12,135
199	7375
199(a)(1)	7375
199(a)(2)	7375
199(b)	7375
199(b)(1)	7375
199(b)(2)	7375
199(c)(4)	7375
199(c)(4)(B)	7375
199(c)(4)(B)(i)	7375
199(c)(7)(A)	7375
199(d)(2)	7375
212	6001; 6115; 6201; 6245; 6301; 6315; 6325; 6725; 8745; 13,001
213	8001; 17,341
213(a)(1)	6775
213(c)	18,015
215(c)	4451
216	11,015
217	6560
217(c)(1)	6560
219(b)	14,601
219(c)	14,601
219(d)(1)	14,625
219(d)(2)	14,625
219(f)	14,601
219(f)(3)	14,601
219(g)	14,625
219(g)(7)	14,625
222	6570; 8665
223	6575
262	6725
263	6245; 6795
263A	13,425; 13,435
263A(b)	13,425; 13,435
264	6765
265	6205; 6765; 17,201
265(1)	6765
265(2)	6765
266	10,101
267	6775; 16,215; 18,381
267(a)	10,225
267(a)(1)	10,035
267(a)(2)	6775
267(b)	6775; 10,225; 14,765; 16;133; 16,355
267(b)(6)	18,381
267(c)	10,225
267(d)	10,225
267(e)	16,133; 16,355
269	1131
274(a)	6755
274(c)	6545
274(h)	6545
274(j)(2)	4335
274(j)(3)(B)	4335
276	6745
280A	7371
280A(c)	7351
280A(d)(2)(A)	7371
280A(g)	7371
280B	6795
280E	6735
280F	6805; 6845
280F(d)(1)	6845
301	4401; 16,241
303	17,117
305	16,241
305(a)	10,125
305(b)(4)	4401

References are to paragraph (¶) numbers

306	16,241
307	10,125
307(b)(1)	4401
311	16,241
312	16,241; 16,275
316	4401
316(a)	4401
317(a)	4401
318	14,205; 14,235
331	16,285
334(a)	16,285
336	16,285
351	11,401; 13,365; 13,685; 16,215
358	16,215
362	16,215
401	14,235
401-418E	14,201
401(a)	14,125; 14,201; 14,255; 14,285
401(a)(3)	14,255; 14,265
401(a)(4)	14,001; 14,205
401(a)(6)	14,255; 14,265
401(a)(7)	14,275
401(a)(9)	14,235; 14,425; 14,635
401(a)(9)(B)	14,235
401(a)(9)(B)(iv)	14,235
401(a)(9)(C)(ii)	14,235
401(a)(10)(A)	14,501
401(a)(10)(D)	14,501
401(a)(11)	14,325
401(a)(13)	14,285
401(a)(14)	14,235
401(a)(16)	14,215
401(a)(17)	14,001; 14,525; 14,545
401(a)(25)	14,110
401(a)(27)	14,115
401(a)(31)	14,425
401(a)(31)(B)	14,235
401(a)(35)(B)	14,285
401(a)(35)(C)	14,285
401(c)	14,501
401(c)(2)	14,601
401(c)(2)(A)	14,501
401(c)(2)(A)(v)	14,501
401(c)(2)(A)(vi)	14,501
401(c)(3)	14,501
401(c)(4)	14,501
401(f)	14,415
401(k)	14,425; 15,715
401(k)(2)	5195
402	14,305
402(c)	14,345; 14,405
402(c)(8)(B)	14,345

402(e)	14,285; 14,345
402(e)(4)(B)	14,335
402(e)(4)(D)(i)	14,301
402(e)(6)	14,345
402(g)	14,215
402(g)(7)	14,425
402(h)	14,401; 14,501
402(h)(3)	14,535
402(A)	14,405
402(A)(c)(3)	14,405
403(a)	14,415
404(a)(2)	14,415
403(b)	14,401; 14,425; 14,435
404(a)(5)	14,765
404(a)(11)	14,765
404	14,305
404(c)(3)(A)(v)(I)	14,401
404(j)(1)(B)	14,501
408	14,601
408(a)	14,601
408(b)	14,601
408(d)	14,535; 14,625
408(d)(1)	14,625
408(d)(2)	14,625; 14,635
408(d)(3)(C)	14,235
408(d)(3)(E)	14,235
408(d)(3)(G)	14,501
408(k)(2)	14,501
408(m)	12,001; 12,301
408(o)	14,625
408(p)(2)(A)(iii)	14,545
408(p)(4)	14,501
408(q)	14,535; 14,545
408A	14,635
408A(d)(2)(B)	14,635
408A(d)(3)(A)(iii)	14,635
408A(d)(4)	14,635
408A(d)(4)(A)	14,635
408A(d)(4)(B)	14,635
409A	14,701
409A(a)(1)(B)	14,701
409A(a)(2)	14,701
409A(a)(3)	14,701
409A(b)(1)	14,701
410	14,001
410(a)	14,255
410(a)(1)	14,255
410(a)(2)	14,255
410(a)(3)	14,255
410(a)(4)	14,255
410(b)	14,265
410(b)(5)	14,265

References are to paragraph (¶) numbers

411	14,001; 14,275
411(a)(1)	14,275
411(a)(2)(A)	14,275
411(a)(2)(B)	14,275
411(a)(4)	14,275
411(a)(5)	14,275
411(a)(6)	14,275
411(a)(7)	14,275
411(a)(8)	14,275
411(a)(11)(A)	14,235
412	14,001
414(i)	14,101
414(j)	14,110
414(p)(1)(A)	14,285
414(p)(1)(B)	14,285
414(q)	14,205; 14,265
414(r)	14,265
414(s)	14,401; 14,425
414(v)	14,215
414(x)(2)(A)	14,555
414(x)(2)(B)(i)	14,555
414(x)(2)(B)(ii)	14,555
414(x)(2)(B)(iii)	14,555
414(x)(2)(B)(iv)	14,555
414(x)(2)(C)	14,555
414(x)(2)(C)(i)(II)	14,555
414(x)(2)(D)	14,555
414(x)(5)(A)	14,555
415	14,001
415(a)	14,215
415(b)	14,215
415(b)(1)(A)	14,501
415(c)	14,215
415(c)(1)	14,401; 14,501
415(c)(2)	14,501
415(f)	14,215; 14,225
421–425	4655
422	14,725
422(a)	14,725
422(b)	4615; 14,725
422(b)(4)	14,735
422(c)	4615
422(d)	4615
423	4625; 14,715
423(b)	4625
441	13,001; 13,015
442	13,015
443(b)(2)	13,165
443(d)	13,165
446	13,201; 13,301
447	13,230
448	13,225; 13,230
448(c)	13,225
451(b)	18,015
453	2035; 13,601
453(b)	10,245; 13,601
453(c)	10,245
453(d)	13,601
453(e)	13,685
453(i)	12,935
453A	13,601; 13,655
453B	13,695
453B(a)	13,685
454	4385
457	14,205; 14,425
457(a)(1)	14,435
457(a)(1)(A)	14,435
457(a)(1)(B)	14,435
457(b)	14,401; 14,435
457(b)(6)	14,435
457(d)	14,435
460	13,501
460(b)	13,501
460(b)(5)	13,501
460(e)	13,501
460(f)	13,501
461(a)	6245
461(g)	6245
461(h)	6245; 13,235
461(h)(3)	13,235
464	13,230
465	7125; 9045
465(b)(4)	7125
465(b)(6)(B)	7125
465(e)	7125
469	7001; 7261
469(a)(2)	7231
469(b)	7215
469(c)(1)	7235
469(c)(2)	7273
469(c)(3)	7231
469(c)(4)	7273
469(e)	7205
469(e)(2)	7231
469(f)	7287
469(g)(1)	7225
469(h)(1)	7235
469(h)(5)	7235
469(i)	7281
469(m)(2)	7211
471	13,415; 13,435; 13,485
472	13,453
472(f)	13,473
474(c)	13,481

References are to paragraph (¶) numbers

481	13,301; 13,325; 13,355; 13,675
481(a)	13,675
481(c)	13,675
483	13,699
501	8301
501(c)(3)	14,425
529	14,815; 15,225
529(c)(2)(B)	17,325
530	14,801; 14,815
531	16,275
532	8,015
532(c)	16,275
541	16,275
545	16,275
611	6795
613	6885
631	12,615
642(a)	18,365
642(b)	18,045; 18,325; 18,365
642(c)	18,357
642(c)(5)	17,225
642(g)	18,365
643(a)	18,301; 18,325; 18,357
643(a)(1)	18,325; 18,357
643(a)(2)	18,325; 18,357
643(a)(3)	18,325; 18,357
643(a)(5)	18,325; 18,357
643(b)	18,357
643(e)	18,381; 18,503
643(e)(2)	18,381
643(e)(3)(A)(iii)	18,381
644	13,015
651	18,325
651(a)	18,325
651(a)(1)	18,209
651(b)	18,325
652	18,325
652(b)	18,325; 18,345
661(a)	18,357
661(c)	18,357
662(a)	18,373
662(a)(1)	18,345
662(a)(2)	18,345
662(b)	18,345
663(a)	18,373
663(b)	18,373
663(c)	18,373
664	17,225
674(b)	18,525
675	18,525
676(a)	18,525
677	18,525
677(a)(3)	17,173
691(a)	18,015
691(a)(3)	18,015
691(c)	18,015; 18,371
704(c)	16,165
704(e)	17,125
705	16,355
706(a)	16,125
706(c)	16,125
706(d)	16,171
707(b)(1)	16,109; 16,133
707(b)(2)	16,133
709(b)(1)	16,109
721	11,401; 16,141
722	16,141
723	16,141
731	16,175
734	16,175
741	12,115
751	16,175
751(a)	12,115
752(c)	16,149
755	16,175
879(a)	4215
901(e)	9035
904(a)	9035
911	14,801
931	14,801
933	14,801
936	1151; 13,115
1001	13,230
1001(a)	10,001
1001(b)	10,015
1011	10,025
1012	10,101
1014(a)	10,175; 11,015; 17,181
1014(a)(1)	17,195
1014(a)(2)	10,175
1014(b)(6)	10,175; 17,157
1014(e)	10,175
1015(a)	10,145; 17,315
1015(c)	17,315
1015(d)(1)	10,145; 17,315
1015(d)(2)	10,145
1015(d)(6)	10,145; 17,315
1016	10,025
1016(a)	10,025
1019	4395
1022(a)	10,175; 17,181
1022(d)(4)(B)(i)	10,175; 17,181
1022(d)(4)(B)(iii)	10,175; 17,181

References are to paragraph (¶) numbers

1031 .... 10,035; 11,345; 11,385; 15,015; 15,425; 17,195
1031(a) 11,201; 11,215; 12,645
1031(a)(3) 11,275
1031(b) 11,201; 11,225
1031(c) 11,225; 12,645
1031(d) 11,245; 11,255
1032 .... 11,401; 16,225
1033 .... 11,265; 11,345; 11,385; 12,645; 15,015; 15,445; 17,195
1033(a) 11,301
1033(a)(1) 11,315; 11,345
1033(a)(2) 11,325; 11,345
1033(a)(2)(B) 11,365
1033(b) 11,015; 11,315; 11,325
1033(d)-(f) 11,301
1033(g)(3)(A) 11,355
1033(g)(4) 11,365
1033(h)(1)(B) 11,365
1033(h)(2) 11,305
1034 11,001
1035(a) 11,415
1036(a) 11,405
1037(a) 11,435
1038 .... 11,455; 13,695
1041 17,345
1060 10,115
1091(a) 10,201
1091(d) 10,201
1202 .... 9425; 9475; 12,301; 12,530
1211 7225
1221 .... 12,025; 16,133; 16,175
1222 .... 10,030; 12,201; 12,301
1223 .... 16,141; 16,215
1223(1) 11,265; 12,215
1223(1)(A) 11,325
1223(2) 10,145; 12,215
1223(4) 10,201
1223(5) 10,125
1223(11) 12,215; 17,181
1231 .... 12,025; 12,301; 12,615; 12,645; 12,655; 12,701; 12,725; 12,755; 12,801; 12,815; 12,825; 12,841; 12,875; 12,935; 13,675; 15,425; 15,465; 16,115; 16,120; 16,133; 16,141; 16,215; 16,275
1231(b) 12,615
1231(c) 12,645; 15,465
1234(a) 12,165
1234(a)(2) 14,735
1235 12,125
1235(a) 12,125
1235(b) 12,125

1236(a) 12,535
1236(b) 12,535
1236(c) 12,535
1236(d) 12,535
1237 12,545
1237(a)(1) 12,545
1237(a)(2) 12,545
1237(b)(1) 12,545
1237(b)(2) 12,545
1239 16,133
1239(a)-(c) 10,225
1241 .... 4395; 12,155
1244 12,525
1244(a) 12,525
1244(b) 12,525
1244(c)(1)-(3) 12,525
1244(c)(1) 12,525
1244(c)(3) 12,525
1244(d)(1) 12,525
1244(d)(3) 12,525
1245 .... 12,701-12,755; 12,815; 12,835; 12,875; 12,901; 12,915; 16,175
1245(a) 12,835
1245(a)(3) 12,715
1245(b)(1) 12,901
1245(b)(2) 12,901
1245(b)(4) 12,915
1250 ...... 12,301; 12,801-12,835; 12,875; 15,425
1250(a) 12,815; 12,825; 12,845
1250(a)(1) 12,815
1250(a)(1)(B)(iii) 12,865
1250(b)(1) 12,301; 12,815
1250(c) 12,801
1250(d)(1) 12,901
1250(d)(2) 12,901
1250(d)(4) 12,915
1253 12,135
1253(a)-(c) 12,135
1253(b)(2) 12,135
1271(a)(1) 13,675
1271(b)(1) 13,675
1301 13,015
1311-1314 13,180
1341 13,180
1361 16,301
1362 16,335
1362(e) 16,335
1363 16,301
1366(a)(1) 16,355
1366(b) 16,355
1367 16,365
1367(a) 16,355

References are to paragraph (¶) numbers

1368(b)	16,375
1368(c)	16,375
1368(e)	16,385
1371	16,301
1374	16,345
1375	16,345
1378(b)	13,015
1396	9045
1411	3405
1411(a)(1)	3405
1411(b)	3405
1411(c)(1)	3405
1411(c)(2)	3405
1411(c)(3)	3405
1411(c)(6)	3405
1411(d)	3405
1433(a)	17,515
1433(b)(2)(A)	17,515
1563	16,245
2001	17,001
2002	17,025
2010	17,009
2011	17,230
2011(b)	17,035
2014	17,035
2031	17,001; 17,181
2031(b)	17,191
2031(c)	17,105
2031(c)(2)	17,105
2032	17,181
2032(a)	17,181
2032(a)(2)	10,175; 17,195
2032(c)	10,175; 17,181; 17,195
2032A	17,117; 17,195
2032A(a)(1)	17,195
2032A(a)(2)	17,195
2032A(b)(1)	17,195
2032A(b)(1)(A)	17,195
2032A(b)(1)(B)	17,195
2032A(b)(1)(C)	17,195
2032A(b)(2)	17,195
2032A(b)(3)	17,195
2032A(b)(3)(A)	17,195
2032A(c)(1)	17,195
2032A(c)(7)	17,195
2032A(d)(2)	17,195
2032A(e)	17,195
2032A(e)(1)	17,195
2032A(e)(2)	17,195
2032A(e)(4)	17,195
2032A(e)(6)	17,195
2032A(e)(7)	17,195
2032A(e)(8)(A)-(E)	17,195
2033	17,101; 17,173; 17,187
2035	17,001; 17,117; 17,141
2035-2038	17,001; 17,165
2035(a)	17,117
2035(a)(2)	17,117; 17,173
2035(b)	17,117
2035(b)(2)	17,117
2035(c)	17,141
2035(c)(3)	17,117
2036	17,117; 17,125; 17,133; 17,141
2037	17,117; 17,133; 17, 141
2038	17,117; 17,141; 17,575
2039(a)	17,149
2039(b)	17,149
2040	10,175
2040(a)	17,157
2041(b)(1)	17,165
2041(b)(2)	17,165
2042	17,173
2043	17,175
2044	17,217
2046	17,255
2051	17,001
2053	17,001
2053(a)(4)	17,195
2053(c)(1)	17,201
2054	17,201
2055	17,001; 17,035; 17,545
2055(a)	17,225
2055(b)	17,225
2055(e)(2)(A)	17,001; 17,225
2055(f)	17,105
2056	17,001; 17,217
2056(b)(1)	17,217
2056(b)(3)	17,217
2056(b)(5)	17,217
2056(b)(6)	17,217
2056(b)(7)	17,217
2056(b)(7)(C)	17,217
2056(c)	17,217
2058	17,001; 17,230
2103(a)	17,101
2501(a)(1)	17,301; 17,405
2501(a)(5)	17,375
2502(c)	17,301
2503(b)	17,315
2503(c)	15,225
2503(e)	17,341; 17,525
2505	17,009
2511(a)	17,405
2513(a)(1)	17,341

References are to paragraph (¶) numbers

2513(a)(2)	17,341
2514	17,165; 17,395
2514(c)(1)	17,395
2514(c)(3)	17,395
2516	17,345
2518	17,255
2519	17,217; 17,375
2522	17,545
2522(b)	17,355
2522(d)	17,355
2523(a)	17,345
2523(c)	17,345
2523(e)	17,345
2523(f)	17,217
2523(i)	17,345
2603	17,565
2604	17,575
2611(b)(1)	17,525
2611(b)(2)	17,525
2612(a)(1)	17,525
2612(b)	17,525
2612(c)(1)	17,525
2612(c)(2)	17,525
2613(a)	17,515
2622(b)	17,575
2631	17,535
2631(c)	17,501
2632	17,535
2641	17,545
2642	17,545
2651(c)(1)	17,515
2651(d)	17,515
2652(c)(1)	17,525
2662	17,565
3121(a)(6)	3405
3121(v)	14,015; 14,701
3121(v)(1)	14,401; 14,501
3306(c)(7)	14,435
3306(r)	14,701
3306(r)(1)	14,401; 14,501
3402	2365
4972	14,305
4973	14,801
4974	14,235
4974(a)	14,235; 14,625
4975(c)	14,285
4975(c)(1)	14,601
4975(e)(2)	14,601
4975(f)(6)(B)(iii)	14,355
6012	3375
6012(a)	18,045; 18,215
6012(a)(1)	18,001
6013(a)	18,001
6018(a)(1)	17,025
6018(a)(3)	17,025
6019(a)	17,341; 17,405
6039D	5201
6075(a)	17,025
6075(b)	17,405
6161	17,025
6161(a)	17,025
6166	17,025; 17,117
6166(g)	17,025
6213(a)	2311
6213(b)(4)	2311
6213(g)(2)	2301
6324(b)	17,301; 17,405
6501(a)	2355
6501(c)(1)-(3)	2355
6501(c)(4)	2355
6501(d)	2355; 18,035
6501(e)(1)	2355
6501(e)(1)(A)(i)	4355
6501(f)	2355
6501(h)	2355
6501(j)	2355
6502(a)	2355
6511(a)	2311; 2325
6511(b)	2325
6511(d)	2325
6513(b)	2325
6532(a)	2311
6601(j)	17,025
6611(e)-(f)	2333
6621(a)	2333
6651(a)	18,209
6651(a)(1)	2365
6651(a)(2)	2365
6651(a)(3)	2365
6651(d)	2365
6651(f)	2365; 18,209
6654(d)(1)	2365
6654(d)(1)(A)-(B)	2365
6654(d)(2)	2365
6654(e)(3)	2365
6655	2365
6655(d)(1)(B)(ii)	2365
6655(e)	2365
6656(a)	2365
6656(b)	2365
6662	2365; 7261
6662(a)	2365
6662(b)	2365
6662(d)(1)	2365

References are to paragraph (¶) numbers

6662(d)(2)(B)	2365
6662(d)(2)(B)(i)	2365; 2370
6662(d)(2)(B)(ii)	2370
6662(d)(2)(B)(ii)(II)	2370
6662(d)(2)(C)	2365
6662(d)(2)(D)	2035
6662(e)	2365
6662(f)	2365
6662(g)	2365
6662(h)	2365
6662(h)(2)(A)	2365
6662(h)(2)(C)	2365
6662A	2365
6663	2365; 18,209
6663(a)	2365
6663(b)	2365
6664(a)	2365
6664(c)	2365
6664(c)(1)	2365
6694(a)	2365; 2370
6694(b)	2365
6695(a)-(c)	2365
6695(d)	2365
6695(e)	2365
6695(f)	2365
6701	2365
6724(d)(3)	4451
6903	18,035
7201	1131; 2365
7202	2365
7203	2365
7204	2365
7205	2365
7206	2365
7207	2365
7463(a)-(b)	2311
7520	17,109; 17,149; 17,185; 17,225
7602	2301
7701(a)(36)	2365
7801(a)	2211
7802	2211
7805	2225
7805(a)	2035
7872(c)	4385

Private Letter Rulings

9015014	6801

Regulations Sections

1.44A-1(c)(1)	9015
1.61-2(d)(2)(i)	10,135
1.61-2(d)(3)	5185
1.61-3(a)	4355
1.61-6(a)	10,115
1.61-12(a)	4485
1.62-1(g)	6535
1.62-1T(f)	8603
1.71-1(e)	4451
1.72-5(a)(2)(i)	5125
1.72-5(c)	5125
1.72-5(d)	5125
1.72-9	5125
1.72-16(b)(2)	14,335
1.83-1(a)	14,735
1.83-1(b)(1)	4601
1.83-1(b)(2)	4601
1.83-2(a)	14,745
1.83-3(c)	4601
1.83-4(a)	14,765
1.83-4(b)	14,745
1.83-7	4655
1.83-7(a)	4655; 14,735
1.106-1	5155
1.125-1	5195
1.127-2(c)	5201
1.132-2	5101
1.162-2(c)	6545
1.162-3	13,215
1.162-4	6795
1.162-5(a)	8665
1.162-5(b)(3)	8665
1.162-6	8665
1.162-17(b)	8603
1.162-17(b)(4)	8603
1.162-20(a)(2)	6745
1.162-20(b)	6745
1.162-21(b)	6735
1.162-21(c)	6735
1.165-1(d)(2)(i)	2147; 7301
1.165-1(d)(2)(ii)	2147; 7301
1.165-7(a)(3)(i)	7301
1.165-7(b)(1)	2147
1.165-8(d)	7301
1.165-9(b)(2)	10,215
1.166-1(c)	12,501

References are to paragraph (¶) numbers

1.166-2(b) 6245
1.166-5(a)(2) 12,501
1.166-5(b) 6245
1.167(a)-3 6865
1.167(a)-5 10,115
1.167(g)-1 .... 6855; 10,145; 10,215
1.167(h)-1(b) 18,331
1.167(h)-1(c) 18,331
1.168-1(d)(3) 6835
1.171-1(b) 10,025
1.174-2(a) 6875
1.183-1(b)(1) 7345
1.183-2(b) 7345
1.212-1(k) 6795
1.213-1(d) 18,015
1.217-2(d)(1) 6560
1.263(a)-1(b) 6795
1.263(a)-2 6795
1.263A-1(b)(2) 13,435
1.263A-1(b)(3) 13,435
1.263A-1(b)(5) 13,435
1.266-1(b) 10,101
1.267(d)-1(c)(3) 10,225
1.274-2(d)(1) 6755
1.274-5 6755
1.301-1 4401
1.301-1(j) 10,135
1.305-1 4401
1.305-1-1.305-7 10,125
1.316-1 4401
1.401(a)-1(b)(1) 14,110
1.401(a)(4)-1(b) 14,205
1.401(a)(9)-5 14,235
1.401(a)(9)-6 14,235
1.401(a)(9)-9 14,235
1.401(a)-14(b) 14,235
1.401(a)(31)-1 14,345
1.401(k)-1(a)(6)(i) 14,501
1.401(k)-11(b)(3) 14,501
1.401-1(b) 14,115
1.401-1(b)(1)(i) 14,130; 14,501
1.401-1(b)(1)(iii) 14,120
1.401-1(b)(5) 14,285
1.401-2 14,285
1.401-11(b)(1) 14,501
1.402(a)-1(a)(2) 14,335
1.402(g)-1(e)(8)(iii) 14,401
1.404(b)-1T 14,765
1.404(e)-1A(f) 14,501
1.408-8 14,625
1.408-8A-6 14,635
1.423-2(d) 14,715

1.423-2(g)(1) 14,715
1.423-2(i) 14,715
1.442-1(b) 13,101; 13,115
1.442-1(e) 13,115
1.443-1(a)(2) 18,025
1.446-1(a)(1) 6245
1.446-1(a)(3) 13,215
1.446-1(a)(4)(i) 13,401
1.446-1(c)(1)(i) 13,215
1.446-1(c)(2)(i) 13,265
1.446-1(d) 13,245
1.446-1(e) 13,301
1.448-1T(b) 13,225
1.448-1T(e) 13,225
1.451-1(a) 13,235
1.451-1(b) 18,015
1.451-2 4125
1.451-2(a) 13,215
1.451-3(a) 13,501
1.453 2035
1.457-7(c)(1) 14,435
1.457-7(c)(2)(i) 14,435
1.460-1(c)(3) 13,501
1.460-4(d)(4) 13,501; 13,540
1.461-1(a)(1) 13,230
1.461-2 13,235
1.469-1T(e)(1)(ii) 7235
1.469-1T(e)(3) 7261; 7273
1.469-1T(e)(3)(B)(ii) 7273
1.469-1T(e)(4)(iv) 7231
1.469-1T(g)(2) 7231
1.469-4(b)(1) 7261
1.469-4(c)(1) 7261
1.469-4(c)(2) 7261
1.469-4(c)(3) 7261
1.469-4(d) 7261
1.469-4(e) 7261
1.469-4(f)(1) 7261
1.469-4(f)(2) 7261
1.469-4(g) 7261
1.469-4(h) 7261
1.469-4(j) 7261
1.469-4(k) 7261
1.469-5T(a) 7235
1.469-5T(c) 7235
1.469-5T(e) 7235
1.469-5T(f) 7235
1.471-1 .... 13,401; 13,415
1.471-2 13,415
1.471-2(c) 13,445
1.471-3 13,425
1.471-4(c) 13,445

References are to paragraph (¶) numbers

1.471-6(a)	13,230
1.471-11	13,425
1.472-2(e)(3)	13,453
1.472-4	13,445
1.472-8	13,473
1.472-8(e)(2)(v)	13,473
1.481-1(c)	13,325
1.611-1(a)	6885
1.611-1(b)	6885
1.611-1(c)(4)	18,331
1.611-1(c)(5)	18,331
1.641(b)(2)	18,035
1.642(b)-1	18,045
1.642(g)-1	18,365
1.642(g)-2	17,201
1.643(a)-0	18,301
1.651(a)(1)	18,209
1.652(c)-4	18,325
1.662(a)-2	18,345
1.662(a)-3	18,345
1.662(c)-4	18,357
1.663(b)-1(a)(2)(i)	18,373
1.664-3(b)	17,225
1.691(a)-2	18,015
1.691(a)-3	18,015
1.691(b)-1	18,015
1.704-1(e)(3)	16,195
1.706-1	13,015
1.1001-1(a)	10,001
1.1001-1(c)(1)	10,001
1.1012-1(a)	10,101
1.1012-1(c)	4401
1.1012-1(c)(1)	10,201
1.1012-1(c)(2)	10,201
1.1012-1(c)(3)	10,201
1.1016-3(a)(2)(i)	10,025
1.1031(a)-1(a)	11,215
1.1031(a)-1(b)	11,215
1.1031(a)-3(g)(4)(ii)	11,275
1.1031(d)-1(e)	11,235
1.1031(d)-2	11,245
1.1033(a)-2(c)(2)	11,385
1.1034-1(b)(4)	11,025
1.1034-1(c)(3)	11,005
1.1036-1(a)	11,405
1.1038-1	11,455
1.1091-1(a)	10,201
1.1091-2	10,201
1.1223-1(a)	11,265
1.1223-1(b)	10,145; 12,215
1.1223-1(e)	10,125
1.1223-1(f)	10,125
1.1234(a)(2)	14,735
1.1235-2(b)	12,125
1.1237-1(a)(4)(i)	12,545
1.1237-1(c)(3)	12,545
1.1237-1(c)(4)	12,545
1.1244(a)-1(b)	12,525
1.1244(b)-1	12,525
1.1244(c)-1(b)	12,525
1.1245-4(a)	12,901
1.1250-1(e)(3)	12,801
1.1250-3(a)	12,901
1.6012-3	18,045
1.6012-3(b)(1)	18,001
1.6013-1(d)	18,001
1.6072-1(b)	18,001
1.6654-2(d)(2)	16,187
1.6661-3	2035
1.6662-3(b)(3)(ii)	2370
1.6662-4(d)(3)	2035
1.6662-4(d)(3)(i)	2035
1.6662-4(d)(3)(ii)	2035
1.6662-4(d)(3)(iii)	2035
1.6662-4(e)(2)(i)	2370
1.6694-1	2365
1.6694-2(b)(1)	2370
1.6694-2(c)(1)	2370
1.6694-2(c)(2)	2370
15A.453-1(c)	13,675
15A.453-1(d)(3)	13,675
20.2013-1	17,035
20.2031-1(b)	17,181; 17,185; 17,191
20.2031-2	17,191
20.2031-2(b)	17,187
20.2031-2(e)	17,187
20.2031-2(f)	17,191
20.2031-3	17,191
20.2031-6(a)	17,185
20.2031-6(b)	17,191
20.2031-8	17,185
20.2031-8(b)	17,185
20.2032-1(c)(2)	17,187
20.2032A-8(a)(3)	17,195
20.2036-1(a)	17,125
20.2036-1(b)(2)	17,125
20.2037-1(c)(2)	17,133
20.2038-1(a)	17,141
20.2038-1(a)(3)	17,141
20.2053-1(a)(1)	17,201
20.2053-1(b)(3)	17,201
20.2053-3(a)	17,201
20.2053-6	17,201
25.2503-3(a)	17,325

References are to paragraph (¶) numbers

25.2503-3(b)	17,325	25.2512-2(e)	17,187
25.2503-3(c)	17,325	25.2513-1(b)	17,341
25.2511-1(a)	17,301	25.2513-1(b)(5)	17,341
25.2511-2(b)	17,301	25.2522(a)-1(a)	17,355
25.2011-2(g)	17,301	31.3121(v)(2)-1(c)	14,701
25.2011-2(h)	17,301	301.6903-1	18,035
25.2511-1(a)	17,301	601.105(c)(1)(ii)	2301
25.2511-2(b)	17,301	601.105(d)(1)(iv)	2301
25.2511-2(g)	17,301	601.106(d)(1)	2311
25.2512-2(b)	17,187	601.201(c)(4)	2225

Revenue Procedures

74-33	13,015	2002-39	13,015
75-120	8655	2003-16	14,345
77-16	8655	2004-64	8315
84-74	13,355	2008-52	13,301; 13,325; 13,355
87-56	6801; 11,215	2009-39	13,301
87-57	6801	2011-14	13,301
88-22	6801	2012-29	14,745
89-46	15,201	2013-13	7351
92-64	14,705	2014-30	6575
94-36	2035	2014-61	17,195
2000-22	13,215	2015-1	2225
2000-30	4385	2015-2	2225
2001-10	13,215	2015-3	2225
2002-19	13,325	2015-7	2225
2002-28	13,215	2015-8	2225
2002-37	13,115	2015-13	13,325
2002-38	13,015; 13,115		

Revenue Rulings

54-135	17,301	66-262	6765
54-569	11,345	67-396	17,301
55-79	12,115	68-37	11,335
55-711	3345	68-125	13,015
56-366	14,501	68-145	18,015
57-244	11,275	68-650	11,025
57-310	18,015	69-188	8255
57-314	11,301	69-292	8665
57-599	8501	69-494	14,285
58-210	10,201	70-413	6245
59-60	17,187; 17,191	72-265	11,405
59-173	11,335	72-440	14,235
59-379	3225	72-456	11,215
60-190	3225	72-545	6325; 6725
63-221	11,301	73-18	11,315
64-31	11,005	73-99	6245
64-237	11,345	74-8	11,301
65-34	3225	74-43	17,325
66-7	12,201	74-175	18,015

References are to paragraph (¶) numbers

74-370	3345	79-229	6245
74-407	6745	79-302	17,157
75-120	8655	79-340	18,015
75-168	6545	80-261	17,325
75-380	2147; 6535	81-7	17,325
76-319	11,345	81-180	11,301
77-16	8655	84-18	14,601
77-264	13,365	84-89	3345
77-282	3225	85-97	5145
77-297	11,275	86-142	14,601
78-39	6245	87-22	6245
78-111	6745	90-23	6545
78-112	6745	92-29	6125
79-173	3225	2010-25	8215

Table of Cases

References are to paragraph (¶) numbers

A

Alderson, J. 11,275
Allen, C. 17,125
Allen, L. 6795
American Automobile Assn. 13,235
American Dental Co.: Helvering v. 4485
Appleman, J.A. 8501
Arkansas Best Corp. 12,101
Austra, J.A. 8501

B

Baird Publishing Co., J.H. 11,275
Barnhill 6545
Bedell, A.M. 13,215
Berland's Inc. of South Bend 1131
Betz 2055
Bishop, C.J. 2365
Blasdel, J.W. 17,325
Blodgett 2055
Bogardus, A.G. 4325
Bolton, D.D. 7371
Bonaire Development Co. 6245
Bowden, F. 4025
Budin v. Comm. 7345
Burke, J.E. 2055
Burnet: North American Oil
    Consolidated v. 1195
Burns, H.F. 8501
Burrett: Doggett v. 6215

C

Californians Helping to Alleviate
    Medical Problems, Inc. 6735
Cameron, J.D.M. 3225
Cartwright, D.B. 17,185
Chandler, E.G. 17,301
Cohan, G.M. 6901
Cohen, M. 6735
Colorado Springs National Bank 6505
Commissioner of Internal Revenue Service—
    See name of taxpayer
Connors, Inc. 13,301
Coupe, L.Q. 11,275
Crummey, D.M. 17,325
Curphey, E.R. 6215

D

Deputy v. DuPont 6225
Doggett v. Burrett 6215
Drye, Jr. 2055
Duberstein, M. 4325
Dunn and McCarthy, Inc. 6225

E

Earl: Lucas v. 1195; 4201
Eisner v. Macomber 4015
Elliott, T.O. 7345
Estate of E.B. Witt v. Fahs 13,215
Estate of O.D. Casey 17,575
Estate of Little 17,165

F

Fahs: Estate of E.B. Witt v. 13,215
Farmers' Loan & Trust Co.: Pollock v. 1151
Fausner 2147
Fleming Est., J.F. 3345
Flint v. Stone Tracy Co. 1151
Frank, M. 6505

G

Gale, D.L. 14,501
Gill 6235
Glick, Eugene B. 2055
Goedel 6225
Golsen, J.E. 2311
Grace Est., J.P. 17,125
Gregory v. Helvering 1195
Grier 6215
Groetzinger, R.P. 8775

H

Haden Co., W.H 11,275
Hamilton National Bank
    of Chattanooga 13,215
Helvering—See name of taxpayer
Higgins 6215
Hoey: National Investors Corp. v. 1131
Hoover Motor Express Co., Inc. 6735
Horst: Helvering v. 4201

References are to paragraph (¶) numbers

Hort, W.M. 12,155
Hughes Properties, Inc. 6245

J

Jenkins, H.L. and T.M. 6225
Johnson, H. 3225
Jones, J.M. 6795

K

Kershaw Mfg. Co., Inc. 1131
Klien, J. 13,710

L

Lessinger, S. 16,215
Levin, S.B. 6215
Lincoln Electric Co. 6235
London Shoe Co., Inc. 5015
Lovett, T. 3225
Lucas v. Earl 1195; 4201
Lutter, H.M. 3225

M

McGowan: Williams v. 12,115
Macomber: Eisner v. 4015
Magill, F.M. 6601
Markarian, F. 3225
Mayo 8775
Microsoft Corp. 2055
Moser, W.L. 7125

N

National Airlines, Inc. 13,301
National Investors Corp. v. Hoey 1131
Newman, S.R. 1131
Noel, M.L. 17,173
North American Oil Consolidated
    v. Burnet 1195

O

O'Donnabhain 8015
Old Colony R.R. Co. 8201

P

Paolini, R. 6535
Patchen, J.C. 13,301
Patrick, et al: U.S. v. 6725
Perry, Jr., Harvey D. 2055
Petrane, G.A. 2055
Pollock v. Farmers' Loan & Trust Co. 1151
Pool, H.A. 2147
Putnam Est., M. 4401

R

Reinhardt 14,235
Richardson Foundation, S.W. 18,357
Riggs National Bank of
    Washington, D.C. 18,357
Robinson 14,701
Ross, L.W. 4125
Rudkin Testamentary Trust 18,365

S

Schall, C. 4325
Scott 2055
Shore, D.R. 13,365
Smoll, J.M. 18,209
Springer 18,525
Stacy, H. 8501
Stidger 6545
Stone Tracy Co.: Flint v. 1151
Sullivan, N. 6735

W

Watson, E.A. 12,115
Weightman, G. 7351
Welch: Helvering v. 6225
Williams v. McGowan 12,115

Y

York 6505

Z

Zaninovich, M.J. 6245

Topical Index

References are to paragraph (¶) numbers

A

Accelerated cost recovery system (ACRS)
nonresidential property........................ 12,835
for Section 1245 property....... 12,735–12,755
for Section 1250 property....... 12,835; 12,855
for tangible property depreciation........... 6801
**Accelerated depreciation
and amortization in AMTI**........................ 9425
Accident and health plan benefits.............. 5155
Accounting methods................. 13,201–13,375
accrual....................... 1195; 13,235–13,240;
13,265; 18,015
adjustments made to items
for changing..................... 13,325
application for change,
time and form of.............................. 13,355
cash 1195; 13,215–13,230; 13,265; 18,015
cash to accrual method......................... 13,301
change of............................... 13,301–13,355
combination of methods...................... 13,301
correction of mathematical errors......... 13,301
denial of change................................. 13,301
for estate.. 18,045
hybrid.. 13,265
overall.. 13,201
for separate sources of income.............. 13,245
tangible property costs........................ 13,275
tax 6245
tax planning for.................................. 13,365
timeliness in electing........................... 13,375
for trust... 18,215
underlying facts, change in.................. 13,301
Accounting periods.................... 13,007–13,180.
See also Tax year
change of............................... 13,101–13,165
tax planning for.................................. 13,175
Accrual accounting method....... 13,235–13,240
for decedent....................................... 18,015
deduction of expenses under.................. 6245
defined.. 1195
disadvantage of.................................. 13,235
hybrid methods including.................... 13,265
tax planning for.................................. 13,240
**Accumulated adjustments account
(AAA)**... 16,385
Adjusted gross income (AGI)
calculating... 3015

deductions for.................... 6101; 6115; 6245;
6401–6585; 8665
deductions from.................. 6101; 6125; 6401
importance of.. 3025
Adoption assistance tax credit........ 9032; 9034;
9125
Adoption expenses................................... 5140
Advertising as business deduction............. 6201
Affordable Care Act (ACT)....................... 8065
Alcohol fuels tax credit............................ 9045
Alien spouse, gifts to............................... 17,345
Alimony
income treatment................................... 4451
recapture.. 4451
**Alternate valuation method,
valuation date for**.............................. 17,181
Alternative MACRS system............. 6801; 6805
Alternative minimum tax (AMT)
carryover of credit for............................ 9455
exemption amounts under....................... 9435
imposition of.. 9401
planning for.. 9475
tax credits under.................................... 9445
of trust.................................... 18,215; 18,371
Alternative minimum taxable income (AMTI)
adjustments to taxable
income for.......................... 9415; 14,725
corporations....................................... 16,255
defined... 9401
of estates and trusts............................ 18,371
items added back
to taxable income in computing........... 9425
Alternative short-period tax.................... 13,165
**American Institute of Certified Public
Accountants (AICPA)**.............................. 2375
American Jobs Creation Act of 2004
automobile depreciation......................... 6845
business incentives created by................. 1101
domestic production
activities deduction under.................... 6585
exclusion of gain on sale
of residence under............................ 11,001
focus of.................................... 1151; 1171
manufacturing deduction created by....... 7375
Section 179 use with autos..................... 6825
American Opportunity Tax Credit............. 5075.
See also Hope Scholarship Credit

References are to paragraph (¶) numbers

American Recovery and Reinvestment Act of 2009
- focus of 1151
- gains on small business stock under 12,530
- income from cancellation of debt exclusion under 4485

American Taxpayer Relief Act of 2012 (ATRA) 1151; 1165
- capital gains and dividends 12,001
- dividend income 4401
- educational assistance plans 5201
- gains on small business stock 12,530

Amortization
- accelerated, in AMTI 9425
- of intangible assets 6865
- of some start-up costs for business 6505

Amount realized defined 11,025

Annuities
- commercial 17,149
- employee 5125
- expected return 5125
- investment in contract, defined 5125
- joint and survivor 5125
- private 17,149
- refund 5125
- single life 5125
- starting date, defined 5125
- taxation of payouts from 5125
- variable 14,755

Annuity distributions 8785; 14,325

Appeals court system 2055

Appeals process of IRS 2311

Applicable credit amount
- for estate tax 17,009
- for gift tax 17,009

Arbitrage bonds 5075

Arrowsmith doctrine 13,180

Assignment of income doctrine 4201
- defined 1195

At-risk rules 7125
- application of 7201

Audits, tax 1121

Automobile expenses, computing deduction for 6535

Automobiles, depreciation for 6845

Awards included in gross income 4335

B

Bad debts
- with accrual method of accounting 13,235
- as business deduction 6245
- nonbusiness 6245; 12,501

Bankruptcy Act of 1980 1151

Basis
- of acquired property in like-kind exchanges 11,255; 11,275
- adjusted 10,025; 11,025
- adjustment for business casualty 7301
- allocated among multiple properties 10,115
- allocated for nontaxable, stock dividends 10,125
- cost as original 10,101
- defined 1195
- determination of, for property transactions 10,101–10,245
- equal to estate tax value 17,181
- as fair market value 10,135
- of nontaxable stock rights 10,130
- of property acquired by gift 10,145
- of property acquired from decedent 10,175
- of property converted from personal to business use 10,215
- of shares in stock transactions 10,201
- survivor's 10,175
- for transfer of property by gift 17,315

Below-market interest loans 4385

Blue Books 2021

Bonds, estate tax value of 17,187

Bond transactions 4385

Bonus depreciation 6835; 6845

Boot in like-kind exchanges of property
- giving 11,235
- receipt of 11,225

Bribes, disallowance of deduction for 6735

Business deductions 6001; 6201–6245
- common 6201
- disallowed 6735–6745
- for interest 8235
- related to capital expenditures 6801–6901

Business expenses
- criteria 6205
- employee 6601; 8601
- ordinary and necessary 6225
- reasonable 6235
- trade or business activity requirement 6215

Business gifts deduction 6515

Business losses 7301–7371
- casualty and theft 7301
- deduction of 6401
- hobby loss rules for 6715; 7345
- home office expenses as 7351
- net operating losses for 7331
- vacation home expenses as 7371

References are to paragraph (¶) numbers

Business organization 16,001–16,385
   choice of 16,001
   corporation 16,215–16,285
   limitation of liability 16,005
   partnership 16,101–16,195
   S corporation 16,301–16,385
Business property
   personal-use property converted
     to use as 10,215; 11,005
   trade-in of property used partly as 11,215
Business purpose defined 1195
Business start-up expenses deduction 6505
Business tax credit, general 3065
Business year
   natural 13,175
   tax year coinciding with 13,015
Buy-sell agreements, advantages of 17,193

C

C corporations
   cash basis accounting not allowed for ... 13,225
   taxable income of 13,001
Cafeteria plans of benefit packages 5195
Capital asset
   classification under IRS Restructuring
     and Reform Act of 1998 of 1151
   defined 1195; 12,025
   holding period of 10,030
   installment sales of. *See* Installment sales
Capital asset treatment
  vs. ordinary treatment of property
   for franchises 12,135
   for inventory 12,101
   for lease cancellation payments 12,155
   for options 12,165
   for patents 12,125
   for sale of business 12,115
Capital expenditures
   business deductions related to 6795;
     6801–6885
   cash method rules for 13,230
   cost recovery of 13,180
   for medical care 8025
Capital gain property,
  charitable contribution of 8325
Capital gains
   corporate tax returns 16,225
   on Section 1244 stock 12,530
Capital gains rates
   baskets of 12,301

changed under Taxpayer Relief Act of 1997
   and later acts 12,001
   corporate taxpayer 12,401
   establishment of 1151
   holding period required
     for long-term 12,001; 12,201–12,215;
     13,710
   of individuals 12,301–12,401
   special provisions for 12,501–12,545
   for taxable lump-sum distributions 14,335
Capitalization of expenses for long-term
  contract 13,535
Capital losses
   baskets for different terms of 12,301
   carryovers of 12,315
   corporate tax returns 16,225
   deduction of 6401
   nonbusiness bad debts as 12,501
   on Section 1244 stock 12,525
   worthless securities as 12,515
Carryback and carryforward
  of unused credits 9045
Cash accounting method 13,215–13,230
   for decedent 18,015
   deduction of expenses under 6245
   defined 1195
   hybrid methods including 13,265
   limitations on use of 6245; 13,225
   tax rules for 13,230
Casualty and theft losses, business
   basis adjustment for 7301
   computation of deduction for 7301
   deduction of 6401
   year of deduction for 7301
Casualty losses
   of estate 17,201
   personal 6401; 8501; 12,655
Charitable contributions 8301–8355
   for complex trusts 18,357
   corporations 16,235
   deduction from gift tax for 17,355
   deduction from income tax for 8275; 8355
   estate tax rules for 17,225; 18,357
   filing and substantiation
     requirements for 8355
   limitations on 8325
   percentage limits 8325
   qualified organizations for 8301
   recapture rules for 12,925
   steps in determining individual 8325
   tax planning, contributions 15,545

References are to paragraph (¶) numbers

tax planning, gifting............................. 15,547
valuation of... 8315
Charitable remainder trusts
CRAT 17,225
CRUT 17,225
Checks, deductible payment by 13,230
Child tax credit............. 1151; 3065; 9001; 9032
Circuit court of appeals, U.S. 2055
Civil Services Retirement System
(CSRS) 14,445
Claim of right defined.............................. 1195
Claim of right doctrine 13,180
Closely held business realty,
special use valuation for 17,195
Closely held corporations
passive activity rules applied to 7231
Closely held stocks, valuation of 17,191
CODA plans.
See 401(k) plans
Code Sec. 179 expensing 1151
election of.. 6825
not applicable to property converted
from personal to business use................ 6855
College tax planning................................. 15,225
American Opportunity Credit 15,225
campus rental property 15,225
custodial accounts/nongrantor trusts.... 15,225
IRAs 15,225
Lifetime Learning Credit 15,225
qualified tuition programs (QTPs) 15,225
services compensation.......................... 15,225
universal life policies 15,225
Commercial loans...................................... 4385
Community property, basis of................ 17,157
Community property income..................... 4215
Community Renewal Tax Relief
Act of 2000 1151
Compensation for services 4315
Compensation vs. gift................................ 4325
Completed-contract method
for long-term contracts 13,501; 13,515
Condemnation of property
in involuntary conversion 11,355
Conduits
defined.. 1195
Conservation easements,
tax advantages of................................. 17,101
Consolidated Appropriations Act 1151
Constructive receipt doctrine........ 4125; 14,705
defined.. 1195
Contested liabilities under
accrual method of accounting 13,235

Co-ops, ownership requirement
for gains exclusion for 11,015
Co-ownerships of property 17,157
Corporate exchanges of property 11,401
Corporate tax avoidance 1131
Corporation Excise Tax of 1909 1151
Corporations.
See also C corporations; Personal service
corporations; S corporations
alternative minimum tax (AMT) 16,255
charitable contributions 16,235
closely held 7231
debts 4485
distributions 16,241
dividends received deduction 16,225
formation 16,215
income, deductions, credits.................. 16,225
liquidations.. 16,285
minimum tax computation.................. 16,265
organization expenses.......................... 16,225
penalty taxes 16,275
personal service.................................. 16,250
taxable income of.................. 13,001; 16,245
tax year of.................. 13,015; 13,115; 13,175
Cost allocation procedures
for inventory 13,435
Cost depletion method
for natural resources............................... 6885
Cost recovery for capital expenditures ... 13,180
Court of federal claims, U.S....................... 2055
Coverdell education
savings accounts 14,801; 14,815; 15,701
Crummey trusts 17,325
Current Tax Payment Act (1943)............... 1151
Customs tax 1101

D

DB/K plans (defined benefit
and 401(k) combined)........................... 14,555
Death taxes on prior transfers
as credit against estate tax 17,035
Debts
bad 6245
deductible from gross estate 17,201
Decedent, final tax return of 18,001–18,015
Deductions .... 6001–6901.
See also individual type
additional standard, for age
and blindness.. 3035
for adjusted gross income........................ 3015

References are to paragraph (¶) numbers

business. *See* Business deductions

capital losses 16,225

categories of allowable.................. 6001–6125

classification of 6001

dividends received.............................. 16,225

of estate 17,201–17,255

factors affecting allowance of 6201–6245

on final tax return of decedent 18,015

general rules for 6725

italicizing.. 13,240

itemized. *See* Itemized deductions

itemized vs. standard............................... 3035

limitations on expenses 6701–6795

marital. *See* Marital deduction

married taxpayers filing separately........... 3035

personal. *See* Itemized deductions, personal

standard.. 3035

substantiation of 6901

tax planning.. 15,025–15,035; 15,501–15,605

   acceleration 15,025

   business and educational travel 15,595

   business meals and entertainment...... 15,585

   charitable contributions..................... 15,545

   charitable gifting............................... 15,547

   deferral.. 15,025

   hobby losses...................................... 15,601

   home office expenses 15,605

   investment interest 15,575

   itemized.................. 15,035; 15,501; 15,515

   medical expenses 15,525

   personal interest 15,555

   qualified residence interest................. 15,565

   standard 15,035

   state and local taxes 15,535

**Deductions in respect of decedent
(DRD)** 18,015

Deferred compensation plans ... 14,001–14,015.
See also individual type

Deficit Reduction Act of 1984 1151

Defined benefit plans.............................. 14,110

   and 401(k) combined (DB/K) 14,555

   limitations on benefits from................. 14,501

Defined contribution plans

   catch-up contributions to 14,215

   defined benefit plans

      compared to 14,110; 14,501

   limitations on contributions to 14,110;
      14,215–14,225

   types of......... 14,101; 14,115–14,130; 14,525

De minimis fringe benefits 5101

Dependent care

   assistance programs............................. 5235

   tax credit.. 3065

Dependents

   children as, exemption for...................... 4451

   children as, kiddie tax for...................... 3365

   death of 3225

   eligibility of 3225; 3365

   gross income test................................. 3225

   of heads of households 3345

   relationship or member
      of household test 3225

   standard deduction for......................... 3365

   support test... 3225

Depletion of natural resources................... 6885

Depletion preference in AMTI 9425

Depreciation

   averaging conventions for 6801

   bonus... 6835; 6845

   in determining AMTI.................. 9415; 9425

   of MACRS property 6801; 11,395

   of nonresidential
      real property 12,825–12,841

   of real property 6815

   of residential real property 12,845–12,861

   Section 179 election to expense 6825

   of Section 1245 property 12,735–12,755;
      13,601

   of Section 1250 property 12,801–12,875;
      13,601

   of tangible property as
      business deduction 6801

Depreciation classes............................... 13,301

Determination letters of IRS........... 2035; 2225

Disabled persons access tax credit............. 9045

Disaster, property damaged in 11,305

Disaster loss deduction election 8501

Discharge of debt 4485

**Disclaimers against estate gift
or bequest**... 17,255

Distributable net income (DNI)

   for estate or trust..................... 18,301–18,345

   to avoid double taxation of income...... 18,301

   computed for complex trusts
      and estates 18,345

   computed for simple trust.................... 18,325

   concept of... 18,301

   first and second tiers for...................... 18,345

   separate share rule for determining 18,373

Distributions, corporate

   cash 16,241

   corporations...................................... 16,241

   property received 16,241

   retirement plan, from.......................... 15,725

   S corporations................................... 16,375

   stock dividends 16,241

References are to paragraph (¶) numbers

Distributions from estate or trust........... 18,345
District court, U.S.................................. 2055
Dividend income.............. 4401; 10,125; 16,225
Divorce
    alimony payments............................. 15,255
    custodial parent exemption following 3225
    dependent exemption
      for parents following.......................... 3225
    front-loading provisions...................... 15,255
    income treatment.................................. 4451
    legal expenses related to 6725
    personal and dependency exemptions 15,255
    residence transferred to taxpayer
      incident to, period of ownership for.... 11,015
    settlements, tax planning 15,255
    termination of payments...................... 15,255
    transfers to spouse as free
      of gift tax in connection with 17,345
Dollar-value LIFO inventory method...... 13,473
Domestic production gross receipts
  (DPGR)... 7375
Double deductions, preventing.............. 13,180
Double taxation
    preventing............................... 13,180; 18,301
Drugs, medical expense deductions for 8055

E

Earned income tax credit........ 1151; 3065; 9125
Economic benefit doctrine 4101; 14,705
Economic Growth and
  Tax Relief Reconciliation Act of 2001....... 1151
    basis changed for estate property under 17,181
    graduate education exclusion of.............. 5201
    repeal of GST tax for 2010 by 17,501
    retirement plans added by................... 14,001
Economic income 4001
Economic Recovery Tax Act of 1981
  (ERTA) 1151; 2021
    investment credit at-risk limitation in 9045
Educational assistance plans.................... 5201;
                       14,801–14,815
Educational (Series EE) savings bonds
  exempt from gross income 5075
Education credit 3065
Education expenses
    classification of 8665
    for maintaining or improving skills......... 8665
    to meet employer or
      minimum standards of job 8665
    for new trade or business 8665
    tax planning, travel 15,595

Elderly and disabled persons
  tax credit.. 3065; 9025
Electing special use valuation 17,195
Emergency Economic Stabilization
  Act of 2008 .... 1151; 4485
    exclusion for debt forgiveness
      extended by... 4485
    qualified disaster losses under................. 7331
Employee benefits, taxable vs. nontaxable.
  See individual benefits
Employee business expenses............ 6601; 8601
Employee discounts, qualified.................... 5101
Employee expenses
    for job seeking 8655
    reimbursed... 8603
    unreimbursed 8605
    for work clothes and uniforms 8675
Employee Retirement Income Security
  Act of 1974 (ERISA) 1151; 14,001
Employee stock ownership plans
  (ESOPs) 14,125
Employee stock purchase plans 4625; 14,715
Employer identification number 3405
Employer-provided child care
  expenses credit 9045
Employer social security tax credit 9045
Employer-sponsored deferred
  compensation plans 14,001–14,545
    nonqualified. *See* Nonqualified deferred
      compensation plans
Employer-sponsored
  retirement plans .... 14,101–14,445.
  See also individual type
    contribution limits for, table of............ 14,435
    portability of........................... 14,345; 14,435
Employment taxes 1101
Empowerment zone employment
  tax credit... 9045
Energy Policy Act of 1992....................... 1151
Energy Policy Act of 2005 .... 1151; 9045
Energy-related tax credits......................... 9045
Energy Tax Act of 1978 1151
Enhanced oil recovery tax credit 9045
Entertainment expenses
    partial deduction of 6755
    substantiation of.................................... 6755
    tax planning... 15,585
Entity defined.. 1195
Estate
    accounting method for 18,045
    alternative minimum tax for 18,371
    created at death of decedent................. 18,025

References are to paragraph (¶) numbers

deductions for 18,331
determining taxable income of 13,001
distributions by 18,373; 18,381
DNI system for 18,301–18,345
duration of 18,025; 18,387
executor of 18,035; 18,045
fiduciary responsibilities for 18,035
income in respect of decedent
   included in 18,015
personal exemption on
   estate tax return for 18,045
as separate taxable entity 18,025
tax year of 13,015

Estate assets, probate vs. nonprobate 17,201

Estate tax.
See also Gross estate, deductions from
   applicable credit amount for 17,009
   charitable contribution rules for 17,225;
                             18,357
   computing 17,001; 17,009
   credits against 17,035
   filing requirements for 17,025
   generation-skipping trust to avoid 17,501
   impact of present and
     future interests in property of 17,109
   revenue from 1101
   tax rate for 18,045
   unified transfer tax applied to 17,015

Estate tax return 18,015; 18,045

Estimated tax payments
   for estate 18,045

Estimated tax payments tax credit 9165

Ethics rules for practitioners 2375

Exchanges of services 13,230

Excise tax
   credit for gasoline and special fuels for 9155
   for gifts 17,405
   revenue from 1101

Exclusions from gross income.
See individual types

Expenses
   with accrual method of accounting 13,235
   administrative estate 17,201
   capitalization of,
     for long-term contract 13,535
   deductible from gross estate 17,201
   funeral 17,201
   limitations on deductibility 6701–6795
   prepaid 13,235
   production of income, for 6301–6325

F

Fair market value (FMV) of property
   acquired from decedent 10,175
   basis as 10,135
   defined 10,015
   for gifts 17,365
   in gross estate 17,181
   for transfers by gift 17,315

Fair market value of service received 13,230

Fair tax 1101

Family Support Act of 1988 1151

Family tax planning 15,201–15,255
   college 15,225
   divorce settlements 15,255
   income-shifting 15,201

Family transfers of property,
lifetime 17,125–17,133

Farm and Military Tax Acts of 2008 1151

Farmers
   cash basis tax rules for 13,230
   income averaging for 13,015

Farming
   passive losses for 9415

Farmland, special use valuation for 17,195

Federal Employee Retirement System
(FERS) 14,445

Federal income tax,
underlying rationale of 1171–1187
   economic factors in 1175
   objectives of tax law for 1171
   political factors in 1185
   social factors in 1181

Federal Insurance Contribution Act
(FICA) business credit 9045

Federally declared disaster areas 8501

Federal Social Security Act 1151

Federal taxation
   administrative authority for 2035
   fundamental aspects of 1101–1175
   legislative process for 1161
   statutory authority for 2021

Fellowships excluded from gross income
of degree candidates 4345

FIFO inventory valuation method 13,435;
                             13,453

Filing requirements for tax returns 3355; 3375

Filing status 3301–3365

First-time homebuyer, credit for 1151

Fiscal year.
See Tax year

References are to paragraph (¶) numbers

Fishing businesses,
income averaging for 13,015
529 plans 14,815
Fixed assets tax planning 15,401–15,465
expensing election 15,401
involuntary conversions 15,445
leasing vs. buying 15,411
like-kind exchanges 15,425
residence sale 15,435
Section 1231 rules 15,465
"Flat" basis bonds 4385
Flat tax 1101
Foreign death taxes,
credit against estate tax for 17,035
401(k) plans
catch-up contributions to 14,405; 14,545
contribution limits for 14,401; 14,405;
14,435
elective deferrals in 14,415
requirements for 14,001; 14,401; 14,435
Roth 14,001; 14,405
SIMPLE plan within 14,545
for small businesses 14,501
solo 14,001; 14,501–14,515; 14,545
tax planning 15,715
403(a) qualified annuity plans 14,415
403(b) tax-sheltered annuity
(TSA) plans 14,001; 14,425; 14,435
elective deferrals in 14,215; 14,425
rollovers to 14,345
457(b) deferred compensation plans,
governmental and nongovernmental ... 14,435
Franchises, transfer of 12,135
Fringe benefits 5101
FSC Repeal and Extraterritorial Income
Exclusion Act of 2000 1151
Functional-use test
of replacement property 11,345
Funeral expenses 17,201

G

Gain realized defined 11,025
Gains and losses on sale
or exchange of property 11,001–11,455
AMTI adjustments for 9415
for installment sales 13,601–13,710
nonrecognition of 11,401–11,455
of personal residence 11,001–11,025
Gasoline and special fuels tax credit 9155
General Agreement on Tariffs
and Trade (GATT) 1151

General business tax credit 3065; 9045
carryback and carryforward of 9045
limitation on 9045
Generation-skipping transfer
(GST) tax 17,501–17,575
applicable fraction for 17,545
computing 17,555
credits and deductions for 17,575
direct skip under 17,525; 17,535; 17,555
exemptions from 17,535
inclusion ratio for 17,545
nature and purpose of 17,501
rate of tax for 17,545
repeal for 2010 of 17,501
skip person defined for 17,515
taxable events under 17,525; 17,555
taxable terminations
of trusts under 17,525; 17,555
tax liability for 17,565
transfers to skip person under 17,525
Gift loans 4385
Gifts
to alien spouse 17,345
business 6515
for co-owned property 17,385
disclaimers of 17,255
effective date of 17,301
excluded from gross income 5001
of life insurance 17,117
powers of appointment as 17,395
present vs. future interest in 17,325
of property 10,145; 12,215;
17,301–17,415
recapture rules for donee of 12,901
within three years of death, exceptions
to adjusted taxable gifts of 17,117
valuation of 17,365
Gift-splitting 17,341
Gifts to minors, conditions
for avoiding future interests in 17,325
Gift tax 17,301–17,415
applicable credit amount for 17,009
computing 17,415
deductions for 17,345–17,355
divorce settlements not subject to 17,345
exclusions from 17,341; 17,535
gratuitous transfers not subject to 17,375
history of 1151
impact of present and future interests
in property of 17,325
increase in basis for paid 10,145
liability for 17,405

References are to paragraph (¶) numbers

paid as includible in gross estate........... 17,117
revenue from... 1101
unified transfer tax applied to 17,015
Gift tax return 17,405
**Grantor of grantor trust, rules
for control of property for** 18,525
Gross estate, deductions from ... 17,201–17,255
for administration expenses................. 17,201
allocation of... 17,201
for casualty losses of estate 17,201
for charitable contributions................. 17,225
for claims against estate....................... 17,201
for debts 17,201
for disclaimers...................................... 17,255
for funeral expenses............................. 17,201
marital 17,217
Gross estate, property for .... 17,101–17,173.
See also individual type
co-ownership of.................................... 17,157
in excess of probate estate 17,101
powers of appointment for.................... 17,165
special deduction for family-owned
business for.. 17,101
types of.. 17,185
Gross income.......................... 3011; 4001–4655.
See also individual items
defined... 1195
derived from business 4355
exclusions from............................ 5001–5255
list of income items included in 4301
valuation of............................ 17,181–17,195
Gulf Opportunity Zone Act of 2005........... 1151

H

Heads of households, tax liability for 3345
**Health insurance plan costs,
deduction of**...6575
**Health Insurance Portability
and Accountability Act (1996)** 1151
Health plan benefits................................... 5155
**Health savings account (HSA),
deduction for**..6575
High-deductible health insurance plans 6575
High-income phaseout of exemptions 3227
Highly compensated employees
defined... 14,205
discriminatory plans for 14,701–14,765
**Hiring Incentives to Restore Employment
(HIRE) Act, focus of** 1151
Hobby losses 6715; 7345
tax planning....................................... 15,601

Holding period
for capital gains to be considered
long-term 12,201–12,215; 13,710
defined.. 1195
for property 10,030
for property acquired from decedent.... 10,175
for property acquired
in nontaxable exchange...................... 11,265
Home office expenses 7351
tax planning.. 15,605
Hope Scholarship Credit............... 9031; 14,801;
14,815
Hospital care, deduction for 8035–8045
Household and dependent care tax credit 9015
**Household and personal effects,
valuation of**.. 17,185
Household employers, employment taxes ... 3405
**Housing Assistance
Tax Act of 2008** 1151; 11,005
**Hurricane Katrina employees,
tax credits related to**................................ 9045

I

**Incapacitated taxpayers, period
of ownership for sale of residence by**.... 11,015
Incentive stock option (ISO) plans............. 4615
Incentive stock options
adjustment to AMTI for exercising........ 9415;
14,725
requirements for 14,725
Income
accelerating.. 13,240
accounting... 4025
in cash method of accounting.............. 13,215
community property............................... 4215
corporations... 16,225
deferring... 13,240
defined.. 1195
dividend 4401
divorce and separation 4451
economic.. 4001
expenses incurred for production
of income 6301–6325
on final tax return of decedent............. 18,015
for installment sales 13,655; 13,710
legal/tax concept of................................. 4015
for passive activity rules, active,
passive, or portfolio 7205
prepaid 13,235
S corporation....................................... 16,355
tax-exempt, expenses and interest on....... 6765

References are to paragraph (¶) numbers

Income averaging for farmers 13,015
Income in respect of decedent 18,015
Income recognition,
  tax planning 15,001–15,015
    acceleration 15,015
    avoiding 15,001
    deferral 15,015
Income-shifting
    defined 1195
    employment in family business 15,201
    family tax planning 15,201
    government bonds 15,201
    intrafamily loans 15,201
    land 15,201
    life insurance 15,201
    municipal bonds 15,201
    stock 15,201
Income tax, federal.
  See also Federal income tax,
  underlying rationale of; Federal taxation
    corporate 1101
    history of 1151
    individual 1101
    of trusts and estates 18,001–18,525
Income tax, state and local
    deduction of 8101; 8115
Income Tax Law of 1894 1151
Indexing adopted in Tax Reform
  Act of 1986 1165
Indian employment tax credit 9045
Individual retirement accounts (IRAs)
    catch-up contributions to 14,535; 14,601
    conversion among 14,635
    Coverdell Education Savings accounts 15,701
    deemed 14,535; 14,545; 14,601
    inherited 14,235
    premature distributions from 14,245; 14,625
    rollovers to 14,235; 14,345; 14,401; 14,635
    Roth 14,345; 14,601; 14,635; 15,701
    self-directed 14,601
    SEP 14,345; 14,501; 14,535;
                      14,545; 14,635
    SIMPLE 14,001; 14,345; 14,501; 14,545
    spousal 14,601
    tax planning 15,701
    traditional 14,235; 14,245; 14,301; 14,435;
          14,445; 14,601–14,625; 14,635; 15,701
Inheritances
    excluded from gross income 5001
    recapture rules for 12,901
Injuries, compensation for 5145

Installment method of reporting.
  See Installment sales
Installment payouts from estate
  or trust 18,373
Installment sale of property
    depreciation recapture in 12,935; 13,540
    reporting of 10,245
Installment sales 13,601–13,710
    advantages and disadvantages of 13,710
    computation of gain for 13,655
    defined 13,601
    disposition of installment obligation
      prior to maturity in 13,685
    electing out of reporting 13,675
    interest on 13,699
    repossession of personal
      property under 13,695
    taxpayers qualifying for use of 13,601
Installment Sales Revision Act of 1980 1151
Installment Tax Correction Act of 2000 1151
Insurance contract exchanges,
  gain or loss not recognized for 11,415
Insurance premiums
  as business deductions 6245
Intangible assets, amortization of 6865
Intangible drilling costs in AMTI 9425
Interest
    AMT deductions for 9415
    on government obligations
      excluded from gross income 5075
    on installment sales 13,699
    investment 8225; 15,575
    passive investment 8245
    for payment of services 8255
    personal (consumer) 8205; 15,555
    prepaid 6245; 8265; 13,235
    qualified residence interest 15,565
    received as included in gross income 4385
    requirements for deduction of paid 8201
    on residence loans 8215
    on savings bonds 5075
    on student (qualified education) loans,
      deduction of 6570; 8210
    tax-exempt, in AMTI 9425
    trade or business 8235
    on under- or overpayments of taxes 2333
Interest payments
  as business deduction 6201; 6245
Internal Revenue Code of 1939 1151
Internal Revenue Code of 1954 .... 1151; 2021;
                            18,373

References are to paragraph (¶) numbers

Internal Revenue Code of 1986

citing sections of 2021

subtitles of 2021

Tax Reform Act of 1986

redesignated as.................................... 1151

Internal Revenue Service (IRS)

accounting method prescribed by 13,301

actuarial tables of 5125

Appeals Office of 2211; 2311

audits by... 1121

changes directed by............................. 13,301

Chief Counsel, Office of....................... 2211

Communications and Liaison................. 2211

criminal investigation 2211

homepage of... 2075

national office of................................... 2211

National Taxpayer Advocate.................. 2211

operating divisions................................ 2211

organization of...................................... 2211

permission or consent 13,301

permission to change accounting

period from 13,101–13,115

Privacy, Governmental Liaison

and Disclosure, Office of 2211

Professional Responsibility, Office of....... 2211

representation of taxpayers for 2215

Restructuring and Reform

Act of 1998 .... 1151; 2211

return preparer office 2211

rulings programs of................................ 2225

taxpayer compliance assistance by 2245

tax returns processed by 1121

user fees for requests to 2225

Whistleblower Office............................. 2211

Internet-based tax research systems 2075

Inventories 13,401–13,481

advance payments for future sale of...... 13,235

capital asset treatment for 12,101

cost of merchandise m

ethods for 13,425–13,445

uses of.. 13,401

valuation of............................. 13,415–13,481

Inventory shrinkage, estimates of........... 13,485

Investment expense deductions....... 6301–6315

itemized...................................... 8701–8785

Investment income

tax on net 4401

Investment interest deduction.................. 8225

tax planning... 15,575

Investment tax credit 9045

Involuntary conversion of property 11,015;
11,301–11,395

condemnation of real property in......... 11,355

deferring gain in 11,301

defined.. 11,301

elective rules

for replacement property in 11,325

exchanges of stock for 11,345

mandatory rules

for replacement property in 11,315

qualifying replacement property for 11,345

recapture rules for 12,915

reporting requirements for 11,385

rules for property damaged

in disaster for.................................. 11,305

severance damages in 11,335

tax planning.. 15,445

time limit for replacement

with qualified property in.................. 11,365

**IRS Restructuring and Reform
Act of 1998**.................................... 1151; 2211

Itemized deductions, personal 8001–8785

allowed in computing AMTI................. 9415

of beneficiaries of income

in respect of decedent 18,015

of charitable contributions............ 8301–8355

as deductions from AGI 6101; 6125

of education expenses 6565; 8665

of employees 6535; 8601–8655

of interest paid............................. 8201–8265

of investment expenses.................. 8701–8785

of medical expenses...................... 8001–8065

miscellaneous.................... 8601–8680; 9415

of mortgage insurance........................... 8275

of personal casualty

and theft losses 6401; 8501–8525

of rent and royalty expenses 8701

of tax counsel and tax preparer's fees 8680

of taxes 8101–8115

tax planning............... 15,035; 15,501; 15,515

of wagering losses.................................. 8775

J

**Job Creation and Worker Assistance
Act of 2002** 1151

**Jobs and Growth Tax Relief Reconciliation
Act of 2003 (2003 Tax Act)**

capital gains tax rates reduced under 12,001

dividends tax rates reduced under 4401;
12,001

purpose of.. 1151

Job-seeking expenses, deduction of 8655

References are to paragraph (¶) numbers

Jointly owned property,
survivor's basis in 10,175
Joint returns
for married individuals filing jointly 3301
tax year as same for both spouses for 13,115
Joint tenants 4235
married 17,157
unmarried 17,157
Judicial authority in interpreting Code 2055
Jury duty pay 4331

K

**Katrina Emergency Tax Relief
Act of 2005 (KETRA)** 1151
**Keogh plans for self-employed
individuals** 14,001; 14,501;
14,525–14,545
Kickbacks, illegal 6735
Kiddie tax 3365

L

**Lease cancellation payments, capital
vs. ordinary assets treatment of** 12,155
**Leasehold improvement,
depreciation rules** 6815
Leasing vs. buying, tax planning 15,411
Legal fees as business deduction 6201
Letter rulings of IRS 2225
Life estates, valuation of 17,185
Life insurance
gifts of 17,117
group-term 5115
incidents of ownership in 17,173
includible in gross estate 17,173
reversionary interest in 17,173
valuation of 17,185
**Life insurance proceeds excluded
from gross income** 5015
Lifetime Learning Credit 5075; 9031;
14,801; 14,815
Lifetime transfers of assets 17,125
LIFO inventory method 1151; 13,415;
13,435; 13,453
dollar-value 13,473
simplified dollar-value 13,481
**Like-kind exchanges
of property** 11,201–11,275
assumption of liabilities in 11,245
basis of acquired property in ... 11,255; 11,275
defined 11,201

giving boot in 11,235
holding period for property
acquired in 11,265
qualifying property for 11,215
recapture rules for 12,915
receipt of boot in 11,225; 12,915
tax planning 15,425
three-party 11,275
**Limited partners not considered
material participants** 7235
Liquidations, corporations 16,285
**Listed and reportable transactions,
penalties for** 2365
**Loan service payments
not deductible as interest** 8255
**Lobbying activities,
limited deductions for** 6745
Local tax planning .... 15,535.
See also individual types of taxes
Lodging expenses for medical care 8035
**Lodging furnished to employee
as compensation** 5185
Long-term care insurance
prepaid 8065
qualified 5165
Long-term contracts 13,501–13,540
alternative accounting methods for 13,501
AMT adjustments for 9415
capitalization of expenses for 13,535
special tax regulations for 13,540
**Look-back method
for long-term contracts** 13,501
Losses deductions 6245; 6401
disaster 8501
from gross estate 17,201
of individual taxpayers 6401
**Lower-of-cost-or-market
(LCM) inventory method** 13,415; 13,445;
13,453
**Low-income housing
depreciation recapture** 12,865
Low-income housing tax credit 9045
**Lump-sum payouts from estate
or trust** 18,373
**Lump-sum pension
or qualified plan distributions**
five-year forward averaging of 13,180
tax consequences of 14,301; 14,325;
14,335
ten-year forward averaging of 14,335

References are to paragraph (¶) numbers

M

Making Work Pay credit............................ 1151
**Manufacturing deduction
and tax rates** 6585; 7375
Marital deduction
  history of.. 1151
  for QTIP trust 17,345
  for surviving spouse from estate tax...... 17,217
  for surviving spouse from gift tax......... 17,345
Married individuals
  filing jointly... 3301
  filing separately 3035; 3315
Meals
  as business expenses, deduction of.......... 6755
  furnished to employee as compensation .. 5185
  tax planning.. 15,585
Medical expenses 8001–8065
  capital expenditures for medical care as 8025
  for decedent's medical care deducted
    from decedent's final return 18,015
  as deductible for AMTI 9415
  for hospital and institutional care 8035–8045
  for medical care 8015
  for medical insurance premiums 8065
  for medicines and drugs.......................... 8055
  requirements for deducting..................... 8001
  tax planning.. 15,525
  unlimited exclusion for qualifying........ 17,341
**Medical insurance premiums
deduction of**... 8065
**Medicare Catastrophic Coverage Repeal
Act of 1989**.. 1151
Medicare surtaxes 3405
Medicines and drugs, deductions for 8055
Membership dues, prepaid 13,235
Method of accounting. *See* Accounting methods
Military benefits..................................... 5255
Mining exploration, AMT for 9415
**Modified accelerated cost recovery
system (MACRS).**
  See also Alternative MACRS system
  nonresidential real property 12,841
  for Section 1245 property....... 12,745–12,755
  for Section 1250 property....... 12,841; 12,861
  for tangible property depreciation........... 6801
Money purchase plans................ 14,130; 14,525
**Mortgage Forgiveness Debt Relief
Act of 2007** 1151; 4485
  gain on sale of
    principal residence under................... 11,015

**Mortgage loan interest paid,
deduction of**... 8215
  under AMT 9415
Moving expenses
  classification of 6560
  qualification requirements
    for new job location for 6560
  time and distance requirements for 6560
  year of deduction of............................... 6560
**Municipal bond interest excluded
from gross income** 5075
Mutual funds
  differences between variable
    annuity contracts and 14,755
  valuation of... 17,185

N

Net investment income tax........................ 4401
Net operating losses (NOLs).................. 13,301
  carryback and carryforward
    periods for 7331; 13,180
  computation of.. 7331
  to offset AMT income 9415
  recomputation of tax liability
    in carryback year of 7331
Net tax due... 3075
Net tax liability, calculating 13,001
New markets tax credit............................... 9045
Newsletters of tax information 2075
No-additional-cost services 5101
Nonbusiness bad debts 12,501
**Nonqualified deferred
compensation plans** 14,015; 14,435;
                            14,701–14,765.
  See also Deferred compensation plans;
    individual type
Nonqualified stock options...................... 14,735

O

**Options on property, gain
or loss from sale or exchange of** 12,165
**Ordinary income property,
charitable contribution of** 8325
Organizational cost.
  See Start-up costs
Orphan drug tax credit............................... 9045
Owner-employees.
  See also Self-employed persons
  loans to...................... 14,355; 14,501–14,545

References are to paragraph (¶) numbers

qualified retirement plan,
contributions for 14,501–14,545

P

Partners

qualified retirement plans for 14,501

Partnership, taxable year of 13,015; 13,115; 16,125

basis allocations 16,165

contributions to 16,141

debts 16,149

deductions 16,120

determining taxable income of 16,125

distributions 16,175

estimated income tax 16,187

exchange of 16,181

family 16,195

income 16,120

liabilities, contributed property 16,157

new partner admission 16,171

organizing 16,101; 16,109

partner's basis in 16,115

related parties rules for partners and 16,133

reporting income of 16,125

sale of 16,181

start-up costs 16,109

tax year of 16,125

Partnership exchanges of property 11,401

Partnerships

cash basis accounting not allowed
for some 13,225

determining taxable income of 13,001

family 17,125

sale of 12,115

taxable income taxed to partners of 4375

tax year of 13,015; 13,115

Passive activity

death, gift, and other transfers 7225

defined 7235

disposition of 7225

Passive activity loss rules 7201–7287

application of 7201

change of activity from passive
to nonpassive under 7287

classification of income under 7205

identifying activity under 7261

material participation in business under 7235

participation standard for 7235

rental activities under 7273

rental real estate activities under 7281

significant participation
in business under 7235

suspended losses under 7215

Passive investment interest, deduction of 8245

Passive losses

for farming 9415

or credits, disallowance of 7211

taxpayers affected by 7231

Passive loss rules

application of 7215

Patents, capital gain treatment of 12,125

Pay-as-you-go tax system defined 1195

Penalties assessed by IRS

accuracy-related 2365

for aiding understatement
of tax liability 2365

civil fraud 2365

criminal fraud 2365

delinquency 2365

for early withdrawals from
457(b) plans 14,435

for early withdrawals from qualified
deferred compensation plans 14,001

for early withdrawals
from qualified retirement plans 14,535;
14,545; 14,625

for estate or gift tax
valuation understatements 2365

for estimated taxes 2365

for excess nondeductible retirement
plan contributions 14,305; 14,401

for failure to make deposits of taxes 2365

for failure to make required
minimum distributions 14,235

fraud 2365

generally 1121

negligence 2365

as nondeductible, government 6735

for substantial overstatement
of pension liabilities 2365

for substantial understatement
of tax liability 2365; 2370

for substantial valuation misstatement 2365

for underpayment of taxes 2365

Penalty taxes 16,275

accumulated earnings tax 16,275

personal holding company tax 16,275

Pension plans

money purchase 14,130

qualified. *See* Qualified retirement plans

rollovers from 14,345

References are to paragraph (¶) numbers

Pension Protection Act of 2006 .... 1151; 14,555
Percentage depletion method
for natural resources 6885
Percentage-of-completion method
for long-term contracts 13,501; 13,515
Personal deductions 6001; 6725
Personal exemptions 3045; 3201–3225
for dependents 3225
history of 1151
not claimed against AMTI 9415
for taxpayer and spouse 3201
**Personal (consumer) interest paid,
nondeductibility of** 8205
tax planning 15,555
**Personal Responsibility
and Work Opportunity Reconciliation
Act (1996)** 1151
Personal service corporations 16,250
passive activity loss rules applied to 7231
tax year of 13,115
**Personal travel combined
with business travel** 6545
**Personal-use casualty
and theft gains and losses** 12,655
**Personal-use property converted
to business use**
basis of 10,215
exclusion of gain provision
not applied to 11,005
P.L. 101–140 1151
Points, deductibility of 8265
**Political contributions
as nondeductible** 6745
**Pollution control facilities,
AMTI calculations for** 9415
Pooled income funds 17,225
Powers of appointment 17,165; 17,395
Prepayments of services 13,230
Private activity bonds 5075
Private letter rulings 2035
Prizes included in gross income 4335
Production of income deductions 6001;
6301–6325
Profit-sharing plan
as defined contribution plan 14,115
included in estate 17,149
paired or unpaired Keogh plan as 14,525
Property, terminable interests in 17,217
Property acquired for resale 13,435
Property acquired from decedent
alternative valuation of 10,175
by gift 10,175; 12,215

holding period for 10,175
survivor's basis in 10,175
**Property acquired through exchanges
and conversions, holding period for** 12,215
Property exchanges 13,230
Property taxes
deduction of 8101; 8105
**Property transactions, capital
and Section 1231 assets in** 12,001–12,935;
13,601; 13,675
rules and limitations on 12,001–12,025
**Property transactions,
gains and losses in** 10,001–10,245;
11,001–11,455
AMTI adjustments for 9415
Property transfers
by gift 17,301–17,315
part-sale, part-gift 17,175; 17,405
Public policy doctrine for deductions 6735
Purchase money debts 4485

Q

Qualified annuity [403(a)] plans 14,415
**Qualified deferred
compensation plans** 14,001; 14,205;
14,301–14,315
Qualified disaster losses 7331
Qualified dividends, tax rates for 12,001
**Qualified domestic relations order
(QDRO)** 14,285; 14,345
Qualified heir for special use valuation 17,195
**Qualified higher education expenses
for Coverdell ESA** 14,801
**Qualified production activities income
(QPAI)** 7375
Qualified residence interest 8215
tax planning 15,565
Qualified retirement plans.
See also individual types
contributions to 14,301–14,315; 14,501
coverage requirements for 14,265
credit for contribution to 9033
credit for plan startup costs
of small employers for 9045
defined 14,001
distributions from 14,235–14,245;
14,301; 14,325–14,345
divorce or separation as
prompting distributions from 14,285
early retirement option of 14,235
employer-sponsored 14,101–14,130

References are to paragraph (¶) numbers

loans and withdrawal benefits for........ 14,355; 14,501
nontax benefits 14,001
partial distributions........................... 14,325
participation requirements for............. 14,255; 14,501

penalties for.
    See Penalties assessed by IRS
prohibited transactions for................... 14,285
requirements of....................... 14,201–14,285
sections of Code pertaining to 14,201
tax benefits.. 14,001
tax treatment of 14,245; 14,325–14,335; 14,501
types of.................... 14,101–14,130; 14,335; 14,401–14,425; 14,501
vesting in 14,275

Qualified retirement plan types
defined benefit.
    See Defined benefit plans
defined benefit
    and 401(k) combined (DB/K)........... 14,555
defined contribution.
    See Defined contribution plans
employer-sponsored................ 14,101–14,130
for large businesses.................. 14,401–14,445
for self-employed individuals..... 14,501–14,545
for small businesses................. 14,501–14,545

Qualified state tuition programs (QTPs). 17,325
**Qualified terminable interest property
  (QTIP) trust**.. 17,217
**Qualified transportation
  fringe benefits of**...................................... 5101

R

Rabbi Trusts.. 14,705
Real estate
subdivided 12,545
valuation of... 17,185
Realized gain or loss
defined.. 10,001
factors in determining............. 10,001–10,035
recognized gain or loss vs. 1195
Real property
nonresidential, depreciation of.............. 6815; 12,825–12,841
reacquisition of 11,455
residential, depreciation of.................... 6815; 12,845–12,861
special use valuation method for 17,195

Recapture
alimony or separate
    maintenance payments 4451
in relation to special use valuation........ 17,195
Recognition of gain or loss
for installment sales 13,685
nonrecognition and 10,035
realization of gain or loss and................. 1195
Recovery of tax benefit items 5035
Refunds, claims for 2325
Registered bonds.................................... 5075
Related-party transactions 6775; 16,133
Remainder interests, valuation of 17,185
**Renewable electricity production
  tax credit**.. 9045
**Rental activities under passive
  activity loss rules** 7273
Rental payments as business deduction....... 6245
**Rental real estate activities
  under passive activity loss rules** 7281
Rent and royalty expenses 8701
Rent and royalty income 4395
**Replacement property
  in involuntary conversions**
elective rules for 11,325
mandatory rules for 11,315
qualifying 11,345
**Repossessions of personal property
  sold in installment sales** 13,695
**Required minimum distributions
  from qualified retirement plans**
commencement of.................. 14,235; 14,625
penalty for failure to make...... 14,235; 14,435
rules for 14,235; 14,625
**Research and experimental
  (R&E) expenditures**................................. 6875
Research tax credit 9045
Residence, sale of principal.
    See Sale of residence
**Residence (mortgage loan) interest paid,
  deduction of**.. 8215
under AMT 9415
tax planning.. 15,565
Residential energy property tax credit....... 9042
Restaurant property, depreciation rules 6815
Restricted stock plans 4601; 14,745
Retail improvement, depreciation rules 6815
Retained life estates................................ 17,125
Retirement income
distributions 15,725
gross income exclusion of....................... 5055
individual retirement accounts (IRAs)..... 15,701

References are to paragraph (¶) numbers

planning 15,701–15,725
Section 401(K) plans 15,715
Revenue Act of 1913 1151
Revenue Act of 1916 1151
Revenue Act of 1938, exclusion
of business property as
capital asset under 12,615
Revenue Act of 1962 1151
Revenue Act of 1964 1151
Revenue Act of 1971 1151
Revenue Act of 1978 .... 1151; 14,001
Revenue Act of 1987 1151
Revenue procedures 2035; 7351
Revenue Reconciliation
Act of 1989 .... 1151; 2021
Revenue Reconciliation Act of 1990 1151
Revenue Reconciliation
Act of 1993 .... 1101; 1151
losses and credits from rental real estate
activities excluded from passive loss
limitations under 7281
Revenue rulings 2035
Revenue sources 1101
Reversionary interests
in grantor trust 18,525
valuation of 17,185
Reversions of lifetime transfers 17,133
Revocable lifetime transfers of property 17,141
Rollovers
of 457(b) plans 14,435
of 529 plan assets 14,815
of Coverdell ESA assets 14,801
of government plans 14,445
of qualified plan balances 14,235; 14,335;
                  14,345; 14,405; 14,501; 14,625
of reconverted IRAs 14,635

S

S corporations
accumulated adjustments account
and other adjustments account
(AAA) for 16,385
allocation of income, deductions,
credits 16,355
distributions 16,375
election of status of 16,315
losses 16,365
tax treatment 16,301
tax year of 13,015; 13,115; 16,325
termination of election of 16,335

S corporations, taxable income of
allocation of income, deductions,
credits 16,355
determining 13,001; 16,345
taxed to shareholders 4375
Safe, Accountable, Flexible,
Efficient Transportation Equity Act 1151
Salary reduction SEPS (SARSEPs) 14,535
Sale of business considered
sale of assets 12,115
Sale of property
amount realized from 10,015
installment 10,245
between related parties 10,225
terminology for, definitions of 11,025
Sale of residence 11,001–11,025
exclusion of gain from... 5025; 11,005; 11,015
general rules for 11,001
as involuntary conversion,
exclusion of gain from 11,015
pro-ration of exclusion of gain for 11,015
Taxpayer Relief Act of 1997
treatment of 11,001–11,015
tax planning 15,435
time of ownership for 11,001
by widowed spouse,
ownership period for 11,015
Sales tax and state and local
income tax deduction 8101; 8115
Savers' credit for qualified
retirement contributions 14,601
Savings bonds interest as taxable 5075
as income in respect of decedent 18,015
Savings incentive match plans
for employees (SIMPLE) 14,001; 14,345;
                                                          14,501
contribution limits for 14,545
elective deferrals in 14,215
as IRAs 14,001; 14,345; 14,501
premature distribution penalty for 14,235;
                                                          14,545
Scholarships excluded from gross income
of degree candidates 4345
Section 179 election to expense 6825; 6845
Section 401(k) plans
tax planning 15,715
Section 1202 (small business) stock
gain on sale or exchange of 12,301
Section 1231 assets 12,601–12,655
computing gains
and losses on 12,645–12,655
defined 12,615

References are to paragraph (¶) numbers

installment sales of.................. 12,935; 13,675
personal-use casualty and theft
   gains and losses excluded from........... 12,655
tax planning.............................. 15,465

Section 1245 property
charitable contributions of.................... 12,925
computing gains and losses on 12,725
defined.. 12,715
depreciation methods for 12,735–12,745
depreciation recapture for 12,701–12,755;
                                         13,601
difference between recapture
   for Section 1250 property and........... 12,815
gifts and inheritances of........................ 12,901
property types included in 12,715
rules for 12,701

Section 1250 property
charitable contributions of.................... 12,925
defined.. 12,801
depreciation recapture for 12,801–12,875;
                                         13,601
difference between recapture
   for Section 1245 property and........... 12,815
gifts and inheritances of........................ 12,901
low-income housing............................. 12,865
nonresidential real................... 12,825–12,841
residential real........................ 12,845–12,861

Securities
defined.. 12,535
held by dealers 12,535
worthless, as capital loss 12,515

Self-employed persons
deduction limit for retirement
   plan contributions by 14,305; 14,501
earned income of 14,215; 14,501
health insurance plan costs
   deductible by........................... 6575; 15,101
matching contributions on behalf of.... 14,215
qualified retirement plan concepts for 14,501
tax planning, vs. employee 15,101–15,115
trade or business expenses 15,115
transportation expenses of...................... 6535

Self-employment tax 3405; 6101
Selling expenses defined 11,025
Services, prepaid................................. 13,235
Settlement agreements for tax disputes.... 2315
Short-term informal arrangements 14,765
Sickness, compensation for....................... 5145
Simplified dollar-value
 LIFO inventory method................... 13,481
Simplified employee pension
 (SEP) plans 14,001; 14,501;
                                         14,535

elective deferrals in.............................. 14,215
as IRAs 14,345; 14,501
Simplified production method
 of cost allocation 13,435
Simplified retail method
 of cost allocation 13,435
Single individuals, tax liability for 3325
Sixteenth Amendment 1151
Small Business and Work Opportunity
 Tax Act of 2007 1151
Small businesses
cash basis accounting method for......... 13,225
retirement plans for 14,501–14,545
start-up costs for pension plans of.......... 9045
Small Business Job Protection
 Act of 1996................................. 1151; 14,001
Small Business Jobs Act of 2010
excluded gains on small business
   stock under....................................... 12,530
focus of...................................... 1151
Small business (Section 1202) stock
gain on sale or exchange of.................. 12,301
Small business (Section 1244) stock
gains on sale of.......................... 9425; 12,530
loss deductions for 12,525
Social Security Act Amendments of 1983 1151
Social Security Domestic Employment
 Reform Act of 1994................................ 1151
Social Security tax refunds tax credit......... 9115
Sole proprietors
calendar-year accounting period for 13,015
qualified retirement plans for 14,501
Sole proprietorship
sale of 12,115
Special assessments, deductibility of......... 8105
Special use valuation method
 for real property................................. 17,195
Spending Reduction Act of 1984 1151
Standard deduction.......................... 3035; 3365
Start-up costs
business investigation expenses 6505
for pension plans of small employers,
   credit for 9045
State bond interest excluded
 from gross income 5075
State death taxes, deduction for 17,230
State tax planning 15,535
Statute of limitations on tax collections.... 2355
Stimulus Plan.
See American Recovery and Reinvestment
Act of 2009
Stock bonus plans 14,120; 14,125
distributions from................................ 14,335

References are to paragraph (¶) numbers

Stock exchange

in involuntary conversion 11,345

Stock option plans.

See also individual type

nonstatutory 4655

Stock rights 4401

allocation of basis for nontaxable 10,130

Stock shares

estate tax value of 17,187

wash sales of 10,201

Stock transactions

basis for 10,201; 11,405

corporate gain or loss 16,225

Student (qualified education) loan interest,

deduction of 6570; 8210

Student loans, discharge of 4485

Subchapter S Revision Act of 1984 1151

Subscription income, prepaid 13,235

Substance vs. form 1195

Supreme court, U.S. 2055

Surviving spouses

decedent's medical expenses paid by 18,015

eligibility of 3355

gain on sale of principal residence by ... 11,015

marital deduction

in computing taxable estate for 17,217

minimum required interest

in property of 17,217

passing of property to 17,217

Suspended losses under

passive activity rules 7215

T

Tangible property costs 13,275

Taxable income

defined 1195

determining C corporation's 13,001

determining estate or trust's 13,001

determining individual's 12,301; 13,001

determining partnership's 13,001

determining S corporation's 13,001

Tax accounting 13,001–13,710

Tax Adjustment Act of 1966 1151

Tax administration 2211–2245

Tax and Trade Relief Extension

Act of 1998 1151

Tax avoidance

tax evasion vs. 1131

Tax benefit rule defined 1195; 13,180

Tax brackets 3055

Tax collections 1121

Tax computation,

corporation minimum 16,265

Tax concepts, basic 1195

Tax counsel, deduction

of expenses incurred for 8680

Tax court, U.S.

federal 2055; 2311

redetermination of deficiency through 2311

Tax credits .... 3065; 9001–9165.

See also individual type

for AMTI 9445

at-risk limitations 9045

compensation and retirement 14,601

extension in 1998 of 1151

foreign 9035

nonrefundable 9001–9045

recapture 9045

refundable 9105–9165

tax laws addressing 1151

types of 9001

Tax Equity and Fiscal Responsibility

Act of 1982 (TEFRA) 1151; 2021

Taxes

as business deduction 6245

deductions of 8101–8115

not allowed in AMTI computation 9415

payable of another taxpayer's 6785

preference items 9425

types of 1101

Tax evasion 1131

Tax Extension Act of 1991 1151

Tax formula, components of 3001–3085

Tax institutes 2075

Tax law

economic factors of 1175

objectives of 1171

political factors of 1185

social factors of 1181

sources for, analysis of 2075

Tax liability

assessment of 1131

calculating net 13,001

of decedent 18,035

deferred through installment sales 13,710

filing status types for determining 3225

for generation-skipping transfer tax 17,565

for gift tax 17,405

recomputed in carryback year of NOL 7331

of trust 18,215

Taxpayer Bill of Rights 2 (1996) 1151

Taxpayer Relief Act of 1997 (TRA '97) 1151

applicable credit amount named in 17,009

References are to paragraph (¶) numbers

conservation easements made
more attractive under 17,101
exclusion of gains from sale,
of residence changed by 11,001
home office expenses 15,605
long-term contract rules under 13,501
NOL carryback periods
changed under 7331
taxation rate of capital gains
changed under 12,001; 12,815;
12,865–12,875

Taxpayer Relief Act of 2012.
See American Taxpayer Relief Act of 2012 (ATRA)

Taxpayers
classification of 3085
compliance assistance for 2245
obligations of 1131
representation for IRS of 2215

**Taxpayer-use test
for replacement property** 11,345

**Tax payments, installment method
for deferring** 13,180

Tax planning
for accounting method 13,365
for accounting period 13,175
for accrual method 13,240
for AMT 9475
for Code Sec. 179 expensing election 6825
deductions 15,025–15,035; 15,501–15,605
family 15,201–15,255
fixed and other assets 15,401–15,465
income recognition 15,001–15,015
individuals 15,001–15,725
retirement 15,701–15,725
self-employed vs. employee 15,101–15,115

**Tax planning and
compliance expenses** 6301; 6325

Tax policy 1187

Tax practice and procedure 2301–2375

Tax preparer
fees 8680
penalties 2365

Tax rates 3055
schedules of 3395

Tax Reduction Act of 1975 1151

**Tax Reduction and Simplification
Act of 1977** 1151

Tax reference materials 2001
primary 2021–2055
research methodology for 2125–2147
secondary 2075

Tax reform 1165

Tax Reform Act of 1969 1151
Tax Reform Act of 1976 1151
Tax Reform Act of 1984 .... 1151; 2021
Tax Reform Act of 1986
scope of 1101; 1151; 1165
tax rules for generation-skipping
transfers under 17,501; 17,515
Tax reform measures 1187
**Tax Relief, Unemployment
Insurance Reauthorization,
and Jobs Creation Act of 2010** 12,530
Tax Relief and Health Care Act of 2006 1151
Tax Relief Extension Act of 1991 1151
Tax research situations 2125–2147
Tax research systems, Internet 2075
Tax return, decedent's final 18,001–18,015
Tax return, estate 18,015; 18,045
Tax return, examination of 2301
appeals process following 2311
audit reconsideration during 2301
by correspondence examinations 2301
by district office examinations 2301
by field office examinations 2301
Tax return, filing requirements for 3355
Tax return, gift 17,405
Tax return, number of 1121
Tax return, trust income 18,215
Tax return preparer fees, deduction of 8680
Tax services, published 2075
Tax shelters 7001
cash basis accounting not allowed for 13,225
defined 13,225
farming 13,230
Tax tables 3385
Tax terminology, definitions of 1195
Tax year
corporate 13,015; 13,115; 13,175
defined 13,007
election of 13,015
of husband and wife 13,115
individuals 13,015
short 13,007; 13,165
tax principles affecting 13,180
Technical advice letters of IRS 2035; 2225
**Technical and Miscellaneous Revenue
Act of 1988** 1151
Technical Corrections Act of 1982 1151
Tenancy by the entirety 4225
Tenants in common 4235; 17,157
Term certain interests, valuation of 17,185
**Terminable interest in property,
requirements for** 17,217

References are to paragraph (¶) numbers

Theft losses, business
basis adjustment for 7301
computation of deduction for 7301
deduction of 6401
year of deduction for 7301
Theft losses, personal 8525; 12,655
of individual taxpayers 6401
Thrift savings plans 14,445
**Top-hat plans for
highly compensated employees** 14,435
Trade deductions .... 6001.
See also Business deduction
for interest 8235
Transfer of property by gift
basis computed for 17,315
defined 17,301
Transportation expenses, deductions for
of employee 6535
for medical care 8035
of self-employed taxpayer 6535
Travel expenses, business deductions for ... 6545
substantiation of 6545
when combined with personal travel 6545
Treasury regulations 2035
Trust income tax return 18,215
Trusts
accounting method for 18,215
administration fees for 18,365
alternative minimum tax for ... 18,215; 18,371
beneficiaries of 18,209; 18,365; 18,387
cash basis accounting not allowed
for some 13,225
charitable remainder 17,225
charitable remainder annuity (CRAT) .. 17,225
charitable remainder unitrust (CRUT) 17,225
complex 18,209; 18,345; 18,373
creation of 18,209
Crummey 17,325
deductions for 18,331; 18,365
defined 18,209
determining taxable income of 13,001
DNI system for 18,301–18,345
fiduciary responsibilities for 18,035
generation-skipping 17,501–17,535
grantor 18,525
inter vivos 18,209
multiple 18,503
nature of 18,209
qualified retirement 14,001
qualified terminable interest property
(QTIP) 17,217; 17,345
revocable 18,503
separate share rule for 18,373
simple 18,209; 18,325
sixty-five day rule for distributions of 18,373
taxable distributions from 17,525; 18,373;
18,381
taxation of 18,209–18,381; 18,503–18,525
tax credits for 18,365
tax rates for 18,215
tax year of 13,015
termination of 18,387
testamentary 18,209
trustee of 18,215
uses of 18,209
Tuition reduction plans 5215
**Tuition to qualifying educational
organization, unlimited exclusion of** 17,341

U

**Uniform capitalization (UNICAP) rules
for real or personal property** 13,425–13,435
Uniform Lifetime Table 14,235
Uniforms, deduction of cost of 8675
**U.S. obligations exchanges,
nonrecognition of gain or loss on** 11,435

V

Vacation home expenses, deductions for ... 7371
Valuation
of charitable donations 8315
of commercial annuities 17,149
of decedent's property 10,175
of farm 17,195
of gifts 17,365
of gross estate 17,181–17,195
of inventory 13,415; 13,453
of present and future interests
in property 17,109
Value-added tax (VAT) 1101
Vesting requirements
of pension and retirement plans 14,115;
14,275; 14,501
of qualified deferred
compensation plans 14,001
of self-employed plans 14,435
Vow to Hire Heroes Act 9045

W

Wagering losses, deduction of 8775
Weighted average inventory method 13,453

References are to paragraph (¶) numbers

Wherewithal to pay.................................... 1195
Widowed taxpayers,
   sale of residence by.............................. 11,015
Windfall Profit Tax Act (1980) 1151
Withholding of tax at source tax credit..... 9105;
                                             9135
Work clothes, deduction of cost of 8675
Worker, Homeownership, and Business
   Assistance Act of 2009, focus of 1151
Working condition fringe benefits.............. 5101
Working Families Tax Relief Act of 2004
     focus of... 1151; 1171
Working interest in oil and gas properties,
   passive activity rules not applied to 7231
Work opportunity tax credit 9045

Filing Requirements

For 2015, Code Sec. 6012 requires a tax return to be filed if gross income for the year is at least as much as the amount shown for the categories in the table below.

Filing Status		Gross Income 2015
Single	Under 65	$10,300
	65 or older	11,850
	Dependent with unearned income	1,050
	Dependent with no unearned income	6,300
Married Filing Joint Return	Both spouses under 65	$20,600
	One spouse 65 or older	21,850
	Both spouses 65 or older	23,100
Married Filing Separate Return	All	$4,000
Head of Household	Under 65	$13,250
	65 or older	14,800
Surviving Spouse	Under 65	$16,600
	65 or older	17,850

Personal Exemption

The personal exemption reduces taxable income by $4,000 in 2015.

High-Income Taxpayers. The deduction for personal exemptions is reduced or even eliminated for certain high-income taxpayers. When adjusted gross income exceeds one of the following threshold amounts, the deduction for exemptions is reduced by 2 percent for each $2,500 ($1,250 for a married person filing separately) or fraction thereof by which adjusted gross income exceeds the threshold amount.

Filing Status	Adjusted Gross Income Threshold Amount 2015
Single	$258,250
Married Filing Joint Return	309,900
Married Filing Separate Return	154,950
Head of Household	284,050
Surviving Spouse	309,900

The deduction for personal exemptions is fully eliminated when adjusted gross income exceeds the threshold amount by more than $122,500; in no case can the deduction for exemptions be reduced by more than 100 percent.